COMMERCIAL REAL ESTATE TRANSACTIONS: A Project and Skills Oriented Approach

Second Edition

LEXISNEXIS LAW SCHOOL ADVISORY BOARD

COMMERCIAL REAL ESTATE TRANSACTIONS: A Project and Skills Oriented Approach

Second Edition

James Geoffrey Durham
Professor of Law
University of Dayton
School of Law

Debra Pogrund Stark
Professor of Law
The John Marshall Law School

Thomas R. White, III
John C. Stennis Professor of Law
University of Virginia
School of Law

2009

LexisNexis

978-1-4224-0746-2

Library of Congress Cataloging-in-Publication Data

Durham, James Geoffrey.
Education law : an interactive, problem-based approach / Scott F. Johnson, Sarah Redfield.Commercial real estate transactions : a project and skills oriented approach / James Geoffrey Durham, Debra Pogrund Stark, Thomas R. White III. -- 2nd ed.
p. cm.
Includes bibliographical references and index.
ISBN 978-1-4224-0746-2 (Casebook)
1. Vendors and purchasers--United States. 2. Commercial leases--United States. 3. Real estate investment--Law and legislation--United States. I. Stark, Debra P. II. White, Thomas R. (Thomas Raeburn) III. Title.
KF665.D87 2009
346.7304'37--dc22 2009037558

Editorial Offices
121 Chanlon Rd., New Providence, NJ 07974 (908) 464-6800
201 Mission St., San Francisco, CA 94105-1831 (415) 908-3200
www.lexisnexis.com

MATTHEW BENDER

(2009–Pub.3117)

Dedications

To my loving and understanding spouse, Joan Drake Durham

J.G.D.

To my father, whose love of the law and good deeds inspired me to become a lawyer; to my mother, whose constant "you can do it" inspired me to become a law professor; and to my now grown children and my partner Jessica, for bringing me more joy than words can convey

D.P.S.

To my wife Maria, for her patience and support.

T.R.W.

Acknowledgements

Together we gratefully acknowledge the contributions of our colleague, David L. Cameron, who was a co-author of the First Edition. Chapters 12-15 were conceived by David, and the extensive text he wrote remains in the Second Edition, primarily changed by our updating. After the First Edition was published, David moved from Willamette University College of Law to become Associate Director of the Tax Program, and Senior Lecturer, at the Northwestern University School of Law. His new position took him far enough away from real estate transactions that he decided not to be a co-author of this Second Edition. We thank him for his excellent work on the First Edition, and we also thank him for being so gracious in allowing us to use his work without restriction in preparing the Second Edition.

J.G.D., D.P.S. and T.R.W.

I would like to thank the many people without whom I could not have completed my work on this book. First, I thank Debra Pogrund Stark, who conceived the book and found the rest of us to help her carry it out. Second, I thank the several research assistants at the University of Dayton School of Law who made significant contributions to the book: Edward Brutscher '00, David Herier '97, Thomas Larsen '99, Sara Mills '00, Charles Rittenhouse '11, Therese Schumacher '07, and Matthew Shad '01. All made noteworthy contributions, but David Herier deserves special thanks for his work on helping me to conceive, research and draft Chapters 7 and 8.

J.G.D.

I would like to thank Anne Abramson, reference librarian at The John Marshall Law School, for the excellent research assistance that she has provided to me over the years, and to thank Marie Clear, a former student and research assistant, for her assistance and useful suggestions on the first edition of this textbook. I would also like to thank the following students at The John Marshall Law School who provided research assistance for this second edition: Brian Flores, Greta Hendricks, Amy Keller, and Andrew Yassan. I am also grateful to John Corkery, Dean of The John Marshall Law School, and Ralph Ruebner, Associate Dean, for their generous support of my various research projects. Finally, I am grateful to my friend Doug, who graciously permitted me to utilize his real estate project as a teaching tool. I hope all of my students have clients as pleasant to work with. I also wish to thank my outstanding colleagues at the Real Property, Trust and Estates Section of the American Bar Association and at the American College of Real Estate Lawyers, for sharing with me their "war stories" and helping me to stay current in what is happening in the commercial real estate market; in particular, I thank Steve Davidson, Kenneth Jacobson, and John C. Murray.

Finally, I would like to thank my co-authors for continuing to work on this project with me. In particular, I want to thank James Geoffrey Durham for his many substantive contributions that helped to make the book better than I could ever have imagined.

D.P.S.

There are many who have contributed to my part in these materials, and it is nearly impossible to single out any one of them. I do want specifically to acknowledge: the University of Virginia Law School Foundation, for research support for me and for providing funds which support the teaching of real estate finance; many real estate professionals who have contributed generously of their time and knowledge to advance both the teaching of specific topics and my knowledge of real estate finance in general;

and those anonymous students who suffered through many problems designed to apply the principles set out in these materials.

T.R.W.

PREFACE

A COURSE FOCUSED ON A PROJECT, PROBLEMS AND SKILLS

It is the aim of this book to enable students to develop the knowledge and the skills they need to competently represent the myriad of parties involved in the field of commercial real estate. Students must not only master the legal issues surrounding real estate transactions, they also must appreciate the business issues. In addition, students need to be exposed to and have the opportunity to develop "transactional skills" (skills in communicating with clients, negotiating, drafting, problem spotting, and problem solving). Based upon our collective experiences in private practice and in teaching, it is our belief that the best way to accomplish these objectives in a real estate transactions course is through a project-oriented approach, with exercises that stimulate the development of transactional skills.

In order to achieve this ambitious goal, this book is organized around the "life-cycle" of a single commercial real estate project, the Fox Valley Auto Care Center in Aurora, Illinois. In using an actual specialty shopping center, we feel that we can illustrate and describe how a real estate project is developed, from the raw land into the finished project. In addition to covering the key legal and business issues involved in developing the Fox Valley Auto Care Center, the materials also include exercises in which the students will engage in client counseling, negotiations, drafting, problem spotting, and problem solving. Through these exercises, students will be exposed to the real world activities of real estate lawyers and will become aware that in the commercial real estate context, to a large extent, they will create the applicable "law" through the agreements and documents that they draft. By focusing on the development of an actual specialty shopping center, the book exposes students to the basic legal and business problems that generally arise during the life-cycle of any commercial real estate development, taking into account differences in end use.

We will follow the legal work done by the law firm, Kaplan & Miller, which represents the developer, the Regent Real Estate Development Corporation. The partner in charge of Kaplan & Miller's work for Regent is Donna Smith, who has assigned to her an associate, Samuel Nader. Sam's job is like that of most young associates in law firms — he is often called upon to review or draft the legal documents proposed for a transaction and to research the thornier legal rules underlying some of the business decisions which Regent has made and now intends to implement. The problems he uncovers will be examined, in some cases as he discussed them with Donna, who must then decide how to proceed on Regent's behalf. You will often find yourself reviewing Sam's work and discussing it in class. For example, Sam will be assigned to review the draft of an agreement to purchase the land necessary for Regent's planned shopping center development, taking into account the concessions Regent has made with the seller in reaching agreement and Regent's objectives for the use of the land. What issues will he have to resolve in order to make the acquisition effective for Regent's specific purposes of developing a specialty shopping center devoted to the accessories for and the maintenance of automobiles?

Part I begins with an introduction of the Fox Valley Auto Care Center and the financial and tax analysis necessary in any real estate development project. Following the description of the site proposed for the Fox Valley Auto Care Center, Chapter 1 provides information on understanding the business of real estate developments generally. Chapter 2 then engages in an analysis of present value concepts, and Chapter 3 focuses on income tax issues and how they affect the developer's choices. Finally, Chapter 4 discusses choice of entity issues (including a discussion of a limited liability company set up to own the Fox Valley Auto Care Center).

Once the basic decision is made to build a specialty shopping center in a specific location, the developer typically enters into purchase agreements to acquire the land desired. Part II focuses on this phase, the acquisition of the land for the Fox Valley Auto Care Center. In Chapter 5, students will have the opportunity to review the purchase agreements entered into to acquire the land, as well as the closing escrow utilized to coordinate the multi-party transactions necessary to close the deals. Students will also be asked to critically analyze what has been drafted to determine if it is adequate to meet Regent's needs, and if not, what should be done. Chapter 6 contains a summary of the key issue of assuring good title to the land. Chapter 7, governmental control of the use of land, and Chapter 8, environmental issues, review other important issues that arise in the acquisition of vacant land and contain both general information and some of the actual documentation utilized in the development of the Fox Valley Auto Care Center. In keeping with the project-oriented focus of the book, in Part II students will have the opportunity to review the purchase and sale agreements, the survey and title insurance policy that Regent relied upon when it purchased the land, the annexation agreement Regent entered into with the city from which it was seeking services and rezoning, and the environmental report Regent received with respect to the property it was planning to acquire.

Part III focuses on the topic of financing the acquisition and construction of real estate generally and the Fox Valley Auto Care Center specifically. Chapter 9 discusses the basic legal and business issues that arise in real estate financing. Chapter 10 investigates the critical issue for any lender, the security for the loan. Finally, Chapter 11 addresses the due diligence the lender performs in evaluating the project and the developer, and what the lender will require to document and fund the loan. As is done in other sections, Part III incorporates actual documents utilized in the featured project. These documents include the promissory note, mortgage and loan agreement required by the lender, the certificate of insurance provided for the project, and the opinion of counsel required to close the loan. In keeping with the problem and skills focus of the book, Part III also sets up various problems related to the financing of the project for Sam and Donna to work through, and provides students with opportunities to negotiate and draft some of the key terms of the loan documentation.

Continuing with the theme of the life-cycle of a real estate project, Part IV addresses construction issues generally, as well as how they arose in the Fox Valley Auto Care Center project, viewed from the perspective of the owner/developer, the architect, the general contractor, sub-contractors, and the lender. Chapter 12 provides an overview of the construction process. Chapter 13 takes an in-depth look at the process of contracting to have the project's improvements designed and built, along with the rights and responsibilities of the various parties. Part IV also contains the proposal by the architect that designed the Fox Valley Auto Care Center and poses problems for Sam and Donna to handle.

Part V covers the topic of leasing the real estate development by identifying the most significant issues that arise, and analyzing how these issues were handled in the actual leases of the Fox Valley Auto Care Center. Chapter 14 is a review of business and legal issues in leasing, while Chapter 15 is a thorough exploration of the leasing of the Fox Valley Auto Care Center, examining issues that did arise and could have arisen. Part V also contains thorny issues for Sam and Donna to deal with, as well as student negotiation and drafting exercises.

PREFACE

To complete the life cycle of a real estate development, Part VI covers the disposition of the real estate investment. Chapter 16 addresses the topic of loans in default, including the Fox Valley Auto Care Center financing, and the rights, remedies and options available to the lender and the borrower in this situation. Chapter 17 explores the tax consequences to various dispositions of the real estate investment, including the forced sale of the property by the lender.

The topics covered in this book are not limited to those actually encountered in the Fox Valley Auto Care Center development. Throughout the book we raise issues that did not become part of the Fox Valley Auto Care Center story so that the student may learn about the most important issues facing real estate attorneys in any type of real estate development.

Let us make one more point before we begin with the story of the Regent Real Estate Development Corporation and its Fox Valley Auto Care Center. The development occurred in 1989, which for real estate lawyers (and law students) seems "long ago in a galaxy far, far away." For the second edition, we considered using a newer development, but the development of the Fox Valley Auto Care Center still provided an almost ideal platform to discuss the issues we thought relevant. In addition, the situation in 1990 when the project's construction loan matured is remarkably similar to the situation real estate developers face in 2009 — a real estate recession and credit crunch in which very few new commercial real estate loans are being made and those being made are under much higher standards that most developers can not satisfy. Since 1989, many cases have been decided, statutes passed, regulations issued, and new insights offered by attorneys in their writings. Because time has not stood still, we always endeavor to bring the reader current law. It makes telling the story of the Fox Valley Auto Care Center more complicated at times, but we hope that you will bear with us. The students who have used these materials in draft form for three years and in the first edition for eight years have found the effort most worthwhile!

Let us now turn our attention back to the matter at hand and introduce you to the Fox Valley Auto Care Center, the real estate development project that will be the subject of our attention for the semester.

TABLE OF CONTENTS

Chapter 6 ASSURING GOOD TITLE TO THE PROJECT SITE . . . 247

Chapter 7 PUBLIC CONTROLS ON THE USE OF THE PROJECT SITE . . . 279

Part I

UNDERSTANDING THE BUSINESS OF REAL ESTATE DEVELOPMENT

Chapter 1

INTRODUCTION TO THE PROJECT, THE DEVELOPER, AND THE ROLE OF THE DEVELOPER'S LAWYER

§ 1.01 FOX VALLEY AUTO CARE CENTER

[1] A Story

Unlike the texts used in most law school courses, this one has a single story running through it, a story that involves real people and entities, real places, real events, and real money. As a law student, you have read and analyzed cases and problems that we as law professors hope will show you that real people have real needs for legal advice. With this book, we endeavor to be more direct. We present to you the law of real estate transactions through the review of an actual transaction, and we hope that you will better see how the parties' needs for legal advice and legal services arise and how lawyers can best respond to their clients' needs.

The story involves a small specialty shopping center called the Fox Valley Auto Care Center located on State Route 59 in Aurora, Illinois, a suburb of Chicago. We have changed many of the names of people and business entities, but not all. We changed some names not to mask what really happened, but so that we will not intrude on any person's privacy. We have endeavored to present the transaction at the center of the story as realistically as possible. For example, one of the parties involved in the transaction is the national company Turtle Wax and, as of 2009, there is a Turtle Wax car wash on the site in front of the Fox Valley Auto Care Center. The Auto Care Center is in the area surrounding the enclosed mall called the Westfield Fox Valley Shopping Center.

Now we get to the part where we made some changes. Most of the names have been changed, but keep in mind that we did not change what the real people did. Only rarely did we change the substance of the documents you will be reading (each updated document is noted, with one of the biggest changes being that we have changed the entity formed to own the Fox Valley Auto Care Center from a limited partnership to a limited liability company). If people (including the lawyers involved!) made mistakes, we have left them in. If the documents are not as concise or thorough as we, in hindsight, would like (and we all know that hindsight is 20/20), we left them alone.

The developer we will call the Regent Real Estate Development Corporation, a smaller developer in the Chicago area that also had an affiliated construction company, the Regent Construction Company. Regent had developed other specialty shopping centers as well as residential apartments and condominiums. The principal in Regent on whom we usually will be focused is David Delaney. Regent is an Illinois corporation that had elected Subchapter S status under the federal tax laws. Regent was represented by the Chicago law firm of Kaplan &

Miller through its partner Donna Smith and associate Sam Nader. The rest of the parties are set forth as you read through this Section 1.01. Our focus, however, usually will be on Regent, Delaney, Smith and Nader.

[2] Retail Shopping Centers

The first step in our journey is to establish some common points of understanding about retail developments like the Fox Valley Auto Care Center. Retail centers are everywhere. Drive down any major thoroughfare and you will see a wide variety of these centers, from the very large regional or even "super regional" center, usually with an enclosed mall, to the small neighborhood center clustered around a single important store, usually a supermarket, to the still smaller "strip shopping center." As retailing business changes, the character of these centers must also change. Large, regional shopping centers may no longer command the market advantage they once did, while new concepts have influenced design of newer centers.

The more traditional type of center usually has some smaller stores clustered around one or more "anchors," a larger store intended to be the draw which attracts customers into the center for itself and potentially as customers for the smaller stores. In the 1990's a trend emerged that employed a "big box," such as those epitomized by Wal-Mart stores, but used by many other retailers such as home improvement centers, discount stores, electronic and appliance super stores, and grocery warehouses. Sometimes, several of these big box stores are grouped into a "power center," which may include smaller local stores. As another example, one of the more recent shopping center concepts is the center with mixed uses (retail and office, and sometimes residential) that has the appearance of a older downtown. Keep in mind that each center is built to exploit the commercial potential of its particular location, as that potential was understood by the developer and using what the developer frequently views as "cutting edge" concepts (although as one travels around the U.S., it frequently is hard to distinguish between what is cutting edge and what is copycat).

Shopping centers involve the business of retail merchandising, which is more difficult for the developer and her "team" to analyze than apartment rents or office rents. We say "team" because every developer directly employs or retains a variety of professionals including architects, engineers, business consultants, accountants, and, yes, lawyers. It is important that each of these professionals not only understand what her role is but also the developer's overall goals. Without basic understanding of what the developer is trying to accomplish, the professional cannot economically render effective professional services.

Shopping center developments are more difficult to analyze than office or apartment developments for one simple reason: historically, one can project both the market for and the attainable rents of new apartments and offices, but one has great difficulty projecting retail sales for a shopping center. Of course, shopping centers exist in order to make retail sales, and retail sales also dictate attainable rents because rents are only attainable at a level that will be supported by the retail sales of the tenants.

While understanding current retail markets is essential for successful development of a shopping center, in many cases the nature of the development for which a particular tract of land is best suited is sufficiently clear to support the development decision without the need for much further research. This can occur, for example, when the tract lies in the path of ongoing, significant future development. It is less clear for larger centers that must draw customers from a wider surrounding area. The Fox Valley Auto Care Center is an example of the former situation. The area surrounding the Westfield Fox Valley Shopping Center included a well-established enclosed shopping center (a typical enclosed mall with several department stores as anchors), and the Fox Valley Auto Care Center was built on the outskirts of the shopping center area facing a major thoroughfare, State Route 59.

[3] The Concept

[a] Specialty Centers and the Auto Care Center Concept

Regent had been looking for an interesting new concept in the development of shopping centers when Delaney and another of its officers attended a conference on shopping center development. Conferences such as these are regularly presented by several organizations, such as the International Council of Shopping Centers or the Urban Land Institute, and are attended by developers as a way to make contacts with others in the business and to learn new concepts. At this conference, the concept of a center presenting clustered car care uses was discussed.

The idea of a specialty shopping center is to focus on shoppers who have a specific shopping interest:

> One of the first subcategories to evolve after the principal types [of shopping centers] were established was the "specialty shopping center." Initially, the term was applied to any center that failed to meet the traditional definitions. Although the term is widely recognized in the shopping center industry as an appropriate classification for nontraditional shopping centers, the industry never has agreed on a clear definition of it and so it means different things to different people. One salient characteristic that has often differentiated a specialty center from a conventional center is the absence of a traditional anchor tenant. The role of the anchor tenant might be played by another type of tenant or by a group of tenants that together might function as an anchor tenant or by any number of other variations. In a neighborhood specialty center, for example, a combination of gourmet food shop, delicatessen, meat market and greengrocery might function in lieu of a supermarket. A food cluster, several restaurants, and a cinema complex might also serve as anchor tenants. Specialty centers, especially those that have a special architectural character or environmental ambience, have sometimes been referred to as "themed centers" or "themed specialty centers." Since the advent of "urban entertainment" and "lifestyle centers," however, the term "themed center" has fallen into disuse.
>
> In any case, "specialty center" is no longer an adequate description of the numerous disparate shopping center subcategories, and the format needs to be more precisely defined to be meaningful. Today, with shopping center specialization becoming the norm and with market segmentation dividing the retail pie into more complex and overlapping segments,

> specialty centers need to be characterized as what they are: "entertainment," "fashion, " "off-price," "outlet," "megamall," "home improvement," "lifestyle," "power" and other qualifiers that more precisely define their character, focus and targeted retail segment.

URBAN LAND INSTITUTE, SHOPPING CENTER DEVELOPMENT HANDBOOK 13–14 (3d ed. 1999).

The "anchor" tenant is intended to be the draw for customers who would then be attracted to the other stores which might not by themselves have been sufficiently attractive to draw enough customers. In the specialty center, the other retail stores typically are closely related to the principal attraction.

Regent explored the auto care center concept with retailers to determine whether the retailers had sufficient interest for Regent to proceed. Regent's adaptation of the auto care center concept was to have a car wash with an adjacent strip center that would have other stores dealing with related items. Regent approached Turtle Wax, a nationally known and respected seller of products used to clean and protect automobile finishes. Regent viewed Turtle Wax as an ideal anchor tenant because its name and reputation would serve as the attraction for customers for the other stores in the center. The discussions with Turtle Wax proved to be fruitful.

[b] Questions About an Auto Care Center as a Specialty Shopping Center

1. What do you think should be the characteristics of the area in which an auto care center would be successful? What would you look for in particular?

2. What kinds of stores do you think would fit the concept, and where would you find these tenants? Obviously, the concept of what stores will fit in an auto care center will change. For example, Cellular Communications was one of the first tenants of the Fox Valley Auto Care Center, and it seems kind of quaint to think of bulky cell phones and their antennas installed into autos (the prime market for cell phones in 1989) while today most middle schoolers likely have tiny handheld cell phones in their backpacks!

3. What information would you seek out to assure yourself that the location you have selected will be likely to succeed?

[4] The Site

[a] Identifying the Site

What type of location does an auto care center need? A site with a lot of automobile traffic passing by, *slowly*, with easy access from the highways, and close to a magnet which will attract that traffic from a wide area. Intrigued by the auto care specialty shopping center concept, David Delaney drove around the suburban area west of Chicago, looking for likely sites. He found what appeared to be a suitable site with a "For Sale" sign on it and negotiated with the owner to purchase it. Regent got Turtle Wax on board and engaged in promising negotiations with several potential tenants to lease the space in the center. Regent's development of its first auto care center was shaping up as a success.

After Regent's first auto care center development had begun, Metropolitan Diversified Properties, Inc. ("Metropolitan"), the developer of the Westfield Fox Valley Shopping Center and the owner of still undeveloped land around it, became intrigued with the auto care center concept. One of Metropolitan's people suggested to Delaney that the property Metropolitan owned near the Westfield Fox Valley Shopping Center also might be a good site for Regent to build an auto care center.

Stop and consider, from Regent's and Delaney's perspectives, the situation presented to them at this point in the story. Regent had adopted a concept that others had made successful elsewhere in the United States and its first attempt, in a growing suburb of one of the county's largest metropolitan areas, was shaping up to be a success. Then Metropolitan, a Connecticut based developer of shopping centers nationwide, approached Regent and proposed that Regent duplicate that success on what had the appearance of being an ideal site: in a thriving mall area and on a major thoroughfare.

There were some problems with the site, however, that made its development by Regent problematic. The site Metropolitan suggested was a piece of a larger property located in the Fox Valley area. That piece by itself was not large enough for the center, but adjacent to it was a residential tract that Metropolitan had been unable to acquire in assembling its larger development parcel when it built the Westfield Fox Valley Shopping Center. The tract was owned by Alan and Barbara Johnson and, since the Johnsons had refused to deal with Metropolitan, Metropolitan had excluded the tract from its development plan for the Fox Valley area. The Johnsons' tract had not been annexed by the City of Aurora and was not zoned for retail commercial uses. For the auto care center development to be successful, this property (the "Johnson tract") would have to be acquired. Metropolitan also wanted a portion of the Johnson tract to complete the overall plan it had developed for the area, including its tentative layout for streets.

Figure 1.1: Site of Fox Valley Auto Care Center

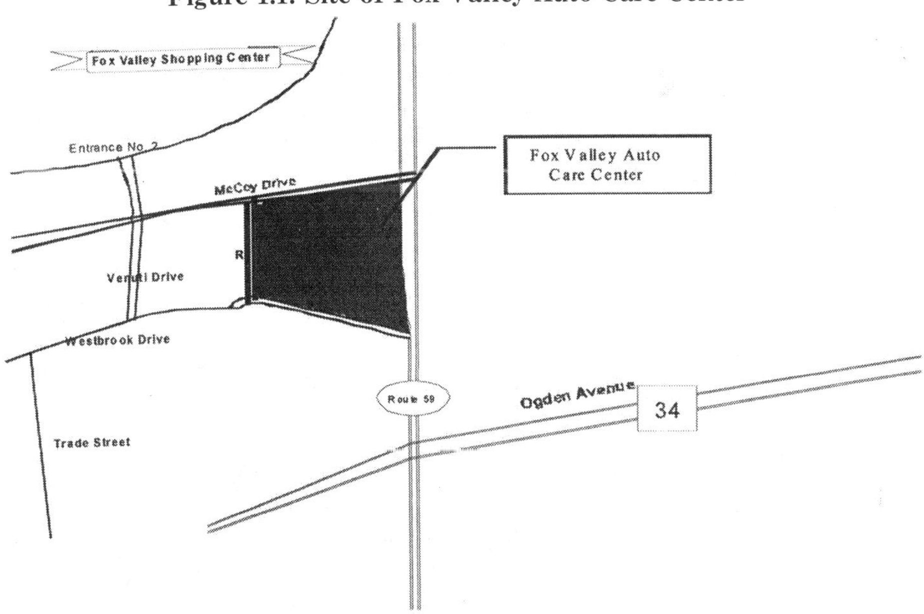

The site was promising. *See* Figure 1.1. Right across McCoy Drive, a main thoroughfare, is the Westfield Fox Valley Shopping Center, a large, well established enclosed regional shopping mall. There were then undeveloped areas adjacent to the mall, including the parcels assembled by Metropolitan. Metropolitan had gone so far as to plat its land and include it in a development plan approved by the City of Aurora, which had annexed much of the area. Some streets had been constructed, although a portion of Metropolitan's land was partially cut off from State Route 59 by the Johnson Tract and could not be fully developed for that reason.

The selected portion of the Metropolitan land was located at the corner of McCoy Drive and State Route 59, the main north-south connector in that area of DuPage County. At the time that Metropolitan and Regent were engaging in discussions the entire area was undergoing substantial retail development. With so much development underway, Regent decided that a market study of the potential of the site for development as an auto care center was unnecessary.

Many developers do not rely on market studies. For a regional center, which to be successful would have to draw customers from a large area, a market study is essential. But for smaller community or neighborhood centers, a local developer may believe that he or she knows the area well enough to dispense with the cost (and the delay, which itself is a cost) of the study. The center is then built, but success is sometimes slow in coming. Advisors to developers on financial matters observe that this often happens when the developer fails to ask enough hard questions: what value does this transaction add to the plan as a whole?

[b] Questions About Selecting the Site

1. Was the decision by Regent not to obtain a market study wise? To Regent, this was a business decision, made from experience. The first auto care center was shaping up as a success. Of course, we are not asking you, as Regent's lawyer, to make business decisions for Regent. However, as a lawyer, you need to understand what your client is doing so that you know how sophisticated your client is and what type of legal protections your client might need. If your client takes risks without engaging in industry recognized risk management (any new shopping center is risky, but the developer can take steps to lessen the risk), then you, as the lawyer, are on notice that you may need to take additional steps necessary to better protect the client.

2. What would you want to know about the first auto care center? Many factors go into the success of a retail center, and one of them is the symbiosis of the collection of shops that draws customers who otherwise would not necessarily come to any of the individual stores.

3. Thinking of your own experiences (most of you own automobiles, after all), why would you be drawn to shop in an auto care center? Or, why would you not be drawn to shop in it? How much do you trust your own responses? Again, the point is not for you to do the analysis of the business decision, but for you to have some understanding of what types of protections you may need to provide your client.

[5] Assembling the Site and Maintaining Control

Figure 1.2: Existing Parcels at the Site

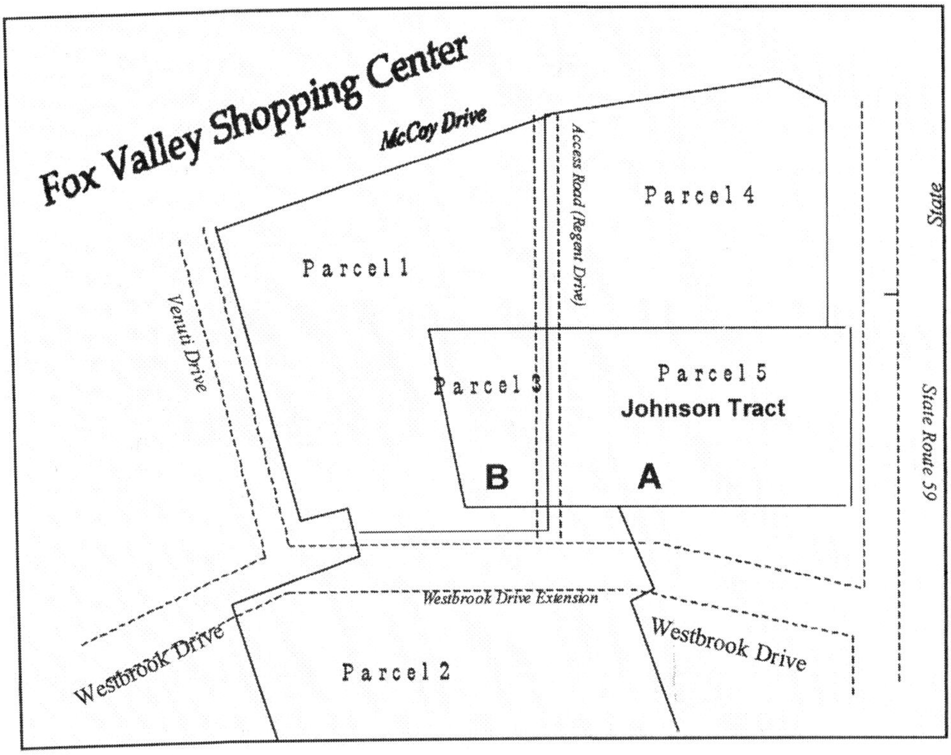

Regent now entered into a three-cornered negotiation. Acquisition of the Johnson tract (Parcels 3 and 5 on Figure 1.2) was the key to success of the project. David Delaney found it easier to develop a rapport with the Johnsons than had Metropolitan, and Delaney and the Johnsons were able to agree on a price, so the first piece of the puzzle was in place. Metropolitan, which had control of the second piece of the puzzle, was interested in the ability of Regent to purchase the Johnson Tract for two reasons: (1) it was interested in Regent's ability to develop the corner tract (Tract A or Parcel 5) along with Metropolitan's land (Parcel 4) into the proposed Auto Care Center; and (2) it wanted to acquire part of the Johnson Tract (Tract B or Parcel 3) to further its own plans for development of the surrounding area (Parcels 1 and 2). Turtle Wax, in turn, was interested in purchasing its part of the Auto Care Center development and constructing a car wash that it would operate. Turtle Wax's minimum land requirements would include most of the Johnson Tract and some of the property then being acquired by Regent from Metropolitan. See Figure 1.3.

Figure 1.3: The Proposed Reconfigured Parcel Plan

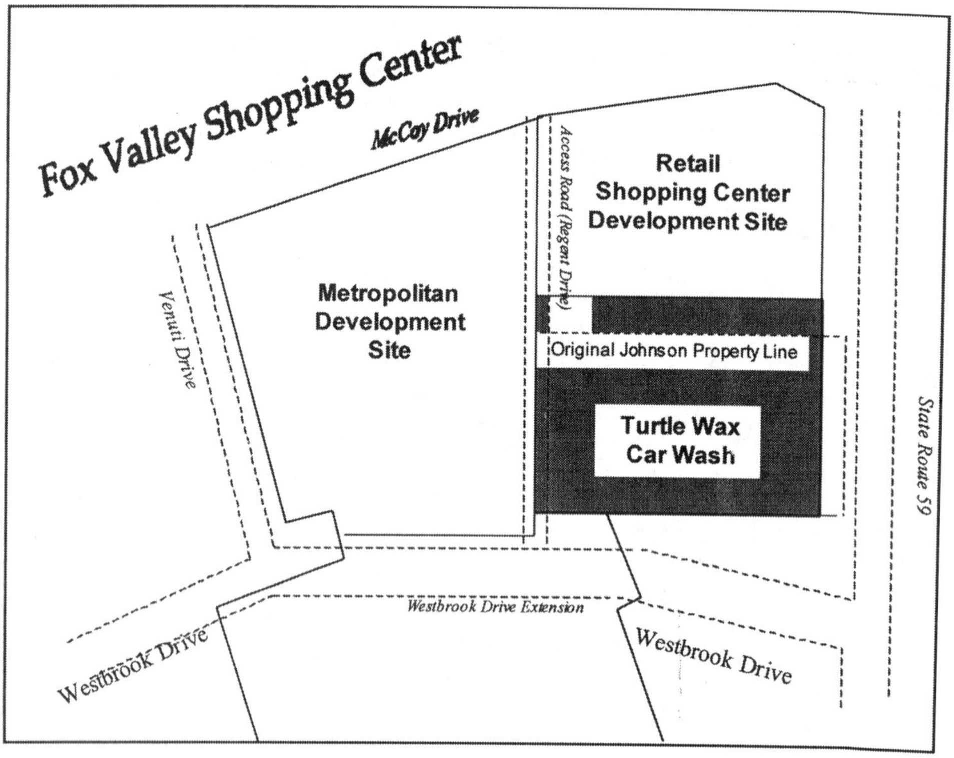

Consider these transactions from the perspective of each of the players. Regent wanted to have control over the necessary pieces and, failing that, would not want to proceed further. When negotiations commenced, Regent did not have any agreements that assured it that the other piece would be available on terms that would permit the development to proceed. The Johnsons, too, had personal interests in how the property was ultimately developed because they would be able to obtain a higher price for their land if the end use had a higher value. Metropolitan wanted the development of the Auto Care Center to be compatible with its own development, and, because the land it had first acquired was subject to restrictions, wanted to assure itself that the development conformed to those requirements. Further, Metropolitan wanted Regent's development to be successful, which it felt would increase the value of the land it was retaining, with its new dimensions and access (sometimes, however, things do not work out as intended, as you will see in the photographs at the end of this chapter, because Metropolitan appears not to have attracted a high-level retail use to its retained land). Regent, Metropolitan and, of course, Turtle Wax wanted to be sure that access to these properties was consistent with what they planned for their respective parcels. Turtle Wax also wanted to be sure that it would be able to operate the car wash efficiently and successfully, and it viewed the rest of the Auto Care Center as necessary for that operation. Finally, the project as a whole would have to receive approval from public authorities, which would zone it appropriately and authorize the issuance of the necessary permits.

Consider how these various interests might be protected in the negotiations that follow. You should keep this question in mind: how would you set the deal up to accomplish Regent's (or, for that matter, any other parties') objectives?

§ 1.02 UNDERSTANDING THE BUSINESS OF SHOPPING CENTER DEVELOPMENT

The following discussion is focused on the development of retail properties. Retail development is different in some important ways from other types of real estate projects. It is true that a shopping center project needs tenants, and just as with other commercial rental property, the tenants need customers. However, to make the retail project work, the developer must understand who those customers are and where they come from. Unlike residential or office properties, which can be analyzed more from straightforward demographic data, the developer needs to know more than the simple fact that customers for the tenants in its proposed center exist; he also needs to have a concept about how to attract those customers to his project and into his tenants' stores. The shopping center developer has to know more about business conditions and retailing trends than do developers of other types of real estate projects. To put financial decision-making in perspective in order to analyze Regent's development of the Fox Valley Auto Care Center, it is necessary to think about these business objectives more broadly.

[1] A Developer's Perspective

The first part of the following article sets the stage for the work that the developer must do in making his financial analysis of the project. In a later portion of this same article, which appears in Chapter 2, *infra*, the authors apply financial principles to explain how they decide when to undertake a proposed shopping center development.

Ron Sher & Merritt Sher,
Developing and Investing in Local and Community Centers and Highway Retail,
***in* Shopping Centers and Other Retail Properties**
(John R. White & Kevin D. Gray eds., 1996)*

There are rapid changes taking place today that impact local and community center and highway retail development in many ways. The changes range from environmental and land use regulations, to the flexibility of credit markets and the availability of financing. Consumer demands and attitudes are driving retailers to change their formats, as are changes in technology and distribution. Customers demand more every day as they seek better values, improved systems, more convenience, and more sophisticated presentation. This means that today's retail developer must understand marketing, merchandising, critical mass, circulation, synergy, and aesthetics in addition to the more traditional aspects of the development process.

---

* This article is reprinted from Shopping Centers and Other Retail Properties, edited by John R. White and Kevin D. Gray in association with the Urban Land Institute. Copyright © 1996 John Wiley & Sons, Inc., Publisher. Reprinted by permission of John Wiley & Sons, Inc.

These rapid and ongoing changes can have a profound effect on the viability of retail property. The retail property that just a few short years ago was considered a valuable asset that would only increase in value may now be a vacant property with little hope for the future. On the other hand, some properties have appreciated dramatically in the midst of all this change, thriving as they adapt to the forces that mold the evolution of retail.

Today's developer is challenged at every turn throughout the entire investment and development process. One way to better understand the complexities and hazards of the developer's journey from land acquisition to the establishment of a thriving shopping center is to relate the retail development process to the categories in a pro forma statement of development expense and operating income. These familiar tools will serve as especially useful metaphors, since they quantify all aspects of the development process and are applicable to an assortment of retail types. Simplified pro formas for a hypothetical neighborhood shopping center are included as exhibits in this chapter. As much as 95% accuracy can be achieved with such pro formas if the information they convey is supplied by a knowledgeable decision maker, with adequate due diligence.

HISTORICAL PERSPECTIVE

Starting after World War II, the downtown core was comprised of department stores, small retailers, restaurants, service businesses, and public buildings. People shopping and gathering at that time were to a large extent centered downtown. When automobile usage became so widespread after World War II, the nature of retail started to change dramatically. First to evolve were the highway commercial stores, which opened at random locations for the convenience of motorists. Later, the shopping center developed. This was an agglomeration of stores that usually included a place to purchase food.

Actually, retail merchandising and retail real estate development evolved in tandem — when one changed, so did the other. For example, as retailers moved out of the downtown core, suitable real estate became more plentiful and less expensive. People had more mobility. Stores grew. A small grocer had a 10,000-square-foot supermarket. The 10,000-square-foot supermarket then grew into a 25,000-square-foot supermarket. This 25,000-square-foot model was basically the retail standard for the 20-year period from about 1955 to 1975. It became the anchor for retail commercial development and marked the birth of the neighborhood center, which was closer to the suburban population. As these communities grew, the neighborhood center was joined by the community center; it was distinguished not only by size, but also by the range of services supplied. Principally, the arrival of this type of center meant that merchants now sold soft goods as well as services and food. The first neighborhood centers were approximately 6 to 8 acres, while community centers were approximately 20 to 30 acres. The large regional center . . . was the next to evolve.

At first, as the neighborhood and community centers grew, other elements of downtown retail moved to them, especially the small retailers, or "mom-and-pop" stores. There would be one, two, perhaps three large anchors (in those days totaling 20,000 or 25,000 square feet) in a center, while stores of 1,000 to 3,000 square feet would be plentiful. Generally, the small spaces paid considerably higher rent than did the anchors. There would be some intermediate-size tenants

(5,000 to 10,000 square feet) and they would pay rents between the small stores and anchors. The profit in a project generally came from the small stores.

Changes continued in retail, and the small stores began to disappear. Over time, specialty stores grew from 2,000 to 5,000 square feet, then climbed to 10,000 or 20,000 square feet. Today, for example, the new sporting goods prototypes are 43,000 square feet. This change and growth played havoc with many small mom-and-pop stores. Even within the sporting goods category, specialty retailers have split up into stores of 5,000 feet or more that specialized in categories such as golf or bicycles. Some small, individual stores, such as fly fishing shops or climbing shops, continue to exist, but even these very specialized stores are finding it harder and harder to compete.

As the nature of the tenants continued to change, so did the shopping centers. Some of the stores that began to specialize in categories derived from the department stores started moving from downtown out to the highway commercial areas. Then in the mid-1960s came the concept of taking those category tenants, which we called promotional tenants, and aggregating them in a promotional center, a term that Terranomics (the authors' company) trademarked. The promotional tenants were the forerunner of the "category killer." They specialized in categories of 5,000 to 10,000 square feet; occasionally they were smaller, as in the case of Wallpapers to Go. The promotional center usually took these tenants, all destination retailers, and grouped them in a dynamic retail center that ranged from 20,000 to 100,000 square feet. This was one of the first centers that was not anchored by a market or drugstore of 30,000 square feet or more, and it set the tone for some of the more recent developments. As the size of those specialty retailers grew, they acquired the name category killer. The name reflected both function and form: They specialized in a category, had a complete selection at a good price, provided knowledgeable service, and were destination retailers. They also were "killer" competition for other tenants.

BIRTH OF THE POWER CENTER

With the growth in size of category killers, the power center was born. In 1984, 280 Metro in Colma, California, was developed by Terranomics, the first "power center." This was the next logical step: Assembling a collection of larger tenants on a big piece of property. The power center also came to include a limited number of smaller interest tenants, such as restaurants and yogurt shops, as a convenience for customers. The result was a center with the power and strength to draw people from a long way for destination shopping. Power centers were generally located near freeways on a high-visibility site, which encouraged people to travel long distances to shop there.

After power centers came the "big boxes," which include Price/Costco, Home Depot, and Sam's. (Big boxes are sometimes called power parks when they exist in clusters designed to make them more attractive to city dwellers.) Offshoots of the various categories also were developed. Some promotional centers focused on one product type, such as home, apparel, or recreational products. Then came the outlet center, most often located far from regionals since the tenants were usually manufacturers, and department stores did not want to compete with their manufacturers.

Originally, shopping centers were defined as neighborhood, community, and regional shopping centers, but these definitions no longer work today. Community centers and power centers are now the two dominant terms for shopping centers in the industry. There are far more community shopping centers than power centers, which have received the bulk of public attention because they are so innovative. Yet, the community center, anchored by a supermarket, drug chain, and (in some instances) a junior department store, remains a strong and viable competitor. The old regional center of less than one million square feet often has been reconfigured to become a form of community center. A power center, on the other hand, is more than 300,000 square feet, and serves a trade area of 100,000 people or more. Its principal tenants are the large promotion retailers and the big boxes.

Lifestyle centers — a concept that we believe to be one of the biggest shopping center development opportunities through the year 2005 — is basically a type of center or store where consumers can purchase items that define who they are, how they live, and what they believe in. The Grove at Shrewsbury, developed by Terranomics in Shrewsbury, New Jersey, is a 145,000-square-foot lifestyle center that offers activities and merchandise that are personally relevant to shoppers. The stores there include Williams Sonoma, Victoria's Secret, the Limited, Gap Kids, Ann Taylor, and Eddie Bauer — all typical of lifestyle retailers. This constellation of retailers appeals to a strong market segment comprised of shoppers with discretionary income who are attracted to these products.

For the purpose of this chapter, everything other than community centers, power centers, outlet centers, and regional centers will be considered convenience retail, highway retail, or special situation retail. Centers need not be true to type. A good developer can mix, and often should, components of each.

WHAT MAKES A GOOD LOCATION

Because the initial investment decision is so important, consider some factors that influence it. The first might be location, but to mention location alone is simplistic: what is a great location for one type of project might not work at all for another. Location is so complex it could be the subject of an entire book.

Some of the simple fundamentals of location include visibility, access, proximity to neighborhoods, and traffic patterns: Is it on the going-home or going-to-work side of the street? What is happening in and to the neighborhood? It is important to know if a location is right for a particular project. It must be convenient to the neighborhood and accessible to the population it serves. The size, demographics, and the amount and quality of the competition are also important.

With location, there is a trade-off between convenience and regionality. It generally is better to be convenient. However, when a larger trade area is being served, the location must be reasonably convenient to the expanded trade area. Major shopping trips are encouraged when both the project and the stores are larger. Big stores do well in destination locations serving larger trade areas; whereas small stores do not unless they are well located in an integrated regional shopping experience. Stores that are frequented more often can exist in smaller trade areas, but that same location may be too small a trade area for a larger store. A good location for either type of retailer is generally in a commercial pocket. In some cases, the project itself may be large enough to create the pocket. This, for example, explains why the power center needs to locate in a larger trade area at an interstate highway site.

The process of choosing a location can begin several ways. The developer may begin with a project in mind, then look for a location; or begin with a location in mind and look for a project. To effectively maximize economic gain and create a development that will endure, the site should be matched with its best use. A small project in the heart of a community would generally be a neighborhood site. A large piece by a freeway interchange would more often be a power center, entertainment center, location for big boxes, or a combination thereof.

Retail property with the best location is generally the most valuable. This rule usually applies unless the more powerful tenants locate elsewhere. Then the property that has the strongest critical mass is the most valuable. If better retailers locate on a lesser property, the owner of the best real estate could be in trouble. You have a better chance to recover when you have the best property. There are many times when weaker retailers survive on the best property, but they prevent the best location from functioning as the best property.

Other than the requirement (in some instances) for different types of sites, the guidelines for the location of community centers, power centers, and other retail projects are similar. However, there are very few absolute rules — only guidelines.

When identifying sites for successful shopping centers, the proposed use must be considered. In addition, the following criteria are important:

1. *Appropriate Critical Mass.* Is the project big enough to draw the traffic necessary to make it successful? Size is very much a function of use. Is it big enough for its intended use (*i.e.*, can it accommodate enough tenants to provide the consumer with a selection)? This determination is based on the subsequent site selection criteria. Sometimes a project that is too small for the site will fail but would have succeeded had it been larger.

2. *Traffic Circulation.* How accessible is the site? How fast is the traffic? Is it too fast? Or too slow? Is it on continuous right turn or is it a difficult left turn? Also, how easy or difficult is it to exit?

3. *Visibility.* Can the property easily be seen to allow enough time to turn in? Even if the use is a known destination, the shopper likes to be able to see where he or she is going. Does the location of the building itself have a presence and an ease about it that makes it a comfortable destination?

4. *Site Planning.* This involves circulation on the site. It must be relatively easy to park near the stores. There must be enough parking, so that customers will expect to find a space. It must be very easy to get in and out and must not be dangerous. This does not mean that all of the people must be able to park all of the time. The ratio of parking to retailers will vary.

5. *Signage.* The signage must have appropriate impact. Signs should be easily visible, and they must be of the size and graphic presentation to reflect the appropriate store image. This includes balancing the needs of tenants with the scale of the center. The signs must relate in a way that makes the store entrances and the stores appear inviting and hospitable. They must relate to the building so that the store looks large enough and

the relationship with its neighbors appears appropriate. Signage that is too uniform tends to make the center look dull and boring. Pylon signs should be located to draw attention to the center and major tenants. They are not necessary unless visibility is weak.

6. *Exterior Elevations.* The major stores should have a strong individual identity, but that identity should relate in an interesting way to adjacent stores. The customer should be able to get a slightly different feeling in different parts of the center. Smaller stores that have similar markets can be grouped together with similar types of building design and signage elements. The colors and the elevations should add interest to the center. Even the smaller stores, if possible, should have interesting, individualized characteristics. The big stores should be designed to have a presence that reflects their size, and the smaller stores to look inviting but smaller. Visibility is very important to tenants, as is presence, and it is difficult to lease a large store that does not look large. Only so much presence can be provided, and it should be allocated to the greatest square footage.

7. *Tenant Mix.* Does the project have a unique authority that gives it drawing power beyond what would normally be expected on this site? A number of factors influence the draw. The strongest concentration of the best retailers that appeal to the same customers will expand it. A center with a specialty focus tends to boost the draw. The more interesting the tenant mix, the more unique the identity and the larger the draw. Mix also can serve to fill the deficiencies in nearby shopping centers. This will make all of the centers stronger and tends to create a shopping district comprised of several shopping centers. As a corollary, shoppers like to get used to driving in the same traffic patterns. If there is a good mix, they will drive it more often.

8. *Security.* Do people feel secure going to this property day and night? Lost night-time business can cause a project to fail.

9. *Environment/Site Feasibility.* You must determine whether the site can be developed. Will you be able to get the zoning approvals and buildings permits that you require? Is it a site that will be controversial? Was it a toxic waste dump? Will there be flood plain issues? Traffic issues also should be considered. Ask yourself if the use you have in mind is one that the community will accept. Do you intuitively think that? Here your gut feeling is very important. Time is money, and working on a project — especially if you have put hard money down — can be a mistake. Trust your intuitions and don't pursue a project that you doubt will work.

10. *Zoning and Enactments.* Zoning and enactments can take a long time and may involve a great risk, but when successful can be very profitable. The best approach is to buy the property only if successful in obtaining the desired zoning and enactments, but this strategy requires controlling the property with an option or contingencies for a long time. The process can tie up capital and organization. It is almost a separate business operation in many cases; and projects requiring re-zoning, changes in a comprehensive plan, variances and enactments should be carefully considered.

11. *Pre-Leasing.* If a project meets the criteria described in (9) and there is a very strong confidence level, a pool of equity or a lot of cash, and a very tight market, then a developer might consider going ahead without pre-leasing. But when financing is necessary, or any doubts remain, then pre-leasing is a necessity. Sixty percent pre-leasing on a project is usually sufficient, but on rare occasions an exceptional site may be purchased without a tenant.

MODERATING RISK

When considering development, you must consider risk. The more risk, the more return will be required. Also, the more risk, the more difficult it is to obtain financing. Many believe that there is a direct relationship between risk and reward in development. This relationship, in fact, often is not the case. Usually the use for a parcel and the rents a retailer can pay in a project have a maximum level, and the development risks can be mitigated with little impact on return. Control risks: zoning, environmental, leasing, construction, financing. Controlling these risks does not necessarily mean less return.

The best way to control most of these risks is to have a sufficient feasibility period, under a purchase option with extension provisions, when buying the property. Hopefully, the developer will be able to build the project as planned, while discovering environmental problems, zoning and traffic problems, and often building-permit problems, before assuming ownership. A purchase option also allows pre-leasing during the option period; this is the time to arrange financing.

Usually it is not possible to have everything perfectly arranged prior to closing. At some point, you must assess the risks and close the purchase, pay significant nonrefundable dollars, or possibly lose the property. Often a quick purchase results in a better price. This usually increases your return, but it also increases risk. If concessions are wanted from the seller, you normally have to make a reciprocal concession, and frequently that concession is to pay more for the property — often the full asking price. One tactic when negotiating the purchase of land for a new development is to offer the full asking price and negotiate on the terms and conditions. The developers who have done well are the ones who controlled their risks and built sound projects, rather than those who speculated on land.

TYPES OF DEVELOPERS

For the sake of explanation, we will distinguish between the proactive and reactive developer. (Most developers are a mix.) Usually the proactive developer operates from one of the following perspectives when looking for land:

1. *Project-Driven.* These developers want to do a project in a certain area, and thus look for a parcel of land there. In this case, developers usually have in mind the type and size of investment and property they are looking for, and this will guide the search. For example, you may feel that there is a need for a small automotive center in a certain neighborhood, so you would look for a site of up to 2 acres. You may just be motivated by a general shortage of retail, higher than normal rents, low cost, strong demand, or a shortage of services. There would be a specific reasons for identifying a certain area as the right site for a profitable project. A key player in this arena is Homart, which builds more power centers nationally than any other

developer. Its ties to Sears provide this company with a built-in system for developing many projects and also keep it well capitalized.

2. *Tenant-Driven.* Here, the developer is working with a tenant. This can either be seeking a location for a tenant or even sites specified by the tenant. It may be a build-to-suit, a remodel, or a purchase. This potential site could incorporate additional tenants. In fact, the tenant may wish to anchor a center, or at least be the catalyst for one. In this case, the demographics and selection criteria would be based on the needs of the tenant. Often, the developer can create business by working with a tenant to help them penetrate areas. At times the tenant may even be a partner with the developer on these projects. We have worked on joint ventures with The Gap, Starbucks, and Millers Outpost. Kornwasser Friedman is a tenant-driven developer that works in tandem with Price Club, developing new outlets nationally for this warehouse store. The alliance enables Kornwasser Friedman to raise money for development by soliciting Price Club shareholders, thus leveraging off of a publicly traded company to fund major projects nationally.

3. *Land-Driven.* This is the perspective of the developer who may own, control, or be fascinated by a piece of land that is sitting fallow and who wants to determine how to make it productive. How often have we seen the sign, "Will Build to Suit"? Possibly the developer knows something advantageous about the land or has a relationship with the owner, a neighbor, or government officials. Or the site can have a special characteristic like a view or water setting. Alexander Haagen, for example, is a land-driven developer in Southern California skilled at identifying and transforming intriguing pieces of land to interesting power and community centers. This developer has a given sense of what interests retailers and can put together projects with unique characteristics determined by a specific marketplace. An example of this is the old Sears building on Geary Street in San Francisco, which was transformed into a promotional center offering major retailers that included Mervyns, The Good Guys, and Toys R Us.

Instead of being proactive and looking for land, the developer also can be reactive — as when an interesting and available piece of land or project is presented to you. Then the developer may ask such questions as, "Is this the type of ground I would want to use for the kind of project I would like to build?" or "Is it right for a tenant I know?"

A piece of property doesn't always come in a nice, neat package. In fact, if it did it probably wouldn't be there anymore — at least not if it is in the path of development or obvious fill-in. Usually there are problems, such as zoning, access, easement, environmental, and ownership. It may be too small, not have enough frontage, or the configuration may be wrong. It may have environmental or title issues. However, overcoming these problems also creates opportunities, especially if you see a solution that is obvious to no one else. Controlling a piece of property gives you a comparative advantage. It may be necessary to assemble two- or three-piece parcels. Is one parcel key to the assemblage? Can you tie up that property long enough to acquire the other two or three? Possibly a building can be torn down. A tenant's lease may be expiring. Can you relocate a tenant to help recapture a building and create an assemblage? Can you arrange joint-use parking with an adjacent parcel? Sometimes there are special costs attached to land acquisition, including buying out existing tenants, demolishing existing buildings, or being in a situation where the buyer rather than the seller pays the commission. Despite such costs and the many questions that always should be asked, when you spot the opportunity you must do what is necessary to capitalize on it. Remember that parcels rarely come in nice neat packages, and problems can create opportunities.

In-Fill Development

Certainly one example of this is in-fill development, that is, filling in after the obvious sites are done and development has been substantially completed. In-fill development presents interesting possibilities and often results in some of the best projects. However, it usually requires more creativity. Generally such a property has unusual circumstances and often is in its second or third incarnation. This often leads to special problems, including environmental issues, demolition, lease encumbrances, municipal covenants, and multiple ownerships. But in-fill properties, if chosen wisely, are less likely to be subject to variations in the economy or future over-supply of retail, which in the long term can be harmful to retail's strength and value. We, particularly in our lending company, prefer in-fill or urban locations — projects in dense areas without more competitive rates available for retail. Projects in the path of development often are more of a commodity. There is plenty of land available and only so much rent a retail site can command. Thus margins will be tighter, and you are faced with competition from others possibly doing a similar project.

Are Pads a Sound Idea?

Another item to consider with local, community, and highway retail development is whether or not to sell pads. Pads are small outparcels, but part of the major tract, which are usually located at curbside and which may be sold or leased. Selling off pads is often short-sighted and can be detrimental for many reasons, including a loss of control. Future purchasers will want to control the entire property, and this will affect the price. If you lose control of what happens on the pad, pads can devalue the entire center. The amount of square footage on the pad is usually only a small fraction of that of the center, but it can block visibility and make the land less efficient for parking. While the sale of pads may provide more equity, in terms of the overall project, it is usually very expensive equity in the long term. A poorly developed pad in front of a center can negatively affect the state of the entire property behind it.

Free-Standing Retail

Developing a free-standing retail building for a single user on a highway may appear simple, and there is no doubt that it is less complicated than developing a shopping center. However, many of the same issues arise, including a decision on the location, determining the feasibility, controlling the property, and determining who the tenant is before construction begins and preferably before the property is purchased. Permitting has become a major problem for developers. Certainly one of the most important considerations is to re-lease such a building. To speculatively build a free-standing building rarely makes sense. Financing would be impossible, and the building might not be exactly right for the tenant that does come along. There may be no cash flow for a significant time, and the use of borrowed money means a negative cash flow.

When constructing a free-standing retail building it is extremely important to consider the tenants' credit. Credit becomes less important as the tenants' proportion of the project decreases. The terms of the lease also are important, and the tenant should not have kick-outs. In the greatest extreme, leases should be true triple net, with all operating costs and taxes the responsibility of the tenant. Even if the tenant is strong, but particularly if they are not, it is important that the building generally be useable for another tenant. It is hard to lease a White Castle, a Shari's, or an IHOP to just anybody. When determining if a building with rent substantially above market rent is a profitable investment, always discount the over-market rent due to the cost of any specialized tenant improvements paid by the landlord.

The dollars-per-square-foot cost of a free-standing retail building can sustain the market value of the building. There is a limit to what price per square foot a certain project or market can sustain. So, when determining the value of a property, rent should be discounted significantly, which is achieved by landlord concessions such as high tenant improvement allowances or free rent. However, because there is an income stream, rent should not be discounted completely. Tenant inducements increase the cost per square foot of a project, and lenders and investors are more comfortable with a lower cost per square foot.

[2] Note on What Motivates a Developer

As we consider the development of the Fox Valley Auto Care Center, think about the motivations of the two developers, Regent and Metropolitan. Metropolitan, on the one hand, is clearly interested in the land. It originally assembled a very large parcel on which it built the Westfield Fox Valley Shopping Center, which is a regional shopping mall. Now, it is interested in developing the land that it owns in the area immediately contiguous to the mall. Regent, on the other hand, is an end use developer that is interested in leasing up the retail space it plans to build. They are both "developers," but their goals are quite different.

§ 1.03 THE ROLE OF THE DEVELOPER'S LAWYER

We now address the related issues of just how much the developer's lawyer needs to understand about the deal and what the lawyer should do with that knowledge.

[1] Making Lawyers Deal Lawyers

Tina L. Stark,
Thinking Like a Deal Lawyer,
54 J. Legal Educ. 223 (June, 2004)*

I am a former corporate partner at Chadbourne & Parke, where I had a broad-based transactional practice with an emphasis on acquisitions, dispositions, recapitalizations, and financings. There I was repeatedly frustrated by the new associates' lack of sophistication about business and business deals. One day I

---

made the mistake of articulating that concern at a corporate partners' meeting. The Powers That Be swiftly assigned me the task of turning the neophytes into sophisticates. It was then that I first began to develop a model for teaching students and associates to be transactional lawyers.

That model begins with the proposition that doing deals is fundamentally different from litigating, in terms of both the skills used and the substantive knowledge required. This applies at the most basic level — that is, what it means to think like a lawyer. Although the academy prides itself on teaching students to think like a lawyer, for the most part we teach students to think like litigators. To teach our students to be deal lawyers, we must teach them to think like deal lawyers. . . .

I. Translating the Business Deal into Contract Concepts

The analytic skill that litigators use is different from the one that deal lawyers use. Specifically, litigators use the analytic skill that we teach in our first-year courses. There we teach students to take the law and apply it to the facts to create a persuasive argument. That argument is then memorialized in a brief or a memo or is otherwise used to sway another, be it the other party or the court. The paradigm is one in which the litigators seek a certain legal result by working backwards from the law to a static set of facts. The analytic skill of deal lawyers stands this paradigm on its head.

Deal lawyers start from the business deal. The terms of the business deal are the deal lawyer's facts. The lawyer must then find the contract concepts that best reflect the business deal and use those concepts as the basis of drafting the contract provisions. I call this skill "translating the business deal into contract concepts." Mastering it is the first steppingstone to becoming a deal lawyer. All else flows from this skill. It is the foundation of a deal lawyer's professional expertise and problem-solving ability. Without it, negotiating and drafting are abstractions.

Two simple hypotheticals bring the different skills into relief. Imagine that a driver is going eighty miles an hour and hits a pedestrian; the pedestrian dies, and his heirs bring a lawsuit against the driver. The legal issue is whether the driver was negligent. To determine that, we teach students to look at the components of the cause of action for negligence and then to see whether each of the components can be matched up with the facts. The law is applied to the facts. That is the litigator's analytic skill.

To illustrate the deal lawyer's analytic skill, I will use an exercise from my drafting course. The exercise entails two students negotiating the purchase of a used car. . . .

The negotiation begins with the buyer asking basic questions about the car. What make and model is it? How many miles has it been driven? Has the car been in any accidents? Once the seller has answered all the buyer's questions, I ask the students how they would incorporate the seller's responses into the contract. Stated otherwise, how would they translate the business deal into contract concepts?

Inevitably, the students are taken aback and give me blank stares — if they even dare lift up their eyes from their papers. But they are not at fault for not knowing that the answer is representations and warranties. Unfortunately, most of them have never discussed these concepts in the context of a sophisticated commercial agreement. Instead, they undoubtedly learned about misrepresentations in torts and about warranties in connection with the Uniform Commercial Code Article 2. The students are also at a loss because the way of thinking is new to them.

To further see the translation skill in action, imagine that the seller has told the buyer that the car has been driven exactly 50,000 miles. Imagine further that the buyer tells his lawyer that he does not want to buy the car on the closing date if the car has been driven more than an additional 500 miles. Once again, there is a business goal, and the question is how to translate that goal into contract concepts and then into contract provisions.

To answer the question, the deal lawyer must analyze the goal from both a business and a legal perspective. The answer requires that the contract have three separate provisions, each interlocking with the next. Each provision implicates a different contract concept.

First, the seller would need to represent and warrant to the buyer the number of miles the car has been driven as of the signing date. This representation and warranty provides a base-line measurement, induces the buyer to enter into the transaction, and provides a basis for a cause of action if it is false. The seller is at risk of liability if its statement is false.

Next, the seller would have to covenant that the car would not be driven more than 500 miles between the signing and the closing. This covenant picks up on a timeline at the point where the representation and warranty left off. The representation and warranty spoke as of a moment in time (the signing of the contract). The covenant goes forward in time from the signing until the closing. It protects the buyer because it is a promise which, if broken, gives the buyer the right to sue for damages.

Finally, the contract would need to include a condition precedent that the buyer would not be obligated to close unless all of the covenants had been performed; that is, the buyer would not have to buy the car on the closing date if the car had been driven more than 500 additional miles. Thus, to protect the client properly, the deal lawyer must have analyzed the business transaction and recognized that there were three different points on the timeline from the signing to closing and that adequate protection for the client required a different contract protection at each point on the timeline. Again, the desired business result determines the contract concepts to be used. The law and business are inextricably intertwined.

Upon completing the car purchase exercise, students can understand a point that is fundamental to their education as transactional lawyers: there is an underlying similarity to all contracts. Their structure is composed of representations, warranties, covenants, and conditions precedent. They are the contract's building blocks. Therefore, the translation skill applies not only to a car purchase agreement and an employment agreement, but also to a multibillion-dollar acquisition agreement, a license agreement, and a construction contract.

When learning the translation skill, students must learn not only the legal aspects of a contract concept, but also its business purpose. So the class studies the role of representations and warranties as a risk allocation mechanism.

Initially, the students look at risk allocation in the context of the car seller's representation and warranty that the car has been driven exactly 50,000 miles. That representation and warranty is what deal lawyers call "a flat representation." It is precise and without any wiggle room, and it is a high-risk statement for the seller. If the number of miles is even slightly wrong, the seller is potentially liable for damages. To reduce the seller's risk, the representation and warranty must be qualified. For example, the seller could state that the car had been driven *approximately* 50,000 miles. Now, a minor difference in the number of miles will not impose liability on the seller. Because this change reduces the seller's risk, more risk has now been allocated to the buyer. If the car has been driven 51,000 miles, the buyer may or may not be able to make a successful claim for misrepresentation and breach of warranty. It all depends on what "approximately" means.

Because of the importance of the risk allocation concept, the class also looks at a more sophisticated example — a series of alternative representations and warranties that show how a buyer and seller might negotiate a "no litigation" representation and warranty. The first representation is flat. It states as an absolute that the seller is not a party to any litigation and that there are no threatened litigations against the seller. This representation and warranty, of course, puts all the risk on the seller. If there is even one threatened litigation, the seller is liable.

The next representation and warranty refers to a disclosure schedule that lists any existing or threatened litigations. ("Except as set forth on Schedule 3.10, there are no existing or threatened litigations.") The remainder of the representations and warranties gradually shift the risk with respect to threatened litigations from the seller to the buyer.

- To the knowledge of the Seller, there are no threatened litigations.
- To the knowledge of the officers of the Seller, there are no threatened litigations.
- To the knowledge of the executive officers of the Seller, there are no threatened litigations.
- To the knowledge of A, B, and C, there are no threatened litigations.

In each instance, the pool of knowledge for which the seller is responsible becomes progressively smaller; the seller's risk diminishes and the buyer's risk increases. As the students work through this exercise, they begin to see that the translation process is not a mechanical one. Thinking like a deal lawyer is nuanced. . . .

II. Adding Value to the Deal

Translating the business deal into contract concepts is only one aspect of thinking like a deal lawyer. The better deal lawyers are able to look at a transaction from the client's perspective and add value to the deal. Looking at a contract from the client's perspective means understanding what the client wants to achieve and the risks it wants to avoid. "Adding value to the deal" is a euphemism for "finding and resolving business issues." These skills are problem-solving skills and are an integral component of a deal lawyer's professional expertise. They require a sophisticated understanding not only of substantive law, but also of business, the client's business, and the transaction at hand. At a law firm, having these skills is generally the province of the partners, and not necessarily all of them.

In a totally unscientific survey, I asked partners how they identified business issues. These are some of the responses:

- Identifying business issues requires a sixth sense.
- A business issue is any issue you find that the client should resolve.
- You know one when you see one.

The gist of these answers is that the partners learned how to discern business issues from experience. If this is so, how do we teach law students to find business issues? Aren't the business issues in an acquisition agreement different from those in an employment agreement? What could we possibly teach students that would enable them to find business issues in agreements as diverse as a license agreement and a power purchase agreement?

Such pessimism is unwarranted. A careful analysis of a cross-section of agreements reveals that five business issues recur in most agreements. With an understanding of these issues, the student (or lawyer) is better able to analyze the transaction and to recognize how each of the issues manifests itself in a particular agreement. The five issues are money, risk, control, standards, and endgame. They are the five prongs of the business issue framework. . . .

Virtually all agreements have issues related to *money*: purchase price, interest rates, time value of money, or earn-out calculations. Lawyers can often add value by using their practice-specific expertise. For example, if a corporation is entering into a broker arrangement in connection with the purchase of a jet, the lawyer may be able to draw upon her expertise and note that the brokerage fee is outside the normal range.

The second prong is *risk*. Representations and warranties, covenants, and conditions precedent are all risk allocation mechanisms. How they are negotiated directly affects a client's risk in a transaction. Risk can also manifest itself in multiple other ways in a transaction. First, a contract can raise the specter of tort liability — fraudulent inducement, product liability, or tortious interference with contract. Second, the provisions can create contract risk. For example, a noncompete, liquidated damages, or an indemnity provision could be unenforceable. Third, a contract could create the risk of statutory liability. A classic example is liability under the securities laws. Finally, risk could be inherent in the transaction. Credit risk is a salient example.

Ferreting out risks is not usually a problem for most lawyers. They have been taught issue spotting. But if that is all that a lawyer does, she will justly earn a reputation as a deal killer. To be effective, she must assess the probability that a risk will occur and, if it is significant, find a way to limit it.

The third business issue is *control*. In analyzing control as a business issue, the initial inquiry must be whether having control is good or bad from a client's perspective. The answer is fact dependent. For example, limited partners are entitled to limited liability because they exercise no control over the limited partnership. In this context, lack of control is good. But limited partners generally do not want to abdicate to the general partner all control over their investment. They want the right to make decisions to protect their investment. Therefore, the limited partners will seek as much control as the general partner will tolerate and as much as they can accrete without becoming general partners under the relevant state law. Control is a two-edged sword for limited partners.

Control is always an issue when there is risk. To add value, a deal lawyer must recognize the risk and then determine how to control or diminish it.

The fourth prong of the framework is *standards*. Virtually every word in a contract is a standard. There are both macro and micro standards. For example, every representation and warranty establishes a standard of liability. If the standard is not met, the recipient of the representation and warranty may sue the maker. This is a macro standard. But that macro standard can be changed at the micro level. By changing a word or a phrase in a representation and warranty, the standard changes. Are property, plant, and equipment in *good* repair, *customary* repair, or *in compliance with industry standards?*

Covenants and conditions precedent are also standards, as is every adjective (*material* contracts) and adverb (*promptly* deliver). Definitions are also standards (how a financial ratio is defined determines the standard to be incorporated into a loan covenant). A deal lawyer adds value by recognizing when a standard is inappropriate and by negotiating an alternative that more accurately reflects the client's business goals.

The last prong is *endgame*. Every transaction ends. It may end happily or unhappily. The relationship between a banker and its borrower can end with the loan repaid in full (happy) or with the borrower in default (unhappy). If a trademark license agreement ends, the contract must provide for, among other things, a mechanism for determining how and when the licensee should make the final payments, as well as instructions for what the licensee should do with any remaining merchandise. Endgame provisions are some of the most significant provisions in a contract because they often involve money — a topic near and dear to most clients' hearts.

[2] Real Estate Lawyers

M. Jay Yurow, *Commercial Real Estate Transactions*, 14 The Compleat Lawyer 42 (Spring, 1997)*

Whether a client is buying or selling, lawyers who handle commercial real estate transactions need much more than a firm handshake. They need a solid grasp of the issues — financing, taxes, titles, surveys — as well as an almost omniscient ability to assess the other side's intentions.

Representing the Seller

The range of the issues to be considered when representing a seller typically is more limited than those that must be addressed when representing a purchaser. Unlike the purchaser, the seller does not have the burden of determining whether the property is suitable. Nor does the seller have to worry about how to finance the acquisition of the property or what form of entity is most appropriate for holding title.

In many instances, the fundamental concerns of the seller are actually rather straightforward. Virtually all sellers would like the sale to be on an "as is" basis to minimize the risk that the purchaser might have claims for defects that are not discovered until after the closing. For much the same reason, sellers also prefer to limit the representations and warranties they make in the contract. Because retaining the deposit is often the seller's only remedy for a purchaser default, sellers want the deposit posted by the purchaser to be as large as possible and "at risk" at the earliest possible date. Finally, because most contracts provide that the seller bears the risk that the property will suffer no damage between the date the contract is signed and the closing, sellers generally want the closing to occur as quickly as possible.

Transaction costs. While the division of transaction and other costs is often based on local custom, there is usually no reason these costs cannot be shared in some other manner. Because the amounts involved can be substantial, you and your client should pay particular attention to the allocation of costs associated with roll-back taxes, special assessments, proffers, and broker commissions. It will be helpful if you can discuss the allocation of all costs with your client before contract negotiations begin. Otherwise, you run the risk of having to deal with an angry or disappointed client who receives a smaller check than anticipated.

Taxing matters. Before contract negotiations become too involved, you should discuss the tax implications of the transaction with your client. If your client does not understand the tax consequences of the sale and you are not able to advise your client on this topic, you and your client should meet with a tax lawyer or accountant to determine whether adverse tax consequences can be mitigated by structuring the transaction in a particular fashion.

Financing. One of the more difficult dynamics for an inexperienced client to comprehend is that the timing of a transaction is often dictated by a third party — the lender. If your client, as the seller, is willing to offer purchase money financing to the purchaser, it can retain greater control over the closing date, but must understand and be prepared to accept both the risk of being a lender and the added complexity of introducing the lender/borrower dimension into the negotiations.

A second advantage of seller-financing is that it removes one very significant variable from the contract negotiations — the financing contingency. This contingency is commonly required by purchasers who have not already secured a commitment for financing. If the purchaser cannot obtain financing, the contingency is not satisfied, the deposit is generally returned, and the purchaser is relieved of its obligation to complete the transaction. If a financing contingency is included in the contract, make sure that it contains specific guidelines about the financing terms that the purchaser must accept and the time period in which the purchaser must satisfy the contingency. . . .

Be realistic. Perhaps the most difficult and overlooked task confronting a seller is the need to realistically assess the degree to which the purchaser desires to own the property. Before negotiating a contract, your client should have a clear indication that the purchaser is serious about acquiring the property, has the capacity to perform — that is, to complete the transaction — and has the ability to pay the purchase price at the appropriate time. Ultimately, if the purchaser cannot or will not perform, your client has wasted time and money and may have lost other opportunities that were available.

The Purchaser's Position

A frequent misconception of both clients and lawyers who are not experienced in commercial real estate matters is the belief that the value of a property is ascertained by adding the worth of the land and the improvements. In fact, unless a client intends to use the property for his own purposes, the income generated by a commercial property is at least as important an ingredient in determining its value. If your client intends to finance the acquisition of an income-producing property, be assured that a lender will be as concerned with the quality of the tenants and the leases as it is with the value of the land and improvements.

What form to choose. One of the first issues lawyers for the purchaser must address is how the client should hold title to the property once acquired. Lengthy articles have been written about the advantages and shortcomings of the various entities (partnerships, corporations, and limited liability companies, to name a few) commonly used for holding title to real estate. Make sure you understand both the tax consequences and the liability protections afforded by each in order to help your client select the entity that best suits its needs. Lawyers also should advise the client on whether to commingle the property with other assets or to acquire title to the real estate in the name of a separate, single-purpose entity.

Warranties. A number of issues arise during the negotiation of a sales contract that are of particular concern and interest to the purchaser. While sellers loathe making representations and warranties, purchasers are comforted by the existence of such representations and warranties in the contract. Aside from the breadth and scope of the representations and warranties themselves, also consider the length of time that representations and warranties made by the seller should continue after the closing. Further, remember that the seller (or some person or entity with assets associated with the seller) must be available after closing to answer for any actionable misrepresentations or for the breach of any warranty. The best and most fiercely negotiated representations and warranties will do your client little good if the seller has already distributed all of the cash from the sale and dissolved.

The study period. Before deciding to acquire a property, most purchasers endeavor to collect as much information about the property as they can. While some of your client's due diligence can be done prior to executing a contract, most buyers are understandably reluctant to expend significant sums to investigate a property before it is under contract. Accordingly, much of the due diligence that the purchaser must perform to satisfy itself that the property is desirable or suitable for its purposes is done during that period of time commonly called the "feasibility period" or "study period." There is usually a tension between what the seller wants (a short study period) and what the purchaser desires (a lengthy study period). Counsel your client to be realistic when assessing the length of time that it will need in order to determine that the property satisfies its requirements.

Closing conditions. Understandably, many purchasers desire to instill as much certainty in the acquisition process as possible. While it is helpful that your client have a study period to determine whether or not a rezoning of the property is likely to be approved, it will usually take far more time to actually complete the rezoning. A common solution is to make certain events that are fundamental to the purchaser conditions precedent to the purchaser's obligation to acquire the property. Depending upon the characteristics of the property, and the intended and current uses of the property, the purchaser may want to condition its obligation to acquire the property on the procurement or satisfaction of subdivision, site plan, and zoning approvals, or approval by architectural review boards. If the conditions precedent are not satisfied, your client may have incurred some out-of-pocket expenses, but can be assured that its deposit will be returned and that it will have no further liability to the seller for failing to close.

Title review. Among the studies that your client should undertake during the study period is a review of title. Title reviews are done either by a title abstractor or title company. In either case, an abstractor searches the land records to determine what matters burden or benefit the property and prepares a report of title or a title commitment that lists encumbrances, exceptions, and other matters of record.

Your client can often shift some of the risks of ownership to the title company by obtaining specific endorsements to address particular concerns. For instance, a title company can provide assurance that the property has access to and from a dedicated roadway, or if the property is comprised of two or more parcels, the company can issue an endorsement insuring that the parcels are contiguous. The cost of the endorsements will vary depending upon the jurisdiction and the type of coverage requested. You also should require that beneficial easements (such as an easement over an adjoining parcel that permits access to the property) be included in the description of the insured property, and that all existing mortgage liens, judgments, and similar encumbrances be satisfied and released prior to closing.

The survey. To fully understand the title report or commitment, it may be necessary to have a survey of the property prepared. . . .

Environmental assessments. Unless your client is going to finance the acquisition of the property itself, it will almost certainly need to obtain an environmental site assessment to assure the lender that there is no environmental contamination present. Environmental engineers or consultants can be hired to prepare an environmental audit for the property. If the audit reveals the presence of any hazardous material, you also will need to counsel your client about the risks of owning a property that has environmental defects. If the property is already developed, your client also may want to obtain an architectural or structural engineering report to ensure that the improvements are sound.

Many lenders have a list of approved title companies, surveyors, environmental consultants, and structural engineers. Before you or your client engage a contractor to perform any of these services, make certain that the contractor is on your prospective lender's approved list or is acceptable to the lender. Otherwise, your client runs the risk of having to pay to duplicate the study.

Review of leases. If the property is occupied by tenants, obtain a current rent roll, together with copies of all leases from the seller. Your client will need to review the leases to determine whether the rents being paid by the tenants will cover the costs of owning and operating the property. A review of the leases also is essential in determining what rights the tenants have to renew their leases, expand, or purchase the property. Finally, your client should take a hard look at the identity of the tenants to ascertain whether the tenants are creditworthy and otherwise able to honor the obligations described in their leases. It also is imperative that the purchaser discover whether any of the tenants are in default under their leases and the extent to which the seller has, in the past, alleged the existence of defaults or initiated litigation to deal with the tenants. Frequently, these questions are answered by representations made by the seller in the contract.

Development. If the property is not yet developed, a number of development issues must be considered, including:

- Is the property subdivided?
- Has the property received site plan approval from local officials?
- Is the current zoning appropriate for the purchaser's intended use or does the property need to be rezoned?
- Is the density adequate?
- Does the property have access to and from dedicated roadways?
- Are utilities available to the site and are they in adequate quantities?

Unless each of these questions can be answered affirmatively, your client should understand that it may prove more costly and time consuming to complete the project than was anticipated.

Financing. One concern that all purchasers share is how they will finance the acquisition of the property and, if the site is not developed, the subsequent development and construction. A client that has not secured a commitment for financing should begin discussions with lenders at the earliest possible date. Because the financing terms offered by lenders can vary significantly, the client should meet with at least several lenders to discuss the project and the essential terms on which each lender would agree to make financing available.

To the extent that the purchaser can identify a source of financing early and ascertain the requirements of a particular lender, the purchaser should enlist the assistance of the seller in satisfying some of the lender's requirements. Because the seller has a vested interest in whether the loan closes, it should, within limits, be willing to help the purchaser by providing information and permitting the lender's representatives to have access to the property. You would also do your client a great service by including in the contract a covenant that the seller will cooperate with the lender and the purchaser in satisfying the lender's requirements.

[3] Why the Lawyer Needs to Know the Deal

It is helpful to have a list of possible problem areas before beginning the work of creating the legal structure for the client-proposed transaction. Tina Stark writes about deal lawyers in general, and many of Jay Yurow's points are specific to real estate transactions. Many of the specifics relate to the use which the developer plans to make of the property, and how the proposed use fits with existing uses and restrictions on all or a portion of the property. While the client may have a clear idea of the proposed development, its structural details — the possible versus the ideal — will inevitably require compromises. The message from Tina Stark and

Jay Yurow for real estate transactions is simple: it is essential to know about these problem areas in advance, while the component parts of the proposal can be adjusted without impairing the financial requirements to make the deal work. And if the deal, in the end, will not work, at least not in the way that the parties had planned, it is better to make adjustments up front or even, as a last resort, to call it off. The developer's effort to make certain that the development it has planned will meet its expectations *before* committing to the purchase will inevitably conflict with the wish of the seller of the to-be-developed land to make the sale binding as early as possible.

The legal documents provide the structure for the deal; they will have to reflect the objectives not just of the lawyer's client, but those of the parties with whom the client must deal as well. Consider the parties involved in the transactions to enable Regent to develop the Fox Valley Auto Care Center:

(1) The Johnsons, of course, must agree to sell their property to Regent. While the property has been used for rural residential purposes, the Johnsons may have objectives which, in negotiating with them, you as the representative for the purchaser will have to solve, and do so in a way which is effective for Regent's purposes.

(2) Metropolitan is willing to sell a parcel of land to Regent but only if Metropolitan can buy from Regent some of the Johnson land. Metropolitan also intends that Regent's development will meet the criteria Metropolitan has established for its own development. Moreover, Metropolitan has negotiated approval of its site plan with the local authorities, so Regent's plan will have to meet similar criteria.

(3) Regent intends to develop the site with Turtle Wax, and Turtle Wax's participation in that development is essential. Regent will have to make deals with the Johnsons and Metropolitan (not to mention the local authorities) which will satisfy Turtle Wax as well.

(4) Regent intends to finance the Auto Care Center with a bank loan. In making the agreements with these other parties, Regent must necessarily keep the requirements of a potential lender in mind. Because Regent is searching for a permanent lender while these other negotiations are taking place, it may be difficult to predict what impact the other agreements will have on Regent's ability to make the best deal for debt financing.

If the specifics of this one, fairly simple project (as shopping center developments go) seem convoluted, think ahead about the legal questions which the project will raise. It has been said that real estate development is the most regulated industry in the United States, and you are just beginning to see why that is so. Land use controls by local government inevitably involve not just the specifics of the development, such as the location of roads and utilities and how these elements interact with existing roads and utilities, but significant political questions as well. Often the politics of obtaining approval for a development will require a series of political steps, culminating in the approval by the governing body of the jurisdiction in which the development is located. We will address these directly in Chapter 7. There are also significant environmental control issues, involving both the federal government and local government. We will address the federal regulations in Chapter 8. These requirements mean that Regent must take specific steps in qualifying its development plan, each of which requires planning, research and negotiation, all skills which the real estate lawyer will be expected to bring to the table.

An essential element in this planning is the financial structure of Regent's development. This requires financial planning, making arrangements for financing or contributions by investors, and designing and implementing the legal structure within which the financing is made available for the project. Each step will require knowledge of (or information about) specific legal fields, such as the state law relating to the entity chosen as the vehicle for the development (usually a limited partnership or limited liability company), federal and state laws regulating the issuance of securities and, in particular, federal and state income tax laws. The client may ask for the lawyer's judgment about the value of using one financial arrangement or structure over another, or may rely on the lawyer's knowledge of and experience in the financial markets for guidance about the best way to finance all or part of the project.

For the real estate lawyer, this is a tall order. Often, the lawyer must rely on her own contacts with experience, special expertise or both to develop the information needed to provide the advice requested by the client. At each step, the lawyer's interest should be to advance the client's project — to add value to it. Sometimes, it is helpful merely to ask how a step proposed by the client will do this. We are not suggesting that the lawyer take over the deal. What we are suggesting is that the lawyer needs to understand what the client is doing in order to well represent the client.

§ 1.04 WHY AN AUTO SERVICE CENTER?

As we take you through the creation of the Fox Valley Auto Care Center, from the time the opportunity to do it first appears to disposition, we will show you how and where the special knowledge of the real estate lawyer as planner, negotiator and advisor can advance the client's interest. As we will see, the lawyer's role cannot be limited to acting just as the drafter of the documents, although drafting is a not inconsiderable part of the lawyer's job. First, however, it is time to introduce some more specific characteristics of the type of project involved, and to consider whether the overall concept was a good one.

[1] The Concept that Regent Adopted

Debra Pogrund Stark,
Rules of the Road for Developing a Successful Auto Service Center,
5 J. Real Est. Dev. (Summer, 1989)*

Introduction

An auto service center is similar to a shopping center except that all of the tenants in an auto service center engage in various forms of automotive service and/or repair work. A typical auto service center contains between 15,000 to 45,000 square feet of space and between 5 to 20 retailers. . . .

The Appeal of Auto Service Centers

Consumer Demand

Several developments have occurred which have led to consumer demand for this type of center. The first such development has been the decline in the number of gas stations in America, and in particular, the number of gas stations which offer automotive repair or service work. A second development is that consumers are holding on to their automobiles longer, increasing the age of the average automobile in the United States and, consequently, increasing the demand for repairs. Moreover, increased technological advancements in automotive systems created a need for more specialization in automotive maintenance and repair. One retailer could no longer do it all. Thus, there currently exists an increasing demand for automotive service and repair work, but a declining supply of persons to do such repair and service work. Consumers are seeking new places to have their automobiles serviced and repaired and real estate developers have stepped in to fill this gap.

To make such centers more appealing to consumers, developers should:

1. Locate the centers near other retail areas or near residential areas rather than locating them in fringe industrial areas;

2. Offer such amenities as car washes, common waiting rooms (complete with lounges, TV and coffee), restaurants, beauty shops, and movie theaters;

3. Provide convenient one-stop shopping for all automobile care needs (a typical auto service center includes a car wash, tire store, auto parts store, muffler and brake shop, tune-up shop, oil and lube shop, transmission repair shop, and ancillary stores such as auto glass repair, mobile phone, car stereo and car alarm products, insurance claim center, automotive detailing and car rental); and

4. Provide an aesthetically pleasing atmosphere through landscaping and meticulous cleaning of the centers.

Retailer Demand

A variety of factors make auto service centers attractive to automotive service and repair retailers. The first factor is the location of the centers. In the past, municipalities viewed automobile repair and service retail establishments as an eyesore. Through zoning laws, municipalities prevented such establishments from being located in residential or even commercial areas. Developers, however, have been more successful in convincing municipalities to allow development of auto service centers in residential and commercial locations by creating a neat, clean and attractive center. Second, developers contend that sales by various retailers at the auto service centers will be greater than in their stand-alone stores due to the synergy among the various tenants. Consumers may come to the center for one purpose, but once there they may utilize some of the other services available. Third, by becoming a tenant in an auto service center, the retailer can avoid expending a large capital outlay to build a stand-alone store. In addition, by being a tenant in an auto service center, the retailer can lease precisely the space it requires; while in a stand-alone situation, retailers were sometimes forced to acquire larger space than they needed to satisfy applicable zoning laws. Finally, the factors which cause auto service centers to be appealing to consumers discussed above cause service centers to be appealing to retailers due to the increased traffic to the center.

Developer Interest

The main attraction of auto service centers to real estate developers is that if done properly the return on the developer's investment can be very high. Auto service centers are less complicated and thus cheaper to build than traditional strip malls. With pre-engineering and pre-structuring, auto service centers can be constructed in less than six months for about $50 per square foot, enabling the developers to charge the tenants between $10–$20 per square foot in rent. Assuming that a developer puts in 20% of the project cost as equity and that there is a high level of occupancy, the return on one's investment of $70–$90 per square foot can be in the 16%–25% range.

[2] Notes and Questions About the Auto Service Center Concept

1. Do you think Regent should have more information about the market for this kind of "specialty" center? Where would you look for it? Do you need to be an expert on market research to evaluate the information you think is important?

2. Will the location itself cause problems of its own? What might they be? It will help to make a list of the questions you have about this plan, and then keep track of them as the development of the center and implementation of the developer's plan are analyzed.

§ 1.05 DEVELOPMENT REQUIREMENTS

We now turn to the basic financial parameters facing Regent. These will be central to your consideration of the next two chapters.

Before proceeding, Regent would have to be assured that it would be able to acquire the development tract at a price that would make the development economical. Regent also would have to determine that it could finance (1) the purchase of the tract, and (2) the construction and lease-up of the retail center it proposed to build. These each would require the prices to be negotiated and a preliminary financing commitment to be obtained. For the purpose of analyzing this process, consider the decision point to be March of year 1 (in the actual case, 1989, but for analysis, the years will be referred to as year 1 = year of acquisition, with numbering sequentially thereafter), and assume the following:

- Regent can purchase the Johnson Tract (Parcels 3 and 5 in Figure 1.2, *supra*) for a price of $580,000, cash at closing. The contract between the parties conditions the closing on Regent obtaining 90% financing at 11% interest, 30-year amortization, 10-year term.

- Metropolitan will sell its portion of the development tract (Parcel 4 in Figure 1.2) to Regent for two forms of consideration: $325,000 in cash and the transfer to Metropolitan of a portion of the Johnson Tract (Parcel 3 in Figure 1.2). Regent will be responsible for the construction of the access road and the extension of Westbrook Drive to the access to State Route 59, subject to reimbursement from Metropolitan of 50% for the access road and 80% for Westbrook Drive.

- In order to construct and operate the car wash, Turtle Wax will require 87,700 square feet, or just over two acres (Parcel 5 and a portion of Parcel 4 — see Figures 1.2 and 1.3). Regent has determined that a site this size located in a shopping center would be sold to a "credit tenant" (a national company like Turtle Wax) for $825,000, and Turtle Wax is willing to purchase the site for this amount, cash at closing, provided its requirements for construction and operation have been met. Regent will prepare the site at its expense, and Turtle Wax will be responsible for construction of its facility.

- On the remaining site, 94,200 square feet, Regent will be able to construct two buildings to house retail shops with 20,000 leasable square feet. Actual construction cost for the buildings, which are basic shell structures with access to utilities and subject to tenant improvements as Regent and the tenants might agree, will be $45 per square foot. Including $40,000 for the cost of tenant improvements and signage, Regent Construction Company, Regent's affiliate construction company, will serve as the general contractor for all the necessary work, including site preparation (except for the construction of the access roads), at a fixed price of $1,240,000. Construction will begin on August 1 (the projected closing date for the land acquisition transactions), and is scheduled for completion within one year. The cost of constructing the access roads and the Westbrook Drive extension is estimated to be $250,000, subject to partial reimbursement by Metropolitan.

- Regent has determined that the probable market rental value of the retail shops, assuming that the tenant will be responsible for tenant improvements, is an annual rent of $15 per square foot. The rent can be adjusted to reflect differences in whether Regent bears the cost of the tenant build-out. Leases will be "triple net leases," which means that the tenants will be required to pay their own utilities and their proportionate share of all common area costs, including real estate taxes and insurance (leaving the developer responsible only for providing the capital and for the tenant costs attributable to any vacant space). In addition, tenants will pay management fees and a capital reserve allowance. The smallest bay will be 1,375 square feet, with respect to which Regent has reached a leasing agreement with Cellular Communications at $15 per square foot, or $20,625 per year. In addition, Regent plans to construct a lubrication bay (1,800 square feet), which it proposes to lease for an annual rent of $30 per square foot (this will be the most expensive space to construct because of the necessary basement for the lubrication bay). Regent expects lease-up of the Auto Care Center to require two years, with a vacancy loss of 25% in year 2 and 7.5% thereafter.

- Regent estimates the balance of its costs to be as follows:

Architectural/Engineering Cost	$40,000.00
Legal & Accounting	$40,000.00
Insurance	$15,000.00

Survey & Closing	$30,000.00
Marketing/Leasing Fees	$80,000.00
Construction Period Real Estate Taxes	$35,000.00
Contingency/Operating Deficit (3% of costs)	$60,000.00

- Regent has obtained a construction loan from First Mortgage Bank at an annual interest rate of prime plus 100 basis points (100 basis points equal 1%). The rate will be adjusted quarterly. The construction loan to Regent (or Regent's nominee) is with recourse (three shareholders of Regent Real Estate Development Corp. will guarantee payment of the loan) and will mature seven months after completion of construction (about 20 months from the first draw). If all goes according to schedule, this will be on February 28, year 3. Regent has decided not to get permanent financing for the completed center because it would like to see if more favorable loan terms will be available at the time the construction loan must be paid off.
- Regent will take a developer's fee for its work in assembling the project, and keep in mind that Regent's developer's fee is a cost of developing the Fox Valley Auto Care Center which will be reflected in the financials for the development and be part of the costs that any investor will have to take into account. The fee is normally 5% of the aggregate construction cost of the project, including soft costs, and is taken as the construction loan is drawn down. For purpose of the analysis of the transaction, assume the fee to be $100,000.
- Regent proposes to syndicate shares in this center, as it has for other shopping centers it has constructed, to local investors to whom it normally offers shares for investment. The investors will be accredited investors for securities law purposes,* thus considerably simplifying the securities requirements with which Regent must comply. It would like to offer 40% of the deal (economics and tax attributes) through a limited liability entity. The terms are negotiable, but Regent believes that a cash payment of $50,000 plus credit enhancements (to satisfy the lender) should be sufficient to make the deal work for Regent. The enhancements would be in the form of irrevocable letters of credit drawn to the order of the lender subject to a maximum term and a maximum amount. For a deal this size, the credit enhancement should be 10% of the loan.

There is a lot to digest in these numbers. You should take some time to familiarize yourself with them.

---

* An accredited investor includes a natural person who has *either* a net worth of $1,000,000 or more *or* income of $200,000 in each of the two preceding years with reasonable expectation of earning the same amount in the current year. *See* CFR § 230.501(a)(5), (6). The offering of securities to such investors is exempt from registration under the Securities Act of 1933 and from certain disclosure requirements under Reg. D. *See* CFR § 230.506(b)(2)(ii). Securities Act registration and disclosure requirements can be quite burdensome, so qualification for the private offering (and small issue) exemptions is important.

§ 1.06 PHOTOGRAPHIC OVERVIEW OF THE FOX VALLEY AUTO CARE CENTER

As you read through this material, you may find it helpful and illuminating to see photographs of the actual site. Real estate development projects such as this one involve many important visual elements that are not always apparent when considering the issues from a wholly theoretical and academic perspective. For example, rules regarding parking, stacking and loading and common area maintenance that are discussed in the easement documents take on heightened meaning when you can see the site as it was actually developed.

These photographs were taken in the spring of 2009. The design of the auto care center today is surprisingly close to the plan as originally conceived. Regent did not know how Metropolitan was planning to use its site. Do you think that Regent would have been pleased with the recreational uses that Metropolitan developed on its land? Why or why not?

The map below is an overview of the center and its environs depicting the relationship of the various businesses and public roads. The following pages contain both photographs of the site and corresponding maps. The maps orient you to the property and buildings, illustrating the position and direction from which each photograph was taken.

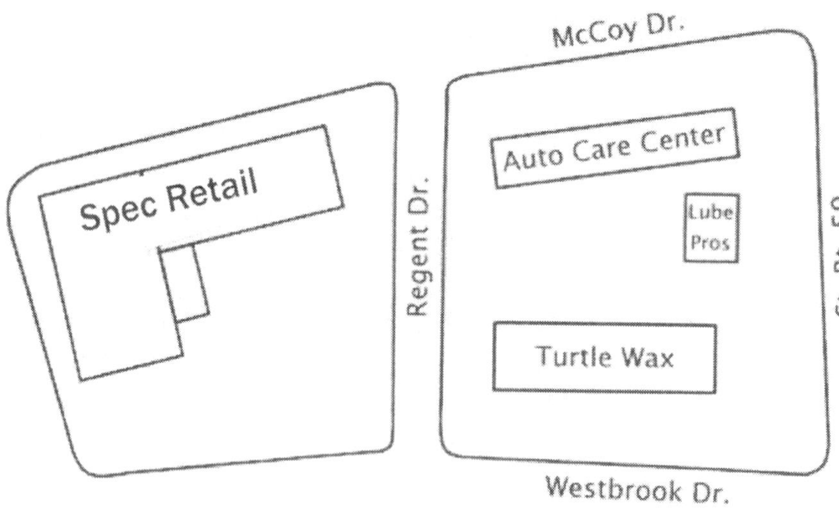

FOX VALLEY
AUTO CARE CENTER
STERLING AUTOMOTIVE
LubePro's
10 MINUTE
OIL CHANGE
Muffler & Brake Man
Allstate
Blackie's

TurtleWax
CAR WASH
ENTRANCE

Auto Care
Lube Pros

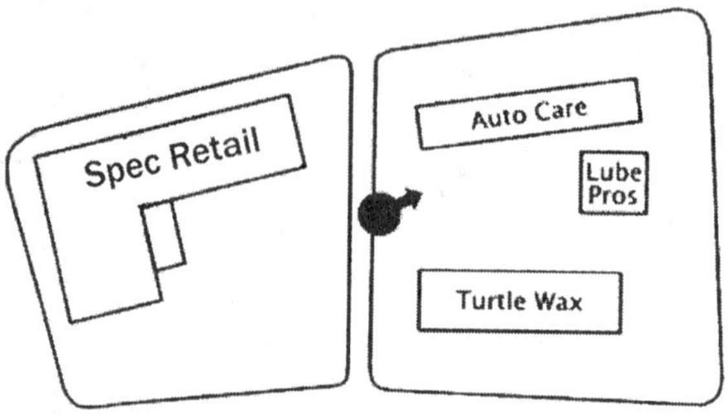
Spec Retail
Auto Care
Lube Pros
Turtle Wax

Lube Pros
Turtle Wax
Entrance

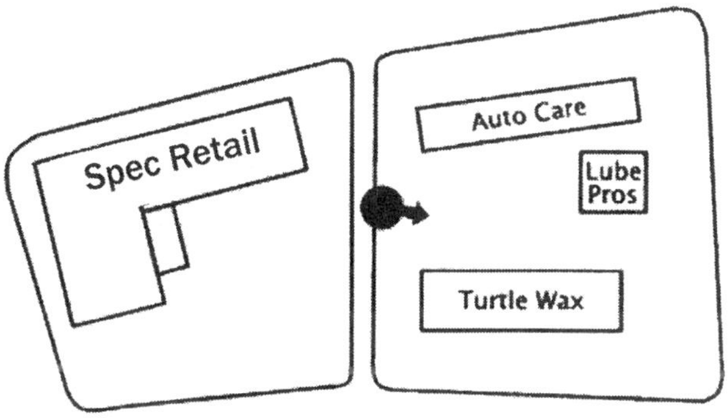
Spec Retail
Auto Care
Lube Pros
Turtle Wax

Auto Care (Front)

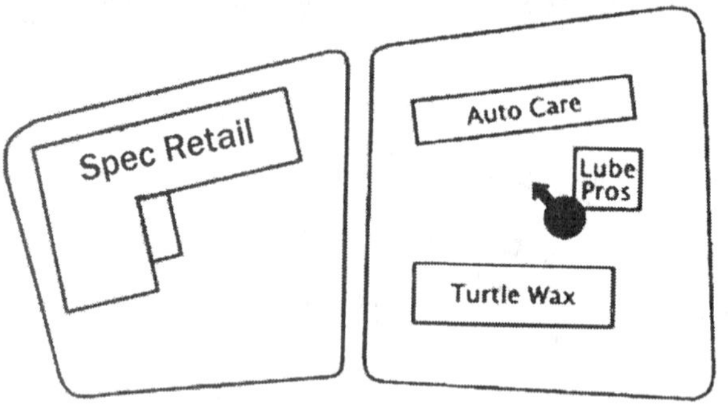
Spec Retail
Auto Care
Lube Pros
Turtle Wax

Auto Care (Back)

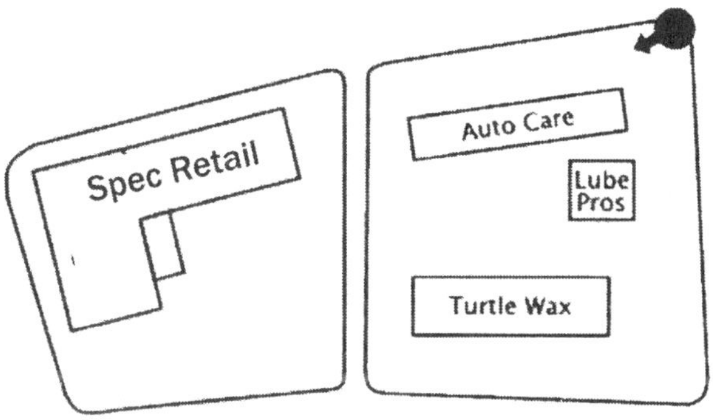
Spec Retail
Auto Care
Lube Pros
Turtle Wax

Turtle Wax

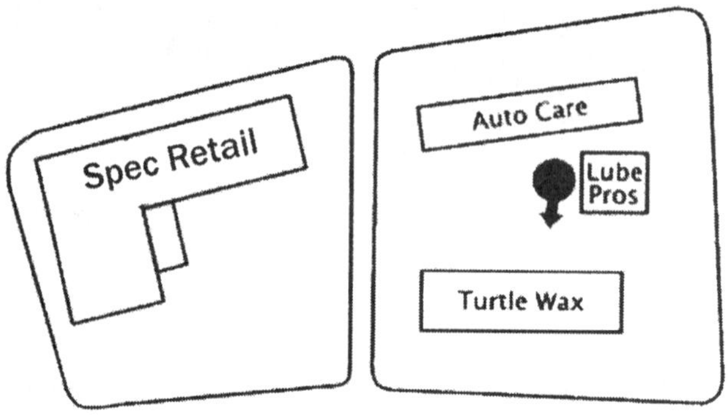
Spec Retail
Auto Care
Lube Pros
Turtle Wax

Auto Care
Regent Dr
Spec Retail

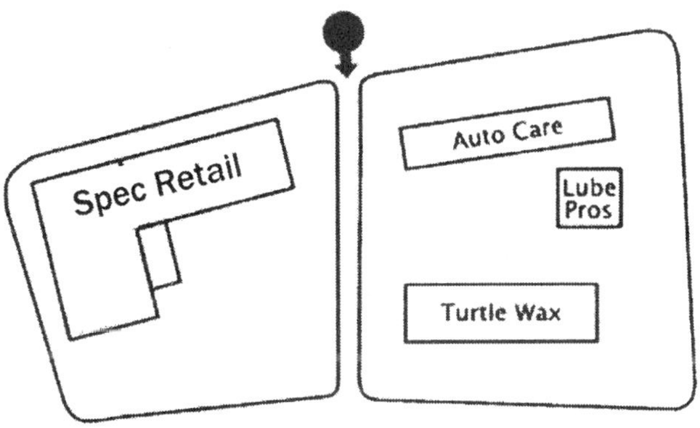
Spec Retail
Auto Care
Lube Pros
Turtle Wax

Spec Retail

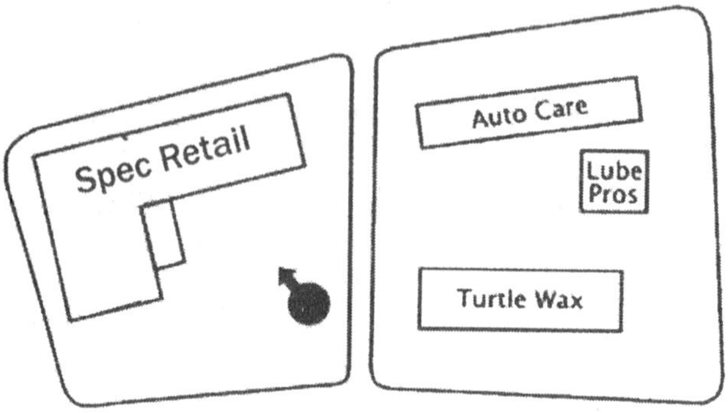
Spec Retail
Auto Care
Lube Pros
Turtle Wax

Spec Retail
Auto Care

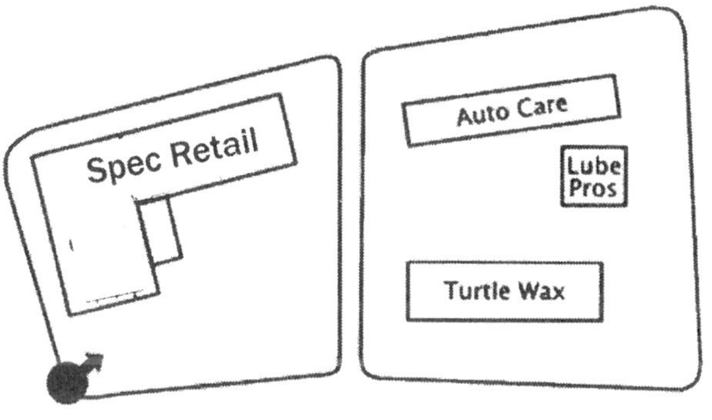
Spec Retail
Auto Care
Lube Pros
Turtle Wax

Chapter 2

APPLYING PRESENT VALUE CONCEPTS TO ANALYSIS OF REAL ESTATE PROJECTS

§ 2.01 OVERVIEW: IDENTIFYING THE INTERESTS

[1] Discounted Cash Flow Analysis

Real estate projects provide developers and their investors with relatively predictable cash flows over long periods of time. The value of a project depends upon the present value of the cash flow, which is derived by, first, forecasting the cash flow in each year that investors are likely to hold their investments in the project. Next, the annual cash flows are discounted to the present, usually using the rate of return which the investors predict they can earn on alternative investments. The result is then compared to the cost of creating or purchasing the project in question at the time that the decision is to be made. If the sum of the present values of these future cash flows exceeds the cost of the project, we say that the investment has a "net present value" which can then be compared to the net present value of other possible investments. Reliance on present value concepts to determine the present value of the project is referred to in the following material as "discounted cash flow analysis" or simply "DCF."

While many factors affect the value of a real estate project, the personal computer makes it possible to construct the financial anatomy of such a project quickly and then to manipulate the factors to show how each factor influences the value. One should not be seduced, however, by the apparent precision which the use of computers introduces to this analysis. A financial work-up or "pro forma" is based on assumptions, and an awareness of the importance of those assumptions is essential if the valuation determined by using this analysis is to be properly understood. As we will show in this chapter, important financial decisions rest on accurate application of these concepts. The problems associated with making the calculations are discussed next.

[2] The Players

Consider a simple model of the real estate project described in Chapter 1. Basically, it involves three players: the developer; one or more lending institutions ("the lender"); and one or more investors ("the investor"). The role of the developer in creating the plan and setting it in motion was the focus of Chapter 1. To proceed with its plan, the developer must obtain the capital to finance the construction and initial operating costs of the project from the other two players. To do this, the developer will, in effect, sell to each of the capital participants, the lender and the investor, a share of the projected future income of the project. The income that the project is expected to produce is referred to here as the project's "economics," and the problem for the developer is how much of the economics will the developer need to sell to these other players in order to obtain the capital necessary to accomplish the development.[1]

To accomplish this objective, the project, meaning the land and various commitments which enable the project to be built, will be transferred to an entity. When the Fox Valley Auto Care Center was developed, the entity usually was a limited partnership, and the entity which owned the FVACC was, in fact, the Fox Valley Auto Care Center Limited Partnership. Today, however, the entity most likely will be a limited liability company, or LLC. Since the entity necessarily will be taxed as a conduit under the income tax rules governing partnerships (so that the investor gets the benefits of mortgage interest, property tax and depreciation deductions), we choose, for purposes of Chapters 2 and 3, to refer to the entity as the "operating partnership."[2] We know that for those not familiar with intricacies of the tax rules (which is most of us!) that references in the text to "partnership" when we really mean "LLC" can be confusing, but we ask you to trust us that, as we discuss the financial structure of real estate investments generally and the Fox Valley Auto Care Center in particular, it will make more sense for us to refer to the operating partnership, and for you to think "LLC."

The developer will likely be the managing partner in the partnership, which will borrow as much capital from the lender as the developer can negotiate. The lender's share of the project's economics is traditionally a fixed annual amount determined by the loan documents and secured by an interest in the project itself (the "mortgage") which is senior to other interests in the project. The partnership will agree to make the loan payments, and the lender will have rights to enforce its interest directly against the property and usually the rents if the operating partnership defaults. In return for seniority and other rights to accelerate the loan in default, and to collect the proceeds from the assets of partnership,[3] the lender will generally not have any right to future increases in income and value (the "residual" interest).

When the project increases in value as rents increase, we hope as projected, the increase in value will be allocated *entirely* to the residual interest. This is what the

---

[1] Looking ahead, you will see that this is a circular problem. The developer has a design in mind for this project. To build the project, the developer will need capital equal to $x. Once built and rented to tenants, the developer forecasts that the project will produce $y in net income, referred to below as "net operating income" or the "free and clear," this being the cash flow which will be used to obtain financing. In turn, the income must support the financial structure (the capital) needed to complete the project. If the projected rents are inadequate to support the design, then the design of the project must be adjusted, but if adjusted, the income may be reduced, and that, in turn, may support less capital, and so on. The question will always be where to break the circle.

[2] Partnerships are taxed under subchapter K of the Internal Revenue Code. §§ 701–777. The objective is to achieve the distribution of cash flow to investors with a *single layer of tax*, and that tax to be imposed at the investor level. A "tax conduit" is an entity from which the tax consequences of its operations are allocated to the members of the entity and reported on their tax returns. Partnership taxation is a straightforward idea with very complicated rules. These issues are discussed in Chapter 4.

[3] In the real estate industry, long term loans (referred to as "permanent financing") are normally non-recourse as to operators and investors of the real estate project. Current market conditions may sometimes make permanent financing difficult to achieve, as the auto care center vividly demonstrates. In order to obtain the capital necessary to build the project, the developer may agree to a "mini-perm." This loan product is a construction loan which typically converts to a non-recourse loan for a limited term once the project is completed and often after it has attained specified operating benchmarks. The developer is then taking the risk that it will be able to refinance the original loan when it matures. This situation is discussed in the text below.

investor purchases with its capital contribution. We say that the investor has "leveraged" its interest because increases in value attributable to the capital obtained from the lender are allocated to the investor.[4] Because the lender has priority, payments required by the loan must be made first; the cash flows remaining after those payments have been made will then be distributed to the partners, in the paradigmatic example, the developer and the investor.[5] When the income, and thus the value of the project, increases, as the parties anticipate that it will, all of the increases will be shared by the partners in accordance with their partnership interests. Because the lender's right is limited to fixed payments, a portion of the increase received by the investor will derive from that part of the project which was financed by the loan. Enhancing the investor's share of the income from the project in this way is what we mean by "*leverage*."

The concepts introduced here in the context of our paradigmatic example play a major role in the financing of real estate projects. What ties them together is the valuation of the projected income streams that permits the interests of the players to be determined relative to each other. The following discussion is intended to provide you with the tools to do this work.

§ 2.02 INTRODUCTION TO VALUATION OF REAL ESTATE PROJECTS

To obtain long-term financing, the developer will approach a lender with a specific plan for the project. The lender may be a life insurance company, a commercial bank or another financial intermediary[6] which may then "securitize" the loan by "packaging" it with other loans and selling the packaged loans on public capital markets. The plan will include a projection of the cash flows the project is expected to produce when up and running and fully leased (the "pro forma"). Relying on this plan, the traditional pattern is for the developer to negotiate a binding commitment from the lender to make a non-recourse loan for a fixed amount of money upon completion of the project (the "permanent loan"). Then, the developer will use the permanent lender's commitment to negotiate financing for construction and lease-up from a commercial bank (the "construction loan"). This arrangement would have been formalized in a three-party agreement in which the permanent lender agreed to buy the construction loan and the mortgage securing the loan from the construction lender (referred to as a "take out" of the construction loan) when construction was completed and other requirements specified in the agreement, such as reaching certain stated goals in leasing up the project, had been met.

---

[4] This works both ways. If rents decline, then the investor's share is disproportionately reduced because cash flow required to pay the lender will come from the investor's share.

[5] "Cash Flow" available for distribution may be reduced by other amounts given priority, including, for example, the creation of reserves against future costs, or account maintenance fees. Distributable cash flow is always a quantity defined by the terms of the deal made by the developer with its investors and memorialized in the Partnership Agreement, or the Management Agreement for a limited liability company.

[6] Long term real estate loans are often arranged through mortgage bankers, such as Capmark Finance, Inc., *see* www.capmark.com, which "originate" loans by financial institutions such as Freddie Mac to real estate projects. These loans may then be resold on public markets by securitizing them, although turmoil in the securities markets since 2007 has made securitization more difficult, even for loans to sound income producing projects.

Because of conditions in the mortgage markets, negotiation of a permanent loan may not be possible, and then the construction lender, which may have done other similar deals with the developer, will agree to a "mini-perm."[7] The construction loan will be a business loan because of the risk involved in completing the construction of the project, and will therefore be with recourse to borrower. Once construction has been completed and benchmarks specified in the loan documents met, the loan will then be converted into a non-recourse loan, usually with a more limited term than that found in permanent financing. The converted loan may have terms similar to the traditional self-amortizing permanent loan which require curtailment of principal, or it may not. With the Fox Valley Auto Care Center, the construction lender did agree to extend the term of the construction loan to give the developer time to refinance it, but this arrangement does not seem to have been a typical mini-perm.

To attract the investor's capital into the partnership, the developer will provide the investor with a description of the project and a financial analysis similar to that provided to the lender. From a review of this document and its own evaluation of the financials provided by the developer, the investor must decide whether or not to invest in this particular project. The underwriting requirements for most lenders will limit the amount which can be loaned to a percentage of the project's *value*, in current markets probably 70 to 75%, and may in addition require that a percentage of the project's *cost* be provided as equity. Note that value and cost are different quantities. Value depends upon valuation of the future cash flows,[8] while cost means the actual outlay required to build (or buy) the project and begin operations. When credit becomes tighter, as in the financial crisis beginning in 2007, equity required may range from 25% to 35% of the *cost* of the project, depending upon current economic conditions, and the lender may require that all or a significant part of the equity be contributed to the project *before* any portion of the loan proceeds can be used.

The developer will usually be a partner in the partnership, so for the developer, the question will be how much of the project's economics must be offered to the investor in order to induce it to contribute the capital needed by the project. The greater the share of the economics that must be offered to "sell" the project, the less is the prospective value of the developer's interest.

In making its investment decision, an informed investor will consider factors in addition to the numerical rates of return which can be predicted — such factors as the possibility that land values will rise or fall significantly, that rent control regulations may freeze its rents, or that competition will depress rents while costs continue to rise, and the like. Nevertheless, based on its best estimate of what will happen to the project, the investor will use financial analysis to evaluate the profitability of the project by computing the rate of return which it expects the cash flow from the project to produce, and comparing that measure against projected rates of return from other, alternative investments.

---

[7] *See* note 3, *supra*.

[8] As we are about to explain, valuing the future cash flows that are projected in the developer's pro forma depends upon assumptions about the normal return a project of that type and quality will produce under current market conditions. The lender and the investors will make their own assumptions about these multiples, which may produce a *lower* value than that advocated by the developer, thus reducing the amount of capital which each player would be willing to contribute to the project. *See* note 11, *infra*.

[1] Rates of Return

[a] General Measures of Rates of Return

[i] "Cap" Rate

The traditional and relatively simple method of measuring the rate of return for a given real estate investment is to divide the net operating income produced by the project (net rents, or gross rents less operating expenses) by the cost.[9] This figure, usually referred to as the capitalization rate or simply the "cap rate," gives a measure of the project's profitability before taking into account the current state of the financial markets and the particular investor's situation. This method is often used by real estate brokers because of its relative simplicity, both in determining it and in using it to compare different real estate investments. For this number to be useful, however, it must be based on operating results for a normal year — viz., the "stabilized net operating income" for the project.[10] Moreover, using this number as the measure of an investment's performance ignores any consideration of the period of time over which the project will produce this annual rate of return, and it also does not take into account any estimate of the project's eventual selling price.

The cap rate has a similar function to earnings multiples in the financial markets. Experienced developers and most lenders have a good sense of what capitalization rate a project should attain, given its type, size and location, and the current state of the real estate markets. Lenders and investors usually rely on the capitalization rates similar projects have experienced, or new projects are expected to experience, sometimes without much data to support their conclusions. Future projections are no better than the assumptions made to produce them, and sometimes these assumptions are nothing more than educated guesses. If the developer cannot demonstrate that the project as planned will produce a cap rate at least as good as that expected by its lenders and investors, it will be difficult to fund the project.[11]

[ii] "Cash on Cash"

Developers may sometimes rely on the rate of return measured by the first stabilized year's cash flow available for distribution to the partners (net operating income less the debt service, often referred to as "cash flow after finance," or "CFAF"), divided by the amount of equity required ("cash-on-cash"). This measures the return experienced by the investor on its actual investment.

---

[9] Net operating income ("NOI" or "free and clear") is the operating *cash flow* produced by the project. Because the entity which will own and operate the project will not itself pay income tax, this cash flow is available to be used for all project costs, including financing costs. The tax consequences will be considered later.

[10] For new construction, the "stabilized income" may be difficult to predict accurately, particularly for shopping centers. In these projects, success depends upon the retail business conditions in the area where the center is located, and often on the identity and business success of an anchor tenant. This may be particularly true for a specialty center like the Fox Valley Auto Care Center.

[11] For example, a mortgage banker in negotiating the loan will use the cap rate it thinks is appropriate for the project to determine value. The maximum loan available for the project, as we shall see, is a function of this value. If cost exceeds value, that is, the cap rate likely to be produced by the project is lower than the cap rate expected by the lender, the maximum loan that the developer can negotiate with that lender will be less than the developer's financials have projected.

Although this approach takes into account the cost of financing for the specific project, so that favorable loan terms may offset the effect of a low cap rate, the cash-on-cash return may be less useful to the decision whether to invest than the capitalization rate.

The interesting result for the investor will be the *after-tax* return, and this depends on the relationship between the investor's individual income tax characteristics, the cash flow distributed from the project, and the tax effects produced by the project. In the United States, taxpayers will pay tax on their taxable income, but for this purpose recall that a tax conduit does *not* pay tax on its income, which is instead allocated among its members according to percentages or "shares" set out in the agreement. Each member must then report its share of income reported by the partnership.[12] The partnership determines its taxable income as if it were an individual,[13] and thus may take deductions for expenses incurred by it in operating the project. These expenses include normal operating costs,[14] such as salaries of employees, insurance premiums, advertising or promotional cost, normal repairs, utilities, rent charged under a land lease, and similar costs; interest charged by the lender;[15] real estate taxes;[16] and, most importantly, cost recovery deductions, typically depreciation.[17] Cost recovery deductions are important to this analysis because these deductions are allowed without an offsetting expenditure, referred to here as "non-cash deductions." By cost is meant the amount paid to construct or acquire the asset involved, including the proceeds of a loan made to the operating partnership for this purpose. Cost

---

[12] The operating partnership will file an "information return" with the Internal Revenue Service on Form 1065, and will provide to each of its partners a "schedule K." The share of each partner in specific tax items reported by the partnership will be set out in this schedule and must be entered on that partner's income tax return in the appropriate place, where it is taken into account in computing that partner's tax liability.

[13] INT. REV. CODE of 1986 § 703(a) (hereafter "IRC").

[14] IRC § 162.

[15] *See* IRC § 163. Section 163 imposes limitations on the deductibility of interest from certain types of investments for individual taxpayers. Thus, for example, the deduction for "investment interest," defined as interest "paid or accrued on indebtedness properly allocable to property held for investment," IRC § 163(d)(3)(A), is limited to net investment income. However, the operation of a real estate project is, in general, the operation of an active business, so this limitation will not apply to interest paid or accrued by the operating partnership in the typical real estate deal. As far as the analysis in this book is concerned, you need not concern yourself with this kind of limitation, although there are other limitations on the deductibility of net losses, which we discuss in a later chapter. If the taxpayer directly owned an interest in an income producing real estate asset, rather than an interest in the operating partnership, then the limitations on the deductibility of interest would apply.

[16] IRC § 164(a)(1).

[17] IRC § 168. Cost recovery (depreciation) is a statutory concept. In each year, the taxpayer may take a deduction for a percentage of the cost of a depreciable asset, in this case, the building, land improvement costs (parking lots, landscaping), and some furnishings. Because the allowance varies depending on the type of asset involved, an issue we explore at some length in Chapter 3, cost must be allocated among these assets. For purposes of this discussion, assume that the only asset is an apartment building. The statute prescribes the method (straight line in the case of real property, meaning that cost is allocated pro rata in each year over the prescribed period), § 168(b)(3)(B), and the period (for residential real estate, the prescribed period is 27.5 years), § 168(c). The deductible amount is then the reciprocal of the prescribed period, or 1/27.5 = 3.636%. The Internal Revenue Service requires that the depreciation be determined using a convention for the month of the year in which the asset was put in service or acquired by the taxpayer, although this calculation can be done using a table, Rev. Proc. 87-57, Sec. 8, Table 5, 1987-2 C.B. 687, 700. Similar rules apply to the calculation of cost recovery deductions for commercial property, although in that case the prescribed term is 39 years.

recovery deductions are computed using the *original* cost basis of the asset, although the cost basis of the asset must be reduced by cost recovery deductions as they are allowed.[18]

Rents are taxed as ordinary income, and a partner's share of the taxable income (or loss) of the partnership will be taxable to (deductible by) that partner according to rates applicable to ordinary income under section 1 of the Internal Revenue Code. To determine the partner's return *after tax*, the tax incurred because of the inclusion of partnership net income, or the tax reduction resulting from the partner's deduction of its share of partnership net loss, must be subtracted from (or added to) cash distributions to that partner.[19]

These elements are developed more fully in the application of discounted cash flow ("DCF") analysis to the investor's interest in the project, rather than as the rate of return for a one year period. The cap rate, however, may be compared to cap rates for other projects or to the expectations of the other players. This provides a rough measure of the value of the project, compared to other projects, but one should note that cap rates themselves are only a crude measure of value, and usually are adjusted by the person who is making the comparison for current market conditions, type of project, location, etc.

[iii] Other measures

There may be other methods to express in short-hand terms the value of a project for purposes of comparison to other projects. Gross rents, for example, might serve as a proxy for value, which would be determined for the purpose of the person making this calculation by applying a "factor" or multiplier to the effective gross rent produced by the project. One would have to use such a factor with great care, being aware that it ignores not only the timing of cash flows but also the efficiency of the project, that is, the relationship of effective gross rents to net operating income.[20]

[b] Capitalization of the Rental Income Stream

A more sophisticated method of evaluating a real estate project uses DCF analysis to capitalize the project's income stream over the expected investment period (the "investment horizon"). This method applies the concept of the present value of a dollar to be received at a future time to discount future cash flows to the present. No one believes that an obligation to pay $100 one year in the future is worth $100 today. The value today of a future obligation depends upon the rate of interest the payee expects to receive on investment of its money. If it expects to

---

[18] IRC § 1016(a)(2). We say that the *basis* of the asset is *adjusted* for allowable cost recovery deductions, and it is this *adjusted basis* which is used to determine gain or loss on a taxable disposition of the asset.

[19] As you will see, DCF analysis assumes that the project will be sold (and the partnership liquidated) at the end of the investment period, usually ten years. This final cash flow includes the cash from the hypothetical sale, and that amount must be adjusted for capital gain resulting from the sale. We discuss this issue later in this Chapter.

[20] Proprietary data bases collect cost factors in the operation of rental properties by type of property, age, size, etc., which can then be compared to effective gross rent which would be useful in determining how the particular property is being operated when compared to competing properties. *See, e.g.*, Building Owners and Management Institute, which collects this data and will make available through its on-line store. www.BOMI-edu.org/.

receive a 10% return on its money, for example, it should be indifferent between having $90.90 today and $100 at the end of one year.[21] The value today of a series of annual cash flows is the sum of the present values of each cash flow.

Suppose, for example, that an investor is contemplating the purchase of an interest in an asset that will produce cash flows of $25 a year for five years and $100 at the end of the sixth year, assuming the payments are assured and there are no other factors which must be taken into account. Our hypothetical investor will decide how much to offer for these cash flows based on the rate of return she believes she can realize on the funds to be invested. Frequently, this rate of return is referred to as the investor's *"hurdle" rate of return*, as that is the rate of return which must be earned by a new investment before the investor will invest. The valuation issue as a function of the expected return can be depicted as shown in Figure 2.1, in which the present values of the cash flows have been calculated for discount rates shown in the table.

Figure 2.1

Present Value of Future Cash Flows at Various Discount Rates

Year	Cash Flow	8%	10%	12%
1	25.00	23.15	22.73	22.32
2	25.00	21.43	20.66	19.93
3	25.00	19.85	18.78	17.79
4	25.00	18.38	17.08	15.89
5	25.00	17.01	15.52	14.19
6	100.00	63.02	56.45	50.66
Total	**225.00**	**162.83**	**151.22**	**140.78**

You can see that an investor who would otherwise earn a return of 10% (or more) on its investments will not pay more than $151.22 for the cash flows shown in the left-hand column. As the investor's required return *increases*, the value of a set of given future cash flows *decreases*, or conversely, if rates of return earned on investments fall, the current price at which those cash flows can be purchased should rise.[22]

---

[21] Thus: $90.90 + (10% × $90.90) = $90.90 + $9.10 = $100.

[22] More broadly, cap rates can be thought of as an extension of discount rates used to value income producing real estate assets. In the recent real estate "bubble," cap rates have been declining to a point well below the historical average, which is just under 8 percent. The lower the cap rate, the higher the value of the asset in real estate markets. Cap rates for commercial real estate projects of less than 4% have been reported, which, in comparison to the historical averages, implies that income producing real estate has been overvalued, a conclusion supported by recent increases in the cap rate. The cap rates experienced in actual transactions as distinguished from those used in appraisals tend to be more conservative, and this at least has been observed since 2007.

[2] Application of Rates of Return Methods to Real Estate Investments

The evaluation of a real estate project by using the capitalization of income technique is no different from the example described above. The investor decides what rate of return she expects to earn on her investments. She can then analyze the cash flows which the project is predicted to produce each year during its useful life, and compute the present value of each of those amounts. The sum of the present values of each year's annual net distributable cash flow is the present value of the investor's interest in the project at the required rate of return. This number is then compared with the asking price. If it exceeds the price, there is a "*net present value*" ("NPV"), and investment at the asking price may, other things being equal, be acceptable.

This is the best method of evaluating a project if one's purpose is to decide its maximum value as an investment. Note that it takes into account all the factors ignored by the methods previously discussed: it considers the *amount* of money to be received each year in the future, *when* that amount will be received (the more distant in time the payment, the less its value), the *period* of time over which the project will be useful, and, finally, its *projected value at the end* of the investment period (the project's "residual value"). The net sales price at a projected future time is an amount which can be added to that year's distributable net income (*i.e.*, treated as a cash flow from the project) and then discounted at the required rate of return to produce its present value. Many large institutional lenders use this method of valuation to determine the value of the project, and thus the amount of money which they are willing to lend or invest.

[a] The Internal Rate of Return

Capitalizing a project's projected income stream tells an investor how much she should pay for a project given the investor's required rate of return. Suppose she wanted to know what rate of return the project will earn, assuming that the projection of future cash flows is accurate and she will acquire the right to those cash flows for the offering price. This would be useful information for her to compare with the return provided by other investments in her portfolio. Since we know what it will cost her to purchase the cash flows, we need to reverse the calculations in the capitalization process described above. In that process, we assumed a discount rate as the return the investor would expect to earn on investments in her portfolio, computed the present value of the cash flows and compared the result to the cost. Instead of doing that, we will find the discount rate which, when applied to the investor's share of the future cash flows, will result in a present value equal to the price which she is being asked to pay. Although this is simply another discount rate, it is *the discount rate* which yields a value precisely equal to the purchase price. We call this discount rate *the internal rate of return* or simply the "IRR."

The investor, of course, is only concerned with analyzing her share of the project's economics compared to the amount of her equity investment, while a lender will want to know the value of the entire project in order to determine its maximum loan as a percentage of value. Hence the internal rate of return for an investor is generally computed after financing costs have been taken into account, whereas the capitalized value of the project is generally computed using the project's net operating income, which includes financing cash flows (the *debt service*) to which the lender's own hurdle rate has been applied.[23] The internal rate of return, then, is a rate of return specific to the investor for whom it has been calculated.

The investor is also interested primarily in her net, *after-tax*, cash flow. Recall that a share of taxable income or loss realized by the operating partnership will be allocated to investor, and taken into account by her in computing her income tax liability.[24] This requirement will either increase her tax liability (an additional cost associated with her investment in the project) or decrease her tax liability (an additional cash flow produced by her investment in the project). The internal rate of return therefore is computed with reference to the investor's own income tax characteristics. Furthermore, this analysis assumes that the property will be sold after it has been held for a set period of time (the "investment horizon"), usually ten years, and that the investor's interest in the project will be liquidated for a cash payment. Disposition of the property at an assumed price will result in a taxable gain or loss, and the investor must also be treated as having taken that gain or loss into account on her personal tax return.[25] The tax liability will be treated as a cost which reduces the cash payment or, if a loss has resulted in a tax deduction, an increase in the cash payment. In this analysis, the net liquidating distribution is simply another cash flow.

Because real estate investing has distinctive tax effects and because some investors desire to use these effects to enhance the value of their investment relative to alternatives, this aspect of DCF techniques may seem to be particularly difficult.[26]

One way to picture the mechanics of the internal rate of return method is to visualize the investment as producing a series of future cash inflows to the investor

---

[23] As we discuss later, the lender is interested in comparing the cost of financing with the operating characteristics of the project itself. This informs the lender's *underwriting* of the loan proposal, which is the financial analysis of the soundness of the project and whether the lender has the margin of safety which its underwriting policy requires.

[24] *See* text at notes 12–17, *supra*.

[25] The determination of the amount of taxable gain on disposition of the property is complicated by the requirement that the mortgagee be paid the balance due on the mortgage at that time. We examine this issue in Chapter 3, *infra*. More generally, recall that as cost recovery deductions are allowed to the partnership, the tax basis of the project is reduced ("adjusted"). *See* text at notes 17-18, *supra*. The investor's share of the tax gain is then measured by the amount realized on the transaction minus the project's adjusted tax basis. IRC § 1001. The "amount realized" for this purpose includes the consideration paid by the buyer plus the balance due on the mortgage. The gain is then subject to tax, first, to the extent of cost recovery deductions claimed by the taxpayer, at a maximum rate of 25%, IRC § 1(h)(1)(D), (h)(3), and the balance of the gain at the capital gains rate, equal at this writing to 15%. If the tax computed under the ordinary income tax rates is less, not often the case for real estate investors, then the taxpayer will pay the lesser amount.

[26] Real estate investments are generally viewed as tax shelters, *see* IRC §§ 448(a)(3), 448(d), 461(i)(3), 1256(e)(3)(B), requiring partnerships with limited partners having in the aggregate more than a 35% interest in losses to use the accrual method of accounting. These partnerships include, as a practical matter, every real estate project owned by an investment entity, which will invariably be a tax conduit (referred to here as a partnership). Individual taxpayers who invest in operating partnerships then face added complexities in reporting the returns from their investments, such as the alternative minimum tax (IRC §§ 55–59), limitations imposed by the at risk rules (IRC § 465), or the passive loss limitation (IRC § 469). These limitations are discussed in chapter 3, *infra*, although for purposes of this book, the impact of these rules on the individual tax liabilities of investors will be disregarded.

which she can purchase at a given price. The inflows are the annual *after-tax* profits produced, and include the net cash proceeds received by the investor from the sale of the investment in the year of its sale. Thus, if the investor were to sell her interest at the end of the third year, the cash inflows for the first two years would be the project's after-tax profit (cash distributed to her minus her income tax liability) for each year, and the third year's inflows would be the sum of the third year's after-tax profits plus the net after-tax proceeds of the sale. If the project is profitable, the sum of the three inflows will be greater than the purchase price of the investment, and the internal rate of return will be that discount rate which, when applied to the three inflows, will result in a present value which is just equal to the purchase price. As the holding period lengthens, the sum of the aggregate cash inflows will increase, but since the largest payment occurs in the year of sale, and since that time has now been deferred, the *present value* of the proceeds of sale is less. Thus, the fact that the sum of the cash flows is greater the longer the investor holds the project does *not* mean that the rate of return will necessarily increase as the holding period increases.

[b] Importance of the Internal Rate of Return

Using the internal rate of return as a measurement of the project's rate of return has two major advantages over the one-year snapshot techniques used by some real estate brokers. *First*, it allows the investor to take into account the timing factor. Money received in the early years has greater value than money received later on; a quick look at a present value table (Table A, appearing at the end of this chapter) which provides the present value of $1 to be received at the specified time in the future for various discount rates will indicate the importance of this factor.[27] For example, at a discount rate of only 6%, the present value of a dollar to be received ten years from now is only about 50 cents; discounted at 10%, its present value is only 39 cents. In addition, by taking the time factor into account, the internal rate of return method allows the investor to compute her rate of return on the assumption that she will sell at a particular time in the future. She can thus compute her rate of return using different assumptions about when she will sell her interest; by looking at the trend of these rates of return, she can then determine the optimum year in which to sell. These conclusions depend on the reliability of assumptions about changes in net operating income and in the value of the project.

A *second* advantage of the internal rate of return method is that it forces the investor to carefully specify *all* of the assumptions and predictions which she is making when she evaluates the investment. To perform the analysis, she must construct a cash flow table over the time period she expects to hold the investment on which projected rents and expenses will be shown. Thus, it forces her to project her eventual sales price, any future increases in rents and costs, and the income tax liability which she will incur upon sale of the project. The importance of these assumptions to the return which the investor is seeking to predict can then be tested by varying the assumptions, a process which can be performed easily and quickly with a personal computer.

---

[27] The formula for deriving the present value of a cash flow at a specific time is provided at the end of this chapter. If you need to review it, you should turn to it now.

[c] Use Caution When Relying on the Internal Rate of Return

Relying in the internal rate of return also has some weaknesses. To begin with, reliance on such detailed calculations may lull the investor into a false sense of security. The rate of return which the calculation produces is no better than the assumptions upon which it depends. These weaknesses are described more fully in the articles that follow this general discussion. But since the assumptions can be varied, it does allow the investor to see what the impact would be if her assumptions prove incorrect. More importantly, however, it is essential to understand exactly what the rate of return figure does and does not say. It does tell the investor what rate of return an institution such as a bank would have to pay her on her equity capital in order to produce the series of cash inflows which the project will produce. Note, however, that at the end of the holding period of the project, the investor does not "get her money back" upon receipt of the net proceeds from the sale. The cash inflow in the year of sale is simply that — another cash inflow. Thus, the rate of return produced by this method is *not equivalent* to putting one's money in the bank and earning an annual return upon it with the original investment being returned in the year of sale.

The cash inflows in the first year or so may be large and involve some return of capital; on the other hand, it is conceivable that they could be small enough to require further investment of capital. In order to compare the rate of return generated by the internal rate of return method with a compound interest rate quoted by a bank, the investor would have to be able to invest the cash flows distributed from the project in *another investment yielding the same rate of return*. The internal rate of return is thus more directly comparable to a simple interest rate since simple interest does not contemplate the reinvestment of earned interest but rather assumes that the interest is immediately payable. To determine accurately the return actually earned over the investment period, the future value of each cash flow from the date of distribution to the end of the period should be calculated, using the investment yield selected by the investor, and the yield to maturity of the investment from the date of the original investment in the project to the end of period determined. The result is a modified or blended rate of return which reflects both the return produced by the real estate project and the return earned on the cash distributed from the project.

[3] Example

The workings of the valuation model which employs the internal rate of return technique can perhaps best be understood by carefully looking at an example. In setting up this example, a prospective investment by one investor will be analyzed. The methods illustrated here are equally applicable to a more complicated example with more than one investor, although in that case the interest of each investor must be separately analyzed.

[a] Set-up

Consider an apartment building[28] which has 100 units and will cost $10,000,000 to buy.[29] Assume that the value of the land on which the project is built is 10% of the total cost, or $1,000,000.[30] Assume also that cash flow from the operation of the project will produce a cap rate of 9% (or $900,000 of net operating income after paying all expenses, other than federal income taxes and mortgage payments). Assume that a first mortgage of $7,500,000 at 8% interest can be negotiated, with payments sufficient to fully amortize the loan over 30 years.[31] This loan will require the borrower to pay fixed monthly payments totaling $629,293 annually, each payment to be applied first to pay interest on the unpaid principal balance and then to reduce principal. To acquire the apartment building, our investor must therefore provide $2,500,000 of equity (cost ($10,000,000) minus the mortgage ($7,500,000)). Assume, initially, that current (2009) federal income tax law applies, and thus, for cost recovery purposes, the residential building will have a useful life of 27.5 years for the calculation of tax depreciation on the straight-line method (annual depreciation therefore is 3.636% of the *building's* original cost, $9,000,000).[32] First year operations can then be projected as shown in Figure 2.2.[33]

---

28 This model will be used to determine how to determine the return which an investor in a project like the Fox Valley Auto Care Center can expect. For this purpose, we use the simplest type of project with uniform rents per unit, generally required by market constraints. In a retail center, rents for each unit will typically be separately negotiated, with terms and conditions applicable to that specific unit, but the general principles explained here will apply in making the decision whether to proceed with the FVACC.

29 By "cost" we mean the actual cost of purchasing the building itself, including transaction costs. For a discussion of cost allocation issues, see Chapter 3, *infra*. When acquiring an income producing real estate project, there will be costs allocable to evaluation of the project, acquisition of the land and the formation of the operating entity. For purposes of this illustration, we ignore these costs, although they can be substantial, and usually are incurred before the project has been acquired and produces any income.

30 The value of the land is important, because land is not a depreciable asset, and therefore will not produce cost recovery deductions. Control over the land, however, may have a significant effect on the residual value of the project at the time it is projected to be sold. In some cases, the land on which a project is built will be leased from the owner of the land, who then controls the residual value of the land. Lease payments on long-term (35 years or more) land leases tend not to be capitalized into the value of the land, and are therefore low relative to the value of the land. The *purchase* of an existing project, such as we are discussing here, with a land lease in place might then command a somewhat higher price for the building to reflect the capital value of a land lease with favorable terms. Perhaps more important for this analysis, payments under a land lease are currently deductible for tax purposes as an operating expense.

31 Note that the "term" of the mortgage loan may be shorter than the amortization period. The lender usually will want to refinance a permanent loan at current market rates after a relatively short period. In past years, this implied a term of ten years, although under current market conditions, the lender may require a shorter term. In contrast, the amortization period is determined as that period over which equal monthly payments will fully retire the principal of the loan (a "self-amortizing loan"). This period is used to determine how rapidly the principal of the loan should be reduced ("curtailed"), and, as we shall see, plays an important role in how the benefits of tax leverage can be achieved. When the amortization period exceeds the term of the loan, a principal balance will be due at maturity (the "balloon payment"). In some kinds of loans, particularly loans insured by the Federal Housing Authority, the term of the loan will be the same as the amortization period.

32 Straight-line depreciation means that the building's cost is allocated pro rata over the period ("useful life") set by statute, and the allocated portion deducted in each year. *See* note 17, *supra*. As noted earlier, the amounts deductible in the first and last years of the period are adjusted because of certain conventions.

33 By first year operations, we mean the first year in which projected operational levels have been

Figure 2.2
First Year Operations Summary

Cash Flow			Taxable Income		
Net Operating Income		900,000	Net Operating Income		900,000
Interest	(560,155)		Interest	(560,155)	
Principal	(69,138)	(629,293)	Depreciation	(313,560)	(873,805)
Cash Flow after Finance		270,707	Taxable Income		26,195

The before-tax cash flow in the first year is $270,707, or 10.46% of our investor's equity investment ($2,500,000) ("cash-on-cash").[34] Taxable income, however, is much less, reflecting the substantial cost recovery deductions which offset or "shelter" otherwise taxable rental income produced by the property. The investor will be required to include this income on her personal income tax return and pay tax, in this case at her marginal income tax rate (35%), and her total cash return (her cash inflow) in the first year would then be $261,539, or approximately 10.5% of her net $2,500,000 investment.

By making the same calculations for each future year in the investment period, the investor can project her inflow for each year that she intends to own the investment. In making these projections, it is usually assumed that rents and expenses[35] will tend to rise while the property is held by the investor, and that it can be sold for more than its initial purchase price. These assumptions may be only informed guesswork but are usually consistent with experience.[36] As a result of these calculations, we can produce the set of numbers shown in Figure 2.3.

achieved. This projection is referred to as "stabilized net income." The importance of achieving this projection is discussed in the following material, but one should remember that this achievement requires that the project be "rented up," and that the tenants are paying the projected market rents.

[34] This assumes that all of the cash flow is distributed to the investor. When a project is operated in a partnership with more than one investor, some of the cash flow may be retained as operating capital or in capital replacement reserves. The analysis described here assumes that the cash flow is available to the investor for other investments.

[35] Operating expenses are the cost of operating the project and include the items you might expect, such as maintenance costs, administrative or "office" expense, promotional or advertising expense, insurance premiums, real estate taxes, security, and utilities. *See* text at note 14 *supra*. Expenses also usually include a fee paid to the manager of the project, which may be a professional management concern, and is usually a percentage (4–5%) of Effective Gross Income. *See* note 36, *infra*.

[36] A more sophisticated analysis will include an analysis of the rents and the potential loss due to vacancy (usually assumed to be 5%). Vacancy loss is the loss of rental income because the rental unit is not occupied by a rent-paying tenant. Even fully rented apartment projects will incur vacancy loss as tenants leave and the apartment is prepared for a new tenant. Rent net of the vacancy loss ("Effective Gross Income") is then inflated at an assumed rate. Operating expenses may be broken out by category, with assumed inflation rates (usually greater than the rate used for income) for each type of expense. Income and expenses would then be netted for each year in the investment period, resulting in increased net operating income, but not at a uniform rate. The example discussed here shortcircuits that process by assuming an inflation rate for net operating income.

Figure 2.3

Text Example: Cash Flow Table

Current Law

Year	*Free And Clear*	*Depre-ciation*	*Debt Payments*		*Cash Flow After Finance*	*Taxable Income*	*Net Aftertax Cash Flow*	*Cash from Sale*	*Aggregate After-tax Cash Flow*
			Interest	*Principal*					
-									(2,500,000)
1	900,000	313,650	560,155	69,138	270,707	26,195	261,539		261,539
2	918,000	327,240	554,788	74,505	288,707	35,972	276,117		276,117
3	936,360	327,240	549,004	80,289	307,067	60,116	286,026		286,026
4	955,087	327,240	542,771	86,522	325,794	85,076	296,018		296,018
5	974,189	327,240	536,054	93,239	344,896	110,895	306,083		306,083
6	993,673	327,240	528,816	100,477	364,380	137,617	316,214		316,214
7	1,013,546	327,240	521,015	108,278	384,253	165,291	326,401		326,401
8	1,033,817	327,240	512,610	116,683	404,524	193,967	336,635		336,635
9	1,054,493	327,240	503,551	125,742	425,200	223,702	346,905		346,905
10	1,075,583	327,330	493,790	135,504	446,290	254,464	357,228	3,318,109	3,675,337
	9,854,749	3,258,900	5,302,555	990,376	3,561,818	1,293,294	3,109,165		6,427,274

IRR: 13.72%

*Assume that net operating income (free and clear) increases by 2.0% per year

In generating the cash flow table, net operating income was inflated by 2% per year. This may be a fairly conservative assumption, as the articles following this discussion show. In this chapter, and for the most part throughout this work, we accept the assumption that rents will increase over time, since this is the general historical pattern. How rapidly they will rise, particularly for shopping centers, is anybody's guess, and experience, at the time we write this in mid-2009, suggests that decreases in rents (and therefore value) will occur, even severe decreases, from time to time.

With traditional financing, the mortgage payments remain constant over the term of the mortgage. As net operating income rises, the net cash yield also rises modestly over time. The amount of the debt service payment which is deductible for tax purposes, however, depends on the amount of interest paid on the mortgage. Since the interest paid in each payment is calculated on the remaining unpaid principal at the beginning of the payment period, the amount of deductible interest included in each payment will decrease each year as payments are made on the mortgage. Because tax depreciation is calculated on a pro rata basis over the investment period, that deduction will remain constant. The amount of rental income not offset by deductible expenses will rise over time, therefore, with the investor's tax cost increasing.

You may notice that the portion of the mortgage payment which is applied to reduce principal benefits the investor because her equity increases as the principal due on the mortgage decreases. Payment of the mortgage principal, however, is not a distribution to the investor but rather has the effect of an additional contribution of capital.[37] An increase in the equity investment means additional funds have been *committed to* the project and should not be treated as a return on that equity investment (funds *withdrawn* from the project). Principal payments are eventually repaid to the investor when the property is sold, the mortgage is paid, and the net sales proceeds are distributed, in the same manner as the investor's original capital contribution may be recovered.

[b] Some Calculations

Our investor's cash inflows over the projected ten year investment period are shown in Figure 2.3. If the investor sells her interest in the project after ten years, her cash inflow for the tenth year will be increased by the net proceeds of the sale. To complete the picture drawn here of the full cycle of the investment, therefore, it is necessary to estimate a future sales price. Because this estimate is inherently unreliable, a number of different prices can be projected, and the effect of a sale at each price on the rate of return is determined. For purposes of illustration, assume that a capitalization rate higher than the initial cap rate, say by one percentage point, will be required by a purchaser in the year of sale, and use that rate to capitalize the net operating income shown on our cash flow table for the tenth year of operation.[38] In the example, net operating income projected for year 10 is

---

[37] The additional investment is itself derived from the property and not independently paid by the investor from an outside source. Therefore, it does *not* reduce the investor's rate of return. As the text notes, nor does it increase the investor's rate of return.

[38] The best practice is to increase the cap rate in order to estimate a sales price. An increased cap rate may be appropriate for the project because it is older, perhaps subject to increased competition or in need of improvement. This indicates that a prospective purchaser would likely pay *less* for the same cash flows, that is to say, would require a greater return to compensate for increased risk. Of course, we do

$1,075,583 approximately, and the cap rate would be 10% (initial cap rate = 9% + 1%). This yields an estimated sales price of $10,755,830 ($1,075,583 ÷ 10%), which is, we hope, conservative. Because sales proceeds are larger than operating cash flows, estimates of the future selling price of the property frequently have disproportionate effects on the rate of return calculation and should be approached cautiously. *See* Figure 2.5, *infra*.

In the sale, the unpaid balance of the mortgage must be paid out of the gross sales price, and the federal income tax paid on the profit from the sale. In the example, the remaining unpaid mortgage balance will be $6,509,624. The taxable gain will be the difference between the price (assumed to be $10,755,830) and the adjusted tax basis[39] for the apartment project (original cost ($10,000,000) minus accumulated depreciation ($3,258,900) = $6,741,100). Taxable gain on the projected sale of the project at the end of the tenth year is then: $10,755,830 (the "amount realized") less $6,741,100 (the "adjusted basis") equals $4,014,743 (the "gain realized").[40] Since our investor has held the project for the production of income (a "capital asset"), the gain will be taxed as capital gain, and the amount of the tax will be subject to certain maximum limits. For sales occurring after the effective date of the 1997 Tax Act, the tax cannot exceed 25% of the gain attributable to previously deducted depreciation (.25 × $3,258,900 = $814,725),[41] plus 15% of the gain in excess of that amount (.15 × $755,833 (market capital gain) = $113,375).[42] The after-tax cash proceeds will thus be $3,318,109 ($10,755,833 (sales proceeds) − $6,509,624 (balance due on the mortgage) − $814,715 (tax on previously deducted depreciation) − $113,375 (tax on the balance of the gain)), which, for purposes of this analysis, is treated as an additional cash inflow at the end of the tenth year.

---

not know what the situation will be ten years in the future, so this is just an approximation of what we believe is likely to be the situation.

[39] "Adjusted basis" is a tax concept. It refers to the investor's original cost, IRC § 1012, plus additional capital expenditures (*e.g.*, capital improvements to the building), minus "adjustments" prescribed by section 1016. Cost recovery deductions are the only "adjustment" with which we need to be concerned here. *See* note 18, *supra*.

[40] IRC § 1001(a).

[41] The recent history of maximum tax rates applicable to capital gains is interesting. Although depreciation is deducted from ordinary income, the gain resulting, at least in part, from the basis adjustments will be taxed as capital gain from depreciable real estate. When the capital gain deduction was repealed in 1986, the maximum marginal tax rate applicable to capital gains was set at 28%. In 1997, capital gains rates were lowered in the so-called "Taxpayer Relief Act of 1997," but in a very complex manner. For depreciable real estate (that is improvements to real estate, since land is not depreciable) held for at least one full year, the rate is 25% on "unrecaptured section 1250 gain," IRC § 1(h)(1)(D), but "unrecaptured section 1250 gain" is defined to include an amount equal to *all* depreciation taken with respect to the real estate asset, with no phase out. IRC § 1(h)(7)(A). Thus, although the investor would ordinarily pay income tax at a marginal rate of 35%, the gain from the sale of the project would be taxed, at most, at 25%, a modest although significant differential (10%). This effect, achieving a rate arbitrage for the depreciation deductions is generally referred to as "conversion." The marginal variations in the capital gains rate have little effect on rates of return for real estate assets, so one might well wonder why our political policymakers have been so convinced that changing the rate of tax on capital gains could produce a dramatic improvement in the economy.

[42] IRC § 1(h)(1)(C). The 15% maximum rate on capital gain was enacted in 2003, by the Jobs and Growth Tax Relief and Reconciliation Act of 2003, P.L. 108-27, § 301(b)(1)(A). This provision expires at the end of 2010, along with the other "Bush Tax Cuts," after which the previous maximum rate, 20%, would apply. It seems clear that there will be significant tax legislation before the 15% rate expires, but what that legislation will provide is anybody's guess. We have made the calculations assuming that the current maximum rate will continue to apply in 2018, although uncertainty in what the tax will be at that time is another risk to take into account when making these projections.

[c] The Internal Rate of Return

If the timing of the inflows were disregarded, the total return would be the sum of the annual inflows ($3,109,165) plus the net proceeds on sale ($3,318,109) or $6,427,274 on an initial investment of $2,500,000 — a profit of $3,927,274. Spread evenly over ten years, this would be an average of $39,000 per year, or about 15.7%. But dollars received early are worth more than dollars received later, and it is this fact which creates the necessity for the calculations needed to determine the internal rate of return. Using a present value table (Table A, at the end of this chapter) our investor can find an interest rate which will make the present value of all the inflows equal to his outflow.[43] This calculation has been done in Figure 2.4.

Figure 2.4

Text Example: Present Value of Cash Inflows

Year	Cash Inflows	Present Value of $1 at	Present Value of inflow at 13%	Present Value of $1 at	Present Value of inflow at 14%
	Discount Rates:	*13%*		*14%*	
1	261,539	0.885	231,450	0.877	229,420
2	276,117	0.783	216,240	0.769	212,463
3	286,026	0.693	198,231	0.675	193,060
4	296,018	0.613	181,553	0.592	175,266
5	306,083	0.543	166,129	0.519	158,970
6	316,214	0.480	151,883	0.456	144,063
7	326,401	0.425	138,740	0.400	130,442
8	336,635	0.376	126,629	0.351	118,011
9	346,905	0.333	115,479	0.308	106,676
10	3,675,337	0.295	1,082,711	0.270	991,399
	6,427,274		2,609,047		2,459,769

In making the calculation, the sum of the present values for each cash inflow at a discount rate of 13% does not reduce the present value of the inflows to $2,500,000, which means that the rate of return must be greater than 13%. At 14%, the present value of the inflows is less than $2,500,000, which means that the rate of return must be less than 14%. Interpolation (which is not wholly accurate because present discounted value does not vary linearly in relation to the rate of return) indicates that the projected inflows would have a present value of $2,500,000 if discounted at 13.73%, which is then the approximate internal rate of return for the example, a determination which accords well with the computer generated number shown in Figure 2.3, which was calculated on a personal computer. The interpolation is shown below. Remember that the accurate discount rate is greater than 13% which means that the interpolation calculation begins at 13% (the higher present value shown in figure 2.4):

[43] Using a spreadsheet on a personal computer, discounting to present value is relatively simple, and can be done quickly for any interest rate. The mechanical operation of finding the internal rate of return is done here to help you to see what you are trying to do with a spreadsheet, so that you can understand what is being done, and how assumptions affect the calculations.

$$\frac{\$2{,}609{,}047 - \$2{,}500{,}000}{\$2{,}609{,}047 - \$2{,}459{,}769} = \frac{109{,}047}{149{,}277} = 0.73$$

As pointed out in the discussion, the unadjusted internal rate of return assumes, in the comparison with rates of return generated by other investments, that the cash inflows received by the investor from the project are in fact reinvested and continue to earn at the same rate. This is never true. The return on other investments is often less than the return generated by the real estate investment, so some adjustment is required in order to determine the effect of the investment on the investor's return for the full investment period. Assuming that each cash inflow is immediately reinvested by the investor at a 6% *after-tax* return, the "adjusted internal rate of return" would be reduced to 11.4%.[44]

[4] Issues in Making Cash Flow Projections

In the following material, we discuss some problems in generating accurate results from cash flow projections and the impact of these problems on value. The Securities and Exchange Commission generally forbids the use of cash flow projections in registration statements to determine value. Can you see why? The conclusions presented by pro formas which have been generated through the use of computerized spreadsheets provide the illusion of precision As you now understand, projecting cash flows into the future is not scientific, as no one can predict what economic conditions will be even a short time into the future, and the precision suggested by the pro forma is not any more reliable than the assumptions made about those conditions in making the calculations. Investors who do not question these assumptions may easily be misled about the risks they would take in making an investment in reliance on the pro formas.

[a] Residual Value

The investor's share of the net distributable proceeds from the projected sale of the project at the investment horizon is treated as a large cash flow in the final year of the investment period. Because this cash flow is much larger than operating cash flows, it can have a disproportionate effect on the internal rate of return. The effect of varying the sales price on rates of return is shown in Figure 2.5. As you see, the effect is substantial. This problem can be more fully explored through a spreadsheet by determining the present values of the various components which contribute to the return earned on the investment. It is not difficult to demonstrate that assumptions as to the sale price can contribute *as much as 50% of the value* taken into account in determining return on investment.

---

[44] For a discussion of the methodology to adjust the internal rate of return by analyzing return on other investments, see C.Edward Chang & Robert W. Owens, *Modifying the Internal Rate of Return Method for Real Estate Investment Selection*, 29 REAL EST. REV. No. 3, 36 (1999).

Figure 2.5 Text Example: Internal Rates of Return

Compared for different assumed sales prices

Sales Price	*Unadjusted*	*Adjusted*	*No Tax*
$1,000,000	12.435%	10.374%	15.289%
$1,100,000	14.107%	11.699%	16.866%
$1,200,000	15.553%	12.896%	18.246%
$1,300,000	16.832%	13.988%	19.475%
$1,400,000	17.980%	14.994%	20.585%

* "Adjusted internal rate of return" means investor's assumed return on investment of cash flows = 6%

[b] Tax Leverage

The cash flow tables and the various rates of return were generated by making assumptions about the tax position of the individual investor and by subtracting her projected income tax liability. To understand the history of real estate investing, one must know a lot more about changes in the income tax law. Before 1986, when the Congress removed many of the incentives which had made real estate so attractive to tax sensitive investors, rates of return would be higher *after-tax* than in the absence of any tax. This meant that the tax law had *subsidized* investment in real estate and had, because returns are invariably calculated after-tax, enhanced the capitalized value of all real estate investments. Sudden removal of the tax incentives contributed to the real estate recession in the late 1980s and early 90s. Because of the adverse effects of these incentives on the markets, it seems unlikely that such substantial incentives will again be provided for investment in real estate, but income tax considerations remain an important consideration in real estate investment decisions.

Most traditional real estate syndications have substantial leverage, meaning that the amount of debt the syndication carries is a high percentage of the project's cost, sometimes as much as 100%. The treatment of debt, for both financial and tax purposes, explains this result. Equity owners have been able to increase return to equity on an investment by using debt-financing with fixed costs and a claim limited to a fixed portion of the project's capital. When the return to the project (the capitalization rate) exceeds the fixed cost of the debt, the difference on the debt-financed portion of the project's cost is captured by the investors who own the residual interest in the project. This is called *financial leverage*. For positive leverage to exist, the payment rate on the debt (the "constant") must be less than the capitalization rate for the project, a fact which may not always be true, as recent experience in the real estate markets has shown. The illustration used in the text assumes an interest rate of 7.5% on the debt, which, with level payments over 30 years, produces a "constant" of.0839, and a cap rate of 9%. Financial leverage in this project is therefore positive: a portion of the return on the *debt* portion of the project enhances the return to the holders of the *equity*. The effect of leverage is illustrated by Figure 2.6.

Figure 2.6 Text Example: Variation in Relative Mortgage Size

Comparison of the effect on return on equity and after-tax internal rate of return for a 7.5%, 30 year standard mortgage

mortgage percentage	*value equity*	*debt service*	*cash flow after finance*	*debt constant*	*cash-on-cash*	*after-tax internal rate of return*
90.0%	$1,000,000	$ 755,152	$ 144,848	0.0839	14.5%	23.8%
80.0%	$2,000,000	$ 671,246	$ 228,754	0.0839	11.4%	15.6%
75.0%	$2,500,000	$ 629,293	$ 270,707	0.0839	10.8%	13.7%
60.0%	$4,000,000	$ 503,434	$ 396,566	0.0839	9.9%	10.7%
50.0%	$5,000,000	$ 419,529	$ 480,471	0.0839	9.6%	9.6%

In this example, note that as the size of the mortgage in relation to total project cost increases, *pre-tax return on equity* (cash-on-cash for first normal year) also increases.

When the *after-tax return* is considered, however, under the assumptions made for this project, the *internal rate of return* increases much more rapidly as the relative size of the debt increases. This results from the interplay of two factors. First, it was assumed that net operating income would *increase* at the rate of 2% per year over the life of the project. Debt service on the first mortgage remains constant. Thus, the *equity share* of the cash flow from the project *increases* over time. As a relative matter, the larger the debt (*i.e.*, that portion of return on the property which is fixed), the higher the return to the equity investor. Second, taking tax into account tends to enhance cash flow early in the project while reducing cash flow at the end of the investment period, that is, by *deferring* payment of tax on a portion of the project's operating income until the project is sold. This *deferral* (the effect of tax leverage) increases the internal rate of return as the proportion of the project financed with fixed debt increases.

From Figure 2.6 the effect of leverage is readily apparent in the internal rate of return, particularly for a more highly leveraged project. A 12.5% increase (from 80% to 90%) in the amount of the mortgage brings about a 52% increase in the return to equity (from 15.6% to 23.8%). Another way of analyzing the leverage is to note that because there is a spread between the cost of debt and the 9.0% return on total assets, the investor's return must be greater than 9.0%. For example, in the case of a 7.5%, 30 year mortgage for 75% of the cost:

9.0% of investment ($2,500,000) produces:	$225,000.
+.6% (9.0%-8.4%) × principal of the mortgage:	+ $45,000
Net cash flow to equity investors:	$270,000

The example demonstrates why the advantage of financial leverage *increases* as the proportion of debt increases, thus showing the benefit of arranging a mortgage that is as large a percentage of the total asset cost as possible.[45] In the case illustrated here, as you can see, the effect of financial leverage is greatest at very high leverage.

---

[45] The difference between the return on the debt portion and the overall cap rate on project cost enhances the investor's cash-on-cash return. As principal on the debt is paid, this advantage diminishes, slowly at first. The proportion of the project cost (and later, value) which consists of debt is important, and this increases the incentive to stretch out payment terms (lengthen the amortization period) as much as possible. It is also an incentive to refinance as rents, and therefore value, increase.

Figure 2.7 Text Example: Variation in Loan Term

Comparison of effect on return on equity and after-tax internal rate of return for 7.5%, 75% mortgage

Time to pay down	*debt service*	*cash flow after finance*	*debt constant*	*cash-on-cash*	*after-tax internal rate of return*
40	$ 592,264	$ 307,736	0.079	12.3%	14.2%
30	$ 629,293	$ 270,707	0.084	10.8%	13.7%
25	$ 665,092	$ 234,908	0.089	9.4%	13.3%
20	$ 725,034	$ 174,966	0.097	7.0%	12.6%
15	$ 834,311	$ 65,689	0.111	2.6%	11.7%

Figure 2.7 provides the same information about the return on the project as the repayment term is varied. Obviously there are benefits to having a long-term mortgage (or, more accurately, a mortgage under which level payments are required as if the mortgage had a long term).[46] In this case, the mortgage constant exceeds the capitalization rate for terms shorter than 30 years. The 15-year term, for example, illustrates a case of *negative leverage*. In that case, some of the return on the *equity* portion of the project is used to pay some of the debt service. The analysis used above indicates what has happened:

9.0% of investment ($2,500,000) produces:	$225,000.
−2.1% (9.0%-11.1%) × principal of the mortgage:	– $157,500
Net cash flow to equity investors:	$67,500

In the negative leverage case, the investor is *not* losing money, but compared to the 9.0% return on assets, she is *building up her equity position* at the rate of $157,500 per year, as a glance at the IRR for the project with such a loan shows. Because equity build-up cannot be realized until sale or refinancing of the building, it is not included in the calculations of return from operations.

Finally, Figure 2.8 illustrates the effect of varying the interest rate.

---

[46] Recall that the amortization term is the number of years over which level payments, at the specified interest rate, would fully amortize or pay off the loan. *See* note 31, *supra*. Most real estate loans have a shorter maturity date, at which time the remaining unpaid principal of the loan is due and payable (the "balloon"). Up until the financial credit crunch beginning in 2008, most real estate developers were not concerned with a shorter term to maturity, as they fully expected to be able to refinance the first mortgage loan, usually for a large amount which would be used to, first, repay the balance due on the existing mortgage, and, second provide additional proceeds which could, *inter alia*, be distributed to investors. The tax implications of refinancing are discussed in Chapter 3.

Figure 2.8 Text Example: Variation in Interest Rate

Comparison of effect on return on equity and after-tax internal rate of return for 30 year, 75% mortgage

interest rate	*debt service*	*cash flow after finance*	*debt constant*	*cash-on-cash*	*after-tax internal rate of return*
12.00%	$ 925,751	$ (25,751)	0.123	-1.0%	6.2%
11.50%	$ 891,262	$ 8,738	0.119	0.3%	7.1%
11.00%	$ 857,091	$ 42,909	0.114	1.7%	7.9%
10.50%	$ 823,265	$ 76,735	0.110	3.1%	8.8%
10.00%	$ 789,814	$ 110,186	0.105	4.4%	9.7%
9.00%	$ 724,160	$ 175,840	0.097	7.0%	11.3%
8.00%	$ 660,388	$ 239,612	0.088	9.6%	12.9%
7.00%	$ 598,772	$ 301,228	0.080	12.0%	14.5%
6.00%	$ 539,595	$ 360,405	0.072	14.4%	15.9%

As the interest rate on the debt is reduced, it should be obvious why the net advantage for the equity investors increases.

Developers almost always seek to increase the amount of leverage on their projects, and in good economic times they are able to. If the first mortgage lender required a 70% debt-to-value ratio,[47] for example, the developer might then negotiate to obtain "mezzanine" financing, in which the lender would take a security interest in the equity interests of the investors in the project.[48] The mezzanine loan would be made to owners of the investment interests in the project, and not to the entity which owned the project, with the understanding that the loan was secondary financing for the project. Mezzanine lending is not true debt, but rather a form of equity with debt characteristics. Because of the risk involved, mezzanine loans require much higher interest. Analysis of these financing techniques requires a more complex analysis of sharing rental income streams, which is beyond our focus here (on the more traditional capital structure typically found in real estate transactions).

§ 2.03 APPLYING PRESENT VALUE CONCEPTS TO ANALYSIS OF REAL ESTATE PROJECTS

DCF analysis is a powerful analytic tool for determining the value of real estate projects to inform the developer's decision whether to proceed with the project and, subsequently, the investor's decision whether to contribute capital to the project. This analytic technique is used to make private investment decisions, because the public markets, which now play an important role in financing U.S. real estate, use different methods to measure the value of an investment. It is important now to evaluate the reliability of the conclusions that are based on the application of the method.

---

[47] After the real estate recession in the late 1980s through the early 1990s, first mortgage lenders became more wary of secondary financing, and often required provisions in mortgage loan documents which prevented loans secured by a secondary lien on the project itself, such as, for example, "due on encumbrance" provisions. These provisions have led to more creative financing which has contributed to the current economic situation.

[48] *See* James D. Prendergast, *Secured Real Estate Mezzanine Lending (With Form)*, 23 PRAC. REAL EST. LAW. NO. 2, 35 (2007); Andrew R. Berman, *"Once a Mortgage, Always a Mortgage" — The Use (and Misuse of) Mezzanine Loans and Preferred Equity Investments*, 11 STAN. J.L. BUS. & FIN. 76 (2005).

The personal computer has lent an aura of precision to the analysis which, perhaps, it does not deserve. Certainly, as the articles explain, anyone who is relying on DCF analysis in making significant investment decisions must proceed with caution.

[1] Using DCF Techniques

[a] A Cautious Approach to DCF Analysis

J. Douglas Timmons & Wayne R. Archer,
Discounted Cash Flow Analysis and Unpredictable Cash Flows
18 REAL EST. REV. No. 3, 26–30 (1988)[*]

Discounted Cash Flow (DCF) techniques have arrived in the world of real estate, but their welcome has been mixed. Many question whether these techniques improve real estate decisions, and the answer is less than obvious.

Two years ago, this question was pressed in *Real Estate Review* by Hugh Nourse who, considering the uncertainty that he observed in real estate cash flows, came to a negative verdict.[1] In place of DCF analysis, Nourse argued for "behavioralist analysis" that involves three types of decision skills:

1. Interpreting clues about a project, location, site, building, finance, and management;
2. Avoiding some common risks; and
3. Improving negotiating skills.

Nourse is persuasive, but his verdict appears too sweeping. The investor should approach each investment problem using the tools that appear to be most effective for the particular case. The first question to be addressed should be, "What kind of analysis will be useful for analyzing this particular problem?" This article examines this basic question. It then asks, "If DCF analysis appears to be a useful option, how may one achieve better real estate decision making through its use?"

CASH FLOW PREDICTABILITY AND THE METHOD OF ANALYSIS

Investment analysis of real estate involves computing both quantitative returns and the management of risk. So a circumspect investor tries to assure that risk is reduced as far as it is cost effective to do so. From this perspective, Nourse's "behavioralist" steps are integral to any prudent approach to real estate investment, regardless of whether the investor uses DCF analysis. Thus, there actually is no conflict between prudent use of DCF analysis and a "behavioralist" approach to real estate investment. One is not a substitute for the other.

---

[*] J. Douglas Timmons is an Assistant professor in The College of Business at the University of Texas at San Antonio. Wayne R. Archer is an Assistant Professor in the College of Business Administration at the University of Florida, Gainesville. This article is reprinted with the permission of the West Group, Inc.

[1] Nourse, "Improve Investment Decisions by Breaking the DCF habit," 15 Real Est. Rev. 75–80 (Winter 1986).

But the question still remains, when is DCF analysis useful in the investment-decision process? The applicability of any analytical approach to the real estate investment problem depends on the predictability of the property cash flows. The polar cases, of course, are those in which the cash flows are either completely certain or completely uncertain. But real-world cash flows lie between these extremes. The more predictable the cash flows from an investment, the more useful are the refinements of DCF analysis. At a moderate level of certainty, such as in a case in which distant cash flows are unpredictable but immediate cash flows are reasonably sure, DCF sensitivity analysis is still useful. In contrast, when cash flows are highly uncertain, say, in the development of highly innovative projects, it is doubtful that any projection of cash flows is fruitful.

Underlying the predictability spectrum, of course, is a risk spectrum. The less predictable the cash flows, the greater the risk that the investor takes in making the investment. Similarly, cases in which the method of analysis must be rudimentary, are also those in which the risk is high.

Elements That Determine Investment Risk

It is possible to identify seven dimensions of real estate that affect the riskiness of a property and the investor's ability to predict its cash flows:

1. Stability of the local economy;
2. Durability of project location;
3. Predictability of tenant(s);
4. Terms of the leases;
5. Uniqueness of the project concept;
6. Maturity of the project; and
7. Capacity of management.

An additional determinant of risk is the quality of information available to the investor. Quality of data can be a factor apart from the risk characteristics of the property itself that reduces the certainty of cash flow predictions.

- *Stability of the local economy*. Some communities, because of the nature of their economic bases, tend to have steady growth, modest employment fluctuations, and only small annual changes in the character of their basic economic activities. This stability is reflected in local real estate demand. Many real estate markets are local in character. They are dependent on the local economy, which in turn depends on money generated from the "export" activities of the community. Stable "export" activity tends to translate into stable demand for retail, residential, and commercial properties.

- *Durability of project location*. There are nodes within almost any community where the economic activity has remained robust and steady over many years. Certain commercial locations have remained fully built up, and when one land use becomes obsolete it is quickly replaced by another. Examples of these locations include areas adjacent to major universities or civil service centers, the land around key freeway intersections and central commuter routes, and the areas around major airports. Finally, residential locations that are attractive, are fully built up, have good commuter access, and are well buffered from deleterious intrusions can hold their attraction for decades.

- *Predictability of tenants.* Properties that serve unpredictable tenants, even if located within a stable local economy in a durable location, can have cash flows that fluctuate from year to year. Extreme examples are clubs or "trendy" restaurants. Yesterday's "in" place can be tomorrow's vacant building. Fast-food restaurants, motel chains, and many real estate firms are examples of less explosive but still volatile tenants.

- *Lease terms.* Lease terms are also factors in cash flow stability. Cash flow is more certain as the lease payment is less dependent on tenant income. It is also more certain if some expense changes can be passed through to the tenant by means of pass-through clauses or "expense stops."

- *Uniqueness of project concept.* The more unique a real estate venture, the greater the chance that it will be either a great success or a significant failure. Innovations like central-city conversions, "festival" shopping centers, "off-price" shopping malls, "food courts," condominium retail centers, and innovative condominium apartments are examples of these "unique" concepts.

The authors recently examined a new food court occupied strictly by local fast-food vendors, located on the back side of a new off-price shopping center in an "oil patch" community. DCF analysis of the property would have been an overly precise decision-making technique.

- *Maturity of the project.* Before a project is fully occupied, it faces risks that could delay the achievement of projected operating income. Similar risks arise whenever the stage is set for high tenant turnover, because of extensive rehabilitation and rent increases, change in use of the property, or changing neighborhood.

- *Capacity of management.* The quality of a property's management team affects both its performance and its economic stability. An owner who lacks experience or financial strength may fail to maintain good management, causing a property to become vulnerable over time to sharp changes in its operating cash flows.

- *Information failure.* Poor market information will reduce cash flow predictability. If, in a local apartment market, data on current vacancy rates, new apartment construction, condominium conversion activity, or local employment changes are incomplete or inaccurate, the developer will be unable to produce accurate forecasts of otherwise fairly predictable cash flows. Unfortunately, data in many local real estate markets are incomplete and their quality is difficult to evaluate. Thus, the possibility of information failure may reduce the investor's confidence in the accuracy of cash flows that normally are readily predictable.

THE BENEFITS OF DCF ANALYSES

The higher a property is on the scale of cash flow predictability, the greater is the benefit of using DCF analysis to make property decisions. DCF analysis has been questioned broadly, but it is popular because of the following potential advantages:

1. It uses explicit projections of cash flows;

2. It accounts for the time value of money;

3. It makes real estate decision making comparable with the decision techniques used for other assets; and

4. It has fewer unstated assumptions than other decision techniques.

• *DCF utilizes explicit projections of cash flows.* Although it has been argued that the explicit cash flow forecasts required for DCF analysis are a weakness of the technique, this criticism is valid only if better information is available for other forecasting techniques. The major alternative "data" are market-derived capitalization rates. These "cap" rates contain implicit expectations about future cash flows. In order to serve as a substitute for an explicit projection, however, a cap rate must reflect the experience of comparable properties for which the investor has comparable expectations about risk, growth in income, effect of taxation, economic life, financing, etc. Such comparables have always been difficult to discover. They are even more difficult to find today. Tax reform has reduced the appropriateness of pre-tax reform cap rates. Elimination of the capital gains exclusion tends to discourage sales that will generate new evidence. In more and more markets, there are no valid substitutes for explicit income forecasts.

• *DCF analysis accounts for the value of time.* Since real estate decisions generate benefits and costs that occur at different times, it is necessary to adjust for the timing differences to make them directly comparable. The economic rationale for time adjustments (time-value-of-money theory) is well-known and does not require lengthy defense. Since the timing of cash inflows and outflows is a major element in the comparative desirability of investment alternatives, time-adjusted measures of return are an essential tool of rational investment analysis. Its ability to compare and evaluate projects in which the cash inflows and outflows are differently timed is the true strength of the DCF method.

• *DCF analysis is a decision-making technique that parallels techniques used in making other capital budgeting decisions.* DCF analysis makes real estate decisions comparable with a larger set of corporate asset management decisions or with other asset portfolio decisions.

To categorically forsake the use of DCF analysis in investment decision making would be a step backwards. Using comparisons of net present value that attempt to determine which projects are expected to add most to investor wealth is preferable to using less sophisticated techniques even under conditions of some uncertainty. Although investors cannot consider all possible opportunities, they still can maximize investment value within the limited investment universe that they do consider.

• *DCF requires more explicit assumptions, but fewer unstated assumptions, than traditional analysis does.* Discounted cash flow analysis requires the understanding of more technical methods of analysis, the acquisition of additional data and estimates, and extra time and effort on the part of the analyst. The payoff, however, is the ability to make analysis more specific.

By contrast, the simpler ratio analysis, which is traditional in real estate, is subject to many limitations. Problems with using capitalization rates were alluded to previously. Using equity dividend rates (cash on cash returns) to choose among projects also is troublesome because using this ratio as a "hurdle rate" confuses the effects of investor attributes with the effects of project attributes. On the investor side, the appropriate equity dividend rate depends on the investor's required yield and income tax situation. On the property side, the required equity dividend rate depends on the expected growth of cash flows, the degree of financial leverage, the income tax characteristics of the property, and the expected selling price.

For highly leveraged real estate, the expected rate of appreciation is a particularly critical determinant of the required equity dividend rate. When all else is equal, differences in expected (forecast) appreciation can cause the required equity dividend rate to range from negative to, say, more than 10%.

THE RISKS OF DCF ANALYSIS

The major risks of using DCF analysis are (1) that the investor may misinterpret the results or (2) the process requires a lengthy expenditure of time and attention. The former most likely would result from a failure to conduct adequate risk assessment beforehand, which could be a serious failure for any approach to real estate investment. The second would occur if time and attention were diverted to futile forecasting of unpredictable events at the expense of better risk management.

Both errors are possible, but neither is necessary. Adequate attention to risk assessment and risk management at the beginning of the investment process is probably the prescription for avoidance of both errors. The better the understanding of the risk character of the property, the better the sense of what additional refinements in analysis are useful. There is never a substitute for good judgement in real estate analysis; focusing on the risk characteristics of the property at the onset should help to make the judgment come more easily.

PROPER USE OF THE DCF TECHNIQUE

Rather than abandoning DCF analysis, as some real estate analysts suggest, the real estate investor should seek to use the technique more appropriately. Many investors who employ DCF tend to short-cut the technique (possibly because they are overwhelmed by the mathematics and computations associated with the model). For example, many analysts use single-point (best-guess) estimates of input variables, and their analysis is based solely on that one scenario.

The purpose of DCF models is not to foresee the future but rather to help investors determine the implications of plausible futures. In those circumstances where future operating results can be predicted with considerable certainty, the DCF technique is an appropriate tool for making investment decisions, such as accepting or rejecting a project, ranking projects, or evaluating alternative methods of financing. Even when the cash flows of a project have limited certainty, however, DCF sensitivity analysis can serve as a means for determining where risks lie and what impact those risks may have on profitability. Frequently, sensitivity analysis can bring to light important considerations that have been neglected.

The DCF Process

The objective of the process is to use DCF analysis prudently. The following five steps suggest how this might be accomplished:

• *Gather data.* All data, whether quantitative or qualitative, that have a bearing on the potential cash flows of the investment should be sought.

• *Evaluate the data/estimate input variables.* Estimation of future cash flows requires that the analyst convert the gathered data into quantitative form. Since this is the most important step in proper DCF analysis, the analyst *must* carefully evaluate all data and then consider how those data will affect the input variables required by the model. Plausible five-to-ten-year projections should be developed for various economic scenarios, perhaps (1) most likely, (2) worst case, (3) best case. These first two steps normally will be the most time-consuming portion of any real estate investment analysis.

• *Calculate DCF values.* Depending on the model being used, values like NPV and IRR most likely will be determined for all scenarios.[2]

• *Interpret results.* Under which scenarios does the project have a positive NPV or an IRR that satisfies investor requirements? *Why* does the project meet or fail to meet investor requirements? Sensitivity analysis may help to pinpoint those variables that affect profitability most. Another useful analysis is partitioning of IRR to determine which type of cash flow benefits a project most depends on.[3] These techniques not only clarify how and why a project may or may not work, but also serve as basic risk analysis. Other more sophisticated types of risk analysis, such as the certainty-equivalent approach, decision trees, and Monte Carlo simulation, also could be incorporated into the DCF process. For most real estate projects, however, careful sensitivity analysis is probably the most useful method of detecting key variables and identifying the risks they create.

• *Making the decision.* After careful interpretation of all output generated, the analyst makes a decision whether to accept or reject a specific investment proposal. When DCF analysis is properly used, the decision evolves around all of the data generated by the model. Projects that may have appeared to be promising based on single-point estimates often appear too risky when worst-case scenario and sensitivity analysis show specific causes for concern. Decision making, even when DCF is used, requires judgment.

CONCLUSION

Discounted cash flow analysis can be valuable, but only if two conditions are met:

1. There must be enough certainty about future cash flows to make projections worthwhile; and

---

[2] The extremely rapid evolution of microcomputer software for DCF analysis has now made it possible to set up all the computations of a DCF analysis in minutes and to recompute new scenarios in seconds. Spreadsheet-based DCF "templates" are especially flexible approaches to computation. The authors will provide more information on these templates on request.

[3] Zerbst, "Evaluating Risks by Partitioning the IRR," 9 Real Est. Rev. 80–84 (Winter 1980).

2. The technique must be used as an aid to thought rather than as a substitute for thought.

If these conditions are satisfied, then DCF analysis, especially when performed in the modern computer spreadsheet environment, can be a cost-effective aid for many real estate decisions.

[b] The Potential to Abuse DCF Analysis

Vernon Martin III,
Nine Abuses Common in Pro Forma Cash Flow Projections,
18 REAL EST. REV. No. 3, 20–24 (1988)*

The advent of personal computers and software packages for real estate investment analysis has made it so simple for analysts to perform computerized analyses of cash flows from income-producing properties over multiyear holding periods that real estate proposals using these projects have proliferated. The final computer output appears authoritative and precise and gives the impression that it is the result of thorough analysis on a lease-by-lease basis. These computer analyses, replete with estimated cash flows and internal rates of return, are now common in applications for real estate loans and in promotional packages from real estate brokers. Interestingly, these "computer analyses" never fail to justify asking prices or desired loan amounts.

THE MERITS AND DANGERS OF DISCOUNTED CASH FLOW ANALYSIS

One common feature of almost all cash flow projections is a discounted cash flow (DCF) analysis, preferably based on a lease-by-lease examination but often based on summary estimates of annual income by year, over a multiyear holding period. Lease-by-lease DCF analysis examines the cumulative flows from current leases and the expected flows from new leases executed under expected re-leasing conditions and shows the effect of these flows on a multiyear income stream. A present value of the income stream is computed by discounting cash flows according to an equity yield rate or internal rate of return (IRR) typically required by investors for similar properties. One of the reasons for the growing use of DCF analysis is the impressiveness of the presentation. Moreover, unstable markets have caused many to prefer multiyear DCF analysis over stabilized single-year capitalization.

Critics of DCF analysis decry the number of unverifiable assumptions that must be made in the course of a DCF analysis and the fact that the conclusions may be altered by manipulating variables and changing key assumptions such as growth rates and rates of return. Because computer technology has only recently made lease-by-lease analysis practical, many of the working analysts are recent college graduates who have little real estate experience. Without supervision, these young analysts are likely to produce unrealistic cash flow models. DCF analyses should be scrutinized and made to pass rigid tests.

---

* Vernon Martin III, MSRE, CFE, Certified General Appraiser, and is a Principal with American Property Research. This article is reprinted with the permission of the West Group, Inc.

EXHIBIT 1

Ten-Year Pro Forma Cash Flow Projection

(in $000)

	1	2	3	4	5	6	7	8	9	10	11
Base rental income	2,654	2,787	2,926	3,072	3,226	3,387	3,557	3,734	3,921	4,117	4,323
Expense recovery income	663	690	717	746	776	807	839	872	907	944	981
Gross potential income	3,317	3,477	3,643	3,818	4,002	4,194	4,396	4,606	4,828	5,061	5,304
Less: Rental concessions	-149	-233	-61								
Less: Vacancy/collection loss	-606	-174	-182	-191	-200	-210	-220	-230	-241	-253	-265
Effective gross income	2,562	3,070	3,400	3,627	3,802	3,984	4,176	4,376	4,587	4,808	5,039
Less: Expenses											
Management fee	-102	-123	-136	-145	-152	-159	-167	-175	-183	-192	-202
Taxes	-126	-129	-131	-134	-136	-139	-142	-145	-148	-151	-154
Insurance	-38	-39	-40	-42	-43	-44	-45	-47	-48	-50	-51
Utilities	-585	-608	-633	-658	-684	-712	-740	-770	-801	-833	-866
Other expenses	-287	-298	-310	-323	-336	-349	-363	-378	-393	-408	-425
Total expenses	-1,138	-1,197	-1,250	-1,302	-1,351	-1,403	-1,457	-1,515	-1,573	-1,634	-1,698
NOI	1,424	1,873	2,150	2,325	2,451	2,581	2,719	2,861	3,013	3,174	3,341

	noi year of sale	cap rates	
Reversion:	$ 3,342,258	8.50%	$39,320,682
less: closing costs		2.00%	-786,414
Net sales proceeds			$38,534,269
Present value of the reversion			$10,861,468
IRR =		13.50%	
Present value of NOI			$12,105,768
IRR =		13.00%	
	Total present value:		$22,967,236
	rounded to		$23,000,000

Note: Reversion occurs at the end of year 10

AN INSTRUCTIVE PRO FORMA

Exhibit 1 is a pro forma cash flow statement for a 12-story office property encumbered by "full service" or "gross" leases (with expense stops). It calculates the present value of its net operating income (NOI) and a reversion by discounting these flows at an equity yield rate or IRR. It illustrates some of the problems often found in cash flow projections.

Inflation of Income and Expenses

One obvious feature of the analysis in Exhibit 1 is the fact that income grows with perfect regularity (exactly 5% per year), indicating that a lease-by-lease analysis was probably not performed. The reader must immediately ask some obvious questions. Are there long-term leases that limit the upside rental income potential? What are the assumptions concerning market rents? Are they based on quoted rental rates or effective rental rates? Have rental statements and other concessions (such as moving allowances or extra interior finish) been accounted for? The creators of Exhibit 1 used quoted rents rather than effective rents and inflated them at 5% per annum. They have phased out rental concessions after the first three years. As a result, effective rents are rapidly increasing. Comparison of eleventh year rental income of $4,323,000 to first year "Gross *effective* rental" income (gross potential income adjusted for rental concessions) of $2,505,000 produces a compound growth rate of 5.6%. Although the difference between 5% and 5.6% seems slight, this treatment of rent concessions accounts for 10% of the rental growth over the holding period (72.44% versus 62.89%).

Growth of Operating Expenses

The rates of growth that the pro forma assigns to cash flow categories affects the outcome of the analysis. The observer must compare the relative growth rates assigned to income and expenses. It is a truism that expense growth exceeds income growth over the long term because operating expense ratios usually increase as a building ages. Exhibit 1 assumes a 5% growth rate in rental income and a 4% growth rate in expenses. Because these rates are compounded over a ten-year period, rents grow 62.9% while expenses grow only 49.2%. Thus, they drive the expense ratio for this property down at a time when it should be going up.

	Base Rental Income (in $000)	**Expenses** (in $000)	**Ratio of Expenses to Income**
Year 1	2,654	1,138	42.9%
Year 11	4,323	1,698	39.3%

The Building Owners and Managers Association publication, *1986 B.O.M.A. Experience Exchange Report: Income/Expense Analysis for Office Buildings*, gathers national data on income and expenses for office buildings. It compares mean income and expenses for various categories of office buildings and includes in its calculations comparative expense-to-income ratios for buildings of various ages. These are summarized in Exhibit 2.

Exhibit 2

RATIO OF EXPENSES TO NET OPERATING INCOME IN BUILDINGS OF VARIOUS AGES AND VARIOUS BUILDING HEIGHTS

Age	5–9 Stories	10–19 Stories	20–29 Stories
0–9 years	.396	.398	.428
10–19 years	.571	.471	.538
20–29 years	.584	.564	.500
30–39 years	.849	.607	.630

If the 12-story building of Exhibit 1 were typical of National BOMA data and had a precisely average relationship of expenses to income, it would be incurring 39.8 cents of expenses for every dollar of income early in its life, 47.1 cents of expenses per dollar of income ten years later, and 56.4 cents per dollar of income 20 years later. If expenses grow at 5% per year as assumed in the pro forma, what should be the expected income growth to produce the proper income expense ratios in ten years and 20 years?

The value of \$.398 growing at 5% per year for ten years is [$.398 \times 1.05^{10}$] or \$.648. If 64.8 cents is 47.1% of income, the income that it produces is

$$\frac{0.648}{.471} = \$1.37643$$

Thus, a dollar of expenses in year ten will produce \$1.40 of income. If \$1 of year 1 income is to produce \$1.40 in ten years time, income need grow at an average annual rate of only 3.2%.

The same set of calculations applies to the second ten years. BOMA averages indicate that year 10 expenses per dollar of income are 47.1 cents. The value of \$.471 growing at 5% per year for ten years is [$.471 \times 1.05^{10}$] or .76721.

$$\frac{.76721}{.564} = \$1.36$$

Thus, a dollar of year 20 expenses produces \$1.36 of year 20 income. If a dollar of year 10 income is to grow to \$1.36 by year 20, the growth rate is 3.125% per year.

Obviously, the income expense ratio of no individual building stays at exactly national averages. The relationships may diverge sharply in unusual market situations in which supply is restricted relative to demand. Especially in this day of competition among developers, these restricted market situations are comparatively few. In any case, reviewers should be exceedingly skeptical of any DCF analysis in which income growth exceeds or even is equal to expense growth. if income growth is expected to be stable, expenses should usually increase at a rising rate.

Digression on Percentage Rent

The reviewer who is examining the pro forma of a property in which the leases call for percentage rent should be aware of percentage rent characteristics. The landlord's percentage rental income does not necessarily increase at the same rate as either the building's base rent growth or the tenant's sales growth. If sales breakpoints are "natural breakpoints" (i.e., they are established by dividing the percentage rate into the minimum rent), then the sales overages (on which the tenant pays percentage rent) will decline as the parties negotiate new, higher rent leases.

For example, a tenant pays $12 per square foot and pledges to pay 6% on sales overages above a breakpoint. The natural breakpoint is $12/.06 = $200 per square foot. If the tenant has sales of $250 per square foot, he pays 6% of the $50 per-square-foot sales overage, or $3 per square foot. Assume that he renegotiates rent at the end of the lease term for a new rent of $18 per square foot. The new breakpoint is $18/.06 = $300 per square foot. Because the $300 breakpoint exceeds his sales income of $250 per square foot, percentage rent falls from $3 per square foot to zero. Thus, percentage rental income can decrease while all other growth trends are positive. Because percentage rental income is a residual, however, it can also grow much faster than sales growth or rental growth.

Expense Stops and Expense Recovery Income

Exhibit 1 improperly inflates expense recovery income at 4% per annum. When a property is encumbered by full-service or "gross" leases, tenants whose leases expire may be able to negotiate new leases with higher expense stops. If renewing tenants are able to get new expense stops equivalent to their pro rata share of prior-year operating expenses, they reduce their contribution to the building's expense recovery income and consequently total expense recovery income increases at a rate less than the expense growth of the property.

Vacancy and Collection Losses

The vacancy and collection loss line in Exhibit 1 is estimated as 5% of gross potential income, starting in year 2. Observers should scrutinize this assumption for its relevance to the building's current and future market situation. How competitive is the subject property, given its proposed rents? What is the quality and duration of tenancies? What competitive properties currently exist, and what competition is expected to be built in the future? In many markets today, the rule-of-thumb 5% deduction for vacancy and collection losses is inadequate.

Most real estate software today allows one to program void periods between tenancies to add precision to the estimation of vacancy losses. The crucial questions to ask are: (1) Are these void periods realistic given market conditions; and (2) What is the probability of tenant turnover?

Analyzing the Expense Lines

Expenses typically include taxes, insurance, utilities, management fees, cleaning, maintenance and repair, trash removal, landscaping, and parking lot maintenance. Growth in each expense category must be examined. Expenses should reflect any unusual inflationary cycles, such as the recent rapid increase in insurance costs in many markets or the rapid increase in fuel costs during the 1970s.

The subject property in Exhibit 1 is located in California. West Coast observers should recognize that property tax expenses are incorrect in the pro forma. In California, assessed value is adjusted to market value upon sale and assessments are generally 1% of value in addition to any special assessments.

In those markets in which space cannot be rented unless the property owner undertakes substantial tenant improvements at the property owner's expense, those who examine DCF proposals must look for a line in the "Expense" category with a title like "Tenant Improvements" or "Replacement Allowance." Most real estate software programs are capable of considerable precision in this area and allow one to plug into the model tenant improvement costs between tenancies. Once again, the observer must examine the probability of tenant turnover, the inflation of tenant improvement costs, and whether subsequent improvements will be as extensive. These expenditures are often erroneously classified as capital items and are deducted below the net operating income line in DCF analyses. Consequently, these tenant improvement expenses are omitted from the calculation of net operating income.

Leasing costs at the beginning of a project are usually treated as capital items, but re-leasing costs that are incurred in addition to management fees should be expensed rather than capitalized.

The Reversion Calculation

Many assumptions must go into the calculation of the reversion sales price. Typically, sales price is established by capitalizing the net operating income of the final or subsequent year of analysis. The resulting sales price is an influential determinant of overall present value in any DCF analysis of ten years or less. For this reason, much care should go into selecting an ending capitalization rate or "overall rate" (OAR). If the property being analyzed is already at stabilized occupancy, the observer would not ordinarily expect a lower capitalization rate in the year of reversion than in the first year. In Exhibit 1, the ending capitalization rate is 8.5%, which is lower than the initial stabilized rate of 8.75% (based on 95% occupancy).

	NOI[1]	*Price*	*OAR*
Year 1	2.013	23,000	8.75%
Year 10	3.341	39.306	8.50%

Many analysts typically add at least one-half a percentage point to current cap rates when they capitalize tenth- or eleventh-year income. If the property has an

---

[1] The year 1 net operating income (NOI) used here is not the $1.424 thousand of Exhibit 1. It is a stabilized NOI calculated by subtracting from gross potential income of $3.317 thousand, a stabilized 5% vacancy, and total expenses of $1.138 thousand.

especially limited economic life (say, it is a metal industrial building), one must make a stronger adjustment.

Californian properties present a unique reversion situation. Assessments are limited to 2% annual growth and properties are reassessed at market value upon sale; thus, the eleventh year's expenses should reflect greatly increased property tax expenses. Net income is consequently lower, but a slight downward adjustment can be made to the ending capitalization rate.

Observers should also examine sales costs upon reversion. Although it is true that investment-grade properties can be sold at commission rates as low as 1.5%, other closing costs (legal fees, prepayment penalties, and fix-up costs) may be incurred that may be equal to the cost of sales commissions.

Choosing the Internal Rate of Return

Finally, the chosen internal rate of return bears scrutiny. Is it consistent with market evidence for similar properties? Observers may want to interview clients or contacts in real estate investment firms for their investment criteria.

Observers who examine an IRR should be cognizant of relationships between current rates of return (such as the overall capitalization rate) plus rates of appreciation, perceived gradations of risk, and the resultant IRR. The IRR can be equated to the capitalization rate plus an adjustment for expected growth. When both income and value are expected to change at a constant ratio the relationship can simply be stated as: "IRR = OAR + a," where a is the rate of annual appreciation.

When income-to-value ratios are changing, similar but more complicated equations must be used. The overall capitalization rate should be based on stabilized net operating income or the IRR analysis technique described previously can lead to confusion.

Risk is an important element in IRR analysis. A real estate IRR should exceed the rates of return possible in investments less risky than real estate. If anything else were the case, there would be little incentive to develop or invest in real estate. Likewise, the IRR should exceed the mortgage loan interest rate. If anything else were the case, real estate developers and investors would leave their line of work to get into the lending business!

A CORRECTED CASH FLOW MODEL

Exhibit 3 is an 11-year pro forma cash flow projection that avoids the errors and misleading rates of change included in Exhibit 1. The projection of rental growth and expense recovery income is based on a lease-by-lease analysis. Effective market rents are inflated at 3.5% per annum and expenses rise at 5% per annum. The vacancy and collection loss line assumes a general collection loss rate of 1.5%, six-month void periods between tenancies, and 35% tenant turnover upon lease expiration. This combination of assumptions results in an average vacancy rate of 8.5%.

EXHIBIT 3

Corrected Ten-Year Pro Forma Cash Flow Projection

(in $000)

	1	2	3	4	5	6	7	8	9	10	11
Base rental income	2,505	2,556	2,850	2,900	2,798	2,808	3,022	3,199	3,345	3,420	3,734
Expense recovery income	663	663	645	664	684	768	746	752	806	869	895
Gross potential income	3,168	3,219	3,495	3,564	3,482	3,576	3,768	3,951	4,151	4,289	4,629
Less Vacancy/collection loss	(606)	(250)	(370)	(225)	(181)	(194)	(658)	(460)	(287)	(286)	(307)
Effective gross income (EGI)	2,562	2,969	3,125	3,339	3,301	3,382	3,110	3,491	3,864	4,003	4,322
Less: Expenses											
Management fee	(102)	(119)	(125)	(134)	(132)	(135)	(124)	(140)	(155)	(160)	(173)
Taxes	(140)	(143)	(146)	(149)	(152)	(155)	(158)	(161)	(164)	(167)	(187)
Insurance	(38)	(40)	(43)	(45)	(48)	(51)	(54)	(57)	(61)	(64)	(68)
Utilities	(585)	(614)	(645)	(677)	(711)	(747)	(784)	(823)	(864)	(908)	(953)
Other Expenses	(287)	(302)	(315)	(331)	(348)	(366)	(384)	(404)	(424)	(445)	(467)
Reserves for replacements and commisions	(150)	(158)	(166)	(174)	(181)	(189)	(196)	(206)	(216)	(227)	(241)
Total Expenses	(1,302)	(1,376)	(1,440)	(1,510)	(1,572)	(1,643)	(1,700)	(1,791)	(1,884)	(1,971)	(2,089)
Net Operating Income (NOI)	1,260	1,593	1,685	1,829	1,729	1,739	1,410	1,700	1,980	2,032	2,233

		Cap. Rate	
Reversion:	$ 2,233,456	12.00%	$ 18,612,133
Less : closing costs:		4.00%	$ (744,485)
Net sales proceeds			$ 17,867,648
Present value of the reversion.			$ 4,819,667
IRR =	14.00%		
Present value of the NOI.			$ 9,086,009
Total Present Value:			$ 13,905,676
rounded to			$ 14,000,000

Note: reversion occurs at the end of year 10

Initial overall rate ("OAR" or "Cap. Rate") = 11.4% (based on stabilized occupancy of 91.5%)

Ending OAR (Cap. Rate) = 12%

Property taxes are computed at 1% of market value for the first year after purchase and for the year after reversion. Consequently, a sharp increase in taxes occurs between years 10 and 11, while in previous years increases are limited to 2%. Although all other expenses were inflated at 5%, insurance expenses were inflated at 6% per annum, reflecting current trends.

A reserve allowance for tenant improvements and leasing commissions was added to the pro forma. Given the forecast of 35% turnover, an averaging of all such costs over the holding period required a reserve of 13% of all other expenses combined.

An examination of the first year of income on a vacancy-stabilized basis yields an initial OAR of 11.4% (versus an actual rate of 9%). This corresponds well with the ending capitalization rate of 12%.

NINE TEST AREAS

This article has identified nine problem areas that may mislead those who wish to evaluate pro forma cash flow statements and DCF analyses. In summary, they are the following:

- Mismatched growth rates between rental income and expenses, which become particularly misleading when they are compounded over a long period of time. For most types of properties, expense ratios should increase over time.
- Failure to consider rental concessions and effective rents and the substitution of quoted rents. Failure to use proper market rates.
- Absence of lease-by-lease analysis in properties encumbered by long-term leases (leases that extend beyond the period of analysis).
- Figures that project that expense recovery income will increase at the same growth rate as other expenses in a property encumbered by gross leases with expense stops.
- Projections for vacancy and collection losses that are not synchronized with market conditions.
- Use of operating expense categories that do not include all cost items. Common omissions are tenant improvements and leasing commissions.
- Use of ending capitalization rates that are lower than starting capitalization rates. Reversion capitalization rates should be related to the subject's property's age and remaining economic life.
- Underestimation of sales and other reversion costs.
- Use of an inappropriate internal rate of return.

This basic checklist enables observers to scrutinize pro forma cash flow statements for obvious errors, but it should by no means be considered exhaustive. Observers should seek some type of verification for every assumption used in the analysis, and the suggestions in this article should be considered merely as a prelude to proper due diligence.

[2] Questions and Notes About the Value of DCF Analysis

[a] Questions

1. How confident are you of a value obtained by using DCF analysis? How heavily would you rely on this method in deciding whether to advise a client to incur personal liability on a construction loan to build, *e.g.*, the Fox Valley Auto Care Center? In many projects, the parties first negotiate an agreement on the financial statements which they will use in creating the financial structure for their deal, and it will be helpful for you to know what to look for in reviewing a set of financials which are the foundation for the transactions the lawyers are documenting.

2. In light of the "abuses" identified by Martin which, in his view, lead inevitably to too high a value, do Timmons and Archer make a persuasive case for the use of DCF analysis? They argue that the method is not useful when cash flows are "unpredictable." Cash flows from shopping centers may be less predictable than cash flows from other types of real estate projects. How much unpredictability can be tolerated? The personal computer permits the analysis to be tested quickly and easily by varying the assumptions made in constructing cash flow tables, even tenant by tenant. "Sensitivity analysis," so-called, can be used to show which variables are likely to have the most effect on value. A knowledge of the other, less quantifiable, elements important in making investment decisions is then necessary to evaluate how significant the sensitive factors may be.

3. DCF analysis is helpful in focusing on timing factors in the analysis of the value of rent producing real estate. Notice that it values the projected income stream and not the underlying real estate itself. Obviously, however, the physical characteristics of the underlying project are centrally important to a final determination of value. Projects with the same financial characteristics may well be dramatically different types of investments, which appeal to investors with different risk/reward characteristics. To evaluate a project, then, the developer, or, for that matter, an investor, will necessarily review a variety of information much wider than the simple numerical quantities employed in the spreadsheet analysis we do here. This observation may underlie the willingness of experienced developers to rely on single multiples, such as the "cap rate," or the cash-on-cash return. This one number, adjusted to reflect the perception of risk by the professional making the analysis, may adequately convey *to that person* the return on investment expected for this particular project, but without more information, quite likely is meaningless to someone else. The point so often made in the material is that, however important spreadsheet analysis will prove to be, it is not a substitute for the developer's experience and judgment.

4. Whatever may be the case for existing properties which a purchaser investigates for the purpose of negotiating a price, how does this process work in the planning stage for a project to be constructed? What comparable information would you want to see before proceeding with the decision to construct the project? Is it the same for the investor considering whether to provide capital to the project as it is for the developer? What

information would you, as an adviser to the developer, want to have about the market segment on which success of the center depends before recommending that construction go forward? Would a lender considering a construction loan application want to have the same information? . . . more or less?

[b] Notes

Consider the following alternative approach to valuation.

Donald Liteplo, *Cap Rate Valuation Must Yield to Intensive Multi-Factor Analysis*, 24 REAL EST. REV. No. 3, 36, 40–42 (1994)*

Experience indicates that major investors become fully committed to an available income-producing property only after their search, negotiation, and subsequent due diligence efforts indicate that the property satisfies a considerable number of criteria. These include several quantifiable measures and several nonquantifiable measures.

Quantifiable measures. The most common quantifiable measures are the following:

- Estimated annual cash flow yield;
- Estimated average annual cash flow yield;
- Estimated payback (from cumulative cash flow);
- Estimated annual breakeven point;
- Estimated average annual breakeven point;
- Estimated "before-tax" IRR; and, occasionally,
- Estimated "after-tax" IRR.

Significantly, these are calculated for a defined "projected period of investment hold," generally a time span of 5 to 20 years (most typically, 10 years). The major players do not seriously consider the artificial and silly presumption of a "perpetual" investment. Even if some of them expect that the investment may be held for 50 years or longer, their financial projections reflect expectations of performance that can be realistically anticipated in the reasonably near future. Even though the investment is judged for its probability to survive and compete for a number of decades (physically, functionally, etc.), the "number crunching" relates to a much shorter period . . . a period for which forecasts can be made with some degree of confidence. These forecasts include predicted lease renewals, vacancies, occupancy cost, inflation, etc.

Sometimes, the property must meet established minimum standards for each measure. At times, a property will still be considered if certain critical measures are met and other measures are not missed by a significant amount.

Nonquantifiable Measures. Following are examples of commonly considered nonquantifiable measures:

- Quality of tenants (creditworthiness);
- Mix of tenants (complementariness);
- Life of leases (Are remaining terms substantial; are the leases well staggered?);
- Quality of lease agreements (Are the documents in good legal form? Are they complete?);
- Strength of location (Is there good exposure and access? Is it known in the community?);
- Quality of improvements (Are they structurally sound? Is the property functionally and aesthetically above average?);
- Expansion potential (Is there unused density or surplus land?);
- Market area stability (What is the expectation for population growth, the growth of competition?);
- Covenant/guarantees (Head lease? Construction warranties?); and
- Attractiveness of financing (Investors have preferences for certain types and terms of financing).

All of these qualitative measures reflect the investment's riskiness and its near-future prospects as well as its ability to remain competitive over the long haul. The nonquantifiable measures will often be greater in number, and occur in a greater variety of combinations than the quantitative. It is generally more difficult to establish specific qualitative standards (e.g., the minimal, or unacceptable, tenant mix). For some investors, in some markets, the nonquantifiable measures will be critical (producing a "go" or "no go" decision); for others, failure to satisfy the nonquantifiable measures may simply demand the application of more stringent quantifiable measures.

THE DECISION-MAKING MATRIX

The matrix is currently in use as a decision-making tool. Simple matrices are used to assess the desirability of a given investment property. Assume, for example, that a realtor has provided information about a newly listed property to a prospective investor (a major financial institution). Generally, after the institution has inspected the premises and after it has gathered financial and other pertinent information to supplement the initial sales (promotional) packet, appropriate investment officers review the key quantifiable and nonquantifiable factors to determine whether or not the property satisfies critical/minimal standards.

If not, the property is usually rejected out of hand. If it passes the initial tests, the common practice is to conduct further analysis.

During this more detailed analysis, the property may or may not be tied up by a signed interim agreement (usually an option or a conditional offer).

The analytical procedures of both the initial and subsequent analysis occur within a grid (matrix). Property desirability and maximum price are determined by the weighting of two sets of factors . . . quantifiable and nonquantifiable. In some way (most probably by a system of "ranking"), the procedure is made to produce a decision.

"APPRAISAL/ANALYSIS TOOL"

If the property has met the critical non-quantifiable standards, the investor assesses his chances of completing a transaction at the indicated maximum price. If he believes that the vendor will "deal," he makes an offer. If negotiation produces a final agreement, the elements of the transaction constitute "market evidence."

The process is quite easily applied as an appraisal system:

1. Through the analysis of such actual transactions, obtained from interviews with marker participants (mainly the purchasers), the appraiser identifies the key nonquantifiable and quantifiable measures and standards applicable to a particular type of property in a given locale on or about the date of appraisal.
2. The appraiser analyzes the property for its corresponding characteristics and qualities.
3. The appraiser applies the market measures and standards using an analytical approach, which includes a "trial and error" set of calculations, to determine the probable maximum price that would be paid. (The trial and error calculations are relatively simple to conduct with computer spreadsheets.)

Some market participants compare the estimated price in step 3 above with the estimated depreciated replacement cost for the property to ensure that the former is no greater than the latter.

If the appraiser/analyst is in possession of "standards" extracted from actual sales and could support and/or adjust the standards with "survey" evidence of current investor requirements (which may have changed since the last known sale), so much the better. Estimates of value arrived at in this manner should certainly be superior to those that are the result of capitalization in perpetuity.

Even if there have not been many, or any, recent transactions for a given property type in a given market area, the appraiser/analyst may be able to produce a credible valuation. Knowing the prevailing standards established and imposed by prospective investors for a given property type in a given market area could be enough — actual sales may not be needed. In other words, the evidence of investor "requirements," found via a documented canvassing of known active investors, can make possible reasonable appraisal/analysis where otherwise an appraisal would not be credible.

Does Liteplo's discussion help you to understand the valuation process? Certainly, he seems to be interested in accumulating a lot of information which does not appear in the financial analysis we have been discussing here. The process he describes may be nothing more than the accumulation of experience by successful developers. In the end, he concludes with the suggestion that "those who depend on the services of appraisers . . . enter into dialogues, exchange information, and assist appraisers in incorporating the measures with which the industry is experimenting in day-to-day work."

[3] Using DCF Techniques to Evaluate Shopping Center Proposals

Chapter 1 contained the first part of an article by Ron and Merritt Sher, describing the business of developing shopping centers. In the following portion of the article, the authors use financial techniques to explain how they decide whether to proceed with a shopping center project. We will then apply the process they describe to the Fox Valley Auto Care Center, to explore how the decision to proceed with this project may have been made.

Their discussion begins with an analysis of the cost of developing the site for the proposed center.

Ron Sher & Merritt Sher,
Developing and Investing in Local and Community Centers and Highway Retail,
***in* Shopping Centers and Other Retail Properties**
(John R. White & Kevin D. Gray eds., 1996)*

SITE COSTS

We usually break site costs down into on-site and off-site. Off-site costs are those expenditures required of the developer by the city. The developer may have to widen an overpass because traffic counts are too high, or perhaps contribute to the cost of traffic signals. Significant storm drainage fees may be required, or the widening of a street. There are a myriad of things that could happen here. The city may have extensive improvement plans that include requiring the developer to pick up a share of a local improvement district. (This expense occasionally can be passed on to the tenant — but not always.)

On-site construction costs also must be factored into the retail real estate development equation, for example, bringing in or exporting dirt, retaining walls, environmental cleanup, demolition of existing buildings, and provision for or relocation of utilities. The developer must ascertain all of the many on-site variables that can drive up the cost of getting the land into buildable shape. Some cities have large landscaping provisions and parking requirements. All of these factors will effectively cut down land productivity and force up your land price on a per square foot basis.

On-site costs also involve parking lot construction. How fancy do you want to make the parking lot? We believe in cutting some costs, but not too many, for example, double striping is more expensive than single striping but it helps to keep people in the middle of parking spaces, making the parking lot function better. Scrimping on lighting is false economy. Sufficient lighting enhances the appearance, increases the desire to shop, and will discourage crime. If you want to

---

* This article is reprinted from Shopping Centers and Other Retail Properties, edited by John R. White and Kevin D. Gray in association with the Urban Land Institute © 1996 John Wiley & Sons, Inc., Publisher. Reprinted by permission of John Wiley & Sons, Inc.

build projects that will sell at low capitalization rates to institutional buyers (discussed later), you must also have excellent landscaping. Other kinds of projects require lower on-site costs; much depends on the neighborhood, tenants, and your personal goals.

BUILDING COST FACTORS IN DEVELOPMENT PLANNING

After determining general site costs, which cannot entirely be done without a plan, you next need to conceptualize your shopping center. (These steps don't necessarily come in this order, but tend to evolve simultaneously.) When planning a shopping center, it is important to know what you want — rather than relying solely on consultants. Many projects where developers assumed that consultants, including architects, were knowledgeable and relied on them resulted in serious mistakes. The developer should check the work of consultants and consider their input but remain the ultimate decision maker. Site planning is an extremely important part of the development process. Not only is it necessary to lay out the center to maximize the gross usable area, but the space must be leasable. This means that the areas must have visibility, access, sufficient parking, and reasonable dimensions. Also, circulation in the center must be viable, with easy ingress and egress. We do countless sketches, changes, and fine-tuning before we end up with our ultimate site plan.

Once the plan is in place, you need to determine what to build. However, it is important to gauge the cost and quality of the building of your needs and the project needs. Building a very inexpensive building is, we believe, nearly always false economy. Essentially, most shopping center buildings are boxes with different kinds of facades. The incremental cost of making a project look attractive is very little compared to the advantages gained by positioning it well in the market — to say nothing of one's responsibility to the neighborhood. The pay off is two-fold: signed leases and a positive reputation in the community. Often developers will overbuild. This is when money is spent that will affect neither the income nor the long-term success.

It is possible to divide building costs into three categories: Base Shell, Vanilla Shell Improvements (VSI), and Tenant Improvements (TI). The shell is basically the box with a facade. For one redevelopment project in Bellevue, Washington, the first part of our redevelopment involved constructing a new building on the prime corner. We felt this was so important to the image and momentum of the project that we built a shell and facade far beyond the demands of the tenants.

Vanilla Shell Improvements (VSI) involve taking the store from a base shell to a vanilla box — an industry term that means a store with walls ready to be painted, a concrete floor, a drop ceiling with lights, electrical outlets, HVAC, and restrooms. The amount allocated for this varies somewhat according to the store size, but runs approximately $10 per square foot.

A Tenant Improvement (TI) allowance is given to a tenant for work they intend to do on the store. This can be from $2 per square foot for flooring or a partition wall and painting, to more than $75 per square foot for an important image tenant with strong credit that will be a strong draw for the center. The amount of the TI will vary greatly with the type and size of the project, the store, and the landlord negotiating leverage. The line where the VSI ends and the TI begins is often blurred during budgeting. If the developer does the construction and goes beyond the vanilla shell, then TI has shifted to VSI. On the other hand, if the tenant takes the building in base shell condition the VSI has become TI. Actually, the sum of the two is the most important number.

Landlord improvements and rent are clearly a trade-off. Tenants usually want the landlord to finance their store improvements and are willing to pay interest and amortization in the form of higher rent. If lenders treat the rent as over-market then most of the additional tenant subsidy will be in the form of additional developer equity. We always budget some TI money. This is "mad money," enabling us to entice the right tenants into the project. Unless you make some money available, you cannot be a major player and bid for the key tenants that will create the nucleus for a dynamic shopping center.

Soft Costs

Another category listed on our pro forma is that of soft costs. This is actually a catch-all for items not included elsewhere. It includes leasing commissions — which could be the subject of another book. As developers also involved in the brokerage business, we value brokers and pay commissions gladly. Good brokers work hard and deserve to be well-compensated. Maintaining a good relationship with the broker and promptly paying fair, but not excessively high, commissions is recommended. In the long run, this will help position the developer favorably in the market. Soft costs also include loan fees and legal fees, which tend to be under budgeted in pro formas. Other soft costs include architectural and engineering fees and the development fee, which constitute development overhead. We tend to budget development fees as more than our time, assuming development fees must cover office overhead. Permit fees vary greatly from jurisdiction to jurisdiction. We also include marketing as a soft cost. Sometimes it is included with commissions if it is the responsibility of your agent. Ideally, all soft costs should be identified and included, no matter how small. Ordinarily, construction interest and lease-up, which we describe below, also are included in soft costs.

Construction/Development Interest

A very important part of the retail real estate pro forma, and probably the most difficult to pinpoint, is the construction interest. This can be divided into (1) the land carry and cost of money during the construction period and (2) the time during which the center is not earning sufficient income to cover debt service. In terms of the first, purchase of a property that doesn't generate income means that interest on the acquisition price must be carried. Mainly this is during the planning and entitlement stage, but could be longer. Certainly it is preferable to plan and obtain permits prior to closing, but that is the exception rather than the rule. There also is the period when the center is under construction, where construction expenditures generate a substantial amount of interest. Construction interest is a significant charge, which illustrates the importance of minimizing the time from purchase of the ground to completion of the store.

The second part of construction interest occurs during the time that the center is not earning full income. Most projects take 3 to 12 months to fully lease after construction is completed. Even if this leasing is completed right away, time usually must be allowed for the tenant to perform tenant improvement work, stock the store, and train employees. Sometimes there is a period where the tenant must be given free rent. It is important to identify an interest number that reflects the income shortfall during the lease-up period.

This entire area is one of the most difficult to estimate, and often in real cost it is the greatest problem to the developer. Interest cost is real. Working quickly to control interest is very important to success, because time costs money. We recommend breaking contingency down by category. As you hone in on your pro forma you also can hone in on and reduce your contingency. Hopefully, it will be realistic in terms of total project costs.

INCOME AND EXPENSES

Another important part of the pro forma is the income and expenses breakdown. The income statement for determining the value of property has changed greatly. Now when determining income value, buyers are including re-leasing commissions and tenant improvement allowances as expenses. Deferred maintenance is a bigger issue when inflation and the ability to refinance capital improvement cost do not exist. Design has become more important, resulting in the need to remodel centers more often. How predictable is the upside? With rents in many places only equal to and often less than those of ten years ago, it is very hard to predict appreciation. Hence yields have increased. Greater equity is required than before — often 40% or more. Capitalization rates on market drug centers and freestanding buildings have ranged on first-year rents from 7% to 12% return. The yields on less stable properties have increased in the last five years more than with other types of properties, principally due to the lack of institutional buyers and lenders. More properties than ever before have become obsolete. Essentially, it is the stability and predictability of the income stream that has had the principal effect on value.

Income primarily consists of minimum rent. Percentage rent is not much of a factor for the pro forma, because with few exceptions it is difficult to project. It can affect the cap-rate, however, and is important with a property that has a history of percentage rent. Historic percentage rent will be counted, but may be discounted when a property is sold. Other miscellaneous income comes from sources such as fireworks stands, telephones, rides, and billboards.

When discussing income, it is important to understand the development of retail as it also affects pricing and rental structure. The sector of retail industry that is growing most rapidly and appears to be the most profitable can pay the most for land or rent. But the developer also must look at competition. A shortage of large retail space occurred in the mid-1990s. The obsolete 25,000-square-foot supermarkets, which were supplanted by the 35,000- and 50,000-square-foot supermarkets, have been absorbed. There is more than sufficient small retail space, because there is not much demand. But there is great demand for large space. Thus it appears that when developing a center today, the rents you can get for large spaces are often as high as they would be for small ones. Another source of income is reimbursement by tenants for expenses such as property taxes, insurance, the cost of maintaining the shopping center common area and buildings, and security. Leases should be structured so that nearly all of the costs of operating the shopping center are reimbursed. Management fees are not usually reimbursed by the tenants of strip centers.

The expense portion of the income statement includes the costs of maintaining the common area and buildings, insurance, property tax, and management fees.

These fees can be paid to an outside management company or be used to cover the developer's cost of managing the center. Partnership expenses are another consideration and are not reimbursed by tenants. Other expenses attached to a property are levies from local improvement districts, off-site parking, and leases. For pro forma purposes, expenses are deleted. The assumption is made that the tenant leases require the tenant to reimburse the landlord expenses, so that they don't affect the income statement. However, in most long-term cash projections, it is customary to report all expenses on a line-item basis as well as the line items for reimbursement of expenses.

Vacancy must be considered and shown as an expense. It is unrealistic to assume 100% occupancy. There will be tenant turnover. Even if the spaces don't stay vacant long, there is lost rent during lease-up time, and the construction period to be calculated, along with a possible rent-free period.

Re-leasing costs must also be included. They are particularly important when considering an existing rather than a new project. Re-leasing usually requires remodeling the space, providing tenant improvements, the cost of commissions, and possibly marketing — all costs that frequently are ignored or underestimated on the expense side of the pro forma. Another cost that has been ignored over the years, but is especially important to include when buying a project, is the amount of money required to keep that property in the vanguard and positioned well ahead of the competition. Too many people think that once you build a shopping center you don't need to go beyond merely maintaining it. It is essential to keep a shopping center contemporary and competitive, and the cost of doing so must be included.

IMPORTANT PRO FORMA FORMULAS: RETURN ON INVESTMENT TO RETURN ON EQUITY

These formulas are shown in Figure C and are applied to our hypothetical example. The presentation here is simplistic, but works very well. A sophisticated analysis might involve a 10-year projection of net operating income (NOI), discounted according to the cost of capital and any risk factors. While this type of analysis is good, it is not imperative. After calculating income and expenses, the NOI can be determined by subtracting nonreimbursed expenses from income.

Dividing NOI by total project costs will yield return on investment (ROI) — an extremely important number for the retail real estate developer. We want it to be higher than our interest constant so as to avoid negative leverage (despite amortization). We know it must be higher when interest rates are higher, higher for risky projects, and for projects that will not be of institutional quality.

In analysis of the project's potential profit, you divide NOI by a capitalization rate to determine market value. Once the market value is determined, selling costs must be subtracted to yield a number representing net market value. Net market value minus the costs of the project results in projected pre-tax profits. The capitalization rate is perhaps best described as the rate of return the project would yield if sold on the open market. A project is considered investment grade if it meets the following criteria: low vacancy, strong credit, excellent location, good neighborhood, well-maintained and nice looking, high sales per square foot, and little competition. It usually is the type of property that a conservative institution will purchase. The value of the property will be higher if it is attractive to that type of purchaser. This means that they would buy it to yield less, thus at a lower capitalization rate. To develop such a property requires a smaller ROI, as it sells at a higher price. Conversely, if a property is in a lower income area, is leased to noncredit tenants, and is in an area of oversupply with high vacancy rates, it will need to sell to yield a higher return on investment (at a higher capitalization rate).

To analyze the profitability of a project, a developer must consider the end result. A lower sale price means the development's profit expectations at the outset must be much higher. This is important to remember, for in the development "equation" one eventually compares the net market value to the initial cost in order to determine profit. When determining how to develop, you need not consider whether you are going to sell the project, but you should ask yourself these important questions: Would it be saleable if we need to sell, and to whom and for how much? We build and lease to the same standard, whether it is our intent to sell or keep the property.

When we undertake a project we always ask ourselves if this will be something that an institutional investor would want to own. If we don't feel that a properly developed and leased property will have the quality to be valued at a lower than market cap rate (i.e., higher price), we pass on that project — unless the profit potential seems outstanding or there is another special reason. With development, something unexpected always surfaces — and usually it is negative.

When beginning a project, the developer has a tendency to think that everything is going to go well and be positive, but always consider risk, downside, and what will happen if things don't go as expected. The rate of return on investment also must be considered. What rate of return will be necessary? The return depends on a lot of factors, including the capitalization rate at which the project should be or may be valued. It involves the cost of capital, which is generally a reflection of current capital markets. Clearly, the rate of return has to be above the cost of capital so that positive leverage exists. How much positive leverage is necessary? Again, it all depends on where interest rate levels are historically: If they are higher, less positive leverage is necessary since expectations of an increase in rates would be less than for a decrease. Another consideration is the relationship of equity to debt. More equity means less positive leverage is necessary — even negative leverage is possible at some point, because the equity portion has a greater effect and returns required on equity are not as interest-rate sensitive. Much depends on your opportunity cost of capital (the higher it is, the higher the return you need). It may also be affected by how long you intend to hold the property, or how soon you need your capital. Sometimes, too, there are noneconomic considerations.

Projects rarely are built for all equity; even if this does occur, there is usually an intent to finance later. There are two measures to determine how much of the project costs can be financed. One is based on debt service coverage, and the other is based on loan to value. One must compare the calculated amount of financing based on debt service coverage with that based on loan-to-value ratio, and then take the lesser amount of the two. Lenders usually will require a certain debt service coverage ratio, which depends on a number of factors including the project, lender, developer, and whether the loan is recourse or non-recourse. The ratio required generally is in the range of 1.25 to 1. To determine the amount available for debt service, divide NOI by the debt service coverage ratio, a rate that takes into consideration the amortization period and interest rate. To compute the loan amount available, divide the amount available for debt service by the debt service constant. For example, if there is a 10% interest rate and 20-year amortization, the amortization constant would be the amount of money necessary to amortize the loan at 9% [*sic*] over 20 years. In this case, it is 10.80% per annum, paid monthly. The other way to arrive at the value of the loan is to take the project value and multiply this by the maximum percentage loan to value permitted, generally from 60% to 75%.

The final steps in the pro forma analysis are to determine the equity needed in the project by subtracting the amount of the loan available from the cost of the project and to identify return on equity by dividing the cash flow after debt service by the equity required; the latter also is called the cash on cash return.

THE PRO FORMA IN DEVELOPMENT PLANNING

The pro forma is designed to determine the feasibility of a development. Each development is very different, and the pro forma in a sense is a synopsis of the development. It details how a development is expected to go — with a contingency, of course. Throughout the process, developers need to do their best to achieve or exceed the pro forma. This goal is never without problems; developers are in the business of problem solving.

A typical pro forma for a simple neighborhood shopping center is shown in Figures A and B.

The line items in both exhibits are the important factor, rather than the costs, for these line items and their subcategories are the main aspects of the project for discussion. Assume that the land is already zoned retail commercial. One street is a main arterial, and the other feeds directly into the neighborhood. Figure D is a site plan of the shopping center. The 36,800-square-foot building is pre-leased to a strong grocery chain. A 4,000-square-foot restaurant is committed for the corner building. A building is also planned to have a 6,400-square-foot video store and 7,100 square feet of small stores perpendicular to the market. There is also a lease to a 12,000-square-foot drugstore, and 6,700 feet of additional small stores between the market and the drugstore. Prospective tenants for the stores include a dry cleaners, mail box store, hair salon, and a beauty supply store. The project has a good mix; not too many shops in relation to the major, but enough for it to work. We have provided the parking field required by the market and ample parking for all the stores. The restaurant is placed so that the view of the in-line store is not blocked too much. The land price of $2,704,000 reflects a good usable site without unusual problems or the requirement of excessive on- or off-site work.

Figure A
Development Pro Forma

	Area in square feet	$/square foot	Total
LAND:	6.21 Acres	$10.00	$2,704,000.
SITE COSTS			
On Site			
Grading & Site Preparations			80,000.
Retaining Wall			10,000.
Parking Lot Lighting & Landscaping		2.50	494,000.
Off Site			
Stop Light Contribution			35,000.
Storm Water			100,000
CONSTRUCTION			
Allowance for Market	36,000	$40.	1,472,000.
Allowance for Restaurant	4,000	45.	180,000.
Video Stores	13,500		
Shell		42.	567,000.
Tenant Improvements		10.	135,000.
Drug Stores	18,700		
Shell		38.	710,600.
Tenant Improvements		10.	187,000.
TENANT IMPROVEMENT ALLOWANCE			
	32,500	5.	161,000.
CONSTRUCTION CONTINGENCY			
5% Not Including Market & Restaurant			
Market Allowance			125,000.
SOFT COSTS			
Leasing Commissions	73,000	3.5	256,000.
Loan Fees		1.25%	78,000.
Legal & Consultants			80,000.
A&E			120,000.
Permits			35,000.
Marketing			5,000.
Development Fees			180,000.
TOTAL EXPENSES			$7,745,000.
INTEREST			
Construction Interest (Land Amounts @ 10%)			125,000.
Negative Cash Flow to Break-Even Leaseup			125,000.
TOTAL PROJECT COSTS			$7,995,000.

The site costs reflect a slightly uneven site that requires some leveling work, so there is money in the on-site category for exporting dirt and building a retaining wall. The other on-site costs at $2.50 per square foot on the land not occupied by buildings covers the cost of the paving, landscaping, all the standard utilities, lighting, and so on. Off-site costs include one-quarter of the cost of a traffic signal and a storm water contribution to the city. Normally storm water shows up as a cost for retention on-site or as a contribution off-site.

Figure B
Pro Forma Income Statement

Tenant	Area in square feet	$/square foot	Total
Market	36,800	11.00	$404,000.
Restaurant	4,000	24.00	96,000.
Video	6,400	19.00	121,600.
Stores/Video Building	7,100	16.50	117,150
Drugstore	12,000	14.00	168,000
Stores/Drug Store Building	6,700	16.50	110,500.
TOTALS	73,000		$1,018,100.

Other Income—	
Telephone, Xmass Trees, Fireworks	$1,500.
Less:	
Management Fee (4%)	(40,700.)
Vacancy (5% excluding Market)	(30,700.)
Reserve for structural, releasing and tenant improvements (5% excluding Market)	(30,700.)
TOTAL EXPENSE	($ 102,100.)
Net Operating Income:	$ 917,500.

We presume that all common area costs are reimbursed, as well as taxes and insurance, and that there are no owner payments not reimbursed to the landlord as local improvement districts. Although most leases will have percentage rental provisions, on a project of this type they probably should be included when determining the feasibility of the project.

The deal with the supermarket in this example is for them to build their building, with an allowance from the developer. The same applies to the restaurant. This is usually disbursed as monthly draws through our loan, but sometimes it is a reimbursement to the tenant upon opening for business. In this case, for simplicity the market and restaurant will front their costs. The video building, which also has space for other uses, is estimated at $42 per square foot to complete.

It's more expensive than the other building because it is smaller and shallower, with more demising walls. The other 18,700 square feet is estimated at $38 per square foot for base shell. To these estimates is added $10 per square foot for completing the building through a plain, or vanilla, shell.

Tenant Improvement (TI) allowances should be in the budget. Budgeting for them allows much more flexibility when dealing with tenants. When you budget this expense you also can expect, on the income side, to get more rent. The $5 per square foot TI will probably allow you to average 75 cents per square foot more in rent for those tenants receiving them, but the main thing is to be able to use it to make deals.

Figure C Pro Forma Formulas

	Formula	Example
1.	N.O.I. (Net Operating Income) / Total Project Costs = Return on Investment	917,500 / 7,995,00 = 11.48%
2.	(Net Operating Income) / (Capitalization Rate) = Sales Price	917,500 / 0.095 = $9,657,895
3.	Sales Price less Sales Cost @ 4%= Net Sales Price	9,657,895 – 386,000 = $9,271,895
4.	Net Sales Price less Project Cost = Before Tax Profit	9,271,895 – 7,995,000 = $1,276,895
5.	Net Operating Income / Required Debt Service Coverage = Maximum Debt Service	917,500 / 1.25 = $734,000
6.	Maximum Debt Service / Debt Service Constant = Maximum Loan Amount	734,000 / 0.109044 = $6,731,228
7.	Sales Price × Loan to Value** = Maximum Loan Amount	9,657,895 × 65% = $6,277,632
8.	Amount of the Loan = Lower of (6) or (7)	$6,277,632
9.	Project Cost Less Amount of Loan = Equity Required	7,995,000 – 6,277,632 = $1,717,368
10.	N.O.I. less Debt Service = Cash Flow	917,500 – 734,000 = $ 183,500
11.	Cash Flow / Equity Required = Return on Equity or Cash on Cash	183,500 / 1,717,368 = 10.68%

*Assume 10% interest and 25-year amortization
**Assume loan to value required by the lender = 65%

A 5% construction contingency for items (not including the market and restaurant) has been included. This is a "safety net," and is strongly recommended. Leasing commissions have been estimated at $3.50 a foot. They will be higher on the small stores and lower for the supermarket; this is an average number. The 1.25% loan fee is an estimate based on the loan amount of $6.25 million. The other soft costs are reasonable estimates for a project of this size. Interest costs in this case are based on the following: a land-hold of eight months from the time of purchase through completion of construction with a construction loan interest rate of 10%; a six-month construction period with a 22 month outstanding average on the other construction costs, and payment of the market and restaurant TI allowances upon their opening for business. We have also provided $125,000 to cover debt service shortfall during the lease-up period. It is presumed that $1.75 million in equity is contributed day-one, and does not accrue interest. On the income side, we assume pre-leasing of the market, the video store, drugstore, and the restaurant. After taking out management, vacancy and reserve, you are left with $917,500 in net operating income. This, divided by the cost of $7,995,000 provides an 11.48% return.

After reviewing the implications of this investment (Figure C), it is evident that nearly $2 million in equity is required to accomplish this project: for those of us who are used to working with other peoples' money, the required equity is considered to be a substantial sum for a project of this size. The debt service constant at 10.9% is not much less than the return on investment of 11.48%. This means that there is almost no positive leverage, including amortization. Unless the developer has a lot of cash, this project would generally not be a good idea if the intention is to hold. Thus, it might make sense to build this project with construction financing and sell it upon completion, thereby making a profit.

The preliminary pro forma can also be used for sensitivity analysis. What would happen if more rent could be obtained? Can we get more rent? What is the risk? How much pre-leasing is necessary? Can we do a pre-sale of the project by identifying a buyer before we build? On the cost side, is a contingency necessary? How much certainty can be attached to costs? Can firm contractor bids be obtained for some work, that is, can money be taken out of the site-work estimate or any of the other cost projections? With this pro forma, a developer might pursue this project and still not know whether to go forward. This type of project has many advantages; it is attractive to lenders, and very marketable (if well located). On the down side, it requires much equity and has a marginal profit. It is very typical of initial pro formas.

DEVELOPING FOR THE FUTURE

Today, it is more important than ever to assess the long-term value of retail real estate. It is not merely a question of capitalization rates, but also a question of identifying the underlying characteristics that determine long-term stability and future increase in value. Traditionally, institutional investors have been most interested in purchasing regional centers. However, many of these centers once thought to be invulnerable have become financial disasters. As a result, there is more demand for supermarket drugstore-anchored centers and freestanding, net leased property. The stronger the tenant, the lower the yield. Markets have changed and residual values have disappeared. Even some of the seemingly strongest retailers have gone through reorganization, allowing them to terminate leases.

Retail changes so quickly. The changes have to be anticipated. The developer must interpret retailers' advertising and other signs to understand the latest merchandising concepts and how they are affecting retail real estate development. Prior development formulas aren't necessarily helpful. Retail changes quickly, and if the developer or retailer is not changing or going forward, they will be going backward, resulting in loss of value and market share. View the big picture and build projects that will not only be successful, but will, with constant attention, maintain and increase their value in the future.

Figure D Neighborhood Shopping Center Site Plan

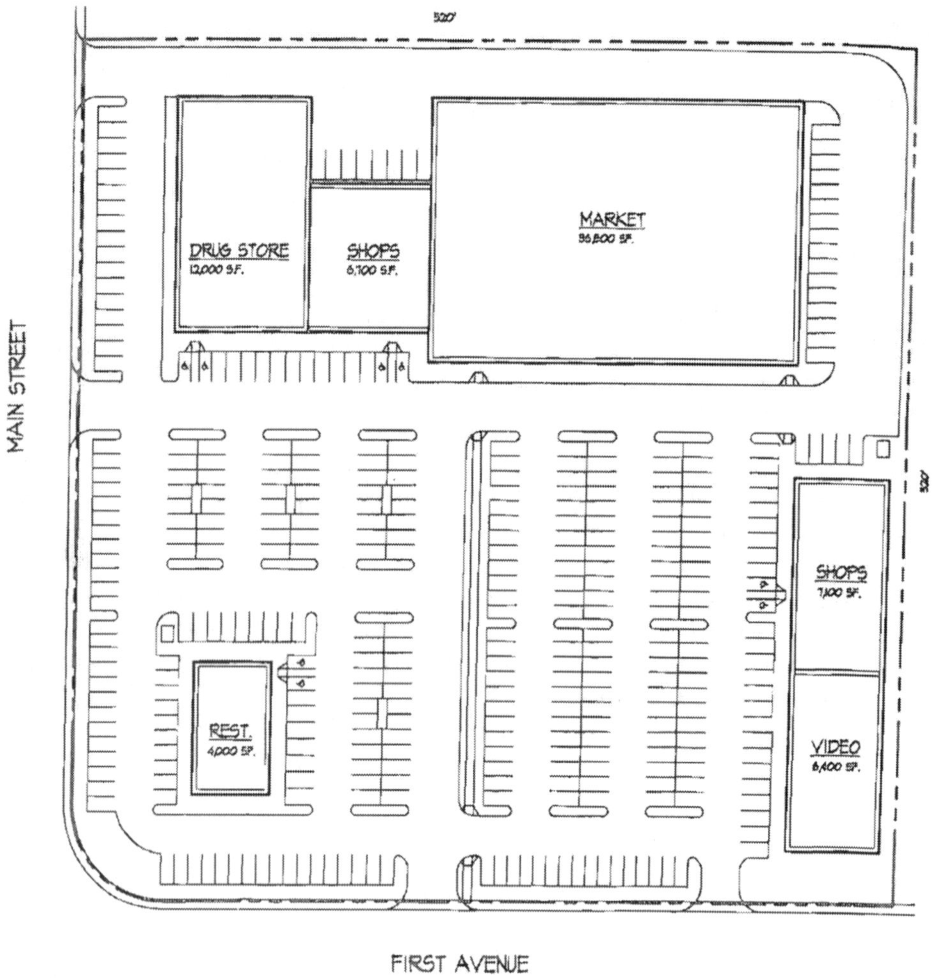

§ 2.04 CONSTRUCTING THE *PRO FORMA* FOR THE FOX VALLEY AUTO CARE CENTER

Review the financial information about the acquisition and construction of the Fox Valley Auto Care Center in Section 1.05 in Chapter 1. Our next step will be to put the DCF analysis to work to help Delany and Regent decide whether to proceed. For this purpose, the sample *pro forma* described by the Shers will be useful. The numbers on the *pro forma* will be calculated using the present value techniques explained in Section 2.02. First, however, the real cost of completing the project will have to be determined. Next, the projected rentals for the project should provide the information needed to create the capital structure required to support construction and operation of the project. This includes the amount which can be borrowed (depending on the criteria used by the lender to evaluate real estate projects) and, when the amount of the loan is known, how much capital will have to be invested by the developer, or by outside investors, to complete the project.

At the outset, note that there is an inherent circularity in many development decisions.[49] The projected rents will depend upon the ability of the project to attract tenants at that rent level, and this depends in turn on the design of the structure. How the structure is designed, as the Shers point out, will affect the cost of construction. The ability of the Developer to negotiate the mortgage and to attract capital contributions from investors in order to fund those costs then depends upon the rents. Successful developers know from experience where to cut the circle, and what information they will need to make that decision. Once the decision is made, and the cost of raising the capital needed to implement the plan determined, it will be up to the lawyers and accountants to fill in the details. So, let's get started.

[1] Capitalizing the Costs of Acquiring and Constructing the Project

[a] Site Acquisition Costs

The first step will be to determine the cost of the site for the Auto Care Center. This has both financial and tax dimensions. For financial purposes, the cost of acquisition is often funded from the construction loan, and that is what happened with the Fox Valley Auto Care Center. For tax purposes, an accurate allocation of cost among the components of the project is important for two reasons: the allowance of depreciation deductions and the determination of taxable gain or loss on disposition of the Center. Before analyzing the sources of funds and how these funds were expended in acquiring and constructing the Center, it will be useful to consider some basic tax points.

Gain or loss from the disposition of property is included in taxable income. To calculate the gain, the "tax basis" of the property must be known.[50] Tax basis is defined to be the "cost" of the property. IRC § 1012(a). Cost means the amount expended to acquire or construct the property and includes borrowed funds. When a portion of a single tract is sold, as was the case here, basis must be allocated between that portion sold and the balance retained, usually in proportion to the market value of each portion. Under Regent's development plan, about half of the original tract (the land Regent acquired from Metropolitan and the Johnsons) was sold to Turtle Wax for cash. When that happened, part of the original cost of the tract had to have been allocated to the car wash site. At this stage of the project, cost has the same meaning for financial purposes as it does for tax purposes, although this will not always be true as the Center is developed and operated.[51]

---

[49] As we noted earlier, *see* note 1, *supra*, the design-build circularity will always be present when new construction is planned. When the purchase of an existing project is analyzed, as in the example examined earlier in this chapter, the rent structure of the project is known, and the financing problem resolves to a determination whether that structure will support the capital required to complete the purchase.

[50] *See* text at note 40, *supra*.

[51] When the Limited Liability Company which will be formed to acquire the project pays cash for the land, the land will be shown on its books at a "book value" equal to the amount paid for the land. Since, in this case, the book value and the tax basis for the land are the same, we can refer to the property's "book value" in discussing the tax consequences of the project. You should be aware, however, that "book value" and adjusted tax basis are different concepts and in many cases, will have different values.

Regent acquired the development tract in two stages: first, by purchase of the Johnson tract; and second, by exchanging a small piece of the Johnson tract plus cash for the corner lot from Metropolitan. The cost of acquiring these two chunks must be aggregated and then reallocated among the two parts of the tract. Regent also incurred a contractual obligation to do some site preparation work, a part of which was reimbursed by Metropolitan. The unreimbursed cost incurred in general grading and road preparation has been treated here as part of the cost of the full development tract.[52] Next, the development tract was itself subdivided, and a two acre portion was sold to Turtle Wax for cash. The cost of the whole development tract can be allocated on the basis of the area of each portion, which in this case is a good proxy for market value. *See* Figure 2.9.

Figure 2.9 Allocation of Land Acquisition Costs

determination of the purchase price	area square feet	total cost			
Johnson Tract:		$ 580,000			
Metropolitan Diversified Services:		$ 325,000			
		$ 905,000			
Cost of Tract (book value or tax basis)					
		allocation by land area	allocated purchase price	road construction	original cost
Turtle Wax car wash site:	87,700	48.21%	$ 436,330	$ 44,265	$ **480,595**
retail stores site:	94,200	51.79%	$ 468,670	$ 47,545	$ **516,215**
total land area (development tract):	181,900		$ 905,000	$ 91,810	

The gain on the sale is then calculated by subtracting Regent's cost from the cash consideration received from Turtle Wax (in tax parlance, the "amount realized").[53]

How should the sale to Turtle Wax be treated for financial purposes? Regent has no obligation to use the proceeds from the sale to Turtle Wax in the development of its shopping center, and, in fact, it seems to have treated the two transactions as separate. Assume that Regent used the cash proceeds for other purposes and did not account for them as a recovery of part of the cost of the overall development. It will have both a financial and a tax gain to report from the sale. This is consistent with real estate development practices generally, where the objective in most cases is to minimize the amount of the developer's own funds which must be committed to the project. But in thinking about Regent's investment return from its development in the Fox Valley Auto Care Center, can the Turtle Wax transaction really be viewed as a distinct transaction? After all, it would not have occurred but for the plan to build the FVACC.

In calculating the financial results of the Fox Valley Auto Care Center, the cash proceeds remaining *after* the payment of income taxes on the gain derived from receipt of the Turtle Wax proceeds is the interesting amount. The objective in evaluating real estate projects is always to determine the amount invested and the

[52] Site preparation may be a depreciable asset when it results in land improvements, the cost of which will have to be separately identified. Land improvements include the construction of parking lots, outside lighting and landscaping, even though these elements appear to be permanent additions to the site. *See* Rev. Proc. 87-56, *supra* note 17, asset class 00.3. Site improvements are depreciable over a term of 15 years, and may be depreciated under the Modified Accelerated Cost Recovery System ("MACRS") using the 150% declining balance method. IRC § 168(b)(2).

[53] *See* text at note 41, *supra*.

cash flow actually received by investors after payment of *all* costs, and specifically the tax cost. If this is not done, evaluation of the financials for any project will be incomplete, for, as you will see, the tax issues play a central role in practically all of the planning decisions for a real estate project. Technically, both state and federal income taxes should be determined, but to reduce the complexity of the discussion, state income taxes will be put to the side, although in an actual case you would not do so. Because state income taxes vary from state to state, and because many state income tax systems follow the federal system, analysis of the federal income tax issues should give you the information you need to do your own evaluation of the income tax in your state.

The after-tax gain from this transaction could have been netted against the aggregate cost of the Johnson and Metropolitan transactions, and the net result treated as the acquisition cost of the land. In many shopping center developments, the "anchor," that is, the business whose presence in the center is intended to draw customers into the center, will make its own deal with the developer. The anchor's store may be constructed by the developer and leased at a rental favorable to the tenant. The anchor's premises may, however, be acquired by the anchor, either outright, as did Turtle Wax in the Fox Valley Auto Care Center, or under a ground lease, and the anchor would then construct its own premises. Regent's development plan takes the latter form, even though Turtle Wax's car wash does not resemble a typical anchor. It is consistent with development practices in smaller center developments despite its somewhat unusual features.

[b] Site Preparation Costs

Site preparation, as the article written by the Shers makes clear, involves several different steps. There is the physical preparation of the site for construction of the following: roads and utilities; the buildings themselves; parking areas and lighting; and finally, landscaping. In this case, the work was done under a fixed price contract, and the information available in the problem does not attempt to allocate the actual cost of each element. More realistically, each element will have a separate cost which must be evaluated in determining whether that particular design feature (such as how the parking lot is arranged, and the parking spaces delineated) adds value to the project from the developer's point of view sufficient to justify the cost of including it. The contractor, Regent Construction Co., an affiliate of Regent Development Co., would keep careful records of the cost of each element. An important question, both for financial purposes and for tax purposes, is how to allocate these costs to each feature of the development.

The tax cost will be reduced by tax depreciation. Recall that the cost of an asset which produces income over time cannot simply be deducted from income when the asset is purchased or built; instead that cost must be allocated to and deducted over the years in a specified income producing period (the asset's "useful life"). Under current law, the useful lives of assets in different "classes" are prescribed by statute, as is the allocation method. *See* IRC § 168. Because buildings and other structures decline in value as time passes and, theoretically at least, must eventually be replaced, they may be depreciated.

Because the land itself is considered not to decline in value with use, however, the acquisition cost of the land (as distinguished from the construction cost of a structure or site preparation to build a structure) cannot be depreciated. Developers sometimes structure the land acquisition phase of the development to minimize its nondepreciable cost, as in the use of long term land leases, for example. With the Fox Valley Auto Care Center, the acquisition of the land was a straight cash deal, albeit financed with a generous construction loan, and followed by the resale to Turtle Wax of a portion of the original development tract at a significant gain.

The cost allocation decisions made here have important tax consequences. It is desirable to allocate as much of the cost as possible away from the land on which the Fox Valley Auto Care Center was built and either to the tract sold to Turtle Wax (in order to offset gain[54] on that sale) or to a depreciable asset other than the land itself. These decisions involve cost elements other than the actual cash payments made to acquire the land, and it is to these questions that we now turn.

In its agreements with Metropolitan, Regent agreed to make certain improvements to the land. Some of this work involved general improvement of the site, such as grading to prepare it for building or the construction of roads and other infrastructure which will be more or less permanent. The cost of this work is treated in the tax law and in the allocations made here as a cost of acquiring land for development, and thus must be capitalized and included in the non-depreciable basis of the development tract. Other improvements to the land, however, relate specifically to the Fox Valley Auto Care Center building[55] and can be expected to retain their usefulness only so long as the FVACC operates. These improvements include access roads for the FVACC itself, parking and exterior lighting and landscaping costs. The depreciable nature of these costs is recognized administratively as expenditures within a depreciable class of assets separate and distinct from the building itself. Oddly, these costs are treated as having a useful life which is much shorter than the useful life imposed on commercial real estate structures by statute, 15 years as compared to 39 years.[56] Moreover, land improvement costs specifically related to the construction of the FVACC may be depreciated using 150% declining balance depreciation, a method which provides a faster write-off of the costs than does straight line, although this method would probably not be used because it produces adverse tax consequences when the property is finally sold.[57]

---

[54] Because the sale to Turtle Wax occurred very soon after the land had been assembled, and while it was still owned by Regent, the gain will probably be short term capital gain as it occurred within one year after Regent's acquisition of the land. IRC § 1222(1). Short term capital gain will be taxed as ordinary income, probably to Regent's shareholders, because Regent is an electing subchapter S corporation. The sale took place before the Fox Valley Auto Care Center LLC was formed and the shopping center tract transferred to it.

[55] The cost of site work which is actually part of the construction of the building, however, such as excavation or grading for the foundations of the building, is part of the cost of constructing the building and is included in the basis of the building and depreciated as such.

[56] *See* note 52, *supra*.

[57] IRC § 168(b)(2). 150% declining balance depreciation is calculated by taking the straight line depreciation (the reciprocal of the useful life), multiplying that rate by 150% and the applying the result to the adjusted tax basis of the asset involved. Because the tax basis of the asset is adjusted each year by subtracting the depreciation allowed from the basis for the asset at the beginning of the year, allowable depreciation in succeeding years will decline as the tax basis of the asset is reduced (hence, "declining balance"). Because the initial rate applied to the tax basis of the asset is greater than the straight line rate, more depreciation deductions are allowed sooner than under the straight line rate, so 150% declining balance depreciation is viewed as accelerated depreciation, and gain attributable to the depreciation which has been claimed is subject to "recapture," *i.e.*, taxable as ordinary income under section 1245. In any event, as the allowable depreciation declines, eventually the allowable amount will

[c] Building Construction Costs

A portion of the contract price for the construction of the Fox Valley Auto Care Center has been arbitrarily allocated to site preparation, and the balance will be used to build the building itself. The building will be a simple shell as in warehouse construction with internal bays for individual tenants. As the Shers put it, this will be a "vanilla shell." Would it help to divide the cost among the basic shell, vanilla shell improvements and tenant improvements (using the Shers' terminology)? It would make a difference to the tenants if Regent provided them with a budget for tenant related improvements, and this does seem to have been in the Fox Valley Auto Care Center project for some tenants. One might think that an improvement to the building for a specific tenant which has a relatively short-term lease could be depreciated over a period no longer than the lease itself, and for many years the law did permit tenant improvements constructed by the lessor to be depreciated by the lessor over the tenant's lease term. The law now provides, however, that any improvement to a building must be depreciated over the same useful life as applied to the building when first acquired, that is, 39 years.[58] Any undepreciated cost for a tenant improvement may be deducted by the lessor as a loss if the improvements are abandoned when the tenant's lease terminates.[59] Thus, there would be no immediate tax advantage to differentiating cost between the shell and tenant improvements.

From a summary of the rents, you will see that the rent projected for Lube Pros, whose premises include the lubrication bay, is significantly greater than the rents for other spaces in the Fox Valley Auto Care Center: $14–$17 annually per square foot for the other tenants and $30 annually per square foot for Lube Pros. (See the summary of the lease terms for Lube Pros in the Document Book). Construction of a lubrication bay requires some special features and more expense than preparation of the other bays. If Regent bears this cost, it would negotiate a higher rent for the lubrication portion of the building in order to be compensated for its higher construction cost. In effect, Regent has financed the construction of assets needed by Lube Pros in its business, and Lube Pros has agreed to compensate Regent by paying more rent.[60] Would you want to know this

---

be less than would be allowed using the straight line method (ratable deductions) over the remaining useful of the asset. At that point, declining balance depreciation converts to the straight line method. The actual percentages applied to assets for which this method has been elected are prescribed by tables promulgated by the Internal Revenue Service, depending on when during the taxable year the asset is placed in service (that is, when the project opens for business and the site improvements are used by paying customers of the Center). *See* Rev. Proc. 87-57, 1987-2 C.B. 687, *amplified and clarified*, Rev. Proc. 89-15, 1989-1 C.B. 816, Tables 1 – 4, prescribing rates which apply to the unadjusted basis of the asset.

58 The Internal Revenue Service takes the position that any improvement which is attached to the structure such as, for example, plumbing fixtures, is part of the structure and is depreciable as such. This position applies both to lessors and to lessees. More recently, "qualified tenant improvements" made during 2008 and 2009 are 15 year property subject to certain conditions. IRC §§ 168(e)(iv), (ix); 168(k)(3). These rules do not apply to the Fox Valley Auto Care Center, and even if they did, the improvement must have been made more than three years after the building was first placed in service. Some of these provisions were enacted in recent legislation which extended favorable treatment for leasehold improvements, so one might expect to see similar extensions in the future.

59 The tenant improvement must have been "irrevocably disposed of or abandoned." IRC § 168(i)(8)(B).

60 Lube Pros might prefer to make this arrangement with Regent, as financing costs for Regent

information, as a prospective purchaser, in order to analyze the rent structure of the Center?

[d] Soft Costs

In preparing plans and obtaining permits which enable the Center to be built, Regent must incur significant costs for a variety of professional services. These include legal fees paid to lawyers who implement the developer's decision to acquire the tract and construct the Center, as well as fees paid to architects, engineers, accountants, etc. These costs, all of which are necessary to complete the plan and construct and begin operating the Center, are referred to as "soft" costs.

Regent has also charged one or more fees for its services. The practice on charging development fees varies among developers. Some will charge as much as 10 to 15% of the project cost. These fees compensate the developer for the work done in creating the project and implementing the developer's plan. It is not unusual for a successful project to require several years of planning, doing research, negotiating with owners, lenders, investors, government agencies, and others. This is time consuming, difficult work, albeit well rewarded when the project is successful.

How should soft costs be allocated for tax and/or financial purposes? Note that an element of value is added to the project by *each* cost. Most of the work is tied up in the Fox Valley Auto Care Center itself and so can justifiably be allocated to, and included in the tax basis of, the building, but some obviously relates to the acquisition of the site and its preparation for use as a shopping center. For example, how do you as a future attorney think the "legal" cost should be allocated among these different elements?

There is a long history in the tax law about the appropriate treatment of many soft costs. At an early stage in the tax shelter industry, promoters took aggressive positions in asserting the deductibility of many of these costs (including, naturally, all of their fees, which were payable up-front, out of the capital contributed by investors). That is to say, a large portion of the initial capital contributions by investors was used to pay imaginatively created fees to developers, promoters, brokers, etc., for which immediate tax deductions would be claimed. These deductions would be allocated by the partnership agreement to the investors, who used the deductions to reduce their incomes from other sources (*e.g.*, salaries, investments, etc.) for what would otherwise be a nondeductible, capital investment. *See, e.g., Egolf v. Commissioner*, 87 T.C. 34 (1986). This practice produced large tax savings in the first two years of the project, and may have been the source of the term "soft" because of the tax savings potentially available through deductions. In 1986, Congress amended the rules governing capitalization of expenses for tax purposes to make plain that such costs are not deductible. IRC § 263A.

Today, virtually none of these up-front planning and arranging fees can be deducted immediately, and some (so-called, "syndication" fees or expenses incurred in selling partnership interests to investors) are never deductible.[61]

---

might be less than financing costs for Lube Pros, and the additional rent obligation would not appear on Lube Pros' balance sheet.

[61] *See* IRC § 709(a). Selling expenses must be added to the *investor's* tax basis for the investor's interest in the partnership. The major exception to this rule is provided for "organization" expenses, which are costs incurred in forming a partnership. These expenses would have been amortizable over the

Instead, most such costs must be added to the tax basis (book value) of the building or other asset (or, if appropriate, to the basis of the land), and then recovered for tax purposes through depreciation, if at all. Fees incurred by the developer to arrange financing, such as loan origination or commitment fees or legal fees incurred in negotiating and closing on a loan, are associated with the financing to which they relate and must be included in the cost of the financing. These fees must then be "amortized" or allocated pro rata over the term of the financing for tax deduction purposes.[62]

[e] Interest and Taxes

Interest paid during planning (usually to exercise control over the land under a conditional sales contract), construction and lease-up is a capital cost, and must be capitalized and added to the tax basis of the building.[63] Do you understand why? In an historic case, the U.S. Supreme Court held that depreciation claimed on machinery used to construct power lines must be capitalized, added to the tax basis of the *power lines* and recovered for tax purposes as depreciation on the power lines (a very long-lived asset when contrasted with trucks, compressors, cranes, etc.). *Commissioner v. Idaho Power Co.*, 418 U.S. 1 (1974).[64] Since that decision, virtually every period charge incurred in aid of construction (or, more technically, "production") has been required to be capitalized.[65] Real estate taxes incurred during the construction period are treated in the same manner as interest.

Construction loans are almost always recourse loans against which funds are drawn as expenditures are made, as provided in the loan documents. Sometimes, the draw is based on reaching a specified stage in the construction of the project rather than whether the expenditures have actually been incurred. These issues are discussed in depth in the section dealing with mortgages. Interest is charged on the actual amount borrowed as the funds are drawn down, so an allocation of interest charges to the construction and lease-up period will be required. These costs are capital costs for both financial and tax accounting purposes.

---

life of the partnership only if it had limited life. If the taxpayer elects, however, these expenses may be "amortized" (deducted ratably) over a 60 month period. *Id.*, § 709(b).

62 *See* Enoch v. Commissioner, 57 T.C. 781, 794–95 (1972), *acq.*, 1974-2 C.B. 1; Sleiman v. Commissioner, 1997 RIA T.C. ¶ 97,530, *aff'd on other issues*, 187 F.3d 1352 (11th Cir. 1999) (fees incurred for one-year construction loan amortized over one year).

63 *See* IRC § 263A(f); Treas. Reg. § 1.263A-8. The interest to be capitalized is determined by the "avoided cost" method, see *id.*, § 1.263A-9(a), meaning that any interest payment which the taxpayer would have avoided had accumulated production expenditures (very broadly defined) been used to pay down the debt must be capitalized. These rules are by now well established.

64 A more recent Supreme Court case, *Indopco, Inc. v. Commissioner*, 503 U.S. 79 (1992), is the underlying authority for an inclusive rule on capitalization of production period (and pre-opening) expenses.

65 Reichel v. Commissioner, 112 T.C. 14 (1999); Von-Lusk v. Commissioner, 104 T.C. 207 (1995) (soft costs, incurred in obtaining public approvals, are pre-operating capital costs). For a useful summary of the multifarious capitalization rules applicable to the acquisition or construction of real estate projects, see L. Weld, C. Price & C. Edmonds, *Tax Aspects of Acquiring Business or Investment Real Estate*, 24 Real Est. Rev. No. 1, 27 (1994).

[f] Lease-up

Operating expenses are deductible from operating income once the "production period" has ended, which, according to the regulations, means that physical construction activity has been completed.[66] Prior to that point in time, operating costs must be capitalized as a cost of acquiring, constructing and putting into service the rental business represented by the project.[67]

[2] Costs in the Fox Valley Auto Care Center

Having explored the cost allocation issues involved in a real estate project like the Fox Valley Auto Care Center, it is time to prepare a set of "*pro forma* financials" for use in deciding whether to proceed with the project, and to obtain financing and capital contributions from investors. These financials are "*pro forma*" because they are not the actual costs which will be incurred, but rather budgets and projections provided for planning and solicitation purposes. The first step is to determine the acquisition and construction costs and how those costs are to be allocated.

[a] Acquisition Cost

Regent has agreed to pay $580,000 cash for the Johnson Tract, and then an additional $325,000 cash for the corner lot of the Metropolitan Tract. Actually, part of the consideration paid for the Johnson Tract should be allocated to the second portion, but we do not need to cut the allocation questions quite so finely. Regent acquired the entire site for aggregate cash payments of $905,000 and then proceeded to divide it into two parts, one of which it sold to Turtle Wax. The allocation of cost has been made in proportion to the relative areas of the two parts of the development tract, as shown in Figure 2.9, *supra*.

[b] Access Road Construction

As part of the transaction, Regent agreed with Metropolitan and then, subsequently, with Turtle Wax, to construct access roads subject to certain cost sharing arrangements. The net cost, assumed to be $91,810, has also been allocated between the two portions of the original development tract as shown in Figure 2.9, *supra*. Construction costs for roads servicing the Metropolitan developments will be reimbursed, and are transactions separate from Regent's development of the Center.

[c] Sale to Turtle Wax

Determination of the tax basis (and the book value) of the *land* to be used in the development of the Fox Valley Auto Care Center is shown as "book value" of the retail store site in Figure 2.9, *supra*. The effect of the sale of the car wash site to Turtle Wax for cash has previously been discussed. Because the construction budget and other documents do not reflect the use of these proceeds in the development of the FVACC, it appears that Regent used the net proceeds for

---

66 Treas. Reg. § 1.263A-12(d)(2).

67 Blitzer v. United States, 684 F.2d 874 (Ct. Cl. 1982); *see generally* IRC § 196 (denying deductions for "start-up expenses").

other projects. Accordingly, this transaction will not be reflected in the financials for the FVACC.

[d] Construction and Other Production Costs

The construction contract has a fixed price of $1,240,000. This price is assumed to include all costs incurred in the actual construction of the Center, including site preparation and tenant fix-up, but not construction of the access roads. It is now necessary to allocate the construction contract cost and the "soft costs" to be incurred in completing the Center among the elements to which they apply. This allocation is shown in Figure 2.10.

Figure 2.10
Allocation of Budgeted Costs for Construction of Fox Valley Auto Care Center

Fox Valley Auto Care Center			cost	*Allocations*	depreciable basis		*amortizable*
	square feet	$PSqFt	book value	*land*	*site*	*building*	*cost*
LAND:	94,200	4.98	468,670	468,670			
SITE COSTS:							
On Site							
Grading & Site Preparations		1.90	178,980		178,980		
Parking Lot Lighting & Landscaping			121,000		121,000		
Off Site							
contractual road work			47,545	47,545			
Access Road Improvements			50,000		50,000		
Storm Water							
CONSTRUCTION:							
Construction of Shops	20,000	45.00	900,000			900,000	
TENANT IMPROVEMENT ALLOWANCE:			40,000			40,000	
CONSTRUCTION CONTINGENCY:							
5% for total construction costs			60,000			60,000	
SOFT COSTS:							
Leasing Commissions	20,000		80,000				80,000
Loan Fees			25,000				25,000
Legal & Accounting			40,000	20,000		20,000	
A&E			40,000	10,000		30,000	
Survey & Closing			30,000	30,000		-	
Insurance and Real Estate Taxes (construction)			50,000			50,000	
Development Fees			100,000			100,000	
TOTAL EXPENSES			2,231,195	576,215	349,980	1,200,000	105,000
INTEREST:							
Budgeted Construction Interest (@ 12%)			185,000			185,000	
Reserve for Negative Cash Flow to Break-Even Leaseup			60,000			60,000	
			245,000			245,000	
TOTAL PROJECT COSTS:			2,476,195	576,215	349,980	1,445,000	105,000

To make the allocations under the construction budget, a cash flow table, Figure 2.11, shows when the cash requirements for the construction of the Fox Valley Auto Care Center occur and how the timing of the expenditures would be reflected in draws from the construction loan and how other sources of capital would be applied. It will also show how expenditures relate to different phases of the construction. In actual practice, a chart such as this, known as a "Sources and Uses" table, would show more detail than the chart reproduced here.

Figure 2.11 Sources and Uses: Construction Budget

Fox Valley Auto Care Center
The Regent Development Group
Fox Valley Car Care Center Construction Cash Flow Projections

Uses		1989						1990						
	Project Total	July	August	September	October	November	December	January	February	March	April	May	June	July
Expenditures														
Land	468,670	468,670												
Access Roads	47,545			47,545										
Grading & Site Preparations	178,980	89,490	89,490											
Parking Lot Lighting & Landscaping	121,000					24,200	12,100	12,100	12,100	30,250	30,250			
Construction Contract	1,050,000			160,000	160,000	135,800	147,900	107,900	107,900	52,625	52,625	52,625	52,625	20,000
Architectural/Engineering	40,000	25,000	5,000	2,000	2,000	2,000	2,000	2,000						
Development Fees	100,000			20,000	20,000	20,000	20,000	20,000						
Legal & Accounting	40,000	25,000	10,000	2,500	2,500									
Insurance	15,000	10,000						5,000						
Survey & Closing	30,000	20,000	5,000	5,000										
Construction Loan Fee	25,000	25,000												
Leasing Commissions	80,000	20,000	10,000	10,000				20,000		20,000				
Interim Interest (at 12%)	185,076		5,582	6,882	9,572	11,562	13,548	15,553	17,429	18,853	20,121	21,200	21,989	22,785
Real Estate Taxes:	35,000	25,000		10,000										
Contingency/Operating Deficit	60,000		5,000	5,000	5,000	5,000	5,000	5,000	5,000	5,000	5,000	5,000	5,000	5,000
Total Project Costs:	2,476,271													
Cash flow requirement:		708,160	130,072	268,928	199,072	198,562	200,548	187,553	142,429	126,728	107,996	78,825	79,614	47,785
Sources														
Equity Capital:	150,000	150,000												
cumulative construction draw:		558,160	688,231	957,159	1,156,230	1,354,793	1,555,341	1,742,894	1,885,323	2,012,051	2,120,047	2,198,872	2,278,486	2,300,000
construction interest rate:	12.0%													
cumulative construction deficit:												-	-	(26,271)

A developer must have a chart of this kind to identify the sources of capital and to match those sources to the capital outflow. The cost of capital, as you have seen, is an essential element in determining the final project costs.

Note that this chart correlates the draws on the construction loan, and therefore the amount of construction interest, with budgeted costs, some of which have been allocated arbitrarily to times within the construction period. Interest on the construction loan is shown as "interim interest" as it accrues. When the draws occur will depend on the construction loan documents. This chart also shows that "equity capital" has been contributed to the Limited Liability Company and will be used in the construction of the Fox Valley Auto Care Center.[68]

[3] Income and Expense

In order to finance these costs, the cash flow from the project must be sufficient to sustain the capital structure from which the costs are paid, and to provide the necessary returns to lenders and investors. The next stage is to develop the information needed for construction of a cash flow table, just as in the opening discussion on present value.

[a] Rents

How do you find out about rents when much of the project is yet to be leased? The sample project used by the Shers to illustrate their creation of a *pro forma* demonstrates how rents will vary with the type of tenant, the importance of the tenant to the success of the project, and the amount of tenant-specific investment which the developer must make in order to obtain the tenant's lease. With the Fox Valley Auto Care Center, this seems relatively straightforward, or does it? As construction began, there were some tenants already under lease or involved in leasing negotiations. Ideally, Regent would want to have "credit tenants,"[69] but this may be difficult for an auto specialty center. A major cellular phone company, or perhaps a "Jiffy Lube" in the lubrication bay, is the type of tenant which the developer, and the developer's lender, would prefer, but the tenants in the Fox Valley Auto Care Center mostly were "local," that is, small businesses with only one or two locations in the immediate area.

Can you think of other credit tenants that might be attracted to an auto care center? What about an auto parts store? The Fox Valley Auto Care Center does not seem to have attracted such a tenant. What might have been the problem there? To answer this question, you will need to reconsider the deal Regent made with Metropolitan, which, in turn, must have been affected by the deals Metropolitan would have made with other developers, as well as Regent's contract with Turtle Wax. One of the most difficult problems for the developer of a retail center is what kind of center to build. The Shers discuss this problem, which is a "design" problem. There is a close relationship between the tenants and the

---

68 When lending becomes tight, lenders will usually require a developer to contribute capital to the project *first*, before any loan proceeds may be used, and the amount required will be a percentage of the *cost* of the project (and its value). In the actual case, it appears that the construction funding was available to Regent before any equity capital was required, although according to the budget, the cost does exceed the construction loan. In the sources and uses chart, equity capital is shown as an initial contribution but may have been contributed to the project as the need for this capital appeared.

69 A credit tenant is usually a national retailer, such as, say, The Gap, although some regional chains can meet the requirements as well. The credit rating of these tenants, rather than the rental income potential of the rental space, on a five year (or more) lease will support most debt financing. Most local tenants do not have the same credit standing. For a discussion of these issues, see T. Boyce, *Recent Developments in Credit Tenant Loans*, 26 Real Est. Rev. No. 4, 5 (Winter 1997).

building; where there is an anchor, the nature of the anchor will have a major impact on the design decisions. This impact, for purposes of this discussion, goes further than restrictions or obligations which might be imposed by and incurred in the leases; because the rent will determine the financial structure of the project, and because the financial structure will, in turn, determine how much can be spent in construction costs, the ability of a shopping center to attract the right tenants is essential.

Consider the criteria explained by the Shers as indicia of a successful shopping center. How many of these does the Fox Valley Auto Care Center seem to meet? Consider critical mass, that is, the right density of shops to attract customers, and the tenant mix. These factors tend to be influenced by the quality of the building. Here, Regent decided to build what the Shers refer to as a "Vanilla Shell." Is the design of the buildings at the Fox Valley Auto Care Center one that will attract tenants? Will the "anchor," the Turtle Wax car wash, attract the right customers, that is, customers who might shop for more than just a car wash and car wash products? What do customers do while their automobiles are being washed or serviced? Why do you think some major department stores, such as Sears, have automobile service departments associated with their retail stores?

These are design and business issues for Regent, and it would not be appropriate for lawyers to raise questions about the business decisions their developer client makes in planning and building such a project. Lawyers can help, however, by identifying contractual restrictions which might hamper the developer in the implementation of its plan. In this case, Metropolitan was the principal developer of the large regional shopping mall just across the street from the location of the Fox Valley Auto Care Center. In signing leases with tenants, Metropolitan or its affiliate may have agreed to restrictions on leases with existing tenants in the mall or in nearby developments in which it participates. Radius restrictions like these, if imposed on Regent by its contracts with Metropolitan, could have limited the activities in which Regent's tenants could engage, and might then have made finding tenants more difficult than Regent might have expected.

Considerations like these may be relevant for an offering memorandum intended to attract investors. In these memoranda, the risks that the Center might not succeed need to be accurately disclosed, and you might find the factors discussed in the Sher article helpful as they relate to the specifics of the development of the Fox Valley Auto Care Center. This will require you to relate the expected tenant mix to the rental structure which will provide the capital necessary for the long term success of the project

In analyzing the leases, improvements to the building may be necessary for the tenants to conduct their respective businesses. For most, the cost of tenant improvements does not seem to have been particularly heavy, involving partitions and some basic fit-up. The cost of construction of the lubrication bay is a different problem, as pointed out earlier, and may have been "fronted" by Regent (that is, Regent paid to have the improvements constructed for the tenant), financing the tenant improvement in return for increased rent. Lube Pros, the actual tenant, may not have had much capital and so could not have paid for the construction itself. Repayment of Regent for doing this would be made out of future rents, which, because of the special construction necessary for proper operation of a lubrication bay, should not be viewed as premium (above market) rents. How do you think that a lender would want to account for the increased rent on this part of the Fox Valley Auto Care Center?

The leases are for a specified rent, with annual rental increases built in to the basic rent structure. There is no percentage rent. The Fox Valley Auto Care Center may be too small for such a rental structure, and its growth potential limited. In larger centers, which typically have an anchor store or stores, the leases often require the payment of a percentages of sales above a benchmark number. Percentage rents are discussed in the Sher article.

[b] Expenses

The leases are net leases. In a net lease, the tenant pays its aliquot share (usually determined by floor area ratios) of all the operating costs of a center, including real estate tax but not the debt service.[70] In the leasing arrangement for the Fox Valley Auto Care Center, the tenant also paid management fees and an additional fee to Regent for its administration of common area maintenance charges ("CAM"). Moreover, each tenant paid an additional amount determined by the area subject to its lease into a reserve for capital improvements. As a result, there are no operating expenses for which Regent, which will manage the FVACC, is responsible, except for its aliquot share (attributable to vacant space) of CAM expenses. In most real estate projects, there will be some expenses for which the developer/landlord remains liable, and tenants may object to loading all expenses onto the rental structure, including future increases in these costs. The *pro forma* for the Fox Valley Auto Care Center is, however, quite a bit simpler because of the way these expenses are handled in this project.

[c] Pro forma

The Shers calculate the numbers they propose to use in analyzing their projects based on a "stabilized net operating income." They comment further that cash flow statements of the kind discussed earlier in these materials are unnecessary. Do you agree? Think back to the DCF discussion on valuation methodology. Experienced developers often rely on the single year numbers which the Shers discuss, but it is their experience which in turn lends meaning to their numbers. The DCF methodology should force the inexperienced analyst to think hard about the underlying assumptions one must make to give the single year numbers significance.

Are the "formulas" the Shers use helpful in helping you to reach a conclusion about the propects for the Fox Valley Auto Care Center? What additional information do you think you need in evaluating their methodology? With the FVACC, the assumptions about rents and other relevant items should be accepted as reasonable, but you might want to find out what happens in your model as these assumptions are varied, which is the main reason why DCF analysis is helpful.

At this point, there is enough information about the Fox Valley Auto Care Center to plug the necessary values into the *pro forma* formulas used by the Shers

---

[70] A net lease is intended to provide the owner with constant (here increasing by the factors built in to the leasing formulas) net operating income over the term of the lease. *See* Phillip S. Scherrer & Timothy J. Mathison, *Net Leases as Real Estate Investments*, 27 Real Est. Rev. No. 2, 51 (1997). A triple-net lease is a lease under which the tenant pays all property charges including real estate taxes A ground lease would typically be a triple-net lease.

in their analysis to determine how much permanent financing will be available to the FVACC. See their chart, Figure C, *supra*. The results are shown in Figure 2.12.

Figure 2.12 Fox Valley Auto Care Center Pro Forma Formulas

1.	$\frac{\text{N.O.I. (Net Operating Income)}}{\text{Total Project Costs}}$ = Cap rate (at cost)	$\frac{300{,}975}{2{,}476{,}195}$ = 12.73%
2.	$\frac{\text{(Net Operating Income)}}{\text{(Capitalization Rate)}}$ = Market Value	$\frac{300{,}975}{0.095}$ = \$3,168,158
3.	Sales Price less Sales Cost @ 4%= Net Sales Price	3,168,158 – 126,726 = \$3,041,432
4.	Net Sales Price less Project Cost = Before Tax Profit	3,041,432 – 2,481,113 = \$560,319
5.	$\frac{\text{Net Operating Income}}{\text{Minimum Debt Coverage}}$ = Maximum Debt Service	$\frac{300{,}975}{1.25}$ = \$240,780
6.	$\frac{\text{Maximum Debt Service}}{\text{Debt Service Constant}}$ = Maximum Loan Amount	$\frac{240{,}780}{0.1007}$ = \$2,390,978
7.	Market Price × Loan to Value = Maximum Loan Amount	3,041,432 × 65% = \$1,976,931
8.	Amount of the Loan = Lower of (6) or (7)	\$1,976,931
9.	Project Cost Less Amount of Loan = Equity Required	2,476,271 – 1,976,931 = \$499,340
10.	N.O.I. less Debt Service = Cash Flow	300,975 – 199,084 = \$101,891
11.	$\frac{\text{Cash Flow}}{\text{Equity Required}}$ = Cash on Cash	$\frac{101{,}891}{499{,}340}$ = 20.41%

Notes:

Item 2: Assume market capitalization rate for a constructed strip center = 9.5%.

Item 3: Assume constructed center could be sold at cap rate = 9.5%

Item 5: Assume mortgage lender requires debt cover = 1.25

Item 6: Assume 9.0% interest and 25-year amortization to calculate debt constant = 1.007.

Item 7: Assume loan to value required by the lender = 65%

Figure 2.13 is a mortgage table showing the annual cost of debt service using the Sher formulas to calculate the amount the Developer can expect the bank will lend on a long-term basis ("permanent financing"). In applying the formulas shown in the Sher chart, we have used conservative underwriting standards. A loan at 9% with a 25 year amortization period would, assuming that projected stabilized net operating income can be achieved, provide enough loan proceeds to retire the construction loan. However, if the lender will apply the 9.5% cap rate to the income from the project, and limit the amount of its loan to 65% of value, loan proceeds are less. Interest rates are, as of this writing (early 2009), low, so it is likely that both the loan interest and the market cap rate have been stated at higher values than we might expect to find in the current market. Adjustment of these numbers, assuming a loan-to-value requirement of 75%, for example, yields a more satisfactory conclusion. In the markets of 2009, however, retail trade has fallen off, so lenders require larger margins of safety for their loans, and the assumptions we have made here are consistent with that position.

Figure 2.13 Mortgage Table

Fox Valley Auto Care Center

Debt service calculation

	actual mortgage
Principal of take out loan:	1,976,931
Interest rate:	9.0%
Term:	25
Monthly payment:	16,590
Annual debt service:	199,084
Loan constant:	0.1007
commencement date:	1-Aug-90
months in short period	4

Year	*Principal: beginning*	*ending*	*annual debt service*	*principal paid*	*interest paid*
1	1,976,931	1,962,448	66,361	14,483	51,879
2	1,962,448	1,939,034	199,084	23,414	175,670
3	1,939,034	1,913,424	199,084	25,610	173,474
4	1,913,424	1,885,412	199,084	28,013	171,071
5	1,885,412	1,854,771	199,084	30,640	168,444
6	1,854,771	1,821,256	199,084	33,515	165,569
7	1,821,256	1,784,598	199,084	36,659	162,425
8	1,784,598	1,744,500	199,084	40,097	158,987
9	1,744,500	1,700,642	199,084	43,859	155,225
10	1,700,642	1,652,669	199,084	47,973	151,111

The debt level provided by these formulas is purely hypothetical and stated here for discussion purposes. The actual amount that can be borrowed depends on the *lender's* criteria, and the lender's criteria are subject to the "golden rule" (them as have the gold, make the rules). Moreover, these numbers predict an equity commitment by Regent of about $170,000, which does not seem to have occurred.

They also depend upon the ability of Regent to lease up the Fox Valley Auto Care Center at the projected rents, which in this case was not achieved within the time frame necessary to refinance the construction loan.

What do the results of these formulas tell you? Is it useful? The capitalization rate, from line 2 of Figure 2.12, has a function similar to that of a price/earnings ratio in the financial markets, and defines the anticipated current yield from a property with an investment cost equal to the project cost, at least if the projected rents can be realized. It can be compared with the current yield from other similar properties located in the same market area. With the Fox Valley Car Care Center, there are other developments in progress, so this information could be useful for comparison.

In computing the "price" or value, we use a *capitalization rate* which is different from current yield, and then use that rate to project a value from stabilized net operating income. Because the Fox Valley Auto Care Center had not rented up at the time these pro forma financial statements were prepared, current yield is calculated using a projected rental schedule with vacancy loss estimated at the time when the FVACC is expected to be in full operation, so-called stabilized net operating income, which is projected in Figure 2.14.[71]

This capitalization rate could then be compared to the returns on comparable properties in the same geographic area, and if it appeared high, that could be a warning that projected rents have been overstated. Remember from the present value discussion that the *lower* the discount rate, the *higher* the value, and *vice versa*. In projecting a *value*, a different (lower) capitalization rate has been used, perhaps chosen as representative of the returns similar projects have produced. In determining loan values, the lender would substitute the cap rate which it believes represents the experience of projects like this one, but here a *reduced* capitalization rate means that the calculated value (on line 2) will be *greater* than the cost of acquiring the land and constructing the project. In the early 1980s, this was a frequent experience for Developers, who optimistically predicted rising rents. Calculations like this one supported high financing limitations which ultimately undermined the security for the loans and contributed to the real estate recession that occurred in the late 1980s and early 1990s.

---

[71] *See* Marisa Timm, *Real Estate's Flawed Paradigm: Stabilized Income*, 23 REAL EST. REV. No. 4, 17 (1994). The actual experience of the Fox Valley Auto Care Center shows a high capitalization rate (over 12%) when compare to the cost of acquisition and construction. This might imply an optimistic rental projection, although by 1992, the third year of operation, 85% of the space had been rented and rental cash flow exceeded the projections. For a developer of shopping centers, a high cap rate on construction (efficient allocation of cost to produce the projected rental cash flow) and a significantly lower market cap rate for sale or financing purposes is the objective, as this produces a large profit. Compare cost to market value, assuming a cap rate of 9.5%, Figure 2.12, item 4. This assumes, of course, that the financial markets permit sale or refinancing.

Figure 2.14 Stabilized Net Operating Income

Pro Forma Income Statement			
Tenant	**Sq.Ft.**	**$PSqFt**	**Total Base Rent**
Cellular Communications	1,500	15	22,500
Globe Glass	3,500	15	52,500
Master Werks	2,000	15	30,000
Casey Muffler & Brake	2,750	15	41,250
Sparks Tune-up Centers	2,500	15	37,500
Lube Pros	1,800	30	54,000
New Tenant	2,000	15	30,000
New Tenant	2,000	15	30,000
New Tenant	1,950	15	29,250
Projected rental:	20,000		327,000
Other Income:			-
Vacancy (30% first year; 7.5% long range)			(24,525)
Other expenses (nonreimbursed CAM):			(1,500)
Reserve for Structural Repair (paid by tenants):			-
Stabilized net operating income:			300,975

This capitalization rate (9.5%), which is higher than the cap rates experienced until late 2008, projects a *value* which is then used to make predictions about the level of financing that can be achieved. In Figure 2.12, line 7, the lender's loan-to-value limitation is assumed to be 65%, and applying this limitation to the projected value produces a maximum loan amount of $1.98 million, approximately, which is considerably less than the budgeted cost to buy and build the project. As noted above, underwriting standards in 2009 have contracted in the face of a financial crisis, when lending to projects like the Fox Valley Auto Care Center has almost completely ceased. In the early 1990s, however, when Regent was attempting to negotiate a permanent loan, real estate markets were just beginning to recover from the recession, and lenders, understandably concerned about the security for making real estate loans, as they are now, had set unrealistically high underwriting standards. This, and the reduced rent produced by the FVACC because it had not rented up, made it very difficult for Regent to find a permanent loan which would refinance the construction loan on the property without requiring a capital infusion.

A problem for the Fox Valley Auto Care Center may be found in the rental projections. The alternative limitation imposed by lenders on the amount that can be financed is found in the debt cover ratio. This calculation is made on line 5 of Figure 2.12. Here, it is assumed that the lender will require a debt cover ratio of 1.25, which means that net operating income from the Fox Valley Auto Care Center must be 25% greater than the debt service required to pay the debt. Dividing net operating income by the debt cover ratio yields the maximum amount of projected income from the Fox Valley Auto Care Center that the lender will accept as debt service. The remaining 25% is viewed as a cushion or margin of error to protect the lender against the potential failure of the Fox Valley Auto Care Center to produce the anticipated income. Once stabilized net income is known, and if the loan terms have been negotiated, the maximum amount to be financed by this lender can be found by applying the loan constant (the ratio between annual debt service and the original mortgage principal) to the maximum available debt service. This calculation is done on line 6 for a 25-year, self-amortizing loan at 9% interest. An improvement in the loan terms, such as a lower interest rate, would yield a higher financing limitation. In this case, however, the loan is subject to the loan-to-value limitation anyway, so working with the debt cover limitation will not improve the leverage for the FVACC.

Note how much these calculations depend upon an accurate prediction of the rent potential for the project. This is really where the developer's experience in assessing the likelihood of success for the project plays a critical role, as most of the other variables are known within narrow margins of error. If the projected current yield from a property yet to be built is much higher than the capitalization rate for comparable properties, it would be advisable to proceed with caution.

The *pro forma* financials for the project, which we are now creating, will be essential to obtain the necessary long term financing. You can expect the accuracy of the *pro forma* to be the subject of hard bargaining with the lender, and the making of a loan commitment inevitably begins with agreement on the financials. So, this will be an important step in the planning to create the capital structure for Regent's project.

You should create your own cash flow table, just as was done in the initial discussion on present values, making the necessary assumptions in building it and then varying those assumptions to see how changes in the assumptions affect your financial estimate of value. See Figure 2.15, where such a cash flow table has been created using the formulas described in the Shers' article to determine the permanent loan expected for the Car Care Center (see Figure 2.13), using projected stabilized net income from Figure 2.14, and assuming that additional equity has been contributed to the Fox Valley Auto Care Center LLC to finance the completion of the project.

Figure 2.15 Fox Valley Auto Care Center
Pro Forma Financials

rental inflator:	3.0%	Where year 1 = 1990
expense inflator:	4.0%	
CAM expense:	40,000	
Investor tax rate:	35.0%	

Year:		1 1990	2 1991	3 1992	4 1993	5 1994	6 1995	7 1996
Gross rental income:		136,250	327,000	336,810	346,914	357,322	368,041	379,083
vacancy factor:		-50.00%	-30.00%	-7.50%	-7.50%	-7.50%	-7.50%	-7.50%
vacancy loss:		(68,125)	(98,100)	(25,261)	(26,019)	(26,799)	(27,603)	(28,431)
Net rental income:		68,125	228,900	311,549	320,896	330,523	340,438	350,651
Other income:		-	-	-	-	-	-	-
Income:		68,125	228,900	311,549	320,896	330,523	340,438	350,651
common area expense (includes real estate taxes)		16,667						
owner's share (vacant space):		(8,333)	(12,000)	(3,120)	(3,245)	(3,375)	(3,510)	(3,650)
Net operating income (free and clear):		59,791	216,900	308,429	317,651	327,148	336,929	347,001
Less debt service:		(66,361)	(199,084)	(199,084)	(199,084)	(199,084)	(199,084)	(199,084)
Cash Flow:		(6,570)	17,816	109,345	118,567	128,064	137,845	147,917
Distributable cash flow from the partnership:		-	17,816	109,345	118,567	128,064	137,845	147,917
Taxable Income:								
Add principal paid:		14,483	23,414	25,610	28,013	30,640	33,515	36,659
Subtract amortization:		(17,000)	(17,000)	(17,000)	(17,000)	(17,000)	(1,000)	(1,000)
Subtract depreciation:		(30,179)	(60,393)	(60,393)	(60,393)	(60,393)	(60,393)	(60,393)
Taxable income:		(39,267)	(36,164)	57,562	69,186	81,311	109,966	123,183
Tax cost (benefit):		(13,743)	(12,657)	20,147	24,215	28,459	38,488	43,114
After tax cash (entire project):		7,173	30,473	89,199	94,352	99,605	99,357	104,804
Investment (Sales Proceeds)(from figure 3.1):								1,177,971
Assume that Regent sold investor 40% of project economics:								
Equity Required:	499,264							
Investor Capital:	199,736							
Percentage interest:	40.0%							
Aggregate Cash Flows:	499,264	7,173	30,473	89,199	94,352	99,605	99,357	1,282,775
[1] Investor Interest:	(199,736)	2,869	12,189	35,679	37,741	39,842	39,743	513,110
Internal rate of return:	22.2%							
[2] Developer Interest:	(299,529)	4,304	18,284	53,519	56,611	59,763	59,614	769,665
Internal rate of return:	22.2%							

Figure 2.15 shows the kind of return Regent can expect if it would be willing to invest the amount of equity capital our financial analysis implies, approximately \$500,000, and investors would be willing to contribute an aliquot share of this capital for a proportionate share of the project's economics, in this case 40%.

The calculated internal rate of return on the equity in the Fox Valley Auto Care Center over the seven year investment horizon shown in Figure 2.15 is more than 22%, within the range of the cost of capital for this type of project. To make this calculation, we had to estimate how much cash proceeds a sale of the project at the end of the investment would bring. In making this calculation, we capitalized year seven net operating income at a cap rate of 10.5%, 100 basis points greater than the assumed market capitalization rate at the time the Center was built. The result is shown in Figure 3.1 in Chapter 3, *infra*. When the need for this additional capital became apparent as Regent attempted to refinance the construction loan, what would you have advised? How does a developer evaluate the risk involved in making substantial additional investment in a project like the Fox Valley Auto Care Center when the financial markets are frozen by poor market conditions?

In more complicated situations, the cash flow table, and its underlying assumptions, will provide the information necessary for dividing cash flow between investors and the developer/manager of the project. This will require calculating the tax burden on the cash flows distributed to the investor. To do that, it will be necessary to discuss more of the tax aspects of investing in real estate, to which we turn in Chapter 3.

§ 2.05 EXPLANATION OF PRESENT VALUE CALCULATIONS

Suppose A invests $\$X$ in an investment from which A is guaranteed to receive interest = $i\%$. At the end of one year, A will have accumulated the following amount:

$$\$Y = \$X \times (1 + i)$$

where $\$Y$ = the future value of the accumulation, or simply "*FV*" and $\$X$= the *present value* of the investment, or simply "*PV*." In this example, i is taken to mean the annual simple interest rate. Suppose A does not withdraw any funds, and leaves the investment, plus the interest, to accumulate additional interest at the same rate for one more year. Then, substituting the symbols used above, at the end of the second year, A will have accumulated an investment (or *FV*) of —

$$FV = PV \times (1 + i) \times (1 + i)$$

or

$$FV = PV \times (1 + i)^2$$

This expression can be generalized for any number of periods ("n") during which the investment (*PV*) will earn income at the rate of i during the period:

$$FV = PV \times (1 + i)^n$$

If the future value of the investment is known (that is, the projected cash flow for any year which is n years from now) and you want to solve for the present value of that cash flow (CFn), the formula will be —

$$PV_n = \frac{CF_n}{(1+i)^n}$$

And the present value of the cash flows through the investment period (that is, to year "n", when the project would be sold) is simply the sum of all these values. Or —

$$PV_{1..n} = \frac{CF}{(1+i)} + \frac{CF_2}{(1+i)^2} + \frac{CF_3}{(1+i)^3} + \ldots + \frac{CF_n}{(1+i)^n}$$

The "net present value" of the investment, at the selected discount rate = i, is the difference between the sum of the present values of the cash flows and the price of the investor's interest = C.

$$NPV = \left\{ PV_{1..n} = \frac{CF}{(1+i)} + \frac{CF_2}{(1+i)^2} + \frac{CF_3}{(1+i)^3} + \ldots + \frac{CF_n}{(1+i)^n} \right\} - C$$

With a personal computer and any one of the modern spreadsheet programs widely available, these numbers can be easily computed. In most spreadsheets, there will be "functions" which, by filling in the appropriate quantities (or "arguments"), will calculate the present value of an annuity (periodic cash flows) or the net present value of irregular cash flows. Much of the discussion of present values in the evaluation of real estate projects depends on these calculations.

Table A

Present Value of $1

Years Hence	Discount rates 5%	6%	7%	8%	9%	10%	11%	12%	13%	39%	40%	41%	42%	47%	48%
1	0.952	0.943	0.935	0.926	0.917	0.909	0.901	0.893	0.885	0.719	0.714	0.709	0.704	0.680	0.676
2	0.907	0.890	0.873	0.857	0.842	0.826	0.812	0.797	0.783	0.518	0.510	0.503	0.496	0.463	0.457
3	0.864	0.840	0.816	0.794	0.772	0.751	0.731	0.712	0.693	0.372	0.364	0.357	0.349	0.315	0.308
4	0.823	0.792	0.763	0.735	0.708	0.683	0.659	0.636	0.613	0.268	0.260	0.253	0.246	0.214	0.208
5	0.784	0.747	0.713	0.681	0.650	0.621	0.593	0.567	0.543	0.193	0.186	0.179	0.173	0.146	0.141
6	0.746	0.705	0.666	0.630	0.596	0.564	0.535	0.507	0.480	0.139	0.133	0.127	0.122	0.099	0.095
7	0.711	0.665	0.623	0.583	0.547	0.513	0.482	0.452	0.425	0.100	0.095	0.090	0.086	0.067	0.064
8	0.677	0.627	0.582	0.540	0.502	0.467	0.434	0.404	0.376	0.072	0.068	0.064	0.060	0.046	0.043
9	0.645	0.592	0.544	0.500	0.460	0.424	0.391	0.361	0.333	0.052	0.048	0.045	0.043	0.031	0.029
10	0.614	0.558	0.508	0.463	0.422	0.386	0.352	0.322	0.295	0.037	0.035	0.032	0.030	0.021	0.020
11	0.585	0.527	0.475	0.429	0.388	0.350	0.317	0.287	0.261	0.027	0.025	0.023	0.021	0.014	0.013
12	0.557	0.497	0.444	0.397	0.356	0.319	0.286	0.257	0.231	0.019	0.018	0.016	0.015	0.010	0.009
13	0.530	0.469	0.415	0.368	0.326	0.290	0.258	0.229	0.204	0.014	0.013	0.011	0.010	0.007	0.006
14	0.505	0.442	0.388	0.340	0.299	0.263	0.232	0.205	0.181	0.010	0.009	0.008	0.007	0.005	0.004
15	0.481	0.417	0.362	0.315	0.275	0.239	0.209	0.183	0.160	0.007	0.006	0.006	0.005	0.003	0.003
16	0.458	0.394	0.339	0.292	0.252	0.218	0.188	0.163	0.141	0.005	0.005	0.004	0.004	0.002	0.002
17	0.436	0.371	0.317	0.270	0.231	0.198	0.170	0.146	0.125	0.004	0.003	0.003	0.003	0.001	0.001
18	0.416	0.350	0.296	0.250	0.212	0.180	0.153	0.130	0.111	0.003	0.002	0.002	0.002	0.001	0.001
19	0.396	0.331	0.277	0.232	0.194	0.164	0.138	0.116	0.098	0.002	0.002	0.001	0.001	0.001	0.001
20	0.377	0.312	0.258	0.215	0.178	0.149	0.124	0.104	0.087	0.001	0.001	0.001	0.001	0.000	0.000

Chapter 3

INCOME TAXES AND REAL ESTATE INVESTING

§ 3.01 OVERVIEW OF THE CHAPTER AND LIMITATIONS ON ITS SCOPE

[1] Overview

Investment returns are calculated on the net cash flow to the investor after the effect of income taxes has been taken into account. Because income tax liabilities, and, sometimes, benefits are significant, and often vary depending upon the capital structure of specific projects, this approach is essential if the value of the investment is to be accurately determined. This chapter will examine the income tax issues involved in the development of the Fox Valley Auto Care Center in some depth.

[2] Limitations on Tax Deferral and Avoidance

This chapter does not address in detail limitations on tax advantages which have played a prominent role in real estate investing. These limitations were enacted to prevent the use of tax shelters by investors who were less interested in the economic advantages of real estate investing than they were in the tax benefits. The limitations include the "at risk" rule under IRC § 465 and the limitation on the deduction of "passive losses" imposed by IRC § 469. The "at risk" rule limits the capital which will be taken into account in determining the investor's tax basis to the amount which she puts "at risk" in the venture. There is an exception, however, for "qualified nonrecourse financing," which is financing provided by an independent lending institution on commercially reasonable terms.[1] The increasing use of Limited Liability Companies as the entity of choice for real estate investing, which we discuss in Chapter 4, implicates "at risk" limitations on the ability of the members of an LLC to use the otherwise favorable tax treatment of interests in conduit entities, and will require some discussion.[2]

The passive loss rule limits the amount of tax deductions for tax losses from an investment in a trade or business in which the taxpayer does not "materially participate" to the amount of passive income which the investor realizes from other, similar investments. We assume that any nonrecourse loan to the Fox Valley Auto Care Center LLC will be "qualified nonrecourse financing" because it will be made by an independent lender and secured by a mortgage on the Center[3] and further, that any net loss deductions allocated to investors in the LLC will be offset by passive income realized by these investors from other passive investments.

---

1 IRC § 465(b)(6).

2 *See* Chapter 4, note 20, *infra*.

3 *See* Treas. Reg. § 1.465-27, T.D. 8777, 1998-2 C.B. 219.

§ 3.02 DEPRECIATION

Depreciation is a tax concept. How it applies to the Fox Valley Auto Care Center has been discussed in Section 2.04 of Chapter 2 where the allocation of the cost of acquisition and construction of the Center was analyzed. When we examined the viability of the Fox Valley Auto Care Center as an investment, we broke down the overall cost of acquiring the land and building the Center into component parts, and then allocated some to depreciable assets (some of which were depreciable as improvements and some as land preparation costs), and some to nondepreciable land. In this chapter, depreciation is treated as an essential element in the tax make-up of the Fox Valley Auto Care Center from the investor's perspective, and the role of depreciation in making real estate a tax favored investment is analyzed.

[1] Depreciation Recovery Periods

The Internal Revenue Code specifies how depreciation is calculated for real estate assets. IRC §§ 168(b)(3)(A)–(B); 168(c)(1); 168(e)(2). For commercial structures, such as those at the Fox Valley Auto Care Center, tax depreciation must be calculated using the straight-line (equal annual amounts) method over a 39-year cost recovery period (a structure's "useful life") using a mid-month convention (all structures placed in service during a particular month are treated as having been placed in service on the fifteenth day, whether they were or not). The Internal Revenue Service has published Tables to be used in calculating depreciation (Rev. Proc. 87-57, 1987-2 C.B. 687), and for real estate with a 39-year useful life, allowable depreciation will be 2.564% (100% divided by 39 years = 2.564%) of the Center building's unadjusted tax basis (see Figure 2.10, *supra*) per year, except for the first and last years in the period, which must be interpolated from Table 13.[4] Depreciation on "residential" structures is 27.5 years, calculated on the straight line basis (Table 6); the 39 year period applies to all real estate which is not residential property.[5] IRC § 168(e)(2)(B).

Despite the length of the recovery period, it appears shorter than the expected productive lives for most real estate assets,[6] and the value of most productive real

---

[4] As discussed in section 2.04[1], *supra*, the cost of a real estate development is allocated among different elements with a different cost recovery period for each element. Thus, the cost of land improvements is treated as a separate asset with a cost recovery period of 15 years. *Id.* While most fixtures and interior finishes, including tenant improvements, are treated as part of the structure, and depreciable in the same manner as the structure, some finishes, such as floor coverings and window treatments, may be treated as personalty, depreciable over 5 years and under a declining balance method. *See* Chapter 2, note 57, *supra*. Allocation of cost to movable personal property must be supported by a cost segregation study which would be done by a professional engineer, and may be expensive. The Internal Revenue Service has published a Cost Segregation Audit Techniques Guide, http://www.irs.gov/businesses/article/0,,id=134180,00.html (revised December 2007), which examines issues involving the allocation of cost to personal property in depth. Some advantage may be gained for residential projects which usually have more finish work, but this would not be true for a project like the Fox Valley Auto Care Center, where tenant spaces were provided as vanilla shells.

[5] In 1993, the depreciation period for real estate other than residential property was lengthened from 31.5 years to 39 years. OBRA 1993, § 13151(a), effective for property placed in service after May 13, 1993. This was frankly admitted to be an increase in the effective income tax rate applicable to commercial real estate, and was done to increase tax revenues.

[6] The Treasury Department's Report to Congress on Depreciation Recovery Periods and Methods, issued on July 28, 2000, discussed at some length the 39-year recovery period set for nonresidential improvements to real estate, noting that the length of the recovery period may exceed that for economic

estate does tend to rise. As discussed in Chapter 2, the value of the "residual" or resale price has major significance in analyzing the value of investment in real estate. Calculations of the return on investment are premised on the expectation that the value of real estate will increase, not decline, during the holding period for the investment. Allowing *any depreciation* deductions for real estate assets may, therefore, seem anomalous. Economically, however, the value of a real estate investment at the present time will decline over a future period, a phenomenon described as economic depreciation, which can be demonstrated with DCF analysis. Thus, the value of the rental stream produced by the asset declines, in terms of the current cost of the asset, as the holding period lengthens. So, tax depreciation is justified in terms of investment decisions made today, and, under the current rules, may actually be less than economic depreciation would support.

Depreciation, unlike interest expense, is a "noncash deduction." This means that the owner of the project need not make a current cash payment in order to obtain a current tax deduction. Interest, on the other hand, usually involves a cash outlay in the year for which the deduction is taken. Payment of interest, therefore, will reduce net operating income (that, is the project's operating cash flow); depreciation will not. As an aside, a non-tax element is the payment of principal on any loan. It reduces the project's cash flow, but is not deductible for tax purposes.

The investor's tax liability will result from her share of the project's taxable income or deductible loss which is allocated to her under the LLC operating agreement. In computing taxable income, a depreciation deduction has the effect of reducing the investor's tax liability without changing her share of the project's cash flow. We say that the investor's income has been *sheltered* by the depreciation deduction, at least to that extent. In today's tax world, the amount of "shelter" for a commercial real estate project is relatively low, because tax depreciation has been spread over so long a period, but it is nonetheless real. Although the project may generate positive taxable income when rents exceed expenses, interest and depreciation, it may still have a significant amount of shelter for the cash flow it produces. Compare this to an investment in a stock or a bond. Financial assets are almost never depreciable, so the cash flow generated by the asset is equal to its taxable income. But with a real estate asset, a portion of the capital invested in the project may be deducted each year, so that the cash flow from the property is inevitably greater than its taxable income. By using large amounts of *tax leverage*, a concept explored in depth below, it is possible to shelter significant positive cash flow from income tax for investors in real estate projects.

Depreciation is calculated using the tax basis of the property, and this will require a cash outlay at some time to support the determination of the property's cost on which the tax basis depends. The objective will be to postpone the time when that cash outlay will have to occur. This will be done by borrowing as much of the purchase price as the developer can persuade the lender to lend and deferring repayment of the loan for as long as the lender will agree.

---

depreciation because the marginal tax rate on nonresidential real estate exceeded the marginal tax rate on the same assets subject to economic depreciation. A recovery period of 30 years seemed appropriate. The Report noted, however, the tendency of real estate assets to rise in value and the ability of investors to use high leverage, which was said to offset the view that 39 years is too long. While major tax legislation is certain to occur in the next few years, there is no indication that the cost recovery period for real estate is under consideration.

[2] Tax Basis

Depreciation is calculated using the rate prescribed above and applying the rate to the original cost of the depreciable asset, here the Fox Valley Auto Care Center building. The original tax basis of the building is the cost of construction, including allocable "soft costs," which is referred to as "unadjusted [tax] basis" because no "adjustments" to basis have yet been made.[7] The determination of tax basis was discussed earlier when the book value of the constructed building was derived in Figure 2.10, *supra*. This amount is shown in the column labeled "depreciable basis," and this is the number we will use in calculating the tax depreciation for purposes of determining cash flow.

Tax basis is a technical term: it means those costs which have previously been accounted for in the tax system and which are allocated to the acquisition, construction or improvement of the asset in question.[8] After a cash receipt has been included in taxable income, it should not be taxed a second time to the taxpayer who had received it. For example, suppose Taxpayer ("T") received $1,000 as compensation for personal services. T reported this income on her tax return and paid the income tax assessed on the return. Later, she used the cash to purchase 100 shares of Acme Corp. stock. T will be credited with a tax cost of $1,000 (her "basis"), which will be applied to prevent her from having to pay tax a second time on the same dollars. The Acme stock has a *tax basis* in T's hands of $1,000. Later, T sold the Acme stock for $1,500, paid in cash. She will "realize" a taxable gain equal to the difference between the $1,500 she received from the sale (the "amount realized") and her tax basis. Thus, $1,500 (the "amount realized") – $1,000 (tax basis) = $500 ("gain realized"). IRC § 1001(a). The gain realized must be included in her taxable income ("gain recognized"), unless there is a specific statutory exemption or exclusion[9] which excuses T from having to do so. IRC § 1001(c).

When the asset is depreciable, as are the Fox Valley Auto Care Center buildings, depreciation is calculated using the same tax basis. This is illustrated here using a simple example. Although the example may seem oversimplified, the concepts introduced here, and elaborated on later, are central to an understanding of the tax advantages of investing in real estate.

Example 1: Depreciation

Suppose that B bought a building instead of corporate stock. The building is "depreciable," meaning that, as it produces income (rent), its value, theoretically at least, diminishes. Therefore, a portion of the value has been converted into rent. To recognize this result for tax purposes, B

---

[7] *See* text at Chapter 2, note 18, and note 39, *supra*.

[8] The most important exception to this rule is the treatment of property passing on the death of a taxpayer. The tax basis of that property is not its "cost," as we are discussing this concept here; rather it is the fair market value of the property at the time of the death of the taxpayer. IRC § 1014. Since most property has increased in value while held by the decedent, date of death value will be greater than tax cost, and we say that the basis of the property to the heirs has been "stepped up" or increased, thus *exempting* from tax any untaxed gain at the time of death.

[9] In real estate investing, the most common statutory exclusion is allowed for "exchanges" of property of "like kind." IRC § 1031. This type of provision manipulates basis to permit a deferral of the gain and not an exemption because the tax basis of the property being exchanged is moved over to the property being received in the exchange.

may claim a depreciation deduction in each year that B holds the property for rent. The tax law has assigned a "useful life" [permitted depreciation period] of 39 years to B's building. Because depreciation on real estate *must* be calculated only by the straight line method, the depreciation deduction to which B is entitled is calculated at a rate of 1/39 (2.56%) per year.

To put some numbers on this example, suppose B used $1,000 of savings (amount saved from after-tax income) to buy the building (all equity). B may claim a depreciation deduction equal to 2.56% of $1,000 in year 1, when B receives rental income for that year, assuming B has held the building for rent for the full year. So, Depreciation = 2.56% × $1,000 = $25.64. This amount is deductible as an expense of earning income (*see* IRC § 167(a)), but when *allowable* as a deduction, depreciation must also reduce the tax basis of the property (*see* IRC § 1016(a)(2)). This is because, in theory at least, 1/39 of the property has been converted into income. Basis is then "adjusted" by subtracting the amount deductable for depreciation to produce the building's "adjusted basis." IRC § 1011(a).

In this example, B's adjusted tax basis for the Building in year 2 will be $1,000.00 − $25.64 = $974.36.

§ 3.03 BORROWING TO CREATE TAX BASIS

In general, cost means the cash outlay required to acquire or construct the asset. So, if the developer must pay the construction cost in cash, has there not been a cash outlay? And since this cost may be recovered for tax purposes only through depreciation, has not the deduction for that cash payment by the developer been deferred? This seems to be the worst of all worlds: an immediate cash outlay but only a deferred (and, for commercial real estate, *deferred over 39 years*) cash benefit.

In most single asset projects, a substantial part of the cost is borrowed ("leveraged"), and the permanent loan is nonrecourse.[10] What does it mean for a loan to be "nonrecourse"? The borrower in the Fox Valley Auto Care Center case would be the Fox Valley Auto Care Center LLC. The LLC would sign a note that would provide that the lender would agree not to proceed against the LLC or its members to enforce the loan; rather, the lender would agree to limit its enforcement to the real and personal property of the LLC.

Construction loans are different, however, because of the contingencies involved in construction. A construction loan is a normal business loan, at the risk of the business, so to speak, and so, almost invariably, recourse to the developer.[11] For a

---

[10] Traditionally, the permanent loan for income producing real estate would be nonrecourse, although "credit enhancement" techniques were frequently negotiated to make the lender comfortable. As you will see, letters of credit provided by the investors to the lender in the Fox Valley Auto Care Center project would have been used to improve the terms of the anticipated permanent loan. Under difficult financial conditions, lenders become reluctant to make nonrecourse loans, which then become more costly. Various techniques may then be negotiated to provide the credit enhancement desired by the lender while limiting exposure of the investors to liability and simultaneously supporting the tax advantages which make real estate a desirable investment. We discuss this problem in greater depth in chapter 4.

[11] The project may be owned by an entity, all the members of which have no personal liability for any of the entity's debts, including a construction loan. In that case, the developer, promoter or syndicator

loan to be recourse means that the lender can proceed against the borrower or guarantor, individually, and usually against assets other than the project, for repayment when the loan is in default.[12] For a completed, leased-up real estate project, which is the security for the loan, how valuable do you think the ability of the lender to pursue the individual participants will be? In the competitive world of real estate lending, most projects are owned by an entity (which, for simplicity, we will refer to as the "partnership" or "LLC," depending on the context) in which no member is liable for more than her original capital contribution. Because of the tax issues, the permanent loan *must* be nonrecourse for the members of the partnership or LLC to share in the tax advantages of real estate investing. This factor is most important in influencing the lender to make a nonrecourse loan, and the tax system has obliged with a set of rules that confer the same tax advantages which a recourse loan would provide. This is the point at which our analysis begins.

[1] Income Tax Treatment of Borrowing and Repaying Loans

The proceeds of a loan are not considered taxable income to the borrower when received from the lender. Yet these proceeds are like any other cash receipt and have all the tax characteristics of taxable cash flow ("savings"). The developer, therefore, can use borrowed funds to purchase or construct a capital asset, and report cost equal to the actual cash expenditure. In Example 1, B could have achieved the tax result shown in the example whether B used savings (all equity) or the proceeds of loan (all debt) to acquire the building.

In tax theory, not taxing the receipt of the loan proceeds is justified on the ground that the borrower's receipt of the loan proceeds is offset by the borrower's obligation to repay the loan. The taxpayer has not realized any "income." Because the proceeds are not taxed when received, no tax benefit is allowed for funds used to repay the loan; that is, principal payments are not deductible. Repayment of the loan will be made with funds that have been previously taxed — the normal justification for increasing basis by the amount of a capital expenditure. Therefore, if the financing is available, the developer can borrow the full amount of the cost, use it to pay the cost of construction, and take cost recovery deductions against the full unadjusted cost basis which now *includes* the loan proceeds.

Consider the situation in the Fox Valley Auto Care Center. Regent was able to borrow enough to pay practically all acquisition and construction cost out of the proceeds of the construction loan. These funds were received by the LLC and applied to acquire and construct the Center, as shown in figure 2.10, *supra*. A significant portion, $1.8 million approximately, was used to construct depreciable assets. The LLC has the right to retain project income in excess of the debt service, which, because the project was, in fact, highly leveraged, may be a relatively small number. Yet, the LLC will be allowed to take cost recovery deductions against its taxable income for the cost paid with funds borrowed from someone else. Such heavy financing ("overleveraging") does have risks,

---

will be required separately to guarantee payment of the construction loan. With the Fox Valley Auto Care Center, FMB required three of the principals in Regent to guarantee the construction loan. *See* "Payment Guaranty" in the Document Supplement.

[12] Sometimes an agreement of guarantee will authorize the lender to proceed against the guarantor directly following default on the loan by the borrowing entity without having to foreclose against property first. Payment Guaranty, paragraph 5.

particularly if the construction loan cannot be refinanced, but the tax benefits of doing it this way mean that deductions are being claimed now for an expenditure which will not actually be made until some time in the future.

In the traditional real estate project, there will have been a nonrecourse permanent loan, the proceeds of which will be used to pay or "take out" the recourse construction loan.[13] The lender will have the first mortgage on the project, and the mortgage is an interest in real estate. Funding the permanent loan and paying off the construction loan may appear to have the effect of a sale by the borrower of an interest in the real estate project to the lender. That is not the case, however. For tax purposes, the developer is treated merely as having borrowed the funds derived from the nonrecourse loan secured by the property and may treat these funds (for tax purposes) in the same way as the funds from a recourse loan and therefore as part of *the developer's cost* for the project. Thus, the closing of the permanent loan for the project is not a taxable event. There is a long history to this tax treatment, as will be explained shortly.

In deriving the cash flow table for the Fox Valley Auto Care Center (see *supra* Figure 2.15), the cost allocations shown in Figure 2.10, *supra*, have been used. Since virtually *all* of these costs have been paid from the construction loan, you can now see why the depreciation deductions are referred to as "noncash deductions." For the purpose of this discussion, assume that Regent was able to negotiate a permanent loan based on the criteria explained in the Sher article, *supra*. This assumption is reflected in Figure 2.15, in which the cash flows have been determined, beginning with the projected completion date for the Center and using a permanent mortgage in the principal amount of $1.98 million at 9% interest with payment terms based on an amortization period of 25 years. Annual debt service, including interest and principal, of $199,084 is shown in the cash flow calculation. These calculations also result in an equity requirement of approximately $500,000.[14]

To pay the debt service on the permanent loan, the Fox Valley Auto Care Center LLC will have to use cash proceeds generally available from taxable sources. Because the loan proceeds would not have been taxable on receipt, funds used to repay principal will have been included in taxable income. In the typical real estate project, and on the *pro forma*, principal is paid from taxable rent or more generally, out of the proceeds from the sale of the property.

---

[13] Although nonrecourse financing may be difficult to obtain in the credit markets of 2009–10, and perhaps later, nonrecourse lending can be expected to return, in part because the predominant organizational structure of the typical income-producing real estate project demands it. As explained earlier, *see* text at Chapter 2, note 7, following the real estate recession in the late 1980s and early 1990s, the older practice of negotiating a permanent or take-out loan before beginning construction declined and was replaced by different financing arrangements, often referred to as "mini-perms," which contemplated refinancing and replacement of the original loan within a relatively short period of time. The construction loan in the Fox Valley Auto Care Center project was negotiated with the expectation that it would be refinanced and replaced with a nonrecourse permanent loan.

[14] As the formula values in Figure 2.12 show, more favorable loan terms would have reduced the equity required. In the actual case, Regent would have negotiated to obtain a take-out loan at least equal to the amount of the construction loan, so no additional equity would be required at the closing of the permanent loan.

[2] Taxing the Residual Value: Conversion

At the investment horizon (the end of the anticipated holding period on which projections for the real estate investment are based), which is assumed to be seven years for the Fox Valley Auto Care Center, the project will be treated as having been sold, and the net cash proceeds from the hypothetical sale will be included as a distributable cash flow. To determine the sales price, we have chosen a capitalization rate that is over two percentage points *less than* the initial current yield for this project (10.5%), a relationship suggested in the Sher article, *supra*, and that cap rate has been applied to capitalize the net operating income projected for the year of sale. See Figure 2.12, *supra*. The initial projected yield on the Fox Valley Auto Care Center is determined there to be 12.7%, which may seem high. That rate depends on the relationship between achievable market rents and the cost of constructing the Center. Cap rates in today's real estate markets are lower, and a cap rate in the 9–10% range would probably be acceptable, as suggested in the Sher analysis. The high capitalization rate suggests that the projection of stabilized net operating income may also be inaccurate.

In determining residual value, it is usually recommended that the cap rate used be higher than the initial cap rate for the project. That is, because the project is older when sold at the end of the investment period, a prospective buyer will likely perceive that it is a riskier investment than it would have been originally and will require a higher risk premium. Because the residual value is sensitive to rates of return, calculating residual value in this way for use in the projections may not have provided an accurate forecast of the return on this project.[15]

When the property is sold, the "amount realized" equals the projected sales price, which may be paid in cash at closing or in installments and by taking the property subject to the existing loans. Taxable gain is the difference between the amount realized and the project's "adjusted basis," that is, the project's original cost reduced by the depreciation deductions allowable to the owners and increased by any subsequent capital expenditures.

---

[15] Net operating income in the final year of the investment project was projected by inflating the original stabilized net operating income. If stabilized net operating income at inception is inaccurate, then final net operating income is also likely to be inaccurate, and residual value determined by capitalizing final year net operating income will also be inaccurate.

Figure 3.1
Determination of net cash on sale

Sales Price (amount realized):			3,339,537	[1]
assume capitalization rate for year of sale:	10.5%			
Tax basis Land:		576,215		
Cost Improvments:	1,794,980			
less depreciation	(392,540)	1,402,440		
Adjusted tax basis for purposes of determing gain on sale:			(1,978,655)	[2]
Taxable gain:			1,360,882	[3]
Capital GainsTax:				
Tax on depreciation recovered:	392,540		98,135	[4]
Rate:	25.0%			
Tax on market gain:	968,342		145,251	[5]
Rate:	15.0%			
Pay the balance due on the mortgage:			1,784,598	[6]
Sale commission:	4.0%		133,581	[7]
Costs associated with the sale (sum of lines [4] through [7]):			2,161,566	[8]
Net cash proceeds from the sale (line [1] minus line [8]):			1,177,971	[9]

It will be helpful to think of the cash flow from sale of the project in the following way: first, the amount realized offsets the remaining undepreciated tax basis for the property (line [2], Figure 3.1) and to that extent is derived from after-tax income; second, it replaces that portion of the tax basis reduced by depreciation deductions ("unrecaptured depreciation") and to that extent, results in taxable income (line [4]);[16] and third, the balance of the proceeds represents the increase in the value of the project since its acquisition or construction (line [5]), hence "market gain."[17]

Depreciation deductions reduce ordinary taxable income otherwise taxable to the developer or, through the partnership or LLC, to other investors in the project. When the property is sold, the proceeds replace the amount deducted and, while taxable, are taxed as capital gain at the special maximum rate of 25% applicable to unrecaptured depreciation. In determining the tax benefit or cost to investors, it is generally assumed that the marginal income tax rate for them will be the maximum rate on ordinary income, or approximately 35%.[18] Referring to Figure 2.15, *supra*,

16 Gain which replaces depreciation deductions is defined in IRC § 1(h)(6)(A) as "unrecaptured section 1250 gain." When this gain is derived from a sale or exchange of a project "held" by the taxpayer for one year or more, it is taxed as capital gain subject to a maximum 25% marginal rate. *Id.*, § 1(h)(1)(D).

17 This gain, when derived from the sale or exchange of the project held for one year or more, is taxed as capital gain subject to a 15% marginal rate (or less, depending on the taxable income of the taxpayer). *Id.* § 1(h)(1)(C). The 15% maximum rate on market capital gains is scheduled to increase to 20% at the end of 2010, assuming that Congress does not legislate otherwise.

18 At the end of 2010 the 35% marginal rate (the result of the "Bush tax cuts") is also scheduled to increase to the rate that applied before enactment of the 2001 Tax Act, or 39.5%. The calculations made

the allowable depreciation for the second year in the projection, for example, will be approximately $60,000. This deduction will reduce the income tax liability of the individual LLC members on rents produced by the Center by 35% × $60,000 = $21,000. In the seventh year, when it is assumed that the Center will be sold for an amount in excess of its original cost, the amount of the depreciation allowed as a deduction in year 2 will be recovered as part of the sales proceeds. It will be taxed at the maximum rate of 25%, so the tax cost of realizing the gain is 25% × $60,000 = $15,000, resulting in a $6,000 saving. This tax saving is a permanent reduction in the tax liabilities of the LLC members. The tax rate arbitrage produced by the tax treatment of capital gain is referred to as "conversion," and it is valuable, albeit less so than the effects of tax leverage.[19]

[3] Tax Leverage

"Tax leverage" occurs when the tax basis of the depreciable asset includes borrowed funds, thus increasing the corresponding depreciation deductions and reducing the amount of equity which the developer is required to contribute.

Example 2: Leverage Effect of Depreciation Deductions

B purchased the project in Example 1 for $1,000. Assume that B can earn noi of $100 (10%) on this property. The project is commercial real estate, so depreciation will be allowed on the straight line method over 39 years (2.56% per year). B's marginal tax rate is 35%:

- Assume first, that B did not borrow to buy Project, and paid the full price from B's own savings. Then taxable income = $100.00 less depreciation ($25.60), or $74.40, tax is $26.04 and B takes home $25.60 (the amount of cash flow offset or "sheltered" by the depreciation deduction) plus $48.36, or $73.96, a cash on cash return of 7.4%, where investment = $1,000.

- Assume, on the other hand, B borrowed $750 (75% of the Project cost), at 8% interest, and paid the difference. Disregard principal amortization on the loan. Interest due is $60.00. Tax basis is the same as before. Now, taxable income = $100.00 − $60.00 [interest] − $25.60 [depreciation] = $14.40, resulting in a tax liability of 5.04. Cash flow is then $40.00 (cash flow after finance) − $5.04 = $34.96. This represents a 14.0% cash on cash return because *investment* has been reduced to $250 as a result of the loan.

The effect of tax leverage nearly doubles B's cash on cash return in the example because it reduces B's cash outlay without affecting the amount of B's depreciation deductions. This effect has previously been discussed in Chapter 2, and at this point, the mechanism for producing the benefit can be plainly seen. Note that the tax leverage effect will occur so long as B has not actually paid the principal on the loan;

---

here reflect the marginal rates in effect at the time of writing, and obviously would need to be adjusted when (and if) they change.

[19] The ability to convert real estate depreciation deductions into capital gain is now cited as an important reason for *not* reducing the recovery period for nonresidential real estate. Depreciation on personal property such as machinery may be allowed at a more rapid rate (shorter recovery periods, accelerated depreciation methods), but any gain produced on sale of the property will be fully "recaptured" and reported as ordinary income. IRC § 1245. Only real estate assets produce conversion.

a principal payment is simply additional equity. Including the proceeds of indebtedness in the depreciable tax basis of the Project in effect defers the income tax liability which B must eventually pay when B repays the loan. The deferral is valuable only to the extent that it is reflected in a tax benefit (the depreciation deductions), so the objective will be to delay repayment of the loan as long as possible. So long as the amortization of the principal of the loan occurs more slowly than the depreciation of the tax basis produced by the loan, there will be a tax leverage effect.

Ultimately, the loan will have to be taken into account for tax purposes, but this will not occur until the end of the investment period. It will be necessary to examine the principal income tax cases which provide the doctrinal support for the tax effects described here, but first it will be helpful to complete the presentation of the Fox Valley Auto Care Center project for use in persuading investors to join Regent as members in the Fox Valley Auto Care Center LLC.

§ 3.04 COMPLETING THE CASH FLOW TABLES

[1] Net Operating Income

Now that we have explored the income tax effect of investing in a real estate project, it is time to complete the cash flow table for the Fox Valley Auto Care Center. With the projected cash flows determined for the investment period, DCF analysis is applied to find the net present value for prospective investors at their required "hurdle rates" and the internal rate of return they would receive for this project. As described in Chapter 2, the beginning point for this analysis is stabilized net operating income, with lease-up assumed to have been attained within a three-year period at Regent's forecast market rents. *See* Figure 2.14, *supra*. Actual cash flow is adjusted by subtracting the projected vacancy loss attributable to difficulties in attaining lease-up.

The cash flow table is shown in Figure 2.15, *supra*. Because the leases are net leases, the only operating expense that the Fox Valley Auto Care Center LLC, discussed below, incurs will be the common area cost for vacant portions of the Center building. The rent inflator (3%) is the actual inflator applied to rent in the leases. This produces net operating income, or the "free and clear," for each of the years in the investment period.

[2] Cash Flow After Finance

The debt service results from the mortgage shown in Figure 2.13, *supra*, which was assumed to be the amount calculated in the pro forma evaluation at 9%, with a 25-year amortization period. *See* Figure 2.12, *supra*. Debt financing is a variable which may remain in play up to the time for the loan to close, so in a period during which loan underwriting standards loosen, the actual loan terms may become more favorable and may therefore improve the return on the property. More typically, the developer will want to be certain about the financing cost, and therefore will negotiate a loan commitment in which both the developer and the lender have made a binding agreement on the terms of the loan. That, of course, was not the case with the Fox Valley Auto Care Center. For purposes of this discussion, however, assume that a permanent loan was negotiated under the terms described in the text.

Debt service normally consists of level payments that include both interest and principal. Debt service must be paid before cash available for distribution is determined. Certain other set asides may also be made at this point in the analysis. The most common would be a contribution to a reserve for replacement of parts of the building which are likely to wear out, such as heating and air conditioning equipment or the roof. Other possible reserves might include a reserve for renting expenditures, tenant fix-up or commissions, or capital improvements to access roads, parking, lighting or landscaping. These cash reserves are additional assets of the Center, even though contractual commitments to the lender may require the maintenance of certain cash reserves.

Reserve commitments are not operating expenses as such and therefore are not deductible for tax purposes, but do reduce cash flow. Typically, the authority to establish and maintain reasonable cash reserves will be delegated to the manager by the LLC operating agreement.

[3] Taxable Income or Loss

To calculate the tax burden (or benefit) from cash flow after finance ("CFAF"), it is necessary to add back the amount of loan principal paid during the year and amounts set aside in operating reserves (both nondeductible cash expenditures), and to subtract tax amortization[20] and depreciation (noncash tax deductions). The income tax liability (or refund, if taxable income is negative) is then calculated for the investors using the selected marginal rate, here 35%. Finally, the proceeds from the sale of the project at the end of the investment period (here 7 years) are calculated as shown in Figure 3.1, *supra*.

Note that the LLC does *not* pay income tax. Instead, income or loss is calculated as if the LLC were an individual, with certain adjustments, IRC § 703(a), and the result is then allocated among the LLC members as provided in the LLC operating agreement. IRC § 704(a). The LLC will prepare a tax return and an information return setting out these quantities, which will then be included on the individual tax returns of the LLC members. The LLC members, therefore, will receive the tax benefit of the tax rules applicable to real estate investing, and will bear whatever tax liability is generated by taxable income or gain realized by the LLC. The LLC will be taxed as a "conduit entity," because its income or loss will be passed through the LLC and out to the LLC members.

Taxable quantities ("items" in the language of the tax law) will be allocated among the LLC members whether any cash is distributed to them or not. As you can see, the net distributable cash flow from the Fox Valley Auto Care Center LLC is projected to be substantially greater than taxable income, and all LLC members anticipate hefty cash distributions, which should not then attract any further tax. This will be explained further below, but at this point it is advisable to insert a *caveat*. The partnership tax rules which govern these consequences are very

[20] Tax amortization refers to deductions allowed for expenditures which are not current expenses but are not attributable to depreciation of tangible property. Some common examples of amortizable expenditures include costs of acquiring leaseholds or loan origination costs. *Cf.* Sleiman v. Commissioner, 1997 RIA T.C. ¶ 97,530, *aff'd on other issues*, 187 F.3d 1352 (11th Cir. 1999) (fees incurred for one year construction loan amortized over one year); Chapter 2, text at note 62 *supra*. Organizational expenditures are amortizable over 60 months, IRC § 195, and purchased intangible assets such as customer lists and goodwill are now amortizable under IRC § 197, a provision which may have significant impact on acquisitions by partnerships.

difficult; real estate lawyers not steeped in these rules are well advised to have tax counsel close by as transactions are set up and the LLC agreements drafted.

[4] Interests of the LLC Members

Regent proposes to sell a 40% interest in the Fox Valley Auto Care Center LLC to investors. By a 40% interest is meant 40% of all of the project economics initially owned by Regent, and therefore the same percentage of each of the economic quantities and tax items realized by the LLC. These would include: operating cash flow; the right to a share of refinancing proceeds; the residual value, after payment of then existing liens; and, last but not least, the tax characteristics for the project, and, in particular, the right to claim depreciation deductions. How much are these economics worth? To answer that question, the cash flow pro forma has to be extended to show the *after-tax* results to the investors.

In deriving the after-tax cash flows in Figure 2.15, *supra*, income tax liabilities have been calculated for the project as a whole by assuming that the maximum marginal tax rates will apply no matter how the income or loss is allocated. Then, the *net figures* have been allocated as Regent has proposed, 40% to the investors (line [1]) and 60% to Regent (line [2]). This permits comparison of the returns for the project and for its participants, although, technically, it is not how the process actually works. The individual LLC members will report the tax items allocated to them on their own individual income tax returns and calculate their tax liabilities accordingly, so it would be more accurate to make the tax calculations and determine the after-tax cash flows separately for each LLC member based on the tax character of the amounts allocated to each member. That qualification should not detract from the comparison of returns described here.

Assume that Regent has offered to sell a 40% interest in the project economics to the investors in return for (1) a capital contribution to the LLC of $200,000, and (2) credit enhancement in the form of a letter of credit for $200,000 against which the construction lender may draw if the construction loan is in default.[21] The letter of credit would be for a period of at least one year, renewable for one additional year. The letter of credit is essentially a loan made by the bank issuing the letter of credit to the LLC members for which they will provide security and which results in a net cost to the members even though that cost will not be reflected in LLC capital; obligations to make future capital contributions, which is what a letter of credit represents, are not themselves capital contributions. If the return earned by the investors were to be accurately determined, the cost of acquiring and maintaining the letter of credit would be taken into account, but these costs will vary with the transaction and the credit position of each investor, and so are

---

21 In reality, the offer was made on the basis of sources and uses, assuming Regent would be able to refinance the construction loan at par. *See* Figure 2.11, "sources and uses," which projected an equity requirement of $150,000. For a 40% share, the investors would have been asked for a $60,000 capital contribution. The capital markets changed, however, and Regent was not able to lease up the Center. Available refinancing fell short, requiring a capital contribution of approximately $500,000 instead of the projected $150,000. *See* Figures 2.12, Item 9, and 2.15. If we assume that Regent and its investors were willing to contribute the additional capital needed, then Figure 2.15 projects the expected rate of return over a 7 year investment horizon. That period should be sufficient to allow the financial markets to clear, and, with improved operating numbers from the Fox Valley Auto Care Center, refinancing could be expected to result in enough proceeds to retire the original loan and repay a significant portion of the investors' capital contributions. We discuss refinancing later in this chapter.

difficult to quantify. For purposes of this analysis, they will be ignored with the caveat that the return derived for the LLC members will have to be adjusted to reflect that undetermined cost.

[5] Problem

Donna Smith comes into Sam Nader's office and asks Sam to draft a memorandum explaining the value of investing in the Fox Valley Auto Care Center to investors to whom a presentation will be made. "I know you've never done one of these before, Sam, and I'll be happy to go over it with you when you are finished. Your memo should outline those parts of the analysis where there is risk of error, and make plain what the risk is. Above all, no investor, however sophisticated, should be misled by your memo. It's tough to do, but the best way to learn is to have to do one."

Sam is somewhat disconcerted, because he has never seen a memo of the type Donna described to him. He decides to go over the numbers for the Fox Valley Auto Care Center and the way in which they were derived, come to the best conclusions he can, and take a shot at the memo. He figures that Donna knows what she wants and that her goal is for him to analyze the deal so that she then can put the memo into a form that can be presented to potential investors. Please prepare Sam's memo.

[6] The Internal Rate of Return

The cash flow table (Figure 2.15, *supra*) shows projected cash flows distributed to each of the members in Fox Valley Auto Care Center LLC. In addition, it would show the tax items allocated to each LLC member, an allocation usually made *pro rata*, and these allocations would then be used to determine the tax cost or benefit for each member and thus the net, after-tax receipt by that member. As explained above, this was done in this case by assuming that each individual LLC member would pay tax at the maximum marginal federal income tax rate (35.0%) and would have no special tax characteristics, an assumption which in practice would be tested for each individual member. At the bottom of the cash flow table, the capital contribution made by each interest is entered as a cash contribution at the end of the year preceding the first year on the projection, and the spreadsheet function (in Excel, "IRR") is used to generate an internal rate of return.

Calculation of the internal rate of return was done manually in Chapter 2. *See supra* Figure 2.4. To carry forward that illustration, a manual calculation of the internal rate of return is shown in Figure 3.2.

Figure 3.2
Internal Rate of Return

Present Value of Investor Cash Inflows

Year	Cash Inflows	Present Value of $1 at	Present Value of Inflow @ 22%	Present Value of $1 at	Present Value of Inflow @ 23%
Discount Rates		*22%*		*23%*	
1	2,869	0.8197	$2,352	0.8130	$2,333
2	12,189	0.6719	$8,189	0.6610	$8,057
3	35,679	0.5507	$19,649	0.5374	$19,174
4	37,741	0.4514	$17,036	0.4369	$16,489
5	39,842	0.3700	$14,742	0.3552	$14,152
6	39,743	0.3033	$12,053	0.2888	$11,477
7	513,110	0.2486	$127,553	0.2348	$120,469
	$681,173		$201,574		$192,150

For this purpose, the cash flow shown in Figure 2.15, *supra*, as allocated to the investors will be treated as fully distributed to them. Note that, while the cash flow allocated to the investors is derived on the table, it does not necessarily show cash distributions, which will depend upon the terms of the LLC operating agreement. Moreover, Figure 2.15 accepts as accurate a capital contribution by the investors approximately equal to $200,000, and as noted above, the investors are obligated to have purchased a standby letter of credit for the project. In computing the rate of return for their benefit, the investors will have to include these costs as well.

The manual calculation done in Figure 3.2 results in the following interpolation, and an internal rate of return of 22.2%:

$$\frac{\$201{,}574 \; - \; (\$200{,}000)}{\$201{,}574 \; - \; (\$192{,}150)} = \frac{\$1{,}574}{\$9{,}425} = 0.167$$

The internal rate of return yielded by this analysis is what an investor in a real estate project like the Fox Valley Auto Care Center might expect. If Regent had been able to refinance the Fox Valley Auto Care Center as Regent had anticipated (that is, for a take-out loan of $2,300,000 at the original terms), the internal rate of return would doubled.[22] The reason for this would have been Regent's ability to

[22] This also assumes that 1) cost overruns and operating deficits resulting from the larger debt

borrow almost the entire cost of construction and lease-up. The capital required to acquire an interest in the project's cash flows would, therefore, have been low, and the return correspondingly high. Note, however, that the IRR calculation can be deceptive, as it assumes that the cash withdrawn can be invested at the same rate of return, an assumption that is often inaccurate. Nonetheless, the IRR is useful to a potential investor for purposes of comparing the opportunity that investing in the Fox Valley Auto Care Center presented with other investment opportunities.

[7] Net Present Value

The last thing to be done in completing the preliminary financial analysis is to determine the net present value of this investment at the *investor's* hurdle rate of return, as was discussed in the introductory discussion of present value calculations. Assume that an investor requires a 12% after tax return as the minimum expected return on other investments she would make with funds available for this purpose.

Figure 3.3
Fox Valley Auto Care Center
Investor's Position:

hurdle rate of return= ***12.0%***

Year		*cash flow*		*present value*
1	$	2,869	$	2,562
2	$	12,189	$	9,717
3	$	35,679	$	25,396
4	$	37,741	$	23,985
5	$	39,842	$	22,607
6	$	39,743	$	20,135
7	$	513,110	$	232,105
Total Present Value:			$	336,507
Investor's capital contribution:			$	(199,736)
net present value:			$	136,771

The result shows a high present value, when compared to the modest cash outlay which the investors have been asked to make. To the extent that one has confidence in the numbers, this shows that the investment in the Fox Valley Auto Care Center would be superior to other investments at the investors' expected return on those alternative investments. This calculation depends upon the accuracy with which the future cash flows have been projected and on the discount rate chosen by the investors to make the calculation. Although these numbers are very favorable, it

service payments required to support the larger loan would have been absorbed by the budgeted contingency and 2) the Fox Valley Auto Care Center would have achieved lease-up in the third year of operations.

should be clear that these financial results are merely the start of the analysis; much more needs to be done to evaluate the soundness of the investment.

This concludes the preliminary analysis of the investment. Actual experience with this project turned out to be different from that projected, a result which is not unusual. Financial analysis of real estate projects involves educated guesses and assumptions, and at bottom, rests on the individual judgment of the person making the analysis. The developer may not have accurately forecasted how well the project would perform in operation, and often lease-up will take longer and require more rental concessions *ex post* than considered judgment took into account *ex ante*. All of these things affect the actual return the developer and the investors in the project realize at the end of the day.

We now turn to examine some basic questions for investing in real estate, beginning with the logic of tax leverage and underlying tax law principles which support it.

§ 3.05 TAX LAW PRINCIPLES IN DETERMINING "TAX LEVERAGE"

You will recall that the developer could borrow as much of the acquisition and construction cost as he could persuade the lender to lend and obtain a tax basis equal to the sum of his capital contribution and the amount borrowed. Depreciation for the entire property, not limited to the developer's equity interest, would then be calculated on this tax basis even though the loan proceeds themselves had not yet been included in taxable income. This tax treatment of indebtedness appears to have been accepted by the Commissioner of the Internal Revenue at an early date, long before modern financial principles were applied to real estate investing. It was not until property values declined in the 1930s, and properties were sold for less than unpaid mortgage balances, that the courts explored the tax theory supporting this result. Obviously, these issues will be critical to real estate and tax lawyers as the severe downturn in real estate values which started in 2007 plays out.

Because receipt of the loan proceeds is not taxable, funds applied to repay the loan are not deductible. This result is sensible, of course, as the tax cost for the depreciation deductions would, in theory, have to be paid by the borrower at some point in time. Consider for a moment what might happen if this basic premise were not true. T would borrow an amount necessary to build the depreciable building, and the amount borrowed would not be taxable. T would then use her cost, including the loan proceeds, to calculate depreciation deductions which would reduce her taxable income. Suppose, then, T compromised the indebtedness, and repaid less than the amount borrowed. Unless T were required to include in income the difference (that is, the amount by which T's obligation was reduced), or otherwise account for it in the tax system,[23] T would have taken a deduction for a loss which, economically and in tax theory, was borne by someone else — the lender. In tax language, it would be said that T would have *both* an exclusion (for cancellation of a portion of the indebtedness) *and* a deduction (for depreciation deductions calculated on that part of the basis funded with the debt) for the *same* tax item, which is a violation of fundamental tax theory. How to solve the problem,

[23] *See* IRC § 108, which provides the tax treatment of "cancellation of indebtedness" income in a wide variety of settings.

particularly when the loan is obtained without recourse — that is, the risk of loss is borne by the lender — may not be so clear.

[1] The *Crane* Case

The treatment of a nonrecourse mortgage on disposition of the property first reached the Supreme Court in the famous case of *Crane v. Commissioner*, 331 U.S. 1 (1947). Mrs. Crane inherited an apartment house from her husband in 1932. The apartment house was encumbered by a nonrecourse mortgage equal to the value of the apartment house, which had been reported on Mr. Crane's estate tax return. Then, as now, the property received a tax basis equal to its market value as reported on the estate tax return, and Mrs. Crane claimed depreciation deductions with respect to that tax basis. *See* IRC § 1014.

Six years later, unable to earn a profit from the apartment house rents, Mrs. Crane sold the property for $3,000 to a third party, subject to the mortgage, none of which had been paid. Although Mrs. Crane had taken $28,000 in depreciation deductions, she asserted that she had sold only her equity in the apartment house and so realized a gain of $2,500 ($3,000 – costs of sale, $500). The Commissioner, conceding that Mrs. Crane's method for calculating depreciation deductions was correct, took the view that the amount she realized on the sale had to include the unpaid balance of the mortgage which had been included in the value of the property in the first place. Recalculating the amount realized and offsetting that by the tax basis for the entire property, adjusted now for the depreciation deductions Mrs. Crane had taken, resulted in a taxable gain of approximately $24,000. The Tax Court sustained the Commissioner, but the court of appeals reversed.

The U.S. Supreme Court in *Crane* reviewed depreciation methodology in the case of mortgaged property. It concluded that the basis of the property had been properly determined, and with it the depreciation deductions. Since her depreciation had been calculated on the whole property, and not just Mrs. Crane's equity, it was the whole property that had been sold. Accordingly, the amount realized by Mrs. Crane had to include the mortgage; otherwise the tax result would not make sense. It is essential here to recognize that the Court endorsed the Commissioner's acceptance of the depreciation calculations and from that point, concluded that inclusion of the amount of the nonrecourse mortgage to which the property was subject in the amount realized from the sale was essential.

Central to the Court's reasoning was its conclusion that a *nonrecourse* mortgage in an amount less than the value of the property would be viewed by the mortgagor interested in retaining her equity in the property in the same manner as a *recourse* mortgage, pointing out in its often cited footnote 37 that a case in which the mortgage exceeded the value would be a different case. When the mortgage is recourse, the taxpayer's personal liability to pay the mortgage would have to be discharged in some way, so when the buyer accepts the property subject to the mortgage, the transaction is equivalent to the buyer's payment of cash to the mortgagee, thereby discharging the debt. In *Crane*, the Court observed that Mrs. Crane had in fact received cash and so the property must have been worth more than the mortgage. This conclusion was often questioned in commentary, but it took another 30 years for the issue to be resolved.

[2] Commissioner v. Tufts

In *Tufts*, there was no dispute: the property was worth considerably less than the amount of the nonrecourse mortgage, which had been made just a few years earlier. This is the issue which the Court had thought would make a different case from *Crane*. In *Tufts*, the Court carefully discussed its earlier precedent and concluded that not only was it bound to follow *Crane*, but also that *Crane* controlled the result in the case before it. As you read the opinion, consider: why did the Court think it was bound by that precedent? Why did the Court think that it decided *Crane* the way it did? *Crane*, and particularly its footnote 37, is often referred to as the foundation for the tax principle that nonrecourse indebtedness must be included in the tax basis of the owner of the property, which is why this material appears at this point in this book. If so, how would you characterize the origins of the doctrine? As incidental to another problem which the Court thought it was addressing in *Crane*?

COMMISSIONER OF INTERNAL REVENUE v. TUFTS

461 U.S. 300 (1983)

Justice Blackmun delivered the opinion of the Court.

Over 35 years ago, in *Crane v. Commissioner*, 331 U.S. 1 (1947), this Court ruled that a taxpayer, who sold property encumbered by a nonrecourse mortgage (the amount of the mortgage being less than the property's value), must include the unpaid balance of the mortgage in the computation of the amount the taxpayer realized on the sale. The case now before us presents the question whether the same rule applies when the unpaid amount of the nonrecourse mortgage exceeds the fair market value of the property sold.

I

On August 1, 1970, respondent Clark Pelt, a builder, and his wholly owned corporation, respondent Clark, Inc., formed a general partnership. The purpose of the partnership was to construct a 120-unit apartment complex in Duncanville, Tex., a Dallas suburb. Neither Pelt nor Clark, Inc., made any capital contribution to the partnership. Six days later, the partnership entered into a mortgage loan agreement with the Farm & Home Savings Association (F&H). Under the agreement, F&H was committed for a $1,851,500 loan for the complex. In return, the partnership executed a note and a deed of trust in favor of F&H. The partnership obtained the loan on a nonrecourse basis: neither the partnership nor its partners assumed any personal liability for repayment of the loan. Pelt later admitted four friends and relatives, respondents Tufts, Steger, Stephens, and Austin, as general partners. None of them contributed capital upon entering the partnership.

The construction of the complex was completed in August 1971. During 1971, each partner made small capital contributions to the partnership; in 1972, however, only Pelt made a contribution. The total of the partners' capital contributions was $44,212. In each tax year, all partners claimed as income tax deductions their allocable shares of ordinary losses and depreciation. The deductions taken by the partners in 1971 and 1972 totaled $439,972. Due to these contributions and deductions, the partnership's adjusted basis in the property in August 1972 was $1,455,740.

In 1971 and 1972, major employers in the Duncanville area laid off significant numbers of workers. As a result, the partnership's rental income was less than expected, and it was unable to make the payments due on the mortgage. Each partner, on August 28, 1972, sold his partnership interest to an unrelated third party, Fred Bayles. As consideration, Bayles agreed to reimburse each partner's sale expenses up to $250; he also assumed the nonrecourse mortgage.

On the date of transfer, the fair market value of the property did not exceed $1,400,000. Each partner reported the sale on his federal income tax return and indicated that a partnership loss of $55,740 had been sustained.[1] The Commissioner of Internal Revenue, on audit, determined that the sale resulted in a partnership capital gain of approximately $400,000. His theory was that the partnership had realized the full amount of the nonrecourse obligation.[2]

Relying on *Millar v. Commissioner*, 577 F.2d 212, 215 (3d Cir.), *cert. denied*, 439 U.S. 1046 (1978), the United States Tax Court, in an unreviewed decision, upheld the asserted deficiencies. 70 T.C. 756 (1978). The United States Court of Appeals for the Fifth Circuit reversed. 651 F.2d 1058 (1981). That court expressly disagreed with the *Millar* analysis, and, in limiting *Crane v. Commissioner, supra*, to its facts, questioned the theoretical underpinnings of the *Crane* decision. We granted certiorari to resolve the conflict. 456 U.S. 960 (1982).

II

Section 752(d) of the Internal Revenue Code of 1954, 26 U.S.C. § 752(d), specifically provides that liabilities incurred in the sale or exchange of a partnership interest are to "be treated in the same manner as liabilities in connection with the sale or exchange of property not associated with partnerships." Section 1001 governs the determination of gains and losses on the disposition of property. Under § 1001(a), the gain or loss from a sale or other disposition of property is defined as the difference between "the amount realized" on the disposition and the property's adjusted basis. Subsection (b) of § 1001 defines "amount realized": "The amount realized from the sale or other disposition of property shall be the sum of any money received plus the fair market value of the property (other than money) received." At issue is the application of the latter provision to the disposition of property encumbered by a nonrecourse mortgage of an amount in excess of the property's fair market value.

---

[1] The loss was the difference between the adjusted basis, $1,455,740, and the fair market value of the property, $1,400,000. On their individual tax returns, the partners did not claim deductions for their respective shares of this loss. In their petitions to the Tax Court, however, the partners did claim the loss.

[2] The Commissioner determined the partnership's gain on the sale by subtracting the adjusted basis, $1,455,740, from the liability assumed by Bayles, $1,851,500. Of the resulting figure, $395,760, the Commissioner treated $348,661 as capital gain, pursuant to § 741 of the Internal Revenue Code of 1954, 26 U.S.C. § 741, and $47,099 as ordinary gain under the recapture provisions of § 1250 of the Code. The application of § 1250 in determining the character of the gain is not at issue here.

A

In *Crane v. Commissioner, supra*, this Court took the first and controlling step toward the resolution of this issue. Beulah B. Crane was the sole beneficiary under the will of her deceased husband. At his death in January 1932, he owned an apartment building that was then mortgaged for an amount which proved to be equal to its fair market value, as determined for federal estate tax purposes. The widow, of course, was not personally liable on the mortgage. She operated the building for nearly seven years, hoping to turn it into a profitable venture; during that period, she claimed income tax deductions for depreciation, property taxes, interest, and operating expenses, but did not make payments upon the mortgage principal. In computing her basis for the depreciation deductions, she included the full amount of the mortgage debt. In November 1938, with her hopes unfulfilled and the mortgagee threatening foreclosure, Mrs. Crane sold the building. The purchaser took the property subject to the mortgage and paid Crane $3,000; of that amount, $500 went for the expenses of the sale.

Crane reported a gain of $2,500 on the transaction. She reasoned that her basis in the property was zero (despite her earlier depreciation deductions based on including the amount of the mortgage) and that the amount she realized from the sale was simply the cash she received. The Commissioner disputed this claim. He asserted that Crane's basis in the property, under § 113(a)(5) of the Revenue Act of 1938, 52 Stat. 490 (the current version is § 1014 of the 1954 Code, as amended, 26 U.S.C. § 1014 (1976 ed. and Supp. V)), was the property's fair market value at the time of her husband's death, adjusted for depreciation in the interim, and that the amount realized was the net cash received plus the amount of the outstanding mortgage assumed by the purchaser.

In upholding the Commissioner's interpretation of § 113(a)(5) of the 1938 Act,[3] the Court observed that to regard merely the taxpayer's equity in the property as her basis would lead to depreciation deductions less than the actual physical deterioration of the property, and would require the basis to be recomputed with each payment on the mortgage. 331 U.S., at 9–10. The Court rejected Crane's claim that any loss due to depreciation belonged to the mortgagee. The effect of the Court's ruling was that the taxpayer's basis was the value of the property undiminished by the mortgage. *Id.*, at 11.

The Court next proceeded to determine the amount realized under § 111(b) of the 1938 Act, 52 Stat. 484 (the current version is § 1001(b) of the 1954 Code, 26 U.S.C. § 1001(b)). In order to avoid the "absurdity," *see* 331 U.S., at 13, of Crane's realizing only $2,500 on the sale of property worth over a quarter of a million dollars, the Court treated the amount realized as it had treated basis, that is, by including the outstanding value of the mortgage. To do otherwise would have permitted Crane to recognize a tax loss unconnected with any actual economic loss. The Court refused to construe one section of the Revenue Act so as "to frustrate the Act as a whole." *Ibid.* Crane, however, insisted that the nonrecourse nature of the mortgage required different treatment. The Court, for two reasons, disagreed.

---

[3] Section 113(a)(5) defined the basis of "property . . . acquired by . . . devise . . . or by the decedent's estate from the decedent" as "the fair market value of such property at the time of such acquisition." The Court interpreted the term "property" to refer to the physical land and buildings owned by Crane or the aggregate of her rights to control and dispose of them. 331 U.S., at 6, 67 S.Ct., at 1050.

First, excluding the nonrecourse debt from the amount realized would result in the same absurdity and frustration of the Code. *Id.*, at 13–14. Second, the Court concluded that Crane obtained an economic benefit from the purchaser's assumption of the mortgage identical to the benefit conferred by the cancellation of personal debt. Because the value of the property in that case exceeded the amount of the mortgage, it was in Crane's economic interest to treat the mortgage as a personal obligation; only by so doing could she realize upon sale the appreciation in her equity represented by the $2,500 boot. The purchaser's assumption of the liability thus resulted in a taxable economic benefit to her, just as if she had been given, in addition to the boot, a sum of cash sufficient to satisfy the mortgage.[4]

In a footnote, pertinent to the present case, the Court observed: "Obviously, if the value of the property is less than the amount of the mortgage, a mortgagor who is not personally liable cannot realize a benefit equal to the mortgage. Consequently, a different problem might be encountered where a mortgagor abandoned the property or transferred it subject to the mortgage without receiving boot. That is not this case." *Id.*, at 14, n. 37.

B

This case presents that unresolved issue. We are disinclined to overrule *Crane*, and we conclude that the same rule applies when the unpaid amount of the nonrecourse mortgage exceeds the value of the property transferred. *Crane* ultimately does not rest on its limited theory of economic benefit; instead, we read *Crane* to have approved the Commissioner's decision to treat a nonrecourse mortgage in this context as a true loan. This approval underlies *Crane*'s holdings that the amount of the nonrecourse liability is to be included in calculating both the basis and the amount realized on disposition. That the amount of the loan exceeds the fair market value of the property thus becomes irrelevant.

When a taxpayer receives a loan, he incurs an obligation to repay that loan at some future date. Because of this obligation, the loan proceeds do not qualify as income to the taxpayer. When he fulfills the obligation, the repayment of the loan likewise has no effect on his tax liability.

Another consequence to the taxpayer from this obligation occurs when the taxpayer applies the loan proceeds to the purchase price of property used to secure the loan. Because of the obligation to repay, the taxpayer is entitled to include the amount of the loan in computing his basis in the property; the loan, under § 1012, is part of the taxpayer's cost of the property. Although a different approach might have been taken with respect to a nonrecourse mortgage loan,[5] the Commissioner has chosen to accord it the same treatment he gives to a recourse mortgage loan.

---

[4] Crane also argued that even if the statute required the inclusion of the amount of the nonrecourse debt, that amount was not Sixteenth Amendment income because the overall transaction had been "by all dictates of common sense . . . a ruinous disaster." Brief for Petitioner in *Crane v. Commissioner*, O.T.1946, No. 68, p. 51. The Court noted, however, that Crane had been entitled to and actually took depreciation deductions for nearly seven years. To allow her to exclude sums on which those deductions were based from the calculation of her taxable gain would permit her "a double deduction . . . on the same loss of assets." The Sixteenth Amendment, it was said, did not require that result. 331 U.S., at 15–16.

[5] The Commissioner might have adopted the theory, implicit in *Crane*'s contentions, that a nonrecourse mortgage is not true debt, but, instead, is a form of joint investment by the mortgagor and the mortgagee. On this approach, nonrecourse debt would be considered a contingent liability, under

The Court approved that choice in *Crane*, and the respondents do not challenge it here. The choice and its resultant benefits to the taxpayer are predicated on the assumption that the mortgage will be repaid in full.

When encumbered property is sold or otherwise disposed of and the purchaser assumes the mortgage, the associated extinguishment of the mortgagor's obligation to repay is accounted for in the computation of the amount realized.[6] . . . Because no difference between recourse and nonrecourse obligations is recognized in calculating basis,[7] *Crane* teaches that the Commissioner may ignore the nonrecourse nature of the obligation in determining the amount realized upon disposition of the encumbered property. He thus may include in the amount realized the amount of the nonrecourse mortgage assumed by the purchaser. The rationale for this treatment is that the original inclusion of the amount of the mortgage in basis rested on the assumption that the mortgagor incurred an obligation to repay. Moreover, this treatment balances the fact that the mortgagor originally received the proceeds of the nonrecourse loan tax-free on the same assumption. Unless the outstanding amount of the mortgage is deemed to be realized, the mortgagor effectively will have received untaxed income at the time the loan was extended and will have received an unwarranted increase in the basis

---

which the mortgagor's payments on the debt gradually increase his interest in the property while decreasing that of the mortgagee. Note, *Federal Income Tax Treatment of Nonrecourse Debt*, 82 Colum.L.Rev. 1498, 1514 (1982); Lurie, *Mortgagor's Gain on Mortgaging Property for More than Cost Without Personal Liability*, 6 Tax.L.Rev. 319, 323 (1951); *cf.* Brief for Respondents 16 (nonrecourse debt resembles preferred stock). Because the taxpayer's investment in the property would not include the nonrecourse debt, the taxpayer would not be permitted to include that debt in basis. Note, 82 Colum.L.Rev., at 1515; *cf. Gibson Products Co. v. United States*, 637 F.2d 1041–1048 (5th Cir. 1981) (contingent nature of obligation prevents inclusion in basis of oil and gas leases of nonrecourse debt secured by leases, drilling equipment, and percentage of future production). We express no view as to whether such an approach would be consistent with the statutory structure and, if so, and *Crane* were not on the books, whether that approach would be preferred over *Crane*'s analysis. We note only that the *Crane* Court's resolution of the basis issue presumed that when property is purchased with proceeds from a nonrecourse mortgage, the purchaser becomes the sole owner of the property. 331 U.S., at 6. Under the *Crane* approach, the mortgagee is entitled to no portion of the basis. *Id.*, at 10, n. 28. The nonrecourse mortgage is part of the mortgagor's investment in the property, and does not constitute a coinvestment by the mortgagee. *But see* Note, 82 Colum. L. Rev., at 1513 (treating nonrecourse mortgage as coinvestment by mortgagee and critically concluding that *Crane* departed from traditional analysis that basis is taxpayer's investment in property).

[6] In this case, respondents received the face value of their note as loan proceeds. If respondents initially had given their note at a discount, the amount realized on the sale of the securing property might be limited to the funds actually received. *See Commissioner v. Rail Joint Co.*, 61 F.2d 751, 752 (2d Cir. 1932) (cancellation of indebtedness); *Fashion Park, Inc. v. Commissioner*, 21 T.C. 600, 606 (1954) (same). *See generally* J. Sneed, The Configurations of Gross Income 319 (1967) ("[I]t appears settled that the reacquisition of bonds at a discount by the obligor results in gain only to the extent the issue price, where this is less than par, exceeds the cost of reacquisition").

[7] The Commissioner's choice in *Crane* "laid the foundation stone of most tax shelters," Bittker, *Tax Shelters, Nonrecourse Debt, and the* Crane *Case*, 33 Tax.L.Rev. 277, 283 (1978), by permitting taxpayers who bear no risk to take deductions on depreciable property. Congress recently has acted to curb this avoidance device by forbidding a taxpayer to take depreciation deductions in excess of amounts he has at risk in the investment. Pub.L. 94-455, § 204(a), 90 Stat. 1531 (1976), 26 U.S.C. § 465; Pub.L. 95-600, §§ 201–204, 92 Stat. 2814–2817 (1978), 26 U.S.C. § 465(a) (1976 ed., Supp. V). Real estate investments, however, are exempt from this prohibition. § 465(c)(3)(D) (1976 ed., Supp. V). Although this congressional action may foreshadow a day when nonrecourse and recourse debts will be treated differently, neither Congress nor the Commissioner has sought to alter *Crane*'s rule of including nonrecourse liability in both basis and the amount realized.

of his property.[8] The Commissioner's interpretation of § 1001(b) in this fashion cannot be said to be unreasonable.

C

The Commissioner in fact has applied this rule even when the fair market value of the property falls below the amount of the nonrecourse obligation. Treas.Reg. § 1.1001-2(b), 26 CFR § 1.1001-2(b) (1982);[9] Rev.Rul. 76-111, 1976-1 Cum.Bull. 214. Because the theory on which the rule is based applies equally in this situation, *see Millar v. Commissioner*, 67 T.C. 656, 660 (1977), *aff'd on this issue*, 577 F.2d 212, 215–216 (3d Cir.), *cert. denied*, 439 U.S. 1046 (1978);[10] *Mendham Corp. v. Commissioner*, 9 T.C. 320, 323–324 (1947); *Lutz & Schramm Co. v. Commissioner*, 1 T.C. 682, 688–689 (1943), we have no reason, after *Crane*, to question this treatment.[11]

---

[8] Although the *Crane* rule has some affinity with the tax benefit rule, *see* Bittker, *supra*, at 282; Del Cotto, *Sales and Other Dispositions of Property Under Section 1001: The Taxable Event, Amount Realized and Related Problems of Basis*, 26 Buffalo L.Rev. 219, 323–324 (1977), the analysis we adopt is different. Our analysis applies even in the situation in which no deductions are taken. It focuses on the obligation to repay and its subsequent extinguishment, not on the taking and recovery of deductions. *See generally* Note, 82 Colum.L.Rev., at 1526–1529.

[9] The regulation was promulgated while this case was pending before the Court of Appeals for the Fifth Circuit. T.D. 7741, 45 Fed.Reg. 81743, 1981-1 Cum.Bull. 430 (1980). It merely formalized the Commissioner's prior interpretation, however.

[10] The Court of Appeals for the Third Circuit in *Millar* affirmed the Tax Court on the theory that inclusion of nonrecourse liability in the amount realized was necessary to prevent the taxpayer from enjoying a double deduction. 577 F.2d, at 215; *cf.* n. 4, *supra*. Because we resolve the question on another ground, we do not address the validity of the double deduction rationale.

[11] Professor Wayne G. Barnett, as *amicus* in the present case, argues that the liability and property portions of the transaction should be accounted for separately. Under his view, there was a transfer of the property for $1.4 million, and there was a cancellation of the $1.85 million obligation for a payment of $1.4 million. The former resulted in a capital loss of $50,000, and the latter in the realization of $450,000 of ordinary income. Taxation of the ordinary income might be deferred under § 108 by a reduction of respondents' bases in their partnership interests. Although this indeed could be a justifiable mode of analysis, it has not been adopted by the Commissioner. Nor is there anything to indicate that the Code requires the Commissioner to adopt it. We note that Professor Barnett's approach does assume that recourse and nonrecourse debt may be treated identically. The Commissioner also has chosen not to characterize the transaction as cancellation of indebtedness. We are not presented with and do not decide the contours of the cancellation-of-indebtedness doctrine. We note only that our approach does not fall within certain prior interpretations of that doctrine. In one view, the doctrine rests on the same initial premise as our analysis here — an obligation to repay — but the doctrine relies on a freeing-of-assets theory to attribute ordinary income to the debtor upon cancellation. *See Commissioner v. Jacobson*, 336 U.S. 28, 38–40 (1949); *United States v. Kirby Lumber Co.*, 284 U.S. 1, 3 (1931). According to that view, when nonrecourse debt is forgiven, the debtor's basis in the securing property is reduced by the amount of debt canceled, and realization of income is deferred until the sale of the property. *See Fulton Gold Corp. v. Commissioner*, 31 B.T.A. 519, 520 (1934). Because that interpretation attributes income only when assets are freed, however, an insolvent debtor realizes income just to the extent his assets exceed his liabilities after the cancellation. *Lakeland Grocery Co. v. Commissioner*, 36 B.T.A. 289, 292 (1937). Similarly, if the nonrecourse indebtedness exceeds the value of the securing property, the taxpayer never realizes the full amount of the obligation canceled because the tax law has not recognized negative basis. Although the economic benefit prong of *Crane* also relies on a freeing-of-assets theory, that theory is irrelevant to our broader approach. In the context of a sale or disposition of property under § 1001, the extinguishment of the obligation to repay is not ordinary income; instead, the amount of the canceled debt is included in the amount realized, and enters into the computation of gain or loss on the disposition of property. According to *Crane*, this treatment is no different when the obligation is nonrecourse: the basis is not reduced as in the cancellation-of-

Respondents received a mortgage loan with the concomitant obligation to repay by the year 2012. The only difference between that mortgage and one on which the borrower is personally liable is that the mortgagee's remedy is limited to foreclosing on the securing property. This difference does not alter the nature of the obligation; its only effect is to shift from the borrower to the lender any potential loss caused by devaluation of the property.[12] If the fair market value of the property falls below the amount of the outstanding obligation, the mortgagee's ability to protect its interests is impaired, for the mortgagor is free to abandon the property to the mortgagee and be relieved of his obligation.

This, however, does not erase the fact that the mortgagor received the loan proceeds tax-free and included them in his basis on the understanding that he had an obligation to repay the full amount. See *Woodsam Associates, Inc. v. Commissioner*, 198 F.2d 357, 359 (2d Cir. 1952); Bittker, 33 Tax.L.Rev., at 284. When the obligation is canceled, the mortgagor is relieved of his responsibility to repay the sum he originally received and thus realizes value to that extent within the meaning of § 1001(b). From the mortgagor's point of view, when his obligation is assumed by a third party who purchases the encumbered property, it is as if the mortgagor first had been paid with cash borrowed by the third party from the mortgagee on a nonrecourse basis, and then had used the cash to satisfy his obligation to the mortgagee. Moreover, this approach avoids the absurdity the Court recognized in *Crane*. Because of the remedy accompanying the mortgage in the nonrecourse situation, the depreciation in the fair market value of the property is relevant economically only to the mortgagee, who by lending on a nonrecourse basis remains at risk. To permit the taxpayer to limit his realization to the fair market value of the property would be to recognize a tax loss for which he has suffered no corresponding economic loss.[13] Such a result would be to construe "one section of the Act . . . so as . . . to defeat the intention of another or to frustrate the Act as a whole." 331 U.S., at 13.

In the specific circumstances of *Crane*, the economic benefit theory did support the Commissioner's treatment of the nonrecourse mortgage as a personal obligation. The footnote in *Crane* acknowledged the limitations of that theory when applied to a different set of facts. *Crane* also stands for the broader proposition, however, that a nonrecourse loan should be treated as a true loan. We therefore

---

indebtedness context, and the full value of the outstanding liability is included in the amount realized. Thus, the problem of negative basis is avoided.

[12] In his opinion for the Court of Appeals in *Crane*, Judge Learned Hand observed: "[The mortgagor] has all the income from the property; he manages it; he may sell it; any increase in its value goes to him; any decrease falls on him, until the value goes below the amount of the lien. . . . When therefore upon a sale the mortgagor makes an allowance to the vendee of the amount of the lien, he secures a release from a charge upon his property quite as though the vendee had paid him the full price on condition that before he took title the lien should be cleared. . . ." 153 F.2d 504, 506 (2d Cir. 1945).

[13] In the present case, the Government bore the ultimate loss. The nonrecourse mortgage was extended to respondents only after the planned complex was endorsed for mortgage insurance under §§ 221(b) and (d)(4) of the National Housing Act, 12 U.S.C. § 1715l(b) and (d)(4) (1976 ed. and Supp. V). After acquiring the complex from respondents, Bayles operated it for a few years, but was unable to make it profitable. In 1974, F&H foreclosed, and the Department of Housing and Urban Development paid off the lender to obtain title. In 1976, the Department sold the complex to another developer for $1,502,000. The sale was financed by the Department's taking back a note for $1,314,800 and a nonrecourse mortgage. To fail to recognize the value of the nonrecourse loan in the amount realized, therefore, would permit respondents to compound the Government's loss by claiming the tax benefits of that loss for themselves.

hold that a taxpayer must account for the proceeds of obligations he has received tax-free and included in basis. Nothing in either § 1001(b) or in the Court's prior decisions requires the Commissioner to permit a taxpayer to treat a sale of encumbered property asymmetrically, by including the proceeds of the nonrecourse obligation in basis but not accounting for the proceeds upon transfer of the encumbered property. *See Estate of Levine v. Commissioner*, 634 F.2d 12, 15 (2d Cir. 1980). . . .

When a taxpayer sells or disposes of property encumbered by a nonrecourse obligation, the Commissioner properly requires him to include among the assets realized the outstanding amount of the obligation. The fair market value of the property is irrelevant to this calculation. We find this interpretation to be consistent with *Crane v. Commissioner*, 331 U.S. 1 (1947), and to implement the statutory mandate in a reasonable manner. *National Muffler Dealers Assn. v. United States*, 440 U.S. 472, 476 (1979).

The judgment of the Court of Appeals is therefore reversed.

It is so ordered.

JUSTICE O'CONNOR, concurring.

I concur in the opinion of the Court, accepting the view of the Commissioner. I do not, however, endorse the Commissioner's view. Indeed, were we writing on a slate clean except for the *Crane* decision, I would take quite a different approach — that urged upon us by Professor Barnett as *amicus*.

Crane established that a taxpayer could treat property as entirely his own, in spite of the "coinvestment" provided by his mortgagee in the form of a nonrecourse loan. That is, the full basis of the property, with all its tax consequences, belongs to the mortgagor. That rule alone, though, does not in any way tie nonrecourse debt to the cost of property or to the proceeds upon disposition. I see no reason to treat the purchase, ownership, and eventual disposition of property differently because the taxpayer also takes out a mortgage, an independent transaction. In this case, the taxpayer purchased property, using nonrecourse financing, and sold it after it declined in value to a buyer who assumed the mortgage. There is no economic difference between the events in this case and a case in which the taxpayer buys property with cash; later obtains a nonrecourse loan by pledging the property as security; still later, using cash on hand, buys off the mortgage for the market value of the devalued property; and finally sells the property to a third party for its market value.

The logical way to treat both this case and the hypothesized case is to separate the two aspects of these events and to consider, first, the ownership and sale of the property, and, second, the arrangement and retirement of the loan. Under *Crane*, the fair market value of the property on the date of acquisition — the purchase price — represents the taxpayer's basis in the property, and the fair market value on the date of disposition represents the proceeds on sale. The benefit received by the taxpayer in return for the property is the cancellation of a mortgage that is worth no more than the fair market value of the property, for that is all the mortgagee can expect to collect on the mortgage. His gain or loss on the disposition of the property equals the difference between the proceeds and the cost of acquisition. Thus, the taxation of the transaction in property reflects the economic fate of the property. If the property has declined in value, as was the case here, the taxpayer recognizes a loss on the disposition of the property. The new purchaser then takes as his basis the fair market value as of the date of the sale. *See, e.g., United States v. Davis*, 370 U.S. 65, 72 (1962); *Gibson Products Co. v. United States*, 637 F.2d 1041, 1045, n. 8 (5th Cir. 1981) (dictum); *see generally* Treas.Reg. § 1.1001-2(a)(3), 26 CFR § 1.1001-2(a)(3) (1982); B. Bittker, 2 Federal Income Taxation of Income, Estates and Gifts, ¶ 41.2.2., at 41-10–41-11 (1981).

In the separate borrowing transaction, the taxpayer acquires cash from the mortgagee. He need not recognize income at that time, of course, because he also incurs an obligation to repay the money. Later, though, when he is able to satisfy the debt by surrendering property that is worth less than the face amount of the debt, we have a classic situation of cancellation of indebtedness, requiring the taxpayer to recognize income in the amount of the difference between the proceeds of the loan and the amount for which he is able to satisfy his creditor. 26 U.S.C. § 61(a)(12). The taxation of the financing transaction then reflects the economic fate of the loan.

The reason that separation of the two aspects of the events in this case is important is, of course, that the Code treats different sorts of income differently. A gain on the sale of the property may qualify for capital gains treatment, §§ 1202, 1221 (1976 ed. and Supp. V), while the cancellation of indebtedness is ordinary income, but income that the taxpayer may be able to defer. §§ 108, 1017 (1976 ed. Supp. V). Not only does Professor Barnett's theory permit us to accord approriate treatment to each of the two types of income or loss present in these sorts of transactions, it also restores continuity to the system by making the taxpayer-seller's proceeds on the disposition of property equal to the purchaser's basis in the property. Further, and most important, it allows us to tax the events in this case in the same way that we tax the economically identical hypothesized transaction.

Persuaded though I am by the logical coherence and internal consistency of this approach, I agree with the Court's decision not to adopt it judicially. We do not write on a slate marked only by *Crane*. The Commissioner's longstanding position, Rev.Rul. 76-111, 1976-1 C.B. 214, is now reflected in the regulations. Treas. Reg. § 1.1001-2, 26 CFR § 1.1001-2 (1982). In the light of the numerous cases in the lower courts including the amount of the unrepaid proceeds of the mortgage in the proceeds on sale or disposition, . . . , it is difficult to conclude that the Commissioner's interpretation of the statute exceeds the bounds of his discretion. As the Court's opinion demonstrates, his interpretation is defensible. One can reasonably read § 1001(b)'s reference to "the amount realized *from* the sale or other disposition of property" (emphasis added) to permit the Commissioner to collapse the two aspects of the transaction. As long as his view is a reasonable reading of § 1001(b), we should defer to the regulations promulgated by the agency charged with interpretation of the statute. . . . Accordingly, I concur.

[3] Comments and Questions on *Tufts*

[a] The Transaction

Sketch out the original transaction by which Pelt, the developer, and his colleagues, Tufts, Steger, Stephens and Austin, acquired the Duncanville complex. What were the elements that made it work economically? Note that they were able to borrow practically every last dollar of the construction cost. Why? These commitments were all made in advance, so how did the lender know what the income of the project would be? Although the loan was nonrecourse, did the lender care?

[b] Valuation

In the statement of facts, it is said that, when the parties agreed to dispose of their interests in the project, the property was worth only $1,400,000. How did anybody know that? Value, of course, is a conclusion. Using DCF analysis, value is derived from analysis of the rental income stream generated by the property. If the rents do not support the capital structure of the project (viz., the loan plus the equity contributions), what then happens to that capital? Is it true that the developer lost nothing, except for the relatively small amount of cash invested, because the loan was nonrecourse? If the property were foreclosed, should the tax result be any different? *See* IRC § 7701(g) (providing that, in determining gain or loss on disposition of property subject to nonrecourse indebtedness, the value of the property "shall be treated" as not less than the amount of the mortgage); Reg. § 1.1001-2(a)(4)(i); (c) *Example (2)*.

[c] Cancellation of Indebtedness

Is there an alternative way of analyzing the tax problem in *Tufts*? This is suggested in Justice O'Connor's concurring opinion which endorsed the position urged by the *amicus*: divide the value attributed to ("realized in") the sale between (i) the then value of the property and (ii) the amount of the debt in excess of the property value. The tax treatment of excess debt would be determined by cancellation of indebtedness ("COD") principles, as if the excess had been "canceled" by the elimination of the partnership's responsibility (such as it was) to pay it. Are you persuaded by Justice O'Connor's opinion? *See* IRC §§ 108(a)(1)(D); (c)(3); 1017. Would it make sense in analyzing the tax consequences of the disposition of property to bifurcate a nonrecourse loan secured by the property when the value of the property is less than the face amount of the loan? Consider again IRC § 7701(g) and the implications for *2925 Briarpark, Ltd v. Commissioner, infra* section 17.02.

In *Frazier v. Commissioner*, 111 T.C. 243 (1998), the lender foreclosed on a residence, which the taxpayers had held for rent, and bid the property in at the foreclosure sale for $570,000. At that time, the mortgage, which was recourse as to the taxpayers, was $585,000, but the property had a value of only $375,000. The taxpayers' basis for the property was then $495,000. Treas. Reg. § 1.1001-2(a)(2) provides that the indebtedness should be bifurcated, with an amount equal to the then value of the property attributed to the foreclosure sale and the balance taxed under the cancellation of indebtedness rules. *See* Rev. Rul. 90-16, 1990-1 C.B. 12. The Commissioner asserted that the lender's bid, the amount of which was unexplained, should be treated as the amount realized, despite the taxpayer's proof of a lower market value, and contrary to the position taken in Revenue Ruling 90-16. The Tax Court concluded, however, that the contrary authority was distinguishable because of the proof of market value, and held that the taxpayers realized a capital loss of $120,000, equal to the difference between their adjusted tax basis ($495,000) and the value of the property ($375,000). The balance of the mortgage ($585,000 – $375,000 = $210,000) was taxable, if at all, under COD rules of section 108. Section 108, as you might expect, provides a number of exceptions and a means to defer the potential tax liability. "Tax leverage" is an essential element in the formation and operation of conduit entities for real estate projects, and the tax effect of foreclosure will be discussed further in Chapter 17. Why treat recourse mortgages differently from nonrecourse mortgages?

[d] "Phantom Gain"

In *Tufts*, the project had a cost basis for tax purposes almost equal to the amount of the first mortgage because the developer was able to borrow 100% of the actual cost. You might say here that the result yielded by the DCF method of valuing the property for the purpose of underwriting the loan was not consistent with construction costs, or more truthfully, that the underwriting criteria for the loan were rather loose. If there has been no curtailment of principal (as was true in *Tufts*), then including the unpaid balance (the original principal amount, increased by unpaid accrued interest and other costs) in the "amount realized" for tax purposes approximates the original cost (tax basis) of the project. But, as you have seen, the tax basis for the project must be "adjusted" (reduced) by the depreciation allowed to the owners. The gain on disposition, therefore, results from the fact that the tax basis has been reduced. This result, in a case like *Tufts*, produces a *tax cost* to the owner but no offsetting proceeds, as typically would be generated by a sale of the property.

As we have demonstrated, tax leverage is valuable because it produces a cash flow which is sheltered, temporarily, from tax — which is to say that the tax liability on the income offset by the depreciation deductions has been deferred.[24] When the property is disposed of, the deferral ends, and a taxable gain results. Of course, the tax sheltered cash that produced the gain has already been withdrawn from the project and so *realized* by the investor. Memories are short, however, and the taxable gain on disposition is not usually associated by the taxpayer/investor with the earlier cash withdrawals (or the deductions which "sheltered" income from an external source). Hence, the gain resulting from a transaction like *Tufts* appears artificial, a "phantom gain," albeit accompanied by a real tax liability.

Deferral results when the depreciation deductions attributable to tax basis derived from the use of debt are allowed more rapidly than the principal of the debt is repaid. A long amortization period for the debt, at least in privately syndicated projects, is therefore valuable, even if the term of the loan (when it reaches maturity and must be repaid) is shorter. Insured FHA loans often have an amortization period of 40 years, even today, so the amount of deferral may be substantial, and the so-called "phantom gain" correspondingly large. The presence of this overhanging gain frequently inhibits disposition of real estate projects, and has given rise to a complex set of strategies for the disposition of such "overleveraged" properties with minimum tax impact.[25]

---

[24] In *Tufts*, the project did not produce any cash flow; instead, there were losses. The deductions were valuable, nonetheless, because, at that time, they could be used to offset income from some other source. In Tufts' case, that would have been income from Tufts' law practice. The tax on this income was deferred, not forgiven, and "stored," if you will, in the adjustments to the tax basis of the real estate project.

[25] It is not necessary to have conditions under which there is a significant amount of tax sheltering for there to be substantial deferred gain. Straight-line depreciation and long amortization periods for a

[e] Refinancing

Suppose that D constructed a project, Golden Acres Shopping Center, at a cost (depreciable tax basis) of $10,000,000. D borrowed $7,500,000, on a nonrecourse first mortgage, to construct Golden Acres. D operated Golden Acres for 10 years, at which point, D (or D and D's investors) had taken $2,600,000 in depreciation deductions. D's adjusted basis for Golden Acres was then $10,000,000 – $2,600,000 = $7,400,000. Suppose D had also paid $600,000 in curtailment of the principal of the first mortgage, so the unpaid balance of the loan was then $7,500,000 – $600,000 = $6,900,000. Rents had, however, risen markedly during this period of time, and interest rates had fallen. These favorable conditions permitted D to negotiate a new loan for $12,000,000, also nonrecourse. Assume that D could prepay the original mortgage without penalty. D then received loans proceeds of $12,000,000, paid the existing mortgage, $6,900,000, and executed a new first mortgage in favor of the refinancing lender. D then found himself with cash on his hands of $5,100,000, which he promptly distributed to his investors for their individual use. What is the tax effect of this transaction?

First of all, it is clear, is it not, that changing the amount of the loan, whether by curtailing principal out of current cash flow or by refinancing, has no effect on the tax basis for the property. Naturally, the loan proceeds could be used to make capital improvements to the property (thus increasing tax basis to the extent of the cost of any improvements), which will often happen in rehabilitation work, but assume they are not so used. Second, receipt of the proceeds is not taxable. The cash proceeds may be used by the borrowers (D and D's investors) for any purpose without incurring tax. Acquisition or construction of a new project will result in a tax basis equal to cost for that project. Recall that the reason for this tax result is that the proceeds are offset by the obligation to repay. Even though the loan is nonrecourse, the tax authority supporting this result is well established.[26]

The result is overhanging gain. Golden Acres now has an adjusted tax basis of $7,400,000 but is subject to debt of $12,000,000. Neither D nor D's investors has any personal liability, under the assumed facts, to repay the loan, but they are charged with the deferred gain on the project, which we can call the "*Tufts*" gain.[27] When disposition of the property occurs, there will be a large "phantom gain" for D and D's investors to worry about. In privately syndicated, successful projects, the debt is often re-upped as the income generated by the project increases to support it, with the cash proceeds available for distribution but with the tax consequences deferred. In many projects, the tax cost of the gain is so substantial that the parties will take any reasonable step to defer the day of reckoning.

---

highly leveraged property, however sound economically, will produce the effect. So will refinancing, as we discuss next.

26 *See* Woodsam Associates v. Commissioner, 198 F.2d 357 (2d Cir. 1952). When the full value (or cost) of the property can be borrowed, the taxpayer is said to have "mortgaged out." That is, the taxpayer has withdrawn the value of the property in cash (or has not expended any of her own funds), without incurring tax.

27 When this phenomenon occurs in a partnership context, the partnership tax allocation rules define the "*Tufts*" gain as "minimum gain," and require that it be allocated to the partner who took the deductions or received the borrowed proceeds. The gain is "minimum gain" because it is the minimum amount of taxable gain that will be allocated among the partners if foreclosure occurs.

[f] Partnership Tax Issues

Note that Pelt and his companions sold their *partnership interests* to Bayles. The tax result for them, however, turns out to be the same, whether the project itself or their interests in the partnership are what is sold. This happens because, for a partnership, the tax basis consequences of leveraging flow through the entity and out to the partners. The partners, therefore, will have, in general, the same tax basis, albeit allocated among their interests by some complex rules, as does the project, and they will have to adjust basis for their interests in the partnership as the tax deductions are allocated to them. Similarly, on disposition of their partnership interests, the partnership indebtedness also must be allocated among the partners and included in the amount each will have realized on the sale of his or her interest.

[4] Recycling Tax Basis

What about Bayles, the buyer of the Duncanville project in *Tufts*? Why would he pay *anything* for the property? Assuming that he could operate the project to support the debt and ultimately generate enough cash flow to make the project successful, he would rely on tax rules which permit him to include in his tax basis the debt secured by the project. But should he be permitted to "recycle" the basis for the project by including the full amount or any part of the original nonrecourse loan in *his cost basis* for depreciation purposes?

In a variety of tax planning schemes, promoters sought to use the *Crane* doctrine to create tax basis (as well as interest deductions) which could then be turned into depreciation deductions which were channeled to high income taxpayers. In the typical transaction, the promoter, P, would purchase the subject property from a third party for a negotiated price, usually making a down payment, giving a nonrecourse, second mortgage note and taking the property subject to existing senior indebtedness. Presumably, this transaction reflected fair market valuc. Then, usually simultaneously, P would resell the property, sometimes retaining the underlying land (which, you will recall, is nondepreciable), to a syndicate composed of P, as the general partner or manager, and investors, who held their interests as limited partners. The resale price would be much greater than the price paid by P, and would include a substantial cash payment, usually two or three times the cash down payment P had paid, and a large, nonrecourse wraparound mortgage (the underlying mortgage would not be paid off and the seller would accept a new larger mortgage that "wrapped around" the smaller existing mortgage). The cash payment (and up front fees) would be paid from the capital contributions by the investors, and the required debt-service payments would be set approximately equal to the rent derived from the property. Apart from the cash payment, very little cash would change hands, sometimes even with the original seller.

The investors would realize substantial tax losses. At a pre-1986 marginal rate of 50%, these losses would fully offset, within a short period of time, their net cash investment. This type of tax shelter arrangement makes no sense today, in large part because marginal tax rates have been reduced, depreciation periods lengthened and deductions for excess "passive losses" disallowed. (*See* IRC § 469.) In the early 1980s, the "at risk" rules were amended to apply to real estate projects, and under these rules nonrecourse seller take-back financing, essential to making the tax shelter arrangements work, is excluded from tax basis. (*See* IRC § 465(b)(6)(D)(i), referring to § 49(a)(1)(D)(iv)(II).) So, these schemes do not work today, and cannot be sold to investors. Nonetheless, the principles on which they were founded remain good law, and in the wake of the recession in real estate values in 2008 and later years, there will, no doubt, be circumstances under which a Fred Bayles will acquire a real estate project subject to a nonrecourse debt possibly greater than its apparent value. The question remains, whether *any* of that debt can be included in the purchaser's tax basis.

[5] Mortgages in Excess of Value

[a] Abusive Use of Excessive Mortgages for Tax Purposes

In several cases growing out of the private syndication of real estate projects to achieve tax benefits, in which purported nonrecourse indebtedness was created between buyer and seller (now disallowed by the at-risk rules) or between related entities, courts held that the debt could be disregarded in its entirety when the amount of the debt did not reasonably approximate the value the property subject to the debt. *See Bergstrom v. United States*, 37 Fed. Cl. 164 (1996); *Estate of Franklin v. Commissioner*, 544 F.2d 1045 (9thCir. 1976). The rationale of these cases is based on economic substance: when the nonrecourse mortgage is disproportionate to the value of the property, the entire transaction lacks substance and should not be given effect. In one case, *Pleasant Summit Land Corp. v. Commissioner*, 863 F2d 263 (3d Cir. 1988), *cert. denied*, 493 U.S. 901 (1989), the Third Circuit held that a nonrecourse debt in excess of the value of the property could be included in tax basis up to the value of the property, but no other court Circuit Court has reached the same conclusion.

Cases like *Bergstrom* address the use of nonrecourse indebtedness to create artificial tax basis for investors, using a real estate project as the subject and manipulating the financial information on which the valuation of the project is based. The remedy is drastic: disregard the nonrecourse debt for tax purposes altogether. How useful is such a remedy for the more likely case today in which the value of the underlying project has declined below the balance due on the debt? That is what had happened in *Tufts* at the time the project was purchased by an unrelated third party, and it is happening again as real estate markets falter. *Bergstrom* is different from cases like *Tufts*, because the transaction in *Bergstrom* was *designed* to make the nonrecourse debt greater than the value of the underlying property solely for the purpose of inflating the tax basis and providing the investors with larger depreciation deductions than could be justified by the real value of the property. In *Tufts*, on the other hand, the nonrecourse debt was originally supported, ephemerally, by the value of the property. It became excessive when the value of the property declined. Is the rule in these cases simply irrelevant for purchasers like Bayles?

The problem exemplified by these cases will probably not recur as lenders would resist the purchase of an overleveraged property by an unrelated third party except, perhaps, in the context of a work-out of the debt. See *Regents Park Partners v. Commissioner*, 63 T.C.M. (CCH) 3131 (1992), a case with facts that are so unusual that they will not likely be repeated. In *Regents Park Partners*, the taxpayer and its mortgagee, HUD, had a long history of dealing over the mortgage. The debts were originally bona fide nonrecourse debt when they closed, but the value of the underlying projects, two apartment towers in Chicago, declined dramatically when serious construction defects were revealed. The loans were insured FHA loans, and when the original developer defaulted, HUD fulfilled its insurance obligation and acquired the loans from the original mortgagee, thus becoming the mortgagee. Subsequently, the developer gave possession of the projects to HUD, and HUD awarded the taxpayer a temporary management contract. The projects continued to experience structural problems, necessitating significant investment by the taxpayer, who sought to negotiate a longer term arrangement with HUD. HUD apparently had assured the taxpayer that it would renegotiate the mortgages if the workout arrangement with the taxpayer met certain criteria, which it did, by reducing the principal amount to the level that the project economics would support. When HUD refused to renegotiate the mortgage, it was prevented from foreclosing by the judgment of the Federal District Court.

The taxpayer sought to include the unpaid balance of the mortgages in the tax basis of the projects, and to deduct interest accruing on this balance. The Commissioner relied on *Estate of Franklin* and kindred cases to argue that no part of the mortgage could be treated as real indebtedness, and further that the taxpayer was not the owner of the apartment projects for tax purposes. The Tax Court, in a Solomonic judgment, concluded that the taxpayer could treat that portion of the debt equal to the "fair market value" of the projects as real debt, both for tax basis and for accrual of interest expense.

If the tax avoidance principles expressed in *Franklin's Estate* are not relevant, and the purchaser and the mortgagee do not negotiate over the debt, as they did in *Regents Park Partners*, the tax rule is left unresolved. It is not clear today how Fred Bayles would be permitted to treat the nonrecourse debt encumbering the property he acquired from the partnership in *Tufts*. But one might observe that the regulatory practices to which most institutional holders of first mortgage real estate loans are subject would preclude the mortgagee from carrying a nonperforming debt on its books at its original face amount.

[b] Problem

Suppose that Regent was successful in persuading Bank that its pro forma was an accurate statement of value. The Bank then approved a nonrecourse loan for $2,300,000, at 9% interest, 25-year amortization, and with a 10-year term (the "permanent loan").[28] The permanent loan was used to take out the construction loan at the end of year two. Prospective tenants did not line up, however, and 70% lease-up was the best that Regent could do. Regent obtained an appraisal for the Center, then with only 70% of rentable area under lease, for a value of $1,900,000.

In year four, Second Square, Ltd., which operates by buying underperforming shopping centers and making them successful, expressed interest in acquiring the Fox Valley Auto Care Center for a cash payment of $100,000 and taking the property subject to the mortgage. Assume that Regent has paid $40,000 of principal on the mortgage, and that the mortgage is assignable without penalty.

---

[28] With the Fox Valley Auto Care Center, Regent was not able to refinance the construction loan at $2,300,000. See our analysis of this problem as shown in Tables 2.12 and 2.15, *supra*. The problem asks you to assume that Regent did persuade the Bank's loan committee to refinance the entire construction loan.

Second Square has inquired into the circumstances under which the permanent loan was negotiated because it would like to be assured that it will have a tax basis, in the aggregate, for the Fox Valley Auto Care Center equal to $2,360,000 ($2,260,000 (balance due on the mortgage) + $100,000 (cash payment)).

Regent would like to do the deal. Donna asks Sam to tell her how firm the basis determination will be, as a "talking point." Draft a short memo from Sam to Donna that gives her the scope of the "talking point" she has asked for.

[c] Bottom-Feeders and Other Compromises

In the fallout of projects from the savings and loan debacle, the Resolution Trust Corporation organized the loan portfolios it inherited from defunct S&L's into financial packages which it sold on the capital markets. Purchasers of the loans, which might carry a face value much greater than the purchase price, could "restructure" the loan to match the then-existing economics of the underlying project, sometimes by reducing the balance due but also by adjusting payment terms and interest rates. Because the purchase price would have been less than the face value of the loan, these restructurings would be consistent with the purchaser's financial position with respect to the project. Sometimes, the original lender (or a participating lender) would "work out" the loan with the borrower, again by adjusting the terms of the loan to fit the project economics. Failure of work-out negotiations could result in foreclosure or bankruptcy or both. These are topics explored later in Part VI, Chapters 16 and 17.

A foreclosure sale, or a transfer by deed in lieu of foreclosure, is a taxable sale, and the amount realized on that sale would not be less than the face amount of the nonrecourse mortgage encumbering the property. *See* § 3.05[3][d], *supra* and 17.02, *infra*. When overhanging gain is present, foreclosure or transfer by deed would result in "phantom gain" in exactly the same way as would a more successful disposition of the property, particularly when the debt is nonrecourse. In cases where this has occurred, the result is tax liability on the economic failure of the investment, and the investors will think it unfair to incur a tax liability at the same time that they lose the property. On the other hand, loss of the property terminates the arrangement under which the investors may take depreciation deductions on a tax basis derived from the nonrecourse debt, thus cutting short the deferral period. As we have seen, imposition of tax at that time is perfectly consistent with the structure of the investment, whether or not it succeeded in economic terms.

Consider the tax effect of a foreclosure instead of a sale in the Second Square transaction described above. At a time when Fox Valley Auto Care Center has an appraised value of $1,900,000, the balance due on the mortgage is $2,260,000. Assume that the Fox Valley Auto Care Center LLC has an adjusted tax basis of $2,125,000. Economically, the project may appear not to have succeeded, at least not yet. But, with an original cost of $2,300,000, the LLC members have taken $175,000 in depreciation deductions while paying only $40,000 of the principal on the debt. The net tax benefit is $135,000. What will be the tax effect of the foreclosure?

The taxable gain is computed as follows:

Amount realized (face amount of the debt)[29]:	$2,260,000.
Adjusted Tax Basis:	$2,125,000.
Gain realized (and recognized):	$135,000.

Note that the current fair market value of the Fox Valley Auto Care Center has absolutely nothing to do with this calculation, which is based on what we can now call the "*Crane* system," a kind of Newton's law of real estate investing. This depends upon the amount of the mortgage and the total depreciation deductions taken by the investors. A larger equity investment might affect the numbers somewhat, but in private syndications, the objective almost always will be to keep the equity investment low and thus to obtain as much leverage as possible.

[6] Restructuring the Loan

The loan can be "restructured" to reduce the borrower's obligation to an amount supported by the project economics. This subject will be addressed more fully in Part VI, Chapters 16 and 17, but we broach it here to complete the tax picture at the outset of the transaction. There are tax consequences to restructuring the loan. Recall that loan proceeds are not taxable to the borrower when received, and, as a consequence of this rule, that the borrower must repay the loan out of after-tax income. The loan proceeds may be used to acquire or construct the project, in which case the expenditure becomes part of the tax basis for the project and produces favorable tax treatment to the developer or investor. What should happen when the amount due on the loan is reduced? Recall that in the context of a loan on which the taxpayer has personal liability, a compromise of the debt will produce cancellation of indebtedness income. Should a reduction in the amount of a nonrecourse debt, the tax effect of which the *Tufts* rule suggests should be tied to the fate of the property, produce the same tax result? Or, should the debt reduction be reflected in a basis adjustment? This problem was addressed in the following ruling.

[a] Revenue Ruling 92–99.

Rev. Rul. 92–99, 1992-2 C.B. 35

ISSUE

If the principal amount of an undersecured nonrecourse debt that arose out of the purchase of property is reduced by the holder of the debt who was not the seller of the property, does the debt reduction result in discharge of indebtedness income under section 61(a)(12) of the Internal Revenue Code, or is the debt reduction treated as a purchase price adjustment that reduces the basis of the property securing the debt?

FACTS

[29] IRC § 7701(g)

In 1988, individual A purchased an office building from B for $1,000,000, its fair market value. To pay for the building, A signed a note payable to C, a third-party lender, for $1,000,000. The note bore interest at a fixed market rate payable annually and was secured by the office building. In 1989, when the value of the office building was $800,000 and the outstanding principal on the note was $1,000,000, C agreed to modify the terms of the note by reducing the note's principal amount to $800,000. C's reduction in the note was not based on an infirmity that clearly related back to B's original sale (B's inducement of a higher purchase price by a misrepresentation of a material fact or by fraud). The modified note bore adequate stated interest within the meaning of section 1274(c)(2) of the Code.

The facts here do not involve the bankruptcy, insolvency, or qualified farm indebtedness of the taxpayer. Thus, the specific exclusions provided by section 108(a) of the Code do not apply.

LAW AND ANALYSIS

Section 61(a)(12) of the Code provides that gross income includes income from the discharge of indebtedness. Section 1.61-12(a) of the Income Tax Regulations provides that the discharge of indebtedness, in whole or in part, may result in the realization of income.

Section 108(e)(5) of the Code permits a debt reduction to be treated as a purchase price adjustment under certain circumstances. Section 108(e)(5) provides that if (A) the debt of a purchaser of property to the seller arising out of the purchase is reduced, (B) the debt reduction does not occur in a title 11 bankruptcy case or when the purchaser is insolvent, and (C) the reduction would be treated as income to the purchaser from the discharge of indebtedness but for paragraph (e)(5), then such reduction will be treated as a purchase price adjustment. This purchase price adjustment treatment will result in a reduction in the basis of the property securing the debt rather than discharge of indebtedness income.

The debt in this case was reduced by an agreement between C (the third-party lender) and A (the purchaser) of the property. Even though the debt arose in connection with the purchase of the property by A from B, it was not a debt of the purchaser (A) "to the seller" (B), as required by section 108(e)(5)(A) of the Code. Thus, the debt reduction by C does not qualify as a purchase price adjustment under section 108(e)(5) of the Code.

In addition, the debt reduction by C is not considered a purchase price adjustment under common law. *See Fifth Avenue-Fourteenth Street Corp. v. Commissioner*, 147 F.2d 453, 456–57 (2d Cir. 1945), in which the court stated that a purchase price adjustment is limited to a case where the seller-mortgagee agreed to the debt reduction. The Service generally will not follow cases permitting a purchase price adjustment by third-party lenders, such as *Hirsch v. Commissioner*, 115 F.2d 656 (7th Cir. 1940), and *Allen v. Courts*, 127 F.2d 127 (5th Cir. 1942). An agreement to reduce a debt between a purchaser and a third-party lender is not a true adjustment of the purchase price paid for the property because the seller has received the entire purchase price from the purchaser and is not a party to the debt reduction agreement. The debt reduction relates solely to the debt and results in discharge of indebtedness income to the debtor.

Hirsch and *Allen* relied on *Bowers v. Kerbaugh-Empire Company*, 271 U.S. 170 (1926), to conclude that no discharge of indebtedness income resulted from a reduction of third-party debt. These cases reasoned that the proceeds of third-party debt should be traced to the investment for which the proceeds were used, and any loss (realized or unrealized) on that investment may be used to offset any income from the discharge of the debt.

However, subsequent Supreme Court decisions and other court cases, when viewed together, have discredited *Kerbaugh-Empire*. *See Burnet v. Sanford & Brooks Co.*, 282 U.S. 359 (1931), which established the annual accounting period concept; *United States v. Kirby Lumber Co.*, 284 U.S. 1 (1931), which held that the discharge of an indebtedness resulted in gross income; *Commissioner v. Glenshaw Glass Co.*, 348 U.S. 426 (1955), which held that gross income included all accessions to wealth from whatever source; *Commissioner v. Tufts*, 461 U.S. 300 (1983), which held that the amount realized on the sale of property encumbered by a nonrecourse obligation (that exceeded the fair market value of the property) included the amount of the obligation discharged; and *Vukasovich v. Commissioner*, 790 F.2d 1409 (9th Cir. 1986), which held that the discharge of an indebtedness resulted in gross income, notwithstanding the loss that the taxpayer incurred on the underlying transaction. Citing the above Supreme Court cases, the Ninth Circuit in *Vukasovich* stated that *Kerbaugh-Empire* was inconsistent with those decisions, and concluded that when an accession to wealth resulting from the discharge of indebtedness was otherwise includible in gross income, *Kerbaugh-Empire* did not prevent the taxation of that income.

Further, the Service will not follow *Commissioner v. Sherman*, 135 F.2d 68 (6th Cir. 1943), involving a third-party lender, to the extent that it relied on *Kerbaugh-Empire* to permit a purchase price adjustment. The Service will, however, treat a debt reduction in third-party lender cases as a purchase price adjustment to the extent that the debt reduction by the third-party lender is based on an infirmity that clearly relates back to the original sale (e.g., the seller's inducement of a higher purchase price by misrepresentation of a material fact or by fraud). *Cf. Commissioner v. Sherman*, 135 F.2d 68, 70 (6th Cir. 1943). No other debt reduction by a third-party lender will be treated as a purchase price adjustment.

The reduction in the note by the third-party lender (C) in this case was not based on an infirmity that clearly relates back to the original sale, so A cannot treat C's debt reduction as a purchase price adjustment. Thus, A realizes $200,000 of discharge of indebtedness income in 1989 under section 61(a)(12) of the Code.

HOLDING

If the principal amount of an undersecured nonrecourse debt that arose out of the purchase of property is reduced by the holder of the debt who was not the seller of the property, this debt reduction may not be treated as a purchase price adjustment (in the absence of an infirmity that clearly relates back to the original sale), but results in discharge of indebtedness income under section 61(a)(12).

[b] Compromise of Nonrecourse Debt

Recall that nonrecourse debt incurred to purchase or construct income-producing depreciable property, such as the Fox Valley Auto Care Center, will be included in and increase the tax basis of the property. Cost recovery deductions will then be calculated with reference to that basis, that is, it will be used to create tax deductions for the owner of the property. Repayment of the debt must then be made from after-tax income or gain. Because the proceeds have not been taxed when received, use of the proceeds to support tax deductions will cause a deferral of tax on the income used to make the repayment, and, as we have seen, the objective in most leveraged real estate transactions will be to postpone repayment of the debt for as long a period as possible.

Suppose, however, that the amount of the debt is reduced, as is often the case in a work-out. The lender agrees to a smaller repayment or some other adjustment which gives the borrower more time to improve the operation of the project. With less debt to repay, some adjustment to the tax advantages which the borrower may have gained from the proceeds of the debt will have to be made. There is a choice for the typical real estate project: immediate inclusion in the income of the borrower of the amount of the adjustment as cancellation of indebtedness income, IRC § 61(a)(12), or a reduction in the remaining tax basis of the property. The former approach views the reduction in the amount of the debt as if it were a repayment, and treats it as taxable income; effectively, this terminates the deferral period which the original debt might otherwise have provided. The latter reduces the opportunity for future deferrals, but does not result in taxable income. This treatment for debt restructuring had been permitted in an early Board of Tax Appeals decision. *Fulton Gold Corp. v. Commissioner*, 31 B.T.A. 519 (1934), a result which was explicitly rejected by the IRS in Rev. Rul. 91-14, 1991 C.B. 18. The IRS takes this holding a step further in Rev. Rul. 92–99.

What does the Ruling hold? If reduction in debt incurred to acquire property also reduces the tax basis of the property, hasn't the taxpayer also surrendered the tax benefit which the debt had produced? It may be true that the cost recovery deductions allowed to the taxpayer with respect to the original basis of the property were greater than would have been allowed had the debt been equal to the balance due after the debt was restructured, because then tax basis would have been less from the inception of the project. But why would this incremental benefit cause inclusion of the full amount of the debt reduction in the taxpayer's taxable income? The following example will help to explain the alternative solutions.

Example 3: Loan Restructuring

Developer D constructed Golden Acres Shopping Center on leased land at a cost of $10,000,000, borrowing $9,000,000 nonrecourse to finance the project. D then operated Golden Acres for 10 years, during which D claimed cost recovery deductions equal to $2,600,000, and distributed all cash flow. D did not pay any principal on the loan. After 10 years of operation, the Center had a tax basis of $7,400,000 and was subject to a nonrecourse debt of $9,000,000. Economic conditions caused some of D's tenants to fail, resulting in a decrease in the net operating income of the Center. At the point where the value of Golden Acres was $7,000,000, the lender agreed to reduce the amount due on the mortgage to the value of the Center, a reduction of $2,000,000.

As Revenue Ruling 92–99 concluded, under the law in effect from 1986 to 1993, the reduction in the principal of the nonrecourse loan resulted in COD income of $2,000,000, taxable as ordinary income, unless D qualified for one of the exceptions in IRC § 108(a). *See* Rev. Rul. 91-31, 1991-1 C.B. 19. The alternative would have adjusted the tax basis of the Center down from $7,400,000 to $5,400,000, with the result that annual cost recovery deductions would been reduced from $260,000 to $190,000, thus deferring the tax effect of the debt reduction over the remaining useful life of the property. This approach could be viewed as an adjustment of the purchase price of the property since the adjustment is to the original third party debt incurred to construct the Center. D just did not have to pay as much as he originally agreed to pay, but D did get to keep all of the cost recovery deductions taken in the preceding ten years. Cases like *Hirsch* and *Allen v. Courts*, referred to in the ruling, so held.

[c] Statutory Exceptions: The Purchase-Price Adjustment

IRC § 108(e)(5) provides that an adjustment in the debt incurred by the buyer of property to the seller will be treated as a price adjustment and not cancellation of indebtedness income. The price adjustment naturally requires corresponding adjustment to the basis of the property. This exception is limited, however, to an adjustment which results from direct negotiations between the *original* buyer and seller, and does not apply the reduction in third party debt, as discussed in the example. Because of the application of limitations imposed by the at-risk rules, which require the lender to be unrelated to the seller, this exception is generally not available in the real estate development context. Older judicial authority which implied a different conclusion was disapproved by the Internal Revenue Service in Rev. Rul. 92–99.

[d] Statutory Exceptions: "Qualified Real Property Business Indebtedness"

In 1986, Congress decided that permitting the "cancellation of indebtedness income" ("COD income") which resulted from the reduction of the taxpayer's repayment obligation in a business context to be deferred by basis adjustments was "too generous," and so repealed the exclusion (then IRC § 108(a)(3)) which had provided this result. Tax Reform Act of 1986, § 822(a). The IRS then took the position expressed in Revenue Ruling 92–99. Later, in light of the major problems stemming from the savings and loan crisis, Congress relented, and in 1993 reinstated a more restrictive version of the deferral rule. OBRA 1993 § 13150.

Under the law in effect now, the debt, incurred to construct or acquire an income producing real estate project, would be "qualified real property business indebtedness,"[30] and D could exclude $2,000,000 from income if he elected to reduce the basis of Golden Acres Shopping Center by $2,000,000. IRC

[30] IRC § 108(c)(3). To meet this definition, the indebtedness must be secured by depreciable real property "used in [the taxpayer's] trade or business" and must have been "incurred or assumed to acquire, construct, reconstruct or substantially improve" the property. IRC § 108(c)(4). It is not entirely clear when rental real estate is used in the owner's "trade or business" of operating the property, but significant management responsibilities would seem to qualify. *See* PLR 9426006 (July 1, 1994). This appears to be the case in the example.

§§ 108(a)(1)(D), (c). Making the election, therefore, would reduce the adjusted tax basis of the Center from $7,400,000 to $5,400,000.[31] Annual cost recovery deductions would be reduced from $260,000 to $190,000. You should recognize that this is equivalent to including an additional $70,000 in D's income over the remaining 29 year depreciation period, thus deferring the tax on the COD income, in just the same way that the purchase price reduction would have operated.

The election to reduce the basis of depreciable property requires that the taxpayer have basis in depreciable property which is subject to reduction, and the exclusion is limited to the amount of depreciable basis available for this purpose as of the beginning of the taxpayer's taxable year following the year in which the COD income is realized.[32] Basis reduction then follows the rules set out in IRC § 1017. Generally, the reduction must first be applied to the property which is security for the restructured debt,[33] and then to any other depreciable property owned by the taxpayer, but only if the adjustment actually reduces the taxpayer's depreciation deductions.[34] If the property is subsequently sold at a gain, the amount of the basis reduction is then treated as recapture income under IRC § 1245 and taxed as ordinary income.[35]

[e] Statutory Exceptions: Partnerships and LLCs

In real estate developments, the real estate assets will be held by an entity which is taxable as a conduit, as discussed earlier. The debts involved in these restructuring situations will be entity level debt, but, as you know by now, the partners or members of the entity will report the income and losses of the entity on their individual tax returns. The law is clear that whether a debt adjustment results in COD income will be determined at the entity level, and if the entity does realize COD Income, it will be allocated to the partners or members according to the governing agreement. IRC § 108 provides a number of exclusions from the taxation of COD income, but these exclusions are available to the partners or members in the entity and not to the entity itself. IRC § 108(d)(6). For example, COD income realized by a bankrupt taxpayer, or by a taxpayer who is insolvent, is excluded from the taxpayer's income. IRC §§ 108(a)(1) & (2). Once an LLC has

---

[31] The amount of COD income which may be excluded under § 108(c) is limited to the difference between the principal amount of the debt immediately before it is restructured and the fair market value of the property at that time. IRC § 108(c)(2)(A). Here, the principal amount of the debt before reduction is $9,000,000 and the value of the property at the time of the reduction is $7,000,000, so the full amount of the COD income may be excluded. Generally speaking, lenders would not agree to reduce the debt below the agreed fair market value of the security, that is, to create equity for the debtor, so this limitation reflects the usual workout situation.

[32] IRC § 108(c)(2)(B).

[33] Treas. Reg. § 1.1017-1(c)(1). This requirement means that the taxpayer must continue to own the qualifying property. Disposition of the property terminates the election.

[34] IRC § 1017(b)(3)(B). If an exclusion of COD income results because the debt was discharged in bankruptcy, or the debtor is insolvent, the statute requires the reduction of "tax attributes," such as net operating loss deductions and including the basis of depreciable property. IRC § 108(b). The taxpayer may elect under § 108(b)(5) to apply the attribute reduction rules to the basis of depreciable propery before other tax attributes. These reductions are applied *first* before any reduction under the election discussed in the text. This is a further complication not discussed here because, in the main, the investors with whom we are concerned in this book will not be bankrupt or insolvent. You should be aware, however, that bankruptcy or insolvency adds another layer of complexity to an already difficult process.

[35] IRC § 1017(d). This prevents the conversion of COD income deferred by making the election into capital gain on a subsequent disposition of the property.

realized COD income, therefore, even if the LLC is itself bankrupt or insolvent, the COD income must be allocated to the members of the LLC according to the Management Agreement, and each member's share of the COD income may then be excluded by that member only if he or she is bankrupt or to the extent that he or she is insolvent. We need to think about this rule in applying exclusions which are more likely to be available to investors in real estate projects.[36]

To see the problem and explain the solution, return to our example, but assume that Golden Acres Shopping Center is owned by Golden Acres, LLC. The members of Golden Acres, LLC are Developer, who owns 50%, and Elaine Investor ("E"), who owns the remaining 50%. The debt reduction has occurred in the debt of the LLC, which is secured by the Center. LLC will continue to own the Center, which is encumbered by the debt with the reduced principal amount, resulting in COD income of $2,000,000. The COD income is allocable under the Managing Agreement of the LLC, 50% to D and 50% to E. E does not directly own any depreciable real property, and E is solvent. The exclusion is available to D and E, if at all, and *not* the LLC.

Can E elect to reduce basis and thus exclude her share of the COD income? Here, the statute requires E's interest in the LLC (a tax partnership) to be treated as depreciable property to "the extent of [her] proportionate interest in the depreciable property held by [the LLC]." IRC § 1017(b)(3)(C).[37] E could elect, therefore, to reduce the basis of her interest in the LLC *provided*, the LLC agrees to an equivalent reduction in its basis in the Center property. The regulations permit E to decide whether or not to request the LLC to reduce the basis of its property with respect to her interest, and allow the LLC discretion whether to comply with E's request.[38] If E does not make this request, or the LLC refuses to comply, E may apparently still qualify for the exclusion if she owns other depreciable real estate with adequate basis to absorb the reductions on the first day of the following taxable year.[39] Under our assumed facts, this would not help E. However, if D joined E in making the request, the regulations require the LLC to agree to the adjustment since D and E together own more than 80% of the interests in the LLC.[40]

These rules are not simple and are not easy to understand, let alone apply. They are important, however, in a world where deleveraging is occurring, especially in real estate. This may not be the case for the Fox Valley Auto Care Center, which has a different problem; the construction loan cannot be refinanced in the current

---

[36] It may be that a member in an LLC which is in financial difficulty also faces bankruptcy or is insolvent, but remember that the use of an LLC to organize a real estate venture is to protect financially solvent investors from liability for the debts of a floundering project. In this situation, an unsuccessful project can produce COD income which results in income taxable to the members of the LLC which owns the project, and thus a tax cost without any distributed cash.

[37] The regulation requires the taxpayer to treat her share of COD income as attributable to "discharged indebtedness secured by [her] interest in the partnership." Treas. Reg. § 1.1017-1(g)(1).

[38] *Id.* § 1.1017-1(g)(2)(ii). The idea here is that the member desiring to use the exclusion and the LLC would be able to negotiate an appropriate solution. Because the inside basis adjustment would be attributable *solely* to the member requesting it, accounting for reduction may be expensive, so the LLC might require the member to bear part of the cost.

[39] E apparently could not purchase a depreciable asset for the purpose of qualifying for the exclusion and include that asset as depreciable real property for the exclusion, *see* IRC § 108(c)(2)(B), but interests in other real estate owning partnerships or LLCs may also qualify.

[40] Treas. Reg. § 1.1017-1(g)(2)(C).

market for the current principal amount even though the FVACC itself retains significant value.

[f] The "Cottage Savings" Regulations and the Election to Defer COD Income

While we are considering the effect of restructuring or "working out" the debt on over-leveraged property, it is necessary briefly to discuss another aspect of this problem: *when* might a borrower realize cancellation of indebtedness income? In a straightforward case, a reduction in the outstanding principal balance due on the loan is COD income. This is understandable, because the loan proceeds had been received by the borrower without having to pay income tax; repayment or cancellation required recognition of a tax effect. Suppose, however, that the adjustment is not quite so clear. That is, suppose the parties agree to adjust the terms of the debt without reducing the principal amount, and the result of deferring payment or adjusting interest is to reduce the present value of the loan. Is there COD income as a result? To see how this problem can occur, we need to digress briefly.

In the U.S. Supreme Court case of *Cottage Savings Ass'n v. Commissioner*,[41] the taxpayer made long term loans which it continued to own and service. In the late 1970's, however, market interest rates rose substantially, making it difficult for the taxpayer to continue to finance its investment in these loans, the market value of which had declined significantly.[42] This was before the days of "mark-to-market," so that as long as the taxpayer held the loans, and they were not in default, the lender was not required to write down the value of its loan portfolio, which would have caused it serious regulatory problems. However, the taxpayer did need tax relief, and the Federal Home Loan Bank Board stepped in to help. The FHLBB promulgated a rule permitting the taxpayer to exchange its loan portfolio for a comparable loan portfolio of another bank. The rule held that this exchange would not be a disposition requiring the taxpayer to recognize the losses on its portfolio for regulatory purposes. So, the taxpayer did as advised, and exchanged its interest in its portfolio for an interest in the portfolio of another bank which, in economic terms, was practically identical to the portfolio it had relinquished. But the debtors, mostly homeowners, were different persons and the security for these loans were different properties, so the taxpayer asserted that it had "realized" the economic loss for tax purposes, and claimed significant loss deductions.

The IRS rejected the taxpayer's deductions. The IRS argued that because the portfolios were substantially economic equivalents, the taxpayer had not realized any loss. But the Supreme Court thought differently. Because the identity of the obligors and the security for the loans were different, it concluded that the difference was material and a realization had occurred. So, the IRS lost. But, behind every cloud there is a silver lining, and the IRS exploited its loss by promulgating Treas. Reg. § 1.1001-3. Under this regulation, changes in the terms

---

[41] 499 U.S. 554 (1991).

[42] Suppose the taxpayer had a portfolio of loans which earned an average interest rate of 6.5%. If the market interest rate for such loans rose to 9%, the market value of this portfolio would decline by more than 20%. That is, in order to earn the equivalent amount of interest, the bank would need to lend approximately 20% less money.

of the debt may result in a "significant modification," which causes a deemed exchange of the original debt instrument for the modified debt instrument. The exchange would be taxable under IRC § 1001, and could result in the realization of COD income by the borrower.[43]

The regulation provides that if a modification of the original debt occurs, and if the modification is significant, the original debt is deemed to have been exchanged for a new debt having a value equal to its "issue price."[44] If stated interest on the modified debt exceeds the current federal rate, the issue price of the modified debt instrument will be the stated principal amount of the loan.[45] The regulatory definition of the circumstances in which these arcane rules apply provides some very specific rules as to what is a modification and when the modification is significant. The important thing to note is that COD income can result from relatively minor changes in the terms of the original instrument, including the lender's forbearance in enforcing the terms of the loan for more than two years.

So, why is this important for projects like the Fox Valley Auto Care Center? Consider how negotiations between Regent and First Mortgage Bank over a workout of the loan might have proceeded. Assume the term was extended at least once, or other variances in the original terms of the loan agreed to, including changes in the yield of more than 25 basis points[46] or a deferral in payment exceeding 50% of the original term of the loan.[47] It would not have been difficult to cross the threshold and cause a deemed exchange. This would be more important for a project the value of which had declined below the then balance due on the mortgage than for a project like the Fox Valley Auto Care Center, which seems to have retained value in excess of the principal due on the loan, but the fact that these rules are in effect and that it is relatively easy to cross the realization threshold means that attorneys engaged in work-out projects must keep them in mind.

Concern over the ease with which the application of the *Cottage Savings* regulation might be triggered may have provided the impetus for a short term relief provision permitting a deferral of COD income resulting from a deemed exchange.[48] This very complicated provision applies to debt for debt exchanges

---

[43] IRC § 108(e)(10). There would be tax consequences for the lender as well. The original lender might realize a loss, but the loss might be treated as original issue discount under the tax rules, and lender's deduction would then be deferred over the remaining term of the loan.

[44] *Id.* "Issue price" is a technical term defined in IRC § 1274, and for our purposes usually means the stated redemption price at maturity, that is, the principal due at maturity. § 1273(b)(4). If the debt instrument is "regularly traded on an established market," then the issue price of the new (modified) debt is the value of the old (unmodified) debt. § 1273(b)(3). Do these rules have any application here? "Regularly traded" is broadly defined; one should think about securitized debt, which has been a common practice in the recent past.

[45] The "applicable federal rate" is determined monthly by the IRS from interest on government obligations. As this is being written, these interest rates are very low. For April, 2009, the long term federal rate (maturity of 9 years or more) is 3.69%, so it would be very unusual to find a debt interest carrying an interest rate less than the federal rate. For maturities of less than 9 years (such as the loan from First Mortgage Bank to Fox Valley Auto Care Center, LLC), the federal rate would have been 2.14%.

[46] Treas. Reg. § 1.1001-3(e)(2).

[47] Treas. Reg. 1.1001-3(e)(3)(ii).

[48] IRC § 108(i), added by American Recovery and Reinvestment Act of 2009 ("ARRA"), Pub. L. No. 111-5, § 1231(a).

("releveraging") which occur in 2009 and 2010.[49] Basically, it authorizes the partnership (the LLC in our example) to elect to defer COD income realized in a covered transaction with ratable inclusion of that income over five taxable years beginning in 2014, unless "acceleration" of the inclusion occurs sooner. Deferred COD income is allocated to members on the day immediately preceding the exchange, or deemed exchange, in which the COD income was realized. Interest deductions and basis adjustments resulting from the transaction are also deferred until the COD income is included on the members' tax returns. This provisions now represents short term relief, but we mention it here because there is the possibility that the availability of this type of relief may be extended.

[g] Other Tax Deferral Mechanisms

Disposition of highly leveraged real estate projects will produce "phantom gain," and investors will then incur tax liability without having received any cash with which to pay the tax. In casting about for strategies to postpone the day of tax reckoning, many tax savvy investors have reinvested sales proceeds in another real estate project under the nonrecognition rules provided by IRC § 1031. Under this provision, gain or loss realized in an exchange of properties of "like kind" will not be recognized, except, in the case of realized gain, to the extent the taxpayer receives nonqualifying property ("boot"), usually cash.[50] In a qualifying exchange, the basis of the replacement property will be equal to the basis of the exchanged property ("substituted basis"), adjusted for any taxable gain realized because of the receipt of boot or for additional consideration paid by the taxpayer. Manipulation of basis preserves the unrecognized gain in the replacement property.

Although the statute calls for an "exchange," this requirement has been loosely interpreted to permit multi-party transactions which also qualify. And indeed, after *Starker v. United States*, 602 F.2d 1341 (9th Cir. 1979), the replacement property need not have even been identified when the original property is sold. A multi-party exchange is now done under statutory rules Congress enacted to authorize and limit so-called *Starker* transactions. *See* IRC § 1031(a)(3). The transaction is done through a "qualified intermediary," often a title insurance company, which receives the proceeds from and deeds to the properties involved, and distributes the deeds and proceeds according to a previously negotiated set of escrow instructions. So, if the Fox Valley Auto Care Center LLC had agreed to sell the FVACC in year four, for example, it could have contracted with a qualified intermediary to hold the funds, use them to acquire another real estate project, and distribute that asset to the LLC in "exchange." The replacement would have to have been identified within 45 days of the sale of FVACC, and the replacement property acquired within 180 days. As long as the replacement property has a cost at least equal to the sales price of the FVACC, and the amount of debt incurred on the replacement property is not less the amount of debt on the Center at the time of its sale, this technique will work.

---

[49] *See* Monte A. Jackel, Jeffrey W. Maddrey & Robert J. Crnkovich, *New COD/AHYDO Legislation: Needed Relief Adds Complexity*, 123 Tax Notes 198 (2009).

[50] IRC § 1031(b). For highly leveraged property, the extent to which debt to which the property is subject exceeds debt to which the replacement property is subject is treated as the receipt of cash by the taxpayer. Reg. § 1.1031(d)-2 (including very helpful examples).

Section 1031 transactions have become popular, and the practice much refined. Note an important factor, however: the same taxpayer that sold the original property, in this case the Fox Valley Auto Care Center LLC, must be the taxpayer that makes the replacement under section 1031. Not all LLC members may agree that reinvestment is the best strategy, and the practice has evolved to the point where it may be possible for individual members to invest in a replacement fund to achieve a satisfactory tax deferred result.

Chapter 4

CHOICE OF ENTITY CONSIDERATIONS

§ 4.01 FACTORS AFFECTING THE CHOICE OF ENTITY

At the outset, Regent had to choose the entity that would own the Fox Valley Auto Care Center and provide the financial structure necessary to support the Auto Care Center's capital requirements. This entity would need to be flexible enough to permit investors to hold the capital interests which they had negotiated and to participate in the expected returns from the Auto Care Center. Income tax treatment of profits and losses, and cash distributions, are central issues. For tax purposes, three elements must be present: (1) There must be a single layer of tax (*i.e.*, the taxable return from the Center must be subject to federal and state income tax only once). If these returns are taxed both to the entity and then a second time, on distribution, to the investor, the marginal tax rate becomes sufficiently high to eliminate the competitive advantage for real estate investing. (2) The tax benefits associated with real estate investing must be made available to investors. The principal tax benefit is that provided by tax leverage. For this to work, the benefit of depreciation deductions must be allocable in some way to the investors, including the allowance of tax deductions for tax losses (deductions exceed income) and the ability to distribute refinancing proceeds without immediate tax consequences. (3) There must be flexibility in allocating the tax consequences of the cash distributions for which investors have negotiated.[1] These elements may vary, and the entity will need to have enough flexibility to permit adjustment of the tax effect for individual investors to reflect this variation.

When Regent developed the Fox Valley Auto Care Center, the entity of choice was the limited partnership: Regent, a Subchapter S corporation, acted as the General Partner and the investors were Limited Partners. Since the late 1980s, however, the entity of choice has become the limited liability company, or "LLC." As part of our goal to bring you current law and current development forms, we have converted the Fox Valley Auto Care Center Limited Partnership into the Fox Valley Auto Care Center, LLC. This complicates things, as you soon will see, but it better prepares you for how today's real estate lawyers and real estate developers are operating.

---

[1] While there are important business considerations in selecting the form of the entity which will own and manage the project, the most significant considerations are the tax consequences to the investors. In fact, the choice of entity for real estate investments is almost completely tax driven. This relates to the *tax system* under which the entity will be operated, and that permits, as we shall explain, a choice among several types of entities, each of which is a tax conduit. Principally, the choice will be between a limited liability company (as assumed in the earlier chapters of this book) and a limited partnership. There are differences between these two entities, which we will explain after discussing the basic choices and why these choices are tax driven.

[1] Limited Liability: Corporate Attributes

Investors will not invest unless their exposure to loss is limited to the amount invested ("limited liability"). Limited liability is the classic attribute of corporate stock. For most investors, the corporation might seem to be an ideal way to structure the investment: shareholders are not personally liable for the debts of the firm, beyond the amount of capital they may have contributed to the firm; shares of stock are easily transferred; the corporation's capital structure can be organized into classes of stock and various kinds of debt to reflect the differing interests of investors and developers; the corporation's business is centrally managed; and the existence of the entity will not be affected by anything that might happen to a shareholder. While this is true for financial or business purposes, the *tax* characteristics of a corporation (a "regular corporation" or a "C" corporation) disqualify the corporation as an appropriate form of entity for real estate investing. The reason for this conclusion is illustrated next.

[a] The Corporate Tax

Assume that Regent is organized as a corporation and, contrary to the actual situation, has not elected to be taxed under Subchapter S of the Internal Revenue Code.[2] This form of organization is not satisfactory for tax purposes for the following reason: a corporation is a separate taxpayer, and as such, is subject to a separate, corporate level tax on its taxable income. I.R.C. § 11. The corporation can retain its income, and pay that tax, which may or may not be less than the tax imposed on income taxed to an individual.[3] If the corporation distributes its income (which may, in general, approximate "earnings and profits") to its shareholders, the distributions are taxable to the shareholders as dividends[4] and are not deductible by the corporation from its income.

Example: Tax Effect of Incorporation

Assume that U, an individual, purchased a building for $10,000,000. The building produces $1,000,000 in net rents (net of all other cash expenses) and can be depreciated over a 39 year period (rate = 2.56%). Assume that U's marginal income tax rate is 35%.[5] This year, U will be able to deduct $256,000 in depreciation, and will pay tax of $260,000. U's net cash receipt is $740,000. The average tax rate on U's income from the building is:

---

[2] I.R.C. §§ 1361–1379.

[3] The marginal tax rate for very large corporations is 35%. *See* I.R.C. § 11(b)(1)(D). For corporations with taxable income between $75,000 and $10,000,000, the marginal rate is 34%. Taxable income less than $75,000 is taxed at lower rates. The maximum marginal rate for individuals is 35%, I.R.C. § 1, or actually a little more for taxpayers who itemize deductions. *See* I.R.C. § 68(a). At the maximum rates, therefore, corporate business income which is retained in the business may actually be subject to tax at lower marginal rates than if the enterprise were organized as a partnership or proprietorship.

[4] I.R.C. § 316(a).

[5] The highest marginal income tax rate for individuals at the time this is being written. The Obama Administration proposes to increase this marginal rate to the rate that applied prior to the "Bush tax cuts," so this rate may be increased. A similar caveat is necessary for the corporate tax rates used in this example, as corporate tax rates may also be changed. The essential point made by the example, however, is not contradicted by variations in the applicable income tax rates.

$$\frac{(\$1,000,000 - \$740,000)}{\$1,000,000} = 26\%$$

Now assume that V Corp., U's wholly owned corporation, purchased the building for $10,000,000. Assume that V Corp.'s marginal tax rate is 34% (*see* I.R.C. § 11(b)(1)(C)). V Corp. will pay income tax of $253,000 [($1,000,000 – $256,000 = $744,000) × .34 = $253,000]. After payment of tax, V Corp. will have current earnings and profits of $497,000 (current earnings and profits are computed by subtracting the tax paid, $744,000 – $253,000). (Note that a corporation must apply a useful life of 40 years in computing depreciation for purposes of determining its earnings and profits. I.R.C. §§ 312(k)(3)(A); 168(g)(2)(C). Therefore, in determining the owner's taxable dividend the equation is: $1,000,000 – $250,000 (40 year depreciation, 2.5%) – $253,000 (tax paid by the corporation) = $497,000, the owner's taxable dividend.).

V Corp. intends to distribute all after tax cash, $747,000, to its sole shareholder U. Based on current earnings and profits, the distribution would be taxed as a dividend to U of $497,000, on which U would then pay tax at tax rate on dividends of 15%,[6] or $75.000. Result: U has received $672,000 cash after tax (an average tax rate of about 32.7%, as compared to an average tax rate of 26% on rental income received by U directly). The nondividend portion of this distribution is a return of capital, and will reduce the basis for the U's stock.[7] If the amount of the nondividend distribution exceeds the shareholder's adjusted basis, the excess will attract additional income tax, usually at capital gains rates.[8]

The example illustrates the effect of the corporate level tax on cash flow distributed from a real estate project operated by a corporation. In this illustration, use of a corporate entity results in at least a 25% increase in the effective tax rate on cash distributions, and that is under the most favorable circumstances.[9] This is the effect of the "classical" corporate tax structure, of which the American income tax is the most fully developed example in the world today. So, because the essence of the game in the real estate business is distribution of tax-sheltered cash to investors, the classical corporate tax structure will inevitably produce too much tax. However, the use of an entity to protect the developer from potential liability in the operation of the project is essential. In addition, the developer will ask Investors to provide capital to the project in return for a share of the equity, and for them, limited liability is no less essential. The task is to create an entity which *preserves* the tax benefits of investing in real estate but provides the equity participants with

---

6 The maximum tax rate on dividends is at the time of this writing 15%, I.R.C. § 1(h)(11)(A) (qualified dividends included in "net capital gain"). This rate terminates at the end of 2010, at which time, unless Congress acts sooner, dividends would be included in ordinary taxable income subject to U's marginal tax rate, as proposed by the Obama Administration.

7 I.R.C. § 301(c)(2).

8 If V Corp. in the illustration had accumulated earnings and profits from past years, or additional current earnings and profits from other transactions, the distribution would be taxed as a dividend. The tax (at 15%) would then be $112,000 and the effective tax rate, 36.5%.

9 As you can see, this conclusion is sensitive to the tax treatment of corporate dividends, which, at this time, is unsettled.

the protection against liability to limit their exposure to loss to the amount of their investment.[10]

[b] Special Corporate Tax Elections

It is possible to use a corporation that will result in a single layer of tax on distributed cash flow by electing a passthrough status. There are two such elections available to real estate projects, although neither will work for the type of real estate project represented by the Fox Valley Auto Care Center. These are explained next.

[i] Subchapter S

A corporation and its shareholders may elect to be taxed under Subchapter S of the Internal Revenue Code (§§ 1361–1379). The effect of this election is to have corporate income, loss and certain other items with favorable tax characteristics allocated and taxed to its stockholders, *pro rata*, thus achieving the single layer of tax which is necessary for real estate investing. An S election, while useful, for example, when a corporation serves as the general partner in a limited partnership, has drawbacks that limit its use as the vehicle for the project itself. To make the election, the corporation must meet some restrictive definitional requirements (I.R.C. § 1361). In particular, the corporation may have only one class of stock. In the simpler real estate ventures, where the project economics are shared *pro rata* throughout the life of the enterprise, this may not be a serious problem, but when there are investors with different interests and different rights to cash flow distributions, the one class of stock requirement would effectively preclude use of Subchapter S.

Moreover, the rules governing the allocation of the S corporation's tax items among its shareholders do not provide enough flexibility, even in relatively straightforward real estate projects. Even though specific tax items retain their tax characteristics when allocated to shareholders and reported on their income tax returns, all of them must be allocated in proportion to the number of shares owned by each shareholder on each day of the year. I.R.C. § 1366. When corporate income or deduction is allocated to a shareholder, the shareholder's tax basis for her stock is adjusted to reflect that tax effect. I.R.C. § 1367. Later, when cash flow is distributed to the shareholder, the cash distributed is, in general, treated as a return of the shareholder's investment, which reduces the tax basis in the shareholder's stock. I.R.C. § 1368. In this way, income is taxed once, to the shareholder, when received by the corporation, and not a second time when distributed. However, unlike a partnership, the corporation remains a separate taxable entity, and the *corporation's* tax basis for its assets is not reflected in the outside basis of the *stockholder's stock*. Cash distributions, therefore, which are made from income sheltered by depreciation deductions or directly from the proceeds of borrowing, may exceed outside basis and will then, to that extent, be taxable on receipt by the shareholder. This means that the leverage effects so

---

[10] Under Limited Liability Company statutes, an LLC, all of the interests in which are owned by one member, is "disregarded." For an individual, the "disregarded entity" is taxed as a sole proprietorship, that is, as if the entity did not exist and its property were owned by the individual. These rules are discussed later in this chapter. Note that entity classification for tax purposes has no effect on state law, so that an individual may create a single member LLC to own a real estate project, be taxed as if that individual owned the project directly, and yet be protected from liability for the debts of the entity.

important to the taxation of real estate investments are not available to the shareholders of an S corporation.[11]

Regent Real Estate Development Corp., which is the Manager in the Fox Valley Auto Care Center, LLC, is an S Corporation, but it is an operating entity which will have no need to use tax leverage. Income or deductions allocated to it will, in turn, be reallocated to and among the corporate general partner's stockholders.[12]

[ii] Real Estate Investment Trusts ("REITs")

There are a variety of passthrough entities, each with its own definitional rules and passthrough techniques, of which the S Corporation is only one.[13] Real Estate Investment Trusts (REITs) are another. A REIT is an entity defined solely in the tax law. I.R.C. §§ 856–859. It is, in general, a state law corporation, which would otherwise be taxed for federal income tax purposes as a corporation. To qualify, the REIT must have its capital invested primarily in real estate assets, and the ownership of its stock must be spread among a relatively large group of stockholders. A qualifying corporation achieves the single layer of tax at the corporate level by deducting the dividends it pays to its shareholders,[14] who then are taxable on the dividends they have received.[15] Like mutual funds, REITs may allocate capital gain among its shareholders but this is the only type of tax item which retains its tax character when allocated to shareholders. A qualifying REIT must distribute 90% of its taxable income to be entitled to any dividends paid deductions, a requirement which can hamper the ability of REITs to raise capital.[16]

---

[11] A corporate electing to be taxed under Subchapter S remains a corporation for all purposes of the income tax *except* as provided in Subchapter S. This may have significance if the corporation owns appreciated assets, for example, which are distributed to its shareholders, as this would trigger gain at the corporate level. I.R.C. § 311(b)(1). In addition, an electing Subchapter S corporation may have corporate earnings and profits, which could, under certain circumstances, cause cash distributions to be taxed as dividends. These rules can make use of an S election deceptively complicated.

[12] The difference between a limited partnership and an LLC is that a limited partnership must have a general partner which is liable for the debts of the partnership. Use of an electing Subchapter S corporation as the general partner in a limited partnership, therefore, is useful in protecting the principals who own the general partner from liability for the debts of the partnership, and yet permits the income, and the cash flow, to be realized by them with tax imposed only at the individual shareholder level.

[13] There are other entities which perform the same function as the REIT, which is taxed in the same manner as a Regulated Investment Company ("RIC"). These include Real Estate Mortgage Investment Companies ("REMICs") and Financial Asset Securitization Investment Trusts ("FASITs"). These entities are taxed, as is a REIT, by allowing the entity to deduct distributions of taxable income to its shareholders. These entities have been useful in the securitization of investments in mortgages and other financial assets.

[14] I.R.C. §§ 857(b)(2)(B); 561(a)(1).

[15] Subject to limited exceptions, taxable dividends paid from a REIT are not "qualified dividends" which would be included in net capital gain under I.R.C. § 1(h). I.R.C. § 857(c)(2)(B).

[16] In the financial difficulties beginning in 2008, REITs experienced restricted cash flows which hampered the ability of publicly traded REITs to make qualifying distributions with respect to their stock. The IRS then issued Rev. Proc. 2008-68, 2008-52 IRB 1373, which permitted a REIT to declare a dividend payable in its own stock or in cash, at the option of the shareholder, but subject to a cap of at least 10% on the maximum amount of cash which the REIT would be required to distribute. A dividend issued in this manner would be treated as a distribution of property equal to the cash into which distributable shares were nominally convertible, and would qualify as a taxable (and deductible) REIT distribution for qualification purposes. This ruling permitted a REIT, in 2009 at least, to avoid

The REIT's taxable income, after taking into account depreciation deductions, is usually less than its cash flow, which is a typical feature of real estate investing. The REIT remains a taxable corporation, and suffers from the same problem that makes Subchapter S corporations a poor choice as an entity to own and operate real estate projects. In the first place, corporate-level losses are not passed through to shareholders; the only tax benefit for the REIT is the dividend paid deduction, and it must have taxable income for the deduction to work. Second, corporate level debt will not be reflected in the tax basis of its shareholders. High leverage, therefore, may produce sheltered cash flow, but the distribution of that cash flow will be an offset to basis, which may not be sufficient to absorb it. Some REITs are publicly held entities, and the value of the stock of a publicly traded REIT on the capital markets will be determined by its dividend rate and not by the real estate market value of its real estate assets. This confluence of rules and practice have created a useful and valuable niche for REITs, but basically disqualifies them from use by the smaller enterprises with a few private investors that the Auto Care Center represents.

[2] Partnerships and Corporate Attributes

The entity of choice for real estate projects is a conduit entity which is taxed under the partnership tax rules of the Internal Revenue Code (a "tax partnership"), such as a limited liability company. This kind of entity has more flexibility built into it than does the S Corporation, since its governing document is usually a contract which can be drafted to achieve the many different purposes which real estate entities may be called upon to serve.[17] The stated purpose of the tax rules is to require the tax consequences to follow the economics, although in deals with any degree of complexity, the rules are so complicated and abstract that how this purpose is achieved may be difficult to understand. Before exploring what these entities are and how their tax status is determined, it is important to understand what the partnership tax rules accomplish and why that is so important to real estate investing. These elements are explored here in relation to the advantages which income tax rules provide for real estate investments.

[a] Tax Leverage

The central element in the tax rules applicable to real estate projects is the ability to borrow money without personal liability and use the borrowed funds to create tax basis for depreciation purposes. Further, the essence of the real estate tax advantage is the ability to claim depreciation deductions before the debt is repaid, often long before repayment. When this was analyzed in Chapter 3, capital was invested directly into the Fox Valley Auto Care Center project by Regent and the investors, and it was assumed that the same tax consequences would be available to members in the limited liability company to which the project had been

---

disqualification for failing to make qualifying distributions of cash equal to at least 90% of its taxable income.

[17] Limited Liability Companies and Limited Partnerships are defined by state statutes, which usually permit the controlling agreement to vary substantive provisions of the statute, excepting those provisions which generally define the legal duties of members or partners to the entity and therefore to other members or partners. *See, e.g.*, 805 Ill. Comp. Stat. 180/15-5 (2009). A statute like that enacted in Illinois provides a set of "default" rules which apply unless the operating agreement provides otherwise, and these rules are typically very basic.

transferred. The transition of these concepts from direct ownership to the ownership of interests in a tax partnership is explained next.

When the developer borrows money to finance the construction or acquisition of a real estate asset, as the owner of the asset, he will be allowed to include the loan proceeds in his tax basis for the property, and then to claim depreciation deductions based on the overall tax basis, rather than depreciation being limited solely to his equity in the project. *See* Section 3.05 in Chapter 3. Income or gain used to repay the loan will be taxed to the borrower. *Commissioner v. Tufts*, 461 U.S. 300 (1983), also discussed in Section 3.05[2], *supra*. When the project has been transferred to a limited liability company, however, the LLC is the borrower and the indebtedness becomes part of the LLC's tax basis. At this point, there are *two separate tax bases* to consider: first, the entity's tax basis, which will be used to generate the tax deductions through depreciation ("inside basis"); second, the members' aggregate tax bases for their partnership interests ("outside basis").

Because the advantage from tax leverage generally follows the basis, the extent to which the *investors in the entity* can include the LLC's indebtedness in the bases for their partnership interests, *as if* they owned the project directly, will be of central importance. There are several reasons for this. First, the project may generate tax losses when depreciation deductions exceed net operating income plus the amount of principal paid on the mortgage.[18] Remember that depreciation deductions are not cash expenditures,[19] so these tax losses are deductions which can be allocated to members of the LLC and deductible on their personal returns even though the project has positive cash flow. In order to take these deductions, however, the member to whom these deductions are allocated must have sufficient outside basis to absorb the deductions, which, when claimed by the member, reduce his tax basis. Deductible losses which have been allocated to the member in excess of his outside basis are not immediately deductible by him but instead are deferred until his basis has been increased enough to claim them. I.R.C. § 704(d). To be sure, the member's capital contributions to the LLC will increase the tax basis for his interest, I.R.C. § 723, but in highly leveraged projects a member's actual capital contributions may, relatively speaking, be only a small percentage of the value of the project. Without the additional tax basis attributable to the member's share of the LLC's debt, these deductions will be deferred or even lost.[20]

---

[18] Net operating income = the "free and clear," which is project cash flow in excess of cash expenditures. *See* text at Chapter 2, note 9. Expenditures include payments which are not deductible for tax purposes. Most important, payments of principal on the mortgage are not deductible. Additions to reserves for capital improvements or future expenditures are not deductible either, so these types of payments would be included in income for purposes of this analysis.

[19] *See* text at Chapter 2, notes 17–18.

[20] The "at-risk" rule is important at this point. A member is not "at risk" with respect to money borrowed by the LLC unless that member has personal liability to repay the loan. *See* text at notes 42–43, *infra*. The statute provides an exception for "qualified nonrecourse financing" in a real estate activity. I.R.C. § 465(b)(6). Under the regulations, a recourse loan to an LLC for which no member has personal liability will be treated as "qualified nonrecourse financing" if the predominant activity of the LLC is holding real estate. Treas. Reg. § 1.465-27; *see* Chapter 3, note 4, *supra*. The recourse liability of the LLC will be ignored. Such a liability will be allocated among the members of the LLC for at risk purposes according to the partnership tax rules. I.R.C. § 465(b)(6)(C). Note that the at risk amount is reduced by cash distributions to the member from the partnership, Prop. Treas. Reg. § 1.465-22(b), and if the amount at risk for a member is reduced below zero, a "recapture" (inclusion of the amount by which the member's at risk amount is less than zero in ordinary income) can result. I.R.C. § 465(e).

Second, the primary objective in real estate investing is distribution of cash flow. In the LLC taxed as a partnership, all *tax* items are allocated to members for tax purposes. The actual cash flow is not itself, at least not at the entity level, allocated to members. And when made, cash distributions are not separately taxed as if they were, for example, dividends, but they do offset the distributee member's outside basis. Distributions in excess of basis produce taxable gain to the member. I.R.C. § 732.[21] This gain is *in addition to* the taxable income of the LLC, and is to be avoided at all costs. If entity level indebtedness were *not* included in the member's outside basis, avoidance of tax on distributions in the typical leveraged real estate deal would be very difficult.[22]

Note that when entity-level debt is included in the member's outside basis and that basis is an offset for tax purposes to cash distributions, the LLC may borrow additional funds which in turn will increase the outside basis of its members;[23] the increased outside basis will then offset subsequently distributed loan proceeds which will not be taxed to the distributee members. In the typical real estate project which has been refinanced, distribution of loan proceeds from the entity on a refinancing causes debt overhang which ultimately will be taxed to the members who received the distributions.[24]

The rules under which these calculations are made are almost as complicated as the tax allocation rules, which may appear to the real estate lawyer (and to many real estate developers) to inflict serious damage to brain functions.[25] Indeed, restrictions on the deductibility of passive losses and limitations on the amount of depreciation which can be claimed, particularly for commercial projects, may make this basis manipulation seem relatively unimportant, yet in long term real estate projects, which have been refinanced over and over again, with the excess proceeds distributed to investors at each refinancing, the lack of investor level tax basis is more than a nuisance; it defeats the entire purpose of the investment.

---

21 The gain is taxed as if it resulted from the sale or exchange of the member's interest (viz., in the same manner as a return of capital). I.R.C. § 741. Generally, the gain will be taxed as capital gain, but there are complicated rules under which unrealized gain or income of the partnership may be allocated to distributee members and affect the character of the gain in their hands.

22 Recall that in *Commissioner v. Tufts*, 461 U.S. 300 (1983), *supra* § 3.05[2], the partners contributed relatively small amounts of cash but were allocated depreciation deductions several times greater. To be able to claim these deductions, the partners needed to have enough outside basis to absorb them. That basis was supplied by the nonrecourse debt to which the project in that case was subject.

23 At this point, it is enough to understand that the basis increase occurs. The exact mechanism by which this is accomplished is explained later in this chapter.

24 *See supra* § 3.05[3][d].

25 One might well ask why the tax rules need to be so complicated. Consider, however, the objectives of the tax provisions as we describe them here: flexibility in allocating tax advantages and concomitant economic incidents among the members of the entity, year-by-year, taking into account variation over time in the interests of the members; and all the while preserving the single layer of tax required for successful real estate investing which permits the distribution of cash without additional tax cost. Add to these objectives the sophistication of modern real estate practice, and you can see the source of the complexity. Simplification would compromise these objectives. While many in the tax bar observe that the partnership tax rules are an invitation to manipulation and thus tax avoidance, the political support for Subchapter K of the Tax Code seems secure, much of it coming from the real estate industry.

[b] Allocations of Tax Quantities

The partnership tax rules are more valuable to the real estate developer than would be the use of an electing S corporation because of the flexibility these rules provide for allocating partnership tax attributes among partners. Recall that tax character of items of income and deduction for an S corporation are allocated *pro rata* among its shareholders. Allocation of one category of income or loss to one investor, and a different category to another investor, or different categories in different percentages, is not permitted. Moreover, cash distributions, except for payments of interest or principal with respect to qualifying debt ("straight debt") must be distributed, in the main, as dividends. Because a qualifying S corporation may have only one class of stock, the corporate capital structure cannot be adjusted to accommodate different investment interests.[26] Partnerships and limited liability companies, on the other hand, are defined by contract, with the governing statutes generally providing a series of default rules that can be changed in the governing agreement. The economic incidence of cash flows, types of income, categories of loss deductions, refinancing proceeds, and ultimately liquidation distributions can be varied among members of the entity as they may agree. And the tax characteristics of these various items are required to follow their apparent economic incidence, or, to state this point a bit differently, the transaction can be designed so that the *economics* of the deal follow the *desired tax allocations*.[27]

Think of a partnership structure as a black box. Rent, refinancing proceeds, sales proceeds and other economic inputs are rearranged, allocated and distributed to investors at the other end. The genius of the whole arrangement is the way it is possible to make the tax rules work to help make the economic deal. As wonderful as this sounds, any set of rules this flexible is bound to be complex. And the partnership "economic effect" regulations under which this is accomplished are among the most complex and abstract regulations ever promulgated. *See* I.R.C. § 704(b); Treas. Reg. §§ 1.704-1(b) ("economic effect" regulations); 1.704-2 (allocation of "nonrecourse deductions"). If you are the lawyer negotiating a complex economic arrangement in a privately financed real estate deal (publicly financed deals are a whole different order, to which an understanding of the role played by REITs is essential), and if you are not steeped in the refinements of the economic effect regulations, you will certainly require the services of a partnership tax lawyer.

[3] Electing Partnership Tax Status

These two reasons are good enough to justify all the attention focused on entities taxed as partnerships. It is vitally important to have the entity which owns and operates the real estate venture qualify to be taxed as a partnership. Before 1995, large limited partnerships, formed under the Uniform Limited Partnership

---

[26] *See* I.R.C. § 1361(b)(1)(D), Reg. § 1.1361-1(*l*)(1) (identical rights to distribution and liquidation proceeds).

[27] This is one of the main criticisms of the partnership allocation rules, that they encourage allocations solely for tax purposes, which do not have much economic substance. Remember the nonrecourse character of much of partnership operation. In actual experience, the rules under which this is done are so complicated that partnership tax lawyers despair of explaining them to clients. As a result, most real estate transactions, where a lot of this maneuvering would be relevant, are structured to make allocations in a straight *pro rata* manner.

Act, and its later revisions, however, appeared closely to resemble corporations. Indeed, in regulations under I.R.C. § 7701(a)(3), the so-called "Kintner regulations," tax partnerships were differentiated from corporations (or more accurately, "associations") by a series of arbitrary and formalistic tests, which, if observed, made partnership tax status practically unavoidable.

From today's vantage point, that would have seemed nonsensical, given the prominent role that modern partnerships have played in the tax shelter industry, but the bias in the old definitional rules was intentional. In the late 1950s, when the Kintner regulations were issued, the Treasury Department was attempting to limit the ability of professionals to incorporate their practices in order to use the qualified employee benefit plan rules to provide themselves with tax sheltered retirement funds. Since the professionals in question would be organized into service partnerships, and partners were not "employees" as required by the qualified employee benefit plan rules, the Treasury's objective was to recharacterize professional "associations" as partnerships. Almost immediately, however, every state legislature responded by enacting professional incorporation laws, so Treasury lost that war. Later, when the immense value of these regulations to formally structured tax shelter arrangements became clear, efforts by the Treasury Department to backtrack and revise the regulations were defeated politically. There is a long and interesting history to this, particularly in the fight by the Treasury to protect the corporate tax base from organizing into large, publicly held, partnerships. For your purposes, the history is now irrelevant, although some limited liability company statutes still have provisions specifically intended to meet the requirements of the old definitional rules.

Many commentators thought that, in applying the formalistic Kintner rules, the lack of "limited liability" was essential to partnership status. The primary attribute of the corporation is often said to be the limited liability of its stockholders to the amount invested. In contrast, the general partner in a limited partnership is personally liable for the debts of the partnership to outsiders, although the general partner was often itself a corporation. The Kintner regulations, however, treated limited liability as just another factor, without giving it a more prominent significance than the three other factors: centralized management, indefinite continuity of life, and free transferability of interests. The regulations provided that the corporate attribute of limited liability would be lacking for most limited partnerships that had a real general partner with full, unlimited liability for all partnership debts, and the general partner had significant net worth. This was a strange concept in itself because liability in real estate investments, at least, was attenuated through the medium of nonrecourse indebtedness and insurance, so it was not clear for what the general partner was supposed to be liable.

In the 1980s, however, Wyoming pressed for the IRS to characterize an entity formed under its statute as a "limited liability company" ("LLC"), a relatively old organizational concept, particularly in Europe, as a tax "partnership," and, to some surprise, the IRS responded with a favorable ruling. Rev. Rul. 88-76, 1988-2 C.B. 360. Within a very short time, practically every state legislature had enacted a statute authorizing the formation of a limited liability company. By definition, these statutes provided that no member of a limited liability company would be held liable for the LLC's debts.[28] The IRS soon had issued many rulings conferring

[28] *See* 805 Ill. Comp. Stat. 180/10-10 (2009).

partnership tax status on the limited liability company statutes of individual states. *See, e.g.*, Rev. Rul. 93-3, 1993-1 C.B. 209 (Virginia); Rev. Rul. 93-49, 1993-2 C.B. 308 (Illinois).

In 1996, the Treasury concluded that insisting that partnership tax entities continue to meet the artificial requirements of the old regulations was futile, probably because, since it was unable to change the entity classification rule for political reasons, it was evident that high-priced lawyers had better things to do than write the stilted, stylized (expensive) opinion letters called for by the Kintner regulations. Hereafter, unless the state statute under which the entity is organized actually states that the entity formed under its provisions is a "corporation," partnership tax status is not only elective, but also is the default choice.

[4] The Regulation

SIMPLIFICATION OF ENTITY CLASSIFICATION RULES

T.D.8697
61 FR 66584
Wednesday, December 18, 1996

BACKGROUND

On April 3, 1995, 1995-1 C.B. 297, Notice 95-14), relating to classification of business organizations under section 7701 of the Code, was published in the Internal Revenue Bulletin. A notice of public hearing was published in the Federal Register on May 10, 1995 (60 FR 24813). Written comments were received and a public hearing was held on July 20, 1995.

On May 13, 1996, the IRS and Treasury issued a notice of proposed rulemaking (61 FR 21989 [PS-43-95, 1996-24 I.R.B. 20]) under section 7701. The regulations proposed to replace the existing regulations for classifying certain business organizations with an elective regime. Comments responding to the notice were received, and a public hearing was held on August 21, 1996. After considering the comments that were received in response to the notice of proposed rulemaking and the statements made at the public hearing, the proposed regulations are adopted as revised by this Treasury decision. The revisions are discussed below.

EXPLANATION OF PROVISIONS

Section 7701(a)(2) of the Code defines a partnership to include a syndicate, group, pool, joint venture, or other unincorporated organization, through or by means of which any business, financial operation, or venture is carried on, and that is not a trust or estate or a corporation. Section 7701(a)(3) defines a corporation to include associations, joint-stock companies, and insurance companies.

The existing regulations for classifying business organizations as associations (which are taxable as corporations under section 7701(a)(3)) or as partnerships under section 7701(a)(2) are based on the historical differences under local law between partnerships and corporations. Treasury and the IRS believe that those rules have become increasingly formalistic. This document replaces those rules with a much simpler approach that generally is elective. . . .

A. Summary of the Regulations

Section 301.7701-1 provides an overview of the rules applicable in determining an organization's classification for federal tax purposes. The first step in the classification process is to determine whether there is a separate entity for federal tax purposes. . . . Whether an organization is treated as an entity for federal tax purposes is a matter of federal tax law, and does not affect the rights and obligations of its owners under local law. For example, if a domestic limited liability company with a single individual owner is disregarded as an entity separate from its owner under § 301.7701-3, its individual owner is subject to federal income tax as if the LLC's business was operated as a sole proprietorship.

An organization that is recognized as a separate entity for federal tax purposes is either a trust or a business entity. . . . The distinctions between trusts and business entities, although restated, are not changed by these regulations.

Any business entity that is not required to be treated as a corporation for federal tax purposes (referred to in the regulation as an eligible entity) may *choose its classification* under the rules of § 301.7701-3. Those rules provide that an eligible entity with at least two members can be classified as either a partnership or an association [taxable as a corporation]. . . .

In order to provide most eligible entities with the classification they would choose without requiring them to file an election, the regulations provide *default classification rules* that aim to match taxpayers' expectations (and thus reduce the number of elections that will be needed). The regulations adopt a passthrough default for domestic entities, under which a newly formed eligible entity will be classified as a partnership if it has at least two members, or will be disregarded as an entity separate from its owner if it has a single owner. . . . Finally, the default classification for an existing entity is the classification that the entity claimed immediately prior to the effective date of these regulations. An entity's default classification continues until the entity elects to change its classification by means of an affirmative election.

An eligible entity may affirmatively elect its classification. . . .

C. Discussion of Comments Relating to the Elective Regime

Most of the commentators agreed that the default rules included in the proposed regulations generally would match taxpayers' expectations. . . .

Par. 7. Sections 301.7701-1, 301.7701-2, and 301.7701-3 are revised to read as follows:

§ 301.7701-1 Classification of organizations for federal tax purposes.

(a) Organizations for federal tax purposes —

(1) In general. The Internal Revenue Code prescribes the classification of various organizations for federal tax purposes. Whether an organization is an entity separate from its owners for federal tax purposes is a matter of federal tax law and does not depend on whether the organization is recognized as an entity under local law. . . .

(b) Classification of organizations. The classification of organizations that are recognized as separate entities is determined under §§ 301.7701-2, 301.7701-3, and 301.7701-4. . . .

§ 301.7701-2 Business entities; definitions.

(a) Business entities. For purposes of this section and § 301.7701-3, a business entity is any entity recognized for federal tax purposes . . . that is not properly classified as a trust. . . . A business entity with two or more members is classified for federal tax purposes as either a corporation or a partnership. . . .

(b) Corporations. For federal tax purposes, the term corporation means —

(1) A business entity organized under a Federal or State statute, . . . if the statute describes or refers to the entity as incorporated or as a corporation, body corporate, or body politic; . . .

(c) Other business entities. For federal tax purposes —

(1) The term partnership means a business entity that is not a corporation under paragraph (b) of this section and that has at least two members.

§ 301.7701-3 Classification of certain business entities.

(a) In general. A business entity that is not classified as a corporation . . . can elect its classification for federal tax purposes. . . . An eligible entity with at least two members can elect to be classified as either an association (and thus a corporation under § 301.7701-2(b)(2)) or a partnership, and an eligible entity with a single owner can elect to be classified as an association or to be disregarded as an entity separate from its owner. . . . [E]lections are necessary only when an eligible entity chooses to be classified initially as other than the default classification or when an eligible entity chooses to change its classification. An entity whose classification is determined under the default classification retains that classification . . . until the entity makes an election to change that classification under paragraph (c)(1) of this section. . . .

(b) Classification of eligible entities that do not file an election

(1) Domestic eligible entities. Except as provided in paragraph (b)(3) of this section, unless the entity elects otherwise, a domestic eligible entity is —

(i) A partnership if it has two or more members. . . .

[5] Comments on the Regulation

The language of the regulation has been edited down to the bare minimum, but you should be able to grasp the important features of this development: for most business entities, except for those which are specifically organized under a state "corporation" statute, the basic tax regime is the partnership tax regime. This will permit the manipulation of the entity concepts to achieve the maximum amount of flexibility, and the long running debate over how far the corporate tax regime should extend is largely over. Serious problems remain, particularly for many entities formed under the law of another country. More importantly, the partnership tax rules are very complicated and can produce serious and unexpected consequences for the unprepared. Unless you have a working knowledge of these tax rules, you will need expert tax advice whenever you are asked to draft a partnership agreement for a real estate transaction.

Now that the entity classification rules are elective, the choice of entity is easily and quickly made. Indeed, all entities other than those formally classified by state law as "corporations," *by default*, are taxed as partnerships. This result is desirable for real estate investment entities, because for them, application of the partnership tax rules is essential. Despite the passthrough tax treatment, however, entities taxed as partnerships are not invisible, and will be treated as separate entities for tax purposes as the occasion requires.

The operating agreement for the Fox Valley Auto Care Center, LLC is in the Document Book. It is based on an older agreement which was drafted as a limited partnership agreement to comply with the pre-1996 definition. Some provisions may reflect requirements imposed by the pre-"check-the-box" regulations in order for the Limited Partnership to be taxed as a partnership. The provisions of the LLC Operating Agreement, and the reasons for them, are discussed next. Unhappily, even in a limited liability company as straightforward as is the Fox Valley Auto Care Center, LLC, as you can see from looking at the operating agreement, the structural issues are anything but simple.

[6] Organizational Issues for the Future

Where a "check-the-box" test for partnership tax status will lead, particularly for real estate firms, is an open question. If no member of the organization has personal liability, lending institutions may take a different view of nonrecourse loans, and that could have serious consequences for the partnership allocation rules.

The consequences of elective tax status have already been considered in several forums. Professor George Yin, reporter for the ALI study of Pass-Through Entities, comments:

> If an explicit classification election is adopted, it will likely increase the number and variety of firms qualifying as partnerships for tax purposes and therefore subject to the operating rules of Subchapter K. The Treasury's view is that implementation of an explicit election should not have any substantive consequences because classification is already functionally elective. But this view overlooks two key points.
>
> First, although partnership status may be functionally elective under current law, the existing classification standards exact a price for making that election. The principal cost is the required selection by the firm of suboptimal governance rules relating to the firm's transferability of interests, centralization of management and continuity of life. In addition, there are the transaction costs to obtain the partnership classification, and the cost of uncertainty about that status, at least where the organization opts not to follow standard-form formation conditions. All of these costs would be reduced considerably, if not completely eliminated, under an explicit classification election scheme, thereby facilitating a partnership tax election for greater numbers and types of firms. For example, most observers believe an LLC is presently an unsuitable form for widely-held ventures because of the existing tax classification standards, but there is no particular reason that would be true under an explicit election scheme.

Indeed, following replacement of the corporate resemblance test, one might expect further evolution of permissible organization forms at the state level, with perhaps movement towards common adoption of "unincorporation" statutes. The goal would be to authorize the most flexible and efficient set of business organization rules consistent with the conditions of the tax classification election [citing Larry E. Ribstein, *Statutory Forms for Closely Held Firms: Theories and Evidence from LLCs*, 73 WASH. U. L.Q. 369, 432 (1995)].

Second, the explicit classification election may help to create a "snowball" effect in the utilization of the new business form. As use of such form becomes more widespread because of the election, concerns about the state law acceptance and ramifications of that form would lessen. This, in turn, might persuade more firms presently organizing as limited or general partnerships, as well as S or C corporations, to organize under the new form instead. Though already taxed under subchapter K, limited and general partnerships might see advantage in the new form if, like an LLC, it offered limited liability for all owners plus the ability of owners to be actively involved in management. Firms presently organizing as S or C corporations might select the new form because of its tax advantages. Of course, the snowball effect would be even more pronounced if the Treasury were to ease the tax consequences of conversions of existing corporations into the new form. . . .

The foregoing discussion is not intended to comment upon the desirability of the anticipated developments. Indeed, some have welcomed the popular emergence of LLCs, whereas others are more wary. But welcome or not, the use of LLCs and, possibly, even further evolutions of business forms will no doubt increase and accelerate as a result of a shift to an elective tax classification regime. These developments will, in turn, place greater stress on the operating rules of subchapter K.

George K. Yin, *Reporter's Memorandum No. 1*, ALI FEDERAL INCOME TAX PROJECT; TAXATION OF PASS-THROUGH ENTITIES 65–68 (1995).

The ALI Study culminated in a detailed report, published as a "Reporters Study," GEORGE K. YIN & DAVID SHAKOW, AMERICAN LAW INSTITUTE, TAXATION OF PRIVATE BUSINESS ENTERPRISES (1999), rather than as a recommendation, because many of the Reporters' recommendations did not command agreement by the steering committee. It does agree with the basic policy decision to make tax status elective, at least for private business firms, and then goes on to make recommendations to simplify the rules for small firms and to fix certain problems in the operation of the rules. The report is a careful analysis of the present system for taxing conduits, and reflects an enormous amount of work, but its failure to command agreement demonstrates the political staying power of the current partnership tax system. Then and now, the votes are not there to change them.

§ 4.02 PARTNERSHIP TAX ISSUES

Before analyzing the Fox Valley Auto Care Center, LLC operating agreement, a brief explanation of some of the salient partnership tax rules will help you to understand what is sought to be accomplished. Although investment in the Fox Valley Auto Care Center is a straightforward *pro rata* deal between the developer and the investors, with no "special allocations" or guaranteed payments to make use of the flexibility of the partnership tax rules, the value of using an entity form that will be treated under the federal tax laws as a partnership can readily be seen.

[1] The Tax Basis for the Investors' Partnership Interests

The Fox Valley Auto Care Center is owned by a limited liability company organized under Illinois law. Investors have acquired interests as members that will entitle them to receive 40% of the project economics. Regent, as a Subchapter S corporation, will be the Manager of the LLC, and will retain 60% of the project economics.[29] The investors have contributed $60,000 cash and provided credit enhancement to the construction lender through the use of standby letters of credit in the amount of $200,000.[30] Regent will contribute the land and assign the various agreements allowing the development to proceed to the LLC; Delaney and two other principals in Regent have personally guaranteed the construction loan and made other commitments to complete the Auto Care Center and operate it.[31]

The tax basis of the LLC for the Auto Care Center (its "inside basis") will be primarily attributable to the construction loan. This loan is a recourse loan to the LLC which has been personally guaranteed by Regent's shareholders. Delaney anticipated that he would be able to negotiate a nonrecourse permanent loan secured by a first mortgage on the Auto Center to pay off ("take out") the construction loan. The basis allocation rules for both types of loans are important, and will be mentioned here.

[a] The Mechanism

Entity level indebtedness is allocated to partners or members in two steps:[32] each member's share of the change in entity level indebtedness is first determined, then that share is treated as either a *contribution* of cash by the member to the

---

[29] Fox Valley Auto Care Center, LLC, is designated in its articles of organization as a "Manager-managed company," and Regent is the designated manager of the company. *See* 805 Ill. Comp. Stat. 180/1-5 (definition of "manager-managed company"), 180/5-5(a)(4). If not so designated, then the LLC would be a "member-managed company," with each member empowered to act as the LLC's agent. Ill. Comp. Stat. 180/13-5 (agency of members). Then, decisions would be made by a majority of the members, meaning each member is counted individually regardless of the member's percentage interest in company. *Id.*, 180/15-1(a). These are default provisions and can be varied in the operating agreement.

[30] Construction loans are invariably recourse loans, which is why the construction loan in this case was personally guaranteed by the individual shareholders of the general partner and "enhanced" by the letters of credit provided by the Investors. Regent probably would not have anticipated these "enhancements," to have been necessary to secure a permanent nonrecourse loan had it been negotiated by Fox Valley Auto Care Center LLC. Because the construction period is usually short and does not produce much in the way of current tax effects, the allocation of inside debt to the outside bases of the interests of the members of the LLC did not have as much significance as it would have had for a longer term loan.

[31] Regent Development Co. is the designated "Manager" of the LLC, and, in the typical case, would have been created to do this specific development, that is, it would be referred to as a "special purpose entity." Because no member of an LLC is liable for the debts of the LLC (805 Ill. Comp. Stat. 180/10-10(a)), the use of another limited liability entity for this purpose is not necessary. The organizational form used in this case may produce an anomalous result under the partnership tax rules, as we observe below. Note, also, that the financial analysis explained in Chapter 2 has assumed that the general partner did contribute $90,000 to the LLC. See figure 2.11, *supra*.

[32] In this discussion, we refer to a limited liability company as the entity to which the partnership tax rules apply because the Auto Care Center has been organized as an LLC.

LLC (I.R.C. § 752(a)), if the member's share of the change is positive, or a *distribution* of cash from the LLC to the member (I.R.C. § 752(b)), if the member's share is negative. A contribution of cash causes an increase in the member's basis for his interest (I.R.C. § 723), and a distribution produces a decrease (I.R.C. § 733(1)), unless the amount of the distribution exceeds the member's adjusted basis for the member's interest, in which case a taxable gain results just as if a real distribution of cash had occurred.

Note that, although the contribution or distribution is constructive in the sense that the member did not actually contribute cash or receive a cash distribution, as the case may be, the tax effects are real. Therefore, a *decrease* in a member's share of the entity level debt can result in a taxable gain, that is, a real tax liability, obviously not a desirable result. Moreover, a member's *share* of partnership level debt can change when, for example, the character of the debt changes from recourse to nonrecourse (or vice versa), even though the aggregate amount of partnership level debt is itself unchanged. These rules can be tricky and produce unexpected results if care is not taken in establishing the partnership's debt structure.

[b] Determining the Partner's Debt-Share

The important determination will be the amount of each member's share of the entity level debt. This determination depends on whether the debt is recourse or nonrecourse *to the members*.[33] For this purpose, a debt is recourse for tax purposes if any member (or a person related to the member), taking into account the operating agreement of the LLC and all related arrangements such as personal guarantees, is liable to pay it. The debt is then allocated to the members who bear the economic risk of loss. *See* Treas. Reg. § 1.752-2(a). In the abstract, this makes sense, as the debt is theoretically allocated to the members who would actually be called upon to pay it if it goes into default. To test this proposition, however, the Treasury regulation creates a hypothetical disaster, makes some (usually unrealistic) assumptions, and asks which member is at the end of the line in terms of legal liability to pay the debt (the "payor of last resort"). To a practical real estate developer, this may not make much sense, but it has the advantage of providing a definite result not dependent on an assessment of whether a member who is legally liable will actually be able to pay.

Nonrecourse entity-level debt is the converse: it is entity-level debt for which no partner or member has personal liability.[34] A nonrecourse entity level debt (up to the recent past, the normal case in real estate investing) will be allocated for debt-

---

[33] Teas. Reg. § 1.752-1(a). "Recourse" as used in the regulation is defined to mean that the person "bears the economic risk of loss." For purposes of these tests (and the application of the "at risk" rules), for a person to bear the "economic risk of loss" means that the person is the "payor of last resort." *See* Hubert Enterprises v. Commissioner, T.C. Memo. 2008-46 (applying the "payor of last resort" test to determine whether the taxpayer is "at risk"). Because no member of an LLC is liable for the debts of the entity, a debt which is *recourse* as to the entity may be *nonrecourse* to the members of the entity. This kind of debt is referred to as an "exculpatory" liability. *See* Treas. Dec. 8385 preamble part V.B., 1992-1 C.B. 199, 203.

[34] In the case of a limited liability company ("LLC"), a debt which is recourse to the LLC is nonetheless (by definition) nonrecourse as to all of its members. In an attempt to clear away some of the confusion as to application of the at risk rules, the IRS promulgated a regulation under the "at risk" rules to specify that such a debt will be treated as a "qualified" nonrecourse debt, meaning that it is subject to the rules governing debt which is nonrecourse by its terms. Treas. Reg. § 1.465-27(b)(4).

share purposes under a completely different set of rules. Although the rules themselves, see Treas. Reg. § 1.752-3, are too complicated to be described here, the general principle under which these rules operate is not difficult to understand. In the first place, you should note that, by definition, no member is liable to pay the debt. Instead, the lender's right to collect the debt is limited to the property, which is the security for the debt (or to the assets of the entity), so that an economic risk analysis is simply irrelevant. Now recall that repayment of a debt must be made from after-tax income or gain. The reason is that receipt of the debt proceeds is not taxable, so no tax benefit is allowed for repayment. Nonrecourse debt, therefore, is allocable to the member to whom would be allocated the taxable income used to repay the debt. This may, of course, be the regular taxable income of the entity, used to pay down the mortgage in the ordinary course (that is, the member's percentage share of the LLC's profits).

In the typical case, the debt will be "paid" when the property is sold. Again, please recall the *Tufts* case in Section 3.05 of Chapter 3. Very little cash changed hands in that transaction, although the debt was treated as having been paid, and a taxable gain resulted. This gain was allocated to the partners in the Tufts partnership, and was taxed as a gain or profit realized by them and used to pay the debt. Another fact should be clear: once the tax basis of the property has been reduced, usually by taking depreciation deductions, and an overhanging debt has been created, the partners or members who shared in the tax benefit created by the debt (the depreciation deductions) *cannot escape liability* for the tax on the gain.[35] So, the difference between the unpaid balance of the mortgage and the adjusted tax basis of the property will be taxable at some time to those partners or members,[36] even if foreclosure should occur. This gain is defined as the "minimum gain,"[37] or the *Tufts* gain. When the overhang is created, this "minimum gain" *must* be allocated to the partners or members who have received the tax benefit (depreciation deductions or distributed refinancing proceeds) from the debt. And the debt, which is how the amount of taxable gain will ultimately be determined, must itself be allocated to those same partners.[38] *See* Treas. Reg. § 1.752-3(a)(1).

[c] A Practical Application

With the Fox Valley Auto Care Center, LLC, the entity level debt (the construction loan) is a recourse loan to the LLC. The loan was personally guaranteed by Regent's shareholders, and would have been guaranteed by Regent

---

[35] Overhanging debt can result from refinancing. In this case, the excess proceeds, not needed to pay off the previous mortgage or for other partnership or LLC business purposes, will be distributed to the partners or members. The distribution will not be taxable immediately, which is a tax benefit to the distributee partners or members. Instead, the tax on cash withdrawal is deferred. The same principles described here for achieving tax leverage (depreciation deductions), therefore, will apply to the distribution of refinancing proceeds.

[36] Unless death intervenes. *See* I.R.C. § 1014.

[37] Treas. Reg. § 1.704-2(d).

[38] This is a vast oversimplification. Minimum gain is a book concept; that is, it is allocated comparing the unpaid balance of the mortgage to the book value of the entity property. Because book value (the value carried on the books of the entity) can (and often does) vary from adjusted tax basis, minimum gain (and its counterpart, section 704(c) gain) is one of the most difficult concepts in the tax law. Unhappily for the real estate professional, it may commonly be present in many highly leveraged real estate partnerships or LLCs.

as well had the Auto Care Center been originally organized as an LLC.[39] Under the partnership tax rules, the loan must be allocated, for purposes of determining the outside basis of a member, to the member who bears the "economic risk of loss." Treas. Reg. § 1.752-2(a). This means that *none* of the tax basis attributable to the construction loan can be allocated to the investors, whose tax basis for their interests will be limited to their cash contributions ($60,000).

The investors did provide standby letters of credit for the benefit of the construction lender. These letters of credit were clearly available for the lender to draw against if the construction loan ever went into default. Because the letters of credit had to be approved by the construction lender, there is little doubt that the lender was permitted by the terms of the letters to draw against them if the loan was in default without first having to try to collect from the entity or on the personal guaranty provided by Regent or any one of its shareholders. Will this provide an additional amount of basis for the interests of the investors, who are otherwise shielded from liability? The Treasury regulations do not address this question directly, but do provide, generally, that a partner who "pledges" property as additional security for a partnership loan (a "direct pledge") will be treated as being at risk to the extent of the value of the property pledged as security. Treas. Reg. § 1.752-2(h)(1). The "direct pledge" is not further explained, and there is some question whether it applies to a recourse loan (for which another member already bears the risk of loss[40]) or simply to a portion of a loan which is otherwise a nonrecourse loan.

The effect of the letter of credit on the basis allocation question discussed here will depend, assuming the regulation does apply to authorize the allocation, on the terms of the letters and whether the members who provided it are entitled to reimbursement under the guarantee provided by Regent and its shareholders. This is a legal issue, and does not depend in any way on the practicalities of the situation. If, under Illinois law, FMB, the construction lender, draws on the letters of credit and the investors reimburse the issuer, then the investors would be subrogated to the rights of FMB and could proceed against the guarantors; whether or not the investors would actually do so, liability to make the ultimate payment would remain with Regent, and the debt would be entirely allocated to the outside basis of Regent's interest in the LLC.

In the actual case, the LLC's ownership of the Fox Valley Auto Care Center terminated at the end of year three, at which time it appeared that the LLC's net

---

[39] While we have introduced the LLC as the entity of choice for a real estate development, the original transaction was done using a limited partnership, with Regent as the general partner. Regent would have been personally liable as the general partner for the recourse debts of the partnership, and thus its guarantee would have been unnecessary. When the LLC is substituted for the partnership, Regent would not be liable for the debts of the LLC, but, with the personal guarantee of all of its shareholders, there would be no point in preserving Regent's freedom from liability. So, we assume that Regent has joined in guaranteeing payment of the construction loan. Had Regent not done so, its shareholders collectively would not have been a "related party" for this purpose because no one of them owned 80 percent or more of Regent's stock. *See* Treas. Reg. § 1.752-4(b)(1). And then their guarantees would have been ignored in the analysis described in the text. Treas. Reg. § 1.752-2(b)(3) (final sentence).

[40] The Treasury regulations assume that all partners or members with personal liability to make a payment will do so, whether or not they actually can do so. Treas. Reg. § 1.752-2(b)(6). In this case, the lender probably can draw on the letter of credit if the LLC defaults, without having to proceed against the guarantors first. Both sets of liabilities are secondary, so the allocation question should turn on the subrogation issue described in the text.

taxable loss (deductions in excess of income) allocated to the investors exceeded their cash contributions by nearly $25,000. Assuming, for the moment, that these deductions could have been allocated to the investor members, the deductible amount would have been limited to the basis attributable to their capital contributions. *See* Section 4.02[2][b][v], *infra*.

To generate additional outside basis, the Limited Partners would have been required to assume some personal liability for payment of the construction loan, or make sure that they have waived whatever right of reimbursement they otherwise have had from a draw against the letters.

[d] Nonrecourse Loans

Although a nonrecourse permanent loan was not negotiated by Regent for the Fox Valley Auto Care Center, it is worth noting that the tax benefits from the use of debt can be allocated to members of a limited liability company. Investors in these entities have no liability beyond the amount of their original contributions. The allocation principle, however, does not require personal liability, and, in fact, requires instead that the loan used to create these tax benefits in the hands of the individual investors *must* itself be nonrecourse. This works by an allocation of the taxable income or gain, under the partnership allocation rules, used to pay the loan to members with limited liability. When there is any personal liability, of any kind, of a partner or member, or of a person related to a partner or member, the nonrecourse allocation rules do not apply at all. This explains, in part, why the typical real estate loan is nonrecourse; if lenders were unwilling to make nonrecourse loans, and investors required protection from liability for debts of the enterprise, as they normally would, the partnership tax rules would not work for investors in real estate entities. To be a player in the game, therefore, a lender must be ready to make loans on a nonrecourse basis. At the present time (summer 2009), however, whether the real estate investment game will continue to operate in this way is not clear.

In some cases, often involving the admission of new investors or the acquisition of the project by another entity, it will be essential for existing investors to retain the shares of debt they had when the deal was set. In such a case, the debt principles can be manipulated by adjusting personal liability for a *portion* of the debt in order to preserve the investor's debt share. This might be done, for example, by a partial guarantee of the bottom portion of the debt (viz., the last part of the debt to be paid). Usually, there is very little risk, but the ultimate liability rules under which recourse debt-shares are determined will nonetheless attribute a debt-share to the investor making the guarantee.

In a world where nonrecourse lending is not available, investors with limited liability may be asked to guarantee a portion of the enterprise debt in proportion to each investor's share of the project's economics. There is some authority supporting allocation of amounts at risk (to satisfy the requirements of I.R.C. § 465) and shares of the guaranteed debt (for outside basis purposes) by means of such guarantees. As noted in the text, this technique converts what is nonrecourse debt (that is, an exculpatory indebtedness[41]) into a recourse debt allocated to a member who or which is the "payor of last resort." In *Abramson v.*

---

[41] *See* note 33 *supra*.

Commissioner,[42] the taxpayers invested as limited partners in a limited partnership which purchased the distribution rights to a feature motion picture. Each investor signed a guarantee under which, in the event of default by the partnership, he or she promised to pay directly to the lender a stated percentage of the outstanding balance of the nonrecourse debt incurred by the partnership to acquire the film. The Tax Court held that the guarantee both provided grounds for an allocation of the inside debt and for an at risk amount to each guaranteeing partner:

> The guarantee of an otherwise nonrecourse note places each guaranteeing partner in an economic position indistinguishable from that of a general partner, with liability under a recourse note — except that the guaranteeing partner's liability is limited to the amount guaranteed. While recognizing that under State law there may be differences between the obligations of a general partner and those of a limited partner guarantor, such differences should not be controlling for Federal tax purposes. Each is obligated to use his personal assets to satisfy, pro rata, the partnership liability. In effect, the limited partners are the equivalent of general partners to the extent of their pro rata guarantees especially since, as to this obligation, the liability of the general partners is limited. Economic reality dictates that they be treated equally, and we so hold. Consequently, both general and limited partners will be entitled to include such liabilities in their bases to the extent of their pro rata guarantees.[43]

[2] Allocations

The tax items derived from the operation of the partnership's assets (for example, depreciation deductions, interest deductions and rents) may be separately allocated among the partners. Allocations that vary from a partner's percentage share are referred to as "special allocations," but these are not a common feature of real estate ventures. Most have allocation rules similar to those found in the Fox Valley Auto Care Center, LLC operating agreement. Even in a straightforward *pro rata* deal, like this one, however, there may be problems that must be attended to in the agreement. The following article discusses these problems in a generally helpful manner.

---

[42] 86 T.C. 360 (1986).

[43] *Id.* at 374. The court noted that there was no right of reimbursement, a situation which is likely to be present when the liability is that of an LLC, the assets of which are deemed to be worthless in the application of the regulatory test for recourse loans. In a later case, the Tax Court held that a promissory note given to a limited partnership by a limited partner which was pledged to a bank which made a recourse loan to the partnership created personal liability for the limited partner to the extent of that partner's pro rata share of the bank loan: "The critical inquiry should be who is the obligor of last resort, and in determining who has the ultimate economic responsibility for the loan, the substance of the transaction controls." Melvin v. Commissioner, 88 T.C. 63, 75 (1987). These are older cases, decided before the final regulations under § 752 were promulgated, but there is nothing in these regulations which contradicts the holdings in these cases.

[a] Partnership Allocations in a Real Estate Venture

Jeremiah Luxemburger, Allocation of Partnership Income and Losses, 12/1/92 REAL EST. REV. 30–34*

If there is one area of a partnership agreement that is shrouded in confusion and mystery, it is that section of the agreement that allocates partnership income or loss. Much to the confusion of lesser mortals,[1] the clauses are replete with tax law mumbo jumbo like *minimum gain chargeback, nonrecourse deductions, qualified income offsets*, and *partner nonrecourse deductions*. This article attempts to rephrase these concepts in basic English.

THE TWO CAUSES OF COMPLEXITY IN ALLOCATING INCOME AND LOSS

Two characteristics of partnership agreements make the allocation of income and loss and the drafting of the allocation sections exceedingly complex:

- A limit on the requirement that a partner with a deficit in his or her capital account must contribute additional capital in the amount of that deficit.
- Partnership borrowing on a nonrecourse basis.

A deficit in a partner's capital account exists when the sum of the losses allocated to him or her plus the money distributed to him or her exceeds the capital the partner contributed plus the profits allocated to him or her. But a limited partner's liability (by definition) does not exceed his or her capital contribution. Therefore, the partner is not required to make up any capital account deficit by an additional contribution.

Nonrecourse loans exist in either general or limited partnerships that have borrowed money on a nonrecourse basis. They exist in almost all partnerships that own substantial amounts of real estate or tangible property. Such loans cause complexity in partnership loss allocation because when a property secured by a nonrecourse loan produces an economic loss that is greater than the partnership's equity in the property, the excess loss is borne by the lender and not by the partnership or its partners.

THE CAPITAL ACCOUNTS OF A PLAIN VANILLA GENERAL PARTNERSHIP

All partnerships have capital accounts that keep track of their constituent partners' interests in the partnership. Generally, these accounts reflect the amounts contributed by the partners to the partnership, the income or loss charged to each partner, and each partner's withdrawals from the partnership.

Assume a typical service partnership between Midas, a money partner, and Fisher, a service partner. Midas begins with a capital account of $100 and Fisher

---

* This article is reprinted with the permission of West Group, Inc.

[1] To a tax lawyer, a lesser mortal is any layperson or an attorney whose specialty is not the Federal Tax Code.

with a capital account of zero. They agree to divide profits and losses equally. So, if there is a profit of $100, each partner's capital accounts would be increased by $50. Midas's capital account would become $150, and Fisher's capital account $50. But if there is a loss of $100, each partner's capital account is decreased by $50. Midas's account becomes $50, and Fisher's has a $50 deficit. If the partnership is liquidated after the profitable year, the $200 cash in the partnership is distributed $150 to Midas and $50 to Fisher. If the liquidation occurs after the loss year, there is no cash in the partnership because Midas's $100 capital contribution was used to pay expenses. Fisher must contribute $50 to the partnership to make up the $50 deficit in his capital account, and the partnership distributes that $50 to Midas to pay Midas the $50 balance in his capital account. Both capital accounts have been brought to zero, and each partner has borne half the losses.

Treatment of Noncash or Tax Losses

Suppose the partnership's losses had been tax losses. Tax losses are noncash losses, usually losses arising from the depreciation charges against real property. Partners once allocated these losses recklessly because they were not considered real. (The partners assumed that the property would not really depreciate in value, so depreciation was not a real loss but just a tax loss.) Many partnerships believed that these noncash losses could be allocated to whoever needed them most; this is not always so.

Assume that the Midas-Fisher partnership purchases a depreciable asset with Midas's cash, and the partnership has depreciation of $100 and a profit of $100. If, on liquidation, the property is disposed of for its depreciated value (zero), the partnership has $200 cash,[2] and it can distribute $150 to Midas and $50 to Fisher. If the partnership has a loss of $100, the result is the same as in the first example when the loss was a cash loss. The allocation of half the loss to Midas and half to Fisher reduces Midas's capital account to $50 and Fisher's to a $50 deficit. What then happens on liquidation? If the depreciable asset is disposed of for its depreciated value (zero), the partnership has no cash. Fisher must again contribute $50 to eliminate his capital account deficit and to supply the partnership with $50 cash, which will be paid to Midas to reduce his $50 capital account to zero. If the asset is sold for its original cost of $100, that $100 gain is allocated $50 to Midas and $50 to Fisher. Their respective capital accounts are now $100 and zero, and on liquidation, the partnership pays the $100 cash to Midas to reduce his capital account to zero.

Enter Cash Flow

Assume that the Midas-Fisher partnership uses Midas's $100 to purchase depreciable property and that during the first year the partnership receives cash that is $100 in excess of cash expenses. The noncash depreciation deduction on the asset is $100. This means that the partnership has $100 in cash flow but no income or loss.[3] Midas and Fisher agree to take equal distributions of the cash flow, so Midas's capital account is reduced to $50 and Fisher's to a $50 deficit. If the

---

2 The $100 profit consists of $200 revenue less $100 depreciation.

3 A $200 gross income less $100 cash expenses less $100 depreciation (a noncash expense) equals zero income but $100 cash flow.

partnership is then liquidated and the asset is sold for its book value (zero), Fisher must return to the partnership the $50 previously distributed to him in order to eliminate the deficit in his account. The partnership will then pay the $50 to Midas, reducing the $50 balance in his capital account to zero.

THE CAPITAL ACCOUNTS OF A LIMITED PARTNERSHIP

The neat, symmetric results of a general partnership allocation disappear if Fisher is a limited partner. The limited partnership by its terms protects Fisher, a limited partner, from loss beyond what he has invested as capital in the partnership. If, in each of the foregoing examples, Fisher were a limited partner instead of a general partner, he would not have had to pay money to the partnership in order to make up any deficit in his capital account. The partnership, in turn, would have had no money to pay to Midas to return to him the balance in his capital account. Instead of suffering losses of $50 or one-half of the losses in each case, Midas would have suffered losses of $100 or all of the losses.

In the tax loss examples, Fisher as a limited partner would not have to pay $50 on liquidation to reduce the deficit in his capital account. He would not have suffered any economic loss because of the tax loss. Consequently, the tax law prohibits a limited partnership from allocating losses to limited partners if such allocation creates a deficit in a limited partner's capital account but requires them to go to the general partner who will suffer the economic losses if there are any.

In the preceding cash flow examples, in which Midas and Fisher each received $50 in cash flow, the tax laws do not prohibit Fisher as a limited partner from getting his share of the cash flow. If a distribution of $50 to Fisher results in a $50 deficit in his capital account, then Fisher must recognize $50 in income.

For example, assume that the Midas-Fisher limited partnership has $100 in cash flow and $200 in gross income but no income because of deductions of $100 depreciation and $100 other deductible expenses. (Net income after noncash deductions is zero.) Even if the partnership agreement says that Midas and Fisher are to share profits, losses, and cash flow 50/50, the tax law will not permit the partnership to allocate any losses to limited partner Fisher, who has a zero capital account.

If the partnership does distribute cash flow to Fisher and the distribution reduces Fisher's capital account to less than zero, the partnership must also allocate gross (not net) income to Fisher so that the cash distribution is accompanied by a corresponding allocation of partnership income. This is how the scenario plays out.

The partnership distributes $50 cash to Fisher and allocates $50 gross income to his capital account with the result that his capital account stays at zero. Now the partnership must allocate the remaining $150 gross income less $200 in expenses (a $50 loss) between the partners, $25 to Midas and $25 to Fisher, according to the partnership agreement. But such an allocation would reduce Midas's capital account to $25 and Fisher's capital account to negative $25. Because Fisher, as a limited partner, is not obligated to contribute $25 to the partnership on liquidation, the tax law requires that the entire $50 loss be allocated to Midas. This reduction, together with the $50 reduction due to the cash flow distribution, reduces Midas's capital account to zero. If the partnership is now liquidated and the building is disposed of for its zero depreciated book value, Midas has a zero capital account that reflects his initial $100 investment reduced by $50 he received and a $50 economic loss he suffered. Fisher has a zero capital account that reflects and increase from zero to $50 by the addition of $50 of taxable gross income and the reduction from $50 to zero by virtue of the cash flow distribution. In a limited partnership, the tax law interferes with the partner's agreed-on 50/50 allocation of losses, cash flow, and profits when it is not consistent with the economic results. Had Fisher, even though he is a limited partner, made or been required to make a $50 contribution (e.g., by giving his note) to the partnership's capital in each of the preceding situations (either originally or on liquidation), the partnership would have been allowed to distribute $50 to him without allocating him gross income.

TREATMENT OF NONRECOURSE LOANS

It is common in real estate transactions for a lender to lend money against the security of real estate and to agree that if the loan is not repaid, the lender will not seek to collect any amount in excess of the fair market value of the property. The essence of nonrecourse loans is that there is no recourse against the borrower's general assets, only against the encumbered asset.

Plain Vanilla General Partnerships with Nonrecourse Loans

Assume that when Midas and Fisher set up their general partnership, Midas contributed $20 to capital and the partnership purchased depreciable property for no cash and a $100 nonrecourse loan. During the first three years, the partnership had cash expenses equal to income and a total of $100 in tax losses (depreciation) allocated half to Midas and half to Fisher. At the beginning of the fourth year the lender foreclosed on the property, which was therefore worth nothing to the partnership.

Midas and Fisher divided the $100 of tax losses as the partnership allocated $50 in losses to each, but on foreclosure they had no economic loss. The partnership still has the $20 cash that Midas contributed; the lender has absorbed the $100 economic loss. Midas and Fisher each have a $50 tax gain because the partnership surrendered an asset with a basis of zero to the lender in satisfaction of a $100 debt, and his gain was allocated equally to each partner. The allocation of this gain has the effect of restoring Midas's capital account to $20 and Fisher's to zero. The partnership has income of $100 but no cash. The tax law allowed the partners to deduct depreciation losses that economically were borne by the lender because the partnership agreement provides that the partners receive the taxable gain created by the surrender of the property to satisfy the debt.

If the general partnership had used all of Midas's cash (e.g., $20) for a down payment on the property and had financed the balance with an $80 nonrecourse loan, the result would have been the same. Each partner would have been charged $50 in losses, and the lender's loss would have been $80 instead of $100. The partnership would recognize an $80 gain (because it satisfied an $80 debt with property having a basis of zero), which is allocated half to Midas and half to Fisher. Midas and Fisher would each lose $10 (one-half of the down payment for the property). On liquidation, Fisher would have to contribute $10 to the partnership to cover the deficit in his capital account and bring it to zero. The partnership would distribute Fisher's $10 to Midas. Midas would receive the $10, and his capital account would be reduced to zero.

Limited Partnerships with Nonrecourse Loans

Capital accounts of limited partnerships with nonrecourse loans are treated no differently than those of general partnerships with nonrecourse loans except for the differences imposed by the relief of limited partners from making up deficits in their negative capital accounts. In the first nonrecourse loan example, the partnership suffered no economic loss, so the allocation treatment is the same whether the partnership is general or limited. However, in the second example, in which the partnership invested $20 to acquire an equity in the property, if Fisher is a limited partner, the tax laws do not permit the partnership to allocate any losses to him until the losses equal to the $20 partnership's equity that Midas furnished have been allocated to Midas's capital account. After Midas's $20 equity is reduced by the first $20 in losses both Midas and Fisher can be allocated losses attributable to nonrecourse debt as long as they are allocated gains on the sale or foreclosure of the property securing the nonrecourse loan equal to the amount of losses allocated.

TREATMENT OF PARTNER LOANS

It is common for a partner to make loans to his partnership. In general partnerships, these loans are usually recourse loans; if Midas lends $100 to his 50/50 partnership with Fisher, the latter will owe Midas $50 if the loan is not paid. In limited partnerships, however, these loans are often made by a partner (or an affiliate) and are, by their nature, nonrecourse, that is, there is no source for their repayment except partnership assets, because limited partners have no obligation to contribute capital to make up losses allocated to them in excess of their capital.

Assume that in the Midas-Fisher general partnership, neither partner contributes any capital, but Midas lends $100 on a recourse basis. If the partnership loses $100, both parties have negative $50 capital accounts. On liquidation, each general partner must contribute $50 to bring his capital account to zero as each partner suffers a $50 economic loss. The partnership uses the $100 to repay Midas, as lender, $100.

Now assume that Midas made a recourse loan to the Midas-Fisher limited partnership and Fisher is the limited partner. Fisher is not required to contribute $50 to repay Midas's $100 partner recourse loan, and Midas will suffer the entire $100 economic loss as general partner. The same would be true if the loan were nonrecourse. For this reason, the tax law does not allow any losses attributable to a nonrecourse partner loan to be allocated other than to the lending partner. No loss can be allocated to Fisher; the entire $100 loss must be allocated to Midas. The result achieved is the same if Midas and Fisher were in a general partnership and Midas's $100 partner loan was expressly nonrecourse. Because only Midas, as the nonrecourse partner lender, will bear the economic loss if the loan is not paid, only Midas may be allowed the loss attributable to the nonrecourse partner loan and then only if the partnership agreement ensures that any taxable income recognized by the partnership as it repays the loan is allocated to Midas in the amount of such losses.

DEFINING THE TERMS

No matter what a partnership agreement says, under most circumstances the tax law prohibits it from allocating losses to a limited partner who is not required to contribute money to make up deficits in his capital amount that were occasioned by those losses. The tax law holds that such losses do not have *substantial economic effect*. The only exception to this rule involves nonrecourse loans. The tax law permits tax losses to be allocated to partners when the economic loss is incurred by unrelated nonrecourse lenders, as long as the taxable income attributable to the repayment of those loans is allocated to the same partners who were allocated the losses related to the loan. The tax law calls such losses *nonrecourse deductions*; it identifies the taxable income that must be allocated to partners who take such nonrecourse deductions as *minimum gain* and the provision that allocates this minimum gain as a *minimum gain chargeback*.

When an allocation of losses (other than nonrecourse deductions) creates a deficit capital account for a limited partner, the tax law specifies that if the deficit is foreseeable, the partnership may not allocate losses creating the deficit to the limited partner, and that if the deficit is unexpected, the partnership must immediately allocate gross (not net) income to the limited partner in the amount of the deficit. This requirement is referred to as a *qualified income offset*.

Finally, when a partner makes a nonrecourse loan to the partnership, the tax laws prohibit the allocation of losses with respect to that loan to any partner but the lending partner because the lending partner is the only partner who will bear the economic loss if the loan is not repaid. In addition, the tax law requires the partner taking the losses to receive the taxable gains when the nonrecourse loan is satisfied. These losses are called *partner nonrecourse deductions*, and the allocation of taxable gains to the lending partner is called the *partner minimum gain chargeback*.

By each of the means previously described, the tax law seeks to implement the requirement that a partner who gets tax losses ends up with an economic loss. If no partner suffers an economic loss because it is borne by a nonrecourse lender, the law requires the partners to whom the loss is allocated to pay income tax on the amount of loss that is suffered by the lender.

[b] Notes on Partnership Allocations

[i] Leverage and Limited Liability

As Luxemburger makes clear, the problem posed for most real estate partnerships is the degree of leverage typically found in real estate enterprises. In these cases, it is inevitable that the partnership books will run deficits; that is, the partnership's debts will exceed the *book value* (but, hopefully, not the *market value*) of its assets. After all, that is how tax leverage works. When the amount due on the debt exceeds the book value of the partnership's assets, the partners' capital accounts, which is how accountants keep track of the partners' equity in the partnership, will be negative, and implicitly the partners will have an obligation to make good the deficit at the end of the day (a "deficit restoration" obligation). But, of course, these partnerships all provide limited liability, so a real deficit restoration obligation is never present. Because the tax theory supporting the allocations of the tax quantities is that there will be an economic effect to each such allocation, there is a problem: how to support an allocation which creates a deficit which, in turn, could not possibly have an economic effect?

The "minimum gain" system supplies the answer. Taxable gain realized from the inclusion of the amount of the mortgage in the amount realized, as happened in *Tufts*, is also a "book gain"; that is, it will be treated as income for book purposes and will offset the deficits created in the partners' capital accounts. If deficit-creating events occur, the system requires allocation of the minimum gain that results to the partners who receive the tax benefit resulting from the deficit-creating event. You need not fully understand the mechanics to see immediately what is happening: the tax benefit allocated to partners today (the system works because tax liability is deferred) is offset by a binding agreement, explicitly provided in the partnership agreement, to pay the tax when income realization occurs. The system is completely circular, and can, if the parties wish to design it this way, be set up to work effectively *without regard to the actual economics of the underlying deal.*

You should not be discouraged by the apparent level of complexity these rules create; in most cases, the arrangement is self-correcting. The minimum gain rules require the tax allocations to make up the deficits, which will occur almost automatically when the property is finally sold. Moreover, most agreements contain a provision authorizing the general partner to make whatever adjustments are necessary to comply with the tax rules. In effect, the agreement says to the general partner: "Make sure you do what the accountants tell you is necessary to protect our tax benefits and realize the economic deal we made."

The tax rules were designed with a limited partnership owning a single asset, one real estate project, as the paradigm. The partnership's asset would be security for, and therefore subject to, a nonrecourse loan, and the balance due on the nonrecourse loan could then be compared to the adjusted book value of the asset to determine the amount of minimum gain present in the partnership. Applying these rules to limited liability companies, as we have done, adds more complexity. All limited liability company statutes permit the members to make an operating agreement which can vary any of the relevant provisions (the default rules) in the statute, and thus can apply the tax rules to accomplish the same result as with a partnership.[44] One should note, however, that a loan which is recourse as to the LLC may, by definition, be nonrecourse as to all of the members of the LLC. The loan may not be secured by any specific asset of the entity, leaving the comparison between the balance due on the loan and the adjusted book value of an asset or assets, as the paradigm requires, unclear. The Treasury regulations do permit the LLC to make a "reasonable" allocation of a single debt to or among several assets which are security for payment of the debt for this purpose as long as the allocation is not changed while any portion of the debt remains unpaid.[45]

---

44 Note that the general partner of a limited partnership has, by definition, unlimited liability, so that the loan, if it is to meet these conditions, must be nonrecourse, and a nonrecourse loan would be secured by a specific asset (or assets).

45 Treas. Reg. § 1.752-3(b). What is not clear is whether a loan that is recourse to the LLC would be treated in the tax law in the same way that a loan which is nonrecourse, in the sense that the lender has agreed to limit its remedies to the asset secured by its mortgage. If the lender pursues its remedies under the loan agreement against the LLC personally, would there be an exchange for tax purposes in the same sense as foreclosure in *Tufts* would have been treated as an exchange? *See* I.R.C. § 7701(g), providing that in determining the amount of gain or loss, property shall be deemed to have a value "not

[ii] "Safe-Harbors"

These rules create what is known as a "safe-harbor." If the LLC operating agreement satisfies the requirements described in the tax regulations, the allocations it provides for tax purposes will not be disturbed. On the other hand, if the rules are not observed, the regulations provide a "facts and circumstances" test,[46] or an "economic effect equivalence" test.[47] In simple entities where all allocations are made *pro rata*, and distributions, including distributions in liquidation of a member's interest in the LLC, are made consistently with the allocations, compliance with the regulatory tests would not seem to matter.[48] After all, how would allocations be made if not *pro rata*? No one knows, and that is the problem. Besides, why not include the magic words, as most operating agreements do, and then make all allocations *and distributions pro rata*? That is basically what is done in most real estate deals.

[iii] Design Elements and Capital Accounts

The central ingredient in the tax rules is the maintenance of capital accounts. A partner's capital account is basically a way of keeping score by stating what share the partner has in the equity shown on the partnership books. Every partnership level transaction must be recorded in the capital accounts of the partners, and the regulations are very specific about how this is to be done. *See* Treas. Reg. § 1.704-1(b)(2)(iv) (specifying how capital accounts must be maintained for tax purposes). Furthermore, the partnership agreement must provide that, in liquidation of a partner's interest, that partner is to be paid the amount shown in his or her capital account.[49] Of course, by that time partnership assets will have been sold, or the partnership will have entered into some kind of transaction which will justify increasing (or decreasing) the book value of the partnership's assets to reflect their market values (a "book-up"), with the resulting gain or loss allocated to capital accounts in the same manner that realized gain or loss would have been allocated under the agreement. This ultimate check on the economic effect of partnership allocations may require capital account adjustments, which the agreement will have to provide. Remember, the capital account must be the benchmark for

---

less than the amount of any nonrecourse indebtedness *to which such property is subject*." (Emphasis supplied.) If the debt is treated as a recourse debt for this purpose, then Treas. Reg. § 1.1001-2 would apply, and the amount of the debt in excess of the value of the property of the LLC would result in cancellation of indebtedness income to the LLC. *Cf.* Frazier v. Commissioner, 111 T.C. 243 (1998), discussed in § 3.05[3][c], *supra*. While there is no authority on how entity level recourse debt would be treated for minimum gain purposes, the at-risk regulation treating such debt as "qualified nonrecourse financing," Treas. Reg. § 1.465-27(b)(4), note 34, *supra* (disregarding the recourse liability of partnerships), and § 1.752-3(b)(1) (permitting the allocation of a single liability among multiple properties) are suggestive.

46 *See* Treas. Reg. § 1.704-1(b)(3) ("manner in which the [members] have agreed to share the economic benefit or burden (if any) corresponding to . . . the . . . allocated [items].")

47 *See* Treas. Reg. § 1.704-1(b)(2)(ii)(*i*).

48 By "pro rata" we mean in proportion to some measure (usually, the amount of capital contributed to the project) stated in the agreement. In the absence of a provision in the operating agreement so stating, however, the LLC statute could require that allocations and distributions be made in equal shares. *See* 805 Ill. Comp. Stat. 180/25-1(a) (2009).

49 Treas. Reg. § 1.704-1(b)(2)(ii)(*b*)(*2*). The corollary is that a member with a deficit balance in that member's capital account, must pay ("restore") it to the LLC. If the member is not obligated to restore a deficit (a "DRO"), no allocations can be made to that member which would create a deficit which is not offset by a share of minimum gain. *Id.* at paragraph (*d*).

distributions in liquidation of a partner's interest.

Partnership allocations can be manipulated to achieve the desired economic result. For example, allocations might be made according to an initial sharing arrangement until some point, specified in the agreement, has been reached. At that point, the sharing percentages may change or "flip" to allocate more to one partner, typically the developer, and less to the others.[50] This is how allocations can be used to insert more flexibility into the deal negotiated by the parties. In some cases, the design of partnership allocations may reach the level of an art form, although in practical terms, the imagination of the draftsman will be bounded by his or her ability to explain the result to the client.

[iv] Distributions and Allocations

The LLC operating agreement will have to provide for distributions and allocations separately. A distribution is a real event, and can cause unexpected tax consequences. To meet the safe-harbor for tax allocations, the operating agreement must contain a provision defined in the regulations as a "qualified income offset." See Treas. Reg. § 1.704-1(b)(2)(ii)(*d*)(*6*). A member's capital account must be reduced by the amount of any distribution made to the member. If the reduction causes the deficit in the member's capital account to fall below the permitted level (viz., that member's share of minimum gain of the LLC), then the member must have agreed in advance to receive an allocation of gross income from the LLC until the deficit has been eliminated. In effect, the operating agreement must specify that deficit cash distributions constitute a direct distribution of taxable income.[51]

Allocations, on the other hand, are just that, allocations of tax quantities. An allocation can always be changed, although, because of the effect on capital accounts, there may be secondary tax effects.

[v] Allocations Under the Fox Valley Auto Care Center, LLC Operating Agreement

The original Fox Valley Auto Care Center Limited Partnership Agreement did not contain the necessary provisions for the economic effect "safe-harbor." We have inserted these provisions in the operating agreement for the LLC to conform it to the typical provisions you would expect to find in a properly drafted agreement for a real estate project. In the actual agreement, all distributions, including liquidating distributions, were to be made according to sharing percentages specified in the agreement (40% for the Investors and 60% for the General Partner), so these provisions should not make any difference in the actual deal. The minimum gain system was not installed either, but this can be explained because the nonrecourse allocation regulations had not been promulgated when the

---

[50] In the arrangement described in the text, the developer's interest is referred to as the "carried interest" (viz., carried by the investment of the Investors). The use of carried interests for the benefit of managers in Hedge Fund agreements has led to proposals to tax allocations to managers as compensation.

[51] *See* Section 4.6(e) of the Fox Valley Auto Care Center, LLC Operating Agreement (in the Document Book). This provision also contains a "look ahead" rule under which distributions which are planned to be made the following year must be anticipated in order to preserve enough in the distributee member's capital account to absorb the amount of the planned distribution.

original agreement was negotiated. Treas. Dec. 8385, published in the Federal Register on December 26, 1991. Moreover, a permanent nonrecourse loan was never put in place, so the minimum gain system would not have been needed. Instead, the partnership operated over a three-year period with a recourse loan, under which the three principals in the general partner had personally guaranteed the loan. There was, therefore, never any minimum gain which could be used to support deficit allocations to the limited partners.

Under those circumstances, an allocation of a tax quantity could *not* have been made to an investor if the allocation would have created a deficit in that investor's capital account. Here, too, the original partnership agreement failed to respect capital accounts, because it did not appropriately limit the tax allocation of losses. That could have been a problem for the Fox Valley Auto Care Center Limited Partnership, as the maximum amount of tax losses (depreciation deductions in excess of cash flow after finance) which could have been allocated to the limited partners would have been the sum of their capital contributions. Reallocation of some of those tax losses to the general partners could have upset the "economic equivalence" on which the partners would have had to rely.

We have created the basic documents for the Fox Valley Auto Care Center, LLC. This entity has been created under the Illinois Act, which was enacted in 1994. As pointed out earlier, the operations of the LLC are governed by an "operating agreement" which can override any provision in the Act with certain limited exceptions. In order to form an LLC, articles of organization must be filed with the Secretary of State, along with certain other formalities. This is a basic document which rarely would contain the substantive provisions required to make the tax rules work for the LLC. The articles must state, however, whether the LLC is a member-managed LLC or a Manager-managed LLC. We have chosen to designate the Fox Valley Auto Care Center, LLC as Manager-managed because of the authority this designation confers on Regent, which had similar authority as the General Partner in the original limited partnership. And we have inserted in the LLC's Operating Agreement provisions necessary to apply the "safe harbor" rule to support tax allocations in the event that permanent financing could be negotiated to take out the construction loan.

§ 4.03 THE FOX VALLEY AUTO CARE CENTER, LLC OPERATING AGREEMENT

The Operating Agreement is in the Document Book. The following discussion, which examines some of the specific provisions included in the agreement, is keyed to that document, and you should refer to it for the context of the provisions discussed here.

[1] General Comments

Each state has enacted a Limited Liability Company Act.[52] These statutes provide default rules governing the obligations of the members to each other, to the LLC and to outsiders with whom the LLC transacts business. Most of these rules can be (and usually are) superseded by the operating agreement.[53]

As familiarity with the LLC form has increased, so has its use. For this reason, we have chosen to restructure the arrangement for the Fox Valley project as an LLC. The thing to keep in mind is that these entities are recent creations, and the legal doctrines which will govern the relationships among the members in the future are undeveloped. Will the LLC effectively shield all members from liability for the debts of the enterprise? How will these doctrines interact with the partnership tax rules on which the success of real estate ventures rest? Questions such as these have not been resolved. Perhaps the difficult economic conditions of the past few years will result in litigation or in the promulgation of additional tax authority that will provide more certainty.

[2] Definitions

Many of the terms used in operating agreements to make the allocations required by the negotiated deal between the parties do not have a technical meaning. Thus, a provision which divides the "profits and losses" of the LLC really does not provide as much information as members or their accountants need to know in order to implement such a provision. Accordingly, these terms must be defined. In addition, as previously discussed, the tax rules *require* the insertion of some very technical provisions in the agreement. The drafting of these provisions can be considerably simplified (and made more elegant) through the judicious use of definitions. As a result, the "Definitions" article of virtually every operating agreement should contain vital information affecting the substance of the deal negotiated by the parties to the agreement. You should *always* study this part of the operating agreement with care, as a lot of the "custom" work done in the agreement has been done in the definitions.[54] And you can usually tell when a defined term is encountered because, as a widely accepted convention, the term is capitalized for no apparent reason.

---

52 As one example, see 805 Ill. Comp. Stat.180/Art. 1-60 (2009), effective January 1, 1994.

53 For a limited partnership, the partnership agreement can also override most of the statutory provisions governing the formation and operations of limited partnerships, with the statute serving as a set of "default" rules. While one might think that the entity formation issues for the two types of entities are similar, there are enough differences between the two to make correlations difficult. The most significant difference is that no member of an LLC is liable for the debts of the company merely by being a member, whereas a limited partnership must have a general partner, which is liable for the debts of the partnership. When capital account deficits occur in an LLC, as they often do for real estate ventures, the tax rules require that some member be ultimately liable to pay the debt. When that feature is lacking, the tax rules may prevent use of the tax advantages these rules would otherwise allow. *See* note 33 *supra*.

54 There are many "forms" which are provided as references for the drafting of operating agreements, and most law firms will have some which they use as the beginning point for the drafting of agreements for specific deals. One should always take care in using a form, and never use a provision without knowing precisely what it is intended to accomplish. Many of these forms, however, omit a provision defining terms used in the agreement. To us, this is a missed opportunity, as the definitions will provide the inexperienced draftsperson with cues as to where the important operative issues are to be dealt with.

You should read through Article II of the Operating Agreement. A few of the more important definitions are discussed below:

[a] "Adjusted Capital Account Deficit"

This is defined in § 2.2, and § 3.4 spells out how each member's capital account will be determined. The Treasury Regulations are very specific about how each adjustment to the account should be made, and the safe harbor rules require that these adjustments follow precisely the regulatory provisions. Rather than specify all of the technical steps required, here as in other provisions meant to conform to the tax rules, the definitions refer to the regulation involved (and to the "Allocation Regulations" generally), and state that these rules are to be followed. In the application of the nonrecourse debt rules, a deficit in a member's capital account may arise, as we have described, but will be covered by a chargeback rule that automatically offsets the apparent deficit. It is difficult to describe how this process works, and to avoid excessive technical verbiage which is meaningless to most real estate lawyers, the definition incorporates the offset and permits a much simpler expression of the intended result (to permit technical capital account deficits which are offset by other provisions in the rules).

[b] "Capital Contributions"

"Capital Contributions" is defined in § 2.7, and capital contributions by the members are more fully provided for in Article III, which spells out the initial obligations of the parties to contribute to the LLC. The provisions in Article III go further and include all subsequent contributions to the LLC.

[c] "Capital Transactions"

The definitions identify two types of transactions, for which different distribution provisions are made. In the "capital transaction" (§ 2.8), loans to the LLC from lending institutions (generally) or proceeds from the sales of assets are identified as cash available for distribution from the disposition or refinancing of the LLC's assets. In many real estate projects, there would be different priorities in making distributions from this type of transaction than from operating cash flow, and this would be reflected in the distributional allocations. *See* §§ 4.2 and 4.3 of the Operating Agreement.

[d] "Cash Flow"

> § 2.9 "Cash Flow" — See Net Cash Receipts.
>
> § 2.10 "Cash Funds from Operations" means gross receipts and other income derived from the development, ownership and operation of the Property (other than funds received as Capital Contributions, Financing Proceeds or Sales Proceeds).

The definitions frequently refer to other defined terms. You can sense here the complexity of these provisions by noting that "cash" is defined in different ways. A reference to cash outside of these definitions would be ambiguous. In this deal, cash flow from operations (viz., mainly from rent) is treated differently than cash derived from sales or financing of the LLC's assets. Often, cash derived from asset transactions would be treated as a rearrangement of the capital interests in the firm, as contrasted with interests in return from operations.

[e] "Financing Proceeds"

Read this definition in § 2.13 with care. To what does it specifically refer? Look at Article IV, which provides how *distributions* are to be made, and § 4.3, which specifies how Proceeds from Capital Transactions (which includes Financing Proceeds and Sales Proceeds) are to be treated. Generally, refinancing and sale result in a withdrawal of capital from the enterprise, and these distributions may be used to achieve different investment objectives (such as reimbursement for Contributions to Capital) than distributions of regular operating funds.

[f] "Gross Asset Value"

As part of the "safe harbor" for tax allocations, the LLC's assets must be initially included in Capital Accounts at fair market value. Thereafter, the assets are stated at a book value which will be this initial value adjusted for depreciation calculated with respect to the original book value. The tax rules require that Capital Accounts provide for each member's entitlement out of the assets of the LLC, so occasionally restatement of the book value may be necessary to preserve a member's economic interest in the deal. This may occur, for example, when a new member makes a capital contribution and is admitted to membership in the LLC. At that time, existing members would be concerned that the value of their interest in the assets of the LLC be preserved relative to the amount contributed by the new member. To accomplish this objective, the value of the assets on the books of the LLC will then be increased ("booked up") to market value ("Gross Asset Value") and the amount of the increase allocated among the existing members in proportion to the way in which those members would have shared in the gain if the assets had actually been sold to a third party. This process is stated in § 2.14, the definition of "Gross Asset Value," and references to this term then include references to the process without the need to restate it.

The increase in value has the effect of deferral of tax on the gain in which the members have shared in the book-up. For tax allocation purposes, this deferred gain must be taken into account in making tax allocations and corresponding adjustments to the members' capital accounts. Hence, the definition of "Depreciation" in § 2.12 requires that depreciation be computed for capital account adjustment purposes using the book value of the assets, even if the amount of depreciation for tax purposes is less. *See* Operating Agreement § 2.31 (defining "Profits and Losses" to include book gains and losses). This problem is discussed in section 4.03[4][f], *infra*.

[g] "Net Cash Receipts" or "Net Cash Flows"

This term in § 2.20 corresponds generally to Cash Flow After Finance ("CFAF") which is the cash flow available for distribution to owners of the equity (viz., the members). Notice the authority of the Manager over decisions about what expenses to pay and which reserves to create and fund.

[h] "Nonrecourse Debt or Nonrecourse Liability"

It is not entirely settled how a recourse liability incurred by an LLC should be defined for purposes of the tax rules. Section 2.21 cites the provisions of the regulations that control this question, and this definition is intended to apply the interpretation of the regulatory provisions which supports the application of the nonrecourse debt system to the LLC's operations.

[i] "Nonrecourse Deductions"

Nonrecourse debt at the company level is often used to provide tax benefits, usually in the form of depreciation deductions, to members in the LLC. In § 2.22 these deductions are allowed before the proceeds of the loan which supports the deductions have been taxed. As we have discussed in this and earlier chapters of the book, the allowance of these deductions is the tax benefit which flows from the use of nonrecourse indebtedness. This (as well as the distribution of financing proceeds from a refinancing of nonrecourse debt) can result in a deficit in members' capital accounts. When that happens, a "Minimum Gain" is created or increased, and this "minimum gain" represents a deferred taxable gain which offsets the tax benefit which the members have been allocated. To keep track of which members are responsible for reporting the taxable income that the minimum gain will produce in the future, it is allocated among the members according to the manner in which they share the tax benefit (the Nonrecourse Deductions). The regulations permit this allocation to be made differently from taxable income or loss generally, hence the definition.

[j] "Partner Nonrecourse Debt"

A member may become liable to make a payment on an entity-level debt which is in form nonrecourse. Recall that Regent and its principals guaranteed the bank loan for the Center.The tax regulations continue to treat this debt as if it were a nonrecourse debt, but all of the tax incidents related to that debt are then allocated to the member(s) who bear the "economic risk of loss," meaning that, in the end, they will be required to pay the debt. *See* Treas. Reg. §§ 1.704-2(b)(4), -2(i). The nonrecourse rules (minimum gain, etc.) apply to this type of debt (and deductions and other tax benefits associated with it) in the same way that they apply to Partnership Nonrecourse Debt, except that all of the tax incidents flowing from this debt are allocated to the members who bear the risk of loss. Hence, in §§ 2.26, 2.27 and 2.28 the terms "Partner Nonrecourse . . ." etc. *See* Operating Agreement § 4.6(d).

[k] "Partnership Minimum Gain"

This definition in § 2.29 refers to the tax gain that would be realized on the foreclosure of LLC assets by the lender, or the disposition of LLC assets in lieu of foreclosure, a tax issue presented and resolved in *Commissioner v. Tufts, supra* Section 3.05[2]. Minimum gain is a deferred taxable gain which each member to whom a "Share of Partnership Minimum Gain" has been allocated has agreed to report and pay tax. *See* Operating Agreement, § 4.6(c) ("minimum gain chargeback").

[1] "Sales Proceeds"

The definition in § 2.35 is similar to the definition of "Financing Proceeds" and has been inserted in the Agreement, most likely, to reserve to the Manager control over the size of any contingency reserves. In a single project real estate entity, like the Fox Valley Auto Care Center, LLC, sale of the property signals the termination of that particular project, and distribution will liquidate the interests of the members.

[3] Capital Contributions and Capital Accounts (Article III)

This article specifies the members' "Participating Percentages" in the LLC. The meaning of these percentages depends on how allocations and distributions are defined, although it is useful to set these percentages early in the agreement, particularly where all items are shared by the same percentage.

[a] "Capital Contributions" of the Manager (§ 3.4(b))

The Manager, Regent Real Estate Development Corporation, would have transferred the contract right to acquire the "Property" to the LLC, which would have been shown on the LLC books as having a value of zero, although the purchase contract, paid for by other properties (including a portion of the Johnson Tract), clearly had value. Regent had negotiated this contract, and the contracts with the other parties, on its own behalf (recall the discussion in Chapter 2 of how the proceeds from the sale of the Turtle Wax portion of the tract would be handled) as well as for the LLC. This, along with the development work necessary to bring the shopping center plan to fruition and to obtain the construction loan from First Mortgage Bank ("FMB"), was essential for the success of the venture, but there is no indication in any of the records whether that value was shown on the books of the entity and included in Regent's capital account. *See United States v. Stafford*, 727 F.2d 1043 (11th Cir. 1984). One of the requirements of the "economic effect" regulations for tax purposes is that "property" contributed to the capital of the entity be reflected in the capital account of the contributing member *at its fair market value*. Treas. Reg. § 1.704-1(b)(2)(iv)(*d*)(*1*). In this case, the Operating Agreement states that the Manager had used its own funds to begin the development of the Fox Valley Auto Care Center (the "Property"), intending to be reimbursed by the construction loan (the "Loan"), and implicitly the nonrecourse take-out loan. To the extent that the loan proceeds were not sufficient, the Manager's unreimbursed expenditures would be specifically included as a Capital Contribution, and therefore in the Manager's capital account.

[b] The "Letter of Credit" (§§ 3.3(b)–(f))

The obligation of the members, other than the Manager, (the "investors") to provide the agreed upon Letter of Credit is included in their obligation, specified in the Operating Agreement, to provide capital to the enterprise. An investor who does not comply with this requirement becomes a "Defaulting Member," and the other investors are then obligated to perform. The terms of the Letter of Credit are stated, and it is made clear that the Letter of Credit is intended solely as credit enhancement for the construction loan. The agreement specifies that a draw against the Letter of Credit will be treated as a capital contribution and therefore an increase in the Capital Accounts of the investors, § 3.4(b)(iii), a provision that is consistent with the tax law. Finally, the Operating Agreement authorizes the Manager to take steps to remedy the failure or refusal of an investor to comply with his or its agreement to provide the Letter of Credit, and to extend it (§ 3.5). These provisions will have been negotiated for the purpose of protecting both the LLC and the investor, who might be unwilling to proceed past a certain point. Typically, these provisions include the right to buy out the investor for his or its out-of-pocket cost minus expenses of correcting the problem. Members other than the Manager in a Manager-managed LLC do not have opt-out rights under the Illinois statute, but these rights can be provided in the operating agreement.[55]

[c] "Capital Accounts" (§ 3.4)

The obligation to maintain Capital Accounts is spelled out, with appropriate cross references to the allocation and distributions provisions of the Operating Agreement. The Operating Agreement then states that Capital Accounts are to be maintained "with all other adjustments required for the proper maintenance of capital accounts for Federal income tax purposes." This statement is essentially a direction to the LLC's accountants to do what is necessary to comply with the tax law rules on capital account maintenance.

[d] Additional Capital (§ 3.7)

The Manager is authorized to raise additional capital if it decides that such action is required. If new members are admitted, in exchange for a participating percentage determined by the Manager in its discretion, then the participating percentages for the existing members (viz., the Manager *and* the investors) are reduced proportionately. This is a common provision in these agreements intended to permit the Manager, that is the developer, to revise the capital structure if the initial capitalization proves to be insufficient. There is an anti-dilution provision to protect a Non-Defaulting member from being squeezed out. Under the anti-dilution provision, any reduction in any member's percentage interest in the LLC must occur pro rata between the Manager and the investors. If interests in the LLC are represented by Units, as is proposed here, issuance of additional units to a new member would automatically have that effect.

[4] Distributions and Allocations (Article IV)

In order to comply with the economic effect test for tax purposes (the "safe harbor"), proper maintenance of capital accounts is essential. Distributions must be made from capital accounts, which means that, when no member has a deficit restoration obligation, no distribution can properly be made which has the effect of reducing the distributee member's capital account below zero. Therefore, the provision on *allocations*, which is the method by which capital accounts are manipulated to assure that economic effect rules are not violated, comes first, subject to a series of special prescribed adjustments. Once the capital account values have been determined, then the distributions can be made, with the limit on distributions measured by the amounts included in the capital accounts. A distribution, however, is a real event and has economic significance, so that the allocations, to have economic effect for tax purposes, will have to take the facts on

[55] 805 Ill. Comp. Stat. 180/35-50(a).

the ground (viz., distributions) into account and be adjusted accordingly. The adjustment of allocations to correct for economic issues is made in § 4.6, and all allocations are subject to these provisions. The Operating Agreement has provisions which are intended to assure this result.

Before discussing these provisions in more detail, we note that the allocation and distribution provisions of an operating agreement represent the heart of the economic deal the parties have made. The draftsperson of these provisions (the so-called "waterfall") should test them by making a series of assumptions about how the project will operate and applying the allocation and distribution provisions to those assumed fact situations. Only in this way can the actual effect of a set of allocation and distributions provisions be seen and unhappy surprises avoided.

[a] Allocation of Operating Profits and Losses (§ 4.1)

Profits and Losses are defined as tax items, and appropriate adjustments are made relative to these tax items. *See* § 2.31. These items are allocated to members (and reported on their income tax returns) and reflected appropriately in each member's Capital Account. In making the calculations, positive adjustments are made before distributions are subtracted. Note, however, that if the lender draws against the Letters of Credit of an investor, cash flow will then be distributed to the investors whose Letters of Credit were drawn down to repay the investor. Under the allocation rule, Operating Profit is allocable, first, to cover the repayment, that is, the repayment is treated for tax purposes as having been made, first, from taxable income. You should think carefully about this allocation. If you represented the investors, is this the arrangement you would recommend?

[b] Allocation of Profits and Losses from a Capital Transaction

Capital Transactions usually affect the capital interests of the members. This allocation occurs after application of the special allocation provisions, including the Minimum Gain Chargeback (§§ 4.6(c) and (d)). In most cases, a chargeback will occur when assets are sold and the minimum gain with respect to that asset is eliminated. Since the chargeback applies first, gain or loss may already have been allocated to offset negative balances in the capital accounts of the members. Once the chargeback has been applied, additional gain realized in the capital transaction will be used, first, to bring all capital accounts to zero, and then to make positive adjustments to capital accounts to realize the economic deal negotiated by the parties, in this case, sharing in the economics in proportion to their "Participating Percentages." Remember that the capital accounts are intended to implement, in the final analysis, the economics of the deal, and to provide for each member the share that member expects to receive. The operating agreement should provide that liquidation of the LLC will follow positive balances in the members' capital accounts. *See* § 4.4(a)(ii).

Losses from Capital Transactions are allocated proportionally among members with positive balances in their capital accounts (to absorb the losses). No member, however, has a deficit restoration obligation, apart from the deemed restoration obligation arising from minimum gain. *See* § 4.4(b). What happens if losses exceed the aggregate positive values in all capital accounts? If calculations are accurate, this contingency should not occur, as these losses would, presumably, be borne by the lender (or by the guarantors).

[c] Operating Distributions (§ 4.2)

Operating distributions are distributions of "Net Cash Receipts," which is a defined term. It includes the entire cash flow through the entity, other than Capital Transactions, less debt service payments, and all other operating expenditures including additions to reserves, except payments made from Capital Contributions and Financing Proceeds. That is, distributions of operating cash (assuming that this is what is intended) must be made according to the following priorities: (1) reimbursement of draws against the Letter of Credit; (2) repayment of Developer unreimbursed capital expenditures; and (3) the excess according to Participating Percentages. Operating Distributions do not explicitly include repayment of capital contributions, although this might reflect an assumption that capital has been contributed in the same proportion as Participating Percentages.

Because no member has a deficit restoration obligation, distributions may not cause an "Adjusted Capital Account Deficit" in any member's capital account. You might expect distributions to be covered by the nonrecourse debt system, which has the effect of creating deemed deficit restoration obligations. But consider the guarantees made by the Manager and its principals. This may skew allocations in the minimum gain system to them, and that would potentially expose the investors to unexpected tax effects. Distributions which exceed the positive balance in the distributee member's capital account automatically become distributions of gross income. This is the effect of the "qualified income offset." *See* § 4.6(e). The effect is to *shift* taxable income from the Manager to the investors.

[d] Distributions from Capital Transactions (§ 4.3)

This provision establishes a system of priorities for the distribution of the proceeds from capital transactions (viz., a refinancing or a sale of the property). It is clear that these priorities were negotiated: (1) reimbursement of draws against the Letter of Credit, proportionately; (2) repayment of additional capital contributions, proportionately; (3) reimbursement of additional capital provided in the development process by Regent, less any amount previously reimbursed; (4) return of initial capital contributions; and (5) the balance, if any, according to participating percentages. This system tracks positive additions to the capital accounts as provided in the agreement, and allocates the remaining proceeds in excess of the priority amounts according to the Participating Percentages. This excess may represent gain or loss on sale. In the case of a refinancing, it would represent *unrealized* gain, which, most likely, had not been booked into capital accounts. The distribution of the proceeds of a refinancing may represent the distribution of minimum gain and would then increase the distributee member's share of entity minimum gain.[56] This protects the distributee from immediate tax effects. Note also that when the distribution of the proceeds of a capital transaction results in the liquidation of the LLC and in making the distribution in accordance with the positive balances in capital accounts, as required by Section 4.4(a)(ii), the Manager is authorized, with the approval of the members, to make adjustments in distributions (presumably also affecting the allocation of taxable gain or loss) in order to realize the economics of the original deal. In a straightforward pro rata

[56] Treas. Reg. § 1.704-2(h).

arrangement like this one, no one expects this kind of adjustment to be necessary.

[e] Special Allocation Provisions (§ 4.6)

These provisions implement a series of special adjustments the tax rules may require in order for the operating agreement to comply with the safe-harbor. We have already discussed the "minimum gain chargeback," § 4.6(c), and the "qualified income offset," § 4.6(d). Nonrecourse deductions and "excess nonrecourse liabilities," § 4.6(j), may be allocated in a different manner than the basic allocation provisions, but that is not done here. Note that "Partner Nonrecourse Deductions" and other comparable items are allocated under the nonrecourse liability system. The special allocation provisions also make clear that a loss may not be allocated to a member if the effect of the allocation would be to cause an Adjusted Capital Account Deficit for that member. While there is a gap in the application of these rules to the LLC, in most cases like this, the gap will not matter. Losses have to be funded somehow, and that usually means that a creditor is bearing the risk that the loss will ultimately be realized.

[f] I.R.C. Section 704(c) (§ 4.6(h))

Section 4.6(h) requires that unrealized gain or loss on LLC property at the time the property is contributed to the LLC ("precontribution gain or loss") be allocated to and taxed to the member who contributed the property. Its purpose is to prevent precontribution gain or loss from being shifted and taxed to a different taxpayer, a strategy which was possible in the early days before Congress required allocations to meet the economic effect test. The statute specifically applies to property contributed to an LLC at a time when that property's fair market value differed from its tax basis. When that happens, the economic effect test requires that the capital account of the contributing member be increased by the fair market value of the contributed property. Because the member will have a tax basis for his interest equal to the basis of the contributed property, the contribution has created a "book-tax disparity," which the statute requires be resolved as quickly as possible. The problem creates a battery of tax effects, which are now dealt with in an elaborate regulation. *See* Treas. Reg. § 1.704-3. When there is a § 704(c) problem, you truly do need to consult a tax lawyer.

The Fox Valley Auto Care Center, LLC was created with cash contributions, or the equivalent, and it then constructed the Auto Care Center. There is no precontribution gain, and § 704(c) has no apparent application. One should not assume that this is the end of the problem. Book-tax disparities can also be created when additional capital contributions are made to the LLC which have the effect of changing the sharing percentages, or when there is a distribution to a member as consideration for all or part of that member's interest in the LLC. Booking up the LLC accounts to reflect the then value of its assets, which is permitted (and usually recommended), *see* Treas. Reg. § 1.704-1(b)(2)(iv)(*f*)(5), Operating Agreement § 2.14(b), will create a book-tax disparity which must be resolved using § 704(c) principles even if § 704(c) does not literally apply. Even if the accounts are not "booked up," the economic effect regulations require allocations to be made using § 704(c) principles.

[g] Corrected Allocations (§ 4.6(k))

As you have seen, the drafting technique used to apply the technical allocation rules of the Treasury Regulations is to use a cross reference to the regulations themselves rather than restate the requirements in the technical jargon of the tax rules. The allocation provisions of operating agreements are intended to meld application of these requirements with the economic deal made by the parties, but sometimes this does not work out very well. Application of the tax rules, and the requirement that the operating agreement specify that liquidating distributions follow positive balances in capital accounts, may produce distortions in the members' interests. In this case, for example, the guarantees are likely to cause the bank loan to be characterized as "partner nonrecourse indebtedness," which would require the allocation of deductions and losses attributable to the debt specifically to the members who made the guarantees despite the objective to share these items equally. Most agreements, therefore, include a provision, similar to § 4.6(h) of the Fox Valley Operating Agreement, authorizing the Manager to modify the allocation rules in order to qualify the allocations for the safe-harbor while preserving the economics of the original deal. Correcting distortions, when they occur, is not a simple task, so these allocation rules generally represent a set of instructions to the Manager (and the LLC's accountants) to do the best they can to conform to the rules. When the deal is a straight pro rata deal, like the one here, assuming that the construction loan, subject to the guarantees and credit enhancements frequently required by the construction lender, has been taken out by a typical nonrecourse permanent loan, distortions are less likely to occur

[5] Books, Records, Reporting (Article VI)

These are standard provisions, imposing upon the Manager the duty to prepare reports, chief among them the Schedule K, which provides information to the members needed by them to file their tax returns. For tax purposes, partnership tax returns (Form 1065) are audited separately from the returns of the individual members, even though the LLC as a tax partnership is not a "taxpayer," and adjustments proposed on that return will be applied automatically to the returns of the individual members. *See* I.R.C. §§ 6221–6231. The partnership audit rules do not apply to "small partnerships," but, because Regent, the Manager, is an S Corporation, the exception for small partnerships will not be available to the Fox Valley Auto Care Center, LLC. Regent is expressly appointed to be the "Tax Matters Partner" under I.R.C. § 6231(a)(7), with authority to negotiate with the IRS over any tax issue involving the LLC and with the obligation to keep the members informed about any tax question that might arise. *See* § 7.11 of the Operating Agreement.

[6] Powers, Rights and Obligations of the Manager (Article VII)

This part of the Operating Agreement authorizes the Manager to handle all business matters for the LLC and sets out its obligations to do certain specified things. Typically, it is authorized to engage in other real estate transactions (that is, to continue its normal business operations) without incurring liability to the LLC. Under the Agreement, the members agree that the authorizations it contains constitute special powers of attorney specifically authorizing the Manager to deal with the Property and their interests in the LLC by executing the documents required to create, operate and ultimately dispose of the Property. *See* Article VII.

In a typical LLC, or limited partnership, established to develop real estate, it is common for the investors to agree that the manager has the power and authority not only to manage the entity's affairs on a day to day basis, but also to have sole authority to make major decisions as well. The investors usually do not have as much expertise in real estate development as the manager does and they are looking to the manager to operate the investment knowing that if it should act in a fraudulent manner, they will have recourse against the manager. However, sometimes, if an investor has invested a substantial amount of the equity in the deal, or the investor has extensive experience in real estate development, the investor may try to negotiate to be involved in certain "major decisions." This involvement could be in the form of requiring consent from all of the members or a majority of the members for certain actions. Examples of possible major decisions include: refinancing the debt, sale of the property, amendment of the operating agreement, the filing of a law suit, or liquidation of the LLC's assets. If a limited partnership was used as the vehicle for the transaction, a limited partner had to be careful not to require too much of a say in the operation of the partnership or it could lose its limited liability. This is not a problem when the investment vehicle is a limited liability company, but one should check the state statute authorizing the formation of a limited liability company to make sure that this is the case.

Article VII also contains exculpation (§ 7.7) and indemnification (§ 7.8) provisions for actions taken by the Manager on behalf of the LLC unless done "in bad faith, recklessly, negligently or in breach of . . . the Agreement." Section 7.6 authorizes the Manager to borrow money on behalf of the LLC from itself or from an affiliate, and states the maximum interest rate which can be charged. There is no provision here dealing with priority cash distributions used to repay such loans, a provision which is often found in agreements of this kind. None of these provisions is unusual. In a situation where there are more outsider investors, one would expect to find a more thoroughly negotiated set of warranties by the Manager, and corresponding limitations on the exercise of the Manager's authority.

[a] The Letter of Credit

If the LLC is dissolved by an act of the Manager which breaches the agreement, Regent is obligated only to use its "best efforts" to secure the return of the Letter of Credit, to the extent not drawn upon. This provision seems intended to protect Regent from liability for damages if it does not succeed, for example, in obtaining necessary financing.

[b] Valuation Issues

Sections 7.9 and 7.10 deal with valuation issues that frequently occur when a member dies. In § 7.9, the Manager has reserved the discretion to make or revoke an election under I.R.C. § 754, and may do so at the "reasonable request" of a member, "*provided* the member agrees to pay the incremental [accounting] costs." Recall that the LLC has an inside basis for its assets and the member has a separate outside basis for his interest in the LLC. As described, it is desirable for these two bases to be determined in the same manner, so that the inside basis is equal to the sum of the outside bases for all of the members. There are occasions, however, when a transaction involving a member's interest will not affect the basis of LLC assets, such as a taxable sale of a member's interest or the death of a member with transmission of the interest to the member's heirs. When that happens, the member's successor will have an outside tax basis which is, usually, higher than that member's share of the inside basis for LLC assets. *See* I.R.C. §§ 1012 (basis for purchased property is cost), 1014 (basis for inherited property is fair market value at date of death). Because gain or loss, and depreciation, is determined at the company level, a lower inside basis will produce more taxable income than the successor member should receive. Inside basis is not changed (viz., increased) *unless* an election under I.R.C. § 754 is made, and then complicated allocations and bookkeeping will be required to comply with the law. These additional accounting burdens can be substantial, which is why the LLC agreement requires the member requesting the election to agree to pay the incremental cost.

The valuation issue dealt with in § 7.10 is similar. This provision obligates the Manager to cooperate in determining a value for a membership interest for transfer tax purposes, again *provided* that the member requesting the valuation agrees to pay the incremental cost, most likely an appraisal fee. In addition, because tax partnership allocations will be affected by a transfer in the middle of the LLC's taxable year, the Manager is authorized to require the member requesting the accounting services to agree to pay, and perhaps even to prepay, the cost of these services, including an hourly fee for the accounting work. The allocations required result from dividing the LLC's Fiscal Year into two portions, and allocating tax items in an appropriate way between those two portions. *See* I.R.C. §§ 706(c)-(d) and § 4.2(d) of the Operating Agreement.

Provisions which specifically authorize the Manager to require payment (and even prepayment) of the cost of additional accounting services needed to comply with the rules regarding partnership tax elections when an interest is transferred are, again, not unusual. What does seem to be different here is the specificity with which this provision is made. It appears that these elections have been discussed by the parties, either for this LLC or in other similarly structured deals.

[7] Transfers of Interests (Article IX)

Restrictions on transfer are common in limited partnership agreements or operating agreements of limited liability companies. While the agreement cannot prevent the transfer of the economic interest to a transferee, it will usually place conditions on the "substitution" of a member by the transferee. Article IX of the operating agreement is typical. The concern here is that a transfer not cause problems for the LLC with the securities laws or by causing a constructive liquidation of the LLC for tax purposes.[57] Moreover, if a person is to be admitted as a substitute member, the person will be asked to agree to the terms and conditions imposed on a member by the operating agreement. Remember that the LLC is a tax partnership, and the tax effects of transactions at the partnership

[57] Under I.R.C. § 708, a sale or exchange of 50% or more of the "total interest" in a tax partnership within a twelve month period causes a constructive liquidation of the partnership for tax purposes. This would cause a readjustment of all of the important tax quantities for the partnership, and, as this agreement makes clear, is a consequence to avoid.

level will be allocated to and reported by the transferee on the transferee's tax return.

Moreover, compliance with the tax regulations to assure the intended tax effect of allocations made under the agreement may also result in the imposition of tax liabilities or other restrictions on distributions. Most agreements also permit the original investors to make transfers to family members or to further an estate plan. The Operating Agreement enforces these conditions by giving authority to the Manager to approve the substitution of a member in its "sole and absolute discretion," except for family transfers by the original investors where the member agrees to remain personally liable for agreed upon capital contributions and renewal of the letters of credit. Perhaps this grant of authority goes too far and the Manager should only be able to reject a potential substitute member on a reasonable basis; it is possible that some of this language was influenced by the prior tax law that required a limited partnership to have non-corporate characteristics (free transferability being a corporate characteristic). In the event there is a dispute about a specific transfer if there is only a small group of investors, the agreement may provide a right of first refusal to the remaining members, with carefully negotiated conditions on the offering and exercise of such a right. Remember that these are exit provisions, which can prove to be vitally important under some unknown future circumstances. And in all of these cases, the agreement will assert that the transfer is "void" unless it complies with conditions specified in the governing provision.

The Agreement provides that the Manager cannot transfer its interest without the consent of the members except for a transfer of a security interest for a loan to the LLC, or a transfer to an entity which is wholly owned by the current Manager or the owners of the current Manager. *See* § 9.2(c) of the Operating Agreement. This restriction makes sense, since the members are relying on the expertise of the specific Manager, Regent, and the individuals who comprise this entity. The exception allows the Manager some flexibility in its corporate structure without effecting any real change as to who is in control and liable, and also clarifies that a transfer to secure a membership obligation is acceptable.

[8] Dissolution (Article X)

"Dissolution" is a state law concept that applies to partnerships but not necessarily to other types of entities, such as a limited liability company, or at least not in the same way. When a partnership is "dissolved," its theoretical existence (an agency relationship) ceases. A partnership which is dissolved, usually by the exit of the general partner (exit of a limited partner cannot cause a dissolution) may nonetheless continue, although the successor entity is, abstractly, a new partnership.

For a limited liability company, dissolution, meaning termination of the LLC's juridical existence, is defined by statute and generally means that the LLC has ceased to do business, although the operating agreement can specify the circumstances in which a dissolution can occur. Actual liquidation of the enterprise (that is, the sale of its assets followed by a distribution of the proceeds to members) can result from a dissolution, although this question, also an exit right, is usually treated as a different issue. The conditions under which physical liquidation would occur are often carefully negotiated, particularly since modern statutes do provide certain exit rights by default, which would usually be superseded by the agreement. The Operating Agreement does not contain detailed dissolution or liquidation provisions, providing instead that the Manager has authority to decide whether the LLC should be dissolved. While this does seem to confer a lot of authority on Regent, in deals like this one, the developer and its investors usually will be repeat players, and the developer will be motivated to protect the interests of its investors.

[9] Member "Representations and Warranties" (Article XVI)

This provision is meant to comply with requirements of Federal and State Securities Laws. The LLC has offered membership interests to the investors, which are "securities" for purposes of these regulatory statutes, under an exemption from registration which requires that the members be "accredited investors." *See* § 16(h). Moreover, as this provision makes clear, Regent did not prepare an "offering memorandum" which would make the necessary disclosures about the formation and operation of the LLC. The investors acknowledge the lack of formal disclosure, § 16(g), and warrant that they have carefully reviewed the operating agreement with the help of any advisors they might select, § 16(e), and with an understanding of the financial and other matters provided in the Operating Agreement, § 16(d). They also warrant that they are purchasing interests in the LLC for their own account and solely for investment purposes. (§§ 16(a) and (b).) This part of the Operating Agreement is designed to protect Regent from liability under the securities laws, but, since the actual disclosure is not documented, if a question arises, it may not be effective by itself.

[10] Drafting Assignment — Revisions to the Fox Valley Auto Care Center, LLC Operating Agreement

An LLC operating agreement is a blueprint that governs the ongoing relationship of the members to the LLC relating to the operation of the real estate project. It not only has to address how to treat current matters, it must also anticipate future issues that can arise and provide guidance on how these matters can be handled. In light of what you have read, if you represented the investors, what changes, if any, would you suggest be made to the Fox Valley Auto Care Center, LLC Operating Agreement? In answering this question, what further information would you want from your client? What changes would you suggest be made to the Operating Agreement if you represented the Manager, Regent?

Part II

REACHING AGREEMENT TO PURCHASE THE FOX VALLEY AUTO CARE CENTER SITE AND CLOSING THE DEAL

Chapter 5

PURCHASE OF THE SITE

§ 5.01 REACHING AGREEMENT TO PURCHASE THE SITE

[1] The Contract as the "Constitution" of the Deal

The purchase agreement is the most important of the legal documents that are prepared in connection with the purchase and sale of real estate. It establishes or modifies the rights and obligations of the parties, including any conditions to the obligations of each party to close the transaction, and it includes the parties' representations, warranties, promises, and indemnifications. The agreement typically also establishes the remedies available in the event of a breach of the agreement. While state law may provide certain protections to parties, such as the implied condition of marketable title, many of these protections can be modified by the terms of the purchase agreement. In short, the purchase agreement "sets" the deal in many ways and thus becomes the "constitution" of the deal.

Many larger developments will involve the acquisition of more than one parcel of land, and Regent's development, though not large, required the acquisition of two parcels. The purchase agreements used were quite different, and the reasons for the differences should become apparent as you read the two agreements and consider them in the context of the parties' relationships. You are going to need to closely read both of them. First, we give you a perspective on what a good contract for the sale of real estate should include. We follow that by asking you to read the two purchase agreements that Regent entered into, the first with the Johnsons and the second with Metropolitan. Following the first agreement, we present a number of questions, as well as a litigator's perspective on interpretation of contract terms. We also raise an ethical issue which arises in one of the terms of the Regent-Johnson agreement. We ask you to consider these questions and materials in between your reading of the two agreements so that you might reconsider what you have just read in the shorter Regent-Johnson agreement, and as preparation for what you are about to read in the longer Regent-Metropolitan agreement.

[2] Crafting a Purchase and Sale Agreement

In addition to being the "constitution" of the deal, the purchase agreement also is the "blueprint" for how the rest of the deal will proceed, who will absorb the risk of certain identified losses, how the costs of the closing will be allocated, and a myriad of other matters. For example, look ahead to Paragraph 10 of the Regent-Johnson agreement in the Document Book. Paragraph 10 involves when Regent was to get possession of the Johnson tract and appears to be the result of some fairly hard bargaining on a matter that concerned both parties. Reading Paragraph 10 gives you an idea of how what would seem to be a small point can become important enough to be the subject of hard bargaining and result in some difficult drafting and review issues.

The following article gives you an outline of typical provisions in a purchase agreement. The author also gives you brief descriptions of each of those provisions, which should help you anticipate some of the issues facing the lawyers for Regent, the Johnsons and Metropolitan. One of the keys to representing your client well in the drafting or review of a real estate purchase agreement is anticipating future concerns so that the agreement can well protect the parties and limit any future surprises.

Richard Ridloff, How to Prepare a Contract of Sale for Commercial Real Property,

THE PRACTICAL LAWYER (July 1979)*

The first function of an attorney when confronted with the sale or purchase of a commercial property, whether it is a shopping center, office structure, warehouse, or multifamily residential building, is to ascertain the factual data pertaining to the transaction. The attorney has an obligation of due diligence in this regard, and the importance of a thorough preliminary investigation cannot be overemphasized.

Perhaps the first point to be determined is whether a broker is involved. A brokerage agreement does not always have to be in writing and, absent language to the contrary, the brokerage commission is earned when either the contract of sale is signed or when a ready, willing, and able purchaser accepts the terms of the seller. Thus, a brokerage agreement should be concluded prior to a "meeting of the minds" between the buyer and seller and, certainly, before a contract of sale is negotiated.

The brokerage agreement between the broker and the party responsible for the payment of the brokerage commission — usually the seller — should provide that the brokerage commission be earned only if and when title actually passes under the terms of the contract of sale and the consideration is paid. No commission or remuneration should be due the broker if a contract of sale is not executed or if a contract is executed but title is not closed for any reason other than the willful default of the seller. The unmarketability of title or the inability of the seller to convey title in accordance with the terms of the contract of sale should not be considered a willful default.

Mortgages and Ground Lease

Another fact that should be ascertained is the existence of any mortgages and ground leases affecting the property. Restrictions contained in the mortgage or ground lease documents with regard to sale of the property or transfers subject to the mortgage may preclude any sale at this time or, at the very least, necessitate the waiver of the restrictions by the mortgagor or ground lessor. Further, possible restrictions on additional financing may preclude the seller from taking back a purchase money second mortgage, thus causing a renegotiation of the sale terms.

In addition to possible restrictions in covenants, a purchaser who intends to take title subject to the mortgage or ground lease should also focus upon:

- The remaining terms of the mortgage or ground lease, including provisions in the mortgage and renewal rights in the lease;
- The interest or rental rate, whichever is applicable, including percentage interest or rent;
- The default provisions, particularly the notice and grace periods;
- The application of insurance or condemnation proceeds;
- Prepayment rights with regard to mortgages; and
- The restrictions on dealing with space tenants or entering into new leases.

Title

Since mortgages and ground leases are not the only matters that may affect or restrict the use of a property, the conditions of title to the property should be reviewed prior to entering into the contract of sale. If possible, the existing survey and title report should be procured, as well as copies of all easements and restrictions. If these documents are not available, a new report and survey might be obtained prior to entering into the contract of sale. Despite protestations to the contrary by many title companies, a title report can be prepared in 24 hours, if necessary.

Service Contracts

Trash removal, laundry room, elevator, heating, ventilating, air-conditioning, and parking lot maintenance, painting, and any other so-called "service contracts" affecting the property should be studied. The important factors are whether the contracts are cancelable and the applicable service charges.

Employees

The persons who are employed directly by the seller in connection with the property should be ascertained, and whether their employment can or should be terminated. It may be necessary to obtain union contracts or private agreements that may materially differ from industry standards. If any employees are to be retained, applicable contract provisions with regard to wages, benefits, and vacations, as well as union membership, must be verified, and a detailed list of the employees, along with their job descriptions, addresses, social security numbers, seniority, and other details must be secured from the seller. The amount of vacation time accrued is important, since appropriate adjustments with regard to compensation will have to be made between the seller and purchaser at closing. If any employees are to be terminated, provision for severance pay, if applicable, must also be arranged between the parties.

Governmental Regulations

The purchaser's attorney should be certain that the property and its present use — or intended use, if that is to differ from its present use — complies and will continue to comply with all applicable zoning and other governmental regulations. Copies of the Certificate of Occupancy and other required licenses and permits should be examined.

Management Contracts

Any management contract covering the property should be reviewed and a determination made whether the contract is assignable or whether it can be canceled without penalty, what the notice provisions for termination are, and whether the terms are adequate. Since a managing agent can be of immeasurable assistance in procuring the information necessary for the title closing and in aiding the new purchaser after closing, it is always best to maintain good relations with present management, even if a later change is contemplated.

Space Leases

A current rent roll should be obtained along with copies of the leases, which must be inspected for:

- The remaining terms;
- Rental provisions, including escalations and percentage rent;
- Option provisions, whether, *e.g.*, to renew or terminate, purchase the property, expand the building, or exercise a right of first refusal on additional space;
- The landlord's obligations for repair and maintenance; and
- Special tenant requirements, such as parking, restrictive covenants, and so forth.

Expenses

Which party is to be responsible for the payment of title company charges, survey fees, transfer taxes, recording fees, leasing commissions, and similar charges should be established.

The attorney should have his answers before a contract of sale is signed. Laxity may lead to a contract of sale that omits many important provisions, resulting either in disputes at the time of title closing, the noncompletion of the transaction, or the closing of a transaction the parties would not have made had all the facts been assessed prior to the closing.

LETTERS OF INTENT

"Letters of intent," those seemingly innocuous agreements to agree in the future, which are usually executed before an attorney is consulted, can have devastating results. If the agreement is signed by both parties and sets forth the purchase price, description of the property, terms of the sale, and a closing date, the seller may become obligated to pay a brokerage commission. Even if some of the necessary contractual elements are missing, a court may interpret the document as a binding contract and compel the parties to go ahead with the sale or pay damages in the event of default. For these reasons, letters of intent should be avoided if possible. When, however, one or both of the parties insist upon executing this agreement before proceeding with the preliminary investigation, it should be carefully drawn so as to negate any inference that the parties have entered into a binding contract. The agreement should be labeled "letter of intent," and should expressly state that no liability or obligation is intended and which conditions or terms are left for future negotiation.

THE CONTRACT OF SALE

As soon as the attorney's preliminary investigation has been completed and the parties have agreed on the basic economic issues involved in the sale, the contract of sale should be prepared. Since there is no such thing as a standard contract for a commercial transaction, the initial draft of the contract may bear little resemblance to the final executed contract of sale.

Execution Date

Because of the hectic nature of many contract closings, the execution date of the contract of sale is sometimes left out. While this omission generally will not affect the validity of the contract, the date should not be ignored, especially if contract clauses dealing, for instance, with notices of violations are tied to the date, litigation may result from the contract, or eminent domain proceedings may occur after the contract date.

Parties

The parties to the contract of sale should be properly identified by name, description, and address, as well as by the capacity in which they are executing the contract, *e.g.*, attorney-in-fact, executor, or general partner. Thus it will be possible to determine who is to be bound by the terms of the contract.

Assignment

The named purchaser in a commercial transaction is generally given the right to assign the contract to a third party, particularly when there is no purchase money mortgage or the purchaser's credit rating or ability to manage the property will not be a factor. If the seller is concerned about the identity or ability of the third-party assignee, the customary practice is not to prohibit the assignment of the contract to a third party; rather, the purchaser is permitted to assign the contract, but only to an entity in which he has a specified interest or with the seller's consent, which consent the seller may not withhold unreasonably.

Legal Description

The legal description of the property to be conveyed should be specific and cover the land and buildings, appurtenances such as easements and tunnel and railroad sidetrack agreements, fixtures, and personal property included in the sale. If applicable, the rights of the seller as lessee under ground leases should be included. Since ambiguities will be construed against the seller, his attorney should carefully examine the legal description and, when possible, take the description from the existing deed or title policy.

Purchase Price

Down Payment

Since the contract of sale will be void unless a consideration is stated, reference to the purchase price must be made in the contract. The customary "10 per cent down payment" required for the purchase of single-family residences has no relation to a commercial transaction involving millions of dollars, where the down payment is strictly a matter for negotiation between the seller and purchaser. Whatever this amount may be, the purchaser's attorney should insist that it be held in escrow, with the specific terms of the escrow stated in the contract or in a separate agreement. Preferably, the escrowee should be a third party, although in many cases the seller's attorney will serve. From a purchaser's viewpoint, it is advisable for the escrow provisions to specify that the escrowee is an agent of the seller, and that the seller guarantees the return of the down payment to the purchaser if the purchaser becomes entitled to the money.

If the down payment is substantial and there is to be a fairly long interval between the signing of the contract of sale and the closing of title, the purchaser should seek to have the down payment invested in an interest-bearing account, with the accrued interest applied toward the balance due under the contract of sale.

The Purchase Money Mortgage

If the seller is to give a purchase money mortgage as part of the purchase, it is advisable to attach as exhibits to the contract of sale the proposed note and purchase money mortgage, as well as any other documents intended to secure the note, such as an assignment of the lessor's interest and a financing statement. If this is not possible, all major terms of the purchase money mortgage documents should be set forth in the contract. Although the personal liability of the purchaser for the repayment of the note is a matter for negotiation, purchase money mortgages are usually non-recourse in commercial transactions.

The Existing Mortgage

When an existing mortgage is to be assumed by the purchaser, it may be appropriate to put a specific restriction in the contract prohibiting the seller from prepaying or modifying the mortgage between the time of the contract signing and the closing of title. The approximate mortgage balance at the time of title closing should be stated, and provision should be made for the seller to procure an estoppel certificate from the mortgagee. The form of estoppel certificate should be attached as an exhibit, and the certificate preferably should be drafted by the purchaser's attorney and cover as much ground as possible. It should include, among other things, the following items:

- A certification as to the amount of principal and interest still to be paid;
- The maturity date and rate of interest;
- The date from which interest accrues;
- A representation that the payments due under the mortgage are current; and
- A representation that the sale will not permit an acceleration of maturity, be considered a default under the mortgage, or change any other term of

the documents.

Most institutional lenders have their own form of estoppel certificate or letter and may refuse to consider the form preferred by the seller and purchaser. In that case, or in the event the mortgagee refuses to give an estoppel certificate altogether, the purchaser should consider accepting as a substitute an affidavit from the seller covering the same points together with substantiating evidence, like canceled checks.

The parties should also decide whether the purchaser must put down more cash at the title closing in the event the mortgage balance is reduced at that time below the amount stated in the contract of sale.

Satisfaction of Existing Obligations

The contract of sale should also require the purchaser, upon request within a reasonable time prior to the closing date, to provide at the title closing separate certified or bank checks to satisfy any existing liens or other matters affecting title that the seller would otherwise be obligated to pay and discharge. These matters will thereupon no longer be deemed objections to title, provided:

- The seller delivers to the purchaser at the closing instruments in recordable form that are sufficient to satisfy such matters, together with the cost of recording or filing the instruments; or
- Satisfactory arrangements have been made with the purchaser's title insurer to deposit sufficient monies with it to enable it to issue its policy of title insurance either free of such matters or with insurance against the enforcement of these matters against the insured property.

Closing Adjustments

Rents

Provisions for closing adjustments are usually relatively simple when they involve the sale of residential real property or vacant land. In the case of sales of commercial real property, closing adjustments are much more complicated and often give rise to disputes between the parties.

For example, how should fixed tenant rentals in arrears at the time of title closing be treated? Assuming that the tenant will pay the arrears, the seller will want either a credit for their amount or the first rental receipts after the title closing. The purchaser will be reluctant to give any credit for funds not in hand and that may not be forthcoming, and will want the rental receipts to be applied initially against current rentals due the purchaser, with only the excess, after deduction for the purchaser's reasonable collection expenses, going to the seller to cover the arrears.

A possible solution to this dilemma, common in the New York City area, is to apply one month's rental receipts to cover the arrears due the seller, with the balance being collected either by the seller, who is empowered to take direct legal action against the tenant but without the right to use summary proceedings, or by the purchaser, who will collect and pay the arrears, but only after the current rentals are subtracted and the reasonable expenses of collection deducted. Under this arrangement, the purchaser will usually not be required to institute legal action against the defaulting tenant.

This problem will, of course, not arise if fixed tenant rentals are current at the time of title closing. Also, percentage rentals and escalation charges for increases in real estate taxes and operating expenses will not present much difficulty, for the purchaser will usually agree to collect and pay the seller's proportionate share of percentage rentals and escalation charges, less the reasonable expenses of collection. The contract of sale should state, however, the time within which the purchaser is to remit the seller's share to the seller, and what action, if any, is to be taken in the event of a tenant default.

Space Leases

In the case of space leases, adjustments with regard to matters other than rentals can be complex and require negotiation between the parties. For instance, a purchaser will often take the position that prior to the closing of title, any charges incurred in connection with space leases, like tenant finish work or brokerage charges, are part of the purchased rent roll and should be paid by the seller without any right to reimbursement from the purchaser. The seller, on the other hand, usually asserts that the purchaser should bear the burden of these costs, since he will get the benefit of the leases for which the costs were incurred. There is merit to the arguments of both parties and some sort of compromise is usually desirable. A common compromise provides that the purchaser:

- Pay for the costs incurred for space leases commencing after the date of title closing;
- Be responsible for the brokerage commissions on the renewals of existing leases; and
- Share with the seller the cost of charges incurred with regard to leases made after the execution of the contract of sale that commence prior to the date of title closing in proportion to the time which the lease term bears to the period of ownership of the property by the seller and the purchaser.

Because the purchaser will take title subject to new leases whether he pays for the costs involved or not, he should seek to prohibit the seller from leasing the property to any tenant between the time the contract of sale goes into effect and the closing of title without the purchaser's consent. The seller will usually agree to this clause, provided the purchaser's consent is not to be unreasonably withheld or delayed. In the alternative, the seller may be allowed to lease the property according to certain guidelines, *e.g.*, leases for not more than 3 years made on standard forms and calling for specific rentals may be permitted, with only leases outside the guidelines requiring the prior approval of the purchaser. The purchaser should also seek to restrict the seller's right during this period to commence eviction proceedings against defaulting tenants, accept surrenders of leases, or enter into modifications of existing leases without the purchaser's consent.

To verify the accuracy of the rent roll and the amount of rentals that are in arrears at the time of closing, provision should be made in the contract of sale for estoppel statements [also referred to as "estoppel certificates" — Eds.] to be obtained from the space tenants by the seller. Because of the time, effort, and difficulty involved in obtaining these statements, this requirement is sometimes limited to major tenants. The form of the estoppel statement to be used should be attached as an exhibit to the contract of sale and, as in the case of estoppel certificates from mortgagees, the purchaser should consider accepting an affidavit from the seller with regard to those space tenants for which estoppel statements cannot be obtained.

Real Estate Taxes

Adjustments for real estate taxes generally do not present much difficulty. Attention should be paid, though, to multiple tax jurisdictions with differing fiscal years and to jurisdictions in which real estate taxes are paid in arrears. In addition, if an existing mortgage will be assumed by the purchaser, provision should be made for the assignment to him of any tax or insurance escrows held by a mortgagee, which sums are to be credited to the seller at the time of title closing.

Insurance

Adjustments for insurance premiums are also easy to make, although the purchaser will want to decide whether, if the seller's insurance policies are transferable, he will want to take over the seller's policies or obtain new ones. In certain high-risk areas where new policies are not readily available, it may be advisable for the purchaser to assume the seller's policies. In most situations, the purchaser will prefer to obtain his own policies.

Other Adjustments

Provision should be made in the contract of sale for all other items that need to be adjusted at title closing. These items may consist of:

- Interest on existing mortgages or rent under ground leases;
- Water and utility charges;
- Employees' wages and benefits;
- Payroll and similar taxes;
- Fees payable to the landlord under state laws for administering tenant security deposit accounts;
- Fees and dues payable by the landlord to local landlord-oriented organizations;
- Sewer rents;
- Vault charges;
- Building supplies; and
- Fuel.

With regard to building supplies, only unbroken cartons or unused materials are usually adjusted, with all other supplies, such as fire extinguishers and lobby furniture, being included in the purchase price.

Warranties and Representations

Perhaps the most hotly negotiated provisions in the contract of sale will be those relating to the warranties and representations to be given by the parties. The seller will attempt to restrict its liabilities as much as possible, and will almost certainly insist upon a representation by the purchaser to the effect that "the purchaser is relying upon its own examination, investigation, and inspection of the financial aspects of the transaction and of the physical nature of the land, buildings, equipment, and any other improvements agreed to be sold under the contract," and that "the purchaser agrees to take the same 'as is' without warranty or representation by the seller or any agent, employee, or representative of the seller, except for matters expressly warranted or represented in the contract." This provision puts the onus on the purchaser to be sure that any warranties or representations of the seller upon which the purchaser is relying are expressly set forth in the contract.

The purchaser will most likely look for warranties and representations from the seller regarding:

- Space leases;
- Employees;
- Appliances and other equipment included as part of the purchase price;
- Service and other contracts;
- Licenses and permits;
- Maintenance of the property;
- Completion of, and payment for, work to be performed by the seller;
- The authority of the seller to enter into the transaction; and
- The pendency or threat of litigation that may adversely affect the property.

The specific warranties and representations relating to these various matters are subject to negotiation between the parties. As a general rule, however, the purchaser should insist that it receive warranties and representations with regard to any matter which will materially affect the lawful operation of the property, its economic value, or the potential liabilities of the owner.

Space Leases

The seller should certify the accuracy of a rent roll, to be attached as an exhibit to the contract, that identifies the various space tenants and the leased space, makes specific reference to the tenant leases, and sets forth the salient terms of the leases — expiration dates, rentals, whether current or in arrears, renewals or other options, concessions, and security deposits, if any. The seller should also represent that all brokerage commissions earned with respect to the leases have been paid. Further, the seller should agree to restrictions on leasing or dealing with existing tenants between the time the contract of sale is signed and title closed.

Employees

A list of the employees, certified by the seller, should be attached as an exhibit to the contract, setting forth the important information regarding their wages and benefits. The purchaser should attempt to restrict the seller's right prior to title closing to terminate or lengthen the term of any employees, raise existing wages or benefits, or hire new employees without the consent of the purchaser.

Personal Property

A detailed listing of the personal property included as part of the purchase price should be attached as an exhibit to the contract, and a differentiation made between property that is fully owned by the seller or only leased to or mortgaged by him. The seller should certify the all-inclusiveness of the list, and, where pertinent, represent that the property will be in "good working order" at the time of title closing. If the seller agrees to such a representation, deletion of the word "good" before the words "working order" may be requested. The deletion should be acceptable to an average purchaser, although the full phrase is preferable and essential when the equipment is necessary for the operation of the property, as an elevator in a high-rise office building.

Contracts

Only those contracts that the purchaser is assuming need be set forth as an exhibit to the contract of sale and certified as correct by the seller. The names of the parties, the subject matter, and the terms of the contracts should be stated, and the seller's right to amend the terms or cancel the contracts without the consent of the purchaser should be restricted.

Licenses and Permits

The various licenses and permits in the seller's possession should be set forth in the contract. The purchaser' s attorney should not be satisfied with a listing, but he should press for a representation from the seller that the licenses and permits were duly issued and continue in full force and effect, and that they are all the licenses and permits needed for the lawful operation of the property in accordance with its present and intended use.

Maintenance of the Property

Provision should be made for the seller to maintain the property between the time of the contract of sale and the title closing in the same manner as the seller maintained it before the contract of sale. The purchaser should seek to obtain a representation from the seller as to the accuracy of listed expenses for repairs and maintenance incurred by him during the preceding year or years.

Representations relating to the completion of, and payment for, work to be performed by the seller should extend to tenant finish work and substantial general maintenance work, such as painting, as well as to capital improvements.

Authority of Seller

The authority of the seller can be established by requiring a corporate resolution or an opinion from seller's counsel to be furnished at the title closing.

Litigation

Representations in regard to litigation will probably be limited by the words "to the best of seller's knowledge."

Mutual Representations

Both parties should represent that they have had no dealings with any broker except the one specified, and one party, usually the seller, should agree to pay the broker's commission pursuant to a separate agreement.

Survival of Representations

Regardless of what warranties and representations are forthcoming from the seller, the purchaser's attorney should insist that they be true as of the date of execution of the contract of sale, if that be the case, as well as on the date of the title closing. Warranties and representations covering matters that cannot be ascertained until after the title closing should survive the delivery of the deed. The purchaser's attorney will often suggest a survival period of 2 years, and the seller's attorney will counter with 6 months; a compromise of one year is often made.

Damages for Breach of Warranty

The seller's attorney should insist on provisions in the contract limiting the seller's liability for damages in the event of a breach of warranty. Thus, to preclude the purchaser from rescinding the contract in the event the rents set forth in the rent roll are in excess of the rents actually due under the tenant leases, he should be entitled only to damages based upon a capitalization at going rates of the difference between the rents projected in the rent roll and the actual rents due, plus any amounts the purchaser may have to refund to the tenants in the event of prior overpayments.

On the other hand, the purchaser's attorney should resist, where possible, the seller's attempts to limit its liability. In certain cases, the principals of the seller, should the seller be a corporation, ought to guarantee the seller's obligations under the contract of sale, including the seller's liability for breach of warranty.

Violations

The term "violations" in a contract of sale may have different meanings, depending upon the jurisdiction whose laws govern the transaction. The word may refer to a condition that would cause a government agency to shut down the operation of the property. It could also apply to a breach of publicly or privately-imposed restrictions and be the basis for damages, fines, or injunctions. The attorneys should be familiar with the customary usage of this word in the applicable jurisdiction prior to using it in the contract of sale.

The purchaser's attorney should request that the seller be responsible for curing violations until the title closing. However, this is not the customary practice, and usually the seller is responsible only for violations noted or issued prior to the signing of the contract of sale. Any violations noted or issued after that date become the responsibility of the purchaser.

The seller should not be required to remedy violations for whose cure the space tenants are responsible. In addition, if the seller is responsible for curing any violations, he may desire the option to cancel the contract, rather than correct the default, in the event the violation will be too costly to remedy. In that case, a specific dollar amount may be given as a benchmark, so that only if the cost of curing the violations will exceed this amount would the seller have the option to cancel the contract. The purchaser, on the other hand, should have the option of taking the property subject to the violations, but with an equitable price reduction.

Failure to Cure

If the seller fails to cure violations for which it is responsible, the simplest solution is to allow the purchaser a credit against the purchase price at the time of title closing equal to the cost of correcting the violations. The cost can be estimated by an architect or contractor appointed by the seller but subject to approval by the purchaser, which approval may not be unreasonably withheld. If the parties cannot agree to this arrangement, an alternate, but more complicated, procedure would place in escrow the estimated cost of remedying the violations pending their cure by the seller or a third party. The seller would be responsible for any deficiencies in the escrow account and be entitled to any excess remaining. A specific date should be set for performance, and if the deadline is not met, the purchaser should have the option of drawing upon the escrowed funds to cure the violations.

Default Provisions

The seller will seek to limit its liability upon default to the return of the down payment — with or without interest, depending upon whether arrangements were made to have the down payment placed in an interest-bearing account — together with the reasonable costs expended by the purchaser for title examination and survey charges. The purchaser may agree to this provision if it does not apply to a willful default by the seller; otherwise, the purchaser could be subject to a contrived default.

In turn, it is customary in commercial transactions to limit the liability of the purchaser to the retention of the down payment by the seller as liquidated damages. The seller should consider this fact when the amount of the down payment is being negotiated. Specific performance is indicated when the defaulting party can, but will not, cure the default.

Risk of Loss

In many jurisdictions there are statutory provisions covering the risk of loss as between the purchaser and the seller during the period between the signing of the contract of sale and the title closing. If the statutory provisions do not properly express the intent of the parties, overruling provisions should be added to the contract.

The seller should be required prior to the delivery of the deed to repair any damage to the property, or any damage not exceeding a specified amount. An alternative should permit him to assign to the purchaser the rights to any insurance proceeds due as a result of the property damage. Similarly, the seller should assign to the purchaser the rights to any condemnation proceeds that may be paid. The purchaser should have the option to cancel the contract in the event a substantial part of the property, perhaps worth a specific dollar amount, is destroyed or condemned or if the property cannot be repaired within a specified amount of time from the date title is closed.

If, in the event of damage to the property, insurance proceeds are to be assigned to the purchaser, the purchaser's attorney should insist that the property be adequately insured, with a minimum amount set forth in the contract, and that the seller maintain rental insurance.

If, for one reason or another, the parties cannot agree on how to handle damage to, or destruction of, the property, provided there is good faith between the parties, the seller and the purchaser may execute the contract of sale, absent the provisions relating to risk of loss, simultaneously with the closing of title. . . .

Closing Arrangements

The parties should specify a date in the contract when the title closing is to take place. If either party is concerned about having the right to adjourn the closing date or fears that the other party will unduly delay the closing, the contract should specify the number and length of adjournments that are available to each party.

Conditions to Closing

Any conditions to the title closing should be expressly set forth. The seller should not accept any conditions that, for all practical purposes, leave the closing to the discretion of the purchaser, and he should insist that all inspections of the property or investigations into the financial aspects thereof be conducted by the purchaser prior to entering into the contract of sale.

On the other hand, many matters that should be handled prior to title closing can only be satisfied after the contract of sale is executed. For example a purchaser may be unable to obtain a mortgage commitment or governmental approval of the sale unless and until there is an executed contract of sale, a zoning variance or rezoning may be necessary, or pending litigation may have to be completed satisfactorily. In those cases, provisions in the contract conditioning the purchaser's obligations upon the proper resolution of these matters are not only appropriate but necessary.

One prerequisite to closing that should not be ignored relates to the state of the seller's title to the property. The seller should be required to convey to the purchaser marketable or insurable title to the property — the terms "marketable" and "insurable" may have different meanings in different jurisdictions — subject only to certain permitted exceptions specified in the contract, that any responsible and reputable title insurance company in the jurisdiction will insure.

If the seller is unwilling to accept certain conditions to closing upon which the purchaser insists and the conditions can be satisfied without the existence of an executed contract of sale, the parties may let events take their natural course and, if the contested conditions no longer present a problem, execute the contract of sale and close title at the same time.

Closing Documents

The contract of sale should specify what documents each party is to bring to the title closing. It is customary to set forth these items in considerable detail. By doing so, the title closing is greatly facilitated.

Most items to be delivered at the title closing are in the control of the seller. The seller's attorney must usually prepare and bring to the closing or previously deliver:

- The deed;
- The bill of sale;
- An affidavit of title, if required;

- Corporate resolutions, if applicable;
- Assignments of service contracts, transferable licenses and permits, warranties, space leases, the ground lease, if any, and the security deposits;
- Architectural or engineering plans, if available;
- The certificate of occupancy and other licenses and permits;
- Current bills for taxes and water and sewer charges;
- The original leases and manually-executed counterparts of any ground leases or mortgages affecting the property;
- Transferable insurance policies;
- Estoppel certificates or letters from space tenants, ground lessors, and mortgagees;
- The tenant security deposits; and
- Letters to parties in interest, such as tenants, ground lessors, mortgagees, or contractors, informing them of the sale.

The managing agent, working with the seller's attorney in obtaining many of these items, can offer invaluable assistance in this regard.

The form of the deed to be executed by the seller should be specified in the contract, although in commercially-oriented states it is almost always a special warranty deed — or, in New York, a bargain and sale deed — with covenants only against the grantor's acts. The purchaser is expected to look to the title insurer for further assurances pertaining to title.

The bill of sale will either be in warranty or quitclaim form, depending upon the nature of the personal property being conveyed. Any applicable sales tax imposed upon the sale of the personal property should be apportioned by the parties at contract time, with each party undertaking to indemnify the other in the event a sales tax is imposed when the parties agreed that no tax was due. If any insurance policies are to be transferred, arrangements should be made through a reliable broker and the form of assignment should be approved by the insurer. The insurance company may have its own form of assignment, which should be procured. Similarly, the approval of any assignment form should be obtained from the ground lessor and mortgagor.

The delivery of the tenant security deposits to the purchaser may be made in the form of a credit to the purchaser, a separate check from the seller, or an assignment of the bank account wherein the funds are deposited, depending upon the local rules relating to co-mingling of funds.

The responsibility of the purchaser to deliver items at the title closing is not nearly as broad as that of the seller. Generally, the purchaser will bring the balance of the cash portion of the purchase price, usually in the form of a wire transfer or a certified or bank check, and documents assuming the seller's obligations under the ground lease, space leases, and service contracts. In addition, the purchaser should receipt for the tenant security deposits and, if requested, indemnify the seller against claims for the security deposits to the amount of the funds actually received by the purchaser.

Closing Expenses

The allocation of closing expenses should be set forth in the contract of sale. These expenses may include:

- Real property transfer taxes;
- Documentary stamps for the deed;
- Mortgage recording taxes;
- Sales taxes;
- Survey costs; and
- The cost of title insurance.

Which party usually bears the burden of various expenses depends upon the particular jurisdiction. The attorneys should be familiar with the customary practice in the applicable jurisdiction prior to determining who pays for what. However, notwithstanding any customary practice, the relative strength of the bargaining positions of the parties may be decisive in this regard — and in regard to many other matters in the contract as well.

Miscellaneous Provisions

The contract of sale should provide that it is the entire agreement between the parties, forbid oral modifications, cover text variations, make the singular also mean the plural, and so on. These "boilerplate" provisions can be found in any form book and are self-explanatory. More important, the contract should include all special arrangements that relate to the particular property involved in the sale or to the negotiations between the parties.

CONCLUSION

Once the contract of sale has been executed, the parties must direct their efforts toward the closing of title. The difficulties encountered in achieving this objective will, to a great extent, be determined by the time and effort that went into the preparation of the contract of sale. A well-drawn agreement that covers most of the contingencies that may arise prior to title closing will facilitate the attorney's work. It will prevent arguments, delays in closing, and sometimes, even failures to close.

The importance of the contract of sale cannot be overestimated. It is only a means to an end — the title closing; but if done properly, it will greatly enhance the probability that the end will become a reality easily.

[3] Note on Drafting and Reviewing Real Estate Purchase Agreements

Now that you have been exposed to the typical and complex considerations to drafting a real estate purchase and sale agreement, we would like you to keep one more thing in mind as you review the purchase agreements. In order to draft the purchase and sale agreement, or review and make suggested revisions to a draft agreement prepared by another party or her attorney, one must have a firm grasp of the goals and expectations of his client.

- What, generally speaking, are the goals and expectations of a buyer or seller of real estate? In considering that question, consider more than just "to buy" and "so sell." A Seller may have more goals than merely to sell the land for the highest price. And a buyer certainly may have more goals than merely buying the land for the lowest price. These goals will have real impacts on the financial and other terms of the resulting contract.
- What, specifically, are the goals of Regent, the Johnsons, and Metropolitan? There are many. If you take the time to think through them (and perhaps make lists of them) now it will help you as you review the contracts and as you consider the possible reasons that different terms were included in the contracts. The role of the lawyer for any party, after all, is to know his client's goals and, to the extent possible, accomplish them.

§ 5.02 THE REGENT AGREEMENT WITH THE JOHNSONS

[1] The Agreement

We have given you all of the Regent-Johnson agreement, but with only one of its four exhibits. We included Exhibit A, the legal description of the parcel of land, because it is short (for a legal description) and, if you had never read a legal description, we wanted you to see what one looks like. The other attachments (the unsigned Regent-Metropolitan agreement, the preliminary title insurance commitment, and the Johnsons' prior title insurance policy) were either not informative for our purposes at this point or redundant. As a note as to the difficulty facing Regent in putting the deal together, the Regent-Johnson agreement also became an attachment to the Regent-Metropolitan agreement that you will read next.

You need to closely read the entire agreement, but we would like you to specifically consider several issues raised in the Ridloff article (all paragraph references are to the Regent-Johnson agreement):

- Ridloff notes that in a brokerage agreement, the seller typically does not owe her broker a commission if the transaction does not close unless the reason for the failure to close is a willful default by the seller. Do you see why? See Paragraph 14 and consider why the seller agrees to indemnify the buyer.
- Ridloff points out that the parties have to be specific about what liens will or will not be allowed. In many transactions, this issue involves little bargaining: the parties usually require all liens of record to be released at the time of closing, except, possibly, for any mortgages the buyer intends to assume or take subject to (which means that the buyer only will pay to the seller the difference between the purchase price and the amount of any mortgage(s) left in place). The issue is larger than that in the Regent-Johnson agreement, however. See Paragraphs 5B, 6A, and 7.

- Beyond any liens, Ridloff also notes that the contract must deal with the general issue of title to the subject property. Title is the subject of Chapter 6. See Paragraphs 5 and 6A(i).

- Virtually all property is subject to some form of government regulation that will affect how it can be used, and Ridloff points out that these issues should be anticipated in the contract. Chapter 7 deals with governmental land use regulations and Chapter 8 deals with governmental environmental regulations. See Paragraphs 4A(ii), 5, and 7. These paragraphs also deal with what Ridloff terms "Conditions to Closing."

- The parties will have to pay many different costs and expenses, and Ridloff notes that the contract should allocate responsibility for them. See Paragraphs 5, 7, and 10, and Paragraph 8E and 8F. Ridloff also notes that these costs and expenses frequently will be prorated between the parties. See Paragraph 8F.

- Ridloff warns that what is meant to be a "Letter of Intent" could be construed by a court to be a binding contract. As you will soon see, Regent was faced with at least one "chicken and egg" problem in the overall transaction: Regent needed both the Johnsons' and Metropolitan's land in order to build the Fox Valley Auto Care Center, but neither by itself was useful to Regent. Regent had to reach agreement with both the Johnsons and Metropolitan before it irrevocably bound itself to either. The Regent-Johnson agreement you are about to read was the only signed document between those two parties. Consider the "chicken and egg" issue as you read the agreement and also see Paragraph 4A(iv).

  Note that Regent elected to use conditional purchase agreements rather than letters of intent as a means to tie up the property it desired to purchase as it determined the viability of its project. Why do you think Regent did not use letters of intent? For a detailed discussion covering various issues that arise with the use of letters of intent, see David C. Camp, Hazel I. Lee, Joel S. Rosenstein, Mark A. Sen, *Letters of Intent in Sale Transactions and Loan Commitments*, 439 PLI/Real 527 (April/June 1999).

  Another possibility was to obtain an option to purchase the real estate. Under a typical option to purchase, even if the party does not exercise the option to purchase it will lose the fee it paid to obtain the option. For more information on options to purchase real estate and the legal issues that arise in this context, see John C. Murray, *Dressing Up a "Naked" Option* (from "Commercial Real Estate Financing: What Borrowers and Lenders Need to Know Now"), 457 PLI/*Real* 79 (May 2000).

- Another issue highlighted by Ridloff is the typical requirement that the buyer make an "earnest money" payment at the time the contract becomes binding on the parties in order to assure the seller that the buyer will complete the transaction and to provide a fund from which the seller may collect damages for any breach by the buyer. See Paragraph 3 and Paragraph 15B. See also *infra* § 5.02[4] for a discussion about who held the escrow money in the Regent-Johnson transaction.

- Ridloff also discusses "Violations" and "Default." One potential violation involved any environmental conditions on the land. See Paragraph 7. As for defaults, see Paragraph 15B.
- If the land being purchased is improved, Ridloff points out that the contract should allocate the risk of loss. See Paragraph 9A.

You now should be ready to read the Regent-Johnson agreement. Please consider these issues, but also look for others.

[2] Notes and Questions on the Regent-Johnson Agreement and the Parties' Bargaining Positions

1. Who do you think prepared the purchase agreement between Regent and the Johnsons? Does it appear that the agreement was heavily negotiated?
2. If you had represented Regent at the time its agreement with the Johnsons was entered into, would you have wanted to prepare the agreement or at least review it before it was signed by Regent?
3. If you had represented Regent, are there any terms you would have wanted to change?
4. If you had represented the Johnsons, are there any terms you would have wanted to change?
5. Why do you think the Johnsons were required to deposit a warranty deed into escrow at the beginning of the transaction rather than right before closing?
6. Do you think the financing contingency adequately protected the parties? In considering this on behalf of Regent, do you think that the contingency in any way reflected how Regent intended to finance the purchase of the Johnsons' land? If not, and we obviously think not, then what was the point of the contingency as it was stated?
7. In the Regent-Johnson agreement, do you think it was wise for Regent to allow the Johnsons to retain possession after closing? Did Regent make any provisions to mitigate any negative effects from the Johnsons retaining possession after closing?

[3] Interpretation of Contract Terms

Consider the following excerpt from an article by a litigator who has many opinions on what transactional lawyers do when negotiating, drafting and modifying contracts. As we have stated already, the Regent-Johnson agreement that you have read and the Regent-Metropolitan agreement that you are about to read are very different documents. The author has some words of wisdom for transactional lawyers, and you may conclude that Regent's lawyers were in both positions described by the author.

David G. Steuer,
A Litigator's Perspective on the Drafting of Commercial Contracts,
in Drafting Corporate Agreements (1998–1999)*

I. Introduction

By the time litigators examine a commercial agreement, drafters generally have formed the contractual landscape on which the parties' struggle will commence. Foresight therefore dictates that negotiators of business agreements consider their clients' potential litigation risks at the drafting stage. This paper presents drafting considerations based on both a client's prospective posture as defendant or plaintiff and on its sophistication and bargaining power; offers suggestions for drafting choice of law and choice of forum provisions, including recommendations for selecting arbitration or litigation; and highlights several drafting perils which frequently degenerate into litigation. In the absence of successful commercial dealings, favorable contractual fortifications tend to console clients. . . .

III. Client's Bargaining Power and Sophistication

The doctrine of *contra proferentum* specifies that, in cases of contract ambiguity, where a term's meaning remains uncertain after application of other rules of interpretation, courts interpret the ambiguous term in the manner least favorable to the party who drafted the provision. Since the party with greater bargaining power usually chooses the words of the contract, *contra proferentum* chiefly amounts to a rule of public policy favoring the underdog. Accordingly, a lawyer's drafting strategy should vary depending on the relative sophistication of her client and her opponent.

A. Representing the Stronger Party in Drafting an Agreement

If the stronger party's lawyer drafts an agreement, she should negate the effect of *contra proferentum* by inserting a clause stating that the agreement is the product of negotiation. One example of such a boilerplate clause appears below:

> "Mutual Drafting: This Agreement is the joint product of [Company A] and [Company B], and each provision hereof has been subject to the mutual consultation, negotiation, and agreement of [Company A] and [Company B], and shall not be construed for or against any party hereto."

However, regarding adhesion contracts, the attorney for the party with superior bargaining power need not even attempt to vitiate *contra proferentum*, since the doctrine applies "with peculiar force" in such contexts.

Even if a contract appears unambiguous, when the stronger party drafts a contract, it should avoid overreaching. Courts resist strict enforcement of onerous agreements favoring the more sophisticated party, effectively applying *contra proferentum* to unambiguous terms. Furthermore, oppressive provisions requiring the cooperation of the weaker party, such as a term obliging a defaulting software

---

company to surrender its source code, will inevitably be ignored by the weaker party and end in litigation, rendering the provision of little real world value to the drafting party. As a final disincentive to overreaching, western courts will refuse to enforce contractual provisions that infringe on rights provided by federal statute.

B. Representing the Weaker Party in Drafting a Commercial Agreement

If a client lacks significant bargaining power, or for some other reason would likely have the weaker legal position should litigation arise, its lawyer should retain the option of having a jury trial. Unpredictability of juries, jurors' sympathy for the underdog, and delay involved in litigation — particularly in the era of "three strikes and you're out," which has greatly expanded the criminal docket — all give leverage to the weaker party. Furthermore, the weaker party's advocate should ensure that dispute resolution between the parties involve notice, cure periods, and cooling-off periods. For example, the attorney could seek to require 30 days of mediation before either party commences dispute resolution, on the rationale that delay creates uncertainty which enhances the weaker party's bargaining position. As a cautionary note, however, if the weaker party will probably stand as plaintiff in future litigation, weaving delay into the dispute resolution mechanism could result in significant financial hardship. . . .

VI. "Tickets to the Courthouse," or, How to Get Your Agreement into Litigation

Commercial contracts end up in litigation for a variety of reasons. Altered boilerplate, an oral promise in contradiction to a writing, an unwritten modification of an agreement, an ambiguous or undefined critical term, or unsigned signature pages may all cause parties to seek judicial vindication. This section considers these few avenues whereby partners to a contract become courtroom adversaries. . . .

D. Undefined or Ambiguous Critical Terms

Carelessness in failing to define key terms explicitly may come back to haunt the drafter. In order to avoid litigation, critical terms must be defined in a manner that does not leave room for misinterpretation.

A variant of the undefined or ambiguous term, provisions arrived at by artificial compromise also provide negotiators with admission to the courthouse. For example, party X may obtain a contractual provision stating that he can terminate the contract at his sole discretion at any time without any payment or obligation of any kind to Y; as a compromise, X may concede to a term holding that prior to termination, X must consult in good faith with Y concerning any matters regarding the contract that would lead X to terminate. Potential disputes abound in such illusory meetings of the minds of the parties.

[4] Notes and Questions on the Ethics of Acting as an Escrow Agent

Do you think that the Seller's and Buyer's attorneys were good choices to act as escrow agents at the beginning of the transaction (Regent's attorneys) and at the end of the transaction (Johnsons' attorney), if the Johnsons remained in possession after closing? This issue is a sub-issue of the larger consideration of when a lawyer may represent more than one party in a matter. As we consider all the transactions that Regent engaged in as it developed the Fox Valley Auto Care Center, you will see other instances of lawyers (Regent's and others) representing more than one party.

[a] A Practitioner's Perspective

In his very informative, and highly readable, book, REAL ESTATE LORE, MODERN TECHNIQUES AND EVERYDAY TIPS FOR THE PRACTITIONER (published by the ABA Real Property, Probate and Trust Section in 2006), retired Blank Rome partner Harris Ominsky includes as Chapter 51, LAWYERS AS ESCROW AGENTS (pages 302–304). To put it bluntly, Ominsky doesn't like it when lawyers act as escrow agents. To make the point, he cites a Connecticut case, *Galvanek v. Skibitcky*, 738 A.2d 1150 (Conn. App. 1999), in which the appellate court held that a lawyer was barred from serving as an escrow agent when one of the escrow parties also was the lawyer's client, although he notes that Connecticut lawyers who want to act as escrow agents ultimately won by getting the legislature to authorize the practice.

Ominsky advises lawyers who want to act as escrow agents to only do so with a written agreement that gives an objective basis for any action to be taken by the escrow holder: "For example, instead of the attorney having to make a decision about whether certain repairs have been made, the triggering event should be the receipt of a letter from a designated party certifying the repairs have been made."[1] In addition, Ominsky advises lawyers to insist that acting as an escrow agent have as little impact on a lawyer's relationship with her client as possible: "[I]f there is a dispute, attorneys should be able to continue to represent their clients, and should be able to either deposit the escrowed item into court in an interpleader, or hold it until a court order is received. Also, the attorney should be indemnified against any costs or expenses by the parties to the escrow."[2]

Ominsky sets out a recognizable scenario: in the sale of a home, the lawyer represents the seller and acts as the escrow holder. At the closing, money is retained to fund the seller's repair of the roof. The lawyer may face the wrath both 1) of his client, the seller, if the seller completes the repair but the buyer is not satisfied, or 2) the unsatisfied buyer, if the lawyer decides to release the money to his client, the seller. The answer, again, is that the escrow agreement must have no subjective duties for the escrow holder, but even if every duty has an objective standard, the escrow holder still may be faced with the wrath of either escrow party, and be faced with being a party to a lawsuit or a disciplinary action (and likely losing a client!).

Finally, Ominsky also points out that the escrow holder might be responsible for the money if the institution into which he deposits the money becomes insolvent, either losing all or part of the money or delaying its being paid. Ominsky's answer is to be careful, and our answer is to get the parties to agree as to the bank or other financial institution in which the money will be deposited (and with a statement that the parties are relying on government depository insurance for any loss caused by failure of the bank or other financial institution).

---

[1] HARRIS OMINSKY, REAL ESTATE LORE, MODERN TECHNIQUES AND EVERYDAY TIPS FOR THE PRACTITIONER 303 (2006).

[2] *Id.*

[b] ABA Model Rules of Professional Conduct

Consider the following provision of the American Bar Association's Model Rules of Professional Conduct (which are in effect in Illinois and the vast majority of other states):

Model Rule § 1.7 — Conflict Of Interest: Current Clients

> (a) Except as provided in paragraph (b), a lawyer shall not represent a client if the representation involves a concurrent conflict of interest. A concurrent conflict of interest exists if:
>
> (1) the representation of one client will be directly adverse to another client; or
>
> (2) there is a significant risk that the representation of one or more clients will be materially limited by the lawyer's responsibilities to another client, a former client or a third person or by a personal interest of the lawyer.
>
> (b) Notwithstanding the existence of a concurrent conflict of interest under paragraph (a), a lawyer may represent a client if:
>
> (1) the lawyer reasonably believes that the lawyer will be able to provide competent and diligent representation to each affected client;
>
> (2) the representation is not prohibited by law;
>
> (3) the representation does not involve the assertion of a claim by one client against another client represented by the lawyer in the same litigation or other proceeding before a tribunal; and
>
> (4) each affected client gives informed consent, confirmed in writing.

The lawyers involved in the Regent-Johnson agreement needed to consider MR § 1.7 in deciding whether to act as escrow agents in the transaction. They needed to answer several questions:

a. By acting as escrow agents, were they representing both parties to the transaction? Likely, they would have concluded they would not be representing the other party.

b. By acting as escrow agents, did they have responsibilities to the other party? Undoubtedly they did. An escrow agent is a fiduciary who owes a fiduciary duty to all the parties to the escrow.

c. By acting as escrow agents, were their fiduciary duties to the other party such that it would make it impossible for them to continue representing their own clients? Likely they would conclude it would not.

d. If they conclude that they will act as escrow agents, should they reveal the potential for conflict (engage in a "consultation" with them) and receive their clients' consents?

Questions

1. The issue of client consent is a tough one. Some would suggest that any time the lawyer goes through the suggested analysis that she should consult with the client and obtain the client's consent before going forward; the theory is that if something should happen in the future, no matter how remote, no surprise is the best surprise. Others would argue that only if the lawyer felt she had divided loyalties should she consult with the client; the theory being why raise unnecessary problems in the middle of what likely already is a complex set of considerations for the client. Which do you think the lawyers should have done?

2. In our opinion, any negative consequences from the attorneys acting as escrow agents would have been much greater for James Mallory, the Johnsons' attorney, than it would have been for Donna Smith and Sam Nader in their representation of Regent. Do you understand what those consequences would have been and why we are of the opinion that any negative consequences would have been greater for Mallory than for Smith and Nader?

§ 5.03 THE REGENT AGREEMENT WITH METROPOLITAN

[1] The Agreement

As with the Regent-Johnson agreement, in the Regent-Metropolitan agreement we have given you all of the agreement along with the attachments that you need to interpret the agreement and to understand its full scope. Some of the attachments will not seem of much importance at this point, but as we bring out the broader issues raised by them, their importance will become apparent.

Many of the issues present in the Regent-Johnson agreement are present here. As with the Regent-Johnson agreement, it is important to keep in mind which party has the upper hand, either as to the agreement as a whole or as to specific issues. In almost all agreements, no party gets everything it wants, and you should be thinking about what these parties likely wanted but were willing to negotiate away in order to make the deal work.

Let us again highlight some of the points raised in the Ridloff article and give you references to the Regent-Metropolitan agreement (the text of our references are shorter in most instances to avoid being redundant with our references to the Regent-Johnson agreement):

- Brokerage agreements and indemnification. See Paragraph 9.
- Liens. See Paragraphs 1 and 5.
- Title. See Paragraphs 1, 4, and 5.
- Government regulations. See Paragraphs 3 and 5, and § e of Paragraph 14.
- Costs and expenses. See Paragraphs 3, 4, 5, and 10.
- Letter of intent or "chicken and egg" problem. See Paragraph 14.
- Escrow of earnest money. See Paragraph 2.

- Default. See Paragraph 12, and § c of Paragraph 7.
- Ridloff also mentioned another issue that is a subject of the Regent-Metropolitan agreement, assignment of the contract by Regent. See § b of Paragraph 16.

At this point you should read the Regent-Metropolitan agreement. As when you read the Regent-Johnson agreement, you should keep these issues in mind and many others.

[2] Notes and Questions on the Regent-Metropolitan Agreement

1. It is interesting to note that Regent's purchase agreement with Metropolitan is quite different from the purchase agreement with the Johnsons. How do they differ? In what respects are they similar?
2. Who do you think prepared the purchase agreement between Regent and Metropolitan?
3. What might explain the presence of more representations and promises by the seller in the agreement with the Johnsons and more promises on the part of Regent in the agreement with Metropolitan?
4. What are some of the different promises that Regent makes in its agreement with Metropolitan, and why would Metropolitan insist on those promises?
5. In the Regent agreement with Metropolitan, how has Regent protected itself from being obligated to close on the purchase of the property if it looks as if Regent will not be able to develop the Fox Valley Auto Care Center on the site?
6. In the Regent agreement with Metropolitan, what is the effect of the different contingencies, for annexation and zoning, financing, and environmental review?
7. Has Metropolitan protected itself from letting Regent walk away from the deal too easily?
8. Why does the Regent agreement with Metropolitan require the use restrictions contained in Paragraph 8 to also be included in the deed from Metropolitan to Regent?
9. Why does the Regent agreement with Metropolitan list which obligations will survive closing?
10. Why does Paragraph 11b of the Regent agreement with Metropolitan deal with the implications of the division of the parcels?
11. Are the remedies provisions in Paragraph 12 of the Regent agreement with Metropolitan fair and reasonable to the parties? Why or why not?
12. Note again that the first earnest money was deposited with Regent's attorneys. Do you think that this was a risk that Donna and Sam should have taken? Even if you think that the risk was small (and we think it was), would they have been better off opening an escrow account with

Title Services?

[3] Problem

Like most transactional lawyers, Donna Smith and Sam Nader have periods of time when they are busy, and then other periods of time when they are very busy. As the Regent-Metropolitan agreement was being negotiated, Donna was very busy. Donna went to Sam's office and asked him if he had time to thoroughly review both the signed Regent-Johnson agreement and the draft of the Regent-Metropolitan agreement and to write a memo to her on any problems he saw in the Regent-Metropolitan agreement, particularly problems arising from any inconsistencies between the two agreements. Sam, like most young associates, gulped, and then, like only some associates (the ones more sure in their positions), asked Donna if there were any particular areas she was interested in. She responded that at this point she mostly was interested in getting the two agreements to "mesh" and that Sam's memo should focus on what it was going to take for Regent to meet its obligations under the two agreements and close the deal as well as making suggestions as to possible changes in the Regent-Metropolitan agreement.

If you were Sam, what would your memo highlight? What section(s) of the Regent-Metropolitan agreement do you think might be modified and what modifications would you suggest?

§ 5.04 CLOSING THE DEAL

[1] The "Four-Party" Closing

The mechanics of how to close a moderately complex transaction are well illustrated in the Escrow Agreement for the "four-party" closing among Regent, Metropolitan, the Johnsons and Turtle Wax. It was this closing that allowed Regent to move forward with the Fox Valley Auto Care Center. "Four-party" is in quotation marks because there were more parties to the closing than just the four among whom land was transferred. There also were parties who did not have a direct interest in the transaction but who were selling services to the principal parties: attorneys and law firms; the escrow holder, Title Services, Inc.; and the title insurer, Commonwealth Title Insurance Co. And then there is, arguably, the most important party of all, at least in terms of funding the entire transaction, and a true "principal party" as well: Regent's lender, First Mortgage Bank ("FMB"). You will learn much more about FMB in Part III.

Due to the complicated set of closings for the project, as well as the numerous conditions to closing, it made sense to close the various deals through a deed and money escrow arrangement. The Escrow Agreement refers to a "New York style closing." A "New York style closing" is also referred to as a "table closing," and it is one in which the parties gather in one place, usually around a conference table (hence the name "table closing") at the same time, and the escrow holder moves documents and money around the table to close the transaction. Contrast with that a "deed and money" escrow closing where the parties submit the documents and funds to the escrow holder who then "closes" the transaction by delivering some documents to the party(ies) designated, recording other documents, and transferring funds to the party(ies) designated. Despite the Escrow Agreement calling for a New York style closing, the closing was so complicated that little would have been accomplished by having multiple parties and their attorneys gathered around one table. In fact, the closing was a deed and money escrow closing, as we are sure you now can understand why.

Because this was to be a complex closing, we have included the Escrow Trust Instructions in addition to the Escrow Agreement. Under the Escrow Agreement, the parties deposited all of the closing documents and funds with Title Services, Inc., a title and escrow company, which, once all the required documents and monetary deposits were made to it, was instructed to "close" the various transactions. Title Services had to do many things to effect the closing, including issuing title policies, recording numerous documents, disbursing monies, and delivering documents to the parties.

The Escrow Trust Instructions set forth the exact terms on which Title Services was to act on behalf of each of the principal parties. It is also in the Escrow Trust Instructions that FMB, the "fifth" party, gets into the act: it is FMB's money that will close the transactions. In most real estate closings, the lender drafts the instructions and sends them to the escrow holder, and FMB did, in fact, draft the Escrow Trust Instructions.

In addition to outlining the transaction, an Escrow Agreement also will state what happens if the closing does not occur. Consider whether the provisions in the Escrow Agreement and the Escrow Trust Instructions go far enough to protect the parties.

[2] The Complexity of Closing the Deal

The Ridloff article does a good job of laying out what documents and monies will be necessary to close a typical transaction. Below is the list from the article which we have annotated to include items that became part of the closing in our transaction:

- The deed [and all other transfer instruments reserving or creating other interests such as easements or servitudes]
- The bill of sale [of personal property]
- An affidavit of title [or other title documents such as title insurance exceptions and endorsements, FIRPTA affidavit, ALTA statements, and utility letters and GAP undertakings], if required
- Corporate resolutions [and certification of legal existence of seller], if applicable
- Assignments of service contracts, transferable licenses and permits, warranties, space leases, the ground lease, if any, and the security deposits
- Architectural or engineering plans, if available
- [Certified survey or subdivision plat]
- The certificate of occupancy and other licenses and permits
- Current bills for taxes and water and sewer charges [including evidence of payment of current utilities and real estate taxes]

- The original leases and manually-executed counterparts of any ground leases or mortgages affecting the property [including any assignment(s) of rents]
- Transferable insurance policies
- Estoppel certificates or letters from space tenants, ground lessors, and mortgagees
- The tenant security deposits
- Letters to parties in interest, such as tenants, ground lessors, mortgagees, or contractors, informing them of the sale
- [1099-S certifications]
- [New financing documents including notes, mortgages and UCC-1 and UCC-2 Financing Statements]
- [Proceeds disposition, including any wiring instructions]
- [Closing Statements]

In addition, the Ridloff article also lists the funds necessary to close a typical transaction:

- [Sufficient funds for transfer]
- Real property transfer taxes
- Documentary stamps for the deed
- Mortgage recording taxes
- Sales taxes
- Survey costs
- The cost of title insurance

[3] The Escrow Agreement and the Escrow Trust Instructions

[a] The Documents

You now should read both the Escrow Agreement and the Escrow Trust Instructions. You should have a good idea of what you are looking for.

[b] Notes and Questions About the Escrow Agreement and the Escrow Trust Instructions

1. You should become familiar with all the terms mentioned in the Escrow Agreement and the Escrow Trust Instructions. There are a few that may not be all that obvious:

   FIRPTA Affidavit is to fulfill the requirements of the federal Foreign Investment In Real Property Transfer Act under which the buyer must withhold 10% of the purchase price if the seller is a foreign person or entity. The seller provides the completed form to the buyer to avoid the withholding.

Gap undertakings are the seller's representation and warranty to the title company that it has not encumbered the property since the last title search.

Transfer stamps typically are placed on the deed by the county to signify that the appropriate transfer tax has been paid.

2. Did Title Services, Inc. receive clear instructions as to all aspects of the transaction? If not, which party was, or parties were, placed at risk over which issue(s)?

[4] Land Trusts

Note that the title to the property is held by a land trust. Several states (Illinois, Florida, Virginia, North Dakota, Indiana, and Hawaii) by statute recognize this type of entity as capable of holding title to real property, and holding title in this manner can be beneficial to an owner. The trustee of a land trust does not operate the property but simply signs documents as directed by the person or entity with the power of direction. A land trust agreement typically is boilerplate — with only a few blanks filled in concerning the identity of the beneficiary and the person(s) or entity(ies) with the power of direction

There are a variety of reasons to hold title in a land trust. Some owners become the beneficiaries of land trusts so that their interest in real property is not of public record (the recorded documents, such as the deed and mortgage, can be signed by the trustee of the land trust rather than by the beneficiary). In addition, several individuals or entities who would have interests in the property can agree that one individual can hold the power to direct the land trust to execute agreements respecting the property.

There also may be a tax reason for holding property in a land trust. In some jurisdictions, while a transfer of fee simple title is subject to a transfer tax, a transfer of a beneficial interest in a land trust would not be subject to a transfer tax. This was the case in Illinois for many years, and many people utilized land trusts in order to avoid paying such transfer taxes. Illinois law was changed, and transfers of beneficial interests in land trusts are now also subject to transfer taxes. Note, however, that land trusts are ignored for federal tax purposes and the beneficiary of the trust is treated as the owner.

Finally, another reason for an owner to employ a land trust arises when the owner seeks to obtain a loan secured by the property. Having title to real property in a land trust can be beneficial to the owner's lender, and the lender may insist that title be transferred to a land trust as a condition to the lender making the loan. A lender might be able to more quickly and cheaply recover on the collateral when the title is held by a land trust. This will be discussed in more detail in Part III.

[5] Problem

After the Escrow Agreement and the Escrow Trust Instructions are delivered to Kaplan & Miller, Donna Smith again comes to Sam Nader's office. Donna asks Sam to review them and to write her a memo that lays out what Regent will have to do in order to close the multiple transactions. Sam again asks the next question,

"On what do you want me to focus?" Donna is less patient this time (she is starting to rely on Sam and she expects him to rise to the occasion) and responds, "Tell me what I need to tell David Delaney the next time I speak with him. He doesn't need all the picky little details, after all he has been doing this for years. I need to make him aware of anything unusual in this deal, you know, the things he might not be anticipating. And I need to know if what FMB and Title Services have put together will get the job done."

If you were Sam, what would your memo highlight? What section(s) of the Escrow Agreement and/or the Escrow Trust Instructions might be modified and what modifications would you suggest?

Chapter 6

ASSURING GOOD TITLE TO THE PROJECT SITE

§ 6.01 THE IMPORTANCE OF TITLE

We suppose that you think it is obvious that Regent needs to get good title to the project site. It is obvious, but there is more to it than you may realize. If Regent does not get good title to the site, beyond losing the overall purchase price for the site, it also may lose any financing it has arranged and it could lose the value of any improvements it makes.

To guide you through the title process, we begin by discussing what is good title, how a buyer of land can determine if he is receiving good title, and how a buyer of land can obtain insurance that he is receiving good title. We finish the chapter by discussing the title implications of the various easements and restrictions that Regent had to agree to with both Metropolitan and Turtle Wax.

§ 6.02 MARKETABLE OR GOOD TITLE*

[1] Definition of Marketable Title

Most real estate transactions are predicated upon the ability of the seller to deliver, and the willingness of the buyer to accept, a "marketable" title. Marketable title has been described as "[that which] embrace[s] the entire estate or interest sold, and [which is] free from the lien of all burdens, charges, or encumbrances which present doubtful questions of law or fact."[1] It has also been defined as that "which imports such ownership as insures to the owner the peaceful enjoyment and control of the land, as against all others."[2] The purpose of a title examination is to determine the marketability of a title and the presence of any liens or encumbrances against the title to the property.

[2] Effect of Liens and Encumbrances

Even though title may be marketable in terms of the ownership, the title may be subject to encumbrances that materially affect its value. A property that is encumbered by a restrictive covenant which prevents its future development, or by a gas pipeline easement that severely hinders its use, is less "marketable" to potential buyers. Nevertheless, from a technical standpoint, the presence or absence of encumbrances should be considered an issue separate from the marketability of the title itself. A title examiner is expected to determine whether

---

* Adapted from Robert M. Curry & James Geoffrey Durham, Ohio Real Property Law and Practice (6th ed. Lexis 2006), Chapter 6, Title to Real Estate. Most citations have been omitted.

1 Frank v. Murphy, 64 Ohio App. 501, 505, 29 N.E.2d 41, 43 (1940).

2 McCarty v. Lingham, 111 Ohio St. 551, 558, 146 N.E. 64 (1924).

the record title is marketable and to list all encumbrances, but the title examiner is not in a position to determine whether the encumbrances affect the value of the property. In addition, errors, irregularities and deficiencies in property descriptions in the chain of title do not impair marketability unless, after all circumstances of record are taken into account, a substantial uncertainty exists as to the land which was conveyed or intended to be conveyed, or the description falls beneath the minimal requirement of sufficiency and definiteness which is essential to an effective conveyance.

Not all real estate contracts recognize the technical distinction between a marketable title and one that is free from encumbrances. The contract may use the term "marketable title" in a more general sense, implying not only a marketable title, but also one that is not subject to encumbrances which materially impair its use or value. This is a question of interpretation that is beyond the scope of the title examination itself. In many states, the courts also will imply a covenant of marketable title even if the parties have not included one. Attorneys drafting purchase contracts should not leave this issue to interpretation, but rather should address not only the quality of title (marketable) but also the types of liens and encumbrances to which the property may be subject.

[3] "Good," "Clear," or "Insurable" Title

Although most real estate purchase contracts call for the seller to deliver and the buyer to accept a marketable title, some contracts will require "good," "clear," or "insurable" title. "Good" title or "good and marketable" title may imply a higher standard than mere marketability. However, if a title is marketable, it is, by definition, good enough that a buyer or examiner should not object to it. Therefore, unless the context indicates a different intent, "good" title and "marketable" title probably should be considered synonymous. "Clear" title, on the other hand, usually refers not to the title itself but to the absence of liens or encumbrances against the real estate.

"Insurable" title generally refers to the quality of title that a title insurance company would accept in determining whether to insure the title to the property. Title insurance policies insure the marketability of title, so that, in most instances, the terms "marketable" and "insurable" are synonymous. Differences may emerge, however, if a title insurer elects to assume the risk that a particular title defect will not be asserted, and agrees to "insure over" that defect, or if the insurer takes a more conservative view and refuses to insure against a defect which a title examiner deems not to impair marketability.

[4] Points for the Buyer's Attorney

A buyer's attorney has to keep at least two points in mind. First, if her client is considering using a form contract, many form contracts state that the buyer will accept title with "encumbrances of record." That statement, of course, turns the concept of marketable title on its head because the buyer, in theory, is bound to accept recorded encumbrances. An attorney always should be mindful of the effect of such form provisions and be prepared to counsel her client both as to suggested modification and as to why the modification is necessary. Second, the buyer's attorney has to be aware of her client's intended use of the property, because an encumbrance that might not render title unmarketable might prevent or inhibit her client from engaging in the intended use.

§ 6.03 TITLE REVIEW*

[1] Title Search

Title is searched by a thorough review of the records of the jurisdiction; in most states title records are kept on a county by county basis. It varies by jurisdiction as to who will perform the title search. In some states the traditional practice is that attorneys, or more frequently members of their staffs, will perform the title search. In other states, a title abstractor or an employee of a title insurance company will perform the title search.

The title searcher must review the index to find documents relating to the subject parcel of land and then read each document. In addition to documents recorded in what is typically called the county recorder's office, other documents may pertain to title. Some of these other documents that may not be recorded by the county recorder include probate documents, judgment liens and bankruptcy filings. It varies from state to state, and sometimes from county to county, as to where the title searcher must inquire and as to how those documents are filed and indexed.

[2] Abstract or Opinion of Title

An abstract of title is a concise statement of the substance of documents or facts, appearing on the public records that affect title.[1] An abstract of title may be described as a methodically written history of the title to a specific tract of land. Abstractors should keep in mind that the purpose of an abstract is to enable the examiner to make a complete opinion on the record title from the abstract alone.

A certificate of title (sometimes referred to as an opinion of title, title examination, or report of examination of title) is the written opinion of a lawyer that the title to the land described in the certificate is marketable and unencumbered as appears of record, except for the defects and encumbrances set forth. It may be based upon an abstract of title or upon a direct examination of the public records.

For example, Ohio State Bar Association Ohio Standards of Title Examination § 2.3 states that the certificate or opinion should include:

(1) The period of time of the examination.

(2) That the opinion is based on an abstract of title or is based on an examination of the public records of ____________ County, Ohio, as disclosed by the public indexes relating to the premises.

(3) That the opinion or certificate does not purport to cover the following: (a) Matters not of record, (b) Rights of persons in possession, (c) Questions

---

* Adapted from Robert M. Curry & James Geoffrey Durham, Ohio Real Property Law and Practice (6th ed. Lexis 2006), Chapter 6, Title to Real Estate. Most citations have been omitted.

[1] State *ex rel.* Doria v. Ferguson, 145 Ohio St. 12, 60 N.E.2d 476, 478 (1945).

which a correct survey or inspection of the premises would disclose, (d) Rights to file mechanics' liens, (e) Special taxes and assessments not shown by the county treasurer's records, (f) Zoning and other governmental regulations, (g) Liens asserted by the United States and State of Ohio, their agencies and officers under the Ohio Solid and Hazardous Waste and Disposal Act and Federal Super Fund Amendments, and under Racketeering Influence and Corrupt Organization acts and receivership liens, unless the lien is filed in the public records of the County in which the property is located.

[3] Effect of Recording

The effect of recording is to give constructive notice to all persons dealing with the land of properly recorded instruments in the chain of title. Accordingly, an unrecorded deed, land contract, or other instrument is unenforceable as against a subsequent bona fide purchaser for value without actual knowledge of the prior unrecorded instrument. As between the parties to the unrecorded instrument, however, in most states, recordation is not a prerequisite to enforceability. However, an unrecorded deed, land contract, or other instrument fails to provide constructive notice to subsequent purchasers. Therefore, in true "race-notice" jurisdictions, the first to record will prevail, assuming, again, that any subsequent purchaser for value who is first to record received his interest without notice of the prior but unrecorded instrument. However, in a "notice" jurisdiction, it does not matter whether the subsequent grantee records at all as to his rights over the prior unrecorded grantee (but it would matter as to yet subsequent grantees), and in a "race" jurisdiction, it does not matter that the subsequent purchaser has knowledge as long as he records before the prior grantee.

Priority of a mortgage is determined according to the order of recordation. The first mortgage presented for record shall be the first recorded and thereafter have priority over subsequently recorded mortgages. Until a mortgage is filed for record, it remains invalid and unenforceable against any subsequent buyer unless the subsequent buyer has actual knowledge of the mortgage.

[4] Documents Entitled to Recording

Recording an instrument not authorized by statute to be recorded typically has no effect on the rights of third persons. Recording an instrument not entitled to be recorded does not serve as constructive notice to subsequent bona fide purchasers, although it may show an equitable right and be actual notice.

A deed or other interest in real property must be signed by the grantor, mortgagor, vendor, or lessor, and such signing by the grantor, mortgagor, vendor, or lessor must be "acknowledged." In all states, a deed must be "acknowledged" by a notary public or other government official, and in some states a deed must be "witnessed" (much like a will, the witnesses must be present when the deed is signed). The notary public, and, if required, the witnesses, shall attest to the signing and subscribe their names to the attestation. The later addition of witnesses' signatures, outside of the presence of the grantor, renders the deed ineffective to convey legal title. The effect of a defectively executed deed or other instrument is that recording will not provide constructive notice to subsequent bona fide purchasers.

[5] Possession as Actual Notice

The benefits of the recording act are available only to subsequent bona fide purchasers who had, at the time of the purchase, no constructive or actual notice of a prior, unrecorded conveyance or encumbrance. In most states, the possession of property by a third person is notice to a buyer of the legal and equitable rights claimed under the possession to the extent that the rights may be disclosed by a reasonable investigation or by inquiry of the occupant. Actual notice of the possession is not necessary, unless required by statute, but the possession must be visible. Possession, however, gives no notice of any rights of a third person in the property obtained previously through the possessors if those rights are not actually known or entitled to constructive notice through the public records. Moreover, there is no duty to inquire of a possessor as to the rights of third parties claiming through him.

The majority of cases hold that a title acquired by adverse possession is marketable and relates back to the commencement of the possession. An adverse possessor, however, can only establish a record title by judgment of the court. Generally, an unrecorded easement is not enforceable against a bona fide purchaser for value who has no actual or constructive notice (including that which would be known if an inspection of the land were made) of the easement; assuming, again that in a "race-notice" jurisdiction, the subsequent buyer records first. An easement not recited on any deed in the owner's chain of title results in no constructive notice of the encumbrance for subsequent buyers, but a buyer may be subject to "notice to make inquiry" based on the obligation that the buyer inspect the land. Thus, if there is no actual knowledge of the unrecorded easement, or facts supporting notice to make inquiry, then such encumbrance is unenforceable as against third parties.

§ 6.04 TITLE REVIEW, TITLE INSURANCE AND SURVEYS

[1] Title Insurance

The following article raises issues about the necessities for and considerations in obtaining title review, title insurance, and a survey in developing the Fox Valley Auto Care Center.

David E. Snediker,
Surveys and Title Insurance,
39 THE PRACTICAL LAWYER NO.3*

Title insurance policies are contracts of indemnity that protect the policy holder against actual monetary loss up to the policy limits and subject to the policy coverage. Title insurance policies are not guarantees that automatically obligate the insurer to pay money if a title defect is later discovered. The insured must show an actual loss in value or actual damage to insured interests, and the insurer then has the option to pay money to the insured or litigate against or settle with third parties to protect the insured's interests. *See* D. BARLOW BURKE, JR., LAW OF TITLE INSURANCE § 1.3 (Little, Brown & Co., Boston, 1986 & Supp. 1992).

POLICY FORMS

Until recently, title companies were using various policy forms throughout the country, and in some cases such as New York, multiple policy forms within the same state. It is now possible to obtain an American Land Title Association ("ALTA") policy in each state except Texas, which requires title insurance companies to use policy forms that have been adopted by the Texas State Board of Insurance. (The Texas policy forms are based on the 1990 ALTA form.) Iowa is unique in prohibiting the issuance of title insurance except by the state through the Iowa Title Guaranty Fund. The policies used by the fund are, however, ALTA forms. In addition, private insurers issue ALTA policies "out-of-state" based on Iowa attorney title certifications.

The ALTA Policy. The 1990 ALTA policy forms in use nationwide are substantially similar in coverage, subject to differing regional exceptions for survey matters, water rights, mechanic's liens, rights of parties in possession and other "off record" issues. Many ALTA regional exceptions, especially survey exceptions, can be deleted or "endorsed over" if appropriate documentation, and in some cases additional premiums and further underwriting considerations, are provided.

The CLTA Policy. In California and several western states, both ALTA and California Land Title Association ("CLTA") policies are available. The primary difference between the basic CLTA policy and the standard ALTA policy used in these states is that the ALTA policy does not have coverage exceptions for certain survey issues and various "off record" matters. However, the California ALTA policies are more expensive and generally require an ALTA survey to provide "extended coverage" over the basic CLTA policy. Numerous CLTA policy endorsements are available (subject to certain additional cost, documentation and underwriting considerations) that can significantly "upgrade" the basic CLTA policy coverage. For a discussion of the ALTA and CLTA policy forms, their coverages and differences, see Robert C. Barnes & Eric B. Salter, *A Practical Guide to Title Insurance in California*, 8 Cal. Real Prop. J. 1, 4 (Fall 1990).

COVERAGE

Subject to stated exclusions from and exceptions to coverage (and the policy's general conditions and stipulations), the basic 1990 ALTA lender's policy ("Lender's Policy") insures against loss or damage by reason of:

- Title to the estate or interest insured being vested other than as stated in the policy;
- Any defect in or lien or encumbrance on the title;
- Unmarketability of the title;
- Lack of a right of access to and from the land;
- The invalidity or unenforceability of the lien of the insured mortgage;
- The priority of any lien or encumbrance over the lien of the insured mortgage;
- Lack of priority of the lien of the insured mortgage over statutory liens for services, labor or material (a) arising from improvements or work related

to the land which is contracted for or commenced before the policy date or (b) arising from an improvement or work related to the land which is contracted for or commenced after the policy date and which is financed in whole or in part by proceeds of the indebtedness secured by the insured mortgage which at the date of the policy the insured has advanced or is obligated to advance; and

- The invalidity or unenforceability of any assignment of the insured mortgage shown in the policy or the failure to vest title to the insured mortgage in the named assignee free and clear of liens.

The standard form 1990 ALTA Owner's Policy ("Owners Policy") provides only the first four coverages offered by the Lender's Policy. For a detailed discussion of the 1987 ALTA policy forms, which are virtually identical to the 1990 ALTA forms except for a new creditor's rights exception, see *Title Insurance, The New Policy Changes* (PLI Real Est. L. and Prac. Course Handbook Series No. 300, 1987).

Short Form Residential Policy. In addition to the Owner's Policy and the Lender's Policy, there is a 1988 short form ALTA residential loan policy (the "Short Form Residential Policy"). Unlike the basic Owner's Policy or the basic Lender's Policy, the Short Form Residential Policy also provides insurance against loss or damage by reason of any violation, variation, encroachment or adverse circumstances affecting title that would be disclosed by an accurate survey. The Short Form Residential Policy is not available from all insurers in all states. For example, as of last summer [1997] Lawyers Title Insurance Company had only filed for use of the Short Form Residential Policy in Arizona, Georgia, Hawaii, California, Louisiana, Ohio, Tennessee and Mississippi.

EXCLUSIONS

The Owner's Policy excludes coverage for loss or damage, costs, attorneys' fees or expenses that arise by reason of:

- Laws, including zoning and environmental laws, which relate to occupancy or enjoyment of land, the character, dimensions or locations of improvements, separation in ownership or change in dimensions of parcels of land, or environmental protection;
- Eminent domain;
- Defects, liens, or encumbrances agreed to by the insured or known to the insured and not known to the company (which are not matters of public record) or which result in no loss or damage which would not have been sustained if the insured had paid value for the insured estate; and
- Creditor's rights matters.

The Lender's Policy excludes these items and lien enforcement problems caused by a lender's failure to comply with "doing business," [Some states require that an out-of-state corporation register to do business in the subject state. — Eds.] usury, or consumer protection laws, as well as statutory liens arising from services, labor, or materials contracted for and commenced after the policy date unless they are financed by indebtedness which has been, or must be, advanced.

SURVEYS

In a land survey, an engineer measures and plots dimensions and areas on or near the earth's surface for a stated purpose and in conformity with an agreed-upon standard of accuracy. There are various types of surveys which can be performed depending upon the intentions of the parties (aerial, perimeter, tape location, "as-built," topographical, and so on). The surveyor's field efforts are usually portrayed graphically in the form of a map, plat, chart, or other agreed-upon medium reflecting details required by the person ordering the survey. For a helpful discussion of surveys and survey language, see Gary York, *Surveys in Real Property Transactions* (pts 1 & 2), 5 Cal. Real Prop. L. Rep. 7, 8 (1982).

ALTA/ACSM Land Title Surveys. An "ALTA/ACSM Land Title Survey" (commonly referred to as an ALTA survey) is a land survey conducted in accordance with minimum standard detail requirements (the "Minimum Standards") jointly adopted in 1992 by the Board of Direction, American Congress on Surveying and Mapping and the American Land Title Association. The Minimum Standards were established to promote a distinct and clear understanding among the insured, the title insurer, and the surveyor. The Minimum Standards require, among other things, that when the survey is ordered the surveyor must be advised that an "ALTA/ACSM Land Title Survey" is desired. Additionally, the surveyor must be provided with "Record Documents" (as defined in the Minimum Standards). When the survey is ordered, the surveyor must also be told what class of accuracy is desired (Urban, Suburban, Rural or Mountain/Marshland), and the surveyor must be given various other specified information (such as the names and deed data for adjacent owners) as available.

If an ALTA/ACSM Land Title Survey is performed the surveyor must provide at least two sets of prints of a plat or map representing field work conducted on the ground surveyed, with the notations and information required by the Minimum Standards. The prints must be certified as required by the Minimum Standards and the surveyor's seal must be affixed.

Minimum Standards. The Minimum Standards require that the plat or map show differences between record bearings, angles, or distances and those actually measured and whether the record description "closes." In addition, the surveyor must show:

- Significant detail regarding recorded and measured beginning points and distances from corners of the property to the nearest right-of-way lines in the street;
- The names and widths of streets and highways abutting the property;
- Monuments found or placed;
- The location of buildings;
- Recorded and observed easements, the character and location of walls, buildings, and fences within five feet of either side of boundary lines;
- Encroachments by or onto adjoining property streets, easements, and record setback lines, and driveways or alleys on or crossing the property;
- Cemeteries and burial grounds disclosed in the process of surveying or searching title; and

- Ponds, lakes, springs, or rivers bordering on or running through the property.

The surveyor must also point out streets adjoining the premises which are legally defined but not physically opened.

Significant additional detail may be obtained by agreement between the surveyor and the insured, including such things as flood zone designation, land area, contours, setback and height restrictions imposed by applicable law, "substantial visible" improvements (such as signs, swimming pools, landscaping and the like), parking areas and striping, curb cuts, and utility locations.

SURVEYS AND TITLE INSURANCE

Title surveys are used to identify property and extract relevant information from a physical inspection that might affect the property's marketability of title. Although surveys are helpful — and indeed critical — for many real estate transactions, keep in mind that surveys are not instruments of conveyance. They provide information about physical facts to the impression of the surveyor. They do not create or convey title. For an informative discussion of the effect of matters discernible from surveys on marketability of title see Bernard M. Rifkin, "The Land Survey, a Survey of the Law of New York, California, Florida, Illinois and Texas as of 1987" in J. Pedowitz, Title Insurance 1989: Negotiating Additional Coverages, at 285 (PLI Real Est. L. and Prac. Course Handbook Series No. 331, 1989).

Survey Exceptions. Title policies usually contain coverage exceptions in addition to the standard coverage exclusions. The exceptions are generally set forth on Schedule B to the policy and can consist of standard printed exceptions (which will differ regionally as discussed above) and specific additional exceptions based on relevant facts. One standard exception, which normally may be removed, insured over, or modified if a current survey (or in certain cases relevant affidavits) is provided, is the "survey exception." The standard survey exception negates insurance for encroachments, overlaps, boundary line disputes, or other matters which an accurate survey or inspection of premises would disclose.

Regional Variation. The precise wording of the standard survey exception may differ from region to region and among insurers. Typical language in a case where no survey exists would be:

> "Rights or claims of parties in possession and easements or claims of easement not shown by the public records, boundary line disputes, overlaps, encroachments and any matters not of record which would be disclosed by an accurate survey and inspection of the premises."

A short form exception frequently set forth is:

> "Such state of facts as would be disclosed by an accurate survey and inspection of the premises."

If an older survey is provided, the insurer may rewrite the exception as:

> "Such state of facts occurring subsequent to ____________ [date of the old survey] as would be disclosed by a current accurate survey and inspection of the premises."

Survey-Specific Language. If a current acceptable survey is provided, the insurer will frequently replace the standard survey exception with language keyed to the survey, such as:

> "Matters shown on survey of ____________ prepared by ____________ dated ____________."

A better approach for the insured would be to have problems disclosed by a survey specifically identified, such as:

> "Encroachment upon the insured premises of ____________ as shown on the survey of ____________ prepared by ____________ dated ____________."

The best approach for the insured would be to have the survey exception deleted in its entirety if there is no apparent problem.

Problem Areas. There are many reported cases dealing with title insurance coverage litigation, but the total number of cases is probably less than one might initially expect since the insured needs to show "actual loss" arising out of matters insured against to be able to sustain a claim. Also, under the conditions and stipulations of the Owner's Policy and the Lender's Policy, the title companies may settle matters with third parties once a claim is raised, and they can pay the policy limit to the insured and cancel the coverage.

Survey Error Exceptions. Although the total number of title insurance coverage cases may be less than one would expect, perhaps the most commonly litigated issue is whether coverage may be denied because of an exception in the policy relating to survey matters. The list of title problems that could arise which would potentially be discernible from a "correct" or "accurate" survey is a long one. Representative examples include:

- Discrepancies between recorded and measured courses and distances;
- Discrepancies between measured and "actual" courses and distances (including record information and "off-record" information such as the location of improvements, natural monuments, etc.);
- Discrepancies between recorded and measured area;
- Discrepancies between measured and "actual" area;
- Encroachments of buildings, stoops, vaults, walls, fences, landscaping or other improvements onto the property insured or by the property insured;
- Encroachments of driveways, streets, highways, and other rights-of-way or easements onto the property insured or by the property insured;
- Appurtenances, such as access, water, and utility rights; and
- Matters observable by physical inspection which are suggestive of rights of others, such as signs, tenancies, prescriptive rights, and adverse possession.

Limits. Not every title problem creates title company liability. For example, although certain encroachments might constitute "title defects" (for example, an encroachment of a stoop, vault, wall, window, etc., onto a public street) the defects may be permitted by statutes, adverse possession, or prescriptive rights. If there is no "actual loss" there is no liability for the insurer.

Legal Access. It is also important to remember that the basic Lender's Policy and the basic Owner's Policy do not insure appurtenances other than legal access. Accordingly, if the dispute involves an insured's claim to property or rights beyond the boundary described in the policy, the insurer can deny coverage, absent special affirmative insurance to the contrary. *See, e.g., Offenhartz v. Heinsohn*, 30 Misc. 2d 693, 150 N.Y.S. 2d 78 (1956). In *Offenhartz* the insured was not allowed to recover against a title company when it was denied the right to use a pipeline that crossed adjoining property since the policy did not provide affirmative insurance for continued use of the pipeline even though the survey showed the pipeline as "location unknown."

Reasonable Expectations. While the older cases have tended to allow title insurers to avoid liability for wrongly describing matters beyond boundaries, modern courts are more likely to hold the insurer liable for damages resulting from reliance on surveys read into a policy which wrongly refer to matters beyond the boundary lines on the theory that insurance companies should be liable for reasonable expectations of lay purchasers of insurance. *See MacBean v. St. Paul Title Ins. Corp.*, 169 N.J. Super. 502, 405 A.2d 405 (1979); *see also* Burke, *supra* at § 13.3 (describing current trends in comparison to older cases).

Guaranteed Results? Keep in mind that title companies do not warrant the complete accuracy of surveys even when they are "read into" a policy. For example, specific reference in a title policy to a survey as "insured," when the survey correctly shows boundary lines but incorrectly locates the building, thereby leading the insured to believe that zoning setback lines were not violated, would not create liability for the insurer (absent special affirmative insurance) since loss arising from the operation of governmental laws is excluded from coverage and mislocation of the building does not, itself, create a title defect that is otherwise insured against. On the other hand, if the survey read into the policy failed to show that the building impermissibly encroached upon adjoining property, the insurer would be liable for damages incurred to remove the encroachment. *Broadway Realty Company v. Lawyers Title Insurance and Trust Company*, 226 N.Y. 335, 123 N.E. 754 (1919).

Endorsements. Litigation involving survey matters may be generally categorized into two groups: those cases where a problem exists that would have been shown by a "correct" survey, but no survey was tendered and the policy contained a "correct survey exception"; and those cases where a defective survey was read into the policy. The purpose of the survey exception is to exclude from coverage problems that cannot be discovered from a search of public records but which can be discovered from an accurate survey. *Walker Rogge, Inc. v. Chelsea Title & Guaranty Company*, 116 N.J. 517, 562 A.2d 208 (1989). In those states where "extended coverage" is available only at an extra charge and with a current survey, courts seem to be more strict in denying coverage for matters which could have been learned by a correct survey. *See Muench v. Oxley*, 90 Wash. 2d 637, 584 P. 2d 939 (1978); *see also Conti v. Western Title Ins. Co.*, 40 Cal. App. 3d 536, 115 Cal. Rptr. 257 (1974).

Deleting the Exception. To be safe, an insured should always have the survey exception deleted and should obtain affirmative coverage on survey-related matters of interest to it. Representative affirmative endorsements that may be available include:

- Insurance that the property insured is the same as the property shown on a referenced survey;
- Insurance that multiple parcels are contiguous if so shown by the survey;
- Insurance on acreage or, if refused by the insurer, a limitation on acreage exceptions with affirmative insurance on boundary courses and distances;
- Insurance on specified access (identified public street or specified easement);
- Insurance on specific locations of easements and improvements (when blanket easements are involved, insurance against loss of use of the easements by the insured, or from use of the easements by others, sometimes may be obtained); and
- Insurance that no encroachments of improvements by or onto the property, easements, or setback lines (insurance against zoning setback violations may require a zoning opinion). For a helpful discussion of survey-related endorsements, see James L. Lipscomb, et al., "Survey Type Coverage Desired by the Institutional Investor," in Title Insurance 1989: Negotiating Additional Coverages, at 331 (PLI Real Est. L. and Prac. Course Handbook Series No. 331, 1989).

CONCLUSION

Title insurance policies, like most insurance products have undergone significant change in recent years. The standard policies now widely available offer considerable predictability and uniformity. You can make the best use of the policies by taking advantage of the built-in opportunity to tailor them to your client's specific needs by judiciously choosing from standard endorsements and coverages.

[2] Endorsements on Title Insurance Policies*

Title insurance policy endorsements are amendments or supplements that clarify or expand its coverage. The granting of these endorsements is at the discretion of the title company, although some states regulate the types of endorsements that a title insurance company may include to its policies. The title company will usually charge a fee for an endorsement which can be a nominal amount or quite expensive, depending on the nature of the endorsement sought.

Legal description endorsements can be obtained so that the policy insures that the land described in the policy is the same land as that shown on a particular survey. A "contiguity" endorsement insures that when a property consists of multiple parcels, the parcels are contiguous along their common boundaries so as to constitute a single parcel of land. If a structure on the property encroaches onto an easement, a neighboring property or a set-back area, the policy may be endorsed to insure against loss, or to insure that the owner will not be forced to remove the encroaching structure.

Several forms of zoning endorsement are available, ranging from a simple endorsement confirming that a parcel of land is in a particular zoning classification

---

* Adapted from Robert M. Curry & James Geoffrey Durham, Ohio Real Property Law and Practice (6th ed. Lexis 2006), Chapter 6, Title to Real Estate. Citations have been omitted.

and identifying the uses permitted under that classification, to a detailed endorsement which insures that the property conforms with all applicable zoning requirements. The latter endorsement may, when the title insurance policy insures the lender on a construction loan, also include zoning compliance when the development is built according to the plans reviewed and accepted by the construction lender and the title insurer.

Condominium and PUD endorsements insure that the property consists of a parcel in a properly formed condominium or planned unit development and that there are no current violations of the condominium or PUD restrictive covenants. In addition, a comprehensive endorsement is available to insure against loss or damage due to any violation of a restrictive covenant, set back line or easement affecting the property.

Numerous endorsements are available to insure a lender against claims affecting the priority of its lien. Common endorsements include a Truth-in-Lending endorsement (insuring against impairment of the lien due to a claimed violation of the Truth-in-Lending law); a usury endorsement (insuring against the impairment of the lien due to a claim of usury); a variable rate endorsement (insuring that the lien priority will not be affected merely because the loan calls for changes in the rate of interest); a revolving credit endorsement (insuring the validity and priority of future advances made under a revolving credit); and a comprehensive endorsement, covering loss due to a breach of restrictive covenants, set back lines or easements, or due to encroachments.

§ 6.05 TITLE INSURANCE AND THE FOX VALLEY AUTO CARE CENTER

[1] The Fox Valley Auto Care Center Title Insurance Policies

Title insurance, like all insurance, is a contract between the insurance company and the insured. The insurance company endeavors to carefully define for what exactly it is insuring, and the insured should carefully consider what protection she is obtaining in purchasing the policy. For Sam Nader, as it is for many lawyers who may have not read their own auto or homeowner's/renter's policies, the process of reading a title insurance policy is an introduction to the world of insurance.

In the Document Book we have included two title insurance policies. The first is the Owner's Policy; the second is the Lender's Policy. The owner and the lender have similar, but different, interests that need to be insured. There is cross-over between the two, both in the terms of the title insurance policy provisions and in the premiums. If a title insurer issues an owner's policy, likely it will issue the lender's policy for a much lower premium than if there were no owner's policy, and vice versa. Do you see why?

As the Snediker article points out, title insurance policies are relatively uniform across the country. The structure of the ALTA forms is typical: first are two form sections, "Covered Risks" (the insuring clause) and "Exclusions From Coverage"; next are two "schedules" with the relevant information about the policy, Schedule A (the amount of the policy, the stated insured(s), and legal description of the insured parcel(s)) and Schedule B (any specific exclusions pertaining to the insured parcel); these are followed by the part of the policy that every lawyer needs to know, "Conditions," the form section that describes and defines the true coverage of the policy; and last are any endorsements (modifications or expansions on the terms or coverage).

Although we will not be considering Regent's financing for the Fox Valley Auto Care Center until Chapter 9, we have included the provisions of the Lender's Policy so that you may see the different interests of the owner and the lender, which highlight how each is trying to protect its investment in the Center. You will be able to highlight some of those differing interests as you read the two policies by comparing the following sections:

- The Owner's Policy includes coverage for encroachments which would be shown by a survey (#2. (c)).
- The Lender's Policy includes four additional terms of coverage relating to the validity and enforceability of the mortgage (#9. through #12.).
- The Exclusions from Coverage in the Lender's Policy has a different #4. and a different #5., both relating to the validity and the enforceability of the lien of the mortgage.
- In the Conditions section of the two policies, there are different definitions of "insured" in paragraph 1. (subparagraph (a) in the Owner's policy and subparagraph (e) in the Lender's policy); Paragraph 7. of the Lender's Policy gives the title insurer the option of buying out the lender if there is a title problem; Paragraph 8. of the Lender's Policy includes several additional limits on the title insurer's liability; Paragraph 10. is greatly different; Paragraph 11 in the Owner's policy is not in the Lender's policy; and Paragraph 12. in the Lender's policy (Paragraph 12. in the Owner's policy) includes additional terms.
- In Schedule B, Paragraphs 9 and 10 are changed to reflect that the Lender's Policy covers a construction loan that will be disbursed as the construction proceeds rather than totally when the loan closes.

Finally, as you read the two policies, do not be confused by the stated insureds, because in each policy it is First Mortgage Bank. As we pointed out in Chapter 5, First Mortgage Bank is both the trustee for Regent as the owner of the property, and, obviously, the lender.

[2] Questions About the Fox Valley Auto Care Center Title Insurance Policies

1. Why do you think that the purchase agreements both called for the obtaining of title insurance policies rather than relying on an abstract of title and/or an attorney's opinion of title?
2. What does a title insurance company insure when it issues an owner's title insurance policy?
3. What does a title insurance company insure when it issues a lender's title insurance policy?
4. How do the two policies differ? Are the differences something that should concern Regent's attorneys?

5. What title problems are excluded from coverage?

[3] The "Fairway" Problem — Transfer of Partnership Interests and Title Insurance

Many real estate development projects are undertaken by partnerships that obtain title insurance policies in the name of the partnership. That was not the case with the Fox Valley Auto Care Center, because title to the land was held by a land trust rather than the Fox Valley Auto Care Center Limited Partnership. If the partnership is thought of as an entity separate from its partners, you might think that changes in the members of the partnership would have no effect on the partnership itself or on any contracts that the partnership may have entered into. However, the court in *Fairway Development Co. v. Title Insurance Co. of Minnesota*, 621 F. Supp. 120 (N.D. Ohio 1985), thought otherwise.

In *Fairway Development Co.*, Fairway, a general partnership under Ohio law, sued Minnesota Title for damages when an easement was discovered encumbering property insured by Minnesota Title under a policy that did not list the easement as one of the excepted encumbrances on Schedule B. Minnesota Title defended itself in the action by claiming that the named insured under the policy, which Minnesota Title referred to as Fairway I, no longer existed because two of its three partners had transferred their interests to the remaining partner and a third party, thereby terminating Fairway I and resulting in a new partnership, Fairway II. Minnesota Title maintained that it was not in privity of contract with Fairway II and, thus, could not be held liable under the policy. Relying on Ohio law, which followed the Uniform Partnership Act, the court agreed with the title insurer and concluded that the assignment by two of the original three partners of their "entire respective bundles of partnership rights" dissolved Fairway I and that Fairway II was not a continuation of Fairway I but a new partnership. Consequently, Minnesota Title was not liable under the title insurance policy.

Although the decision in *Fairway Development Co.* might suggest that a new title insurance policy must be obtained every time the membership in an insured general partnership changes, an endorsement to an original title insurance policy could achieve the same result. Indeed, following this decision, title insurance companies began providing so-called "Fairway endorsements" under which successor partnerships would continue to be insured under the original policy. Similar or related issues exist in connection with corporations, limited partnerships, and limited liability companies, particularly upon the conversion of one type of entity into another. The important point is that these issues be considered and discussed with the title insurer at the time the policy is issued or at least before any transfer of ownership in the insured entity occurs. For further discussion of these issues, see Joyce Dickey Palomar, *Limited Liability Companies, Corporations, General Partnerships, Limited Partnerships, Joint Ventures, Trusts — Who Does the Title Insurance Cover?* 31 REAL PROP., PROB. & TR. J. 605 (1997); Marc Weinreich, *Commercial Transactions: Who Does the Title Insurance Cover?* 6 PROB. & PROP. 42 (March/April 1992). SEE GENERALLY D. BARLOW BURKE, JR., LAW OF TITLE INSURANCE §§ 5.1.1 and 17.8 (2d ed. 1993).

§ 6.06 THE SURVEY

[1] The Fox Valley Auto Care Center Survey

The Document Book includes a copy of one of the surveys for the Fox Valley Auto Care Center. Its reduced format likely will make it difficult for you to examine. Most surveys are on much larger paper than a page in the Document Book (8-1/2 by 11), and the survey in the Document Book was on a single 24 x 36 inch sheet. Despite its reduced size, you should study it to start to become familiar with surveys in general. The survey was prepared prior to construction of the buildings at the Auto Care Center.

There are different reasons for having a survey done. Some surveys are done for the purpose of establishing title to a parcel when the parcel is going to be transferred from one party to another, perhaps from a seller to a buyer. These surveys will either be by "metes and bounds" or according to a previously filed subdivision map. A metes and bounds survey will take the description of the parcel from the most recent title document (usually the deed received by the current owner) and seek to determine whether the described boundaries of the parcel can be established and whether there are any problems with the description of improvements on the parcel and improvements on adjoining parcels (whether, for example, there are any encroachments by the improvement on one parcel onto the other parcel). A survey based on a subdivision map seeks to do the same thing, but its beginning point is the subdivision map rather than a metes and bounds legal description.

Another typical reason for having a survey done is to establish the boundaries and topography of a site in order to subdivide the plat into lots or parcels. A survey for a subdivider usually will serve as the basis for a subdivision map which will have to be reviewed and approved by the governing municipal jurisdiction before it may be recorded. The subdivision process is discussed in more detail in § 7.01, *infra*.

[2] Reviewing a Survey Map

R. Lee Hixson,*
What to Look for When Examining a Survey Map,
Probate & Property, September/October 2004, pages 54–56**

Most people are aware of the existence of malpractice in the legal and medical professions, and they have at least some clue about what steps can be taken to avoid becoming a victim of lawyers or doctors who do not follow accepted practice. But what about surveyors? Are lawyers working with survey maps even remotely aware of what constitutes surveying malpractice? When unfolding a map for the first time, do most lawyers have any idea what to look for to determine whether the boundary resolution shown on the map is a good one? Is it possible for a nonsurveyor to spot a weak boundary on a map?

---

* R. Lee Hixson is a licensed surveyor in Yuba City, California.

** Copyright © 2004 by R. Lee Hixson. Reprinted by permission.

The answer to the last question is "yes" and the purpose of this article is, first of all, to alert lawyers to the possibility that some maps are deficient and, second, to give them some guidance in differentiating between a map with a good boundary and one with a weak or poorly resolved boundary.

Boundaries are the single most important facet of any map produced by a surveyor. Most maps, if not all, show a boundary. Conditions vary from state to state, but, of the large variety of maps that surveyors prepare, virtually all contain the boundary lines of the parcel in question and the boundary lines relate to all the other data on the map. The boundary defines the relationship of the subject parcel to the adjoining parcels. The boundary purports to represent the limits of the vesting deed of the subject parcel. Even with topographic surveys (which contain a wealth of information about utilities, terrain features, structures, and easements), none of the data shown on the map makes any sense without that crucial spatial relationship to a boundary.

And yet most state laws do not even begin to spell out the ingredients of a properly resolved boundary. California law, for example, sums up the entire matter in 19 words. In discussing the technical requirements of a survey map, the statute states that the survey shall show "[t]he relationship to those portions of adjacent tracts, streets, or senior conveyances which have common lines with the survey." Cal. Bus. & Prof. Code § 8764.

It is, of course, impossible to condense the entire accumulated wisdom of boundary law and precedent into a single sentence. All the good intentions of those who wrote the law aside, it is simple human nature that, if the law does not lay out the principles to be followed, then a great deal can be saved by choosing the path of least resistance. Many surveyors — even county and city surveyors — have reported that the only requirement for "treating adjoining deeds" is that the book and page references be noted on the map. But to conduct a thorough study of the deeds for the subject parcel and each adjoining parcel to make sure that there are no conflicts between any of them takes many hours, sometimes days, and clearly would result in a much larger bill for the client.

Definition of a Boundary Resolution

The resolution of a boundary refers to the entire process of analyzing all available, pertinent information about the location of the boundary of a given subject parcel *in its relationship to the boundaries of the parcels (and/or rights-of-way) that surround it*, with an eye to determining whether inconsistencies or incompatibilities exist between any of those boundaries.

A parcel is rarely, if ever, an island unto itself. Its existence and location are integrally related to the parcels that surround it. "Resolving" a boundary necessitates a consideration of the parcels and rights of way that border it on every side. A good map will present the evidence and analysis relied on to conclude where these boundaries lie.

What to Look For

Some surveyors might be lazy, or cheap, or ignorant, or perhaps even fraudulent. Given surveyors' varying competence, and given that some state laws do little to enforce a standard of competence, what can individuals in the allied professions do when examining a map to get a better idea of how good the boundary is? What follows are suggested guidelines. Remember that surveying is, indeed, a highly complicated art and science and that this short article cannot do justice to its many subtleties. Nevertheless, some general principles should be kept in mind when examining a map.

Most nonsurveyors do not know what questions to ask when they look at a map. If the surveyor who prepared the map is available, ask him or her to describe the evidence used to place the boundary of the subject parcel where it is located on the map.

Every angle point — or every beginning and ending point of a particular line — should be justified on the map. The map reader should realize that the surveyor should have a reason for the location of every angle point and every end point of a line or curve. Some surveyors are more conscientious than others as to how clearly they display this data, but the data should be there in some form. If the map cannot be adequately interpreted by itself, then ask the surveyor to explain the rationale behind his or her resolution.

Usually, the best justification for locating a line will be that the surveyor found a good monument in the field that marks one or both ends of the line (or curve) in question. If a map symbol indicates a "found monument" at each end of a line, then that means the surveyor has decided those monuments are good and will control the position and length of the line. These monuments can serve this purpose because they have a good pedigree (for example, they have been accepted by many surveyors on prior recorded maps) or because the surveyor found a deed that specifically mentions the existence of the monuments. Other justifications can be used for accepting a monument, but the point is that it was found in the field and, in the surveyor's professional judgment, it should be used to control the position of the line.

The more found monuments there are at the angle points of the parcel boundary, the more solid is the resolution of the map. But that is not always the case. What controls a boundary if there are no found monuments anywhere around the boundary?

A line can be located for other very good reasons. It might be because a remote monument was found down the street and the surveyor held a record distance from that monument to locate a point on the subject parcel boundary. This justification is an acceptable alternative for setting the position of a line and includes two elements: (1) a monument was found and (2) a record distance was used to measure from that monument to the point that the surveyor needed to locate. These are good reasons for making a decision about locating a particular line or angle point.

But what about that "record distance" mentioned above? How would the map reader know that the surveyor had used a record distance to locate a point on the subject parcel boundary? A typical way would be to show the record distance inside parentheses, with a number or letter behind it, like this: "(135.34')R3." The "R3" refers to a record reference. A table of "Record References" will appear somewhere on the map, and the surveyor is calling attention to the third reference in the list. The table entry for R3 might be the book and page of a recorded deed. It might be a previously recorded map of some type. Thus, what the surveyor is saying is: "I found the distance of 135.34 feet mentioned in a deed and determined that this distance should be held in order to arrive at the position of one of the angle points in the boundary of the subject parcel."

Such language is drafting shorthand used by surveyors. Drafting styles vary around the country, and there are many other ways of indicating that the surveyor has "used" (relied on) a record distance to control a point or line.

Another possibility is to add an explanatory note. Suppose that some monuments were found and used to establish the right of way line along a street. Then, coming off of this line, the map shows one of the side lines of the subject parcel. Questions arise: What angle is formed between this side line and the right of way line? Why does the side line have the bearing (the angle) that it does? Sometimes surveyors will draw an arc between the two lines, then add a note stating: "Record angle held, per R2." This indicates that, because a monument was not found at the back end of the side line, the surveyor determined that the next best justification for establishing the bearing of the side line was to "hold" a record angle between the two lines according to some other recorded document or map.

Sometimes a note will be so long and complex as to deserve a special statement off to the side of the map. A surveyor may have gone through a lengthy analysis of a line or point and needed to summarize his or her thinking by describing in some detail how that part of the boundary was resolved. Such a summary is always a good sign, because it shows that the surveyor takes the resolution of the boundary seriously and wants to make sure that anyone examining the map can understand that resolution.

The bottom line is that, no matter which method is used, the map reader should be able to decipher the rationale behind each and every decision made in the location of a line, curve, or point. The more explanatory data on the map, the better the map, and the more defensible its resolution.

If a map reader is examining a map and cannot tell why a line is located where it is, there is nothing wrong in calling the surveyor to ask for an explanation. It may be uncommon, but it should be no less acceptable than if a patient were to ask his or her doctor to explain exactly why a certain prescription was given or why a test was ordered. If the lawyer is using a map that has important implications for a project or a case, he or she can, and should, ask to meet with the surveyor to secure a complete breakdown of the reasoning that went into the boundary shown on the map.

Look at it this way: a boundary has to be built on a strong foundation, and ultimately that foundation is based on the monuments that were located in the field. The perfect situation would be for a monument to be found at each angle point going around the boundary. But if only some (or even none) were found along the boundary, then remote monuments come into play and the boundary can be built from them. As the web of parcel lines is constructed from the remote monuments, the surveyor calculates the way back to the subject parcel and eventually is able to position the boundary from them. But each step along the way needs to be justified, and if that justification is not obvious on the map, asking the surveyor to explain things makes sense.

Alternatively, seek a second opinion. As with a doctor's diagnosis, a map depicts the professional opinion of a particular surveyor on where a parcel lies relative to the parcels surrounding it and relative to the monuments located in the field. Many times this author has been brought a map and asked to analyze it and explain what the surveyor did. It is not that hard for an experienced surveyor to study the information on a map and then to describe what it tells about how the other surveyor resolved the boundaries it shows. Summarizing the strengths and weaknesses of the map is also possible.

The best maps are those that faithfully present a summary of the evidence found and all the key decisions that link the subject parcel boundary to that evidence. Because the record of those decisions is often lacking on maps with which they work, lawyers are forced to question the quality of the map's resolution. Is it because the surveyor, for whatever reason, elected to simplify and therefore did not add enough notes to explain the resolution to the reader? Or is it because the surveyor is doing shoddy work and hiding behind the brevity of the law, thus producing a map with little or no justification for the decisions it represents?

Conclusion

Ideally, a map should show the basis for the surveyor's determination of the boundaries. The basis, however, is not always evident from looking at the map. Because the law does not require the surveyor to show a complete resolution on his or her map, how is the map reader to know that the map is accurate? The answer is that one cannot know the answer. And this realization is what prompts the recommendation that the map reader go beyond merely trusting that a surveyor does competent work. If a map appears to be lacking in documentation or analysis, the lawyer should contact the surveyor who prepared it and ask him or her to fill in the blanks. And depending on the circumstances, consider obtaining a second opinion from another surveyor.

[3] Questions About the Auto Care Center Survey

1. Since Regent was obtaining an owner's title insurance policy, why was a survey needed?
2. When representing a buyer in ordering and reviewing a survey, what should you be looking for?
3. Do you see any potential title problems based upon your review of the title insurance policy and the survey that Regent received?
4. Remember that there also are issues from the Trustee's Deed and Declaration of Easement that Regent had to agree to in the Regent-Metropolitan contract that you read as part of the contract review in Chapter 5. Are there any aspects of the Trustee's Deed or Declaration of Easement (which are exhibits to the Regent-Metropolitan contract in the Document Book) that you find problematic? The next section addresses this issue.

§ 6.07 EXTENDED CONTROL OVER ADJOINING LAND

[1] The Issue of Being One Part of a Larger Development

As we have already seen, one of the reasons that the site was so attractive to Regent was that it was part of a much larger planned commercial development which had at its center the Westfield Fox Valley Shopping Center enclosed mall.

Being part of the greater whole comes at a cost, however, and it is a cost in addition to any premium Regent paid for the land. The Fox Valley Auto Care Center must fit into the overall Fox Valley development. We now turn to evaluating the agreements that make all of this possible, which the title of the following article shortens to REAs, or "Restrictions and Easements Agreements." We have included the entire article, but have omitted all of its exhibits except for two that should be helpful to you in evaluating the two agreements Regent entered into, one with Metropolitan that covers the entire Fox Valley area and the other with Turtle Wax which only covers the Auto Care Center.

Kenneth M. Jacobson, *The Lender Looks at REAs and Co-Tenancy**

A. The Scenario

You are outside counsel to Widows, Widowers and Orphans Insurance company ("WWOIC"), which has recently returned to the real estate lending market after a long hiatus. WWOIC's inside counsel calls you and asks for your help in analyzing some issues in connection with a potential loan that WWOIC is considering. The loan will be secured by real estate comprising the developer's portion of a retail shopping center. WWOIC's inside counsel usually handles these issues directly, but, in this particular instance, is unable to do so. WWOIC's inside counsel is an "old hand" at retail shopping center mortgage lending, but in this particular instance, the loan production officer for WWOIC has not had substantial experience with this type of mortgage lending. You are asked to provide your experienced hand in guiding the loan production officer through the basic issues that mortgage lenders need to concern themselves with in connection with REAs and co-tenancy arrangements. WWOIC "faxes" a copy of a generalized sketch of the center. Naturally, you consider this to be a wonderful opportunity to assist your client.

B. The Context

The foregoing example highlights the context in which consideration of these issues may arise. The mortgage lender looks at retail real estate as a package. In this regard, the lender will analyze the benefits and burdens that affect the real estate in question. In the example, the shopping center in question is a relatively large piece of real estate, consisting of one or more "outlots," and interior and exterior common areas that include areas devoted to parking and access. In the example, as in many real estate settings, the ownership of the center has been split. Accordingly, the largest parcel of the center is owned by a developer and the remainder of the real estate in question is owned by the anchors. A variation of this arrangement might find ownership of the parcel vested in the developer, with the anchors leasing their parcels on relatively long term lease arrangements. The economic issues are very similar and, although this particular presentation [These materials were prepared in connection with a program presented at the 1997 American Bar Association Annual Meeting. — Eds.] will focus on bifurcation of ownership, bear in mind that the analysis has some application in the single-owner context as well.

The retail shopping center is operated as a common enterprise in that the developer tries to create value by leveraging off the "traffic" generated by the anchors.[1] This concept of multiple ownership is not unique to retail shopping centers and may apply to other contexts (*e.g.*, mixed-use facilities). In the retail shopping center arena, the entire center may not be owned by a single borrower, and the lender will be asked to limit its security to the portion of the center owned by the developer, rather than the entire center. For example, the borrower may own the in-line stores, most of, or significant portions of, the common areas and, perhaps, some, but not necessarily all, of the department store pads and outparcels. The portions of the retail center not owned by the developers will be owned by the anchors and outlot owners.

C. Legal Issues with Multiple Ownership

Most of us can appreciate the complexity which the multiplicity of ownership creates for the owners and their lenders. The owners must rely on each other to satisfy their parking requirements, their utility requirements, their pedestrian and vehicular access requirements, and their concerns regarding construction and control over construction, operation, appearance, visibility, structural integrity and maintenance. Furthermore, the parties must adopt rules to govern what happens in the event of a casualty loss.[2] For new construction, each owner wants an affirmative obligation imposed on the other to construct and complete its portion of the project in accordance with mutually acceptable plans and by mutually acceptable dates.[3]

In looking at these particular situations, one must give due regard to the time at which one analyzes the situation. Vacant land that is about to undergo development presents a different set of issues than a "seasoned" center. In the center that is about to begin development, the construction lender is concerned that at the end of the date it will have a completed center, that the improvements to be located on the department store pad (or leased department store pad) are completed and that the anchor has opened for business. Under those circumstances, analysis will focus on making certain that there are sufficient contractual (and economic) incentives for completion and opening of the project.

D. Definitions

Before we can analyze what the lender is looking at, we should agree on definitions.

A "REA" is a shorthand way of referring to a "Restrictions and Easements Agreement," although it is sometimes referred to as "CCREA," that is, "Covenants, Conditions, Restrictions and Easements Agreement," "Development

---

[1] James P. McAndrews, *Operating Agreement: Control Within Shopping Center Complex*, Real Prop. Prob. & Tr. J. (Winter 1972), at 812.

[2] *See generally*, Susan B. Hoffnagle, *et al.*, *Reviewing a Shopping Center REA*, Real Prop. Prob. & Tr. J. (Winter 1983), at 651–77.

[3] Development obligations may be set forth in a separate "companion" agreement.

and Operating Agreement" or "DOA," or "CCRs" or "Covenants, Conditions and Restrictions Agreement."[4] This is a document which is almost invariably recorded and which establishes the respective easements and other agreements which will bind the center and its respective owners. In essence, the REA is the governing document for the common enterprise. The REA establishes utility, parking, access, structural support and encroachment easements across the properties to be located in the shopping center. The REA also imposes obligations upon certain parcels and confers benefits on the same or other parcels. The documents may also provide for the imposition of liens on one or more of the parcel owners as a means to secure the performance of parcel owners.

A "Co-Tenancy Agreement" is an agreement which may be found in a REA or in a lease among parcel owners (or between a landlord and tenant) which conditions the opening and continued operating status of one store upon the opening and continued operating status of one or more other stores. The instrument will typically be recorded, or a memorandum will be recorded, placing third parties on record notice of the provisions of the co-tenancy agreement. Again, going back to the fact that the shopping center is a common enterprise where the success of one depends upon the success of the other, the co-tenancy agreement provides a legal backstop to the economic concerns which attend the common enterprise concept.

The shopping center developer looks at these agreements as necessary for the development of the center. Without these agreements, the developer would not be able to attract anchors. Without anchors, it cannot viably lease the remainder of the center and generate the return it is looking for. The anchors look at these as critical because (a) without the REA the anchor is an island without access or control over the balance of the development and (b) the anchor would not wish to remain open (or at least be obligated to open or remain open) unless other "key" stores were open. The anchor looks at its role as critical and without the anchor being comfortable with the governing agreements for the center it will not agree to participate in the common enterprise.

The lender, on the other hand, looks at itself as the funnel through which the money flows. The lender will look at the REA and the co-tenancy agreement from three related perspectives, namely what exposure does the lender have in the event it forecloses its mortgage and becomes an owner, how will the burdens and benefits of these agreements affect the ability of the borrower to service the loan and how will the REA and co-tenancy arrangements affect its exit strategy, that is, how will prospective purchasers and lenders view these arrangements. The lender review process starts with the due diligence phase of the project. Examination of the relevant leases will occur in which the interrelationship of the REAs and the major leases is considered. What issues will the lender consider in analyzing these documents? We will briefly review the lender's "spin" on the following:

1. Covenants to Open, Covenants to Operate and Co-Tenancy;
2. Allocation of Payment and Performance Obligations:
    a. Who Pays for What? Is it a Fair Allocation?
    b. What are the Burdens Imposed on the Developer's Parcel?
3. Easement Issues

---

[4] *See* McAndrews, *supra*.

4. Insurance and Casualty

5. Taxes

6. Self-Help and Lien Rights

7. Miscellaneous Issues

   a. Personal Liability

   b. Successor Liability

   c. Estoppel Provisions

E. Covenants to Open, Covenants to Operate and Co-Tenancy

These covenants are related to each other. Each of these obligates a parcel owner to perform an obligation and confers a benefit upon one or more other parcel.

Covenants to open obligate a particular pad owner to open. They do not necessarily obligate that particular owner to continue to operate its facility. These covenants are important because (a) with the common enterprise, all profit when all open (and remain open) and (b) some tenants and pad owners will condition their opening and/or will have termination rights (as to operating covenants in a REA, or a lease, or a right to terminate the lease) in the event that a pad owner does not open as it has agreed to do. Indeed, occasionally, the developer will be required to covenant or represent that it has obtained such covenants from the other anchor. Covenants to operate obligate the pad owner (or tenant) to operate (usually for a specified term) a particular type of business, and, in some cases, under a particular name (although, these will often provide some relief for the obligated party to change the name under which it operates in the event that the pad owner changes the name it uses on a regional or other level). Co-tenancy covenants, explained above, obligate a tenant or owner to operate or to stay in business unless other tenants or occupants depart. These co-tenancy arrangements may entitle a department store owner (or tenant) to terminate its lease or occupancy covenant in the event one or more anchors terminate(s) its (their respective) lease(s) or cease(s) to operate.

The reason for the covenant to open should be obvious. If we are dealing with a department store, the owner and lender need the store to open in order to generate customer traffic which will utilize the in-line stores and increase the ability of the landlord to sign and retain tenants. The increased traffic flow generates sales which allow the tenants to pay rent. The lender and the owner also desire that the tenant or pad owner covenant to operate as a particular type of store or under a particular name for a given duration. This assures the owner and the lender of the viability of the center for at least the period of the covenant. The concern is that the tenants, who in a sense are parasitic to the department store, will suffer declining sales and may vacate their premises if the department store goes dark. Key tenants or pad owners may not accept any restriction on their ability to conduct their business, that is, while they may agree to open, they may not agree to operate for a particular period of time, let alone conduct operations under a particular name or, for that matter, as a particular operation at all. Given the changing nature of retailing, no one can predict what the future will bring, and these stores may not commit themselves for any extended period of time. The developer will be concerned about the possibility of an anchor going dark and will try to negotiate for recapture rights, that is, the right to take the space back if the tenant or department store owner ceases operations for a given period of time, and may also try to restrict the ability of the tenant to carve up the space in connection with possible subleases. Obviously, from a lender's point of view, the possibility that the tenant may go dark is not a desirable one, but due diligence progresses by analyzing store sales, attempting to discuss the potential future with store managers, etc. This is a risk, but, in a viable center, with several anchors, the lender may take the risk on the theory that it would be unlikely that sevral spaces would go dark at once.

How does the lender look at co-tenancy arrangements? Certainly, the retail shopping center market is a dynamic business and centers often change to meet different conditions. In addition, department stores want the flexibility to abandon their premises in the event that the premises does not generate the profitability that they seek (or if their business plan changes). Indeed, it was not too long ago that many retailers were in significant financial distress and one could almost have filled an entire center with all-bankruptcy court tenants (certainly this would have been a unique marketing concept). The lender recognizes this reality in most instances and looks at how well the sites which might be abandoned are positioned with respect to potential substitute tenants and alternative uses and would hope to see provisions in the operative documents which allow for recapture of the sites in question should a store vacate its premises. With respect to co-tenancy, the lenders will try to avoid situations where the departure of only one anchor will trigger the right of another anchor to depart. (Perhaps two or more anchors might cease operations.) This would avoid the potential domino effect that might result. Remember the effect of a co-tenancy provision is not only a loss of an operating tenant or department store owner, but the tenant or department store owner with the benefit of this provision may also be entitled to terminate its lease (or operating covenant) and this would also deprive ownership of the basic rent that the owners seek. In addition, provisions which activate the co-tenancy right only after an extended period would be favored. Furthermore, the lender would prefer to see provisions that preclude activation of a co-tenancy provision because of a breach of another owner's or tenant's occupancy covenant until the expiration of a reasonable time for the developer to enforce the operating covenant.

F. Allocation of Payment and Performance Obligations/Restrictions

REAs often obligate the various owners to maintain different portions of the center. Usually, the developer is obligated to maintain the parking, landscaping, access and other common areas of the shopping center. Often, the developer is required to maintain these facilities to a particular standard. The question of who performs the obligations is related to, but different than, the question of who pays for the performance of these obligations. The developer will seek to allocate the costs among the various parcel owners in some proportion to their benefit. The lender reviewing this issue will not only analyze what burdens are imposed by the covenants relating to maintenance (discussed below), but will pay close attention to the allocation of payment responsibilities among the parcel owners (and the mechanism for recapturing those payments). Among other things, the lender tries to analyze whether the payment responsibilities are fairly allocated so that the parcel which is encumbered by its mortgage bears a financial responsibility proportionate to the benefit which it derives and which is capable of satisfaction from the income stream from the parcels encumbered by the lender's liens. Among other things, this necessitates analysis of lease provisions to determine whether these expenses are properly passed on to the developer's tenants. To the extent that the financial burden disproportionately falls on the developer's parcel, a situation is created where it will be difficult, all other things being equal, to attract and keep tenants.

The burdens imposed on the developer's parcel are varied. Among other things, the developer's parcel may bear the obligation (as mentioned above) to take primary responsibility for maintenance and repair of the common areas of the center. This can be addressed from the financial perspectives considered above. In addition, other burdens may be imposed on the portion of the center owned by the developer, including provisions respecting aesthetics, no-build areas and maintenance of an agreed upon common area plan. Each of these limitations makes sense from the pad owner's perspective. As a common enterprise, the pad owner desires a certain level of maintenance and a certain level of aesthetic condition (including signage). The pad owner is also concerned about the agreed upon common area plan as, among other things, the location, number of parking spaces, no-build areas and access plans are of critical importance to it. The developer (and its lender) similarly is concerned that the parcel owner pay its share of liabilities and maintain its pad.

The lender looks to determine whether the burdens of the REA are proportionate and may be achieved within the cash flows generated by the developer's parcel. In addition, the lender reviews the REA to determine if any restrictions have been violated and whether the restrictions imposed are reasonable. For example, restrictions in no-build areas will limit the ability of the developer to construct additional parking the center requires. In addition, the lender is concerned whether the restrictions unduly limit leasing efforts with respect to the center. For example, limitations on the ability to change access configurations may be unduly restrictive. Other examples include restrictions with respect to potential uses of the center. The lender will seek comfort through estoppel letters, a review of the site plan and an analysis of the business plan. The lender will also review the leases to determine if the leases of the developer's parcel impose obligations which are inconsistent with obligations or restrictions imposed by the REA. In this regard, the lender might insist on a variant of a "stacking plan" requiring a listing by area of restrictions, exclusives, etc. The lender will also require, in its loan documents, that changes to the REA will require its approval. In addition, the lender will review the REA to determine if the parking requirements imposed by the pad owner can be satisfied and whether the parking requirements are such that they are consistent with the balance of the uses. In addition, the developer parcel may be limited with respect to future expansion and development. This may adversely impact future development.

G. Easement Issues

The lender's concern with this issue should be obvious. Because of the multiple ownership of the center, the lender needs to know that the parcel which secures its loan is entitled to access to and from a public street, that such a parcel has the right to parking throughout the center, that such parcel's site has access to electric, gas, telephone, sanitary sewer and other utilities, that water drains from such parcel, etc. The lender will review the easements and the plans and specifications for the center to verify that utilities serve its site and that such utilities are located either entirely on its site or by appurtenant easements on the department store sites. The lender will insist that these easements be perpetual and appurtenant and insured as insured parcels on title insurance parcels. In addition, the lender will insist that the easements which benefit the department store sites are not encroached upon by improvements located (or to be located upon) the developer's parcel and do not unduly restrict the developer's use of its parcel. The easements should be appurtenant (and insured by the title insurer as appurtenant) and perpetual (surviving termination of the restrictions and other covenants in the REA). The lender will seek assurances that the easements benefitting its collateral cannot be extinguished by the foreclosure of a "superior" lien interest encumbering the servient estates.

H. Insurance and Casualty

The lender will review the REA to determine if the owners of the other pads are required to obtain insurance and/or restore improvements following a casualty loss. Typically, the lender will want an obligation on the part of the pad owner to maintain casualty insurance with an affirmative obligation to rebuild following the casualty loss in question. The lender will prefer to avoid circumstances where the rebuilding obligation is asymmetrical, as for example, where the developer is obligated to rebuild its parcel without a symmetrical obligation on the part of the pad owner. Indeed, the developer (and its lender) will be very concerned if it may be obligated to rebuild without an operating covenant in place for an anchor. Because the REA will have a superior priority vis a vis a mortgage, provisions which permit a lender to avoid restoration obligations by paying down its indebtedness would not excuse an owner from restoring property damaged by a casualty.

In addition to the casualty insurance requirements, the lender will also look at whether or not the REA imposes liability insurance requirements on the owners and whether those requirements have been satisfied.

I. Taxes

This is not necessarily an REA issue, but it is related. The lender wants to be certain that the pads are separately taxed so that it will not suffer adverse tax consequences with respect to failure by the pad owner to pay its share of taxes.

J. Self-Help and Lien Rights

To the extent that an REA imposes affirmative obligations on one parcel or another to maintain and repair its parcel, the owners of the other parcel will have an interest in assuring themselves that those covenants are complied with. Because the center is a common enterprise, poor repair and maintenance for one part of the center may have negative consequences for other parts of the center. Accordingly, the lender wants to know that the owner of the other pads has affirmative obligations to maintain its parcels and will also want to understand and underwrite for the obligations imposed upon its parcel.

The parties to the REA may not be satisfied with a right to sue for injunctive relief or for damages in the event one party or the other fails to perform its obligations under the REA. The REA may provide for self-help remedies. The lender will typically want to know when those remedies can be activated and will often desire a mechanism to obtain prior notice of (and a right to cure such failure prior to) the exercise of those remedies. The REA may grant the party having performed its obligations with lien rights to collect the costs of self-help and for collection of expenses that are to be billed to the owners of other pads. The lender is, obviously, concerned about the priority of its mortgage. The REA may assuage the lender's concerns by providing that these liens are subordinate to the liens of the mortgages of record, although this is sometimes limited to first mortgages and/ or mortgages granted to institutional investors. Furthermore, such liens should also be subordinate to leases of the parcel in question in order to preserve the lease if the lien is foreclosed. The lender may request an estoppel letter confirming that there are no sums owning to, or by, the pad owner.

K. Miscellaneous Issues

The lender who acquires a project prefers not to incur personal liability for nonperformance of REA provisions and will review the REA to determine whether it will be exculpated from personal liability following acquisition of the property. In a similar vein, the lender reviewing an REA would generally prefer an REA provision that makes an owner liable only to the extent of liabilities that accrue during ownership by that particular owner. This may be difficult to get (especially for the developer), but institutional lenders may get some relief with respect to these issues. The lender looks to determine if the REA provides for estoppel letters which may be relied upon by lenders, prospective lenders and by purchasers. Finally, provisions which afford lender notice of a breach and an opportunity to cure that breach are important. Provisions that require the consent of one party or the other to the REA to mortgages or sales of the real estate in question would generally be considered unacceptable (making the project unfinanceable).

L. Summary

In summary, the lender looks at REAs much like prospective purchasers will look at an REA and co-tenancy agreements. The market dynamic has changed and the lenders and purchasers of the world recognize that things are different. The multiplicity of ownership with a center creates additional underwriting issues for the lender and often results in the lender requiring its approval for changes in the REA.

[Exhibits A-F are omitted and Exhibit H has been presented in part.]

Exhibit G.

General Restrictive Covenants

Developer and _____________ covenant and agree that no building or buildings or improvements, other than Common Area Improvements, shall be created or expanded on the _____________ Parcel, except within the designated Permissible Building Areas, and that the exterior wall or walls, as the case may be, of buildings erected on all such Parcels shall be along the fixed building lines thereof, to the extent shown on Exhibit B, and such buildings shall be located as shown on said Exhibit B, provided, however, that exterior walls of any such buildings may be moved and relocated within the designated Permissible Building Area.

Size of Buildings

No Store of any Major Tenant or the Developer shall be constructed or expanded other than within the respective Permissible Building Area and as otherwise required by this REA.

Height Limitations

No building shall be constructed or expanded which exceeds the height limitations set forth in Exhibit D.

Payment on Default and Lien

If under this REA a Party is compelled or elects to pay any sum of money or do any acts that require the payment of money by reason of the other Party's failure or inability to perform any of the provisions of this REA to be performed by such other Party, the defaulting Party shall promptly upon demand reimburse the paying Party for such sums, and all such sums shall bear interest at the rate of ____________ percent per annum over the then existing ____________ by ____________ (but in no event exceeding the maximum rate per annum permitted by ____________ law) from the date of expenditure until the date of such reimbursement. Any other sums payable by any Party to any other Party under this REA that shall not be paid when due shall bear interest at the rate of ____________ per annum over the then existing ____________ by said bank (but in no event exceeding said maximum annual rate) from the due date of payment thereof.

If Developer is required by the terms of this REA to pay ____________ any sum, then in addition to interest of said sum as aforesaid ____________ shall have and is hereby given as security to pay for such sum and interest due it, a valid and enforceable lien (hereinafter sometimes called "lien") upon Developer's right, title and interest in and to the Shopping Center Site and all the Improvements at any time and from time to time situated upon the Developer Parcel (hereinafter sometimes called "Developer's Property") and ____________ shall have the right to foreclose the ____________ Lien in the manner provided by law, it being understood and agreed that the ____________ Lien shall be superior to any other lien and encumbrance on the Developer's Property created or arising after the date of this REA, excepting only the lien of any first mortgage or first deed of trust (hereinafter in this Section ____________ called "First Mortgage") and/or any assignment of Developer's interest in Leases in connection therewith heretofore or hereafter placed upon the developer's Property or any part thereof, and as to any such First Mortgage, the ____________ Lien shall be subordinate; provided, however, that the aforesaid subordination of the ____________ Lien shall not in any manner be deemed to constitute a subordinate of any other of ____________ rights, privileges and immunities created pursuant to this REA, which said rights, privileges and immunities shall be at all times prior and superior to the lien of any such First Mortgage. Anything hereinbefore in this Section ____________ contained to the contrary notwithstanding, it is expressly understood and agreed that the ____________ Lien is subject to the following conditions:

(1) ____________ agrees that its lien shall be expressly subject and subordinate to any and all advances in whenever amounts and whatever made with interest thereon and to any expenses, charges and fees incurred

thereby including any and all of such advances, interest, expenses, charges and fees which may increase the indebtedness secured by such First Mortgage above the original principal amount thereof, provided the same are advanced or incurred under any of the express provisions of such First Mortgage or any extension, consolidation, modification or supplement thereto or under any assignment of leases or otherwise in connection with such First Mortgage intended to be secured thereby.

(2) ____________ agrees that its lien shall be subject and subordinate to any and all Leases upon all or any part of the Developer's Property to which the lien of such First Mortgage shall have been made subject and subordinate.

(3) ____________ agrees to execute and deliver any further assurances of the subordination of the ____________ Lien to the First Mortgage as provided in this Section.

Exhibit H.

Easements for Use of Common Area

Each Party hereby grants to the other Party easements in the Common Area on its (Grantor's) Parcel for:

(1) ingress to and egress from the Grantee's Parcel;

(2) the passage and parking of vehicles;

(3) the passage and accommodation of pedestrians on such portions of the Common Area of Grantor's Parcel as is set aside, maintained and authorized for such use under this REA; and

(4) the doing of such other things as are authorized or required to be done on Common Area under this REA.

Enjoyment of the easements granted by this Section shall commence on the date the Common Area in question is completed.

Each Party hereby reserves the right to eject from the Common Area on its Parcel any persons not authorized to use the same. In addition, each Party reserves the right to close off the Common Area of its Parcel for such reasonable periods of time as may be legally necessary to prevent the acquisition of prescriptive rights by anyone; provided, however, before closing off any part of the Common Areas as provided above, such Party must give notice to the other Party of its intention to do so and must coordinate its closing with the activities of the other Party so that no unreasonable interference with the operation of the Center occurs.

The easements provided for in this Section are subject to the rights to use the Common Area for other purposes provided for in this REA; however, except as otherwise herein provided, no changes shall be made in the Common Area or in location or design of Common Area Improvements prior to the Expiration Date.

The easements granted under this Section shall terminate on the Expiration Date of this REA notwithstanding any other provision of this REA.

. . . .

[2] Questions on REAs

1. What is a restrictions and easements agreement? What is a co-tenancy agreement? What functions do these types of agreements serve?
2. How is multiple ownership of a common enterprise involved in the Fox Valley Auto Care Center project?
3. What are the key areas of the restrictions and easements agreements and co-tenancy agreements that attorneys should focus on when reviewing these agreements?

[3] The Easement Agreement with Turtle Wax

Regent, as the developer of the Fox Valley Auto Care Center, and Turtle Wax, as the purchaser of the center's "outlot," entered into an agreement concerning the use of the paved areas of the Fox Valley Auto Care Center. In the Easement Grant in the Document Book, Regent is the owner of lot 1 and Turtle Wax is the owner of lot 2 (the area just south of lot 1). Turtle Wax intended to build and operate a car wash on lot 2. The easement grant not only created a grant of easement but also spelled out the agreements the parties reached relating to the paving of the easement area along the boundary line of the two parcels for ingress and egress to the two parcels as well as the maintenance of this paved area. Each party was concerned that the other party could take advantage of the other, both in use of the easement area and in the sharing of the costs of maintaining the easement area. A big issue was that the easement area needed to be kept clear, so the agreement prohibits the easement area from being used for parking, "stacking" (allowing cars to wait in line, likely for entry into the car wash), and loading and unloading. You should now read the Easement Grant.

[4] Client Counseling Exercise

Now that you have read the Jacobson article and the easement grant between Regent and Turtle Wax, review once more the Declaration and Trustee's Deed attached to the Regent-Metropolitan purchase agreement which we asked you to read as part of your contract review in Chapter 5. Assume you represent the construction lender. Would any of these encumbrances trouble you? Why or why not? Are there any changes you would require, as a condition to funding the loan, in the relationships between the developer and its two "neighbors"? Once again, keep in mind that sometimes the most difficult task in reviewing a document is to identify what important points are missing. Draft a memo to your client explaining any concerns you have and what can be done to address your concerns.

Chapter 7

PUBLIC CONTROLS ON THE USE OF THE PROJECT SITE

§ 7.01 ZONING

Before any financial analysis, before any contract drafting, before undertaking any feasibility studies, comes the analysis involving the potential to be able to use specific land as intended by your client. The first question then, is "what is the property zoned?" If the current zoning would not allow the Auto Care Center use, then the next question is: "can the property be rezoned to allow for an Auto Car Center use?"

In answering the second question, it is quite often the attorney's call. A "yes" answer is not easily given. There is no such thing as a lay down when it comes to rezoning. Significant time and money is going to be spent by your client with you and other consultants (e.g., civil and traffic engineers; building architects; lighting engineers, etc.), before the first spade of dirt can be turned. Your answer then, is very important to the client.

There are two documents that are absolutely crucial to the analysis of the rezoning question: 1, the Land Use Plan and 2, the Zoning Code. The Land Use Plan is a view from 20,000 feet of how different land uses ought to be grouped within the boundaries of the governmental entity where the property is located. The Zoning Code implements the LUP vision through detailed rules and regulations as to how and where specific land uses may be developed within the governmental entity.

This section focuses on seven issues: 1. the states' power to zone; 2. the state enabling acts which give municipalities the power to zone; 3. the requirement that zoning be "in accordance with a comprehensive plan"; 4. the process for the enactment and amendment of zoning ordinances and "spot zoning"; 5. variances; 6. nonconforming uses; and 7. takings with a focus on historic and landmark preservation ordinances. After this general discussion of zoning, there is an article that discusses how zoning is administratively implemented. Finally, there are two additional sections which deal with issues directly raised by the Fox Valley development: the related issues of contract zoning and conditional zoning, and annexation of land by a municipality and the use of annexation agreements.

[1] The States' Power to Zone

Zoning is the regulation by districts of the development of, building on and use of real property. Typically, different uses are allowed in each of the districts, but some uses may be allowed in more than one district. A normal zoning regime will include districts for industrial, commercial, business, and residential uses. In some cities, typically larger ones, there also may be "mixed use" zoning. A "mixed use" zoning district would allow two or more different uses, such as retail business on the first floors of buildings in a multi-family residential district, in order to allow for "vertical" separation of uses. In most zoning regimes, the separation of uses is entirely "horizontal," that is only like uses are allowed in a given zoning district. Although in 1926 the U.S. Supreme Court upheld the general validity of zoning ordinances in *Village of Euclid v. Ambler Realty Co.*, 272 U.S. 365 (1926), just two years after that, in *Nectow v. City of Cambridge*, 277 U.S. 183 (1928), the Court allowed a zoning challenge where the attack was on the zoning ordinance as it applied to a particular parcel of land.

Zoning is carried out under a state's police power; therefore zoning ordinances must be substantially related to public health, safety, morals and welfare. A zoning ordinance, including an ordinance which zones a particular parcel, therefore, is invalid and unconstitutional if it is arbitrary and capricious, having no substantial relation to public health, safety, morals and welfare of the people. In *Gunderson v. Village of Hinsdale*, 508 N.E.2d 1212 (Ill. App. Ct. 1987), and *Palatine Nat'l Bank v. Village of Barrington*, 532 N.E.2d 955 (Ill. App. Ct. 1988), two Illinois courts used the following factors in determining whether a zoning ordinance was arbitrary and without substantial relation to health, safety, morals and welfare:

1. The existing uses and zoning of nearby property;
2. The extent to which property values are diminished by the particular zoning restrictions;
3. The extent to which the destruction of property values of the plaintiff promotes the health, safety, morals or general welfare of the public;
4. The relative gain to the public as compared to the hardship to the property owner;
5. The suitability of the subject property for the zoned purposes;
6. The length of time the property has been vacant as zoned, considered in the context of the development in the vicinity of the subject property;
7. Community need for the proposed use; and
8. The care with which the community had undertaken to plan its land use development and aesthetic factors.

[2] A Municipality's Power to Zone

The police power gives the states the power to engage in the use zoning of land as well as to regulate the intensity of the use through the regulation of building height and bulk, open space and yard requirements, and restrictions on the number of people who may live, work or shop in a building at the same time. In order for a local government to have the power to zone, the legislature of a state must delegate the power to zone to the local government. In the overwhelming majority of states, the power to zone is exercised exclusively by local governments, likely because local government bodies have the advantage of knowing the neighborhoods, the existing uses, and other related considerations.

Most states have enacted zoning enabling acts generally modeled on the Standard State Zoning Enabling Act ("SSZEA"), which was first promulgated by the U.S. Department of Commerce in 1926. The SSZEA allows municipalities or other local government entities to enact zoning ordinances. The SSZEA is divided into eight main sections.

[a] Grant of Power

Section One gives the municipal legislature the power to zone to promote health, safety, morals or the general welfare. The types of restrictions allowed include: the height of buildings; the number of stories of buildings; the size of buildings; the portion of a lot that may be filled with structures (lot coverage); the size of yards; the allowable population density; and the location of buildings based on their use. This allows for two distinct types of restrictions. The first is based on the physical aspects of the buildings and the land, commonly referred to as bulk restrictions, while the second type of restriction is based on the use of the property, called use restrictions. Use restrictions are based on splitting up areas into districts, such as single family residential, commercial, industrial or any number of other districts.

As an example, consider Illinois' enabling legislation which permits both types of restrictions:

65 Illinois Compiled Statutes, 5/11-13-1. Objectives; classification, regulation and location of uses; nonconforming uses

To the end that adequate light, pure air, and safety from fire and other dangers may be secured, that the taxable value of land and buildings throughout the municipality may be conserved, that congestion in the public streets may be lessened or avoided, that the hazards to persons and damage to property resulting from the accumulation or runoff of storm or flood waters may be lessened or avoided, and that the public health, safety, comfort, morals, and welfare may otherwise be promoted, and to insure and facilitate the preservation of sites, areas, and structures of historical, architectural and aesthetic importance; the corporate authorities in each municipality have the following powers:

(1) To regulate and limit the height and bulk of buildings hereafter to be erected;

(2) to establish, regulate and limit, subject to the provisions of Division 14 of this Article 11, the building or set-back lines on or along any street, traffic-way, drive, parkway or storm or floodwater runoff channel or basin;

(3) to regulate and limit the intensity of the use of lot areas, and to regulate and determine the area of open spaces, within and surrounding such buildings;

(4) to classify, regulate and restrict the location of trades and industries and the location of buildings designed for specified industrial, business, residential, and other uses;

(5) to divide the entire municipality into districts of such number, shape, area, and of such different classes (according to use of land and buildings, height and bulk of buildings, intensity of the use of lot area, area of open spaces, or other classification) as may be deemed best suited to carry out the purposes of this Division 13;

(6) to fix standards to which buildings or structures therein shall conform;

(7) to prohibit uses, buildings, or structures incompatible with the character of such districts;

(8) to prevent additions to and alteration or remodeling of existing buildings or structures in such a way as to avoid the restrictions and limitations lawfully imposed under this Division 13;

(9) to classify, to regulate and restrict the use of property on the basis of family relationship, which family relationship may be defined as one or more persons each related to the other by blood, marriage or adoption and maintaining a common household;

(10) to regulate or forbid any structure or activity which may hinder access to solar energy necessary for the proper functioning of a solar energy system, as defined in Section 1.2 of The Comprehensive Solar Energy Act of 1977;

(11) to require the creation and preservation of affordable housing, including the power to provide increased density or other zoning incentives to developers who are creating, establishing, or preserving affordable housing; and

(12) to establish local standards solely for the review of the exterior design of buildings and structures, excluding utility facilities and outdoor off-premises advertising signs, and designate a board or commission to implement the review process.

[b] Districts

Section Two of the SSZEA allows for division into districts as are deemed best suited to carry out the purposes of the Act. Further, Section Two requires regulations to be uniform if they are applied to like buildings in the same district, but allows one district's regulations to differ from another district's regulations.

[c] Purposes in View

Section Three requires that regulations shall be made "in accordance with a comprehensive plan." Section Three goes on to outline the general purposes of regulations, including: promoting general welfare; providing adequate light; preventing overcrowding of land; avoiding undue concentration of population; and facilitating adequate transportation, water, sewage, schools and parks. Section Three also requires that in making the regulations, consideration should be given to encouraging the most appropriate use of the land. Some of these purposes are included in the above example from Illinois.

[d] Procedure

Section Four allows the municipal legislature to determine the manner in which the regulations are to be determined, enforced, amended and supplemented. Section Four also sets out the requirement of a public hearing. Notice of fifteen days of the place and time of the public hearing is required as well as published notice in a local newspaper of general circulation.

[e] Changes

Section Five allows adjacent landowners to have some input into changes in the zoning of property proximate to theirs. It allows for landowners who live within a certain distance, as prescribed by statute, the ability to petition their fellow neighbors who are in the requisite proximity to protest the change.

[f] Zoning Commission

Section Six establishes a process for the municipal legislature to appoint a commission to recommend the boundaries of the districts and the uses allowed in those districts. This commission shall have public hearings and issue a final report to the municipal legislature. The final report is to be used by the legislature in its final determination of the issues involved.

[g] Board of Adjustment

Section Seven allows for a five-person board which is to make special exceptions in proper cases. The board has both original and appellate jurisdiction. The appellate jurisdiction is for cases in which a landowner or citizen seeks to appeal a decision by a department, board, bureau or officer of the municipality.

[h] Enforcement and Remedies

Section Eight provides for enforcement of the Zoning Act and declares that any violation of the Zoning Act is a misdemeanor. Section Eight also allows for the legal remedy available to the municipality.

[3] Comprehensive Plan

The Standard State Zoning Enabling Act requires that zoning ordinances be "in accordance with a comprehensive plan." A "comprehensive plan" can be found either in a formally adopted ordinance, frequently labeled a "master" or "comprehensive" plan, or through review of the zoning ordinance itself. A few states require a locality to adopt a formal comprehensive plan as a prerequisite to imposing land use controls, such as zoning or subdivision regulation. Once adopted, there are widely varying concepts of the effect of the comprehensive plan.

[a] Comprehensive Plan as a Guide

In some states, the comprehensive plan is seen only as a guide for the legislature to consult in making its decisions. In *Saenger v. Planning Comm'n. of Berks County*, 308 A.2d 175, 176 (Pa. Commw. Ct. 1973), the court noted that "a comprehensive plan is abstract and recommendatory, whereas a zoning ordinance is specific and regulatory." This conceptualization makes the comprehensive plan something to consult rather than giving the enactment of the comprehensive plan any real effect. This is the traditional view, from which many states are moving away.

[b] Comprehensive Plan as a Constitution

Many states have enacted statutes which elevate the comprehensive plan to the level of a land use or zoning constitution. This is generally known as the consistency doctrine, because land use actions must be consistent with the comprehensive plan in order to be valid. One such state is Florida, which now considers a comprehensive plan to be a statutorily mandated legislative plan to control the development of land. Florida Statutes § 163.3194(3)(a) states:

> A development order or land development regulation shall be consistent with the comprehensive plan if the land uses, densities or intensities, and other aspects of the development permitted by such order or regulation are compatible with and further the objectives, policies, land uses, and densities or intensities in the comprehensive plan if it meets all other criteria enumerated by the local government.

[c] Questions

1. How does bringing the comprehensive plan up to the level of a "zoning constitution" affect the power of a local legislative body?
2. Does making the comprehensive plan the "zoning constitution" add flexibility to the local government's zoning power or take flexibility away?
3. Should a developer be concerned about whether the zoning of his land, either currently or as proposed, comports with the comprehensive plan?

[4] Adoption and Amendment of Zoning Ordinances and Spot Zoning

[a] Adoption and Amendment

The adoption of a zoning ordinance and the amendment of a zoning ordinance bring forth similar issues. As with the initial zoning of a parcel, an ordinance which rezones a parcel or an area from one zone to another can be held invalid if it is arbitrary or an irrational exercise of the police power with no substantial relation to health, safety and welfare. Some states go farther and require that any zoning amendment address either a mistake in the original zoning ordinance or demonstrable changed conditions that would mandate a change in the zoning. There is a practical side to this, however, especially in cases involving rezonings. In allowing a rezoning of property on the basis that the current zoning bore no substantial relationship to the public health, safety or welfare, the court in *Frank DeMarie v. The City of Lake Forest*, 417 N.E.2d 641, 647 (Ill. App. Ct. 1981), found it significant that none of the adjacent property owners appeared at the public hearing to protest the consideration of the new zoning ordinance.

[b] Spot Zoning

Spot Zoning is singling out a small area of land, perhaps a single parcel, for treatment different from surrounding parcels. In *Reskin v. City of Northlake*, 204 N.E.2d 600, 603 (Ill. App. Ct. 1965), the court stated: "To constitute spot zoning the two requisites which must coexist are: a change of zone applicable only to a small area, and a change that is out of harmony with the comprehensive planning for the good of the community as a whole." It is spot zoning if a zoning ordinance treats the "spot" differently from other areas which are similar, without any reason for the different treatment. In *Bartram v. Zoning Comm'n. of the City of Bridgeport*, 68 A.2d 308, 311 (Conn. 1949), the court stated that giving special treatment to a single lot or a small area is generally against sound public policy and obnoxious to the law. The court then explained when singling out a specific spot is allowable:

> It can be justified only when it is done in furtherance of a general plan properly adopted for and designed to serve the best interests of the community as a whole. The vice of spot zoning lies in the fact that it singles out for special treatment a lot or a small area in a way that does not further such a plan.

There are several ways to defend against allegations of spot zoning, other than showing how the change furthers the general plan. Because a rezoning usually gets a presumption of validity, any rezoning which is "fairly debatable" likely will be upheld by the courts. Therefore, if there is a valid public purpose for the rezoning, it is likely to be upheld. In addition, a significant change of conditions in the area rezoned may be a valid reason for the different treatment of the parcel. If the area rezoned is different from the surrounding area in some way, courts are less likely to hold that the change constitutes spot zoning. Also, the rezoning is likely to be allowed if it meets the criteria of the zoning ordinance for a conditional use or a variance.

[5] Variances

There are two general types of variances, area and use. An area variance allows deviation regarding the placement or size of structures, while a use variance allows use of existing property in a manner not permitted by the ordinance, and generally inconsistent with the surrounding property. The typical requirement for a use variance is a showing that the rigid enforcement of the zoning ordinance will result in "unnecessary hardship." By contrast, for the area variance, the landowner need only show "practical difficulty." Variances typically are granted as administrative actions by an administrative body appointed to decide cases involving inconsistencies in the application of a zoning ordinance, such as a zoning board of appeals, or by an administrative body with general jurisdiction over zoning matters, such as a zoning or planning commission.

A variance gives relief to an owner whose land cannot be used as zoned. One of the most prevalent fears is that a variance will be given for reasons that do not constitute a hardship to the landowner. Variances should not be granted because of the financial plight of the applicant or the lack of any protestors at a hearing. In general, a variance can be granted if the grant of the variance will not be contrary to the public interest, the enforcement of the zoning ordinance will result in practical difficulty or unnecessary hardship, and the grant of the variance will preserve the spirit of the ordinance.

Some localities have very specific criteria that must be followed in order for a variance to be granted. In *Burke v. Village of Glenview*, 628 N.E.2d 465, 467 (Ill. App. Ct. 1993), the court approved of a municipality's use of the following factors:

1. The physical surroundings (topography and shape of the land);

2. The uniqueness of the piece of property in comparison to other property in the area;
3. That the purpose of the variance cannot rest solely on a desire for economic gain;
4. The difficulty has not been created by any person with an interest;
5. That granting the variance will not be detrimental to the public welfare;
6. The proposed variation will not impair adequate light or air to adjacent property; and
7. The variance will not alter the essential character of the locality.

These criteria amply describe the interests that most courts would hold to be relevant in considering whether a variance was properly granted.

[6] Nonconforming Uses and Structures

When a construction project involves the renovation, or even expansion, of an existing building, issues involving nonconforming uses and structures can arise. Nonconforming uses are uses of a building that are excluded under the current zoning ordinance but which were in existence prior to the time that the ordinance was enacted. Similarly, nonconforming structures are buildings or improvements, the size, dimensions, or location of which are prohibited under the current zoning ordinance, but which were in existence prior to the time that the ordinance was enacted. In many instances, nonconforming uses and structures are permitted to remain until the nonconforming uses are abandoned or the nonconforming structures are demolished. In some instances, municipalities are prohibited under the state's zoning enabling act to terminate nonconforming uses or structures, and, in other instances, the zoning ordinance itself permits the continuation of such uses and structures.

Despite the inconsistency that nonconforming uses and structures bring to the overall zoning scheme within a particular district, they are frequently permitted, based on the belief that the properties will eventually be brought into conformity as uses change and improvements age. However, the nonconformity may make the property more valuable and thereby ensure its continuation. For example, the only existing store in a newly designated residential district may be perpetuated because of the lack of competition from other retailers. The existence of nonconforming uses and structures also creates difficulties when owners wish to renovate a nonconforming structure particularly after a fire or other casualty, expand a nonconforming use, or change from one nonconforming use to another. Numerous examples exist of courts having to determine the rights of the property owners in such situations. *See, e.g., City of Countryside v. Oak Park National Bank*, 223 N.E.2d 293 (Ill. App. Ct. 1966) (upholding an ordinance that required the demolition of a nonconforming structure when damaged by fire in an amount greater than 50% of its replacement cost); *Jasper v. Michael A. Dolan, Inc.*, 242 N.E.2d 540 (Mass. 1968) (distinguishing between an increase in the business of a nonconforming use and an enlargement of a nonconforming use that differs in kind in its effect on the neighborhood and concluding that the sale of liquor by a store previously licensed to sell only beer and wine constituted a new use); *Stevens v. Town of Rye*, 448 A.2d 426 (N.H. 1982) (change from an automobile garage to a bath shop and plumbing supplies shop not a permissible expansion of a nonconforming use). *See generally* Mandelker, Land Use Law §§ 5.68–5.76 (4th ed. 1997); 7 Rohan, Zoning and Land Use Controls, ch. 41 (2000).

[7] Historic and Landmark Preservation and Takings

Notwithstanding that the protection of private property is a basic constitutional tenant, *Euclid* tells us that zoning is a proper exercise of the police power. Two years after *Euclid*, in the case of *Nectow v. City of Cambridge*, 277 U.S. 183 (1928), the United States Supreme Court set down certain constitutional standards by which a zoning code is to be judged. There are two basic challenges to a zoning ordinance: 1) the specific zoning clause which regulates a use is so broad and vague as to be unconstitutional as written; and 2) the zoning provision, perfectly acceptable on its face, is being applied to a specific piece of property, which because of factors relating to the property itself make the application of the zoning provision unconstitutional.

The regulation of land uses by government can sometimes result in the denial of all reasonable use of the land by the landowner. Government has the right to "take" private property for public use, *but* only after the payment of just compensation. It is not uncommon in zoning litigation to include a "take" claim — the zoning provision in question effectively denies the property owner all reasonable use of the property. The take claim opens the door for the award of monetary damages not ordinarily available in traditional zoning litigation. The jurisprudence of eminent domain/condemnation is beyond the purview of this book. Nevertheless, the close, sometimes overlapping connection, between zoning litigation and "takings" jurisprudence is omnipresent in the zoning analysis process.

A seminal U.S. Supreme Court case, *Penn Central Transportation Co. v. City of New York*, 438 U.S. 104 (1978), is critical to the consideration of these two subjects, historic and landmark preservation on the one hand, and takings on the other. In *Penn Central*, the Court gave its approval to historic preservation legislation while at the same time stating that over-regulation by government could constitute a taking under the Fifth Amendment to the U.S. Constitution, thereby voiding the statute and/or requiring the government to pay the landowner just compensation. We use *Penn Central* as a focus because it is the modern beginning of the Court's takings jurisprudence. Over-regulation is a not infrequent complaint by land developers, and, although it was not raised by Regent in the development of the Fox Valley Auto Care Center, the principles should always be considered when evaluating the regulation to which almost any real estate development is subjected. Regent faced no issues of historic or landmark preservation in the development of the Auto Care Center, but, just as with other subjects, we use the connection to a relevant subject (takings) to introduce you to a subject faced by many developers, especially those engaging in development on previously used sites in urban areas.

In *Penn Central*, the City of New York enacted a landmark preservation ordinance pursuant to a New York state enabling statute. The City's ordinance allowed for the designation of historic districts, historic sites, and historic buildings. After enacting the ordinance, the City proceeded to designate many districts, sites and buildings as landmarks, including Penn Central's building, Grand Central Terminal. Designation involved an elaborate process including extensive documentation and study by city agencies and several public hearings in which the landowner could appear, present witnesses and evidence, and present its arguments before designation was granted or denied. The designation procedure also provided relief from the strict application of the ordinance, up to and including permission to demolish the landmark if the landowner could not earn a sufficient return from use of the building as protected by the landmark ordinance. Many states and cities have enacted landmark and historic preservation statutes and ordinances, many of which are similar to New York State's and the City of New York's.

After opposing the landmark designation of the Terminal, rather than appealing the designation, Penn Central sued the City in New York state court alleging that the landmark designation of the Terminal was a taking. The New York courts, including its highest court, the New York Court of Appeals, and the U.S. Supreme Court all upheld the City's landmark preservation ordinance and the landmark designation of the Terminal for many reasons, but the prime one arguably was that Penn Central could still use Grand Central Terminal for the purpose for which it was built. As a landmark or historic preservation case, the case was significant because the U.S. Supreme Court accepted preservation of landmarks and historic buildings and sites as encompassed within the police power and sufficiently important that a landowner could be forced to bear a significant loss to further the public purpose of historic or landmark preservation.

As a takings case, *Penn Central* was even more important. The Court had flirted with the concept of a regulatory taking in the 1922 case of *Pennsylvania Coal Co. v. Mahon*, 260 U.S. 393 (1922). It was not until 56 years later in *Penn Central* that the Court began to give form to the concept. Many cases have followed, including *Agins v. City of Tiburon*, 447 U.S. 255 (1980) (the Court held that a parcel of land could be so regulated in its use that most of its value was lost without constituting a taking); *Lucas v. South Carolina Coastal Council*, 505 U.S. 1003 (1992) (the Court held that if a regulation stripped property of all value, it did constitute a taking unless the regulation was one based on historical legal limits on the use of the property, which would mean that the property owner had no right to engage in the use and the regulation therefore took nothing that the owner had); *First English Evangelical Lutheran Church v. County of Los Angeles*, 482 U.S. 304 (1987) (the Court held that a regulation could effect a temporary taking if it denied the owner all use for a period of time, and that the owner must be compensated for the period of time between enactment of the regulation and its invalidation or repeal); *Nollan v. California Coastal Commission*, 483 U.S. 825 (1987) (the Court held that there had to be an "essential nexus" between the effect of a regulation requiring an exaction and its stated purpose, and, if not, it would effect a taking); and *Dolan v. City of Tigard*, 512 U.S. 374 (1994) (the Court held that even if there were an essential nexus between effect of a regulation requiring an exaction and its stated purpose that the burden on the property owner must be "roughly proportional" to the harm caused by the property owner's proposed development).

Our goal with this recitation of some of the Court's takings cases (believe it or not, there are more!) is not to make you a takings expert, but to make you aware of the issue and some of the major cases decided by the Court on the issue. These cases, and how they interrelate with each other, are much more complex than our simplistic recitation would make them appear, and to add to the complexity many state courts also have decided takings cases. For the developer's attorney, a takings claim is always a consideration when a governmental agency seeks to restrict use or demands a payment or deed of land in exchange for approving the client's project.

§ 7.02 PRACTICAL APPROACH TO ZONING

[1] Administrative Implementation

Richard S. Dalebout,[1]
Utah Zoning Law: The Zoning Ordinance,
UTAH BAR JOURNAL, April, 2001

Introduction[2]

Enabling Acts. The Municipal Land Use Development and Management Act empowers cities and towns in Utah to divide or "zone" the territory within their boundaries into districts and to regulate land uses therein. The County Land Use Development and Management Act similarly empowers counties. Subject, of course, to constitutional limitations, these two acts — commonly referred to as "enabling" acts — are the controlling law of zoning. They are worth reading: an experienced land use planner (and a non-lawyer) once commented that he could often out-maneuver local lawyers in zoning matters simply because he read and understood the applicable enabling act and they didn't.

Zoning Ordinance. The enabling acts permit cities and counties to use their law-making power to adopt a "zoning ordinance" consisting of a map and a text. The map illustrates the territory of the city divided into districts which have names such as "Agricultural (A-1)," "Single Family Residential (R-1)" or "Neighborhood Shopping Center (SC-1)." The text describes what can and cannot be done within each of these districts. For example, in an R-1 zone, as the name suggests, single family residences are allowed and more intensive uses such as duplexes and four-plexes are prohibited. It is left to the city or county to decide on the names for the zoning districts and the uses allowed within each of these districts — these are not prescribed in the enabling acts.

The Planning Commission

Organization and Procedure. The process of adopting a zoning ordinance starts with a planning commission, which is created by the governing body and is required for the exercise of zoning powers. (Commission members are local residents who are appointed by the governing body and usually serve without compensation.)

---

[1] Richard S. Dalebout, a member of the Utah Bar, teaches local government law in the Marriott School at Brigham Young University. He is a member of the Utah County Board of Adjustment. Copyright © 2001 by the Utah State Bar Association. Reprinted by permission.

[2] Because of space constraints, only cursory endnotes are used. Unless otherwise indicated, all statutes quoted or referred to are found in The Municipal Land Use Development and Management Act (Utah Code Ann. § 10-9-101) or the County Land Use Development and Management Act (Utah Code Ann. § 17-27-101). Case references are limited to identifying significant cases and identifying the source of quotations.

Powers and Duties. A planning commission has no law-making authority and, in general, it performs only the planning and administrative functions specified by the governing body. There are, however, three things it must do:

- *General Plan.* The planning commission must prepare "a comprehensive, long-range general plan" for the development of land in the city, which it recommends to the governing body. This general plan is the foundation on which the zoning ordinance is built. Any subsequent amendments to the general plan must likewise be routed through the planning commission for its recommendation.
- *Zoning Ordinance.* The zoning ordinance (map and text) must be reviewed by the planning commission before adoption into law by the legislative body. Amendments must be reviewed by the planning commission.
- *Subdivisions.* Any subdivision ordinance must be recommended by the planning commission. Amendments to the subdivision ordinance must also be reviewed by the planning commission. A subdivision plat may not be filed or recorded until the officer or body designated to approve subdivision plats has received the recommendation of the planning commission.

In the processes above, the governing body cannot proceed without first receiving the recommendation of the planning commission. However, the planning commission is completely subordinate because the governing body can modify any of the recommendations before enacting them into law (the general plan, zoning ordinance and subdivision ordinance)[3] or approving them (subdivision plats).

An example of the administrative work that may be handled by a planning commission (if authorized by the governing body) is holding a public hearing and deciding whether to grant a conditional use permit. In *Stucker v. Summit County*,[4] the local ordinance required a proposed use to be compatible with neighboring uses. Because compatibility was at issue, the ordinance authorized the planning commission to hold hearings and make a decision resolving the issue. The ordinance provided:

> When a developer and affected property owners cannot reach a consensus of opinion regarding compatibility of the proposed land use, *the Planning Commission holds a public hearing prior to making a decision and listens to the concerns of all affected property owners* and interested parties regarding the proposed project's compatibility.[5]

Although a planning commission (like that above) may hold a hearing and consider the opinions of local land owners, it crosses the line when it allows itself to be controlled by what the Utah Court of Appeals has characterized as "public clamor." In *Davis County v. Clearfield City*,[6] the Utah Court of Appeals noted: "[This] clamor is typified by the curious action taken at the Planning Commission hearing, where citizens in attendance were asked to vote on the application. Only one person

---

[3] *See* Gardner v. Perry City, 994 P.2d 811 (Utah App. 2000).

[4] 870 P.2d 283 (Utah App. 1994).

[5] *Id.* at 285 (emphasis added).

[6] 756 P.2d 704 (Utah App. 1988).

voted for the facility and all others in the audience voted against it."[7] (Application denial was later overturned on appeal.)

The Zoning Ordinance

Legislative Action. The zoning ordinance (map and text) is adopted as law by the governing body. This legislative action is in derogation of the common law and is an exercise of police power. It is traditional to say that police power is exercised to promote the health, safety, morals and general welfare of the community. As long as the legislative judgment of the city council is within reasonable bounds, the courts usually will not overturn it. As the Utah Court of Appeals stated in *Sandy City v. Salt Lake County*[8]:

> It is well established in Utah that "courts of law cannot substitute their judgment in the area of zoning regulations for that of the governing body." Instead, the courts afford a comparatively wide latitude of discretion to administrative bodies charged with the responsibility of zoning, as well as endowing their actions with a presumption of correctness and validity, because of the complexity of factors involved in the matter of zoning and the specialized knowledge of the administrative body. Thus, the courts will not consider the wisdom, necessity, or advisability or otherwise interfere with a zoning determination unless "it is shown that there is no reasonable basis to justify the action taken."[9]

"Spot" Zones. There is a theoretical limitation on the power of the governing body to adopt a zoning ordinance — in this case the zoning map. The enabling act requires that territory on the map be divided into districts, and the Utah Supreme Court has recognized that such language seems, by definition, to prohibit a division of territory into very small pieces or islands which are sometimes referred to as "spot" zones. Although seemingly clear in concept about spot zoning, the Utah courts have in practice deferred to the discretion of local governing bodies. The result is that the courts have thus far been unwilling to acknowledge the existence of a prohibited "spot" zone, even when the zoning district is no bigger than a commercial corner lot.[10]

Permitted Uses. For each zoning district there is language in the text which describes the uses which are *permitted*. These are so-called "permitted" uses, and that language is usually accompanied by language stating that no other uses are allowed.

For example, an R-1 (single family residential) district might be accompanied by language in the text which allows the construction and use of a residence for a "single family," and no other uses. A well-crafted zoning text will include a list of definitions. In this case, the text should include a definition for "family." If there is not a "family" definition, the absence thereof will lead to disputes. (For example, are an unmarried man and woman living together a "family?" If the answer is yes, are two university students living together a "family?" If the answer to that is yes, are

---

[7] *Id.* at 711–12 n. 9.

[8] 794 P.2d 482 (Utah App. 1990).

[9] *Id.* at 485–86 (citations omitted).

[10] *See* Marshall v. Salt Lake City, 141 P.2d 704 (Utah 1943).

three, five or seven university students living together a "family?" And so on.)

Conditional Uses. Increasingly, the uses allowed in a district are uses known as "conditional" uses. The city and county enabling acts define a "conditional use" as "a land use that, because of its unique characteristics or potential impact on the [municipality/county], surrounding neighbors, or adjacent land uses, may not be compatible in some areas or may be compatible only if certain conditions are required that mitigate or eliminate the detrimental impacts."

For example, the governing body may create a Professional Office (P-O) zone and in the zoning text allow a convenience store (including the sale of gasoline) as a conditional use. The (abbreviated) text might be something like this:

> 21.15.000 Conditional Uses. A convenience store (including the sale of gasoline) is permitted only on the following conditions:
>
> (1) that the building lot shall not be less than 30,000 square feet in size,
>
> (2) that Utah Department of Transportation approval be obtained for any ingress or egress onto a state road, and
>
> (3) that the applicant consent to any additional term or condition necessary to prevent harm to the health, safety or general welfare of persons working or residing in the vicinity.

At an imaginary hearing on the question of issuing a conditional use permit for a convenience store (including the sale of gasoline) there is testimony that noise and light from the convenience store will cause problems at a nearby office building. Therefore, when the permit is issued, it contains the following requirements: "a fence not less than six feet high shall be maintained along the east convenience store boundary line. Parking lot lighting shall not illuminate past the east boundary line." The permit is subject to these conditions.

Elderly and Persons with a Disability. The enabling acts provide special protection for residential facilities for the elderly and for persons with a disability. Implicit in this protection is the assumption that cities and counties, under pressure from unhappy residents,[11] may not voluntarily authorize the use of such facilities. Thus, the enabling acts provide that each city and county "*shall* adopt" ordinance provisions that permit the use of facilities for the elderly and persons with a disability which meet standards described in the enabling acts.

Subdivision Regulations

Subdivision Plats. A subdivision plat is a map illustrating the division of real estate into building lots, open spaces, roads, utilities and the like. Property described in a subdivision plat is sold by reference to the plat. Thus, the deed for a building lot described in a subdivision plat might contain a description something like this: "Lot 10, Plat A, Elmwood Subdivision, according to the plat on file with the Urbana County Recorder." The enabling acts place the platting process within the control of cities and counties, and land which must be platted cannot be sold or developed until a subdivision plat is approved.

---

[11] *See generally* Bangerter v. Orem City Corp., 797 F. Supp. 918, 920 (D. Utah 1992).

Cities and counties guard the subdivision plat approval process jealously because it is by controlling this process that they ensure that each new development fits into the overall plan for the city. Through this control a city or county enforces a variety of exactions such as connection fees, impact fees, dedications of land, and fees in lieu of dedications of land, all of which are part of the conditions of approval.[12] (For example, the plat will not be approved if the developer does not install — at the developer's expense — roads, sidewalks, sewer and water lines, and electric utilities.[13])

"Subdivision" Defined. Meeting the demands of a city or county in the platting process can be very expensive; thus, some land owners try to avoid the process. That raises the question: when can real estate be sold using a simple "metes and bounds" description, and when must the subdivision platting process be followed? The answer is that cities and counties may require land to be platted if the land is in a "subdivision" as defined in the enabling acts. The word "subdivision" has a comprehensive definition. It means, in general, any division of land into two or more smaller pieces for the present or future purpose of "offer, sale, lease, or development."

The "subdivision" definition has several exceptions. Of particular significance in counties is the exception that "a bona fide division or partition of agricultural land for agricultural purposes" is not within the subdivision definition. The effect of this exception is that land which is divided for agricultural purposes is not subject to platting requirements. If such a division of land is not subject to platting requirements it is not subject to the requirements and exactions normally associated with the subdivision process. Historically, counties have had difficulty with abuses in relation to this exception. As so-called "agricultural" parcels get increasingly smaller through the process of division, it becomes apparent that the real use of the resulting parcels is non-agricultural (for example: a house and three acres for a horse). To avoid arguments about when a land use has ceased to be truly "agricultural," and thus subject to the subdivision process, some counties place minimum standards for what is a "bona fide division of agricultural land" in their subdivision ordinance.

Zoning Procedure

Follow the Ritual. The adoption of zoning ordinance provisions requires that the governing body follow a specific ritual of notices and hearings. Unfortunately, some cities and counties (often smaller ones) sometimes fail to follow the ritual and the result is that in a moment of crisis they find their zoning ordinance is invalid. (Knowing this, experienced land use litigators always check the public record, looking for a technical defect that will give them an easy win.)

Some years ago the City of West Jordan failed to follow the ritual. In *Call v. City of West Jordan*,[14] the city adopted an impact fee pursuant to its power to enact subdivision ordinances; however, evidence showed that the city failed to conduct a

[12] *See generally* Michael J. Mazuran, *Evolution of Real Estate Development Exactions in Utah*, Utah Bar J., Aug.-Sept. 1990, at 11.

[13] *See generally* Home Builders Ass'n v. City of North Logan, 983 P.2d 561 (Utah 1999).

[14] 727 P.2d 180 (Utah 1986). *See also* Hatch v. Boulder Town Council, 2001 UT App. 55 (Utah App. 2001).

required public hearing. Nevertheless, the city argued that the public hearing requirement was satisfied "because the ordinance was adopted at a regularly scheduled city council meeting which was open to the public." The Utah Supreme Court disagreed and invalidated the impact fee ordinance:

> [W]e hold that because the statute calls for a *public hearing* our legislature contemplated something more than a regular city council meeting held, so far as the record here discloses, without specific advance notice to the public that the proposed ordinance would be considered. Notice, to be effective, must alert the public to the nature and scope of the ordinance that is finally adopted. *Failure to strictly follow the statutory requirements in enacting the ordinance renders it invalId.*[15]

Standard for Review. The process of changing the zoning text or map is a *legislative* process and should be distinguished from *administrative* processes such as, for example, the approval of a conditional use permit or a planned unit development. In *Bradley v. Payson City*[16] the Utah Court of Appeals noted that judicial review of legislative acts "is highly deferential to the municipality's decision." The legislative act of a municipality will be upheld as long as the decision is "reasonably debatable."

Initiative/Referendum. The processes of initiative or referendum may only be used to alter a zoning ordinance when the change is a significant change of zoning policy; they cannot be used to make otherwise routine zoning amendments. Article VI, section 1 of the Utah Constitution explicitly authorizes the use of initiatives and referenda by voters "of any legal subdivision of the state." However, the Utah Supreme Court has held that some decisions by a legislative body, although cast in the form of a legislative act, are in substance an administrative decision. Thus, for example, in *Wilson v. Manning*,[17] the plaintiffs were refused the use of a referendum with respect to their objection to the rezoning of ten acres of land from residential to commercial. According to the court:

> This ruling does not mean that an amendment to a zoning ordinance can never be the subject of a referendum. Some amendments can constitute such a material variation from the basic zoning law of the governmental unit as to constitute, in effect, the making of a new law rather than merely, as this Court [has] said . . . "implementing the comprehensive plan and adjusting it to current conditions."[18]

This case law has been codified and the statute regulating initiatives and referenda refers to a routine zoning amendment as an "individual property zoning decision" and prohibits the use of initiatives and referenda to accomplish those decisions.[19]

Temporary Regulations (Moratoria). There is no provision in the acts for a moratorium on development as such, but in the case of a "compelling, countervailing public interest," the legislative body is permitted to adopt temporary zoning regulations without a public hearing. These temporary regulations may operate as

15 *Id.* at 183 (emphasis added).

16 Bradley v. Payson City, 413 Utah Adv. Rep 13 (Utah App. 2001).

17 657 P.2d 251 (Utah 1982). *See also* Citizen's Awareness Now v. Marakis, 873 P.2d 1117 (Utah, 1994).

18 *Wilson v. Manning* at 254.

19 Utah Code Ann. §§ 20A-7-101 and 102.

moratoria because they may, for up to six months, "prohibit or regulate the erection, construction, reconstruction, or alteration of any building or structure or subdivision approval." The authors of this provision were understandably reluctant to use the word "moratorium" or to extend the restriction beyond six months because the United States Supreme Court has held that if zoning regulations "deny a landowner all use of his property," even temporarily, the landowner may have a cause of action for compensation.[20] . . .

[2] Advice on How to Represent a Client Before a Local Board

H. Stanley Riffle
Winning Game Plans For Local Board Appearances,
GPSOLO, October/November 2008[*]

There will likely come a time in the career of each general practitioner when a client will ask for assistance in appearing before a local governmental board. Although there is no "one-size-fits-all" approach to a local board appearance, there are some general practice guidelines that will provide the best opportunity for success. Key elements in the successful approach include understanding the proposed project, understanding the law, pre-hearing preparation, and conduct of the hearing itself.

Understanding the Proposed Project

It is impossible to present your case to a local board unless you fully understand the nuances of the project your client is undertaking. This may seem very basic, but if you do not understand the project, you will not be able to explain it to the board. Thus you need to be completely conversant with all aspects of the proposal. You should insist on meeting with any client, employee, consultant, engineer, or architect that had any part in the plan preparation. Always take time to review the development site. Keep in mind that in all likelihood, the board members have a general understanding of the site, and they will expect you to have the same or better familiarity. By viewing the site, you can accomplish a number of things, including:

- determining what, if any, neighbors are in the vicinity;
- getting a feel for the lay of the land;
- finding out if there is any obvious history of use of the land, such as quarry operations, junkyards, environmental concerns, etc.;
- discovering any obvious wetland issues; and
- identifying potential traffic or access problems.

---

[20] *See* First English Evangelical Lutheran Church of Glendale v. County of Los Angeles, 482 U.S. 304, 318 (1987).

[*] Copyright © 2008 by H. Stanley Riffle. Reprinted by permission. H. Stanley Riffle is a partner in the firm of Arenz Molter Macy & Riffle SC in Waukesha, Wisconsin, and is the Budget Officer of the ABA General Practice, Solo and Small Firm Division. He may be reached at srifftel@aol.com.

Understanding the Law

Once you have a general understanding of the project, you must determine the statutory and code provisions that apply to the project. Enabling statutes set forth not only the composition of the membership of the board but often its jurisdiction, general procedures, and rules. Determining the jurisdiction of the board is very important; it would be quite embarrassing to appear with your client before the wrong body, and malpractice insurance rates do not appear to be shrinking.

With regard to understanding the applicable local ordinances, you will be far ahead if you read the entire code instead of relying on the short section that appears applicable. Many municipal codes have provisions pertinent to a project scattered throughout the book (undoubtedly owing to revisions and codifications made without input of the municipality's attorney). Most ordinances include a general section on the intent of the ordinance. Although the "Purpose Section" (as it is generally titled) may appear to be boilerplate, it can become the most important language for your case, especially on appeal.

Once you have identified all applicable substantive code provisions, you then must determine exactly what approvals are needed from the local board(s) and what procedures must be followed. Generally, the clerk or secretary of the board will be very helpful and may save you a good deal of time in translating code to practice. I recommend that you get to know this person well.

Once you have a firm handle on legal and procedural fronts, sit down with your client and set goals. Discuss with the client what he or she is willing to live with. Know what specific conditions are acceptable to your client. Because there may be requests for tradeoffs, you need to know your bottom line. Thus, the goals should include a worst-case acceptable outcome and a time frame for reaching the goal. Be realistic. Municipal approvals take time.

Pre-hearing Preparation

Pre-hearing preparation is often the most important factor in obtaining board approval. If you have the municipal staff and, perhaps, individual board members nodding "yes" before the meeting even begins, your time before the board will be a pleasurable one. Some "best practice" tips to help accomplish this follow.

Communicate with staff and consultants. You should become familiar with the staff members with whom you will be dealing. Not only will they be able to assist you in learning the board's procedures, but they may give insight as to how the board generally thinks, identify known obstacles, point out need for additional information, and communicate positive information to board members in the form of a staff report or otherwise. If the board uses any professional staff, such as a municipal engineer, lawyer, or planner, pay them a courtesy call prior to the hearing to determine what, if any, position they have in regard to the project. Should you meet with any of the professional staff, memorialize the discussions in writing. A brief note to the professional staff person thanking him or her for the meeting and summarizing the discussion and issues raised will be of great assistance to you in the long run.

Obtain copies of recent board minutes. Although prior minutes may contain nothing more than the actual decisions of the board, even this may be helpful. It also can be helpful to listen to the tapes of prior meetings. Most local boards tape their proceedings and retain those tapes for a specific period of time. The staff may be of assistance to you in determining if any specific taped proceeding is similar in nature to your request.

Talk to other applicants. If at all possible, talk to someone who has been before the board previously. Any insight into how the board reacted to the presentation will be most helpful, especially if the application was approved.

Application process. Determine if a specific application must be filed. Many times the board does not have such a form. In other instances a very specific application is needed. If a written application is needed, prepare it yourself. Although it is wise to ask the staff to review the application once you have completed it, do not rely on the staff to prepare the application for you. The staff may not fully understand your project.

Make sure the application is placed on the agenda. Many projects are delayed because the specific action requested of the board was not properly noticed, so no action could be taken. Check to see whether or not other notices are required and whether they have been properly published and served.

Analyze potential opposition. Determine in advance whether there is opposition to the project. Generally, this can best be determined by knocking on doors. Find out if your opposition is totally opposed to the project or whether some reasonable conditions would satisfy their concerns. Offer to meet with them prior to meeting with the board, if at all possible, to analyze their strength, listen to their concerns, and determine if they have any legitimate legal issues that you will be required to address. Obviously, a great deal can be learned from the opposition prior to the meeting.

Ex parte contacts. If you will be appearing before a legislative or quasi-legislative board, there are generally no rules prohibiting contact with board members individually. Keep in mind that many board members are contacted by the opposition prior to the meeting. If you do not contact them, they may come to the meeting with very one-sided background information. As volunteers, board members may have very little time to spend with you. A mere offer to meet and/or tour the site with them prior to the meeting will be well received whether or not your offer is accepted. A quorum of the board should not ordinarily be present at one time. Often you will not be able to contact each and every board member prior to the meeting. Nonetheless, it pays to determine who the strong members of the board are and who the naysayers may be.

Meeting Considerations

As a general rule, always introduce yourself and each member of your party prior to commencing your presentation. Most board members want to know who is in the audience and why. If possible, hand out a list of the names and titles of the individuals who will be involved in the presentation. This will help to supplement your record and will be appreciated by the board members.

Of course, you already will have learned the specific procedures attendant to the meeting. As the applicant, you will in almost all instances be making your presentation first. You will have determined whether the proceeding is a public hearing or merely a meeting. Some local boards are very strict about allowing other members of the public to make statements if it is not a public hearing.

Develop a record of your presentation or testimony. Determine in advance from the clerk of the board whether the meeting will be taped, whether the tape will be preserved, and how detailed the minutes will be. If this "record" is of concern, you may consider arranging for a transcript at your client's expense. Although the board may be somewhat intimidated by a court reporter or video camera, these are becoming more commonplace. Be sensitive to the board's feelings while balancing your need to record the proceedings. Keep in mind that intimidating the board to the extent that they do not comment on your presentation will be of little benefit to your client in the long run.

A well-prepared handout is always well received. Make sure you have enough copies so that there is one for each board member as well as the entire professional staff and clerk. It also is appreciated if you have enough for the press and the public. A handout is almost always made part of the record, and on any review by a court, it is part of the file sent up. The trick, of course, is to have a well-prepared handout that will be of assistance to the board and important for the record but that is not confusing. A confused board with unanswered questions will, in most instances, either table your request for a month or deny it outright.

In almost all instances, the "burden of proof" is on the applicant. Again, this is where the applicable codes become important. In almost all situations there will be some general language setting forth the standards by which the board is to rest its decision. Direct the board's attention to the applicable code (unless for strategic reasons you want the board to make its decision without such reference).

Be available to board members before and after the public meeting to clarify your particular request. Most boards are not impressed if you show up just for your matter and leave immediately: Unless the meeting is exceptionally long, it looks much better if you appear at the start of the meeting and stay throughout. This way; you will be available to the board members prior to the meeting and immediately thereafter to discuss your project. Your opposition may be taking advantage of this opportunity to lobby the board members.

Make sure that the board takes clear action. Often, there can be confusion as to what the board is actually approving or what conditions it has placed on the approval. Also, if there is a denial, you may ask for the board's reasons for not approving the project. Some boards will be receptive to a draft of a proposed motion. If at all possible, have it available in advance of the meeting for the municipal lawyer because he or she often is asked to word the motion. Don't be afraid to be presumptuous — draft a proposed motion for the approval of your project with reasonable conditions that are acceptable to your client.

Appearing before local boards is much like appearing before a jury; and the means to achieving the goal are identical. Knowing the facts, knowing the law, and articulating the reasonableness of your position are key: These suggestions should aid in your preparation, so when you face that one time in your career when a client asks you to appear with him before the Mayberry plan commission, you can confidently tell him, "I charge double for night meetings."

§ 7.03 THE PROBLEMS OF CONTRACT ZONING AND CONDITIONAL ZONING

One of the more difficult distinctions in zoning law is between contract zoning and conditional zoning, yet the distinction is critical: contract zoning is typically invalid because the courts fear that the municipality will "contract away its police power," while conditional zoning generally is valid as long as the basis for imposing conditions is not too vague and does not involve too much discretion. As you will soon read, Regent, along with the Johnsons, entered into a contract with the City of Aurora. The contract involved several issues, including the annexation of the Johnson parcel into the City of Aurora.

The issue for our consideration is whether that contract was valid under Illinois law. The location of the Fox Valley Auto Care Center in the State of Illinois turns out to be fortuitous for us in this part of our study of zoning law. Illinois has an extensive body of case law concerning both contract zoning and conditional zoning. Note, however, that the large number of cases does not mean that the Illinois courts have developed a clear distinction between the two concepts. The cases do give us the result of classifying an ordinance as contract zoning (it is void) versus conditional zoning (it may be valid), but the Illinois courts are not clear as to how we are to distinguish between the two. In addition, the Illinois legislature, like the legislatures in many other large states, has adopted statutes allowing municipalities to enter into annexation agreements with landowners, and Regent did enter into an annexation agreement with the City of Aurora.

[1] Contract Zoning

Contract zoning occurs when there is some sort of a zoning change that is predicated on a promise by the landowner to limit use of the land to a particular use, or fewer uses than allowed by the zoning ordinance. Typically there is a change to a zoning classification that allows for many uses, but the landowner agrees to limit itself to one specific use. Contract zoning binds the municipality and the landowner. The courts are concerned that, taken as a whole, such an agreement between the municipality and the landowner furthers a private interest as opposed to a public interest. The following principal case discusses the issues surrounding contract zoning. As you read the case, keep in mind what it means to a developer who needs to reach agreement with a zoning authority.

[a] A Traditional View of Contract Zoning

CEDERBERG v. CITY OF ROCKFORD

8 Ill. App. 3d 984, 291 N.E.2d 249 (Ill. App. Ct. 2d Dist. 1972)

Defendant City appeals from an order entered in a declaratory judgment action whereby the trial court held valid an ordinance granting local business zoning to certain property owned by plaintiff's predecessor-in-title, but found void a restrictive covenant which limited the otherwise permissible local business uses allowed on that land.

On appeal, the City does not contest the finding that the restrictive covenant is void but argues, generally, that if the restrictions fall so must the zoning ordinances.

* * *

On May 13, 1968, prior to plaintiff's purchase of subdivision lots 16, 17 and 18, an ordinance was passed rezoning lots 17 and 18 from residential to local business. (Lot 16 was rezoned in the same manner on September 3, 1968.) On May 14, 1968, a restrictive covenant, affecting only Lots 17 and 18, was executed by the then-owner and was thereafter recorded. (Evidence indicates that this was done at the suggestion of the zoning committee, coincidental with, and as a condition to, passage of the committee's report recommending rezoning.) The covenant provided that, notwithstanding the granted local business classification (which, by City's ordinance, permits forty-four types of local businesses), use of the land in question would be limited to offices. On February 27, 1969, a waiver of the covenant, approved by the mayor, was filed and a replacement covenant was recorded. The latter's terms, stated within the covenant to be in accordance with a report of the City's zoning committee, provided that twenty-six enumerated uses, otherwise permitted in a local business district, would not be allowed on the lots in question. The trial court found that the restrictive covenant was an improper attempt by the City to control the use of the land. Neither party contests this finding.

Plaintiff began considering purchase of the property in question approximately two years prior to actual acquisition. Negotiating through a realty agency, he informed the agent that he wanted to build a laundry center, including a Laundromat, sales showroom and service department. The record indicates that as a result of representing the vendor in a prior sale of the property, the realtor had knowledge of the restrictive covenant affecting the property, but it is unclear if he knew whether plaintiff's proposed use would be permitted under the covenant. Plaintiff testified that he was informed by the agent that a retail business would not be restricted. The agent testified that, before plaintiff made his formal offer to purchase, the City's building department was consulted concerning the feasibility of constructing the laundry center on the property, and its representative indicated such a use would be allowed. On January 15, 1971, plaintiff made a written offer to purchase the premises contingent upon obtaining financing and a building permit to construct the laundry center.

From February through April of 1971, plaintiff had several conversations with one Roy Hunt, a building department inspector and zoning official. Plaintiff submitted his sketches and plans for the proposed laundry center to the department. Roy Hunt testified that during this time he was unaware that there was a restrictive covenant in existence. At all times during this period, he orally assured plaintiff that the building permit necessary to carry out the plans would be issued. Plaintiff obtained an updated title policy with an effective date of March 20, 1971; the policy did not include a copy of the restrictive covenant although it did indicate the existence of the restriction and gave reference to the microfilm number on which it was recorded.

The real estate closing occurred on April 15, 1971; a temporary building permit was issued on April 20, and a permanent one on April 28. Plaintiff, acting as general contractor, started excavation on April 23. On May 5, a stop order was issued by Roy Hunt, he having been directed by resolution of the City Council to halt construction because of the existence of the restrictive covenant. Although defendant had, in the trial court, asserted the validity of the restrictive covenant, on appeal both parties agree that the covenant was a type of "contract zoning" and, as such, is void. The precise question left for review is what effect, if any, the restrictive covenant bore upon the validity of the ordinance rezoning the property from a residential to a local business district.

The briefs of both parties cite three cases as authority for the conclusion that the restrictive covenant is void: *Houston Petroleum Co. v. Automotive Prod. C. Assn.*, 9 N.J. 122, 87 A.2d 319 (1952); *Hartnett v. Austin*, 93 So.2d 86 (S.Ct. Fla. 1956); *Baylis v. City of Baltimore*, 148 A.2d 429 (Ct. of App. Md. 1959). Each of these cases condemns the practice of regulating zoning through agreements or contracts between the zoning authorities and property owners. While no single basis for the rule against such zoning practices emerges from the cases cited, among the court's reasons are that by entering into agreement with the property owner, the zoning authority might use the zoning power to further private interests in violation of public policy; that such rezoning is a deviation from a basic zoning plan resulting in non-uniform application of the zoning law and inconsistencies within a zoning classification; that when the actual zoning requirements in force are determined by reference to evidence extrinsic to the zoning ordinances, the zoning law is rendered vague.

We agree with the trial judge and the parties to this appeal that the restrictive covenant in question was an invalid attempt by the City to control the use of the land. Evidence is clear that there was an agreement between the City Council and the prior landowner, by which the local business zoning classification would be granted if a restrictive covenant was executed, limiting the business uses permitted on the land. The cases cited support the conclusion that, under these circumstances, the restrictive covenant is void. In addition, although the exact problem presented by this case seems never to have been decided in Illinois, a somewhat similar case has established the rule that "zoning ordinances should not be subject to bargaining or contract." (*Hedrich v. Village of Niles*, 112 Ill.App.2d 68, 77 (1969).) It was there noted that when zoning is conditioned upon collateral agreements or other incentives supplied by a property owner, the zoning officials are placed "in the questionable position of bartering their legislative discretion for emoluments that had no bearing on the requested amendment." (*Hedrich, supra*, at p. 78.) This reasoning is clearly applicable to the instant case. There is no indication in the record that the rezoning was necessary or that it was granted only after a consideration of the appropriate use of the land within the total zoning scheme of the community.

None of the cases cited to us, and none we have found, have, however, resolved the specific question of whether or not, in this case, the zoning ordinance involved is valid. It is to be noted that in *Hartnett v. Austin, supra*, and *Baylis v. City of Baltimore, supra*, the zoning ordinance itself contained the restriction to which the property would be subject. Those cases are thus distinguishable from the instant one and from *Houston Petroleum Co. v. Automotive Prod. C. Assn., supra*, where the ordinances were absolute on their face, making no reference to restrictions. Even in *Houston Petroleum Co.*, where the underlying ordinance was apparently not disturbed when the restrictive agreement was declared void, the court does not supply a rationale for its decision. It is basic that the zoning power of local authorities is derived from the statutes. (*See Park Ridge Fuel Co. v. Park Ridge*, 335 Ill. 509, 516 (1929).) The grant of zoning power is found in Ill. Rev. Stat. 1969, ch. 24, sec. 11-13-1 et seq. Nowhere is there set forth a power by which local authorities may enter into restrictive covenants as found in this case. The entire context of Division 13 of chapter 24, section 11, demonstrates that the zoning power must be exercised through the ordinances of the local authority, and section 11-13-1 indicates that the power may be used only for the promotion of the public health, safety, comfort, morals, and welfare.

We hold the ordinance here in question, void. The ordinance was adopted only because of the limitations contained in the restrictive covenant. The record discloses that the City gave no consideration to the statutory standards of public health, safety, comfort, morals and welfare. The effect of the enactment taken together with the covenant, was to create a classification not set forth in the general zoning ordinances.

We therefore affirm the trial court's decision to void the restrictive covenant, but reverse that part of its decision which found the rezoning ordinance valid. Affirm in part; reverse in part and remand with directions.

[b] Note on Contract Zoning

Contract zoning could have been an issue with the Fox Valley Auto Care Center. The City of Aurora already had zoned the larger Fox Valley development so that Metropolitan could carry out its plan for both the Westfield Fox Valley Shopping Center mall and the surrounding developments. However, the Johnson tract had not been annexed by the City of Aurora and therefore was not in the city. One of the bargaining issues between Regent and the Johnsons was whether the Johnson tract would be annexed into the city so that it could become part of the overall zoning district for the larger Fox Valley development. The Johnsons did not want their land annexed as long as they owned it, and Regent insisted that it be annexed if Regent were going to buy it. We will unfold the story more after you consider materials on both conditional zoning and annexation agreements.

[2] Conditional Zoning

Similar to the issue of contract zoning is the issue of conditional zoning. Conditional zoning involves the rezoning of land that is conditioned on the landowner performing certain acts or abstaining from certain acts. Contract zoning is generally held invalid, while conditional zoning is usually valid. However, as you will see in the following principal case, *Nolan v. The City of Taylorsville*, this is not always true. In order for conditional rezoning to be valid, it must be in accordance with a comprehensive plan (consistent with the municipality's overall zoning scheme) and it must be general (applying to parcels similarly zoned) rather than specific (applying only to the parcel under consideration).

In *Sylvania Electric Products Inc. v. City of Newton*, 183 N.E.2d 118, 122 (Mass. 1962), the court allowed conditional rezoning and gave the following explanation:

> The induced, voluntary action of Sylvania [the landowner], not the vote of the council, imposed the option restrictions; the vote reclassified land which was being subjected to those restrictions. The zoning decision was that the locus, so restricted by its owner, should be made a limited manufacturing district. That, in form, was an appropriate and untainted exercise of the zoning power.

The Massachusetts court focused on the fact that the zoning authority will only rezone after the landowner takes steps to mitigate any potential harm to the surrounding landowners.

[a] The Fine Line Between Invalid Contract Zoning and Valid Conditional Zoning

NOLAN v. CITY OF TAYLORVILLE

95 Ill. App. 3d 1099, 420 N.E.2d 1037 (Ill. App. Ct. 5th Dist. 1981)

This action was brought by neighboring landowners against the City of Taylorville to have two city ordinances invalidated. One rezoned a tract of land from single-family residential to multiple-family residential use, and the other granted a special use on the tract to build a 134-unit apartment building for the elderly and handicapped. The owners of the tract of land and the developer of the high-rise were allowed to intervene as defendants. In a bench trial the court ruled that both ordinances were invalid because they were conditional or contract zoning and were unrelated to the welfare of the community as a whole. The defendants appeal.

The defendants assert that the trial court improperly placed the burden of proof upon them to uphold the validity of the ordinances in question. They also assert that the findings that the ordinances were conditional or contract zoning and arbitrary and capricious were against the manifest weight of the evidence.

The land involved in this case is a tract of approximately two acres known as the Bland tract. It is within the city limits of Taylorville, Illinois, surrounded on all sides by properties which are zoned "R-1," single-family residential use. The "R-1" classification had, until 1980, allowed for the construction of churches and schools without the need for special permission. It had in addition allowed for certain businesses to be operated from a home upon the granting of a special use permit. The properties abutting the Bland tract include a church, three schools, and a number of single-family dwellings, most of which are one or one and a half stories tall. One of the homes, owned by one of the defendants, has a special use permit to allow the owner to operate a real estate brokerage on the premises.

On October 25, 1979, three owners of the Bland tract, William E. Bland, Thomas Bland, and Patricia Jenkins, requested the Taylorville City Council to rezone the tract from R-1 to R-2, multiple-family residential use, in order that a 126-unit apartment building for the elderly and handicapped could be built upon it. The Taylorville City Council held a joint public hearing on the proposal with the Taylorville Planning Commission on November 19, 1979. At the end of the hearing the planning commission voted three to two against the rezoning proposal. The city council, however, passed Ordinance 1942 rezoning the tract from R-1 to R-2 by a vote of seven to one.

The R-2 classification only allows multiple-family units to a maximum of eight families without a special use permit. Also, the general zoning ordinance of the city of Taylorville, Ordinance 1793, has a height limit of 50 feet for any building without prior approval of the planning commission and city council. The owners, therefore, applied for a special use permit to build a 134-unit, six-story high-rise apartment building to house elderly and handicapped people. On January 7, 1980, another public hearing was held jointly by the city council and the planning commission. The commission voted three to two against the special use permit, but the city council passed Ordinance 1947 granting the special use by a vote of seven to one.

The ordinance limited the permitted use to elderly and handicapped tenants because of the limited parking proposed, and it included eight conditions to be performed by the owners and developer of the tract. These were extensive and included widening Cherokee Street, extending sidewalks to a nearby shopping center beyond the end of the property, adding a loop to the water system, and improving storm and sanitary sewer facilities for the area. . . .

On December 7, 1979, a number of owners of property near to or abutting the Bland tract filed a complaint for declaratory judgment against the city of Taylorville, seeking to have Ordinances No. 1942 and 1947 declared invalid. The owners of the Bland tract and the developer of the project were allowed to intervene as defendants and after amendments to the pleadings a two-day bench trial was held. The trial court required written briefs from the parties following the testimony. On April 29, 1980, the trial court held both ordinances invalid as conditional or contract zoning and arbitrary, capricious, and unrelated to the general welfare of the community. The defendants filed a motion for a rehearing. A rehearing was held on June 9, 1980, but the judge did not set aside the order of April 29 as urged by the defendants. On July 8, 1980, the defendants appealed the failure to set aside the order invalidating the ordinances.

In his rulings on petition for declaratory judgment, Judge Slater stated that he was considering Ordinances 1942 and 1947 as a unit "since it appears from the evidence that both ordinances were passed for the purpose of allowing a multiple family residence of 134 units to be built on the premises involved." Defendants challenge that position and assert that each ordinance must be considered separately. Ordinance No. 1942 does not mention the 134-unit elderly and handicapped project, but merely rezones the tract from single-family to multi-family use. The defendants maintain that even if the special use ordinance is invalidated, No. 1942 should survive on its own.

The initial request for rezoning from the owners of the Bland tract made clear the intended housing project use. The testimony at the public hearing on Ordinance No. 1942 went to the proposed project and not to any other multi-family uses, such as low-rise apartments without age or handicap limitations. The Taylorville City Council passed the rezoning ordinance in order to take the first step toward allowing the elderly and handicapped project. The Illinois Supreme Court dealt with a similar question thus:

> "In our opinion, it is appropriate for the court to avoid . . . difficulties by framing its decree with reference to the record before it, and particularly with reference to the evidence offered at the trial. In most of the cases that have come before us in recent years, a specific use was contemplated and the record was shaped in terms of that use." *Sinclair Pipe Line Co. v. Village of Richton Park* (1960), 19 Ill. 2d 370, 379, 167 N.E.2d 406, 411. . . .

Under the circumstances of the case before us it was appropriate for the court to consider the rezoning ordinance and the special use ordinance as a unit in determining their validity.

Zoning ordinances are presumptively valid, and the presumption may only be overcome by clear and convincing evidence. The burden of proof is on the plaintiff. (*LaSalle National Bank v. County of Cook* (1957), 12 Ill. 2d 40, 46, 145 N.E.2d 65, 69.) Conditional zoning ordinances, however, are suspect and subject to special scrutiny. Courts have been concerned that municipalities not surrender their governmental authority to determine sound land use, or improperly try to control the use of land. Conditional zoning can also furnish an avenue for corruption of officials. But conditional rezoning is not invalid per se in Illinois. (*Goffinet v. County of Christian* (1976), 65 Ill. 2d 40, 51, 357 N.E.2d 442, 448.) [For a discussion of *Goffinet* see the note following this case. — Eds.] The conditions in the rezoning ordinance in the *Goffinet* case were general and related to satisfying existing statutes and regulations of environmental protective agencies. The court in *Goffinet* distinguished those conditions from the very specific ones in *Andres v. Village of Flossmoor* (1973), 15 Ill. App. 3d 655, 304 N.E.2d 700. The supreme court said:

> "The *Andres* case was clearly a demonstration of improper conditional rezoning. The conditions placed in the rezoning ordinance introduced elements of contract, which have no place in the legislative process, and showed an abuse of zoning authority." (*Goffinet v. County of Christian* (1976), 65 Ill. 2d 40, 50–51, 357 N.E.2d 442, 447.)
>
> At the appellate level in the *Goffinet* case, this court said:
>
> "Some conditional rezoning may be in the public good, subservient to a comprehensive plan, in the best interest of the public health, safety and welfare and enacted in recognition of changing circumstances." (*Goffinet v. County of Christian* (1975), 30 Ill. App. 3d 1089, 1095, 333 N.E.2d 731, 736.)

We were looking at a situation in that case which indicated no detriment to surrounding landowners, no decrease in property values or danger to health or safety of children or adults. Balanced against that was an unquestionable benefit to the entire region by the granting of the special use with conditions attached.

Unlike *Goffinet*, the case before the court involves admitted detriment to the surrounding homeowners and residents of the neighborhood. The question then becomes: is there a reasonable basis of public welfare which requires the change with its resulting loss to the neighbors? (*LaSalle National Bank of Chicago v. County of Cook* (1957), 12 Ill. 2d 40, 47–48, 145 N.E.2d 65, 69.) The LaSalle case sets out six factors to be taken into consideration in determining the validity of a zoning ordinance. No one factor is controlling.

The trial court in the case at bar considered each of the six factors in ruling on the petition for declaratory judgment:

> (a) The existing uses and zoning of nearby property; (b) The extent to which property values are diminished by the particular zoning ordinance; (c) The extent to which the diminished property values promote the health, safety, morals or general welfare of the public; (d) The relative gain to the public as compared to the hardship imposed on the individual property owners; (e) The suitability of the subject property for the zoned purposes; and (f) The length of time the property has been vacant as zoned considered in the context of land development in the area in the vicinity of the subject property. *LaSalle National Bank of Chicago v. County of Cook* (1957), 12 Ill. 2d 40, 46–47, 145 N.E.2d 65, 69.

Under (a) the court took note of the fact that all of the immediately adjacent property was zoned R-1 and was used for single-family residences, schools, and a church. A substantial portion of the nearby area was also single-family residential, with R-2 and business zoning to the west by the shopping center. Under (b) the court noted the testimony that the surrounding dwellings would be diminished in value by the construction of the proposed building. Under (c) the court acknowledged the testimony of projected increased taxes and Federal Government rent subsidy payments as a result of the building, but pointed out the testimony regarding the pending construction of units of housing for elderly and handicapped people elsewhere in the county, including the city of Taylorville. Under (d) the court indicated concern for the threat to the safety of the school children in the area caused by the logical increase in traffic caused by such a dense population increase. Traffic congestion, loss of privacy by the sheer height of the building, and the aesthetic loss of homogeneity of the neighborhood were hardships acknowledged. Under (e) the court questioned the suitability of the tract for the housing project. The court felt the property was more suitable for single-family dwellings, as originally provided before the zoning change. The court found that the fact that the owners would stand to make more money from the land if it were used for the high-rise was not sufficient reason in itself to change the zoning. Under (f) the court took note of the fact that the properties nearby, especially north of the tract, had sold for single-family dwellings with no problem. Also, the evidence indicated the owner of the tract had not made any active attempt to sell the property.

The court found the ordinances arbitrary and capricious and unrelated to the general welfare of the community for the reasons above.

> "The law does not require that the subject property be totally unsuitable for the purpose classified but it is sufficient that a substantial decrease in value results from a classification bearing no substantial relation to the public welfare." *LaSalle National Bank v. County of Cook* (1957), 12 Ill. 2d 40, 48, 145 N.E.2d 65, 69–70.

The conditional zoning cases, notably *Goffinet*, talk of uniqueness of location of property for a particular use and overriding public benefit to be derived by allowing the rezoning subject to conditions. The evidence in the instant case did not establish a shortage of areas already zoned R-2 in Taylorville and large enough not to need a size variance. On the contrary, four such areas which met the developer's criteria existed, presumably not totally surrounded by single-family single-story structures. The court found that "there is no evidence presented that the zoning as set forth herein unquestionably serves the public health, safety and welfare."

"Where the testimony before the lower court in a bench trial, as here, is contradictory, the weight to be given testimony is a matter for the trial court, and the court's judgment will not be disturbed unless manifestly against the weight of the evidence." *Smith v. County Board* (1980), 86 Ill. App. 3d 708, 716, 408 N.E.2d 452, 460.

We believe the findings and judgment of the trial court are supported by the evidence and should be affirmed.

Judgment affirmed.

[b] Note on Conditional Zoning

Imagine how Regent and the Johnsons could structure their deal so that annexation and zoning by the City of Aurora are part of it. Then you need to add in the involvement of the City of Aurora which, as the municipality, likely will want to have jurisdiction over the entire Fox Valley development, both to control how the development is done and to get the tax revenues from the new retail uses.

[3] Distinguishing Between Contract and Conditional Zoning: *Goffinet v. County of Christian*

One of the casebook authors sometimes answers questions from students with a blank look and the statement "It depends." Unfortunately for Illinois real estate lawyers that is the answer to the question "How do you distinguish between contract and conditional zoning?" Certainly one could argue that the City of Rockford's attorney reasonably thought the zoning of the three lots was conditional zoning, rather than contract zoning, and that Roy Hunt (the zoning official) made an informed and correct decision in ordering Mr. Cederberg to stop construction on his laundry center. Perhaps with a little more difficulty, one could argue the City of Taylorville's position. What is interesting is that the City of Taylorville seemed to come a lot closer to winning than did the City of Rockford. Why do you think that was the case?

The answer may be that courts have a difficult time distinguishing contract and conditional zoning, and that the factual circumstances may well be determinative. The "deal" for the limitations on use in *Cederberg* smacks of a "behind closed doors" special deal (three residential lots), whereas the deal in *Nolan* was made in a much more public manner and had a more public impact; Mr. Cederberg's predecessor was going to build offices whereas in *Nolan* the owners were going to build a 134-unit apartment building for the elderly and the handicapped. The *Nolan* court also cites extensively to an Illinois Supreme Court case in which the court allowed conditional zoning, *Goffinet v. County of Christian*, 30 Ill. App. 3d 1089, 333 N.E.2d 731 (1975). In *Goffinet*, a rural county rezoned a large parcel of land from agriculture to heavy industry to allow the construction of a synthetic fuels plant. The condition was that if the plant were ever closed that the zoning would automatically revert to agricultural.

This sheds some light on why *Cederberg* was an easy case and yet *Nolan* was not. It seems to depend on how much public benefit there is from the deal. There was little or no public benefit in *Cederberg*, some to, arguably, quite a bit in *Nolan*, and the Illinois Supreme Court thought a lot in *Goffinet*. It would seem, therefore, that for a project as small as the Fox Valley Auto Care Center, with little or no direct public benefit, Donna Smith and Sam Nader should be concerned that any agreement with the City of Aurora might be cast as contract zoning. There was an additional factor for Donna and Sam to consider, however: the project site was going to be the subject of an annexation agreement between Regent and the City of Aurora.

§ 7.04 SUBDIVISION REGULATIONS

[1] Regulation of Divisions of Land

As we have noted, Regent was both a buyer and a seller of land as it assembled the land necessary for the Fox Valley Auto Care Center. Regent bought land from both the Johnsons and Metropolitan and then sold land to both Metropolitan and Turtle Wax. In order to effect the two sales of land, Regent had to divide the Johnson parcel into two parcels, selling one to Metropolitan and selling the other to Turtle Wax, and Regent had to divide the land it acquired from Metropolitan into two parcels, selling one to Turtle Wax and retaining the other for the Fox

Valley Auto Care Center. Such a division of land may trigger a state's subdivision map act requirements under which the "subdivider" must file a "subdivision map" with, and gain approval from, the municipal government with jurisdiction over the land.

Although the Zoning Code is comprehensive in its description of how land can be used, the zoning process does not easily deal with the organization and structure of how multiple lots interrelate to public infrastructure and, once lots are created, how those lots become part of the public record so they can be transferred. The Subdivision Regulations are the civil engineer's Bible, but because the Subdivision Regulations also deal with how land can be used they are part of the attorney's zoning analysis.

Below is set forth the relevant section of Illinois subdivision law. Other states' laws will vary, but the Illinois statute is fairly typical. In addition, we have included another Illinois statute, one that requires the platting of land when it is annexed to or "disconnected" from a municipality. You may already have noted that part of the over all transaction was to have the Johnsons' land annexed into the City of Aurora. As you will soon see, annexation also plays into determining what Regent will have to do.

[2] Illinois Subdivision Law

Following are two sections of Chapter 109 of the Illinois Revised Code known as the Plat Act. As you read them consider the following questions:

1. Did any of the conveyances violate the Illinois Plat Act? Do you need additional information to answer this question?
2. Would you have recommended to Regent that it should have sought a subdivision of the land?

Illinois Compiled Statutes

765 Illinois Compiled Statutes 205/1. Subdivision of land into parts of less than five acres; topographic studies; survey; plat; monuments

(a) Except as otherwise provided in subparagraph (b) of this Section whenever the owner of land subdivides it into 2 or more parts, any of which is less than 5 acres, he must have it surveyed and a subdivision plat thereof made by an Illinois Registered Land Surveyor, which plat must particularly describe and set forth all public streets, alleys, ways for public service facilities, ways for utility services and community antenna television systems, parks, playgrounds, school grounds or other public grounds, and all the tracts, parcels, lots or blocks, and numbering all such lots, blocks or parcels by progressive numbers, giving their precise dimensions. There shall be submitted simultaneously with the subdivision plat, a study or studies which shall show topographically and by profile the elevation of the land prior to the commencement of any change in elevations as a part of any phase of subdividing, and additionally, if it is contemplated that such elevations, or the flow of surface water from such land, will be changed as a result of any portion of such subdivision development, then such study or studies shall also show such proposed changes in the elevations and the flow of surface water from such land. The topographical and profile studies required hereunder may be prepared as a subsidiary study or studies separate from, but of the same scale and size as the subdivision plat, and shall be prepared in such a manner as will permit the topographical study or studies to be used as overlays to the subdivision plat. The plat must show all angular and linear data along the exterior boundaries of the tract of land divided or subdivided, the names of all public streets and the width, course and extent of all public streets, alleys and ways for public service facilities. References must also be made upon the plat to known and permanent monuments from which future survey may be made and the surveyor must, at the time of making his survey, set in such manner that they will not be moved by frost, good and sufficient monuments marking the external boundaries of the tract to be divided or subdivided and must designate upon the plat the points where they may be found. These monuments must be placed at all corners, at each end of all curves, at the point where a curve changes its radius, at all angle points in any line and at all angle points along a meander line, the points to be not less than 20 feet back from the normal water elevation of a lake or from the bank of a stream, except that when such corners or points fall within a street, or proposed future street, the monuments must be placed in the right of way line of the street. All internal boundaries, corners and points must be monumented in the field by like monuments as defined above. These monuments 2 of which must be of stone or reinforced concrete and must be set at the opposite extremities of the property platted, placed at all block corners, at each end of all curves, at the points where a curve changes its radius, and at all angle points in any line. All lots must be monumented in the field with 2 or more monuments.

The monuments must be furnished by the person for whom the survey is made and must be such that they will not be moved by frost. If any city, village or town has adopted an official plan, or part thereof, in the manner prescribed by law, the plat of land situated within the area affected thereby must conform to the official plan, or part thereof.

(b) Except as provided in subsection (c) of this Section, the provisions of this Act do not apply and no subdivision plat is required in any of the following instances:

1. The division or subdivision of land into parcels or tracts of 5 acres or more in size which does not involve any new streets or easements of access;
2. The division of lots or blocks of less than 1 acre in any recorded subdivision which does not involve any new streets or easements of access;
3. The sale or exchange of parcels of land between owners of adjoining and contiguous land;
4. The conveyance of parcels of land or interests therein for use as a right of way for railroads or other public utility facilities and other pipe lines which does not involve any new streets or easements of access;
5. The conveyance of land owned by a railroad or other public utility which does not involve any new streets or easements of access;
6. The conveyance of land for highway or other public purposes or grants or conveyances relating to the dedication of land for public use or instruments relating to the vacation of land impressed with a public use;
7. Conveyances made to correct descriptions in prior conveyances;
8. The sale or exchange of parcels or tracts of land following the division into no more than 2 parts of a particular parcel or tract of land existing on July

17, 1959 and not involving any new streets or easements of access;

9. The sale of a single lot of less than 5 acres from a larger tract when a survey is made by an Illinois Registered Land Surveyor; provided, that this exemption shall not apply to the sale of any subsequent lots from the same larger tract of land, as determined by the dimensions and configuration of the larger tract on October 1, 1973, and provided also that this exemption does not invalidate any local requirements applicable to the subdivision of land;

10. The preparation of a plat for wind energy devices under Section 10-620 of the Property Tax Code.

Nothing contained within the provisions of this Act shall prevent or preclude individual counties from establishing standards, ordinances, or specifications which reduce the acreage minimum to less than 5 acres, but not less than 2 acres, or supplementing the requirements contained herein when a survey is made by an Illinois Registered Land Surveyor and a plat thereof is recorded, under powers granted to them.

(c) However, if a plat is made by an Illinois Registered Surveyor of any parcel or tract of land otherwise exempt from the plat provisions of this Act pursuant to subsection (b) of this Section, such plat shall be recorded. It shall not be the responsibility of a recorder of deeds to determine whether the plat has been made or recorded under this subsection (c) prior to accepting a deed for recording.

765 Illinois Compiled Statutes 205/1.02. Area annexed to, or disconnected from, municipality; filing and preparation of plats

When any city, village, municipal corporation or political subdivision in the State annexes or disconnects territory, a plat of the land included in the disconnection or annexation must be filed with the recorder in the county or counties where the territory is located. In counties where the county clerk is not also the county recorder, a copy of the plat shall also be filed with the county clerk. Each plat shall state a legal description or descriptions sufficient to identify the boundaries of the annexed or disconnected territory, by reference to government surveys or by metes and bounds, including the section, township and range in which the territory is located. Such a plat must be prepared by a Registered Land Surveyor or in the case of cities, villages and incorporated towns by a Registered Land Surveyor or a duly employed municipal engineer registered under the laws of the State of Illinois, provided such engineer has had training in the field of civil engineering.

[3] Questions About Subdivision Requirements

1. Did the conveyances contemplated for the Project require a subdivision of the land?

2. Did all of the contemplated conveyances fall within the exemptions in § 1(b)?

3. What happens if a landowner such as Regent does not comply with the Act?

§ 7.05 ANNEXATION OF THE JOHNSON TRACT

[1] Annexation and the Developer

Although we include annexation in the zoning section, it really is not a zoning issue, but it is part of the zoning analysis. Knowing the location of the property is mandatory in order to undertake a zoning analysis. Regent may have been unaware that the Johnson parcel was in the township. Even if David Delaney did know, he likely was not familiar with the process or the timing of the needed annexation. Donna and Sam had to be aware of the need to annex the Johnson parcel in order for Regent to be able to develop the Fox Valley Auto Care Center.

Annexation may become an issue for a developer planning a new development in one of two situations. In one situation, the parcel under consideration is located in two different jurisdictions, one incorporated and the other unincorporated. In the second situation, the parcel is in an unincorporated jurisdiction which is adjacent to one or more incorporated jurisdictions. An example of an "incorporated" jurisdiction is a city, town, or village to which the state has delegated the power to zone. An example of an "unincorporated" jurisdiction is an area in a county or township over which the county or township has general jurisdiction but which is not in a city, town, or village. If the parcel is in two different jurisdictions, it likely will be easier to gain approval for development, and to obtain municipal services for the finished development, if the portion of the parcel in the unincorporated area is annexed into the incorporated jurisdiction. If the parcel is in an unincorporated jurisdiction, there may be significantly different services (police, fire, schools, etc.) available in the incorporated jurisdiction, or zoning in the incorporated jurisdiction may be more conducive to the planned development than in the unincorporated jurisdiction. In either case, the developer may consider having the land annexed into the incorporated jurisdiction as one option in obtaining approval for the development.

If the incorporated jurisdiction which is annexing the parcel has statutory authority to zone the land at the time of annexation, zoning can be included as part of the annexation ordinance. Zoning can be a proper condition and circumstance of annexation. If, however, the annexing jurisdiction does not have the power to include zoning as part of the annexation ordinance, or if the developer has not decided which zone would be best for the planned development, the developer and the annexing jurisdiction may want to enter into an annexation agreement which includes their ongoing agreement about zoning and other issues.

Under Illinois law, annexation agreements may include the amending or continuing in effect on the part of the annexing jurisdiction of the zoning status of the area to be annexed. In addition, the annexation agreement can also limit increases in fees that the annexing jurisdiction can charge, establish the developer's contributions of land or money to the annexing jurisdiction, allow for the annexing jurisdiction to grant abatement of property taxes, and provide for the granting of utility franchises for the parcel. One Illinois court of appeal has held that the annexation agreement therefore can allow for the construction of public improvements, the conveyance of land by the developer to the annexing jurisdiction, and the developer's payment of funds to school districts. Finally, successor landowners and municipalities are bound by the annexation agreement.

[2] Interpretation of Annexation Agreements

The following principal case should be read together with the Illinois statutes following it and the "Annexation Agreement for Fox Valley Auto Mall," which is in the Document Book.

[a] *Village of Lisle v. Action Outdoor Advertising Company*

VILLAGE OF LISLE v. ACTION OUTDOOR ADVERTISING COMPANY

188 Ill. App. 3d 751, 544 N.E.2d 836 (Ill. App. 2d Dist. 1989)

Plaintiff, Village of Lisle (Village), brought this action against defendants, Action Outdoor Advertising Company, Chester H. Smith, Judith M. Smith, and Michael St. Onge, seeking to enjoin defendants from constructing an outdoor advertising sign on the Smiths' property. The Village's action was based upon an "Annexation Agreement" between the Village and the Smiths providing for the future annexation of the Smiths' property by the Village. After the Village's motion for a temporary restraining order and petition for preliminary injunction were denied, the parties filed cross-motions for summary judgment. The trial court denied the Village's motion for summary judgment and granted defendants' motion for summary judgment. The Village now appeals from the trial court's order granting summary judgment in favor of defendants. We affirm.

The Village is an Illinois municipal corporation located in Du Page County. Defendants Chester and Judith Smith are the owners and holders in joint tenancy of property located at 25 W. 241 and 25 W. 253 Ogden Avenue, in unincorporated Du Page County. The Smiths' property is not contiguous to the Village and is located approximately 648 feet from the Village's corporate limits.

In late 1985 or early 1986, the Smiths obtained approval from Du Page County to have a parcel of the subject property rezoned as a community business district. At that time, the Smiths were asked if they were interested in tapping into the Village sewer system. The Smiths subsequently contacted the Village and expressed their interest in doing so. At the same time, the Smiths agreed to enter into a preannexation agreement. The Smiths subsequently filed a petition for annexation with the Village requesting annexation of their property.

On February 16, 1987, the Village and the Smiths entered into an annexation agreement which provided for the future annexation and zoning of the Smiths' property when the property becomes contiguous to the Village. The agreement was signed by the Village president and the Smiths and was attested to by the Village clerk. Paragraph 2 of the annexation agreement provided that the Smiths would install, or otherwise construct all landscaping, parking areas, lighting, signage, utilities, structures, or improvements of any kind upon the property in accordance with plans appended to the annexation agreement and determined to have been in accordance with the Village's code. The agreement further referred to the Smiths' petition for annexation and provided that the Smiths would not seek annexation by any other municipality and would object to any other municipality's attempt to annex their property. The Village subsequently passed and approved a resolution authorizing the execution of the annexation agreement.

On October 2, 1987, the Smiths entered into a lease with defendant, Action Outdoor Advertising Company (Action), allowing Action to erect and maintain an outdoor advertising display on the Smiths' property. Action subsequently obtained a building and use permit from Du Page County for the construction of a 14-foot by 48-foot double-faced sign.

On January 13, 1988, Action began construction of the outdoor sign on the Smiths' property. Agents of the Village became aware of the construction and immediately served Action with a stop-work order instructing Action to cease and desist from constructing and installing the outdoor sign at that location. Action refused to comply with the stop-work order.

On January 14, 1988, the Village filed the instant action for injunctive and other relief against the Smiths, Action, and Action's president, Michael St. Onge. The Village's complaint alleged that construction of the sign on the Smiths' property was in violation of the annexation agreement executed between the Smiths and the Village. The Village's complaint further alleged that the construction of the sign at that location frustrated and interfered with the aesthetic and safety goals of the Village and violated the terms of the annexation agreement. The Village sought a preliminary and permanent injunction, damages for breach of contract, and, as against Action and St. Onge, an award of punitive damages. Contemporaneously with filing its complaint for injunctive and other relief, the Village filed an emergency motion for a temporary restraining order. The Village's motion alleged that the continued construction and installation of the outdoor sign would cause the Village immediate and irreparable injury. The trial court denied the temporary restraining order after a hearing and continued the cause for further proceedings.

On January 27, 1988, the trial court held a hearing on the Village's motion for entry of a preliminary injunction. At that hearing, the Village dismissed Michael St. Onge as a party defendant. The trial court subsequently entered an order providing for further briefing by the parties and continuing the cause for further proceedings. On February 4, 1988, the trial court entered an order denying the Village's motion for a preliminary injunction and setting the cause for trial.

The parties subsequently filed cross-motions for summary judgment. On July 21, 1988, the trial court held a hearing on the motions at which time it continued the cause to August 31, 1988, for status and a ruling.

On August 31, 1988, the trial court entered an opinion and order ruling on the cross-motions for summary judgment. In that opinion, the trial court defined the issues as (1) whether the annexation agreement under present circumstances was valid and enforceable; (2) whether the sign restriction provision of the annexation agreement was valid and enforceable; and (3) whether the Village was entitled to injunctive relief. The trial court concluded that the annexation agreement was valid but unenforceable on the basis that the Smiths' property was not contiguous to the Village's boundaries and contiguity was a contingency of the annexation agreement's enforceability. As an alternative basis for ruling in defendants' favor, the court concluded that section 7 of the Highway Advertising Control Act of 1971 (Ill. Rev. Stat. 1987, ch.121, par. 507) precluded the Village from prohibiting the sign's construction. The court noted that the Village could impose regulations on a sign's size, lighting, and spacing, but concluded that the Village was not entitled to injunctive relief because it failed to establish that the outdoor sign violated any size, lighting, or spacing restrictions. Accordingly, the trial court denied the

Village's motion for summary judgment and granted summary judgment in favor of defendants. The Village then brought this timely appeal. . . .

The Village contends that the trial court erred in holding the annexation agreement unenforceable. The Village argues that the annexation agreement is valid and therefore enforceable on its terms absent a good defense. We disagree.

Section 11-15.1-1 of the Illinois Municipal Code (Code) (Ill. Rev. Stat.1987, ch. 24, par. 11-15.1-1) provides the statutory authority for corporate authorities to enter into annexation agreements. Pursuant to section 11-15.1-1, "[t]he corporate authorities of any municipality may enter into an agreement with one or more of the owners of record of land in any territory *which may be annexed to such municipality as provided in Article 7.*" (Emphasis added.) (Ill. Rev. Stat. 1987, ch. 24, par. 11-15.1-1.) Section 7-1-1 of the Code defines "territory which may be annexed" as "[a]ny territory which is not within the corporate limits of any municipality *but which is contiguous to a municipality.*" (Emphasis added.) Ill. Rev. Stat. 1987, ch. 24, par. 7-1-1.

In the instant action, the Smiths' property is not contiguous to the Village and therefore could not be annexed pursuant to article 7 of the Code. (*See* Ill. Rev. Stat. 1987, ch. 24, par. 7-1-1; *People ex rel. City of North Chicago v. City of Waukegan* (1983), 116 Ill. App. 3d 88, 93.) Since section 11-15.1-1 of the Code (Ill. Rev. Stat. 1987, ch. 24, par. 11-15.1-1) only authorizes municipalities to enter into annexation agreements for property "which may be annexed to such municipality as provided in Article 7," only an agreement regarding contiguous property would be valid.

In addition, the validity of an annexation agreement that purports to allow a municipal authority to exercise its police powers over a noncontiguous tract of property fails when examined in light of the purpose behind the contiguity requirement. The fundamental notion of a municipal corporation is that of unity and continuity, not separated or segregated areas. (*People ex rel. Village of South Barrington v. Village of Hoffman Estates* (1964), 30 Ill. 2d 385, 387.) This necessity for unity of purpose and facilities forms the very basis for the requirement of contiguity. (30 Ill. 2d at 387.) The purpose of the contiguity requirement is to permit the natural and gradual extension of municipal boundaries to areas which adjoin one another in a reasonably substantial physical sense. (*People ex rel. County of St. Clair v. City of Belleville* (1981), 84 Ill. 2d 1, 12; *People ex rel. Village of Long Grove v. Village of Buffalo Grove* (1987), 160 Ill. App. 3d 455, 462.) In that way, delivery of services is more convenient for the city and more efficient for its citizens. *City of Belleville*, 84 Ill. 2d at 12.

Similarly, the statutory authorization of preannexation agreements serves to further important governmental purposes, such as the encouragement of expanding urban areas and to do so uniformly, economically, efficiently, and fairly with optimum provisions made for the establishment of land use controls and necessary municipal improvements, including streets, water, sewer systems, schools, parks, and similar installations. (*Village of Orland Park v. First Federal Savings & Loan Association* (1985), 135 Ill. App. 3d 520, 526.) This approach also discourages fragmentation and the proliferation of special districts. 135 Ill. App. 3d at 526.

By allowing the Village in the instant action to enforce its ordinances on a property owner through an annexation agreement where it could not do so through actual annexation would permit the Village to do indirectly what it is prohibited by statute from doing directly. In other words, while the Village cannot annex the Smiths' property because it is not contiguous to the Village, it nonetheless seeks to exercise the same control under an annexation agreement which contemplates future contiguity. It is axiomatic that a party cannot circumvent the purpose of a statute by doing indirectly what it cannot do directly. (*In re Petition of the Village of Kildeer to Annex Certain Territory* (1988), 124 Ill. 2d 533, 547.) Accordingly, we hold that the annexation agreement in the instant action is invalid and unenforceable as the property which is subject to the agreement is not contiguous to the Village and, as such, is not a proper object of annexation. . . .

The Village nonetheless asserts that section 7-1-8 of the Code authorizes corporate authorities to enter into annexation agreements for noncontiguous property. Section 7-1-8 of the Code provides that territory not within the corporate limits of a municipality "but which is contiguous to a municipality *at the time of annexation*" may be annexed to the municipality. (Emphasis added.) (Ill. Rev. Stat. 1987, ch. 24, par. 7-1-8.) The Village argues that the language "contiguous . . . at the time of annexation" implies that a municipality may enter into annexation agreements for noncontiguous property. The Village concludes that, since agreements to annex noncontiguous property are valid pursuant to section 7-1-8, the terms of such agreements are enforceable regardless of whether the property is contiguous at the time of enforcement. In other words, contiguity is not a condition precedent to enforcement of an annexation agreement. Although the Village concedes that such a rule could result in extraterritorial grants of power, the Village asserts that the Code's provisions "in and of themselves specifically grant extraterritorial power over property contemplated for annexation." We disagree.

We note that the underlying basis for the Village's argument that section 7-1-8 authorizes parties to enter into annexation agreements for noncontiguous property is faulty and inapplicable to the instant action. The language "contiguous . . . at the time of annexation" was added to section 7-1-8 after our supreme court decided *People ex rel. County of St. Clair v. City of Belleville* (1981), 84 Ill. 2d 1. In *City of Belleville*, the city sought to annex three adjacent tracts of property, only one of which was contiguous to the city. (84 Ill. 2d at 4–5.) The court invalidated the ordinances purporting to annex the two noncontiguous tracts, stating:

> "We realize that this construction requires a municipality desirous of annexing several parcels, only one of which is contiguous to the municipality, to annex each parcel at separate times. In some situations this requirement may appear cumbersome. We can only conclude that the General Assembly has imposed this limitation to prevent a municipality from conducting a wholesale annexation of successive parcels of property where each parcel, other than the first, is not contiguous to, and is more remote from, the original corporate limits." *City of Belleville*, 84 Ill. 2d at 11.

After the opinion in *City of Belleville* was filed, the legislature adopted Public Act 82-211, which added the words "at the time of annexation" in the first sentence of section 7-1-8 and also added section 7-1-48 to the Code. (*See* Pub. Act 82-211, eff. Aug. 14, 1981.) Section 7-1-48 authorizes the annexation of multiple parcels of property in a single annexation proceeding; however, that section further provides that an annexation of property which does not comply with the section 7 requirements would not invalidate annexation of the "remainder of the annexed territory, *unless the exclusion or disconnection of the non-complying area would destroy the contiguity of the remaining territory.*" (Emphasis added.) (Ill. Rev. Stat. 1987, ch. 24, par. 7-1-48(b).) In other words, section 7-1-48 authorizes the annexation of multiple parcels in a single annexation proceeding as long as at least one parcel is contiguous to the annexing municipality and the remaining parcels are contiguous to each other. (*See* Ill. Rev. Stat. 1987, ch. 24, par. 7-1-48(b).) Thus, while Public Act 82-211 authorized the procedure invalidated in *City of Belleville*, it did not, as the Village suggests, do away with the requirement of contiguity. The instant action does not involve the annexation of successive parcels, and the Village does not argue or otherwise comment on the fact that another parcel of property which is not subject to the annexation agreement separates the Smiths' property from the Village.

Under these circumstances, enforcement of the zoning provisions of the annexation agreement in the instant action would permit the Village to exercise extraterritorial power over the Smiths' property. Absent an express grant of statutory authority, a municipality may not exercise extraterritorial governmental power. (*Commercial National Bank v. City of Chicago* (1982), 89 Ill. 2d 45, 77–78.) The Code's provisions do not, as the Village contends, grant such authority. We agree with defendants that the practical effect of such a finding would authorize a municipality to enter into an annexation agreement for property anywhere within the State and, pursuant to the agreement, exercise its police power over that property. We do not think such a result was intended by the legislature. Having concluded that the annexation agreement in the instant action is invalid and unenforceable as it is not authorized by statute, we need not address the alternative basis relied upon by the trial court in entering judgment for defendants. However, it is necessary to comment briefly on the Village's remaining argument that equitable estoppel precludes defendants from challenging the validity of the annexation agreement. The Village asserts that estoppel should apply since the Smiths, as parties to the agreement, have derived substantial contractual benefits from the agreement. We disagree.

Contracts entered into by a municipality which are expressly prohibited by law are void and cannot be rendered valid by estoppel. (*Ligenza v. Village of Round Lake Beach* (1985), 133 Ill. App. 3d 286, 291; *Stahelin v. Board of Education, School District No. 4* (1967), 87 Ill. App. 2d 28, 41–42.) Section 11-15.1-2(f) of the Code provides that annexation agreements may not incorporate any provisions inconsistent with the Code or forbidden by law. (Ill. Rev. Stat. 1987, ch. 24, par. 11-15.1-2(f).) As we have noted above, the annexation agreement in the instant action was invalid and not authorized by statute as it did not relate to property contiguous with the Village and therefore resulted in allowing the Village to exercise extraterritorial police powers. Accordingly, the Village cannot now argue that defendants should be estopped from asserting its validity.

Moreover, even if the Village was authorized to enter into the agreement, equitable estoppel would not apply. Estoppel refers to the reliance by one party on the words or conduct of another so that the party changes his position and suffers harm. (*Gary-Wheaton Bank v. Meyer* (1984), 130 Ill. App. 3d 87, 95–96.) The record in the instant action, while establishing that the Smiths did receive water and sewer service, also indicates that they paid the Village for those services and, in fact, paid double the normal fee since their property was located outside the Village limits. The Village argues that this payment "does not vitiate the fact that [the Smiths] received substantial benefits under the annexation agreement" since the Smiths "would have never obtained [the benefits] without agreeing to the express terms of the agreement." This assertion is not supported by the record.

Accordingly, for the reasons set forth above, we affirm the judgment of the circuit court of Du Page County granting defendants' motion for summary judgment.

Affirmed.

[b] Illinois Annexation Agreement Statutes

Village of Lisle v. Action Outdoor Advertising Company was "overruled" by the Illinois legislature in 1990. We ask you to read the following statutes to determine issues about the annexation agreement for the Johnson parcel and the development of the Fox Valley Auto Care Center, and you will see that the issue critical to the court's holding in *Village of Lisle v. Action Outdoor Advertising Company* (but not relevant to the annexation of the Johnson parcel) is directly addressed.

65 Illinois Compiled Statutes 5/11-15.1-1. Agreements with owners of record

The corporate authorities of any municipality may enter into an annexation agreement with one or more of the owners of record of land in unincorporated territory. That land may be annexed to the municipality in the manner provided in Article 7 at the time the land is or becomes contiguous to the municipality. The agreement shall be valid and binding for a period of not to exceed 20 years from the date of its execution.

Lack of contiguity to the municipality of property that is the subject of an annexation agreement does not affect the validity of the agreement whether approved by the corporate authorities before or after the effective date of this amendatory Act of 1990.

This amendatory Act of 1990 is declarative of existing law and does not change the substantive operation of this Section.

65 Illinois Compiled Statutes 5/11-15.1-2. Contents and scope of agreements

Any such agreement may provide for the following as it relates to the land which is the subject of the agreement:

(a) The annexation of such territory to the municipality, subject to the provisions of Article 7.

(b) The continuation in effect, or amendment, or continuation in effect as amended, of any ordinance relating to subdivision controls, zoning, official plan, and building, housing and related restrictions; provided, however, that any public hearing required by law to be held before the adoption of any ordinance amendment provided in such agreement shall be held prior to the execution of the agreement, and all ordinance amendments provided in such agreement shall be enacted according to law.

(c) A limitation upon increases in permit fees required by the municipality.

(d) Contributions of either land or monies, or both, to any municipality and to other units of local government having jurisdiction over all or part of land that is the subject matter of any annexation agreement entered into under the provisions of this Section shall be deemed valid when made and shall survive the expiration date of any such annexation agreement with respect to all or any part of the land that was the subject matter of the annexation agreement.

(e) The granting of utility franchises for such land.

(e-5) The abatement of property taxes.

(f) Any other matter not inconsistent with the provisions of this Code, nor forbidden by law.

Any action taken by the corporate authorities during the period such agreement is in effect, which, if it applied to the land which is the subject of the agreement, would be a breach of such agreement, shall not apply to such land without an amendment of such agreement. . . .

65 Illinois Compiled Statutes 5/11-15.1-3. Procedure

Any such agreement executed after July 31, 1963 and all amendments of annexation agreements, shall be entered into in the following manner. The corporate authorities shall fix a time for and hold a public hearing upon the proposed annexation agreement or amendment, and shall give notice of the proposed agreement or amendment not more than 30 nor less than 15 days before the date fixed for the hearing. This notice shall be published at least once in one or more newspapers published in the municipality, or, if no newspaper is published therein, then in one or more newspapers with a general circulation within the annexing municipality. After such hearing the agreement or amendment may be modified before execution thereof. The annexation agreement or amendment shall be executed by the mayor or president and attested by the clerk of the municipality only after such hearing and upon the adoption of a resolution or ordinance directing such execution, which resolution or ordinance must be passed by a vote of two-thirds of the corporate authorities then holding office.

65 Illinois Compiled Statutes 5/11-15.1-4. Effect of agreement; enforcement; limitation of actions

Any annexation agreement executed pursuant to this Division 15.1, or in conformity with Section 11-15.1-5 hereof, shall be binding upon the successor owners of record of the land which is the subject of the agreement and upon successor municipal authorities of the municipality and successor municipalities. Any party to such agreement may by civil action, mandamus, injunction or other proceeding, enforce and compel performance of the agreement. . . .

[3] Questions About Annexation of the Fox Valley Auto Care Center

1. Do you think that the Annexation Agreement for Fox Valley Auto Mall is valid under Illinois law?

2. What changes would you have made to the agreement if you had been representing Regent?

3. What type of zoning relief and governmental approvals did Regent seek and obtain prior to closing on the acquisitions?

4. Which of the approvals necessary to operate the center were not obtained prior to closing?

5. What conditions must be met and what challenges could be raised? Are these challenges likely to be successful?

[4] Drafting Exercise

Donna Smith comes into Sam Nader's office late one Friday afternoon. She is not happy. "I just received this draft of the Annexation Agreement for the Fox Valley Auto Care Project. I took a quick look at it, and I am no expert on these things, but some of it just does not seem right. I want you to take a shot at it. Can you have it back on my desk on Monday morning?"

Like most associates, Sam has learned that he can look a little pained upon being asked, but he better have a good reason for saying "No." Lacking a good reason, he agrees. He knows that Donna wants a "mark up," that is she wants him to indicate what changes he would make by using a red pen on a copy of the draft to delete and add provisions. Sam thinks this is kind of quaint, but he hates doing it. Since they don't have the draft on disk, Sam decides to write a memo to Donna outlining the changes he thinks should be made along with short explanations for the changes. Please draft Sam's memo.

Chapter 8

THE IMPACT OF ENVIRONMENTAL REGULATIONS ON THE PROJECT SITE

§ 8.01 THE BASICS OF CERCLA LIABILITY

The Comprehensive Environmental Response, Compensation and Liability Act ("CERCLA") was enacted to provide for the clean-up of hazardous substances. The Act allows for clean-up of such substances either under government direction (42 U.S.C. §§ 9604 and 9606) or by private parties (42 U.S.C. §§ 9607(a)(4)(B), 9613(F), and 9659). CERCLA establishes a fund (42 U.S.C. § 9611) known as "Superfund," to pay for a clean-up in the event that the responsible parties are yet to be ascertained or are no longer available. Superfund can be used by the Environmental Protection Agency ("EPA") in both private clean-ups and government clean-ups. We will focus on direct property owner liability under CERCLA rather than recovery from Superfund, because Superfund has had such huge demands placed on it that imposition of liability upon property owners usually will be the more effective avenue for relief.

In *State of New York v. Shore Realty Corp*, 759 F.2d 1032 (2d Cir. 1984), the Second Circuit held that CERCLA liability can be imposed on the current owner of property without any showing of wrongdoing by the current owner. This provision makes CERCLA a critical concern for the developer of land, including Regent as the developer of the Fox Valley Auto Care Center. The potential liability could be very significant, and could affect both the short-term profitability of the project and the long-term value of the developed land. CERCLA imposes true strict liability. The current owner need do nothing wrong and can be held liable just as if that owner was the wrongdoer who caused the contamination. You will see this principle applied in the next principal case, *Edward Hines Lumber Company v. Vulcan Materials and Osmose Preserving*, 861 F.2d 155 (7th Cir. 1988), in which the Seventh Circuit held liable both the current owner, who had nothing to do with the disposal of the hazardous substances, as well as the owner at the time of the disposal of the hazardous substances. In addition, in *United States v. Monsanto*, 858 F.2d 160 (4th Cir. 1988), the Fourth Circuit held that CERCLA holds all parties jointly and severally liable. Thus, where the history of a parcel of land is unclear or where there is known activity that could have involved the use of hazardous substances, the potential developer must determine whether ownership of the land will subject it to liability under CERCLA.

The materials that follow focus on three threshold issues raised by CERCLA which need to be considered in the acquisition of land for development: (a) what substances are covered by CERCLA and what constitutes a release of those substances; (b) the different mechanisms used to impose liability; and (c) CERCLA's statutorily defined defenses. This discussion is followed by two sections that deal with the parties who are subject to CERCLA liability, the type of liability imposed, and the special provisions in CERCLA for imposing liability on lenders.

[1] Covered Substances and What Constitutes a Release

CERCLA defines hazardous substances and what constitutes a release of a hazardous substance in very broad terms. The definition of hazardous substances in 42 U.S.C. § 9601(14)(B) includes those hazardous substances identified by other environmental statutes, and then adds several others. Thus, hazardous substances include those solid wastes, both by character and specifically enumerated hazardous wastes, listed in the Resource Conservation and Recovery Act ("RCRA"); the hazardous air pollutants listed in the Clean Air Act; the toxic pollutants listed in the Clean Water Act; and other substances designated by CERCLA. CERCLA specifically excludes petroleum from its listing of hazardous substances. The court in *Southern Pacific Transportation v. California*, 790 F. Supp. 983 (C.D. Cal. 1991), held that this exemption applies even if the substances found in the petroleum are otherwise hazardous under CERCLA. RCRA presents a possible route around the petroleum exclusion, discussed *infra* in § 8.01[4].

CERCLA imposes liability for costs of clean-up when there is a release. A release includes the spilling, leaking, pumping, pouring, emitting, emptying, discharging, injecting, escaping, leaching, dumping or disposing of a hazardous substance into the environment. In *United States v. Alcan Aluminum Corp.*, 990 F.2d 711 (2d Cir. 1993), the court held that no minimum quantitative amount of a substance needs to be released in order for it to be a "release" of a hazardous substance under CERCLA. The amount released therefore can be a very small amount and still result in liability.

[2] Mechanisms Used to Impose Liability

There are four main mechanisms that can be used to make a party pay for a mandated clean-up. First, under 42 U.S.C. § 9604, the EPA can assume the Superfund financed response costs and then assess the costs against the responsible parties. This action is limited by CERCLA. The action is not allowed if: (a) the substance is a natural substance in its natural unaltered form and natural location; (b) the substance is part of a structure on the land; or (c) the substance is in private or public drinking water which is already deteriorated due to ordinary use.

Second, under 42 U.S.C. § 9606, if there is an imminent and substantial endangerment to public health and welfare because of actual or threatened releases, the EPA may seek abatement through a prohibitory or mandatory injunction.

> Subsection 106(a) [§ 9606(a)] will continue to serve a minor interstitial role in hazardous waste cases. The provision has been invoked to justify the appointment of a receiver in an appropriate case, to derive authority for a nationwide service when that was in doubt, and to fill a legal gap by giving settling generators access to a site for purposes of implementing a settlement remedy.[1]

Third, under 42 U.S.C. § 9607(a), a cost recovery action can be maintained in order to recoup the costs of clean-up. This may be either a government action or an action by a private party. According to the Fifth Circuit (*see Amoco Oil Co. v.*

---

[1] William H. Rodgers, Hazardous Wastes and Substances 534 (1992).

Borden. Inc. 889 F.2d 664, 668 (5th Cir. 1989)), this action requires five elements: (a) the site must be a facility (42 U.S.C. § 9601(20)(A)(ii) defines a "facility" as including any place where hazardous substances have "otherwise come to be located"); (b) the defendant must be a responsible party under CERCLA; (c) there must be a release or the threat of a release; (d) there must be a hazardous substance; and (e) the plaintiff must have incurred response costs.

Fourth, under 42 U.S.C. § 9613(f), a private party who has been held liable for the costs of a clean-up may bring a contribution suit against a jointly liable party. This type of action generally is brought after there has been liability established under one of the preceding mechanisms. This allows a party that has been held liable the opportunity to seek contribution from any other person who is potentially liable. A court may allocate among liable parties using such equitable factors as the court may determine are appropriate. With CERCLA's joint and several liability this is an important feature of the statutory scheme.

[3] CERCLA's Statutorily Defined Defenses

In 42 U.S.C. § 9607(b), CERCLA specifically allows three defenses to be raised by a party who otherwise would be liable for clean-up costs. The first two defenses are very limited in their application and thus rarely used: an act of God or an act of war. The third defense is called the "innocent landowner defense." The "innocent landowner defense" is stated as being an act or omission of a third party who neither (a) is an employee or agent of the defendant nor (b) has a contractual relationship with the defendant, and when the defendant can establish by a preponderance of the evidence that he exercised due care with respect to the hazardous substance and took precautions against foreseeable acts or omissions of third parties.

In order to assert the "innocent landowner defense" the landowner must show that he did not have any reason to know of the contamination. The Seventh Circuit has held (*see Kerr-McGee Chemical Corp. v. Lefton*, 14 F.3d 321 (7th Cir. 1992)) in interpreting 42 U.S.C. § 9601(35)(B) that to qualify as an innocent landowner, the person must establish that at the time of acquisition, he used good commercial standards in determining what inquiries he should make into the previous ownership and use of the property. This requires that the landowner use due care and take precautions against third party acts or omissions. Government entities that acquire land through escheat, involuntary transfer or eminent domain are innocent for the purposes of this defense. In addition, people who inherit property are innocent for the purposes of this defense.

[4] Possible Ways to Get Around CERCLA's Petroleum Exemption

As stated before, CERCLA provides a cause of action to recover cleanup costs incurred when there has been a release of a hazardous substance, but it specifically excludes petroleum from its listing of covered hazardous substances. While that may not be an issue for Regent in the acquisition of land for the Fox Valley Auto Care Center, tenants of the auto care center may well use hazardous substances, including petroleum. This illustrates the point that a developer must be concerned both about what it is getting when it purchases a development site, and also what the users will do on the site after the development is completed and occupied.

The CERCLA petroleum exclusion does not exclude all situations where petroleum is present. When petroleum products are "mixed" with other products, it may cause loss of the exemption. Courts have held CERCLA's petroleum exclusion inapplicable if petroleum is unnaturally contaminated with hazardous substances other than those substances which are constituents of petroleum products, and that the petroleum exclusion is no help even if petroleum constituents are found in concentrations exceeding naturally occurring levels.

In addition, RCRA regulates the treatment, storage, and disposal of both solid and hazardous wastes, including petroleum, primarily through a permit system. RCRA has a special section devoted to underground storage tanks. RCRA also provides a cause of action that can be used to compel a landowner, such as Regent as the owner of the completed Fox Valley Auto Care Center, to clean up wastes, including petroleum. To qualify under RCRA, the wastes, including petroleum, must be shown to present an "imminent and substantial danger." In one case, the court held that, since the risks associated with a petroleum spill at a particular location were minimal, it was not shown that the property posed an "imminent and substantial danger."

A landowner who first cleans up a petroleum spill, and then tries to bring an action under RCRA, will likely not recover, because there no longer is an "imminent and substantial danger" after the cleanup. Courts have held that RCRA offers the private citizen only injunctive relief — either a mandatory injunction to make the defendant clean up or a prohibitory injunction to stop the releasing of wastes into the environment. Neither remedy contemplates the award of already expended cleanup costs.

§ 8.02 OWNER LIABILITY FOR USE OR DISPOSAL OF TOXIC SUBSTANCES

[1] Liability Issues in General

42 U.S.C. § 9607 of CERCLA holds four groups potentially liable for their actions: (a) the current owner and operator of the facility; (b) the owner or operator of the facility at the time of disposal of the hazardous waste; (c) a party who arranged for the disposal of the hazardous waste; and (d) any transporter of the hazardous waste. Under CERCLA, a "facility" is a place where hazardous substances end up, not necessarily a specific waste site.

The first two types of liability are incurred when one is found to be an owner or operator. Owners need not be "operators" in order to have CERCLA liability. If an owner leases out land, the owner can be held liable even if the owner did not know that the lessee was using or disposing of hazardous substances on the land. In addition, the lessee can be held liable as an "operator" even though the lessee did not own the land.

Defining what an "operator" is has been left to the courts, because the statutory definition gives no real guidance. One U.S. District Court (*see United States v. New Castle*, 727 F. Supp. 854 (D. Del. 1989)) has outlined four areas to look to in making the determination: (a) who controlled the financing of the facility; (b) who managed the everyday operations of the facility; (c) who was responsible for the environmental maintenance of the facility; and (d) who has had any economic benefit conferred on it because of activities at the facility.

A past owner can escape liability, but only if there was no release or addition to the contamination by that past owner. Note, however, that with the broad definition of what is a "release" of a hazardous substance, it is difficult for a past owner to take advantage of this exception if there is any hazardous substance that has been disposed of on the land. For example, if there were closed containers of hazardous waste on the land that were leaking, even though a past owner did nothing with the containers (or did not even know of them because the containers were buried or concealed), the past owner would be liable because of the "release" of hazardous waste during the past owner's period of ownership.

"Arranger" or "generator" liability is limited to those who actually do take part in the arranging of where hazardous substances are used or disposed of. However, the courts have been unwilling to impose liability on companies who make products that include hazardous substances. As the U.S. District Court for the Western District of Oklahoma held in *United States v.* Hardage, 750 F. Supp 1444, 1458 (W.D. Okla. 1990):

> "Generator" liability under [42 U.S.C. § 9607(a)(3)] is imposed on "any person who by contract, agreement, or otherwise arranged for" disposal, treatment, or transport to a hazardous waste facility. Courts have construed this section broadly. A generator need not have selected the site. Generator defendants can be liable for disposal of wastes at a particular site "even when defendants did not know the substances would be deposited at that site or in fact believed they would be deposited elsewhere." As far as the waste is concerned, the United States must present evidence that a "generator defendant's waste was shipped to a site and that hazardous substances similar to those contained in the defendant's waste remained present at the time of release." [citations omitted]

"Transporter" liability is imposed on those who transport hazardous waste. As the *Hardage* court also held, 750 F. Supp at 1458:

> Liability of transporters is not as broad as the above-discussed generator liability. "Transporter" liability under [42 U.S.C. § 9607(a)(4)] is imposed on: "any person who accepts or accepted any hazardous substances for transport to disposal or treatment facilities, incineration vessels or sites selected by such person, from which there is a release, or a threatened release which causes the incurrence of response costs, of a hazardous substance. . . ." Transporters are liable under CERCLA if they selected the particular site for disposal of hazardous substances. [citations omitted]

[2] Determining Who Is An Owner or An Operator

[a] *Hines Lumber v. Vulcan Material*

In the following case, Judge Frank Easterbrook of the Seventh Circuit deals with a claim by an owner that another party is jointly liable as an "operator" of a facility. As you read the case, consider what this means for Regent as it both acquires the land and plans for its ultimate use.

EDWARD HINES LUMBER COMPANY v. VULCAN MATERIAL COMPANY

861 F.2d 155 (7th Cir. 1988)

EASTERBROOK, CIRCUIT JUDGE.

After the Edward Hines Lumber Co. sold its wood processing plant in Mena, Arkansas, to Mid-South Wood Products, Inc., the Environmental Protection Agency concluded that the site had been contaminated by toxic substances. Invoking its powers under the Comprehensive Environmental Response, Compensation, and Liability Act of 1980, 42 U.S.C. §§ 9601-75 (CERCLA or the Superfund Act), the EPA first put the Mena site on the national priority list for attention, 42 U.S.C. § 9605(a)(8)(B), and then asked Hines and Mid-South to remove the offending chemicals, 42 U.S.C. §§ 9604(a), 9606. They signed a consent decree promising to do so and have almost completed work, at a cost close to $5 million. Hines filed this suit to recover from the suppliers of wood preserving chemicals the expenditures it has lavished on decontamination. The only supplier remaining in the case is Osmose Wood Preserving, Inc., which designed and built the portion of the plant that treated wood with chromated copper arsenate, and sold Hines its requirements of that chemical. The district judge granted summary judgment in Osmose's favor. 685 F. Supp. 651 (N.D. Ill. 1988).

* * *

Hines now wants to recover contribution from Osmose solely under § 113(f)(1) of CERCLA, 42 U.S.C. § 9613(f)(1), a provision added by the Superfund Amendments and Reauthorization Act (SARA), Pub. L. 99-499, 100 Stat. 1613, 1647, in 1986. It provides:

> Any person may seek contribution from any other person who is liable or potentially liable under section 9607(a) of this title, during or following any civil action under section 9606 of this title or under section 9607(a) of this title. Such claims . . . shall be governed by Federal law. In resolving contribution claims, the court may allocate response [= cleanup] costs among liable parties using such equitable factors as the court determines are appropriate. Nothing in this subsection shall diminish the right of any person to bring an action for contribution in the absence of a civil action under section 9606 or section 9607 of this title.

Hines may require Osmose to chip in to the decontamination effort only if Osmose is a "person who is liable or potentially liable" under the Act. Osmose's potential liability arises, if at all, under § 107(a)(2) of CERCLA, 42 U.S.C. § 9607(a)(2), which provides that (with some defenses and exceptions) "any person who at the time of disposal of any hazardous substance owned or operated any facility at which such hazardous substances were disposed of" must pay the costs of getting rid of them.

So everything turns on whether Osmose "owned or operated" the Mena plant. At this point the statutory chain comes to an end, for § 9601(20)(A)(ii) informs us that "the term . . . 'owner or operator' means . . . in the case of an onshore facility or an offshore facility, any person owning or operating such facility." This is circular, although it does imply that if Mena is neither "onshore" nor "offshore" — perhaps because in outer space? — then an owner or operator is not a statutory "owner or operator." The definition of "owner or operator" for purposes of earthbound sites must come from a source other than the text. The circularity strongly implies, however, that the statutory terms have their ordinary meanings rather than unusual or technical meanings.

A pause for the facts will put the question in perspective. Hines had been preserving wood at its 57-acre site using several different chemicals for nine years before it contracted with Osmose to build an additional plant. Osmose is experienced in using chromated copper arsenate, which, when applied under heat and pressure, makes wood suitable for prolonged exposure to the elements. (The principal product of the plant Osmose built at Mena is 2x4 beams used in the construction industry.) For $135,840, Osmose designed and built a plant for Hines's use at Mena; Osmose trained Hines's employees to operate the machinery; it also licensed Hines to use its trademark in connection with treated wood. Hines promised to buy its next five years' requirements of chromated copper arsenate from Osmose and gave Osmose "full and immediate access to the plant and to all chemical processes and products located thereon or produced thereby for the purposes of insuring quality control according to the Osmose standards." Osmose promised to construct a closed-loop system, so that the toxic preservative would not escape; it also built the plant on a concrete platform, the better to trap any leaking chemicals. Hines operated the plant between 1976 and 1978; Mid-South has run it since. In 1981 the Arkansas Department of Pollution Control and Ecology found residues of chromated copper arsenate and other toxic substances in the groundwater near the plant. The EPA's tests in 1984–85 confirmed this finding and identified Mena as the source. Getting rid of the chemicals (while avoiding new deposits) has been expensive.

Osmose designed and built the plant, furnished the toxic chemical, trained Hines's employees, and reserved a right to inspect ongoing operations. This must be enough, Hines submits, to make Osmose an "operator" within the meaning of the Superfund Act. It is easy to see the attraction of sweeping Osmose into the category of responsible persons. Since the facts and inferences must be taken favorably to Hines, the party resisting the motion for summary judgment, we must assume that Osmose came up with a defective design, did not build the plant to standard, trained Hines's employees poorly in how to control the toxic chemicals, and hid all of this from the management at Hines and its successor Mid-South so that they omitted steps that could have rectified the problem sooner and cheaper. When the liability may be large — it is costly to clean up polluted sites — there is a chance that one or more of the firms that have caused the problem will not have the assets necessary to set things right. The prospect of a shortfall in assets means that someone else (the public at large) must incur cleanup costs; victims may be left to bear their own losses; thinly-capitalized firms may take too few precautions. The designation of additional firms as responsible ameliorates this problem and so helps to achieve statutory aims. The prospect of liability under CERCLA would induce a firm in Osmose's position to take greater care in design, construction, and training, all of which would be beneficial (if it did not lead to excessive precautions, which it might).

It is not our function to design rules of liability from the ground up, however. We are enforcing a statute rather than modifying rules of common law. Osmose surely was not an "owner" of the Mena site, so it is potentially liable only if it was an "operator." The statute does not fix liability on slipshod architects, clumsy engineers, poor construction contractors, or negligent suppliers of on-the-job training — and the fact that Osmose might have been all four rolled into one does not change matters. The liability falls on owners and operators; architects, engineers, construction contractors, and instructors must chip in only to the extent they have agreed to do so by contract. To the point that courts could achieve "more" of the legislative objectives by adding to the lists of those responsible, it is enough to respond that statutes have not only ends but also limits. Born of compromise, laws such as CERCLA and SARA do not pursue their ends to their logical limits. *See Covalt v. Carey Canada, Inc.*, 860 F.2d 1434 (7th Cir. 1988), slip op. 10. A court's job is to find and enforce stopping points no less than to implement other legislative choices.

The statute does not define "operator," and we turn to common law analogies, as the sponsors of the legislation anticipated. *See Colorado v. ASARCO, Inc.*, 608 F. Supp. 1484, 1488–89 (D. Colo. 1985) (quoting statements on the floor of the House and Senate). *See also New York v. Shore Realty Corp.*, 759 F.2d 1032, 1052 (2d Cir. 1985), *United States v. Northeastern Pharmaceutical & Chemical Co.*, 810 F.2d 726, 742–43 (8th Cir. 1986), and *United States v. Dart Industries, Inc.*, 847 F.2d 144 (4th Cir. 1988), the only other appellate decisions dealing with the definition of "operator" — none of which is helpful in assessing the status of Osmose.

One potential analogy is the distinction between co-venturer and independent contractor. At common law, the employer of an independent contractor is not liable for the contractor's torts, and the contractor is not liable for the employer's. (SARA has turned that outcome 180 degrees, for if the analogy is sound the independent contractor is not an "operator" of the offending facility and therefore escapes liability, but the wisdom of this choice is not ours to question.) The dominant characteristic of the independent contractor is day-to-day control of its own operations. *United States v. Orleans*, 425 U.S. 807, 96 S. Ct. 1971, 48 L. Ed. 2d 390 (1976); Restatement (Second) of Agency § 2(3) (1958). This Osmose had. It designed and built the plant, a turnkey operation on behalf of Hines, which became the operator of the finished facility. Thereafter Hines had day-to-day control, hiring employees, deciding how much to produce, where to sell it and at what price. Osmose hovered in the background, concerned about the quality of the finished product, which could affect its reputation, but did not interfere with operational decisions. So Hines was the operator of the plant as well as its owner, Osmose the independent construction contractor.

A different analogy is the joint venture, which is the one Hines favors. We may assume that the principal operator's co-venturer would be a statutory "operator." Hines thinks that Osmose was so wrapped up in the chromated copper arsenate process that it must be a joint venturer. It offers as the clincher Osmose's contractual right to inspect the plant. The common law definition of a joint venture has at least three elements missing from the arrangement between Hines and Osmose, however: willingness to be joint venturers, shared control, and division of the profits and losses. For cases reciting these elements, among others, see, e.g., *Secon Service System, Inc. v. St. Joseph Bank & Trust Co.*, 855 F.2d 406, 416 (7th Cir. 1988); *Steinbeck v. Gerosa*, 4 N.Y.2d 302, 317, 175 N.Y.S.2d 1, 151 N.E.2d 170, 178–79 (1958); *Boyer v. First National Bank*, 476 N.E.2d 895, 897–98 (Ind. App. 4th Dist. 1985). *Cf. Forsham v. Harris*, 445 U.S. 169, 180, 100 S. Ct. 977, 63 L. Ed. 2d 293 (1980). The contract specified that Osmose was not a partner or joint venturer with Hines. Osmose had no control of the work at the Hines plant, no right to choose employees, direct their activities, or set prices; it had at most a limited veto power

— if the product was not up to snuff, Osmose could stop selling chromated copper arsenate and deny Hines the right to use its trademark. The contract assigned exclusively to Hines the responsibility for keeping the plant in compliance with environmental rules. ("Both parties hereto understand and agree that all blowdown and condensats from steam-conditioned charges and outfall of effluent from steam-conditioned charges shall be the responsibility of OWNER.") Osmose had no right to share in the profits and was not required to contribute to the losses, or any other expense. Hines does not allege that Osmose paid part of its workers' compensation claims, for example, or shared in the benefits of improved safety. Hines could have shut the plant or revamped its operation in order to reduce emissions; Osmose could not require Hines to do either. *Cf. Dart*, 847 F.2d at 146 (an agency with a veto power over waste disposal practices is not an "operator" when it does not control the employees or finances of the facility); *Northeastern*, 810 F.2d at 743 (suggesting, without expressly discussing § 9601(20), that "the authority to control the handling and disposal of hazardous substances" is "critical" to the statutory scheme).

So neither the analogy to independent contractors nor the analogy to joint venturer assists Hines. Its reply brief asks us to come up with a new definition, blending elements of common law doctrines to produce one more favorable to Hines. Such efforts often produce nothing but confusion, however. *See Kungys v. United States*, 485 U.S. 759, 108 S. Ct. 1537, 1545–47, 99 L. Ed. 2d 839 (1988). A series of small variations on established rules makes law more complex and less predictable. The independent contractor and joint venturer categories have been functional and hence stable. We are unwilling to ring variations on established themes.

The desire of operators to minimize their own liability will lead them to pay close attention to their designers and suppliers. When they lack the expertise to supervise closely, they can induce their contracting partners to take care by insisting on warranties and indemnification. To the extent they anticipate the risks involved — as Hines and Osmose surely knew of the risks of contamination — the outcome of this process is not fundamentally different from the outcome produced by a rule of liability. R.H. Coase, *The Problem of Social Cost*, 3 J.L. & Econ. 1 (1960). The Superfund Act places liability on the "owner or operator" of the facility. Large potential obligations concentrate the mind wonderfully, leading the owner-operator to assign duties and liabilities by contract to those who can best take precautions. Hines had a warranty and could have bargained for indemnification; if it did not, or if it chose not to enforce the rights it had, Hines has only itself to blame.

AFFIRMED.

[b] Questions About Owner and Operator Liability

1. In purchasing land for a new development, how concerned should a developer be about hazardous waste that may have been disposed of on the site? If you represent the developer, how would you address these concerns?
2. After reviewing the Phase I Environmental Property Transfer Assessment for the Johnson tract in the Document Book, would you advise Regent to

proceed?

3. Given the nature of the Fox Valley Auto Care Center, do you think Regent should be concerned about future liability under CERCLA or RCRA? If so, how would you address these concerns? Part of the answer to this question will have to wait until you have considered Regent's leasing of space in the Auto Care Center in Part V.

§ 8.03 LENDER LIABILITY FOR OTHERS' USE OR DISPOSAL OF TOXIC SUBSTANCES

[1] Why Lender Liability Matters to Developers

Almost every developer borrows money to finance the development being undertaken, and, in virtually every situation, the developer will use the land as security for the loan. As with any other loan, a lender making a loan to a developer must be concerned about the security being given for the loan. If the security is subject to CERCLA liability, its value will be reduced by the amount of the liability, since any owner will be jointly and severally liable for any clean-up costs. Therefore, at the outset, a lender has to be concerned about the impact of CERCLA liability on the value of the security. A lender frequently will demand not only that an environmental review of the site be undertaken but also that the developer make specific warranties and agree to indemnify the lender for any loss (which, for at least that purpose, would make any loan recourse rather than non-recourse). For that reason, we are going to take a diversion into the issue of lender liability, an issue that becomes critical if a lender becomes an owner or an operator, and therefore an issue with which the lender is concerned at inception in evaluating the land as security. If the lender is concerned, so must be the developer.

CERCLA liability could cause the owner of the land to intentionally abandon the land, thereby leaving the lender with the equally unattractive choices of foreclosing on land with known CERCLA liability attaching to any future owner, or abandoning the security of the land and pursuing its borrower personally. In order to sell the land, the lender will be forced to clean up any hazardous waste or sue responsible parties for the clean-up costs. With the cleaned-up property, the lender may still face problems, because of the stigma attached. Many potential purchasers will know of the problems with the land and may look elsewhere to buy.

[2] Lender as an Owner or an Operator

CERCLA, as it was originally drafted, arguably imposed liability on a lender which engaged in certain actions (or, according to some courts, merely had the power to take those actions) related to the ownership or operation of a facility which secured its loan. In response to the concern of lenders, the EPA promulgated rules which took the position that in most situations a lender would not be liable under CERCLA. In *Kelley v. EPA*, 15 F.3d 1100 (D.C. Cir. 1994), the D.C. Circuit held that the EPA's rules were invalid because the rules were substantive and therefore exceeded the EPA's rule-making authority. Congress responded by amending CERCLA to include the substance of most of the EPA's rules.

The amendments to CERCLA in 42 U.S.C. § 9601(20)(E) & (F) make it clear that those who hold indicia of ownership primarily to protect a security interest are exempted from liability. The statute now reads so that the holder of the interest can foreclose, sell, re-lease and the like without losing the exemption if certain conditions are met.

In order to maintain this exemption, the lender must not participate in management of the facility. The statute allows the lender to have some influence over the borrower in how the borrower goes about managing the facility, but the lender cannot exercise decision-making control over the environmental compliance or control at the level of a manager of the facility.

Chapter 11, "Due Diligence, Documenting and Closing the Loan," deals more fully with the issue of lender liability.

§ 8.04 ENVIRONMENTAL REVIEW IN THE PURCHASE OF THE JOHNSON TRACT

[1] How the Environmental Assessment Was Done

The Phase I Environmental Property Transfer Assessment for the Johnson tract is in the Document Book, and at this point you should read it. We have not included either the aerial photographs of the site (taken several times in the past and at the time of the assessment), or the tables listing materials found at the Johnson Tract. We felt that both the photographs and the findings were adequately described in the text of the report.

A Phase I assessment is the lowest level assessment which is done. If the Phase I assessment reveals evidence of potentially larger problems, or if larger problems are known of before any assessment is undertaken, then the assessment necessarily will be of a more thorough nature. A Phase I assessment was undertaken because no one anticipated any unusual problems with the Johnson tract. As you read the Phase I assessment for the Johnson Tract, you should consider whether the issues raised in it should be of concern to Regent and whether you would advise Regent to proceed with the purchase of the Johnson tract.

[2] Assignment

After the Phase I assessment for the Johnson Tract was delivered to Donna Smith's office at Kaplan & Miller, Donna sent it to Sam Nader with the following note:

> Sam:
>
> Attached is the Phase I assessment for the Johnson tract. It looks pretty clean, but I don't have time to thoroughly review it. Please review it and get back to me with any concerns that we should raise with Regent.
>
> Donna

Please prepare a short memo from Sam to Donna that summarizes the results of the Phase I assessment and gives Sam's opinion on whether Donna should communi cate any concerns to Regent.

Part III

FINANCING A REAL ESTATE DEVELOPMENT

Chapter 9

BASIC BUSINESS AND LEGAL TERMS AND ISSUES

§ 9.01 THE FINANCING PROCESS

[1] Introduction

In a typical commercial real estate deal, the developer seeks to finance the maximum amount of the funds necessary to develop the real estate project in order to take full advantage of anticipated positive leverage from the project. Indeed, at the height of the commercial real estate market in 2006 and early 2007, borrowers were able to obtain financing of close to 100% of the project costs/value through a combination of a conventional first mortgage loan and a "warehouse loan" (a loan where the warehouse lender received as collateral an interest in an entity that has an interest in the real estate project rather than an interest in the real estate directly). But even before the securitization of commercial real estate and use of warehouse loans, a developer would ordinarily obtain financing of between 70–90% of the project costs/value from a conventional first mortgage loan on the real estate and would attempt to raise most of the remaining 10–30% (the equity portion) through the sale of interests to passive investors. These passive investors would later recapture this equity through the refinancing or sale of the project once the project was built and operating. Because of this high degree of leverage, one could argue that the lender has a greater interest in the success of the development than the real estate developer. Of course, the developer is the party who conceives of the project and takes all of the actions necessary to turn the conception into a reality (including providing letters of credit and/or guarantees of payment and completion in the context of a construction loan) and then manages the property. The developer would argue that due to this "sweat equity," it has the strongest interest in the success of the project. In addition, to the extent that the project is a success, the developer and investors typically realize the gains of any appreciation of the value of the property in excess of the debt on the property, but sometimes more immediately realize on that appreciation in value by obtaining a junior mortgage on the property representing this appreciation in value.

Although both the developer and the lender have an interest in achieving a successful real estate project, the lender will want and need to independently verify the viability of the project and the lender's security interest in the property. This is because the lender initially advances far more funds into the project than the developer and the developer can usually recover much of its sweat equity in the form of developer's fees or overhead costs early on in the construction draw process. A lender that makes a loan secured by income producing real estate will typically look primarily to the property as the means of recovery of its investment in the event that the borrower defaults in paying back the loan. After a borrower defaults, a lender can foreclose on the mortgaged property as a means to recover the outstanding debt owed to it.

In order to verify the viability of the real estate project, lenders engage in a process called "due diligence" whereby they examine the numerous issues relevant to a successful project. This examination will vary somewhat, depending upon the stage in the project in which the lender's funding occurs (*i.e.*, at the acquisition and construction phase, or after the project is built and leased). The due diligence the lender should perform includes a review of many of the issues addressed in Parts I and II of this book. The lender should focus on three basic issues in a construction loan: (i) that the cash flow from the property can adequately service the debt and other expenses of owning and operating the property, (ii) that the property and project when completed will comply with all zoning, subdivision and title restrictions, and (iii) that there is no or little potential liability for environmental matters. Lender's counsel must also carefully review the construction documents that the developer contemplates entering into. This is because, if the developer defaults under the construction loan, the lender may need to exercise its right to step into the shoes of the developer under the various contracts the developer has entered into and complete construction. The topic of construction of the project's buildings and other improvements is covered in Part IV, *infra*.

Due diligence also requires a review of any leases that the developer has entered into and the preparation of a standard form of lease for any future tenants. It is not adequate for the lender to merely assume a certain cash flow based upon the rents from the leases; the lender's counsel should carefully review the leases to make certain that the terms of the leases will not permit a disturbance of this cash flow in certain circumstances. This topic is discussed further in Part V, *infra* which deals with leasing generally. Thus, through the due diligence process, almost every aspect of the real estate development project may be viewed as a "finance" issue.

The due diligence process then leads to the inclusion of various conditions in the loan commitment and loan documents that the borrower must agree to before the lender will fund the loan. More likely than not, whether FMB was represented by house counsel or an outside law firm, a senior lawyer would be assigning to a junior lawyer the task of initially reviewing all these matters, much in the way that, in representing Regent, Donna assigns matters to Sam. The junior lawyer would then raise any potential problems he sees with the senior lawyer, who would, in turn raise any serious concerns with FMB. The loan documents that the junior lawyer would prepare would include various representations, warranties, and indemnifications from the borrower relating to the due diligence matters. The documents will also contain various covenants from the borrower, delineation of events of default, and remedies available to the lender in the event of default. In terms of covenants from the borrower, the lender's main concern is that the borrower properly pay project expenses when due and that the borrower prudently operate the project. If, after conducting its due diligence, the lender discovers that a condition to funding is not satisfied (*e.g.*, there exists a serious title or zoning problem that can not be corrected prior to the scheduled closing date), then the lender can elect not to fund the loan. If after the loan is made, the borrower breaches a covenant, or the lender discovers a material misrepresentation, then the lender can declare the borrower to be in default under the loan. The lender can then exercise its rights and remedies as agreed to in the loan documents, subject to any common law or statutory protections provided to borrowers.

In addition to these due diligence and related matters, there are numerous business issues that the lender and borrower must address. These matters include the amount of interest that the lender can charge for the moneys advanced, the timing of repayment of the principal by the borrower, and legal limitations upon what bargain the parties may strike, such as the prohibition against usury and limitations on election of remedies. One prime concern to lenders is the reliability and consistency of the return on their investment. This arises, for example, when making a fixed interest rate loan on a completed and leased project. In this situation, the lender will want to structure the loan transaction so that it will receive a certain return on its investment over a specified period of time. The lender will frequently provide in the loan documents that the borrower is not permitted to repay the debt before the loan matures (referred to as a "prepayment lock"). The loan documents also typically provide that, in the event of a default and the lender's election to require that the entire unpaid debt be repaid immediately (referred to as an "acceleration of the debt"), the borrower must pay a special charge. The charge (referred to as a "prepayment charge") is typically equal to the amount necessary to allow the lender to reinvest the sums repaid to yield the same rate of return the lender would have received under the loan if the loan had not been paid off earlier than its stated maturity date.

Lender's counsel typically drafts the loan documents using the lender's standard form (if they have standard forms) or using a form with which lender's counsel is familiar and satisfied. A senior lawyer typically would assign the task of creating this first draft of the loan documents to a junior lawyer, who might even be the first one to respond to comments on the loan documents from borrower's counsel. Of course, any changes to the form would have to be approved in some fashion by the lender. Some lenders establish (and advise their attorneys of) standard approved deviations to their forms, and some do not. The negotiation and approval process can occur in many ways, but the key to a successful process is good communication among the attorneys and their clients.

[2] Overview of Part III

In keeping with the project-oriented focus of this book, this chapter begins with a term sheet relating to the acquisition/construction loan for the Auto Care Center project. The term sheet was created by the lender and delivered to the borrower to summarize the basic business and legal terms of the construction loan. This chapter then presents an overview of the commercial loan process, the special issues that arise in the context of construction and take-out loans for new construction, how these issues are addressed at the loan commitment stage, and the enforcement of loan commitments. This chapter then devotes considerable attention to the basic loan terms of a construction loan.

Chapter 10, Security for the Loan, focuses on the topic of establishing the security for the construction loan and how this collateral can be seized upon by the lender in the event of a default by the borrower. Although the security for the loan is an element of the basic terms of the loan, it is such a fundamental and, at times, complicated term that it deserves an entire chapter of its own, especially when covering the enforcement of the collateral granted upon the borrower's default. Chapter 11, Due Diligence, Documenting and Closing the Loan, highlights the due diligence a lender must exercise in evaluating the project. It then provides materials on closing a loan by examining the conditions to funding the loan in the loan agreement entered into for the Fox Valley Auto Care Center, and analyzing the opinion of counsel required to close the loan. Chapter 17, Loans in Default, appearing in Part VI, Termination of the Real Estate Investment, focuses on the strategies that borrowers and lenders engage in when a borrower is in default under the loan, with an emphasis on bankruptcy options, lender liability claims, and tax considerations.

§ 9.02 TERM SHEET FOR THE FINANCING OF THE ACQUISITION AND CONSTRUCTION

As you read through the Term Sheet, put yourself in Sam Nader's shoes. What problems, if any, do you see with the proposed loan terms from the perspective of the borrower? Also, jot down any terms that you do not understand and make sure that your questions are answered in the Comments and Questions section that follows the Term Sheet.

[1] The Terms for the Fox Valley Auto Care Center Construction Loan

MEMORANDUM

TO: Sam Nader

FROM: Donna Smith

RE: Construction loan for the Fox Valley Auto Care Center

Date: June 25, 1989

This deal is heating up again. Please review the attached cover letter and term sheet to become familiar with the basic terms of the loan and let me know if you see any issues that we should address with David when we meet with him next week.

Mr. David Delany

415 West North Avenue

Chicago, Illinois 60610

Re: Proposed Construction Loan for the Fox Valley Auto Care Center

Dear David:

It was good seeing you. I am attaching a term sheet that summarizes the terms we discussed for the captioned loan. I plan to ask our attorneys to begin the paperwork for the loan so please let me know as soon as possible if you have any questions or concerns regarding the terms outlined in the term sheet.

I look forward to working with you on this project.

Very truly yours,

Bruce McDill, V.P.

First Mortgage Bank

Term Sheet

1.	Loan Amount:	$2.3 million
2.	Maturity Date:	January 31, 1991 (seven months from the anticipated completion of construction)
3.	Interest Rate:	Floating at "prime" plus 1% per annum
4.	Amortization:	None; a "balloon" payment of the entire principal balance due at maturity
5.	Liability for Debt:	Recourse Loan
6.	Structure of the Ownership/Borrower:	A land trust owns fee simple title to the property. The beneficiary of the trust will be a limited partnership or an LLC. The general partner of the limited partnership/manager of the LLC is an S-corporation.
7.	Security/Collateral:	A first mortgage lien on the land and improvements, an assignment of rents and leases, a collateral assignment of the beneficial interest in the land trust, a first security interest in the personal property, an assignment of plans and specifications, general contractor's agreement, engineer's agreement and other contracts relating to construction of the project.
8.	Credit Enhancements:	Payment guaranty and completion guaranty from the principal shareholders of the corporate general partner/manager of the beneficiary of the land trust and either (i) a letter of credit in the amount of $200,000 for the benefit of the lender or (ii) a certificate of deposit and a pledge agreement relating to the certificate of deposit
9.	Construction Commencement Date:	October 30, 1989
10.	Construction Completion Date:	June 30, 1990
11.	Leasing Requirements:	Subordination, non-disturbance and attornment agreements from Casey Muffler, Lube Pros and Sparks Tune-Up
12.	Loan Fee:	$23,000 (1% of the loan amount)
13.	Allocation of the Loan Proceeds:	For the acquisition and construction of the Project as detailed in the approved budget
14.	Payment of the Loan:	Payment through a construction escrow with a title company

[2] Comments and Questions Regarding the Term Sheet

1. How do you think the lender arrived at the loan amount of $2.3 million? In answering this question, recall the valuation materials in Chapter 2 and the two-step approach lenders utilize in determining the maximum loan

amount (the lesser of the debt service coverage ratio and the loan to value ratio). You should also review § 9.04[1] which describes the different typical loan-to-value ratios for different types of real estate investments. What loan-to-value ratio did the lender apply in agreeing to loan up to $2,300,000?

2. Note the scheduled date of completion of the construction and the scheduled maturity date (a seven-month gap). Why do you think the loan was structured to mature seven months after the scheduled completion of construction?

3. Note that the interest rate is not fixed but will float based upon the "prime" rate (the rate lenders charge to their good customers) and that no portion of the principal amount of the loan will be paid until the maturity date. This is a standard structure for a construction loan. Had this been a long-term loan, the interest rate would more likely be a fixed interest rate with some level of amortization (payment of a portion of the principal debt) of the loan being made in each payment period. Had this construction loan been for a larger project (a construction loan of at least $3 million), the lender may have required that the borrower enter into an interest rate swap to reduce the risk that the floating rate will increase to such a degree that it makes the loan become "out of balance." A loan is out of balance when the interest which accrues on the loan exceeds the amount budgeted for the payment of that interest, causing the loan proceeds to be inadequate to meet all project expenses. The topic of interest rate swaps is covered in § 9.04[3][a][i], *infra*.

4. Note that the debt is "recourse" (*i.e.*, that all of the borrower's assets are liable for the payment of the debt), as compared with a "non-recourse" debt in which only the borrower's interests in the property pledged to the lender can be recovered by the lender to pay the debt. It is typical in the context of a construction loan for the loan to be recourse rather than non-recourse. Why do you think this is the case? Which type of loan is more speculative from the perspective of the lender, a construction loan or a permanent loan? Although permanent loans for built and leased-up projects are typically structured to be "non-recourse," lenders in recent years have carved out situations where their non-recourse loans will become "recourse" when certain situations arise (such as default by the borrower based upon committing waste or fraud). This topic is covered in § 9.04[3][c], *infra*.

5. Note that the title to the property is held by a land trust. As previously discussed in § 5.04[4], *supra*, certain states (Illinois, Florida, Virginia, North Dakota, Indiana, and Hawaii) by statute recognize this type of entity as capable of holding title to real property, and holding title in this manner can be beneficial to borrowers. Holding title to real property in a land trust can also be beneficial to the lender. A lender might be able to more quickly and cheaply recover on the collateral when the title is held by a land trust. When title to land is held in a land trust, one potential piece of collateral for the loan is a collateral assignment of the beneficial interest in the land trust, which is a personal property interest. Consequently, the lender may be able to recover on this type of collateral through a U.C.C. sale, rather than a mortgage foreclosure. This is beneficial to the lender, because the lender will be able to avoid the rights of redemption associated with a

mortgage foreclosure. In order for a court to enforce the collateral assignment of beneficial interest, the court must find that the land trust is genuine and not established as a disguised real estate mortgage. In *Melrose Park National Bank v. Melrose Park National Bank*, 123 Ill. App. 3d 282, 288 (1984), the court outlined a four-part test to determine whether the parties intended to create a security interest in personal property rather than an equitable mortgage. The test is whether: (1) the trust agreement contains no provision for the sale of the real estate in the event of a default under the loan; (2) the land trust is set up for purposes other than as security for a debt; (3) the pledge of the beneficial interest is subsequent to the creation of the trust; and (4) the pledged security for the transaction is of the trust beneficial interest only. Non-compliance with these four factors may result in a finding of a real estate mortgage.

6. The collateral for the Fox Valley Auto Care Center acquisition/construction loan is consistent with what a lender would typically require for this type of loan. In essence, the lender wants to be able to step into the shoes of the borrower in the event of a default by the borrower. If the default occurs before construction is completed, the lender will want to be able to finish construction of the project.

   Importantly, the lender requires a mortgage of the land trust's fee simple title to the real property that is prior in right to any other liens so that if the lender forecloses on the mortgage, it can extinguish any other liens on the property. The lender also requires a separate security agreement whereby the borrower (the limited partnership or the LLC) pledges the equipment and any other personal property owned by the borrower in connection with the project. The land trust does not sign this security agreement, because it does not hold title to such non-real estate property. In the event of a default by the borrower, the lender can recover against this collateral through a U.C.C. sale since the collateral is in the form of personalty rather than realty.

7. The lender requires an assignment of leases and rents, so that during the period from the default until the foreclosure sale, it can attempt to recover income from the property and apply that income to pay necessary expenses of the project. By so applying the rents, the lender can prevent the borrower from pocketing the rents and not applying them to such necessary expenses. In addition, to the extent that certain leases will be in place before the mortgage lien is recorded, lenders will require that the tenants under such leases sign subordination, non-disturbance and attornment agreements ("SNAs"). SNAs typically provide that in the event the lender forecloses on the property, the tenant will "attorn" to the lender as the new owner (*i.e.*, agree to become tenant to the new owner). It also provides that the lease is subordinate in priority to the loan, but that the lender will not terminate the tenant's leasehold interest so long as the tenant is not in default under the lease.

8. As previously discussed, one reason the lender requires a collateral assignment of the beneficial interest in a land trust is for the possible election to perform a quick U.C.C. sale. Another possible benefit is that, through this document, the borrower and land trust agree that the land trust will not execute any document without the lender's consent. This

agreement prevents the land trust from executing other mortgages, leases, etc. without the lender's knowledge and consent.

9. First Mortgage Bank required Regent to obtain either an unconditional and irrevocable letter of credit in the amount of $200,000 for the benefit of First Mortgage Bank or a certificate of deposit in that amount as Regent's equity in the project, although, actually, it was the investors in the Fox Valley LLC who were responsible to obtain either the letter of credit or the certificate of deposit. The letter of credit and certificate of deposit serve as "credit enhancements," a topic that is covered in § 10.05, *infra*.

10. It is also typical for a lender to require guarantees of payment and completion of the project when the lender makes a construction loan. These are not usually required with a long-term loan that follows construction and completion of the real estate project (known as a "take-out" or "permanent loan"). These long-term loans usually bear interest at a fixed rate, are non-recourse, and do not require guarantees. This is because the take-out lender steps into the project after construction is completed and the project is leased up. The lender can look to the real and personal property pledged to recover the principal amount of the loan. If the borrower defaults when a project is under construction and not yet fully leased and the lender forecloses on the collateral pledged, the construction lender is less likely to be able to quickly resell the property to recover the loan made. Hence, the construction lender requires payment and completion guarantees from creditworthy persons or entities related to the borrowing entity as additional protection in the event of a default by the borrower.

11. Payment of the construction loan is not made in one lump sum to the developer. Instead, construction lenders will pay the loan in increments that relate to the phase of construction to make sure that the proceeds of the loan are applied to construction of the project pledged as security to the lender. In many states, contractors have special lien rights that provide a mechanism for them to be paid for the work they have performed. As will be discussed in Chapter 10, lenders will often require that payment of the loan proceeds be made through a construction escrow agreement with a title company as the escrowee. Under the terms of the escrow agreement, the disbursement is not made until the title company is willing to issue to the lender insurance that the amount of the loan disbursed is senior in right to any mechanic lien claims for work performed to that date.

12. Sometimes the most difficult aspect in evaluating a document is to ascertain what important points are missing. This Term Sheet was a very "bare-bones" summary of the terms of the proposed loan. If you were representing the lender in this deal, what additions would you consider making to it and why? Does the term sheet adequately address the critical aspects of the acquisition/construction loan? Consider this as you read the rest of this chapter, which provides an overview of the commercial loan process generally and the key issues borrowers and lenders must focus on at the loan commitment phase.

§ 9.03 BASIC LEGAL AND BUSINESS ISSUES

[1] Overview of the Commercial Loan Process

[a] "Tailoring" the Loan

The Robbins article below provides a good overview of the commercial loan process and an explanation of the key documents which evidence and secure the debt. The article also provides helpful suggestions in negotiating the terms of the loan transaction and provides some answers to question 12 above.

Martin B. Robbins,[*]
One Size Doesn't Fit All:
Negotiating Commercial Loan Transactions for Borrowers
CBA Record, May 1997, at 24[**]

It's (Not) Only a Letter — The Loan Commitment

Once the key economic terms are agreed on by the lender and borrower, they are often set forth in a commitment letter or term sheet signed by both parties. It is essential that the parties understand whether the commitment is intended to be binding. Much litigation has resulted from ambiguity. The document is often prepared by non-lawyer bankers or brokers, with the consequence that it is either unduly vague and/or flatly erroneous. If the document is considered binding, serious problems may result: a banker may be offended if the borrower balks at proceeding based on the letter, or the borrower may be forced to proceed with an unintended structure or pay a fee in order to avoid doing so. *The lesson is to determine, at the time the borrower is asked for its signature, whether the commitment is to be binding.* If so, the counsel should negotiate the document to the point that it reflects the agreed-on deal. Conversely, if it is not to be binding, this should be clearly stated. Of course, the borrower should understand the risk associated with a non-binding document: the lender may back out of the transaction.

Legal concerns aside, the transaction will proceed more smoothly if the borrower has carefully considered, and the commitment reflects, all of the fundamental economic terms. These would normally be (1) amount borrowed or available; (2) interest rate; (3) commitment duration; (4) repayment terms; (5) applicable fees; (6) collateral (including whether the loan is full or limited recourse); and (7) financial or operating covenants. While the loan documents will address all of these points and more in detail, *it is critical that the borrower be fully counseled, at an early stage, as to its obligations.*

Finally, the lender will desire to include the basis on which it may avoid its obligation to proceed. Even with a signed commitment, the borrower is not guaranteed to receive the funds. Among other things, the lender will usually have no obligation if final documents are not executed and conditions precedent satisfied by a date certain.

---

[*] Adjunct Professor, Depaul University College of Law.

Usually, the lender's counsel will prepare and submit to the borrower and its counsel a first draft of the loan documentation. At a minimum, there will be a promissory note, loan/security agreement, proceeds disbursement letter, and incumbency certificate or other evidence of the authority of the borrower and its officers or employees that sign the documents. In a secured financing, there will be numerous other materials, depending on the nature of the collateral and the service capability of the lender and borrower. If real estate is being pledged, a mortgage or deed of trust will have to be executed and recorded in the public records.

The Source of All Liability — The Note

The promissory note should be carefully scrutinized because it is the source of all of the borrower's obligations under the other documents. *It is critical that the appropriate borrower be named at the beginning of the note and the signature line.* In most cases, the note should do little more than state several of the key economic provisions, such as amount borrowed, interest rate and repayment schedule; however, *if the obligation is intended to be anything other than full recourse, then that intention must be explicitly stated in the note.* If the document is silent, the obligation is full recourse. A borrower's right to prepay the obligation must also be expressly stated in the note. Whatever the note's content, the borrower must sidestep duplicative notes to avoid potential multiple liability resulting from an erroneous or fraudulent transfer or theft of the instrument.

Meat on the Bones — The Loan Agreement

The loan agreement will normally address (1) the total amount of the financing and any formulas for advances . . . ; (2) interest rate computation; (3) the mechanics of borrowing and repayments, including minimum amounts and maximum frequencies for either; (4) in secured transactions, creation and preservation of the lender's security interest in the collateral (there may be a separate security agreement limited to this purpose); (5) conditions precedent to the obligations of the lender to disburse funds; (6) representations of the borrower concerning its business and finances, on which the lender will rely; (7) covenants of the borrower as to the operation of its business — these may pertain to its financial condition (*e.g.*, debt/equity ratio not to exceed a certain amount), or its operations (*e.g.*, reject risky types of orders), or to the collateral (*e.g.*, pay all taxes applicable to it); (8) events of default and lender remedies; (9) indemnities of the borrower in favor of the lender, such as protection against lawsuits involving the collateral (*e.g.*, environmental exposure) and agreements to pay legal and other costs associated with the drafting and enforcement of the loan documents; and (10) so-called "housekeeping" matters, such as significance of section captions, amendment procedures, supersession of prior oral and written agreements, and governing law. There may also be a separate definitional section if the volume of defined terms is large enough to warrant it.

The Bottom of the Pit — Amount and Duration of Financing

In connection with the total amount of the financing, the duration of the lender's commitment to advance funds must be checked. . . .

It is also essential to characterize the arrangements (1) a revolving facility [Editor's Note: This is a loan where the amount borrowed can be repaid and then re-borrowed]; (2) a line of credit with no re-borrowing of amounts that are repaid; or (3) a term loan with only one advance.

The Damage Estimate — Interest Rate Determination

If the facility calls for an adjustable interest rate, the borrower must understand and agree with the timing and extent of the adjustments. For any financing involving either a floating rate and/or multiple advances, the interest rate will probably be the sum of an "index" such as the Prime Rate, Treasury Bill Rate or London Interbank Offered Rate, and a "spread" of some negotiated amount, which is usually expressed in "basis points" or hundredths of a percentage point. *As long as the borrower agrees with the applicable index and spread, the only documentation concern should be the inclusion of a verifiable standard for their determination.*

A Technicality — Moving the Money

The borrowing and repayment mechanics section is rarely controversial; however, language should provide for fundings with sufficient frequency to meet the borrower's cash needs. . . . Similarly, extensive procedural requirements for fundings may have the same effect. Prepayment premiums should be carefully scrutinized, especially if they are in excess of a so-called "make whole" amount intended to compensate the lender for interest rate declines.

Your Firstborn Child — Collateral

Lenders will often seek to draft the grant of the security interest broadly so that it encompasses all obligations of the borrower to the lender. Thus, a satisfaction of one note does not result in a release of collateral. This is called "cross-collateralization." *It is preferable for the borrower to provide in the agreement for the staged release of collateral as obligations are satisfied.* The borrower should insist on the independence of each item of collateral, *i.e.*, a given item secures the borrower's obligations under a particular promissory note so its assets will be free to serve as collateral for other loans.

A second area of contention is likely to be collateral administration. The lender will usually demand some sort of control over the collateral. This may range from simple periodic reporting on status, to elaborate requirements for the holding of inventory in bonded, public warehouses (with the lender's approval needed to authorize any releases), to requirements for the obligors under leases to make payment directly to the lender. Apart from reporting requirements, collateral administration provisions may prove troublesome in connection with the conduct of the borrower's business. It is a rare company that wishes to involve its customers in the details of its banking arrangements; however, the borrower should always expect to furnish some level of assurance as to the continued existence of the collateral. Apart from requirements for the prepayment of taxes and insured premiums and provision of certificates of insurance in favor of the lender, this assurance will encompass limitations or prohibitions on collateral sales or modifications.

When Do We Get the Money? — Conditions Precedent

Conditions precedent may include both deliverables, such as legal opinions and lien searches, and substantive requirements, such as third party consents or the borrower's financial condition. In addition, it will almost always be required that the borrower's representations and warranties be true at the time of any subsequent funding. Deliverables are intended to establish that the borrower, as an entity, actually intends to and is able to perform its obligations under the loan agreement. *If other creditors exist, counsel must review their documentation to determine if their consent is required.*

The borrower's financial management must be consulted to ensure that the proposed substantive requirement provide sufficient latitude to accommodate fluctuations in its business. A potentially problematic standard is the customary provision that any "material" adverse change in the borrower's business, operations or financial condition not have occurred. A quantitative standard for "materiality" will vary with the nature and size of the borrower and must be negotiated into the definitional section.

Not Their Business! Yes It Is! — Use and Misuse of Representations and Warranties

The significance of this topic goes well beyond conditions. The material inaccuracy of the borrower's warranties will invariably constitute grounds for the lender to call a default. Thus, the borrower's management must approach the negotiation of this section with the utmost care.

Through this section, the borrower will be asked to "flesh out" the financial statements it provided to the lender. The warranties will, among other things, elaborate on many of the line items in the financials. This will often be accomplished through a disclosure schedule that will be attached to the loan agreement. This schedule will either request exceptions to a general statement or request a full enumeration. The warranties will address the borrower's assets and its fixed and contingent liabilities. They will encompass not only litigation that is then pending but also situations that may give rise to future litigation and/or governmental claims. For example, environmental violations have lately emerged as a "hot" subject for warranties.

Counsel should also advise the borrower as to the potential loss of confidentiality (attorney/client privilege and otherwise) associated with exceptions to otherwise "clean" warranties. In all cases, *borrowers must make complete and accurate disclosures* of the matters that are addressed and *attempt to negotiate the deletion of matters that would involve a great burden on the borrower to compile.*

It is often said that borrowers should err on the side of over-disclosure to avoid a future assertion of default by the lender. From a legal standpoint, this is true; however, the borrower is not well served if an unnecessary disclosure results in the lender either calling off the transaction or re-pricing it to the borrower's detriment. In cases of genuine uncertainty, counsel must thoroughly advise client management of the risks associated with each alternative and defer to its decision, without knowingly participating in or encouraging the borrower to perpetrate a fraud on a lender or anyone else.

An additional potential problem area is the customary request for "global" warranties pertaining to financial statements. The usual request will be for confirmation that the statements fairly present the borrower's financial condition and results of operations and are in accordance with generally accepted accounting principles. For a borrower that customarily obtains audited financial statements, this is less of a problem. Even then, the delivery of unaudited interim financial statements requires special scrutiny to ensure that no material differences occur between the audited and unaudited statements.

When the borrower does not deliver audited statements, this issue becomes more problematic. It is unreasonable for the borrower to take responsibility for the application of specialized expertise when this has not in fact been the case. In this situation, the borrower should confine its warranty to an acknowledgment that it is unaware of any material inaccuracies in the statement on which the lender relies. Support for this warranty will still require a conservative analysis of the borrower's finances, with an emphasis on areas involving discretion. For example, the balance sheet maintenance of the goodwill of an acquired company requires a determination that the acquired company still has material going-concern value above the value of its individual assets. Similarly, management must exercise discretion regarding reserves for impaired receivables and contingent liabilities.

When the borrower has previously been a party to other financings with a different lender, *counsel should also closely review any warranties as to the non-encumbrance of assets to ensure that an asset currently being pledged is not already subject to a blanket lien.*

I'll Pay Back the Money — What's This Other Stuff? — Covenants

The topic of covenants is closely related to the topic of warranties. In both cases, the items included in the loan agreement must be customized to fit the borrower's present and anticipated circumstances. A breach of a covenant will permit the lender to call a default and accelerate the outstanding loan balance while ceasing further advances.

Covenants sections traditionally include three types of items: boilerplate (matters such as maintenance of the borrower's corporate existence and place of business), operating provisions (pertaining to the decisional process for certain matters and permissible and prohibited activities), and financial covenants (pertaining to the borrower's ongoing financial condition).

Boilerplate items typically have little impact on the conduct of the borrower's operations. Operating items may significantly impact the borrower's operations if they slow down its decisional cycle or involve the lender or someone else (such as a board of directors) in operations to a cumbersome event. Counsel must consult with the borrower to evaluate these ramifications and negotiate appropriate modifications.

Financial covenants often prove to be the most significant and controversial material in the loan agreement. . . . For example, covenants might limit the incurrence of additional debt or the expenditure of additional capital; they might do this directly or through requirements governing the income or cash that must be generated and retained relative to interest payments and other fixed charges. If these covenants are unduly restrictive, the firm may not be able to pursue the often risky ventures needed to penetrate new markets. . . . Thus, while it is reasonable for the lender to insist on assurances that the borrower's financial condition will permit it to make the required payments, the borrower must insist on retaining the flexibility needed to permit business expansion. Even if the borrower will be able to comply with a particular covenant proposed by a lender, its management still must question whether it is desirable to do so.

Covenant compliance should not be taken for granted. The borrower should reflect on its margin of error in the event that it suffers adversity. While it is impossible to craft covenants that will be met in the event of a total marketplace or natural disaster, it is imprudent to disregard the possibility of market downturn or seasonality.

To the extent that the borrower either has a long business relationship with the lender or has an objectively strong financial condition, the lender's need for restrictive financial covenants is reduced. The reverse is also true — if the borrower has not dealt with the particular lender or is in questionable financial circumstances, it will have to reconcile itself to living with some sort of substantial covenants, but must fully understand their import and reasonably expect to comply.

Oops! I Blew It! Now What? — Default and Remedies

The loan agreement must be negotiated with the intention that the borrower will fully comply with it, and the default section must be specifically addressed to avoid inadvertent noncompliance and to mitigate the consequences of any noncompliance that does occur. The borrower will be in default if it fails to make the required payments. While this concept is non-controversial in cases in which the borrower does not have the funds, the borrower must also be cognizant of situations in which the funds are available but a deadline is missed because of an outright error. Although the lender's desire for a good business relationship will normally permit this situation to be resolved with a phone call, this may not be the case if interest rates have risen since the loan was written or if the lender and borrower have been in conflict. The lender may seize on any seemingly trivial breach by the borrower to try to recover its money and lend it elsewhere. *The lesson is that the borrower should insist on the provision of written notice of and an opportunity to cure any occurrence that would constitute a default.* Lenders invariably extend this provision on request, with payment cure periods ranging from five to twenty days.

It is also customary for loan agreements to include as events of default the borrower's failure to comply with covenants or the inaccuracy of representations and warranties at the time they were made. A cure period is essential here, but in practice, it will have to be longer than the payment cure period to give the borrower enough time to take whatever action is required. To avoid needless controversy, a materiality standard should be inserted.

A different type of event is the cross-default, under which a default on one lender's obligation constitutes a default on that of another. This can have the effect of turning a manageable predicament involving one lender into a catastrophe involving all of a company's debt-holders, which is likely to push it into bankruptcy. [Editor's note: To try to avoid this situation, real estate lenders require that the entity that owns the real estate be a "single purpose entity" with the entity only owning the real estate project and no other assets, thereby reducing the chances that there are other lenders with other obligations that the borrower could be in breach of.] When borrowers have debt with several lenders, the bankers will request such provisions to avoid tying the hands of one lender while the others push a troubled borrower into default. While the bankruptcy law contains "preference" provisions intended to mitigate the effect of such a scenario, any rational lender would greatly prefer to avoid it. *Cross-default provisions should be avoided wherever possible. If their omission is not possible, a dollar threshold should be included.*

The nature of the lender's remedies on default may determine if a default situation is just an undesirable event or if it is the beginning of the end for the borrower. While all loan agreements will provide that a missed payment will entitle the lender to accelerate the principal balance, in a secured financing, other consequences may ensue. The lender may be entitled, immediately and without legal process, to seize assets and sell them. *To the extent possible, the borrower should always require some legal process before the lender can enforce its lien on collateral.* This will give the borrower some time to try to refinance with another lender.

No matter what an agreement may say about when collateral may be seized, there is also the question of which items may be seized. A high degree of cross-collateralization may impede the borrower's efforts to obtain other financing. It also exacerbates the consequences of a default. Accordingly, a borrower will want collateral released on satisfaction of the corresponding obligation so that it may be sold or used without restriction. To have this right, the loan agreement must expressly assign specific collateral to a specific obligation.

The remedies analysis must be conducted by reference not only to the remedies section of the loan agreement but also to the granting clause of the collateral section and to the granting clause and remedies sections of the separate security agreement, if one exists. *Borrower's counsel should be alert for seemingly innocuous granting clauses that recite that a particular asset secures all obligations of the borrower to that lender.* Likewise, special attention should be paid to after-acquired property provisions, which not only grant a lien on currently owned assets but also extend the lien to assets thereafter acquired. Such a provision is inevitable in the event of a receivable or inventory financing, but not otherwise.

You Mean the Interest Isn't Enough — Lender's Expenses

Even worse than having to pay money to a lender in the event of a default is having to make such a payment when no default exists. This, however, is simply part of the financing process. Most loan agreements submitted by lenders require the borrower to pay the lender's legal and other expenses in connection with the negotiation, modification and enforcement of the agreement. There is no reason for a borrower to assume that it must pay any of its lender's expenses, and they are negotiable in contexts other than an enforcement action. Such items should be viewed as a loan pricing issue and negotiated accordingly with a cap on the expenses for which the borrower will be responsible. Also, the borrower should feel free to question whether the expense of particular deliverables must be incurred at all. For example, a lien search will be essential for a first transaction with a noninvestment-grade borrower and will involve a substantial expense, but the same is not necessarily true for a fifth transaction between a given lender and a highly-rated borrower. Similarly, the borrower may be able to persuade the lender to accept an in-house legal opinion in lieu of a law firm opinion. These agreements should be contained in the commitment letter as well as the loan agreement.

Closely related to the borrower's liability for out-of-pocket expenses is the universal demand for the borrower's indemnity for third party claims associated with the financing. While this issue was of largely theoretical significance until recently, the expansion of environmental liability during the past 20 years has justifiably caused real estate and other secured lenders concern that they will be held responsible for some aspect of the borrower's use of the pledged collateral, whether or not they foreclose on it. Borrowers should expect to furnish some indemnity against third party claims. *They should seek to limit it to reimbursing out-of-pocket losses resulting from a final judgment* and should seek to reserve for themselves the authority to conduct litigation and enter into a settlement.

Nuts and Bolts — Housekeeping Provisions and Ancillary Documents

The housekeeping provisions are worthy of the borrower's attention, but only a limited amount. The mechanics for delivery of notice (recipient, medium and timing) should be complied with, regardless of any oral discussion between the parties. Choice of forum and required arbitration clauses should be considered to avoid manifest inconvenience in the event of a dispute. *The borrower may wish to negotiate some special amendment or waiver provision to expedite process in cases in which speed becomes essential,* for example, in situations involving multiple lenders. Apart from a substantive critique of customary legal opinions, which may be found in detail elsewhere in the literature (such as 47 *Business Lawyer* 167 Nov. 1991 "Third Party Legal Opinions and Legal Opinion Accord of the Section of Business Law, American Bar Association"), the best advice with respect to other documents is to address these ancillary materials at an early stage of the transaction to ascertain what is required and procure it on a timely basis. Counsel should pay particular attention to required approvals, such as those of the borrower's board of directors or stockholders.

While the "how to's" of advising a borrower are somewhat involved and technical, they can be easily summarized: borrowers and their counsel must negotiate all material provisions of the structure and documentation to ensure that they are tailored to accommodate the requirements of the particular borrower and that the documentation reflects the parties' actual agreement. Put another way, one size loan does not fit all! [Editor's note: The idea that "one size" of loan documents "does not fit all" is quite valid, yet for commercial real estate loans intended for the secondary market, borrowers were often told that the terms of the loan documents could not be significantly modified since that would adversely affect the ability to sell the loans as part of a pool of mortgage loans. Real estate developer/borrowers often agreed to this approach because the loans intended for the secondary market were often at a lower interest rate/cost than portfolio loans intended to be held by the originating lender.]

[b] Comments on the Overview of the Commercial Loan Process

The Robbins article focused on loans to already operating businesses (both real estate and other asset based loans) and not on the special issues that arise when financing construction of a real estate project. The next two articles, by Garfinkel, will focus on addressing these special construction issues, such as methods to reduce the risk of mechanic's lien claims, at the loan commitment stage.

[2] Overview of the Special Issues Involved in Construction Loans

[a] Addressing Issues at the Loan Commitment Phase

Marvin Garfinkel,
The Negotiation of Construction and Permanent Loan Commitments (Part I),
25 THE PRACTICAL LAWYER No. 1, at 13 (March 1979)*

[Editor's note: Much of the original Garfinkel articles that follow were devoted to the interrelationship between the borrower, the construction lender, and the "permanent" or "take-out" lender. In the 1970s and 1980s, it was common for construction lenders to insist that a permanent lender was lined up to pay off the construction loan when certain conditions were met as a precondition for the construction lender to make the construction loan. This arrangement was created through an agreement among the borrower, the construction lender and the permanent lender entered into prior to funding the construction loan and referred to as a "Buy-Sell Agreement" or "Tri-Party Agreement." By the end of the 1980s, this arrangement was no longer typical and, as recently as the middle of 2007 (prior to the recent credit crunch), rather than insist on a Buy-Sell agreement, construction lenders would make a loan whose term would cover not only the estimated period of construction, but extend to the point when the project was estimated to operate in a stabilized fashion (at which point the borrower was expected to be able to obtain a take-out loan). Because Tri-Party Agreements have been rarely used for so many years, we elected to delete most of those portions of Mr. Garfinkel's article from this chapter, but have retained his discussion of construction issues that should be addressed at the loan commitment and loan documentation stage.]

A primary concern of the construction lender is that the project be completed; hence, with a reasonable margin for safety and contingencies, the cost of completion should at no time exceed the available undisbursed balance of the construction loan. In the language of the industry, the loan at all times must "remain in balance."

To this end, the construction lender will require at the construction loan settlement evidence of the anticipated cost of the completion of construction and proof that any amount — "gap" — by which the anticipated construction costs — including all professional fees, interest, taxes, and other builder's reserve items —

exceed the construction loan will be available. It is not unusual for the construction lender to require that cash equal to the gap be deposited in escrow with it prior to commencement of construction, and that this gap money be disbursed prior to any loan proceeds.

. . . .

The Borrower-Developer

The borrower-developer is seeking to construct one or more buildings or other real estate improvements with a minimum, if any, investment of its own capital. It is important to the developer that, as the project progresses, sufficient funds become available to finance construction and construction-related costs such as interest, overhead expenses, taxes, insurance premiums, professional fees, and marketing expenses. A developer may also try to limit its exposure in terms of liability in excess of its investment in the project. . . .

The investor-developer, on the other hand, is concerned that the project be completed on time in accordance with the approved plans and specifications. . . .

The General Contractor

If a general contractor not related to the developer is employed to build the project, the general contractor will want, as a minimum, to be paid promptly for work in place as construction proceeds, and to be paid all retainage within a reasonable period after substantial completion of construction. Ideally, the general contractor would like to be certain that so long as it performs its obligations under the general contract, the owner-developer will likewise perform its obligations. This requires an owner who has substantial financial resources other than the construction loan and the project that is being developed — a circumstance all too often unattainable.

The general contractor's investment in the project at any point in time prior to the disbursement of the full retainage is equal to the amount by which the sums it has expended or incurred for labor, material and overhead and paid to subcontractors exceeds the sum drawn against the construction loan or otherwise paid by the owner to the general contractor. To these out-of-pocket and accrued expenses must be added the liability of the general contractor under equipment and material purchase orders and to subcontractors for work to be performed at later stages of construction.

To reduce its investment and perhaps even to anticipate profits, the general contractor, and, in turn, its various subcontractors, may seek to "front-end load" the job — that is, structure the payment schedule so that the amount paid during the early part of the job exceeds the actual value, less retainage, of the work done. This attempt tends to defeat the objective of the construction lender — and the developer, if other than the general contractor — that at all times the undisbursed balance of the construction loan must exceed the sum that would probably be required to complete the work. An alternative to front-end loading of the payment schedule is to overestimate the value of work already performed. The owner and construction lender will, however, seek to avoid this by diligent inspection and evaluation of the rate of progress of the job and by exercising corresponding control of the payment vouchers approved during the course of construction.

Risk Shifting

. . . .

The attorney representing each of the parties to a construction loan transaction seeks to shift the risk of the unexpected from his client.

This article will deal with those aspects of negotiation and documentation that relate to the probability of a default and are intended to cushion the effect of the default upon one or another party to the transaction. It will not concern itself with the negotiation of the business terms of the construction loan arrangement, such as interest rates, front end fees (points), and other service charges.

The Construction Loan

A construction loan bank officer will normally base his risk-taking evaluations upon the quality of the project, market analysis, and past experience with, or the reputation of, the developer, the general contractor if other than the developer, and the permanent lender. Offers of personal guarantees and extraneous collateral rarely affect a lender's decision as to whether to make a loan, although collateral is often required by a lender as a condition to granting a construction loan.

A construction lender will often ask for items of security in excess of those demanded by the permanent lender in order to better protect itself during the high risk construction period. It will seek security that is ample to satisfy any loan balance which might remain if the permanent loan closes but fails to produce sufficient funds to repay the entire loan balance. This might occur, for instance, if, as a result of construction delays or a dramatic increase in interest rates, the interest reserve initially established fails to cover the actual interest accruing prior to the closing of the permanent loan. Under those circumstances, if the borrower is unable to cover the gap from its own resources, the construction lender may be forced to increase the loan amount to prevent a default. . . .

A bank's internal procedures often require that its credit department approve all proposed real estate loans that have been structured by a real estate loan officer. Personal guarantees by the individual principals of the developer are usually required by the construction lender to provide a most significant inducement for them to complete the job and deliver the loan to the permanent lender. A personal guarantee is a useful device to prevent a developer from flying away from the aggravations of a project in trouble.

If a project is to be developed by a limited partnership, the general partner, may, for tax reasons, resist becoming personally liable on the construction loan. Under sections 704 and 752 of the Internal Revenue Code, a limited partner's deductions for partnership losses is generally limited to his contribution to the partnership plus his share of the partnership's non-recourse debt. Specifically, a partner's loss allocation for tax purposes is limited to the adjusted basis for federal income tax purposes of his partnership interest at the end of the partnership year in which the loss occurred. An increase in a partner's share of the liabilities of the partnership or any increase in a partner's individual liabilities by reason of his assumption of partnership liabilities is treated as a contribution by him of money to the partnership. Any debt for which the general partner alone is personally liable will generally not be allocated to any of the limited partners for purposes of determining the tax basis of the limited partners' interest in the partnership.

It thus often becomes important that the non-recourse nature of a construction loan be preserved. A properly drafted guarantee of completion by a general partner, or preferably by a general-contractor affiliate of the general partner, rather than by the general partner himself, may satisfy the construction lender that the developer will not lose interest in the project and, at the same time, satisfy the partnership's tax counsel that the loan amount will be allocated among all the partners for basis determination purposes under section 752.

It is unusual for a construction lender not to require some form of personal guarantee unless the actual construction is to be performed by a bonded general contractor. When that happens, the construction lender depends upon the obligation under the performance bond coupled with an adequate holdback as reasonable assurance of completion. Since a performance bond only guarantees performance of the general contractor's obligations under the construction contract, it is most important for a construction lender who is relying upon a performance bond to be sure that, to the greatest extent possible, the general contract actually requires the delivery of a completed building by the contractor for a specified maximum sum without any conditions that are not reasonably within the control of the construction lender.

Even at its best, a performance bond is not security in the true sense of the term. It is a safe document for a loan officer to require in order to complete his file and evidence his due diligence. As a practical matter, a lender seeking to collect under such a bond has a rough row to hoe.

The ability of a contractor to deliver a bond does, at least, qualify him as being considered an appropriate bonding risk by a bonding company. Since a contractor's ability to secure bonds may be his life blood, there is some possibility that he will protect his bonding line of credit by fully performing his contractual obligations under bonded contracts. A corporate contractor's individual principals will often provide security in the form of personal guarantees to their bonding company that go far beyond what an owner would require of a general contractor.

The Construction Loan Commitment

The construction lender will obviously concern itself most deeply with the financial responsibility of the developer. A paramount concern is whether the developer will, if required, be capable of advancing additional funds to protect the project.

Although useful to arrange the basis of the loan arrangement, a formal construction loan commitment is not essential and is oftentimes either completely ignored or so abbreviated as to consist only of a brief memorandum of the salient provisions of the proposed loan. A construction lender with extensive experience and an ongoing relationship with a particular developer will thus often rely upon a relatively informal construction loan commitment. On the other hand, many lenders will use multi-paged detailed commitments.

. . . A final construction loan commitment can generally be fashioned only after . . . an arrangement with the general contractor, if other than the developer, ha[s] been established. Before the construction loan can be concluded, the . . . general contract arrangement [must be] basically completed, and the costs of construction through subcontracts must be settled. [Editor's note: Some level of specified lease achievement may also be a precondition to funding, even by the construction lender, in projects such as hotels, shopping centers, warehouses, industrial parks, and office buildings].

. . . .

The Terms

The actual construction loan commitment, if one is used, will concern itself in more or less detail with such matters as the loan amount, interest rate, service charges and loan fees, term, and security. It will also establish various conditions precedent to closing on the construction loan, including . . . the quality of the title to be provided, a specification of fire, liability, rent loss, and workmen's compensation insurance requirements, and possibly a personal guaranty requirement. The commitment should specify generally the provisions to be contained in the construction loan agreement itself, including a requirement that construction be completed in accordance with certain plans and specifications for a maximum specified sum. If the interest rate is based on a prime rate, the method of determining the applicable prime rate should be stated. The construction loan commitment should also describe the manner in which the difference between the loan amount and the total project cost will be provided by the developer.

Commercial banks and mortgage brokers and other mortgage intermediaries that customarily borrow funds from commercial banks will often relate the interest rate to a prime rate. Although the practice varies throughout the country, the interest rate on loans by insurance companies, savings banks, and savings and loan associations will often be based on the market rates in effect at the time the commitment is issued. [Editor's note: Since this article was written, many other players became the source of real estate financing including investment groups, pension funds, syndicators, hedge funds, and investment banking firms, and the interest rates they charge are still based on market rates in effect prior to the loan being made, and for securitized loans, the rate is not fixed until twenty-four to forty-eight hours prior to when the loan is made.] The dangers inherent in a variable interest loan pegged to a prime rate are obvious. Predictability of total project cost is, from the point of view of both the construction lender and the developer, the keynote of a successful project. A variable rate without a limit injects an unknown factor of possible catastrophic magnitude. The interest is typically paid from the construction loan advances. It is doubtful whether a construction lender would ever proceed with a project if any other cost item were so uncertain. As a rule of thumb, approximately half of the full loan amount will be outstanding for the full term of actual construction. On this basis, if the cost of construction is to be \$5 million and construction is to take 18 months, the interest cost at an 8% rate will be approximately \$300,000 [\$5 million × 1.5 × .08 × .5]. Obviously, a delay in construction time or an increase in interest rates may have a significant effect on the total fund requirements. For instance, an increase of 4 percentage points over the life of the loan will add approximately \$150,000 to the total project costs. If we assume a 10% developer's equity — \$500,000 — this \$150,000 amounts to a 30% increase in equity requirements. [Editor's note: As previously discussed, due to the risk of rising interest rates during the term of the construction loan, some lenders require the borrower to enter into an interest rate swap or cap to mitigate this risk.]

Often, construction lenders will issue letters of intent, rather than loan commitments, because of the number of variables involved and the difficulties of adequately documenting a construction loan commitment. The conditions precedent to settlement on the construction loan that are found in a construction loan agreement provide a good summary of the various items that must be handled by the developer's counsel in preparation for the construction loan settlement.

Construction Related Conditions

The paramount concern of the construction lender is the completion of the facility upon which the loan is predicated. To the construction lender, the facility consists not only of a building such as a single family house, a phase of a condominium project, an apartment house, or a warehouse, but it also includes all onsite and offsite improvements required before the building can be sold or produce its full projected income. . . . There is a significant possibility that the loan may experience serious problems if the physical improvements constructed differ significantly from those contemplated by the loan commitment.

Drawings and Specifications

. . . .

Premature commencement of construction might also be induced by extraneous circumstances, like the imposition of new zoning or environmental regulations in the locality, the possibility of sewer or other utility moratoriums, changes in building codes, the timing of trade union contract terminations, climatic conditions, and backlogs in agency approvals. In certain localities, construction will often proceed on major projects on the basis of foundation building permits only. "Foundation only" permits, if available, will usually be issued subject to the right of the permitting agency to approve or disapprove the final working drawings and specifications. In addition, the permit-issuing agency will reserve the right to require modifications to the previously approved foundation plans in the event that, upon receipt of the final plans for the entire building, it determines that the previously developed foundations are not appropriate to support the structure as finally engineered. Needless to say, the necessity of any modification may have a catastrophic effect on the project. It might, for instance, require a significant design change to accommodate additional footings or perhaps a major redesign of a structural system.

Mechanic's Liens

The commencement of construction prior to the execution of all construction documents presents major problems in those states in which the priority of the lien of the construction mortgage is based upon the "obligatory advance doctrine." Under this doctrine, the lien of a mortgage is established upon each advance of funds as to such advance, not upon the recording of the mortgage, unless the mortgagee is obligated to advance the funds on the basis of the occurrence of circumstances over which it has no independent control. Most obligatory advance states also generally adhere to the "relation back doctrine," pursuant to which a mechanic's lien dates from the commencement of construction on the project even by a contractor or subcontractor other than the one claiming the lien. In those states that apply both doctrines, the lien of the construction mortgagee as to funds advanced after the commencement of construction will have priority over a mechanic's lien only if the construction loan mortgage is recorded prior to the commencement of construction *and* the construction lender is obligated at that time to advance the loan proceeds on the basis of objective criteria that are not subject to his control.

If a construction lender or developer is contemplating activity in a state other than its own, it must, at least prior to the issuance or acceptance of any loan commitment, familiarize itself with the local mechanics' lien laws. Many a developer has seriously jeopardized a project by prematurely commencing construction in a "relation back-obligatory advance" state before an obligatory advance construction loan agreement was executed and the construction loan mortgage recorded.

Progress Payments

The schedule of progress payments may be based upon either designated stages of construction or the percentage of completion by the various construction trades. Under the stages of completion approach, which is the simplest to arrange and is common for smaller or for single family house projects, a specified number of dollars are disbursed at each visible stage of construction. . . .

Under the percentage completion by trades approach, the general contractor or developer submits a schedule to the construction lender that allocates the entire contemplated hard construction cost — the so-called "brick and mortar costs" — among the various construction trades, such as carpenters, masons, excavators, electricians, plumbers, plasterers, and painters. As construction proceeds, progress payments are disbursed on the basis of the estimated percentage completion of each trade. This approach is customarily employed on larger projects, and its use raises the front-end load problem.

It is vital to the construction lender and, if an unrelated general contractor is used, also to the owner, that the progress payments as construction proceeds do not exceed a predetermined percentage — usually 90% — of the actual cost of construction to that point in time. Although now construction contracts and loan agreements sometimes provide for half of the accumulated retainage to be distributed at some point prior to the substantial completion of construction — perhaps, halfway through a job — the undisbursed balance of the retainage, less any "punch-list" reserve [Editor's note: the "punch list" consists of items to be completed or corrected after substantial completion of the construction], is generally distributed only upon substantial completion. . . .

The provisions of the construction loan commitment relating to the physical process of construction will vary according to whether the developer will also function as its own general contractor or whether there will be a financially responsible and possibly bonded general contractor who will build the project under a legally binding contract with the developer. If an unrelated general contractor is involved, the construction lender will often require that the general contract itself be assigned to the construction lender, and if a performance bond is required, that the construction lender be made a joint obligee under the bond. The construction loan commitment will provide for the approval by the construction lender of the general contract and, possibly, also of the prime subcontracts, as well as his acceptance of the performance and payment bonds issued thereunder.

Assignment of Interests

The construction lender will seek to assure that, in the event of a default, either it, or, more practically, its nominee will be in a position to step into the shoes of the borrower-developer in order to complete the construction of the work. The construction lender will secure a contractual right in the event of default to succeed the developer's various project-related rights and assets — including the architectural contract, purchase orders, subcontracts, the building permit, sewer and utility connection authorizations, and leases. In the case of a project such as a hotel, the construction lender may seek to secure from the hotel franchisor the privilege of designating a qualified nominee to operate the project under the franchise in lieu of the developer or its lessee in the event of a default. Nevertheless, the experience of most construction lenders has been that it is far better under default circumstances to work with the defaulting developer in attempting to complete the project rather than for the lender to take over the physical construction.

. . . .

Marvin Garfinkel, *The Negotiation of Construction and Permanent Loan Commitments (Part 2)*, 25 The Practical Lawyer No. 2, at 37 (April 1979)*

. . . .

Credit Lease Requirements

So-called "credit leases" with highly rated tenants generally form the foundation of the economic viability of commercial rental projects, such as shopping centers, warehouses, factories, industrial park type buildings, motion picture theaters, free-standing stores, bank buildings, service stations, tire stores, and restaurants. . . . The form and the terms of the lease are either specified in some detail in the . . . commitment or made subject to the approval of the . . . lender. [Editor's note: In the absence of a take-out loan commitment, construction lenders would typically at least require that a certain percentage of the project is under lease before funding the construction loan to better ensure that once construction is completed, the project will successfully be in operation which will make it easier for the borrower to then obtain a longer term loan.]

. . . .

Default Problems

Construction lenders are becoming increasingly sensitive to the possible use by developers and others with a conflicting interest of the debtor rehabilitation provisions of the Federal Bankruptcy Act. So-called "chapter proceedings" are often initiated to prevent a construction lender seeking to limit its losses from taking control of a defaulting project. The developer will often threaten to utilize these procedures in order to extract from the construction lender concessions in the form of releases from personal liability, cash payments for equity positions of little value, or agreements not to proceed against posted collateral security or under or against performance bonds or third party agreements. To reduce their exposure to demands in the event of trouble, construction lenders will often require assignments absolute on their face of all of the various rights held by the developer. [Editor's note: As is explained in detail in Section 10.03, bankruptcy court decisions have clarified that the assignment of rents does not need to be "absolute" in order to have a "perfected" security agreement that would be enforced in a bankruptcy action (for perfection, the assignment of rents just needs to be properly recorded). Bankruptcy courts have also clarified that a "conditional absolute" assignment of rents will not cause post-petition rents to become the lender's property rather than a part of the debtor's estate, however, the conditional absolute assignment language may still persuade some courts to more favorably treat the rents as "cash collateral" under the bankruptcy code. This topic is discussed in detail in Section 10.03 along with other "bankruptcy proofing" devices lenders now typically require, which originated with loans intended for the secondary market.] A developer is much more likely to subject a corporation he controls to a debtor rehabilitation proceeding than to subject himself. If the lender can foreclose against the stock of the corporation, the developer has little motivation to seek relief on behalf of the corporation. The only relief that would be of value would be a stay of execution against the assets of the developer — i.e., the stock of the corporation — and such a stay would generally be available in the context of a chapter proceeding only if the holder of the stock, and not the corporation itself, were subject to the protection of the bankruptcy court.

Lenders will on occasion require hypothecation of the stock or other evidence of ownership of the entity owning the real estate so as to avoid the necessity of real estate foreclosure proceedings, [Editor's note: In Illinois and other states that recognize land trusts, lenders may require the borrower to have a land trust be the fee simple title holder to be able to perform a simpler U.C.C. sale of the beneficial interest in the land trust to try to avoid a more complicated real estate foreclosure sale.] It is usually more expeditious to proceed under the Uniform Commercial Code against personalty such as stock than to foreclose against real estate. In subjecting the stock to a lien in its favor, the construction lender should be sure that the corporation is more than a mere nominee titleholder, with the real ownership in the developer or some other entity such as a limited partnership. The construction lender will also secure an assignation of all development rights, like building permits and authorizations by governmental authorities, franchises, in the case of hotels and restaurants, leases, and all construction related documents, such as architectural and engineering agreements, the general contract purchase orders, and subcontracts.

Furthermore, many construction lenders require that all subcontractors agree that in the event of a default by the developer under the construction loan, they will complete the work for the unpaid balance due in the subcontracts if requested by the construction lender, and that these undertakings be assignable, subject only to the obligation of the construction lender to pay for work done and materials supplied *after* it takes over the project.

This provision that third parties acknowledge rights in the construction lender may lead to negotiations between the construction lender and the third parties. The general contractor, for instance, often has no choice but to look to the construction loan as its sole source of payment. Hence, it may seek some assurances from the construction lender that in the event the construction lender should take over the job in a default situation, the construction lender will make all payments to which the general contractor is entitled. Most construction lenders will resist such an obligation. A possible alternative for the construction lender is to agree that if it avails itself of the general contractor after taking over the project, it will pay both for work prior to, as well as following, its assumption of the project. Often the commitment will extend to the amount due for work for which construction funds have not been disbursed yet — work not included in vouchers against which advances have actually been made.

When the general contractor understands that the owner has no significant resources other than the funds from the construction loan, the general contractor often will enter into a contract only if the construction lender agrees that in the event the lender takes over the project and proceeds to complete construction, the general contractor will be employed by the construction lender to finish the work. Provisions, however, should be made for renegotiation or escalation of prices in the event of a significant time delay or other major change of circumstances.

[b] Comments and Questions Regarding the Special Issues in Construction Loans

1. The Garfinkel articles focused on the various goals of the borrower/developer, borrower/investor, construction lender, and general contractor in a construction of a real estate project; identifies the key risks to achieving these goals that can arise, and then summarizes methods to address these risks of loss. All of the parties (in particular the construction lender and borrower/investor) have an interest in the construction of the project being completed on time, in accordance with the plans and specifications, within budget and lien free. Of critical concern to the borrower/developer is that there be sufficient funds from the construction lender to pay for the construction. Of particular concern to the general contractor is that she is paid promptly as work progresses in an amount necessary to pay her out of pocket expenses and a portion of the general contractor's hoped for profit.

2. Among the typical key risks that can arise during the construction process that Garfinkel discusses are cost overruns, failure of the contractor or subcontractors to perform all of the work, defects with the work, failure of the borrower/developer to pay the contractor, and bankruptcy of one or more of the players. How do these various risks get addressed through obligations imposed and procedures required under the construction loan agreement? For example, how are progress payments with retainage requirements used to reduce the risk of cost overruns? What is "front loading"? In the event that the borrower/developer is in default under the construction loan, how is the lender able to mitigate its losses? Can you think of any other risks to the lender that arise in a construction loan as contrasted with a "take-out" loan? For example, what if there are defects in the construction that the lender funded. Could the borrower/developer

claim that the lender would be liable to the borrower for the damages from such defects? What if during the course of construction the borrower asked the bank's loan officer to withhold payments due to construction defects detected until the problems were corrected and the bank refused to do so without investigating the truth of the borrower's claims? Do you think a lender should have a duty to exercise care to identify defective construction? *See Davis v. Nevada National Bank*, 103 Nev. 220, 737 P.2d 503 (1987) ("a lender normally has no duty to exercise care to identify unworkmanlike or deficient construction. . . . However, it would be unjust to permit a lender, with impunity, to simply disregard a borrower's complaint of *substantial* construction deficiencies affecting the structural integrity of a project. . . .").

3. Later you will be reviewing some of the key loan documents for the Fox Valley Auto Care Center. Keep the points of the Garfinkel and Robbins articles in mind and the potential lender liability issue discussed above when you review these documents to see how well the lender and borrower protected their respective interests when they negotiated these loan documents.

4. Note that the Garfinkel article was written in 1979. The Fox Valley Auto Care Center was developed ten years after the article was written. One key change that occurred during that period regarding the structuring of loans was the development of what became known as "mini-perm loans" (loans from a commercial bank that often took out its own construction loans). The term of the loan for the Auto Care Center project was scheduled to end seven months after the anticipated completion of construction. During that period, it was anticipated that the developer would be able to secure a take-out loan (this was still during the time when lenders and their money were aggressively chasing after borrowers and real estate projects; this changed in 1990 when a real estate recession hit). In addition, the lender in the project had made oral assurances to the borrower that if the borrower was unable to obtain the take-out loan by the time the construction loan matured, the lender would rollover the loan for another year so the borrower could then secure a permanent loan. Unfortunately, the real estate recession hit right around the time the construction loan became due. What impact do you think that had on Regent's ability to obtain a take-out loan? As previously noted, as recently as the middle of 2007 (just before the liquidity crisis began to emerge), it was still common practice for a construction loan to fund without requiring the borrower to obtain a take-out loan as a precondition. As we enter a period of conservative lending, perhaps construction lenders will start to require the presence of a take-out loan as a precondition to funding the construction loan as conventionally took place in the 1970s.

5. Garfinkel notes in his discussion of the construction loan commitment that, although it is useful to nail down the basics of the loan arrangement, a formal loan commitment is not essential and often is ignored. This is especially the case early in the deal if the construction lender is experienced and has an ongoing relationship with the developer. Why do you think this is so? What risks does this create for a borrower or a lender? For example, many states have statutes that require for a loan

commitment to be enforced, or any other action to be brought in contract or tort regarding the alleged credit agreement, that the loan commitment or credit agreement must be in writing and signed by both parties.

[3] Enforcing the Loan Commitment

As the Garfinkel articles indicate, the main function of the loan commitment is to bind the lender to make, and the borrower to take, the loan contemplated between the parties, subject to any conditions to funding expressed in the loan commitment. In the event that circumstances not covered by these conditions change for the parties, the loan commitment is still binding. Thus, one of the most important aspects of the loan commitment is that it be drafted in a manner that makes it a binding obligation.

[a] Enforceability of Loan Commitments

The case that follows is included not only to illustrate what is necessary for a loan commitment to be binding and enforceable, but also to convey a sense of why a borrower might desire to extricate itself from the commitment and the ramifications of such a decision on a lender.

LINCOLN NATIONAL LIFE INSURANCE COMPANY v. NCR CORPORATION

603 F. Supp. 1393 (N.D. Ind. 1984)

William C. Lee, District Judge.

This matter is before the court for a decision on the merits. Plaintiffs brought this diversity action seeking damages for losses resulting from an alleged breach of contract. This court having considered the entire record and being duly advised, hereby renders and enters the following Findings of Fact and Conclusions of Law pursuant to Rule 52(a) of the Federal Rules of Civil Procedure.

Findings of Fact

1. This diversity action was brought by four life insurance companies. Plaintiff, The Lincoln National Life Insurance Company (hereinafter Lincoln), is organized under the laws of the State of Indiana and has its principal place of business in the State of Indiana. Plaintiff, Provident Mutual Life Insurance Company (hereinafter Provident Mutual), is organized under the laws of, and has its principal place of business in, the State of Pennsylvania. Plaintiffs Provident Life and Accident Insurance Company (hereinafter Provident Life) and Life and Casualty Insurance Company of Tennessee (hereinafter Life and Casualty), are organized under the laws of the State of Tennessee and have their principal places of business in that state. Defendant, NCR Corporation (hereinafter NCR), is a Maryland corporation with its principal place of business in the State of Ohio. . . .

4. This action arises out of a "Mortgage Loan Commitment Letter" (hereinafter loan commitment letter) issued by plaintiff Lincoln as the lead lender for itself and on behalf of the other plaintiffs. The loan commitment was sought by defendant NCR through the services of a mortgage broker, United California Mortgage

(hereinafter UCM), for the purposes of financing the construction of NCR's world headquarters building in Dayton, Ohio. NCR agreed to pay UCM a fee of one-half of one per cent (1/2 of 1%) of the principal amount of the loan for use of UCM's services. [Editor's Note: UCM had requested a $50,000 "good faith" deposit from NCR and a one percent (1%) commitment fee, but NCR did not agree to these requests.]

15. On November 19, 1975, the Board of Directors of NCR adopted a resolution which authorized the officers of NCR to establish a real estate subsidiary to own the land and buildings for the new headquarters. This subsidiary, NCR Realty, was authorized to execute its note and mortgage to plaintiffs-lenders, and further authorized to assign the lease to the mortgagee as additional security for the loan. . . .

17. During the first quarter of 1976, NCR noted a substantial increase in its cash balance. Because of this, questions arose regarding the need for external funding of its world headquarters building.

18. Partly in response to the increase of NCR's reserves, NCR's Treasurer, D.W. Russler, sent a letter to UCM regarding the mortgage loan. The letter included "an amended Letter of Authorization to either renegotiate the mortgage loan for the Headquarters Building or negotiate a reasonable penalty fee for canceling the commitment." (Plaintiffs' Exhibit 15). The letter indicated that an acceptable loan would be one for $13,000,000 (Thirteen Million Dollars) at 9 3/8% interest or alternatively a 1.5% penalty fee. For its efforts, UCM was offered a fee which was on a sliding scale and would increase as the rate of a new loan became less than 9 3/8% or as the proposed penalty fee for cancellation became less than 1.5%.

19. Subsequently, on May 10, 1976, Mr. Russler of NCR sent another letter to UCM indicating that the mortgage loan should not be consummated because (1) the interest rate was above that generally found in the market and (2) NCR's need for such financing was no longer evident. (Plaintiffs' Exhibit 17).

20. UCM in turn notified plaintiff Lincoln by letter of May 14, 1976 and attached a copy of Mr. Russler's May 10, 1976 letter.

21. On May 26, 1976 plaintiff-lenders wrote NCR objecting to its decision not to take down the loan. Mr. Russler responded on July 13, 1976 and confirmed that NCR no longer desired to fund the building of the world headquarters by outside sources. The response further indicated that NCR had no legal obligations to the lenders.

22. Following the July 21, 1976 letter from NCR, plaintiff-lenders deleted the NCR loan from their cash flow charts.

23. The mortgage loan from plaintiff-lenders was never made.

24. Construction of NCR's world headquarters building began in 1974 and it was first put into partial use in the fall of 1976. The building was built for the sum of $12,975,931 (Twelve Million Nine Hundred Seventy-Five Thousand Nine Hundred Thirty-One Dollars). Had the loan been closed, it would have been in Dayton, Ohio for that amount.

Conclusions of Law

This case presents a variety of legal issues — some rather novel — which must be addressed in order to resolve the controversy between the parties. In an effort to sort out and clarify the issues, the remainder of this judgment will be divided based upon the following considerations. First, because there exists complete diversity between the parties and jurisdiction is properly invoked under 28 U.S.C. Section 1332, consideration must be given to a determination of which state's substantive law governs the legal issues. Second, since the parties are in complete disagreement with respect to whether or not the underlying transactions constituted an enforceable contract, analysis of the nature and extent of the agreement is necessary. Finally, consideration must be given to whether or not damages are appropriate and, if so, to what extent. These factors will be considered in turn. . . .

The foregoing review of the five factors in the "most intimate contact" test leads this court to conclude that Indiana law should govern the present dispute over the substantive issues.[1] Admittedly, Ohio law could very well govern the substantive issues. Fortunately, and as both parties recognize, however, which state's law governs is of no great moment in this case for it appears that neither the Indiana courts nor the Ohio courts have been presented with the precise issue before this court. Moreover, a decision on the merits must rest upon an interpretation of fundamental principles of contract law.

The Enforceability of the Commitment

. . . [T]his case revolves around an agreement to finance construction through use of a mortgage loan. . . . Reduced to its most basic element, this case hinges upon the interpretation given the agreement between the parties. It is plaintiffs' position that the agreement conferred a mutuality of obligations[2] so that plaintiffs were committed to lend and defendant required to borrow. Defendant suggests that the agreement only committed the plaintiffs to lend had they been called upon to do so. Taking the respective parties' positions together, the issue is obvious: was the agreement relating to the financing of the World Headquarters Building an enforceable contract? The answer, however, is not so obvious.

The difficulty in answering the question before the court stems, in part, from the fact that no other court has apparently addressed the precise issue presented in this case. Most courts which have addressed mortgage loan commitment letters have done so in two different situations. One situation arises where the lender has

---

[1] As with the substantive issues, this court is of the view that Indiana law should govern the dispute about damages. This is so because it appears that Indiana courts and federal courts applying Indiana law apply the doctrine of lex fori to damages. *See, e.g., Stanish v. Polish Roman Catholic Union of America*, 484 F.2d 713, 721–24 (7th Cir.1973) ("[w]ith respect to the questions of remedies for breach of contract, Indiana courts would apply Indiana law."). *See also, Prudence Life Insurance Co. v. Morgan*, 138 Ind. App. 287, 213 N.E.2d 900 (1966).

[2] The necessity that mutuality of obligations exist in order for a binding contract to be formed has led to two seemingly opposite conclusions by the United States Court of Appeals for the Seventh Circuit. In *Sonnenblick-Goldman v. Murphy*, 420 F.2d 1169, 1173 (7th Cir.1970), the court states that "[a]n enforceable contract requires mutuality of obligation, whereby both parties are bound to perform." Yet one year earlier in *Consolidated Laboratories v. Shandon Scientific*, 413 F.2d 208, 212 (7th Cir.1969), the court indicated that mutuality of obligation, as in the case of a unilateral contract, was not necessary where "executed consideration" exists.

breached and the borrower sues for damages or specific performance, *see, e.g., First National State Bank of New Jersey v. Commonwealth Federal Savings & Loan Ass'n*, 610 F.2d 164 (3d Cir.1980), while the other situation arises where the mortgagor or mortgage broker sues to recover a commitment fee, *see, e.g., In re Four Seasons Nursing Centers of America*, 483 F.2d 599 (10th Cir.1973).[3] Here, as the facts make clear, it is the borrower who allegedly breached and the lenders who seek damages though no commitment fee secured the agreement. Nonetheless, the existent case law, such as it is, coupled with basic tenets of contract law suggests that the agreement between the parties as plaintiffs urge, constituted a bilateral contract instead of the unilateral contract theory advanced by defendant.

The distinction between a unilateral and a bilateral contract is a simple one: A unilateral contract is one in which no promisor receives a promise as consideration for his promise. A bilateral contract is one in which there are mutual promises between two parties to the contract; each party being both a promisor and a promisee. Restatement of Contracts § 12 (1932). That is, "[i]n the case of a unilateral contract, there is only one promisor; and the legal result is that he is the only party who is under an enforceable legal duty," 1A, Corbin, Corbin on Contracts § 21 (1963), for a unilateral contract "as its name implies is a one-sided contract while a bilateral contract confers a mutuality of obligations requiring performance on both sides." Restatement, *supra* § 12. Defendant argues, as previously noted, that the commitment letter was a unilateral contract because NCR made no promises. Defendant further argues that the commitment letter was, in effect, a unilateral option contract[5] whereby NCR's obligations would only accrue upon its compliance with certain terms expressed in the agreement. Plaintiffs, of course, are of the view that binding promises were made which ultimately culminated in the agreed to commitment letter.

Some authority can be found for both parties' positions. Courts and commentators alike have referred to mortgage loan commitments alternatively as unilateral and bilateral contracts. As stated by one commentator:

> It [a commitment letter] can be a unilateral contract: "Upon compliance with the following conditions we will loan you money," or it can be a bilateral contract: "We will lend and you will borrow. . . ."

Wolf, R., *The Refundable Commitment Fee*, 1968 Bus.Law 1065, 1066. *See also Johnson v. American Nat'l Ins. Co.*, 126 Ariz. 219, 613 P.2d 1275 (App.1980) (option contract); *Dubin Weston v. Louis Capano & Sons*, 394 F. Supp. 146 (D.C.Del.1975) (bilateral contract). It is, however, not the least bit surprising that commitment letters have been deemed to be either a unilateral or bilateral contract for, as the above passage suggests, it is the language embodied in the instrument which controls and the parties' intention must be gleaned through application of basic

[3] *See also, Hidalgo Properties v. Wachovia Mortgage*, 617 F.2d 196 (10th Cir.1980); *Plantation Key Developers v. Colonial Mortgage Co. of Indiana*, 589 F.2d 164 (5th Cir.1979); *Stanish v. Polish Roman Catholic Union of America*, 484 F.2d 713 (7th Cir.1973); *Sonnenblick-Goldman v. Murphy*, 420 F.2d 1169 (7th Cir.1970); *Walker v. First Pennsylvania Bank N.A.*, 518 F. Supp. 347 (E.D.Pa.1981); *Weston v. Capano & Sons, Inc.*, 394 F. Supp. 146 (D.Del.1975); *Harding v. Pan Am. Life Ins. Co.*, 452 F. Supp. 527 (E.D.Va.1978).

[5] Though defendant argues that an option can only exist with respect to a unilateral contract, it is clear that "options" can exist with respect to both unilateral and bilateral contracts. 1A Corbin, Corbin on Contracts § 260.

tenets of contract law. It is to those basics which the court now turns.

Absent illegality, unconscionability, fraud, duress, or mistake, parties are generally free to contract as they desire and are bound by the terms of the contract. *See Brokers Title v. St. Paul Fire & Marine Ins. Co.*, 610 F.2d 1174 (3d Cir.1979). In construing a contract so made, "a court's paramount consideration is the intent of the parties." *Mellon Bank N.A. v. Aetna Business Credit*, 619 F.2d 1001, 1009 (3d Cir.1980), *citing O'Farrell v. Steel City Piping*, 266 Pa.Super. 219, 403 A.2d 1319 (1979). It is the objective, not subjective, intent of the parties which controls. *See, e.g., Frigaliment Importing v. B.N.S. International Sales*, 190 F. Supp. 116 (S.D.N.Y.1960). . . .

And it is settled beyond question that, where one party drafts a document, in subsequent litigation, the document will be strictly construed against the drafting party and in favor of the non-drafting party. *See, e.g.*, WILLISTON, WILLISTON ON CONTRACTS § 621 (3d ed. 1961); *First National State Bank of New Jersey v. Commonwealth Federal Savings & Loan*, 610 F.2d 164, 170 (3d Cir.1980) (ambiguity construed against drafter-lender).

Turning to the agreement between the present parties, it is clear that the finalized agreement occurred only after several exchanges between Lincoln as the lead lender and defendant NCR. Though this series of offer and counter-offers modified to a greater or lesser extent certain terms in the agreement, it did nothing to ameliorate what defendant deems to be the ultimate pitfall of the agreement: nowhere does the agreement state that the defendant is required to borrow the money. While the agreement does not, in so many words, explicitly state that "defendant is required to borrow," that requirement is, in plaintiffs' view, implicit within the context of the entire agreement. Particularly important in this regard is the paragraph relating to the date of funding, which reads:

> Funding and Commitment Expiration Dates: It is understood that construction of the subject building is scheduled for completion during the second half of 1976 and that NCR agrees to take the loan funds down no later than the fourth quarter of 1976. Assuming that construction is completed according to schedule, Lenders will be prepared to fund the loan as soon as construction is completed and all of the terms and conditions of this commitment have been fulfilled and would prefer that funding of the loan take place by October 15, 1976. However, in any event, the loan must be funded by no later than December 31, 1976, since this commitment and Lenders' obligations under it shall terminate by that date unless the expiry date is extended in writing by Lenders. (Plaintiffs' Exhibit 1)

and the notation that:

> "THE UNDERSIGNED HAS READ, APPROVED AND ACCEPTED [subject to amendments] THE FOREGOING MORTGAGE LOAN COMMITMENT, INCLUDING THE GENERAL CONDITIONS
>
> AS OF THIS 17th DAY OF November, 1975.
>
> NCR CORPORATION
>
> /s/ D.L. McIntosh
>
> (Name) (Title)

D.L. McIntosh, Vice

President, Finance"

(Plaintiffs' Exhibit 1).

As has been suggested, the interpretation given to the foregoing passages lies at the very foundation of this litigation. And, of necessity, initial consideration must be given to the language embodied in the document. *Mellon, supra.*

Focusing solely upon the document and applying the rule that it is to be strictly construed against the drafter, defendant suggests that no agreement to borrow can be found. While plaintiffs contend that the phrase "NCR agrees to take the loan funds down no later than the fourth quarter of 1976" means defendant commits itself to borrow the money, defendant urges that this construction is vitiated by the remainder of that paragraph for when that phrase is read in the context of the entire paragraph, it places no obligation upon defendant but merely serves to establish an expiration date for plaintiffs' commitment to make the loan. Similarly, defendant contends that the language referring to acceptance is vague and since plaintiffs drafted the letter, no commitment to borrow should be implied.

To be sure, and as has already been ruled upon by this court in response to defendant's motion for summary judgment, the foregoing phrases are ambiguous and susceptible to more than one meaning. Certainly there is an ambiguity in the very fact that one of defendant's officers signed the Mortgage Loan Commitment with the notation "read, approved and accepted." (Memorandum of Decision and Order, Feb. 26, 1980 at p. 4). "If, as defendant contends, it regarded the document only as an offer made to it for a unilateral rather than a bilateral contract, in itself, it seems, at the least, ambiguous that defendant would so sign it." *Id.* At the time of entry of the ruling, the court intimated that resolution of this apparent ambiguity could only be cured through the introduction of parol evidence.[6] *See, e.g., Pennzoil v. Federal Energy Regulatory Com'n.*, 645 F.2d 360 (5th Cir.), *cert. denied*, 454 U.S. 1142 (1982).

As a general proposition, the parol evidence rule bars admission of extrinsic evidence to vary or contradict the terms of an unambiguous written agreement intended by the parties to be an integrated agreement. *See Freeman v. Continental Gin*, 381 F.2d 459 (5th Cir.1967). Where, as here, the written agreement is ambiguous, the parol evidence rule is inapplicable and extrinsic evidence of surrounding circumstances may be admitted to explain an ambiguity. *See Massey-Ferguson v. Bent Equipment*, 283 F.2d 12 (5th Cir.1960). "In determining the intention of the parties to a contract a court may consider the circumstances which existed when the contract was made." *American Fletcher Mortgage v. Cousins Mortgage*, 623 F.2d 1228, 1237 (7th Cir.1980). "It may also consider the nature of the contract and its subject matter and the apparent purpose of making the contract." *Id.; see also Standard Land Corp. of Indiana v. Bogardus*, 154 Ind. App. 283, 289 N.E.2d 803, 823 (1972).

Evidence extrinsic to the commitment letter indicates that the parties sought to enter into an enforceable contract. With respect to the notation "accepted" as it appeared in the final document, several factors indicate that it obligated NCR to

6 "A contract is ambiguous when it is reasonably susceptible to more than one meaning in light of the surrounding circumstances and after applying established rules of construction." *Watkins v. Petro Search*, 689 F.2d 537 (5th Cir.1982).

take down the funds. [Editor's Note: The discussion of this extrinsic evidence is omitted.] . . .

Taken together, the court is of the view that the parties bargained for, and entered into, an enforceable contract. The bargaining process consisted of offers and counter-offers in which both sides exchanged the terms and conditions which they wished to include in the contract. The upshot of the agreement was one in which the lenders agreed to fund approximately fourteen million dollars at 9 7/8% interest for a term of twenty-five years. In consideration of this promise, NCR agreed to take surveys, furnish descriptions, transfer titles, reassign mortgages and the like. (Plaintiffs' Exhibit 1).

In reaching the conclusion that an enforceable contract was entered into, the court is not unmindful of the arguments advanced in opposition by defendant. Particularly worthy of note in this regard are two arguments. First, the absence of a commitment fee suggests that the parties viewed this as a unilateral contract. Second, the lenders did not specifically include language requiring the defendant to borrow though it would have been easy to do so.

With respect to the first argument, it is appealing for one reason — had a commitment fee anchored the deal, the litigation would probably not have arisen and certainly would have been less complex. However, the absence of a commitment fee is not fatal in this case and its absence has been adequately explained. The loan agreement was a financial transaction between institutional lenders and a major domestic corporation. The agreement as struck was a "triple net lease" whereby NCR's credit rating would serve as security for the lease. (Trial Transcript Vol. I, p. 48). While it could be expected that in about 3% of cases a borrower would walk away from such an obligation, (Trial Transcript Vol. I, pp. 63–4, 208) it was virtually unheard of that a borrower of NCR's corporate stature would walk away from such an obligation. Moreover, plaintiffs' assumption that the commitment letter was binding upon all parties further explains the reason behind not requiring a commitment fee. Thus there was no reason to secure the mortgage loan agreement through use of a commitment fee.

In the context of mortgage loan agreements, the reasons for commitment fees are varied. The commitment fee may be intended to constitute liquidated damages, as in *In re Four Seasons, supra*; or it may serve as a consideration, as in *Regional Enterprises, Inc. v. Teachers Insurance & Annuity Ass'n.*, 352 F.2d 768 (9th Cir.1965); or it may be given as a stand-by fee as in *Harding v. Pan American Life Ins. Co.*, 452 F. Supp. 527 (E.D.Va.1978). Since consideration has already been found to exist in this case, and since there existed no stand-by lender, the only valid reason for a commitment fee here would have been to serve as a benchmark for liquidated damages. While such an agreed figure would have eliminated much confusion, it adds nothing to the question of whether or not a valid contract had been entered into by the parties. All such a fee would have done in this context would have been to set a price upon NCR's decision to breach the agreement.

Likewise, defendant's second argument does little to detract from the conclusion that the parties entered into an enforceable contract. Had plaintiffs included words to the effect that "NCR agreed to borrow," perhaps this lawsuit would not have developed. But that argument misses the mark for the issue, as indicated at the outset, is whether or not, even absent such language, an enforceable contract existed. The court has already so found. And, it should be noted that "though not at all controlling, the parties are experienced business people who struck what they considered to be at the time a firm and fair bargain." *Harding, supra* at 528.

Thus far, the court has determined that the parties entered into an enforceable contract and consequently, liability is found in favor of the plaintiffs. There remains the question of damages and it is to that topic which the court now turns.

Damages

. . . .

In order to recover, plaintiffs have the burden of proving that they have suffered damages. *Indiana Bell Telephone Co., Inc. v. O'Bryan*, 408 N.E.2d 178 (Ind.App.1980); *Rauch v. Circle Theatre*, 176 Ind.App. 130, 374 N.E.2d 546 (1978). The damages claimed cannot be based upon conjecture nor subject to uncertainty. *Raco Corp. v. Acme-Goodrich, Inc.*, 126 Ind.App. 168, 126 N.E.2d 262 (1955). With respect to damages for breach of contract, damages are designed to one or more interests of the non-breaching party:

> (a) His "expectation interests" which is his interest in having the benefit of his bargain by being put in as good a position as he would have been in had the contract been performed;
>
> (b) His "reliance interests" which is his interest in being reimbursed for loss caused by reliance on the contract by being put in as good a position as he would have been had the contract not been made; or
>
> (c) His "restitution interest" which is his interest in having restored to him any benefit that he has conferred on the other party.

Restatement 2d Contracts § 344. . . .

With respect to mitigation in this case, it appears altogether clear that this requirement was absolutely met by plaintiffs, for shortly after NCR raised the issue of repudiation, all of the plaintiffs removed the NCR obligation from their respective loan charts and apparently invested the allocated funds elsewhere. Since plaintiffs did in fact mitigate the extent of damages caused by defendant's breach of the agreement, the issue becomes one of determining damages in accordance with plaintiffs' "expectation," "reliance" or "restitution" interests. By a process of elimination, it appears that two of the three types of damages — "restitution" and "reliance" interest — are not at issue in this case. At one point in time plaintiffs did claim "restitution" interest through their request for specific performance. That claim, however, was withdrawn prior to trial.[7] Arguably, plaintiffs may have sustained damages based upon their "reliance" interest to the extent their employees expended efforts from January 20, 1976 when the loan commitment was finalized, to the date NCR terminated the commitment. However, no claim for such damages has been made by plaintiffs.[8] Thus the sole type of damages which plaintiffs are seeking is that relating to their "expectation" interests. As will be seen, plaintiffs have not, in fact, established beyond speculation and conjecture that they were, in fact, so damaged.

---

[7] Record at 61–63.

[8] It appears that in mortgage loan situations, the commitment fee is generally given to cover such types of damages should a breach occur. *See In re Four Seasons, supra.*

The sum total of damages plaintiffs attribute to defendant's breach is $1,783,709 to which must be added prejudgment interest in an amount of eight per cent (8%) per annum. Though simple arithmetic is involved in the ultimate calculation, the process leading up to deriving the separate figures which form the basis for the computation is not so simple.

While the measure of damages for breach of an agreement to lend money is generally the difference between interest on the contract note and interest the non-breaching party incurred or earned in a substitute loan, *see Downing v. Dial*, 426 N.E.2d 416 (Ind. App.1981); *Doddridge v. American Trust & Savings Bank*, 98 Ind. App. 334, 189 N.E. 165 (1934), the substitute loan measure of damages is not feasible in this case because no particular funds were earmarked for the NCR loan. That is, the NCR loan funds were to be derived from the cash flow to plaintiffs resulting from the continued maturing of investments previously made and the availability of funds obtained from other sources. Thus, when the NCR loan funds were removed from each plaintiff's cash flow chart, the newly freed money was reinvested elsewhere, yet it is impossible to tell exactly where. Conceivably, some of the money went to other loans producing higher or lower interest and had longer or shorter yield terms.

Since it is impossible to tell exactly what happened to the NCR funds, plaintiffs argue that the measure of damages is the difference between interest on the NCR loan and a comparable loan after the breach. In this case the difference would be the 9 7/8% interest agreed upon by the parties and the interest rate on a comparable loan at the lower interest rate prevailing after the breach. Using this formula, plaintiffs calculate their damage claim essentially as follows. The total amount to be funded under the agreement was $13,405,931.

This amount was to be loaned at 9 7/8% interest for a period of twenty-five years. Using the 8.5% prevailing rate for a comparable loan, in December of 1976, the damages are calculated as the difference between the interest on the 9 7/8% loan and the interest on the comparable loan with each interest amount reduced to present value as of December 1976.

Graphically, the calculations are as follows:

Present value of interest at 9 7/8%	$11,324,275
Less present value of interest at 8.5%	- 9,536,486
	$1,787,789

Thus, plaintiffs claim entitlement to damages in that amount.[11]

As the above makes abundantly clear, plaintiffs' market damage theory rests upon several important assumptions. In making the calculations, plaintiffs presuppose, among other things, the amount of the loan, the length of time the loan would

[11] At this juncture it should be noted that the figure relating to damages in excess of 1.5 million dollars is the outermost figure of damages requested by plaintiffs. Perhaps anticipating the problems with the many uncertain variables involved in their calculations, plaintiffs, in their post-trial brief, urge that at a minimum, they are entitled to damages of approximately $750,000 which takes into consideration the fluctuating interest rates between July and December of 1976; the amount of the capitalized costs for the building less the amount for the land on which the headquarters was built; and the possibility that prepayment would occur. Yet, as will be seen, even these reductions do nothing to ameliorate what the court views to be the pitfall of plaintiff's damage claims — the preponderance of the evidence does not support a claim to any quantifiable damages.

be outstanding, and the date for determining the comparative market rate with interest computed on a comparable loan as of that date. [Editor's note: The court's discussion of these assumptions and adjustments that need to be made for the assumptions to be valid is omitted.]

Plaintiffs are in the investment business. During calendar years 1975 and 1976 plaintiff Lincoln carried approximately 2.5 billion dollars in investment (exclusive of policy loans); Provident Mutual carried approximately 1.1 billion dollars in investments; Provident Life and Accident approximately 900 million dollars in investments; and Tennessee Life and Casualty 600 million dollars in investments. (Defendant's Exhibits O, P, Q, R). These investments consisted primarily of bonds, stocks, mortgage loans and real estate. (*Id.*). In order to secure funding at the appropriate time, each proposed loan is placed on a cash flow chart. These cash flow projections, for the most part, are simply charts in which estimated lending dates of future investments are listed. Through the use of these charts, plaintiffs are able to predict what their cash needs will be in the future. (Transcript Vol. I, pp. 164–8). Though an item is listed on the cash flow chart, no funding is allocated for that item until shortly before the targeted funding date.

With respect to the inclusion of the NCR loan on each of plaintiffs' cash flow charts, it is altogether clear that no investments were changed as the result of that inclusion. (Transcript Vol. I, pp. 72–4; pp. 165–66.) In fact, the proposed loan to NCR was placed on each of plaintiff's cash flow charts before committee approval. (*Id.*; Vol. I, p. 159; 214). And, the funding was removed from the charts within two months after NCR's notification that it intended not to take down the funds.

The foregoing scenario of inclusion and deletion indicates that the proposed funding for NCR was nothing more than a paper transaction. The inclusion of the NCR loan commitment on plaintiffs' charts was done to prepare for a future contingency — funding — which did not occur. Moreover, plaintiffs were aware that the loan would not be made sufficiently in advance of the targeted funding date that they had not changed any investments in preparation for funding.

So what, in fact, happened to the money which would have gone to NCR? The answer is not altogether clear. It is clear, however, that any money which would have gone to NCR was reinvested elsewhere. (Transcript Vol. I, p. 87; p. 169; pp. 215–21). What those investments were, what the terms of those investments were, and what the yield of those investments were, is impossible to determine. Certainly some were below the rate to be charged NCR and had earlier maturity dates, while other investments of comparable terms in years yielded higher interest rates. (*Id.*). Generally, however, long term loans such as those proposed to NCR have turned out to be bad investments. (Defendant's Exhibit M). In this respect an interesting query arises as to what value it was to plaintiffs in not tying up nearly 13 million dollars for twenty-five years at 9 7/8% interest. It is not idle speculation to assume that part and parcel of plaintiffs' motion to withdraw their request for specific performance stemmed from the fact that in today's market the NCR loan proposal could not be viewed as a good prospect. . . .

In sum, this court is of the view that plaintiffs have not established that they were in fact damaged. While they need not trace the particular funds allocated to NCR, *Pipkin v. Thomas & Hill, Inc.*, 298 N.C. 278, 258 S.E.2d 778 (1979), *supra*, it is nonetheless incumbent upon them to show that damage resulted from NCR's breach. Though they may have been entitled to "reliance interest" damages to the extent that their employees expended efforts subsequent to January 20, 1976 (when the loan commitment was finalized) and the date that NCR terminated the commitment, they have claimed no such damages. And since they have not proven that the NCR breach had any effect upon their investment opportunities they have not shown entitlement to damages for their expectation interest. In short, plaintiffs have wholly failed to show by a preponderance of the evidence that they lost anything as a result of defendant NCR's breach.

Conclusion

On the basis of the foregoing, the court finds that a binding, enforceable contract existed between the parties. Since NCR breached the same the court finds in favor of the plaintiffs and against the defendant. The court further finds that plaintiffs have not met their burden with respect to their claim for damages, and accordingly, no damages will be awarded. Costs assessed against defendant and in favor of the plaintiffs.

[b] Comments and Questions Regarding *Lincoln National*

1. What happened in the *Lincoln National* case so that NCR, the borrower, changed its mind and did not want to borrow the money as originally contemplated? In general, fluctuating interest rate environments are fertile grounds for breaches of loan commitments. Can you see why? A famous example of this is illustrated in *Teachers Insurance & Annuity Association of America v. Butler*, 626 F. Supp. 1229 (S.D.N.Y. 1986), where the court ruled that the borrower had negotiated in bad faith for the deletion of a certain event of default in the loan documents as a means to avoid the consummation of the loan transaction and enter into another loan at a lower interest rate. What evidence do you think the lender presented that induced the court to find that the borrower had negotiated for the change in the event of defaults section of the loan documents in bad faith?

2. What is necessary to create an enforceable loan commitment?

3. What did the lenders do wrong in the drafting of the loan commitment in the *Lincoln National* case that called into question the enforceability of the loan agreement against the borrower?

4. On what basis did the court still rule that the borrower was in fact obligated to borrow as contemplated by the loan commitment?

5. Since the court ruled the loan commitment was enforceable, why did the court deny any remedy to the lenders? Why didn't the lenders seek rescission and restitution-type damages? Why didn't the lenders seek specific performance? What type of remedy did the lenders seek? In general, courts seem reluctant to order specific performance to either party in loan commitment cases and instead rule that damages are an adequate remedy. Does that make sense to you?

6. How did the lenders calculate their expectation damages? Why did the court reject their calculations? What is the substitute loan measure of damages and why did that not apply here?

7. Do you agree with the court's analysis that the lenders failed to prove they were in fact damaged by the borrower's breach?

8. What lessons can one learn from this case when drafting a loan commitment for a lender in terms of (i) ensuring that the loan commitment is binding on both parties (if that is the intent) and (ii) ensuring adequate remedies in the event of breach?

9. As an aside, do you think the loan commitment contained a choice of law provision? Did it matter in this case?

10. *Lincoln National* involved a situation where the borrower breached the loan commitment by refusing to accept the loan. But what if the borrower fails to satisfy a condition in the loan commitment? Should the lender in such circumstance be able to refuse to fund the loan and instead retain a standby deposit of 3% of the loan amount that the borrower had deposited? Even assuming that the 3% figure for damages is not an unenforceable penalty, the question is whether failure to satisfy the condition constitutes not only a condition to funding but also a breach of the loan commitment. How do you determine that question? *See Woodbridge Place Apartments v. Washington Square Capital, Inc.*, 965 F.2d 1429 (7th Cir. 1992) (condition in loan commitment that the project have a 93% occupancy level permitted lender to not fund the loan but did not constitute a breach of the loan commitment by the borrower so the lender was not entitled to keep the 3% standby deposit unless the record reflected that the borrower had failed to meet this condition in bad faith). Do you think a lender can impose a condition to the funding of the loan that is not set forth in the loan commitment and then refuse to fund the loan if the borrower can not meet this additional condition? If a lender may be held liable for breach of the loan commitment if the lender does that, what does this suggest in terms of the drafting of the loan commitment from the lender's perspective?

§ 9.04 BASIC LOAN TERMS

Once the lender and the borrower have entered into a loan commitment, or have at least agreed to the basic loan terms, the next step is for the lender's counsel to prepare a first draft of the loan documents and the closing checklist. While it is true that the terms of the loan documents will have a large impact on the rights and obligations of the lender and borrower, certain rules of law will trump what the parties agree to, such as the equitable right of redemption and certain bankruptcy law protections. In addition, a close scrutiny of these documents in their entirety does not pose the best way to understand the key loan terms. This is because the loan documents and closing requirements are so voluminous that one can easily become buried in them and be unable to see the forest for the trees. Certain aspects of these loan transactions are more critical than other aspects. This chapter focuses on some of the fundamental elements of the loan transaction. The first critical issue is the amount of the loan.

[1] The Loan Amount

As previously discussed in Chapters 2 and 3, if the borrower anticipates a higher rate of return on the funds borrowed than the cost of the borrowed funds, it makes sense for the borrower to obtain the largest loan a lender is willing to make to maximize the borrower's return on its investment. The lender, on the other hand, should limit the amount of the loan to a level where it seems safe that, if there is a default, the lender will be able to recover its investment. Since in a real estate mortgage loan, the real estate pledged is the main source of repayment, the amount the lender is willing to loan is based primarily on the value of the mortgaged property. In the past, and prior to the development of vast securitization of commercial real estate loans, depending upon the type of real estate involved, institutional lenders were willing to loan an amount equal to anywhere from 65% to 85% of the appraised value of the real estate. The following is an example of guidelines some financial institutions used in the past, prior to the development of the securitization of commercial real estate loans:

Type of Real Estate Loan	Loan to Value Limit
Raw Land	65%
Land Development	75%
Commercial Construction, including multi-family residential property, condominiums and cooperatives	80%
Construction Loans for Residential Property for 1–4 Families	85%
Improved Property	85%

As previously discussed in Chapters 2 and 3, a second method lenders utilize in determining the maximum loan amount is applying a debt service coverage ratio. This formula is based on ascertaining the amount of debt that the borrower can safely afford to pay in light of the interest rate under the loan and the projected income from the property. Debt service coverage ratios of 1.25 are common (*i.e.*, net operating income which is 25% greater than the debt service). A loan is then made up to the amount by which the net operating income is 25% greater than the debt service.

The other measure to apply to determine loan amount is the loan to value ratio. The appropriate ratio varies depending upon the type of loan (*i.e.*, how risky it is) and changing standards in the marketplace. Today, during the credit crisis, highly cautious loan to value ratios of 60% are being used even for fully constructed and leased up properties. At the time of the development of the Fox Valley Auto Care Center, the lender would probably have used an 80% loan to value ratio, resulting in a loan amount of approximately $2.4 million (using the other assumptions in Figure 2.12 from Chapter 2, *supra*, to arrive at a fair market value of approximately $3 million). However, lenders typically use the lesser of the loan to value ratio and the debt service ratio. Applying the assumptions in Figure 2.12 regarding the interest rate and amortization of the loan and net operating income, a 1.25 debt service ratio would only allow a slightly lower loan amount of approximately $2.3 million.

[2] The Term of the Loan

Another critical element of the loan transaction relates to the lender's distinct need for assurance that the borrower will continue to make payments of interest on the loan for the entire term of the loan. There are three circumstances where the loan may be paid off prior to its maturity. First, if the borrower is unable to perform the terms of the loan and defaults and the lender accelerates the debt and commences a foreclosure, then the loan will be paid off prior to its original scheduled maturity date. The next two sections discuss the two other situations when loans are paid off early: when the borrower refinances to obtain more favorable loan terms (a lower interest rate, a larger loan amount, a more favorable payment schedule, or some or all of these) and when the borrower transfers the property to another party.

[a] Prepayment Locks and Charges

If interest rates drop during the term of the loan and the loan is a long-term, fixed interest rate loan, a borrower will desire to prepay the loan and refinance at the lower rate. The excerpt that follows explains why prepayments in such circumstances are so problematic to lenders, how lenders have documented their loans to attempt to prevent this (or reduce their losses when this occurs), and how borrowers have responded. Loans are also repaid due to a sale of the property or other default triggering an acceleration of the debt, and in such circumstances, the lender will desire to be covered for its losses if current interest rates at which the lender can reinvest the funds are lower than the interest rate under the repaid loan.

WILSON FREYERMOUTH, JOHN MCNEARNEY, DEBRA STARK & DALE WHITMAN, ANATOMY OF A MORTGAGE (ABA 2001)*

. . . Most real estate secured loans are long term loans (a construction loan is the primary example of a short term loan). Most of these long term loans accrue interest at a fixed rate (e.g., 8% per annum) as opposed to a floating rate (e.g., "prime" plus 1%). If interest rates rise during the term of the loan, a lender would not have the right to demand that the borrower pay off the indebtedness immediately so that the lender could reinvest the loan proceeds in a higher interest rate loan. This is because the typical loan documents provide for monthly payment of interest and some amortization of principal with the balance, if any, due at the maturity of the loan. For the same reason, most courts have ruled that if interest rates have dropped during the term of the loan, a borrower is not entitled to prepay the loan so that they can enjoy a new loan at a lower rate of interest. This is known as the "perfect tender in time rule." If the loan documents are structured in the way described above, and are "silent" on the issue of prepayment, then the majority of courts will apply the perfect tender in time rule and not permit the borrower to prepay the debt. *See* Frank S. Alexander, *Mortgage Prepayment: The Trial of Common Sense*, 72 Cornell L. Rev. 288 (1987); and Debra P. Stark, *New Developments in Enforcing Prepayment Charges*, 26 Real Prop. Prob. & Tr. J. 213 (1991). However, a growing minority of jurisdictions would allow the borrower to prepay the debt if the loan documents are silent on the issue. John C. Murray, *Enforceability of Prepayment Premium Provisions in Commercial Loan Documents*, in Commercial Real Estate Financing (PLI Handbook 1999) and attached exhibits.

Most loan documents are not silent on the issue of prepayment. The form deed of trust and note we are analyzing permit prepayment of all of the loan if the borrower pays to the lender a prepayment premium to compensate the lender for the losses the lender will or may incur in connection with the prepayment (the potential reinvestment loss described above and other losses and expenses the lender may incur). The form deed of trust and note provide that no prepayment charge will be imposed in the event of a casualty or condemnation when insurance proceeds or the condemnation award are applied to the debt (in these two instances the prepayment is beyond the control and fault of the borrower and many lenders have opted not to require a charge in that context) or when a prepayment is made within ninety days before the stated maturity date of the loan (this gives the borrower a window period to obtain and close on a refinancing). The form documents clarify that the prepayment charge applies whether the prepayment is "voluntary" or "involuntary" (i.e., a default by the borrower and acceleration of the debt by the lender). [Editor's Note: The form note and form deed of trust mentioned in this excerpt are the forms utilized by FNMA to document federally insured loans secured by multi-family housing real estate.]

Enforcement Issues

It is important that the loan documents clarify that a prepayment charge will apply in an "involuntary" prepayment situation because, when loan documents have failed to clarify this, courts have refused to enforce the prepayment charges when the borrower has defaulted and the lender has accelerated the debt. *See, e.g., Slevin Container Corporation v. Provident Federal Savings & Loan Association*, 424 N.E.2d 939 (Ill. App. Ct. 1981); and *In re LHD Realty Corp.*, 726 F.2d 327 (7th Cir. 1984). However, when loan documents clearly require a prepayment charge in a default/acceleration situation, courts have enforced the imposition of such charges in such situations. *See, e.g., Pacific Trust Co. TTEE v. Fidelity Federal Sav. and Loan Ass'n*, 184 Cal. App. 3d 817, 824, 229 Cal. Rptr. 269, 274 (1986); *Village of Rosemont v. Maywood-Proviso State Bank*, 149 Ill. App. 3d 1087, 501 N.E.2d 859 (1986); and *Eyde v. Empire of America Federal Savings Bank*, 701 F. Supp. 126 (E.D. Mich. 1988).

The second major issue is how the prepayment charge is calculated. Older loan documents provided for a charge based upon a specified percentage multiplied against the balance of the loan being paid off (e.g., 10%). Typically, the percentage would decline as the loan became closer to maturing (the idea being that as the loan got closer to maturing, the lender's damages from prepayment declined). This method was obviously imprecise (e.g., if interest rates had actually risen, then the lender would have no pure reinvestment losses; conversely if interest rates had dropped significantly, it is possible the lender would suffer losses in excess of 10% of the balance of the loan). Due to this imprecision, and the need to more accurately guarantee that the yields to maturity in the loan documents be maintained even when the loans were paid off early, lenders began to utilize a "yield maintenance formula" to calculate the prepayment charge.

The form note in Schedule A provides for a yield maintenance formula. [Editor's Note: The FNMA form referred to is not included in this book, the note utilized for the construction loan for the Fox Valley Auto Care Center, which contains many similar terms but, is included in the Document Book. The FVACC construction loan promissory note does not include a prepayment clause, however.] Under this formula one multiplies the principal amount being prepaid by the difference between the interest rate on the note and the yield rate on a specified U.S. Treasury Security at the time of the attempted prepayment or acceleration of the loan. The theory behind this comparison is that upon repayment of the debt, the lender can reinvest the amount paid with the purchase of the U.S. Treasury Security. If the U.S. Treasury Security is accruing interest at the same or a higher interest rate than under the note, then no charge is owed. If the U.S. Treasury Security is accruing interest at a lower interest rate than under the note, the borrower is required to pay a prepayment charge equal to that difference in rates multiplied by the balance of the loan to compensate the lender for that difference. Under the terms of the note, this amount is then discounted to its present value (to account for the fact that receiving the money today is worth more than receiving the money ten years from now). It should be noted, however, that the calculation of the prepayment charge in the form note provides for the greater of 1% of the unpaid balance of the loan or the difference in interest rates described above. Consequently, even if interest rates have risen since the loan was made, at least a 1% charge would apply. . . .

There are hundreds of reported cases involving the enforcement of prepayment charges. The most unclear area in the law today on the enforcement of prepayment charges relates to the manner in which they are calculated and challenges that they are unenforceable penalties under a liquidated damages analysis or unreasonable under Section 506(b) of the U.S. Bankruptcy Code. Some courts, usually bankruptcy courts, have applied a liquidated damages analysis to the charge and have ruled that the yield maintenance formula is an unreasonable estimate of the loss a lender will suffer. These courts point out that because U.S. Treasury Securities are a safer investment than first real estate mortgage loans, the treasury rate will be lower than the mortgage loan rate when the loan is first made. It is contended that as a result it is unreasonable to compare U.S. Treasury Security yields with the interest rate under the first mortgage loan and that such comparison gives the lender more than they originally bargained for. *See In re Skyler Ridge*, 80 B.R. 500 (Bankr. C.D. Cal. 1987); and *In re Kroh Bros. Dev. Co.*, 88 B.R. 997 (Bankr. W.D. Md. 1988). Instead, the U.S. Treasury Security yield should be upwardly adjusted to reflect the higher rate then being offered for first mortgage loans. Lenders counter that they may no longer be in the real estate mortgage lending business at the time the borrower prepays the debt and so they will not be reinvesting the loan proceeds in this manner. Lenders also argue that even if they are still in the mortgage lending business, it is difficult if not impossible to find a truly comparable real estate mortgage loan, so the lender will suffer a loss if they must upwardly adjust their formulas in this fashion. Some courts accept the lenders' arguments on this issue. *See New England Mutual Life Insurance Co. v. Stuzin*, No. 86-2740-S, 86-2471-S, 1990 U.S. Dist. LEXIS 13137 (D. Mass. 1990); and *R-D Investment Company v. Mutual Benefit Life Insurance Company*, No. 880–883 (D. Neb. Sept. 19, 1991).

There is also a split of authority on the enforcement of a prepayment charge based upon a specified percentage. Prior to the *Skyler Ridge* decision, courts exercised very little scrutiny of the amount of the charge, and enforced charges of between 5% and 50% of the outstanding balance of the loan. *See, e.g., Northway Lanes v. Hackley Union National Bank & Trust Co.*, 334 F. Supp. 723 (W.D. Mich. 1971), *aff'd*, 464 F.2d 855 (6th Cir. 1972); and *Williams v. Fassler*, 110 Cal App. 3d 7, 12, 167 Cal. Rptr. 545, 548 (1980). In these cases the courts viewed the prepayment charge as the bargained for consideration for the privilege of prepayment. But when courts have applied a liquidated damages analysis, there is a split of authority on the outcomes. One court would enforce a prepayment charge of 10% even when applying a liquidated damages analysis. *See In re Schaumburg Hotel Owner Ltd. Partnership*, 97 B.R. 943 (Bankr. N.D. Ill. 1989). Another court indicated that a charge of 10% takes on the characteristics of a penalty. *See Clinton Capital Corp. v. Straeb*, 589 A.2d 1363, 1371 (N.J. Super., Ch. 1990). Indeed, yet another court held that even a charge of 1% is unreasonable since it presumed a reinvestment loss. *See In re A.J. Lane and Co., Inc.*, 113 B.R. 821 (Bankr. D. Mass. 1990).

Conclusion

It is fairly safe to conclude that in a non-default situation, that a court would and should enforce the prepayment charge in the form note as the "bargained for consideration for the privilege of prepayment." As a practice point, it would help if the form note in fact utilized this type of language in the "voluntary prepayment" section. In a default situation, however, the prepayment charge utilized in the form note is susceptible to challenge as an unreasonable penalty applying a liquidated damages analysis depending upon the precedent the court is bound to follow or that the court finds persuasive. The provision does not upwardly adjust the Treasury Security to reflect the higher first mortgage interest rate. In addition, it provides for a minimum 1% fee which presumes a loss when there is no reinvestment yield loss.

The following are a few additional suggestions to increasing the likelihood of enforcement of the prepayment charge in light of the case law in this area. First, because some courts analyze whether the charge is reasonable in light of the actual losses the lender has suffered, it is very important when enforcing the prepayment charge to provide the court with adequate evidence of the extent of the lender's harm. If you can show that the actual losses equal or exceed the charge, then the charge is more likely to be enforced. It is also a good idea to provide an example of how the prepayment charge would be calculated so that the borrower will be less likely to assert that it did not really understand what it was agreeing to. This type of argument was raised when some prepayment charges utilizing the "yield maintenance formulas" equaled as much as 30% of the loan amount being paid off. Had there been an example of the possibility for such a high charge, this would support the argument that the borrower knew what she was agreeing to. Lenders can also require reasoned opinions on the enforceability of the charge and provide for springing liability if the borrower or related persons or entities challenge its enforcement to reduce the likelihood of a challenge being made. It would also be a good idea to have the borrower acknowledge in the loan documents why treasury yields were being used (that the lender might not be making mortgage loans and the difficulty of finding a comparable mortgage loan to reinvest the prepaid money in) and why there is a minimum 1% charge (e.g., identify the other costs and losses of the lender due to the prepayment which are separate from the issue of a loss in yield upon reinvestment).

[i] Comments and Questions Regarding Prepayment Charges

1. Why did lenders typically impose yield maintenance type prepayment charges in the context of a permanent loan but not typically a construction loan? Under what circumstances would a lender incur losses if a loan is prepaid? With the securitization of commercial real estate and the selling of construction loans to the secondary market, prepayment locks and prepayment charges began to be applied to construction loans as well, and prepayment charges began to be determined based upon "defeasance provisions" rather than yield maintenance type clauses. Under a defeasance provision, the borrower who wishes to pay off the loan purchases a treasury security with the same yield to maturity as the repaid loan, and may even pay less than the balance of the loan amount for this treasury bill if interest rates had risen since the loan was made, but would have to pay more (similar to the alternative yield maintenance premium) in the event that interest rates had dropped since the loan was first made. For a fuller discussion of the use of defeasance provisions with commercial loans intended to be sold into the secondary market, see Section 10.06.

2. Do you think that typical "yield maintenance" charges paid by borrowers are a reasonable charge? What changes might a borrower attempt to negotiate when faced with a typical yield maintenance clause? Are there any features of it that could be claimed to be unfair to the borrower?

3. The construction loan documents which Regent signed for the construction loan freely permitted prepayment of the loan without any charges. Had Regent been signing a note for a take-out, long term, fixed interest rate loan, the loan documents likely would have included prohibitions of prepayment and/or a prepayment charge in substantially the form that is in the following problem.

4. With the development of the securitization of commercial mortgages, shorter term mortgage loans and mezzanine loans (loans secured by the borrower's pledge of its equity interest in the entity that comprises the borrower) with a term of 3–5 years, became subject to an "exit fee" that would be triggered upon the voluntary or involuntary prepayment of the loan or at the maturity of the loan. Case law is contradictory as to whether these exit fees are valid and whether to apply 1) a liquidated damages analysis, requiring that the amount of the exit fee be a "reasonable" estimate of the lender's costs, or 2) a bargained for consideration analysis, which requires that the amount not be unconscionable. It is also unclear whether the charges will be construed as "additional interest" as contrasted with a "prepayment premium" and how the exit fee will be treated by a bankruptcy court. *See Delta Rault Energy 110 Veterans L.L.C.*, 2004 U.S. Dist. LEXIS 15136 (E.D. La. 2004) (exit fee held to be an additional loan charge rather than a prepayment premium or penalty subject to a liquidated damages analysis); *In re Maywood, Inc.*, 210 B.R. 91 (Bankr. N.D. Tex. 1997) (court stated it is not customary in a Chapter 7 case for courts to award termination fees even if the contract provides for

them, and ruled that since the lender failed to show any evidence of damages as the result of its decision to accelerate the loan, the "early termination" fee was unreasonable under Section 506(b) of the Bankruptcy Code).

[ii] Negotiation and Drafting Problem

As previously mentioned, the loan documents for the construction of the Fox Valley Auto Care Center freely permitted prepayment of the loan. If the loan documents were for a permanent loan, they likely would include a prohibition of prepayment for a specified period and include a charge in the event the loan is prepaid due to the borrower's default and acceleration of the debt. The permanent loan documents also likely would grant the borrower the right to prepay the debt after a certain period has expired, provided that the borrower pay a "prepayment charge" to the lender in addition to all of the indebtedness then due.

Assume that you represent the lender in negotiating and closing a permanent loan and that the lender's form note contains the prepayment language set forth below. Draft a memorandum to your client indicating what changes you propose to be made to the language below and explain the reasons for these changes. Next, assume that you represent the borrower and draft a memorandum to counsel for the lender indicating the precise changes you recommend be made to the prepayment clause below.

Be prepared in class to negotiate on behalf of either the borrower or the lender.

Standard Prepayment Charge Clause

If the Loan is prepaid prior to maturity, Borrower shall pay Lender a premium equal to the greater of (i) 1% of the principal sum prepaid, or (ii) the product obtained by multiplying (x) the principal sum prepaid, (y) an interest rate equal to the amount, if any, by which the Note rate of interest exceeds the rate on a United States Treasury security with a term equal to the remainder of the regularly scheduled loan term, and (z) the number of years or fraction thereof remaining in the regularly scheduled loan term.

[b] Due-On-Sale and Due-On-Encumbrance Clauses

[i] Overview

A third common circumstance resulting in loans being paid off prior to their maturity is when a borrower transfers all or part of its interest in the mortgaged property, usually as part of a sale. In this circumstance (and the related one of further mortgaging the property), lenders often desire the right to accelerate the debt through the use of "due-on-sale" and "due-on-encumbrance" clauses. Under these clauses, the entire indebtedness becomes due if the borrower sells or grants a security interest in the mortgaged real estate, or sells or grants any interest with respect to the beneficiary of the land trust, the partnership interest in a limited partnership, the membership interest in a LLC, or the shares of the corporate general partner.

There are two main reasons for a due-on-sale clause. First, the lender in making the loan is relying on the credit and expertise of the specific borrower. Second, the sale situation provides the lender with an opportunity to reinvest the money loaned at a higher interest rate if interest rates have risen since the loan was first made. There are also two main reasons why a lender desires a due-on-encumbrance clause. First, if the borrower borrows additional funds secured by the mortgaged property, the income from the mortgaged property may not be able to adequately service both debts, causing the borrower to be more likely to default on one or both of the mortgage loans. Second, the presence of a junior lien holder makes it more difficult for the borrower and lender to restructure the loan if there is a potential or actual default. Any modifications of the senior loan without the consent of the junior lien holder which prejudices the junior lien holder will cause the senior loan to lose priority against such junior lien to the extent of the prejudice (*see* § 17.03 *infra*). However, under certain circumstances, it may make sense for a senior lender to agree to the creation of a junior lien on the mortgaged property. Can you think of any circumstances when a senior lender would agree to the borrower's obtaining a second loan secured by the mortgaged property? If so, what conditions should a lender impose in granting such consent?

[ii] Sample Clauses

The excerpt that follows includes very comprehensive "due-on-sale" and "due-on-encumbrance" provisions, an explanation of these provisions, and a discussion of their enforcement. After you review the comprehensive provisions and explanation, you will be asked to compare these provisions with the due-on-sale and due-on-encumbrance clauses for the construction loan for the Fox Valley Auto Care Center to see how well First Mortgage Bank and Regent handled this issue.

WILSON FREYERMOUTH, JOHN MCNEARNEY, DEBRA STARK & DALE WHITMAN, ANATOMY OF A MORTGAGE (ABA 2001)*

FORM DEED OF TRUST

[This is the FNMA multi-family housing form deed of trust. — Eds.]

21. *TRANSFERS OF THE MORTGAGED PROPERTY OR INTERESTS IN BORROWER.*

(a) The occurrence of any of the following events shall constitute an Event of Default under this Instrument:

(1) a Transfer of all or any part of the Mortgaged Property or any interest in the Mortgaged Property;

(2) a Transfer of a Controlling Interest in Borrower;

(3) a Transfer of a Controlling Interest in any entity which owns, directly or indirectly through one or more intermediate entities, a Controlling Interest in Borrower;

(4) a Transfer of all or any part of Key Principal's ownership interests (other than limited partnership interests) in Borrower, or in any other

entity which owns, directly or indirectly through one or more intermediate entities, an ownership interest in Borrower;

(5) if Key Principal is an entity, (A) a Transfer of a Controlling Interest in Key Principal, or (B) a Transfer of a Controlling Interest in any entity which owns, directly or indirectly through one or more intermediate entities, a Controlling Interest in Key Principal;

(6) if Borrower or Key Principal is a trust, the termination or revocation of such trust; and

(7) a conversion of Borrower from one type of legal entity into another type of legal entity, whether or not there is a Transfer.

Lender shall not be required to demonstrate any actual impairment of its security or any increased risk of default in order to exercise any of its remedies with respect to an Event of Default under this Section 21.

(b) The occurrence of any of the following events shall not constitute an Event of Default under this Instrument, notwithstanding any provision of Section 21(a) to the contrary:

(1) a Transfer to which Lender has consented;

(2) a Transfer that occurs by devise, descent, or by operation of law upon the death of a natural person;

(3) the grant of a leasehold interest in an individual dwelling unit for a term of two years or less not containing an option to purchase;

(4) a Transfer of obsolete or worn out Personalty or Fixtures that are contemporaneously replaced by items of equal or better function and quality, which are free of liens, encumbrances and security interests other than those created by the Loan Documents or consented to by Lender;

(5) the grant of an easement, if before the grant Lender determines that the easement will not materially affect the operation or value of the Mortgaged Property or Lender's interest in the Mortgaged Property, and Borrower pays to Lender, upon demand, all costs and expenses incurred by Lender in connection with reviewing Borrower's request; and

(6) the creation of a tax lien or a mechanic's, materialman's or judgment lien against the Mortgaged Property which is bonded off, released of record or otherwise remedied to Lender's satisfaction within 30 days of the date of creation.

(c) Lender shall consent, without any adjustment to the rate at which the Indebtedness secured by this Instrument bears interest or to any other economic terms of the Indebtedness, to a Transfer that would otherwise violate this Section 21 if, prior to the Transfer, Borrower has satisfied each of the following requirements:

(1) the submission to Lender of all information required by Lender to make the determination required by this Section 21(c);

(2) the absence of any Event of Default;

(3) the transferee meets all of the eligibility, credit, management and other standards (including any standards with respect to previous relationships between Lender and the transferee and the organization of the transferee) customarily applied by Lender at the time of the proposed Transfer to the approval of borrowers in connection with the origination or purchase of similar mortgages, deeds of trust or deeds to secure debt on multifamily properties;

(4) the Mortgaged Property, at the time of the proposed Transfer, meets all standards as to its physical condition that are customarily applied by Lender at the time of the proposed Transfer to the approval of properties in connection with the origination or purchase of similar mortgages on multifamily properties;

(5) in the case of a Transfer of all or any part of the Mortgaged Property, or direct or indirect ownership interests in Borrower or Key Principal (if an entity), if transferor or any other person has obligations under any Loan Document, the execution by the transferee or one or more individuals or entities acceptable to Lender of an assumption agreement (including, if applicable, an Acknowledgment and Agreement of Key Principal to Personal Liability for Exceptions to Non-Recourse Liability) that is acceptable to Lender and that, among other things, requires the transferee to perform all obligations of transferor or such person set forth in such Loan Document, and may require that the transferee comply with any provisions of this Instrument or any other Loan Document which previously may have been waived by Lender;

(6) if a guaranty has been executed and delivered in connection with the Note, this Instrument or any of the other Loan Documents, the Borrower causes one or more individuals or entities acceptable to Lender to execute and deliver to Lender a guaranty in a form acceptable to Lender; and

(7) Lender's receipt of all of the following:

(A) a non-refundable review fee in the amount of $3,000 and a transfer fee equal to 1% of the outstanding Indebtedness immediately prior to the Transfer.

(B) In addition, Borrower shall be required to reimburse Lender for all of Lender's out-of-pocket costs (including reasonable attorneys' fees) incurred in reviewing the Transfer request, to the extent such expenses exceed $3,000.

(d) For purposes of this Section, the following terms shall have the meanings set forth below:

(1) "Initial Owners" means, with respect to Borrower or any other entity, the persons or entities who on the date of the Note own in the aggregate 100% of the ownership interests in Borrower or that entity.

(2) A Transfer of a "Controlling Interest" shall mean, with respect to any entity, the following:

(i) if such entity is a general partnership or a joint venture, a Transfer of any general partnership interest or joint venture interest which would cause the Initial Owners to own less than 51% of all general partnership or joint venture interests in such entity;

(ii) if such entity is a limited partnership, a Transfer of any general partnership interest;

(iii) if such entity is a limited liability company or a limited liability partnership, a Transfer of any membership or other ownership interest which would cause the Initial Owners to own less than 51% of all membership or other ownership interests in such entity;

(iv) if such entity is a corporation (other than a Publicly-Held Corporation) with only one class of voting stock, a Transfer of any voting stock which would cause the Initial Owners to own less than 51% of voting stock in such corporation;

(v) if such entity is a corporation (other than a Publicly-Held Corporation) with more than one class of voting stock, a Transfer of any voting stock which would cause the Initial Owners to own less than a sufficient number of shares of voting stock having the power to elect the majority of directors of such corporation; and

(vi) if such entity is a trust, the removal, appointment or substitution of a trustee of such trust other than (A) in the case of a land trust, or (B) if the trustee of such trust after such removal, appointment or substitution is a trustee identified in the trust agreement approved by Lender.

(3) "Publicly-Held Corporation" shall mean a corporation the outstanding voting stock of which is registered under Section 12(b) or 12(g) of the Securities and Exchange Act of 1934, as amended.

Explanation

When a lender makes a loan to a specific borrower which is secured by a mortgage on a specific real estate project, the lender does so after performing an evaluation of the creditworthiness, reputation, and experience of the borrower and of the value of the real estate being pledged. Consequently, it is important to the lender that during the term of the loan the entities, and ultimately, the people who control the borrowing entity and sub-entities, do not change without the lender's consent and that these entities and people retain a controlling interest in the mortgaged property.

One way to ensure that this occurs is to prohibit any transfers of the mortgaged property or of any controlling interests in the borrowing entity and sub-entities as is done in Paragraph 21(a) of the form deed of trust. The exceptions listed in Paragraph 21(b) are ones that are commonly requested by borrowers and which lenders can live with since they do not impinge upon the basic protection that the lender is trying to accomplish with the "due-on-sale" provision. Paragraph 21(c) relates to the type of transfer that is potentially of concern to lenders but provides a procedure by which the borrower can seek the lender's consent to the transfer, including the payment of a specified non-refundable review fee, a transfer fee, and reimbursement of the lender's out-of-pocket expenses incurred in review ing the transfer request.

Enforcement

Congress enacted the Garn-St. Germain Depository Institutions Act, 12 U.S.C. Section 1701, et seq., in 1982. The Act provides that a lender's actions relating to due-on-sale situations are governed by the terms of the loan documents. The Act clarified that due-on-sale clauses are enforceable, notwithstanding state law to the contrary. Prior to this Act, the enforcement of due-on-sale clauses was less certain. Some states required the lender to show that its mortgage lien was impaired by the sale or that the risk of default increased due to the sale, in order for the lender to prevent a sale of the mortgage property and an assumption of the loan by the new owner. See, e.g., *Wellenkamp v. Bank of America*, 582 P.2d 970, 977 (Cal. 1978). The Act applies to both residential and commercial loans, with nine exceptions in the residential context. 12 U.S.C. Section 1701j-3(d).

Loan documents sometimes simply provide that the borrower may not sell the mortgaged property without the lender's consent. When a borrower comes to the lender later seeking consent to a proposed sale, the lender sometimes conditions consent on receiving additional collateral. This was the situation in *Destin Savings Bank v. Summerhouse of FWB, Inc.*, 579 So. 2d 232 (Fla. Dist. Ct. App. 1991). The court held that the lender could condition consent to the sale on the borrower providing additional collateral. In *Destin Savings*, appellee, Anderson (president of Summerhouse of FWB), received a commercial loan from appellant, Destin Savings, to enable his development of a restaurant. The mortgage and security agreement prohibited any sale, conveyance, transfer, lease or encumbrance without the mortgagee's written consent and declared any such transfer to be void. It also provided that if any other party obtained an interest in all or any part of the property it would be considered an event of default. In the event of a default, the mortgagee was authorized to declare the outstanding principal and accrued interest due and payable immediately. In 1989, without the mortgagee's consent, appellee Anderson entered into a sales contract for the restaurant with appellee Hobbs. After submitting Hobbs' financial statements to Destin Savings, the bank conditioned the consent of the assumption of the mortgage upon Hobbs pledging a $100,000.00 certificate of deposit which would be opened in the bank or taking out a second mortgage on his home with Destin as the lender. Hobbs refused and they closed the sale without obtaining Destin Savings' approval. The mortgagors filed complaints against the bank seeking declaration as to their rights under the mortgage agreement including the judgment regarding the additional collateral requested. The circuit court did not approve the conditions imposed by the mortgagees after applying a reasonableness standard to them and allowed the assumption. The appellate court reversed. The court held that the Garn-St. Germain Depository Institutions Act, 12 U.S.C. § 1701j-3 could be applied in commercial transactions and that under the Act the lender's actions were governed by the terms of the loan. Since the loan documents did not include language indicating that the lender's consent would not be unreasonably withheld, the court would not impose a reasonableness standard on the lender. *Id.* at 237.

Sometimes the loan documents provide that the lender will not "unreasonably" withhold consent to a sale. A question then arises as to what is reasonable. For example, can the lender condition consent on an increase in the interest rate? There are a line of cases where courts have ruled that a lender can condition consent to a sale on an increase in the interest rate to market rates when the loan documents require the lender not to unreasonably withhold consent to a sale. See, e.g., *Torgerson-Forstrom H.I. of Willmar, Inc. v. Olmsted Federal Savings and Loan Assoc.*, 339 N.W.2d 901, 904 (Minn. 1983) (court stated that there is a dual purpose for a due on sale clause: (i) the protection of the lender's security interest in the mortgaged property [issues of the creditworthiness and expertise of the proposed new owner of the property] and (ii) the lender's interest in protecting its position in the money market [keeping its investments at market rates]); and *Western Life Insurance Co. v. McPherson K.M.P.*, 702 F. Supp. 836 (D. Kan. 1988). See, also, *Rustic Hills Shopping Plaza, Inc. v. Columbia Savings and Loan Association*, 661 P.2d 254 (Col. 1983) (conditioning consent to a sale on increasing the interest rate from 7 to 15% was not unconscionable conduct rising to level of prohibited restraint on alienation where at the time interest rates on a new loan would have been approximately 18–19%).

Since courts will now enforce the terms of the loan documents with respect to due-on-sale clauses, it is important for lenders and borrowers to carefully negotiate the terms of the due-on-sale provision. If the lender would be willing to consent to a sale if it can condition such consent on requiring additional collateral, charging a fee, or increasing the interest rate, then the loan documents should expressly provide for this. Because the form deed of trust does this and appears to be reasonable (as opposed to unconscionable) in its terms (requiring a 1% fee) it should be enforceable. The form deed of trust also wisely provides that the lender does not have to show impairment of the mortgage as the basis for the due on sale clause. The court in *Western Life* stated that "the parties to a loan contract can limit a lender's right to exercise a due-on-sale clause to situations when a change in the ownership would impair the lender's security," but that the clause in question (that the lender would not unreasonably withhold consent) did not do so. *Western Life, supra* at 842.

[iii] Questions Regarding Due-On-Sale and Due-On-Encumbrance Clauses

1. Read paragraphs 7.9, 7.11 and 10(e) of the Loan Agreement in the Document Book. What did the parties negotiate regarding the terms of the due-on-sale clause and due-on-encumbrance clause?

2. Did Regent and First Mortgage Bank adequately address their respective needs?

[3] The Interest Rate

Another critical element of loan transactions involves the rate at which interest will accrue. There are two potential complications relating to the loan's interest rate. First is the issue of the borrower's ability to pay the interest due when the rate is a floating rate (*e.g.*, a loan that bears interest at 1% to 2% in excess of specified U.S. treasury rates, the "prime" rate charged by a lender, or "LIBOR," the London Interbank Offering Rate), since the interest rate may rise significantly during the term of the loan. Second, even for a fixed rate loan, there is the possibility that the interest rate charged might be usurious under the relevant state law, especially when the interest is combined with late charges for late payments or default interest, which is the higher interest rate some loan documents provide for during the period a borrower is in default. These two complications and how they are addressed are discussed below.

[a] Interest Rate Hedges to Address Floating Rate Risks

[i] Overview

Permanent loans on already constructed and operating real estate projects typically accrue interest at a fixed interest rate. However, shorter term construction loans typically accrue interest at a floating rate. If interest rates rise during the term of the construction loan beyond what is anticipated and budgeted for in the construction budget, the developer may be unable to pay the monthly installments of interest. Construction lenders who wish to loan at floating rates but avoid this risk require that the developer enter into a transaction that will "hedge" against this risk. The hedge can be very simple, such as the borrower paying a flat fee to another entity (sometimes an affiliate of the construction lender) who agrees that if the floating interest rate exceeds a certain specified level (such as the monthly amount budgeted for interest payments in the construction budget), then the counterparty will pay to the borrower the overage each month of that interest rate on the unpaid balance of the construction loan, thus capping the developer's interest rate exposure. This simple interest rate hedge transaction is called an "interest rate cap."

Some developers were reluctant to enter into interest rate caps because they would then have to pay what might be an expensive upfront fee for something that they might never use if interest rates do not rise past the specified capped level. These developers preferred instead to enter into a second type of interest rate hedge transaction that would require a smaller or no up-front fee. This second type of interest rate hedge is called an "interest rate swap" in which the developer enters into an agreement with a counterparty (sometimes the counterparty was an affiliate of the construction lender) under which the developer agrees to pay to the counterparty, at certain specified intervals, a payment if the fixed rate specified in the swap agreement is greater than the floating rate specified in the swap (paying the difference to the counterparty), and the counterparty agrees to pay to the developer at certain specified intervals a payment if the floating rate specified in the swap agreement (which should be the same as the floating rate obligation under the construction loan) is greater than the fixed interest rate specified in the swap (paying the difference to the developer). There is no exchange of principal between the developer and the counterparty under the swap agreement, but the interest rate payments are calculated using a "notional" amount (a fictional amount based upon the construction loan amount) to function as a principal amount for purposes of calculating the monthly payments of interest. When one combines the interest rate swap agreement with the underlying construction loan interest rate obligation, the developer is able to basically convert the floating rate construction loan obligation into a fixed rate obligation based upon the fixed rate specified in the interest rate swap agreement.

The illustration in the article below provides a visual explanation of how the construction loan payments and interest rate swap payments can provide a conversion of a floating rate loan into a fixed rate loan.

The counterparty might charge a fee to the developer to enter into the interest rate swap or may be compensated by having the borrower agree to a fixed rate that is higher than current fixed rate loans. The counterparty might be betting under the swap that interest rates will not rise above the fixed rate payments and will receive money from the developer each month that the floating interest rate is less than the fixed rate under the swap agreement but taking a risk if interest rates rise above the fixed rate specified in the swap.[1] But the developer's entry into the interest rate swap (an action typically required by the construction lender) is not motivated by a desire to "bet" on interest rate swings. To the contrary, it is for the purpose of converting an uncertain floating rate construction loan obligation into an agreed upon fixed rate obligation (through the use of the swap agreement and counterparty's agreement to pay the developer when the floating rate exceeds the specified fixed rate in the swap agreement). The ability for the swap agreement to work as intended from the developer's perspective presumes that the counterparty remains solvent and makes any required payments to the developer throughout the term of the swap agreement. In this respect, the interest rate swap is somewhat similar to a "credit default swap" (a topic discussed in Section 10.06 relating to the securitization of commercial real estate finance); the holder of a pool of mortgage loans enters into the credit default swap not as a means to "bet" on the likelihood of default but as a means to protect against the level of defaults rising past a certain specified level; but the counterparty to the credit default swap is gambling on the level of default and when the credit crisis became acute at the end of 2008, these counterparties appear to not be able to live up to their obligations under the credit default swaps.

Thinking about interest rate swap agreements causes many students' heads to spin, but when real estate developers enter into construction loans that exceed several million dollars, it is a common transaction for real estate developers to enter into and hence an important topic for commercial real estate attorneys to understand. The developer in the FVACC deal was not required to enter into an interest rate swap agreement, because the size of the loan in that deal was too low to justify the transaction costs associated with entering into a swap agreement.

The following article provides additional details on the use of interest rate hedge products by real estate developers in the context of a construction loan, including security, bankruptcy, and liability issues that arise.

---

[1] Although some counterparties enter into "mirror" swap transactions, for a fee, that reverses their position under the swap with the developer, to hedge against that risk.

Steven R. Davidson, *Hedging Your Bets with Interest Rate Hedging Products*, PROBATE & PROPERTY, Sept/Oct 1996 at 33*

Over the last 10 years, interest rate hedging products have become an increasingly common feature of real estate financing transactions. . . .

COMMON INTEREST RATE HEDGING PRODUCTS

Interest rate swaps.

An interest rate swap is a transaction with the following structure. One party to the swap contract pays an amount calculated at a specified interest rate and a hypothetical principal amount (sometimes called the "notional amount"), while the other party (sometimes called a "swap counter-party") pays an amount calculated at a different interest rate based on the same notional amount. Although the two interest rates chosen can be different floating rates, the most common type of interest rate swap involves one party making payments based on a fixed interest rate and the other party making payments based on a floating interest rate. When a borrower enters into an interest rate swap, it most frequently makes payments to the swap counterparty based on a fixed rate and receives payments from the swap counterparty based on a floating rate.

Often a borrower will obtain an interest rate swap when its loan is based on a floating interest rate, such as the London interbank offering rate (LIBOR), and the borrower does not want the risk of future increases in the floating rate. By carefully structuring the interest rate swap, the borrower can eliminate most of the risk of increasing interest rates. At the same time, the borrower gives up any savings that would otherwise be achieved if floating interest rates decline. A more detailed review of the swap mechanics will illustrate how a borrower can effectively fix its interest cost.

An interest rate swap is an exchange of interest payments. There is no principal debt owed by either party to the swap (although frequently the counterparty or its affiliate is also the borrower's lender). For that reason, the agreement evidencing the interest rate swap is sometimes called an Interest Rate Exchange Agreement. To compute the interest payments exchanged, the parties must choose a notional amount. When a borrower enters an interest rate swap to hedge the interest cost on a specific loan, the notional amount is typically the principal amount of the loan. For loans having further disbursements or periodic amortization payments, a schedule of notional amounts that vary during the term of the interest rate swap can be used. If the borrower wants to hedge only a portion of the interest rate risk, it can enter a swap based on a notional amount that is only a fraction of the principal amount of the loan.

After choosing the notional amount for the swap, the floating rate must be selected. The typical real estate borrower will pay an amount based on a fixed rate to the swap counterparty and, in return, will receive a payment from the swap counterparty based on a floating rate. The floating rate chosen for the interest rate swap should be as close as possible to the floating rate that the borrower pays the lender under the loan. The payment dates and the dates on which the floating rate is reset under the interest rate swap agreement should also correspond to the dates when payments are due under the loan and the dates on which LIBOR or other interest periods, if applicable, expire under the loan.

For example, assume that the borrower has obtained a $10 million loan with interest payments due on the fifth of each month based on an interest rate of one month LIBOR plus 200 basis points (the so-called "spread"). To use an interest rate swap effectively to convert that loan to a fixed rate loan, the borrower would choose an interest rate swap with a $10 million notional amount, payment dates on the fifth of the month and a floating rate equal to one month LIBOR (the spread is usually not included in the swap agreement). The LIBOR payments the borrower receives under the interest rate swap are passed through to the lender, and the borrower also pays the lender the additional 200 basis point spread. As a result, the borrower's interest cost under the loan does not vary, even though LIBOR may fluctuate substantially during the term of the loan. The borrower effectively pays the fixed rate due under the interest rate swap, plus the 200 basis point spread payable under the loan documents. This assumes that the lender incurs no additional costs related to LIBOR that are then charged to the borrower under the note. The interest rate swap and loan remain separate transactions. The payment streams resulting from these two transactions and the effective fixed rate cost to the borrower are illustrated in the accompanying diagram.

Fixed Rate Achieved Through Swap

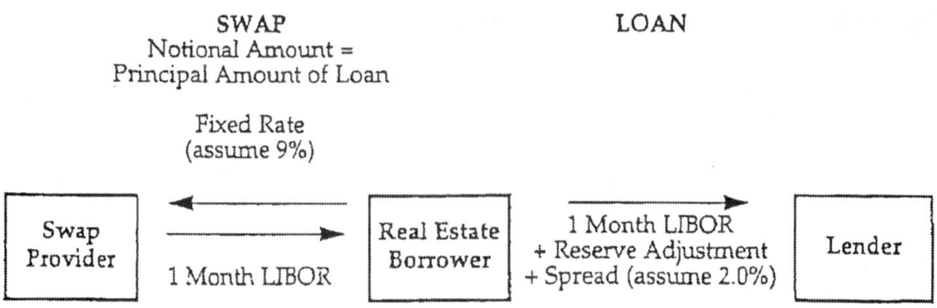

Borrower's Effective Rate = Fixed Swap Rate (9%) + Reserve Adjustment* + Spread (2%) = 11%

*Under current regulations no reserve adjustments apply to LIBOR loans.

36

Although this description implies that each swap party makes a payment to the other each month, typically the payments under the swap agreement are structured as net payments so that each month only one party is obligated to make a payment. Depending on the current rate, the net amount due is paid by one party or the other. Over the life of a swap, payments can change directions many times. The swap is sometimes referred to as being "in the money" or "out of the money" for a party, based on whether, at that time, the party is entitled to receive or is obligated to pay the net payment.

Like the notional amount, payment dates and reference rate, the length of the swap term is important. If the borrower is trying to use the interest rate swap to fix its interest cost on a loan, it will usually choose a swap term that corresponds to the loan term. Although no money is borrowed under the swap itself, the fixed rate quoted for the swap will vary based on the length of the swap. With a normal yield curve, the fixed rate becomes higher as the term goes longer.

Under an interest rate swap, both parties have continuing obligations to make payments throughout the term. Each party's ability to perform is therefore of critical concern. Because many real estate borrowers are single purpose entities, the borrower's credit alone will be insufficient to permit it to enter into an interest rate swap agreement. Unless the borrower's obligations are guaranteed by a satisfactory credit support provider, the obligations under the interest rate swap are often secured by the real estate. Special issues in using real estate to secure an interest rate swap agreement are discussed below.

Many possible advantages result from combining a floating rate loan and an interest rate swap instead of simply obtaining a fixed rate loan. Many lenders are not able to lend money at a competitive fixed interest rate. Historically, insurance companies, pension funds and other long-term lenders have been the providers of fixed rate loans. In contrast, banks have more commonly charged a floating interest rate for their loans. When asked to compete with the fixed rate proposals of long-term lenders, banks often cannot respond with competitive rates because of the way they fund their loans. Many banks have found that, by offering an interest rate swap in combination with a floating rate loan, they can successfully compete with the long-term fixed rate lenders.

Interest rate swaps not only are a tool to obtain a competitive fixed rate but in many cases also provide greater flexibility than fixed rate loans. A fixed rate loan typically will have a period during which the borrower may not prepay the loan, followed by a period during which a premium will apply if the borrower prepays the loan. A floating rate loan combined with a swap can be less restrictive. A floating rate loan usually will have no prepayment prohibition and often will have no prepayment premiums. Although a borrower may have to pay substantial breakage costs to terminate a swap early if interest rates decline, the borrower might actually receive a termination payment to cancel a swap contract if interest rates rise. Furthermore, because the swap is separate from the loan, the borrower does not necessarily have to terminate the swap when the loan is repaid. The borrower could use the swap to hedge the interest rate exposure on a different loan after the original loan has been paid.

In addition, a borrower may choose to enter into a swap after the loan has been made. For example, if floating rates are very low when the loan is closed, the borrower may decide to take the risk of some increase in the rate to take advantage of the low floating rates for as long as possible. Although it is common for lenders to require an interest rate swap to control their credit exposure, a lender may allow its borrower some flexibility on that requirement as long as short-term rates remain low.

Interest rate caps

A second widely used interest rate hedging product is an interest rate cap. This product provides the borrower with protection against rising rates while still allowing the borrower to benefit if rates decline. Under an interest rate cap, the party supplying the cap agrees to make a payment to the borrower if a specified floating rate exceeds the applicable rate cap (sometimes called a "strike rate"). Again, assume that a borrower obtains a $10 million loan at a floating interest rate of LIBOR plus 200 basis points. The borrower may buy an interest rate cap based on LIBOR for a notional amount of $10 million with a strike rate of 10%. If LIBOR goes above 10%, the borrower receives a payment from the cap provider equal to the difference between LIBOR and 10%, multiplied by $10 million. The borrower has therefore effectively capped its interest cost at 10% plus the 200 basis point spread it is paying under the note regardless of how high LIBOR goes. The borrower retains the benefit of declining rates with an interest rate cap. For example, if LIBOR falls to 5%, the borrower pays only 5%, plus the 200 basis point spread.

Typically, the borrower purchases an interest rate cap with an upfront fee. After the borrower pays that fee, it has no further obligation to make payments. This makes the interest rate cap a very attractive product to the cap provider because it takes no credit risk for the borrower. Nevertheless, the fee for an interest rate cap usually is substantial — the lower the strike rate, the higher the fee. As a result, borrowers often are willing to give up all or part of the benefit of declining rates to save the fee.

Interest rate collars

Although used less frequently than interest rate swaps or caps, an interest rate collar is a way for a borrower to reduce the upfront fee of a cap and still retain some of the benefit of declining rates that the borrower would lose with a swap. An interest rate collar sets both a ceiling rate and a floor rate. If the specified floating rate index (again, generally the index used for the borrower's loan) exceeds the ceiling rate, the provider of the collar pays the borrower an amount equal to the difference in those rates multiplied by the notional amount of the collar. If the specified floating rate is less than the floor rate, the borrower pays the other party an amount equal to the difference between the floor rate and the specified floating rate multiplied by the notional amount of the collar. If the floating rate is between the floor rate and the ceiling rate, then no payments are due from either party. Thus, the borrower derives the same protection against rising rates it would have from an interest rate swap or cap agreement. The borrower benefits from declining rates until they are lower than the floor rate. Not surprisingly, the fee payable in connection with an interest rate collar is less than the fee for an interest rate cap but more than the fee, if any, for an interest rate swap.

Other products

Swaps, caps and collars are not the only interest rate hedging products available to borrowers. A "swaption," an option to enter into a swap in the future, is one example of the many additional products available in the marketplace. A discussion of those more exotic products is beyond the scope of this article.

Legal issues for hedging products

The use of interest rate hedging products may raise a number of regulatory, tax and other legal questions. The following discussion focuses on some of the issues that are of greater concern when a real estate borrower obtains a floating rate loan and an interest rate hedging product.

Real estate security

Frequently a borrower secures its obligations under an interest rate swap with a mortgage on the borrower's project. That mortgage will have a priority at least equal to the mortgage securing the underlying loan, although no principal indebtedness is outstanding under a swap agreement. In some states, securing the indefinite swap contractual obligation does not pose any problem and the swap agreement simply can be included in the list of obligations secured by the mortgage. The result in other states is less clear. In those states, as long as the swap provider is the same entity as the lender, the documents are often drafted to recharacterize the amount due under the swap agreement as additional interest.

In many cases, however, the swap provider is an affiliated but separate legal entity. In that case, the lender often unconditionally agrees to advance the affiliated swap provider any amounts due in connection with the interest rate swap agreement and those advances are then secured by the mortgage. Because the advances are obligatory, the priority of the lien usually relates back to the mortgage recordation. If the parties use either of these two methods, the major title insurers are willing to issue special title endorsements (if permitted in the state) insuring that the obligations under the swap agreement are secured with the same priority as the obligations under the loan documents.

Bankruptcy issues

Several important rights in a swap agreement could be affected by bankruptcy. Before 1990, great uncertainty existed about the effect of a bankruptcy on the various rights of the solvent party to a swap agreement. For example, a non-bankrupt swap party might not be able to terminate a swap agreement following the bankruptcy of the other without obtaining relief from the automatic stay. The ability of the parties to offset or net out termination values or payment amounts under multiple transactions between the same two parties was also questionable. Since 1990, § 560 of the Bankruptcy Code makes it clear that both the right to terminate the agreement and the right to offset or net out termination values will be enforceable despite the existence of the bankruptcy proceeding. 11 U.S.C. § 560.

Liability

During the last two years [1994–1996], there have been several well publicized large losses related to derivative transactions. The losses were incurred by large corporations, including Proctor & Gamble and Gibson Greetings, as well as by Orange County, California. With the vast publicity about these cases, it is easy to understand why smaller entities, such as those engaged in real estate financing transactions, are also beginning to assert claims when the derivative products they have purchased allegedly do not produce the results they expected. The claims made have included misrepresentation, breach of fiduciary duty, lack of suitability of the products sold and violation of federal or state securities laws.

Because this is an emerging area of the law, no clear guidance exists on many of the issues raised. In response, many derivative dealers have incorporated into their standard documents provisions comparable to those found in securities offering materials. These provisions include acknowledgments that the party entering into the transaction has consulted its own advisers and fully understands the nature and purpose of the product and is not relying on the product provider as an adviser in connection with the transaction.

Many interest rate swaps are provided by banks in connection with financing transactions. This creates the possibility of claims by borrowers that they were forced to enter into an interest rate swap with the bank or its affiliate as a condition to obtaining credit — a possible violation of the Bank Tying Act. 12 U.S.C. §§ 1971–1978. Congress, when enacting the Bank Tying Act, intended to prohibit banks from extending their economic power for credit extensions into other markets where the banks could force their customers to pay anticompetitive prices for products other than the loan. It is not clear whether a loan and an interest rate swap obtained for the loan are two separate products that could be tied in violation of the Bank Tying Act. Arguably, the swap is an integral part of the loan and not a separate product. The similarities between a fixed rate loan and a floating rate loan with a swap support this position. An interest rate hedging product is becoming a common loan requirement to make a default by the borrower less likely if interest rates rise significantly. Because of the lack of clear authority under the Bank Tying Act and the lack of any reported cases on this issue, a bank should carefully document that the borrower was not required to purchase the swap through the lending bank, but rather was free to obtain the swap from other providers in the market.

Conclusion

The derivative markets have grown dramatically. Although the losses suffered by some and the resulting litigation may have provoked well-deserved caution, the markets can be expected to continue their expansion. The worst losses by parties using derivative products occurred when those products were obtained for pure speculation and not for hedging purposes. As long as interest rates are subject to fluctuations, these derivative products have a legitimate place in the real estate financing market.

[ii] Comments and Questions Regarding Interest Rate Hedges

1. What is an interest rate swap agreement?
2. Why do construction lenders sometimes require borrowers to enter into interest rate swap agreements? Why didn't First Mortgage Bank require Regent to enter into an interest rate swap agreement for the construction loan on the Fox Valley Auto Care Center?
3. When a lender does require the borrower to enter into an interest rate hedge agreement, do you think the lender ever acts as a matchmaker or specifies the entity that the borrower must enter into the swap with? Why might this be a bad idea?
4. What are the advantages to a borrower entering into an interest rate swap agreement? What are the disadvantages?
5. What other options are available to reduce the risk of rising interest rates besides interest rate exchange agreements?
6. What are some of the legal issues one should be cognizant of when representing a party to an interest rate hedge transaction?
7. For a fuller discussion of the legal issues involved when a real estate developer/borrower enters into a swap agreement in connection with real estate finance, see Stark, *Using Interest Rate Exchange Agreements in Real Estate Transactions*, REAL EST. FIN., Fall 1990 at 40, and Stark,

Interest Rate Swaps: A Reassessment, Prob. & Prop., May/June 1997 at 36 (which provides examples of interest rate hedges that proved a disaster to one of the counter-parties and the various defenses that counter-party raised to defend an action to enforce the swap).

8. The Davidson article provides an introduction to the concept and uses of interest rate hedge products. These products are typically documented using standardized forms prepared by the International Swap Dealers Association (ISDA). In order to effectively negotiate the interest rate hedge documentation for your client, it is necessary to be familiar with these standardized forms. For a discussion of these forms generally and an analysis of the key points to negotiate for when using these complicated forms, including damages upon early termination of the transaction, see Stark, *Negotiating Interest Rate Exchange Agreements: A Look at Major Issues That Arise in Drafting Interest Rate Swaps*, Real Est. Fin., Spring 1987 at 93.

9. It appears from cases involving interest rate swap agreements that sometimes parties who have entered into such agreements for the purpose of hedging their floating rate obligations against rising interest rates did not understand the risks and complications that can arise, in particular when a party attempts to terminate the interest rate swap agreement. For example, in *St. Matthew's Baptist Church v. Wachovia Bank National Association*, 2005 U.S. Dist. LEXIS 46607 (N.J. 2005), St. Matthew's had undertaken a short term construction loan, that accrued interest at a floating rate, and sought to refinance that debt with a longer term fixed interest rate loan. Wachovia told St. Matthew's it did not qualify for a fixed rate loan but could enter into a floating rate loan together with an interest rate swap. The swap terms were that St. Matthew's would pay 9.13% under the interest rate swap and receive in return, from its counterparty under the swap, a floating rate based upon the floating rate under the loan with Wachovia. Thus, in essence, St. Matthew's converted its floating rate loan into a fixed rate loan of 9.13% However, after two years, St. Matthew's wished to prepay its floating rate loan with Wachovia and refinance with a more favorable fixed interest rate from another lending source. According to the court, it was not until St. Matthew's sought to prepay the floating rate loan that St. Matthew's learned that if it chose to prepay the loan, and terminate the swap agreement, St. Matthew's would have to pay a very large "termination fee" under the swap agreement. St. Matthew's alleged that, when Wachovia first proposed the floating rate loan and swap to St. Matthew's, Wachovia represented to St. Matthew's that if it cancelled the swap it would only have to pay at most an "unwind fee," which would be smaller than a standard prepayment penalty on a fixed rate bank loan. However, when St. Matthew's two years later tried to prepay the loan and terminate the swap, the swap counterparty claimed a termination fee equal to approximately ten percent of the loan amount. This termination fee was determined based upon "Market Quotations," a defined term in the Master Agreement under the standard ISDA documentation that is very open ended, and that St. Matthew's either failed to read or understand, perhaps due to the verbal representations St. Matthew's had allegedly received

from Wachovia that minimized any termination fees.

One might not be surprised that St. Matthew's Baptist Church, lacking financial sophistication, failed to appreciate how a termination of a swap might be desirable or necessary and failed to realize how high the termination fee under the swap can be. However, even businesses like telephone companies and aircraft servicers have failed to understand these points as well. *See, e.g., Power & Telephone Supply Company, Inc. v. Suntrust Banks, Inc.*, 447 F.3d 923 (6th Cir. 2006); *K3C Inc., Sierra Industries, Inc v. Bank of America*, 204 Fed. Appx. 455 (5th Cir. 2006). It appears from a reading of these cases that even if these two businesses had hired attorneys to review the swap and loan documentation they entered into, that their attorneys also failed to understand and caution their clients on the issue of early termination and the possibility of very high termination fees, perhaps because the termination fees are not conspicuously spelled out in the very lengthy and difficult to read ISDA Master Agreement documentation.

The disappointed parties in these three interest rate swap cases raised similar legal claims for relief from the high termination fees charged to them, including breach of fiduciary duty and duty of disclosure, fraud, and negligent misrepresentation. All three claimants were unsuccessful, with the courts ruling in each case that ordinarily there is no fiduciary duty between a bank and a borrower, or between swap counterparties, and that there could be no "reasonable" reliance (a necessary element for fraud or negligent misrepresentation) when the alleged parole false statement (that there would be at most a small termination fee or that the swap counterparty would act as the other party's financial advisor and only have them enter into suitable swap transactions) was contradicted by the terms of the loan and swap documentation.

Do you agree with the courts that the parties that sought to terminate the swaps should not be permitted to raise any fraudulent representations if they were contradicted by the terms of the swap documentation on the grounds that they did not thereby "reasonably" rely on those false representations? Whichever way you come down on that issue, these cases underscore the need for an attorney to be well versed in the voluminous and complicated ISDA swap documentation and in the special risks and complications that can arise when a client is attempting to hedge a floating rate obligation through the use of interest rate swaps.

[b] Usury Laws and Other Challenges to the Enforcement of the Interest and Other Loan Charges

Another issue of concern to lenders regarding interest rates is whether the effective rate violates a usury law. Many states have enacted laws that limit the amount of interest that can be lawfully charged with respect to a loan. In some cases, the penalty for violating the usury laws is not only forfeiture of the usurious amount of interest, but forfeiture of all interest due under the loan. *See, e.g.*, N.Y. Gen. Oblig. Law § 5-511 (McKinney 1997). This issue becomes even more complicated when a loan is secured with mortgages on properties in more than one state. Whenever representing a lender who is making a loan secured by properties located in many states, it is important to ascertain whether the interest charged would be considered usurious in the jurisdictions where the mortgaged property is located. One should also ascertain whether it is possible to obtain an endorsement to the lender's title insurance policy to insure that the real estate mortgage will not be invalid or lose its security if the loan is deemed usurious. Since the "usury endorsement" does not insure that a loan will not be deemed usurious, if a lender is unsure of this issue, it should require an opinion of counsel on this point as a condition to funding the loan.

[i] Overview

Many, but not all, states provide an exception to the application of usury laws with respect to "business loans." *See, e.g.*, Cal. Fin. Code § 3707 (1997) (loans made to a corporation, loans greater than a specified amount, or some combination of these factors); *Hopfenspirger v. West*, 949 So. 2d 1050, 1053 (Fla. App. 5 Dist. 2006) (statute prohibited a commercial loan borrower, and a similarly situated guarantor, from asserting a usury defense when the commercial loan amount exceeded $100,000). In order to reduce the risk of the interest rate (including any late charges and default interest) from being construed as usurious, lenders commonly insert a "savings" clause in their loan documents that directs a court to enforce the charges only to the extent permitted by law. In addition, if a loan has a natural connection to more than one state's laws (for example if the mortgage property is in one state that may have applicable usury limitations, but the lender is located in another state where there are not applicable usury limitations), the lender may have the loan documents provide that the choice of law is different from where the mortgage property is located as a means to reduce the chances of a successful usury challenge. *See, e.g., Land-Cellular Corp. v. Zokaites*, 463 F. Supp. 2d 1348 (S.D. Fla. 2006) (lender provided in the loan documents for a choice of law in Pennsylvania, where the mortgage lender was located and from where the loan funds were disbursed, rather than Florida law, where the mortgaged property was located, because the interest rate on the loan violated Florida's usury statute, which prohibited interest rates in excess of 18% per annum for loans less than $500,000; the court enforced the choice of Pennsylvania law as having a normal relation to the transaction and enforced the interest due on the loan, since under Pennsylvania law usury limitations do not apply to commercial loans that exceed $50,000). The excerpt which follows provides an example of a typical "savings" clause, discusses case law regarding its enforceability, and raises non-usury challenges which can be made to the interest and other loan charges. After reading this excerpt, you will be asked to think about how these issues apply to the construction loan from First Mortgage Bank.

WILSON FREYERMOUTH, JOHN MCNEARNEY, DEBRA STARK & DALE WHITMAN, ANATOMY OF A MORTGAGE (ABA 2001)*

FORM DEED OF TRUST

[This is the FNMA multi-family housing form deed of trust. — Eds.]

25. *LOAN CHARGES.* If any applicable law limiting the amount of interest or other charges permitted to be collected from Borrower is interpreted so that any charge provided for in any Loan Document, whether considered separately or together with other charges levied in connection with any other Loan Document, violates that law, and Borrower is entitled to the benefit of that law, that charge is hereby reduced to the extent necessary to eliminate that violation. The amounts, if any, previously paid to Lender in excess of the permitted amounts shall be applied by Lender to reduce the principal of the Indebtedness. For the purpose of determining whether any applicable law limiting the amount of interest or other charges permitted to be collected from Borrower has been violated, all Indebtedness which constitutes interest, as well as all other charges levied in connection with the Indebtedness which constitute interest, shall be deemed to be allocated and spread over the stated term of the Note. Unless otherwise required by applicable law, such allocation and spreading shall be effected in such a manner that the rate of interest so computed is uniform throughout the stated term of the Note.

Explanation

Paragraph 25 mainly addresses the issue that the interest being charged under the loan is usurious. It provides for a general "savings" clause (to the extent that any interest or other charges under the loan might violate any law as being too excessive it is reduced to the extent necessary to eliminate a violation) and for specific methods to avoid a violation of law (spreading the amount paid over the term of the loan or applying it to the principal portion of the debt).

It should be noted, however, that in addition to interest, other loan charges (such as late fees and default interest) are susceptible to challenge. See *Metlife Capital Financial Corporation v. Washington Avenue Associates, L.P.*, 313 N.J. Super. 525, 713 A.2d 527 (N.J. Super. App. Div. June 23, 1998) (in a commercial mortgage loan, court held that a 5% late fee and a default rate of interest equal to the greater of 5% per annum in excess of a defined "prime rate" or 15% were unenforceable penalties because they were not related to any damages the lender suffered in connection with the borrower's defaults in making payments), *rev'd*, 159 N.J. 484, 495–497, 732 A.2d 493, 499–500 (N.J. 1999) (court applied a liquidated damages analysis which allows an amount which is reasonable in light of the totality of the following: the anticipated harm caused by the breach, the difficulty in assessing damages, the intention of the parties, the actual damages sustained, and the bargaining power of the parties [the court also noted later that due to the difficulty in assessing damages attributable to a specific late payment, courts may look at what is permitted by statute and what constitutes common practice in a competitive industry] and ruled that the late charge and default interest were reasonable under this standard).

Enforcement

Some courts have enforced the specific "savings" techniques utilized in Paragraph 25. *See, e.g., In re Wright*, 144 B.R. 943 (Bkrtcy. S.D. Ga. 1992) (loan fee spread over life of loan not applied exclusively to first month of loan); and *Pentico v. Mad-Wayler, Inc.*, 964 S.W.2d 708 (Tex. App. 1998) (can spread interest over the term of the loan to avoid usury). However, some courts will not enforce this type of savings clause. *See, e.g., Swindell v. Federal Nat. Mortg. Ass'n*, 409 S.E. 2d 892 (N.C. 1991) (court held that usury savings clause in the mortgage note could not shield mortgagee from liability for charging usurious late payment fee). In *Swindell*, the court noted that there were two purposes behind late payment fees: to encourage the borrower to pay on time and to compensate the lender for the period of the delay. The court ruled that in light of this second purpose, the 5% late charge imposed for payments made more than 15 days late was "interest" within the meaning of the North Carolina statute, *id.* at 894, and that the rate charged exceeded the maximum rate permitted under the usury statute. *Id.* at 895. The court held that the usury savings clause in the note could not shield the lender from liability for charging usurious rates because such a holding would be inconsistent with the policies behind the usury statute (to protect borrowers by putting the burden of compliance on the lender). *Id.* If the usury savings clause were valid, the court asserted, then this would shift the onus back to the borrower to determine that the contract rate was invalid when the burden should be on the lender, the more sophisticated party in the business of making loans. The court's remedy was not to invalidate all interest due on the note, just the entire late charge amount. *Id.* at 896.

Although the *Swindell* case appears at first blush to not be favorable to lenders, some of its dicta could, in fact, be useful to lenders. As noted, the court in *Swindell* stated that there were two purposes to a late charge, one of which was to encourage the borrower to pay on time. If this is a legitimate purpose, then lenders can argue that the charge should not be invalidated as an invalid liquidated damages penalty (unless the amount is unconscionable). *See Dacon Bolingbrook Associates Ltd. Partnership v. Federal Nat. Mortg. Ass'n*, 155 B.R. 467 (N.D. Ill. 1993) (court acknowledged that a valid purpose of late charges is to encourage borrower's to make timely payments and court enforced a 4% late charge); and *Travelers Ins. Co. v. Corporex Properties, Inc.*, 798 F. Supp. 423 (E.D. Ky. 1992) (court enforced a 4% late charge as reasonable).

Conclusion

Due to the strong public policies behind usury laws and the different approaches jurisdictions take to this issue, it would not be helpful to generalize on the enforceability of Paragraph 25 of the form deed of trust. One must always look to the laws of the jurisdiction whose law controls with respect to any specific loan transaction on any issue, but in particular on this issue.

[ii] Enforcement of the Interest Rate, Late Charges and Default Interest in the Fox Valley Auto Care Center

Would the interest due under the construction loan for the Fox Valley Auto Care Center violate Illinois' usury law? Are any late charges or default interest under the Auto Care Center loan documents (see Paragraphs 2(c) and (d) of the Promissory Note in the Document Book) susceptible to attack on the basis of usury laws or some other grounds? In answering these questions, think about (1) *MetLife Capital Financial* and the enforceability of savings clauses discussed in the previous excerpt and (2) the Illinois usury statute that follows.

815 Illinois Compiled Statutes 205/4; General interest rate

(1) In all written contracts it shall be lawful for the parties to stipulate or agree that 9% per annum, or any less sum of interest, shall be taken and paid upon every $100 of money loaned or in any manner due and owing from any person to any other person or corporation in this state, and after that rate for a greater or less sum, or for a longer or shorter time, except as herein provided.

The maximum rate of interest that may lawfully be contracted for is determined by the law applicable thereto at the time the contract is made. Any provision in any contract, whether made before or after July 1, 1969, which provides for or purports to authorize, contingent upon a change in the Illinois law after the contract is made, any rate of interest greater than the maximum lawful rate at the time the contract is made, is void.

It is lawful for a state bank or a branch of an out-of-state bank, as those terms are defined in Section 2 of the Illinois Banking Act, to receive and collect interest and charges at any rate or rates agreed upon by the bank or branch and the borrower.

It is lawful to receive or to contract to receive and collect interest and charges as authorized by this Act and as authorized by the Consumer Installment Loan Act and by the "Consumer Finance Act," approved July 10, 1935, as now or hereafter amended. It is lawful to charge, contract for, and receive any rate or amount of interest or compensation with respect to the following transactions:

(a) Any loan made to a corporation;

(b) Advances of money, repayable on demand, to an amount not less than $5,000, which are made upon warehouse receipts, bills of lading, certificates of stock, certificates of deposit, bills of exchange, bonds or other negotiable instruments pledged as collateral security for such repayment, if evidenced by a writing;

(c) Any credit transaction between a merchandise wholesaler and retailer; any business loan to a business association or copartnership or to a person owning and operating a business as sole proprietor or to any persons owning and operating a business as joint venturers, joint tenants or tenants in common, or to any limited partnership, or to any trustee owning and operating a business or whose beneficiaries own and operate a business except that any loan which is secured (1) by an assignment of an individual obligor's salary, wages, commissions or other compensation for services, or (2) by his household furniture or other goods used for his personal, family or household purposes shall be deemed not to be a loan within the meaning of this subsection; and provided further that a loan which otherwise qualifies as a business loan within the meaning of this subsection shall not be deemed as not so qualifying because of the inclusion, with other security consisting of business assets of any such obligor, of real estate occupied by an individual obligor solely as his residence. The term "business" shall be deemed to mean a commercial, agricultural or industrial enterprise which is carried on for the purpose of investment or profit, but shall not be deemed to mean the ownership or maintenance of real estate occupied by an individual obligor solely as his residence;

(d) Any loan made in accordance with the provisions of Subchapter 1 of Chapter 13 of Title 12 of the United States Code, which is designated as "Housing Renovation and Modernization";

(e) Any mortgage loan insured or upon which a commitment to insure has been issued under the provisions of the National Housing Act, Chapter 13 of Title 12 of the United States Code;

(f) Any mortgage loan guaranteed or upon which a commitment to guaranty has been issued under the provisions of the Veterans' Benefits Act, Subchapter II of Chapter 37 of Title 38 of the United States Code;

(g) Interest charged by a broker or dealer registered under the Securities Exchange Act of 1934, as amended, or registered under the Illinois Securities Law of 1953, approved July 13, 1953, as now or hereafter amended, on a debit balance in an account for a customer if such debit balance is payable at will without penalty and is secured by securities as defined in Uniform Commercial Code-Investment Securities;

(h) Any loan made, guaranteed, or insured in accordance with the provisions of the Housing Act of 1949, Subchapter III of Chapter 8A of Title 42 of the United States Code and the Consolidated Farm and Rural Development Act, Subchapters I, II, and III of Chapter 50 of Title 7 of the United States Code;

(i) Any loan made, guaranteed, or insured in accordance with the provisions of the Housing Act of 1949, Subchapter III of Chapter 8A of Title 42 of the United States Code and the Consolidated Farm and Rural Development Act, Subchapters I, II, and III of Chapter 50 of Title 7 of the United States Code;

(j) Any loan by an employee pension benefit plan, as defined in Section 3(2) of the Employee Retirement Income Security Act of 1974 (29 U.S.C. Sec. 1002), to an individual participating in such plan, provided that such loan satisfies the prohibited transaction exemption requirements of Section 408(b)(1) (29 U.S.C. Sec. 1108(b)(1)) or Section 2003(a) (26 U.S.C. Sec. 4975(d)(1)) of the Employee Retirement Income Security Act of 1974;

(k) Written contracts, agreements or bonds for deed providing for installment purchase of real estate;

(l) Loans secured by a mortgage on real estate;

(m) Loans made by a sole proprietorship, partnership, or corporation to an employee or to a person who has been offered employment by such sole proprietorship, partnership, or corporation made for the sole purpose of transferring an employee or person who has been offered employment to another office maintained and operated by the same sole proprietorship, partnership, or corporation;

(n) Loans to or for the benefit of students made by an institution of higher education.

Amended by P.A. 89-208, § 45, eff. Sept. 29, 1995.

[c] Recourse Versus Non-Recourse Liability for the Debt

Another important feature to a real estate secured loan is whether the borrower's liability for payment of the debt and performance of any enumerated additional obligations within the loan documentation is recourse (*i.e.*, all of the borrower's assets are liable for the debt) or non-recourse (only the pledged assets of the borrower are liable for the debt). As previously discussed, construction loans are usually recourse loans, because until the project is built and in operation, it is less likely in the event of the borrower's default for the lender to be made whole from a sale of the project. Longer term take-out loans usually have been non-recourse for tax reasons, as discussed in Chapter 2 (in order for interest and depreciation deductions to flow through to limited partners and LLC members, all partners or members must have the same status, recourse or non-recourse, under the terms of the loan) and because the collateral, a fully constructed and operational project, is more likely to have sufficient value upon sale to pay off the loan should the borrower default in making loan payments. However, lenders encountered several problems with non-recourse loans on fully built and operational projects. One problem they encountered was that some borrowers failed to apply all of the rents and other income from the project to the payment of real estate taxes and operating expenses for the project and instead applied it to other projects, especially after a default under the loan. Some borrowers used the money from the project as a "war chest" to battle lenders in the courts after a default had occurred. Borrowers also aggressively used the bankruptcy courts to prevent the lender from exercising its rights to swiftly foreclose and take control of the project. To provide an incentive to borrowers not to take these actions, lenders began to draft exceptions or "carve-outs" to the non-recourse language of their permanent loans making the borrower, and even its key principals, personally liable for any fraud or acts of waste or misapplication of funds. To discourage borrowers from filing a bankruptcy action, lenders also provided for recourse liability on the debt to the borrower and, sometimes even its principals, in the event of a bankruptcy of the borrower or for taking certain other enumerated steps (such as failing to maintain their status as a single purpose/asset entity) which could make bankruptcy more likely.

[i] Exceptions to Non-Recourse Liability

The next excerpt will provide an example of typical exceptions to non-recourse liability in loan documentation for long-term real estate secured loans. It will also address the nature of these exceptions, explain why lenders have added these exceptions to their loan documents, and analyze cases that have addressed the issue of personal liability in a non-recourse loan setting. Make sure you understand these points, because after you finish the excerpt, you will be asked to be prepared to represent either a borrower or a lender in negotiating exceptions to a non-recourse loan.

Wilson Freyermouth, John McNearney, Debra Stark & Dale Whitman, Anatomy of a Mortgage (ABA 2001)*

FORM DEED OF TRUST

[This is a paragraph from the FNMA multi-family housing form note. — Eds.]

9. *LIMITS ON PERSONAL LIABILITY.*

(a) Except as otherwise provided in this Paragraph 9, Borrower shall have no personal liability under this Note, the Security Instrument or any other Loan Document for the repayment of the Indebtedness or for the performance of any other obligations of Borrower under the Loan Documents, and Lender's only recourse for the satisfaction of the Indebtedness and the performance of such obligations shall be Lender's exercise of its rights and remedies with respect to the Mortgaged Property and any other collateral held by Lender as security for the Indebtedness. This limitation on Borrower's liability shall not limit or impair Lender's enforcement of its rights against any guarantor of the Indebtedness or any guarantor of any obligations of Borrower.

(b) Borrower shall be personally liable to Lender for the repayment of a portion of the Indebtedness equal to any loss or damage suffered by Lender as a result of (1) failure of Borrower to pay to Lender upon demand after an Event of Default, all Rents to which Lender is entitled under Section 3(a) of the Security Instrument and the amount of all security deposits collected by Borrower from tenants then in residence; (2) failure of Borrower to apply all insurance proceeds and condemnation proceeds as required by the Security Instrument; (3) failure of Borrower to comply with Section 14(d) or (e) of the Security Instrument relating to the delivery of books and records, statements, schedules and reports; (4) fraud or written material misrepresentation by Borrower, Key Principal or any officer, director, partner, member or employee of Borrower in connection with the application for or creation of the Indebtedness or any request for any action or consent by Lender; or (5) failure to apply Rents, first, to the payment of reasonable operating expenses (other than Property management fees that are not currently payable pursuant to the terms of an Assignment of Management Agreement or any other agreement with Lender executed in connection with the Loan) and then to amounts ("Debt Service Amounts") payable under this Note, the Security Instrument or any other Loan Document (except that Borrower will not be personally liable (i) to the extent that Borrower lacks the legal right to direct the disbursement of such sums because of a bankruptcy, receivership or similar judicial proceeding, or (ii) with respect to Rents that are distributed in any calendar year if Borrower has paid all operating expenses and Debt Service Amounts for that calendar year).

(c) Borrower shall become personally liable to Lender for the repayment of all of the Indebtedness upon the occurrence of any of the following Events of Default: (1) Borrower's acquisition of any property or operation of any business not permitted by Section 33 of the Security Instrument [Ed. Note: Section 33 is intended to keep the Borrower as a single purpose/asset entity in order to make it less likely the Borrower will be dragged into a bankruptcy due to matters unrelated to this project and this loan]; (2) a Transfer that is an Event of Default under Section 21 of the Security Instrument [Ed. Note: Section 21 contains a "due-on-sale" and "due-on-encumbrance" type clause previously discussed in this Chapter].

(d) To the extent that Borrower has personal liability under this Paragraph 9, Lender may exercise its rights against Borrower personally without regard to whether Lender has exercised any rights against the Mortgaged Property or any other security, or pursued any rights against any guarantor, or pursued any other rights available to Lender under this Note, the Security Instrument, any other Loan Document or applicable law. For purposes of this Paragraph 9, the term "Mortgaged Property" shall not include any funds that (1) have been applied by Borrower as required or permitted by the Security Instrument prior to the occurrence of an Event of Default, or (2) Borrower was unable to apply as required or permitted by the Security Instrument because of a bankruptcy, receivership, or similar judicial proceeding.

10. *EXCULPATION.* Borrower's personal liability for payment of the Indebtedness and for performance of the other obligations to be performed by it under this Instrument is limited in the manner, and to the extent, provided in the Note.

Explanation

Prior to the 1990s, long term, commercial real estate loans were typically made on a "non-recourse" basis (the property mortgaged was the sole asset the lender could look to in the event that the borrower defaulted in performing its obligations under the loan documents). Lenders were willing to make non-recourse loans to real estate projects that were fully constructed and profitably operating, loaning typically up to 80% of the appraised value of the property. In the event of a default, the lender could accelerate the debt, foreclose on the property, and recover her investment.

During the real estate recession of the early 1990s, numerous real estate projects began to fail and numerous real estate loans went into default. Lenders learned many lessons as they attempted to enforce the loan documents they had entered into. One common problem lenders encountered was borrowers who would take income from the mortgaged project and not apply it to the expenses of the mortgaged project. The borrowers might be applying that money to other projects that the lender did not have a mortgage on, or purchasing other assets that the lender did not have a security interest in, or developing a "war chest" to fund a defense to the lender's foreclosure action (in particular, filing for bankruptcy relief). In reaction to this, lenders have since revised their loan documentation to provide "carve-outs" to the non-recourse nature of the loan (situations which if they arise will cause the borrower to become personally liable to the lender for the repayment of a portion of the debt equal to the loss or damage suffered by the lender as a result of the circumstance).

Paragraph 9(a) of the form note provides for the basic non-recourse nature of the loan. Paragraph 9(b) contains the carve-outs to the non-recourse nature of the loan, including, the borrower's misapplication of the rents, insurance proceeds or condemnation proceeds, or fraud or written material misrepresentation by the borrower. Paragraph 9(c) provides that the borrower becomes personally liable for the entire debt if (i) the borrower changes its status as a "single asset borrower" (by mixing in additional properties it increases the possibility that the borrower could be subject to a bankruptcy filing-a possibility that secured lenders assiduously seek to avoid) or (ii) the borrower makes a prohibited transfer of the mortgaged property or of the borrowing entity under paragraph 21 of the deed of trust. These carve-outs could prove very useful to lenders who in the past had only the carve-outs for "waste" or "fraud" to their non-recourse loans.

Enforcement

While there were no reported decisions interpreting the detailed carve-out language utilized in the form note, there are reported cases where lenders attempted to recover against borrowers' personal assets in a non-recourse loan setting by arguing that the borrowers' failure to pay interest on the loan or real estate taxes on the mortgaged property constituted "waste" or "fraud." In *Chetek State Bank v. Barberg*, 489 N.W.2d 385 (Wis. Ct. App. 1992), the appellee, various lenders (hereinafter referred to as the bank), held a collective commercial mortgage on appellants' property. The mortgage and note contained non-recourse language absolving the various mortgagors (general partners and companies) of any personal liability to the bank on any money judgment with no "carve-outs." The mortgage subsequently went into default and the property was sold at a sheriff's sale that resulted in a deficiency of over $1 million. The bank's complaint in the foreclosure contained a cause of action alleging tortious waste committed by the appellee's failure to pay real estate taxes and interest on the note as the mortgage required. The circuit court granted a default judgment against appellant Barberg and summary judgment against appellant Stucky. The court held that the nonpayment of taxes and interest constituted tortious waste and held them personally liable for the total of both notwithstanding the non-recourse language. The appellate court reversed stating that the nonpayment of interest and taxes did not satisfy the elements of tortious waste. The court stated that the three elements of tortious waste were unreasonable conduct by the possessor of the property that results in physical damage to the property and substantially diminishes its value. The court held that the appellants' failure to pay the taxes and interest was not per se unreasonable conduct. The court also stated that the nonpayments were also not the kind of physical damage that would sustain the second element of tortious waste. Without finding a cause of action for tortious waste, the court concluded that it did not need to consider whether the tort claim was sufficiently independent from the previous foreclosure action to impose personal liability notwithstanding the nonrecourse language.

Even when the loan documents provide for a carve-out for "fraud" or "waste," it is uncertain whether a court would find that the nonpayment of interest or real estate taxes would be deemed to be an act of fraud or waste. *See FGH Realty Credit Corp. v. Bonati*, 641 N.Y.S.2d 12 (N.Y. App. Div. 1996) (court held that the nonpayment of the real estate taxes by the mortgagor did not constitute fraud within the meaning of the exception to the non-recourse provision in the mortgage); *but see Travelers Insurance Company v. 633 Third Associates*, 973 F.2d 82 (2d. Cir. 1992), 14 F. 3d 114 (2d Cir. 1994) (the dissenting opinion did point out that there is case law in Wisconsin, California, and New Jersey, that a mortgage lender can not bring an action against the mortgagor for waste based upon the failure to pay real estate taxes). Even in the *Travelers* case, where the court ruled that under certain circumstances a mortgage lender could bring an action for waste against the mortgagor (in a non-recourse loan with carve-outs for fraud or waste), there are obstacles which can arise which will impede the lender's efforts.

In *Travelers*, the plaintiff (Travelers), loaned $145 million to defendant (Associates), secured by a mortgage on an office building in New York City. The Associates defaulted on the loan and Travelers foreclosed on the property. In addition, Associates had not paid the taxes on the property that resulted in a tax lien. The Note and Mortgage contained an exculpation clause which stated in part "notwithstanding anything to the contrary contained in this Note or the Mortgage, the liability and obligation of the Exculpated Parties to perform and observe and make good the obligations contained in this Note and the Mortgage shall not be enforced by any action or proceeding wherein damages or any money judgment shall be sought against any of the Exculpated Parties, except a foreclosure action against the Mortgaged Property. . . ." Travelers sued and asked the court to set aside a $4 million cash distribution by the defendant to its two partners as a fraudulent conveyance under the New York Debtor and Creditor Law § 270–281 (McKinney 1990) and to enjoin such future conveyances. The district court held that because the loan was non-recourse the plaintiff had no entitlement to the transferred money and therefore the conveyance could not have caused Travelers' injury. Travelers appealed the decision. The U.S. Court of Appeals held that the exculpation clause banned "a tort action seeking money damages for waste of the secured property, however, it [did] not bar an equitable action to prevent waste." *Id.* at 85. The court then concluded that New York courts would find that willful nonpayment of property taxes would constitute waste for equitable relief. *Id.* at 86. The court stated that "the plaintiff may nonetheless have standing under New York's Fraudulent Conveyance Act to set aside the conveyance if the conveyance caused a diminution in the value of the real property, to which plaintiff is entitled to look in the event of default." *Id.* at 86. Consequently although the plaintiff could not collect the $4 million conveyance as damages the court could apply the money to the waste (the taxes). The court remanded the case and granted the plaintiff leave to amend the complaint to assert the claim for equitable relief.

On remand, Travelers filed its amended complaint which included a claim for equitable relief from waste and for specific performance of the Associates obligations along with its original claims for equitable relief from distributions the defendants made to its partners under the law of fraudulent conveyances. The district court dismissed the entire amended complaint stating that because the court appointed a receiver for the property Travelers was no longer in possession and an equitable action for waste would only apply to a mortgagor in possession. The court also added that it was not persuaded that New York law would recognize a willful failure to pay property taxes as waste. The U.S. Court of Appeals reversed the dismissal regarding the claims of waste occurring before appointment of the receiver. The court also reversed the decision regarding the fraudulent conveyance law insofar as the claims related to a portion of the distribution against which Travelers could have brought an equitable action for waste. *Id.* at 126. The court stated that New York courts recognized two general categories of waste: an action against one in control of property who allows the property to deteriorate and decrease in value and an action for waste by a mortgagee against a mortgagor who impairs the mortgage. *Id.* at 120. The court then cited *Union Mortgage Co. v. Nelson*, 275 A.D. 1028 (N.Y. App. Div. 1949), which it found suggested that the second category for waste could be found "for failure to pay taxes where that failure occurred in violation of the mortgagor's obligations or where the failure was willful, intentional, fraudulent, or the like." *Id.* at 122. Consequently, the court held under New York law that where the nonpayment of taxes was fraudulent or where there was an intentional failure to pay under obligation to do so would constitute waste. *Id.* at 123. However, the court did qualify the holding by stating that not every failure to follow the loan obligations would constitute waste. The court reiterated the need for the action to be fraudulent or intentional and more importantly that it had to impair the mortgage. *Id.* at 123. The court found that the intentional nonpayment of taxes would impair the mortgage because it necessitated the mortgagee to pay the tax lien and any accrued interest before being able to assume clear title to the property. *Id.* at 123. The court also defined a willful nonpayment of taxes to be any failure to pay by the mortgagor who is presumed to have knowledge of such taxes and their prior lien status as against the mortgage lien.

Conclusion

The above described cases underscore the need to be more specific in the carve-outs than utilizing the phrases "fraud" or "waste" if trying to recover against the personal assets of a borrower when the borrower has failed to apply the income of the property to the expenses of the property. When there is no carve-out language at all, and a lender sues on a tort theory of waste, some courts will not allow the lender to recover without a showing of physical damages. *See Chetek State Bank, supra*. Even when there is a carve-out for fraud, some courts will not consider the nonpayment of real estate taxes as such. *See FGH Realty Credit Corp., supra*. Finally, even the most favorable decision on this issue, *Travelers Insurance Company, supra*, noted that an action against the mortgagor could not be maintained with respect to rents which the receiver handled (apparently, the receiver had mistakenly paid four million dollars to the partnership instead of towards the real estate taxes).

Since the form deed of trust more specifically and clearly explains the situations in which the non-recourse loan will become a recourse loan, lenders utilizing this form stand a far better chance of recovering against the borrower's personal assets when the borrower fails to apply the income from the property to the expenses of the property. Under this language, the lender should not have to show impairment of the mortgage, fraud, or the elements of tortious waste.

[ii] Comments Regarding Personal Liability for the Debt

1. As noted, when the loan documents only contain carve-out liability for fraud or waste, lenders need to claim that the actions of the borrower that are problematic, such as failure to pay real estate taxes or maintain the property, constitute "permissive waste." The court in *Boucher Investments, L.P. v. Annapolis-West Limited Partnership*, 141 Md. App. 1 (2001), provided a useful definition of what type of failure to act by the borrower would be considered permissive waste: the borrower must fail to act in a way that increases the debt secured by the property, impairs the security of the mortgage by permitting an additional lien on the property, fails to preserve the property, or fails to satisfy a long-recognized duty. The court then ruled that failure to secure off-site parking through renegotiating a contract with an adjacent owner did not constitute permissive waste.

2. One might wonder whether a court would enforce a clause which provides for recourse liability if the borrower files a bankruptcy action, since this might be construed as impeding achievement of the basic policy goal behind bankruptcy law which is to provide the debtor with a clean start and chance to reorganize its debts. However, courts have in fact enforced a carve-out to non-recourse liability based upon the borrower filing a bankruptcy action. *See, e.g., First Nationwide Bank v. Brookhaven Realty Associates*, 223 A.D.2d 618 (N.Y. App. Div. 1996); *FDIC v. Prince George Crop.*, 58 F.3d 1041 (4th Cir. 1995) (although this particular challenge was not raised in either of those two cases).

3. Another possible defense to recourse liability from a carve-out exception to non-recourse liability is a claim that the carve-out is an invalid liquidated damages clause that exacts a penalty. This defense was raised in *Heller Financial, Inc. v. Lee*, 2002 U.S. Dist. LEXIS 15183 (N.D. Ill. 2002), but the court held that the carve-out at issue in the case (for permitting a lien on the mortgaged property without contesting and bonding it over after notifying the lender), did not constitute a liquidated damages clause because it created personal liability for the deficiency judgment, which involves the mortgage lender's actual damages.

4. The Fox Valley Auto Care Center construction loan was a full recourse loan as was typical for construction loans. As such, there was no need for the lender in that deal to create a laundry list of matters that would create recourse liability to the borrower (*i.e.*, the non recourse carve-outs discussed above). However, some lenders create and require a "springing guaranty" for the principals of the borrower (even on a recourse loan) to sign that creates liability on them in the event certain matters occur, such as the filing of a bankruptcy action or certain other events, some covered by the carve-outs, to discourage the principals from allowing those events to occur. Springing guarantees were not typically used at the time of the FVACC construction loan, but soon thereafter started to become a common feature that lenders employed to dissuade the principals of a borrower from taking certain actions that impair the value of the project or impede the lender's ability to foreclose and take over the project after a default.

5. In distinguishing recourse loans from non-recourse loans, it is important to know when a loan has been set up as a recourse loan as contrasted with a non-recourse loan. The key document to look at to determine what type of loan was created is the promissory note. If the promissory note is silent on whether it is recourse or non-recourse, then it is a recourse note. Consequently, if a deal is supposed to be a non-recourse loan, then the attorney representing the borrower should make sure that the note explicitly so indicates and, to prevent later claims of ambiguity on this point, should make sure that all of the rest of the loan documents clarify that the borrower's obligations under each such document are non-recourse to the borrower.

[iii] Negotiation and Drafting Assignment

Assume that you represent the lender of a permanent loan and that the lender's form of non-recourse language and carve-outs to the non-recourse language is the FNMA form quoted earlier. Draft a memorandum to your client indicating what changes you propose to be made to the language and explain the reasons for these changes. Next, assume that you represent the borrower to a permanent loan and that the lender's loan documents contained the non-recourse language of this same FNMA form. Prepare a memorandum to lender's counsel indicating what changes you propose be made to the non-recourse language and provide an explanation of why these changes are reasonable.

As guidance to you in determining how to modify the FNMA non-recourse language and carve-outs, keep in mind the original reasons why lenders provide for these carve-outs to non-recourse liability. If any of the carve-outs in the FNMA form are not really confined to bad faith actions taken by the borrower, then when representing a borrower, one should attempt to negotiate for any such provision to be deleted as inappropriate to a generally non-recourse loan. If representing the lender, consider whether the list of carve-outs adequately covers the various type of bad faith or other problematic actions the borrower could take that would impair the value of the project or prevent the lender from exercising its rights after a default. If any such actions are not covered in the list or not broadly enough covered, suggest modifications to the carve out language in the FNMA form to correct that.

Be prepared in class to negotiate on behalf of either the borrower or the lender.

Chapter 10

SECURITY FOR THE LOAN

§ 10.01 OVERVIEW

The security for the loan is a critical piece in putting together the puzzle of a loan transaction. By definition, a "real estate loan" is a loan secured by a mortgage on the land and on any improvements built or to be built on the land. A mortgage is a pledge by the mortgagor (the borrower) in favor of the mortgagee (the lender) of the borrower's interest in the pledged real estate to secure the debt of the borrower to the lender. If the borrower defaults in performing the terms of the loan, the lender can accelerate the debt and foreclose on the mortgage as a means to recover the debt due the lender. If the loan in default is a recourse loan, the lender can also sue the borrower for the amount still owing to the lender and can recover against any of the borrower's assets in addition to the borrower's interest in the pledged real estate. If the loan in default is guarantied, the lender can also sue the guarantor for the amount still owing to the lender. Therefore, the lender has a number of possible ways to recover the amount owed to it. However, as will be discussed later in this chapter, in some states, lenders might be forced into an election among various remedies or may be required to pursue one remedy before exercising another remedy.

When the loan in default is a take-out loan secured by already built and leased real estate, the lender typically will resort to the real estate pledged to the lender as the principal if not sole means of being repaid the amount still due and owing to it. In addition, during the period between the occurrence of the default and the foreclosure sale, the assignment of rents becomes a critical piece of collateral. Lenders will try to use the assignment of rents as a means to prevent the borrower from failing to properly apply the rents to the expenses of the project, including making payments to the mortgage lender. As will be discussed later in this chapter, depending upon the jurisdiction in which the mortgaged property is located, and the wording of the assignment of rents, the lender may or may not receive protection from the borrower "misusing" the rents.

When the proceeds of the loan are being utilized to finance construction of the real estate project, then the lender not only needs a mortgage of the land, but also, a pledge of the borrower's interest in the contracts the borrower has entered into to construct the project. The goal with a construction loan is for the lender to be able to step into the shoes of the borrower and complete construction of the project. Thus, with a construction loan, a lender will also receive collateral assignments of the borrower's interest in the architect's agreement and construction contracts, as well as assignments of the borrower's interest in various plans and specifications, and permits and licenses. This chapter discusses the various types of collateral mentioned above and the use of credit enhancements like letters of credit as a means to address any "shortcomings" in the project.

§ 10.02 MORTGAGES OF REAL ESTATE

[1] Mortgage Provisions

We begin with the basics and focus on the requirements to create a valid real estate mortgage. On the surface, these requirements appear to be easy to satisfy. For example, the Illinois statutory form of mortgage that follows contemplates the creation of a valid real estate mortgage in a single sentence.

735 Illinois Compiled Statutes Annotated 5/11; Mortgage — Form — Effect

Mortgages of lands may be substantially in the following form:

The Mortgagor (here insert name or names), mortgages and warrants to (here insert name or names of mortgagee or mortgagees), to secure the payment of (here recite the nature and amount of indebtedness, showing when due and the rate of interest, and whether secured by note or otherwise), the following described real estate (here insert description thereof), situated in the County of ____________ in the State of Illinois.

Date ____________
(signature of mortgagor or mortgagors)

The names of the parties shall be typed or printed below the signatures. Such forms shall have a blank space of 3 1/2 inches for use by the recorder. However, the failure to comply with the requirement that the names of the parties be typed or printed below the signatures and that the form have a blank space of 3 1/2 inches by 3 1/2 inches for use by the recorder shall not affect the validity and effect of such form.

Such mortgage, when otherwise properly executed, shall be deemed and held a good and sufficient mortgage in fee to secure the payment of the moneys therein specified; and if the same contains the words "and warrants," the same shall be construed the same as if full covenants of ownership, good right to convey against incumbrances of quiet enjoyment and general warranty, as expressed in Section 9 of this Act were fully written therein; but if the words "and warrants" are omitted, no such covenants shall be implied. When the grantor or grantors in such deed or mortgage for the conveyance of any real estate desires to release or waive his, her or their homestead rights therein, they or either of them may release or waive the same by inserting in the form of deed or mortgage (as the case may be), provided in Sections 9, 10 and 11, after the words "State of Illinois," in substance the following words, "hereby releasing and waiving all rights under and by virtue of the homestead exemption laws of this State." . . .

Many other states provide for a similar type of short statutory form of real estate mortgage. *See, e.g.*, Section 57-1-14 of the Utah Code Annotated (Form of Mortgage — Effect); Section 2101 of the Delaware Code Annotated (Form of mortgage; effect); and Section 61.12.020 of the West's Revised Code of Washington Annotated (Mortgage — Form — Contents — Effect).

Mortgages can secure not only a promise to pay a debt, but also any other type of promise that can be expressed or reduced to a monetary equivalent, such as a promise to complete a construction project or to indemnify or guaranty for the acts or monetary promises of another. In a construction loan, the amount secured by the mortgage is advanced in stages and the loan amount increases during the term of the loan; while in a permanent loan, the loan amount secured by the mortgage is usually advanced in one lump sum and it is typical for the borrower to repay portions of principal each month (along with accrued interest) where by the end of the term of the loan, the entire principal debt is paid off in full (*i.e.*, a fully amortized loan) with no balloon payment when the loan matures. In a "revolving credit mortgage," the amount secured by the mortgage will vary depending upon the current amount owed; the borrower is provided a line of credit up to a maximum specified amount and can freely repay amounts drawn and then borrow additional amounts thereafter. In a typical "reverse mortgage" (a technique used by the elderly or terminally ill), the lender makes a lump sum payment or monthly payments to the borrower which the borrower can use as she wishes, for example to pay living expenses or medical bills. With a reverse mortgage, the lender must determine what the amount of the lump sum or a monthly payment amount will be for the life of the borrower; the lender 1) uses an actuary to ascertain the expected number of years that the borrower will continue to live and 2) has an appraisal of the fair market value of the home prepared. If the borrower opts for monthly payments, the payments will cease upon the death of the borrower, the sale of the home, or if the borrower moves from the home. The money advanced as of that event, plus interest, then becomes due and can be repaid from a sale of the home; any remaining equity in the home would go to the borrower's designated devisee or heir.

[2] Priority of the Mortgage

The Illinois statutory form of mortgage, like other statutory form mortgages, highlights the bare essentials necessary for a document to create a valid mortgage of real estate by the owner in favor of a lender. Notwithstanding the apparent simplicity in creating a valid real estate mortgage, there are some problems that can arise relating to the issue of the priority of the mortgage as against other interests granted with respect to the property. The issue of loss of priority to intervening liens comes up particularly with construction loans and revolving credit loans, due in part to the fact that future advances are made after the mortgage is recorded and might not relate for priority purposes to the date when the mortgage was recorded. Mechanic lien claims are particularly likely to arise during a construction loan but also can arise at any time thereafter if repair work or renovations take place, and in some states, can even gain priority over a prior fully advanced recorded mortgage loan. This section will address in detail how these priority issues can arise and be addressed.

[a] The Impact of Mortgage Provisions on Priority

Under the English common law, priority between two lien claimants was based on which lien-holder received its mortgage or other lien interest first. In America, recording laws were enacted that focus on recording as the means to achieve priority in interest. In general, priority among lien-holders is based on when each lien is recorded rather than when the lien was created, with highest priority being accorded to the lien which is recorded first. This treatment is based on the idea that the recording provides constructive notice to all future lien-holders of the nature and extent of the prior interest that was recorded. However, as the next case illustrates, if the terms of the recorded mortgage fail to provide adequate notice to future lien-holders of the amount of the indebtedness secured by the mortgaged property, this could cause the prior recorded mortgage to lose its priority against subsequently created liens unless the holder of such subsequent lien had actual notice of the prior interest at the time the subsequent lien-holder took its interest in the real estate.

NORTHRIDGE BANK v. LAKESHORE COMMERCIAL FINANCE CORPORATION

365 N.E.2d 382 (Ill. App. Ct. 1977)

Downing, Presiding Justice.

This appeal concerns the priority of mortgage liens. The defendant, Lakeshore Commercial Finance Corporation (Lakeshore), is appealing from an order of the circuit court of Cook County granting priority to the mortgage held by the plaintiff, Northridge Bank (Northridge), on certain real estate located in Cook County, Illinois over that held by Lakeshore and ordering that the proceeds of an escrow fund held by defendant Schroeder, et al. be paid over to Northridge. The trial court stayed the latter portion of its order pending the outcome of this appeal.

On September 16, 1974, Howard Bloom executed a mortgage deed in favor of Lakeshore. The mortgage identifies Bloom as the mortgagor and Lakeshore as the mortgagee, states that the mortgage is to secure the principal sum of $30,000, sets forth the legal description of the real estate, and then, amongst other language, states:

> "This mortgage is given to secure the following note, or other obligation or obligations, hereinafter called the Debt Instrument: *To secure all obligations of Mortgagor to Mortgagee.* * * *
>
> "COVENANTS OF MORTGAGOR: The Mortgagor covenants and agrees as follows:
>
> * * *
>
> "2. The Mortgaged property shall stand as security for the Debt Instrument and for the performance by the Mortgagor of its covenants and agreements therein, and the lien of this mortgage, subject only to the exceptions noted above, shall be a valid and continuing lien upon all of the Mortgaged Property to secure the prompt payment of the Debt Instrument and the performance of each and every obligation therein, provided The Mortgaged Property *shall also be security for any additional and subsequent advances by the Mortgagee to the Mortgagor, and all other obligations due from, or guarantied by, the Mortgagor to the Mortgagee, at any time prior to the satisfaction of this mortgage.*" (Emphasis supplied.)

The next following language, included on the printed form, has been crossed out on the mortgage held by Lakeshore:

> "It is provided, however, that the total indebtedness outstanding at any one time and secured hereby shall in no event exceed __________ DOLLARS."

On October 4, 1974, Bloom executed another mortgage on the same described real estate in favor of Northridge. The relevant portions of that document read as follows:

"THE MORTGAGOR, Howard Bloom, Mortgages and Warrants to Northridge Bank, * * * , to secure the payment of a certain promissory note, executed by said mortgagor bearing even date herewith, payable to the order of said mortgagee the following described real estate (the legal description of the real estate follows) situated in the County of Cook, in the State of Illinois."

It is to be noted that nowhere on the face of the Northridge mortgage document is there a statement or description of the amount of indebtedness it secures.

Northridge recorded its mortgage at 9:28 a.m. on October 25, 1974. On that same date, at 3:07 p.m., the prior mortgage executed in favor of Lakeshore was recorded.

Subsequently, it became apparent to all of the parties concerned that the value of the real estate was insufficient to fully satisfy both the encumbrances. A buyer having been found, Lakeshore and Northridge entered into an escrow agreement with defendant Schroeder, et al., as escrow agent on April 4, 1975. By the terms of this agreement, the parties agreed that the land would be sold and both parties would deliver to the escrow agent satisfactions of their respective mortgages. The escrow agent would deliver them to the buyer of the land at the time of closing. In consideration for the satisfactions, the proceeds of the sale would be given to the escrow agent pending the outcome of a declaratory judgment action to be commenced by Northridge.

The sale was completed according to the terms of the agreement. Northridge then commenced this action for a declaratory judgment, alleging the superiority of its right to the escrow fund over the claim of Lakeshore. Lakeshore's answer admitted the material allegations of the complaint and raised as an affirmative defense that because the Northridge mortgage failed to state the amount of the debt it secured, nor facts by which the amount of the debt could be ascertained, it was insufficient in law to impart constructive notice of Northridge's interest and was therefore unenforceable as against Lakeshore. Northridge replied to the affirmative defense, asserting that the Lakeshore mortgage suffered the same defect, "contrary to the requirements of Chapter 30, § 10 (Ill. Rev. Stat. 1975)."

Both parties then moved for judgment on the pleadings. The trial court granted Northridge's motion for judgment on the pleadings, denied the motion of Lakeshore, declared that the interest of Northridge in the escrow fund is superior to that of Lakeshore, and ordered the fund be turned over to Northridge, permitting the escrow agent to retain the fund pending the outcome of this appeal.

I.

The sole issue to be determined in this appeal is which of these parties has a superior interest in the escrow fund. Lakeshore argues that the mortgage executed by Bloom in favor of Northridge, while recorded prior to the recording of its mortgage, is insufficient as a matter of law to impart constructive notice of the lien claimed to creditors and subsequent purchasers because it fails to state the amount of the indebtedness it purports to secure or enough information for further inquiry as required in Ill. Rev. Stat.1975, ch. 30, par. 10.[1] Lakeshore contends that it is a

---

[1] Chapter 30, § 10, in pertinent part, reads:

"Mortgages of lands may be in the following form, substantially:

"subsequent purchaser without notice" within the meaning of section 30 of the Conveyancing Act (Ill. Rev. Stat.1975, ch. 30, par. 29), and that because it had neither actual nor constructive notice of the Northridge lien at the time its mortgage was recorded, it is entitled to the escrow fund.

Northridge, conceding that its mortgage is insufficient as a matter of law to impart constructive notice, affirmatively argues that Lakeshore's mortgage suffers the same defect. The factual basis for this argument is that while Lakeshore's mortgage initially states that it secures an indebtedness of $30,000, other language on the printed form states that the mortgage was given to secure:

> " * * * all obligations of the Mortgagor to the Mortgagee * * * , any additional and subsequent advances by the Mortgagee to the Mortgagor, and all other obligations due from, or guarantied by, the Mortgagor to the Mortgagee, at any time prior to the satisfaction of this mortgage."

Northridge's claim to the escrow fund is based upon (a) the doctrine of equitable mortgages,[2] through which the intent of the parties to create a mortgage is given effect where a mortgage instrument is otherwise legally defective, and (b) the equitable maxim, "first in time is first in right." (*See* 2 Pomeroy's Equity Jurisprudence (5th ed. 1941), §§ 413 *et seq.*) Northridge argues that as between two recorded equitable mortgages, the mortgage recorded first in time should receive priority.

In reply to this argument, Lakeshore, urging the complete validity of its mortgage, argues that even if Northridge is correct, the equitable maxim should be applied to give effect to Lakeshore's mortgage, as its interest was created prior in time.

Both of the documents in issue fail to state the amount of the indebtedness secured. In *Bullock v. Battenhousen* (1883), 108 Ill. 28, our supreme court held that a trust deed which failed to state the amount of indebtedness secured was insufficient under the recording laws to impart constructive notice, and said, at page 37:

> "The policy, though not the letter, of our statutes requires, in all cases, a statement upon the record of the amount secured. Thus, in section 11, Chapter 30, Rev. Stat. 1874, page 274 (now Ill. Rev. Stat.1975, ch. 30, par

---

> "The Mortgagor (here insert name or names), mortgages and warrants to (here insert name or names of mortgagee or mortgagees), to secure the payment of (here recite the nature and amount of indebtedness, showing when due and the rate of interest, and whether secured by note or otherwise), the following described real estate (here insert description thereof), situated in the county of ____________, in the state of Illinois. Dated this ____________ day of ____________
>
> "A.D., 19____________. A.B.
>
> "Every such mortgage, when otherwise property executed, shall be deemed and held a good and sufficient mortgage in fee to secure the payment of the moneys therein specified. . . ."

2 The doctrine of equitable mortgages was discussed in *Trustees of Zion Methodist Church v. Smith* (4th Dist. 1948), 335 Ill. App. 233, 236, 81 N.E.2d 649, 650, where the court stated:

> "The doctrine of equitable mortgages is based upon the principle that equity will interpret an agreement according to the intent of the parties as evinced therein, and if not contrary to some positive rule of law or public policy, will give it effect even though it does not meet the technical requirements of the law; hence where an instrument manifests an intent to charge or pledge property as security for a debt, and the property as identified, a lien will be recognized in equity."

> 10), the form of mortgage there given requires the mortgage to 'recite the nature and amount of indebtedness.' * * * A statement upon the record of the amount claimed to be due informs all what lien is claimed. They know what they must contest, or subject to what they must take, in subsequently dealing with the property. It prevents secret conspiracies between mortgagors and mortgagees as to the fact and amount of indebtedness to the prejudice of subsequent purchasers and creditors, by compelling them to at once make known the real claim. In some instances, subsequent dealers with mortgaged property could not have information from the holders of indebtedness secured by mortgage, because they could not be found, as in the case of negotiable securities running for a long time, and negotiated many times before maturity; and it might often be, as in the instance before us, perilous to rely on the word of the mortgagor."

The court in *Battenhousen* also quoted the following language from *Metropolitan Bank v. Godfrey* (1860), 23 Ill. 531, 532:

> "The spirit of our recording system requires that the record of a mortgage should disclose, with as much certainty as the nature of the case will admit, the real state of the encumbrance. If a mortgage is given to secure an ascertained debt, the amount of that debt should be stated; and if it is intended to secure a debt not ascertained, such data should be given respecting it, as will put any one, interested in the inquiry, upon the track leading to a discovery. If it is given to secure an existing, or a future liability, the foundation of such liability should be set forth. *North v. Belden*, 13 Conn. 376; *Hart v. Chalker*, et al., 14 (Conn) 77."

In *Flexter v. Woomer* (5th Dist. 1964), 46 Ill.App.2d 456, 197 N.E.2d 161, the Fifth District, citing *Battenhousen*, held that a mortgage which failed to state either the amount of indebtedness or maturity date was insufficient as constructive notice, and granted priority to a subsequently recorded mortgage.

Lakeshore argues that its mortgage states on its face the amount of the indebtedness, citing *Dunn v. Burke* (lst Dist. 1907), 139 Ill.App. 12; *Metropolitan Life Insurance Company v. Kobbeman* (2d Dist. 1931), 260 Ill.App. 508; *Farrar v. Payne* (1874), 73 El. 82; and *Babcock v. Lisk* (1870), 57 El. 327. However, we find nothing in those cases to support Lakeshore's position under the facts of this case. Here, the Lakeshore document initially states that it secures a debt of $30,000. Other language in the form used describes the debt in much broader terms. The language allows Lakeshore to make an unlimited amount of future advances under the same instrument, and language which would set a ceiling on the amount of any future advances has been deleted. Thus, the mortgage executed in favor of Lakeshore not only fails to state the amount of the present indebtedness, it also is completely open-ended as to future indebtedness. It is impossible, from a reading of the Lakeshore mortgage, to ascertain the amount of indebtedness secured thereby.

While we agree with Northridge's assertion that both of the documents are legally insufficient to impart constructive notice of the amounts of their respective liens, we do not believe it is necessary to resort to the doctrine of equitable mortgages to resolve this case. Our recording statute, Ill. Rev. Stat.1973, ch. 30, par. 29, provides ample authority for our conclusion that Northridge has a superior interest in the escrow fund. Ill. Rev. Stat. 1973, ch. 30, par. 29 provides:

"All deeds, mortgages, and other instruments of writing which are authorized to be recorded, shall take effect and be in force from and after the time of filing the same for record, and not before, as to all creditors and subsequent purchasers, without notice; and all such deeds and title papers shall be adjudged void as to all such creditors and subsequent purchasers, without notice, until the same shall be filed for record."

Applying this statute to the facts of this case, at the time Northridge filed its mortgage in the County Recorder's office, it had no constructive notice of the Lakeshore mortgage.[3] Therefore, if the mortgage had stated the amount of the indebtedness it secured, it would be entitled to priority over any instrument subsequently recorded outside of the chain of title. However, as we have concluded that the Northridge mortgage failed to impart constructive notice of the lien claimed, it was subject to being subordinated to a subsequent mortgage by a "subsequent purchaser" without actual notice.

Lakeshore strongly urges that it is a "subsequent purchaser" within the meaning of the statute. Most of the discussion, however, misses the point and deals with the issue of the precise moment in time when a person may be said to have constructive notice, and not whether that party is a "subsequent purchaser." *Doyle v. Teas* (1843), 5 Ill. 202, cited by Lakeshore, dealt with the claim of one Munson that at the time he received his deed to the disputed land from Doyle, he had no actual or constructive notice of a prior contract of sale executed by Doyle in favor of Teas. Under the recording act, Munson argued, even though Teas' contract of sale was recorded prior to Munson's deed, Munson should have priority because of his lack of notice at the time he "subsequently" purchased from Doyle. The supreme court held that Teas had priority because Munson had a duty to examine the record at the time he recorded his deed and could not rely on the state of the record at the time of purchase. Thus, even though Munson was a subsequent purchaser, at the time he recorded he had constructive notice of the claimed interest in Teas, because Teas had recorded first. At that point, it made no difference who had purchased first from Doyle because Munson had notice. The other cases cited by Lakeshore in its brief are all cases in which the issue was solely constructive notice and not, as here, whether the "subsequent recorder" was also a "subsequent purchaser." If anything, the discussion in Lakeshore's brief which defines "subsequent purchaser" strongly supports Northridge's claim of priority. As an illustration, Lakeshore's brief states, at page 10: "In order to effectuate a system upon which a purchaser can rely, the recording act provided for a system that results in protecting a creditor or subsequent purchaser, without notice, who duly records a deed, mortgage, or other instrument authorized to be recorded and penalizing a party who does not duly record his instrument so authorized." This statement clearly supports the Northridge position and provides little support for Lakeshore.

Bloom's mortgage in favor of Lakeshore was executed on September 16, 1974, but was not recorded until 3:07 p.m. on October 25, 1974. In the interim, another mortgage was executed by Bloom in favor of Northridge on October 4, 1974, which was recorded at 9:28 a.m. on October 25. Thus, Lakeshore is a "prior purchaser" who failed to duly record its instrument, while Northridge, the "subsequent" purchaser was completely without constructive notice due entirely to Lakeshore's

---

[3] Neither of the parties to this cause has argued any actual notice on the part of the other. We therefore assume that there was no actual notice.

failure to promptly record. In addition, Northridge duly recorded its mortgage. Had Lakeshore promptly recorded even its defective mortgage, this dispute may never have arisen, for although Northridge would still have been without constructive notice, there is no way of knowing whether the presence of the Lakeshore mortgage on the record would have caused Northridge to exercise caution in extending credit to Bloom.

Our decision here is in accord with the Illinois Supreme Court's 1853 decision in *Kennedy, et al. v. Northup* (1853) 15 Ill. 148, where an interest in land was created, but not recorded until 32 years later. In the interim, another interest in the same land was created and duly recorded. The case turned upon the court's construction of the term "subsequent purchaser." The court held for the party whose interest in the land was created later in time, but recorded first in time, stating:

> "By the fault of some one the land has been twice sold, from which some one must suffer; and is it not right, is it not in harmony with every principle of law, that he who is in fault, in not notifying the world by recording his deed, shall suffer the loss which has resulted from such negligence?" (15 Ill. at 157.)

Accordingly, the decision of the circuit court of Cook County is affirmed.

Affirmed.

Stamos and Perlin, JJ., concur.

[b] Comments and Questions on *Northridge Bank*

1. What was the defect with respect to the Lakeshore mortgage? What was the defect with respect to the Northridge mortgage? Since both mortgages were defective in terms of imparting constructive notice, on what basis did the court rule that the Northridge mortgage was superior in right to the Lakeshore mortgage? Do you agree with the decision?

2. Why do courts require that the amount of debt secured by the mortgage and the maturity date of the loan be specified in the mortgage? What is the impact if the amount of the debt or its maturity date are not adequately described in the mortgage?

3. *Northridge Bank* underscores the importance of indicating a maximum debt which the real property secures in order for the mortgage to maintain a prior level of priority against any subsequent lien-holders and the inadvertent drafting errors which can cause a potential loss of priority. Review the "Recitals" section (it is not labeled "Recitals" but it follows the first "Whereas" and continues up to the granting clause) of the Mortgage in the Document Book. Has the amount of interest, the amount of the debt secured by the mortgage, and the maturity date of the loan been specified in a manner that will maintain the priority of the mortgage in the event that any subsequent liens are created? What types of subsequent liens could arise in the context of the construction and operation of the Fox Valley Auto Care Center?

§ 10.03 ASSIGNMENT OF RENTS AND LEASES

In addition to the note, which is a promise to pay by the borrower serving as evidence of the debt, and the mortgage, which pledges the borrower's fee simple interest in the real estate, lenders will also require borrowers to sign an "assignment of rents and leases." One may wonder why the lender needs this, since the lender's debt either should be paid off by the proceeds from the sale of the property at the foreclosure sale or the lender will be the high bidder at the sale and become the new owner of the real property. However, as previously discussed, during the period between the borrower's default and the foreclosure sale, the borrower might not properly apply rents from the project to project expenses, including making payments on the mortgage loan.

The main purpose of the assignment of rents and leases is to allow the lender to gain control of the rents during this period and prevent the borrower from "bleeding the project" and "building up a war chest" to fight the lender's foreclosure action. State law and practice will govern the proper method to create and exercise the assignment of rents. There are three types of assignment of rents: an absolute assignment, an absolute assignment conditioned on default with a revocable license of the borrower to collect rent prior to default, and an assignment as additional security for the debt. Depending on the type of assignment created and the laws of the relevant jurisdiction, the lender may or may not be able to collect the rents after a borrower defaults by simply notifying the tenants to deliver future rents to the lender. Sometimes the lender will have to acquire possession of the property or petition a court to appoint a receiver in order for the lender to exercise its assignment of rents. State law will also determine whether the lender has a right to the rents collected after the borrower has filed for bankruptcy.

[1] Overview of Assignments of Rents and Leases

The next excerpt explains: (i) the process of creating the assignment of rents, (ii) the kinds of assignments mentioned above and the consequences of each, (iii) the difficult but critical process of enforcing the assignment of rents after the borrower has defaulted in its performance of the obligations of the loan, (iv) potential liability to the lender in exercising the assignment of rents, and (v) the purposes behind an assignment of leases (as contrasted with an assignment of rents). The excerpt also includes the provisions utilized in a form deed of trust relating to an assignment of rents and leases and comments on these provisions.

**WILSON FREYERMOUTH, JOHN MCNEARNEY,
DEBRA STARK & DALE WHITMAN,
ANATOMY OF A MORTGAGE (ABA 2001)***

FORM DEED OF TRUST

[This is the FNMA multi-family housing form deed of trust. — Eds.]

3. *ASSIGNMENT OF RENTS; APPOINTMENT OF RECEIVER; LENDER IN POSSESSION.*

(a) As part of the consideration for the Indebtedness, Borrower absolutely and unconditionally assigns and transfers to Lender all Rents. It is the intention of Borrower to establish a present, absolute and irrevocable transfer and assignment to Lender of all Rents and to authorize and empower Lender to collect and receive all Rents without the necessity of further action on the part of Borrower. Promptly upon request by Lender, Borrower agrees to execute and deliver such further assignments as Lender may from time to time require. Borrower and Lender intend this assignment of Rents to be immediately effective and to constitute an absolute present assignment and not an assignment for additional security only. For purposes of giving effect to this absolute assignment of Rents, and for no other purpose, Rents shall not be deemed to be a part of the "Mortgaged Property" as that term is defined in Section 1(s). However, if this present, absolute and unconditional assignment of Rents is not enforceable by its terms under the laws of the Property Jurisdiction, then the Rents shall be included as a part of the Mortgaged Property and it is the intention of the Borrower that in this circumstance this Instrument create and perfect a lien on Rents in favor of Lender, which lien shall be effective as of the date of this Instrument.

Reasons for taking an assignment of rents. Lenders would not bother to take assignments of rents if foreclosure were always swift and certain. However, state law foreclosure proceedings may take from a few months to a year or more, with lengthy periods especially common in urban areas of states that still require foreclosure by judicial action. In addition, borrowers often file bankruptcy when faced with impending foreclosure. Even in a Chapter 7 liquidation bankruptcy, the "automatic stay" will probably delay foreclosure for a number of months; in a Chapter 11 reorganization, the delay may be even longer.

During the period between default and foreclosure, the borrower is unlikely to make any debt service payments at all. Hence, the accrual of interest on the loan will cause its balance to increase. At the same time, the borrower may "milk" the property, deferring maintenance expenses, taxes, and other operating costs while capturing the entire rental cash flow. Thus, the property's value may be declining at the same time the loan balance is rising. Property that was adequate security for the loan when the default occurred may quickly become inadequate in these circumstances.

The lender's chief remedy for this problem is to attempt to capture the rental cash flow and apply it toward operating expenses and debt service. Even if the cash flow is inadequate to meet the full debt service, capturing it will prevent "milking" and make at least some contribution toward the accruing interest. See Julia Forrester, *A Uniform and More Rational Approach to Rents as Security for the Mortgage Loan*, 46 Rutgers L. Rev. 349 (1993).

Why is the assignment absolute in form? An assignment of rents might be expressed in at least three different ways. First, it could, by its terms, be an assignment "as additional security" for the mortgage debt. This might be termed a "collateral assignment," since the rents would be described as collateral in addition to, and distinct from, the real property itself. Under Restatement (Third) of

Property (Mortgages) § 4.2 (1997), this sort of assignment is referred to as a "mortgage on the rents." The clause, in simplified form, might read as follows:

> Mortgagor hereby grants to mortgagee a security interest in the rents, issues and profits paid by tenants in the property. Upon default in the payment of the indebtedness secured hereby, the mortgagee may, at its option, either with or without taking possession of the property, collect all rents, issues, and profits paid by tenants in the property and apply them toward the indebtedness secured hereby.

Second, the assignment could be a *true* "absolute" assignment, in which the lender would *immediately* begin collecting the rents from the inception of the loan. Sometimes a bank "lockbox" arrangement is used in such assignments, with the tenants paying their rents into the lockbox and the lender having exclusive access to it. Of course, most borrowers strongly resist such an absolute assignment, since it means they must give up control of the rents from the outset. A lockbox arrangement is sometimes employed as part of a "workout" on a defaulted loan, but it is not common to see it implemented in an original loan agreement.

The third type of rents assignment is the type represented in the Fannie Mae form reproduced above, and is the type nearly always employed in modern mortgages on income-producing properties. The assignment is described in "absolute" terms, as in subsection (a) above, but the borrower is granted a "license" to collect the rents until a default occurs, as in subsection (b) below. Thus, before default, the borrower is expected to pay the debt service and operating expenses, but may retain any excess cash flow. This sort of assignment is sometimes described as "conditionally absolute," since actual enforcement by the lender is triggered by the arising of a condition of default.

For all practical purposes, it is obvious that this third and most common type of rents assignment is, like the first kind described above, a collateral or security assignment or, as the Restatement puts it, a "mortgage on the rents." To say, as does subsection (a) of the Fannie Mae form above, that the assignment is a "present, absolute and irrevocable transfer," when in the next breath the borrower is given the right to collect the rents until default, is a transparent sham. This fact has often been recognized by the courts. "The fact that the assignments are conditioned upon default and will terminate upon satisfaction of the debt indicates that they are merely additional security for the loan and not an absolute transfer of the Debtor's interest in the rents." In re Lyons, 193 B.R. 637 (Bankr. D. Mass. 1996). Yet this sham is found in virtually all modern mortgages.

What does the lender expect to accomplish by using "absolute assignment" language to describe what is plainly a security assignment? There are several objectives. The first derives from the state law rule, widely followed, that requires a lender to take some "affirmative action" to enforce a security assignment of rents. The states vary as to what action is required, but typical examples include the mortgagee's taking direct possession of the property, getting a receiver appointed, or obtaining a court order sequestering the rents for the mortgagee's benefit. *See, e.g.*, Oryx Energy Co. v. Union Nat'l Bank, 895 S.W.2d 409 (Tex. Ct. App. 1995); Comerica Bank — Illinois v. Harris Bank, 673 N.E.2d 380 (Ill. Ct. App. 1996); Galleria Towers, Inc. v. Crump Warren & Sommer, Inc., 831 P.2d 908 (Colo. Ct. App. 1991); In re Raleigh/Spring Forest Apartments Assoc., 118 B.R. 42 (Bankr. E.D.N.C. 1990). Some states are a bit more liberal, requiring the lender only to notify the borrower. *See* In re Fluge, 57 B.R. 451 (Bankr. D.N.D. 1985); Cal. Civ. Code § 2938 (1996); Restatement (Third) of Property (Mortgages) § 4.2 (1997).

But whatever affirmative action is required, it will inevitably be somewhat time-consuming, and any delay means that some rents will be lost to the lender. By using the "absolute assignment" language instead, the lender hopes courts will treat the "affirmative action" requirement as inapplicable, and will recognize the lender's right to all rents paid after the date of default. Sometimes this argument works; *see, e.g.*, Credit Lyonnais v. Getty Square Associates, 876 F. Supp. 517 (S.D.N.Y. 1995). Many state courts, however, regard this approach with scepticism; *see* Oryx Energy Co. v. Union Nat'l Bank, *supra*. For that reason, the concluding sentence of subsection (a) of the clause above concedes that if under state law the assignment is not regarded as absolute, it will nonetheless be effective to create a security interest — a mortgage or lien on the rents.

Rents in bankruptcy. When the owner of rental real estate files bankruptcy, all of his or her (non-exempt) assets become the property of the trustee in bankruptcy (or in a Chapter 11 proceeding, the Debtor-in-Possession (DIP), who has all of the powers of a bankruptcy trustee). Since a mortgage lender's ability to obtain the rents from the trustee or DIP is problematic (as we will see below), the lender who has used a "conditionally absolute" assignment of rents clause may simply argue that the rents had been transferred to the lender before the bankruptcy petition was filed, and hence never came into hands of the trustee or DIP. As noted above, this [Editor's Note: "this" meaning the view that due to the "conditionally absolute" language in the loan document, the rents were transferred to the lender prior to the bankruptcy and thus not part of the debtor's estate] is an unrealistic and somewhat silly view of the "conditionally absolute" assignment, but it has prevailed in a few cases, mainly in states following the "title theory" of mortgages. *See, e.g.*, Commerce Bank v. Mountain View Village Inc., 5 F.3d 34 (3d Cir.1993); In re Galvin, 120 B.R. 767, 770–72 (Bankr. D. Vt. 1990); Jason Realty, L.P. v. First Fidelity Bank, 59 F.3d 423 (3d Cir. 1995) (New Jersey law). This result is more likely to be reached if the lender has taken some pre-petition steps, such as obtaining a receiver or actually intercepting the rents, to enforce the rents clause.

Most bankruptcy courts, however, have rejected this view and concluded that the rents remain assets of the debtor despite the presence of a "conditionally absolute" assignment. *See* In re Guardian Realty Group, L.L.C., 205 B.R. 1, 3 (Bankr. D. Colo. 1997); Lyons v. Federal Savings Bank, 193 B.R. 637, 649 (Bankr. D. Mass. 1996); In re 5028 Wisconsin Avenue Associates Ltd. Partnership, 167 B.R. 699, 704–05 (Bankr. D.D.C. 1994); In re Willows of Coventry Ltd. Partnership, 154 B.R. 959 (Bankr. N.D. Ind. 1993); In re Foundry of Barrington Oaks Partnership, 129 B.R. 550 (Bankr. N.D. Ill. 1991) ("[The creditor] can call this arrangement an 'absolute assignment' or, more appropriately, 'Mickey Mouse.' It's still a lien, and the rent is still the debtor's property, subject to that lien").

Perfection of the assignment of rents. A number of bankruptcy cases in the late 1980s and early 1990s confused the concepts of "perfection" and "enforcement" of assignments of rents. They held that a security interest in rents was not *perfected* until the taking of the "affirmative action" required by state law (e.g., appointment of a receiver, a court order sequestering the rents, the taking of possession by the mortgagee, or the like). They seemed not to realize that these acts were required for *enforcement* of the security interest, not for its *perfection*, and that perfection was accomplished simply by recording the assignment of rents. Hence, they held that a trustee in bankruptcy or DIP could assume the role of a perfected lien creditor under the "strong-arm" powers of § 544 and set aside the assignment of rents. *See, e.g.*, In re Bond, 122 B.R. 39 (D.Md. 1990). Lenders concluded that this result was much less probable if they used a "conditionally absolute" form of assignment than if they employed a "security assignment." This provided an additional rationale for lenders to use "conditionally absolute" assignments.

This unfortunate episode is now ended. During the latter part of the 1990s, the vast majority of bankruptcy court decisions have recognized that *perfection* of an assignment of rents (whether of the "security assignment" or "conditionally absolute" type) is accomplished simply by recording it. *See, e.g.*, In re Fairview-Takoma Ltd. Partnership, 206 B.R. 792 (D. Md. 1997). In addition, a number of states have recently enacted statutes providing that recording constitutes perfection. Thus, this reason for using a "conditionally absolute" form of assignment has lost much of its significance.

Rents as cash collateral. If the rents are still the debtor's property, an undersecured mortgage lender may nonetheless get control of them (or "adequate protection" in lieu of them) if they are recognized as "cash collateral" by the bankruptcy court under § 363(a). It is clear that in general, cash collateral includes rents. Section 363(a) provides that:

> "cash collateral" means, cash . . . or other cash equivalents whenever acquired in which the estate and an entity other than the estate have an interest and includes the proceeds, products, offspring, rents, or profits of property subject to a security interest as provided in section 552(b) of this title, whether existing before or after the commencement of a case under this title.

Ordinarily, under § 552 a pre-petition lien won't cover "after-acquired property" — that is, property the debtor receives after the bankruptcy petition is filed. However, rents are different from other after-acquired property. Section 552(b) recognizes the effectiveness of a *pre*-petition security agreement to govern *post*-petition rents "to the extent provided in [the] security agreement." Prior to the Bankruptcy Reform Act of 1994, § 552(b) included a further phrase after that just quoted: ". . . and by applicable nonbankruptcy law." Lenders generally believed that using a "conditionally absolute" assignment of rents would help them convince the bankruptcy courts that their security interests in rents were recognizable under state law, and hence met the last-quoted standard. The 1994 act deleted the reference to nonbankruptcy law, and in the view of some commentators, federalized the law with respect to validity of assignments of rents as governing post-petition rents. Whether this is so is unclear; *see* Freyermouth, *The Circus Continues — Security Interests in Rents, Congress, the Bankruptcy Courts, and the"Rents are Subsumed in the Land" Hypothesis*, 6 J. Bankr. Law & Prac. 115 (1997). Thus, use of a "conditionally absolute" form of assignment may still strengthen the lender's argument for treating post-petition rents as cash collateral.

> *(b) After the occurrence of an Event of Default, Borrower authorizes Lender to collect, sue for and compromise Rents and directs each tenant of the Mortgaged Property to pay all Rents to, or as directed by, Lender. However, until the occurrence of an Event of Default, Lender hereby grants to Borrower a revocable license to collect and receive all Rents, to hold all Rents in trust for the benefit of Lender and to apply all Rents to*

pay the installments of interest and principal then due and payable under the Note and the other amounts then due and payable under the other Loan Documents, including Imposition Deposits, and to pay the current costs and expenses of managing, operating and maintaining the Mortgaged Property, including utilities, taxes and insurance premiums (to the extent not included in Imposition Deposits), tenant improvements and other capital expenditures. So long as no Event of Default has occurred and is continuing, the Rents remaining after application pursuant to the preceding sentence may be retained by Borrower free and clear of, and released from, Lender's rights with respect to Rents under this Instrument. From and after the occurrence of an Event of Default, and without the necessity of Lender entering upon and taking and maintaining control of the Mortgaged Property directly, or by a receiver, Borrower's license to collect Rents shall automatically terminate and Lender shall without notice be entitled to all Rents as they become due and payable, including Rents then due and unpaid. Borrower shall pay to Lender upon demand all rents to which Lender is entitled. At any time on or after the date of Lender's demand for Rents, Lender may give, and Borrower hereby irrevocably authorizes Lender to give, notice to all tenants of the Mortgaged Property instructing them to pay all Rents to Lender, no tenant shall be obligated to inquire further as to the occurrence or continuance of an Event of Default, and no tenant shall be obligated to pay to Borrower any amounts which are actually paid to Lender in response to such a notice. Any such notice by Lender shall be delivered to each tenant personally, by mail or by delivering such demand to each rental unit. Borrower shall not interfere with and shall cooperate with Lender's collection of such Rents.

Notifying tenants. Whatever the law says about how to enforce an assignment of rents, it's clear that as a practical matter, when a default occurs the tenants must be notified and instructed to pay rent to the lender. In many cases, there is no assurance that the tenants will cooperate. The clause authorizes the lender to send a notice to the tenants, and makes it clear that the tenants are justified in paying rent directly to the lender. However, some tenants may find the notice confusing or annoying, and may simply refuse to pay anybody until faced with a court order.

Some lenders use an additional technique to make the transition work more smoothly. They require the borrower to prepare and execute letters to the tenants, advising them to begin paying their rents to the lender. These letters are held by the lender "in escrow" until default, and are then mailed or delivered to the tenants. Of course, this approach is not foolproof; each time a new lease is entered into, the borrower must sign a new letter and put it in the lender's hands. In a multifamily apartment project this is probably impractical, but it may make sense in a loan on an office building or shopping center, in which there are fewer leases and their terms are much longer.

A tenant will be protected in continuing to pay rent directly to the landlord until the tenant is notified that the assignment of rents is being enforced. *See* Restatement (Second) of Contracts § 338.

(c) Borrower represents and warrants to Lender that Borrower has not executed any prior assignment of Rents (other than an assignment of Rents securing indebtedness that will be paid off and discharged with the

proceeds of the loan evidenced by the Note), that Borrower has not performed, and Borrower covenants and agrees that it will not perform, any acts and has not executed, and shall not execute, any instrument which would prevent Lender from exercising its rights under this Section 3, and that at the time of execution of this Instrument there has been no anticipation or prepayment of any Rents for more than two months prior to the due dates of such Rents. Borrower shall not collect or accept payment of any Rents more than two months prior to the due dates of such Rents.

Conflicting assignments of rents. Rents are a property right distinct from the real estate itself. Assignments of rents are conveyances of interests in real property, and presumably subject to the recording acts. Hence, if the borrower had made a previous assignment of rents, but it was unrecorded, the lender who had no notice of it and recorded its own mortgage with an assignment of rents would take priority over the previous unrecorded assignment. The foregoing covenant by the borrower that no competing assignment of rents has been executed is simply designed to give the lender a bit of extra comfort on this point.

Incidentally, the same priority principles govern appointment of receivers. Hence, a receiver appointed at the request of the holder of a junior mortgage will be supplanted by a receiver appointed at the request of a senior mortgage holder. *See* Restatement (Third) of Property (Mortgages) § 4.5 (1997).

Prepaid rents. A landlord who recognizes that foreclosure and loss of the building is inevitable may be tempted to "milk" the property by collecting prepaid rents from the tenants for many months in the future, often at a large discount. The foregoing clause limits the landlord to collection of two months' worth of advance rent, but there is no way for the lender to ensure that the landlord will comply with this limitation. If the landlord enters into an agreement with a tenant that is not "commercially reasonable," a subsequently-appointed receiver may disaffirm it. *See* Restatement (Third) of Property (Mortgages) § 4.4 (1997). Accepting prepaid rent at a large discount would probably be regarded as "commercially unreasonable"; *see* New York City Community Preservation Corp. v. Michelin Assoc., 496 N.Y.S.2d 530 (N.Y. App. Div. 1985). However, if rent were prepaid at the normal rental rate or something close to it, it is doubtful that a receiver would be permitted to disaffirm it; *see* Chemical Bank v. Evans & Hughes Realty, 613 N.Y.S.2d 239 (N.Y. App. Div. 1994).

(d) If an Event of Default has occurred and is continuing, Lender may, regardless of the adequacy of Lender's security or the solvency of Borrower and even in the absence of waste, enter upon and take and maintain full control of the Mortgaged Property in order to perform all acts that Lender in its discretion determines to be necessary or desirable for the operation and maintenance of the Mortgaged Property, including the execution, cancellation or modification of Leases, the collection of all Rents, the making of repairs to the Mortgaged Property and the execution or termination of contracts providing for the management, operation or maintenance of the Mortgaged Property, for the purposes of enforcing the assignment of Rents pursuant to Section 3(a), protecting the Mortgaged Property or the security of this Instrument, or for such other purposes as Lender in its discretion may deem necessary or desirable. Alternatively, if an Event of Default has occurred and is continuing, regardless of the

adequacy of Lender's security, without regard to Borrower's solvency and without the necessity of giving prior notice (oral or written) to Borrower, Lender may apply to any court having jurisdiction for the appointment of a receiver for the Mortgaged Property to take any or all of the actions set forth in the preceding sentence. If Lender elects to seek the appointment of a receiver for the Mortgaged Property at any time after an Event of Default has occurred and is continuing, Borrower, by its execution of this Instrument, expressly consents to the appointment of such receiver, including the appointment of a receiver ex parte if permitted by applicable law. Lender or the receiver, as the case may be, shall be entitled to receive a reasonable fee for managing the Mortgaged Property, Immediately upon appointment of a receiver or immediately upon the Lender's entering upon and taking possession and control of the Mortgaged Property, Borrower shall surrender possession of the Mortgaged Property to Lender or the receiver, as the case may be, and shall deliver to Lender or the receiver, as the case may be, all documents, records (including records on electronic or magnetic media), accounts, surveys, plans, and specifications relating to the Mortgaged Property and all security deposits and prepaid Rents. In the event Lender takes possession and control of the Mortgaged Property, Lender may exclude Borrower and its representatives from the Mortgaged Property. Borrower acknowledges and agrees that the exercise by Lender of any of the rights conferred under this Section 3 shall not be construed to make Lender a mortgagee-in-possession of the Mortgaged Property so long as Lender has not itself entered into actual possession of the Land and Improvements.

Becoming a mortgagee in possession. This section identifies two specific mechanisms for enforcement of the assignment of rents. The first allows the lender to take possession of the property, and the second authorizes the appointment of a receiver to take possession and operate the property. These mechanisms are not the lender's exclusive remedies, since in most states the lender could begin collecting rent, or could get a court order forcing the borrower to turn over all collected rents to the lender, without either taking possession or obtaining a receiver.

Even without mortgage language authorizing possession, in a title theory or intermediate theory state a mortgagee may take possession as soon as a default occurs. In lien theory states, however, the mortgagee may take possession only when the mortgagor has abandoned the property or gives consent to the lender's taking of possession. [Editor's Note: Under a title theory, the mortgage grant is viewed as if the lender was granted fee title to the property with the condition that once the loan is repaid it is reconveyed to the borrower; in a lien theory state, the mortgage is viewed as a grant of a lien interest only; an intermediate theory state falls somewhere in between a title and lien theory.] In effect, the clause above constitutes an advance consent.

Risks of Mortgagee-in-Possession Status. In most cases, the lender will prefer to get a receiver appointed rather than taking direct possession. The reason is that there are extreme risks to a mortgagee who takes possession prior to foreclosure. Such a mortgagee is held to a very high standard of conduct in managing the property. *See* G. Nelson & D. Whitman, Real Estate Finance Law § 4.24ff (3d ed. 1993). Liabilities imposed on the mortgagee include:

a. Strict accounting for all rents and other revenues collected, with duties to the mortgagor that are tantamount to fiduciary in nature. Johns v. Moore, 336 P.2d 579 (Cal. Ct. App. 1959). These duties may be asserted by the mortgagor or by junior lienholders; *see* Shadow Lawn Sav. & Loan Ass'n v. Palmarozza, 463 A.2d 384 (N.J. Super. App. Div. 1983). The mortgagee is entitled to apply rent receipts to repairs, taxes, and other necessary operating expenses; *see* Gomez v. Bobker, 508 N.Y.S.2d 215 (N.Y. App. Div. 1986); Herman v. Herman, 707 P.2d 1374 (Wash. Ct. App. 1985); Martinez v. Continental Enterprises, 697 P.2d 789 (Colo. App. 1984).

b. A duty to manage the property in a reasonable prudent and careful manner, use reasonable means to prevent damage to it, and to keep it productive. *See* ComFed Sav. Bank v. Newtown Commons Plaza Assoc., 719 F.Supp. 367 (E.D. Pa. 1989).

c. Liability in tort to third parties injured on the premises. City of Newark v. Sue Corp., 304 A.2d 567 (N.J. Super. 1973). *Cf.* Briglia v. Mondrian Mortg. Corp., 698 A.2d 28 (N.J. Super. A.D.1997) (mortgagee in possession was not a "commercial landlord" for purposes of sidewalk maintenance ordinance). *See also* Central Heights Condominium Ass'n, Inc. v. Little Falls Sav. and Loan Ass'n, 598 A.2d 233 (N.J. Super. A.D. 1991) (mortgage in possession who completed construction of condominiums was liable to unit purchasers for construction defects); Castillo v. Carver Federal Sav. & Loan Ass'n, 508 N.Y.S.2d 574 (N.Y. App. Div. 1986) (mortgagee in possession could be liable for injuries due to fire on premises if causation were shown).

d. Liability under statutes imposing duties on owners. *See, e.g.*, Hausman v. City of Dayton, 1993 Ohio App. LEXIS 6303 (Ohio App. 1993) (duty to clean up asbestos contamination); Craig v. Mohyde, 1997 Conn. Super. LEXIS 1049 (Conn. Super. 1997) (duty to residential tenants to make repairs under a residential landlord-tenant statute).

e. Liability for all goods and services furnished by third parties to the property. *See* Essex Cleaning Contractors, Inc. v. Amato, 317 A.2d 411 (N.J. Super. 1974).

f. Liability for breach of any covenants running with the land, or covenants running with the ground leasehold estate if the project is built on a ground lease. *See* U.S. Fidelity and Guar. Co. v. Old Orchard Plaza Ltd. Partnership, 672 N.E.2d 876 (Ill. Ct. App. 1996); Moffatt v. Smith, 4 N.Y. 126 (1850); Cockrell v. Houston Packing Co., 147 S.W. 1145 (1912). This includes the duty to make repairs at the behest of tenants if the lease so provides; *see* Touma v. St. Mary's Bank, 712 A.2d 619 (N.H. 1998).

Few lenders have staff members well qualified to carry out these duties, and fewer are willing to accept the associated liabilities. Employing a receivership instead avoids the liabilities, and if the receiver is a professional rental property manager, he or she will probably do a better job than the lender would do. Receiverships have one additional advantage: they do not terminate subordinate leases, while the taking of possession by the mortgagee arguably will do so, at least in title theory states. In a residential rental project, the possibility of terminating subordinate leases unwittingly is not likely to be a major concern. However, in a commercial building it can be a serious problem, and provides another reason that receiverships are generally preferable to direct possession by the mortgagee. *See*

HRPT Advisors, Inc. v. MacDonald, Levine, Jenkins & Co., P.C., 686 N.E.2d 203 (Mass. Ct. App. 1997) (mortgagee's taking of possession won't terminate junior leases if mortgagee does so in its capacity as assignee of rents rather than its capacity as a foreclosing lender).

A lender does not become a mortgagee-in-possession merely by collecting the rents, unless the lender also takes physical possession and begins operating the property. Prince v. Brown, 856 P.2d 589 (Okla. Ct. App. 1993). Nonetheless, it is all too easy for a mortgagee to take possession unwittingly. For example, the lender who enters into a new lease with a tenant is almost surely "in possession." *See* Skolnick v. East Boston Sav. Bank, 29 N.E.2d 585, 130 A.L.R. 1519 (1940). A lender who undertakes to evict a tenant for non-payment of rent, or makes repairs at the request of a tenant, may well be considered to have taken possession. *Cf.* Blackstone Valley Nat. Bank v. Hanson, 445 N.E.2d 1093 (Mass. Ct. App. 1983) (mortgagee who visited the property a few times, asked a tenant to "take care of it," and made emergency repairs was not "in possession.") Cultivating and harvesting a crop on the land is likely to be deemed possession as well; *see* Nelson v. Bowen, 12 P.2d 1083 (Cal. Ct. App. 1932). Counsel should caution their lender clients about taking actions that will result in possession status. The final sentence in the Fannie Mae form quoted above is designed to ward off the argument that the mere presence of a clause allowing the mortgagee to take possession upon default somehow puts the mortgagee in possession automatically.

Receiverships. Since a receiver is an officer of the court, it is not possible for lenders to dictate in absolute terms the conditions upon which a receiver will be appointed. State law varies, but typically requires that one or more of the following factors be present before a court will appoint a receiver:

1. A continuing default on the mortgage debt
2. Inadequacy of the property as security
3. Ongoing commission of waste on the property
4. The mortgagor's insolvency

See, e.g., Dart v. Western Sav. & Loan Ass'n, 438 P.2d 407 (Ariz. 1968).

Hence, the language of the Fannie Mae form, stating that a receiver can be appointed when there is a continuing default "regardless of the adequacy of Lender's security, without regard to Borrower's solvency," may or may not be enforced by the courts. However, it does no harm, and may well influence a court to appoint a receiver even if insolvency or inadequacy of the security are missing. *See* Barclays Bank v. Superior Court, 137 Cal. Rptr. 743 (1977) (mortgage language authorizing a receiver creates a *prima facie*, but rebuttable, showing of entitlement to receiver). Restatement (Third) of Property (Mortgages) § 4.3 (1997) may be helpful to mortgagees in this respect, since it specifically approves the appointment of a receiver if a default exists and the mortgage "contains either mortgage on the rents or a provision authorizing appointment of a receiver to take possession and collect rents upon mortgagor default."

***Ex parte* receiverships.** The form above provides for *ex parte* appointment of a receivership if local law so permits. It does in many states. One might ask whether such a judicial action violates procedural due process? The limited case law on the point suggests that it does not (*see* Friedman v. Gerax Realty Associates, 420

N.Y.S.2d 247 (1979); Hartford Fed. Sav. & Loan Ass'n v. Tucker, 491 A.2d 1084 (Conn. 1985)), or that the language in the form authorizing *ex parte* appointment acts as a waiver of the borrower's due process rights (*see* Manufacturers Life Ins. Co. v. Patterson, 554 N.E.2d 134 (Ohio. Ct. App. 1988)).

(e) If Lender enters the Mortgaged Property, Lender shall be liable to account only to Borrower and only for those Rents actually received. Lender shall not be liable to Borrower, anyone claiming under or through Borrower or anyone having an interest in the Mortgaged Property, by reason of any act or omission of Lender under this Section 3, and Borrower hereby releases and discharges Lender from any such liability to the fullest extent permitted by law.

Relief from strict duties. Ordinarily a mortgagee in possession has a duty to use reasonable diligence in leasing the premises and collecting rents. This subsection attempts to relieve the lender to some degree from this duty, but it is unclear whether the courts will enforce it against the borrower. The exculpation of the lender for "any act or omission" is likewise of doubtful enforceability. For example, if the lender in possession created a dangerous condition on the land and a third party, injured as a result, sued the borrower (who is, after all, still the landowner), it is difficult to imagine that a court would use this clause to relieve the lender of liability.

(f) If the Rents are not sufficient to meet the costs of taking control of and managing the Mortgaged Property and collecting the Rents, any funds expended by Lender for such purposes shall become an additional part of the indebtedness as provided in Section 12.

Expenditures on the property. In general, mortgage lenders have a common-law right to make necessary expenditures to protect their security, and to add those expenditures to the loan balance. *See* Restatement (Third) of Property (Mortgages) § 2.2 (1997). Since under the Restatement, failing to perform reasonable maintenance is waste (§ 4.6), and since lender expenditures to prevent or correct waste are recognized under § 2.2 (*see* § 2.2, Reporters' Note (e)), courts should readily enforce this subsection. *See* Thompson v. Kirsch, 677 P.2d 490 (Idaho Ct. App. 1984) (advances for maintenance could be added to mortgage balance, where mortgage authorized lender to make such advances).

(g) Any entering upon and taking of control of the Mortgaged Property by Lender or the receiver, as the case may be, and any application of Rents as provided in this Instrument shall not cure or waive any Event of Default or invalidate any other right or remedy of Lender under applicable law or provided for in this Instrument.

4. *ASSIGNMENT OF LEASES; LEASES AFFECTING THE MORTGAGED PROPERTY.*

(a) As part of the consideration for the Indebtedness, Borrower absolutely and unconditionally assigns and transfers to Lender all of Borrower's right, title and interest in, to and under the Leases, including Borrower's right, power and authority to modify the terms of any such Lease, or extend or terminate any such Lease. It is the intention of Borrower to establish a present, absolute and irrevocable transfer and assignment to

Lender of all of Borrower's right, title and interest in, to and under the Leases. Borrower and Lender intend this assignment of the Leases to be immediately effective and to constitute an absolute present assignment and not an assignment for additional security only. For purposes of giving effect to this absolute assignment of the Leases, and for no other purpose, the Leases shall not be deemed to be a part of the "Mortgaged Property," as that term is defined in Section I(s). However, if this present, absolute and unconditional assignment of the Leases is not enforceable by its terms under the laws of the Property Jurisdiction, then the Leases shall be included as a part of the Mortgaged Property and it is the intention of the Borrower that in this circumstance this Instrument create and perfect a lien on the Leases in favor of Lender, which lien shall be effective as of the date of this Instrument.

(b) Until Lender gives notice to Borrower of Lender's exercise of its rights under this Section 4, Borrower shall have all rights, power and authority granted to Borrower under any Lease (except as otherwise limited by this Section or any other provision of this Instrument), including the right, power and authority to modify the terms of any Lease or extend or terminate any Lease. Upon the occurrence of an Event of Default, the permission given to Borrower pursuant to the preceding sentence to exercise all rights, power and authority under Leases shall automatically terminate. Borrower shall comply with and observe Borrower's obligations under all Leases, including Borrower's obligations pertaining to the maintenance and disposition of tenant security deposits.

Assignments of leases. Why does the lender want an assignment of *leases* in addition to an assignment of rents? Because the right to rents, *per se*, probably will not authorize the lender to modify the terms of a lease, or to extend or terminate a lease. For example, if the lender commences collecting rents under the assignment of rents, and a particular tenant is delinquent, the lender would like to have the power to renegotiate the lease terms in order to help the tenant cure the delinquency, or to terminate the lease if no satisfactory workout can be achieved. Note that this is far from being a complete authority to manage the property, since it does not permit the lender to enter into new leases with respect to vacant space. In order to do that, the lender will probably have to either become a mortgagee-in-possession or get a receiver appointed.

The assignment of leases is phrased in absolute terms for the same reasons discussed above regarding assignments of rents. The statement that the assignment of leases is not "an assignment for additional security only" is as fictitious here as in the assignment of rents, since the lender's power over leases is conditioned upon, and can only be exercised in the event of, a default. Hence, it is in reality a security assignment.

(c) Borrower acknowledges and agrees that the exercise by Lender, either directly or by a receiver, of any of the rights conferred under this Section 4 shall not be construed to make Lender a mortgagee-in-possession of the Mortgaged Property so long as Lender has not itself entered into actual possession of the Land and the Improvements. The acceptance by Lender of the assignment of the Leases pursuant to Section 4(a) shall not at any time or in any event obligate Lender to take any action under this Instrument or to expend any money or to incur any expenses. Lender

shall not be liable in any way for any injury or damage to person or property sustained by any person or persons, firm or corporation in or about the Mortgaged Property. Prior to Lender's actual entry into and taking possession of the Mortgaged Property, Lender shall not (i) be obligated to perform any of the terms, covenants and conditions contained in any Lease (or otherwise have any obligation with respect to any Lease); (ii) be obligated to appear in or defend any action or proceeding relating to the Lease or the Mortgaged Property; or (iii) be responsible for the operation, control, care, management or repair of the Mortgaged Property or any portion of the Mortgaged Property. The execution of this Instrument by Borrower shall constitute conclusive evidence that all responsibility for the operation, control, care, management and repair of the Mortgaged Property is and shall be that of Borrower, prior to such actual entry and taking of possession.

Avoiding mortgagee-in-possession status. Once again the form attempts to give the lender the maximum possible authority over the landlord-tenant relationship without imposing the substantial risks of mortgagee-in-possession status. However, it's unclear (and doubtful) whether a court will take this disclaimer language at face value. While the mere *acceptance* of the assignment of leases probably will not make the lender a mortgagee in possession, *exercise* of authority over the leases (e.g., renegotiation of their terms or the like) probably will, whether the lender has physically possessed the property or not. *See* Prince v. Brown, 856 P.2d 589 (Okla. Ct. App. 1993).

Likewise, it is clear that a mortgagee in possession is liable for personal injuries to third parties caused by the mortgagee's management activities. *See* Skolnick v. East Boston Sav. Bank, 29 N.E.2d 585, 130 A.L.R. 1519 (1940). It is extremely unlikely that a disclaimer of this duty in the mortgage would preclude a court from imposing liability on the lender.

(d) Upon delivery of notice by Lender to Borrower of Lender's exercise of Lender's rights under this Section 4 at any time after the occurrence of an Event of Default, and without the necessity of Lender entering upon and taking and maintaining control of the Mortgaged Property directly, by a receiver, or by any other manner or proceeding permitted by the laws of the Property Jurisdiction, Lender immediately shall have all rights, powers and authority granted to Borrower under any Lease, including the right, power and authority to modify the terms of any such Lease, or extend or terminate any such Lease.

(e) Borrower shall, promptly upon Lender's request, deliver to Lender an executed copy of each residential Lease then in effect. All Leases for residential dwelling units shall be on forms approved by Lender, shall be for initial terms of at least six months and not more than two years, and shall not include options to purchase. If customary in the applicable market, residential Leases with terms of less than six months may be permitted with Lender's prior written consent.

Lender control of leasing activity. Lenders have a strong and legitimate interest in the leases their borrowers enter into. The value of a rental building is heavily dependent on the quality of its tenants and their obligations under the leases. In mortgages on retail and office properties, the lender may insist on reviewing and approving each tenant and lease. In residential properties, where there are more tenants and greater turnover, individualized lender review and approval isn't practical, so the clause above is a substitute for it.

(f) Borrower shall not lease any portion of the Mortgaged Property for non-residential use except with the prior written consent of Lender and Lender's prior written approval of the Lease agreement. Borrower shall not modify the terms of, or extend or terminate, any Lease for non-residential use (including any lease in existence on the date of this Instrument) without the prior written consent of Lender. Borrower shall, without request by Lender, deliver an executed copy of each non-residential Lease to Lender promptly after such Lease is signed. All non-residential Leases, including renewals or extensions of existing Leases, shall specifically provide that (1) such Leases are subordinate to the lien of this Instrument (unless waived in writing by Lender); (2) the tenant shall attorn to Lender and any purchaser at a foreclosure sale, such attornment to be self-executing and effective upon acquisition of title to the Mortgaged Property by any purchaser at a foreclosure sale or by Lender in any manner; (3) the tenant agrees to execute such further evidences of attornment as Lender or any purchaser at a foreclosure sale may from time to time request; (4) the Lease shall not be terminated by foreclosure or any other transfer of the Mortgaged Property; (5) after a foreclosure sale of the Mortgaged Property, Lender or any other purchaser at such foreclosure sale may, at Lender's or such purchaser's option, accept or terminate such Lease; and (6) the tenant shall, upon receipt after the occurrence of an Event of Default of a written request from Lender, pay all Rents payable under the Lease to Lender.

Subordination and attornment of non-residential tenants. If a project covered by this mortgage includes some commercial (e.g., retail) space, the lender will wish to treat it differently from the residential space. The lender will indeed review and exercise an individualized approval right, and will retain a copy of each lease.

The borrower is required to include in each non-residential lease two of the three clauses found in a "Subordination, Non-disturbance, and Attornment Agreement." The two clauses are the subordination and attornment clauses. Subordination is useful because it allows the foreclosure purchaser to terminate the lease and evict the tenant if the purchaser views the lease as undesirable. Attornment is useful because it allows the foreclosure purchaser, in the same situation, to insist that the tenant remain on the lease if the purchaser views the lease as desirable. In effect, the lender can choose whether to have its cake or eat it. There is, however, no non-disturbance clause protecting the tenant from eviction in the event of foreclosure; indeed, provision (5) expressly provides that the lease may be terminated after foreclosure.

Some commercial tenants, especially those with significant bargaining power, may find the absence of a non-disturbance clause unacceptable. Pressure from such a tenant may force the landlord/borrower to go back to the lender and seek special approval to grant the tenant a non-disturbance covenant.

(g) Borrower shall not receive or accept Rent under any Lease (whether residential or non-residential) for more than two months in advance.

Prepaid rent. This is simply a recapitulation of the provision in Clause 3(c) discussed above prohibiting the collection of prepaid rent for more than two months. Of course, a borrower who is under severe financial stress may be tempted to "milk" the property by collecting additional prepaid rents notwithstanding this prohibition.

[2] Comments and Questions Regarding Assignments of Rents and Leases

1. Why is it so important after a default for the lender to be able to control how the rents from the project are applied? What steps can the lender take to make sure that the rents are applied to the operating expenses and debt service of the project? What are the advantages and drawbacks to the lender becoming a mortgagee in possession? What can the lender do to control the rents without becoming a mortgagee in possession? When would it make sense for the lender to ask the court to appoint a receiver to handle the rents and expenses from the project?

2. Why do lenders want to characterize the assignment of rents and assignment of leases as "absolute" as contrasted with "conditionally absolute," or a "security assignment"? Why do most courts consider the "absolute" characterization as a "sham"? You may have noticed that there is a lack of uniformity among the states on many of their laws relating to matters covered by a typical assignment of rents and leases. Why are courts in "title theory" states more likely to accept the characterization that an "absolute" assignment is truly absolute than do "lien theory" states or "intermediate" states?

3. In 2005, the National Conference of Commissioners on Uniform State Laws promulgated a uniform act governing the creation, enforceability, and enforcement of security interests in rents entitled the "Uniform Assignment of Rents Act." In an excellent analysis of the Uniform Assignment of Rents Act (UARA): *Modernizing Security In Rents: The New Uniform Assignment of Rents Act*, 71 Mo. L. Rev. 1, Appendix (2006), R. Wilson Freyermuth summarized the following rules established by the UARA on some of the thornier legal issues that have arisen where there is currently inconsistency in state and bankruptcy court decisions:

   (a) hotel room charges are deemed as rents even though there is no "lease";

   (b) a mortgage automatically creates a security interest in rents arising from the mortgaged real property unless the mortgage expressly provides otherwise;

   (c) the recording of the assignment of rents is sufficient to perfect the mortgage lender's interest in rents and make it enforceable against subsequent creditors and purchasers (so a bankruptcy trustee can not set it aside under its strong-arm power);

   (d) the security interest in rents is separate from the security interest in the underlying real estate, so the debtor must provide "adequate protection" (a term discussed in the summary of bankruptcy laws in Chapter 16) of the assignee's security interest in rents in a mortgagor/assignor's bankruptcy;

(e) there is no such thing as an "absolute assignment of rents" in the context of a mortgage transaction — an assignment of rents creates only a security interest in the rents (a rule that is consistent with reality);

(f) a provision granting the assignee the right to obtain a receiver following the assignor's default in a mortgage or assignment of rents is enforceable;

(g) upon default by the assignor (or as otherwise agreed by the assignor), the assignee may collect all rents that have accrued but remain unpaid, and all rents that accrue thereafter;

(h) the assignee may enforce an assignment of rents (*i.e.*, start collecting rents) by obtaining the appointment of a receiver, by notification to the assignor, by notification to the assignor's tenants, or by any other method permitted by other law (such as becoming a mortgagee in possession);

(i) the assignee's enforcement of its rights and remedies under the UARA does not render the assignee as a mortgagee in possession or trigger other adverse statutory consequences (such as constitute an election of remedies or violate a state's one-action principle or trigger the application of a state's anti-deficiency statute — examples of limitations on lender's ability to recover on the debt owed from the note, guarantees, and collateral that exists in some states such as in California);

(j) an assignor that collects rents after it receives notification that the assignee has enforced its security interest in rents must turn over to the assignee the rents collected and, if the assignor fails to do so, it is liable to the assignee for the entire amount not turned over (as contrasted with only the amount that the lender can show its lien was impaired due to such action);

(k) most tenants that receive notification to make rent payments to the assignee cannot thereafter discharge their rental obligation by paying the assignor (there is an exception if the tenant occupies the premises as its primary residence, in which case, the tenant can satisfy its rent obligation by paying either the assignee or the assignor);

(l) an assignee that collects rents from the tenants or the assignor can apply the collected sums to the mortgage debt and need not apply the rents to the payment of expenses of maintaining the mortgaged real property, unless otherwise agreed by the mortgagee, but the tenant still has a claim or defense by virtue of the landlord's nonperformance of the lease and can seek appointment of a receiver if the assignee's nonpayment of property-related expenses causes or threatens harm to the tenant's interest in the mortgaged real property; and

(m) the UARA creates coordinating priority rules to govern priority disputes under real property law versus Article 9 with respect to cash monies and the deposit accounts in which cash is typically maintained, which are both personal property under Article 9 and are cash proceeds of rents under real property law.

Although the UARA provides much needed clarification of these thorny legal issues and a uniform approach, as well as a helpful persuasive authority for state courts and bankruptcy courts to consider, it must, of course, be adopted by a state legislature to become binding law for that state.

4. How is an assignment of leases different from an assignment of rents?

5. Take a look at the Assignment of Rents and Leases for the FVACC (the "AOR") in the Document Book. Does it create an "absolute," "conditional absolute," or a "security assignment" of rents? What steps, if any, does the AOR require the lender to take before the lender is authorized to capture the rents and apply them to operating expenses and the debt service? Why do you think the AOR does not provide for the appointment of a receiver in the event of a borrower default? Would a lender risk becoming a mortgagee in possession if it exercised the rights specified in the AOR? What rights, if any, does the lender in the FVACC have to modify the terms of or terminate any of the leases under the assignment of leases? Why should First Mortgage Bank be careful before exercising any such rights?

6. The commentary on the FNMA form deed, which contains the assignment of rents and leases language (rather than in a separate document solely containing an assignment of rents and leases), notes that many of the provisions relating to the assignment of rents and leases are probably not enforceable. Why would a standard form contain terms that might not be enforceable? Is a lender worse off by having terms in its loan documents that are likely not enforceable than if the loan documents were silent on those terms? In Chapter 11, you will see that it is common for the lender to require as a condition to the funding of the loan that the borrower provide the lender with an "opinion of counsel" that states that the loan documents are valid, binding and enforceable. If you were asked to provide such an opinion, what would you do in light of the enforceability issues with several of the terms in the assignment of rents and leases? If the lender knows that some of these terms are likely not enforceable, why does the lender require this opinion of counsel?

§ 10.04 SECURITY INTEREST IN PERSONAL PROPERTY

A borrower who owns and operates a real estate project may own or lease items of personal property which are utilized in the real estate project. The developer of a retail center, such as Regent, may own landscaping maintenance or snow removal equipment. The developer of an apartment complex may own laundry machines. The developer of an office building may own fire prevention equipment and cleaning equipment. The developer of a hotel will own personal property such as furnishings, appliances, exercise equipment, and linens. In addition, hotel revenues, nursing home revenues, parking lot receipts, golf course fees, and other similar items may not be construed as rents and hence not covered by the assignment of rents, but instead be construed as personal property. It is important for the lender to take a security interest in all of the items of personal property owned or leased by the developer/borrower and a security interest in any judgments, awards of damages or settlements from a condemnation. This is because after a default and mortgage foreclosure, the lender will want to be able to take over and operate the project.

In order to create a security interest in these items of personal property, the lender will require the borrower to execute a security agreement. When the borrower is a land trust, the beneficiary of the trust should sign the security agreement, not the land trust, because the land trust only owns the real property, not the personal property. When you review the Loan Agreement in the Document Book you will see that First Mortgage Bank required Fox Valley Auto Care Center LLC, rather than the land trust, to sign the security agreement.

[1] Uniform Commercial Code Searches

The lender's job does not end with the borrower signing the security agreement. The lender also needs to determine if the borrower has previously pledged any interests in the personal property. The next article explains how a lender can determine if the borrower has granted prior security interests and what the lender must do to perfect its security interest in the personal property as against other potential creditors.

Donald A. Wochna,
Personal Property and Security Interests: The Duty to Search,
PROBATE & PROPERTY, May/June, 1995 at 43*

Security Interests in Personal Property

Security interests in personal property generally are created in transactions in which the borrower pledges its personal property to a lender as collateral. A security interest is usually documented by a security agreement that, like a mortgage on real estate, grants the lender an inchoate right to possess and dispose of the collateral. Generally, this inchoate right matures on default, giving the secured party the right to seize the collateral, sell it in a commercially reasonable manner and apply the proceeds in full or partial repayment of amounts due.

For a security interest in personal property to be enforceable against third parties (such as another lender or a trustee in bankruptcy), notice of the security interest must be properly filed in one or more UCC offices. This requirement is set forth in UCC §§ 9-302, 9-304 and 9-305, which have been adopted, without significant modification, by every state. Notice is provided by filing a document, called a financing statement, that identifies the borrower and secured lender and contains a description of the personal property collateral. The financing statement does not constitute the granting of security interest in the collateral, does not give the secured lender any rights in collateral, and does not evidence ownership. The financing statement merely serves as notice that the party identified as the "secured party" on the financing statement may have rights in the collateral. As a result, UCC systems do not offer a practitioner a way to determine ownership of collateral ostensibly pledged by a borrower in a particular transaction.

Variances Among UCC Offices

Differences due to legislative mandate. Each state has developed its own UCC filing system to implement the legislative mandates of the UCC as adopted in that state. The mandates, however, are not uniform from state to state. For example, in some states, the state created the UCC filing system to collect taxes related to the filing of an interest in personal property. UCC filing officers in these states have an important tax collection function, but they are not primarily charged to maintain accurate UCC records.

Other states have mandated that the UCC filing officer create a valid and accurate database that reflects interests in personal property. In these states, maintaining the integrity of the data is of paramount concern to UCC filing officers. These filing officers often reject filings for a variety of reasons to enhance and protect the integrity of the data in the filing system.

Finally, some states have defined the filing officer's authority as a ministerial function. In these states, the filing officer is not responsible for maintaining the integrity or accuracy of the filing database. Instead, the filing officer is charged merely with accepting and filing documents presented.

These differing legislative mandates, combined with political considerations, have resulted in each state creating, maintaining and implementing its own filing system. The result is that 4,283 UCC filing offices now exist in the United States. Each state has created its own form of financing statement on which to report, among other things, security interests in collateral, modification of security interests and termination of those interests. Each of the 4,283 filing offices is permitted, by statute, to charge a fee for filing a financing statement. Filing offices charge separate fees for searching the database to discover adverse interests in the name of a borrower and for copying that information.

Differences in data capture rules and rejection. Lawyers trying to deal with one or more UCC offices face non-uniform data collection and draconian results for failure to comply with the local offices' data capture "rules." Because each filing office collects information using its own unique procedures, no two offices use the same forms or collect exactly the same information. For example, some offices require employer identification (EIN) or social security numbers; others require codes identifying the collateral. The lack of uniformity in data capture is potentially very costly because it allows a filing officer to reject a financing statement.

All filing offices maintain the ability to reject submitted financing statements for failure to comply with local published or unpublished rules. Perhaps the most egregious example of a filing officer's power to reject financing statements is found in *In re Fidler*, 24 UCC Rep.Serv. (Callaghan) 465 (Bankr. D. Or.1978), in which a filing officer retroactively rejected a two year old financing statement during the pendency of a bankruptcy because the $6 filing fee had not been paid. Although the lawyer responsible for documenting the transaction proved that the filing fee had been paid with two separate checks that had been cashed, the bankruptcy court held that the financing statement had never been accepted by the filing officer and, therefore, could be rejected two years after being submitted. As a result, the secured lender was denied a secured claim in the collateral.

The scope of a filing officer's right to reject financing statements has become a topic of considerable attention. The Permanent Editorial Board Study Group on the Uniform Commercial Code, Article 9, in its Dec. 1, 1992 report, suggested that various changes be made to Article 9 to clarify the extent of a filing officer's ability to reject filings. These suggestions confirm the filing officer's ability to reject financing statements that do not conform to the requirements established by the filing office.

Searching the database or index. The second hurdle in the UCC filing system is searching the database. Generally, the actual financing statements that have been filed are not physically searched. Instead, the filing office creates an index of financing statements according to the name of the borrower. Data processing errors in the creation of the index are a concern. Moreover, the index does not reproduce all information on the financing statement. For example, the index does not reproduce the description of collateral contained on the financing statement. Some states create an index in which a code or a letter is assigned to the collateral by either the data processor or the document preparer to describe the type of collateral encumbered by the security interest. Most practitioners, of course, would not rely on these codes or cryptic descriptions to identify accurately the collateral.

A searcher may examine the index manually or, depending on the system searched, by computer. Some filing offices insist that their own employees perform manual searches, while others allow search companies to perform the search. In either case, the practitioner is at the mercy of either an employee of the filing system or an employee of the search company to determine accurately whether any filing of record identifies an interest for a particular borrower.

Generally, financing statements are indexed in the UCC system according to the borrower's name. To determine whether a potential borrower has made a prior pledge of personal property as collateral, a lender must search the proper UCC system in the name of the borrower. This search is more difficult than it seems. For example, any borrower that conducted business in a name or structure different from its current name and structure may have created prior security interests in collateral that are noticed by financing statements filed in the borrower's prior name. Some UCC recordation systems cross-reference name changes, while other systems do not have this capability. Thus, depending on the UCC system involved, a lawyer may need to search the borrower's prior name separately to discover any interest of other lenders. A similar search strategy might be required whenever the borrower misspells or is unaware of its legal name.

The gap period. Searching is further complicated because of delays in processing the financing statements used to compile the index. For example, financing statements that have been received by the filing office but not yet entered on the index are not available to be searched. This may be a significant departure from real estate recordation practice in some jurisdictions. In some real estate recordation systems, filings not yet recorded in the index are said to be "in the basket" and can be searched. Most UCC filing systems, however, do not permit searches of financing statements that have been received but not yet indexed. This creates a "gap" period that must be monitored for every jurisdiction and for each filing office to determine the time within which a filed financing statement will appear in the index and be discoverable by a later searcher.

To facilitate index searches and to decrease the gap period, many filing offices have computerized the index. To search a computerized index accurately, however, one must understand the filing logic of that UCC system. For example, some systems are "exact match" systems and require an exact match between the name under search and the name in the computerized index. Some systems ignore periods or spaces between letters and some do not recognize name variations or abbreviations.

The software to run these computerized systems is developed in-house and is unavailable to the public. As a result, changes in the filing logic that would alter search strategies are generally unknown to the public. And because UCC offices do not share software or other forms of system data management, search logic employed in one system may not achieve accurate results in other systems.

Lenders who create their own searches must be aware of the computer search and file logic of the system they are searching. In *In re Paramount Int'l, Inc.*, 154 B.R. 712 (Bankr. N.D. Ill.1993), the court determined that the lender's security interest in the debtor's accounts receivable, perfected by a filed financing statement in the name "Paramount Attractions," remained perfected after the debtor changed its name to "Paramount International," because a properly constructed search of the Illinois UCC system would have revealed the Paramount Attractions financing statement. The court defined the legal issue as whether the debtor's name change from Paramount Attractions to Paramount International was seriously misleading in light of the computerized search capabilities of the UCC system in Illinois. "The question of whether a filed financing statement becomes seriously misleading depends on whether a reasonably diligent searcher would discover the financing statement." *Id.* at 715. The court relied on testimony of the paralegal with the lender's law firm that a properly constructed search of the Illinois UCC filing system, using only the name "Paramount," recovered over 180 documents, including the financing statement filed in the name "Paramount Attractions."

Based on this evidence of the Illinois UCC system's search response capability, the court held that "a reasonably diligent searcher would discover the [lender's] filed financing statement, and therefore the financing statement was not seriously misleading." *Id.* at 717. The court rejected the debtor's contention that a reasonably prudent later creditor would search only in the borrower's corporate legal name.

The scope of a reasonable search strategy was also the issue in *In re Thriftway Auto Supply, Inc.*, 156 B.R. 300 (Bankr. W.D. Okla.1993), *aff'd*, 39 F.3d 1193 (10th Cir.1994), wherein the court was presented with a lender's search of the Oklahoma UCC system that did not reveal the existence of a filed financing statement in the trade name of the borrower. The court held that the lender had not conducted a reasonable search because it searched only in the borrower's legal corporate name. The court analyzed the capabilities of the Oklahoma UCC filing system, noting that a search of root names other than just the borrower's legal name would have revealed the trade name financing statement. The court reasoned that by limiting the search to the borrower's legal name, the lender "unreasonably hindered itself with electronic blinders." *Id.* at 302.

These cases strike a balance between a duty to construct a reasonable search strategy and the computerized search response characteristics of the UCC filing system in issue. The rationale supporting these cases clearly rests on the technological capabilities of the UCC system in issue. These courts were impressed by the evidence that the UCC system accurately revealed filed financing statements when properly accessed by a reasonable search strategy.

The challenge for the real estate lawyer is to construct a reasonable search strategy — a task that may not be as easy as case law seems to suggest. The cases discussed above assume that the UCC filing systems are precise (produce indexed information identical to financing statement data actually filed) and reliable (produce the same information in response to the same search strategy time after time). Unfortunately, not enough is empirically known about the precision and reliability of the UCC filing systems. At least one noted authority on the UCC has estimated that "the secured lender only has a 90% chance of getting correct information from a public filing officer in a search request. If two searches are made, there is a 20% chance that two different results will be received." Barkley Clark, The Law of Secured Transactions Under The Uniform Commercial Code (rev. ed. 1993).

In light of the disparity among systems, any lawyer's ability to create accurate and reliable search strategies for more than one or two jurisdictions may be doubtful. In some instances this may be because the lawyer does not know the capabilities of the system, does not have the time to monitor the changes to the system and cannot pass to the client the costs to remain proficient in the characteristics of the UCC filing systems. In other instances a search strategy may fail because of systemic errors.

These challenges have opened the door for a fledgling business: personal property lien priority insurance. Some companies are now offering to insure the accuracy of a search of a given UCC recordation system, as well as the perfection and priority of a security interest. The search must be conducted by a reputable search firm with whom the insurer is willing to conduct business. Although not as extensive as title insurance in the coverage afforded (for example, no method to determine ownership of the collateral is available), such insurance may offer comfort to those unwilling to rely on the search results alone.

Conclusion

It seems inevitable that the duty to construct accurate and reliable search strategies will be borne by the lawyers in a transaction. The technological improvements already incorporated into the various UCC filing systems and those on the horizon will prove to be a double-edged sword: on the one hand, these improvements should enhance the UCC system's capabilities; on the other, these improvements continue to create a patchwork quilt of disparate system capabilities, precision and accuracy. The use of search companies, by itself, offers the lawyer no protection because these companies neither create the search strategy nor accept responsibility for the precision and reliability of the UCC filing system data.

In any personal property transaction, a lawyer should take several steps to discharge the duty to construct a reasonable search. The lawyer should:

- deal only with search companies that demonstrate considerable knowledge of the UCC filing system being searched;

- ask the filing companies for assistance in constructing a search strategy, explain to them the nature of the transaction and try to create a search strategy that, in retrospect, will be reasonable given the characteristics of the UCC filing system in issue; and
- determine whether the search company is insured or if it can obtain insurance for the accuracy of the search information purchased.

By being aware of the nuances and problems associated with UCC records, lawyers may better assist their lender clients in obtaining accurate personal property lien searches.

[2] Comments and Questions Regarding Security Interests in Personal Property

1. How do lenders create and perfect security interests in personal property?
2. How can the lender determine if an item of personal property has been previously pledged to secure a debt?
3. What sorts of difficulties might a lender encounter in searching the appropriate database? One problem raised is if the name of the debtor is incorrect on the financing statement (such as "Paramount Attractions" versus "Paramount International"). Under Article 9, a financing statement is not rendered ineffective by an error in the debtor's name unless the error makes the financing statement "seriously misleading." If a reasonably diligent searcher could not find a financing statement due to the error in the debtor's name, courts would deem the name "seriously misleading" and ineffective to perfect the security interest. If the security interest is not perfected, then it is not valid against subsequent takers of interests. Even more problematic, if the debtor files or has filed against it a bankruptcy action, the trustee in bankruptcy or debtor in possession can strike down the unperfected security interest granted, causing the secured creditor to become an unsecured creditor and therefore much less likely to be repaid on its claim in the bankruptcy action. One problem with this approach to defining "seriously misleading" is that it is unclear what type of search a reasonably diligent person would do. In response to this problem, the Revised Article 9 (enacted in each state and in the District of Columbia in 2001 and 2002) clarified that a name error will be considered seriously misleading unless a search under the correct name using the filing office's standard search logic would disclose the defective financing statement. This new standard, although less vague, can be highly problematic since even minor deviations in the name (the use of a knickname such as "Terry" versus "Terence," or the use of a "doing business as" type name versus the name in the organizational documents) might not be picked up in some states' filing systems. *See* John C. Murray, *Sufficiency of Debtor's Name for Valid UCC Filing — Recent Cases, in* TITLE INSURANCE 2006: MASTERING CRITICAL ISSUES FACING BUYERS, SELLERS & LENDERS, REAL ESTATE LAW AND PRACTICE COURSE HANDBOOK SERIES, PLI Order No. 8646, October, 2006.

   Mr. Murray raises several areas of concern for secured lenders, including 1) when the name of the debtor is different in the filed articles of incorporation versus on the Secretary of State's website, 2) whether the exact legal name or correct name for individuals is based upon a birth certificate or a drivers license, 3) whether a person's name should include the first, middle and last name or should use an initial for the middle name, and 4) the variability among state filing systems in terms of the search logic used (*i.e.*, very liberal, strict, or something in between). "Beginning in 2001 the International Association of Corporate Administrators promulgated Model Administrative Rules (MARS) which created standard rules for search logic that tend toward the strict end of the spectrum. . . . Although the MARS search logic [Editor's Note: adopted by a majority of the states] ignores punctuation, case, accents, capitalization, spaces, and other noise words (such as the word "the" at the beginning) as well as words or abbreviations indicating the nature of the organization at the end of the name (e.g., Corp., Co., Ltd., and Attorneys at Law) it does not treat common variations, minor misspellings, or typographical errors as equivalent to the correct name." Mr. Murray cited to a study that concluded that if the filing office provides standard search logic according to the revised UCC § 9-506(c), 25% of financing statements will be deemed ineffective. Thus, the "lowly task" of preparing financing statements and conducting UCC searches, routinely delegated to the most junior attorney on a project or a paralegal, is, in actuality, much more complicated than most realize and can lead to major problems in the event of a bankruptcy (especially if the collateral covered by the financing statement is a valuable component of all the collateral pledged, as in an asset based deal). Due to these complexities, some of the large land title insurance companies now offer UCC search and filing services and insurance policies, which may minimize or eliminate the risk of an incorrect or misleading name in a financing statement, by insuring the attachment, perfection, and priority of the lender's security interest (or the buyer's interest).

4. How well did First Mortgage Bank in the FVACC deal address the issues of (i) creating a security interest in the personal property of the Project (ii) perfecting their interests in the personal property, and (iii) ascertaining if the personal property had previously been pledged? Note that Section 5.1(c) of the Construction Loan Agreement provides that it is a condition to the first advance that the lender receive the "Loan Documents," which defined term makes reference to a list of loan documents attached as Exhibit B. Since the Construction Loan Agreement in the Document Book does not include Exhibit B, take a look at the table of contents of the Document Book to determine which of the documents listed could create a security interest in personal property. Which loan document in the FVACC creates a security agreement pledging the borrower's interest in the personal property for the project and which terms in that document create this interest? Which of the loan documents in the Document Book facilitates "perfection" of the security interest? On the issue of checking if the personal property have been previously pledged, review § 5.1(w) of the Construction Loan Agreement in the Document Book. It refers not only to Uniform Commercial Code searches covering each party comprising Borrower and the Guarantors, but also refers to "federal and state tax lien and judgment searches" covering them. Why do you think it is also

important for the lender to have these latter two searches run? What happens if the search reflects a prior granted interest, lien or judgment?

§ 10.05 CREDIT ENHANCEMENTS

The borrower may be required to provide "credit enhancements" in order to increase the assets the lender can turn to if the debt is not paid when due, or with a construction loan, to pay for completion of the improvements if the costs exceed the budgeted amount. Credit enhancements also can be utilized to cover more limited circumstances, such as to pay for various costs that are at risk of exceeding the amounts budgeted (such as interest on the loan, real estate taxes, insurance, or maintenance charges). They can also serve as leverage to the lender if the borrower later defaults in performing under the loan. A borrower is more likely to agree to "voluntarily" deed the property to the lender after a default if some of the individuals who have invested in the project have personally guarantied the debt.

Two principal forms of credit enhancements are guaranties and letters of credit. Indeed, for the Fox Valley Auto Care Center, First Mortgage Bank required guaranties of payment and completion of improvements from the three principals of Regent. First Mortgage Bank also required a letter of credit in the amount of $200,000, which Regent obtained from the investors. In order for the credit enhancements to "work" (*i.e.*, be enforceable and cover the anticipated risks), they have to be properly drafted and exercised. The materials that follow address these basic issues.

[1] Guaranties

[a] Overview of Guaranties

The following article provides suggestions to the borrower and lender on the drafting of the terms of a guarantee in the context of a construction loan, from the perspective of each participant. The lender desires a guarantee whose obligations are clear and enforceable. The guarantor desires a guarantee that is clear on what is being guarantied and what must occur for the guarantee obligation to terminate.

Kathleen S. Cook,
Guaranties in Construction Loans,
PROBATE & PROPERTY, January/February, 1991 at 6*

A completion guaranty has become a standard item on a list of construction loan documents. In a typical completion guaranty, a guarantor promises a construction lender that the improvements the lender is financing will be completed by a specified completion date, lien-free and in accordance with the plans and specifications that the lender has pre-approved.

In a completion guaranty, as with any guaranty, the guarantor promises to perform certain obligations if the primary obligor (in this case the borrower) fails to do so. Often, as drafted, this is a guaranty of performance rather than payment. The obligations guarantied are not the payment of money but instead the delivery of a completed construction project.

Completion Guaranty Components

Improvements. A lawyer should carefully define the scope of the improvements that the guarantor is agreeing to complete if the borrower fails to do so. The lender should ensure that the work being guarantied includes everything necessary to obtain a certificate of occupancy. The goal of every construction lender is to finance successful projects that get refinanced or sold in a timely fashion, repaying the construction lender in full at or before the loan matures. This simple goal is especially highlighted in these times of increasingly troubled real estate projects when hardly a day passes without a newspaper article on the grave condition of this industry. Physical completion of the financed improvements is a critical first step to achieving the basic goal of repayment. Rarely does a purchaser or permanent lender want to step into an unfinished project. The improvements that the guarantor is guarantying to complete should be the same as those that the borrower is agreeing to build. The guarantor's liability is only secondary: the guarantor promises to complete the project if the borrower fails to build it as agreed. The loan documents must fully and accurately define the improvements, with the guaranty serving as an additional backstop if the borrower does not perform its obligation to construct a project.

The definition of improvements in the completion guaranty should specify the obvious — *e.g.*, the exact number and mix of units (studio, one-bedroom, two-bedroom) in a residential rental or condominium project; the number of houses in a suburban, residential subdivision project; and the square footage, gross and rentable, in an office project or shopping center.

The definition of improvements should include more than just the basic elements of the project. It should also encompass the additional elements necessary to obtain a certificate of occupancy for the project and to make it financially successful. In a suburban shopping center or office complex, both municipal building codes and tenant leasing requirements typically will demand the provision of a minimum number of parking spaces. The exact number is usually based on a ratio of parking spaces to square footage in the building. Depending on the availability and cost of the surrounding land, surface parking or a parking deck can provide the spaces to fulfill the parking requirement. If the project requires a parking deck, the expense will obviously be significant and the physical completion of that structure should definitely be covered by the completion guaranty. By contrast, with surface parking the lender can protect itself by ensuring that the borrower owns the necessary parking area before it closes on the loan. In these deals, the completion guaranty need only address the installation of the requisite number of surface Parking spaces.

If the lender is financing the construction of a residential subdivision or any project in an undeveloped area, elements of the infrastructure (*e.g.*, sewers, roads and utility lines) are necessary components of the improvements. Depending on the location of the project and the targeted market, a subdivision's plans may also include such amenities as a clubhouse, tennis courts, swimming pools, jogging trails and, in some cases, even a golf course. The improvements guarantied should include these elements with specificity.

In some projects the borrower may have obtained a building permit allowing a project of greater density on a site in return for undertaking off-site work for the municipality. This work may be project-related or project-necessitated because of the additional strain that the project will put on the existing infrastructure. These types of related infrastructure improvements include roadway widening and traffic flow enhancements such as jug-handle turns, installation of signal lights and turn signals or rehabilitation of nearby subway stations. In some cases, the borrower may agree to build a school in a residential project.

Sometimes the off-site work has no direct link to the borrower's project but instead results from the needs of the local municipality. For example, the borrower may have agreed to construct or rehabilitate structures to be used for low-income housing in some other part of the municipality. These elements are far beyond the scope of what is traditionally thought of when the term "improvements" is used for purposes of a completion guaranty in a construction loan. However, they should be included in the scope of work that the completion guaranty covers. They are necessary elements for the success of the project and are especially critical if the certificate of occupancy is "held hostage" to the completion of this type of off-site work.

All elements that comprise the improvements in a particular transaction should be based on plans and specifications that the lender has had reviewed by technical experts. The lender should require that the borrower obtain the lender's consent before making any significant change to the previously approved plans and specifications. To prevent the guarantor from later raising defenses based on allegations of changes in the nature of guarantied obligations, the lender's approval to any modification of this nature should be conditioned on the guarantor also acknowledging and approving the modification in question.

The exception to the rule of carefully reviewing plans and specifications before building is the "fast-track" project. *See* Fisher, *Fast-Track Construction — A Legal Quandary*, 4 Prob. & Prop. 28 (Mar./April 1990). In those projects, which seemed far more common in the inflationary real estate markets of a few years ago, the lender closed on the construction loan and made advances without having a set of complete plans and specifications prepared by the borrower's architect in place and approved. The approach of making up the plans and specifications as the project goes along creates a number of risks. The task of clearly and specifically defining the improvements to be built becomes a difficult one. This approach also adds considerably to the budget risk on a project. In a fast-track project, the design and building processes are going on at the same time, making it impossible to have the subcontracts bid out before closing. The hard-cost budget for the project can only be a best guess of what actual expenses will be.

Subject to the enforcement problems discussed below, some of the uncertainty created for a lender in a fast-track project can be allayed by the existence of a completion guaranty. One benefit of a completion guaranty is the requirement that a creditworthy party, the guarantor, agree to deliver a project if the borrower fails to do so. The guarantor obviously desires to ensure that the budget is sensible and provides sufficient funds to assure completion of the financed improvements. Otherwise, the guarantor faces liability for the cost overruns.

Completion. In a completion guaranty, the guarantor should promise the lender that the improvements, however defined and including whatever necessary elements, will be physically completed. Because a completion guaranty terminates on completion of the improvements, the lender must set forth in detail the elements that make it comfortable declaring a project complete and the completion guaranty terminated.

An important objective criterion for proving completion of a construction project is the issuance of a certificate of occupancy by the applicable governmental authority. If the scope of improvements includes only the base building, then the certificate of occupancy should only be required for the shell. If tenant work is part of the definition of improvements, then the required certificate of occupancy should include that work.

Because of the guarantor's desire to be relieved of personal liability sooner rather than later, the lender may receive a request that the required certificate of occupancy be a temporary rather than a permanent one. Bureaucratic lassitude is the usual basis for the request. Although not the norm or the preferable position for a lender, the lender may be willing to accept the issuance of a temporary, rather than permanent, certificate of occupancy. This will depend on the nature of the project, the previous track record of the developer that owns the borrower and the lender's familiarity with the regulations of and bureaucracy in the municipality in which the project is being built.

Another component of determining completeness is the lender's receipt of a certificate from the borrower's architect that the improvements have been completed in accordance with the plans and specifications that the architect prepared and the lender previously reviewed and approved. The certificate should also specify that the improvements are ready for occupancy. The lender will typically require such a certification from the outside professional retained by the lender to monitor the construction progress and review the borrower's draw requests.

Another typical requirement used to determine completion of improvements is the approval and acceptance of the improvements by any ground lessor or lender providing take-out financing. In deals where pre-leasing is required, completion should include tenants' acceptance of the leased premises.

Before determining that the improvements are complete, the lender typically requires receipt of an as-built survey. The original plans for the project will show the proposed location of the improvements and the pre-closing boundary survey will describe the exact location of the premises. The lender will review those plans and the survey to verify that the project will be built on the borrower's property and will be in compliance with all set-back requirements. The as-built survey serves to confirm those facts.

Lien-Free Completion. No lender wants to finance the same improvements twice. When construction is finished, the improvements should be free of liens, other than the lender's and any liens to which the lender has specifically consented. The lender is entitled to receive assurance from the guarantor that no supplier or construction trade has filed a lien against the improvements. The construction lender has already provided funding for the payment of these items. If any liens are filed against the project, the lender should be entitled to look to the guarantor to expunge them, instead of having the lender provide the money to discharge these liens.

Completion Date. The construction loan documentation should specify a date by which the improvements are to be completed and the completion guaranty should serve to put the guarantor's credit behind this promise. The lender should establish this date based on the construction schedule and the contractor's estimate of physical completion of the improvements.

Typically, the completion date definition or the covenants requiring the borrower to build the improvements on an on-going and diligent basis will provide a force majeure (*e.g.*, strike and acts of God) grace period permitting a delay in the expected completion of the project.

The completion date is of tremendous importance to the construction lender and, consequently, is a significant aspect of the completion guaranty. The lender must carefully examine the completion date and any permitted extensions of this date, including those resulting from force majeure delays, to make certain that the date is feasible in several respects. Clearly, the completion date should satisfy any conditions in any leases required as a condition to closing the construction loan. In any lease of office space in a building under construction, the tenant wants to know that either the space it has rented will be ready for it to take possession and start its finish work by a certain date, or that it can cancel the lease and rent space elsewhere. The lease termination will have an adverse impact on the project and the likelihood of any sale or refinancing, of course.

The same need to have the improvements physically completed by a specified date also arises in the context of a permanent take-out or a purchase by an institutional investor such as a pension fund. The permanent lender or the institutional investor will establish in its commitment a date by which it expects the improvements to be completed and by which it can fund its loan or investment. If that date is missed, the commitment terminates and the construction lender is left without its take-out financing.

Even in loans in which there are no pre-leasing or permanent take-out requirements, the completion date remains significant because the accuracy of the budgeting process is based on that date. For example, in a so-called "mini-permanent" loan in which the maturity date is postponed for some considerable time after the completion of the improvements, the typical budget of a construction loan will only provide funding for such items as debt service, taxes and insurance until some fixed point in time after the scheduled completion date. At that time, the improvements are expected to generate sufficient revenues from operations to cover these expenses. A project that is not finished by its scheduled completion date obviously will not meet this goal and will be over budget.

In certain projects the date is even more critical. A shopping mall may miss an entire Christmas season if it is not finished in time to allow the retail tenants to be in place and have their businesses established before Thanksgiving. A hotel or condominium project in a resort area may miss the tourist season if the project is delayed. A month's delay in completion of improvements of these types of projects may mean the loss of significant revenues for an entire year.

Enforcement of Completion Guaranty

Despite the widespread use of completion guaranties in commercial real estate construction loans, there is very little case law or legal commentary dealing with them. *See* Sung, *Issues in the Enforcement of Carry Guaranties and Completion Guaranties: Anti-Deficiency Rules, Suretyship Statutes, and Common Law*, 37

UCLA L. Rev. 225 (1989) (guaranty enforcement problems resulting from California's anti-deficiency statutes and single action rule).

The author found only one California case squarely dealing with enforcement issues related to a completion guaranty. *See Glendale Federal Savings and Loan Ass'n v. Marina View Heights Development Co.*, 66 Cal. App. 3d 101, 135 Cal. Rptr. 802 (1977). In that case, the lender, Glendale Federal Savings and Loan Association, agreed to lend funds to the corporate developer, Marina View Heights Development Co., to finance its acquisition of a parcel Glendale had acquired by deed-in-lieu of foreclosure. The principals of Marina View guarantied the completion of these improvements and grading work within 18 months of the close of escrow. As part of the overall financing, Glendale also agreed to lend funds to correct an unstable soil condition. The principals guarantied completion of this work. The project got into trouble. Glendale eventually foreclosed non-judicially on the property and sued Marina View and the principals.

Within 18 months of the close of escrow, $609,930 in loan proceeds had been expended for grading work and $623,000 had been diverted by Marina View for uses unintended by the loan documents. The court concluded that the principals had breached their guaranty of completion. The court, however, refused to hold the principals liable for damages in the amount of the cost of completing the work. The court instead awarded compensatory damages of $700,000 "for the loss of security occasioned by the diversion of funds." Although an owner of the property could recover damages equal to the "reasonable cost to the plaintiff of completing the work," according to the court, the mortgagee was only entitled to recover the difference in the value of the property with and without the completed improvements.

A damage award based on the cost of completion of the improvements would have resulted in a larger recovery for Glendale than one based on the difference in the value of the property with and without the completed improvements. In reaching its conclusion regarding the proper measure of damages, the court stated:

> While the question appears to be one of first impression in California, it has long been the general rule in other jurisdictions that where a mortgagee has made a loan or an advance for the construction of improvements on the mortgaged property and, in order to strengthen his security, has required a surety bond guarantying completion of the improvements, in an action for breach of the bond, recovery is limited to the injury to the mortgagee's security interest which is measured by the difference between the value of the property with and without the completed improvements. The rule is a sound one because, as we have explained, the bargained-for contractual benefit of which the mortgagee has been deprived is the value which the improvements would have added to the security. (66 Cal. App. 3d at 124–126, 135 Cal. Rptr. at 815 [citations omitted]).

Glendale also argued that it be awarded the higher measure of damages based on the cost to complete the work guarantied on the theory that Glendale, having taken title to the property at a foreclosure sale, was in the same position as an owner suing for breach of a contract to construct improvements on its property. The court rejected this analysis based on the "settled principle" that damages resulting from a contract breach should be based on what might have been "reasonably contemplated or foreseen by the parties at the time they contracted, as the probable result of the breach." 66 Cal. App. 3d at 125, 135 Cal. Rptr. at 816 (citations omitted). At the time that the loan transaction closed, the Glendale court concluded that Marina View's promise to complete the financed improvements and the completion guaranty "were intended as additional security devices only, not a contract to construct improvements on Glendale's land." *Id.*

A construction lender may find *Glendale* troubling because of its review of the evidence on the award of damages for the failure to complete the offsite improvements. Glendale argued that the difference in value was the cost of completing the improvements. In upholding the trial court's rejection of this argument, the appellate court accepted the guarantor's argument on valuation without requiring any expert or even objective testimony to support it.

Because the scant case law concerning completion guaranties in the context of a construction loan is not at all reassuring from the lender's perspective, the question becomes whether these types of guaranties should continue to be a standard requirement on closing document lists. The answer is a reasoned yes. Guaranties of this type can serve as a useful item in negotiating a restructuring of a troubled loan. They also serve to focus attention on what the necessary elements are to make a project an economic success. Finally, from a purely practical standpoint, no lender wants to be the first to eliminate the requirement of a standard loan closing document that might later prove to be of benefit to it. By contrast, it is important to caution lender clients that these guaranties are largely untested in the courts and that they are no substitute for carefully analyzed, underwritten and monitored construction projects.

Guaranties Related to Environmental Hazards

In addition to a completion guaranty, a guaranty providing the lender with assurances against environmental hazards has also become a standard item on a checklist of construction loan documentation. This guaranty is required because the lender is looking for assurances that the improvements and the property on which they have been built are free of environmental hazards. The requirement by construction lenders of guaranties related to environmental liabilities is a fairly recent development and results from increasing lender concern about exposure to liability for environmental problems on financed properties.

One way to document this type of guaranty is to expand the completion/construction guaranty to include the obligations for environmental risks by reference to the relevant provisions contained in the loan documents. Or, these obligations can be put in a separate guaranty that sets forth in full the guarantor's liability.

No matter what form the environmental recourse obligation takes, typical provisions include representations that the mortgaged property is free from contamination by enumerated substances defined as "hazardous material" (or some similar phrase) and that the property is not in violation of any statutes or regulations concerning the hazardous material. These provisions also include covenants in which the borrower promises compliance with environmental protection statutes and regulations and grants to the lender self-help remedies if the borrower fails to comply. In addition, the provisions give the lender the right to enter on the mortgaged property to conduct environmental audits and provides for the borrower's cooperation with the lender or its agents during these audits.

Whether the provisions are in the loan documents or in a guaranty, they typically provide that the borrower or the guarantor, or both, will reimburse the lender for costs that the lender has incurred because of the imposition of any lien by relevant governmental authorities against the mortgaged property resulting from the borrower's failure to comply with environmental protection statutes and regulations. Also included in indemnified costs are those incurred by the lender to remove any lien of that kind, claims paid by the lender to private third parties for the borrower's failures in this regard, costs of environmental audits ordered by the lender, and costs incurred by the lender to defend itself from the assertion of claims related to the borrower's hazardous material.

The related problem of asbestos often is treated in separate provisions. Usually the borrower promises not to install any friable asbestos in the improvements located or being built on the mortgaged property and to remove any asbestos that may have been installed in these improvements. The documentation will include the same type of recourse as that provided for other environmental hazards, whether those provisions are found in the loan documents, the guaranty or both.

Other Guaranties

Another type of guaranty frequently found in construction loans is one in which the guarantor promises to pay interest on the loan, real estate taxes, insurance and maintenance charges. The loan budget will provide for payment of these items during the construction phase. Therefore, during the construction of the financed improvements, this type of guaranty covers the difference between the budgeted sums advanced by lender and the actual expenditures. After completion, this sort of guaranty covers the difference between the amount of cash that the improvements are able to generate and the actual costs for those items.

Guaranties of these items provide the lender with credit support for the loan that would be absent without such a guaranty. In the so-called "mini-perms," these guaranties often provide underwriting justification for the post-construction feature of the financing. These types of guaranties assure the lender that there is a creditworthy source to pay these charges between the end of construction funding for these costs and the point when the completed project will generate sufficient revenues to cover these costs.

These guaranties also give the lender some protection against the occurrence of unforeseen increases in interest rates during the life of the loan. The loan budget will provide for the cost of interest to a specified point based on assumed interest rates. If the rates exceed expectations, the guarantor is liable for the difference.

A frequent topic of negotiations when these guaranties are being used in transactions is whether these guaranties should end at a specified time. The lender will want to have the guarantor obligated to pay these expenses until its loan is fully repaid. However, many guarantors will object because the lender will have no incentive to resolve a problem loan situation by either foreclosing on the property or taking a deed-in-lieu of foreclosure. With a guarantor paying debt service, taxes, insurance premiums and maintenance costs into the indefinite future, the lender would be under little pressure to bring such a situation to a quick resolution.

The guarantor, by contrast, may request that this guaranty end at an unrealistically early date, such as on the loan's maturity date, leaving the lender with little leverage when the loan matures without loan repayment. A compromise solution that takes into account the concerns of both the lender and the guarantor is one where the guarantor's obligations cease once the lender has title to the property, whether by deed-in-lieu of foreclosure or foreclosure. A theoretical justification for this approach is that when the lender made the loan, the bargain was for repayment in full of its principal and interest on the loan until repayment occurred. Failing repayment, the lender is entitled to get the property and interest through the time that it takes title to the property.

Conclusion

Further refinements on this approach can require the lender to begin its foreclosure action within a reasonable time, such as a year, of the loan's having become due and payable. The time for beginning a foreclosure action also should be extended if an intervening bankruptcy by the borrower prevents commencement of a foreclosure action because of the effect of the automatic stay.

[b] Comments and Questions Regarding Guaranties

1. When drafting a "completion guaranty," Cook raises the following elements that should be included as part of the definition of "completion" of the project: (i) issuance of a certificate of occupancy for the improvements, (ii) approval of the improvements by the architect (and even the tenants or buyer, if any), (iii) improvements made in accordance with the approved plans, (iv) completed by a specified date, and (v) lien free work. Why are each of these elements so important, and how does including them in the definition of "completion" in the guaranty of completion aid the construction lender?

2. What other types of guaranties are typically used when a lender makes a construction loan?

3. What special risks arise in making a "mini-permanent" loan or "fast-track" loan and how can guarantees from the principals of the borrower help to address those risks?

4. Rather than have the principals of the borrower provide a guaranty of completion, a lender could instead require that the borrower obtain a surety bond instead. What are the advantages and disadvantages to the lender and to the borrower in replacing the guaranty of completion from the principals of the borrower with a surety bond that the principals of the borrower obtain from a bonding company?

5. Review the Guaranty of Payment and Performance in the Document Book which the three principals of Regent supplied to First Mortgage Bank. Did First Mortgage Bank's guaranty of completion incorporate the five components of completion described above? Did Regent effectively negotiate for a reasonable termination of the guaranteed obligations? What did the principals guaranty besides completion of construction?

6. Did the summary of the *Glendale* case in the Cook article make sense to you? The lender in that case was not able to recover from the guarantors the cost to complete the improvement guaranteed (approximately $900,000) but instead was limited to the amount by which the security was impaired

due to the failure to complete the improvements guaranteed (about $700,000). How often do you think there would be a difference between the two amounts? Under what circumstances would the impairment of value to the security be less than the cost to complete the guaranteed improvement? If the guarantee clearly stated that the guarantor agrees to pay for the costs to complete the improvement if the borrower fails to do so, why should a court provide the lender with a potentially lesser recovery based upon level of impairment of security?

[c] Enforcement of Guaranties

The case that follows also underscores that guaranties are not always enforced according to their terms. If, as Cook points out in the article you just read, construction lenders typically require guaranties, then why do you think there is such a paucity of case law involving the enforcement of guaranties? Consider the outcome in the following case in answering this question.

NATIONAL BANK OF WASHINGTON v. EQUITY INVESTORS

506 P.2d 20 (Wash. 1973)

This particular cause involves a written guaranty of the loan, which the court found unenforceable against the Minnesota estate of one of the guarantors — whose death occurred after his appearance in the case — and the decedent's widow, also a guarantor.

In May, 1969, when the National Bank of Washington and General Mortgage Investments entered into a construction loan agreement with Equity Investors to lend $1,750,000, the borrowers gave the lenders a promissory note in the sum of $1,850,000, secured by a first deed of trust on the real property. Performance of the loan agreement and payment of the promissory note was guarantied in writing by Richard L. Brama and Eileen D. Brama, M. Richard Walsh, Gloria L. Walsh and Brama Construction Company, a Minnesota corporation. The bank, as we have noted, made periodic disbursements on the loan through February 9, 1970, on requests by Brama Construction Company, the contractor, and Equity Investors, owner. From time to time the bank inspected and obtained written reports of the project to ascertain if the work had progressed so as to warrant the requested advances. In October, 1969, however, the bank's inspectors found that, although the project was about 63% complete, the requested advance would exhaust about 65.6% of the loan fund. Accordingly, the bank indicated it would require what the record describes as additional equity funds before making further advances. Walter Stepnitz at that point contributed $75,000. In October, General Mortgage Investments audited the project and calculated that construction costs would run to $1,988,475, instead of the earlier estimated $1,750,000. It agreed to advance an additional $100,000, and helped institute a procedure for waiver of liens in September or October, 1969, for all lien claimants receiving payment from the National Bank of Washington.

Then, on or about December 16, 1969, after the bank and General Mortgage Investments had disbursed a total of $1,386,659.21 in performance of the construction loan agreement, the defendants directly involved in this phase of the action executed the guaranty agreement upon which this particular action was brought. The guaranty agreement, by its terms, provided that the signatories, or new guarantors, as the instrument called them, jointly and severally guarantied the collection of the note upon which the advances contemplated by the construction loan agreement would thereafter be made for completing the project. In pertinent part, the guaranty stated:

> [T]he New Guarantors hereby jointly and severally and Unconditionally guaranty to the Interim Lender (Bank) and Participant (General Mortgage Investments) that:
>
> > (a) The Note (in the full amount advanced up to $1,850,000 plus interest) will be fully paid by May 31, 1970 unless by that date it is purchased by the permanent lender for the floor amount, namely $1,480,000;
> >
> > . . . .
> >
> > (c) By May 31, 1970 the following things will have happened (i) the Project will be completed in accordance with the plans and specifications therefor approved by the Permanent Lender and in accordance with the Construction Contract and (ii) all the conditions of the Permanent Lender for the purchase by it of the Note will be met; and
> >
> > (d) The New Guarantors will hold Interim Lender and the Participant harmless from any and all loss due to advances made under the Note or on account of the Participant's purchase of an interest therein.
>
> Each of the New Guarantors hereby expressly (i) waives presentment, demand, notice of non-payment, protest and notice of protest with respect to the Note and (ii) agrees that as to him or it this guaranty shall continue in full force and effect notwithstanding the death of any of the guarantors or the release of, or any extension of time granted with respect to any of the guarantors or the Borrower or the security for the Note. So long as any portion of the Note is unpaid, none of the New Guarantors will collect from Borrower the claim, if any, by subrogation or otherwise, acquired through payment by any of the New Guarantors of any part of the Note. The liability of each of the New Guarantors hereunder shall not be affected or impaired by any failure, neglect or omission to realize upon the Note or the security therefor.

Signing this guaranty agreement as new guarantors were Walter F. Stepnitz, Evelyn Stepnitz, M. Richard Walsh, Gloria Walsh and Brama Construction, Inc. When construction activities ended with the project still uncompleted, estimated costs of completion ran from $135,000 to $150,000 with only $107,000 remaining in the loan account still undisbursed. National Bank of Washington and General Mortgage Investments brought this action against Equity Investors and the guarantors of the loan to recover upon the guaranty agreement and also to foreclose the deed of trust given by Equity Investors as security for the loan. Concluding that the bank and General Mortgage Investments had negligently administered the loan funds so as to impair what the record describes as the guarantors' security, the trial court exonerated the new guarantors from liability under the new guaranty agreement. On another issue, the court also held that it was without jurisdiction to enter judgment against the estate of Walter F. Stepnitz, one of the new guarantors, whose estate was in probate in Minnesota — an issue which we will subsequently consider.

The first question, then, is whether the bank so negligently administered the loan funds and disbursements as to release the new guarantors from liability on their written guaranty. In other words, did the bank and General Mortgage Investments breach any duty owed to the new guarantors upon which negligence could be found? If they did not, then there can be no demonstrable negligence upon which the new guarantors could be discharged.

Arguing the merits, Defendant Stepnitz contended and the court ruled that affirmative detrimental action in handling loan proceeds operated to release the new guarantors from their guaranty. Cited as leading authority on this point is *Fidelity Sav. Bank v. Wormhoudt Lbr. Co.*, 251 Iowa 1121, 104 N.W.2d 462 (1960), along with *Nolan v. Colorado Mortgage Co.*, 137 Colo. 103, 322 P.2d 98 (1958), and *Black Masonry & Contracting Co. v. National Sur. Co.*, 61 Wash. 471, 112 P. 517 (1911). In essence, the new guarantors contend that the lenders advanced to the builder and lien claimants more than that to which they were entitled under the construction loan agreement, that this tended to deprive the guarantors of part of their security and, as a matter of law, operated to release them from liability as guarantors. But we are unable to find in this record evidence of such dereliction or breach of duty. That other banks may have followed different procedures in advancing construction loan funds does not establish that this bank, in administering this loan, failed to act with reasonable prudence. Whatever may be the general rules of guaranty and suretyship, we think in the absence of fraud, deceit and overreaching that the principles of law upon which the new guarantors rely have no application to the present contract. There are several reasons those principles do not apply here, not the least of which is that the parties to the new guaranty explicitly contracted against the contentions here made.

First, the guaranty agreement itself militates against defendant's contentions. It provides that, in consideration of releasing Richard L. Brama and Eileen Brama individually from the earlier guaranty, the new guarantors "hereby jointly and severally and unconditionally guaranty" that "The Note (in the full amount advanced up to $1,850,000 plus interest) will be fully paid by May 31, 1970," and that the "Project will be completed." Being unconditional by its terms, this guaranty amounts in law to an absolute guaranty and constitutes an unconditional promise to pay on default of the principal obligor. *Sherman, Clay & Co. v. Turner*, 164 Wash. 257, 2 P.2d 688 (1931); *Amick v. Baugh*, 66 Wash.2d 298, 402 P.2d 342 (1965). In the absence of fraud, if a guarantor unconditionally promises payment or performance of the principal contract, the guaranty is deemed absolute, unless by its terms a condition precedent to liability of the guarantor is created. *Sherman, Clay & Co. v. Turner, supra*. We stated the distinction between an absolute and conditional guaranty in *Robey v. Walton Lbr. Co.*, 17 Wash.2d 242, 255, 135 P.2d 95, 145 A.L.R. 924 (1943), as follows:

> "The contract of guaranty may be absolute or it may be conditional. An absolute guaranty is an unconditional undertaking on the part of the guarantor that the debtor will pay the debt or perform the obligation. A conditional guaranty contemplates, as a condition to liability on the part of the guarantor, the happening of some contingent event other than the default of the principal debtor or the performance of some act on the part of the obligee. Where the guaranty is conditional, the obligation of the guarantor may not be enforced unless the event has occurred or the act has

> been performed. . . . A guaranty of the payment of an obligation, without words of limitation or condition, is construed as an absolute or unconditional guaranty." 24 Am.Jur. 885, § 16.

The written guaranty contained no conditions either subsequent or precedent to its taking effect nor did it place any qualifications upon the imposition of liability. It contained no conditions operating to relieve the new guarantors of liability except that the borrowers pay the note according to its terms and conditions. Upon the default of Equity Investors as the principal debtor or obligor, the duty of the guarantor to pay became absolute.

An additional reason those principles do not apply here is that, although we do not find in this record evidence supporting the court's conclusion of negligence in administering the loan, we think that the contract of guaranty here anticipated the possibility that such a claim might be made, and the parties by contract laid to rest the possibility of such a defense. The guaranty agreement thus contained the following provision:

> The New Guarantors will Hold Interim Lender and the Participant Harmless from any and all loss due to advances made under the Note or on account of the Participant's purchase of an interest therein.

The liability of each of the New Guarantors hereunder shall not be affected or impaired by any failure, neglect or omission to realize upon the Note or the security therefor. We do not assume the fact of negligence, but if there were negligence in administering the loan, a hold harmless clause such as the guaranty amounted to in these circumstances would not in public policy be void as a contract to immunize another against his own negligence. RCW 4.24.115. In the absence of fraud and deceit, the new guaranty, in our opinion, does constitute an enforceable contract which must be upheld. *Griffiths v. Henry Broderick, Inc.*, 27 Wash.2d 901, 182 P.2d 18 (1947); *Fleming v. Stoddard Wendle Motor Co.*, 70 Wash.2d 465, 423 P.2d 926 (1967); *Tucci & Sons, Inc. v. Carl T. Madsen, Inc.*, 1 Wash.App. 1035, 467 P.2d 386 (1970).

A guaranty agreement of this kind is in essence a contract of indemnity, an undertaking to hold harmless made for a valuable consideration and as an inducement to the entering into and performance of another contract. It does not belong to that class of agreements alluded to by defendant here involving disclaimers of negligence or landlord liability where one in advance seeks to exonerate himself from the consequences of his negligence or misconduct. These agreements were held unenforceable as a matter of public policy in *Baker v. Seattle*, 79 Wash.2d 198, 484 P.2d 405 (1971); and *McCutcheon v. United Homes Corp.*, 79 Wash.2d 443, 486 P.2d 1093 (1971).

An absolute and unconditional guaranty should be and is enforceable according to its terms. The courts are to enforce it as the parties meant it to be enforced, with full effect given to its contents, and without reading into it terms and conditions on which it is completely silent. *Poggi v. Tool Research & Eng. Corp.*, 75 Wash.2d 356, 451 P.2d 296 (1969); *Dopps v. Alderman*, 12 Wash.2d 268, 121 P.2d 388 (1942); *Kanaskat Lbr. & Shingle Co. v. Cascade Lbr. Co.*, 80 Wash. 561, 142 P. 15 (1914).

Here, the new guaranty agreement provided that:

> The liability of each of the New Guarantors hereunder shall not be affected or impaired by any failure, neglect or omission to realize upon the Note or the security therefor.

As a matter of law, the bank acted with reasonable dispatch to preserve its security. It neither neglected nor failed to sue upon the note or foreclose its interest in the property, and it did not otherwise impair the security supporting the debt. We do not believe, as the new guarantors now contend, that the bank's disbursement of substantially all the loan funds, rather than retaining 10%, impaired the security of the loan, for the loan funds were not the new guarantors' security but rather were authorized to protect the bank. Additionally, the expenditure of the funds into the project would necessarily operate to enhance the security by adding to its value or reducing the claims against it. We find unacceptable the new guarantors' argument that the bank's retention of an additional sum of about $70,000, or about 3% of the project's total cost, constituted a condition, either precedent or subsequent, to guarantors' obligation to make good on their guaranty.

There was no claim here of fraud, misrepresentation, deceit or overreaching. At the time when the new guarantors bound themselves to the guaranty agreement, the project was well along. $1,386,659.21 of the loan funds contracted to be disbursed had already been advanced and projections already showed cost overruns. Whatever duty the plaintiff bank may have owed to the defendant new guarantors with reference to the method, manner and time of disbursing the remainder, we cannot find in this record that it breached that duty and, thus, we must conclude as a matter of law that the bank was without negligence toward the guarantor in making the postguaranty advances.

Outside the contract, the major duty which a construction lender owes to any other party is the duty of good faith; though a loan may be inefficiently managed and with adverse consequences, neither inferior lienors nor absolute guarantors have any recourse against the lender unless it is alleged and proved that the lender acted in bad faith. *Brooklyn Trust Co. v. Fairfield Gardens, Inc.*, 260 N.Y. 16, 182 N.E. 231 (1932). The decisions of the trial court releasing the new guarantors from the agreement is reversed. . . .

[d] Questions and Comments Regarding *National Bank of Washington*

1. On what basis did the guarantors in *National Bank of Washington* claim that they were released from liability under the guaranty?
2. How did the court rule on the claim of release? Even if there were evidence of negligence by the mortgage lender in how the loan was disbursed, would the court have found this as the basis for release of the guarantor under the guaranty? Why or why not? Would the result be different if the lender's actions were in "bad faith"? What would constitute "bad faith" by a lender in exercising its rights? Is it the same as "fraud, misrepresentation, deceit, or overreaching?
3. How well did First Mortgage Bank address in the Guaranty of Payment and Performance the possibility that the guarantors would raise as a defense to liability the manner in which FMB made disbursements of the loan or any other claim of negligence?

4. In Chapter 17, Loans in Default, we will return to the topic of enforcement of guarantees and consider how First Mortgage Bank utilized the guaranties it received when the mortgage on the Fox Valley Auto Care Center went into default and what defenses the guarantors could raise.

[2] Letters of Credit

A second form of credit enhancement is a letter of credit. Letters of credit can be utilized to cover special risks in a manner similar to the use of guaranties, but, because payment under a letter of credit is more certain and easier to accomplish, lenders prefer receiving a letter of credit to a guaranty. A borrower may prefer a limited guaranty over a letter of credit, however, because the borrower will have to pay a fee to the bank that issues the letter of credit as well as pledge assets (typically cash or securities deposited with the issuing bank) on which the issuing bank may draw if the lender draws on the letter of credit. First Mortgage Bank required that Regent provide to it a letter of credit in the sum of $200,000 as additional security for the loan. While the sum of $200,000 is a small percentage of the construction loan (less than 9%), it constituted the most meaningful "equity contribution" of the borrower into the project.

[a] Overview of Letter of Credit

The following article describes what a letter of credit is, the complications that can arise when attempting to draw on a letter of credit, and ways to draft the letter of credit and draw on it to avoid these potential complications.

Kathleen S. Cook,
Jumping Through the Hoops with Standby Letters of Credit,
PROBATE & PROPERTY, March/April 1994 at 24*

Standby letters of credit are becoming more common in all sorts of transactions, including real estate deals. They are tremendously flexible tools that can be shaped for seemingly countless purposes. The overall growth in the face amount of outstanding standby letters of credit has been phenomenal — from $5 billion in 1973, to $38 billion in 1980, and to $140 billion in 1992.

Under a standby letter of credit, the issuer has a primary obligation to the beneficiary, but the credit may be drawn on only when the account party fails to perform its obligations to the beneficiary. Beat U. Steiner, *A Letter of Credit Primer for Real Estate Lawyers*, 28 Real Prop. Prob. & Trust J. 125, 131 (1993).

Standby letters of credit routinely appear in ever varying forms as important components of deals. Consider the following examples of their uses in real estate transactions:

- A letter of credit may serve as credit support for part of a mortgage loan because payment under a letter of credit is more certain and easier to collect than under a payment guaranty.
- As a condition to issuing a building permit, a municipality may require a letter of credit to ensure completion of off-site work promised by a

developer in exchange for project approval.

- Under a real estate sales contract the seller may permit the purchaser to post a letter of credit in lieu of making a cash deposit into an escrow account.
- A landlord may take a letter of credit under a lease in place of a security deposit.
- A joint venture party may require a co-venturer to support its promise to contribute additional capital in the future with a letter of credit.

Typically, standby letters of credit are viewed as equivalent to cash in hand. However, categorizing letters of credit as "good as gold" can disguise the many complex issues that inevitably will haunt the lawyer who ignores the unique and unyielding rules that apply to them. Although standby letters of credit are commonly used and can be molded to serve many purposes, in practice they are subject to rigid, inflexible rules. Violation of those rules may be perilous. Missteps can result in delay, expense or even the letter of credit not being honored at all.

Errors occur in transactions involving letters of credit in part because they usually are taken with the expectation that they will not have to be drawn on. Standby letters of credit are designed to provide the beneficiary with quick, easy and inexpensive access to a specified sum of money if things go wrong. Because they are intended to be drawn on only in the context of failed expectations, a draw on a standby letter of credit almost always occurs in a crisis after the underlying deal has gone sour.

Strict Compliance

The chaos that often accompanies the drawing on a letter of credit can lead to mistakes. Unfortunately, this area of the law allows little tolerance for errors. Perfection, or something very close to it, is required for a beneficiary to get paid. The documentation presented to the issuer must strictly comply with that required under the letter of credit. The following oft-quoted statement of Lord Sumner from *Equitable Trust Co. of New York v. Dawson Partners, Ltd.*, 27 Lloyd's List Law Rep. 49, 52 (H.L. 1927), summarizes well just how rigorous this standard is: "It is both common ground and common sense that in such a transaction the accepting bank can only claim indemnity if the conditions on which it is authorized to accept are in the matter of the accompanying documents strictly observed. There is no room for documents which are almost the same, or which will do just as well."

This standard of strict compliance is not defined in the two main bodies of law governing letters of credit in the United States, the Uniform Commercial Code (UCC) and the Uniform Customs and Practice for Documentary Credits (1994 Revision), but instead is found in case law.

Common Drafting Errors

Lawyers confront numerous practical problems when working with standby letters of credit. The cases discussed below establish useful guidelines to help lawyers avoid costly mistakes. Although these cases do not directly concern real estate, they nevertheless provide valuable guidance for the real estate lawyer working with letters of credit.

Details, details. Often the impediments to drawing under a standby letter of credit were created long before the time of the draw and are a result of errors made when the initial transaction closed and the letter of credit issued. Consequently, a successful drawing under the letter of credit can be extremely difficult or even impossible.

One drafting error is the omission of a ground that permits a drawing. In *Waidmann v. Mercantile Trust Co.*, 711 S.W.2d 907 (Mo. Ct. App. 1986), the underlying stock purchase agreement provided that the failure of the account party to supply a letter of credit was a default under the notes. The notes provided for default if the account party failed to pay on the notes. Unfortunately for the beneficiaries, the notes omitted the default for non-renewal of the letters of credit in the stock purchase agreement. The letters of credit simply provided that they would be available by drafts at sight accompanied by the beneficiaries' signed statement that the borrower had defaulted in payment of the notes.

The account party kept payments current on the notes but failed to renew the letters of credit. On the day the letters of credit were set to expire (the expiry date), the beneficiaries presented a statement asserting that the account party "has defaulted pursuant to the terms of said note *and stock purchase agreement*" (emphasis added). The court found that the attempted draws were invalid. Because of the addition of the phrase "and stock purchase agreement" in the drawing statement, the documents as presented did not strictly conform to the requirements of the letters of credit.

When receiving letters of credit, it is important to double-check all details in any referenced documents that may change at the last minute, such as the final date of the documents. In *American Coleman Co. v. Intrawest Bank of Southglenn*, 887 F.2d 1382 (10th Cir. 1989), the letter of credit provided that the issuer would make funds available to the beneficiary on presentation of a signed statement that the borrower was in default on a note and security agreement dated November 21, 1984. Unfortunately, no note and security agreement dated November 21, 1984 ever existed. The note and deed of trust were dated November 16, 1984 and were recorded on November 21.

The letter of credit issuer paid on two drafts accompanied by a statement describing a default under documents dated November 21, 1984.

A third draft, presented two days before the letter of credit was set to expire, was accompanied by a statement describing a default on the note and security agreement dated November 21, 1984, and the promissory note dated November 16, 1984. The trial and appellate courts upheld the issuer's notice of dishonor. Technically, the letter of credit referenced non-existent documents because there were no notes and security agreements dated November 21, 1984. The courts found that the beneficiary's request for payment was not in strict compliance with the express terms of the letter of credit. The reference to two notes could have misled the issuer. Thus, the minor drafting error in the letter of credit resulted in non-payment to the beneficiary.

Anticipate presentation difficulties. Thinking through the mechanics of drawing under a standby letter of credit before taking it is crucial. When the time comes to make a draw, it is simply too late to change the details. If problems exist and the draw is attempted very close to the expiry date, the beneficiary may lose the benefit of the letter of credit.

Two types of difficulties are highlighted in *Occidental Fire & Casualty Co. of North Carolina v. Continental Illinois Nat'l Bank & Trust Co.*, 718 F. Supp. 1364 and 725 F. Supp. 383 (N.D. Ill. 1989), aff'd, 918 F.2d 1312 (7th Cir. 1990). The first involves the difficulties that arise when the beneficiary and the issuer are in two distant locations. The second is the problem created by having two beneficiaries named on the same letter of credit. In-fighting between co-beneficiaries is always a potential problem creating the risk that any differences between co-beneficiaries may not be resolved in time to draw successfully on the letter of credit before it expires.

In *Occidental,* the letters of credit named as co-beneficiaries two insurance companies, one located in New York and the other in North Carolina. The letters of credit were issued by Continental Bank in Chicago. One beneficiary was taken over by the New York Superintendent of Insurance, who acted as liquidator. The liquidator and Occidental, the other beneficiary, disagreed over their rights under the letters of credit. Occidental attempted two unilateral draws that Continental rejected. Finally, close to the eve of expiry, Occidental and the liquidator agreed to draw jointly and place the proceeds into escrow until the beneficiaries resolved the matter.

Because the beneficiaries and issuer were located far apart, the logistics of the draw were difficult. A lawyer brought the papers to the liquidator in New York for signature and then took them to North Carolina for Occidental's signature. Another person physically carried them to Continental's Chicago office for presentation. Unfortunately, the draw documents contained an error. Continental refused to pay on the incorrect documents. The trial and appellate courts upheld Continental's refusal to pay.

The lesson of this case is to avoid naming two beneficiaries on the same letter of credit. Instead, the lawyer should obtain separate letters of credit for each beneficiary or name one beneficiary who can freely draw on the letter of credit and govern the disposition of the letter of credit proceeds under a separate intercreditor agreement. Another lesson from the Occidental case is to try to arrange for local presentation, either by having a local issuer or by having the letter of credit conferred by a local bank.

Avoid designating a specific officer as a required signatory. Businesses and governmental agencies are constantly changing. Titles are modified and eliminated with great frequency. If a letter of credit requires the signature of a specific office that no longer exists or a person who is no longer available when the time comes to draw, unnecessary problems can result. Therefore, one should avoid specifying a particular office or person as the required signatory on drawing documents. Instead, use a generic term such as "authorized officer."

Lawyers Title Ins. Corp. v. First Nat'l Bank of Chicago, 1989 U.S. Dist. LEXIS 5200 (May 3, 1989 N.D. Ill.), illustrates this point. A dispute arose because the office of the person signing the draw certificate differed from that required by the letter of credit. The designated office, "the Area Manager of the Chicago Area Office of HUD," no longer existed at presentation because HUD had reorganized and eliminated the office of the area manager. HUD therefore presented documents signed by its regional administrators. Under regulations published in the Federal Register at the time of the reorganization, HUD had expressly delegated "all authority currently delegated to any HUD officer or employee" to the regional administrator.

After the delay and expense of litigation, the court found in favor of HUD and upheld the draw under the letter of credit. The court reasoned that the draw was proper because the officer who drew had succeeded by operation of law to the duties and authority of the officer named in the letter of credit. Fortunately for HUD, it could produce published regulations to substantiate its position. The more important point, however, is that to obtain payment under the letter of credit the beneficiary was delayed and incurred litigation costs, results that negated much of the benefit usually gained by taking a letter of credit.

Avoiding Errors in Presentation

Often the lawyer preparing the papers for a draw under a standby letter of credit is operating in a crisis atmosphere. Typically, standby letters of credit require the beneficiary to assert that a default has occurred in the underlying transaction before a draw is permitted. The decision to declare a default is often a difficult one, forcing the beneficiary to consider many complex issues under pressure. Yet, despite the other problems that may exist, the lawyer preparing the draw package must make a presentation that perfectly complies with the requirements of the letter of credit. "Almost perfect" will simply not be good enough to ensure a successful letter of credit draw, as the following cases illustrate.

Stick to the script when making presentation. If a letter of credit requires presentation in a remote location do not become creative at the last minute and try to obtain a verbal modification from the issuer to change the place of presentation to a more convenient one. Instead, focus on the logistics of how to get the draw package to the place required by the letter of credit before expiry. In *Bank of Montreal v. Mitsui Manufacturers Bank*, 1990 U.S. Dist. LEXIS 11907 (Sept. 11, 1990 S.D.N.Y.), the beneficiary made presentation at the New York office of an affiliate of the California-based issuer after the beneficiary had obtained verbal authorization from an officer of the California issuer to permit such presentation. This shortcut to presentation proved very costly to the beneficiary.

The letter of credit was prepared on letterhead of Mitsui Manufacturers Bank, the issuer that listed its Los Angeles address. It also required any presentment to be made to the issuer "on or before July 1, 1984 AT OUR COUNTERS." Bank of Montreal, the beneficiary, through its New York City office, first started to make a draw under the letter of credit on the morning of July 2 when it realized that the letter of credit did not contain an automatic extension provision. Luckily for the beneficiary, the expiry date, July 1, fell on a Sunday and standard banking practice gives the beneficiary until the next banking day to present when the expiry date falls on a weekend.

The Bank of Montreal's lawyer spoke with an officer of the issuer's Los Angeles office who agreed to a presentation at the New York office of Mitsui Bank, Ltd., an affiliate of the issuer. Shortly before 5:00 p.m. New York time, an employee of Bank of Montreal made presentation to the New York office of Mitsui Bank, Ltd. The manager of that office refused the presentation on instructions from the same officer in Los Angeles who previously had approved the arrangement.

Finally, after more than six years of delay and the payment of over $140,000 in legal fees, Bank of Montreal received payment of the full letter of credit in the amount of $150,000 plus interest from the date of presentation. This Pyrrhic victory could have been avoided by strictly following the requirements of the letter of credit.

Make sure the certificate presented to the issuer is exactly what the letter of credit requires. In the *Occidental* cases, the certificates presented to the issuer did not exactly match the requirements of the letters of credit. The letters of credit required the beneficiaries to present a certification that any funds drawn would be held apart to reimburse liabilities under the "aforementioned" bonds.

Instead of the required text, the documents presented certified that the funds drawn would be held apart to reimburse liabilities for "any" bonds. The discrepancies between the required certification language and the certifications as presented were enough for both the trial and appellate courts to find that the beneficiaries were not entitled to payment. The trial court found the differences to be "substantial" and, therefore, the beneficiaries had not met the strict compliance standard. The court found that the issuer could have been misled by the certification to its detriment.

In addition, the courts were utterly unforgiving in their treatment of the lawyers who prepared the certifications. One of the findings of the trial court is especially scathing, saying that one lawyer "knowingly or recklessly" allowed the inclusion of the nonconforming language. The letters of credit expired with the errors uncorrected and the beneficiaries never received the payment they had expected under the letters of credit.

Verify drawing certificate accuracy or risk having to give the money back. Although not getting paid under a letter of credit is bad, getting paid and later having to give the money back is worse. Under UCC § 5-111, when making a draw under a letter of credit, the beneficiary "warrants to all interested parties that the necessary conditions of the credit have been complied with." If the beneficiary breaches this requirement, the issuer or the account party can seek return of money paid under the letter of credit.

If a standby letter of credit requires an act by the beneficiary not completed before presentation, the beneficiary risks having to give back money the issuer paid under the letter of credit. Under these circumstances the draw package, though facially correct, contains factual inaccuracies that can give the issuer the right to demand repayment.

In *Mellon Bank v. General Electric Credit Corp.*, 724 F. Supp. 360 (W.D. Pa. 1989), the underlying documents required the beneficiary to issue a default notice to make true a statement required under the standby letter of credit. That necessary default notice was never given before presentation.

The letter of credit provided credit support for equipment lease obligations and required GECC, the lessor, to certify that amounts were "due and owing" to GECC. The draw documents certified that the lessee was in default under the lease. Although the lessee had missed a lease payment, GECC had not given the notice required to declare a default under the lease.

Because the documents presented were facially correct, Mellon Bank, the issuer, paid the draft on the day after presentment. Mellon later learned about

GECC's failure to provide the lessee with the required notice of default and sued GECC for return of the $600,000. Because GECC did not send the default notice, no payment acceleration occurred. GECC was not entitled to the $600,000 in liquidated damages provided for under the lease. Thus the court found that GECC breached its warranty under UCC § 5-111 when it presented a draft for $600,000 along with a statement that such amount was "due and owing."

Conclusion

Standby letters of credit are useful and malleable tools that appear with increasing regularity in all kinds of real estate transactions. They are not, however, the same as having "money in the bank." They demand close attention by the beneficiary so that all documentation they require is technically and factually accurate and arrives at the specified destination on time. Strict compliance with the technical requirements of letters of credit is the only way to ensure that one receives the benefit of these valuable instruments.

[b] Questions Regarding Letters of Credit

1. How are letters of credit utilized as a "credit enhancement"?
2. What must the beneficiary of the letter of credit do to be able to draw upon it?
3. The Cook article emphasized the importance of the way the draw instructions read for the beneficiary of the letter of credit to later successfully draw on the letter of credit. Note that Paragraph 5.1(ac) (conditions for the first draw) in the Construction Loan Agreement states "The Letter of Credit in form and substance satisfactory to Lender." If you were representing First Mortgage Bank in reviewing the Letter of Credit, what kinds of problems would you be on the lookout for in how the Letter of Credit is written, including the draw instructions?
4. Do you anticipate that First Mortgage Bank would have any difficulty in drawing on the $200,000 letter of credit obtained by the investors in the Fox Valley Auto Care Center LLC?

§ 10.06 IMPACT OF "SECURITIZATION" ON STRUCTURING OF REAL ESTATE LOAN ORIGINATIONS

[1] The Birth, Growth and Decline of "Securitization" of Commercial Real Estate Loans

It was estimated in 2008 that 27% of all commercial real estate secured loans outstanding ($900 billion) were sold on the secondary mortgage market, with 55% of all loan originations being sold on the secondary market at the height of the securitization craze. *See* Joseph Phillip Forte, *Disruption in the Capital Markets: What Happened*, PROBATE & PROPERTY (Sept./Oct. 2008) (hereafter "Forte article"). Some of these loans were originated by "conduit lenders" who made loans to borrowers with the initial intent to immediately sell them to investment banks, which, in turn, issued securities based on the income stream from the mortgage loans. Some of these loans were also made by traditional lenders, such as banks, who decided to retain some of the loans they made as part of their portfolio, but desired to sell off some of the loans they made into the secondary market due to the positive impact of a selective sell-off on their balance sheets. This development is commonly referred to as the "securitization" of real estate finance.

The root of this development for commercial real estate loans can be traced to the real estate recession in the early 1990s when life insurers sold many of the long-term commercial real estate secured loans they held in their portfolios at steep discounts. With a dearth of financing available from traditional sources such as life insurance companies and banks in the early 1990s, the securitization of commercial real estate loans began to develop. By 1998, the commercial mortgage backed securities market was in its formative stages and growing exponentially. *See* Forte article, *supra*. As late as the middle of 2007, the capital market still considered real estate securities to be a "safe" investment with high returns, causing tremendous cash flows and liquidity into commercial real estate finance. But starting in the middle of 2007, the capital flows were cut off "due to the sub-prime debacle and a broader concern over commercial mortgage backed securities and overall credit quality." Robert J. Ivanhoe *Acquisition Financing Techniques in the Current Marketplace, in* NEGOTIATING THE SOPHISTICATED REAL ESTATE DEAL 2008: HIGH-STAKES STRATEGIES IN CHALLENGING TIMES, 554 PLI/REAL 103 (2008).

The expansion of the securitization of residential real estate to highly imprudent prime and sub-prime loans was facilitated by rating agencies that rated these pools of prime and sub-prime loans as "AAA" based on unrealistic projections, including that home values would rise each year between 6–8% with no end in sight. Once many of these unaffordable loans began to go into default and home prices to decline, the bubble burst, and as major players in the financial industry began to declare distress, the credit market froze, necessitating emergency federal intervention. Although in early 2008, the commercial mortgage loan delinquency rate remained low by historic standards (at less than 0.5%), due to the large percentage of commercial real estate loans accruing interest at floating rates and with little amortization (in 2007, more than 80% of the commercial loans had an interest only component and more than 45% were interest only through maturity), the delinquency rate is projected to rise in 2009 and in the years to come. *See* Forte article, *supra*. This is especially likely for loans coming due over the next few years if there is a continuing perceived weakness in the fundamentals of the commercial real estate securing these loans and a tightening of underwriting standards for new loans. *Id.* For example, the country's second largest shopping center owner, General Growth Properties, filed for Chapter 11 bankruptcy in April of 2009, primarily, it was reported, because so much of the financing on its shopping centers was short-term and coming due in 2009 and 2010.

Since simple commercial mortgage backed securities based upon prudent commercial real estate loans are not the risky investments that have threatened to bring down the financial system at the end of 2008, once some level of trust returns to the capital markets, we anticipate that the secondary mortgage market will return for this type of simple and conservative investment. However, we are doubtful that the risky "mezzanine financing" (discussed in the notes after the article below), which became a routine feature for commercial real estate loans intended for the secondary market, and which allowed developers to obtain financing as high as 95% of the value of the project, will return in the near future.

In addition, other highly risky investments, that added so much liquidity for commercial real estate loans, are unlikely to return, such as the use of "collateralized debt obligations" that included investments that were so complicated, even former Chairman Alan Greenspan of the Federal Reserve confessed he did not understand them.

[2] Securitized Commercial Real Estate Loans

The following article addresses the impact of commercial real estate securitization on the structuring, negotiation and documentation of long-term real estate mortgage loans. Initially, from the borrower's perspective, this impact was a positive one, since it reduced the costs to the borrower of obtaining a mortgage loan and allowed for a wider range of property types (such as hospitality) to obtain financing. However, the development also had some drawbacks from the borrower's perspective. Pursuant to the requirements imposed by the secondary mortgage market, lenders insisted on the use of "standardized" forms which made it difficult to negotiate any changes to the terms of these forms, and lenders initially imposed tighter credit standards, which led to lower loan amounts. But over time, with the increased liquidity from the capital markets and a perceived "need to put the money out" that existed prior to the middle of 2007, the underwriting for some commercial real estate loans eventually led to riskier commercial real estate loan terms and riskier loan structures such as mezzanine financing, making those loans more likely to have trouble being refinanced once they become due, especially in light of the liquidity crisis that persists in 2009, the time of publication of this edition of the book. Thus, to the extent that the secondary market facilitated these riskier commercial real estate loans that are in jeopardy of going into default, one could argue that the securitization of these loans ultimately harmed many commercial real estate borrowers. Another aspect of the potential harms to borrowers from their loans being sold to the secondary market relates to the speculation that it will be more difficult to do a "work-out" of a loan in default with a servicer of a securitized loan than if the loan remained with the loan originator, who may have had a relationship with the borrower. This hypothesis is sure to be tested during the current real estate liquidity crisis and is a topic of discussion in Chapter 16.

Steven R. Davidson,
Securitized Loans: Understanding the Origination Process,
Program Materials for 1998 ABA Meeting, Toronto, Canada
Commercial Real Estate: Structured Finance Securitization*

I. OVERVIEW

During the last several years there has been a tremendous growth in loans originated with the intention of later securitization. Previously, insurance companies and pension funds made many of the long-term mortgage loans. These Lenders typically held the loans for the entire term. Currently, many of the Lenders financing commercial real estate are originating the loans with the intention of holding them for a relatively short period of time, pooling them with other loans, and then selling off securities based on the income stream from the mortgage loans. The focus of this Article will not be the securitization process itself. This Article will focus on the origination process for these loans, and how it differs from loans made by Lenders who held them for their own account. Even if you have represented many Lenders and/or Borrowers during your career, if those loans were not structured for securitization you may not have previously addressed many of the issues discussed in this Article.

When Lenders originated loans for their own account, there was no need for standardization other than to satisfy the Lender's own internal guidelines. Now, in order to originate loans that can be pooled and end in the sale of rated securities, there are certain guidelines that are generally followed. This is not to say that all of the principles I will discuss in this Article are inviolate. Some can be varied for very small loans. Others may be varied but with some effect on pricing. Also, different securitized lending programs may still have different internal guidelines. However, there are some basic principles that are present in most securitized loans. This Article will begin with a discussion of underwriting considerations and the methodology for pricing these loans. It will then discuss the requirements relating to the types of acceptable borrowing entities and how some of the basic loan terms for securitized loans may differ from other types of conventional mortgage lending. Finally, it will consider different methods that have been used to introduce more flexibility into the process, such as earnouts, reverse earnouts, and mezzanine financing.

II. PRICING AND SIZING

A. Pricing

Securitized loans are fixed rate loans typically priced off treasury rates. While occasionally there are discussions about the precise treasury securities used to determine the treasury rate, most of the negotiation about price concerns the spread that the Lender will charge above whatever the treasury rate is at the time the rate is locked. It is usually possible to lock the rate in advance of the closing but that often involves additional costs and documentation (including guaranties) to protect the Lender against the losses it may incur if the rate is locked and the loan does not proceed to closing in a timely manner. The most common situation is that the rate is not locked until immediately (usually 24 to 48 hours) before the closing. The Lender will typically require that the closing conditions be substantially satisfied so that there is not much risk of the closing failing to occur. In return, the Lender typically agrees to hold the rate for that 24–48 hour period without the additional deposits or personal guaranties that would be required for a forward rate lock occurring a longer period before closing. Only after the pricing has been determined can all of the blanks in the Loan Documents be fully completed. Therefore, the closing procedure for these loans can be a bit frenetic at the time of closing. Some Lenders will wait until the rate is locked, and then send out execution copies of the documents that same day with instructions that they be signed immediately and returned upon receipt. Other Lenders will send out execution documents with blanks for the information that cannot be completed until the rate is locked. In this case, the documents are signed and returned to the Lender's counsel with the blanks. Once the rate is locked (usually the same day the documents are received back from the Borrower) the Lender's counsel will substitute pages in the completed documents based on a letter agreement signed by the Borrower confirming the information to be added to the Loan Documents. The documents to be recorded are then sent to the title company and the closing occurs.

B. Debt Service Coverage is Key

The most important consideration in the sizing of securitized loans is debt service coverage. For this reason, it is not unusual for the principal amount of the loan not to be finalized until right before closing. The reason for this is that until the interest rate is determined the debt service ratio calculation cannot be finalized and therefore the principal amount remains uncertain. This sometimes results in unusual closing logistics described above with the Borrower being asked to sign a note before the principal amount, interest rate, and monthly payment amount can be completed.

While the calculation of a debt service coverage ratio is a familiar concept to most, there are some peculiarities in the way it is calculated for securitized loans. The basic calculation has the net income from the property as its numerator and the debt service (principal and interest) as its denominator. But, calculating net income from the property is not always as simple as looking at actual property revenues and expenses. Certain adjustments will almost always be required on both the revenue and expense side of the calculation. Similarly, the debt service amount used to calculate the debt service coverage ratio may not be the actual amount payable pursuant to the terms of the note.

There are several common adjustments to revenues in the calculation of debt service coverage ratios. First, there will be an assumed vacancy factor for the property that is consistent with the market average. For example, if the property has a 5% vacancy but similar properties in that market are averaging a 10% vacancy, then the property's revenues will be adjusted to reflect the higher market vacancy. A second adjustment is the marking to market of rents. If the property currently has a tenant paying rent at a level that is above what the new rent would be for the space on current market terms, then only the amount of rent that would be paid based on current market conditions will be counted. Third, if revenues from the property include percentage rents or rents from month to month tenants, the rent may not be counted unless the Lender determines that it is stabilized and likely to be recurring.

Property expenses are also subject to certain adjustments in the calculation of the debt service ratio and the following are some of the more common adjustments. Minimum management fees will be assumed. Often, projects are managed by affiliates of the Borrower. The Lender does not want the net income of the property artificially increased by the affiliate manager accepting a below market management fee. Minimum reserves on an ongoing basis are also deducted as current expenses even if not spent. Reserves will be discussed more later and often are required to be deposited with the Lender during the term of the loan. These reserve amounts cover future capital expenses as well as the projected cost of tenant improvements and leasing commissions based on the amount of space for which leases expire during the term.

The denominator of a typical debt service calculation is the amount of interest and principal installments that will be payable during the relevant period of time.

For securitized loans the rating agencies often apply a minimum debt service constant based on property type regardless of how low actual interest rates are. Therefore, the amount of debt service used in the calculation of the debt service coverage ratio is typically the higher of the actual debt service and the amount of debt service that would be payable based on the rating agency's minimum debt service constant. This can result in lower loan amounts especially in today's low rate environment. Current rates for transactions are almost always less than the rate used to determine rating agencies' debt service constant.

III. THE BORROWING ENTITY

Perhaps one of the biggest changes initiated by the growth of the securitized lending market is the required use of bankruptcy remote entities. This is largely a rating agency driven requirement in an effort to assure timely payments to the holders of the securities that are purchased after the loans are pooled and securitized. If a Borrower goes into bankruptcy, even if the loan payments are eventually made in full they will almost always be delayed. One of the purposes of the rating process is to be sure the bondholders not only get paid in full-but that they also get paid on time.

The use of a single purpose entity has been common in real estate transactions for years. But most single purpose entities do not necessarily satisfy the requirements for a bankruptcy remote entity. As is the case with many of the securitized loan requirements, the size of the loan can impact the number of requirements imposed by the Lender in connection with the borrowing entity. For very small loans, sometimes limiting the purpose of the entity to owning and operating the property being financed is enough. But, as loans get larger, some or all of the following requirements will have to be satisfied.

First, the Lender will look for certain provisions to be contained in the organizational documents for the Borrower. Typically, the entity can be whatever form of ownership is chosen by the Borrower. For real estate, limited liability companies and limited partnerships are the predominant forms but Delaware business trusts and corporations are used from time to time as well. There is no universally accepted list of provisions that should be in the organizational documents although many of the rating agencies have promulgated lists of various items that should be covered. Among the most common requirements (in addition to the limited purpose clause) are the following.

Separateness covenants are often included in the organizational documents. These covenants go to the heart of what the bankruptcy remote entity is about. The goal is to isolate the entity owning the property being financed from the risks associated with the business being conducted by other affiliates of the Borrower. While the Lender can't eliminate the credit risk associated with lending against a piece of real estate, it can protect itself against that entity being brought into a bankruptcy because of its relationship to an affiliated entity that is involved in a failed business. These covenants require the Borrower to conduct its business in a way that assures it will be treated as a separate legal entity distinct from any of its affiliates. Although these covenants are usually contained in the loan documents, it is common for the Lender to ask that they be repeated in the organizational documents.

Other requirements for the organizational documents include limitations on the circumstances that could result in a liquidation or dissolution of the entity, limits on the ability of the entity to incur additional debt, subordination of any indemnification obligations contained in the organizational documents pursuant to which the Borrower would be required to indemnify its partners or members, and requirements that all partners/members approve any bankruptcy filing by the Borrower. The requirements of the specific Lender should be consulted before finalizing the organizational documents. If the property being financed has been owned for some period of time and has not been previously financed by a loan that was securitized, expect to have to amend the organizational documents in connection with closing the loan. It is important to anticipate this requirement especially if there are many outside limited partners or members whose consent will be required to amend the organizational documents.

As the loan size gets bigger, there are typically additional requirements relating to bankruptcy remoteness beyond the provisions that must be added to the partnership or limited liability operating agreement. Again, these can vary in different lending programs. A common requirement is that not only must the borrowing entity be a special purpose, bankruptcy remote entity but there must also be a bankruptcy remote, special purpose entity that is the general partner of the limited partnership or managing member of the limited liability company Borrower. In that case, the requirements discussed above for the organizational documents of the Borrower would also apply to the organizational documents of the general partner/managing member. Another requirement (usually required in all of the larger loans) is the use of an independent director. As discussed above, the organizational documents for the Borrower will typically require the consent of all partner/members for the filing of the bankruptcy petition. If an independent director is required, one of those partners/members would typically be a corporation whose articles of incorporation would require that it have at least one "independent" director. The articles of incorporation would further specifically require that the independent director approve any action by the corporation to cause the Borrower to make a bankruptcy filing. The definition of what causes a director to be independent can vary. Simplistically, it is someone that does not have a business relationship (e.g., employee, partner, vendor, etc.) with the Borrower and is not related to anyone with such a relationship. It is not necessarily someone picked by the Lender (although it is common for the Lender to retain the right to approve the identity of the independent director). The documents do not prohibit the independent director from approving a bankruptcy (such a requirement would likely be unenforceable in any event). The goal is to make sure that there is someone who will take into account the interests of the Borrower's creditors when and if a bankruptcy filing is contemplated. As many Borrowers struggle to find individuals who satisfy the requirements for being an independent director and are willing to take on that responsibility, a new industry is beginning to develop as companies provide independent directors for a fee.

A final requirement in some transactions is the delivery of a substantive nonconsolidation opinion from Borrower's counsel. A detailed discussion of these opinions is beyond the scope of this Article. The basic purpose of the opinion is to confirm for the Lender that the goal of isolating this Borrower from the effects of a bankruptcy of any of its related entitles will be achieved. These opinions are usually rather lengthy. They typically begin with a recitation of a number of assumptions of how the Borrower conducts its business and discuss extensively the case law before reaching their conclusion. Lender's counsel should review the opinions carefully to be sure that the stated assumptions in the opinion are consistent with the requirements of the Loan Documents. Often a principal of the Borrower will be asked to provide a certification which states that he or she has reviewed the assumptions and has found them consistent with how the Borrower conducts its business.

IV. LOAN TERMS

In many respects, securitized loans are much like any other real estate secured loans. However, there are some concepts incorporated into the documents to facilitate the rating of the securities that are ultimately issued. Although these can vary by Lender and loan size the following are some of the common provisions you will find in most securitized loans.

A. Optional Prepayment Date — Is it Really Optional?

One of the most prevalent changes in loan terms for securitized loans is the introduction of the concept of having a stated maturity date and an earlier date, often called the optional prepayment date, effective maturity date, or anticipated repayment date, which is the date on which repayment of the loan is expected. The stated maturity date is typically 25 or 30 years from closing, and usually coincides with the amortization schedule used to determine monthly payments on the loan. Although these loans don't mature for 25 or 30 years, it is expected that they will be repaid at an earlier time-typically 10 or 12 years from closing. Instead of making it an Event of Default if not repaid at this time, the documents will typically provide for an increase in the interest rate and for all cash flow from the property after payment of the regular monthly debt service payment, reserves, and operating expenses, to be applied to the debt. While often called the optional prepayment date, the increase in interest rate is usually sufficiently onerous to assure that repayment will occur on time. If not, the cash management provisions (discussed below) effectively provide a prenegotiated workout that gives the Lender control over how cash from the property is spent and assure that any excess cash available from the property will be captured even if there is no default that can trigger a foreclosure.

B. Cash Management Provisions

While cash management provisions have long been used in real estate workouts, it has not been common to see cash management documents signed in connection with the origination of new loans. This is not the case with securitized loans. As recently as a year or two ago, it was common in the origination of larger securitized loans to have active cash management from the outset. Rents would be sent directly to a collection account, various payments such as debt service and reserves would be made, and the remainder would then be released to pay operating expenses, often in accordance with a budget that had to be approved by the Lender. While the documents to implement this type of cash management arrangement are still often signed at closing for the bigger securitized loans, it is now common for the documents to provide that moneys deposited into the Collection Account be immediately released to the Borrower unless certain events (often called "cash trap events") occurred. These events always include an Event of

Default under the Loan Documents or the occurrence of the optional prepayment date, and can include other events tailored to the particular transaction. These arrangements give the Borrower greater control over the cash flow as long as things are ongoing as expected but still protect the Lender by enabling it to unilaterally trigger tighter controls after a cash trap event occurs without first having to get the Borrower to sign new documentation. For smaller loans, it is not uncommon for the documents to simply provide for the execution of cash management documents prior to the optional prepayment date to avoid the time and expense of putting in place arrangements that may never be needed.

C. Reserve Deposits

While reserve accounts are not unique to securitized loans, they are required on a more consistent basis. Larger creditworthy Borrowers that may previously have had more success in getting the reserve account requirements waived may find themselves setting aside cash reserves with the Lender.

The typical reserve accounts cover taxes, insurance, ground rent payments (if applicable), capital expenses, and sometimes lease rollover expenses associated with leasing space in the property if a number of leases expire within a relatively short amount of time. These reserves will sometimes have an initial deposit at closing and then will be funded monthly during the life of the loan. The capital reserve fund will usually be based on a specified amount per square foot and is not earmarked for specific items. In addition, there is usually a separate deferred maintenance reserve set up to pay the costs of addressing any short-term repair items disclosed in the engineering report. Typically, the amount of this reserve will be equal to 125% of the engineer's estimated cost of repair and these funds can only be used for the designated repairs.

D. Defeasance and Lock Out Provisions

Similar to conventional long-term insurance company loans, securitized loans will specify a period of time during which the loan cannot be prepaid at all (sometimes referred to as a "lock out period"). Securitized loans will generally permit prepayment with no yield maintenance starting with the optional prepayment date (sometimes the Lender will agree to a three to six month window before the optional prepayment date during which such payment can be made as well). Between the end of the lock out period and the optional prepayment date the documents usually provide for the possibility of defeasance. A common concept in bond transactions, defeasance provisions were not traditionally found in real estate loan documents prior to the prevalence of securitized loans. The typical long term fixed rate insurance company loan would allow for prepayment of the loan after a lock out period if the Borrower paid a yield maintenance amount. However, a minimum payment would often be due equal to a specified percentage of the amount being prepaid regardless of what had happened to interest rates. The defeasance provisions contained in securitized loans are actually more favorable for the Borrower. While technically the loan is not repaid, the Borrower purchases treasury securities which are pledged to the Lender in place of the real estate collateral. Since the real estate is released from the Mortgage and the borrowing entity can be released from any further obligations in connection with the Loan, the practical effect for the Borrower is generally the same as if the Loan had been repaid. But the substitution of treasury securities has two important advantages. First, it eliminates the fixed percentage of the principal amount repaid as a minimum payment even if interest rates had gone up since the origination of the Loan. Second, the amount of treasury securities the Borrower must pledge is determined by the income stream generated by those securities (which must cover the interest payments due under the Loan and the amount available to pay principal on the optional prepayment date, regardless of the purchase price for such securities). Therefore, if rates have gone up, the Borrower actually receives the benefit of paying less than the face amount of the loan to purchase the requisite amount of treasury securities.

E. Cooperation with Securitization

When insurance companies and pension funds originate loans for their own account there is no need for elaborate provisions concerning the transfer of the loan after closing. For loans that are being securitized, it is important for the Lender to be able to receive the cooperation of the Borrower in connection with the securitization process, including the possible modification of the Loan Documents in ways that do not materially change the business deal that the Borrower has negotiated. The amount of information needed about a specific loan or Borrower in connection with a securitization will depend upon both the size of the loan and the size of the pool of loans that is being securitized. However, except for the very small loans, it is common for there to be some detailed provisions requiring the Borrower to supply information and otherwise cooperate with the Lender in its efforts to complete the securitization. For very large loans, this can include reviewing portions of the disclosure document prepared for the securitization relating to that Borrower's loan. While most Borrowers will agree to cooperate, many draw the line at whether they will incur additional expense. Although Borrowers used to be routinely responsible for these expenses (and sometimes had to fund a reserve at a closing to pay securitization expenses), it is becoming increasingly common for the Lender to agree that the Borrower will not have to incur additional out of pocket expenses in connection with the securitization.

F. Change in Management

Lenders that securitize their loans have historically been more aggressive in seeking rights to force the Borrower to change management if the property is not performing well. It was common to have a test based on a debt service coverage ratio that would determine if the Lender could require a change in management. As is the case with the loosening of the cash management provisions, there has been a trend toward loosening the requirement for change in management. While in many loans, a minimum debt service coverage test is still used, it is becoming more common for the Lender only to have this right if an Event of Default has occurred (and sometimes also if the optional prepayment date has occurred without the loan being repaid).

G. Assumability

Loan Documents always address the issue of whether the property or interest in the Borrower can be transferred during the term of the loan, whether the loan is being securitized or not. However, the securitized Lender has some special concerns with regard to these provisions. It wants to make sure that the rating on the securities that have been sold will not be affected. This will not often be a problem but if the loan is big enough relative to the size of the pool, the identity of the Borrower for a particular loan may be of concern to the rating agency. Loan Documents will often require as a condition to transfers that a confirmation from the rating agency be obtained confirming no change in rating. If a nonconsolidation opinion was obtained as a condition of closing the loan, a new opinion may be necessary pertaining to the new Borrower.

H. Increased Importance of Default Rate and Late Charges

Default rate and late charge provisions are not unique to securitized loans. However, these provisions typically take on greater importance and are less likely to be waived. The reason for this is that if payments are not made in a timely manner on the loan, the servicer in connection with the securitization may have to advance its own funds in order for timely payments to made to the bondholders. The collection of late charges and default rate interest is one way to compensate the servicer for the money it has needed to advance. For a similar reason, a Borrower is less likely to be able to negotiate notice and grace periods for payments on a securitized loan.

I. Nonrecourse Provisions

Most securitized loans are done on a nonrecourse basis. As is the case with conventional loans, there are often a number of nonrecourse carveouts for which there will be personal recourse. There is less consistency on the nature of these carveouts and who is responsible for them. Some deals are being done with a fairly comprehensive list of carveouts, but only the special purpose Borrower is responsible for the carveouts. Since the Lender already has a mortgage on the Borrower's principal asset, this effectively does not give the Lender very much. Other Lenders take the approach of limiting to a greater degree what the carveouts are but requiring that an individual or other financially responsible party (other than the special purpose Borrower) be responsible for these carveouts.

J. Dual Amortization Provisions

On larger, more sophisticated transactions, the Borrower can sometimes negotiate for the inclusion of "dual amortization" provisions in the Loan Documents. The Borrower may prefer a shorter amortization period in order to reduce its total interest cost during the life of the Loan. Normally if a Borrower asked to make its monthly payments based on a 20 year amortization schedule instead of a 30 year schedule the Lender would have no problem. However, as discussed above, the amount of principal that can be advanced is based on the debt service coverage ratio and the debt service coverage ratio is determined in part by the size of the monthly payment. The shorter the amortization schedule, the bigger the monthly payment, resulting in a smaller maximum loan amount. In order to preserve a large enough loan amount, the required monthly payment may have to be based on the longer amortization schedule. Since the Loan Documents prohibit prepayments, the Borrower can't simply pay more each month than provided for in the Loan Documents. The solution to this problem is for the documents to require only the smaller monthly payment but to permit the larger monthly payment based on the shorter amortization schedule. The securitization is then structured to take those into account. While it is not a default if the Borrower fails to make the larger monthly payment it is not uncommon in these situations for the documents to provide that the failure to make the larger payment is a cash trap event triggering the application of the tighter cash management controls described above. . . . [The remaining portion of the article has been omitted.]

V. CONCLUSION

The dollar volume of loans being originated for subsequent securitization is growing exponentially. Rating agencies have assumed a much greater importance in underwriting and structuring typical real estate loans so that the securities later sold can be rated. Many of these transactions involve small loans and counsel who are unfamiliar with the securitization process. An understanding of the issues discussed in this article can help one negotiate the loan documents and successfully complete the closing of these loans.

[3] Comments and Questions Regarding the Securitization of Real Estate Finance

1. Can you describe what is the "securitization" of real estate finance and how it began?

2. What impact did the securitization of real estate finance have on loan originations? Specifically, how did it impact the amount the lender will loan and what the lender will charge to make the loan? What special requirements did lenders impose in response to the needs of the secondary mortgage market? Patricia Frobes and Frank Crance wrote an article entitled *Anticipating the Future in Loan Documentation*, 18 No. 2 Prac. Real Est. Law. 41 (2002), in which they focused on the fact that, due to the securitization of commercial mortgage loans, borrowers and lenders cannot assume the identity, policies, and management of the other will remain the same over the life of the loan. The authors then identified several areas covered in standard loan documentation in which anticipating the future is particularly important (expansion and alteration of the collateral, changes in the identity of the borrower and lender, lease approval, secondary financing, and inter-creditor rights and obligations). The authors then discussed typical starting positions and possible compromise positions between the borrower and lender on these issues. When negotiating the loan documentation for a commercial mortgage loan where the identity of the lender or borrower is likely to be fluid, this article can provide some useful insights.

3. One of the riskiest features to securitized loans was the development of a loan structure called "mezzanine financing." Beginning in the late 1990s, as conditions to highly rating mortgage backed securities, rating agencies required that developers not enter into junior mortgage loans and further required very low loan-to-value ratios for the first mortgage loans (as low as 65%). The goal with these requirements was to reduce the losses that could arise in the event of a default under the mortgage loans by striving to maintain a first priority among all potential claimants to the mortgaged property and its income. However, the rating agencies permitted the

borrowers to obtain further needed capital **from a structure** where the additional debt would be senior in right to the **equity holders** but junior in right to the mortgage lien (hence referred to as a **"mezzanine"** loan). Under the mezzanine loan, the security for the loan was not a mortgage on any real estate, or even a pledge of the equity of the entity that owns the real estate, but instead, a pledge of the borrower's equity in an intermediary entity (usually a limited liability company) that owned the entity that owned the underlying real estate (*i.e.*, a pledge of the equity interest of an entity that has only an indirect ownership of the underlying property). In the event of a default under the mezzanine loan, the mezzanine lender can foreclose on the equity in the intermediary entity and thereby assume control of the mortgage borrower and the mortgaged property, but the mezzanine lender would now be an equity owner and remain subject to the mortgage lien. By having the loan secured by such a remote interest in the real estate, it was thought that it would be less likely that a default under this mezzanine loan could lead to a bankruptcy by the borrower, or a loss of priority under the mortgage loan if the borrower did file, or have filed against it, a bankruptcy. A problem with the development of mezzanine financing is that, under it, real estate developers were able to obtain even higher loan-to-value ratios (as high as 90–105%) than what had typically been permitted when a junior lien was permitted (usually around 85–90%). *See* Andrew Berman, *Risks and Realities of Mezzanine Loans*, 72 Mo. L. Rev. 993, 996 (2007). Thus, although the rating agencies prohibited junior mortgage liens as a means to reduce the risk of loss of priority in payment from a foreclosure of the mortgaged property or in payment from income from the property, allowing such high loan to value debt, even if only indirectly tied to the real estate itself, made default itself more likely to occur. In addition, the typically high loan-to-value ratios, when one combines the mortgage loan with the mezzanine loan, makes such loans more difficult to refinance as a means to avoid default in a more conservative loan-to-value ratio environment.

4. Do you think that the securitization of real estate finance is a positive change in the business of real estate from the perspective of real estate developers? Many borrowers were originally pleased with "securitization" because of the lower cost of borrowing funds it allowed. It remains to be seen how well securitized loans fare in the current real estate recession or when a borrower otherwise encounters difficulties with a real estate project. How well will such developers be protected when they sign the standardized forms without much negotiation of their terms? How well will the entity servicing the loans be able to negotiate creative solutions to loans in default if they do not have free rein to make the best decisions possible? While securitization for the past ten years led to tremendous liquidity in financing commercial real estate development, beginning in the middle of 2007 and through today (2009), securitization led to ever more complicated and risky investments (such as collateral debt obligations and credit default swaps). It could be argued that these complicated forms of securitization contributed to the credit crisis beginning in 2008, which made it very difficult for developers to obtain financing for new developments, or even to refinance loans that matured.

[4] Assignment

Assume that you represent First Mortgage Bank. Bruce McDill, one of the vice presidents of the bank, has told you that FMB wants to make sure that a proposed permanent mortgage loan between FMB and Regent is structured and documented so that it will be easy to sell it on the secondary mortgage market. Bruce has asked you to prepare a memorandum that recommends any changes (including additional requirements) to the loan terms to achieve this goal. You should review the "Term Sheet" at the beginning of this chapter and the Davidson article before you write your memo to Bruce.

Chapter 11

DUE DILIGENCE, DOCUMENTING AND CLOSING THE LOAN

§ 11.01 LENDER'S DUE DILIGENCE IN EVALUATING THE PROJECT

Once the basic loan terms have been agreed to and the loan documents negotiated, the next step in the loan process is for the lender to independently review the key issues that impact on the successful operation of the real estate project. Lenders are concerned with the status of the title to the real estate, not only that the borrower in fact holds good title to it, but also what encumbrances it is subject to. Lenders also need to ascertain the income from the project, not only by reviewing a rent roll but also by reviewing the terms of the leases. The leases may contain burdensome obligations on the landlord or may contain terms that will allow the stream of income to be disrupted, which will affect the ability of the income from the project to service the payments on the loan. In the context of a construction loan, lenders must verify the adequacy of the construction documentation to achieve the goals of completing the project on time, within budget, and in compliance with laws and the approved plans and specifications. If the project is already built and in operation, then the lender will want to confirm that the project complies with all applicable laws, including environmental laws and zoning laws, and that the project is adequately insured in the event of a casualty. All of these due diligence topics are of equal concern to the developer/borrower. Consequently, many of these topics have either already been covered in previous chapters (such as title matters and compliance with laws) or will be covered in later chapters (such as the review of the construction documents and leases). This chapter will thus focus on these topics to the extent that the lender has concerns with respect to these matters that are different in nature from the borrower's concerns.

[1] Review of Title

As previously discussed in Chapter 6, when reviewing title issues, the lender should verify and receive assurance that the borrower owns the land mortgaged and that the lender's mortgage is valid. The lender should also carefully review the encumbrances that apply to the mortgaged property to make sure that they will not interfere with the borrower's intended use of the property. This review will be quite similar to the review that the developer should have performed. The lender, like the borrower, will rely heavily on the title policy it receives and will negotiate with the title company on many of the same points as the borrower.

There are, however, a few special issues for the lender to consider with respect to the title policy it will receive. First, there are additional matters that are insured in the lender's title policy (the validity of the mortgage lien, the priority of the mortgage loan including against mechanic's liens, and the assignability of the mortgage). Second, there are additional exceptions in the lender's title policy. One of these is the invalidity of the mortgage lien based upon violation of usury or "truth in lending" laws. Another is the invalidity of the lien based upon a failure to comply with "doing business" requirements (a requirement for a corporation to pay certain annual franchise taxes to operate within the state). Another exception is the loss of priority of the mortgage lien to construction work contracted for after the date of the policy.

It is important to note, however, that many of these exceptions to title coverage can in fact be insured through the use of endorsements that can be negotiated for with the payment of a charge and the satisfaction of requirements that provide comfort to the title company. For example, one can obtain an endorsement overriding the exclusion relating to violation of usury laws if the mortgage loan fits into an express exemption from the usury statute. If there are special features to the mortgage loan, the validity and priority of the mortgage lien may be insured in light of these features in a special endorsement. Examples of such features include: a floating interest rate, future advances or revolving credit, or shared appreciation (the lender takes some form of an "equity" interest in the project). In addition, there are special endorsements that the lender can obtain from the title insurance company that address the situation where the loan collateral consists of multiple real estate sites in different locations, even different states (such as a "Tie-In Endorsement," "First Loss Endorsement" and "Last Dollar Endorsement"). For details on these three endorsements, see Gurren *Maintaining and Enhancing Title Insurance Coverage*, American Law Institute-American Bar Association continuing Legal Education, ALE-ABA Course of Study, January 12–14, 2006 *in* Real Estate Financing Documentation: Strategies for Changing Times. A lender also will update the title insurance coverage it obtained when it first funded the mortgage loan if the underlying loan is later to be modified, and it will seek in this title update to be assured of the continuing priority of the mortgage lien and the title company's continuing obligation to defend against any title claims.

Of the various issues raised above, the most problematic, in the context of a construction loan, is a mechanic's lien claim. This issue can not be "resolved" at the time the loan documents are signed, or even after the first disbursement. Instead, the issue of mechanic lien claims must be addressed with each disbursement to insure that all moneys paid are applied to work completed up to that point and that lien waivers are obtained for such completed work. This is necessary because without such waivers the real estate will be at risk for mechanic lien claims for work performed with respect to the real estate. Most importantly for lenders, these mechanic lien claims may in some states have priority against the lien of even a prior recorded mortgage and fully disbursed loan. The next section explains how this issue can arise throughout the term of the construction loan, why it is problematic for lenders, and what lenders can do to reduce these risks.

[2] Intervening Liens

Before advancing the mortgage loan funds, the lender will have a title search performed to make sure that no liens are recorded against the property, and will receive a lender's policy from a title insurance company insuring that there are no other liens encumbering the property as of the date of the policy. Any liens that are of record before the mortgage lender has recorded its mortgage will have priority with respect to the allocation of proceeds from any foreclosure or other forced sale of the property. The existence of other liens of record encumbering the mortgaged property is problematic because, if the liens secure too much debt, then the sale proceeds from a forced sale of the property may not be sufficient to pay off the mortgage lender's loan. In general, all or any part of any liens that arise after the mortgage is recorded will be junior in priority to the mortgage (*i.e.*, the senior lender can bring a foreclosure action which will extinguish the junior lien against the mortgaged property). One problematic exception to this under certain states' statutes is what is known as a "mechanic's lien." This is a lien for the payment of work performed by mechanics, subcontractors, trades-people and suppliers, who furnish services and supplies for an improvement on the property, thereby enhancing the property's value. A mechanic's lien claim is problematic for two key reasons. First, if the claim goes unpaid, the property can be sold to satisfy the debt and the lien claim can, in some states, become senior in priority to the mortgage even if the claim is for work contracted for and done, or supplies contracted for and delivered, after the mortgage is recorded. Second, the applicable state statute might permit recovery of interest and attorneys' fees in addition to the claim for work performed.

The next set of cases involves the situation where a mechanic's lien arises after the mortgage is recorded and some or all of the loan proceeds are advanced to the borrower. The cases explore the issue of the validity of the mechanic's lien claim, its priority, and whether the lender is still somehow liable for payment of the mechanic's claims. Lenders typically will fund a construction loan through a construction escrow and will require borrowers to obtain title insurance in favor of the lender that the amount of the construction loan disbursed is prior in right to any mechanic's lien claims. Since the rights of mechanic's lien claimants differ in each state, what the title insurance company will require to issue coverage over these claims will differ as well. In Illinois, for example, a title insurance company typically will require a certificate from the borrower certifying as to which contractors have performed work so far in addition to the borrower's obtaining lien waivers from those contractors for the work they have performed. The contractors submit the lien waivers into an escrow so they will be assured of their payment before they authorize the escrowee to retain the lien waivers. The second major kind of intervening lien occurs when the borrower seeks to extract some of its equity from the property to pay for further improvements to the property through obtaining a second mortgage loan on the property. This important topic is discussed in Chapter 10, *supra*.

[a] The Obligatory-Optional Test

The following cases address how different states handle the issue of mechanic lien claims and the determination of their priority over prior recorded mortgages. We begin by revisiting *National Bank of Washington v. Equity Investors*. *See* § 10.05[1][c], *supra*. The State of Washington follows the majority of states that adhere to a rule that makes critical the distinction between obligatory advances by mortgage lenders, that are protected in priority from intervening liens, including mechanic's lien claims, and optional advances, that are not.

NATIONAL BANK OF WASHINGTON v. EQUITY INVESTORS

506 P.2d 20 (Wash. 1973)

HALE, CHIEF JUSTICE.

Three separate actions consolidated for trial with a fourth added on the appeal were precipitated by the National Bank of Washington's decision to foreclose its security interest in a 220-unit apartment complex construction project called Crestview West, in Federal Way, Washington. The issues now here on appeal come from the details of financing and constructing the project, and involve (1) a materialman's claim of lien against the property for unpaid lumber, (2) the land sellers' claim that the escrow agent breached a fiduciary duty in the closing, (3) the claim of a guarantor that he should in law be released from his guaranty because the lending bank assertedly mismanaged the loan, and also whether the superior court lost jurisdiction over the estate of one of the defendant guarantors whose death occurred after issue joined and whose estate was admitted to probate in Minnesota and given substituted service, and (4) from a different cause and different parts of the same record but joined in this appeal, the propriety of the trial court's fixing of an upset price and its refusal to confirm the foreclosure sale. . . . [Editor's Note: The text of the opinion relating to issues 2 and 4 are omitted; issue 3 was previously covered in our prior use of this case.]

Columbia Wood Products, Inc., vis-a-vis The National Bank of Washington

Columbia Wood Products, Inc., furnished lumber for the apartment house project, commencing deliveries to the site May 26, 1969, and continuing to about August 5, 1969. As earlier noted, it received partial payment, but when construction came to a halt there was still due and unpaid the sum of $119,672 for material sold, delivered and utilized in the nearly completed buildings. The trial court awarded Columbia Wood Products, Inc., a judgment of $119,672.26 on this unpaid bill, with 12% accrued interest from September 5, 1969, in the amount of $28,721.34, and statutory costs. The court decreed, however, that Columbia Wood Products' judgment lien be subordinate and junior to the lien of National Bank of Washington's deed of trust to the extent of all advances made by that bank on its loan for the construction of the apartment house complex. Columbia Wood Products appeals that part of the judgment and decree which rendered its materialman's lien inferior and junior to the bank's total secured loan advanced for the construction.

Columbia Wood Products' lien was declared inferior to the entire amount of the bank's advances on a theory that the National Bank of Washington possessed a prior and superior deed of trust lien in effect before and continuing during the delivery of the lumber. According to the bank's theory, its priority was established as of about May 9, 1969, when Transamerica filed the trust deed of Equity Investors, a limited partnership, naming the National Bank of Washington as beneficiary, securing a promissory note in the amount of $1,850,000 — all in accordance with a construction loan agreement of May 7, 1969, between the National Bank of Washington as lender and Equity Investors as borrower. As work on the project progressed, the bank advanced the funds. On May 8, 1969, the bank delivered in escrow $211,000 to Transamerica Title Insurance Company for disbursement according to the bank's escrow instructions and as agreed upon by Equity Investors and the Macdonald group. Under the various agreements, the bank paid out the loan funds in segments or advances as the construction progressed until it had reached a total loan of $1,742,678.63, nearly the agreed maximum.

Columbia Wood Products began deliveries of lumber to the project on May 26, 1969, and continued supplying material until August 5, 1969, but with the last delivery there was, as earlier noted, still due and unpaid on the lumber bill some $119,672. Its claim of a lien superior in part to that of the National Bank of Washington is based on the contention that the advances made by the bank under the construction loan agreement as the work progressed were optional advances and could not have been legally enforced against the bank.

The issue, we think, is appropriately stated by respondent bank in its brief, as follows:

> "The issue raised on appeal by Columbia Wood Products, Inc. is whether or not the loan advances made by respondents National Bank of Washington and General Mortgage Investments (referred to herein as 'respondents' or 'lenders') to the borrower, Equity Investors, were entitled to priority as against appellant's materialman's lien claim. Appellant contends that respondents' loan advances were optional and not obligatory and that the advances were entitled to priority only as of the date on which they were made. Respondents contend, and the trial court ruled, that the advances were obligatory under the Construction Loan Agreement between respondents and Equity Investors and that the advances were entitled to priority as of the recording date of the Deed of Trust from Equity Investors to respondents."

Were the advances as made by the National Bank of Washington optional? Or, could the bank have been compelled by the courts to make them? If they were optional, then under the principles adopted by this court, Columbia Wood Products' lien for lumber delivered and utilized in the apartment house project should be superior to that of the bank's deed of trust insofar as advances made subsequent to the materialman's perfected lien are concerned. If the bank, however, under the construction loan agreement could have been compelled in the courts to advance the moneys on the loan, then its lien is totally superior and prior to that of Columbia Wood Products.

We think that Columbia Wood Product's contention is sound and that for the purpose of determining lien priorities the advances were in law optional. In the construction loan agreement, the bank made such explicit reservations for the disbursement of the loan as, in our judgment, render the advances of $1,750,000 optional and not obligatory at law. Although such reservation of discretionary authority appears to be a sound banking practice and designed to protect the financial interests of the party to the project which would wind up with the greater sum of money in it, these protective reservations operated, in law, we think, to subordinate the bank's lien for undelivered advances to those of the materialmen and workmen whose work, services and materials went into the project to enhance the bank's security. It has, we realize, long been the rule in this jurisdiction that a mortgage to secure future advances takes priority over mechanics' and materialmen's liens accruing after recordation of the mortgage (*Home Savings & Loan*

Ass'n v. Burton, 20 Wash. 688, 56 P. 940 (1899)), but there is a well-established corollary to the rule that, if under the contract the advances are optional and not obligatory, then the lien priority for the advances is determined as of the time the advances are actually made.

What made the advances optional in law rather than obligatory? The very terms of the construction loan agreement gave the bank discretion as to which of the subcontractor materialmen would be paid from the advances. The construction loan agreement contained a promise to lend Equity Investors the $1,750,000 "upon the terms and conditions set forth below." This agreement provided that, after deducting all fees, charges and expenses agreed to by the borrower, the remaining proceeds of the loan would be credited to the borrower's construction loan account in the lending bank. Thus, the advances were not to be delivered over to the borrower but would remain on deposit in the lending bank as the contract stated to "finance the construction of apartment buildings on property described in the Deed of Trust."

The construction loan agreement specified that, prior to the first advance of construction funds, the bank was to be supplied with a current appraisal satisfactory to it; that all loan funds must be used for payment of material and labor; and that the loan proceeds were to be assigned by the borrower to the bank for that purpose. The borrower, according to this agreement, had to retain an architect satisfactory to the bank, and this approved architect had to supply the bank with periodic progress of construction reports, and before each advance of loaned money certify that satisfactory progress had been made and in the future would be made in keeping with the remainder of the unexpended loan.

The construction loan agreement left the loan moneys largely under the control and dominion of the bank, "to be advanced at such times and in such amounts as the Lender shall determine." It provided, too, that "No advance shall be due unless, in the judgment of the Lender" all work for which the advance had been made had been done in a good and workmanlike manner, and unless the construction be approved by the architect. The lender, at his option, could advance and pay the loan installments before they became due, if he deemed it advisable to do so-but all such advances were to be treated as a performance of the agreement and not a modification of it. Also, according to the construction loan agreement, the lender was not obligated to disburse more than 90% of the loan until the construction was completed and the property free of liens and claims of all kinds except the lender's lien.

There were other provisions in the construction loan agreement, giving control over the funds to the bank, including:

> "If the construction of said building be at any time discontinued or not carried on with sufficient dispatch in the judgment of the Lender to protect the building from depredation or the weather, said Lender may purchase materials and employ workmen to protect the building so that the same will not suffer from depredation or the weather, or to complete said building, so that it may be used for the purposes for which it was designed under the said plans and specifications."

Accordingly, the disbursements of funds by the bank under an agreement placing discretionary controls in the lender over the disbursement of the loan funds with an additional reservation that the loan is "to be advanced at such times and in such amounts as the Lender shall determine," we think left so wide an area of discretion in the bank as to render the amounts to be advanced and the intervals of their advancing optional rather than compulsory as a matter of law. Had the borrowers sought a decree to overcome these reservations and to compel the advances, or to override the bank's discretionary power to advance or withhold the loan funds, they would have met with nearly insuperable obstacles at law. So broad and yet so specific were the bank's discretionary powers under the contract as to the times and amounts of the advances, a court could not properly override such discretion without abrogating the contract.

Although in a given case there may be difficulty in ascertaining from the circumstances and the language of the mortgage and loan papers covering the whole agreement whether the advances are to be regarded as optional or mandatory, we think that the contractual reservations giving the lender the broad discretion of deciding when and in what amounts, or if at all, he must advance the money render the advances optional rather than obligatory where the purpose is to decide construction lien priorities arising after the initial filing for record of the lender's security documents. As a means of protecting its security, the lender retained broad discretionary powers to determine under what circumstances it would advance the money, to withhold the advances any time that it believed its security in jeopardy or doubted the sufficiency or quality of the construction work or felt that an impending insolvency on the borrower's part would threaten the completion of the project or repayment of the loan. There was no hard and fast commitment to deliver the loan money over to the borrower at a given and stated time, nor to advance the money at more or less fixed intervals and in stated amounts. The lender, in reserving such broad protective discretion, thereby rendered the advances optional rather than obligatory for the purpose of determining the priority of liens.

Thus, we are adhering to what we perceive to be the weight of authority embodied in the rule that, where the advances of promised loan moneys are, under an agreement to lend money, largely optional, that is, where the time and the amount of the moneys to be advanced are largely discretionary in the lender, the legal effect of such provisions is to bring the transaction under the rule for optional advances rather than the rule governing mandatory advances for the purpose of determining lien priorities. Optional advances under a construction loan agreement attach when the advances are actually made. Any liens attaching prior to an optional advance would thus be superior to it, and attaching afterwards, junior to it. *Elmendorf-Anthony Co. v. Dunn*, 10 Wash.2d 29, 116 P.2d 253 (1941); *Kimmel v. Batty*, 168 Colo. 431, 451 P.2d 751 (1969); *Peterson v. John J. Reilly, Inc.*, 105 N.H. 340, 200 A.2d 21 (1964); *Lyman Lamb Co. v. Union Bank of Benton*, 237 Ark. 629, 374 S.W.2d 820 (1964).

A contrary rule on that point would allow a lender, having power to allocate the loan moneys in such a way as to insure that those whose work, materials and efforts serve to enhance the value of the security, to sit idly by and watch his security grow, while at the same time potentially leaving the materialmen, subcontractors and workmen in the position of doing their work and supplying materials for little or nothing. The rule here contended for by lender would lead to an inevitable unjust enrichment, enabling the lender to withhold or apply the loan money as he saw fit, all the while knowing that putative lien claimants were furnishing valuable materials and doing valuable work to the enhancement of his security. The bank here had the option of withholding its advances on the loan from the borrower, and the right to apply the money to the account of Columbia Wood Products in payment of the lumber that company was delivering to the construction project.

The rule of optional loan advances for the resolution of construction and security and lien priorities has classic application here, and we would, therefore, apply the principles of *Elmendorf-Anthony Co. v. Dunn, supra.*

This court referred to *Elmendorf* and adhered to this rule in *Cedar v. W.E. Roche Fruit Co.*, 16 Wash.2d 652, 134 P.2d 437 (1943). In *Cedar*, we affirmed the principle of optional advances, but found it inapplicable to a contract to finance and make future advances to be expended in planting, growing and harvesting a fruit crop. In that case, while recognizing the distinction between obligatory and optional advances, we held the advances promised were not, under the agreement, optional but rather were obligatory. In the instant case, however, the lending bank's duty to make the advances was dependent to such a degree upon so many conditions, the occurrence of which lay within its judgment, that it had the option throughout the construction either to pay the materialmen, mechanics and subcontractors from the loan funds or to retain the loan funds within its control, or to deliver the loan funds over to the borrower. The advances being thus optional, they became subject to intervening liens accruing with the lender's knowledge and acquiescence. *Elmendorf-Anthony Co. v. Dunn, supra; Cedar v. W.E. Roche Fruit Co., supra. Accord: Keltch, Inc. v. Hoyt, Inc.*, 4 Wash.App. 580, 483 P.2d 135 (1971). See also, in support of this principle, *Home Savings & Loan Ass'n v. Sullivan*, 140 Okl. 300, 284 P. 30 (1929), and *Akron Savings & Loan Co. v. Ronson Homes, Inc.*, 15 Ohio St.2d 6, 238 N.E.2d 760, 80 A.L.R.2d 179 (1968).

Accordingly, the judgment and decree of the trial court on the claim of Columbia Wood Products, Inc. is reversed.

[b] Questions Regarding *National Bank of Washington*

1. What is the significance of the characterization of the advances as obligatory or optional?

2. Would a court find that the advances of the loan under the Loan Agreement in the Document Book should be deemed obligatory or optional? *See* §§ 4.3, 5.1(aa) and (ab), 5.2, 5.3, 7.9 and 10.1 of the Loan Agreement. Consider the case which follows as well in answering this question and in determining the significance (or lack thereof) of this issue in Illinois.

3. One fact that does not appear in the excerpted version of the case is that there was also a purchase money mortgage that was subordinate to the construction loan mortgage held by National Bank of Washington. The seller of the land on which the apartment complex was to be built agreed to take part of the purchase price in the form of a note and mortgage on the land, but the seller also agreed to subordinate its purchase money mortgage to any construction loan. This fact led to a circular priority problem, because the purchase money mortgage was subordinate to the construction loan but the mechanic's lien claim was subordinate to the purchase money mortgage because the purchase money mortgage was "advanced" (by the seller's agreeing not to receive the entire purchase price) long before the mechanic's lien priority date. How should a court

allocate the proceeds of a foreclosure sale in such circumstances?

4. Although the case does not make this clear, the purpose behind the "obligatory versus optional advance" rule is an attempt to accomplish two different goals. One goal is to protect mortgage lenders by according priority to any obligatory future advances made by them under a previously recorded mortgage loan. The second goal is to enable borrowers to find other mortgage lenders who would be willing to loan to them in the event that the holder of the prior mortgage lien elects not to make any further advances. The concern that created the "obligatory versus optional advance" rule was that the holder of the first recorded mortgage lien would elect not to make future advances under that loan and the borrower would be unable to obtain such desired funds from another lender because the second lender would fear that any advance it made will be junior in right to potential future advances under the prior recorded mortgage loan. By making optional advances under the prior recorded mortgage lose priority to an intervening lien, it was hoped that the borrower would be more likely to be able to obtain the funds, secured by the borrower's untapped equity in the mortgaged property, from a second mortgage lender. *See* Nelson & Whitman, *Rethinking Future Advance Mortgages: a Brief for the Restatement Approach*, 44 Duke L.J. 657 (1995).

It is important to keep these goals in mind in evaluating whether this rule makes sense, or whether it should be replaced or modified, and how best to apply this rule to various fact patterns. For example, if the lender is obligated to make future advances but only if certain conditions outside of the lender's control are met, is the loan "obligatory"? What if the borrower defaults, and now the lender is no longer "obligated" to make future advances; if the lender elects to make future advances anyway are such future advances "optional" such that they lose their priority to any intervening liens? The Uniform Land Security Interest Act provides useful clarification on both of these questions and would make future advances by the first mortgage lender in both of those situations retain their priority (although the ULSIA does not provide comfort on the issue of loss of priority if the first mortgage lender reserves too much discretion or control). Nelson and Whitman argue that the obligatory/optional advance rule fails to adequately advance the second goal and that the approach taken by the ULSIA focuses solely on the first mortgage lender's goal while failing to address the second goal of the obligatory/optional advance rule. Nelson and Whitman offer, as a better alternative in the context of an open-ended loan (not a construction loan), a "cut off notice" that the borrower can send to the first mortgage lender indicating that the borrower will irrevocably agree not to draw down any more funds on the prior recorded mortgage in order to free up the borrower's ability to obtain a loan from a second mortgage lender; after the borrower gives the "cut off notice" (usually by recording it), the first mortgage lender will then only have priority for the advances made prior to the cutoff notice. This approach has been adopted by some states in place of the obligatory/optional advance distinction with some exceptions as necessary to protect the first mortgage lender's legitimate interests (such as construction loans, where the borrower does not have any equity on which it can secure junior financing, or when the lender has duties to third parties and the mortgage secures the borrower's obligation to reimburse the lender's performance of those duties). What do you think about the Nelson and Whitman critique of the obligatory/optional advance rule and as an alternative the cut off notice rule?

[c] Other Remedies for Lien Claimants (An "Unjust Enrichment" Claim)

IRWIN CONCRETE, INC. v. SUN COAST PROPERTIES, INC.

653 P.2d 1331 (Wash. Ct. App. 1982)

WORSWICK, JUDGE.

This litigation arose out of an unfortunate but familiar occurrence: a grand plan for real estate development gone awry.

In 1972, Olympic Mall Co. borrowed $350,000 from Continental, Inc., to purchase and develop 179 acres of land near Gig Harbor. A deed of trust secured the note. In April 1973, Olympic conveyed 7 of the 179 acres to Sun Coast Properties, Inc., to build a shopping center. The sale contract required Olympic to install a water system on its remaining 172 acres to provide water for the center. The water system was also intended to service additional development on the remaining property. Sun Coast then borrowed $1.5 million from Continental for completion of the center. In October 1973, Sun Coast sold the center site to Gig Harbor Properties, Inc., but continued active in construction of the center. Two months later, Sun Coast, Continental, and Traveler's Insurance Co. entered into an agreement whereby Traveler's agreed to pay off Continental's construction loan and make a permanent loan to Sun Coast for $1.5 million upon completion of the center and Sun Coast agreed to prosecute completion of the center diligently.

By April 1974, Olympic was in default on its $350,000 loan from Continental and Continental notified the trustee of default. In September 1974, Continental gave notice of the trustee's sale of the 172 acres to all whose liens were then of record. While these foreclosure proceedings were in progress, Sun Coast, through its president, Michael Fizzolio, continued to let subcontracts for completion of the water system on the 172 acres. In December 1974, Irwin Concrete, Inc., began work pursuant to a contract with Fizzolio and on January 7, 1975 Fox Automatic Sprinkler Systems, Inc., started work under a contract with Sun Coast Water Co., a corporation formed by Sun Coast Properties to complete the water system. David Davis performed work for Fox pursuant to an oral contract. All work pursuant to these contracts was done on various phases of the water system installed on the 172 acres.

At the trustee sale on January 24, 1975, Continental bid in and bought Olympic's interest in the 172 acres. Four days later the shopping center was finished and Traveler's paid off Continental's $1.5 million construction loan. In February 1975, Irwin, Fox, and Davis filed liens on all the land. A fourth claimant, Hernando Chaves and Associates, engineered the water system, working first for Olympic and later for Sun Coast. Chaves filed a lien on all the land on December 5, 1974. The fifth claimant, Active Construction, worked on the water system early in 1974 at the instance of Olympic.

By summary judgment, the trial court dismissed all liens but, after trial, awarded judgment in varying amounts in favor of all five claimants against Continental. Continental appeals. The claimants[1] cross-appeal dismissal of their liens. Primarily at issue is whether the trial court erred in awarding judgment against Continental based on unjust enrichment, in dismissing the liens, in denying pre-judgment interest and in dismissing Chaves' promissory estoppel claim. Other satellite issues are also raised. We find no error and affirm.

Unjust Enrichment

Although the liens were dismissed, the trial court nevertheless allowed a recovery to all claimants on the theory of unjust enrichment. Continental assigns error to this arguing that it did not request any work,that whatever specific benefit it might have received from completion of the shopping center was not proved and that the water system on which claimants worked operates at a loss and therefore constitutes no benefit. We disagree.

Under the doctrine of unjust enrichment, one who receives a benefit must pay for it only if the circumstances of its receipt or retention make it unjust for him to keep the benefit without paying. *Chandler v. Washington Toll Bridge Auth.*, 17 Wash.2d 591, 137 P.2d 97 (1943). A benefit includes any form of advantage. *Chandler*, 17 Wash.2d at 603, 137 P.2d 97. The trial court found that the claimant's work on the water system helped complete the shopping center thereby enabling Continental to close out its $1.5 million construction loan to Sun Coast, and also that the water system increased the value of the 172 acres Continental now owns.[2] These findings are supported by substantial evidence and will not be disturbed on appeal. *Hudson House, Inc. v. Rozman*, 82 Wash.2d 178, 509 P.2d 992 (1973). Plainly, Continental received a substantial benefit because of the work. Would it be unjust to allow Continental to retain this benefit without paying? The trial court concluded it would be and we agree.

The trial court found that the claimants completed the water system at the urging and with consent of Continental, and that Continental knew about and silently acquiesced in the work when it was foreclosing its deed of trust. Substantial evidence also supports these findings. The record discloses, inter alia, that early in 1974, Continental told Chaves that he had to continue his work in order to receive loan funds. In February 1974, Walt Smith of Active Construction Co. worked on the 172 acres. Before Smith started work, David Ballaine of Continental told him that loan funds from Continental to pay for Smith's work were secure. Late in 1974, Continental knew that Chaves was still certifying work by subcontractors. Continental knew that Irwin, Fox and Davis were working on the water system because Chaves certified their completed work. We conclude that under these circumstances it would be unjust for Continental to receive the benefit of the claimants' work without paying.

---

[1] Active did not appeal and did not respond to Continental's appeal.

[2] Continental's argument that the system now operates at a loss begs the question. Continental does not come to grips with the trial court's conclusion that the value of the land is enhanced by a water system.

Damages

Continental asserts that the trial court erred in awarding damages measured by contract prices, arguing that the correct measure is the value conferred. The argument is correct as far as it goes but that is not far enough, because it simply does not follow that a contract price cannot represent that value. A claim for unjust enrichment is a quasi-contractual claim. *Bill v. Gattavara*, 34 Wash.2d 645, 209 P.2d 457 (1949). Quantum meruit — "a reasonable amount for the work done" — is the measure of recovery. *Heaton v. Imus*, 93 Wash.2d 249, 252–53, 608 P.2d 631 (1980). The only evidence presented was that of the various contract prices. It was not error, therefore, for the trial court to conclude, as it did, that the contract prices represented the value of the work in making a quantum meruit award. *See Losli v. Foster*, 37 Wash.2d 220, 222 P.2d 824 (1950).

Liens

Irwin, Fox, Davis and Chaves cross-appeal from a summary judgment dismissing their liens. At the threshold of our discussion we emphasize the obvious distinction between a lien, which provides security for a claim, and the underlying claim itself. *See* RCW 60.04.180. This is necessary because the claimants, in advancing their contentions, appear to confuse these concepts. The trial court's ultimate judgment was based on the underlying claims.

I

The 172 Acres

The lien claims in question were filed under the provisions of RCW 60.04.010, which authorizes a mechanic's lien for work performed ". . . at the instance of the owner of the property . . . or his agent; . . ." RCW 60.04.030 allows a lien "to the extent of the interest of the . . . company, who in . . . its own behalf, or who, through any of the persons designated in RCW 60.04.010 to be agent of the owner . . . caused the performance of the labor. . . ." The agents so designated by RCW 60.04.010 are ". . . every registered or licensed contractor, registered or licensed subcontractor, architect, or person having charge of the construction. . . ." Continental never caused the performance of any labor by Irwin, Fox or Davis. Chaves seems to suggest that Continental caused him to perform work but, except for the estoppel claim discussed below, Chaves claims no lien on Continental's interest.[3] The deed of trust foreclosure operated to deprive Olympic of any interest in the land (*see* RCW 61.24.030(6)(i)) and, to the extent that Olympic or its agents requested the work, also operated to extinguish the liens. *See W.T. Watts, Inc. v. Sherrer*, 89 Wash.2d 245, 571 P.2d 203 (1977).[4]

However, Irwin, Fox and Davis assert that a fact question existed which required denial of the summary judgment. They argue that Fizzolio could have been found to be the agent of Continental and thus, under the lien statute, the liens could have attached to Continental's interest in the property. We disagree. The

[3] Thus, we do not discuss the question of whether a security interest is lienable.

[4] No contention is made here that a surplus was created at the sale which might have been subject to the liens. *See* RCW 61.24.080(3).

summary judgment record is devoid of any facts which would support the conclusion that Fizzolio was ever Continental's agent for any purpose.

II

Chaves Claim of Priority

Chaves contends that his lien was not foreclosed by the trustee sale because it was senior to that of Continental.[5] He argues that the loan agreement between Continental and Olympic made advances optional with Continental; thus, he claims, to the extent of monies advanced after he started work, his lien claim was senior, citing *National Bank of Washington v. Equity Investors*, 81 Wash.2d 886, 506 P.2d 20 (1973). We disagree.

Chaves cites *Equity Investors* for the correct proposition but he does not come within it. In *Equity Investors*, the court restated the Washington rule that a mortgage to secure future advances takes priority over mechanic's liens accruing after recording of the mortgage, unless the future advances are optional. Where the advances are optional, priority is determined when the advances are made.[6] *Equity Investors*, 81 Wash.2d at 897, 506 P.2d 20. The court found that the bank's advances to Equity Investors were optional, because the bank had discretion whether to disburse funds or not, and could not have been compelled by court decree to advance any money. The court came to this conclusion based on language in the contract which stated that money would be advanced to Equity Investors, "'. . . at such times and in such amounts as the Lender shall determine." . . .

Unlike *Equity Investors*, the contract between Continental and Olympic did not allow Continental to disburse funds based on its own criteria. Subsection (2)(c) of the contract stated:

> The remaining $80,000 shall be disbursed after said lease to a national retail grocery chain has been secured and approved by Continental, for the purpose of site developments, plans for which shall be approved by Continental, and disbursements for which shall be made monthly against actual development costs, based on cost verification as site preparation progresses. Disbursements hereunder shall be subject to approval of Continental.

Disbursements were subject to Continental's approval. However, Continental was not free to advance or retain the money as it saw fit. The quoted language specifies the conditions under which Continental could approve or disapprove of disbursements: "disbursements for which shall be made monthly against actual development costs, based on cost verification as site preparation progresses." Continental's control over disbursements was limited to verifying each advance requested for the

---

[5] His related argument that he was entitled to notice of the sale is clearly without merit. At the time of the sale he had not recorded a lien claim. RCW 61.24.040(1)(b). His case citations are inapposite.

[6] In 1973, the Legislature changed the priority rules for interim or construction financing by adding the following section to the mechanic's lien chapter: Except as provided in RCW 60.04.050 or in RCW 60.04.200 through 60.04.220 any mortgage or deed of trust shall be prior to all liens, mortgages, deeds of trust and other encumbrances which have not been recorded prior to the recording of such mortgage or deed of trust to the extent of all sums secured by such mortgage or deed of trust regardless of when the same are disbursed or whether such disbursements are obligatory. RCW 60.04.220.

cost of work completed on the land. If the amount requested of Continental was verified, Continental had no option, but was required to disburse the money. Continental was obligated to loan $350,000 to Olympic. The only control Continental had over future advances was the ability to see that Olympic spent the loan money for improvements to the land. That control did not render the future advances optional.

Because Continental's advances were mandatory, its deed of trust securing the future advances was perfected on June 9, 1972, the date of filing. Chaves' mechanic's lien arose on June 16, 1972, the date he commenced work, and consequently was junior to the deed of trust.

III

Removal of Improvements

Irwin, Fox and Davis contend that because the trial court dismissed their liens on the 172 acres, it was required under RCW 60.04.170 to order the sale and removal of the improvements they placed on the land. This contention is incorrect. RCW 60.04.170 permits but does not require the court to order the sale and removal of improvements when the underlying land cannot be subjected to a lien. Before the court may order the removal, however, the claimants must prove that the improvements are removable without injury to the freehold. *Pioneer Sand & Gravel Co. v. Hedlund*, 178 Wash. 273, 277, 34 P.2d 878 (1934). The improvements in this case involved concrete holding tanks for water, and underground water pipes. Nothing in the record indicates that these improvements were removable without injury to the land. Claimants failed to sustain their burden.

IV

Lien on Shopping Center

RCW 60.04.010 provides that "Every person performing labor upon . . . any . . . well . . . has a lien *upon the same* for the labor performed. . . ." (Italics ours.) In determining whether a lien exists, the statute will be strictly construed so as not to extend its benefit to those who do not clearly come within its terms. *Dean v. McFarland*, 81 Wn.2d 215, 500 P.2d 1244 (1972). The claimants contend simply that they should have a lien on the shopping center because work they performed on the 172 acres benefited the center. This contention is without merit. RCW 60.04.010 grants a lien only upon the property upon which the work was performed. Washington cases cited by the claimants involved single tracts of land rather than separate tracts owned by different people. At the time of this work, the center was a separate parcel in separate ownership from the land upon which the work was done.

V

. . . .

Pre-Judgment Interest

The claimants contend that pre-judgment interest should have been awarded on their unjust enrichment claim. We disagree. Pre-judgment interest may be recovered only if a claim is liquidated or is for an amount which is determinable by computation with reference to a fixed standard without reliance on opinion or discretion. *Prier v. Refrigeration Eng'r Co.*, 74 Wash.2d 25, 442 P.2d 621 (1968). It is the character of the original claim, rather than the court's ultimate method for awarding damages, that determines whether pre-judgment interest is allowable. *See Prier, supra,* at 33, 442 P.2d 621. Here, the claim and resulting award were based upon quantum meruit. Pre-judgment interest is not allowable in a quantum meruit case. *Modern Builders, Inc. v. Manke,* 27 Wash. App. 86, 615 P.2d 1332 (1980).

Attorney's Fees

RCW 60.04.130 authorizes the trial court to award attorney's fees to the prevailing party in a lien foreclosure action. The trial court awarded attorney's fees to Gig Harbor Properties, Ltd., Western Diversified Equities and Traveler's Insurance Company. We affirm that award. Because Gig Harbor Properties and Traveler's have prevailed on the cross-appeal and have complied with RAP 18.1, they are entitled to attorney's fees here. Therefore, we award attorney's fees for the appeal in the amounts of $1,742.50 to Gig Harbor Properties and $3,600 to Traveler's against cross appellants Irwin, Fox, Davis and Chaves.

Affirmed.

PETRIE and PETRICH, JJ., concur.

[d] Comments and Questions Regarding the *Irwin Concrete* Case

1. Although just dicta, the *Irwin Concrete* case provides guidance on what terms regarding disbursement of the construction loan makes a loan advance "optional" versus "obligatory." Why did the court conclude that Continental's loan terms created an "obligatory" advance such that Chaves' lien on the 172 acre site was extinguished by Continental's foreclosure sale of its prior lien on the 172 acre site?

2. The contractors in *Irwin Concrete* could not maintain a lien on the 7 acre shopping center (let alone a lien prior to a mortgage lender's lien) because the contractors did not do any work on the 7 acre shopping center tract. However, the court still ruled that the owner of the 7 acre shopping center benefitted from the work the contractors did on the 172 acre site and the owner of the shopping center was liable to the contractors to the extent that the contractors' work enhanced the value of the shopping center. Does this make sense to you? Do you agree that the contractors' work on the 172 acres provided value to the owner of the 7 acre shopping center such that the owner should be liable to pay that value to the contractors? Also recall that the contractors could not remove the materials they provided without

damaging the land, another reason why the contractors were able to recover in a cause of action for "unjust enrichment."

3. If contractors can recover the value of their work under the doctrine of unjust enrichment against the owner of the property benefitted by the work, or against a foreclosing lender who takes title at the foreclosure sale to such benefitted property, without a valid mechanic's lien claim, why are mechanic's lien claims important to contractors?

4. In *Irwin Concrete*, if the court had rejected the quantum meruit claim, the contractors would not have been able to recover the value of their work on the 172 acres because the lender's foreclosure of its mortgage lien (due to the "obligatory advance" language of the construction loan agreement) extinguished the contractors' liens which arose after the mortgage was recorded. Would this be the case under Illinois law? The next cases address this issue.

[e] Illinois Lien Claimants

MOULDING-BROWNELL CORPORATION v. DELFOSSE CONST. CO.

26 N.E.2d 709 (Ill. App. Ct. 1940)

BURKE, JUSTICE.

During the early part of 1933 Charles W. Trumbull and Grace Sherwood Trumbull, husband and wife, were the owners of certain real estate located at 2257 Silverton Drive. This property was situated just west of the Illinois Central tracks at the 23rd Street entrance of A Century of Progress. The property was subject to a first mortgage, held by the National Fraternal Society of the Deaf, a corporation. The owners entered into an agreement with the Fridstein Engineering Company for the construction of a restaurant building. After the completion of the building, the property was operated at a loss. In August, 1933, a bill to foreclose certain mechanics' liens upon the real estate and improvements was filed. In October, 1933, a separate bill to foreclose the first mortgage was filed. The cases were consolidated. A decree was entered. On appeal, in the case of *Moulding-Brownell Corp. v. E.C. Delfosse Const. Co.*, 291 Ill. App. 343, 9 N.E.2d 459, this court decided that all the lien claimants had agreed to waive their liens, except John A. Scribbins, surviving partner of Graves & Scribbins, who contracted for and provided the architectural work on the property. The opinion pointed out that the right to a lien by Scribbins was not contested, and the court affirmed that part of the decree which found that he was entitled to a lien for $5,200, together with interest at the rate of 5% per annum from August 29, 1933, for the work which he had done. Accordingly, the decree was affirmed as to the foreclosure of the mortgage and as to the lien of Scribbins, and reversed as to the other lien claimants. When the case was redocketed in the Circuit Court a new decree was entered, which disallowed all of the lien claims except that of Scribbins; found that he had a mechanic's lien for $5,200, and that the plaintiff, mortgagee, had a lien for its mortgage indebtedness of approximately $36,000 and interest. A sale was directed, which resulted in a bid of $40,000. The proceeds of the sale, after deductions for master's fees and other costs in excess of $3,000, being insufficient to satisfy both liens, the cause was re-

referred to a master for the purpose of determining the priorities of the parties in the proceeds of the sale and the proper distribution to be made. Defendant offered testimony before the master to establish the relative value of the land and of the improvements, and to determine the enhancement in value of the property caused by his services. The master determined that three-quarters of the proceeds of the sale was realized from the property as it was before the improvement, and that one-quarter was realized from the enhanced value of the property contributed by the improvement. Defendant testified that his lien was based upon a claim for architectural services, and that his fee was 6% of the construction cost. Accordingly, the master determined that 6% of the enhancement in value of the property was contributed by the services of the defendant, and the remaining 94% was contributed by the other lien claimants. The master also determined that the other lien claimants were paid in the manner they contracted for payment, and that "therefore, payment in such manner has the same effect for the purposes of the pending question as if payment in cash had been made by the equity owner; namely, to enhance the security of the mortgagee." The master found that as to the enhancement in value traceable to the material and services of other claimants, plaintiff, as mortgagee, was entitled to be subrogated, and that the defendant could establish priority only in that portion of the total enhancement in value contributed by his services alone, of 6% of the entire enhancement, which is $600. Defendant Scribbins filed objections to the master's report. He did not object to the finding of the master that "the other lien claimants were paid in the manner they contracted for payment, therefore, payment in such manner has the same effect as if payment in cash had been made by the equity owner, namely, to enhance the security of the mortgagee." An order was entered by the Chancellor that the objections stand as exceptions. The court overruled the exceptions, and on June 15, 1939, entered a supplemental decree. Clauses 4 and 5 read:

> That all of the other lien claimants comprising approximately 94% of the lienable services rendered and materials furnished have been paid in accordance with their contract with Charles W. Trumbull and Grace Sherwood Trumbull, owners of the said real estate; that the claim for lien of John A. Scribbins constitutes 6% of the total improvement and that his service has therefore enhanced the value of the said property in the sum of $600.00; that as to the enhancement of value in the said premises caused by the services rendered and materials furnished of all other contractors and sub-contractors whose claims are, by this decree, found to have been paid in accordance with their contract, the plaintiff, National Fraternal Society of the Deaf, is entitled to be subrogated; and such increase in the value of the property has been caused by the said enhancement caused by the services and materials furnished by all the other contractors and subcontractors, should be held to enhance the security of the National Fraternal Society of the Deaf, a corporation, plaintiff herein, as mortgagee;
>
> That since the total enhancement of the value of the said property is in the sum of $10,000.00, $9,400.00 of the said enhancement became additional security for the payment of the mortgage held by the plaintiff, National Fraternal Society of the Deaf, a corporation; that the balance of $600.00 constitutes the only fund and portion of the proceeds of the foreclosure sale upon which the lien of the said John H. Scribbins, defendant and intervening petitioner, is entitled to priority.

The supplemental decree directed the distribution of the fund. The defendant Scribbins prosecutes this appeal from the supplemental decree. . . .

Both parties emphasize the provisions of § 16 of the Mechanics' Lien Act, § 16, chapter 82, Ill. Rev. Stat. 1939 which reads:

> No incumbrance [*sic.*] upon land, created before or after the making of the contract under the provisions of this act, shall operate upon the building erected, or materials furnished until a lien in favor of the persons having done work or furnished material shall have been satisfied, and upon questions arising between incumbrancers [*sic.*] and lien creditors, all previous encumbrances shall be preferred to the extent of the value of the land at the time of making of the contract, and the lien creditor shall be preferred to the value of the improvements erected on said premises, and the court shall ascertain by jury or otherwise, as the case may require, what proportion of the proceeds of any sale shall be paid to the several parties in interest. All incumbrances [*sic.*], whether by mortgage, judgment or otherwise, charged and shown to be fraudulent, in respect to creditors, may be set aside by the court, and the premises freed and discharged from such fraudulent incumbrance [*sic.*].

As between the parties to the contract, the contract price establishes the value of the improvements. As against the mortgagee and all other third persons, the reasonable value of the improvements must be proven to establish the enhancement. While the lien attaches as of the date of the contract, the priorities as between the lienors and the mortgagee are determined under the provisions of § 16. When the proceeds of the sale are substituted for the land and building, both the mortgagee and the lien claimants are entitled to the same proportionate interest in the proceeds that they had in the property before it was sold. Enhancement is the increase in market value of the property by reason of the improvement covered by the claim for lien at the time of the making of the improvement, and is not affected by the cost of labor or material, the original amount of the claim, or the balance due thereupon. Usually, in a decree the Chancellor divides the proceeds of the sale of property into two funds, over one of which the mortgagees have priority, and over one of which the lienors have priority. These two funds bear the same ratio to each other as do the value of the land and whatever was on it immediately prior to the installation of the improvement and the value of the enhancement created by the improvement under the contract.

Defendant places emphasis on the opinion in *Mitchell v. Robinovitz*, 272 Ill. App. 414. Plaintiff relies on *Clark v. Moore*, 64 Ill. 273; *Croskey v. Northwestern Mfg. Co.*, 48 Ill. 481; and *Southern Illinois Contracting Co. v. Launtz*, 169 Ill. App. 87. The *Clark* case involved a situation somewhat analogous to the case at bar. The court said, 64 Ill. Page 282:

> In the case of *North Presbyterian Church of Chicago v. Jevne*, 32 Ill. 214 [83 Am.Dec. 261], it was held that a prior mortgagee had the first lien on the land as it was unimproved, and the mechanic or material-man had a first lien on the building; and that each should be satisfied out of the fund upon which he had the prior lien; that if either fund was more than sufficient to satisfy the prior lien thereon, and the other was insufficient to pay the prior lien on it, then the latter should be satisfied from the surplus remaining of the other fund. The same rule was adhered to in the cases of

> *Croskey v. Northwestern Mfg. Co.*, 48 Ill. 481, and *Howett v. Selby*, 54 Ill. 151; but where, as in this case, there is a large proportion of the enhanced value of the property produced by the owner paying for labor and material furnished by others than the parties to the suit, the question arises whether the mechanics and material-men shall have it appropriated to the payment of their liens, or shall it be applied to the prior encumbrances, or shall it be treated as a fund in which both may participate pro rata. In such a case, the enhanced value produced by the payment of money by the owner, whilst the work was progressing, should be applied to the satisfaction of the mortgages on the property; and if any portion of the fund thus created shall remain, to be applied to the satisfaction of the liens for labor and materials. It has always been recognized the true rule to hold all improvements placed by the mortgagor on the premises as being embraced in and subject to the mortgage. We can not suppose that they were intended, when made, to be for the benefit of other lien holders. They have their lien on the enhanced value they have given to the property, but have advanced neither money nor materials for which the owner has paid; and the subsequent mortgages may have been given to secure the very money paid by the owner for the labor and materials.

We have carefully considered the arguments of the parties and the cases that have been cited, and are convinced that the purpose of § 16 is to protect the lien claimant to the extent of the increased value of the premises by reason of his improvements. It would be inequitable to allow recovery out of part of the property not benefited by the improvement. In the instant case, had the other contractors not been paid and had the liens in their favor been allowed, the lien of the architect would have been limited in priority to 6% of the total enhancement. The fact that the other contractors have been paid neither aids nor injures him. The priority of his lien must be bottomed on its own strength as a contributor to the enhanced value of the property. The evidence shows that the total enhancement by defendant's services contributed 6%.

Finally, the architect urges that the court should have found that the enhanced value by virtue of the services and material of the lien claimants was from $15,000 to $19,300, instead of $10,000, which he did find. After an examination of the testimony of the experts, we are of the opinion that the court was right in deciding that three-quarters of the sale price, or $30,000, represented that portion of the proceeds realized from the original value of the property, and that one-quarter, or $10,000, represented that portion of the proceeds realized from the enhancement of the value of the property, resulting from the improvement.

We are of the opinion that the formula adopted by the Chancellor for the apportionment of the fund between the mortgagee and the architect was in accordance with the law. Therefore, the decree of the Circuit Court of Cook County is affirmed.

Decree affirmed.

Denis E. Sullivan, P.J., and Hebel, J., concur.

[f] Comments and Questions Regarding *Moulding-Brownell*

1. Does it matter in Illinois whether an advance under a loan secured by a real estate mortgage is obligatory or optional in relation to liens created by contractors for work performed with respect to the real estate? Under what circumstances under Illinois law does a contractor's lien have priority over a fully funded and previously recorded mortgage lien?

2. If doing a title search and promptly recording and funding the mortgage loan does not guarantee lien priority to a mortgage lender against a mechanic's lien claim, what other steps can the lender take to reduce the chances of a mechanic's lien claim taking priority over the lender's mortgage lien? One common technique to prevent mechanic lien claims is to condition funding of the construction loan on obtaining lien waivers from all contractors who performed work and were seeking payment on such work. The owner is required to submit a list of all contractors who had performed work or provided materials; the owner is also required to obtain lien waivers from these contractors and suppliers, and an escrow is set up with the title company to hold onto the loan disbursement and lien waivers. Once the title company has reviewed these materials and is ready to provide a "date down" endorsement to the loan policy insuring against any mechanic lien claims for the work represented by the affidavits, the title company is then instructed to make payments to the contractors. This seems like a pretty good way to prevent mechanic lien claims from arising, but do you see any potential flaws, especially when the owner is not also related to the entity serving as the general contractor? Review the conditions to funding in the Construction Loan Agreement for the FVACC to see if it adequately took similar steps to reduce the chances that a mechanic lien claim would be raised in that case. Did FMB adequately address the risk of mechanic lien claims?

3. Another approach to addressing the problem of mechanic lien claims in jurisdictions like Illinois that permit lien priority based upon enhancement in value is raised in the *Ridgeview Construction Company*, case below.

[g] Prospective Lien Waivers as Protection for Lenders

RIDGEVIEW CONSTRUCTION COMPANY, INC. v. AMERICAN NATIONAL BANK AND TRUST COMPANY OF CHICAGO

628 N.E.2d 1060 (Ill. App. Ct. 1993)

Presiding Justice Tully delivered the opinion of the court:

The appellants in this case, Ridgeview Construction Co., David E. McDaniel Company, Inc., Jones & Brown Company, Inc., and J.S. Reimer Inc., seek to have their mechanic's liens on a certain building project declared prioritized over the liens of Appellees, Heller Financial (Heller), the mortgagee of the property and

American National Bank & Trust (the Trustee) as trustee of the property under Trust No. 104943-01.

In December 1980, the trustee purchased the parcel of land at issue under the proviso that a warehouse would be built on said property and it provided further that there would be no liens on the property and "no contractor or subcontractor shall have the right to assert any mechanic's liens or materialman's liens against title to the Premises." The sole beneficiary to the trust, Michael Wellek (Wellek), then entered into a general contract with WWI Corporation (WWI) for the construction of a warehouse.

Subsequently, WWI entered into various subcontracts with appellants. The agreement incorporated "all the terms and general conditions" of the contract between Wellek and WWI. This meant that the subcontractors would not be allowed to hold any liens against the property for their work and materials.

This is the second time this case comes before this court on appeal. In the earlier case of *Ridgeview Construction Co., Inc. v. American National Bank* (1990), 205 Ill. App.3d 1045, 150 Ill. Dec. 859, 563 N.E.2d 986, this court held that the lien claimants at issue were entitled to bring forth evidence whether Heller, the mortgagee bank, knew or should have known of the fraudulent collusion between the owner and general contractor. The trial court had noted that Heller made a mortgage loan in the face of one half million dollars of recorded mechanic's liens.

This case was then remanded for "proceedings consistent with this opinion." However, on remand, the trial court held that summary judgment be entered in favor of Heller. The trial court's order granting summary judgment stated:

> "Defendants' said motion for summary judgment in their favor be, and hereby is, granted as required by the decision of the Appellate Court."

According to plaintiffs, this order made clear that they would not be allowed to conduct discovery or proffer evidence on fraud.

In the original case before this court, the owner and general contractor signed a no-lien contract which provided that "no contractor or subcontractor shall have the right to assert any mechanic's lien or materialman's lien against title to the property." Subsequently, the general contractor entered into contracts with the many subcontractor-plaintiffs which incorporated all the terms and provisions of the general contract. After the general contractor, WWI, failed to pay amounts due and owing the subcontractors, they filed a "Complaint in Mechanic's Lien Foreclosure." Defendant trust motioned for summary judgment on the basis the liens were barred by the no-lien clause of the general contract. This motion was granted.

Subsequently, Heller filed a motion against plaintiffs-subcontractors on the grounds that its mortgage took precedence over any subcontractor claims based on the no-lien contract. The subcontractors then filed a motion for partial summary judgment seeking an invalidation of this no-lien clause. The trial court agreed with the subcontractors, finding the no-lien clause to be invalid on its face and in addition, that it amounted to fraud between the general contractor and owner. The court then entered a second order finding that the subcontractor's mechanic's liens took priority over the bank's mortgage lien.

The mortgagee argued that it would be inequitable to allow the subcontractors to claim they did not know what they were signing in their contract with WWI, the general contractor. Although the subcontractors did not claim that the mortgagee was aware of the alleged fraud and collusion between the owner, Wellek and the general contractor, WWI, they argue that Heller was not an innocent purchaser and, therefore, their mortgage should not be given priority over the subcontractors' liens.

The appellate court then reversed the trial court and held that the subcontractors failed to establish that the mortgage holders knew or should have known about the fraudulent actions of the owner and general contractor in 1982:

> "It is impossible for this court to determine what appellants (mortgagees) would have discovered in December 1982 had they made an inquiry into the bases for appellee's (subcontractors) liens. However, we do not find compelling appellee's (subcontractors') claim that appellants were in a better position to discover the alleged fraud." (*Ridgeview*, 205 Ill. App.3d at 1052, 150 Ill. Dec. at 864, 563 N.E.2d at 991.)

After remand of this case, the circuit court vacated the prior summary judgment in favor of plaintiffs and entered summary judgment in favor of defendants. The basic premise of this holding is that: (1) plaintiffs were subject to and aware of the no-lien provision in the contract they signed; and (2) defendants were never aware of the fraud or collusion between the owner and general contractor.

ISSUES

The following issues are presented for review: (1) Whether the trial court on remand properly followed the mandate of the Appellate Court by entering summary judgment in favor of appellees; and (2) Whether on remand, the plaintiffs should have been allowed to seek discovery and bring forth evidence in opposition to Heller's motion for summary judgment.

OPINION

The consideration of this court's prior mandate and the discovery issue are very much intertwined. The court stated:

> "We find, as the court did [in *Richard's Lumber and Supply Co. v. National Bank*] that because appellees (subcontractors) have failed to rebut the presumption of appellants' innocence (Heller and American), that appellants were aware or should have been aware of the fraud, appellants' mortgage should have priority over appellees' mechanics liens." (*Ridgeview*, 205 Ill. App.3d at 1053, 150 Ill. Dec. at 864, 563 N.E.2d at 991.)

This quotation quite clearly supports the actions of the trial court upon remand in vacating the prior summary judgment and entering summary judgment in appellants' favor. Had the appellate court worded its mandate a little clearer there would have been no basis for the instant appeal. It is fairly clear that the appellate court did not remand this case for further discovery. This would have violated the doctrines of estoppel and res judicata since the discovery issue was fully and fairly litigated by the trial court and affirmed on appeal:

> "We find that appellees have failed to establish that appellants knew or should have known of the fraudulent activities of Wellek (owner) and WWI (general contractor)."

This court specifically referred to the case of *Richard's Lumber v. National Bank of Joliet* (1975), 32 Ill. App.3d 835, 336 N.E.2d 820, wherein the court held that where the bank paid money in reliance on lien waivers and where the lienors sought to show the invalidity of the waivers on the grounds of fraud not involving the bank, there was a basic presumption of innocence by the bank absent some indication from the facts that the bank knew about, or should have known about, the employee's fraudulent conduct. Likewise in this case, appellants never overcame the presumption of Heller's and American's innocence as against the subcontractors. There exists a fundamental doctrine in equity that where one of two innocent persons suffers by the fraud of a third person, loss must fall upon him who by his conduct put it in the power of such third person to cause the injury. *See Decatur Lumber Co. v. Crail* (1932), 350 Ill. 319, 183 N.E. 228.

This case is also a case of several innocent parties, one of whom must bear the loss. What is significant to the ruling herein, is that the appellant-subcontractors could have prevented their loss had they thoroughly read the contract between the owner and general contractor, wherein the no-lien provision was clearly set forth.

Based upon the foregoing facts, it is quite apparent the trial court acted properly. The trial court did not grant nor can this court grant, discovery privileges in a case where there is no new evidence, not otherwise discoverable previously. This case demonstrates that subcontractors are held accountable for knowing, absent fraud or deception, the realities and implications of any agreements they sign with a general contractor and must learn to protect themselves from "no-lien" contractual provisions.[20]

For the foregoing reasons this case is affirmed in all respects.

Affirmed.

Rizzi and Greiman, JJ., concur.

[h] Comments and Questions Regarding the *Ridgeview* Case and Mechanic's Lien Claims Generally

1. The *Ridgeview* case involved a situation where the mortgage lender attempted to enforce a "no lien" provision in the contract between the owner and the general contractor, and the term also was incorporated by reference into the contract between the general contractor and the subcontractors. The court ruled to enforce the no lien provision against the subcontractors, but Footnote 20 of the case refers to the following new provision added to the Illinois statute limiting the enforcement of some

[20] It appears as though subcontractors have already tried to protect themselves. The 87th General Assembly has enacted P.A.-361 which amends a number of sections of the Mechanics Lien Act and has added a new provision as Ill. Rev. Stat. ch. 82, par. 1.1 (1991) which provides:

> "1.1 An agreement to waive any right to enforce or claim any lien under this Act where the agreement is in anticipation of and in consideration for the awarding of a contract or subcontract . . . is against public policy and unenforceable."

The subcontractors have apparently lobbied their way out of this interesting predicament. But have they? Section 21 of the Act still allows the waiver of mechanic lien rights as long as "the waiver is not prohibited by this Act." This language was added at the same time Section 1.1 was enacted. Its meaning and interaction with Section 1.1 can be expected to be the subject of another appellate case in the not-too-distant future.

waivers of mechanic lien claims that would apply to future cases: " 1.1 An agreement to waive any right to enforce or claim any lien under this Act where the agreement is in anticipation of and in consideration for the awarding of a contract or subcontract . . . is against public policy and unenforceable." The court noted that the meaning of this limitation is unclear in light of Section 21, which was enacted at the same time as Section 1.1, and which provides for the enforcement of mechanic lien waivers so long as "the waiver is not prohibited by this Act." A mortgage lender friendly interpretation of the Illinois statute, as amended, is that if a subcontractor receives separate consideration for the lien waiver it will be enforced, as contrasted with agreeing to the lien waiver as a condition to receiving the contract. However, there is no case law that has directly addressed whether this interpretation of the provision is accurate. Another way to interpret section 1.1, that contractors and subcontractors would favor, is that only when the waiver is given after the construction contract is entered into, for example in the context of a settlement of a dispute, is the lien waiver effective. The court in *Brown and Kerr, Inc. v. American Stores Properties, Inc.*, 306 Ill. App. 3d 1023, 715 N.E.2d 804 (Ill. App. 1st Dist. 1999), seemed to apply this latter interpretation of Section 1.1. Which interpretation makes more sense to you? One response to the problem of enforcing a prospective lien waiver in Illinois is to obtain a subrogation agreement from the general contractor (subordinating any mechanic's lien claims to the lien of the mortgage), and this agreement is then incorporated in the general contractor's agreement with the subcontractors.

2. The issue of addressing and reducing the risk of exposure for mechanic lien claims is usually a difficult one for lenders and, as the prior cases illustrate, one that involves different rules in different jurisdictions. In a few states (such as Kentucky, Massachusetts, Minnesota, Mississippi, New York, North Dakota, and Utah), it is not as difficult to get insurance coverage over mechanic lien claims. This is because the law in these states is that the mortgage will have priority over mechanic lien claims as to all disbursements of the loan made prior to the filing of any such claims. Thus, in those jurisdictions, all the title company needs to do is to check for recorded mechanic lien claims before each new disbursement of the loan and if none are detected, the company can insure the priority of the disbursement.

The situation is different in many other states, however. In several states (Arizona, Arkansas, California, Idaho, North Carolina, Ohio, Oklahoma, Pennsylvania, Rhode Island, and West Virginia), the law initially provides protection to the mortgage lender, but this protection can be lost. The initial protection arises when the mortgage is filed before the commencement of any visible work on the insured property. This priority may be lost if the lender makes disbursements that it is not obligated to make. Thus, in these states, a title insurer must make an assessment as to whether the loan advances for the insured loan are obligatory or optional before it can provide an endorsement against mechanic lien claims. This is because if the loan advances are optional, priority is now contingent upon whether the lender has knowledge of intervening rights at the date the loan advance is made. In a construction setting, such knowledge will be presumed by a court, because the lender is obviously aware that other creditors are supplying services, materials and labor to improve the real property.

Finally, in other states (such as Alaska, Colorado, Illinois, Indiana, Maine, Missouri, Montana, Oregon, Virginia, and Wyoming), there is no basis under statutes for the priority of the lien of a construction loan over statutory liens for services, labor or materials. In these states, title insurers are usually willing to issue coverage against mechanic lien claims only if certain conditions are met. First they will perform a new title search and check if any mechanic lien claims have been filed. Second, they will require receipt of sworn certificates from the developer and general contractor certifying as to which contractors have performed work and the amounts owed to them up through the date of the requested title coverage. Third, they will require lien waivers from each of the contractors identified with respect to the work identified. Even then, as *Irwin Concrete* illustrated, a lender may still be exposed to liability under an unjust enrichment claim, unless the lender has secured a release of all claims from the contractor.

3. How was the issue of mechanic lien claims handled in the construction loan for the Auto Care Center? *See* §§ 4.2(b), 5.1(aa) and (bb), 5.2, 5.3, 7.9, and 10.1(i) of the Loan Agreement in the Document Book. Did First Mortgage Bank provide adequate protection on this issue?

[3] Lenders' Review of Environmental Matters Relating to the Mortgaged Property

[a] Impact of Environmental Contamination on the Value of the Mortgaged Property

As discussed in Chapter 8, if the mortgaged property is subject to CERCLA liability, its value will be reduced by the amount of the liability, since any owner will be jointly and severally liable for any clean-up costs. Therefore, at the outset, a lender has to be concerned about the impact of CERCLA liability on the value of the security, even if the lender does not have personal liability for the clean-up costs. CERCLA liability could cause the owner of the land to intentionally abandon the land, thereby leaving the lender with the equally unattractive choices of foreclosing on land with known CERCLA liability attaching to any future owner, or abandoning the security of the land and pursuing its borrower personally. In order to sell the land, the lender will be forced to clean up any hazardous waste and sue responsible parties for the clean-up costs. With the cleaned-up property, the lender may still face problems because of the stigma attached to the property. Many potential purchasers will know of the problems with the land and may look elsewhere to buy. To address this potential problem, mortgage lenders will require an environmental review of the site be undertaken prior to the lenders' funding of the loan in order to assess the likelihood of an environmental problem with the property. The lender may elect not to make the loan to the borrower if the environmental review reflects significant problems. As will be discussed in more detail, an adequate environmental review is also essential for the lender as a defense in the event that the government attempts to hold the lender personally liable for any clean-up costs relating to the mortgaged property (such potential personal liability is discussed in the next section). In addition, as further protection, a lender will require that a developer make specific warranties and agreements to indemnify the lender for any losses the lender may suffer due to a violation of state or federal environmental laws or claims by private third parties relating to environmental contamination.

[b] Lender Liability for Others' Use or Disposal of Toxic Substances as an Owner or an Operator

As it was originally drafted, CERCLA arguably imposed personal liability on a lender that engaged in certain actions (or, according to some courts [*see United States v. Fleet Factors Corporation*, 901 F.2d 1550 (11th Cir. 1990), *cert. denied*, 498 U.S. 1046 (1991)], merely had the power to take those actions) related to the ownership or operation of a facility that secured its loan. In response to the concern of lenders, the EPA, in an action that is at the center of *Kelley v. Tiscornia*, the case below, promulgated rules that took the position that in most situations, a lender would not be liable under CERCLA. In the appeal from *Kelley* [*Kelley v. EPA*, 15 F.3d 1100 (D.C. Cir. 1994)], the D.C. Circuit held that the EPA's rules were invalid because the rules were substantive and therefore exceeded the EPA's rule making authority. Congress responded by amending CERCLA to include the substance of most of the EPA's rules.

The amendments to CERCLA in 42 U.S.C. § 9601(20)(E&F) make it clear that those who hold indicia of ownership primarily to protect a security interest are exempted from liability. The statutory scheme to a great degree codifies the lender liability rule as it is presented in the *Kelley* case below. The statute now reads so that the holder of the interest can foreclose, sell, re-lease and the like without losing the exemption if certain conditions are met.

In order to maintain this exemption, the lender must not participate in management of the facility. The statute allows the lender to have some influence over the borrower in how the borrower goes about managing the facility, but the lender cannot exercise decision-making control over the environmental compliance or control at the level of a manager of the facility.

As you read *Kelley*, consider what potential CERCLA liability means to a lender and its significance in any loan agreement the lender will enter into with a developer. Following the case is an article that may help you to resolve some of the issues.

KELLEY v. TISCORNIA

810 F. Supp. 901 (W.D. Mich. 1993)

HON. DAVID W. MCKEAGUE

This action is brought pursuant to the Comprehensive Environmental Response, Compensation, and Liability Act ("CERCLA"), 42 U.S.C. § 9601. . . . The State is seeking compensations for expenses it incurred cleaning up two sites: the Auto Specialties Manufacturing Company ("AUSCO") facility located in St. Joseph, Michigan (the "St. Joseph Facility") and the facility located in Benton Harbor, Michigan (the "Riverside Facility"). Counts I and II of the complaint seek relief under CERCLA and allege that Manufacturers National Bank of Detroit ("MNB" or the "Bank") operated the sites during times when hazardous substances were released. Counts III and IV are deleted.

This matter is before the Court on cross-motions for summary judgment. Plaintiffs move for partial summary judgment as to the liability of defendant MNB. MNB also moves for summary judgment. The Court has reviewed the pleadings and exhibits, heard oral argument on October 26, 1992, and now finds the matter ready for disposition.

FACTS

The commercial relationship between the Bank and AUSCO began in 1964. MNB president, Roland Mewhort, was a member of AUSCO's board from 1964 through 1978. Lester Tiscornia placed him on the board after he seized control of AUSCO, a feat Tiscornia accomplished with the financial assistance MNB provided during a family fight for control of the company. After Mewhort died, Jim Bunker, Senior Vice President at Manufacturers National Corporation, took a seat and served on the board until 1986. The Board of Directors met once or twice a year and dealt primarily with pension and capital spending issues. The executive committee, which was comprised of inside directors and the plant operating staff, met more frequently and decided daily operational matters.

During this time, the Bank assigned two account officers, J.F. VanProoyer and Hugh Porter, to AUSCO. They kept the Bank's loan committee apprised of AUSCO's status. The communication from AUSCO to the Bank is reflected in various memoranda which have been provided to the Court. The Bank memoranda for AUSCO in the 1979–1985 era describe the operations of the St. Joseph foundry operations (Exhibit 379), criticize AUSCO's other lender, the Harris Bank, and discuss strategies to force Harris to share the risk or bow out (Exhibit S-2), show the Bank knew of labor disputes and the terms under review in the labor negotiation process (Exhibits 382–384), and discuss AUSCO's default on its loan covenants (Exhibit 385).

In September of 1985, the issue of new financing arose. AUSCO presented a consolidation plan to the Bank during discussions of financing. The Bank opted to continue financing AUSCO and executed two loan agreements on September 15, 1985. A revolving line of credit and a liquidation facilities note were executed. The Bank included various provisions to enable it to monitor the finances of AUSCO. The agreement required daily reporting, prohibited outside financing, banned dividends and created a blanket lien on all machinery and equipment. The daily reporting mechanism, used in asset-based lending, authorized the Bank to monitor the cash proceeds from receivables against the outstanding loan on a daily basis.

In early 1986, Bank officers met with AUSCO officers on a more frequent basis to monitor AUSCO's adherence to the consolidation plan that came into existence during loan negotiations. David Day, an MNB employee, participated in monthly meetings with AUSCO. He expressed concerns as to the ability of the management at AUSCO to make the manpower reductions laid out in the consolidation plan. He also expressed concern because AUSCO failed to meet anticipated reductions in utility costs, maintenance costs, overhead costs, inventory, and shipping and freight costs, all of which were monitored by the Bank. On August 6, 1986, David Day and Hugh Porter met with James Tiscornia, head of operations at AUSCO, to discuss these concerns. The Bank's position at the meeting was that if it were to remain involved in financing, certain changes had to be made. First, Lester

Tiscornia should be dropped from the payroll. Second, a turnaround specialist was needed to replace James Tiscornia. The Bank recommended Benjamin Sachs, as well as another candidate, and indicated to James Tiscornia that Loren Gerber, Chief Financial Officer at AUSCO, was not acceptable to the Bank for this position.

AUSCO hired Sachs in September of 1986. Edward and Lester Tiscornia contacted the Bank during their negotiation with Sachs to question the Bank about whether they had to accept Sachs' terms. Embree, a Bank representative, informed the Tiscornias that if outside management were not retained by AUSCO, the Bank would not continue to lend money to the company. The Tiscornias then requested that a $500,000 bonus provision for Sachs be financed by the Bank. Embree rejected the request. The parties eventually agreed to an incentification bonus, structured to provide compensation to Sachs based on his ability to reduce the debt owed to the Bank. The Bank financed this arrangement. Further, the Bank set the same date for termination on advances to AUSCO under the revolving line of credit as the expiration date of Sachs'contract.

As President and Chief Executive Officer of AUSCO, Sachs had responsibility for the day-to-day operations at AUSCO. In the winter of 1986–87, Sachs experienced management problems and he complained to the Bank. Loren Gerber and James Tiscornia testified in deposition that the Bank threatened to make management changes if they did not cooperate with Sachs. Sachs met with Bank representatives frequently during his tenure; over 100 conferences occurred from August of 1986 through June of 1988. There is no dispute that Sachs provided information to the Bank on a regular basis until he was fired by Lester Tiscornia on June 30, 1988.

. . . .

ANALYSIS

CERCLA liability attaches if each of the following elements is established:

(1) There is a release or threatened release of a hazardous substance;

(2) at a facility;

(3) causing the plaintiff to incur response costs; and

(4) the defendant is a responsible party as defined in § 107(a).

42 U.S.C. § 9607(a); *United States v. Aceto Agricultural & Chemicals Corp.*, 872 F.2d 1373 (8th Cir. 1989).

Liability is strict, fault or state of mind is irrelevant. *United States v. Monsanto Co.*, 858 F.2d 160 (4th Cir. 1988). Because the goals of CERCLA are remedial, the court is obligated to construe the statute's liability provision broadly to avoid frustrating its legislative purpose. *Anspec Co., Inc. v. Johnson Controls*, 922 F.2d 1240, 1247 (6th Cir. 1991).

At issue in this motion is the fourth element, whether the Bank is a responsible party. Under 42 U.S.C. § 9607(a)(2), a responsible party is defined as:

> (2) any person who at the time of disposal of any hazardous substance owned or operated any facility at which such hazardous substances were disposed of, . . .

Further, under the Act, an owner or operator is defined as "any person" and any person is defined as "an individual, firm, corporation, association, partnership, consortium, joint venture, commercial entity, United States government, state, municipality, commission, political subdivision of the state, or any interstate body." 42 U.S.C. § 9601(20)(A) and (21).

There are two time periods in question. The first period is from 1964 to August 6, 1986, during which representatives of the Bank were directors of the company. The second period is from August of 1986 through June 30, 1988, during which the work-out specialist recommended by the Bank actually managed the company. The Bank held the first mortgages on the property during both time periods.

CERCLA explicitly excludes from liability persons who "without participating in the management of a vessel or facility, hold indicia of ownership primarily to protect securing interests in the vessel or facility." 42 U.S.C. § 107(a)(2). Accordingly, it is not enough that the Bank held first mortgages to impose liability on the Bank under CERCLA or MERA, and it is necessary to analyze the actual role played by the Bank in the management of the company during these periods.

In analyzing the participation by the Bank in the management of the company, it is also necessary to consider the lender liability rule issued by the EPA effective April 29, 1992, which expands upon the statutory exclusion, and reads as follows:

> (1) Actions that are Participation in Management
>
> Participation in management of a facility means . . . actual participation in the management or operational affairs of the facility by the holder, and does not include the mere capacity to influence, or ability to influence, or the unexercised right to control facility operations. A holder is participating in management, while the borrower is still in possession of the vessel or facility encumbered by the security interest, only if the holder either:
>
> (i) Exercises decision making control over the borrower's environmental compliance such that the holder has undertaken responsibility for the borrower's hazardous substance handling or disposal practices; or
>
> (ii) Exercises control at a level comparable to that of a manager of the borrower's enterprise, such that the holder has assumed or manifested responsibility for the overall management of the enterprise encompassing the day-to-day decision making of the enterprise with the respect to
>
> (A) Environmental compliance or
>
> (B) All, or substantially all, of the operational (as opposed to financial or administrative) aspects of the enterprise other than environmental compliance. Operational aspects of the enterprise include functions such as that of facility or plant manager, operations manager, chief operating officer, or chief executive officer.
>
> Financial or administrative aspects include functions such as that of credit manager, accounts payable/receivable manager, personnel manager, controller, chief financial officer, or similar functions.

40 C.F.R. 300.1100(c)(1).

The EPA rule provides that a finding of actual participation in management must be made in order to impose liability on a lender. If the borrower was in possession of the vessel or facility during the period in question, as is the case here, the EPA rule further provides that a lender is in actual control only if it takes any of three actions. First, the lender will be deemed to be participating in management if it exercises decision making control over the borrower's environmental compliance. 40 C.F.R. 300.1101(c)(1)(i). No such allegation has been made in this case, and this section does not apply. Second, the lender will be deemed to be participating in management if it assumes or manifests responsibility for the overall management of the enterprise encompassing day-to-day decision making of the enterprise with respect to environmental compliance. 40 C.F.R. 300.1101(c)(1)(ii)(A). Again, no party has claimed that the Bank exercised day-to-day decision making with respect to environmental compliance. Third, the lender will be deemed to be participating in management if it assumes or manifests responsibility for the overall management of the enterprise encompassing day-to-day decision making with respect to all, or substantially all, of the operational aspects of the enterprise other than environmental compliance, as opposed to financial or administrative aspects of the business. 40 C.F.R. 300.1101(c)(1)(ii)(B). This third test must be applied to the facts of this case.

The first period of time at issue includes Mewhort's and Bunker's participation on AUSCO's board. Although Mewhort and Bunker served as directors, their status as directors does not alone impose liability. More is required. *See Kelley ex rel. Natural Res. Comm'n v. Arco Industries Corp.*, 723 F. Supp. 1214, 1220 (W.D. Mich. 1989). Mewhort's and Bunker's only involvement with AUSCO occurred during participation in full board of director meetings which only occurred once or twice a year. The full board's function was to deal with pension and capital spending issues. The executive committee dealt with operational issues and environmental compliance. Neither Mewhort nor Bunker sat on the executive board. The Court finds that there are no attenuating facts to support liability on the basis of this limited participation.

Further, the cases cited in plaintiffs' brief as supporting Bank liability, were decided prior to the enactment of the EPA rule and are factually inapposite. For example, the Bank involvement here is not as overreaching as that upon which the court relied to impose liability in *Rockwell Int'l Corp. v. IU Int'l Corp.*, 702 F. Supp. 1384, 1390–91 (N.D. Ill. 1988). In *Rockwell*, the defendant IU was found to participate in management because it hired or approved the hiring of certain corporate officers, some of whom were IU officers who remained in charge throughout various changes in ownership, determined the responsibilities of those officers it appointed, established the procedure for and approved the operational plans, suggested changes in procedures that directly affected the disposal of hazardous substances, and stated in public announcements that it operated the facility. Although it is likely the court would reach the same result today, the recent EPA rule does temper the value of the decision and the others entered prior to its enactment.

The additional evidence presented by the State does not show that the Bank was intimately involved with the day-to-day decision making regarding operational aspects during this first time period. This evidence consists of a series of memoranda prepared by Hugh Porter, the Bank's front line officer for AUSCO. The Bank memoranda in the 1979–1985 era describe the operations of AUSCO, but always in reference to the financial affairs of the business. Additional memos discuss strategies to force the Harris Bank to share the financing risks more equally or force the Harris Bank to withdraw. Similarly, the documents discussing labor disputes do so in the context of their financial impact and benefit to the company. The Bank's involvement, as reflected in these memoranda, falls within the scope of activities permitted by the EPA rule.

Moreover, the Bank's close monitoring of AUSCO does not remove MNB from the lender liability exemption. Nor does Bank encouragement of AUSCO to follow the consolidation plan make the exemption unavailable to MNB. As the EPA rule makes explicit, influence alone does not incur liability; actual control is necessary. Nor do conditions imposed by the Bank for continued financing exclude the Bank from the exemption. The financial health of the company was such that the Bank needed to protect its security interest. There is no evidence of actual decision making by the Bank as is needed to find liability. Accordingly, the Court GRANTS the Bank's motion for summary judgment for the period from 1964 to August, 1986.

The Court now turns to the second time frame at issue, the Sachs era. The Sachs era begins with the August 6, 1986 meeting, at which the Bank advised AUSCO it would not continue financing unless the Tiscornias provided personal guarantees, trimmed expenses such as Lester Tiscornia's salary and retained a turnaround specialist. The Bank's insistence upon outside management under threat of calling the loan does not constitute impermissible control. *See, e.g., In re Badger Freightways, Inc.*, 106 Bankr. 971, 975–77 (Bankr. N.D. Ill. 1989).

Moreover, the company agreed to hire a specialist, and the company negotiated the agreement with Sachs. The company was free to disregard the Bank's advice and gamble that the Bank would not call the loan. These actions indicate the Bank merely influenced, but did not control, the decision making at AUSCO.

Certainly, the terms of the loan agreement gave the Bank the ability to exercise strong influence over AUSCO, as is true with respect to virtually all well drafted commercial loan agreements. At any time, however, AUSCO had the right to disregard the advice of the Bank, and in fact did so when the company fired Sachs 21 months after he was hired.

The Court is also unpersuaded by the State's argument that Sachs' bonus arrangement is concrete evidence that the Bank acted as an owner or operator under CERCLA. The letter of credit that was offered during negotiation of Sachs' contract could be drawn on for payment of the bonus to Sachs as AUSCO's indebtedness to the Bank was reduced. Clearly such an arrangement provided an incentive for Sachs to pay down the company's debt to the Bank, but this arrangement did not empower the Bank with control over the day-to-day decisions of company operations. The EPA rule provides that a person who exerts influence over a "facility manager but who has no power to direct or implement operational decisions is not 'participating in management,' even if the level of influence exerted over the borrower is substantial." 57 Fed. Reg. 18359. Here, the Bank's influence over Sachs, however substantial, remained influence, and did not constitute control.

Additional evidence relied upon by the State as an indicia of control is that the Bank and Sachs met more than once a week to discuss the corporation. The Court does not find that regular communication between Sachs and the Bank constitutes evidence or even an inference of actual decision making. Daily monitoring of the debtor's financial situation or suggestions as to what action the debtor should follow to resolve its financial difficulties does not justify an exemption from the lender liability exclusion contained in the EPA rule. Here, AUSCO agreed when it secured the loan that the Bank would monitor the company's cash flow on a daily basis. Such monitoring reflects valid financial concerns, not operational concerns, and the Bank's actions did not exceed the scope of monitoring authorized in the loan agreement.

Although the Bank and Sachs deny that the Bank was involved in making decisions, the Court notes that there are executive committee meeting minutes that report that Sachs had cleared an expenditure of $120,000 to relocate the general offices of AUSCO with the Bank. Furthermore, Sachs stated at a special meeting of the board of directors that he had discussed at great length with the Bank the recording of an inventory write-down at AUSCO for the purpose of establishing an artificial income stream.

Again, these topics relate to financial transactions and business. There is no evidence that the Bank decided where the offices should be relocated, when the move should take place, and who should move. Consultation with the Bank about an expenditure does not constitute control. Similarly, questions as to whether to create an artificial income stream fall within the area of financial functions of a company, and come within the lender liability exclusion.

The State supports its argument that the Bank participated in the management of the company with evidence that David Day, an employee of the Bank, indicated to both James Tiscornia and Loren Gerber that he had instructed Sachs that Sachs could fire them. This statement by a Bank employee was accurate; as CEO, Sachs had the authority to fire company employees. Day also stated that Lester Tiscornia, owner of the company, could fire Sachs. This statement was also accurate. Neither statement creates an inference of Bank control. They merely reflect Day's understanding of the corporate structure of AUSCO.

Gerber further stated that Day used the term "we" when he made the first statement, thereby creating an inference that the Bank and Sachs could make personnel changes. To vest the Bank with management authority because a Bank employee may have used language inclusive of the Bank, the Court would have to adopt the "Al Haig" theory of power. Just because David Day said he was in charge did not make it so. There is no evidence that the Bank ever fired anyone, including those threatened by Day's announcement. Moreover, the language of the lender liability exemption labels administrative functions as those performed by a personnel manager. 40 C.F.R. 300.1100(c)(1)(ii)(B). Accordingly, even if the Bank had the authority to fire management, it could still potentially be entitled to the exclusion.

In *United States v. R.W. Meyer, Inc.*, 889 F.2d 1497, 1500 (6th Cir. 1989), *cert. denied*, 110 S. Ct. 1527, 108 L. Ed. 2d 767 (1990), the court concluded that in December of 1980, Congress enacted CERCLA "to initiate and establish a comprehensive response and financing mechanism to abate and control the vast problems associated with abandoned and inactive hazardous waste disposal sites." It appears ironic to this Court that the standard of liability the State seeks to impose upon the lender in this case may well result in increasing the number of abandoned and inactive hazardous waste disposal sites. If banks are held liable under CERCLA for actions such as occurred in this case (i.e., suggesting or demanding new management, monitoring the borrower's financial health, and consulting regularly with its customer), it is reasonable to assume that banks will quickly react to such judicial reasoning by refusing to extend additional credit or otherwise continue to work with troubled borrowers. Banks will insulate themselves from liability by calling loans rather than nursing troubled borrowers back to financial health. This anticipated response virtually guarantees an increase in the country's inventory of abandoned and inactive hazardous waste disposal sites. Although imposing liability on the Bank in this case might not yield such a result in and of itself, this Court declines to extend the definition of responsible parties to include the Bank.

The Court has carefully reviewed all of the indicia of Bank participation in the management of AUSCO's business relied upon by the State in support of its motion. The Court finds that individually and collectively, the indicia relate to financial or administrative aspects of the business, as opposed to the operational aspects necessary for a finding of liability under EPA lender liability rules.

There being no evidence before the Court that the Bank crossed the murky line from the ability to influence operational decisions to actually making operational decisions at AUSCO, the State's motion for summary judgment must be DENIED. The Court GRANTS the defendant Bank's motion for summary judgment.

[c] Good News, But Not Great News, for Lenders

The following article provides "good news" to mortgage lenders. However, how well does this "good news" address all of the concerns raised in *Kelley*?

Baxter Dunaway & Andrew C. Cooper,
Good News for Lenders and Fiduciaries Under Superfund,
PROB. & PROP., May/June 1997 at 49*

Congress has removed much of the uncertainty regarding lenders' and fiduciaries' potential liability for environmental claims by its recent adoption of the Asset Conservation, Lender Liability, and Deposit Insurance Protection Act of 1996, Pub. L. No. 104–208, 110 Stat. 1344 (to be codified at 42 U.S.C. §§ 6991b(h), 9601(20) and 9607) (Act). The Act is very significant and resulted from a seven year lobbying effort by lenders and fiduciaries. The Act does not eradicate lender and fiduciary liability. Nevertheless, if lenders and fiduciaries keep to their roles, they generally should not be liable for hazardous waste contamination on properties with which they are involved.

The Act amends the Comprehensive Environmental Response, Compensation and Liability Act, 42 U.S.C. §§ 9601–9675 (CERCLA), and clarifies the situations in which lenders and fiduciaries will be liable for cleaning up hazardous waste. 110 Stat. at 1344–60. The Act similarly limits liability for leaking underground storage tanks (USTs) under the Resource Conservation and Recovery Act, 42 U.S.C. §§ 6901–6992k (RCRA). 110 Stat. at 1360–62. The Act is applicable to any claim that has not been finally adjudicated as of its effective date of September 30, 1996. *Id.* at 1363.

The Act provides the circumstances under which lenders, as broadly defined, will be liable for the contamination of property they hold as collateral. The law follows the EPA lender liability rule, 40 C.F.R. pt. 300(L) (removed from C.F.R. pursuant to 60 Fed. Reg. 33,912–13) (EPA Rule), and essentially codifies a portion of it. In promulgating the EPA Rule, EPA attempted to interpret the secured

* Copyright © 1997 Baxter Dunaway and Andrew Cooper. Reprinted by permission.

lender exemption contained in CERCLA § 101(20)(A). In *Kelley v. EPA*, 15 F.3d 1100, 1108–09 (D.C. Cir. 1994), *cert. denied sub nom. American Bankers Ass'n v. Kelley*, 115 S.Ct. 900 (1995), the court held that EPA exceeded its authority in promulgating the EPA Rule.

The Act also limits the potential liability of fiduciaries, such as trustees and receivers. The EPA Rule had not addressed the liability of fiduciaries, and CERCLA did not contain a liability limitation for fiduciaries that was equivalent to the secured lender exemption. Therefore, fiduciaries were more at risk than lenders.

Key CERCLA Provisions

With limited exceptions, CERCLA § 107(a)(1) makes "the owner and operator of . . . a facility" strictly liable for the government's cleanup costs. 42 U.S.C. § 9607(a)(1). A "facility" is broadly defined to include any place where hazardous substances have "otherwise come to be located." 42 U.S.C. § 9601(9). "Owner or operator" is defined in CERCLA § 101(20)(A) as any person owning or operating a facility, but "such term does not include a person, who, without participating in the management of a . . . facility, holds indicia of ownership primarily to protect his security interest in the . . . facility." 42 U.S.C. § 9601(20)(A)(ii). This provision is known as the secured lender exemption. The Act does not change this definition but does define what is meant by "participating in the management."

Participating in Management

A lender loses the secured lender exemption if it participates in management. Under CERCLA, as amended by the Act, to participate in management "means actually participating in the management or operational affairs of a vessel or facility; and does not include merely having the capacity to influence, or the unexercised right to control, vessel or facility operations." 110 Stat. at 1352 (to be codified at 42 U.S.C. § 9601(20)(F)(i)). This definition nullifies the decision in *United States v. Fleet Factors Corp*, 901 F.2d 1550 (11th Cir. 1990), *cert. denied*, 111 S.Ct. 753 (1991) (mere capacity to assert control sufficient for lender liability). One who is a lender and holds indicia of ownership primarily to protect a security interest in a vessel or facility will be considered to participate in management only if, while the borrower is still in possession of the vessel or facility encumbered by the security interest, the person:

> (I) exercises decision making control over the environmental compliance related to the vessel or facility, such that the person has undertaken responsibility for the hazardous substance handling or disposal practices related to the vessel or facility; or
>
> (II) exercises control at a level comparable to that of a manager of the vessel or facility, such that the person has assumed or manifested responsibility —
>
>> (aa) for the overall management of the vessel or facility encompassing day-to-day decision making with respect to environmental compliance; or

> (bb) over all or substantially all of the operational functions (as distinguished from financial or administrative functions) of the vessel or facility other than the function of environmental compliance.

110 Stat. at 1352–53 (to be codified at 42 U.S.C. § 9601(20)(F)(ii)).

The term "participating in management" does not include performing an act or failing to act before a security interest is created in a vessel or facility. The term also does not include holding a security interest; abandoning or releasing a security interest; or including in the terms of an extension of credit (or in a contract or security agreement relating to the extension) a covenant, warranty or other term or condition that relates to environmental compliance. In addition, the lender does not lose the secured lender exemption by:

- monitoring or enforcing the terms and conditions of the extension of credit or security interest;
- monitoring or undertaking one or more inspections of the vessel or facility;
- requiring a response action or other lawful means of addressing the release or threatened release of a hazardous substance in connection with the vessel or facility before, during or on the expiration of the term of the credit extension;
- providing financial or other advice or counseling;
- restructuring, renegotiating or otherwise agreeing to alter the terms and conditions of the extension of credit or security interest or exercising forbearance;
- exercising other remedies that may be available under applicable law for the breach of a term or condition of the extension of credit or security agreement; or
- conducting a response action under CERCLA § 107(d) if the action does not rise to the level of participating in management as otherwise specifically defined in the Act.

110 Stat. at 1354–55 (to be codified at 42 U.S.C. § 9601(2)(F)(iv)).

Lender's Right to Foreclose

Before the Act, some courts had held that if a lender foreclosed and took title, it could lose the secured lender exemption. *See Guidice v. BFG Electroplating & Mfg. Co.*, 732 F.Supp. 556, 562–63 (W.D. Pa. 1989). By refining the definition of who is an "owner and operator" subject to CERCLA liability, the Act gives guidance on what a foreclosing lender can do without losing the secured lender exemption. As revised by the Act, an owner or operator:

> does not include a person that is a lender that did not participate in management of a vessel or facility prior to foreclosure, notwithstanding that the person —
>
> (I) forecloses on the vessel or facility; and
>
> (II) after foreclosure, sells, releases (in the case of a lease finance transaction), or liquidates the vessel or facility, maintains business

> activities, winds up operations, undertakes a response action under section 9607(d)(1) of this title or under the direction of an on-scene coordinator appointed under the National Contingency Plan, with respect to the vessel or facility, or takes any other measure to preserve, protect, or prepare the vessel or facility prior to sale or disposition, if the person seeks to sell, re-lease (in the case of a lease finance transaction), or otherwise divest the person of the vessel or facility at the earliest practicable, commercially reasonable time, on commercially reasonable terms, taking into account market conditions and legal and regulatory requirements.

110 Stat. at 1350–51 (to be codified at 42 U.S.C. § 9601(20)(E)(ii)).

These provisions overrule the much-criticized *Fleet Factors* decision in which the Eleventh Circuit held that a lender could be liable as an "owner" if it participated in the financial management of its debtor and had the ability to influence decisions on hazardous waste management. 901 F.2d at 1558. The provisions of the Act also overrule cases, such as *Guidice*, holding that the secured lender per se loses the secured lender exemption when it forecloses and takes title.

Adoption of Part of EPA Rule

In 1992, to alleviate the uncertainty in the financial industry that resulted from the *Fleet Factors* decision, EPA issued the EPA Rule to clarify the standards for lender liability under CERCLA. In *Kelley*, the court held that EPA exceeded its authority in promulgating the EPA Rule. Section 2504 of the Act specifically states that 40 C.F.R. § 300.1105 is deemed to have been validly issued under the authority of CERCLA and to have been effective according to the terms of the EPA Rule. 110 Stat. at 1362. Section 300.1105 relates to "[i]nvoluntary acquisition of property by the government." Further, judicial review of the EPA Rule, as enacted, was preempted, but the Act is not to be construed to preclude judicial review of any amendment to the EPA Rule. 110 Stat. at 1362–63.

The Act does not adopt 40 C.F.R. § 300.100, which is the secured lender exemption. Thus, Congress did not adopt the most important provision of the EPA Rule. Was it because of the pressing need to exempt governmental acquisitions or because Congress was rejecting the more specific provisions of the EPA Rule's secured lender exemption? Another possibility is that Congress considered the language of the Act to be more permissive than the EPA Rule.

The EPA Rule's secured lender exemption is very similar to the lender liability provisions of the Act, and obviously the Act was drafted with the EPA Rule as a guide. With regard to foreclosure, however, the provisions of the EPA Rule are more specific than the Act. As noted above, under the Act the security holder will not be liable after foreclosure "if the person seeks to sell, re-lease (in the case of a lease finance transaction), or otherwise divest the person of the vessel or facility at the earliest practicable, commercially reasonable time, on commercially reasonable terms." 110 Stat. at 1351. In contrast, under the EPA Rule, a holder of a security interest could avoid being considered an "owner or operator" after foreclosure by listing and advertising the property for sale within 12 months after foreclosure. The EPA Rule also provided that the holder of an interest would lose the exemption if, within six months following foreclosure, it rejected or failed to act within 90 days on a written, bona fide offer of fair consideration for the property.

As to EPA's authority to readopt the omitted portion of the EPA Rule, the legislative history is confusing. On September 30, 1996, Senator Alphonse D'Amato, chairman of the Banking Committee, and Senator Robert Smith engaged in a colloquy in the Senate. Senator D'Amato confirmed that "title V [of the bill] does not in any way disturb the central holding in the *Kelley* case, namely that absent a specific delegation, that CERCLA, today, or as amended by this act, does not authorize EPA to issue rules defining the scope of CERCLA liability." 142 Cong. Rec. S11886, S11896 (daily ed. Sept. 30, 1996). On October 3, 1996, however, Senator Frank Lautenberg, ranking member of the Superfund Committee, and Senator Max Baucus, ranking member of the Environment Committee, engaged in another Senate colloquy disavowing the earlier colloquy and in which Senator Lautenberg responded that "this legislation recognizes EPA authority to promulgate rules in this area." 142 Cong. Rec. S12292 (daily ed. Oct. 3, 1996). The Act was sent to the President on September 30, 1996 and he signed it on that day. Thus, the October 3 colloquy was after the date of enactment. Nevertheless, the Act itself recognizes EPA's authority to amend the EPA Rule. As noted above, the section of the Act adopting a portion of the EPA Rule precludes judicial review of any amendment by EPA made after the date of the Act. 110 Stat. at 1363.

Conforming Amendment to UST Rule

The Act also contains a conforming amendment to the UST provisions of RCRA. Section 9003b(h) of the Solid Waste Disposal Act, 42 U.S.C. § 6991b(h), is amended so that "the terms owner and operator do not include a person who, without participating in the management of a UST and otherwise not engaged in petroleum production, refining or marketing, holds indicia of ownership primarily to protect a security interest." 110 Stat. at 1360 (to be codified at 42 U.S.C. § 6991b(h)). The amendment also conforms to the definition of "security interest holders" and fiduciaries in CERCLA §§ 101(20) and 107(n), as amended by the Act. Nothing in the amendment is to be construed as modifying or affecting the final rule on USTs issued by EPA on September 7, 1995 and codified at 40 C.F.R. pts. 280–81. *See* 110 Stat. at 1361 (to be codified at 42 U.S.C. § 6991b(h)(9)(C)).

Fiduciary Protection

Before the Act, fiduciaries were greatly concerned about CERCLA liability because of the broad definition of "owner and operator." *See City of Phoenix v. Garbage Services Co.*, 827 F.Supp. 600 (D. Ariz. 1993) (discussing personal liability of a trustee for response costs). Although it was fraught with interpretational difficulties, at least secured lenders had their exemption. Fiduciaries had no such exemption. Congress remedied this by limiting the liability of fiduciaries, which are broadly defined in the Act. 110 Stat. at 1345–50 (to be codified at 42 U.S.C. § 9607(n)).

The critical issue for fiduciaries is whether the fiduciary can be personally liable for environmentally affected property after the trust assets are exhausted. Congress amended CERCLA § 107 to add subsection (n)(1), which provides that the fiduciary's liability will not exceed the assets held in a fiduciary capacity. 110 Stat. at 1345 (to be codified at 42 U.S.C. § 9607(n)(1)). Additionally, a fiduciary is not liable for administering a "facility that was contaminated before the fiduciary relationship began." *Id.* at 1345–46 (to be codified at 42 U.S.C. § 9607(n)(4)(H)). By contrast, if a lender is liable as an owner or operator, the liability can encompass pre-existing hazardous waste.

The exemption excludes one who acts as a fiduciary for a trust or other fiduciary estate organized for the primary purpose of, or engaged in, actively carrying on a trade or business for profit or one who acquires ownership or control of a vessel or facility for the purpose of avoiding liability of that person or of any other person. 110 Stat. at 1348 (to be codified at 42 U.S.C. § 9607(n)(5)(A)(ii)). Also, the Act does not protect a fiduciary whose negligence causes or contributes to a release or threatened release. *Id.* at 1345 (to be codified at 42 U.S.C.§ 9607(n)(3)). The safe harbor for fiduciary activities is similar to the permitted activities of lenders under the definition of "participating in management." *Compare* 110 Stat. at 1345–46 (to be codified at 42 U.S.C. § 9607(n)(4)) *with* 110 Stat. at 1352–60 (to be codified at 42 U.S.C. § 9601(20)(F)).

Conclusion

The Act provides guidance for secured parties and fiduciaries in avoiding liability under CERCLA and RCRA. The Act gives relief to fiduciaries who have been concerned over choosing between acts that might impose personal environmental liability and acts that carry out their obligations as a fiduciary. The lenders did not get everything they wanted. They would prefer to avoid joint and several liability when they do not qualify for the secured lender exemption. Also, lenders and others are still concerned about the retroactive effect of CERCLA.

The Act does not eliminate the risk of lending to a borrower subject to environmental liability or the risk of foreclosing on contaminated property. The incentive to conduct due diligence is not reduced, but at least guidance now exists on how to avoid triggering CERCLA liability. Fiduciaries must still be wary of holding contaminated property. Unless the fiduciary is negligent, however, personal liability is unlikely.

[d] Questions About Lender Liability and Environmental Due Diligence

1. Even if it is not directly liable under CERCLA, why should a lender still be concerned about whether hazardous substances are present or may be used on the mortgaged property?

2. What can lenders safely do now without losing the protection of the security interest exception? After the EPA rules were invalidated in the appeal of *Kelley*, Congress enacted legislation to once again provide safe harbors for lenders; to what extent does the newly enacted law "codify" the EPA rules and to what extent does it not do so? Which approach (the EPA rules or the law) is better for mortgage lenders?

3. How well did First Mortgage Bank address potential CERCLA liability in its loan documents for the Fox Valley Auto Care Center? See, for example, § 3.1(r) of the Construction Loan Agreement in the Document Book. Where else in the Loan Agreement is the issue of environmental contamination and compliance with environmental laws addressed? Do the loan documents adequately address not only the current situation at the site,

but also changes that will occur once the Fox Valley Auto Service Center is leased up and in operation?

4. As you may recall from Chapter 8, Regent hired a company to perform a Phase I environmental audit on the Johnson's property to make appropriate inquiry into whether there were any likely environmental problems with respect to it. If serious problems were detected, Regent likely would not have closed on the purchase and First Mortgage Bank likely would not have agreed to fund the acquisition/construction loan. But the Phase I environmental audit also potentially serves as a necessary prerequisite to both Regent and First Mortgage Bank defending a CERCLA liability action for the acts that occurred before they took their respective interests in the mortgaged property under the "innocent landowner" or "bona-fide purchaser" status, which requires that such parties conduct "all appropriate inquiries" into the property's environmental status. 42 U.S.C. § 9601(35) In November 2005, the EPA published standards for "all appropriate inquiries" (*see* www.epa.gov/fedrgstr/EPA-WASTE/2005/November/day-01/f21455.htm). These standards are reflected in the American Society for Testing Materials ("ASTM") and are what the real estate industry considers best practices for conducting environmental due diligence. The added clarity in standards was very welcome, but likely will lead to more expensive reports that take longer to prepare than what was customarily done before the publication of these standards. *See* Greene, *Environmental Best Practices For Commercial Real Estate Financing*, 22 No. 5 Prac. Real Est. Law. 41 (Sept. 2006) ("*Environmental Best Practices*").

   It is important to note that certain environmental risks remain outside the scope of these Phase I standards, such as mold, radon, asbestos, lead, and natural resource damage, and so a lender may need to tailor the due diligence scope to include these other matters when appropriate for the applicable real property. *Id.* An even thornier issue is when to perform a Phase II assessment. What if there is a possibility of contamination due to historic uses but no apparent evidence of contamination? What if there appears to be only a minor problem that is detected (for example, if there is staining around new dry cleaning equipment detected in the Phase I): how much soil sampling should take place in response, just in that area, or a more comprehensive soil and groundwater investigation? It is also important to realize that the environmental status of a particular property is potentially ever-changing, and experts therefore advise that Phase I and II assessments should not be relied upon if over 12 months old.

5. Rating agencies generally required that an ASTM assessment be performed for every mortgage loan in a loan pool and that these assessments be not older than 12 months. *Id.* When a Phase II assessment reflected that there were in fact environmental problems with the mortgaged property, a loan might still have been approved for the loan pool if certain "mitigants" were provided, such as an indemnity agreement from a financially acceptable borrower or guarantor, if adequate environmental insurance were provided, or if a remediation action plan approved by the appropriate governmental agency were established. *Id.* For a fuller discussion of these "mitigants" and their effectiveness and

limitations, see *Environmental Best Practices, supra.*

[4] Review of Leases

As previously discussed, one of the methods a lender can use to value the mortgaged property (which, in turn, affects the lender's decision on how much money, if any, to lend when the principal security for the loan is the mortgaged property) is to analyze the income and expenses generated by the property. The developer/borrower will supply the lender with financial statements containing this information. The lender should not solely rely on these statements, however, but should also carefully scrutinize all of the leases entered into to verify the financial information it has received. Moreover, it is not enough to simply look at the lease term and rental figures in the lease. As previously discussed, the lender's counsel should review all of the terms of the lease (at least with regard to the key leases) to determine under what conditions the anticipated revenue from the leases could abate, and to assess under what circumstances the lender, as a potential successor in interest of the borrower, could be exposed to any liabilities under the leases.

[a] Lease Issues for Lenders

Part V, *infra*, will address leasing issues generally, especially from the landlord's and tenant's perspectives. The following article is confined to issues that uniquely concern the lender. It focuses on the relationship between the lender and the tenant, and the methods lenders commonly use to establish rights with respect to the tenants, such as requiring tenant estoppel certificates and subordination, non-disturbance and attornment agreements.

Maura B. O'Connor,

Ten Commandments for Lenders Reviewing Leases*

[The first four rules set forth in this article relate primarily to matters covered in other portions of this work, hence the text which accompanies the first four rules has been omitted and we provide a brief summary of these points here in boldface. — Eds.]

ONE: Start reviewing the leases and related documents early.

TWO: The rental income stream should confirm the property's value.

THREE: The rental income stream should support the borrower's debt service during the entire repayment period.

FOUR: Look out for problem provisions.

FIVE: Get tenant estoppel certificates from every tenant that matters.

Tenant estoppel certificates are not form documents: they are most effectively used if tailored to the specific problems disclosed by your review of the leases. Tenant estoppel certificates are detailed representations about the leases which are typically prepared by lender's counsel for review and execution by each of the tenants of a property. They should provide that the lender and its counsel will rely on the statements in the certificate in making the loan. If a tenant signs such an estoppel, it cannot later deny that the representations made in the estoppel were true and correct when made; in other words, it cannot take a different position later as to facts it affirms in the tenant estoppel.

A tenant estoppel certificate should confirm, at a minimum, each of the following:

- that a true and correct copy of the lease and all amendments, side letters and any other agreements modifying the lease are attached, and the lease as so amended is in full force and effect;
- that the tenant has accepted the premises and is currently occupying them and paying rent and any other charges (such as operating costs and CAM costs), and the amount of such rent and other charges;
- the actual commencement date of the lease;
- the square footage of the premises;
- the amount of any security deposit paid to the landlord by the tenant;
- that the tenant has not paid any amounts to the landlord other than rent and the security deposit;
- that the landlord has not defaulted under the lease, and that the tenant knows of no action or omission which, with the giving of notice or passage of time, or both, would become a default by landlord; and
- that the tenant has no claims or defenses to enforcement of the lease, nor any right to any offsets against rent.

Other provisions can, and should, be added to reflect the specific issues presented by each lease, such as whether all T.I.s [Editor's Note: "T.I.s" or "tenant improvements" are special improvements for a specific tenant that the landlord is obligated to perform under the terms of the lease] have been completed.

Prepare and deliver the tenant estoppel certificates early to find out hidden problems. As a practical matter, most tenants are at best reluctant to review, execute and deliver tenant estoppel certificates to a lender they have never heard of; so most lenders ask the borrower/landlord to take responsibility for obtaining the tenant estoppel certificates. (The leases should provide that tenants must deliver such estoppel certificates within a set number of days after a request by the landlord.) Lenders should require that the borrower deliver the executed certificates well before closing if the timing of the loan allows, so that lender's counsel can carefully review the returned certificates and handle any issues that are highlighted by the tenants.

When the executed estoppel certificates arrive, review them carefully, paying close attention to any modifications of them made by the tenants. If a tenant simply won't provide a tenant estoppel certificate, the lender should investigate further; the landlord may have a big problem with the tenant. The problems that arise sometimes include claims and litigations against the landlord, claims that the landlord has orally modified the lease, previously undisclosed written modifications to the lease, unapproved subleases (sometimes conflicting with other tenants' exclusive rights), releases of environmentally hazardous materials, and excess payments in advance to the landlord.

SIX: Think about your position after a foreclosure.

Many business risks which might be appropriate for a landlord are not appropriate for a lender which becomes a successor landlord through foreclosure. Most lenders' tolerance for risk is different than that of most landlords, and many lenders are not equipped to manage rental properties. In addition, the last thing that most lenders which have foreclosed on real property want to do is spend more money on the tenants of that property.

To avoid such an outcome, analyze the financial terms of the lease, considering which agreements of the original landlord would be so burdensome to the lender after the foreclosure that lender would not be willing to be bound to them. Some of the following types of agreements, for example, might be overly burdensome:

- an agreement by the landlord to provide or finance a T.I. allowance to the tenant or to build T.I.s for any expansion space;
- agreements allowing tenant to use the premises without paying rent during certain periods (usually done early in the term of the lease, but sometimes rent-free periods occur at other times);
- any agreement of landlord to pay the obligations of its tenant under the lease at a different location (usually tenant's former premises);
- agreements concerning payment of broker's commissions;
- any agreements concerning unusually high standards for maintenance of the property or the premises; and
- other agreements to provide further tenant inducements promised by the original landlord which are not provided prior to foreclosure.

The object of this review is to identify obligations which lender is not willing to assume, so that the lender's counsel can draft a Subordination, Nondisturbance and Attornment Agreement in which the lender is absolved from liability for such agreements if it forecloses.

SEVEN: Figure out the priority of the leases and your mortgage.

If the lease documentation does not provide for the subordination of the lease to the loan, determine what leases are senior to the lender's mortgage. The black letter law of real estate priorities is that a mortgage (or deed of trust) recorded in the public records after a notice or memorandum of lease is recorded is junior to the lease. Where a memorandum or notice of a lease is recorded after a mortgage is recorded, the lease is generally junior to the mortgage. However, in some states the tenant in possession is senior to the lender, or has some protections even if the lender records its mortgage and the tenant's lease is not recorded.[7]

If the existing leases contain subordination provisions, find out what their effect will be upon the lender's rights after a foreclosure. Subordination, nondisturbance and attornment may already exist in the leases or lease amendments: check for them when reviewing the lease documentation.

---

[7] Fisher, Jr., Morton P. and Goldman, Richard H., *The Ritual Dance Between Lessee and Lender — Subordination, Nondisturbance and Attornment*, p. 364, Real Property, Probate and Trust Journal, Vol. 30 No. 3 (Fall 1995).

Not all subordination clauses work to a lender's advantage. Many leases contain automatic subordination clauses. These are provisions that make the tenant's lease automatically junior to any lender's mortgage. Such provisions are very dangerous, because they are often too broadly drafted. For example, such a clause can make a tenant's lease junior in priority, or subordinate, to all mortgages, including junior financings. From the senior lender's position, this could lead to the unpleasant situation in which a junior lender which forecloses its mortgage could extinguish leases that the senior lender would prefer to keep in place. Another unintended consequence could occur if the junior lender's mortgage is cross-defaulted or cross-collateralized with another mortgage: then the junior lender could foreclose on the property which is the primary security for the senior lender's note, but only secondary security for the cross-defaulted or cross-collateralized obligation, which would wipe out junior leases, even if the property were otherwise generating enough income so that the borrower could meet its obligations related to the property. For these reasons, any lender which accepts an automatic subordination clause in leases should make sure that the clause operates only to subordinate the lease to its own mortgage.

Determine what would result from the existing priorities if the lender foreclosed. If a mortgage junior to a lease is foreclosed, the lease remains in effect and the purchaser at the foreclosure sale (usually the foreclosing lender) takes title to the property subject to the lease terms. If a mortgage senior to a lease is foreclosed, under most states' laws the junior lease is terminated by the foreclosure, the tenant is no longer obligated under the lease, and the purchaser at foreclosure gets title to the property, but risks losing the tenants. In some states, tenants in possession when the loan is made have certain rights, even if their leases are not recorded and are therefore junior to the foreclosed mortgage, but the obligations of the purchaser as successor landlord are not clear.[8]

In some states, a lender can pick and choose between tenants, and can decide to take title subject to some leases and to terminate others.[9] This gives the lender the ability to terminate below-market leases in a real estate market where rents are going up; or to keep above-market leases in effect in a market where rental rates are decreasing. This result was disapproved by a California court, however, in *Dover Mobile Estates v. Fiber Form Products, Inc.*, 220 Cal. App. 3d 1494 (1990).

California law is muddled. [Editor's Note: The discussion of the complicated law in California has been omitted except for the important questions at the end of this discussion. The key point is to draft an SNDA so as to give the lender a choice about the position of the lease as against the mortgage rather than leaving the question to state law.]

Some of those questions are: what actions must a lender who purchases at foreclosure take to show that it acquires and accepts the premises subject to the lease? What other actions should a lender take if it instead is taking the position that the lease has been terminated by foreclosure and the tenant is now in place on a month to month tenancy? If a lender simply delivers a notice stating that it is now the lender and that the tenants should pay all rents to it . . . , can the tenants treat this as a ratification of the existing lease (or use it to estop the lender from denying that the lease remains in existence after foreclosure)? How, short of

[8] *Id.* at 376 et seq.

[9] *Id.* at 364, 375.

litigating each case, can a foreclosing lender be sure whether or not it has a valid lease? Must any lease guaranties be rewritten to include waivers of any right to challenge the lender's decision to treat the lease as continuing after foreclosure? Since the case leaves these issues open in California, you should deal with them explicitly by drafting a Subordination, Nondisturbance and Attornment agreement that works for your loan and the leases securing it (as discussed below) rather than risking litigation to enforce or terminate a lease.

Determine what obligations of the landlord the purchaser at foreclosure or foreclosing lender must perform in the absence of a subordination, nondisturbance and attornment agreement. If the lender ever were to foreclose, and did not have an agreement expressly stating which obligations of the landlord it would assume, determine if the lender/successor landlord would be obliged for any of the following:

- to pay for or provide maintenance, services, utilities, and the degree and quality required to be provided;
- to pay for tenant improvements in any expansion space;
- to honor tenant's renewal rights provided in the lease after foreclosure; and
- to pay for restoration of the premises after casualty or condemnation, and if so, what percent of the premises must have been destroyed or condemned.

On the last point, a lender should consider whether limiting landlord's own obligations to restore to the amount of insurance proceeds actually collected after a casualty may make sense. To analyze this issue effectively, the lender or its counsel must also consider the insurance coverage that landlord/borrower is required to provide under the loan. In addition, the prudent lender will expect to see lease terms stating that the landlord has the right to retain any award from a condemning authority for the value of the leasehold estate, other than any independent award made to tenant for its moving expenses.

Leases may impose many other obligations on lenders who have become successor landlords due to foreclosure. The law in this area is too complex for the scope of this summary; further, the many confusions in the reported cases create a great opportunity for litigation. For this reason, a lender should enter into a Subordination, Nondisturbance and Attornment agreement with the borrower/landlord and each tenant under a lease that the lender would like to keep in place after a foreclosure.

EIGHT: Enter into Subordination, Nondisturbance and Attornment Agreements with all tenants that matter.

The best way to insure uninterrupted cash flow if lender must foreclose: enter into a Subordination, Nondisturbance and Attornment agreement ("SNDA") with each tenant and with the landlord before the loan closes. Since the ultimate goal of a lender is to achieve uninterrupted cash flow, even after a foreclosure, because such income will allow the lender both to manage the property and to have a better chance of selling it, the best approach for a lender is to enter into a Subordination, Nondisturbance and Attornment Agreement with the borrower/landlord and each tenant that lender would like to keep in place after a foreclosure. Again, the lender's ability to negotiate favorable terms in the SNDA is much better if it is completed well before the loan closes.

Obviously, a lender might do better if it knew that any foreclosure would take place in a rising rental rate market: in that case, the lender's ideal course of action would be to terminate all below market leases, and sign new leases at higher rates. In a failing rental rate market, conversely, the lender would prefer to hold onto existing leases, which often require tenants in a falling market to pay over-market rent rates. Since a lender cannot tell which way the rental market will be headed if it has to foreclose to enforce the borrower's obligation, and since common sense suggests that foreclosures are more likely in real estate markets that are spiraling downward, most lenders would be well advised to enter into a SNDA with each of its borrower/landlord's tenants.

Subordination, Nondisturbance and Attornment Agreements defined. Each of "subordination," "nondisturbance" and "attornment" can be defined separately. "Subordination" is an agreement to allow another's interest in certain real property to have priority over one's own interest: usually lenders require that tenants subordinate their interests to the lien of a first mortgage. "Nondisturbance" in this context means an agreement by lender to recognize the tenant's rights under the lease after a foreclosure. "Attornment" is simply tenant's acknowledgment of its obligation to a new, substituted landlord after any transfer of the landlord's interest; lenders are concerned that a tenant will attorn to a purchaser of the landlord's interest (usually the foreclosing lender) after a foreclosure of the mortgage.

How an SNDA works. An SNDA replaces the confusion in the law about the obligations of a tenant and a lender/successor landlord after a foreclosure with an agreement between the two parties (and often the landlord as well) which spells out their rights after a foreclosure. Usually an SNDA provides that the lease will be subordinated to the loan either (a) if lender so elects, or (b) automatically. Lenders will generally want to have the option to elect to subordinate the lease in question, but if the landlord does not so subordinate before foreclosure actually occurs, the purchaser at the foreclosure sale will end up taking subject to the lease. Either option is acceptable so long as the lender carefully considers what it wants to do. The SNDA agreement should be qualified, so that the lender will not disturb the rights of the tenant under the lease if at the time of the foreclosure the tenant is not in default. Generally, a lender should not worry about delivering a nondisturbance agreement to a tenant as long as the lender obtains in exchange the agreement of the tenant to attorn to it or any other successful bidder after a foreclosure.

Draft the SNDA to limit the obligations of a successor landlord who has acquired the property through foreclosure and to detail the tenant's obligations to the successor landlord. Like the tenant estoppel certificate, the SNDA is not a form document; instead, its usefulness is maximized if it reflects the concerns of the lender specifically raised by the lease to which it relates. Typically, a lender will want the SNDA to provide that a purchaser at foreclosure or the foreclosing lender will not be liable for prior landlord's defaults under lease before foreclosure. The foreclosing lender's liability for performance of its obligations as successor landlord should be limited to the lender's equity in the property. In addition, the lender may try to negotiate a SNDA pursuant to which the successor landlord after a foreclosure will not be liable for any extraordinary or unusually burdensome agreements of the original landlord, including for example exclusive and restrictive covenants, obligations to pay tenant's rent under its prior lease, indirect or consequential damages, or construction or other warranties (*e.g.*, concerning zoning, title, or compliance of the premises with applicable laws) given by the original landlord. A lender should not have to return any security deposits that it has not received to the tenant.

In addition, the SNDA should provide that the tenant will provide to the lender copies of all notices of defaults of the landlord, and an additional time to cure such defaults. As part of this agreement, the tenant should agree to accept performance of lender in place of the original landlord. This is quite important since it is not uncommon for a borrower facing foreclosure to stop performing its obligations as landlord under the leases, leading to a steep slide in the value of the property, and giving the tenants the opportunity to terminate their leases for breach.

The extent to which a lender can obtain the agreement of a tenant to resolve the ambiguities and problems caused by the leases will, of course, depend upon the relative bargaining power of the lender, landlord and tenant. Again, the earlier the negotiations of the SNDA are begun, the more leverage the lender has.

NINE: Amend leases if necessary.

Resolve lease issues that cannot be fixed by the tenant estoppel certificates or in a SNDA by requiring the borrower/landlord to amend the leases. The existing lease may obligate the tenant to enter into amendments to the lease reasonably required by a lender making a loan secured by the property. Even if such a provision is not included, a borrower/landlord seeking a loan is very motivated to persuade its tenant to agree to a lease amendment; if there is no other way to convince the tenant, a borrower about to receive an infusion of loan funds sometimes will grant a tenant concessions, financial or otherwise, in exchange for the tenant's cooperation in modifying the lease to satisfy the lender. However, after the loan funds, most borrowers understand that the lender's leverage is diminished, in part because its remedies are quite limited, expensive and harsh. Like nuclear weapons, the lender's power to foreclose the loan needs to be reserved for very major problems or it loses all value to the lender.

Try to have the leases amended when the problems disclosed in its review are so severe that a carefully drafted tenant estoppel alone won't fix them; for example, when an automatic subordination clause is too broad. Alternatively, the lender and the tenant can enter into a separate agreement that provides that certain obligations and promises of the original landlord will not be binding upon the lender if it forecloses on the property. However, this type of agreement would not necessarily protect the lender's assignee or another purchaser at a foreclosure sale.

TEN: Adjust or amend your loan documents to reflect the terms of the leases.

Get representations and warranties and other assurances if needed from borrower concerning its performance of its obligations as landlord. The loan documents should include the borrower's confirmation that it is not in default as landlord under the leases, and borrower's promises to perform its obligations under the leases. A lender should have the right but no obligation, to cure any breach by the borrower of its obligations as landlord. The loan documentation should provide that the borrower is liable for any amounts so advanced by lender, plus interest on such amounts. Some lenders also require that borrower provide a guaranty or a holdback of some of the loan proceeds to secure such obligations. Additional security can be provided by requiring that borrower provide a letter of credit to secure specific obligations. Of course, if any guaranty or indemnity is provided by a third party, the guaranty or indemnity agreement needs to include waivers of suretyship and guaranty defenses.

Limitations on junior financing. If junior financing is allowed at all by a senior lender, the junior lender should not be able to extinguish through foreclosure leases approved by the senior lender. To this end, the loan documents should provide that any junior lender must recognize all leases approved by the senior lender and provide a mechanism for the same.

Review of standard form leases and creation of leasing guidelines; approval of future leases. The lender or its counsel should review, and the lender should approve, the standard form leases which should under the loan documents be used for all future leases. These standard form leases should include all of the protections that the lender wants from future tenants, including the right to obtain estoppel certificates from them within a certain number of days, the right to require them to enter into a SNDA, the right to require tenants to amend their leases within reasonable limits if required by the lender in certain circumstances (*e.g.*, if required by a lender making a permanent loan). Alternatively, if tenant will not timely enter into such a SNDA or amendment, the form lease should provide that the landlord may terminate tenant's lease. The standard form of lease should also include limitations on the liability of successor landlords after a foreclosure (including the lender and its affiliates) for breaches by the original landlord under the lease. The standard form lease should require that all notices of default, whether from landlord or tenant, should be sent to the lender as well as to the party to whom they are addressed.[10]

A lender will want to have the loan documents give it the right to approve or disapprove all leases and lease amendments over a certain square footage. The loan documents should be very clear about how long the lender has to review such leases and to approve or reject leases. In addition, the loan documents should provide for what happens if the lender fails to approve such a lease.

In summary, a lender which has its counsel perform a careful and timely review of the leases generating the income which is the primary source for repayment of the loan can spot and fix many problems before the loan closes and is funded. It can resolve these problems in advance by judicious use of tenant estoppel certificates, lease amendments, SNDAs, and appropriate modifications of its loan documents. Such care before the loan funds should pay off in better performance of the loans, and less expensive enforcement costs for the loans that must be enforced through foreclosure.

---

[10] In conduit or securitized lending, these issues become very important, as there is no lender available to approve changes to the form leases after a securitized loan closes. After such a loan closes, it is serviced by an entity whose authority is limited to servicing the loan in accordance with its terms. Usually such a servicer will not have the authority to grant waivers of the forms of leases. In order for such a waiver to be obtained, a servicer often will have to have a vote of the note owners, which make such waivers a practical impossibility. It is vital to negotiate the form of SNDA agreements before the loan closes, and try to eliminate any provisions that will later raise tenant objections. Many other issues must also be carefully addressed in advance in such loans, and are outside the scope of this article.

[b] Questions on the Lender's Review of Leases

1. Why do lenders review the leases of the projects they are financing? What are they looking for when they review these leases? "Commandment Four" of the "Ten Commandments" for lease reviews was to "look out for problem provisions." What sorts of provisions do you think would be problematic or would be likely to cause disputes? Calculation of common area maintenance charges and use exclusives are two examples. Did these two issues come up in the leasing of the FVACC?

2. What is a tenant estoppel certificate? How does receipt of a tenant estoppel certificate provide comfort to and benefit the lender with respect to the leases of the project? What should a tenant estoppel certificate include? In answering these questions, consider the facts in *Galleria Towers, Inc. v. Crump Warren & Somer, Inc.*, 831 P.2d 908 (Colo. 1991). The landlord negotiated a cancellation of the lease with the tenant in consideration for the payment of $420,000. The landlord thereafter defaulted on the loan and the lender foreclosed and took title to the property. When the lender attempted to sue the tenant for past due rent and tortious interference with contract based on the provisions of the loan documents which were violated by the actions of the landlord and the tenant, the lender lost. Do you think that the outcome in *Galleria Towers* would have been different if the tenant had signed an estoppel certificate as described in the O'Conner article?

3. What is a Subordination, Nondisturbance and Attornment Agreement? How do lenders benefit from the receipt of such agreements from the tenants in a project? For example, how can an SNDA help a lender when there are potential liability issues in the lease for the lender as a successor owner? Why might a lender not require a general subordination agreement? In answering this question, consider what happens to leases that are junior to the mortgage (due to the leases being entered into after the mortgage is recorded or due to a subordination of the lease) when the mortgage is foreclosed.

4. What due diligence did First Mortgage Bank perform and what did they require relating to the leasing of the Fox Valley Auto Care Center? See Sections 3.1(t) and 5.1(z) of the Loan Agreement in the Document Book. In Part V you will review one of the leases of the Fox Valley Auto Care Center. When you do so, think about how you could use a tenant estoppel certificate or SNA to protect the lender from any problems with respect to this lease. What would your tenant estoppel certificate or SNA provide? What do you think of the SNDA for the FVACC?

[5] Review of Insurance

To get a sense of the type of insurance a construction lender expects to be in place with respect to a real estate project, see Sections 5.1(j) and 7.6 of the Loan Agreement for the Project in the Document Book. Two key concerns are: (1) what if the improvements are damaged or destroyed, and (2) what if during the construction or operation of the project, someone is injured or someone else's property is damaged? Builders' risk and property insurance address the former concern. Risk and liability coverages address the latter concern.

There are many sub-issues involved in addressing these concerns. For example, what should a lender do if the improvements on the land are damaged or destroyed? Should the lender allow the insurance proceeds to be applied to restoring the improvements or should the lender accelerate the debt and apply the proceeds to the debt? See Article 8 of the Loan Agreement and Section 12.c. of the Mortgage, both of which are in the Document Book, with respect to this issue. Another key issue is what documents the lender and its counsel must review in order to know what insurance is in place. Because the insurance policies are so thick and ponderous, it is conventional for lenders to rely on "certificates of insurance." The article that follows discusses certificates of insurance and cautions that some forms of certificates should not be relied upon by lenders when performing due diligence on insurance matters.

Of course, there are numerous other issues to be aware of when reviewing the adequacy of the insurance for a real estate project. These include: using "claims-made" versus "occurrence" policies, shifting from a builder's risk to a permanent policy, determining the amount of insurance, knowing the difference between being an "additional named insured" and an "additional insured," and understanding what insurance the lender would want the other players (tenants, architect, general contractor) to have in place. Indeed, an entire chapter could be devoted to the numerous issues surrounding the insurance of real estate projects. See Steven W. Pottier & Robert C. Witt, *On the Demand for Liability Insurance: An Insurance Economics Perspective*, 72 TEX. L. REV. 1681 (1994) for a detailed analysis of these issues. Real estate attorneys typically rely on insurance experts to review in detail the adequacy of the insurance in place from their client's perspective.

It is also important for the lender to determine whether the insurance requirements and the provisions relating to the payment of the proceeds of insurance after a casualty are consistent in the leases, any reciprocal easement agreements and the loan documents. Finally, lenders should make certain that they have taken the steps required to obtain a valid security interest in the proceeds of the casualty policy.

[a] Can You Rely on Certificates of Insurance?

Alfred S. Joseph III & Arthur E. Pape,
Certificates of Insurance: The Illusion of Protection,
PROBATE & PROPERTY, January/February, 1995 at 55*

Like a magician pulling a rabbit out of a hat, parties to a real estate transaction often pull out a certificate of insurance as evidence that the party has provided the insurance required by the transaction documents. Most real estate transactions, be they a loan, lease, construction contract or reciprocal easement, contain insurance requirements. The lawyer is often faced with reviewing the certificate to determine whether it satisfies the client's needs or is merely an illusion of reality. The lawyer is likely to receive one of two forms:

- an ACORD 25-S (Certificate of Insurance); or
- an ACORD 27 (Evidence of Property Insurance).

Copies of both forms are printed at the end of this article.

ACORD Forms

These forms are published by ACORD, a not-for-profit insurance association affiliated with over 850 property and casualty insurance companies, 35,000 independent agencies and subscribers, and the major insurance agent professional organizations. Among other services, ACORD publishes standard forms approved by a large number of insurance companies. ACORD states that these forms, or substantial equivalents, account for more than 90% of the certificates issued, although other organizations, notably the American Institute of Architects, have developed their own insurance certificate forms. In this article, each of the ACORD forms is called a "certificate," although ACORD uses this term only for the ACORD 25-S. Insurance certificates are generally issued by agents and brokers rather than by the insurance company itself.

ACORD 25-S

The ACORD 25-S is titled "Certificate of Insurance." It purports to evidence existing insurance policies that are identified by number, effective date and expiration date. The form contains a place to describe the policy limits as well as the following three statements:

> This certificate is issued as a matter of information only and confers no rights upon the certificate holder. This certificate does not amend, extend or alter the coverage afforded by the policies below.
>
> This is to certify that policies of insurance listed below have been issued to the insured named above for the policy period indicated. Notwithstanding any requirement, term or condition of any contract or other document with respect to which this certificate may be issued or may pertain, the insurance afforded by the policies described herein is subject to all terms, exclusions and conditions of such policies.
>
> Should any of the above described policies be canceled before the expiration date thereof, the issuing company will endeavor to mail ____________ days written notice to the certificate holder named to the left, but failure to mail such notice shall impose no obligation or liability of any kind upon the company, its agents or representatives.

The ACORD 25-S appears to go out of its way to advise that the recipient of the certificate has no right to rely on the certificate and to make the recipient wonder why he or she accepted the certificate in the first place.

ACORD 27

Unlike the ACORD 25-S, the ACORD 27 is styled "Evidence of Insurance." Like the ACORD 25-S, it purports to evidence existing insurance policies. It appears to be adaptable to any type of physical damage insurance and contains the following statements:

> This is evidence that insurance as identified below has been issued, is in force, and conveys all the rights and privileges afforded under the policy.

> The policy is subject to the premiums, forms, and rules in effect for each policy period. Should the policy be terminated, the company will give the additional interest identified below ____________ days written notice, and will send notification of any changes to the policy that would affect that interest, in accordance with the policy provisions or as required by law.

The ACORD 27 also provides space to identify whether a person with an additional interest is a lender, loss payee or additional insured. Space is reserved to identify persons with other interests in the policy.

Differences with Distinctions?

Note the differences in the ACORD 27 statements and those in the ACORD 25-S. The ACORD 27 conveys all the rights and privileges afforded under the policy; lacks a statement that it does not amend, extend or alter the coverage afforded by the underlying policy; and contains an unconditional obligation to give the certificate holder advance notice of termination and to advise the certificate holder (without specifying how far in advance) of any change to the policy that would affect the interest of the certificate holder. Nevertheless, the ACORD 27 and the ACORD 25-S share the notion that the form is subject to the terms of the underlying policies.

According to the ACORD Forms Instruction Guide (1994 ed.), the ACORD 25-S (Certificate of Insurance) was designed to evidence the existence of insurance and to be delivered to a third party not having an interest in the policy. The Guide states that the ACORD 25-S form should not be used to satisfy a mortgagee or lienholder, waive rights, quote any wording amending a policy unless the policy itself has been amended, quote wording from a contract, or attach to an endorsement. By contrast, the ACORD 27 (Evidence of Property Insurance) was designed to be delivered to a party (such as a lender, loss payee or additional insured) having an interest in the policy.

The format of the ACORD 25-S suggests that the ACORD 25-S is to be used only with liability policies. Likewise, the title of ACORD 27 (Evidence of Property Insurance) suggests that it is to be used only as evidence of property insurance. Many agents believe this to be the case; they often resist using the ACORD 27 to evidence liability insurance. The ACORD instruction guide, however, does not make the property/liability insurance distinction.

In practice, the ACORD 25-S is used for both liability and property insurance. Notwithstanding ACORD's contrary instructions, it is issued both to those having and not having an interest in the policy. When it is used for property insurance, property coverage is dealt with by inclusion of property insurance terms in the "other" space beneath the various specified types of liability insurance. In these cases, the preparer endeavors to include a specification of policy amounts, deductibles and special conditions in the "limits" column.

When both liability and property coverage are listed on an ACORD 25-S, the "certificate holder" box (in which the interest of the certificate holder is identified) may become garbled. For example, a lender typically requires that it be an "additional insured" on liability policies and a "mortgagee" for property insurance. Attempts to explain all this in the limited space afforded by the "certificate holder" box may result in confusion.

When questioned, the issuing agent often indicates a preference for the ACORD 25-S to evidence property insurance because it is the only certificate form with which the agent is familiar. When the agent is pressed to check with its insurer, however, an ACORD 27 becomes available.

Certificates and Case Law

What rights does a certificate of insurance grant to the certificate holder? The Fifth Circuit Court of Appeals held that the insurer had no duty to give to the certificate holder, who was the insured's landlord, notice of cancellation of a liability insurance policy, notwithstanding that it had agreed in the certificate to give a 10 day notice of cancellation. *United States Pipe & Foundry Co. v. United States Fidelity & Guar. Co.*, 505 F.2d 88 (5th Cir. 1974). The *United States Pipe* court held that because the certificate holder had no interest in the policy, no consideration existed for the insurer's promises contained in the certificate. The lease apparently did not require that United States Pipe have an interest in or otherwise benefit from the insurance in question. *United States Pipe* stands for the proposition that a certificate of insurance itself confers no rights on the named holder of the certificate.

In *Lezak & Levy Wholesale Meats, Inc. v. Illinois Employers Ins. Co.*, 460 N.E.2d 475 (Ill. Ct. App. 1984), the plaintiff was an "additional insured" on a policy that insured against "all risk" of physical damage to a cold storage facility and to the personal property stored there. The plaintiff received a certificate of insurance (apparently on the ACORD 25-S form or its equivalent). A breakdown of the cooling machinery spoiled a significant amount of the plaintiff's meat. The policy contained an exclusion from coverage for loss due to equipment breakdown. Although the certificate listed several exclusions from coverage, this one was not listed. Based on the limiting language in the certificate of insurance and on the plaintiff's testimony that he understood that the certificate was not the policy, the court held that the policy exclusion applied.

More recently in *Pekin Ins. Co. v. American Country Ins. Co.*, 572 N.E.2d 1112 (Ill. Ct. App. 1991), a subcontractor delivered to the general contractor (an additional insured) a certificate of insurance containing the ACORD 25-S language, which identified the insurance issued as including "commercial general liability." However, the policy contained an exclusion for claims arising out of "your work," described on a schedule to the policy as "roofing construction." An employee of the subcontractor was injured on the job and sued the general contractor, who tendered defense of the claim to the subcontractor's insurer. The insurer denied coverage. The general contractor had not reviewed the policy but argued that because the policy exclusions conflicted with the plain meaning of the certificate, and because the general contractor was not made aware of the discrepancy, the certificate should prevail. The court held that the general contractor knew it had to look to the policy to ascertain its terms because the certificate disclosed on its face that it was not part of the policy. *Id.* at 1114.

These cases illustrate two general rules: an insured and any other certificate holder has a duty to examine the policy within a reasonable time after receipt of the certificate and to contact the insurer regarding any discrepancies; and a certificate holder is generally charged with knowledge of the terms of the main policy. John A. Appleman, Insurance Law and Practice, Section 9143 (1981).

By contrast, some cases hold that an insured may, through the certificate of insurance, obtain rights greater than those granted by the terms of the policy. Unlike *United States Pipe*, these are cases in which the certificate holder clearly had some interest in the policy. These are generally cases in which an inconsistency between the certificate of insurance and the underlying policy may have misled the certificate holder about its rights under the policy.

Thus, when a mortgagee received a certificate of insurance indicating general coverage for damage caused by the insured's family, but the policy actually restricted the coverage to specific members of the insured's family, the mortgagee recovered for injuries caused by an uninsured family member. *White Motor Corp. v. Northland Ins. Co.*, 315 F. Supp. 689, 693 (D.S.D. 1970). In another case, the indemnity provision of the certificate of insurance provided by a subcontractor to its general contractor stated that the subcontractor would indemnify the contractor against all claims for injury or damage. The policy, which was not tendered to the general contractor, contained an exclusion for rented motor vehicles. The indemnity clause in the certificate controlled, and the insurer provided coverage for an accident involving a rented motor vehicle. *J.M. Corbett Co. v. Insurance Co. of N. Am.*, 357 N.E.2d 125 (Ill. Ct. App. 1976).

These cases reflect the principle that when the certificate is considered to be part of the underlying policy, any inconsistency between the two creates an ambiguity in the policy that courts will construe in favor of the insured. *International Amphitheatre v. Vanguard Underwriters Ins. Co.*, 532 N.E. 2d 493 (Ill. Ct. App. 1988).

The Illinois appellate court, when deciding the *International Amphitheatre* case, was faced with the task of distinguishing its own opinion in the *Lezak* case; it did so by noting that in *Lezak* "the certificate specifically stated that it was not part of the policy; the court found no ambiguity between the certificate and the policy; and the insured admitted knowledge that separate exclusions were contained in the policy." *Id.* at 502.

The same court, when deciding *Pekin Insurance Company*, distinguished it from *International Amphitheatre* and *J.M. Corbett Co.* by reasoning that in *Pekin* there was a "clear showing . . . that the certificate was not part of the policy, and it conveyed no rights to the certificate holder." *Pekin*, 572 N.E.2d at 1114.

After reading these cases, a cynic might conclude that the courts reach the results they think are right and conveniently have two competing lines of cases to assist them in reaching a preconceived result. More likely, the courts recognize that reviewing the original policy is often not practical in the real business world, making reliance on insurance certificates as evidence of insurance necessary. Then the court views the certificate as part of the underlying policy. Any conflict between the certificate and the policy (whether the conflict results from internally inconsistent statements or from the absence of policy provisions in the certificate) will be deemed to create ambiguities in the policy construed for the benefit of the insured and to the detriment of the insurer. When the certificate contains clear language separating it from the underlying policy, the certificate holder will be bound by the underlying policy.

Are Certificates Worth Anything?

Given these conclusions, a practitioner might ask if he or she may ever rely on a certificate of insurance to show that another party has complied with the insurance requirements of the transaction even if, as a practical matter, the underlying policy is unavailable. The prudent answer is "no" when the certificate contains the ACORD 25-S language. ACORD 27, or its equivalent, which conveys the rights afforded under the policy (making it easier to argue that the certificate is part of the policy) is preferred whenever the certificate holder is to have an interest in the underlying policy as additional insured, mortgagee, loss payee or otherwise. In addition, a certificate recipient should consider the following steps:

1. Clearly establish in the underlying transaction documents (*e.g.*, the lease or loan documents) the extent to which the recipient is to have an interest in insurance policy(s) obtained by the other party.

2. Be sure that the recipient's interest in the policy is specifically set forth in the certificate of insurance.

3. If relying on a certificate in lieu of a copy of the policy, use an ACORD 27 rather than an ACORD 25-S, regardless of whether the insurance covers liability or property.

4. If the ACORD 25-S must be used, require the issuing agent to delete (and initial such deletions) any "will endeavor" language and the provisions restricting liability, narrowing the scope of coverage and limiting the obligation to provide notice of cancellation.

5. Have the issuing agent attach to the certificate copies of policy provisions of most concern. For example, the "standard" mortgagee clause varies from company to company, including on matters about which the mortgagee will be given notice, the notice period and non-imputation of the acts of the primary insured.

6. Have the issuing agent either certify that it has authority to make a requested modification to the certificate, obtain a letter from the insurance company ratifying the act of its agent, or obtain a copy of the agent's agreement with its insurance company (because insurance companies differ in the amount of discretion granted to the agent/broker to modify the form).

7. Whenever possible, have the recipient's insurance advisor review the certificate of insurance and any other available information about the other party's compliance with the insurance requirements of the transaction.

8. Provide to the agent a tailored form of certificate that states clearly that it is part of the policy, confers an interest in the policy and incorporates suggestions 2, 5 and 6 above.

9. Consider whether, in light of the distinction between ACORD forms 25-S and 27, transaction documents that require a "certificate" of insurance should be modified to provide instead for "evidence" of insurance.

10. Check state law to determine whether any applicable provisions require specific terms for certificates. *See, e.g.*, California Insurance Code § 384.

Conclusion

Certificates of insurance are not always what they seem. Depending on the form used, often the certificate conveys no rights to the certificate holder and leaves the holder subject to exclusions and other policy conditions. A practitioner who must accept a certificate of insurance should consider requiring the ACORD 27 with the alterations suggested above. To ensure that the certificate reflects reality and not illusion, however, review of the policy itself is the best practice.

ACORD. EVIDENCE OF PROPERTY INSURANCE DATE (MM/DD/YY)

THIS IS EVIDENCE THAT INSURANCE AS IDENTIFIED BELOW HAS BEEN ISSUED, IS IN FORCE, AND CONVEYS ALL THE RIGHTS AND PRIVILEGES AFFORDED UNDER THE POLICY.

PRODUCER | PHONE (A/C, No, Ext): | COMPANY

CODE: | SUB CODE:

AGENCY CUSTOMER ID #:

INSURED | LOAN NUMBER | POLICY NUMBER

EFFECTIVE DATE | EXPIRATION DATE | CONTINUED UNTIL TERMINATED IF CHECKED

THIS REPLACES PRIOR EVIDENCE DATED:

PROPERTY INFORMATION

LOCATION/DESCRIPTION

COVERAGE INFORMATION

COVERAGE/PERILS/FORMS	AMOUNT OF INSURANCE	DEDUCTIBLE

REMARKS (Including Special Conditions)

CANCELLATION

THE POLICY IS SUBJECT TO THE PREMIUMS, FORMS, AND RULES IN EFFECT FOR EACH POLICY PERIOD. SHOULD THE POLICY BE TERMINATED, THE COMPANY WILL GIVE THE ADDITIONAL INTEREST IDENTIFIED BELOW ______ DAYS WRITTEN NOTICE, AND WILL SEND NOTIFICATION OF ANY CHANGES TO THE POLICY THAT WOULD AFFECT THAT INTEREST, IN ACCORDANCE WITH THE POLICY PROVISIONS OR AS REQUIRED BY LAW.

ADDITIONAL INTEREST

NAME AND ADDRESS | MORTGAGEE | ADDITIONAL INSURED | LOSS PAYEE

LOAN #

AUTHORIZED REPRESENTATIVE

ACORD 27 (3/93) © ACORD CORPORATION 1993

ACORD. CERTIFICATE OF INSURANCE DATE (MM/DD/YY)

PRODUCER	THIS CERTIFICATE IS ISSUED AS A MATTER OF INFORMATION ONLY AND CONFERS NO RIGHTS UPON THE CERTIFICATE HOLDER. THIS CERTIFICATE DOES NOT AMEND, EXTEND OR ALTER THE COVERAGE AFFORDED BY THE POLICIES BELOW.
	COMPANIES AFFORDING COVERAGE
	COMPANY A
INSURED	COMPANY B
	COMPANY C
	COMPANY D

COVERAGES

THIS IS TO CERTIFY THAT THE POLICIES OF INSURANCE LISTED BELOW HAVE BEEN ISSUED TO THE INSURED NAMED ABOVE FOR THE POLICY PERIOD INDICATED, NOTWITHSTANDING ANY REQUIREMENT, TERM OR CONDITION OF ANY CONTRACT OR OTHER DOCUMENT WITH RESPECT TO WHICH THIS CERTIFICATE MAY BE ISSUED OR MAY PERTAIN, THE INSURANCE AFFORDED BY THE POLICIES DESCRIBED HEREIN IS SUBJECT TO ALL THE TERMS, EXCLUSIONS AND CONDITIONS OF SUCH POLICIES. LIMITS SHOWN MAY HAVE BEEN REDUCED BY PAID CLAIMS.

CO LTR	TYPE OF INSURANCE	POLICY NUMBER	POLICY EFFECTIVE DATE (MM/DD/YY)	POLICY EXPIRATION DATE (MM/DD/YY)	LIMITS	
	GENERAL LIABILITY COMMERCIAL GENERAL LIABILITY CLAIMS MADE / OCCUR OWNER'S & CONT PROT				GENERAL AGGREGATE PRODUCTS-COMP/OP AGG PERSONAL & ADV INJURY EACH OCCURRENCE FIRE DAMAGE (Any one fire) MED EXP (Any one person)	$ $ $ $ $ $
	AUTOMOBILE LIABILITY ANY AUTO ALL OWNED AUTOS SCHEDULED AUTOS HIRED AUTOS NON-OWNED AUTOS				COMBINED SINGLE LIMIT BODILY INJURY (Per person) BODILY INJURY (Per accident) PROPERTY DAMAGE	$ $ $ $
	GARAGE LIABILITY ANY AUTO				AUTO ONLY - EA ACCIDENT OTHER THAN AUTO ONLY: EACH ACCIDENT AGGREGATE	$ $ $
	EXCESS LIABILITY UMBRELLA FORM OTHER THAN UMBRELLA FORM				EACH OCCURRENCE AGGREGATE	$ $ $
	WORKERS COMPENSATION AND EMPLOYERS' LIABILITY THE PROPRIETOR/ PARTNERS/EXECUTIVE OFFICERS ARE: INCL / EXCL				STATUTORY LIMITS EACH ACCIDENT DISEASE - POLICY LIMIT DISEASE - EACH EMPLOYEE	 $ $ $
	OTHER					

DESCRIPTION OF OPERATIONS/LOCATIONS/VEHICLES/SPECIAL ITEMS

CERTIFICATE HOLDER	CANCELLATION
	SHOULD ANY OF THE ABOVE DESCRIBED POLICIES BE CANCELLED BEFORE THE EXPIRATION DATE THEREOF, THE ISSUING COMPANY WILL ENDEAVOR TO MAIL ____ DAYS WRITTEN NOTICE TO THE CERTIFICATE HOLDER NAMED TO THE LEFT, BUT FAILURE TO MAIL SUCH NOTICE SHALL IMPOSE NO OBLIGATION OR LIABILITY OF ANY KIND UPON THE COMPANY, ITS AGENTS OR REPRESENTATIVES.
	AUTHORIZED REPRESENTATIVE

ACORD 25-S (7/90) © ACORD CORPORATION 1993

[h] And It Gets Worse!

What follows is a brief update, by one of the authors of the prior article, on the situation with certificates of insurance, which has gone from bad to worse. Until the ability to rely on the certificates of insurance improves, real estate attorneys should emphasize to their clients the need to obtain the actual insurance policies and endorsements to truly be protected.

Arthur E. Pape,

A Hot Tip and a Soup Sandwich*

On July 28, 2006, ACORD[1] published new versions of its ACORD 27 (Evidence of Property Insurance) and ACORD 28 (Evidence of Commercial Property Insurance) forms. Copies are attached as Appendix A [omitted — Eds.] and Appendix B [omitted — Eds.]. Prior versions of these forms contained language that conveyed all the rights and privileges contained in the policy and provided an absolute obligation to notify the certificate holder of cancellation of the policy. The new forms for property insurance are like ACORD 25 (the CGL Certificate) and ACORD 26 (Certificate of Property Insurance) forms that were promulgated some years ago. Each of these four ACORD forms, which are typically used by brokers and their insureds to provide "evidence" that the insured has the insurance coverage identified by the form in effect, now contains the statement that it is issued "as a matter of information only" and "confers no rights upon the additional interest named below" and "does not amend, extend or alter the coverage afforded by the policies" identified in the completed form. Thus, while the titles of the new ACORD 27 and 28 forms still contain the word "Evidence," the forms cannot be relied on as proof the insurance exists or that an endorsement naming the mortgagee identified in the Evidence as the holder of an additional interest has actually been issued by the insurer.

To make matters worse, the new ACORD 27 and 28 forms also contain the same language as the ACORD 25 and ACORD 26 forms, stating that if any of the policies described in the certificate is cancelled before the expiration date "the issuing insurer will endeavor to mail" notice to the person identified as having the additional interest specified in the completed form. The number of days notice is blank and must be filled in when the form is completed. Most lenders ask for 30 days prior notice, but under the new language "failure to mail such notice shall impose no obligation or liability of any kind upon the insurer, its agents or representatives."

Publication of these new forms has aroused the lending industry. The Mortgage Bankers Association strongly objects to the new forms on behalf of its membership and is seeking to have the offensive parts rescinded. At least one insurance consultant who represents many of the major players in the collateralized mortgage backed securities (CMBS) market has stated that he will not close a loan on the basis of the new ACORD forms. I understand that certain rating agencies have downgraded loans in which the new ACORD 28 is provided as the evidence of insurance and that other rating agencies have denied investment grade ratings to CMBS loans in those circumstances.

In response to the complaints by the lending industry, ACORD has "organized" a Working Group which meets telephonically for one hour most Wednesday afternoons. The Working Group is comprised of about 45 people representing insurers, agents, lenders and the Mortgage Bankers Association. The purpose of the Working Group is to develop a form of evidence of insurance that will satisfy the objectives and the objections of all parties. Fellow ACREL member, Fred Joseph, and I, since we neither play golf nor have anything else to do on

---

[1] Based in New York, with offices in London as well, ACORD Corporation ("ACORD") is a voluntary membership trade association for the insurance industry.

Wednesday afternoons, have been part of the Group. Some thus far insurmountable hurdles include:

(i) If a new policy is required for the project in question, the policy probably does not exist at closing, because it typically takes the insurance industry anywhere from 2 weeks to 6 months to produce a policy after coverage has been bound. That may be a tough pill to swallow, but thus far, the insurance industry is unwilling or unable to change.

(ii) Binding coverage with a binder like the ACORD 75 form of insurance binder (copy attached as Appendix C) [omitted — Eds.] is also problematic. Binders do not set forth all of the coverage details that the lender wants to know. Although the binder creates an independent contract for insurance, coverage details may be unknown and the binder has a very limited duration, perhaps 30 to 60 days after issuance, at which time the binder expires because it is presumed that the policy will have been issued. As the insurance coverage litigation following the World Trade Center collapse demonstrated so well, insurance policies for large commercial projects are sometimes non-standard or manuscript policies, which means it will be hard to determine exactly what coverage was bound if a loss occurs before the policy is issued.

(iii) State laws and requirements governing insurance policies vary so greatly that it is difficult to set forth the rights of a holder of the ACORD form of Evidence of Insurance to notice of cancellation. A majority of states and the Insurance Services Organization (ISO) Forms require 10 days notice by the insurer if the cancellation is for non-payment of premiums and 30 days notice if the cancellation is for any other reason. These policy provisions automatically apply as part of the ISO form policies if there is a mortgage holder named in the Declarations portion of the policy.

(iv) Another serious defect in the new ACORD 27 and 28 forms is that the "endeavor" language of the new ACORD forms deprives the mortgage holder of the right to notice should the policy be cancelled by the insured. I believe a mortgage holder's right to notice from the insurer of cancellation by the insured was derived exclusively from the old ACORD 27 and 28 which conveyed the rights under the policy and stated that "should the policy be terminated [presumably by either party], the [insurer] will give the [mortgage holder] ____________days written notice." It is important to understand that neither the so-called "New York long form mortgage endorsement" (copy attached as Appendix D) [omitted — Eds.] nor any provision of the ISO policy appears to require notice to a mortgage holder in the event the insured cancels the policy. Appendix E [omitted — Eds.] contains the standard ISO Commercial Property Policy Mortgageholders language that is part of the Additional Coverages built into the Policy, as well as the explanation of the language, which specifically states that "No promise is made to notify the mortgageholder in the event of cancellation at the insured's request." The so-called New York long form mortgage holder endorsement (see Appendix D) [omitted — Eds.] is not any more helpful. Thus, whenever a mortgage holder receives one of the new ACORD forms, if the mortgage holder wants to require notice from the insurer of an attempted cancellation by the insured borrower, it must obtain this right via an endorsement to the policy.

(v) At this point, the Working Group appears to be a long way from even considering the question of the ability of the mortgage holder to rely on the ACORD 28 form. The Working Group has not discussed the ACORD 27.

The situation is as easy to handle as a soup sandwich. I intend to solve the dilemma for myself by developing a form for evidence of insurance for use on behalf of my clients instead of accepting the new ACORD forms. The issue will be whether an insurance broker will be prepared to provide the form.

Everyone seems to agree that one may not amend an insurance policy by using an ACORD certificate. Therefore, no matter what the new ACORD certificates say, the policy will govern. If you have a New York endorsement or a standard mortgage holder clause in the policy, it should override a lot of the limitations of the certificate, except for those relating to notice of cancellation by the insurer to the mortgagee or certificate holder. However, one must review the policy to be sure what rights the mortgagee will have. The author has been advised that one major insurance company is now attempting to insert the "endeavor" language into its policies, which signals a need to watch out for that attempt.

Needless to say, certificates of insurance will be a hot topic for some months to come. The publicity and the wrangling should result in more real estate professionals learning more about certificates of insurance in particular and insurance issues generally.

EPILOGUE

The ACORD Working Group described above stopped meeting regularly in the Spring of 2008. [T]he Working Group, comprised of three factions — insurers, producers and lenders — had come to an impasse on the essential questions of the "information only" language of the ACORD 27 and 28 forms. The Working Group had made some progress in resolving its differences as to the "Notice of Termination" language. After the Working Group went into hiatus, various parties approached the National Association of Insurance Commissioners (NAIC) to request that it conduct a mediation in an effort to reach a resolution of the differences splitting the Working Group. Although the NAIC appeared willing to conduct such a mediation, after nearly a year, no real progress has been made. The Working Group has recently resumed weekly meetings.

AEP

March 24, 2009

[c] Comments and Questions Regarding Certificates of Insurance

1. What functions are certificates of insurance supposed to serve?
2. To what extent can a lender rely on the current forms of certificate of insurance?

3. Review the insurance certificate provided to First Mortgage Bank in the Document Book. Is this certificate of insurance more similar to the Acord 25-S or the Acord 27?

4. If you were representing First Mortgage Bank, what changes would you seek with respect to the certificate of insurance received for the Fox Valley Auto Care Center?

5. What other steps would you take to ensure that First Mortgage Bank's interest in the project is adequately insured?

6. Why do you think insurance companies include provisions in their certificates of insurance that state that the company is not obligated to notify the mortgagee prior to canceling the policy or that the terms of the policy control over the terms of the certificate? Is it reasonable of the insurance companies to include such limitation language in the certificates they issue?

§ 11.02 DOCUMENTING AND CLOSING THE LOAN

Article V of the Construction Loan Agreement for the Fox Valley Auto Care Center contains numerous conditions to the lender's advancing the loan proceeds to the borrower. These conditions mainly involve requiring the borrower to sign various documents that together grant the lender a security interest in all of the facets of the real estate project (such as the real property mortgage, assignment of rents, U.C.C. security agreement, and assignment of the construction documentation). The conditions also relate to providing documentation that addresses the due diligence matters (such as the survey, title insurance policy, U.C.C. searches, certificates of insurance, Phase I environmental audit, construction documents, government permits, and plans and specifications). For a very practical approach to addressing the various conditions to closing the loan already discussed in this chapter, see Joshua Stein, *How to Streamline, Simplify, and Save Money in the Loan Closing Process*, http://www.real-estate-law.com/infoFrame.php?pdf=LOAN_CLOSING_PROCESS_61.pdf

[1] Patriot Act

There is another condition to closing a loan that mortgage lenders now need to add to their closing checklist which was not present when the FVACC deal closed: ensuring compliance with the Uniting and Strengthening America by Providing Appropriate Tools Required to Intercept and Obstruct Terrorism Act of 2001 (the "Patriot Act"). In 2004 several large banks were penalized with fines in the tens of millions of dollars for their non-compliance with anti-money laundering laws. *See* Goodman, *Anti-Terrorism and US Real Estate Lending*, REAL ESTATE FINANCE 21, no. 6 (April 2005).

Banks and other financial institutions are required, according to U.S. Treasury Department rules, to verify the identity of potential accountholders and reject wire transfers or cash transactions with persons on the list of "prohibited persons" (*i.e.*, "Specially Designated Nationals and Blocked Persons" on the list of individuals or entities with whom United States persons are prohibited from doing any kind of business) or entities owned or controlled by prohibited persons. *Id.* The Patriot Act prohibits all United States persons from participating in transactions involving "prohibited persons" or "blocked properties," so a loan to a borrower who is a terrorist or terrorist group that results in a benefit of funds, goods or services to a prohibited person would be a financial benefit that would violate the Order, as would a lender taking possession of a property after an event of default if it is a blocked property. *Id.* Thus, it is imperative that real estate lenders know whom they are dealing with and make sure that the person is not a prohibited person.

This should be done by checking the borrower's name or borrower's owners', shareholders', or investors' names against the US Treasury Department's Office of Foreign Assets Control's "Specially Designated Nationals and Blocked Persons" list, which is over 100 pages long but can be accessed with computer software. Lenders are also being advised to add a representation provision in their loan documents requiring the borrower to represent that prohibited parties are not currently related to the transaction in any way and to covenant that prohibited parties will not be introduced to the deal at any later point in time.

In addition, the Bank Secrecy Act grants the U.S. Treasury Department authority to require financial institutions to maintain records of transactions involving currency and to institute anti-money laundering programs, but, so far, non-banking and non-"financial institution" type real estate lenders (such as a finance company) and "persons involved in real estate closings" (like lawyers and appraisers) have been exempted from the onerous task of creating an anti-money laundering program. However, this may change. *See Anti-Terrorism and US Real Estate Lending, supra,* for a description of the minimum requirements for financial institutions to establish an anti-money laundering compliance program.

[2] Negotiation Assignment

Review Article V of the Loan Agreement in the Document Book. If you were representing First Mortgage Bank, how would you explain each of the items that are conditions to funding the loan? If you were representing Regent, would you object to the wording of any of these requirements? Are there any closing conditions you would try to eliminate or modify?

Assume that you are representing Regent, and prepare a letter to counsel for First Mortgage Bank in which you identify any changes you would like to see with respect to Article V. Be sure to explain in a persuasive fashion the reasons for your suggested changes. Now think about how you would respond to these suggested changes if you were representing First Mortgage Bank. In class, you may be called upon to negotiate this section of the Loan Agreement from either the borrower or the lender's perspective.

[3] Due Diligence and Opinions Relating to Power, Authority, and Enforceability

One of the due diligence items contained in Article V that we have not previously discussed is the issue of the borrowing entity's power and authority to enter into the loan transaction and the enforceability of the documents signed. The case that follows addresses this important issue.

[a] Authority to Enter Into the Loan Agreement

FIRST NATIONAL BANK AND TRUST COMPANY OF WILLISTON v. SCHERR

467 N.W.2d 427 (N.D. 1991)

MESCHKE, JUSTICE.

The First National Bank & Trust Company of Williston appealed from a judgment that Albinus Scherr, a partner, and Scherr and Scherr, the partnership, were not liable on a $65,000 note to the Bank signed for the partnership by only one partner, Pius Scherr, contrary to a restriction in the partnership agreement known to the Bank. We affirm.

Pius Scherr and Albinus Scherr started a general partnership to construct and invest in buildings. On September 15, 1981, this new partnership, Scherr and Scherr, opened a checking account at the Bank. The Partnership Checking Account Signature Card, signed by each of the partners, authorized the Bank:

> "to accept (whether or not payable to the partner who signs the same or to any other partner) checks, endorsements, notes, . . . mortgages or any other instruments for the deposit or withdrawal of funds, for borrowing money and pledging or mortgaging assets of the partnership as security for the payment thereof and for the transaction of any other business with it, when signed by any ____________ of the undersigned."

A separate box adjacent to the partners' signatures on the signature card had in it printed instructions, "Number of Signatures Required," and was filled in with a typed "1." This signature card was kept in the checking account files, not the loan files, of the Bank.

Later a written partnership agreement was completed. It was dated, signed, and acknowledged by Pius on October 1, 1981, and by Albinus on December 21, 1981, when a copy was delivered to the Bank. This agreement included a clause restricting the authority of a single partner to engage in certain transactions for the partnership:

> "Neither partner shall, without the written consent of the other partner, endorse any note, or act as an accommodation party, or otherwise become surety for any person. Without the written consent of the other partner, neither partner shall on behalf of the partnership borrow or lend money, or make, deliver or accept any commercial paper, or execute any mortgage, security agreement, bond or lease, or purchase or contract to purchase, or sell or contract to sell any property for or of the partnership. Neither partner shall, except with the written consent of the other partner, assign, mortgage, grant a security initerest [sic] in, or sell his share in the Partnership or in its capital assets or property, or enter into any agreement as a result of which any person shall become interested with him in the Partnership, or do any act detrimental to the best interests of the Partnership or which would make it impossible to carry on the ordinary business of the Partnership."

The signed copy of the partnership agreement was completed and delivered to the Bank at its request, and was kept in the Bank's loan file for the partnership.

Beginning in November 1981 and continuing into 1984, Scherr and Scherr borrowed large sums from the Bank to acquire property and to construct various buildings in Williston. One venture was construction of a building leased to a Famous Recipe Chicken fast-food franchisee. This project began with a mortgage, signed by both Pius and Albinus, to the Bank on April 29, 1983, for a construction advance of $100,000. Later, Pius alone signed the four notes to the Bank drawing on this short-term loan: One on May 2, 1983 for $10,000; another on June 2, 1983 for $20,000; the third on July 14, 1983 for $15,000; and the fourth note on August 1, 1983 for $55,000. This loan was soon converted to a $100,000 note secured by a long-term mortgage to the Bank, both dated October 26, 1983, and both signed by Pius and Albinus.

The next day, October 27, Pius Scherr alone signed another short-term partnership note to the Bank for $65,000. This note was filled in to say, "THE PURPOSE OF THIS LOAN IS: Final construction on Famous Recipe Chicken." The Bank repeatedly renewed this note through May 1985. Each renewal note was signed for the partnership by Pius alone.

The Scherrs defaulted on their Famous Recipe Chicken obligations to the Bank. The Bank foreclosed the $100,000 mortgage, and then sued the Scherrs to collect the $65,000 note. The trial court entered summary judgment for the Bank against Pius, Albinus, and the partnership for the balance due on the $65,000 note and interest. Pius, Albinus, and the partnership appealed. We affirmed the summary judgment against Pius but reversed the summary judgment against Albinus and the partnership. *First National Bank and Trust Company of Williston v. Scherr*, 435 N.W.2d 704 (N.D.1989) (*Scherr I*). We remanded for trial on the effect of the restriction in the partnership agreement on the liability of Albinus and the partnership to the Bank

After trial on remand, the trial court determined that Pius was not authorized to sign the unsecured, $65,000 note for the partnership because the Bank "had written knowledge" about the specific restriction on his authority in the partnership agreement, and because the Bank "thereafter established a course of conduct of business with the partnership consistent with those restrictions." The trial court felt that it was "arguable but questionable" whether the signature card authorization bound the partnership to a promissory note signed by one partner. The trial court ruled that, "in any event, the restrictive language . . . in the Partnership Agreement . . . overrides and controls the signature card in the event of conflict." The court concluded that Albinus and the partnership were not liable on the note, and entered judgment dismissing the Bank's claim against them. The Bank appealed. This is *Scherr III*.

On appeal, the Bank argues that the signature card authorization was a controlling agreement between the Bank and the partnership, because Albinus thereby consented to Pius's lone signature on the $65,000 note. According to the Bank, any difference between the terms of that authorization and the terms of the later partnership agreement is immaterial. The Bank argues that the partnership's direct authorization to the Bank was not altered by the later restrictive agreement between the partners, even though the Bank knew about it.

In *Scherr I*, we recognized that statutes regulate the authority of a partner to act for the partnership. North Dakota has adopted the Uniform Partnership Act, as have nearly all states. *See* note on Comparative Legislation following NDCC 45-05-01 (Supp.1989). NDCC 45-06-01 (part) says:

> "1. Every partner is an agent of the partnership for the purpose of its business, and the act of every partner, including the execution in the partnership name of any instrument, for apparently carrying on in the usual way the business of the partnership . . . binds the partnership, unless the partner so acting has in fact no authority to act for the partnership in the particular matter, and the person with whom he is dealing has knowledge of the fact that he has no such authority.
>
> . . . .
>
> "4. No act of a partner in contravention of a restriction on authority shall bind the partnership to persons having knowledge of the restriction."

As this statute pronounces, a partner's liability to a third-person is largely fixed by the law of agency. Restatement (Second) of Agency § 14A comment a (1958). Also, NDCC 45-05-03(3) says, "[t]he law of agency applies under this title." Agency law, then, controls this case.

A partner, as an agent of the partnership, normally binds the partnership by executing any instrument that carries on the business of the partnership in the usual way. NDCC 45-06-01(1). But, as with any agent, that is not so if the partner's authority is restricted, and if the restriction is known to the person with whom the partner deals. *Id.* The repetition in NDCC 45-06-01(4) emphasizes that the law commands a different result when a partner acts "in contravention of a restriction on [his] authority" in dealing with someone "having knowledge of the restriction."

Many decisions by other courts have ruled that a person cannot recover from a second partner or the partnership for additional transactions with an acting partner after that person had notice of a later restriction on the acting partner's authority. *Van Dusen v. The Star Quartz Mining Company*, 36 Cal. 571 (1869); *Baxter v. Rollins*, 90 Iowa 217, 57 N.W. 838 (1894); *Dawson Blakemore & Co. v. Elrod*, 105 Ky. 624, 49 S.W. 465 (1899); *Bank of Bellbuckle v. Mason*, 139 Tenn. 659, 202 S.W. 931 (1918); *Dayle L. Smith Oil Co. v. Continental Supply Co.*, 268 S.W. 489 (Tex. Civ. App.1924); *Gladson v. Heagle*, 170 Minn. 166, 212 N.W. 175 (1927); *T.T. Word Supply Co. v. Burke*, 57 S.W.2d 610 (Tex. Civ. App.1933); *DeSantis v. Miller Petroleum*, 29 Cal. App.2d 679, 85 P.2d 489 (1938); *West Side Trust Company v. Gascoigne*, 39 N.J.Super. 467, 121 A.2d 441 (1956); *Arrington v. Columbia Nitrogen Corporation*, 168 Ga. App. 455, 309 S.E.2d 428 (1983). *See also* 59A Am. Jur.2d Partnership, § 267 (1987); 68 C.J.S. Partnership § 143 (1950). *Compare Owens v. Palos Verdes Monaco*, 142 Cal. App.3d 855, 191 Cal. Rptr. 381, 386–90 (1983). These precedents demonstrate that knowledge of a restriction on, or revocation of, an individual partner's authority controls over a preexisting arrangement with a creditor.

In this case, Pius had initial authority to act individually for the partnership in borrowing money from the Bank through the signature card authorization. Afterward, the partnership agreement restricted that authority. When a third person has "previously extended credit" to the principal through the agent "in reliance upon a manifestation from the principal of continuing authority in the agent," that authority can be restricted or revoked by notice to the third person. Restatement (Second) of Agency § 136(2)(a) (1958). N.D.C.C. 3-01-11 (part) says that, "[u]nless the power of an agent is coupled with an interest in the subject of the agency, it is terminated as to every person having notice thereof by: 1. Its revocation by the principal. . . ." The question in this case is whether delivery of the written partnership agreement to the Bank was effective notice that Pius's individual authorization had been restricted. The trial court found as a matter of fact that effective notice of restriction had been given.

One who claims that an agent acted within his authority has the burden of proving the scope of that authority. *Red River Commodities, Inc. v. Eidsness*, 459 N.W.2d 805, 810 (N.D. 1990). The scope of an agent's authority is a question of fact. *Id.* "If a person dealing with an agent has notice that the agent's authority is created or described in a writing which is intended for his inspection, he is affected by limitations upon the authority contained in the writing, unless misled by conduct of the principal." Restatement (Second) of Agency § 167 (1958). No question of fraud on the part of the partnership was raised in the trial court, or pursued on this appeal. "A person has 'notice' of a fact within the meaning of this title when the person who claims the benefit of the notice: . . . 2. Delivers through the mail, or by other means of communication, a written statement of the fact to such person or to a proper person at his place of business. . . ." NDCC 45-05-02 (part). The trial court determined that notice of a restriction had been given to the Bank by delivery of the executed partnership agreement.

The signature card did not stand alone. After the signature card, the Bank sought, received, and knew about a later partnership agreement that restricted one partner's power to borrow for the partnership without the consent of the other partner. There is no claim, in this case, that the partnership subsequently ratified the $65,000 note to the Bank. *Compare Askew v. Joachim Memorial Home*, 234 N.W.2d 226 (N.D.1975). Under agency principles and the Uniform Partnership Act, the trial court's factual determinations that Pius acted in contravention of a restriction on his authority as a partner, known to the Bank, controls this case. . . .

We affirm.

Erickstad, C.J., and Levine, Vande Walle and Gierke, JJ., concur.

[b] Questions and Comments on *Scherr*

1. *Scherr* raises the issue of the possibility that the party signing the loan documents on behalf of an entity does not have the power and authority to sign these documents on behalf of the entity and to bind the entity to the agreements made. Had the lender not received the copy of the partnership agreement, would the signature of one of the two partners on the note for $65,000 been sufficient to bind the partnership? What if there had been no signature card authorization? What is the concept of "apparent authority" and why do you think this concept exists?

2. Would lenders be better off if they simply bury their heads in the sand and not review the organizational documents of the entities that they loan money to? In thinking about this, recall that relying on the agency law concept of "apparent authority" is problematic because the action taken must be within the ordinary course of the entity's business.

[c] The Opinion of Counsel from Kaplan & Miller

One common method that lenders use to address the power, authority and enforceability issue is to require an opinion on these issues (and certain other related issues) from the borrower's counsel. Carefully review the following opinion from the law firm of Kaplan & Miller to First Mortgage Bank with respect to the construction loan for the Fox Valley Auto Care Center to see how these issues are addressed. As you read through the opinion, think about the various reasons why First Mortgage Bank sought this opinion, and what ramifications there are to Regent and Regent's law firm in issuing the opinion to First Mortgage Bank. Also think about what Donna Smith and Sam Nader needed to do to be able to render these opinions to First Mortgage Bank.

Kaplan & Miller
450 Wacker Drive
Chicago, Ilinois 60606

August 12, 1989

First Mortgage Bank

33 North LaSalle Street

Chicago, Illinois 60690

Re: $2,300,000.00 Construction Mortgage Loan (the "Loan") to be secured by a mortgage on property located in the Village of Aurora, County of DuPage, Illinois (the "Property")

Ladies and Gentlemen:

The law firm of Kaplan & Miller has acted as legal counsel to Fox Valley Auto Care LLC ("Fox Valley"), First Mortgage Bank and Trust Company of Chicago Trust No. 108049-04 under Trust Agreement dated April 11, 1989 (the "Trust" and together with Fox Valley sometimes collectively referred to as "Borrower"), Regent Real Estate Development Corp., an Illinois corporation ("Manager") and David Delaney, Andrew Smith, and Michael Mann (collectively "Guarantors"), with respect to the captioned transaction.

As such legal counsel, the undersigned has reviewed the following documents:

1. Construction Loan Agreement dated as of August 2, 1989 executed by and between Borrower and First Mortgage Bank and Trust Company of Chicago ("Lender").
2. Note dated as of August 2, 1989 made by Borrower in favor of Lender in the principal sum of $2,100,000.00.
3. Note dated as of August 2, 1989 made by Borrower in favor of Lender in the principal sum of $200,000.00.
4. Mortgage dated as of August 2, 1989 executed by the Trust in favor of Lender.
5. Assignment of Leases and Rents dated as of August 2, 1989 executed by Borrower in favor of Lender.
6. Collateral Assignment of Beneficial Interest Under Land Trust dated as of August 2, 1989 executed by Fox Valley in favor of Lender.
7. Security Agreement dated as of August 2, 1989 executed by Borrower in favor of Lender.

8. Indemnity Agreement dated as of August 2, 1989 executed by Guarantors in favor of Lender.
9. Guaranty of Payment and Performance dated as of August 2, 1989 executed by Guarantors in favor of Lender.
10. Guaranty of Payment dated as of August 2, 1989 executed by Guarantors in favor of Lender.
11. Loan Affidavit dated as of August 2, 1989 executed by Guarantors in favor of Lender.
12. Pledge and Collateral Agreement dated as of August 2, 1989 executed by Fox Valley in favor of Lender.
13. Collateral Assignment of General Contractor's Agreement dated as of August 2, 1989 executed by Borrower in favor of Lender.
14. Collateral Assignment of Engineer's Agreement dated as of August 2, 1989 executed by Borrower in favor of Lender.
15. Collateral Assignment of Plans and Specifications dated as of August 2, 1989 executed by Borrower in favor of Lender.
16. General Assignment dated as of August 2, 1989 executed by Borrower in favor of Lender.
17. UCC Financing Statements.
18. Letter Agreement regarding Certificate of Deposit and Letter of Credit.
19. Certified copy of Limited Liability Company Agreement relating to Fox Valley and LLC Certificate.
20. Certified copy of Articles of Incorporation of Manager issued by the Secretary of State of the State of Illinois.
21. Certificate of Good Standing of Manger issued by the Secretary of State of the State of Illinois.
22. Certified copy of the By-laws of Manager.
23. Certified copy of Resolutions of the Board of Directors of Manager.

The documents described in Paragraphs 1 through 18 hereof, both inclusive, are herein collectively referred to as the "Loan Documents," the documents described in Paragraphs 19 through 22 hereof, both inclusive, are herein collectively referred to as the "Organizational Documents," and the document described in Paragraph 23 hereof is herein referred to as the "Resolution."

Based upon our review of the Loan Documents, our review of the Organizational Documents and the Resolution, our reliance, with your permission, on the letter from First Mortgage Bank to us dated August 2, 1989 (the "Trustee's Certificate") as to all matters stated therein and our reliance upon such other documents as we deem necessary or desirable, it is the opinion of the undersigned that:

A. Fox Valley is a duly organized and validly existing limited liability company under the laws of the State of Illinois and is authorized to transact business in the State of Illinois;

B. Borrower has full power and authority and legal right to enter into and perform the terms of the Loan Documents and the transactions contemplated thereby;

C. Manager has full power and authority and legal right to enter into and perform the terms of the Loan Documents and the transactions contemplated thereby as Manager of Fox Valley and individually, as the case may be;

D. The Loan Documents which have been executed by the Trust were executed pursuant to a written direction duly authorized, executed and delivered by one of the Guarantors;

E. The execution of the Loan Documents and the performance of the transactions contemplated thereby have been properly approved and authorized by the Manager;

F. The Loan Documents have been fully executed and delivered by, or on behalf of, all signatories thereto, with the exception of Lender, and are legal, valid and binding obligations of said signatories thereto with the exception of Lender, enforceable in accordance with their respective terms;

G. To our knowledge (based solely on the Trustee's Certificate and the letter from Fox Valley to us dated August 2, 1989 [the "Certificate"] attached hereto as Exhibit A), and solely with respect to the signatories thereof with the exception of Lender, no action of, or filing with, any governmental or public body or authority is required to authorize, or is otherwise required for the validity, execution, delivery and performance of the Loan Documents;

H. To our knowledge (based solely on the Trustee's Certificate and the Certificate), we are aware of no violation of any agreement or instrument to which any party to the Loan Documents, with the exception of Lender, is a party; and

I. We do not know of (based solely on the Trustee's Certificate and the Certificate) any suit, action, arbitration or legal, administrative or other proceeding or governmental investigation pending or threatened against or affecting Guarantors, Borrower, or any of the respective businesses, properties or financial or other conditions of Borrower.

The opinions set forth above are qualified as follows:

(i) The enforceability of the rights and remedies provided in any of the Loan Documents against any particular party or parties is subject to applicable federal and state bankruptcy, reorganization, insolvency, moratorium and other similar laws of general application relating to or affecting the enforcement of creditors' rights from time to time in effect;

(ii) The enforceability of the rights and remedies provided in any of the Loan Documents is subject to usual principles of equity (whether enforcement is sought at law or in equity), and the availability of the remedy of specific performance, injunctive relief, other equitable relief and "self-help" lender's remedies, as contemplated by or provided for in the Loan Documents, is subject to the discretion of the court (whether sitting in law or at equity) before which any proceedings therefor may be brought. It is our opinion, however, that the foregoing will not materially interfere with the practical and ultimate realization of the benefits of the security intended to be provided by the Loan Documents;

(iii) Applicable state and federal laws, court decisions and constitutional requirements may limit or render unenforceable certain of the rights and remedies purportedly available to Lender under the Loan Documents and we express no opinion that any particular provision of the Loan Documents will be specifically enforced. It is our opinion, however, that none of the foregoing laws, decisions or requirements will materially interfere with the practical and ultimate realization of the benefits of the security intended to be provided by the Loan Documents;

(iv) We express no opinion with respect to the applicability of the laws of any jurisdiction other than the State of Illinois or governmental subdivisions thereof and all federal laws to the extent substantively or procedurally applicable. This opinion is predicated solely upon statutory and case law in existence as of the date hereof;

(v) We express no opinion as to matters of title, priority of lien or creation, perfection or priority of security interests;

(vi) For purposes of this opinion, we have assumed the following:

(a) That all documents (or photostatic copies thereof) submitted to us are authentic and that all signatures by Lender and the Trust thereon are genuine; and

(b) That Lender will exercise its rights and remedies under the Loan Documents in good faith and in a commercially reasonable manner.

This opinion is rendered solely for your benefit and no other person or entity shall be entitled to rely on any matters set forth herein, nor shall any portion or all of this opinion be quoted or in any way published, without the express prior written consent of the undersigned. This opinion is limited to the matters set forth herein and no opinion is intended to be implied or may be inferred beyond those expressly stated herein.

Very truly yours,

KAPLAN & MILLER

By: ___________

Donna Smith

[Ed. Note: Just below is the "Trustee's Certificate" referred to in the opinion of counsel, coming from First Mortgage Bank as trustee under the land trust set up to hold fee simple title to the real estate. Recall that the LLC is the beneficiary of the land trust. Kaplan & Miller, counsel for the borrower, required the receipt of this Trustee's Certificate in order to give its opinion on the enforceability of the loan documents that the Land Trust signed. This can be confusing, since the land trust trustee happens to be the same bank that is making the mortgage loan, but the land trust could have been set up with a different bank as trustee and that bank would have then been required to issue this Trustee's Certificate to the borrower's counsel instead.]

First Mortgage Bank
423 N. Michigan Avenue
Chicago, Illinois 60690

July 31, 1989

Donna Smith, Esq.

Kaplan & Miller
450 Wacker Drive
Chicago, Illinois 60606

Re: First Mortgage Bank Trust No. 108049-04

To Whom It May Concern:

We hereby certify to you that (a) Fox Valley Auto Care Center LLC, an Illinois limited liability company, is the sole beneficiary of our captioned trust which is validly existing under the laws of the State of Illinois pursuant to a trust agreement dated April 11, 1989 and know as Trust No. 108049-04 (the "Trust Agreement"), (b) the undersigned is a duly organized, validly existing and in good standing national banking association and at all times relevant hereto has had the power and authority to enter into and assume the duties and obligations of the trustee under the Trust Agreement, hold title to the property described in the Trust Agreement and all property to which it, as such trustee, holds title thereunder, and perform and satisfy the duties and obligations of the trustee under the Trust Agreement, (c) the Trust Agreement is in full force and effect without any default thereunder, (d) the undersigned, as such trustee, has the requisite power and authority to execute and deliver the Construction Loan Agreement, Promissory Notes and Mortgage and all other instruments specified in the direction to the undersigned, as such trustee, dated July 31, 1989, (e) all of said instruments have been duly and validly executed and delivered by the undersigned, as such trustee, in accordance with their respective terms and conditions.

Sincerely,

First Mortgage Bank

by: ____________
Gerald Peterson
Vice-President

[Ed. Note: Next is the "Certificate" from the LLC which is referred to in the opinion of borrower's counsel which enables the law firm to provide the opinion on certain matters covered in the Certificate below.]

August 1, 1989

Kaplan & Miller
450 Wacker Drive
Chicago, IL 60606

Re: Fox Valley Auto Care Center (the "Property")

Ladies and Gentlemen:

In connection with the issuance of your Letter of Opinion relating to that certain construction loan for the Property from First Mortgage Bank to the undersigned, we hereby certify as follows:

1. No action of, or filing with, any governmental or public body or authority is required to authorize, or is otherwise required for the validity, execution, delivery and performance of the Loan Documents by the undersigned.

2. There are no violations of any agreement or instrument to which the undersigned or, to the undersigned's knowledge, any Guarantor is a party.

3. There is no suit, action, arbitration or legal, administrative or other proceeding or governmental investigation pending or, to the undersigned's knowledge, threatened against or affecting the undersigned or any Guarantor, or any of the respective businesses, properties or financial or other conditions of the undersigned.

Capitalized terms not otherwise defined herein shall have the same meaning as ascribed to them in your Letter of Opinion.

FOX VALLEY AUTO CARE CENTER LLC

By: REGENT REAL ESTATE DEVELOPMENT CORP.,
its manager

____

Its:____________

[Ed. Note: The matter opined to below was so important to FMB that it required that it be issued in a separate letter to FMB. Why do you think FMB wanted this matter to be separately opined to rather than simply included in the general opinion?]

Kaplan & Miller
450 Wacker Drive
Chicago, Illinois 60606

August 10, 1989

First Mortgage Bank
33 North LaSalle Street
Chicago, Illinois 60690

Re: $2,300,000 Construction Mortgage Loan (the "Loan") from First Mortgage Bank to Fox Valley Auto Care Center LLC ("Fox Valley") and First Mortgage Bank, not personally but solely as Trustee (the "Trustee") under Trust Agreement dated April 11, 1989 and known as Trust No. 108049-04

Ladies and Gentlemen:

This letter is delivered in connection with the Loan and, specifically, in connection with that certain Letter of Opinion dated August 2, 1989 from the undersigned to you delivered in connection with the Loan (the "Opinion"). All capitalized terms not otherwise defined herein shall have the same meaning ascribed to them as in the Opinion.

Based upon our review of the Loan Documents and our reliance upon such other documents as we deem necessary, it is the opinion of the undersigned that the Trustee has taken such actions as are required by the Illinois Mortgage Foreclosure Law of 1987 to waive its statutory right of redemption from a decree or order foreclosing the Mortgage on behalf of Trustee.

Very truly yours,

KAPLAN & MILLER

By: ____________

Donna Smith

[d] Comments and Questions Regarding the Opinion of Counsel

1. How does the opinion from Kaplan & Miller address the legal issue raised in *Scherr*?

2. Why do you think lenders require an opinion from the borrower's counsel as to the power and authority of the borrower to enter into the loan transaction as contrasted with getting an opinion on this matter from the lender's counsel? Is it an appropriate requirement?

3. Why do you think lenders require an opinion from the borrower's counsel as to the enforceability of the loan documents that the borrower has entered into? Is this an appropriate requirement? Some argue that since the loan documents are the lender's form documents, that the lender's counsel should opine as to their enforceability rather than borrower's counsel. One reason why lenders require opinions from borrower's counsel is to try to build an estoppel case against the borrower from later claiming that any of the documents or their terms are unenforceable. It will certainly be more difficult for the law firm of Kaplan & Miller to raise claims or defenses with respect to any matters that they have opined on.

4. What sorts of due diligence must the borrower's counsel engage in to be able to give these opinions? Another function of requiring an opinion is to induce the borrower's counsel to investigate the matters that they are opining on and to take any necessary steps to ensure that the matters opined on are true.

5. What matters did First Mortgage Bank require Kaplan & Miller to opine on in addition to the power, authority and enforceability points? Were there

any terms or phrases in the opinion that you thought were vague or unclear? For example, when the opinion refers to a matter being subject to the opinion giver's "knowledge," what do you think that means? It is important to point out that the opinions that mortgage lenders require from borrowers' counsel have become standardized to a large extent. In 1991, the Business Law Section of the American Bar Association issued a "Legal Opinion Accord" which set forth the standard elements of an opinion such as what has been opined to, what is excluded, and how the opinions are qualified. The Accord also explained the meaning of the terms utilized in the opinion form and the due diligence the opinion giver should engage in to give the opinions described. *See Third-Party Legal Opinion Report, Including the Legal Opinion Accord, of the Section of Business Law, American Bar Association*, 47 Bus. Law. 167 (1991). Since the Business Law Section's form opinion left open how to handle certain matters that related to real estate secured loans, the Real Property, Probate and Trust Law Section of the American Bar Association in 1994 created a follow up report that addressed these issues. *See Report on Adaptation of the Legal Opinion Accord of the Section of Business Law of the American Bar Association for Real Property Secured Transactions, of the Section of Real Property, Probate and Trust Law of the American Bar Association and the American College of Real Estate Lawyers*, 29 Real Prop. Prob. & Tr. J. 569 (1994). The opinion that Kaplan & Miller issued to First Mortgage Bank is substantially in the form referred to in the Accord as adapted as described above, but conformed to the law firm's own approved standard form of opinion. When issuing an opinion as a partner of a firm, the partner should ensure the opinion conforms with the law firm's approved form and due diligence procedures, and if there needs to be any deviation, the partner should make sure to obtain prior approval from her law firm. When an associate is asked to prepare the opinion for the deal for the partner's signature, the associate should keep these precautions in mind and document the due diligence performed to issue the opinion.

6. To what extent can a lender rely on a borrower's counsel's opinion? For example, was the opinion a "flat" or "clean" opinion subject to no qualifications or limitations, or was it a "qualified" opinion? Has Kaplan & Miller opined that every term of the loan documents will be enforceable against Regent and the other parties that have signed the loan documents? Has Kaplan & Miller "guaranteed" to First Mortgage Bank the "opinions" expressed in the opinion letter? In other words, is Kaplan & Miller strictly liable for any misrepresentations or must they have been negligent to be liable? *See Mehaffy, Rider, Windholz & Wilson v. Central Bank Denver, N.A.*, 892 P.2d 230 (Colo. 1995), in which the court held that an attorney may be liable to a non-client they are not in privity with for negligent misrepresentation of material facts. In this case, a bank relied to its detriment on an attorney's legal opinion and the court ruled that the attorney could be liable if it could be shown that he knew that his representation would be relied upon by the non-client for business purposes. *See also Greycas, Inc. v. Proud*, 826 F.2d 1560 (7th Cir. 1987); *Eisenberg v. Gagnon*, 766 F.2d 770 (3d Cir. 1985); *Kline v. First Western Gov't Sec.*, 794 F. Supp. 542 (E.D. Pa. 1992); *Horizon Fin., F.A. v. Hansen*, 791 F. Supp. 1561 (N.D. Ga. 1992); *McCamish v. F.E. Appling Interests*,

991 S.W.2d 787 (Tex. 1999); *Petrillo v. Bachenberg*, 655 A.2d 1354 (N.J. 1995); *Kirkland Constr. Co. v. James*, 658 N.E.2d 699 (Mass. App. Ct. 1995); *Mark Twain Kansas City Bank v. Jackson, Brouillette, Pohl & Kirley*, 912 S.W.2d 536 (Mo. Ct. App. 1995). One issue not addressed in any detail in these cases relates to the apparent requirement that the misrepresentation must be of a material "fact" and not of the law. To the extent that any of the opinions are deemed to be solely opinions of law rather than fact, should a lender still be able to sue the opinion issuer for negligent misrepresentation?

7. Has Kaplan & Miller breached any ethical duties to Regent in providing this opinion to First Mortgage Bank, and does it now have any duties to First Mortgage Bank? In thinking about these issues, recall that First Mortgage Bank required receipt of this opinion as a condition to funding the loan and that Regent certainly knew of, and implicitly consented to, Kaplan & Miller issuing the opinion. In *United Bank of Kuwait PLC v. Enventure Energy Enhanced Oil Recovery*, 755 F. Supp. 1195 (S.D.N.Y. 1989), the court ruled that the borrower's law firm was not liable to the lender for negligent misrepresentation in its opinion to the lender. The court reasoned that since the client had not "instructed [the law firm] to prepare the opinion letter, the imposition of a duty of care upon [the law firm] to [the lender], absent privity of contract, impinges upon the client's privilege of confidentiality, the attorney's ethical obligation to zealously represent its client, and the ethical prohibition on an attorney's representation of an adverse party." *Id.* at 1203. This case suggests that a law firm should obtain explicit direction from its borrower client to issue an opinion on the enforceability of the loan documents to the lender. Are you comfortable with the statement in the Kaplan & Miller opinion that the law firm represents all of the LLC, the bank as Trustee, Regent, and the three shareholders of Regent? Is Kaplan & Miller now representing First Mortgage Bank through issuing this opinion?

8. In addition to the "standard" opinions contained in the Kaplan & Miller opinion letter, lenders sometimes ask for "specialized" opinions relating to land use, environmental, securities or bankruptcy matters. The materials that follow discuss the use of opinions to address compliance with land use and environmental laws and the due diligence the opinion giver must perform to issue these opinions.

[e] Opining on Compliance with Zoning and Environmental Laws: Approaches and Alternatives

In connection with land use and environmental issues, lenders in some jurisdictions will require a formal, written opinion from the borrower's counsel which considers all applicable land use and environmental laws and regulations and concludes that the project, as completed, will comply with all such laws and regulations. In rendering such an opinion, the borrower's attorney must collect extensive factual information about the project. This information will frequently be obtained through responses to questionnaires, and through certificates provided by the borrower's architect, engineer, general contractor, and other parties involved in the construction process. Although the process of preparing an environmental and land use opinion can be time consuming and expensive, it ensures that the attorneys on both sides of the transaction have fully considered the issues and resolved any problems.

[i] Overview of Zoning and Environmental Opinions

The following article addresses the due diligence issue of compliance with applicable land use and environmental requirements. Even if the practice in a particular jurisdiction (such as in Illinois) is not to provide formal opinions with respect to such matters ordinarily, the question of compliance must be still be resolved to the satisfaction of the lender. The article also describes other ways that the borrower and its counsel can provide comfort to the lender that the project complies with land use and environmental requirements.

*Legal Opinions in California Real Estate Transactions,**
22 Real Property, Probate & Trust Journal 373, 426–431 (1987)**

Compliance with Subdivision, Zoning and Environmental Law

A request for an opinion to the effect that a project complies with all subdivision, zoning and environmental laws often presents most California lawyers with one of the most difficult issues in a real property transaction. The many factual (and often technical) determinations which must be made in order to render the opinion may be beyond the lawyer's expertise or the scope of his or her representation of the client. Moreover, environmental laws in particular are often in a state of flux, from the standpoint of judicial and administrative interpretation as well as legislative efforts to amend or clarify such laws. In addition, in many cases the enforcement of such laws is subject to varying unpublished (and at times conflicting or unclear) internal policies of the responsible agencies, and it may not be possible to render opinions as a matter of law regarding the manner in which certain environmental requirements may be applied or enforced in any particular instance.

Notwithstanding such difficulties, an opinion with respect to environmental and zoning matters is often required in order to assure the lender that environmental permits have been obtained and zoning and land use requirements have been satisfied so that the use and value of the property which serves as security for the loan will not be impaired.

The fact that an opinion may be difficult to give, or require extensive investigation by the lawyer, does not necessarily mean that the lender is unreasonable in asking for it. A lender has a legitimate interest in determining that all environmental requirements have been or will be satisfied.[1] Failure to comply with applicable subdivision laws may render the lender's mortgage or deed of trust voidable,[2] and failure to obtain necessary zoning and environmental permits or approvals may delay or prevent the completion of the project. Even if such

---

* Prepared by the Real Property Law Section of the State Bar of California and the Real Property Section of the Los Angeles County Bar Association.

** Copyright © 1987 by Laurence Preble, Myrl Scott, O'Malley Miller & Carl Seneker. Reprinted by permission.

[1] See Schwenke, *Opinion Letters on Environmental Law and Land Use Questions-An Overview*, Am. C. Real Estate Law., Program Material (Nov. 1982) [hereinafter cited as *Schwenke*].

[2] Cal. Gov't Code § 66499.32.

entitlements are eventually obtained, the increased interest expense and other costs associated with the delay may cause the project to fail. In a nonrecourse loan, the lender may bear substantially all of the downside risk. In addition, if the lender forecloses on property upon which hazardous waste is located, the lender may be subject to liability as an "owner" with respect to such waste even though it was not involved in the day-to-day management of the property. For these reasons, zoning and environmental opinions are often an essential part of the lender's underwriting decision with respect to the loan.

Accordingly, it is reasonable to expect that a purchaser or a lender may want some "comfort" with respect to zoning and environmental matters. The degree of comfort which a lender or purchaser may reasonably request may depend, in part, on the nature of the project. A free-standing office or industrial building which has just been completed on a subdivided lot and which has just received a final certificate of occupancy from the appropriate local authority may present very little practical risk of noncompliance with applicable laws. In such instances, a statement in an opinion to the effect that the premises may used for the purposes permitted by applicable zoning laws and which relies upon the issuance of the certificate of occupancy by the appropriate governmental authority and on an officer's certificate of the borrower regarding the present use of the property may present few difficult legal or factual issues. In contrast, a major, multiphased, planned development project which has not yet been completed may present a significantly different situation. In such circumstances, the purchaser and lender may be reasonably interested in knowing which permits and approvals have already been obtained, which future permits and entitlements are required, whether the project has any "vested rights," and whether it may be subject to possible challenges by environmental groups. An opinion with respect to all of these issues may be extraordinarily difficult.

The precise formulation of a zoning, land use or environmental opinion varies with the nature of the project, the involvement of the opining lawyer in the governmental review and permitting process, and the degree of comfort that can be developed through appropriate investigation. If the lawyer has not been intimately involved in the developmental and permitting process for the project, the degree of due diligence required for such an opinion may be extremely burdensome and expensive. Even where the lawyer rendering the opinion has been involved extensively in the developmental and permitting process, he or she may not be able to opine on many of the issues implicitly included in a request for an opinion to the effect that the project complies with "all" applicable laws. For example, how would a lawyer be expected to know whether the project complies with applicable seismic laws? If the lawyer relies solely on a certificate by an architect or an engineer, of what value is the opinion? A conclusion that a project complies with "all" health and safety laws, antipollution laws, and the like, may be so affected by significant factual and technical considerations that the lawyer may be unable to reach a meaningful legal conclusion at a reasonable cost and within a reasonable time. In such instances, the scope of the required opinion and the scope of the lawyer's representation must be established at the inception of the transaction, and the legal issues should be limited to issues which are of legitimate concern to the lender.

The Joint Committee believes that controversies with respect to difficult environmental and zoning opinions may be minimized if the parties focus on the issue at the inception of the transaction. Often, the first issue is to determine whether any opinion at all is required. A loan commitment letter may state that the conditions of closing require "evidence satisfactory to the lender" that the project complies with all applicable laws. Does this language mean that an opinion is required?[3] In many instances, the appropriate "comfort" for the lender may be obtained by including specific representations and warranties in transactional documents and by requiring, as a condition of closing, the delivery of appropriate certificates executed by the project architects, engineers, contractors or other consultants together with copies of relevant governmental approvals and permits. Sometimes a lender may also require the delivery of letters from utility companies and governmental agencies confirming that the project is or will be served by water, sewer, gas, electricity and other utilities. It may also be possible to obtain a zoning endorsement to the lender's policy of title insurance, although the scope of coverage and the degree of "comfort" which such endorsements provide is narrower than one might suppose.

Often, a letter may be requested from an appropriate local governmental official (usually the planning director or zoning administrator) confirming the zoning designation applicable to the particular project and stating, as applicable, that the local agency has no knowledge of any violation of zoning, land use, subdivision or building laws by the project, that applicable environmental review procedures have been completed, and that all required use permits and certificates of occupancy have been approved and issued. Where obtainable in an acceptable form and in a timely fashion, such letters may be of some comfort to the lender with respect to whether there are any present grounds for challenges to the project known to the local agency. However, such letters do not estop the local agency in the event that a violation actually exists, and their value may be limited.

The fact that a lawyer may not be issuing a legal opinion with respect to environmental matters does not mean, however, that the lawyer does not have a significant role or that he or she need not be concerned about whether the project complies with applicable law. As is the case with title matters, the lawyer should normally have the responsibility for obtaining copies of relevant documents, permits, and approvals, preparing or reviewing the various certificates to be delivered at the closing, and ensuring that such documents and certificates satisfy applicable closing requirements.

Of course, the preparation and review of such factual statements or certificates presupposes some degree of familiarity on the part of the lawyer with the project and with applicable subdivision, zoning and environmental laws and other governmental requirements. The lawyer should also understand that he or she may be expected to exercise professional judgment regarding the accuracy and completeness of such statements or certificates. First, the lawyer should verify that the developer and its principal engineering and environmental consultants do not have any material disagreement with the facts as set forth in any such statement or certificates. Second, the lawyer should exercise professional judgment regarding the accuracy of any significant conclusion contained in the statement or certificate. For example, if a letter from the city having jurisdiction over the project recites that the project is exempt from California Environmental

[3] "If environmental concerns are a valid area which the lender wants to have considered, analysis should be handled directly and not by implications." *Schwenke, supra* note [1], at 9.

Quality Act requirements, what due diligence obligations are imposed on the lawyer with respect to his or her reliance on such letter? Ordinarily, a lawyer who was not directly involved in obtaining relevant land use or environmental permits would not be expected to undertake a comprehensive inquiry into the factual basis for such legal conclusion or to perform a detailed review of project applications to validate such exemption. Nevertheless, the lawyer should compare the specific legal requirements for the exemption, as stated in applicable regulations, with the relevant facts related to the project to determine that the conclusion contained in such letter is not legally questionable on its face.

If it is determined that, in addition to the delivery of such documents and certificates, a legal opinion is required, the Joint Committee believes that, in general, a request for an environmental or land use opinion should be limited to issues which have a material relationship to the transaction. In certain circumstances, the lender may agree that the lawyer does not have to reach "ultimate" legal conclusions if the opinion contains a sufficient discussion and explanation of the issues. For example, with respect to a request for an opinion to the effect that the project complies with applicable zoning laws, it may be sufficient if the lawyer identifies the applicable city ordinances and the uses permitted thereunder, states that an application for a zone change was made to the appropriate governmental agency, that notice was given and a hearing held in accordance with applicable requirements, that the application was approved by the appropriate governmental body, and that the time for filing an appeal has expired. Such an exposition, if it describes the governmental approval process undertaken by the developer and the legally relevant elements related thereto, may be sufficient even if it does not reach the ultimate legal conclusion that the project complies with all applicable zoning laws.

There are, of course, other possible ways in which zoning and environmental concerns can be addressed, with the aid of counsel, short of requiring an elaborate or open-ended legal opinion. For example, it is common for loan documents to require representations and warranties of the borrower to the effect that the project complies with all applicable laws and regulations, that all permits have been secured for the lawful construction, operation and use of the property, and that no notices of violation of law have been received. However, such representations may have only limited value if the lender does not receive some level of assurance that the representations are informed conclusions based on a careful review of the factual and legal issues that form the basis of such statements. It is the Joint Committee's belief that the borrower's counsel can reasonably be expected to assist the borrower in understanding the meaning and significance of such representations and in giving the lender an appropriate level of comfort that the borrower's willingness to give such representations is not simply the product of speculation, ignorance or carelessness.

Accordingly, counsel to the borrower could reasonably be expected to discuss with the borrower the content of such representations given in connection with the loan and to assist the borrower in evaluating any potential problems or discrepancies known to the borrower relating to the matters covered by such representation. While counsel may properly disclaim making any independent investigation of the validity, regularity or adequacy of the permits and approvals obtained for the project, counsel will nevertheless need to be generally familiar with the principal land use and environmental permits and approvals typically required for similar projects in order to advise his or her client properly. The lender might reasonably ask that borrower's counsel advise it in writing to the effect that such counsel has discussed the nature, scope and meaning of the borrower's zoning and environmental representations with the borrower and that, in the course of such discussion, nothing has come to the attention of such counsel that would lead him or her to believe that any of such representations are materially inaccurate.

Another approach is to have lender's counsel prepare a list of the principal land use and environmental permits and approvals typically applicable to the type of project in question. Borrower's counsel may then be asked to perform a limited investigation of the applicability and status of such permits and approvals with regard to the particular project, and to render a report thereon (not an opinion) to the lender as a closing condition. In such cases, the report would be limited to the laws and regulations identified by lender's counsel. Borrower's counsel would be expected to conduct a review of the permit status of the project with the appropriate agency officials relating to the property. On that basis, counsel would draw conclusions regarding whether the principal land use and environmental permits identified by lender's counsel appear to be in place and, if any applicable period for challenge has not yet expired, whether there appear to be any significant defects in the permits themselves or in the approval procedures followed by the issuing authority which would create substantial questions regarding the validity or effectiveness of such permits. This approach assumes, of course, that lender's counsel is sufficiently familiar with the project to be able to identify relevant statutes and regulations or that lender's counsel and borrower's counsel are able to prepare a mutually satisfactory list.

In summary, the fact that a commitment letter requires an opinion with respect to compliance with "all" zoning and environmental laws should not, by itself, create controversy or "gamesmanship" between lender's counsel and borrower's counsel. Instead, it should precipitate a discussion between such counsel with respect to the issues to be covered and the scope of the opinion. If the opining attorney has not been directly involved in the developmental process but must become so in order to render the opinion, the fact should be determined at an early stage in the transaction and not left for last minute negotiations. In addition, if the lawyer believes that he or she does not have relevant expertise, consideration should be given to the employment of another lawyer to act as special counsel for purposes of giving the required opinion. In this way the interests of both lender and borrower are served and the transaction may be closed without undue expense or delay.

[ii] Notes Regarding Land Use and Environmental Opinions

1. The importance of the due diligence process was dramatically illustrated in a situation in New York City in which a developer agreed to tear down the top 12 floors of a 31-story apartment building on the Upper East Side of Manhattan after years of litigation. The litigation arose because the building as completed exceeded the height limitations for the zoning district in which it was located. *Dunlap New York City Developer Agrees to Chop 12 Floors from Building*, N.Y. Times (April 23, 1991). The developer received a building permit in 1986 for a 31-story building from the city and started construction. A neighborhood group opposing the project then

demonstrated to city officials that the developer and city had mistakenly located the boundaries of the zoning district. The city issued a stop-work order, but the developer continued construction during the appeal of that order. The order was upheld by the New York Court of Appeals in *In the Matter of Parkview Associates v. City of New York*, 519 N.E.2d 1372 (N.Y. 1988), and a subsequent variance request denied by the city's Board of Standards and Appeals because the hardship was self-created. According to the Board, "reasonable diligence would have uncovered, for a good faith inquirer, the existence of the eastern boundary" of the applicable zoning district. According to the New York Times, the tricky part of the settlement for the developer was to protect the remaining portion of the building while the top 12 stories were demolished and all mechanical systems altered and moved. The Times failed to mention who was ultimately responsible for paying the expenses of construction and the impending demolition. One wonders where the lawyers for the developer and lender were when the question of zoning compliance arose as a due diligence matter.

2. As the previous article points out, the issuance of land use and environmental opinions is not a standard requirement for real estate loans in all jurisdictions or even for all projects in those jurisdictions in which such opinions are more common. Significantly, some state bar associations have recommended that such opinions not be issued because of the technical questions that must be addressed. For example, in Oregon, the state bar has strongly stated that title, land use, and environmental matters should not be the subject of opinions by lawyers.

> These matters should not be the subject of an opinion by the lawyer because they are uniquely within the expertise of professionals other than lawyers. The Committee believes that the factual and technical considerations, particularly in the area of environmental concerns, and to a lesser degree in land use and title matters, are too extensive and require too many assumptions based upon the expertise of others.
>
> In the environmental area, examinations and evaluations of the existence of hazardous substances on-site or the efficiency of a prior cleanup require the opinion of experts. Generally, lawyers do not have the requisite training and background to evaluate such opinions. Reviewing the work of these experts and rendering an opinion based on their work is a fruitless and dangerous exercise for the lawyer. The lender should look to the expert in the field who has done the examination and has the expertise, not to the lawyer. . . .
>
> The Committee recognizes that there may be instances in which the lender will maintain that it is not able to evaluate those issues on its own and will pressure the lawyer to give an opinion. In these cases, the lawyer should suggest that the lender obtain reports or opinions from those experts whose knowledge is relevant to those areas that are of concern to the lender. The lawyer generally should not accept the task of advising the lender as to which experts should be consulted, nor should the lawyer agree to opine or comment on those reports.

Weiner, *Lawyers' Opinions in Oregon Real Estate Transactions*, Or.

L. Inst., Representing Clients in Real Estate Transactions 9-7 through 9-8 (1993). *See also* Holtzschue, *Opinions on Real Estate Secured Transactions in a Post-Accord World: The Opinion Giver's Perspective,* 29 REAL PROP., PROB. & TR. J. 655, 731 (1994) (noting similar concerns by the New York State Bar Association). Although these bar associations may be correct that certain types of factual information are in the domain of other parties, any analysis based on these facts to determine compliance or noncompliance with land use or environmental laws and regulations is uniquely in the domain of the legal profession. The complexity and technical nature of many land use and environmental laws, as well as the technical nature of the factual information upon which any conclusions must be based, does not provide a sufficient basis for an abdication of this responsibility.

3. For further information on land use and environmental opinions, see Grandoff, *Preparing Zoning Opinions*, 13 PROB. & PROP. 29 (Sept-Oct 1999); Holtzschue, *Opinions on Real Estate Secured Transactions in a Post-Accord World: The Opinion Giver's Perspective*, 29 REAL PROP., PROB. & TRUST J. 655 (1994); Hyman, Trapp, & Mitchell, *The Environmental Legal Opinion: Guidelines for Real Estate Attorneys*, 24 REAL PROP., PROB. & TRUST J. 169 (1989); Seneker, *Drafting Environmental and Land Use Opinion Letters (with Forms)*, PRAC. LAW. 39 (Sept. 1988); Holmes, *The Preparation of an Environmental Opinion Letter: A Practitioner's Guide*, 11 B.C. ENV. AFF. L. REV. 413 (1984).

[iii] Questions Regarding Land Use and Environmental Opinions

1. Does the Loan Agreement for the Fox Valley Auto Care Center require that Regent's attorney provide the lender with a land use and environmental opinion? See Article V of the Loan Agreement in the Document Book. If so, what arrangements should the attorney make with the lender regarding the scope of the opinion?

2. To the extent that certificates are required from the project's architect and engineers, what comfort should the lender take in statements under the certificates that the project complies with applicable rules and regulations? When examining the construction contracts between the owner and architect in Part IV, consider what obligations the architect undertakes to provide such certificates to the lender.

3. The Loan Agreement requires that Regent make several representations and warranties concerning compliance with land use and environmental laws and regulations. See Article III of the Loan Agreement in the Document Book. If this is the extent of the "comfort" that the lender requires in connection with these issues, what role does Regent's attorney play, if any?

§ 11.03 BIBLIOGRAPHY OF TOPICS NOT COVERED

Before concluding Part III of this book, we include this bibliography that introduces you to some of the less basic, but important, real estate finance topics not covered at all, or in detail, in this book.

[1] Sale Leasebacks

A sale-leaseback is a common and often complex transaction. In a sale-leaseback, the owner of improved real property agrees to sell that property with the understanding the property will be leased back to it (usually on a long-term basis). The advantage to the seller is that it retains use of the land while acquiring cash for the full value of the property. The buyer, who owns the land in fee simple, will receive rent during the course of the lease and utilize the tax benefits available to owners of real estate.

For a detailed explanation see:

- Joyce and Andre Homburger, Structuring Real Estate Sale-Leasebacks I (1992)

  This is a comprehensive treatment of the sale-leaseback transaction. It discusses the advantages and disadvantages of the transaction to the buyer and seller.

- Thomas C. Homburger & Brian P. Gallagher, *To Pay or Not to Pay: Claiming Damages for Recharacterization of Sale-Leaseback Transactions Under Owner's Title Insurance Policies*, 30 Real Prop., Prob. & Trust J. 443 (1995)

  The article focuses on title insurance liability in the sale-leaseback transaction.

- Marvin Milich, *The Real Estate Sale-Leaseback Transaction: A View Toward the'90s*, 21 Real Est. L.J. 66 (1992)

  This is a short and concise article which explains sale-leasebacks as a financing tool, reviews case law on the subject, and suggests a sale-leaseback outline which comports with the case law.

- John Hastie, *Sale-Leaseback Documents*, ALI-ABA Continuing Legal Ed. (SB08 ALI-ABA 1433) (1996)

  This article contains forms for attorneys setting up sale-leaseback transactions.

[2] Purchase Money Mortgages

A purchase money mortgage is a real estate financing arrangement which is usually sought by a buyer who may be finding it difficult to obtain financing for real property through traditional bank channels or by a motivated seller who is willing to finance the sale of its own property. In a purchase money mortgage transaction, the seller conveys fee title to the buyer. The buyer in return will execute a promissory note secured by a mortgage. The seller holds the mortgage as an institutional lender would.

For more on the subject see:

- Baxter Dunaway, *Priority of Purchase Money Mortgages, in* LAW OF DISTRESSED REAL ESTATE § 27.03 (1996)

  This section gives a clear outline and examples of the priority of a purchase money mortgage holder. It explains that a purchase money mortgage holder may have priority over a judgment holder even if the mortgage is entered into after the judgment.

- David J. Marchitelli, *Construction Mortgagee-Lender's Duty to Protect Interest of Subordinated Purchase Money Mortgagee*, 13 A.L.R.5th 684 (1994)

  This annotation looks at the case law addressing the issue of the priority of construction lenders versus those of purchase money mortgage holders. It discusses the technical facts looked at by courts in determining priority.

- Alvin L. Arnold, *Mortgages: Purchase Money Priority Does Not Extend to Funds Used For Construction*, 24 REAL EST. L. REP. 5 (July 1994)

  This article discusses case law regarding purchase money priority when some of the money loaned is for new construction.

- Juliet Moringiello, *A Mortgage by Any Other Name: A Plea for the Uniform Treatment of Installment Land Contracts and Mortgages Under the Bankruptcy Code*, 100 DICK. L. REV. 733 (1996)

  This article compares the treatment of purchase money mortgages with land installment contracts when the person occupying the land files for bankruptcy. The article provides an excellent explanation of both types of land deals.

[3] Installment Contracts

In an installment contract, the buyer does not receive fee simple title to the real estate until the buyer makes the last payment due under the installment contract, but the buyer has possessory rights to the real estate and is the equitable owner of the real estate. Many installment contracts provide that upon default by the buyer and after any agreed upon cure period, the seller is entitled to possession, the buyer's interest is terminated, and the seller is authorized to retain any payments made by the buyer. This provision may be struck down by a court if, under the circumstances, the result is unconscionable or if it is deemed to be a liquidated damages provision and a penalty. In addition, a court could hold that the entire transaction really is a loan with the property as security, causing the buyer to be accorded the rights of a mortgagor. Oftentimes this type of transaction is entered into when the buyer can not obtain a purchase money mortgage from a mortgage lender, but sometimes a seller desires this structure as a means to defer capital gains.

- Dale A. Whitman, *Transfers by Vendors of Interests in Installment Land Contracts: The Impact of Revised Article 9 of the Uniform Commercial Code*, 38 REAL PROP. PROB. & TR. J. 421 (2003–2004)

  This article explores the impact of revised Article 9 of the UCC on security interests creditors take in a vendor's interest under an installment land contract. Whitman argues that while revised Article 9 helps to clarify some of the questions that existed before, parties to this type of vendor financing will still need to think carefully about how best to protect their interests and will want to ensure the use of proper documentation.

- Henry L. Strong, *Structured Sales: Reducing Risk in Installment Sales*, REAL ESTATE FINANCE 23, no. 2 (Aug. 2006)

  This article addresses ways to improve the likelihood of payment under an installment contract (through assignment of the buyer's interest to a more creditworthy third party) while maintaining the tax advantages of the deferral of capital gains through the installment sale structure.

[4] Ground Leases

A ground lease is a method to obtain control of real property, but not fee simple title to it. It is often used by investors who lack the capital necessary for the purchase of property. The term of a ground lease is usually very long (50–100 years) and enables the lessee to rent the land without a down payment. The conditions of a ground lease usually allow the lessee to make improvements on the land and control the property as it sees fit. The advantage of the ground lease to the lessor is that the lessee is usually required to assume all of the costs associated with the ownership of the land, but the lessor retains the tax benefits of ownership plus the value of the land once the leasehold period expires.

For more on the subject see:

- Richard Casher, *Leasehold Mortgages in Bankruptcy: Look Before You Leasehold*, 390 PLI/REAL 151 (1993)

  This article contains a thorough explanation of a ground lease transaction. It also explains, in great detail, the ramifications if bankruptcy is declared by either party to the ground lease.

- Norton Steuben, *The Income Tax Treatment of Interests Acquired from a Ground Lessor*, 23 FLA. ST. U. L. REV. 863 (1996)

  This article contains a detailed analysis of the ground lease transaction. It focuses primarily on the tax benefits and risks associated with a ground lease. The author also includes a review and critique of existing case law in the area of ground lease law.

- 2 Daniel Kelliher, *Ground Leases, in* LEASII MA-CLE 11-i (1996)

  This chapter discusses the steps necessary to draft a ground lease. It describes the objectives of the parties, and the substantive provisions needed to draft the agreement. The chapter also includes a number of exhibits containing examples of ground lease contract provisions.

[5] Leasehold Mortgages

In a leasehold mortgage, the collateral for the lender is a mortgage of the tenant's leasehold interest. This type of collateral is particularly valuable for a long term lease, such as a ground lease, and one of the key areas of concern for the leasehold mortgagee is the continuing existence of the lease during the term of the loan.

- Joshua Stein, *How Much Protection Does a Leasehold Mortgagee Need?*

(With Model Provisions), 19 No. 6 Prac. Real Est. Law. 7 (November 2003)

This article addresses the premature termination issue and other issues that might make a long term ground lease not "financeable" and provides for a "middle ground" set of mortgagee protections

[6] Synthetic Leases

A synthetic lease is a complex technique used to finance property. The lessee of such property has the advantage of treating the lease as an operating lease for financial accounting purposes, while at the same time treating the lease as a financing device for tax purposes. For more on the subject see:

- John Murray, *Off-Balance-Sheet Financing: Synthetic Leases*, 32 Real Prop., Prob. & Trust J. 193 (1997)

  This article outlines the purpose of the synthetic lease as a financing tool, describes the benefits available to the corporate user of the transaction, and also explains the risks associated with the lease. It also contains an explanation of the documents needed for the transaction.

- Thomas Fileti, *Real Estate Off-Balance Sheet Financing (Synthetic Leases)*, 418 PLI/Real 1021 (1997)

  This article addresses questions that might arise in the study of synthetic leases. It discusses the transaction itself, the kind of entities who can benefit from the transaction, and the pricing involved.

- Evelyn Giaccio, *Synthetic Lease Transactions And "Off-Balance Sheet" Financing*, 424 PLI/Real 563 (1997)

  This article explains the rules relating to the complex accounting process associated with synthetic leases. It also talks about the tax considerations and gives a highly detailed explanation of the synthetic lease itself.

[7] Shared Appreciation Mortgages

While a lender can obtain an equity interest in the mortgaged property in numerous ways, in a typical shared appreciation mortgage, a variable rate of interest is charged by the lender based on the actual appreciation of the property. These agreements generally include at least a minimum level of interest, which is charged regardless of the appreciation. The lender in this agreement has the benefit of earning more interest at the end of the term of the loan if the property appreciates rapidly while the mortgagor borrows money at a lower rate of interest initially.

- Arthur B. Willis, et. al, Partnership Taxation § 5.05 (5th ed. 1995)

  This chapter explains the dangers of these types of loans if they are re-characterized as capital contributions. It explains the severe consequences of such a re-characterization and cites cases illustrating the way the re-characterization is interpreted.

- Hugh A. Brodkey, *Equity Participation, in* FRET IL-CLE 12-1 (1996)

  This article explains the legal ramifications of entering into a shared appreciation mortgage agreement including priority, negotiability, and usury.

- Marc J. Gerson, *Taxation of Equity Participation Rights in Real Estate Held by Foreign Investors*, 24 J. Real Est. Tax'n 391 (1997)

  This article examines the difficulty in assessing the tax considerations to foreign entities who make equity participation loans in the United States. The author points to tax court decisions and tax code provisions that explain how the additional interest received by foreign companies should be characterized.

[8] Loan Participations

A loan participation agreement occurs when a lender sells all or a portion of its interest in a loan to other lenders while still controlling the administration of the loan itself. The original lender is referred to as the "lead lender" and the lenders who purchase interests in the loan are referred to as the "participants." In a loan participation agreement, the lead is usually paid a fee to administrate the loan for the participants who maintain very little control over the loan administration. The lead benefits from being able to sell its interest in the loan, while the participant benefits by not being required to administrate the loan. The can be an "A Lender" and a "B Lender" in which the B Lender's interest is made junior in right to the A Lender in terms of payment and in the event of a bankruptcy.

- Richard D. Jones, *Loan Participation, Syndications, and Co-Lending*

  This article contains a comparison of loan participation to other forms of agreements in which there are multiple lenders. The author explains the complexity and benefits of co-lending.

- Andrew L. Herz, *Loan Participation Agreements*, 429 PLI/Real 483 (1998)

  This article offers a sample draft of a loan participation agreement, which includes a detailed list of clauses that may be necessary to effectuate such an agreement.

- Charles L. Menges, *Minimizing the Lead Lender's Liability to Co-Lenders in Syndicated Loans (with Sample Clauses)*, 19 No. 2 Prac. Real Est. Law. 17 (March 2003)

  This article recommends a few key exculpatory provisions in the loan syndication agreement to save the lead lender "a lot of grief."

[9] Securitization of Real Estate

Although this topic has been addressed in various sections of chapters 9–11, the following articles focus in detail on certain aspects of the securitization of real estate:

- Richard D. Simonds, Jr. & Stephen S. Kudenholdt, *Fundamentals of Mortgage-Backed Securities and Asset-Backed Securities*, 18 No. 3 Prac. Real Est. Law. 39 (May 2002)

  This article covers the basic structures used to issue mortgage-backed securities and asset-backed securities and addresses the complexities of securities and tax law that one needs to understand to properly structure these transactions.

- Marielle Jan de Beur & Susan Berliner, *A Comparison: BBB CMBS and Unsecured REIT Debt*, Real Estate Finance 10 (June 2003)

  This article examines the volatility, ratings history, liquidity, structural differences, the issuer's perspective, the rating agencies perspective, and performance of BBB, CMBS and unsecured REIT debt.

- Kevin J. O'Shea, Peter E. Hein & Peter H. Hoegen, *Senior/Subordinate (A/B) Mortgage Structures: An Easy Entry by German Mortgage Banks into the US Real Estate Market*, Real Estate Finance 25 (June 2003)

  This article reacts to an amendment to the German Mortgage Bank Act that permits German mortgage banks to make first mortgage loans secured by US real estate and provides advice to German mortgage banks on the best way to enter into this market: partnering with US lenders for the benefit of both. Through providing this analysis, the authors also provide a good summary of the different types of co-lending relationships and "top 10" issues for these types of co-lending structures.

- Charles Adelman, *REMIC Amendments Allow Securitization of Reverse Mortgages and HELOCs*, ABI_INFORM_FT (Feb. 2005)

  This article discusses the REMIC amendments designed to facilitate the securitization of "reverse mortgages" and the amendment's application to "HELOC's" (home equity lines of credit).

- E. Kristen Moye, *Non-Consolidation and True Sale/Transfer Opinions in Securitized Real Estate Loan Transactions*, 21 No. 3 Prac. Real Est. Law. 7 (May 2005)

  This article discusses the emergence of rendering reasoned opinions on the treatment of the ownership entities involved in a structured finance transaction in the event of a bankruptcy (*i.e.*, whether those entities will be consolidated or not — consolidation being problematic to mortgage lenders who desire isolation of bankruptcy risk of the single asset entity from its affiliates) and the relevant case law and factors to consider in giving this reasoned opinion. The article also discusses rendering an opinion on whether the sale of the underlying real estate collateral to a special purpose entity borrower will be treated by a court as a sale, rather than a secured financing, and not a fraudulent conveyance as well as the relevant law to consider in order to provide this opinion.

[10] Lender Liability

A lender can incur liability during any part of the loan transaction. The question of a lender's liability can arise in connection with the lender's practices during the drafting of the loan and documentation or when the lender attempts to enforce the loan documents after the loan has been made.

- Stephen Kouri, *An Act in Relation to Credit Agreements: A Statutory*

Defense to Lender Liability, 348 ILL. B.J. (1990)

This article examines the scope of legislation that prohibits borrowers from holding lenders to verbal commitments. It examines the issue from the side of the lender to discuss the law's application to post-breach of contract statements.

- Donald J. Schuller, *Techniques to Reduce Lender Liability*, 6 PROB. & PROP. 16 (June 1992).

  This article examines the pitfalls of loan commitment forms, which may subject the lender to liability. It discusses and suggests clauses designed to lower the lender's exposure and explains the most common mistakes made by drafters.

[11] Miscellaneous Topics

- Douglas P. Selby & Claire Hunter, *Tax Increment Financing: How Public-Private Partnerships are Financing Urban Redevelopment*, ABI_INFORM_FT (Aug. 2004)

  This article explains how "tax increment financing" works (usually with the issuance of bonds to pay for upfront costs of redevelopment that are then repaid from the increase in real estate taxes generated from the improvements), provides examples of how it has been used by municipalities over the past fifty years. and discusses legal challenges to tax increment financing and structuring alternatives.

- Kevin Driscoll, *Credit Tenant Loans*, REAL ESTATE FINANCE 64 (Winter 2002)

  This article discusses why insurance companies seek to make mortgage loans that primarily rely upon the credit standing of a tenant (to benefit from comparatively lower risk based capital charges than with a securitized commercial real estate loan), how they are structured (with an assignment of the lease rental payments to the lender with real estate pledged as collateral), and the regulatory framework insurance companies operate in.

- Cheryl P. Armata, *Financing Tenant in Common Projects*, 22 No. 5 PRAC. REAL EST. LAW. 17 (Sept. 2006)

  This article explains the special risks and ways to address the risks when a lender finances a loan where ownership of the real estate is held as tenants in common (TIC) rather than by a limited liability company. While normally a limited liability company would be the entity that owns fee simple title to commercial real estate, a TIC is sometimes used instead as a better way to facilitate favorable tax treatment under a "1031 Like Kind Exchange."

- Scott E. Fireison, *Financing Affordable Housing: Section 202 Basics*, ABI_INFORM_FT (Aug. 2004)

  This article discusses a program to encourage the development of housing for the elderly instituted under Section 202 of the Housing Act of 1959 through a capital advance and rental subsidy under a multi-year "Project

Rental Assistance Contract" between HUD and the project owner.

- Ray Iwamoto, *Hotel Operator's Agreement with the Owner's Lender (with Forms)*, 22 No. 5 Prac. Real Est. Law. 7 (Sept. 2006)

  This article briefly discusses the lender's need for a subordination agreement and an estoppel certificate from a hotel manager or operator when the owner of the hotel refinances a loan secured by this collateral. The article includes forms of these two documents.

- Richard A. Rosner & Joseph "Jay" Cusimano, *Loans to Condominium Associations*, 22 No. 2 Prac. Real Est. Law. 51 (March 2006)

  This article provides a practical guide to lenders and condominium associations in connection with the provisions in the loan documentation for loans to finance major repairs and replacements to the common elements of condominiums and other common ownership communities.

Part IV

CONSTRUCTION OF THE PROJECT'S BUILDINGS AND IMPROVEMENTS

Chapter 12

THE CONSTRUCTION PROCESS

§ 12.01 OVERVIEW OF THE CONSTRUCTION PROCESS

The construction process involves considerable risk for the parties involved. As one court stated:

> Except in the middle of a battlefield, nowhere must men coordinate the movement of other men and all materials in the midst of such chaos and with such limited certainty of present facts and future occurrences as in a huge construction project. . . . Even the most painstaking planning frequently turns out to be mere conjecture and accommodation to changes must necessarily be of the rough, quick, and *ad hoc* sort, analogous to the ever-changing commands on the battlefield. *Blake Construction Co. v. C.J. Coakley Co.*, 431 A.2d 569, 575 (D.C. Ct. App. 1981).

Viewed from this perspective, one wonders how a construction project of any significant size is ever completed.

In the United States, the most typical scheme of construction contracting follows the Design-Award-Build (D-A-B) system, which may also be referred to as the Design-Bid-Build system. Sweet, Sweet on Construction Law § 3.8 (1997). Under the D-A-B system, the owner contracts with a design professional who designs the project based on the owner's needs or marketing objectives. The design professional is typically an architect, but may be an engineer, depending on the particular project involved. Once the design is completed, a general contractor will be selected who will execute the design and actually construct the project. The selection of the contractor may occur through a competitive bidding process or simply through negotiations with the owner. Once selected, the general contractor will schedule the construction process and supervise and coordinate all of the various specialty trades, such as the excavation contractor, the steel fabricator and erector, the electrical and plumbing contractors, etc., that are necessary to complete the project. In the ideal situation, the project will be completed within budget and on time.

Although relatively straightforward in theory, the D-A-B system has two principal disadvantages. First, the design process is separated from the construction process. When defects occur, responsibility may be difficult to assign, as the architect may claim that the defect occurred through faulty construction techniques or materials and the general contractor may claim that the defect occurred through faulty design. More importantly, however, the specialty trades, those who actually are engaged to construct the project, are not in direct privity of contract with the owner, but are subcontractors to the general contractor. When problems arise, the specialty trades may attempt to bypass the chain of contracts through the general contractor to the owner and the owner may desire to do so as well. Second, the D-A-B system involves considerable time, because it assumes that the general contractor is selected only after the architect has completed the design of the project. On the other hand, the time spent in developing a completed design may be an advantage, since the owner will be able to enter into a contract with the general contractor that will reflect the costs of construction and not the risk of unanticipated design changes.

Numerous methods have been developed to overcome the disadvantages of the D-A-B system. For example, when time constraints require the completion of the project by a particular date, fast-track or phased construction may be used to permit the general contractor to begin construction before the architect has completed the design of the project. In fast track or phased construction, however, the general contractor will not be able to provide a fixed price for construction upon which the owner can rely. Consequently, the owner and general contractor will typically be forced to use a cost-type contract, which may not provide sufficient incentives for the general contractor to control construction costs. In addition, fast track construction can involve considerable scheduling difficulties as designs are revised or are not yet completed when necessary.

Another approach, referred to as design-build, is intended to overcome the division of responsibility between the architect and general contractor under the D-A-B system. Under design-build, the owner enters into one contract with another entity, the Design Builder, to both design and construct the project. Typically, the general contractor will employ or engage the services of the architect in the design build situation. The advantage of the design build approach is that the owner can avoid finger-pointing by the architect and the general contractor for construction defects. However, the owner may sacrifice the benefits of having an independent architect and general contractor overseeing each other's work during the construction process. The design-build approach can often be used in combination with fast track construction.

Yet another alternative to the D-A-B system is to avoid the use of subcontracts and make use of multiple contracts between the owner and the specialty trades. In this situation, the owner assumes the responsibility of coordination and supervision, either directly when the owner has a sufficiently sophisticated technical staff or indirectly through the use of a main contractor, the architect, or a construction manager. Where the owner delegates the coordination function to another but is in privity of contract with the specialty trades, questions of liability may arise when losses result from inadequate coordination.

The use of construction managers has become widespread since the 1970s. Construction management is a flexible concept that may be applied in the D-A-B system or any alternative approach. The construction manager may simply provide general design, cost-estimating, and scheduling advice to the owner to augment that provided by the architect and general contractor. Alternatively, the construction manager may supervise and coordinate the specialty trades on behalf of the owner under the multiple contract approach. Under another approach, the construction manager might replace the general contractor and contract directly with the specialty trades through subcontracts. The widespread use of construction managers in today's construction process indicates the existence of gaps in the traditional D-A-B system or the lack of ability or interest by architects and general contractors to perform certain functions on behalf of the owner.

Importantly, the activities of the parties under the typical D-A-B system, including the owner, the architect, the general contractor, and the subcontractors, are coordinated under the terms of the construction contracts. At a minimum, these contracts should set forth the framework of the design, development, and construction process, and detail the rights and responsibilities of the parties at each stage. The construction contracts should also contain the detailed aspects of the project such as the construction budget, the construction schedule, and the plans and specifications for the completed project. The use of an alternative approach or the presence of a construction manager further emphasizes the need to fully delineate the lines of responsibility and accountability among the other actors in the construction process under the construction contracts.

§ 12.02 OVERVIEW OF PART IV

The purpose of Part IV is to introduce you to the construction process and to give you an understanding of the typical legal relationships that exist among the principal parties: owner, architect, contractor, subcontractors, and the lender. The remainder of this chapter describes the importance of the various types of risks that owners and developers confront in undertaking a construction project and how the details of the financial arrangement between the owner and the general contractor can allocate those risks to the party most capable of reducing those risks. The issue of risk allocation underlies most, if not all, of the contractual provisions that you will encounter in this chapter. Chapter 13 will then describe the legal relationships among the principal parties, including the owner and the architect, the owner and the general contractor, and the general contractor and the subcontractors. Taken together, the two chapters that make up Part IV will provide you with both an overview of the construction process and an appreciation of the lawyer's role in negotiating construction contracts with the specific client's interests in mind.

We do need to point out one aspect of the construction of the Fox Valley Auto Care Center that did not follow the typical pattern. As we have said before, no one project is going to raise every possible issue that can be raised; for example, in our discussion of financing, we had to deal with Regent's failure to obtain a take out or permanent loan commitment. The deviation in the construction process for the Fox Valley Auto Care Center from the typical shopping center development is that the general contractor was an affiliate of the Regent Real Estate Development Corporation. Therefore, as we set out the issues involved in the construction process, we must, at times, assume an element that was not actually present: an independent general contractor and its relationship with the owner.

§ 12.03 RISK AND THE CONSTRUCTION PROCESS

Construction is a risky business. Risk in the construction process can take a number of forms, and the importance of different types of risk varies, depending on the type of construction project. For example, in some construction settings, the greatest concern may be in completing the project on time, while in other settings the greatest concern may be completing the project within budget. In addition, different parties engaged in the construction process may be better able to minimize different types of risk, as well as absorb or insure against any loss that might result from different risks. The minimization of risk through a carefully defined construction process, as well as the shifting of risk from one party to another, should be dealt with in the construction contracts.

Because the significance of different types of risk will depend on the specific characteristics of the construction project, different types of construction contracts have been developed to apply to the varying types of projects. These include fixed price contracts, time-and-materials contracts, and guaranteed-maximum-price contracts.

[1] Identifying and Managing Construction Risks

As the following article explains, owners must be careful to select the proper type of construction contract to reflect the risks of the construction project.

John D. Macomber, *You* Can *Manage Construction Risks*, HARVARD BUS. REV. 155 (March-April 1989)*

Colossal County Hospital was coming apart at the seams. With dozens of newly hired doctors, nurses, and technicians, millions of dollars of equipment on the road, and patient appointments backed up for months, the new facility was impossible to use. For one thing, construction wasn't finished, and much of what was complete was faulty. Worse yet, the contractor had placed liens on the property for nonpayment, preventing occupancy. Costs had greatly outdistanced available financing. The hospital staff was frantic; the bank was apoplectic; the board of trustees was in despair.

How had it happened? The chairman of the board — head of the local branch of a financial services company — was baffled. He tried to trace the history of the project.

Two years earlier, the board members had voted to build an important new facility and renovate an adjoining older one. They hired the best available hospital architect. One group of trustees went on to focus its attention on a special bond issue to provide low-cost financing, while another group put together and executed a detailed marketing strategy to position the hospital as a world leader in several areas of care and research. Working closely with the doctors who would direct the various programs, the architect designed a state-of-the-art medical facility and a splendid building that would serve as a symbol for the hospital and as a landmark for the city.

On the architect's recommendation, a local contractor was retained to begin pricing the preliminary plans. As the drawings and budgeting progressed, the hospital was confident enough to apply for bank financing, and the bank, on the basis of the contractor's estimates and the proposed bond issue, agreed to make the loan.

Then the contractor presented his final budget. To the board's surprise, the estimate had grown by $3.5 million — and the detailed construction drawings still weren't complete. The contractor claimed the architect was upgrading the quality and scope of construction. The architect insisted he was only complying with the growing wish list of the trustees, doctors, and marketing experts hired by the

* Reprinted by permission of *Harvard Business Review. You* Can *Manage Construction Risks* by John D. Macomber, March/April 1989.

board. But the bond issue was based on the original budget, and it wasn't big enough to accommodate the higher price. The hospital could not proceed. The trustees and the doctors held a meeting.

The doctors insisted they had added very little, and they refused to eliminate any of the medical features designed into the building. The trustees were convinced that the overall increase in scope was much smaller than the new price indicated. Everyone suspected the contractor of taking advantage of the hospital. The chairman decided it was time to act.

"In my industry — financial services," he reasoned, "all services are bid for. We give all aspirants a chance to say what they will charge. That's the way to get the lowest price."

A local manufacturer on the board agreed. "I had one of these 'trust me' contractors do my warehouse on a time-and-materials basis, and he soaked me good. He put his worst workers on the job, he didn't fight for purchase discounts, and he did everything he could to get costs up so his fee would go up. Let's not make the same mistake I made."

So the project was put out to bid with no modifications in scope and still without completed blueprints and specifications. Five companies submitted bids. The hospital's chief financial officer awarded the contract to a builder whose price was within the original budget. The original contractor was banished in disgrace, despite his protestations that his estimate was the right price for all the work the hospital would need.

Conflicts developed at once. The new builder had assumed that the space to be renovated would be vacated to work in, but the hospital couldn't do that. The builder threatened to stop work, so the board caved in and gave him an increase. The architect and the contractor fought constantly over interpretation of the drawings and specifications. The trustees, distracted by questions of finance and marketing, did not always make timely decisions. The contractor cut every possible corner to hold down costs, and the architect overruled him again and again.

Just as the building was nearly finished, the board was shocked to receive a huge change-order request from the contractor alleging inaccurate specifications, changed conditions, and decision delays by the owner. The hospital refused to pay. The builder shut the job down and placed mechanic's liens on the property.

This was where the project now stood. The members of the board — successful local businesspeople, educators, and public servants — were angry and embarrassed; the architect was bitter; the original contractor was full of I-told-you-so's for anyone who'd listen. The chairman of the board was still baffled.

This story is exaggerated, of course, but parts of it are familiar to anyone who has been involved in a construction project. Building headaches are a fact of business life. Companies move. Businesses modernize old quarters. Growing organizations need more space. Companies incur some of their largest and longest term debts to finance these investments, while occupancy delays and construction quarrels can rank among the most debilitating problems a company can face. It is often impossible to predict exactly what a project will cost and how long it will take to complete, and it is always difficult to coordinate a dozen professionals — architects, engineers, contractors, bankers, lawyers, consultants, many with their own hidden agendas — and scores of subcontractors, suppliers, and workers.

All in all, the risks involved in a construction project are as great as any a company normally faces, and these risks are very different from the kind companies are used to. Yet many corporate officers and directors who consistently analyze and manage every other controllable risk fail to use all the tools available to control construction risk.

One reason CEOs and directors overlook or underestimate construction risk — and delegate it to subordinates to handle — is that construction is old technology. Buildings have been built before — what's so different about this one? The CFO is the watchdog for other expenses — why can't she watch these dollars too? The company has a department that does its purchasing — why can't it purchase a building? The facilities manager shares a vocabulary with the contractor — why not let him oversee the process? It seems foolish not to delegate a procedure that has been repeated a million times since the pyramids were finished.

But it is the exceptional CFO who can get beyond the first few summary numbers to understand what services a prospective contractor is really proposing; it is the unusual purchasing agent who can oversee completion of a product containing tens of thousands of parts delivered over a period of up to several years; and facilities managers seldom have the expertise to defend their employers against contractors' claims. Finally, most companies do not go through the building process frequently. Construction skills are simply not part of a normal manager's repertoire.

Construction is a confusing process governed by complicated contracts and involving complex relationships in several tiers. The customer is really buying a service, not a product. At one relationship level, the contractor performs an essential service by directing and coordinating the work of dozens or hundreds of subcontractors, suppliers, craftspeople, and laborers. At the next level, someone — sometimes the contractor or the architect — must also coordinate the builder's services with those of the architects, engineers, and consultants. Finally, someone must take control of the entire process and coordinate the coordinators. At this level, the CEO and the board of directors will either manage the project and its risks or let the risks manage them. There is no substitute for responsibility at the top.

There are seven steps in the analysis and management of construction risk:

1. Understanding the types and phases of risk.
2. Assessing the risks of a particular construction project.
3. Matching risks with in-house capabilities and building a construction team.
4. Defining a building strategy.
5. Picking the right kind of contract.
6. Choosing the builder.
7. Monitoring construction.

Understanding the Types and Phases of Risk

There are three kinds of construction risk, and they surface in two phases. The first kind of risk is financial — the project exceeds its budget and endangers the financial health of the company. Budget overruns are not always a matter of poor construction supervision. They are often the result of bad planning, wishful pricing, or poor coordination.

The second kind of risk has to do with time — the building is finished behind schedule. Delays can have devastating financial consequences. What damage will your retail outlet suffer if its space is ready on January 4 instead of November 15? How will your organization function if the computer room is not ready because no one was ever assigned responsibility for ensuring uninterruptible power? What is the toll on your business if your CFO has to spend 40 days in a construction arbitration case?

The third type of risk is design-related — the completed building does not meet the organization's needs. For example, a health care organization with a fixed budget might elect to build a small addition with above-average finishwork and systems, only to discover on completion that it doesn't have enough space. (Perhaps it should have built a larger but plainer facility for the same money.) Or an office developer might pick an air-conditioning system that allows individual controls for each office but turns out to be too noisy. (A better match might have been to sacrifice individual controls to gain acoustic value or perhaps to spend more money to get both.)

All three kinds of risks can be addressed in both the *preconstruction phase* and the *construction-and-settlement phase*. The preconstruction phase is often the most grueling for the owner and often the most important. The organization must now make projections about marketing, budget, space, and schedule, and make actual decisions about design, zoning requirements, financing, traffic, and other environmental concerns. The risks in this phase are small in one sense because no one is actually building anything. But the risks are large in other ways. For one thing, consultants are expensive, and, since the construction loan is not yet in place, the company has to pay them out-of-pocket with unleveraged, highly speculative money. Also, a planning mistake or a piece of budgetary wishful thinking at this moment can cause big problems later on.

At this stage, Colossal County Hospital was already in trouble on three counts. First, the trustees were focusing on their individual specialties in marketing and finance, leaving the other preconstruction responsibilities to subordinates and doctors. Second, the architect dominated the preconstruction team and led it toward a design that would make more architectural and medical history than business sense. Third, the original contractor did not anticipate the growing wish lists, and, once he saw them, he was unable to convince the trustees that his new price was indeed reasonable — in fact, inescapable. The preconstruction team was poorly selected for the real needs of the project, and no one was in a position to monitor the team in detail and with authority.

There is a great deal of uncertainty and ambiguity in the preconstruction phase because the design-cost equation is constantly changing. A lot of hands-on specialists deal poorly with this lack of definition, and a poorly managed team can degenerate into chaos if the participants are allowed to hide behind their disciplines and stonewall or ignore each other.

The design-cost picture that emerges from this phase is the foundation on which great construction-period risk will rest, yet the work done now is the most manageable of the whole. Market and financial risks are external and uncontrollable. Preconstruction risk is internal to the team and can be controlled. The key to success in this phase, as elsewhere, is picking the right team — then providing coordination and central direction. The health care space and air-conditioning noise examples could both be best addressed in the preconstruction phase. Good use of the architect's and contractor's expertise at this juncture can save lots of problems later on.

In the construction-and-settlement phase, the risk factors move from planning to supervision. The design is mostly fixed; time risk no longer depends on creating a realistic schedule but on sticking to it; budgetary risk is no longer a matter of pricing but of cost control.

Yet appearances are deceptive. Depending on the contract, cost control is now mostly or entirely the contractor's responsibility. If your contract specified liquidated damages for late delivery, then schedule is the contractor's responsibility too, although most contracts allow several cost and schedule exceptions. What's more, a construction loan is now in place, so the bank reimburses the contractor directly for construction costs — usually on a monthly basis, always after carefully checking that the work has actually been done and the materials actually delivered, and almost always after holding back 5% to 10% of the total as a kind of performance guarantee until the entire project is complete and final settlement takes place. So where is the owner's risk?

Let's go back to Colossal County Hospital, a large institution brought to its knees at this very stage of the project. First of all, poor planning in the preconstruction phase came home to roost as the project drew to a close. For instance, the trustees had put the project out to bid on the basis of incomplete construction documents (blueprints and specifications), so the contractor had a right to adjust the price as the architect added new details. Second, while the bond issue set a limit on funds, the doctors and the architect fought to spend more, and the trustees never confronted the disparity. Third, the conditions of construction (the hospital's continued use of the space being renovated) and the trustees' repeated failure to make prompt decisions cost the contractor time, and such delays are legitimate grounds for a schedule extension. Finally, the mechanic's lien allows a contractor or subcontractor with a payment dispute to tie up a project in the courts and prevent its use or sale until the dispute is settled. And these are only a few of the problems that can crop up even after price, schedule, financing, payment mechanisms, and delivery date have supposedly been established once and for all.

As complex and as great as all these risks appear — particularly in the egregious case of Colossal County Hospital — it would be a waste of effort to try to eliminate every one of them, because that simply couldn't be done. The goal is to control and manage construction risk within reasonable limits.

Assessing the Risks of a Particular Construction Project

No two projects, no two sites, and no two construction teams are ever exactly the same. In order to pick the right team members, the right group of consultants, the right architect, the right contractor, and the right kind of contract, you need to understand the risks of your particular project. The crucial consideration is project complexity.

What are the company's needs for the project? Is there a rush for occupancy? Do you have time to develop complete blueprints and specifications before you put the project out to bid, or will you have to overlap this document preparation time with the start of construction? Are the mechanical systems routine, or will the contractor need to coordinate their design as well as installation? Is the quality of construction critical, as in a hospital, or do you need only a roof and walls? What about project financing? Some lenders will not make a commitment until they have seen the contracts and all of the completed drawings.

What about the site? There is a world of difference between building on a piece of well-drained farmland and building on a downtown site with an uncertain history and unknown conditions. Hazardous waste and the remains of old foundations are just two of the invisible surprises that are entirely the owner's responsibility in most contracts.

What about the structure? A new building will have many more components than an old one will, but a rehabilitation project will mean more unknowns and greater risks.

Evaluating the risk is the first step to controlling it. The chart, "Assessing Construction Risk," lists the chief risk elements and shows how three hypothetical projects might have rated them.

Assessing Construction Risk

Although many projects will have special risk factors of their own, this table lists the most important things to consider in assessing the risks of your project. Colossal County Hospital is adding a new wing and renovating some older space on a crowded site in the middle of a city. Allperils Insurance is building a new, moderate-rise office structure in a suburban office park. Goodgoods, Inc. is putting up a warehouse on former agricultural land near an interstate highway well away from populated areas.

Risk Elements	**Colossal County Hospital**	**All perils Insurance Company**	**Good goods Warehouse**
Product Site			
Maneuvering room	No staging area	Office park; some constraints	Plenty of room
Neighbors	Residential and politicized	Cooperative	None
Soils	Sand and gravel	Peat and organics	Sand and gravel; some boulders
Traffic	Congested city streets	Coordinate with neighbors	Easy freeway access
Previous uses	Old foundations	Gas station site, buried tanks	None
Foundation			
Excavation	Retaining walls and underpinning	Open cut; some shoring	Open cut
Technology	Backhoe and steam shovel	Pressure injected footings	Simple concrete mat

Risk Elements	Colossal County Hospital	All perils Insurance Company	Good goods Warehouse
Structure			
Design	Beams and floors	Columns, beams, and floors	Bearing walls. Joists, and deck
Materials	Cast-in-place concrete	Steel and concrete composite	Masonry, steel, and concrete
Exterior			
Design	Complex; variety and details	Prefabricated metal panels	Stucco
Materials	Brick, stone, and glass	Stainless steel	Stucco
Dimensional tolerance	Moderate	Low	High
Mechanical and Electrical			
Heating-and-cooling plant	Cogeneration steam and electric	Gas-fired boiler and chiller	Electric heat, no A/C
Distribution	Hot-and-cold-water fan-coil units	Heat pumps	None
Communications	Hospital monitoring systems	Fiber-optic voice and data	None
Finishes			
Complexity	Moderate	Straightforward	Spartan
Materials	Moderate; paint and plaster	Marble and mahogany lobby	Paint, paneling, and drywall
On-site craftsmanship	Durable more than memorable	Close tolerances	Serviceable
Sourcing	Local warehouse stock	Some special-order items	Local warehouse stock
End Uses			
Flexibility intended	No; floor plans fixed	Partitions changeable	Highly flexible
Impact on business	Can't operate without it	Moving day can wait	Can't afford warehouse delay
Special situations	Renovation while space in use	None	None
Process Financing			
Preconstruction sources	Limited	In-house funds	In-house funds
Permanent financing	Reliable but inflexible	In-house funds	Traditional mortgage
Lender requirements	Strict; bonded contractor	Strict but self-administered	Lenient
Time			
Preconstruction time allowed	Years	Months	Weeks
Construction pace	Fast-track	Normal	Selected overtime work
Architecture			

Risk Elements	**Colossal County Hospital**	**All perils Insurance Company**	**Good goods Warehouse**
Complexity of project	High	Suburban office standards	Low
Focus of designer	Make architectural history	Promote client image	Economy and ease of construction
Completeness of plans	Not enough for bid confidence	Complete	Essential items shown
Compensation to architect	High pay for quality designer	Moderate fee	Low fee for standard project
Owner's decision structure	Many committees and users	One small committee	One person
Need for "cooperative" input			
Rethinking of design option	Many preliminary designs	General program known	Few, if any
Relative number of unknowns	Moderate; mostly new construction	Few	Very few
Budgeting expertise needed	Complex schedule and cost issues	Some (atrium, lobby pricing)	None beyond architect
Approvals			
Regulations and codes	Many agencies and rules	Standard life-safety codes	Basic building codes
Politics	Strong community support	Conformity standards	No issues

Matching Risks with Capabilities and Building a Construction Team

Once you've estimated the risks of your project, the next step is to assess your organization's capacities. Building the construction team involves a series of classic make-or-buy decisions: What do we need? Can we provide it in-house? Should we buy it from outside? The chart, "Assessing In-House Capability," will help give you an idea of your organization's capacity to deal with the hundreds of construction headaches that will come up during the project.

Assessing In-House Capability

To make an adequate assessment of how much outside help you will need to get your building built, you need to look at your staff's talents. Basically, more in-house talent means less risk.

Capability	**Colossal County Hospital**	**All perils Insurance Company**	**Good goods Warehouse**
Budgeting talent	One physical-plant veteran	Nobody	One former contractor in-house
Design talent	Nobody in-house	Nobody	Nobody
Team-building talent	No focus on this project	Moderate	One strong CEO
Monitoring talent	Finance experts, no construction experience	Finance experts, no construction experience	Nobody

Capability	Colossal County Hospital	All perils Insurance Company	Good goods Warehouse
Appetite for conflict	Board doesn't like conflicts	Well-developed	CEO happy to knock heads
Fund resources	No money for overruns	Can fund overruns in-house	Need to borrow more for overruns

Everyone knows that building a building requires a contractor and usually an architect, a couple of engineers, a lender, several consultants, and sometimes a lawyer. . . . For the purposes of controlling risk, however, the principal players are your own board of directors, CEO, and senior staff, one or more of whom will actually oversee the entire project.

This person or persons — whom we might call the owner's representative (or even the developer) — will be at the center of a highly charged tangle of big egos, great stress, and high financial stakes. While the architect makes erudite speeches on aesthetics and design, the contractor may communicate mostly in profanities. While the banker speaks financial double-talk in hopes of reducing the lender's risk to zero, the heads of marketing and operations tear their hair out at the prospect of getting the wrong space at the wrong time. It takes a tough leader to coordinate everyone's efforts. If the CEO has the time and expertise, so much the better. If not, then he or she will have to delegate the responsibility to some unusual subordinate with the necessary breadth of knowledge and experience, or carefully assign parts of it to the architect or the contractor. But under no circumstances should coordination be delegated casually. Construction is one of the most argumentative industries on earth and the home of Murphy's Law — "If something can go wrong, it will."

Defining a Building Strategy

The charts have two important implications. First, they show how to identify and address the various individual elements of risk. Second, they define a strategy for the selection of a contractor and consultants. A concentration of high-risk components suggests you should look for the *performance* benefits of *cooperation* and try to find a contractor able to work as a team player. Predominantly low-risk components point instead to the *price* benefits of *competition*. Both kinds of contractors are readily available virtually everywhere.

The construction industry is highly fragmented and comparatively unsophisticated. Company strategies are often more intuitive than deliberate. Still, by choice or accident, construction companies lie somewhere on the spectrum between low-cost product providers at one end of the scale and highly differentiated service providers at the other. The challenge for clients is to identify the objective of each project and to pick the right fit.

Colossal County Hospital had a high-risk job and should have built a strong, cooperative team, including a contractor who would have worked closely with the board to solve problems. Instead, a board oriented too strongly toward competition made a decision solely on the basis of price and suffered the ill effects of an adversarial relationship with the builder. By contrast, the trustee who felt he'd been "soaked" on a time-and-materials contract for a warehouse did in fact waste money on cooperation. He should have had a competitive hard-money bid based on complete construction documents.

If your project is a simple, one-story building on a flat piece of vacant land, a low-cost provider is probably appropriate. The builder will not add much value beyond getting the material to the site and erecting it. If, on the other hand, your project is a complicated, fast-paced rehab, the noncraft services offered by a highly differentiated contractor may have great potential value. Your project may place special requirements on the contractor, like building one phase while the next is still being designed and priced; anticipating discovery of unknown conditions, like concealed rotting timbers; doing a workmanlike job from inadequate design documents; or working around existing occupants. Contractors who can do all this will charge more, but they will also act more like members of your team.

Another service the differentiated contractor can provide is to help you take advantage of the fragmentation of the building business by getting good competition among subcontractors. The commercial building industry is made up of thousands of subcontractors in several hundred specialized trades. These small companies tend to be entrepreneurial and fiercely independent, and their fractiousness can be a problem or an asset. Subcontracts and purchase orders can amount to 70% or 80% of the total cost of a commercial building project. Builders skilled at handling competition at the trade level may charge a higher fee for their own services and still produce the lowest total final cost.

Some contractors are also adept at forming value-adding partnerships with the subcontractors they use most often. Teams like these can gain efficiencies from shared design and production information as well as from a good understanding of each other's work styles. In this kind of cooperative setting, the game can have a sum higher than zero. Teamwork reduces friction, uncertainty, inefficiency, and duplication of effort.

Such teamwork is what Colossal County Hospital needed at every level. Of course, building teamwork requires energy and trust. As always, the question for management is whether the added value is worth the added cost. Colossal County didn't expend the energy or money to build the right team when it should have. Other owners may not need to.

Picking the Right Kind of Contract

The disparities among the levels of service outlined here have led to three main contract types. All three have been around for years, but many owners don't understand their relation to risk control. In most cases, a good evaluation of the kind and level of risk will point clearly to one of these three contracts.

The *lump-sum* contract is easy to understand. Each contractor bidding on the project estimates a total cost, adds a profit margin, and bids a fixed price for the job. The owner picks the lowest bid. If costs go up, the price to the owner remains the same. If costs go down — and the incentive to make them go down by cutting corners can be considerable — the extra margin goes to the contractor. This contract is truly a zero-sum game. Whatever the contractor gets is something you don't get.

With a lump-sum contract, the contractor takes all the visible risk, and the owner takes none. This seems like a good bet for high-risk projects, but just the opposite is true. First, should costs rise unexpectedly above the price that was bid and accepted, your contractor's dedication to the job may abruptly vanish. Second, with a lump-sum contract, the price may be fixed, but so is the scope of the work. Even a small change in the project can throw the whole contract out the window, and you cannot afford to renegotiate that contract once the work is under way. By avoiding risk, you also give up most of your decision making power. In other words, you pay your money and you take your chances — which is no way to build a hospital or any other highly differentiated structure. Still, the lump-sum contract is the right contract for simple jobs where price is more important than collaboration.

Most people are familiar with *time-and-materials* contracts — based on the cost of work plus a fee. Lawyers bill this way, and so do auto mechanics. The builder gets reimbursed for the actual costs of the work, whatever they are, plus a percentage fee or markup. So, in other words, the owner takes all the risk and the contractor none. The customer can be fairly certain that work will be properly done, because there is no incentive to cut corners. Of course, the more the contractor spends, the more the contractor makes — and we know from experience that auto mechanics and lawyers have no particular incentive to hurry.

Despite the obvious disadvantages in terms of risk, there are three fairly common situations — and one fairly uncommon one — where time-and-materials is nevertheless the right contract for the owner. The first is when quality matters more than money. The second is when time is very limited and the contractor will have to work extensive overtime. The third is when construction documents are incomplete or missing, which leaves the contractor nothing on which to base a bid. The fourth situation comes up when owners have so much construction expertise and so much time to devote to supervision that they can get exactly what they want and still hold down costs by directing the location and quality of every brick and nail.

For most situations, one of these two contracts will fit the bill. But for many large construction users, a hybrid form called *guaranteed-maximum-price* is more appropriate. It is often the best contract for performing the work identified as high-risk in the two charts. Like time-and-materials, guaranteed-maximum-price is also based on the cost of work plus a fee, but risk is shared. Up to the predetermined maximum price, the contractor passes along all costs to the owner, but once that price is reached, all risk belongs to the builder.

As in a time-and-materials contract, the owner benefits when direct costs are less than expected. But when costs go up too far, contractors absorb the overrun, as they would in a lump-sum contract. Generally, this arrangement keeps the best features of both other contract types and allows the owner to have his cake and eat it too. Most often, the guaranteed maximum price will be set higher than the lump-sum price for the same project because the contractor's profit is capped.

The goal in this case is to make contractors team players without giving them carte blanche. The construction company's profit does not depend on cost cutting but rather on good performance of this service for the owner. What the customer gets is a limit on exposure and a cooperative relationship instead of an adversarial one.

The exhibit, "Cost vs. Price with the Three Contract Types," shows price in relation to actual construction cost in lump-sum, time-and-materials, and guaranteed-maximum-price contracts.

Cost vs. Price with the Three Contract Types

Assume that the contractor believes your project will wind up costing just about $10 million to build. These three graphs show the price to you and the profit or loss to the contractor for three different kinds of contracts at three different actual final cost levels. At point *a* in each diagram, the contractor has shaved $500,000 for the anticipated costs. At *b*, costs have run as expected. At *c*, there has been a cost overrun of $500,000. Basically, with a *lump-sum*, the contractor gets all the savings and takes all the risk. With *time-and-materials*, the owner takes the savings and takes all the risk. And with *guaranteed-maximum-price*, the owner gets the savings, the builder takes the risk.

Lump-Sum Contract

(Price is fixed at $10,300)

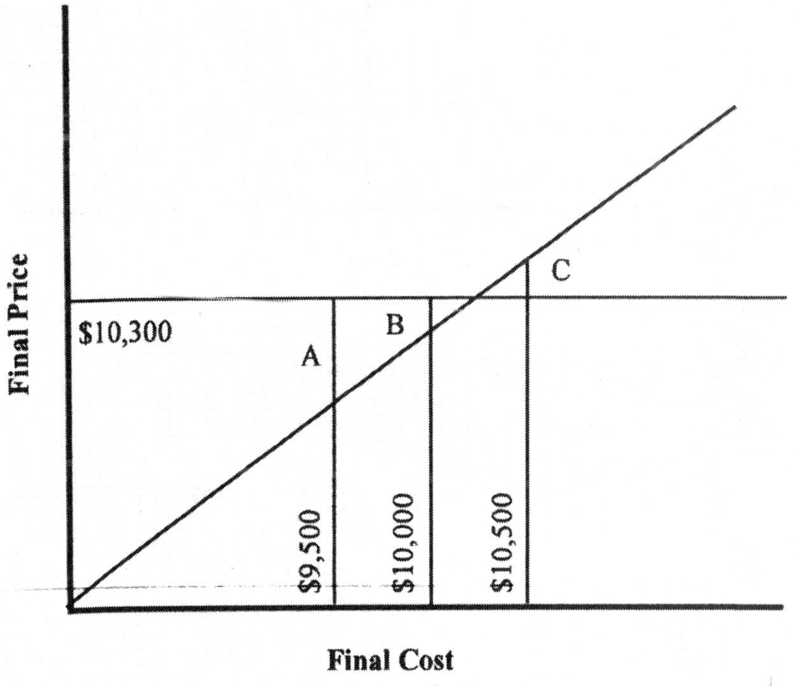

A=If final cost is $9,500, contractor profit is $800 (8.42%)
B=If final cost is $10,000 (as expected), contractor profit is $300 (3%)
C=If final cost is $10,500, contractor loss is $200 (-1.9%)

Time-and-Materials Contract
(Price = cost plus 5%)

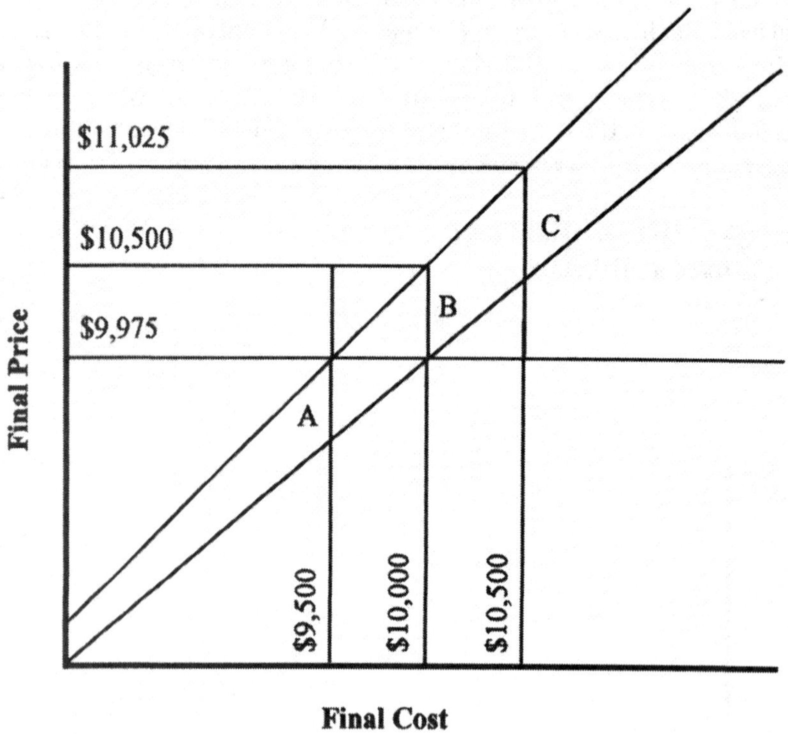

A=If final cost is $9,500, contractor profit is $475 (5%)
B=If final cost is $10,000, contractor profit is $500 (5%)
C=If final cost is $10,500, contractor profit is $525(5%)

Guaranteed-Maximum-Price Contract
(Price = cost of work plus fee of $500 with a maximum price of $10,500)

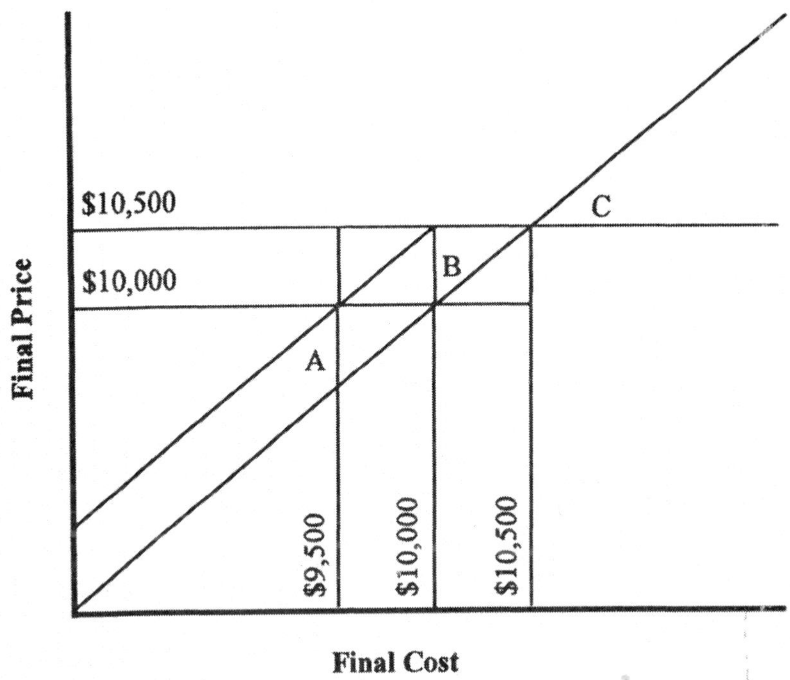

A=If final cost is $9,500, contractor profit is $500 (5.26%)
B=If final cost is $10,000, contractor profit is $500 (5%)
C=If final cost is $10,500, contractor profit is $0 (0%)

These three contract types all assume the traditional owner-architect-contractor configuration. There are three less common ways to assign these roles. With a *turnkey* contract, the owner buys site, design, and finished building as a package. The supplier secures the construction financing and plays the role of owner and contractor (and sometimes architect) during construction. Turnkey contracts are suited to situations where the needs of the user are easily described.

A *design-build* contract is very like a turnkey contract in that the architect and contractor work under one contract, giving one source of responsibility. This fosters cooperation at the cost of eliminating traditional checks and balances. But in design-build, as opposed to turnkey, the owner is responsible for financing.

Construction management, in its simplest form, is merely a consulting service. Construction managers often supplement the owner's in-house construction team by giving advice and providing supervision for a fee. They take no fiduciary responsibility, and they do not guarantee price, results, or schedule. (Be aware that architects, engineers, contractors, and consultants all use the phrase "construction management" a little differently. Before you contract for construction management, make sure you know exactly what you're getting.)

Choosing the Builder

It sounds elementary at this point to say that the way a company chooses a builder should match its project-risk level and contract type. But the old practice of bidding out contracts is so well established that organizations resort to it even when it makes no sense. Each kind of project and contract should have its own selection criteria.

Lump-sum. The builder for a lump-sum contract can be chosen almost entirely by means of an open bid based on construction documents — blueprints and specifications — that clearly define the scope of the work. (Never put partial documents out to bid. In fact, if you must choose a contractor before the documents are done, lump-sum may be the wrong type of contract.) Beyond requiring bidders to satisfy some minimum level of experience, reputation, and financial strength, price is really all you care about.

One warning: Resist the temptation to take advantage of a very low bid. It may be a mistake based on misinterpreted construction documents, and the ensuing fight won't be worth it.

Time-and-materials. For a so-called cost-plus or time-and-materials contract, reputation, ability, and trust are paramount. Check references, look for the right chemistry between all parties, make sure you are comfortable with the builder. Whatever you do, don't try to make a selection on the basis of some kind of estimated bid. If the contract has no cap, the bid means nothing. It can only tempt you to choose the lowest of several meaningless numbers, and that is a good way to pick the least competent candidate.

Guaranteed-maximum-price. The process here is much like the one above. Your guide should be the contractor's experience, references, and integrity, and the chemistry between you. You are planning to pay a fee to a company for its competence in managing construction, meeting schedules, maintaining quality, providing construction services, and treating its clients honestly and fairly. Establishing that competence should be your only criterion.

Any company experienced in the running for this type of contract will be able to give you the names of previous customers who can tell you just how well it performed in the past. Ask about the accuracy of the cost estimates and the extent of the savings returned to the owner (or the size of the overrun absorbed by the contractor). Ask how many serious fights there were and whether they were settled satisfactorily. Find out if the space was delivered on time. Ask for references from former subcontractors as well, and find out what they thought of the company they worked for. You are buying a value-added service. Make sure you will get what you're paying for.

Monitoring Construction

Everybody likes to watch excavating equipment and play sidewalk superintendent when the big steel flies. Monitoring the team and the contract is much less fun — and much more important. Once again, the scope and method of supervision depends on the kind of contract.

On a lump-sum contract, the developer or the owner's representative must monitor both materials and workmanship to make sure the contractor does not pad his or her own profit by delivering less than what was contracted for. This level of attention calls for a construction supervisor who understands specifications, details, workmanship, and materials gradation and handling.

On a time-and-materials contract, the construction supervisor's job is to see that the contractor doesn't waste the owner's money. The builder will not likely cut corners, but cost control probably won't be a top priority either. This kind of contract needs a monitor who understands labor productivity, effective use of raw materials, and cost accounting.

In theory, the structure of a guaranteed-maximum-price contract reduces the degree of supervision the owner will need. The contractor assumes the risk of a cost overrun and earns a predetermined fee to make sure that the work and the materials are right. Still, a prudent owner will keep an eye on workmanship and accounting. The skills of an experienced construction supervisor must still be available, but the need is less urgent.

Clearly, the person who acts as construction supervisor needs experience and expertise. Few CEOs — and few members of the board — would qualify. If the project coordinator is not a construction expert, it may sometimes be worthwhile to hire a construction consultant. Often the architect is used for construction supervision, and sometimes this works very well. But architects are trained to design, and their capacity and willingness to check on workmanship, monitor materials, and oversee accounting is at best uneven.

Then, too, as projects grow more complex, the architect has a progressively greater need to work with, not against, the contractor. There will always be issues of interpretation, aesthetics, even cost, for them to consider together. And in a project with many unknown risks — a building with marine foundations, say, or the renovation of a historic structure — the contractor's experience and judgment are crucial assets for the architect. An owner's insistence on police duty can impair an architect's ability to work with the builder.

Colossal County Hospital survived its ordeal — the city intervened with an emergency loan and a supplemental bond issue — and learned from the experience. For its next addition, the board built a team from the beginning and stayed abreast of the process. The new chairman of the board, head of a local management consulting firm, took on the role of in-house developer. She led the team through a preconstruction analysis of complexity and risk that then drove the choice of contract, builder, financing, and schedule. The chosen contractor had a reputation for accurate pricing and cooperative problem solving. The project came in on time and even slightly under budget.

The manufacturing trustee learned his lesson too. For his new distribution center, he hired an architect who could provide him with dependable, detailed drawings; he put the project out to bid only when all of the specifications and blueprints were complete; and he chose the low bidder from a field of 12 prequalified builders. The space cost him 50% less than with the earlier time-and-materials contract.

Construction is a major obligation for many growing companies. The initial estimates of cost, time, and trouble are bound to change dramatically as work progresses. The construction team itself may be volatile and problematic. But the directors and top management of your company can identify, analyze, and rationally control these risks.

[2] Notes on Controlling Construction Risk

1. For a discussion of the fast track approach, see Bynum, *Construction Management and Design-Build/Fast Track Construction from the Perspective of a General Contractor*, 46 Law & Contemp. Probs. 25 (1983), and Foster, *Construction Management and Design-Build/Fast Track Construction: A Solution Which Uncovers a Problem for the Surety*, 46 Law & Contemp. Probs. 95 (1983).
2. For a discussion of the design-build approach, see Whitlock, *An Argument for Design Build*, 9 Real Est. Fin. 87 (1992), and T.R. Twomey, Understanding the Legal Aspects of Design/Build (1989).
3. For a discussion of construction management, see Spangler and Hill, *The Evolving Liabilities of Construction Managers*, 19 The Construction Law. 30 (Jan. 1999); Schenk, *Construction Wars: Part II; Risk and the Construction Manager: A Continuing Development*, 24 Real Prop., Prob. & Trust J. 593 (1990); Partridge & Noletto, *Construction Management: Evolving Roles and Exposure of Construction Managers and Architect/Engineers*, 12 Amer. J. Trial Advoc. 55 (1988); Conner, *Contracting for Construction Management Services*, 46 Law & Contemp. Probs. 5 (1983); Dieder & Cox, *Construction Management and the Specialty Trade (Prime) Contractors*, 46 Law & Contemp. Probs. 39 (1983); Sweet, *The Architectural Profession Responds to Construction Management and Design-Build: The Spotlight on AIA Documents*, 46 Law & Contemp. Probs. 69 (1983); and Hart, *Construction Management — "CM for Short" — The New Name for an Old Game*, 8 Forum 210 (1972).
4. In addition to the owner, architect, general contractor, and subcontractors, a number of minor actors are necessary to the successful completion of the construction process. These actors include insurers, sureties, suppliers, and unions. Other minor actors, including lenders, lawyers, and trade associations also influence the legal and political context in which construction takes place. *See* Sweet, Sweet on Construction Law §§ 1.6–1.8 (1997).

[3] Questions About Controlling Construction Risk

1. The construction process involves a number of players including the owner, the architect, and the general contractor. What is the role of each of these players in the construction process? What other parties may be involved?
2. Macomber describes three types of risk in the construction process: financial, time, and design risks. How can an owner minimize each type of

risk?

3. Describe the differences between fixed price, cost plus, and guaranteed maximum price construction contracts. In what types of situation is each contract appropriate? What type of construction contract should have been used by Regent to employ an independent general contractor in the construction of the improvements as part of the Fox Valley Auto Care Center? As we have pointed out, in the actual Auto Care Center project, the general contractor was a corporation related to Regent, the developer, which had a significant impact on the terms of the general construction contract. What concerns does such a relationship between the owner and general contractor raise, particular from the lender's perspective? Chapter 13 generally assumes that the owner/developer and the general contractor are unrelated. However, you should keep in mind that the parties in the construction setting may be related and that these relationships may complicate the contractual relationships created under the construction documents.

Chapter 13

CONTRACTUAL ARRANGEMENTS AMONG THE PRINCIPAL PARTIES

§ 13.01 OVERVIEW

As part of the construction team, an owner will typically engage the services of a design professional, frequently an architect, who will work with the owner to design the building and prepare all necessary construction drawings and specifications. The owner will also engage the services of a general contractor who will be responsible for the construction of the building and the supervision of the actual construction process. The terms of the owner's contractual relationship with the architect and general contractor will determine the rights and responsibilities of each of the parties as the construction process unfolds.

Although numerous standardized form-contracts exist which could be used to determine the legal relationship between the owner and architect and the owner and general contractor, the most common form of contracts for this purpose are published by the American Institute of Architects (AIA). The AIA is a nonprofit organization that seeks to

> promote the aesthetic, scientific and practical efficiency of the profession; to advance the science and art of planning and building by advancing the standards of architectural education, training, and practice; to coordinate the building industry and the profession of architecture to insure the advancement of the living standards of people through their improved environment. By-Laws of the American Institute of Architects (quoted in 1 J. Sweet & J.J. Sweet, Sweet on Construction Industry Contracts: Major AIA Documents 5 (4th ed. 1999).

It is ironic, at least for us lawyers, that it is the architects through their professional organization who have co-opted the providing of form contracts for the design and construction industry. Every day across the country, lawyers work with the legal relationships, rights and liabilities established in the forms promulgated by the AIA.

According to the Documents Committee of the AIA, the following axioms serve as the basis for the AIA standard form agreements:

- The AIA documents are intended to reflect the normal, reasonable expectations and actions of the parties to design and construction. To determine these expectations and actions, the AIA considers the customs and practices of the construction industry, aggregated on a nationwide basis.
- Risks are allocated in the documents to the party who has direct control over that portion of the process. Where no party has direct control, the risks are allocated to the party who is best able to protect against an unexpected loss. Where no party has control, the risks are the owner's —

the party who started the project and who is the ultimate beneficiary of the results.

- Risks are allocated along the lines drawn by case law. Where the law is not definite enough, the AIA attempts to provide a solution in the standard forms and model contracts.
- Most AIA documents are standard forms; modifications to them are typically shown in such a manner that all parties may see clearly the additions to, and deletions from, the standard provisions. This approach calls any reallocation of duties, responsibilities, and risks to the attention of all parties using the document.

American Institute of Architects, AIA Documents: An Overview, 2, *in* ARCHITECT'S HANDBOOK OF PROFESSIONAL PRACTICE (12th ed. 1994). *See also* AIA Document M120, Documents Drafting Principles (1995). In addition, throughout the drafting and revising process, the AIA seeks to ensure consensus among all of the parties who may be significantly affected by the documents. Consequently, the AIA documents represent considerable insight and thought on the part of construction professionals on the appropriate allocation of responsibility among the participants in the construction process.

Because AIA documents are so widely used, the delineation of rights, obligations, and risks among the parties serve as a standard against which other form contracts may be compared. Attorneys involved in the construction process, as well as the parties that they represent, need to understand the legal framework that the AIA documents create. In our view, the best way to gain understanding of the AIA form agreements is to review the core basic agreements between the owner and its contractor and the owner and its architect. Document A101-2007, the "Standard Form of Agreement Between Owner and Contractor" ("where the basis of payment is a Stipulated Sum") incorporates Document A201-2007, "General Conditions of the Contract for Construction," and together they set forth the basis for the terms for a contract between an owner and its contractor. Document B101-2007, the "Standard Form of Agreement Between Owner and Architect," along with B101-2007 Exhibit A, "Initial Information," together set forth the basis for the terms for a contract between an owner and its architect. Despite the fact that the architect and general contractor are not in privity of contract, these forms create an integrated relationship among the three parties through the owner. These AIA documents are included in the Document Book and references are to the document and the paragraph within the document.

[1] The Owner and the Construction Process

Although written prior to the most recent revision[1] of Documents A101, A201, B101 and B201 in 2007,[2] the following article describes the general relationships that these documents create and the concerns of the owner in avoiding disputes

---

[1] The AIA updates the form agreements every ten years. Hence, at the time of the building of the Fox Valley Auto Care Center, Regent would have reled on the 1987 versions, which were revised in 1997 and again in 2007. We therefore are using the 2007 versions.

[2] Prior to the 2007 revision of the AIA documents, the owner-architect agreement was designated as B141 (Part 1, the agreement, and Part 2, the scope of the architect's services) or B151 (an integrated agreement), and included all of the subjects that now are consolidated in the B101 and B101 Exhibit A.

with either the architect or general contractor. We have included editor's notes directing you to the relevant paragraphs in the AIA documents in the Document Book.

Paula Marcus.
Building a Construction Contract that Works: The Owner's Role,
44 The Arbitration Journal 3 (1989)*

As a consultant and mediator for the construction industry, the author has had many opportunities to work with owners of major construction projects. It has become clear that many owners (both public and private) believe that hiring an architect and providing the project's financing are their only responsibilities. . . .

Many disputes could be avoided if owners read their contracts carefully, understood the complete range of their responsibilities under the contracts, and checked with their attorneys about the importance and meaning of the various contract elements. Attorneys should explain the significance of the more abstract and intangible aspects of the contracts, as well as the nuts and bolts of payment schedules and the like.

Much of what is written here will be familiar to experienced construction attorneys. This article is meant to be a kind of primer, from a mediator's point of view, for less experienced owners. The primary purpose is to help owners of construction projects deal with some of the complexities of their projects, while minimizing the possibilities of dispute.

Contracts Between Owner and Architect

Schematic Design Phase

In order for the architects to design an appropriate project, they must have a thorough understanding of the owner's needs and budget requirements. Although the architect is not expected to be clairvoyant, he or she should be experienced enough to ask the right questions. A vital part of the design phase is the owner's contractual obligation to furnish a program to the architect. Owners should be aware that analyses of the owner's needs, financial feasibility studies, planning surveys, investigations of existing conditions, and a host of other activities are not part of the Basic Services. [*See* ¶ 3.1 of AIA Document B101-2007. — Eds.] If these or any of the other services listed in the section entitled "Additional Services" should be required, the owner must come to an agreement with the architect, and these services should be spelled out clearly in the section of the contract provided for that purpose. [*See* Article 4 of AIA Document B101-2007. — Eds.]

The owner's program should be presented in as much detail as possible. If, for example, the owner is describing the space allotted for special usage or by a

---

The 2007 versions, however, now include several owner-architect agreements to be used in different situations: B102 (no predefined scope of the architect's services, and must be used with B201); B103 (large and complex projects); B104 (projects of "limited scope"); and B105 (residential or small commercial projects). We have chosen to use the B101 because it likely will be the industry standard, and it will best expose you to what the AIA documents contain, although, arguably, the Fox Valley Auto Care Center is a small commercial project and the B105 might be chosen if it were being constructed today.

particular department, the information might contain the approximate square footage required, the number of people using the space, the type of lighting preferred, the number of outlets needed, special power and media requirements, telephones, computers, plans for future expansion, and the like. The owner and architect together should make a detailed checklist. The owner should recognize that there is a contractual obligation to list constraints as well as criteria.

Lack of owner preparation wastes costly architectural time. When the architect has prepared the preliminary reports, which normally include alternate design approaches and tentative budget requirements, the owner must review these options carefully before permitting the architect to commence with the drawings.

The important question of aesthetics should be thoroughly explored. One hopes that the architect is chosen for his or her aesthetic philosophy as well as for the "right" price. Every building makes an aesthetic statement of some kind, and owners should assure themselves that it is the kind of statement they wish to make.

Where there has been a mutual understanding as to the nature and scope of the project, the architect will prepare schematic design documents, which will allow the owner a first sketchy look at the project. At this time, the architect will prepare a statement of probable construction costs. Owners must understand that although this is a very rough estimate, it should be realistic enough to encourage further work on this scheme. The owner should also get a detailed explanation of how this estimate was reached. The two most terrifying words in the construction industry are "don't worry."

At this stage, if the owner has provided information in a timely fashion and has thoroughly reviewed the work of the architect, the resultant design development documents should enable the owner-architect team to fine-tune the budget to meet the project requirements.

Pre-Existing Conditions and Filing for Approvals

One particular AIA contract states that "the architect shall assist the owner in connection with the owner's responsibility for filing documents required for the approval of governmental authorities having jurisdiction over the project." [*See* ¶ 3.1.6 of AIA Document B101-2007. — Eds.]

This sounds so simple, but it's not necessarily. Does it mean that the architect is supposed to help the owner get a building permit? What are the architect's duties in this connection? [*See* ¶ 3.1.5 and ¶ 3.1.6 of AIA Document B101-2007. — Eds.]

A recent court case involves an owner who did not get prior approval to build on land that he had purchased. The owner had not persuaded the zoning board and the Inland Wetlands Commission that the proposed building would meet their requirements. When the architect requested more money for redesign, the owner was amenable, but when the architect asked for more money based on time spent at all the additional hearings, the owner quoted the above paragraph. There is now a suit pending that includes this particular dispute.

Owners' attorneys should advise their clients as to their responsibilities under the contract for prior conditions. One irate zoning board member can throw an entire project into delay and confusion, and sometimes into court.

These issues should be resolved before the owner and the architect commence discussion of particulars. The owner is responsible for all tests and surveys to determine pre-existing conditions. By contract, the architect is entitled "to rely upon the accuracy and completeness thereof." [*See* ¶ 3.1.2 of AIA Document B101-2007. — Eds.]

Design Development Phase

At this point, the architect is evolving the design development drawings and specifications based on the foregoing discussions with the owner. These drawings should be complete enough to describe the size, shape, and type of construction of the building, including all the structural, architectural, and mechanical elements of the building, although not in their final detailed form.

The owner should *now* determine whether the interior design of the building will be contracted to the architect or to a specialty firm. The placement and quantities of equipment, lighting, and furnishings will determine, to a large degree, the final mechanical plans.

Late changes can be very costly and lead to disputes with the contractors. For example, if a typical floor of an office building has 30 similar offices and, after the final drawings have been issued a decision is made to move the placement of the desks and to add a task light, 30 additional outlets would have to be added to each floor. These outlets must be circuited back to a panel that will probably have to be made larger, and the conduits that collect these panels may increase in size, and so on. The seemingly small decision to add an outlet may end up in a nightmare of extra work and money for all concerned. It cannot be overstated that the owner must try to make the program as complete as possible during the design development stage.

When the design development drawings are complete, the architect should be able to determine the ultimate cost of the project with a fair degree of accuracy. This estimate is then submitted to the owner for further study. [*See* ¶ 3.2.6 of AIA Document B101-2007. — Eds.]

This is one of the most critical points in the life of a project. The owner must now determine whether or not there is going to be a full commitment to the project. This is the last chance to make significant and major changes at no cost to the owner, provided, of course, that there has been no major change in the scope of the work. In order to prevent major disputes with the architect over the proposed budget and the general shape, size, function, and appearance of the projected building, owners must check the design development drawings thoroughly.

Architects are required to perform both basic and additional services in an expeditious manner. The owner is entitled to ask the architect to provide a schedule for the performance of these services. [The 2007 documents require the architect to prepare a schedule at the outset; *see* ¶ 3.2.2 of AIA Document B101-2007. — Eds.] This schedule provides a guideline as to time frames and gives the owner insight into when the various bid packages will be complete. The owner should review this schedule with the architect on a regular basis. This is an often overlooked facet of the owner's responsibilities.

Budgetary Caution

It should be noted here that if a fixed limit of construction costs has been agreed to in writing by the owner and architect, and the lowest bid exceeds that limit, the architect is required to modify the specifications and drawings as necessary to bring the project within the limit. [*See* ¶ 6.6.4 and ¶ 6.7 of AIA Document B101-2007. — Eds.] Owners should know that these revisions will constitute added architectural work unless a fixed limit on construction costs appears in the original contract.

Construction Documents Phase

Based on all of the foregoing, the architect prepares the detailed final construction documents — that is, the plans and specifications which are submitted to the owner for approval.

Even the most inexperienced owner must now realize that there are thousands of small elements which make up any project. It is possible for the most careful architect to forget to record a change or to misplace an added element. Owners should not give pro forma approval to the plans and specifications. The owners' in-house staff and the interior design staff should study the final construction documents with great care in order to ensure that the architectural and mechanical plans are coordinated and agree as to quantities and placement of required services. Specifications should be checked to determine that the owner is getting the necessary type and quality of equipment and that all the information required by the architect has been forwarded.

At this point, the architect is expected to review the estimated budget for the last time before soliciting bids. Any adjustments due to changes or current market conditions should be made here. This is the last chance for a review of the budget by the owner.

Many industry professionals may be familiar with the plaintive cry of owners involved in complex disputes: "But I hired the architect as my expert; he's supposed to do everything." Even though the architect is trusted to perform what is called for by the contract, a great deal of that depends on the performance of the owner.

Bid Document Development

The architect's contract with the owner requires the architect to assist the owner in the preparation of the bid documents. [*See* ¶ 3.5.2.2 of AIA Document B101-2007. — Eds.] Because architects are most familiar with the standard AIA agreements, they will probably suggest their use in drawing up the contracts between the owner and the contractors.[2]

This procedure may or may not be in the owner's best interest. It cannot be recommended strongly enough that the owner seek an attorney with experience in the construction field to prepare the contracts.

---

[2] AIA Document B141, Owner-Architect Agreement, 14th ed. (1987). [As already stated, the American Institute of Architects revised its standard agreements in 1997 and 2007. References to 2007 versions of the revised documents are provided throughout the article. — Eds.]

AIA contracts are prepared by an association of architects for general usage on construction projects. They do not take into account any peculiarities or special requirements of a project. In fact, they may not offer the owner the protection needed because of the nature of the project.

Obviously, the architect will be of great assistance in the preparation of bidding information, bidding forms, addenda, and so forth; however, all documents should be checked by the owner and the owner's attorney before the contracts are sent out for bids.

Specific considerations will be discussed in the sections devoted to the contract between the owner and the contractors.

Construction Phase Administration

Paragraph 2.6.4 of the AIA documents states in part:

> The Architect shall be a representative of and shall advise and consult with the Owner (1) during construction until final payment to the Contractor is due, and (2) as an Additional Service at the Owner's direction from time to time during the correction period described in the Contract for Construction.

This contract provision must carry a lot of unseen weight because inexperienced owners seem to place so much reliance on it. The architect may be a "representative" of the owner, but his or her responsibilities are strictly limited by this contract. The following discussion shows where standard practices of the construction industry are with respect to the architect's responsibilities. [Ed. note: ¶ 2.6.1.3 of the AIA Document B141-1997 still stated that the architect is the "representative" of the owner, but ¶ 3.6.1.2 of AIA Document B101-2007 states: "The Architect shall advise and consult with the Owner during the Construction Phase Services." Nonetheless, Marcus' discussion below still is relevant.]

Inspection

This is the word most frequently cited but least understood. Under the AIA contract, the architect is not responsible for inspection unless the owner specifically contracts for it as an extra service. All the architect is supposed to do is visit the site from time to time to determine "in general" that the finished work is in accordance with the contract documents. [*See* ¶ 3.6.2.1 of AIA Document B101-2007. — Eds.] The fuzzy language is deliberate. A "visit" is not an inspection and "in general" does not imply any degree of compliance. The owner may hire his or her own people or the architect's people to do the inspection of the work. The owner may make suitable arrangements as long as the architect and the contractors understand what these arrangements are. Any understanding should be discussed between the owner and the architect before the contractors come on board. The wise owner will consult with an attorney as well.

If the architect sees substandard work not in accordance with the contract documents, he or she reserves the right to reject the work. [*See* ¶ 3.6.2.2 of AIA Document B101-2007. — Eds.] This does not mean that the architect has an obligation to go searching endlessly for substandard work beyond the normal job site visits.

The architect is supposed to certify the work of the contractor for payment. Based on regular visits, the architect should determine whether the work has progressed to the extent claimed in the contractor's requisition and if it conforms to the contract documents. Needless to say, since inspection is not part of the architect's contract, there are disclaimers.

Inspection is the one activity more than any other where owners have been found to be "penny wise and pound foolish." The author has met owners who have hired a "clerk of the works" as an on-site job presence and then decide later that the clerk can do the work of project inspection as well. This doesn't usually work. The best protection an owner can buy is qualified inspection. A common cause for dispute is when the owner has no real understanding of the contract and has made no provision for inspection, but relies for protection instead upon the architect's visits and/or upon the grace of an unseen higher power.

Some owners are perfectly aware that inspection is an additional service under an AIA contract, but they prefer to take their chances rather than incur the additional expense. Their attorneys should advise them of just how expensive that can get.

The owner must provide expert project inspection and not allow it to become the owner's responsibility by default.

Communications

The following discussion assumes that there is no construction manager in the communications chain. If there is, naturally all communications with contractors should go through the office of the construction manager.

The architect should send the owner copies of all communications and instructions to and from the contractors. It should be unnecessary to state that the owner should have no communication with the contractors that does not go through the architect's office ? unfortunately it is not unnecessary. Some owners do not understand that they have an obligation to see to it that any instructions or communications with the contractors are in writing (or at least backed up by a written copy) and go through the architect's office to the contractor. Any other method of communication leads to confusion and the possible loss of time and money.

Change Orders

Change orders are another topic requiring a discussion of timely action by the owner. Under the General Conditions of the Contract for Construction, which is assumed to be part of the architect's contract,[3] there are three methods of making adjustments to the contract sum. These methods will be discussed in detail under the general heading of "Contract for Construction." At this time, it must be stressed that the owner has an obligation to get information to the architect, review changes in the drawings, evaluate estimates, and make decisions, all as quickly as possible. To delay would cause changes to be made out of sequence; the work of the change order may become concealed by other work in progress; and, as discussed earlier

---

[3] *Id.* at para. 2.6.2. [*See* ¶ 3.6.1.1 of AIA Document B101-2007, which refers to AIA Document A201-2007. — Eds.]

in this article, there are other consequences in making late changes during the design development phase.

Completion Dates

The architect determines the dates of substantial and final completion by inspecting the work solely for this purpose. The owner should remind the architect to collect all warranties and related documents from the contractor on behalf of the owner. If the architect is satisfied that everything is in hand and the work is complete, a final Certificate for Payment is issued. This ends the architect's responsibilities toward the owner. If further work needs to be done, the owner should make agreements to that effect.

Interpretations and Decisions

Owners should be aware that the standard AIA owner-architect agreement reads as follows:

> Article 2 ? Scope of Architect's Basic Services
>
> 2.6.15. The Architect shall interpret and decide matters concerning performance of the Owner and Contractor under the requirements of the contract documents on written request of either the Owner or Contractor. The Architect's response to such requests shall be made with reasonable promptness and within any time limits agreed upon. [*See* ¶ 3.6.2.3 of AIA Document B101-2007. — Eds.]

Article 2.6.16 states, in part:

> . . . When making such interpretations and initial decisions, the Architect shall endeavor to secure faithful performance by both Owner and Contractor, shall not show partiality to either, and shall not be liable for results of interpretations or decisions so rendered in good faith. [*See* ¶ 3.6.2.4 of AIA Document B101-2007. — Eds.]

In addition, paragraph 4.3.2 of the General Conditions of the Contract for Construction at first refers claims *against* the architect for errors or omissions to the architect for decision. [Ed. note: The 2007 versions of the AIA documents create the title of "Initial Decision Maker." ¶ 6.1 of AIA Document A101-2007, "Standard Form of Agreement Between Owner and Contractor where the basis of payment is a Stipulated Sum," now provides space for the owner and contractor to designate another party as the "Initial Decision Maker," but all of the documents designate the architect as the initial decision maker if the owner and contractor do not designate a different party. Therefore, Marcus' statement is correct if the owner and contractor do not designate as "Initial Decision Maker" someone other than the architect, and the default still is the architect.]

Owners should remember that the AIA contracts were written by architects for architects. The owner has no part in the decision making process in this contract, and the only recourse from an architect's decision is arbitration. On the other hand, the contract states that the architect "shall not be liable for results of interpretations or decisions. . . ." [*See* ¶ 3.6.2.4 of AIA Document B101-2007. — Eds.] Owners should be certain that they want to give decisionmaking power to someone who seems not to be fully accountable. [¶ 6.1 of AIA Document A101-2007 provides space for the owner and contractor to do so. — Eds.] Many owners prefer to let the architect make all the decisions.

The architect, however, is not immune from error, and even the least experienced owner is in business and able to make business decisions. You don't have to be an expert in construction to know that you want to have the final word on how to spend your own money.

The author suggests that the owner review with counsel all claims and disputes procedures in the contracts in order to ensure that the final contracts reflect the owner's wishes.

Termination

An owner should terminate the services of an architect only after much thought and after consulting an attorney. If the termination still seems necessary, the attorney should prepare the written notice and see to it that the owner does everything by the book. A common issue in mediation and arbitration is whether there has been a proper termination. When dealing with the contractor, an improper or ill-conceived termination may become even more costly. The use of a "termination for convenience" clause or a termination without cause is discussed later.

Miscellaneous Provisions

The owner should know that if an out-of-state architect is hired, the laws of the architect's principal place of business apply. In the event a dispute arises, the owner may need an out-of-state attorney. [¶ 10.1 of AIA Document B101-2007 makes controlling the law of the location of the Project, but Marcus' comment is appropriate if a dispute arises based on an agreement between the owner and the architect made before they sign the AIA form. — Eds.]

The owner is required to test for, discover, and remove any hazardous substances such as asbestos at the owner's expense.

Payments to the Architect

Payment for an architect's services should be based on direct personnel expenses times a multiplier plus reimbursable expenses within a contract based on a "not to exceed" price. To expect the architect to keep costs down when the fee is based on a percentage of costs may be naive. This applies equally to change orders.

Architects work within much stricter limitations and have lower profit margins than is generally supposed. They are pleased to have a contract in which they are paid for the actual number of hours they work. The owner's attorney may want to expand on paragraph 10.6.1, which deals with the architect's accounting records. [*See* ¶ 11.10.4 of AIA Document B101-2007. — Eds.]

Mediation

Mediation is a good alternative means of dispute resolution between owner and architect, as well as between owner and contractor. One simply includes the following paragraph in the contract documents:

> If a dispute arises out of or relates to this contract, or the breach thereof, and if said dispute cannot be settled through direct discussions, the parties agree to first endeavor to settle the dispute in an amicable manner by mediation under the Construction Industry Mediation Rules of the American Arbitration Association, before having recourse to arbitration or a judicial forum.[4]

While an arbitration proceeding is being set up, nonbinding mediation can be held at very little expense and in short order. If it works, a lot of money is saved. If it doesn't, parties will have gained a good idea of the merits and weaknesses of their cases. . . . [Mediation has been made a part of Documents A201-1997 and B141-1997. *See* ¶ 15.3.1 of AIA Document A201-2007 and ¶ 8.2.1 of AIA Document B101-2007. — Eds.]

Contracts Between Owner and Contractors[5]

Contract Documents

It often happens that by negotiation the owner and contractor reach certain agreements before the contract is signed. These agreements should be spelled out in detail and incorporated into the contract. Unfortunately, these agreements become very large disagreements when the "honeymoon" period of the job is over.

Mediators often hear about precontractual arrangements between the owner and the contractor. When mediators ask to see the written agreements, they are told that at the time of these initial discussions there was a perfect meeting of the minds between "Joe" and "Mike," who are no longer available to testify. Contracts should be checked to ensure that any prior arrangements are incorporated. Owners must remember to tell their architects and attorneys about any arrangements outside the scope of the contract. Better still, owners should not conclude any agreements with the contractors outside of the normal contract procedure.

For multiple contract projects, it is very important that the owner check with the architect to make sure that all trades bid the same revisions of the plans and specifications. If changes have been made between the time of letting one contract and another, the precedent contractor should be made aware of the changes.

If there have been significant or numerous changes during the life of the job, the architect should be instructed to prepare updated drawings that incorporate all the changes to date, clearly marked. If this creates additional work for the architect, the owner should be advised that this is money well spent. Drawings are generally cheaper than legal briefs.

The owner should be sure to keep all versions of all contract documents and not rely on third parties to do this. Copies of the bid set of plans and specifications should be wrapped and stored as if they were the Dead Sea Scrolls. It sometimes happens that a dispute is resolved five or more years after the job is finished. When

---

[4] Construction Industry Mediation Rules (As Amended and in Effect October 1, 1987), at 4. New York-American Arbitration Association, 1988.

[5] AIA Document A201, General Conditions of the Contract for Construction, 14th ed. (1987). [*See* AIA Document A201-2007. — Eds.]

there is no baseline information as to what the owner bought, it is very difficult to build a case.

If there are addenda to the bids, the owner may wish to inspect them in order to make sure that they are in the form that will bring the desired results. If the addenda are to be incorporated into the plans and specifications, it should be done as quickly as possible.

It is important to note that in the AIA documents, the plans and specifications are complementary and no part takes precedence over another. Attorneys may wish to change this. Because any discrepancy will cost the owner money, there may as well be a guideline for change. The plans may be the better criterion because they are singular to one job. Some specifications are used and reused from job to job.

Modifications are mechanisms for making additions to the contracts after the job has been let and before the work has started. The simplest and safest method is the change order, for which there is a well described procedure in the contract. Caution is advised with any other method.

Information and Services Required of the Owner

The owner is obligated to provide "reasonable evidence" before and during the life of the contract that there is sufficient financing for the project. The contractor and the architect alike are entitled to these assurances. The contractor is not required "to execute the agreement or commence the work" without such "reasonable evidence" prior to execution of the contract.[6]

The contract is explicit about the paperwork required of the owner, such as surveys, legal descriptions, utility locations, approvals, easements, assessments, and the like. It also asks for reasonable promptness to prevent delay in the orderly progress of the work. It is obvious that delays in providing this information will cost the owner money.

Owner's Right to Stop the Work

If the architect or the owner finds that there is work being done that is not in accordance with the contract documents and the contractor fails to correct the deficient work, the owner or the owner's agent may stop the work or any part of the work by an order in writing. If the contractor fails *persistently* to perform the work in accordance with the contract documents, the same rule applies.

This is not a step to be taken lightly, however. Any stoppage is bound to be costly and cause acrimonious debate. A stoppage may lead to a dispute resolvable only by legal means. Once all other avenues have been explored and abandoned, or if an immediate question of safety is at stake, the owner should get the blessings of the architect in writing and proceed with care and dispatch. The next step is to order the contractor to stop the work with a clear written order spelling out all the reasons for the order. Careful documentation of such a controversial step goes a long way toward reducing the owner's exposure.

Many large private owners write termination clauses that do not require the owner to show cause. Owners should also ask their attorneys about a "termination

---

[6] *Id.* at para. 2.2.1. [*See* ¶ 2.2.1 of AIA Document A201-2007. — Eds.]

for convenience" clause. The federal government and other governing bodies and owners often have such a clause in their contracts. It permits them to stop work prior to the completion of the project. If the clause is written properly, it may convert an otherwise wrongful termination into a termination for convenience.

The owner holds the purse strings. If a fair method of payment is included in the contract, there should be no reason why the owner cannot terminate the work without having to show cause. This clause, however, should be crafted with extreme care. [An owner's termination for convenience clause was added in the 1997 version of the AIA documents. *See* ¶ 14.4 of AIA Document A201-2007. — Eds.]

Owner's Right to Carry Out the Work

If the contractor defaults or neglects to carry out the work, the owner should send a written notice to the contractor asking the contractor "to commence and continue correction of such default or neglect with diligence and promptness. . . ."[7] After seven days, a second notice can be sent. If the contractor does not correct the deficiencies within the second seven-day period, the owner may perform the necessary work. There is a specified procedure that requires the owner to write a deduct change order, which spells out what happens if the contractor is not owed enough money to cover the work and other possible expenses. Once again, it is imperative that the owner follow all the procedures in the contract documents with the utmost care. We strongly advise the owner to seek the advice of counsel before stopping the work, doing the work of the contractor, or terminating a contractor.

Allowances

If a contract provides payment for allowances for material only, the labor, overhead, profit, and shipping and handling costs are intended to be included in the base contract price.

The owner has an obligation to select the materials under the allowance in a timely fashion. Since labor and other costs are included in the base bid, the owner should be careful not to select materials substantially different from what was anticipated. The quantities should stay in the same ballpark, and the labor for installation should not change radically.

For example, if there is an allowance for vinyl floor tile and the owner decides that marble floor tile is required, then, obviously, the labor and other costs change radically. There is also a substantial difference in material cost. The change in material cost is provided for in the contract by change order. Of course, the increase in labor costs can also be provided for by change order, but both parties would have to agree. This might be a source of friction. It makes more sense to exercise care in the beginning when setting out allowances.

Claims and Disputes

As noted in the previous section dealing with the architect's contract, all decisionmaking power with regard to claims and disputes rests, at first, with the architect and, then, with the panel of arbitrators. The owner, by signing this

[7] *Id.* at para. 2.4.1. [*See* ¶ 2.4 of AIA Document A201-2007. — Eds.]

contract, has checked out of the decisionmaking chain. If the architect fails to make a decision within the stipulated number of days, the dispute goes to arbitration and not to the owner. [Ed. note: The 2007 versions of the AIA documents change this substantially. The 1997 versions of the AIA documents had inserted mediation between the initial decision by the architect and arbitration. Now, the parties may designate an independent Initial Decision Maker (with the architect being the default (¶ 6.1 of AIA Document A101-2007). The decision by the architect or the Initial Decision is final unless 1) the who does not like the decision demands mediation (¶ 15.2.6 of AIA Document A201-2007) or 2) the party who likes the decision gives notice to the other that mediation must be invoked or the decision is final (¶ 15.2.6.1 of AIA Document A201-2007). Finally, binding arbitration no longer is mandated: there is a "check the box" selecting among arbitration, litigation, or other, and the default is litigation (¶ 6.2 of AIA Document A101-2007).]

The author believes that the owner should have the right to final determination before arbitration. It is the owner's money. Suppose the architect and the contractor have irreconcilable differences and cannot settle their disputes. Should the owner not have an opportunity to settle before being forced into arbitration? In these days of rising legal costs, it may be in the owner's best interest to "bite the bullet" and settle the claim as quickly and inexpensively as possible.

In the author's opinion, the owner is better served by having all disputes (with the possible exception of aesthetic disputes) referred back to the owner for a final decision. The architect's interests are not necessarily identical to the owner's. [Ed. note: Marcus' comments still are applicable. The 2007 AIA documents still allow a dissatisfied architect or contractor to drive the owner to mediation and then some binding form of dispute resolution. If the owner wants control, the AIA documents will have to be modified.]

It should be noted here that if the owner decides to take up this responsibility, decisions on claims and disputes should be made as quickly as possible. Disputes cause delays, and delays mean loss of money all around. The architect should be encouraged to render a swift opinion, followed by an equally swift decision from the owner. The time allowed in the contract for the architect to render an opinion is 45 days. That length of time could have disastrous consequences for an ongoing project and should be considered an absolute maximum. [Ed. note: The Initial Decision Maker has 10 days to defer, to decide, or to request more information (¶ 15.2.2 of AIA Document A201-2007). If the Initial Decision Maker requests more information, the parties have 10 days to comply, but then there is no time limit for when the Initial Decision Maker must make a decision (¶ 15.2.4 of AIA Document A201-2007). Presumably, any delay can be resolved by a demand for mediation (¶ 15.2.6 of AIA Document A201-2007).]

The contractor is obligated to continue work on the project pending final resolution of the claim, including any arbitration. The submission of a claim by the contractor, no matter how outrageous, is no reason to stop payment. In this, as in all things relating to the contract, owners should go by the book. Anger will not get the job done.

Permits, Fees, and Notices

The contract should clarify whether the contractor or owner is to pay for the building permit and other permit fees (often, the owner gets the building permit).

These days, this may represent a substantial amount of money. Owners should be aware of this provision and have adjustments to the contract made according to their wishes. Current AIA contracts ask the contractor to pay for the permit. [3.7.1 of AIA Document A201-2007). — Eds.]

Communications Facilitating Contract Administration

The owner should be aware that the architect will receive many requests for interpretation and decisions regarding performance from both the owner and the contractor. There is a specified time limit built into the contract. If the answers are not forthcoming in the time agreed upon or in the maximum time allowed, the contractor may find that he or she has been delayed. These delays may later be inflated to an unmanageable level when the contractor presents a claim.

Since we have already recommended that all communications between the contractors and the architect be copied to the owner, it should be simple for the owner to see to it that there is a system of recording all unanswered questions and other information required by the architect, the owner, or the contractor. Care of the information-tracking log could be the responsibility of the construction manager, if there is one on the project. The owner should check it on a regular basis.

The schedule of a project can also be affected by delays on estimates from the contractor for contemplated changes. The contractor may sometimes have to wait for the owner to decide on a piece of equipment. Prompt decisionmaking by the architect, the contractor, and the owner is critical to the timing and economy of any project. Owners should monitor decisionmaking by others. Turnaround times stated in the contract should be built into whatever system of data monitoring the owner chooses.

Claims for Additional Costs

"What does the contract say?" and "What should the contractor have reasonably been expected to bid?": In almost every case, arbitrators and mediators have to ask themselves these two simple questions. An experienced construction attorney knows how to answer the first question in terms of the actual wording and the standard usages of the trade. The second question is more difficult.

Owners should never be too clever and attempt to cover every contingency in the contract. By asking the contractor to gamble, the owner is setting up a pre-existing cause for dispute. It is better to recognize that a particular project may have unknown conditions and then set up a fair and provable method of payment. The owner should remember that architecture and construction estimating are not exact sciences. The architect has thousands of items to coordinate and fit into the giant puzzle of plans and specs. The contractor estimates by counting and measuring what is shown on the plans and specs, and by praying that all of these items have been counted and measured correctly.

Owners seem to have difficulty with the following concept. If an item is omitted from the plans by the architect or engineer ? and the contractor therefore does not include it ? the bid price is deficient by the price of that item. The owner must pay for it sooner or later, since the owner is the one who will benefit from its use.

Although there is a time limit on claims set forth in the contract, many claims have been successful even when the time limits have not been observed. This is particularly true of claims based on cumulative effects.

Limitation on Consolidation or Joinder[8]

The paragraph of the contract that deals with consolidation can have far-reaching effects in the case of disputes ending in arbitration. For example, the owner may find defective work but may not know if the contractor or the architect is responsible. It is not possible to consolidate both parties in a single arbitration without the architect's permission. The owner may then have to file a separate demand for arbitration for each of the parties. This may make an equitable determination very difficult. A good hard look at this paragraph is in order. [Ed. note: ¶ 15.4.4 of AIA Document A201-2007 now allows for consolidation or joinder.]

Once again, mediation should be considered as an alternative mechanism for dispute resolution. One of the advantages of mediation is that, because of its voluntary nature, one is often able to convince the architect to consolidate with the owner and contractor. The savings in time and money can be enormous. [Ed. note: ¶ 15.3 of AIA Document A201-2007 requires mediation.]

Construction by Owner or by Separate Contractors

The owner may reserve the right to perform work with the owner's own forces or to award separate contracts.

A few years ago, Marcus Associates mediated a large dispute where the parties were five-million dollars apart from a settlement. One of the major causes of the dispute was the fact that the owners let a number of separate contracts without realizing that this action made them their own general contractor. As general contractor, the owners were responsible for, among other things, the coordination of the work of the various trades. Because they were unaware of their responsibilities as general contractor, the scheduling of the trades went awry.

While this is an extreme case, even small, separate contracts can create problems. The author advises against these procedures unless there are very special circumstances or the owner anticipates hiring a construction manager.

Changes in the Work[9]

There is a significant change in this section of the contract, and that is the addition of the construction change directive. [¶ 7.3 of AIA Document A201-2007. — Eds.] It can help the job run more smoothly, but it must be carefully monitored. This method of change is in addition to the more usual change order, which requires a written agreement by the architect, the owner, and the contractor.

The construction change directive is an excellent and flexible instrument that permits the architect and owner (who both sign it) to direct a change in the work that is within the general scope of the contract, but for which there is no agreement

---

[8] *Id.* at para. 4.5.5. [*See* ¶ 15.4.4 of AIA Document A201-2007. — Eds.]

[9] *Id.* at art. 7. [*See* Art. 7 of AIA Document A201-2007. — Eds.]

on price. The contractor is required to proceed with the work of the change subject to a later settlement on the value of the work, either in contract sum or contract time, or both. This can really help to move the job along.

There are a number of methods for determining the value of these changes. The owner should pay close attention to the monitoring. As always, it is preferable to resolve the question of price as quickly as possible.

Time[10]

The owner should be aware that the contract completion time may be a two-edged sword. Although the owner may use it to recover damages due to delays caused by the contractor, similarly the contractor may use it to recover the costs of delays caused by the owner or owner's agents. The owner has a responsibility to encourage the swift flow of responses to inquiries for information ? for example, timely responses to shop drawings.

Certification for Payment[11]

Obviously, payment procedures should be followed scrupulously. The inexperienced owner may not know that under many contracts, the architect has the sole authority to decide whether the work of the contractor has progressed to the degree indicated on the contractor's requisition. If the owner withholds payment after the architect has certified that the requisition is correct, the contractor, after the required notice in writing, may stop the work.

In any case, the owner should insist that requests for payment be sufficiently detailed so that they may be thoroughly checked. The more detail required, the harder it is to "front end load." It is of prime importance that the contractor be paid precisely for the work actually performed-no more and no less. Tipping the balance in either direction is an invitation to dispute.

Substantial Completion

There are a number of activities to be performed by all concerned before a project can be said to be complete. One of the areas in which an owner may reduce the risk of future disputes is "punch lists." The contractor asks for an inspection by the architect when the work is considered to be "substantially complete." The architect inspects the work and draws up a second list of items which remain undone or incomplete. When this work has been inspected, the architect may issue the Certificate of Substantial Completion, which establishes the responsibilities "of the Owner and Contractor for security, maintenance, heat, utilities, damage to the work and insurance, and shall fix the time within which the Contractor shall finish all items on the list accompanying the certificate."[12]

At this stage, the owner must realize that the last punch list has been seen. The owner has probably occupied all or part of the building, and this further complicates the fixing of responsibilities. To request that the contractor return to an area again and again, particularly after the area has been occupied, is asking for a dispute. The

10 *Id.* at art. 8. [*See* Art. 8 of AIA Document A201-2007. — Eds.]

11 *Id.* at para. 9.4.2. [*See* ¶ 9.4.2 of AIA Document A201-2007. — Eds.]

12 *Id.* at para. 9.8.2. [*See* ¶ 9.8.4 of AIA Document A201-2007. — Eds.]

owner is not unprotected, however, because the warranties required by the contract are now in force.

Conclusion

The preceding discussion attempted to address all aspects of the construction project owner's responsibilities that do not involve payments.

With regard to the contract with the architect, the owner and the owner's attorney should decide whether or not the standard AIA contract should be modified to meet the particular needs of the project. The owner should prepare the program and outline the needs of the project carefully and in a timely fashion. All owner reviews and approvals should be completed with dispatch, and all changes to the program should be complete prior to the start of working drawings.

The owner should ask for and receive a schedule from the architect. This schedule should be monitored and coordinated with the owner's work. The architect then asks the owner for approval of the final plans and specs. This review should be more than perfunctory.

When drawing up the architectural and construction contracts, the owner's attorney should consider the consequences of using the standard AIA contracts without considerable amendment. Of particular concern are the paragraphs on "Inspection," "Limitations on Consolidation or Joinder," and "Termination."

The owner should read these contracts carefully. All the action required of the owner should be abstracted from them, and a schedule should be made. This schedule should be followed by the owner, just as the owner expects the architect and contractors to follow their own schedules.

The work of the construction project should be approached in the same professional way that the owner's own work is approached. In this, as in all things, ignorance has a high price.

[2] Note

The traditional major resource for learning about the construction process is J. Sweet, Legal Aspects of Architecture, Engineering and the Construction Process (6th ed. 2000). Professor Sweet provides an exhaustive review of all the major legal problems and issues that arise in construction projects, from basic contract interpretation to design and construction defects, to the resolution of construction disputes. Professor Sweet is the co-author of a two volume treatise on the interpretation of the AIA construction documents as well. J. Sweet & J.J. Sweet, Sweet on Construction Industry Contracts: Major AIA Documents (4th ed. 1999).

[3] Exercise

In thinking about the various parties involved in the construction process from a legal perspective, it is often helpful to graphically depict each party and indicate through the use of arrows drawn between the various parties the existence of contractual relationships. Using such a diagram, depict the contractual relationships that exist among the parties in the construction process, including the owner/developer, architect, general contractor, subcontractors, and the construction lender. Return to this diagram as you consider the legal relationships that exist under the construction agreements among the parties, as described in the following sections.

§ 13.02 OWNER/ARCHITECT AGREEMENT

[1] Overview

Under the traditional Design-Award-Build (D-A-B) system, the architect occupies a central role throughout the design and construction process. The actual role of the architect in any design or construction project will depend on the terms of the agreement reached between the owner and the architect. Although that agreement may be relatively straightforward when a simple construction project is involved, the agreement is often more complicated in the typical commercial context when the exact scope of the architect's responsibilities must be clearly articulated and the legal relationship between the owner, the architect, and the general contractor more fully defined. For purposes of the discussion that follows, the role of the architect will be described based on the AIA documents.

The "Standard Form of Agreement Between Owner and Architect,"AIA Document B101-2007, defines in detail the legal relationship between the owner and architect and the services that the architect will perform. The Standard Form of Agreement Between Owner and Architect, AIA Document B101-2007 is intended to be used in conjunction with AIA Document A201-2007, General Conditions of the Contract for Construction, which it incorporates by reference when the architect's services involve construction contract administration. *See* ¶ 2.6.1.1 of AIA Document B101-2007.

As described in the article by Paula Marcus, the services typically performed by the architect are grouped under the following five main phases of the design and construction process: the schematic design phase (AIA Document B101-2007 ¶ 3.2), the design development phase (AIA Document B101-2007 ¶ 3.3), the construction documents phase (AIA Document B101-2007 ¶ 3.4), the bidding or negotiation phase (AIA Document B101-2007 ¶ 3.5), and the construction phase (AIA Document B101-2007 ¶ 3.6). Each of these phases will be discussed in greater detail.

The owner has obligations in assisting the architect in creating the design of the project. Article 5 of AIA Document B101-2007 details the supporting services that the owner must perform in order to enable the architect to perform the design function. These supporting services include the provision of the owner's program, which will contain the owner's design objectives, schedule, constraints, and site requirements (AIA Document B101-2007 ¶ 5.1). The owner is also responsible for providing a survey and all legal information describing the site, including the location of rights-of-way, easements, and utility services, as well as physical limitations affecting the site such as zoning and deed restrictions (AIA Document B101-2007 ¶ 5.4). The owner is also responsible for furnishing geotechnical engineering services to determine soil and subsoil conditions (AIA Document B101-2007 ¶ 5.5). Based on this owner's program and site information, the architect provides a preliminary evaluation of the proposed project (AIA Document B101-2007 ¶ 3.2.2).

The architect performs the design services for the project in three phases. In the schematic design phase, the architect prepares a conceptual design for the project based on the owner's program. The conceptual design will be reflected in preliminary building plans, sections, and elevations and may include study models and perspective sketches (AIA Document B101-2007 ¶ 3.2.5). Following the owner's approval of the schematic design documents, the architect will move to the design development phase and prepare design development documents that reflect the refinement of the design including plans, sections, elevations, and construction details. At this stage, the quality of the principal materials and systems will be established (AIA Document B101-2007 ¶ 3.3.1). Based on the owner's approval of the design development documents, the architect will move to the construction documents phase and prepare construction documents in sufficient detail to allow a general contractor to construct the project (AIA Document B101-2007 ¶ 3.4.1). During the construction documents phase, the architect will also assist the owner to prepare the documents necessary for the bidding of the project (AIA Document B101-2007 ¶ 3.4.3).

The architect will submit to the owner an estimate of the construction cost of the project (AIA Document B101-2007 ¶ 3.2.5), and then throughout the design process, the architect will update the estimate of the construction cost of the project (*see* AIA Document B101-2007 ¶ 3.3.2 and ¶ 3.4.4). The estimate of the construction cost will typically include contingencies or additional budgeted amounts to cover unanticipated increases in design or construction costs (AIA Document B101-2007 ¶ 6.3). If, during the design phases of the project, any changes in the project or in market conditions result in the estimated construction cost exceeding the owner's budget, the architect will make recommendations to the owner to adjust the size, quality of materials, or budget of the project to bring the estimated construction cost within the owner's budget. The owner and architect may also decide to adjust the scope of the project through the use of design alternates for which separate bids will be requested from contractors in order to determine, following the bidding of the project, whether the owner's budget is sufficient to allow the design alternates to be constructed.

Following the owner's approval of the construction documents, the architect assists the owner in creating a list of prospective bidders for the project and in providing the bidders with the construction documents and bidding information (AIA Document B101-2007 ¶ 3.5.2). The architect may also participate in a pre-bid conference with the prospective bidders in order to answer questions concerning the project and otherwise assist the bidders by clarifying or interpreting the construction documents. Ideally, the bidding process will result in one or more bids that fall within the owner's budget for the construction of the project. The architect then assists the owner in the preparation and awarding of the construction contract.

If the bidding process does not result in the receipt of a bid within the owner's budget, questions have arisen regarding the architect's liability to the owner when the lowest bid received exceeds the architect's estimated cost of construction. As the decision in *Malo v. Gilman*, which follows, demonstrates, the architect may forfeit his fee if the estimated cost of construction was guaranteed by the architect or the estimated cost of construction is unreasonable. *See also Williams Engineering, Inc. v. Goodyear, Inc.*, 496 So. 2d 1012 (La. 1986) (imposing liability against the design engineer where the actual costs of construction exceeded the costs guaranteed by the engineer). Under AIA Document B101-2007, however, this result should be avoided. AIA Document B101-2007 ¶ 6.2 specifically provides that the architect's estimated cost of construction represents the "Architect's judgment as a design professional" and that the "Architect cannot and does not warrant or represent that bids or negotiated prices will not vary from the Owner's budget for the Cost of the Work or from any estimate of the Cost of Work or evaluation prepared or agreed to by the Architect." In addition, AIA Document B101-2007 ¶ 6.6 provides that if the lowest bid exceeds the architect's estimated cost of construction, the owner may (1) increase the budget for the project, (2) authorize rebidding or negotiation within a reasonable time, (3) terminate the agreement with the architect, in which case the architect will still be entitled to be compensated, or (4) revise the project's scope or the quality of the materials to reduce the estimated cost of construction; in the last option the architect will modify the construction documents without additional compensation (AIA Document B101-2007 ¶ 6.7).

Although the D-A-B system suggests that the architect's responsibilities have been completed when the construction process begins, the architect typically remains a major actor along with the owner and general contractor during the actual construction process. For example, the architect may provide the general contractor with additional information about the construction documents and prepare supplemental drawings or specifications (AIA Document B101-2007 ¶ 3.6.4.4). More importantly, however, the architect may serve as a referee in resolving disputes or claims between the owner and general contractor under the construction agreements. AIA Document B101-2007 ¶ 3.6.2.4 states that "[w]hen making such interpretations and initial decisions, the Architect shall endeavor to secure faithful performance by both Owner and Contractor, shall not show partiality to either, and shall not be liable for the results of interpretations or decision so rendered in good faith."

During the construction process, the architect also serves a number of additional important functions. First, the architect has a responsibility to evaluate the progress and quality of the construction work performed to ensure that it is being completed in accordance with the construction documents (AIA Document B101-2007 ¶ 3.6.2.1). Interestingly, the prior versions of the AIA documents stated that this function was carried out by the architect "as the representative of the Owner" (AIA Document B141-1997 ¶ 2.6.2.1). Despite the obligation to evaluate the construction work, the terms of AIA Document B101-2007 attempt to absolve the architect from liability for failing to uncover defective workmanship: "the Architect shall not be required to make exhaustive or continuous on-site inspections to check the quality or quantity of the Work." AIA Document B101-2007 ¶ 3.6.2.1). In addition, AIA Document B101-2007 ¶ 3.6.1.2 states:

> The Architect shall not have control over, charge of, or responsibility for the construction means, methods, techniques, sequences or procedures, or for safety precautions and programs in connection with the Work, nor shall the Architect be responsible for the Contractor's failure to perform the Work in accordance with the requirements of the contract Documents. The Architect shall be responsible for the Architect's negligent acts or omissions, but shall not have control over or charge of, and shall not be responsible for, acts or omissions of the Contractor or of any other persons or entities performing portions of the Work. ¶ 2.6.2.2.

Despite these contractual limitations between the owner and architect with respect to the architect's liability for defective construction work and for defective construction techniques or procedures, the architect's involvement in the construction process itself exposes the architect to potential liability, not only by the owner or general contractor, but by third parties as well. As the decision in *Nicholson v. Turner/Cargile*, in the next section, illustrates, third parties such as the employees of the general contractor or subcontractors may look to impose liability against the architect for losses, including the loss of life. Although the design professional was not held liable in that decision, the potential exposure that the architect confronts dramatically demonstrates the importance of adequate insurance coverage.

During the construction process, the architect must also review and approve all submittals by the general contractor, which typically include shop drawings and product data and samples (AIA Document B101-2007 ¶ 3.6.4.2). Shop drawings are defined under AIA Document A201-2007 ¶ 3.12.1 as "drawings, diagrams, schedules and other data specifically prepared for the Work by the Contractor or a Subcontractor, Sub-subcontractor, manufacturer, supplier or distributor to illustrate some portion of the Work." Product data includes "illustrations, standard schedules, performance charts, instructions, brochures, diagrams and other information furnished by the Contractor to illustrate materials or equipment for some portion of the Work" (AIA Document A201-2007 ¶ 3.12.2). Finally, samples are "physical examples that illustrate materials, equipment or workmanship and establish standards by which the Work will be judged" (AIA Document A201-2007 ¶ 3.12.3). Shop drawings, product data and samples serve to further refine the quality of the construction work or define how the construction work will be completed in conformance with the construction documents. For a discussion of the importance of shop drawings in the construction process, see Ellickson, *Shop Drawings for Construction: Who Is Really Responsible?* 24 REAL PROP., PROB. & TR. J. 611 (1990).

The architect is also a central figure in the preparation of change orders and construction change directives during the construction process (AIA Document B101-2007 ¶ 3.6.5.1). Change orders and change order directives are described in greater detail in the following section. Where change orders or change order directives involve changes in the construction schedule or the costs under the general contractor's contract, the architect will determine the appropriate adjustments and incorporate the adjustments into the change order or other document for negotiation and execution by the owner and general contractor.

Finally, the architect is also involved during the construction process in certifying to the owner that the construction work has been satisfactorily completed as described in the contractor's application for payments (AIA Document B101-2007 ¶ 3.6.3). The architect also retains the authority to reject work that does not conform to the construction documents (AIA Document B101-2007 ¶ 3.6.2.2). Despite the control that the architect exercises in the certification of progress payments to the general contractor, AIA Document B101-2007 ¶ 3.6.3.2 attempts to absolve the architect for any liability for damages if construction has not occurred as claimed on the certificates. *But see State v. Mulvaney*, 72 So. 2d 424 (Miss. 1954) (imposing liability against the architect where the architect undertook the obligation to inspect the work prior to certification of a progress payment). Finally, the architect will inspect the construction work to determine when the project has reached substantial completion and will issue a certificate of substantial completion

(AIA Document B101-2007 ¶ 3.6.6). The architect will also issue a final certificate of payment, including the release of any retainage, based on a final inspection to determine that the project complies with the construction documents.

[2] Liability Issues Involving the Architect

The architect faces the potential of liability, both to the owner and to third-parties, for a breach of the contract or for the rendition of services that falls below the standard of care in the profession. The following two cases address the architect's liability to the owner for construction cost estimates and the architect's liability at the construction site for defective construction methods.

[a] Architect's Design and Cost Estimate

[i] Architect's Liability for Cost Estimates

As previously described, the architect is the key player in working with the developer to design a building that will accomplish the developer's objectives. Under the AIA documents the architect will maintain an estimate of the construction cost of the project throughout the design process in an effort to keep the project cost within the developer's construction budget. However, estimating the cost of a construction project is not an exact science. The question that arises concerns the architect's liability to the developer if construction bids exceed the cost estimates. In an extreme situation, a developer may find that the project as designed cannot be constructed within the proposed budget. In this case, the developer may seek to recover the design costs that will be wasted because of the architect's overly optimistic cost estimates. These are the subjects of the following case.

MALO v. GILMAN

177 Ind. App. 365, 379 N.E.2d 554 (Ind. Ct. App. 1978)

Staton, Judge.

Edward Malo, an architect, completed plans and specifications for Arnold Gilman, who sought to construct an office building. The construction bids received totaled $105,000, 50% more than the preliminary estimated cost of $70,000, which appeared in the contract between the men. Gilman was unable to secure financing and the building was never built. Malo brought an action to recover his fee as architect. Gilman counterclaimed for the $500 he had paid Malo. The trial court found for defendant Gilman and granted his counterclaim. We affirm the judgment.

Malo agreed to provide architectural services to Gilman in the design and construction of an office building. Between May, 1967, and November, 1968, Malo expended considerable time and effort on the project. A verbal agreement was reached on July 28, 1967. Gilman was assured that costs of construction could be kept below $20.00 per square foot. After talking to prospective tenants, Gilman decided he required 3,500 square feet in the building. A standard American Institute of Architects (A.I.A.) form contract was signed on May 14, 1968.[1] Among

---

[1] Since the contract was prepared by Malo, it must be strictly construed against him and in favor of

the terms was the following:

> "It is recognized that this written contract ratifies the similar verbal contract entered into July 28, 1967.
>
> "The preliminary estimated cost of this project is Seventy Thousand Dollars, ($70,000.00)."

The contract also contained the following standard clause:

> "3.4 Statements of Probable Construction Cost and Detailed Cost Estimates prepared by the Architect represent his best judgment as a design professional familiar with the construction industry. It is recognized, however, that neither the Architect nor the Owner has any control over the cost of labor, materials or equipment, over the contractors' methods of determining bid prices, or over competitive bidding or market conditions. Accordingly, the Architect cannot and does not guarantee that bids will not vary from any Statement of Probable Construction Cost or other cost estimate prepared by him."

Malo completed the plans and specifications for the project in September, 1968. In October, 1968, bids were solicited. The lowest total of bids received was approximately $128,000, which was negotiated down to $105,000. The bids were never accepted. Gilman indicated that the bids were unacceptable to him and that he was unable to secure financing. In mid-December, Gilman sold the land on which the building was to have been erected.

Malo demanded payment of his fee for architectural services in the sum of $9,132.60. Gilman refused to pay. Malo brought an action to collect his fee. Gilman counterclaimed for the $500 he previously had paid Malo. The trial court denied Malo's claim, but granted Gilman's counterclaim.

We hold that the judgment of the trial court can be affirmed on either of two alternate theories: (1) that parol evidence was properly admitted to show a maximum cost limitation of approximately $70,000.00, which was exceeded unreasonably by Malo's plans for construction; or (2) that the estimated cost figure appearing in the contract placed a reasonable limit on the actual cost of the project, which limit was exceeded unreasonably.[2] In either event, architect Malo breached the contract and is not entitled to compensation under the contract.

I. Parol Evidence to Show a Maximum Cost Limitation

On appeal, Malo argues that no fixed price agreement appeared in the "fully integrated contract" for architectural services. The only figure appearing in the contract, $70,000.00, was merely a preliminary estimated cost figure which was not binding on the architect.[3] Further, even if the trial court properly allowed evidence

---

Gilman. *Oxford Development Corp. v. Rausauer Builders, Inc.* (1973), 158 Ind. App. 622, 304 N.E.2d 211.

[2] Appellee argued both of these theories in his brief in support of affirming the trial court's judgment. Even though the trial court admitted parol evidence concerning the existence of a maximum cost limitation, the judgment apparently was based on the second theory, that is, that the actual cost would have unreasonably exceeded the estimated cost figure appearing in the contract. See the memorandum by Judge Walton. . . .

[3] For a discussion of the legal issues raised by cost estimates, see: Sweet & Sweet, *Architectural Cost Predictions: A Legal and Institutional Analysis*, 56 Cal. L. Rev. 996 (1968).

of a $20 per square foot cost limitation, Malo claims his final design plans contained 5,400 square feet,[4] 50% more space than originally projected. In that case, the bids totaling $105,000 were in the right price range for a building costing $20 per square foot.

Gilman contends that evidence showing the existence of a $20 per square foot cost limitation (or $70,000 to $78,000 total for the project) was properly admitted, since the contract failed to contain a maximum cost limitation. Further, no significant changes in the project occurred to increase its size or cost.

Normally parol evidence may not be considered if it contradicts or supersedes matters intended to be covered by the written agreement. However, parol evidence may be admitted to supply an omission in the terms of the contract.[5] *Caldwell v. United Presbyterian Church* (Common Pleas 1961), 180 N.E.2d 638, 20 Ohio Ops. 2d 364, 88 Ohio L. Abs. 323; *Spitz v. Brickhouse* (1954), 3 Ill. App.2d 536, 123 N.E.2d 117. Many contracts for architectural services, as here, fail to include specific requirements such as the size, style, and character of the building, the number of rooms, the quality of the materials to be used, and, finally, the maximum cost. Yet, according to section 1.1.1 of the A.I.A. form contract,

> "The Architect shall consult with the Owner to ascertain the requirements of the Project and shall confirm such requirements to the Owner."

Thus, depending on the specific needs of the owner, these requirements may be integral parts of the contract for architectural services. *Standley v. Egbert* (1970), D.C. App., 267 A.2d 365, 367. A contract that fails to set out the details agreed upon, then, is not a complete and integrated statement of the agreement. *See Levy v. Leaseway System, Inc.* (1959), 190 Pa. Super. 482, 154 A.2d 314. Parol evidence may be considered to determine the agreement with respect to these matters. *See* Annot., 69 A.L.R.3d 1353 (1976).

Ordinarily, the maximum cost of a project is agreed upon prior to commencement of design. The owner who plans to construct a building has in mind a figure for the maximum cost of construction, particularly where, as here, he must secure outside financing. The architect must design the project, keeping in mind this maximum cost limitation. Evidence of the maximum cost limitation should be admissible where the contract fails to show that figure.[6] As noted in an annotation to the *Spitz* case, 123 N.E.2d 117, 49 A.L.R.2d 679, 680 (1956):

---

[4] Of this space, less than 3,900 square feet was on the main floor, with the remaining square footage comprising a "partially finished" basement.

[5] Using parol evidence to supply an omission will not modify the written agreement, but merely adds to it. This is consistent with Judge Walton's memorandum, in which he found that there was no modification of the written agreement which would take it outside the Statute of Frauds.

[6] A line of cases, among them *Wick v. Murphy* (1952), 237 Minn. 447, 54 N.W.2d 805, have admitted parol evidence to show the cost of the project agreed upon by the parties, based upon a different line of reasoning. As the courts interpret the contract, the fee for architectural services depends on the actual construction cost. Where no contract has ever been let, the terms of the contract become ambiguous, that is, the fee can not be determined based on actual construction cost. Parol evidence is admissible to resolve the ambiguity.

We note that the contract contains a diagram, with percentage plotted against cost of the project, to determine the architect's fees. The contract utilizes the line marked "Group B." We note that the 7.75%, which is marked on the graph, corresponds to a cost figure of $70,000. This is clearly the figure intended to be used to calculate Malo's fee.

> "In the great majority of the cases where the question has been raised the evidence has been held admissible, usually on the ground that the written contract failed to disclose the parties' intention as to the cost of the structure contemplated, and that such contemplated cost was an element which must have entered into the negotiations."

Indiana has not yet decided a case on this point. However, the following cases allowed the introduction of parol evidence to show a maximum cost limitation when the contract failed to contain one: *Williams & Assoc., Arch. & Eng. v. Ramsey Prod. Corp.* (1973), 19 N.C.App. 1, 198 S.E.2d 67; *Caldwell v. United Presbyterian Church, supra;Petrus v. Bunnell* (1961), Fla. App., 129 So.2d 702; *Spitz v. Brickhouse, supra; Rosenthal v. Gauthier* (1953), 224 La. 341, 69 So.2d 367; and *Food Management, Inc. v. Blue Ribbon Beef Pack, Inc.*, 413 F.2d 716, 726 (8th Cir. 1969), which cited as a general rule "that an oral cost limitation imposed upon an architectural or engineering design, where not contradictory to the express terms of the written contract, may be admitted into evidence. . . ."

We agree that parol evidence of a maximum cost limitation may be introduced where the contract fails to contain such a limitation. The question of fact, whether architect Malo agreed to design a building, the cost of which could not exceed $20 per square foot (or $78,000 for 3,900 square feet), was resolved by the trial court in favor of Gilman. On examining the record, we cannot say that the finding of fact was incorrect as a matter of law.

Gilman testified that, from the beginning, he received repeated assurances that Malo would have "no problem" designing a building costing less than $20 per square foot. The amount of usable space Gilman required was approximately 3,500 square feet. By multiplying the figures, Gilman and Malo arrived at $70,000 as a "firm figure" for maximum cost. Gilman sought to reduce costs, accepting the use of a cost-saving "Uni-Roof" design, and suggesting a cost-cutting relocation of the basement.

Malo testified that he was aware that Gilman was interested in "getting the best price on the market." Yet he claimed that there was no ceiling on the cost of the project, that "it could be as much as a million dollars." Other evidence presented concerning the cost of the project included two bids received on the basis of Malo's preliminary drawings; one was $80,000; the other (which would incorporate the Uni-Roof) was $62,000 to $70,000. Finally, one of plaintiff's witnesses, who was present at a meeting where the bids were tabulated, testified that no specific "cost talk" was discussed, that he did not recall the figure of $70,000, but that $80,000 kept "ringing a bell."

The evidence fails to show that Gilman would have paid any sum of money to construct the proposed building. On the contrary, the evidence clearly shows that he wished to construct the building as cheaply as possible. The trial court correctly resolved the factual question of a maximum cost limitation in favor of Gilman. Under the terms of the agreement, then, Malo lost his right to recover compensation when he designed a building impossible of construction within the maximum cost limitation.

II. Estimated Cost Figure Exceeded Unreasonably

The contract for architectural services contained an estimated cost figure of $70,000. After negotiation, the lowest construction bids totaled $105,000, a figure 50% higher. Appellee Gilman argues that so great a discrepancy should bar Malo from receiving his fee for architectural services.

The court in *Caldwell v. United Presbyterian Church, supra*, supported such a theory. In that case, the building would have cost at least $57,800 to build, or $12,800 (almost 30%) in excess of the $45,000 cost limitation on the project. The court concluded,

> "that plaintiff has not substantially complied with the terms of his written contract and, therefore, is not entitled to recover in this action. . . ."

Id. 180 N.E.2d at 642.

Citing many cases, a federal Court of Appeals decision declared as a general rule

> "that there may be no recovery for engineering or architectural services where the actual cost of the structure substantially or unreasonably exceeds the estimated cost limitation, unless the cost excess is attributable to the owner's action. . . ."

Food Management, Inc. v. Blue Ribbon Beef Pack, Inc., supra, 413 F.2d at 726.

More recently, *Durand Associates, Inc. v. Guardian Investment Co.* (1971), 186 Neb. 349, 183 N.W.2d 246, involved construction bids which exceeded the estimate by 55%. The court interpreted the section of the contract in which the architect explicitly refused to guarantee the cost estimate, declaring that the figure represented a "reasonable approximation of the cost of the project." *Id.* at 250. This did not mean that an architect would never be bound by his estimate. Such a situation would be "contrary to public policy because it would mean that no matter how large the bid for doing the work, defendants would be obligated to pay an architectural fee based on that amount. . . ."[7] *Id.* The court held,

> "that an architect or engineer may breach his contract for architectural services by underestimating the construction costs of a proposed structure. The rule to be applied is that the cost of construction must reasonably approach that stated in the estimate unless the owner orders changes which increase the cost of construction. . . ."

Id. at 251.

III. Conclusion

Under either theory, the trial court could have found that Malo breached his contract for architectural services and denied Malo compensation under the contract, and found that Gilman was entitled to recover the $500 he paid Malo under the contract. The judgment of the trial court is affirmed.

---

[7] See footnote 6 herein.

BUCHANAN, C.J., (by designation), concurs.

HOFFMAN, J., concurs in Part II only.

[ii] Questions About *Malo*

1. What difference would it have made in *Malo* if the architect's contract contained a specific provision that the parties contemplated no maximum cost limitation? Does the court's discussion of the second theory on which the judgment could be based render the actual terms of the contract irrelevant?

2. How is the question of the architect's liability for construction estimates addressed under AIA Document B101-2007 ¶¶ 6.2 and 6.3? Would you advise an owner to modify the terms of the document? How would you advise an architect?

[b] Architect's Tort Liability for Design and Inspection

[i] Architect's Limited Obligation to Inspect

Under the AIA documents, the architect exercises some control over the construction site, at least to ensure that the construction work is completed in accordance with the design specifications. Although the architect will attempt to absolve himself of any liability in connection with construction methods employed by the general contractor, third parties who are injured in the construction process may look to the architect for compensation where the architect knew, or should have known, about defective construction methods. Such claims, as in the following case, can be based on theories of contractual, tort, or statutory duties owed by the architect to the injured parties.

NICHOLSON v. TURNER/CARGILE

107 Ohio App. 3d 797, 669 N.E.2d 529 (Ohio Ct. App. 1995)

PEGGY L. BRYANT, JUDGE.

Plaintiffs-appellants, Beth L. Nicholson, Walter W. Darst, Jr. and Sherri D. Starr, appeal from a judgment of the Franklin County Court of Common Pleas granting summary judgment in favor of defendants-appellees, Robert P. Madison International, Inc. ("Madison"), Korda/Nemeth Engineering, Inc. ("Korda/Nemeth"), and Korda/Nemeth's individual engineers Peter Korda and David A. Holtzapple.

In October 1987, the state hired Madison to provide architectural, engineering, construction management and administrative services for erection of The Ohio State University's Prime Site Computer Building in Columbus, Ohio. To satisfy the structural engineering portions of its contract, Madison subsequently hired Korda/Nemeth.

Plaintiffs assert that on May 18, 1990, David Holtzapple, representing Korda/Nemeth, visited the construction site. On that day, Holtzapple allegedly observed plaintiffs' decedents installing cantilevered beams by utilizing an unsafe leveling procedure. On May 22, 1990, as plaintiffs' decedents were employing this procedure, structural steel collapsed upon them, causing their death.

On May 19, 1992, plaintiffs filed wrongful death claims asserting the negligence of the above-named defendants and other defendants not party to this appeal. In response to a motion for summary judgment filed by Korda/Nemeth, the trial court on March 24, 1994, ruled that the engineering firm owed no legal duty to plaintiffs' decedents. In response to a motion for summary judgment later filed by Madison, the trial court ruled that Madison also owed no legal duty to plaintiffs' decedents. On May 5, 1995, by agreement of the parties, the trial court entered an amended judgment entry granting summary judgment to Peter Korda and David Holtzapple, as the trial court concluded that those individual defendants similarly owed no duty to plaintiffs' decedents. From that entry, plaintiffs brought this timely appeal. . . .

Here, to establish actionable negligence, plaintiffs must prove the existence of a duty defendants owed to plaintiffs' decedents, the breach of that duty, the direct and proximate causation between defendants' breach and plaintiffs' decedents' injuries, and damages. *Sedar v. Knowlton Constr. Co.* (1990), 49 Ohio St. 3d 193, 551 N.E.2d 938; *Johnson v. University Hospitals of Cleveland* (1989), 44 Ohio St. 3d 49, 540 N.E.2d 1370. The trial court premised its decision on the first prong of the four prong test, the lack of any duty defendants owed to plaintiffs' decedents.

Plaintiffs' three assignments of error are interrelated, thus we address them jointly. In them plaintiffs allege that Korda/Nemeth, Korda, Holtzapple, and Madison had contractual, tort, and statutory duties to stop or prevent the decedents' unsafe leveling practices. We first address plaintiffs' assignments of error as they relate to contractual duties.

In arguing that Madison had a contractual duty to stop or prevent the unsafe leveling procedures, plaintiffs focus in particular on sections within Madison's contract with the state which provide that Madison shall visit the work site to "become generally familiar with the progress and quality of the work and to determine in general if it is proceeding in accordance with Construction Drawings and Specifications." (Associate Architect's Agreement, Appellants' Exhibit F, Sec. 1.5.3.) [Ed. note: Compare to AIA Document B101-2007 ¶ 3.6.2.1.] According to the contract, on making these on-site observations, Madison shall inform the Deputy Director of the Division of Public Works of the "progress and quality of the work and shall endeavor to guard the Deputy Director against defects and deficiencies in the work of the Contractor." (Associate Architect's Agreement, Appellant's Exhibit F, Sec. 1.5.3.)

To establish a similar contractual duty for Korda/Nemeth and its individual engineers, plaintiffs focus upon nearly identical language within the contract between Madison and Korda/Nemeth. Paragraph 2.6.3 of the Madison-Korda/Nemeth contract states that Korda/Nemeth shall visit the site "to become generally familiar with the progress and quality of the Work . . . and to determine in general if the Work is being performed in a manner indicating that the Work, when complete, will be in accordance with the Contract Documents." (Madison-Korda/Nemeth Agreement, Appellants' Exhibit E, Sec. 2.6.3.) [Ed note: Compare to AIA Document B101-2007 ¶ 3.6.2.1.] According to the terms of the contract, on making these on-site inspections, Korda/Nemeth shall keep Madison "informed of the progress of the Work . . . and shall endeavor to guard [the state] against defects and deficiencies in such Work." (Madison-Korda/Nemeth Agreement, Appellant's Exhibit E, Sec. 2.6.3.)

Plaintiffs' argument, however, ignores more specific contractual provisions which not only hold the contractor responsible for building processes, but also dictate that Madison is not responsible for the contractor "in the building process." (Associate Architect's Agreement, Appellants' Exhibit F, Sec. 1.5.8.) Indeed, Section 1.5.8 explicitly relieves Madison from certain responsibilities of the contractor, stating that Madison:

> ". . . [S]hall not be responsible for construction means, methods, techniques, sequences or procedures, or for safety precautions and programs in connection with the work and . . . shall not be responsible for the Contractor's failure to carry out the work in accordance with the Construction Drawings and Specifications." [Ed note: Compare to AIA Document B101-2007 ¶ 3.6.1.2.]

The contract between the state and Madison further insulates Madison from responsibility for the contractor's acts, stating that Madison:

> ". . . [S]hall not be responsible for the acts or omissions of the Contractors, their subcontractors or material suppliers, or any of the Contractors or subcontractor's agents or employees or any other persons performing any of the work." (Associate Architect's Agreement, Appellant's Exhibit F, Sec. 1.5.15.) [Ed note: Compare to AIA Document B101-2007 ¶ 3.6.1.2.]

In turn, the contract between Madison and Korda/Nemeth contains similar provisions relieving Korda/Nemeth from responsibility for other's acts. Specifically, Section 1.1.8 of the Madison-Korda/Nemeth contract states that Korda/Nemeth "shall not be responsible for the acts or omissions of the Architect, Architect's other consultants, Contractor, Subcontractors, their agents or employees, or other persons performing any of the Work." (Madison-Korda/Nemeth Contract, Appellants' Exhibit E, Sec. 1.1.8.) Korda/Nemeth also agreed that while visiting the work site, it would "determine in general if the Work [was] being performed in a manner indicating that the Work, when completed, [would] be in accordance with the Contract Documents." (Madison-Korda/Nemeth Contract, Appellants' Exhibit E, Sec. 2.6.3.) As part of those site visits, however, Korda/Nemeth is not "required to make exhaustive or continuous on-site inspections to check the quality or quantity of the Work. . . ." (Madison-Korda/Nemeth Contract, Appellants' Exhibit E, Sec. 2.6.3.) [Ed note: compare to AIA Document B101-2007 ¶ 3.6.2.1.] Korda/Nemeth's approval of plans also does not constitute its approval of safety precautions, "construction means, methods, techniques, sequences or procedures." (Madison-Korda/Nemeth Contract, Appellants' Exhibit E, Sec. 2.6.11.) [Ed note: compare to AIA Document B101-2007 ¶ 3.6.1.2.] Rather, Korda/Nemeth explicitly is not responsible for "construction means, methods, techniques, sequences or procedures, or for safety precautions and programs in connection with the Work. . . ." (Madison-Korda/Nemeth Contract, Appellants' Exhibit E, Sec. 2.6.4), as those activities remain the contractor's sole responsibility. (Madison-Korda/Nemeth Contract, Appellants' Exhibit E, Sec. 2.6.4.)

While plaintiffs' construction of the pertinent contracts ignores the sections limiting the responsibility of architect and engineer ("design professionals") concerning safety, construction means, and techniques, those provisions dictate that

Madison and Korda/Nemeth had no contractual duties to advise the contractor of hazardous construction procedures or to make the site safe. *See Young v. Miller Bros. Excavating Inc.* (July 26, 1989), 1989 Ohio App. LEXIS 2978, Montgomery App. No. 11306, unreported (construing virtually identical language in a contract between the owner and the contractor and concluding that a provision calling for the engineers' on-site inspections did not require them to inspect for hazards). Because Madison's and Korda/Nemeth's on-site inspections were for the purpose of insuring that the construction met with the architect's design specifications, they did not have a contractual duty to make the construction site safe for the general construction workers. *Id.*

Plaintiffs nonetheless rely on their expert engineer who interprets the contracts to impose such a duty on defendants. The contract terms, however, are unambiguous and control; any expert opinion interpreting them has no effect. *See State ex rel. Parsons v. Fleming* (1994), 68 Ohio St. 3d 509, 511, 628 N.E.2d 1377 ("if a contract is clear and unambiguous, then its interpretation is a matter of law and there is no issue of fact to be determined"); *Davis v. Loopco Industries, Inc.* (1993), 66 Ohio St. 3d 64, 66, 609 N.E.2d 144; *P & O Containers, Ltd. v. Jamelco, Inc.* (1994), 94 Ohio App. 3d 726, 731, 641 N.E.2d 794 ("the interpretation of a written contract is a question of law, absent patent ambiguity").

For the foregoing reasons, plaintiffs' assertions that defendants had contractual duties to stop or prevent the unsafe leveling practice are unpersuasive. To the extent the assignments of error relate to contractual duties, those assignments of error are rejected.

Even in the absence of contractual provisions, plaintiffs contend that if Madison's or Korda/Nemeth's on-site representatives actually saw the unsafe leveling practice, defendants had a common law tort duty to stop or prevent the unsafe practice. Because plaintiffs' contentions raise an issue of first impression in Ohio, we look to analogous areas of the law for guidance in resolving plaintiffs' argument.

Ohio case law addresses a similar situation when it develops the duties general contractors owe to the employees of independent subcontractors. Ordinarily, general contractors owe no duty to the workers employed by independent subcontractors. A contractor's duty may arise, however, if it either actively participates in the subcontractor's work or explicitly assumes responsibility for worker safety. As the Supreme Court held in *Cafferkey v. Turner Construction Co.* (1986), 21 Ohio St. 3d 110, 113, 488 N.E.2d 189, "[a] general contractor who has not actively participated in the subcontractor's work, does not, merely by virtue of its supervisory capacity, owe a duty of care to employees of the subcontractor who are injured while engaged in inherently dangerous work." Because erection of a building constitutes inherently dangerous work, general contractors typically owe no duty to employees of independent subcontractors. *Michaels v. Ford Motor Co.* (1995), 72 Ohio St. 3d 475, 478 n.4, 650 N.E.2d 1352.

However, a general contractor owes such workers a duty when it "actively participates in the job operation" performed by the subcontractor. *Cafferkey, supra*, at 112; *Hirschbach v. Cincinnati Gas & Elec. Co.* (1983), 6 Ohio St. 3d 206, 208, 452 N.E.2d 326. Such active participation results when the general contractor "directs the activity which resulted in the injury and/or [gives] or denies permission for the critical acts that [lead] to the employee's injury." *Bond v. Howard Corp.* (1995), 72 Ohio St. 3d 332, 650 N.E.2d 416, syllabus; *Pifher v. Ford Motor Co.* (Aug.

10, 1994), 1994 Ohio App. LEXIS 3589, Lorain App. No. 93CA005581, unreported. Without other activity, however, a general contractor's exercise of his supervisory role does not constitute "active participation" to create a duty. *Bond, supra*, at 335. Thus, a duty does not arise just because the general contractor retains power to monitor and coordinate activities, for the "very nature of the construction business requires a general contractor . . . to 'supervise' a construction job." Michaels, *supra*, 72 Ohio St. 3d at 479, citing *Bond, supra*, 72 Ohio St. 3d at 339.

While a general contractor may also explicitly assume responsibility for workers' safety many contract provisions between general contractors and subcontractors do not give rise to such assumed responsibility. *Cafferkey, supra*, at 113. Contract provisions that do not create such a duty include promises (1) assigning control over safety procedures to the general contractor, *Id.*; (2) retaining a general contractor's right to review details and construction; (3) requiring that the work be finished under an architect's and general engineer's direction and to their satisfaction, *Gilday v. S & R Playhouse Realty Co.* (June 14, 1990), 1990 Ohio App. LEXIS 2440, Cuyahoga App. No. 57022, unreported; (4) promising that a general contractor will have a representative at the job site; (5) requiring that a general contractor specify the work to be done by the subcontractor and specifying the items the general contractor will inspect; (6) requiring a subcontractor to replace personnel found to be incompetent; and (7) promising that material supplied by the subcontractor will meet specifications. *Mount v. Columbus & Southern Ohio Elec. Co.* (1987), 39 Ohio App. 3d 1, 528 N.E.2d 1262, paragraph four of the syllabus. Indeed, in the context of a general contractor's role in safety matters, the Supreme Court considered contractual language similar to that found in this case, and labeled such language "nothing more than standard 'boilerplate' terminology common to virtually all construction contracts." *Cafferkey, supra*, at 113.

If we apply here by analogy the cases concerning a general contractor's duty to a subcontractor's employees, then an architect or engineer generally has no duty to the employees of independent subcontractors, unless the architect or engineer actually participates in subcontractors' work or explicitly contracts for safety responsibilities.

Such a rule is consistent with Ohio law concerning design professionals' liability for third parties' economic damages. Specifically, absent direct contractual privity between a design professional and an injured third party, the design professional sued for professional negligence generally is not liable for a third party's economic damages. *Floor Craft Floor Covering, Inc. v. Parma Community Gen. Hosp. Assn.* (1990), 54 Ohio St. 3d 1, 560 N.E.2d 206. Despite the lack of privity, however, a design professional's significant participation in a contractor's work may create a nexus that substitutes for contractual privity. *Clevecon, Inc. v. Northeast Ohio Regional Sewer Dist.* (1993), 90 Ohio App. 3d 215, 220, 628 N.E.2d 143. Thus, a design professional is not liable for third party economic damages when he or she does not participate in the project or interact with the contractor and signs a standard contract providing the design professional no role in construction means, methods, techniques or procedures; but a design professional who exercises "excessive control over the contractor" through the power to stop the work and give orders about the project is liable for such economic damages. 90 Ohio App. 3d at 220–221.

Because the record lacks evidence suggesting defendants actively participated in the construction at issue or assumed responsibility for safety procedures, defen dants would not be liable in tort to plaintiffs even by analogy. Plaintiffs urge, however, that design professionals have a duty in law to prevent or stop dangerous conditions or practices when they are actually aware of those hazards.

Plaintiffs suggest that design professionals have such a duty because plaintiffs submitted an affidavit of their expert witness, an engineer, who described such a duty and opined that defendants breached that duty. Despite the expert's opinion, issues concerning the existence of duty remain questions of law. *Mussivand v. David* (1989), 45 Ohio St. 3d 314, 318, 544 N.E.2d 265, quoting Prosser, Law of Torts (4th ed.1971) 325–326 ("there is no formula for ascertaining whether a duty exists. Duty . . . is the court's expression of the sum total of those considerations of policy which lead the law to say that the particular plaintiff is entitled to protection"); *Slagle v. White Castle Systems, Inc.* (1992), 79 Ohio App. 3d 210, 216, 607 N.E.2d 45. Thus, deposition testimony, expectations of the parties and expert testimony have no effect upon the determination of duty.

Given the absence of Ohio law concerning design professionals' liability for their work site supervision, plaintiffs next base their argument on Kansas and New Jersey decisions.

For example, the Kansas Supreme Court in *Balagna v. Shawnee County* (Kan.1983), 233 Kan. 1068, 668 P.2d 157, held that an architect-engineer violated his duty to a contractor's employee killed by a collapsing sewer wall. The Kansas court found that although the architect-engineer discovered the safety violations that later caused the collapse, he failed to take action. While the court noted that a design professional's duty to supervise or administer the construction work generally involves only "a duty to see that the building when constructed meets the plans and specifications for which the owner agreed to pay," 668 P.2d at 163, quoting *Hanna v. Huer, Johns, Neel, Rivers & Webb* (Kan.1983), 233 Kan. 206, 662 P.2d 243, paragraph two of the syllabus, it further stated that a design professional may not "stand idly by with actual knowledge of unsafe practices on the jobsite and take no steps to advise or warn the owner or contractor." *Id.*, citing *Hanna, supra*, at paragraph four of the syllabus.

A New Jersey appellate court drew similar conclusions in *Carvalho v. Toll Bros. & Devel.* (N.J. Super. A.D.1995), 278 N.J. Super. 451, 651 A.2d 492, 494, when the on-site engineer had actual knowledge that workers were not employing certain safety precautions. Although the engineer supervising the work site did not have any contractual obligation to inspect for hazards, his actual knowledge of a dangerous condition triggered a duty to take reasonable action. 651 A.2d at 497.

Conversely, defendants cite numerous foreign cases in which design professionals are liable for their on-site supervision only when they actively participate in the work site construction or when they contractually assume responsibility for workers' safety. *See, e.g., Frampton v. Dauphin Distribution Serv. Co.* (Pa. Super. 1994), 436 Pa. Super. 486, 648 A.2d 326, 329 ("an architect, in the absence of a duty specially imposed by contract or course of conduct, has no duty to take affirmative action to protect workers from hazards on the job site which are either known or readily visible"); *Rodriguez v. Universal Fastenings Corp.* (Tex. App.1989), 777 S.W.2d 513, 515 (engineer not negligent for injuries to workers for their failure to use the proper scaffolding because contract provided that contractor was responsible for use of proper scaffolding); *Hanna, supra*, at paragraph three of the syllabus (factors to be considered in determining whether an architect has assumed responsibility for safety practices include (1) actual supervision and control of the work; (2) retention of the right to supervise and control; (3) constant participation in ongoing activities at the construction site; (4) supervision and coordination of subcontractors; (5) assumption of responsibility for safety practices; (6) authority to issue change orders; and (7) the right to stop the work).

While the Kansas and New Jersey cases found the design professional had actual knowledge of the dangerous condition, *Carvalho, supra*, 651 A.2d at 498, *Balagna, supra*, at 164, defendants' citations do not find that the design professional had any actual knowledge of the condition. Plaintiffs' and defendants' cases are best reconciled by concluding that if design professionals have actual knowledge of a hazard, they then have a duty to stop or prevent the dangerous condition or practice. If design professionals, however, do not have actual knowledge, their tort duties arise if they actively participate in the construction or explicitly assume responsibility for worker safety.

Assuming the existence of such a theory which reconciles the cases plaintiffs and defendants rely on and thus creates a duty arising from design professionals' supervision, plaintiffs have not set forth sufficient evidence to establish that Madison and Korda/Nemeth actually breached such a duty. Those decisions holding that design professionals have a duty to workers to stop or prevent hazardous conditions or practices all affirmatively find that the design professional actually saw the unsafe condition or practice and actually recognized its inherent danger. Here, plaintiffs cannot establish a genuine issue of material fact that Madison's or Korda/Nemeth's representatives actually saw the dangerous leveling procedure.

With the conflicting evidence construed in favor of plaintiffs, the record shows Korda/Nemeth's representative, David Holtzapple, visited the work site four working days before the accident for about forty to fifty minutes and walked somewhere on the structural steel. . . . Plaintiffs also presented evidence that sometime during the day Holtzapple visited, plaintiffs' decedents were leveling beams and openly employing the dangerous procedure. . . .

The foregoing evidence, however, does not place Holtzapple within the decedents' proximity as they were using the unsafe leveling procedure. Contrary to plaintiffs' assertions, they need to show more than that Holtzapple was on the structural steel on a day when the decedents were utilizing the unsafe procedure; they must set forth evidence suggesting that Holtzapple actually saw the procedure and recognized it as dangerous. Here, plaintiffs cannot establish a genuine issue of material fact in that regard. Indeed, plaintiffs are forced to rely on speculation to make the bridge between Holtzapple's presence and his knowledge of ongoing procedures. Accordingly, on the evidence before us, reasonable minds cannot conclude that Holtzapple actually saw the procedure and appreciated its danger.

Plaintiffs also allege that Greg Gutman, Madison's field representative, actually observed the unsafe leveling procedure and recognized its danger. With the evidence again construed in plaintiffs' favor, the record shows Gutman observed some of the steel erection, but he did not inspect the structural steel. . . . Gutman's statement that he "really couldn't say" whether he observed the workers performing the unsafe procedure does not constitute evidence that he viewed the procedure, and plaintiffs cannot point to any additional evidence suggesting that Gutman was in a position to see, or actually saw, the unsafe procedure and appreciated its danger. Accordingly, again no genuine issue of material fact exists whether representatives of Madison actually saw the unsafe leveling procedure.

As a result, even if we were to create a duty on the part of these design professionals, plaintiffs have not set forth essential facts giving rise to that duty.

For the foregoing reasons, to the extent that plaintiffs' assignments of error argue a common law duty and breach of that duty, we overrule the assigned errors.

Lastly, plaintiffs argue that Korda/Nemeth's failure to comply with the Ohio Basic Building Code ("OBBC") constitutes negligence per se. Plaintiffs assert that Korda/Nemeth did not comply with OBBC section 1201.3, requiring designs to provide for "temporary stresses."

Initially, failure to comply with the OBBC does not constitute negligence per se; negligence per se involves violations of legislative enactments, not violations of administrative provisions. Thus, failure to comply with the OBBC cannot constitute negligence per se. *Zimmerman v. St. Peter's Catholic Church* (1993), 87 Ohio App. 3d 752, 755, 622 N.E.2d 1184; *Simon v. Drake Construction Co.* (1993), 87 Ohio App. 3d 23, 26, 621 N.E.2d 837, citing *Schwirtz v. Berry* (Sept. 1, 1983), Cuyahoga App. No. 43605, unreported (held building code violation does not establish negligence per se).

Plaintiffs nonetheless argue that Korda/Nemeth also did not meet the standard of engineering care because it did not comply with OBBC Section 1201.3. Plaintiffs again attempt to use their expert witness both to interpret Korda/Nemeth's obligation under OBBC 1201.3 and to establish that Korda/Nemeth breached that obligation.

While expert testimony may be used to establish breach of a standard created by statute or rule, such testimony is not admissible to interpret statutory terms which create the standard. *Payne v. A.O. Smith Corp.* (S.D. Ohio 1985), 627 F. Supp. 226, 228 (expert may not testify as to the rules and procedure of Consumer Product Safety Commission, but expert may testify as to industry practices which are not a matter of law); *see also Eugan v. Marr Scaffolding Co.* (Mass. App.1982), 14 Mass. App. Ct. 1036, 442 N.E.2d 743, 745 (expert could testify whether platform was capable of meeting rules and regulations for prevention of accidents); Henry Wade Rogers, The Law of Expert Testimony (3d ed. 1941) 38, 44, 293 (a qualified witness may testify to methods in general use in a specific type of construction, but the expert may not testify to questions involving points of law). Thus, when a professional's duty is set forth in statutes and regulations, an expert may not define the duty by interpreting statutory and regulatory terms. *State v. Walsh* (1979), 66 Ohio App. 2d 85, 420 N.E.2d (expert may not perform trial court's function of determining legal significance of certain statements within securities offering; expert improperly "addressed very technical legal issues"). To the extent plaintiffs' expert testifies to the meaning of "temporary stresses" within the building code, that testimony is not relevant to a determination of any duty the OBBC requirements impose on Korda/Nemeth.

Absent their expert's opinion, plaintiffs assert that the building code requires Korda/Nemeth to account for temporary stresses, which includes decedents' unsafe construction procedures. We, however, can find no indication that accounting for "temporary stresses" requires a design professional to provide for a potentially unlimited array of unsafe construction procedures. *See, e.g.*, American Institute of Steel Construction, Inc. ("AISC"), Manual of Steel Construction: Allowable Stress

Design (9th ed. 1989) M4 (temporary bracing and leveling shall be in accordance with American Institute of Steel Construction Code of Standard Practice); AISC Code of Standard Practice, *supra*, at 7.9 (temporary supports and other elements required for erection operation shall be determined by the erector and temporary supports shall support loads comparable to those for which the structure was designed, resulting from wind, seismic forces and erection operations, but not the loads resulting from the performance of work by others).

While the trial court opinion does not consider the meaning of "temporary stresses" as a matter of law, the term does not include unsafe construction procedures. Although the OBBC sets forth a duty to provide for "temporary stresses," the code does not create a duty to account for all potentially unsafe construction methods. Korda/Nemeth, therefore, did not breach its duty to account for "temporary stresses" when it failed to predict decedents' unsafe leveling procedure. Thus, to the extent plaintiffs' assigned errors rely on defendants' breach of a duty established under the OBBC, those assignments of error are overruled.

For the foregoing reasons, we overrule plaintiffs' assignments of error and affirm the judgment of the trial court.

Judgment affirmed.

TYACK and HOLMES, JJ., concur.

[ii] Questions About *Nicholson*

1. How relevant should the contractual relationship between the owner and architect and the owner and general contractor be to questions involving third parties injured in the construction process?
2. Are you convinced by the court's analogy between a design professional's liability to a third party for personal injuries and a design professional's liability to a third party for economic damages? Isn't the traditional limit on liability for economic damages based on questions of foreseeability?
3. The court states that "a design professional who exercises 'excessive control over the contractor' through the power to stop work and give orders about the project" could be liable for damages to a third party. Do the AIA documents give the architect such control?
4. What effect would a decision imposing liability against an architect for injuries to a third party have on the construction process? Isn't this really simply a question of who bears the costs of insurance?

[3] The Fox Valley Auto Care Center: The Architect's Contract

As has been done throughout this book, we here examine construction issues in the context of Kaplan & Miller's representation of Regent in the development of the Fox Valley Auto Care Center. This format, however, presents a problem at this juncture caused by the AIA's revision of its documents in 1997 and 2007. This was noted at the beginning of the chapter, but we mention it again here because we have made a choice that may be confusing to you. We are going to present a real document to you, the proposal to Regent by the Chicago architecture and engineering firm of MFH Associates, which was written in 1989. We could have used the 1987 version of the AIA documents, but then we would have been familiarizing you with outdated material. We have chosen, therefore, to have Donna ask Sam to design the folding of MFH's proposal into the 2007 AIA documents, rather than the 1987 AIA documents. The real-life timing may be off, but the time-warp should provide the best learning experience for you.

[a] Donna Sends the MFH Proposal to Sam

MEMORANDUM

TO: Samuel Nader

FROM: Donna Smith

RE: MFH Architectural Services Agreement

I have attached a copy of MFH's proposal for architectural services in connection with the Fox Valley Auto Care Center development with our client, the Regent Real Estate Development Corp. Regent has suggested that this proposal be attached to the 2007 edition of AIA Document B101, *Standard Form of Agreement Between Owner and Architect with Standard Form of Architect's Services* ("AIA Document B101-2007") and has proposed that AIA Document B101-2007 govern the terms of its relationship with MFH except to the extent that the letter provides otherwise.

Regent is familiar with the 1987 edition of the AIA standard form of agreement between the owner and architect ("Document B141-1987") but has never used the 2007 edition. Please review the letter and documents and describe:

1. How the letter should be incorporated into AIA Document B101-2007.

2. The significant changes made in AIA Document B101-2007, as compared to AIA Document B101-1987, that Regent should be aware of.

If I could have your memo by the end of the week, I could then prepare for a meeting with our client at the beginning of next week. Thanks.

[b] The MFH Proposal to Regent

MFH Associates
Suite 1848
20 North Wacker Drive
Chicago, Illinois 60606
312-726-2350

January 16, 1989

Mr. David Delany

The Regent Real Estate Development Company

415 W. North Ave.

Chicago, Illinois

Re: Fox Valley Auto Care Center

Route 59

Fox Valley Shopping Center

Dear Mr. Delany:

I am pleased to submit to you this proposal for Architectural Services on the above listed project. The following is a Description of the Services and the Scope of Services which MFH is proposing to provide and the Fees that will be required:

A. PROJECT DESCRIPTION

The project is to build an Auto Care Center as described in the PROPOSED SITE PLAN in the Regent Group's project prospectus. The site includes an approximately 19,000 s.f. Auto Care Center (2 buildings "A" & "B"), and an approximately 18,750 s.f. Car Wash. Building "B" of the Auto Care Center has a basement.

B. MFH SCOPE OF BASIC SERVICES

The following is a General Description of the work to be performed by MFH as Basic Services. See Sections D through H for a detailed description of items included during each Phase of the Project design.

ARCHITECTURAL — MFH will provide Architectural Services for the two Auto Care Buildings. This will include the placement of demising walls and typical office and bathroom areas. This will also include the design for the basement in Building "B".

STRUCTURAL — MFH will provide Structural design services for the Auto Care Buildings "A" & "B" and their foundations.

C. ITEMS NOT INCLUDED IN MFH'S SCOPE OF BASIC SERVICES

The following items are not in MFH's Scope of Basic Services. These items may be added to MFH's Scope as Additional Services only if agreed by MFH and the Client in writing.

ARCHITECTURAL and STRUCTURAL working drawings will not be prepared for the Car Wash building.

MECHANICAL, ELECTRICAL, PLUMBING, and AUTOMOTIVE WASTE RECOVERY SYSTEMS design for the buildings will not be done by MFH.

CONSTRUCTION COST ESTIMATING

TENANT IMPROVEMENTS including hydraulic lifts and their foundations (except basement for Building "B"), ceilings, & interior finishes will be by others.

SOILS INVESTIGATIONS will be done by others.

SURVEYING for property lines, grade and curb elevations, and location of utilities will be done by others.

CIVIL ENGINEERING for utilities & paving for the site.

LANDSCAPE DESIGN for planting around the site.

D. DESIGN PHASE:

1. During the Design Phase MFH will visit the site and review existing conditions by visual methods.
2. MFH will review Survey and Soils information taken by others.

E. APPROVAL PHASE:

1. MFH will prepare design drawings for the purpose of receiving local city approval for the project's inclusion in the Fox Valley P.D.D.
2. MFH will meet with the client to discuss the basic design of the project. It is expected that up to 4 such meetings be included in basic services.
3. MFH will attend meetings and/or hearings with the Regent Group and the City required to receive approval for the project. It is expected that up to 5 such meetings will be included in Basic Services.

F. WORKING DRAWING PHASE:

1. MFH will provide Working Drawings for the workoutlined in Section B.
2. MFH will not provide HVAC Engineering work for the project. MFH will coordinate the design of HVAC work done by others with the Architectural & Structural work.
3. MFH will not provide Plumbing Engineering work for the project. This will not include sprinkler design. MFH will coordinate the design of Plumbing work done by others with the Architectural work.
4. MFH will not provide Electrical Engineering for the project. MFH will coordinate the design of Electrical work done by others with the Architectural work.
5. MFH will meet with the client to discuss and coordinate their design

with others. It is proposed that up to 4 meetings be included as a part of Basic Services.

G. BIDDING PHASE:

1. MFH will answer questions directed to them from the Client, their Consultants, or Bidding Contractors. A record of all conversations will be kept by MFH.
2. MFH will review alternates to their design which may be proposed by the Client or Contractors as Additional Services.

H. CONSTRUCTION PHASE:

1. MFH will provide permit assistance.
2. MFH will review the following Shop Drawings for items which MFH has designed as Basic Services:

   Structural Steel Shop Drawings

   Metal Floor & Roof Deck

   Steel Bar Joists
3. MFH will make visits to the site when requested by the Client to observe a particular condition as Additional Services. MFH will prepare a visitation report of items observed.
4. If conditions are uncovered during Construction which could not have been foreseen during the Design and Working Drawing Phases, MFH will analyze these conditions and modify their design as Additional Services.

I. FEES:

1. Fees for work described in Section B Basic Services will be a Lump Sum of:

   NINETEEN THOUSAND FIVE HUNDRED ($19,500.00) DOLLARS

   Plus Reimbursables.
2. Fees for Additional Services which may be agreed to in writing by MFH and the client will be billed at the following rates:

Project Manager	$75.00/hr.
Architect/Engineer	$60.00/hr.
Draftsman	$28.00/hr.
Clerical/Office	$21.00/hr.
Plus Reimbursables.	

J. REIMBURSABLES:

1. Costs for the following items which may be incurred in the course of the work will be considered Reimbursable items and be billed in addition to the fees listed above.

   Transportation

   Photos

Prints & Copies

Computer Plots

Delivery Costs

K. BILLING:

1. An Initial Payment will be required upon commencement of the Work of:

   SIX THOUSAND ($6,000.00) DOLLARS

2. MFH will submit monthly summary reports of the amount of work completed during that period.
3. If for some reason the project is canceled or put on hold, the Regent Group will be liable for the work performed up to the cancellation or postponement.
4. The second billing will be made on June 21, 1989 for inclusion in the Regent Group's July 1, 1989 loan opening payment. This billing will include all work performed to that date. Payment will be required within one week of the above loan opening payment date.
5. The third and subsequent billings will be monthly for work performed during that period.
6. Payment for subsequent billings will be required within 30 days of Billing.
7. Payments which are due and outstanding for more that 60 days will be subject to interest charges.

[c] Sam's Analysis of the MFH Proposal and the AIA Documents

MEMORANDUM

TO: Donna Smith

FROM: Samuel Nader

RE: MFH Architectural Services Agreement

This memorandum is in response to your inquiry regarding the architectural services agreement proposed by MFH in connection with the Fox Valley Auto Care Center being developed by our client, the Regent Real Estate Development Company ("Regent"). Specifically, you asked me to review MFH's proposal for architectural services and AIA Document B101-2007 and describe:

1. How the letter should be incorporated into AIA Document B101-2007.

2. The significant changes that Regent should be aware of that were made in AIA Document B101-2007 as compared to AIA Document B141-1987.

INCORPORATION OF MFH's LETTER INTO B101-2007

The AIA envisions that the owner and design professional will develop their agreement through an interactive process in order to reflect the unique goals and needs of the project. The first change in AIA Document B101-2007 is structural: it is an integrated contract that can be used along with AIA Document B101-2007 Exhibit A ("Initial Information"). Previously, in both the 1987 and 1997 versions, the AIA owner-architect agreement was in a modular format that was divided into two parts. Article 1 was an "agreement form" which consisted of specific project information, contractual terms and conditions, and compensation terms. Article 2 was a "service form" which described the architect's services to be rendered on the project.

MFH's letter is generally descriptive of the services it proposes to provide and does little in the way of arranging the legal relationship between the parties. The letter offers a general Project Description in Part A, detailed descriptions of architectural services in Parts B through H, and fee and billing information in Parts I through K. AIA Document B101-2007 provides space, after space to identify the parties, "for the following Project"; we can incorporate Part A of the MFH letter there, or, if Regent and MFH want to include a more complete description of the project, we could attach the optional AIA Document B101-2007 Exhibit A and incorporate Part A of the MDH letter in § A.1.3. Regent should be made aware of the new AIA Document B101-2007 Exhibit A so that it can decide whether it would like to include the greater description of the project and the participants in the design process for which Exhibit A provides. For example, Part C of the MFH letter states that the car wash building is not part of its proposal, and it seems to me that this exclusion would best be stated in an extended description of what the project proposal does include, if Regent decides it would prefer to use the optional AIA Document B101-2007 Exhibit A.

We can then incorporate MFH's description of architectural services from Parts B through H into Article 2 of AIA Document B101-2007. Finally, the new version of AIA Document B101-2007 provides a separate Article 11 into which we can incorporate MFH's fee and billing information.

SIGNIFICANT CHANGES IN B101-2007

AIA Document B101-2007 contains a number of significant revisions to the provisions previously available under the 1987 edition. A number of these provisions significantly affect the legal relationship between the owner and architect and should be brought to the client's attention.

1. Information provided by parties

As mentioned before, the AIA envisions an interactive agreement development process. AIA Document B101-2007 ¶ 1.1 provides a small space for parties to provide general project information, including construction and project budgets, project parameters, team members etc. Regent can provide much of this information after merely reviewing the agreement, but, again, Regent may find it that it is to its advantage to use the AIA Document B101-2007 Exhibit A which provides much more space, and structure, for providing this information. Let me emphasize that it is essential that Regent provide accurate information because AIA Document B101-2007 ¶ 1.3 specifies that, in the event of any subsequent change of the information contained in ¶ 1.1, the owner and architect are to negotiate appropriate adjustments in schedule, compensation, and changes in services. Unless Regent is satisfied with the design concept of the Fox Valley Auto Care Center as currently envisioned, it may wish to amend ¶ 1.3 in order to allow greater flexibility in providing the ¶ 1.1 information.

2. Ownership of design documents

Like Article 6 of AIA Document B101-1987, the intellectual property provision in AIA Document B101-2007 favors the architect, although less than before. Article 6 of AIA Document B101-1987 deemed the architect the owner of the drawings, specifications and other documents prepared by the architect for the project and preserved all common law, statutory, and copyright rights relating to the documents for the architect. Article 7 of AIA Document B101-2007 makes significant changes, but AIA Document B101-2007 ¶ 7.2 still makes the architect and its consultants "the owners of their respective Instruments of Service." Further, under AIA Document B101-2007 ¶ 7.3 the owner's license to use the design documents is only for so long as "the Owner substantially performs its obligations, including prompt payment of all sums when due, under this Agreement." It is therefore advisable that the contract be amended to provide either that Regent will own all rights to the project design documents or that the license to use the design documents does not terminate in the absence of fault by Regent (ideally, fault would only involve an intentional failure to pay rather than the inability to pay). In negotiating changes, Regent also should consider that its construction lender will insist on AIA Document B101-2007 ¶ 7.4 including the construction lender's right to use the drawings and specifications if, for example, Regent defaults on its construction loan. See Report of the Subcommittee of Lender's Concerns When Reviewing Design and Construction Contracts, *The Role of Lender's Counsel in the Design and Construction Process: Contract Review, Conditional Assignments of Contracts, and Related Due Diligence*, 24 Real Prop., Prob. & Tr. J. 557, 563 (1990).

The language of AIA Document B101-2007 ¶ 7.1 is troubling: it has the Owner warranting that the architect is the copyright owner of the Instruments of Service. AIA Document B101-2007 ¶ 7.1 should be redrafted to include express representations and warranties by the architect, on its behalf and its consultants (see AIA Document B101-2007 ¶ 7.2) that the design does infringe on any copyright, and it should impose on the architect an obligation to indemnify and defend Regent against any infringement claims. Neither AIA Document B141-1987 nor AIA Document B101-2007 provides the owner with such protections.

3. Scope of services

As previously noted, AIA Document B141-1987 adopted a modular format that was divided into two parts: an "agreement form" in Article 1, consisting of project information, contractual terms and conditions, and compensation terms, and a "service form" in Article 2, that varied depending on the project. It was anticipated that multiple documents with varying scope of services to be performed by the architect would be published by AIA to be inserted as Article 2.

Article 2 of AIA Document B141-1987 and Article 3 of AIA Document B101-2007 both contemplate a standard scope of services divided into five phases: (1) the schematic design phase as described in AIA Document B101-2007 ¶ 3.2, (2) the design development phase as described in AIA Document B101-2007 ¶ 3.3, (3) the construction documents phase as described in AIA Document B101-2007 ¶ 3.4, (4) the bidding or negotiation phase as described in AIA Document B101-2007 ¶ 3.5, and (5) the construction administration phase as described in AIA Document B101-2007 ¶ 3.6. Apparently Regent is well versed in the intricacies of AIA Document B141-1987 and is comfortable with the scope of services described in that form.

I have one area of concern regarding the standard scope of services outlined in the AIA Document B141-1987 and AIA Document B101-2007: inspection by the architect. Both editions specify that the architect will visit the site in order to become familiar with the progress and quality of the work and to determine if the work is being performed in such a manner that the project will be completed in accordance with the contract documents (AIA Document B141-1987 ¶ 2.6.5 and AIA Document B101-2007 ¶ 3.6.2.1, the latter which also specifies that the architect is to endeavor to guard the owner against defects and deficiencies in the work). Apparently, many owners presume that this provision requires the architect to make detailed inspections and, as a result, shifts the risk liability for defective construction by the contractor onto the architect. See Paula Marcus, *Building a Construction Contract That Works: The Owner's Role*, 44 Arb. J. 3, 7 (1989); Justin Sweet and Jonathan J. Sweet, Sweet on Construction Industry Contracts § 5.13 (3d ed. 1996). However, both AIA Document B1411987 and AIA Document B101-2007 2007 attempt to exculpate the architect from responsibility for the method by which the design is executed and for any failure by the contractor to follow the design. Both AIA Document B141-1987 ¶ 2.6.5 and AIA Document B101-2007 ¶ 3.6.2.1 state that "the Architect shall not be required to make exhaustive or continuous on-site inspections to check the quality or quantity of the Work." See also Marcus, *supra* at 7; Sweet and Sweet, *supra* at § 5.13. If Regent expects the architect to provide greater inspection services during the construction process than called for under the agreement, modifications of the agreement are necessary.

4. "Additional services"

Article 3 of AIA Document B141-1987 provided that the architect would be compensated for "additional services" not included in the basic services specified in the form agreement or listed in Article 12 of AIA Document B141-1987. AIA Document B101-2007 continues to use the concept of additional services. [Ed note: AIA Document B141-1997 introduced the concept of "change of services," which greatly broadened the basis on which the architect could claim adjustment of the fee. AIA Document B101-2007 returns to "additional services," but in doing so continues the broader basis for fee adjustment.]

Regent should be aware, however, of the fact that "additional services" under AIA Document B101-2007 broadens the basis on which an architect may claim an adjustment of the fee. Article 4 of AIA Document B101-2007 is entitled "Additional Services" and provides for a broad array of services that may be performed by the architect for additional fees. Specifically, both as part of Article 4 and in other sections of the agreement, the architect can claim an adjustment of its architectural fee for:

a. According to AIA Document B101-2007 ¶ 1.3, any change to the detailed project information in AIA Document B101-2007 ¶ 1.1 (or the optional AIA Document B101-2007 Exhibit A);

b. AIA Document B101-2007 ¶ 4.1 includes a grid of Additional Services which can be designated as being the responsibility of the owner or the architect, or "not provided," and, if anticipated by the parties to be provided, should be described in AIA Document B101-2007 ¶ 4.2 or in an attached exhibit;

c. AIA Document B101-2007 ¶ 4.3.2 lists many services the architect may undertake for additional fee upon notifying the owner (and the owner is responsible for paying the architect's additional fee unless the owner gives "prompt written notice to the Architect"), including reviewing the contractor's submittals out of sequence (AIA Document B101-2007 ¶ 4.3.2.1) and responding to the contractor's request for information in many cases (AIA Document B101-2007 ¶ 4.3.2.2); and

d. Any of the changes in services provided in AIA Document B101-2007 ¶ 4.3.1.

Regent can avoid unanticipated contractual obligations for payment to MFH resulting from additional services by amending AIA Document B101-2007 in several respects. As mentioned before, Regent should make every attempt to assure that it provides accurate information AIA Document B101-2007 ¶ 1.1 (or the optional AIA Document B101-2007 Exhibit A). Second, Regent should closely consider AIA Document B101-2007 ¶ 4.3.2, and particularly consider deleting, or qualifying differently, the inclusion of the contractor's "request for information" as an "additional service." Third, Regent should thoroughly review AIA Document B101-2007 ¶¶ 4.1, 4.3.1 and 4.3.2 and Parts B through H of MFH's letter (which we recommend Regent incorporate into Article 2 of AIA Document B101-2007). In doing so, Regent should identify those services that it expects the basic architectural fee will cover. Finally, Regent should propose an amendment to AIA Document B101-2007 ¶ 4.3.2 to specify that it is not obligated to compensate the architect for any additional services except those that are pre-approved by the owner.

5. Waiver of consequential damages

AIA Document B101-2007 ¶ 8.1.3 includes a complete and mutual waiver of consequential damages by both the owner and architect [Ed. Note: as did the 1997 version]. Such provisions are generally enforceable against the owner. See, e.g., *Valhal Corp. v. Sullivan Assocs, Inc.*, 44 F.3d 195 (3d Cir. 1995) (enforcing liability limit of $50,000, even though the design professional failed to identify height restriction affecting the planned high-rise and the owner claimed over $2 million in damages). Shifting the risk of loss for consequential damages from the design professional to the owner when design defects are involved may result in reduced initial cost to the owner. See Kenneth M. Cushman & Joyce K. Hackenbrach, *Construction Project Risk Allocation: The Owner's Perspective*, 443 PLI/Real 7, 19 (1999). However, an owner who allows such a provision may be "penny wise and pound foolish," as such a provision will:

a. Expose the owner to significant costs arising from defective design of the facility, without allowing effective recourse to the design professional directly responsible for the defect;

b. Expose the owner to liability to the contractor for damages for its futile efforts to construct the defective design and for related delays, without effective recourse to the design professional; and

c. Create an environment where the design professional is less motivated to do a thorough job because the risk of legal repercussions is greatly diminished. *Id.*

Ultimately, Regent's decision to include or exclude such a waiver is a business decision. However, Regent exposes itself to significant risks if it includes such a provision.

6. Assignment to lenders

AIA Document B101-2007 ¶ 10.3 now recognizes the owner's right to assign the agreement with the architect to a lender. However, the agreement only allows assignment to the lender "if the lender agrees to assume the Owner's rights and obligations under this Agreement." This is potentially problematic because few lenders will agree to such an assumption before the fact. See Penny P. Cobey, *The New B141: An Owner's Manual*, Construction Forum News 2 (Jan. 1998). For this reason, Regent should seek to eliminate this provision.

The lender may also desire contractual flexibility to protect itself against the possibility of the borrower's default. The lender may insist that AIA Document B101-2007 ¶ 10.3 be amended in order to allow it to assign its rights under the design contract to a third party in a workout situation. See Report of the Subcommittee of Lender's Concerns When Reviewing Design and Construction Contracts, *supra* at 566.

7. Termination for convenience

AIA Document B101-2007 ¶ 9.5 provides that the owner may terminate the agreement for convenience and without cause. However, AIA Document B101-2007 ¶ 9.7 provides that, in such cases, the owner will compensate the architect for all lost profits on services not performed. Significantly, AIA Document B101-2007 does not include the percentage-based formula for determining termination expenses that existed in earlier versions of B141. *Id.* It is advisable that Regent propose that the new termination clause be retained because of the flexibility that it provides and delete the lost-profit clause or otherwise provide for liquidated damages in the case of owner termination. This should be acceptable to MFH under paragraph K.3 of its letter to Regent.

8. Free redesign

Unlike AIA Document B141-1987, AIA Document B101-2007 provides a free redesign provision. Under AIA Document B101-2007 ¶ 6.7, if the bids received from general contractors exceed the anticipated construction budget, the architect now must revise the documents without additional charge in order to generate bids that come within budget. However, Regent should note that AIA Document B101-2007 ¶ 6.3 gives the architect unilateral control over the "materials, equipment, component systems and types of construction" to be included in the contract documents, as well as the ability to make "reasonable" unilateral adjustments in project scope. Regent should amend this provision in order to give itself more control over the redesign process.

9. Increased compensation for construction administration

AIA Document B101-2007 ¶ 4.3.3 includes a construction administration provision which invites the parties to place specific numeric limits on reviews of each submittal, visits to the site during construction administration, punch list inspections, and final completion inspections. One author labels the effect of this provision as "nickel and diming" the owner, and suggests that the owners refuse to agree to specific limits and simply insert the word "reasonable" throughout. Cobey, *supra* at 4. It is also advisable that the agreement provide defined periods within which shop drawings and other submittals must be reviewed and approved or rejected by the architect as well as specific contractual provisions specifying the frequency with which the architects and its consultants will visit the project.

10. Necessary additions to AIA Document B101-2007

Regent should propose several additions to the agreement with the architect that address issues not adequately treated in AIA Document B101-2007. First, it should propose language addressing the architect's standard of care in performing the design services and requiring that the architect comply with applicable laws and codes in providing professional services. For the first time, AIA Document B101-2007 ¶ 2.2 includes a basic statement of the architect's standard of care. However, as to complying with laws, codes and regulations, AIA Document B101-2007 ¶ 3.1.5 only requires that the architect "at appropriate times" contact entities that must approve construction documents or provide utility services and that "the Architect shall respond to applicable design requirements imposed by such governmental authorities and by such entities providing utility services," and AIA Document B101-2007 ¶ 3.4.2 states: "The Architect shall incorporate into the Construction Documents the design requirements of governmental authorities having jurisdiction over the Project." Unfortunately, many of the provisions in the AIA documents "generally benefit the architect or serve to diminish the architect's responsibilities." Lord, *Five Things Every Attorney Should Consider Before Approving Construction Contracts for Owners, Developers or Lenders*, 7 The Constr. Law. 5 (Jan. 1987). See also Cobey, *supra* at 4. Regent may also want to include in the provision describing the standard of care an unequivocal allocation of responsibility on the part of the architect for the drawings and specifications and for the content of the work contained in the drawings and specifications. See Report of the Subcommittee of Lender's Concerns When Reviewing Design and Construction Contracts, *supra* at 566.

Second, Regent should propose that an indemnification clause, requiring that the architect indemnify the owner against all claims arising out of professional errors and omissions, be included in the agreement. Finally, for the first time AIA Document B101-2007 ¶ 2.5 requires the architect to maintain insurance, but potentially at the owner's expense and without any requirement for the periods such insurance must remain in effect; Regent may want to modify the insurance requirement as to who bears the cost and adding stipulations regarding length of coverage and the naming of the owner as an additional insured.

[d] Notes on Architect's Design Responsibilities

1. *Housing and Building Codes.* Part of the professional responsibility of the architect in the design process is to ensure that the project will satisfy applicable housing and building codes. *See, e.g., Insurance Co. of North America v. G.M.R., Ltd.*, 499 A.2d 878 (D.C. App. 1985) (architectural firm negligent in not satisfying building code requirements of temporary shoring or bracing during demolition); *Greenhaven Corp. v. Hutchcraft & Associates*, 463 N.E.2d 283 (Ind. Ct. App. 1984) ("if the architect knows the place where it is intended to erect the building he must know the building restrictions of that particular place and must draw the plans and specifications accordingly or else forfeit his right of recovery for his services," quoting 6 C.J.S. Architects § 31 (1975)); *St. Joseph Hospital v. Corbetta Construction Co.*, 316 N.E.2d 51 (Ill. App. Ct. 1974) (architect found liable for damages resulting from use of materials that did not comply with the requirements of the building code); *Mississippi Meadows, Inc. v. Hodson*, 299 N.E.2d 359 (Ill. App. Ct. 1973) (although plaintiff's

evidence insufficient to prove liability, architect may be liable where plans and specifications did not satisfy building code requirements). According to Professor Sweet, "[f]ailure to design in accordance with [applicable building and housing] codes is almost always considered to violate the obligation the design professional owes to her client." J. SWEET, LEGAL ASPECTS OF ARCHITECTURE, ENGINEERING AND CONSTRUCTION PROCESS § 14.05C (6th ed. 2000). As stated by Sam in his memo to Donna, AIA Document B101-2007 ¶ 3.1.5 only requires that the architect "at appropriate times" contact entities that must approve construction documents or provide utility services and that "the Architect shall respond to applicable design requirements imposed by such governmental authorities and by such entities providing utility services," and AIA Document B101-2007 ¶ 3.4.2 states: "The Architect shall incorporate into the Construction Documents the design requirements of governmental authorities having jurisdiction over the Project."

Unfortunately, housing and building codes, which frequently contain design specifications, performance standards, or a combination of the two, "are often difficult to understand and are subject to uneven if not whimsical interpretation." *Id.* Ambiguities in the interpretation of the building code may be resolved through discussions with the local enforcement authority. In *Edward J. Seibert, A.I.A., Architect and Planner, P.A. v. Bayport Beach and Tennis Club Association, Inc.*, 573 So. 2d 889 (Fla. Dist. Ct. App. 1999), the court considered a jury verdict holding an architect liable for failing to design the exits in a residential condominium building in accordance with the applicable building code despite the fact that the design received a building permit after review by the city's chief building inspector who was also the chief code enforcement officer. The jury reached this conclusion based on expert testimony received at trial concerning the interpretation of the applicable code provisions. The appellate court reversed the jury verdict, concluding that the interpretation of the code provision was a question of law, not fact, and that the trial court should have deferred to the interpretation of the enforcement agency where that interpretation was not clearly erroneous.

2. *Americans With Disabilities Act.* Although most building and housing codes are enacted at the state or local level, the Americans with Disabilities Act, 42 U.S.C. §§ 12101 et seq., has created in some ways a type of national building code. The ADA specifically requires that "public accommodations and commercial facilities" constructed after January 26, 1992, be

> readily accessible to and usable by individuals with disabilities, except where an entity can demonstrate that it is structurally impracticable to meet the requirements of . . . standards set forth or incorporated by reference in regulations issued under this subchapter. . . . 42 U.S.C. § 12183(a)(1).

In addition, alterations to an existing facility are to be made accessible "to the maximum extent feasible." 42 U.S.C. § 12183(a)(2). Where alterations are made, the "path of travel" from the altered area to bathrooms, telephones, and drinking fountains serving the altered area are also to be made accessible, provided the additional work required is "not disproportionate to the overall alterations in terms of cost and scope." Furthermore, public accommodations are required to remove existing architectural barriers "where such removal is readily achievable." 42 U.S.C. § 12182(b)(2)(A)(iv).

The definitions of "public accommodations" and "commercial facilities" are expansive and include virtually all nonresidential uses. The following is the definition of "commercial facilities" as contained in 42 U.S.C. § 12181(2):

> The term "commercial facilities" means facilities —
>
> (A) that are intended for nonresidential use; and
>
> (B) whose operations will affect commerce.

The following is the definition of public accommodations as contained in 42 U.S.C. § 12181(7):

> (7) Public accommodation. The following private entities are considered public accommodations for purposes of this title [42 USCS §§ 12181 et seq.], if the operations of such entities affect commerce —
>
> (A) an inn, hotel, motel, or other place of lodging, except for an establishment located within a building that contains not more than five rooms for rent or hire and that is actually occupied by the proprietor of such establishment as the residence of such proprietor;
>
> (B) a restaurant, bar, or other establishment serving food or drink;
>
> (C) a motion picture house, theater, concert hall, stadium, or other place of exhibition or entertainment;
>
> (D) an auditorium, convention center, lecture hall, or other place of public gathering;
>
> (E) a bakery, grocery store, clothing store, hardware store, shopping center, or other sales or rental establishment;
>
> (F) a laundromat, dry-cleaner, bank, barber shop, beauty shop, travel service, shoe repair service, funeral parlor, gas station, office of an accountant or lawyer, pharmacy, insurance office, professional office of a health care provider, hospital, or other service establishment;
>
> (G) a terminal, depot, or other station used for specified public transportation;
>
> (H) a museum, library, gallery, or other place of public display or collection;
>
> (I) a park, zoo, amusement park, or other place of recreation;
>
> (J) a nursery, elementary, secondary, undergraduate, or postgraduate private school, or other place of education;
>
> (K) a day care center, senior citizen center, homeless shelter, food bank, adoption agency, or other social service center establishment; and
>
> (L) a gymnasium, health spa, bowling alley, golf course, or other

place of exercise or recreation.

For a discussion of the cases that have addressed what is a public accommodation or commercial facility, see 136 A.L.R. Fed. 1 (1997). The following are examples of uses deemed to be places of public accommodation under these cases: dentist's office, dental care facility, hospital, theater where musical entertainment is performed, insurance office, doctor's medical office, school, private law school, private school for adolescents, group day care center, department store and movie theater. *Id.* Although the statute appears to exclude only residential uses (other than places of lodging) from the definition of a public accomodation, one court held that a commissary, studio store, and automatic teller machine located on a movie studio's production lot were not "public accommodations" subject to the ADA, even if they fell within the ADA's listed categories of private entities that would be considered public accommodations, because the lot was not open to the public but was restricted to employees and their authorized business guests. *Jankey v. Twentieth Century Fox Film Corp.*, 212 F.3d 1159 (9th Cir. 2000). In light of *Jankey*, how do you think a warehouse would be treated when the only user of the warehouse is a company and its employees?

A tax credit is available to eligible small businesses for expenditures incurred to comply with the requirements of the ADA, including expenditures "for the purpose of removing architectural, communication, physical, or transportation barriers which prevent businesses from being accessible to, or usable by, individuals with disabilities. . . ." 26 U.S.C. § 44(c). The credit is not available, however, for expenditures incurred in connection with new construction.

In addition to the ADA, many states have enacted their own statutory provisions, similar to the ADA, which impose accessibility requirements under existing building codes. Upon the request of a state or locality, the U.S. Attorney General can certify that the building code of the state or locality satisfies the requirements of the ADA, in which case compliance with the building code is rebuttable evidence of compliance with the ADA. 42 U.S.C. § 12188(b)(1)(A)(ii). Finally, the scope of ADA requirements has been the subject of judicial decisions. *See, e.g., Long v. Coast Resorts, Inc.*, 32 F. Supp. 2d 1203 (D. Nev. 1998); *Jankey v. Twentieth Century Fox Film Corp.*, 14 F. Supp. 2d 1174 (C.D. Cal. 1998); *Independent Living Resources v. Oregon Arena Corp.*, 1 F. Supp. 2d 1159 (D. Or. 1998); *United States v. Days Inns of America, Inc.*, 997 F. Supp. 1080 (C.D. Ill. 1998).

Typically, an owner will look to the architect to ensure that the project will comply with all state and federal requirements regarding accessibility. Unlike building code compliance, however, no entity exists to review and approve a design as complying with the requirements of the ADA if the state or local building code has not been certified by the attorney general. This risk has created a market for design professionals who specialize in accessibility issues and compliance. *See* J. SWEET, LEGAL ASPECTS OF ARCHITECTURE, ENGINEERING AND CONSTRUCTION PROCESS § 14.05C (6th ed. 2000).

3. *Potential Catastrophe Averted.* Although design defects and the efforts to correct them seldom make for high drama, the discovery by William J. LeMessurier of a design defect in the structure of the 59-story CitiCorp Center on Lexington Avenue in Manhattan is one exception. LeMessurier, one of the nation's leading structural engineers, had served as the structural consultant in the construction of CitiCorp Center. In 1978, a year after the building's completion, LeMessurier happened to determine that overlooked quartering winds coupled with bolted, rather than welded, joints presented an unacceptable possibility of catastrophic failure in extreme weather. What LeMessurier did and how the defect was corrected is the subject of Joe Morgenstern, *The Fifty-Nine Story Crisis*, THE NEW YORKER 45 (May 29, 1995). As the hurricane season on the East Coast arrived, construction workers ripped open interior walls to reveal the structural steel of the building while metal workers set to work welding two-inch-thick steel plates over each of more than two hundred bolted joints. CitiCorp "brought in drywall crews and carpenters to work from 5 P.M. to 8 A.M., putting up plywood enclosures around the chevrons and tearing Sheetrock; welders to weld from 8 P.M. until 4 A.M., with the building's fire-alarm system shut off; and then laborers to clean up the epic mess before the first secretaries arrived." Depending on who one asked, repair costs ranged from $4.3 to $8 million. In the end, CitiCorp agreed to a $2 million settlement from LeMessurier's liability insurer.

[e] Questions

1. Architects are typically compensated based on a percentage of the construction cost of the project. *See generally* SWEET, SWEET ON CONSTRUCTION LAW § 2.8 (1997). Critics contend, however, that this approach provides the architect with no incentive to control costs. As a result, owners might use a sliding scale under which the percentage fee would decrease if the construction cost exceeds certain benchmarks. In addition, architects might be paid on a cost-based fee arrangement under which the fee is computed as a multiple of personnel expenses or as a flat fee plus personnel expenses. Finally, the architect might receive only a flat fee regardless of the cost of construction or personnel expenses. What are the relative advantages and disadvantages of each payment method? What approach does the AIA Document B101-2007 adopt? *See* AIA Document B101-2007 ¶ 11.1. The architect's fee will typically be calculated independently of certain reimbursable expenses which the owner is obligated to pay. *See* AIA Document B101-2007 ¶ 11.8. What does MFH propose to Regent?

2. What role does the architect have in ensuring that the project complies with all applicable laws and regulations, including zoning ordinances, housing codes, and local, state, or federal environmental laws? *See* AIA Document B101-2007 ¶¶ 3.1.5, 3.4.2, 5.7, and 5.8. What obligation does the architect have to undertake design changes without additional compensation in the event of statutory or regulatory changes? *See* AIA Document B101-2007 ¶ 4.3.1.

3. What obligation does the architect undertake to complete each of the phases in the design process? *See* AIA Document B101-2007 ¶¶ 1.2, 2.2, 3.1.3, and 4.3.4. What is the architect's liability if construction documents are not available on schedule? *See* AIA Document B101-2007 ¶ 8.1.3. To what extent might the architect be able to claim that delay in the completion of the construction documents was due to delay by the owner in the approval of the design or as a result of changes initiated by the owner? *See* AIA Document B101-2007 ¶ 4.3.1.

4. If the owner is unable to secure financing for the project or otherwise decides that the project cannot move forward, what rights does the owner have to terminate the agreement with the architect? Under what circumstances may the architect terminate the agreement? What are the consequences of termination for either the owner or architect? *See* Article 9 of AIA Document B101-2007.

5. What obligation does the architect have to engage in "value engineering"? Value engineering is a process under which the owner, the architect, and perhaps other consultants review the construction documents to determine if construction costs can be saved without adversely affecting the quality of the project. In some instances, the quality of the project may even be improved and construction costs saved at the same time. *See* AIA Document B101-2007 ¶ 3.2.5.2.

6. In another direction, the architect also must present to the owner "the feasibility of incorporating environmentally responsible design approaches." AIA Document B101-2007 ¶ 3.2.3. *See also* AIA Document B101-2007 ¶ 3.2.5.1.

[f] Problem

As would most any young associate, Sam probably felt pretty good when he got his memo to Donna about the MFH proposal off his desk. And, like most any young associate, he was taken aback when Donna's next memo came in. Read through Donna's latest memo and draft Sam's response.

MEMORANDUM

TO: Samuel Nader

FROM: Donna Smith

RE: Regent-MFH Architectural Services Agreement Memo

Thanks for your memo. You were very thorough in your approach, and I particularly appreciated some of your insights into how the AIA Document B101-2007 has some provisions with which the people at Regent likely are not familiar. As a start, your memo is a good piece of work.

But it is just a start. You made several suggestions that changes should be made, but you left it to me to draft the changes. I understand your reluctance to step up and draft those changes because you don't want to waste Regent's money in the event I might disagree with your suggestion and not feel the change is worth making. I am going to tell you what I think is worth changing in this memo, but in the future I would like for you to draft those changes you are confident should be made. I trust your judgment, and you should be willing to risk my criticism.

Please do the following (the numbers correspond to the numbers in your memo):

2. Please draft the language for all three of your points.
3. Regent would like for MFH to make periodic inspections during and at the end of construction (I think we could put in four at this point and then let Regent add or subtract from that) as part of the basic fee agreement and not be subject to MFH's claim for "additional services." Please draft the language necessary to implement this and also to define the nature of the inspections.
4. See my first point in "3." above. Second, please draft the language to implement your suggestions in the second and last points in the last paragraph of this section.
6. You make several good points. FMB is going to want the ability to get the plans, and it is going to want to be able to assign them if there is a default. Please draft language that would do this.
10. All of your suggestions are good. Please draft the necessary changes.

Thanks.

§ 13.03 OWNER/GENERAL CONTRACTOR AGREEMENT

[1] Overview

Under the Design-Award-Build (D-A-B) approach, the general contractor is the principal actor during the construction phase of the project. As previously described, the fee paid to the general contractor for its construction services may be based on a lump sum or fixed price, a percentage of the construction costs, or a percentage of the construction costs with a guaranteed maximum price. As described in the article by John Macomber in Chapter 12, the selection of the fee structure should depend on the risks inherent in the type of project involved.

In a manner similar to that of the owner and the architect, the legal relationship between the owner and the general contractor will be defined under the terms of the construction contract, and, again, typically the AIA form contracts are used. AIA Document A201-2007, General Conditions of the Contract for Construction, details the rights and responsibilities of the owner and general contractor during all phases of the construction process. AIA Document A201-2007 is typically used in conjunction with another AIA standard form agreement, one which is intended to detail the commencement and substantial completion dates for the project, as well as the contract price and method of payment during the construction process. AIA Document A101-2007, Standard Form of Agreement Between Owner and Contractor, is one such agreement and provides for payment to the general contractor as a stipulated sum. AIA Document A101-2007, and AIA Document A201-2007 are in the Document Book. In addition to AIA Document A101-2007, other agreements may be used with AIA Document A201-2007: AIA Document A102-2007 provides for payment to the general contractor on a cost plus fee basis as well as a guaranteed maximum price; AIA Document A103-2007 provides for payment to the general contractor on a cost plus fee basis with no guaranteed maximum price; AIA Document A105-2007 is intended for use in residential or small commercial projects; and AIA Document A107-2007 is intended for use for projects of "limited scope."

Even a cursory examination of Document A201-2007 will show that the legal relationship between the owner and general contractor is a complicated one; the agreement itself is 30 pages long excluding the eight page index! Consequently, the resolution of a legal conflict between the owner and general contractor often requires that a number of provisions be interpreted in concert with each other. The provisions contained in the General Conditions are also coordinated with the terms contained in the agreement between the owner and architect under AIA Document B101-2007 and with the terms contained in the agreements between the general contractor and subcontractors under AIA Document A401-2007. Where controversies arise involving the architect or subcontractors, the terms of each of these contracts must be consulted. The integrated nature of the AIA Documents helps to ensure that overlaps and gaps among the obligations and responsibilities of the various parties in the construction process do not occur. However, the use of these form contracts also requires that changes made in one contract be coordinated with changes in the other contracts where appropriate.

Importantly, the General Conditions provide that the general contractor is the party responsible for overall supervision and direction of the construction work. As stated in AIA Document A201-2007 ¶ 3.3.1:

> The Contractor shall supervise and direct the Work, using the Contractor's best skill and attention. The Contractor shall be solely responsible for, and have control over, construction means, methods, techniques, sequences and procedures for coordinating all portions of the Work under the Contract, unless the Contract Documents give other specific instructions concerning these matters.

In addition, this paragraph provides that the general contractor is "fully and solely responsible for jobsite safety. . . ." AIA Document A201-2007 ¶ 3.3.2 makes the general contractor responsible for acts or omissions of the general contractor's employees, the subcontractors and their agents and employees, and any other persons performing work on behalf of the general contractor. In order to fulfill these obligations, the general contractor is required to have a competent superintendent and necessary assistants on the construction site to supervise and direct the construction work (AIA Document A201-2007 ¶ 3.9.1). The General Conditions also provide that the general contractor will indemnify the owner and architect against any claims, damages, or losses caused by the negligence of the general contractor, a subcontractor, or their employees or agents arising out of or resulting from the performance of the work (AIA Document A201-2007 ¶ 3.18.1).

One of the general contractor's principal responsibilities following the awarding of the construction contract is to prepare and submit to the owner and architect a schedule for the construction of the project (AIA Document A201-2007 ¶ 3.10.1). This schedule must provide and allow adequate time for the architect to review submittals from the general contractor in the form of shop drawings, product data, and samples. The importance of these submittals will be discussed below. This schedule will serve to coordinate the activities of the owner, the architect, the general contractor, and the subcontractors throughout the construction process. Deviations from the schedule may give rise to liability for the party causing the delay, although adjustments can be made to the schedule through change orders and construction change directives.

Although the general contractor is in control of the construction site, the architect retains a central role in the construction process. The terms of the General Conditions provide that the architect will act as the owner's representative on the construction site (AIA Document A201-2007 ¶ 4.2.1). The general contractor is obligated to provide the architect with access to the construction work in progress wherever located on the site to perform this function (AIA Document A201-2007 ¶ 3.16.1). In addition, the owner and contractor agree to communicate with each other through the architect in connection with matters "arising out of or relating to the Contract" (AIA Document A201-2007 ¶ 4.2.4).

As mentioned earlier in the discussion of the architect's role in the construction process, the architect has three principal functions during the construction process. First, the architect will visit the construction site to ensure that the work is completed in accordance with the construction documents (AIA Document A201-2007 ¶ 4.2.2). In this role, the architect has the authority to reject work that does not conform to the construction documents (AIA Document A201-2007 ¶ 4.2.6), and the general contractor has the responsibility to see that the work is corrected at the general contractor's expense (AIA Document A201-2007 ¶ 12.2.1). Second, the architect will review and approve submittals from the general contractor in the form of shop drawings, product data, and samples (AIA Document A201-2007 ¶ 4.2.7). Shop drawings are defined as "drawings, diagrams, schedules and other data specifically prepared for the Work by the Contractor or a Subcontractor, Sub-subcontractor, manufacturer, supplier or distributor to illustrate some portion of the Work" (AIA Document A201-2007 ¶ 3.12.1). Product data includes "illustrations, standard schedules, performance charts, instructions, brochures, diagrams and other information furnished by the Contractor to illustrate materials or equipment for some portion of the Work" (AIA Document A201-2007 ¶ 3.12.2). Finally, samples are "physical examples which illustrate materials, equipment or workmanship and establish standards by which the Work will be judged" (AIA Document A201-2007 ¶ 3.12.3). Shop drawings, product data and samples serve to further define the quality of the construction work or define how the construction work will be completed in conformance with the construction documents. Third, the architect will review and approve applications from the general contractor for periodic payments and for final payment when the construction work is substantially complete (AIA Document A201-2007 ¶¶ 4.2.5, 4.2.9, and 9.3). Although the architect plays a central role in the evaluation of the construction work, the General Conditions attempt to exonerate the architect from any liability that this role may otherwise entail.

The architect is also a central party in the preparation of change orders and construction change directives (AIA Document A201-2007 ¶ 4.2.8). Change orders and construction change directives implement changes to the construction project and serve to amend the construction documents (AIA Document A201-2007 ¶ 7.1.1). Change orders reflect an agreement among the owner, architect, and general contractor to change the construction documents, typically as a result of a design change, which may entail a change in the fee owed the general contractor or an adjustment in the schedule, or both (AIA Document A201-2007 ¶ 7.2.1). A construction change directive, on the other hand, is a written order by the owner and architect to modify the construction documents prior to an agreement with the general contractor concerning an adjustment in the general contractor's fee or the construction schedule (AIA Document A201-2007 ¶ 7.3.1). Where a construction change directive is used, the architect will determine any appropriate adjustments to the general contractor's fee or the construction schedule (AIA Document A201-2007 ¶ 7.3.7). The general contractor can then bring a claim for an adjustment to its fee or to the construction schedule (AIA Document A201-2007 ¶ 15.1).

In the absence of serious conflict between the owner and the general contractor or any unanticipated problems with the weather, subcontractors, suppliers, or laborers, construction should move forward in accordance with the construction schedule. Eventually, the general contractor will consider that the project is substantially complete, which, under the General Conditions, means that the work has been completed in accordance with the construction documents and is ready for the owner to "occupy or utilize . . . for its intended use" (AIA Document A201-2007 ¶ 9.8.1). At this point, the architect will inspect the work to determine if it is substantially complete (AIA Document A201-2007 ¶ 9.8.3 and ¶ 9.8.4). Although the architect may certify to the owner that the work is substantially complete, the general contractor will also typically prepare, and the architect will attached to the certificate of substantial completion, a so-called "punch list," a list of additional items that remain to be completed or defects to be corrected, along with a date by which these items are to be finished (AIA Document A201-2007 ¶ 9.8.4). The certificate of substantial completion will also establish the responsibilities of the owner and the general contractor for "security, heat, utilities, damage to the Work, and insurance" for this transition period. Upon receipt and acceptance of the certificate of substantial completion, the owner will pay the general contractor for the work completed, including retainage (AIA Document A201-2007 ¶ 9.8.5). Final payment to the general contractor will await a subsequent application for final payment by the general contractor and a final inspection and certification by the architect that all work has been completed as required under the construction documents (AIA Document A201-2007 ¶ 9.8.10).

As the previous discussion indicates, the rights and responsibilities of the owner and the general contractor are based on the specific terms of the construction contract. Because the terms of various construction contracts differ, the relationship between the owner and general contractor will differ depending on the contract used. Consequently, a detailed review of the construction contract is necessary to resolve any legal question concerning this relationship.

The relationship between the owner and general contractor described above is based on AIA Document A201-2007, which was significantly revised in 1997 and 2007. One of the major changes in the 1997 edition was the requirement that the parties engage in mediation as a condition precedent to arbitration of any disputes, and this change was carried over to the 2007 edition. This requirement is contained in AIA Document A201-2007 ¶ 15.3.1 which states:

> Claims, disputes, or other matters in controversy arising out of or related to the Contract [with certain exceptions] shall be subject to mediation as a condition precedent to binding dispute resolution.

Prior to the 1997 revisions, disputes between the owner and general contractor were referred first to the architect and then, if one or more of the parties still was dissatisfied, went directly to arbitration. Judicial "suggestion" and recent changes in dispute resolution methodology inspired the addition of mediation. The provision requiring mediation in Document A201-2007 is not without its critics: "Owners who prefer to reserve their options depending on the nature of the dispute at hand may wish to strike this paragraph. Certainly no owner would want to agree by contract to mediate third-party claims or multi-party claims in which other parties have not agreed to mediation." Cobey, *The New B141: An Owner's Manual*, CONSTR. FORUM NEWS 3 (Jan. 1998).

As noted before as a major change in the 2007 AIA documents, AIA Document A201-2007 also provides for possibility that the owner and contractor have designated as Initial Decision Maker a third party other than the architect (AIA Document A201-2007 ¶ 15.2.1). Article 6 of AIA Document A101-2007 provides space for the owner and contractor to identify the name, address and other contact information for a third party Initial Decision Maker (AIA Document A101-2007 ¶ 6.1). Another major change, also noted before, is that litigation is now the default method of binding dispute resolution, but AIA Document A101-2007 also provides a check the box for the parties to choose arbitration or another form of dispute resolution, to be identified by the parties (AIA Document A101-2007 ¶ 6.2).

Another significant change under the 1997 and 2007 revisions of AIA Document A201-2007 is the design delegation provision (AIA Document A201-2007 ¶ 3.12.10). The 1987 version of Document A201 provided little guidance concerning the conditions under which the architect or other design professional could delegate design responsibility to the general contractor. This absence of guidance resulted in blurred lines of responsibility, authority, and liability when construction defects were discovered. Under the 1997 and 2007 versions, the general contractor is not required to provide either architectural or engineering design services unless the construction contract specifically provides otherwise or the services are necessary for the general contractor to carry out the contractor's obligations to determine construction means or methods (AIA Document A201-2007 ¶ 3.12.10). If the contractor is obligated to provide design services, the owner and architect must specify the performance and design criteria that the services must satisfy (AIA Document A201-2007 ¶ 3.12.10). The contractor must then obtain the design services of a licensed professional, who must sign and seal all drawings, calculations, specifications, certifications, shop drawings, or other submittals. If this procedure is followed, the general contractor will be liable for a design defect only if he fails to satisfy the performance or design criteria established by the owner and architect. For further discussion of the design delegation issue, see Potter, *Design Delegation Provisions of AIA Document A201, 1997 Edition*, 18 THE CONSTRUCTION LAW. 27 (July 1998).

Perhaps the most dramatic change in the 1997 and 2007 versions of AIA Document A201-2007, however, is the provision for the mutual waiver of consequential damages (AIA Document A201-2007 ¶ 15.1.6):

> Claims for Consequential Damages. The Contractor and Owner waive claims against each other for consequential damages arising out of or relating to this Contract. This mutual waiver includes:
>
> 1. damages incurred by the Owner for rental expenses, for losses of use, income, profit, financing, business and reputation, and for loss of management or employee productivity or of the services of such persons; and
>
> 2. damages incurred by the Contractor for principal office expenses including the compensation of personnel stationed there, for losses of financing, business and reputation, and for loss of profit except anticipated profit arising directly from the Work.
>
> This mutual waiver is applicable, without limitation, to all consequential damages due to either party's termination in accordance with Article 14 [Termination or Suspension of the Contract. — Eds.]. Nothing contained in this Subparagraph 15.1.6 shall be deemed to preclude an award of liquidated direct damages, when applicable, in accordance with the requirements of the Contract Documents.

The primary reason for adopting a mutual waiver of consequential damages was "to keep claims from taking over [projects]." Shea, *Process of Change: Conceptual Changes to AIA Documents A201, B141, and Beyond*, 9, *in* AIA CONTRACT DOCUMENTS: GENERATION NEXT (1997). For further discussion of this issue, see Ernstrom and Dehmler, *Mutual Waiver of Consequential Damages: The Contractor's Perspective*, 18 THE CONSTRUCTION LAW. 4 (Jan. 1998); Alexroth, *Mutual Waiver of Consequential Damages: The Owner's Perspective*, 18 THE CONSTRUCTION LAW. 11 (Jan. 1998).

A contractor's liability for consequential damages to the owner may frequently be significantly higher than any fee that the contractor would have earned on the project. For example, in *Perini Corp. v. Greate Bay Hotel and Casino, Inc.*, 610 A.2d 364 (N.J. 1992), the New Jersey Supreme Court upheld the $14.5 million award of an arbitrator against the general contractor which represented damages in the form of lost profits to the owner. Perini's fee for the work undertaken was only $600,000. Decisions such as the one in *Perini* may have served as the impetus for the waiver of consequential damages provision under the revised AIA documents. The opinion of the New Jersey Supreme Court, which follows, remains important, as it illustrates not only the court's view of the contractual terms imposing liability against the general contractor but also the court's attitude toward arbitration awards in the construction context.

[2] Contractor Liability for Delay

Delay, whether caused by the owner, the architect, the general contractor, or a subcontractor, can have devastating implications in the construction setting. The numerous parties on a construction site, all with their various, and overlapping, contractual responsibilities, can create difficulties in determining the exact scope of legal liability for delay even when the exact cause of delay can be determined as a factual matter. For a discussion of the liability and causation issues that are inevitably encountered when delay arises in the construction context, see Oles, *The Inexact Science of Delay Analysis*, 17 The Construction Law. 3 (Oct. 1997); Strogatz, Taylor & Craig, *Pricing the Delay: Whom Do I Sue and What Do I Get*, 17 The Construction Law. 4 (Oct. 1997); Kutil & Ness, *Concurrent Delay: The Challenge to Unravel Competing Causes of Delay*, 17 The Construction Law. 18 (Oct. 1997).

[a] Extent of Contractor Liability

When causation and liability can be established, the scope of damages must still be determined under the terms of the construction agreement. The following case addresses these issues.

PERINI CORPORATION v. GREATE BAY HOTEL & CASINO, INC.

129 N.J. 479, 610 A.2d 364 (1992)

O'Hern, J.

This appeal concerns the extent to which a court may invalidate an arbitration panel's award that was allegedly based on a mistaken determination of law. The issue arises in the context of a construction-management contract for an Atlantic City hotel and casino. The principal errors of law asserted are that the arbitrators (1) failed to observe settled principles of contract law by awarding damages that were not in the contemplation of the parties at the date of the contract and (2) awarded damages for lost profits after the date on which the project was substantially completed. We find that the asserted errors of law were not so gross, unmistakable, or in manifest disregard of the applicable law as to warrant judicial invalidation of the award.

I

The matter arises out of a 1983 construction-management contract entered into by plaintiff, Perini Corporation (Perini), and defendant, Greate Bay Hotel & Casino, Inc., trading as Sands Hotel & Casino (Sands). For purposes of this appeal, we adopt generally the version of the facts set forth in Perini's supplemental brief to this Court.

In 1981, Sands's parent company purchased the Brighton Hotel. The Brighton had experienced steadily-declining revenues for several years before Sands purchased it. Sands, however, was able to reverse that trend, making an $8,000,000 profit during its first year of operation. The Brighton's financial troubles had stemmed from several factors: (1) the hotel was a full block from the boardwalk; (2)

there was no entrance visible from the boardwalk; and (3) the company had a poor marketing strategy. Sands realized that in order to increase its revenues, it had to draw a significant number of patrons from the boardwalk.

To achieve that goal, Sands decided to undertake major renovations. On July 21, 1983, it entered into a construction-management agreement with Perini for a partial renovation of the hotel and casino. Under the terms of the agreement, Perini's responsibilities as construction manager were to coordinate with the owner and the owner's architect, supervise the trade contractors, and set a guaranteed maximum price for the project (originally $16,800,000) in exchange for a $600,000 fee plus reimbursement for actual expenses. If the cost of the project exceeded $20,000,000, Perini would be entitled to 4% of the project costs over $20,000,000 in addition to the agreed upon fee. The hotel and casino were continuously open and operating throughout the partial-renovation project.

The project had several component parts: (1) expansion of the existing casino gaming area; (2) creation of a new food court; (3) renovation of the nineteenth and twentieth floors and the addition of a new twenty-first floor to house an executive plaza club and seven luxury "high-roller" suites; (4) creation of an additional entrance at the southeast corner of the building (the new park entrance); and (5) the creation of a $400,000 ornamental, non-functional glass facade located outside of the east wall, which faces the boardwalk. Sands described the latter as a "new glitzy glass facade on the east side of the building which might act as a magnet to lure a new category of customers — strollers who might leave the boardwalk and walk the long block from the beach to the Sands."

The contract contained no completion date and no "time-of-the-essence" clause. At the time the parties entered into the contract, the owner's architect had not completed the plans, drawings, and specifications. Sands concedes that it would have been impossible to fix a completion date at the date of contracting; thus, the contract provided that "[a]t the time a [g]uaranteed [m]aximum [p]rice is established, * * * a [d]ate of [s]ubstantial [c]ompletion of the [p]roject shall also be established."

The contract defines "substantial completion" as "the date when construction is sufficiently complete * * * so the [o]wner can occupy or utilize the [p]roject or designated portion thereof for the use for which it is intended." Perini asserts that "substantial completion" is a term of art in the construction industry with uniformly-understood significance related to performance, warranties, payment, and damages. Most significantly, it asserts that under prevailing law no damages for delay may be awarded after substantial completion.

As noted previously, the contract did not contain a completion date because that date was to be fixed at the time that a guaranteed maximum price was established. However, when the guaranteed maximum price was set (originally at $16,800,000 and later increased to $24,000,000), a substantial completion date had not been placed in the contract.

Sands contends that the parties did agree ultimately to May 31, 1984, as the substantial completion date for the project. The record before the Court shows that the contractual completion dates submitted to the New Jersey Casino Control Commission required substantial completion of the project's three main components (the expansion of the casino, the construction of seven "high-roller" suites, and the new park entrance) on or before June 1, 1984. Significantly, Sands informed Perini that it would postpone the project until 1985 were Perini unable to complete the project before the start of the summer season.

Perini argues that the entire project and various portions thereof reached substantial completion, as defined in the contract, as follows: casino and food court, April 17, 1984; new park entrance and facade, August 31, 1984; suites, September 14, 1984; and the entire project, September 14, 1984. Perini contends that no one disputes that the revenue-producing portions of the work — the expanded casino gaming area and the food courts — were open and operational before Memorial Day and that Perini was entitled to an excusable extension of the completion date for the "high-roller" suites until August 22, 1984. Therefore, for all practical purposes, Perini argues that Sands's only delay claim related to an alleged four-month delay, from May through August 31, 1984, in the substantial completion of the glass facade. After the entire project had reached substantial completion on September 14, 1984, Perini claims that in keeping with the term-of-art meaning of substantial completion, only "punch list" and warranty work remained to be completed at the site. However, Sands sought to terminate the contract by letter dated December 21, 1984, despite an asserted contractual provision that it could not terminate the contract after substantial completion.

After Sands's purported termination of the contract, Perini brought suit in the Superior Court, Atlantic County, Chancery Division. Perini sought a declaratory judgment that Sands could not terminate the contract after the renovation project had reached substantial completion. On Sands's cross-action, the court determined that the termination issue, as well as any other disputed matters, were subject to arbitration under the contract.

Perini and Sands submitted three issues to the arbitrators: (1) lost profit damages alleged by Sands; (2) contract balances due Perini; and (3) wrongful termination of the contract by Sands. By a two-to-one vote, with the attorney-arbitrator dissenting, the panel awarded Sands over $14,500,000 in damages for lost profits. The arbitrators failed to decide explicitly the issue of whether Sands had the power to terminate Perini's contract after substantial completion. During the arbitration proceedings the parties stipulated that Perini would receive $300,000 plus interest as its contract balance.

Sands sought judicial confirmation of the award in the Chancery Division, while Perini sought to vacate the award. . . .

We granted certification . . . limited to the following issues: (1) whether the asserted mistake of law was reviewable by the courts; (2) the continued validity of the principle that mistakes of law are the equivalent of undue means; and (3) the disproportionality of the arbitration award. We now affirm the judgment of the Appellate Division.

II

A.

Judicial attitudes about arbitration have changed significantly. Although originally there was mistrust of the arbitral process, that attitude has been replaced by a strong judicial commitment to arbitration. In *Southland Corp. v. Keating*, 465 U.S. 1, 13–14 (1984), Chief Justice Burger traced the historic reluctance of the courts to support arbitration to the ancient antipathy between equity and specific performance of arbitration agreements. That reluctance has been all but swept away by judicial recognition that the mindless jealousy of the English courts for their own jurisdiction must yield to the needs of a modern society to develop desirable alternatives to litigation. Our guiding principles should strengthen the systems that encourage those alternatives to litigation, not weaken them. . . .

Once an arbitration award has been entered, any party to the arbitration may seek confirmation of the award with the court within three months of the arbitrators' decision. N.J.S.A. 2A:24-7. The award will be confirmed unless "the award is vacated, modified or corrected." *Ibid.* As at common law, the statute narrowly defines the circumstances permitting an arbitration award to be vacated. Those reasons are as follows:

a. Where the award was procured by corruption, fraud or undue means;

b. Where there was either evident partiality or corruption in the arbitrators, or any thereof;

c. Where the arbitrators were guilty of misconduct in refusing to postpone the hearing, upon sufficient cause being shown therefor, or in refusing to hear evidence, pertinent and material to the controversy, or of any other misbehaviors prejudicial to the rights of any party;

d. Where the arbitrators exceeded or so imperfectly executed their powers that a mutual, final and definite award upon the subject matter submitted was not made.

Sections a and d are relevant here and we shall refer to them as the "undue means" and the "exceeded their powers" provisions, respectively.

B.

. . . .

There is little profit in seeking to pigeonhole a mistake of law under either of those statutory sections. Suffice it to observe that "[w]hen the parties intend that their contract be interpreted in accordance with the law, [the arbitrator's] authority is circumscribed by being limited to carrying out that intent." *Kearny PBA Local # 21 v. Town of Kearny*, 81 N.J. 208, 217, 405 A.2d 393 (1979). In this case, Sands does not disagree that the arbitrators intended to interpret the contract and remedy the breach in accordance with law. Specifically, Sands stated that "[t]he arbitrators did intend to apply the law and * * * their award is firmly supported by the applicable legal principles." We do not intend, however, that the arbitrators be judges or that their decisions be subject to the same appellate supervision as those of judges. . . .

Whether the arbitrators are viewed as having acted with "undue means," or having "exceeded their powers," the judicial inquiry must go beyond a search for mere mistakes of law. Were we to decide otherwise, arbitration would simply become another form of private, non-jury trial. A scope of review that allows an arbitration decision to stand when the interpretation of law is reasonably debatable is consistent with the earlier formulation set forth in [*Held v. Comfort Bus Line*, 136 N.J.L. 640, 57 A.2d 20 (Sup. Ct. 1948)]. That formulation requires that the arbitrators must have clearly intended to decide according to law, must have clearly mistaken the legal rule, and that mistake must appear on the face of the award. In addition, the error, to be fatal, must result in a failure of intent or be so gross as to suggest fraud or misconduct. . . .

[W]e believe that the arbitration process is strengthened by having a limited reservoir of judicial review. [*Faherty v. Faherty*, 97 N.J. 99, 477 A.2d 1257 (1984)] is a good example. To let stand an award of alimony that would, on its face, violate New Jersey's statutory law and policy would undermine public confidence in arbitration as a credible system of complementary dispute resolution. We are confident that the limited judicial review that we contemplate will strengthen, rather than weaken, such alternatives to litigation. It is not surprising, in view of the very large sums of money involved in this case and the unusual theory of damages accepted by this arbitration panel, that the arbitral party would seek judicial review.

III

We turn now to the application of those principles to the facts of this case. Perini alleges that several mistakes of law in this arbitration were clear, substantial, and highly prejudicial. We shall address each.

1. Was it a mistake to award damages for lost profits that were not in the contemplation of the parties at the date of contract?

Since *Hadley v. Baxendale*, 9 Ex. 341, 156 Eng.Rep. 145 (1854), lawyers and judges have pondered the difficult issue of harnessing the concept of expectation damages. Should the delay in transit of a crankshaft needed to drive a grist mill have caused a common carrier to be liable for the lost profits of the mill? The rule of consequential damages is said to have been devised to meet the demands of a rapidly-expanding market society. Whatever the doctrine's origins, it is a settled part of our legal landscape.

> "Compensatory damages are designed 'to put the injured party in as good a position as he would have had if performance had been rendered as promised.' 5 Corbin, Contracts § 992, p. 5 (1951)." What that position is depends upon what the parties reasonably expected. It follows that the defendant is not chargeable for loss that he did not have reason to foresee as a probable result of the breach when the contract was made. *Hadley v. Baxendale*, 9 Ex. 341, 156 Eng.Rep.145 (1854); accord *Crater v. Binninger*, 33 N.J.L. 513 (E. & A. 1869). The oft-quoted language in *Hadley* for this proposition is:
>
> Where two parties have made a contract, which one of them has broken, the damages which the other party ought to receive, in respect of such breach, should be such as may fairly be considered either arising naturally, i.e., according to the usual course of things, from such breach of contract itself, or such as may reasonably be supposed to have been in the contemplation of both parties at the time they made the contract, as the probable result of the breach of it. [9 Ex. at 354, 156 Eng.Rep. at 151] [*Donovan v. Bachstadt*, 91 N.J. 434, 444–45, 453 A.2d 160 (1982) (footnote omitted) (citations omitted).]

Lost profits fall under the category of consequential damages. *Seaman v. United States Steel Corp.*, 166 N.J.Super. 467, 471, 400 A.2d 90 (App.Div.), certif. denied, 81 N.J. 282, 405 A.2d 826 (1979); E. Allan Farnsworth, Contracts § 12.14 (1982).

Perini argues that lost profits were not contemplated by the parties at the time of contract most significantly because the parties "specified in their [c]ontract the precise remedies available in the event of a breach by the other side." Perini points to contract clauses 12.1.1 (construction manager agrees to indemnify owner), 12.4 (owner required to purchase property insurance), 13.2.1 (owner may make good on obligations construction manager fails to perform), and 13.2.2 (where construction manager fails to perform duties under the circumstances described, owner may terminate employment of construction manager) in support of its argument. Had either party contemplated damages for lost profits, Perini argues, a provision would have been included in the contract. For example, Sands would have placed a liquidated damages clause in the contract or it would have included a "time-of-the-essence" clause. As one commentator has noted, liquidated damages clauses are included in construction contracts as a "predetermined assessment of compensatory damages for failure to substantially complete the construction project within the contract time." Steven M. Siegfried, *Introduction to Construction Law* § 8.03(d) (1987) (hereinafter Siegfried).

Furthermore, Perini argues that it would not have accepted such a great risk for the minimal fee of $600,000. Thus, Perini argues that because the parties did not mention lost profits as a remedy in the case of late completion, lost profits cannot be awarded, and therefore the award of lost profits was not in accordance with the terms of the contract. Also, Perini contends that the parties could not have anticipated that the failure to complete a non-functional, ornamental facade could lead to damages of millions of dollars. Finally, even if lost profits were contemplated by the parties, they did not intend to allocate the risk of loss to Perini.

However, the testimony of Sands's personnel clearly established that Sands intended to increase its profits by attracting more patrons from the boardwalk. Certainly, Perini had to be aware of Sands's motive at the time it entered into the contract. Also, Sands stressed the importance of timely completion of the project. On numerous occasions Sands informed Perini that it wished to have the project completed prior to the beginning of the summer season, the casino industry's busiest season. Perini was well aware of the projected completion date. In an inter-office memorandum, dated September 26, 1983, Perini's project manager wrote: "The projected completion date is June 15, 1984, which is 12 work days beyond the required completion date on May 31, 1984." Furthermore, Perini knew that Sands would delay construction if the project could not be completed by May 1984. Thus, it appears that the arbitrators had more than enough evidence to conclude that Perini was aware that its failure to complete the project in a timely fashion could lead to a significant loss of income. In fact, a letter written on June 12, 1984, by William Weidner, Sands's president, specifically informed Perini that Sands intended to seek damages. Certainly, based on the evidence submitted to them, the arbitrators could have concluded that the damages were reasonably foreseeable. Thus, Perini's first alleged mistake of law must fail.

2. Was it a mistake to award damages for lost profits after the date when the project was substantially completed?

A.

Perini argues that if the award of lost profits from September through December 1984 is allowed to stand, the well-established rule that limits damages after substantial completion will be violated because the parties agreed that substantial completion of the project occurred on September 15, 1984.

Substantial completion has a definite meaning in the construction industry. Amicus, Associated General Contractors of America (AGCA), tells us that the contract entered into by Perini and Sands is substantially the same as AGCA Document No. 500, which in turn is modeled on forms distributed by the American Institute of Architects (AIA). Those AIA forms are widely used in the construction industry. Justin Sweet, *Sweet on Construction Industry Contracts: Major AIA Documents* § 1.1 (1987) (hereinafter Sweet). The definition of substantial completion that appears in the contract reads as follows: "The date of [s]ubstantial [c]ompletion of the [p]roject or a designated portion thereof is the date when construction is significantly complete in accordance with the [d]rawings and [s]pecifications so the [o]wner can occupy or utilize the [p]roject or designated portion thereof for the use for which it is intended." According to Professor Sweet, the AIA defines substantial completion as "what the owner bargains for, a mostly completed project within the required time." Sweet, *supra*, § 16.15. Professor Sweet also notes that generally AIA contracts contain a clause that requires a contractor, on substantial completion, to submit "a comprehensive list of items to be completed or corrected." That is generally known as a "punch list." *Ibid.* Although the specific clause described by Professor Sweet was not included in the contract here, the definition of punch list and its link to substantial completion will be helpful to our analysis. Generally, the punch list includes those items that restrict the final completion of the project. 2 Steven G.M. Stein, *Construction Law* ¶ 7.09 at 7–78 (1991) (hereinafter Stein).

Another factor that is indicative of substantial completion is the issuance of a certificate of occupancy by the municipality, normally by its building department. *Id.* at 7–77. When an owner attempts to assess liquidated damages, a "certificate of occupancy should arguably determine the date of substantial completion." *Ibid.*

In its amicus brief, AGCA argues that substantial completion in construction law and the common-law doctrine of substantial performance are different, without clearly stating the consequence of that purported difference. It appears that substantial completion is a term used in the construction industry to measure the time commitment portion of the contract. Sweet, *supra*, § 17.4. In any case, the definition of substantial completion used by the parties is similar to the definition of substantial performance used by the courts. *See Jardine Estates, Inc. v. Donna Brook Corp.*, 42 N.J.Super. 332, 337, 126 A.2d 372 (App.Div.1956). Perini in its papers and the case law use the terms interchangeably. Construction-industry authorities agree that the courts use the terms interchangeably. Stein, *supra*, ¶ 6.07[3] & n.13 at 6–18.

B.

As noted previously, Perini contends that it substantially completed the project by mid-September 1984, and therefore should not be liable for lost profits from that date to the date of termination in December 1984. According to Perini, the award of lost profits for that period amounted to approximately $4,000,000.[2] Construction industry treatises agree with Perini. Siegfried states:

> The doctrine of substantial performance can be used as a defense to a breach of contract action for failure to complete a project within the contract time. In fact, unless otherwise specifically agreed, a liquidated damages provision is not enforceable for the period beyond the point of substantial completion. [Siegfried, *supra*, § 8.05.]

As Williston points out, most commonly, the courts have applied the doctrine of substantial performance to cases that involve building contracts. The doctrine has been interpreted to allow a builder who has substantially performed a contract to recover the full price under the contract less any damages suffered by the owner due to the builder's breach. 6 *Williston on Contracts* § 842 (3d ed. 1962). That rule generally is followed in most American jurisdictions. 3A *Corbin on Contracts* § 701 (1960). The case law is in accord. In *Jardine Estates, supra*, the court stated that there is substantial performance of a contract " 'where all the essentials necessary to the full accomplishment of the purposes for which the thing contracted for has been constructed are performed with such an approximation to complete performance that the owner obtains substantially what is called for by the contract.' " 42 N.J.Super. at 337, 126 A.2d 372 (quoting 9 *Am.Jur., Building and Construction Contracts* § 42).

In *Feeney v. Bardsley*, 66 N.J.L. 239, 49 A. 443 (E. & A. 1901), the Court found no error in the lower court's charge to the jury where it stated:

> [I]f the contractor has substantially performed his contract, even though he has failed to do so in some minor particulars, he is entitled to recover the contract price, less what will be a fair allowance to the owner to make good the defects in performance of the contract. [*Id.* at 240, 49 A. 443.]

In *Van Dusen Aircraft Supplies, Inc. v. Terminal Construction Corp.*, 3 N.J. 321, 70 A.2d 65 (1949), this Court, citing *Feeney* approvingly, stated in dicta that the "rule of damages where a building is substantially completed, but is defective in some particulars, is the cost of making good the omitted or defective work." *Id.* at 329, 70 A.2d 65. *Accord Power-Matics, Inc. v. Ligotti*, 79 N.J.Super. 294, 191 A.2d 483 (App.Div.1963); *Winfield Mut. Hous. Corp. v. Middlesex Concrete Prods. and Excavating Corp.*, 39 N.J.Super. 92, 120 A.2d 655 (App.Div.1956); *Amerada Hess Corp. v. Quinn*, 143 N.J.Super. 237, 362 A.2d 1258 (Law Div.1976).

C.

Perini and amicus, AGCA, argue that because the arbitrators awarded damages beyond the substantial completion date allegedly admitted by the parties, they departed from both public (judicial decisions) and private law (the parties' contract) in reaching their decision and thus imperfectly executed their powers, in violation of N.J.S.A. 2A:24-8d.

When assessing damages after substantial completion of a project, courts have treated liquidated damages in a manner similar to that of lost profits. Thus, we have

---

[2] Sands agrees that the award for that period was approximately $4,000,000. That estimate is based on the testimony of Sands's expert. The amount cannot be determined with specificity because the arbitrators failed to delineate how much of the total award covered profits lost during that period.

included several liquidated damages cases in our analysis. Courts have found that liquidated damages may not be imposed after the owner "is able to put the project to its beneficial use or the owner has taken occupancy." Stein, *supra*, ¶ 6.07[3] at 6–18. The rationale behind that policy is that liquidated damages otherwise would become a penalty because those damages are designed to approximate an owner's loss before occupancy. *Id.* at 6–19. The reason for limiting liquidated damages was succinctly stated in *Stone v. City of Arcola*, 181 Ill.App.3d 513, 130 Ill.Dec. 118, 536 N.E.2d 1329 (Ill.App.Ct.1989):

> The trial court found substantial completion on October 10, 1983. Since the project was sufficiently complete at the time to be used for the purpose for which it was intended, then it would seem appropriate to construe the liquidated damages provision to close at the time of substantial compliance, even though there may be minor repairs, adjustments, or finishing work remaining. After all, if the contractor can get paid at substantial compliance, that is the logical time to discontinue the applicability of the liquidated damages clause. If the contractor fails to complete the additional work, the owner's remedy is to have someone else complete it and sue the contractor to recover the expense. [*Id.* at 1338.]

. . . .

Case law also suggests that, like liquidated damages, lost profits can be assessed up to the date of substantial completion. For example, in *D.A. Davis Construction v. Palmetto Properties, Inc.*, 281 S.C. 415, 315 S.E.2d 370 (1984), the court awarded three months' lost rental income to the owner for the builder's failure to substantially complete the project on the date specified in the contract. *Id.* at 372. The owner presented evidence that the property was to have been rented to a beer distributor upon substantial completion. *See also Hemenway Co. v. Bartex, Inc.*, 373 So.2d 1356 (La.Ct.App.) (holding that the owner of retail store should receive the interest it had paid on interim financing and the rent paid on the old building for the period of delay until substantial completion), *cert. denied*, 376 So.2d 1272 (La.1979); *Herbert & Brooner Constr. Co. v. Golden*, 499 S.W.2d 541 (Mo.Ct.App.1973) (awarding delay damages for lost rental on theater and the costs of extending a construction loan until date of substantial completion). *Cf. Brooks Towers Corp. v. Hunkin-Conkey Constr. Co.*, 454 F.2d 1203 (10th Cir.1972) (holding no lost rentals can be awarded where delay in substantial completion was excusable).

Thus, Perini's argument that delay damages cannot be awarded after substantial completion of the contract is amply supported by the case law and construction-industry practice. Had the arbitration panel found that Perini had substantially completed the project, as that term is defined in the contract, by September 15, 1984, then it may have erred in awarding lost profits from that date to the time Sands terminated the contract in December 1984. . . .

We have verified the various transcript references that refer to the condition of the property after September 15, 1984. For example, William Weidner testified that as of Thanksgiving 1984, Sands "had a full-fledged disaster on [its] hands." Also, the lighted, glass-enclosed elevator, which was visible from the boardwalk and was part of the new park entrance, was not completed and operational until late November 1984. Similarly, Perini's work on the glass facade at the vehicle entrance on Indiana Avenue continued through the fall. Perini often had trucks and/or cranes parked on

Indiana Avenue adjacent to or in the new entrance. Thus, it appears, as Sands argues, that although it was able to occupy the new park entrance in the fall while the renovation work continued, it greatly detracted from the building's appearance, obstructed customer access, disrupted operations, and contributed to Sands's loss of business.

At its root, the doctrine of substantial performance "rests on principles of fairness." *Amerada Hess Corp., supra*, 143 N.J.Super. at 253, 362 A.2d 1258. It is intended to avoid the harshness of common-law contract doctrine so that the right of compensation of those who have performed " 'in all material and substantive particulars * * * may not be forfeited by reason of mere technical or unimportant omissions or defects.' " *Ibid.* (quoting *Gillespie Tool Co. v. Wilson*, 123 Pa. 19, 16 A. 36, 37 (1888)).

Sands contracted with Perini in large measure for the construction of an ornamental facade, which was intended to draw people to the casino. To apply the doctrine against Sands might be inequitable because Sands never received what it bargained for-an ornamental glass facade that would attract clientele to its casino. Such an appearance was not entirely achieved by September 15. The arbitrators could have found that the uncompleted work was not a "mere technical or unimportant omission[] or defect[]." Because the doctrine rests on fairness, the arbitrators may have considered it fair to award damages even though the entrance could be used in its uncompleted state. *See Birch Cooley v. First Nat'l Bank of Minneapolis*, 86 Minn. 385, 90 N.W. 789, 790 (1902) (Rule of substantial performance does not apply "where deviations from the contract are such that an allowance out of the contract price would not give the other party essentially what [it] contracted for.").

Perini's argument also fails to take into account the possibility that the public's perception of the Sands building during the critical summer months could have had a significant impact on Sands's operations in the fall. There was evidence in the record concerning the importance of introducing the renovated facility to the public during the peak summer season. A Sands executive testified that the image created by an Atlantic City casino in the summer carries over into the following months. Thus, the situation is not directly analogous to that of a theater owner whose profits resume when the project is substantially completed, *Herbert & Brooner, supra*, 499 S.W.2d 541, or the retail store owner who is able to transfer operations from one store to another, *Hemenway, supra*, 373 So.2d 1356. Here, the arbitrators could have concluded that the delay in completion was an event of non-performance that carried over into the fall resulting in significant consequential damages after substantial completion. In other words, to give the worst case scenario, if, during a renovation, a contractor had left residual materials in a ventilator system that had caused a wide-spread epidemic in a hotel (as in the famous Legionnaire's disease case in Philadelphia, *see* Tom Mathews et al., *The Mystery Fever*, Newsweek, Aug. 16, 1976 at 16), would anyone doubt that after the project had been substantially completed, i.e., fully renovated, the consequential damages incurred by the proprietor would linger long thereafter? An event of non-performance caused a loss of income even after completion. We do not suggest that that is an identical or apt analogy; however, the evidence submitted to the arbitrators suggested that the casino was presented to the public in a poor light due to Perini's delay in completion. That delay and the resulting appearance could have caused profits to lag over the fall. Thus, the arbitrators' decision does not appear to depart from any clear holding that consequential damages cannot be awarded if the residual effects of non-performance of the contract are carried over into a period when the building is operational.

3. Was it a mistake to award damages for lost profits to a new business?

Perini argues that the renovation project amounted to a new business. In *Weiss v. Revenue Building and Loan Ass'n*, 116 N.J.L. 208, 182 A. 891 (E. & A. 1936), the Court stated that lost profits for a new business are "too remote, contingent and speculative to meet the legal standard of reasonable certainty." *Id.* at 212, 182 A. 891. Sands questions that argument. It points out that the casino had a proven track record; the location and nature of the business never changed; and the management team never changed.

However, even were we to consider profits from the 1984 season as those of a new business, the trend in recent cases has been to award lost profits for a new business when they can be proved with reasonable certainty. Robert L. Dunn, *Recovery of Damages for Lost Profits*, § 4.2 (3d ed. 1987); *see also Seaman, supra*, 166 N.J.Super. at 474–75, 400 A.2d 90 (evidence of lost rental value from new operation incorrectly admitted at trial because, among other things, defendant failed to show that a profit would have been made). In *In re Merritt Logan, Inc.*, 901 F.2d 349 (3d Cir.1990), the court predicted that this Court would follow that trend and allow lost profits for a new business if damages were proved with reasonable certainty. *Id.* at 358. That court also relied on comment 2 to N.J.S.A. 12A:2-708(2) (UCC), which states that "[i]t is not necessary to a recovery of 'profit' to show a history of earnings, especially if a new venture is involved." *Ibid.* Given that recent trend, the arbitrators cannot be said to have acted in manifest disregard of the law. Thus, because the arbitrators were presented with enough evidence to decide that Sands had proved its lost profit damages with reasonable certainty, the damage award does not fall.

4. Was it a mistake to award damages greatly disproportionate to Perini's fee?

An excessive or inadequate arbitration award is not grounds in and of itself to warrant judicial interference. Generally, there must be a showing of "misconduct or want of good faith on the part of the arbitrator." *Held, supra*, 136 N.J.L. at 642, 57 A.2d 20.

Perini argues that a damage award of over $14,000,000 is grossly disproportionate to the $600,000 management fee[3] it was to receive under the $24,000,000 contract and is, therefore, in direct violation of this Court's recent decision in *Dixon Venture v. Joseph Dixon Crucible Co.*, 122 N.J. 228, 584 A.2d 797 (1991). Perini states that in *Dixon* this Court was concerned with a damage award that was 16% of the contract price (in *Dixon* the contract price and the "fee" were the same), whereas the damages awarded to Sands were 2400% of the fee received by Perini.[4] Put differently, the damage award to Sands was twenty-four times Perini's fee and the damage award in Dixon was 16 times the seller's price. . . .

---

[3] Sands argues that Perini's actual fee was $771,000 because it was to receive 4% of the contract price if the price exceeded $20,000,000. However, in its Appellate Division brief Sands states that Perini's fee for services was $600,000.

[4] Perini's situation is somewhat different from those found in the cases that address disproportionate damages. In most cases, the fee received is the same as the contract price. Here, Perini's construction-management fee was $600,000 and the contract price was $24,000,000.

Perini argues that the "economic realities" of the situation and the assumptions of the parties at the time of contracting should have been considered by the arbitration panel. Specifically, Perini claims that it would not have entered into the contract if it had assumed it would be liable for over $14,000,000 in damages while receiving only a $600,000 management fee. . . .

Here, . . . the arbitrators had enough competent evidence to determine that Perini was aware of its exposure to liability for lost profits at the time of contracting. The testimony of Sands's witnesses concerning the seasonal nature of the casino business; the need to finish the project before the start of the summer season; and the fact that Sands would have postponed the project until 1985 if Perini were unable to complete it before the start of the summer season led to the inescapable conclusion that Perini would be liable for failure to complete in a timely fashion.

Perini's second disproportionality argument is based on the *Restatement (Second) of Contracts* § 351(3) (1979) (hereinafter § 351(3)). That section, entitled Unforeseeability and Related Limitations on Damages, states:

> (3) A court may limit damages for foreseeable loss by excluding recovery for loss of profits, by allowing recovery only for loss incurred in reliance, or otherwise if it concludes that in the circumstances justice so requires in order to avoid disproportionate compensation. [§ 351(3).]

Based on that section, Perini contends that the doctrine of "disproportionality" allows "a court to avoid extreme unfairness or injustice, by limiting awards of consequential damages, particularly lost profits, in a breach of contract case even where they are foreseeable." Perini argues that even though a consequence may have been foreseeable at the time of contracting, it does not necessarily mean that the parties intended to allocate the risk of loss to one of the parties. That argument tracks comment f to § 351, which in pertinent part states:

> It is not always in the interest of justice to require the party in breach to pay damages for all of the foreseeable loss that he has caused. There are unusual instances in which it appears from the circumstances either that the parties assumed that one of them would not bear the risk of a particular loss or that, although there was no such assumption, it would be unjust to put the risk on that party. One such circumstance is an extreme disproportion between the loss and the price charged by the party whose liability for that loss is in question. The fact that the price is relatively small suggests that it was not intended to cover the risk of such liability. * * *[*Restatement (Second) of Contracts* § 351 cmt.f (1979) (hereinafter comment f).]

Perini argues that because the award is highly disproportionate to the fee received, the parties did not intend to allocate the risk to it. Thus, Perini urges us to follow the Restatement and limit damages.

Although that argument has merit, comment f sets forth several limitations. First, the comment states that damage limitations are "more likely to be imposed in connection with contracts that do not arise in a commercial setting." Second, although it does not appear to be a limitation in and of itself, the comment suggests, through the illustrations that follow it, that a limitation on damages is more likely to be applied where there is an "informality of dealing, including the absence of a detailed written contract, which indicates that there was no careful attempt to allocate all of the risks." That second limitation does not appear to be applicable here because the parties entered into an extensive written contract containing several provisions that addressed damages under certain circumstances. Finally, the section envisions an "*extreme disproportion* between the loss and the price charged by the party whose liability for that loss is in question." (Emphasis added). . . .

Although Perini's argument that it would not have accepted such a great risk for a minimal fee is forceful, it was well aware of the high stakes involved in the Atlantic City casino-construction industry. By contracting with Sands, Perini offered its expertise in this risky endeavor. At the time Perini and Sands entered into the contract, Perini had managed a number of construction projects in Atlantic City. Considering the nature of this project, Perini might have bargained for a "no damages for delay" clause, *see Broadway Maintenance Corp. v. Rutgers*, 90 N.J. 253, 447 A.2d 906 (1982), or a liquidated damages clause in the contract. The only plausible conclusion, then, is that Perini left the resolution of a dispute over non-performance to third-party arbitrators. We cannot say that under those circumstances the arbitrators manifestly disregarded any applicable unmistakable principle of New Jersey law. . . .

IV

As were the courts below, we are troubled by the magnitude of this award. One theory of arbitration, particularly in the construction industry, is that a sophisticated corps of arbitrators can cut through the clutter and reach a just result. Parties who genuinely seek arbitration want a " 'final disposition, in a speedy, inexpensive, expeditious and perhaps less formal manner, of the controversial differences between [them].' " *Barcon Assocs., supra*, 86 N.J. 179, 187, 430 A.2d 214 (quoting *Eastern Eng'g, supra*, 11 N.J.Misc. 508, 510–11, 167 A. 522). They do not simply want three judges. They want three arbitrators with all that that connotes. For those who want a many-tiered review process, it is necessary to preserve those common-law rights. Perini's bitter persistence in challenging this award bespeaks something less than confidence in the arbitral process.

Projects of this magnitude are better left to the agreement reached by the parties in their contract. The theory of lost profits here was most unusual. Sands used its 1985 profits (when it bucked an otherwise declining trend in the industry in Atlantic City) to show what it would have earned over the same period in 1984 but for the delay caused by Perini. Our dissenting members, like the dissenting arbitrator below, are not persuaded. The issue, however, is not whether we are persuaded but whether the arbitrators could have been so persuaded without transgressing any of the statutory restraints on arbitral powers. N.J.S.A. 2A:24-8. We find no statutory basis to vacate the award.

The judgment of the Appellate Division is affirmed.

[b] Questions About *Perini* and the Extent of Contractor Liability

1. The court's decision in *Perini* illustrates the judicial deference accorded to the arbitration process. According to the court, mere mistakes of law are insufficient to set aside an arbitration award. Instead, "the arbitrators must

have clearly intended to decide according to law, must have clearly mistaken the legal rule, and that mistake must appear on the face of the award. In addition, the error, to be fatal, must result in a failure of intent or be so gross as to suggest fraud or misconduct." How comfortable would you be in recommending arbitration as a dispute resolution method if this is the standard for judicial review of an award? Is the court correct when it states "the arbitration process is strengthened by having a limited reservoir of judicial review" and that to be less deferential toward arbitration decisions "would undermine public confidence in arbitration as a credible system of complementary dispute resolution"?

2. Review the mutual waiver of consequential damages provision in AIA Document A201-2007 ¶ 15.1.6. As between the owner and general contractor, who receives the greater protection under this provision? In other words, is a general contractor more likely to experience consequential damages in the event of an owner's breach that will, under this provision, be uncompensated or, as in *Perini*, is an owner more likely to experience consequential damages in the event of a contractor's breach that will, under this provision, be uncompensated?

3. Would a liquidated damages provision in the owner/general contractor's agreement represent a more appropriate compromise between the imposition of full liability for consequential damages and a mutual waiver of consequential damages? How would you determine the amount of liquidated damages so that it would withstand judicial scrutiny?

[3] The Fox Valley Auto Care Center: Conflicts with the General Contractor

[a] Fox Valley Auto Care Center and Contractor Liability for Defects

The following memos between Donna Smith and Samuel Nader ask Sam to examine the general contractor's contract in connection with several potential defects in the construction work. These memos assume that the general contractor is a party independent from the owner. As we stated at the beginning of the chapter, in the actual construction of the Fox Valley Auto Care Center, the general contractor was an affiliate of the Regent Real Estate Development Corp.

[b] Donna's Inquiry About Contractor Liability for Defects

MEMORANDUM

TO: Samuel Nader

FROM: Donna Smith

RE: General Contractor Liability Fox Valley Auto Care Center

As you are aware, the construction process is underway at the Fox Valley Auto Care Center in which our client the Regent Real Estate Development Corp. is the developer. The architect, MFH, has been inspecting the construction undertaken by the general contractor and the roofing subcontractor and has identified what it believes to be a deviation from the construction documents with the materials that the roofing subcontractor is incorporating into the roof system. Although the construction documents do not specify the exact type or brand of materials that are to be incorporated into the roof system, the architect is concerned that the materials and fabrication techniques proposed to be used by the general contractor and subcontractor will not provide the weather protection that the construction documents specify. The general contractor, of course, is claiming that if the architect wants to require that other materials be used at this time, a change order is necessary with appropriate adjustments made to the construction budget and construction schedule. Apparently the materials desired by the architect are not as readily available as those proposed by the general contractor and subcontractor and differing fabrication techniques are more labor intensive. Importantly, Regent is hoping to avoid any further changes to the budget or schedule.

I hope that we can avoid escalating this conflict between the owner and general contractor which might result from a more detailed investigation into the specific types of materials that the general contractor wants to use as compared to those recommended by the architect. I would also like to avoid creating a conflict between the owner and the architect at this time over the question of whether more detailed specifications should have been contained in the construction documents.

Now to the point of my memo. The general contractor claims that its warranties concerning materials and workmanship under the construction contract should fully satisfy Regent and that it, the general contractor, is willing to assume liability under these warranties for failure of the roofing system. My concern is that acceptance of the building upon substantial completion will serve to waive these warranties. I would like you to examine the construction contract which, as you know, incorporates the General Conditions for the Contract for Construction, AIA Document A201-2007 and consider any relevant provisions that may affect this question. Could you prepare your response by the end of the week?

[c] Sam's Memo on Contractor Liability for Defects

MEMORANDUM

TO: Donna Smith

FROM: Samuel Nader

RE: General Contractor Liability Fox Valley Auto Care Center

As you requested, I have examined the construction contract between Regent and the general contractor and focused on the scope of the general contractor's warranties to Regent that survive completion of the project.

AIA Document A201-2007 ¶ 3.5 contains a warranty under which the "contractor warrants to the Owner and Architect that materials and equipment furnished under the Contract will be of good quality and new unless the Contract Documents require or permit otherwise" and "that the

Work will conform to the requirements of the Contract Documents. . . ."[1] AIA Document A201-2007 ¶ 3.5 also provides that the contractor is to "furnish "satisfactory evidence as to the kind and quality of materials and equipment" if required by the architect to do so. I suggest that Regent require that the roofing subcontractor provide the general contractor and the architect with the specifications from the manufacturer of the roofing components along with the manufacturer's recommended fabrication and installation procedure. This information should then be compared with the specifications contained in the construction documents to ensure that the construction documents are being followed.

If the roofing subcontractor's proposal satisfies the specifications contained in the construction documents, the contractor will not be responsible for the consequences of any defect in the design. As a general rule, the owner impliedly warrants the suitability of the design. *See United States v. Spearin*, 248 U.S. 132 (1918) ("if the contractor is bound to build according to plans and specifications prepared by the owner, the contractor will not be responsible for the consequences of defects in the plans and specifications"). If, however, the roofing subcontractor's proposal does not satisfy the specifications contained in the construction documents, the contractor will clearly remain liable under the warranty contained in ¶ 3.5.1.

The General Conditions provide that the owner may accept nonconforming work (AIA Document A201-2007 ¶ 12.3). In this situation, the general contractor's fee is to be reduced "as appropriate and equitable" whether or not final payment has been made.

Under the terms of the General Conditions, the parties need not decide at this time whether the roofing subcontractor's proposal conforms with the requirements of the construction documents. Neither final payment nor the owner's use of the structure will serve to waive the contractor's warranty. AIA Document A201-2007 ¶ 9.10.4 provides: "The making of final payment shall constitute a waiver of claims by the Owner except those arising from. . . . 3 terms of special warranties required by the Contract Documents." Further, AIA Document A201-2007 ¶ 9.9.3 states: "Unless otherwise agreed upon, partial occupancy or use of a portion of the Work shall not constitute acceptance of Work not complying with the requirements of the Contract Documents." Finally, AIA Document A201-2007 ¶ 13.4.2 states: "No action or failure to act by the Owner, Architect or Contractor shall constitute a waiver of a right or duty afforded them under the Contract, nor shall such action or failure to act constitute approval of or acquiescence in a breach there under, except as may be specifically agreed in writing." The Illinois courts have recognized, however, that the acceptance of work can constitute a waiver of defective performance.

> An absolute and unconditional acceptance of the work can act as a waiver or acceptance of defective performance. In order for there to be a waiver, however, the facts must indicate that the injured party intentionally relinquished a known right, and the injured party cannot relinquish that right unless he or she knows or has reason to know of the defective condition. Moreover, "[the] acts relied on by the party in breach must be

---

[1] *See also* AIA Document A201-2007 ¶ 3.1.2 ("The Contractor shall perform the Work in accordance with the Contract Documents."). AIA Document A201-2007 ¶ 3.5 contains an additional warranty from the contractor to the owner and architect that the Work "will be free from defects, Except for those inherent in the quality of the Work the Contract Documents require or permit." The warranty does not extend to "damage or defect caused by abuse, alterations to the Work not executed by the Contractor, improper or insufficient maintenance, improper operation, or normal wear and tear and normal usage."

> inconsistent with an intention by the injured party to insist on rights to performance under the contract." The injured party must also express "assent to accept defective performance in satisfaction and as a complete discharge." The party pleading waiver has the burden to prove it. *Shaw v. Bridges-Gallagher, Inc.*, 528 N.E.2d 1349 (Ill. App. 5 Dist. 1988) (owner did not waive defective performance by accepting an inferior roof) (citations omitted).[2]

Consequently, the parties should enter into an agreement explicitly providing that final payment or use of the project by the owner does not constitute a waiver of the contractor's warranty in this instance.

The architect may be concerned that its review of the product specifications may be subsequently deemed a change in the construction documents imposing design liability on the architect. The architect should be satisfied that under AIA Document A201-2007 ¶ 4.2.7 and AIA Document B101-2007 ¶ 3.6.4.2 the architect's review of product specifications does not serve to shift liability for defective performance from the general contractor to the architect. AIA Document A201-2007 ¶ 4.2.7 states: "Review of such submittals is not conducted for the purpose of determining the accuracy and completeness of other details such as dimensions and quantities, or for substantiating instructions for installation or performance of equipment or systems, **all of which remain the responsibility of the Contractor** as required by the Contract Documents. The Architect's review of the Contractor's submittals shall not relieve the Contractor of the obligations under Sections 3.3, 3.5 and 3.12." [emphasis added]

If the roof system does not perform satisfactorily and the owner can establish that the contractor's performance did not conform to the requirements of the construction documents, the question of the available remedy must be considered. Typically, the owner will be entitled to damages equal to the cost of correcting the defective condition. *Park v. Sohn*, 433 N.E.2d 651 (Ill. 1982); *Brewer v. Custom Builders Corp.*, 356 N.E.2d 565 (Ill. App. 5 Dist. 1976). Nevertheless, the courts, on occasion, have found such a damages remedy unreasonable.

> "If, however, the defects could be corrected only at a cost unreasonably disproportionate to the benefit to the purchaser, or if correcting them would entail unreasonable destruction of the builder's work," the measure of damages then should be the difference between the value of full performance of the contract and the value of performance actually received or, in other words, the amount by which the defects have reduced the value of the property. *Shaw v. Bridges-Gallagher, Inc.*, 528 N.E.2d at 1351 (quoting *Park v. Sohn*, 433 N.E.2d at 657; *Brewer v. Custom Builders Corp.*, 356 N.E.2d at 570).

The application of this rule was at issue in *Shaw v. Bridges-Gallagher, Inc., supra*, in the context of a defectively constructed roof. The roofing contractor, who was found liable for the cost of replacing the defective roof, argued that the cost of replacing the roof would be unreasonably disproportionate to the benefit received by the owner because the roof specified in the 1980 construction contract cost $7,959, while a new roof, for which it was found liable, cost $17,000 in 1987. The owner contended, however, that the cost to replace the

---

[2] In addition, courts frequently discuss whether the alleged defect is patent or latent in determining whether the owner waived the contractor's warranty upon making final payment or taking occupancy of the project. *See* O'Connor, *Warranties, Guarantees, and Correction Remedies Under the AIA Document A201 (1997)*, 18 The Construction Law. 19, n.26 (Jan. 1998).

roof in 1987 was not disproportionate to the $504,989 construction price of the entire building. The court agreed with the owner and concluded that the 1980 contract price of the roof could not be accurately compared to the cost to replace the roof as the replacement cost of a roof would be more in 1987 than in 1980 due to inflation. But see *Witty v. C. Casey Homes, Inc.*, 430 N.E.2d 191 (Ill. App. 1st Dist. 1981) (concluding that the cost-of-repair method for computing damages would be improper because the $50,000 cost to replace the brick would be grossly disproportionate to the $54,566 cost of the building and because replacing the defective brick would seriously damage other parts of the building).

If the parties enter into an explicit agreement concerning the warranty of the contractor's work as noted above, the agreement should also contain a provision describing the calculation of damages as equal to the replacement cost of the roof or the cost of repair, whichever is less, and not the reduced value of the building in order to avoid the type of controversy encountered in *Shaw v. Bridges-Gallagher, Inc.*[4] In addition, Regent should be aware that under AIA Document A201-2007 ¶ 15.1.6, both the owner and the contractor waive claims against each other for consequential damages. Under the terms of AIA Document A201-2007 ¶ 15.1.6.1, the owner waives any and all damages "incurred by the Owner for rental expenses, for losses of use, income, profit, financing, business and reputation, and for loss of management or employee productivity or of the services of such persons. . . ." Consequently, if the tenants suffer damages as a result of a failure of the roof system which are recoverable against Regent under the terms of their leases, Regent would be unable to recover these damages from the contractor under this mutual waiver provision. Any agreement that Regent and the general contractor enter into should address the issue of consequential damages if Regent expects to recover consequential damages from the contractor for failure of the roofing system.

[d] Questions About Contractor Liability for Defects

1. What is the general contractor's responsibility to ensure that the project complies with applicable laws and regulations, including zoning ordinances, housing codes, and local, state, or federal environmental laws? *See* AIA Document A201-2007 ¶¶ 3.2.3 and 3.7.3. Does the owner, architect, or general contractor have the responsibility to obtain all appropriate building permits with municipal authorities? *See* AIA Document A201-2007 ¶¶ 2.2.2 and 3.7.1.

2. One area in which frequent conflicts arise between the owner and the general contractor concerns responsibility for additional expenses when concealed or unknown conditions are found to exist on the site. Often, these

[4] One commentator suggests the following warranty with respect to water penetration:

> The Contractor shall warrant for a period of twelve (12) months that the building(s) shall be watertight and leakproof at every point and in every area, except where leaks can be attributed to damage to the building(s) by external forces beyond Contractor's control. The Contractor shall, immediately upon notification by the Owner of water penetration, determine the source of water penetration and, at its own expense, do any work necessary to make the Building(s) watertight. Contractor shall also, at its own expense, repair or replace any other damaged material, finishes, and furnishings, damaged as a result of this water penetration, to return the building(s) to its (their) original condition.

1 Sweet & Sweet, *supra* at § 12.6 (quoting King & Epstein, *Owner's Counsel Reviews (and Suggests Changes to) the New (1987) AIA General Conditions of the Contract of Construction*, Prac. Real Est. Law. (Part 1) 35 (Mar. 1989)).

situations involve rock formations that interfere with excavation work or inadequate subsurface soil that must be replaced to properly support the building. How are these situations addressed under the General Conditions? *See* AIA Document A201-2007 ¶¶ 2.2.3, 3.7.4 and 3.7.5.

3. Another unexpected or unknown condition that may affect the construction process is the presence of environmental contaminants in the soil or ground water on the construction site. Although environmental consultants and engineers may have examined the site and provided the owner, architect, and general contractor extensive analyses and reports, unexpected sources of contaminants can be discovered during the excavation process. What actions can the general contractor take in such a situation, and what remedies are available to the general contractor where delay or added expenses must be incurred to remediate any contamination? *See* AIA Document A201-2007 ¶¶ 3.7.4, 8.3.1, and 10.3.

4. One of the many factors beyond the general contractor's control that may affect its ability to complete the construction project on time is the weather. How do the General Conditions address the issue of weather? *See* AIA Document A201-2007 ¶ 15.1.5.2.

5. AIA Document B101-2007 describes the contractual relationship between the owner and architect. Because the architect is responsible for the administration of the general contract, Article 4 of AIA Document A201-2007 describes the role of the architect vis-a-vis the general contractor. Describe the relationship between the general contractor and the architect under Article 4 of AIA Document A201-2007.

6. What are the respective obligations of the owner and general contractor concerning the provision of liability and property insurance during the construction process? *See* Article 11 of AIA Document A201-2007. *See also* Bergquist, *A Guide to Insurance Requirement Changes in the 1997 AIA Construction Contracts*, 18 The Construction Law. 25 (Oct. 1998).

7. Under what circumstances can the owner or contractor terminate the construction contract for cause? *See* AIA Document A201-2007 ¶¶ 14.1.1 and 14.2.1. What remedies does the agreement provide for suspension or termination of the contract by the owner for convenience? *See* AIA Document A201-2007 ¶¶ 14.3 and 14.4.

§ 13.04 CONTRACTOR/SUBCONTRACTOR AGREEMENT

[1] Overview

In most projects, the general contractor will engage the services of specialty trade subcontractors that will actually construct most or all of the project. These specialty trades include excavation, foundations, structural steel, and roofing, as well as the trades that specialize in the installation of subsystems within the building such as heating and air conditioning, plumbing, electrical services, and utilities. Under the D-A-B system, the general contractor is responsible for the scheduling, supervision, and coordination of all specialty trades and enters into subcontracts with the specialty trade subcontractors to do so. Subcontractors may, in turn, contract with sub-subcontractors and suppliers.

Although the owner/general contractor/subcontractor approach involves a number of separate relationships and requires a high degree of supervision and coordination, subcontracting, as opposed to an integrated general contractor, provides two principal advantages. First, the general contractor is able to take advantage of specialization of labor by the various subcontractors. When a specific project requires specialized skills in a particular trade, certain subcontractors in that trade may have already developed the skills or have had similar experiences on other projects. The general contractor can select the subcontractor whose employees have the necessary skills rather than having to rely on its own in-house employees. Thus, the general contractor is not prevented from undertaking a project because his employees do not have the specialized skills that the project may require. Second, subcontracting provides the general contractor with certain cost advantages. By subcontracting the work on a project, the general contractor can keep its overhead and personnel costs to a minimum, as well as encourage cost competition among interested subcontractors at the bidding stage of the project. In addition, the general contractor can shift the risk of under bidding on the subcontracted work to the subcontractor.

The advantages of the subcontracting approach are considerable, but disadvantages also exist. Subcontracting adds a new level of contracts that already exist under the D-A-B system between the owner and architect and the owner and general contractor. To ensure that no gaps result in the delegation of responsibilities by the general contractor to the subcontractors, the terms of the subcontracts must be integrated with the terms of the general contract and the architect's contract. Subcontracting also requires extensive oversight and coordination by the general contractor. Difficulties in coordination may arise where various union workers are working together or when union and nonunion workers are involved. When design changes arise during the construction process, cost and scheduling implications will ripple down through the subcontracting layers. Finally, subcontracting raises the risk of nonpayment or delay in payment as disbursements must be made to multiple levels of contractors. Despite these disadvantages, the prevalence of subcontracting in the construction process indicates that the advantages exceed the disadvantages.

In the same way that standardized architect and general contractor contracts have gained popularity in the construction industry, standardized subcontractor contracts have as well. The AIA publishes Document A401-2007, Standard Form of Agreement Between Contractor and Subcontractor. We have not included AIA Document A401-2007 in the Document Book because it is highly repetitive of AIA Document A201-2007, and because we believe we can effectively raise issues involving subcontractors without having you read AIA Document A401-2007. AIA Document A401-2007 details the relationship between the general contractor and the subcontractor and incorporates by reference AIA Document A201-2007, creating an integrated relationship with the other participants in the construction process.

Three issues involving subcontracts have attracted considerable attention by commentators: the enforceability of subcontractor bids, the pay-when-paid controversy, and subcontractor liability for damages in the construction process:

> *Enforceability Of Subcontractor Bids* — The issue involving the enforceability of subcontractor bids concerns the extent to which both the general contractor and the subcontractor are bound when the subcontrac

tor submits a bid to the general contractor during the bidding process. In *Baird Co. v. Gimbel Brothers*, 64 F.2d 344 (2d Cir. 1933), Judge Learned Hand concluded that the subcontractor's bid was not enforceable by the general contractor when the subcontractor revoked the bid before acceptance by the general contractor even though the general contractor had been awarded the construction contract. The California Supreme Court adopted a different rule in *Drennan v. Star Paving Co.*, 333 P.2d 757 (Cal. 1958). Based on a reliance theory, the court concluded that a subcontractor's bid is enforceable if relied upon by the general contractor in the preparation of his bid. Currently, 26 states follow the *Drennan* rule, four follow the *Baird* rule, and the rest have never ruled on the issue. SWEET, SWEET ON CONSTRUCTION LAW § 10.7 (1997). Although the subcontractor is bound to its bid when the bid is relied upon by the general contractor under the *Drennan* rule, the general contractor may not be bound to use the subcontractor and may attempt to renegotiate the bid from an advanta geous position. Of course, this situation can be avoided if the general contractor and subcontractor agree otherwise at the time that the subcontractor's bid is submitted or if bid registries or depositories are used.

Pay-When-Paid — The pay-when-paid controversy concerns the interpretation of the typical provision in the subcontractor's contract, which states that the general contractor will pay the subcontractor if and when the general contractor receives payment for the work. This type of provision, which imposes a condition precedent on the general contractor's obligation to pay the subcontractor, attempts to transfer the risk of nonpayment by the owner from the general contractor to the subcontractor. Unfortunately, the courts have not been consistent in giving effect to these provisions. Some courts have attempted to avoid the problem by distinguished between pay-when-paid provisions and pay-if-paid provisions and concluding that the former provisions do not shift the risk of nonpayment by the owner from the general contractor to the subcontractor. *See* Hill & Evans, *Pay When Paid Provisions: Still a Conundrum*, 18 THE CONSTRUCTION LAW. 16 (April 1998). Other courts have concluded that a pay-when-paid provision must explicitly state that the risk of the owner's insolvency is to be shifted to the subcontractor in order to overcome the presumed intention of the parties that the subcontractor will be paid for services rendered and materials incorporated into a project. *See, e.g., Koch v. Construction Technology, Inc.*, 924 S.W.2d 68 (Tenn. 1996) (concluding that a contractual provision stating that "[p]artial payments . . . shall be made when and as payments are received by the Contractor" did not create a condition precedent but recognizing that the parties could do so explicitly); *A.J. Wolfe Co. v. Baltimore Contractors, Inc.*, 244 N.E.2d 717 (Mass. 1969) (no condition precedent created by a provision stating that monthly progress payments to a subcontractor would be made "within 10 days after . . . [the owner's] payment of such monthly progress payments . . . [has] been received by the [general contractor]. . . ." but acknowledging that an explicit provision could create an enforceable condition precedent); *Thos J. Dyer Co. v. Bishop Int'l Eng'g Co.*, 303 F.2d 655 (6th Cir. 1962) (concluding that a contractual provision stating that "no part of [the payment due the subcontractor] shall be due until five (5) days after Owner shall have paid contractor therefor," was not effective to shift the risk of loss to the subcontractor where the owner failed to pay the contractor but recognizing that an express provision would be effective).

However, even when the subcontract contains an explicit condition precedent under which the general contractor is not obligated to pay the subcontractor until payment from the owner has been received, the courts will frequently limit the application of the provision on equitable grounds, particularly when nonpayment by the owner is the result of the general contractor's late or nonconforming performance. *See, e.g., Midland Eng'g Co. v. John A. Hall Construction Co.*, 398 F. Supp. 981 (N.D. Ind. 1975); *Yamanishi v. Bleily & Collishaw, Inc.*, 105 Cal. Rptr. 580 (Cal. Ct. App. 1972). Importantly, both the California Supreme Court and the New York Court of Appeals have concluded that pay-when-paid provisions, even those containing explicit conditions precedent, are unenforceable as abrogating the subcontractor's right to payment under the state's mechanic lien law. *Wm. R. Clarke Corp. v. SAFECO Insurance Co.*, 938 P.2d 372 (Cal. 1997); *West Fair Electric Contractors v. Aetna Casualty & Surety Co.*, 661 N.E.2d 967 (N.Y. 1995). Finally, the states of Illinois, North Carolina, Wisconsin, Maryland, and Missouri have enacted legislation invalidating pay-when-paid provisions. *See* Ill. Ann. Stat. Ch. 60, para. 21 (Smith-Hurd 1994); N.C. Gen. Stat. § 22C-2 (1991); Wis. Stat. § 779.135 (1994); Md. Real Prop. Code Ann., § 9-113(b) (1995); Mo. Rev. Stat. § 431.183 (1995). The pay-when-paid controversy is sure to continue, given the continuing judicial and legislative involvement with the issue.

Subcontractor Liability for Damages in yhe Construction Process — Finally, subcontractor liability for damages is a significant consideration in the drafting and negotiation of any subcontract. The general contractor will want to pass through to the subcontractor the full extent of the general contractor's liability to the owner or architect for the work undertaken by the subcontractor. This is generally accomplished through the use of a "flow-down," "flow-through,"or "conduit" clause in the subcontract. *See generally* SWEET, SWEET ON CONSTRUCTION LAW § 10.16 (1997). A conduit clause creates obligations between the subcontractor and general contractor that parallel those between the general contractor and owner. Owners, general contractors, and subcontractors are also interested in limiting their risk of loss to each other. Certainly a subcontractor who has only limited control over the project and whose work must be coordinated with the work of other subcontractors will not want to assume responsibility for delays in the performance of its work that it did not cause. In addition, a subcontractor will frequently want the subcontract to contain a liquidated damages clause so that the subcontractor will not be liable to the general contractor for consequential damages caused by the subcontractor's delay. On the other hand, the owner and general contractor will want to limit their liability to the subcontractor for delays that they may have caused. This objective may be achieved through liquidated damages clauses or through "no damage for delay" clauses, which allow the subcontractor only an extension of time to perform for delays caused by the owner or general contractor. *See, generally*, Dunne, *"No Damage for Delay" Clauses*, 19 THE CONSTRUCTION LAW. 38 (April 1999); Reinert, *Limitations on Recoverable Damages*, 18 THE CONSTRUCTION LAW. 5 (April 1998).

[2] Liability Between Property Owners and Sub-Contractors

If there is a dispute between a property owner and a subcontractor, the question is whether one has a cause of action against the other. When a property owner is dissatisfied with a subcontractor, the issue is most often one of poor workmanship, missed deadlines, or incomplete projects, while a subcontractor's most common problem is non-payment. The owner or subcontractor, however, may find it extremely difficult to successfully bring a cause of action against the other.

One possible cause of action is in contract. But if each party's contract is with the general contractor, then the owner and subcontractor have no contractual privity with one another. Traditionally, if there is no privity there is no duty, and a suit by either the owner or the subcontractor could be dismissed on this ground. *See, e.g., H.R. Moch Co. v. Rensselaer Water Co.*, 159 N.E. 896, 897 (N.Y. 1928); *Higgins Erectors & Haulers, Inc. v. E.E. Austin & Son, Inc.*, 714 F. Supp. 756, 760 (W.D. Pa. 1989); *East v. Galebridge Custom Builders, Inc.*, 839 S.W.2d 720, 722 (Mo. 1992).

In the absence of privity, the party bringing the action must initially prove that it is an intended third party beneficiary of the contract. *See, e.g.*, Jean Fleming Powers, *Expanded Liability and the Intent Requirement in Third Party Beneficiary Contracts*, 1993 Utah L. Rev. 67; *J.F., Inc. v. S.M. Wilson & Co.*, 504 N.E.2d 1266 (Ill. 5th Dist. 1987). The case that established this doctrine was *Lawrence v. Fox*, 20 N.Y. 268 (1859). Fox owed a sum of money to a man named Holly, who in turn had an outstanding debt to Lawrence in the same amount. Fox agreed to pay Lawrence directly on Holly's behalf, and when Fox failed to pay, Lawrence brought suit as a third party beneficiary. The court recognized Fox's duty to pay Lawrence. Keep in mind that it would not have been enough for Fox to agree to pay Holly *knowing* that Holly would ultimately give that money to Lawrence. In that event, Lawrence would benefit only indirectly from Fox's and Holly's transaction. Fox had to intend to benefit Lawrence directly by turning the money over to Lawrence himself.

Today, virtually all jurisdictions recognize a third party claim in contract matters (Powers, *supra*, at 67), but this recognition rarely helps our disputing property owner or subcontractor get third party standing. Jay M. Feinman, *Economic Negligence in Construction Litigation*, 15 Construction Law. 34, 35 (Aug. 1995). Judging whether or not someone qualifies as a third party claimant comes down to deciding whether that party was an intended beneficiary or merely an incidental beneficiary of the contract. *See Port Chester Electrical Construction Corp. v. Atlas*, 357 N.E.2d 983, 986 (N.Y. Ct. App. 1976); Restatement (Second) of Contracts, § 302. Section 302 of the Restatement defines the difference between the two as follows:

> (1) Unless otherwise agreed between promisor and promisee, a beneficiary of a promise is an intended beneficiary if recognition of a right to performance in the beneficiary is appropriate to effectuate the intention of the parties and either
>
> (a) the performance of the promise will satisfy an obligation of the promisee to pay money to the beneficiary; or

(b) the circumstances indicate that the promisee intends to give the beneficiary the benefit of the promised performance.

(2) An incidental beneficiary is a beneficiary who is not an intended beneficiary.

One of the Illustrations included in the Restatement proves helpful in unraveling the intended-incidental dynamic defined in § 302:

> 3. B promises A to pay whatever debts A may incur in a certain undertaking. A incurs in the undertaking debts to C, D, and E. If the promise is interpreted as a promise that B will pay C, D, and E, they are intended beneficiaries under Subsection (1)(a); if the money is to be paid to A in order that he may be provided with money to pay C, D, and E, they are at most incidental beneficiaries.

In the case of a disputing property owner and subcontractor, the court looks at the express language of the other party's contract with the general contractor to determine whether or not there appeared to be an express intent to make the aggrieved party a beneficiary. *See, e.g., Beveridge v. New York El. Railroad Co.*, 19 N.E. 489, 496 (N.Y. Ct. App. 1889); *Carson Pirie Scott & Co. v. Parrett*, 178 N.E. 498, 501 (Ill. 1931); *Higgins Erectors & Haulers, Inc.*, 714 F. Supp. at 760. Often, this type of language is not in the contract, and the courts in many jurisdictions will resist finding that the third party is an intended beneficiary in a construction contract. *See Port Chester Elec. Constr. Corp.*, 357 N.E.2d at 986; *North Carolina State Ports Auth. v. Lloyd A. Fry Roofing Co.*, 240 S.E.2d 345 (1978). As you see from the Restatement illustration, above, the intent to benefit the non-contracting party must be very clear, indeed.

While this has traditionally been the holding in most owner-subcontractor disputes, some jurisdictions are increasingly hesitant to look only to the rule. *See* Powers, *supra*, at 86. Jurisdictions in states such as Ohio and Missouri tend to allow third party claims. *See, e.g., Visintine & Co. v. New York, Chicago & St. Louis Railroad Co.*, 160 N.E.2d 311, 314 (Ohio 1959); *Black and White Cabs of St. Louis, Inc. v. Smith*, 370 S.W.2d 669, 675 (Mo. Ct. App. 1963); *Crum v. Lindgren, Inc.*, 564 S.W.2d 544, 547 (Mo. Ct. App. 1978). However, other jurisdictions, such as Illinois and New York, are somewhat more conservative in defining an "intended beneficiary" for the purpose of a construction contract action. *See, e.g., Santucci Construction Co. v. Baxter & Woodman, Inc.*, 502 N.E.2d 1134 (Ill. 2d Dist. 1986); *Port Chester Electrical Construction Corp.*, 357 N.E.2d at 983; Stewart E. Sterk, *The New York Court of Appeals: 150 Years of Leading Decisions*, 48 SYRACUSE L. REV. 1391 (1998).

A second possible cause of action would sound in tort. A cause of action by the owner against the subcontractor and vice versa also faces serious impediments. The party bringing a tort action must overcome the more strict concept of duty implicated in a tort claim. *See, e.g., Redarowicz v. Ohlendorf*, 441 N.E.2d 324, 327 (Ill. 1982). In a contract action, the duty that contracting parties — or third party beneficiaries — are owed stems directly from the agreement. However, in a negligence tort action, the common law duty one party owes another is independent of any contractual agreements: the existence of a contract between two other parties may not be used to heighten the duty of care one of those parties has to a third party outside the agreement. *See, e.g., Wymer-Harris Const. Co. v. Glass*, 171 N.E. 857, 858 (Ohio 1930); *Visintine & Co.*, 160 N.E.2d at 314–15.

The breach of duty in a negligence case, for example, is based entirely on conduct and the concept of "ordinary care." The Missouri supreme court held in *Crowder v. Vandendeale* that allowing negligence as a claim in construction matters would be against policy, would be difficult to support as an implied warranty violation, and would potentially conflict with existing contract law in defenses, remedies, statutes of limitation, and so on. *See Crowder v. Vandendeale*, 564 S.W.2d 879 (Mo.1978). *See also Crum*, 564 S.W.2d at 551; Powers, *supra*, at 79.

Tort claims arising out of construction contract problems face yet another issue in the economic loss doctrine, which examines the validity of the claim by examining the permissible recoveries. The doctrine dictates that a party cannot recover in tort for "economic loss." See W. Dudley McCarter, *Economic Loss Doctrine: Is Privity Required?*, J. MISSOURI B. (Jan./Feb. 1997); Feinman, *supra*, for a thorough discussion of the doctrine. While the concept of "economic loss" is an extremely complex one, the gist of the doctrine is that economic, or contractual, damages are best handled in a contract cause of action. Illinois, for example, is one of the many states that adheres to this doctrine. *See, e.g., Redarowicz*, 441 N.E.2d at 327. More significantly, the U.S. Supreme Court, in discussing an admiralty case involving a products liability issue, held that a party cannot maintain a tort action when a failed product has not damaged other property or injured people:

> [S]ince by definition no person or other property is damaged, the resulting loss is purely economic. Even when the harm to the product itself occurs through an abrupt, accident-like event, the resulting loss due to repair costs, decreased value, and lost profits is essentially the failure of the purchaser to receive the benefit of its bargain — traditionally the core concern of contract law. *East River Steam Corp. v. Transamerica Delaval*, 106 S. Ct. 2295, 2301-02 (1986).

This example epitomizes the difficulty a party can have bringing a torts claim that arises out of a contractual matter.

Traditionally, non-contracting parties in the construction setting were not liable to one another in contract theory due to the lack of privity, or in tort theory due to the economic loss doctrine. However, all jurisdictions recognize the concept of third party beneficiary status and many are increasingly willing to find that the third party was an intended beneficiary of the construction contract. Furthermore, not all jurisdictions recognize the economic loss doctrine. This trend towards allowing claims by non-contracting parties appears to be influenced by policy considerations. There are no easy answers to the question of liability between non-contracting parties, and any particular situation will be governed by its peculiar facts and the approach taken in the relevant jurisdiction.

[3] Subcontractor's Liability for Delay

Questions involving the extent of the general contractor's and subcontractor's liability to each other require careful consideration of often ambiguous contractual documents. Questions of liability frequently involve significant factual controversies concerning causation given the numerous participants in the construction process. As the following decision demonstrates, these legal and factual controversies can lead to extended litigation.

MORSE/DIESEL, INC. v. TRINITY INDUSTRIES, INC.

67 F.3d 435 (2d Cir. 1995)

PARKER, CIRCUIT JUDGE:

Major construction projects generate major construction litigation. Management of either is perilous.

Morse/Diesel, Inc., the general contractor for the construction of the Marriott Marquis Hotel in Manhattan's Times Square, sued the project's structural steel subcontractor, Mosher Steel Company, a division of Trinity Industries, Inc. (collectively "Trinity"), and Trinity's bonding company, Aetna Insurance Company, for damages arising from late performance on the subcontract. Trinity counterclaimed. After a lengthy jury trial in the United States District Court for the Southern District of New York (Loretta A. Preska, *Judge*), judgment was entered in favor of Morse/Diesel against Trinity and Aetna. Trinity and Aetna appeal.

This litigation has gone on for over ten years, and has surely cost millions of dollars in attorneys' fees and imposed innumerable demands on the district court. The jury trial alone lasted six and a half weeks. The work of the district judge in this case appears from our appellate distance to have been, in large part, exemplary. Nevertheless, we find that in one critical respect the jury was prevented from fairly evaluating Trinity's counterclaim. Because the error may have infected the jury's consideration of the case as a whole, we must reverse the judgment and remand for a new trial.

Background to Trinity's Appeal

The steel subcontract for the hotel project was executed in August 1982. It called for Trinity (and its sub-subcontractor, Helena Erectors, Inc., which erected the steel members fabricated by Trinity) to complete the erection work within 13 months, excluding inclement weather. In fact, the job took 20 months, from January 1983 to September 1984, and the final Helena crane was not removed from the site until December 1984. Responsibility for that delay is the central question in this litigation.

Morse/Diesel blamed Trinity, and produced evidence of fabrication errors, shipping mishaps, crane failures, and so on. Morse/Diesel sought damages of over $37 million, consisting primarily of the costs of instituting an acceleration program designed to "recapture" the delay, as well as losses suffered by the hotel owner, the architect, and other subcontractors. The jury substantially agreed with Morse/Diesel and awarded the company almost $26 million in damages, to which the court added an additional $27 million prejudgment interest.

Trinity blamed Morse/Diesel, attributing responsibility for much of the delay to the project's architect (John Portman & Associates) and structural engineer (Weidlinger Associates) (collectively "Architect") who made, in Trinity's estimation, unwarranted demands regarding the installation of certain special steel trusses, known as Vierendeel trusses, and the use of additional bracing during erection. Trinity also argued that inclement weather caused substantial delay. On appeal, Trinity contends that the district court unfairly limited its ability to present these two defenses.

Trinity also counterclaimed against Morse/Diesel for its own damages arising from additional work and delay in completing the subcontract, and appeals on the ground that the district court deprived it of a fair trial on the counterclaim. Further, Trinity claims the district court erred in refusing to allow Trinity's expert to challenge Morse/Diesel's evidence of damages. Finally, Trinity argues that the court miscalculated prejudgment interest.

We agree with Trinity that it was unfairly precluded from presenting its counterclaim to the jury. While it is not necessary to reach the other issues raised by Trinity's appeal, we nonetheless address those issues below in order to provide guidance for proceedings upon remand.

Trinity's Right to Recover Damages

Trinity based its counterclaim for damages against Morse/Diesel on Schedule B, paragraph 53, of the subcontract, which provides:

> Should the Subcontractor be obstructed or delayed in the commencement, prosecution or completion of the work, without fault on his part, by action or inaction on the part of the Owner, Architect, Engineer or Contractor, or by changes in the work, the Subcontractor shall be entitled to include as cost the cost of labor, materials, equipment, supplies and other resultant costs occasioned by such delays and changes *notwithstanding any other provision contained in this agreement.*

(Emphasis added.)

By virtue of the "notwithstanding" clause, paragraph 53 overrides, in part, two "no-damages-for-delay" provisions of the subcontract. Article 16-G of the subcontract's General Conditions provides:

> Should the subcontractor be obstructed or delayed in the commencement, prosecution or completion of the work, without fault on his part, by the act, failure to act, direction, order, neglect, delay or default of the Owner, the Architect, the Contractor or any other contractor employed upon the work, or by changes in the work or by reason of fire, lightning, earthquake, enemy action, act of God or similar catastrophe, or by Government restrictions in respect to materials or labor, or by a strike or lockout beyond such subcontractor's reasonable control, then he shall be entitled to an extension of time for a period equivalent to the time lost by reason of any or all of the causes aforesaid but no claim for extension of time on account of delay shall be allowable unless a claim in writing therefor is presented to the Contractor with reasonable diligence but in any event not later than within four (4) days after the commencement of such claimed delay. The mere presentation of such claim shall not establish the validity of the cause of delay or of the extension of time for completion. *The subcontractor expressly agrees not to make, and hereby waives, any claim for damages*, including those resulting from increased supervision, labor or material costs, *on account of any delay*, obstruction or hindrance for any cause whatsoever, including but not limited to the aforesaid causes, and agrees that the sole right and remedy therefor shall be an extension of time.

(Emphasis added.) And Article 3.4 of the subcontract provides in part:

> All loss or damage arising from any of the Work through unforeseen or unusual obstructions, difficulties or delays which may be encountered in the prosecution of same or through the action of the elements shall be borne by the Subcontractor.

Trinity requested a jury instruction that it could recover damages under paragraph 53 for costs associated with delays caused by others. Judge Preska denied the request. Instead, she explained to the jury that Trinity's "claim for damages on account of delays allegedly caused by Morse/Diesel and its subcontractors" was an "area of ambiguity" in the subcontract. She noted Morse/Diesel's contention "that such damages are not recoverable" because of Article 16-G of the General Conditions and Article 3.4 of the subcontract (both quoted above), and read the pertinent provisions to the jury. Judge Preska then noted Trinity's contention that "these provisions of the subcontract have been negated by paragraph 53 of schedule B," and in turn quoted that paragraph to the jury.

Judge Preska then instructed the jury as follows:

> Once again, it is your job to construe the subcontract in light of all the evidence, to ascertain what the parties intended with respect to [Trinity's] ability to assert claims for damages on account of delay. Whatever understanding you reach you must then apply in evaluating [Trinity's] delay claims.

The fatal flaw in these instructions is that the subcontract in fact contained no ambiguity as to Trinity's right to seek damages for delays caused by others. "Under New York law, a written contract is to be interpreted so as to give effect to the intention of the parties as expressed in the unequivocal language they have employed." *Cruden v. Bank of New York*, 957 F.2d 961, 976 (2d Cir. 1992). "The entire contract must be considered, and all parts of it reconciled, if possible, in order to avoid an inconsistency." *Id.* Whatever tension otherwise would exist among the three contract provisions discussed above is relieved by the "notwithstanding" clause of paragraph 53. By its unequivocal language, paragraph 53 trumps the otherwise inconsistent clauses of Article 3.4 and Article 16-G of the General Conditions. *See In re Gulf Oil/Cities Service Tender Offer Litigation*, 725 F. Supp. 712, 729–30 (S.D.N.Y. 1989) (contract provision containing language "notwithstanding any other provision" explicitly overrides contrary provision). There is no ambiguity.

The precedence of paragraph 53 over contrary language in other provisions is not undermined, as Morse/Diesel contends, by Article 2.1 of the subcontract, which provides that, "in the event of any inconsistency between the terms and conditions" of the subcontract proper and the General Conditions, "the more restrictive provision, as applied to the Subcontractor, shall govern." Because there is no inconsistency once the "notwithstanding" clause is given its necessary effect, there is no reason to resort to the Article 2.1 tiebreaker.

The court thus erred in submitting the contract's meaning on this point to the jury. "Construing an unambiguous contract provision is a function of the court, rather than a jury. . . ." *Cruden*, 957 F.2d at 976. The proper interpretation of the contract is a question of law for the court. *Harris Trust and Savings Bank v. John Hancock Mut. Life Ins. Co.*, 970 F.2d 1138, 1147–48 (2d Cir. 1992), *aff'd*, 114 S. Ct. 517 (1993). The district court should have construed the contract according to its unambiguous terms, and clearly instructed the jury that Trinity had the right under paragraph 53 to recover any costs occasioned by delays in "the commencement, prosecution or completion of the work" that were not its own fault.

The error cannot be deemed harmless. We do not know what the jury would have done had it received a correct instruction on Trinity's counterclaim. The jury returned a general verdict. It certainly concluded that Trinity was at fault for much of the delay and the resulting acceleration damages incurred by Morse/Diesel; the verdict makes that much clear. But Morse/Diesel did not recover all it sought. It is very possible the jury believed that Morse/Diesel (or the Architect or another contractor) was indeed to blame for some of the delay, but that the jury nonetheless did not award damages to Trinity on the counterclaim because it mistakenly concluded that Trinity was not entitled to damages under the "no-damages-for-delay" clauses. Properly instructed on the import of paragraph 53, the jury might also have awarded damages to Trinity for certain additional work, unrelated to delay. The mere fact, therefore, that the jury awarded substantial damages to Morse/Diesel does not necessarily mean that it would not also have awarded offsetting damages to Trinity had it been properly instructed on the significance of paragraph 53.

The question remains whether the error requires retrial of all claims or only the counterclaim. Where, as here, the claim and counterclaim concern essentially the same facts and issues, the question primarily being who is at fault for the delays, we believe it is impossible to isolate the counterclaim for retrial. Although it is apparent that the jury held Trinity accountable for much of the delay, we cannot determine which portions of the ten-month delay were laid at Trinity's feet. It is therefore impossible to identify the "remaining" portions of the delay for retrial solely on the counterclaim. Indeed, the jury might have determined that Trinity was only partly at fault for a particular period of delay, and that the Architect was also partly at fault for the same period of delay, but again did not offset the damages award to Morse/Diesel because of an erroneous interpretation of paragraph 53. Since we cannot know the answers to these questions, it is necessary to reverse the judgment in toto and remand both complaint and counterclaim for retrial.

Remaining Issues in Trinity's Appeal

1. *Extent of the Architect's Authority*

Trinity sought to defend against the claim of late performance, and to establish its counterclaim, by introducing evidence that its proposed methods for erecting the Vierendeel trusses and for temporarily bracing the structure were adequate, and that the Architect's directives to use alternative methods were unreasonable, unnecessary and the cause of substantial delay. Prior to trial, however, the district court granted a motion in limine, ruling that the Architect's decisions with respect to the erection of the trusses and the temporary bracing "must be accepted as final and valid under the contract, unless defendants can show such decisions to have been the product of bad faith, fraud, or palpable mistake equivalent to bad faith."

After reconsideration, the . . . order was reaffirmed. In the second order, the court ruled that Trinity remained free to maintain that the Architect's "decisions to reject their proposed means and methods were taken in bad faith or were palpably mistaken so as to be equivalent to bad faith [but] unless defendants' evidence on this point rises to a level that would allow a reasonable jury to conclude that their claims of bad faith (or the like) were correct, they may not present the evidence at trial."

The ruling was enforced during the trial, effectively curbing the testimony of Trinity's construction expert. In particular, the court curtailed testimony by the expert as to his opinion that there was no "engineering basis" for the Architect's refusal to permit Trinity to use its steel erection methods. The expert testified that the basis for this opinion was his determination that Helena's proposals were "totally adequate." In conformance with the pretrial ruling, the district court declared the opinion inadmissible: "It is insufficient to say that the engineer's rejection of the proposed drawings had no engineering basis. If the basis for that opinion, as I heard the witness state, was that [Helena's] proposal was adequate, that is insufficient." After further colloquy, Judge Preska reiterated her point: "That it would have worked, as we have said 500 times, is not sufficient to show that it was wrongfully rejected." Without more, the workability of Helena's proposals did not go to show that the Architect's rejection of them was "the product of bad faith, fraud, or palpable mistake equivalent to bad faith."

Trinity initially challenges the district court's interpretation of the subcontract provisions that allocate responsibility for the steel erection between Trinity and the Architect. Trinity contends that, read together, these provisions circumscribe the Architect's control over the methods of construction and therefore limit the Architect's authority to reject Trinity's plans. Like the district court, we believe Trinity's reading of the subcontract is one-sided.

Trinity emphasizes Article 3-A of the subcontract's General Conditions, which states:

> The Architect shall, on behalf of the Owner, periodically make on-site inspections of the work to check the quality and progress of the work and to monitor construction activities. Notwithstanding the foregoing, *the Architect will not be responsible for, and will not have control or charge of, construction means, methods, techniques, sequences or procedures or for safety precautions and programs in connection with the work* and he will not be responsible for any subcontractor's failure to carry out the work in accordance with the Contract Documents.

(Emphasis added.) Trinity also points to Article 3-B of the General Conditions:

> The Architect shall be the interpreter of the plans and specifications. In the event of dispute, the Architect shall side with none of Owner, the Contractor or the subcontractor, and the Architect shall also render a decision as to the items to be included within the scope of the work, *which decision is advisory only.*

(Emphasis added.)

But other broad provisions in the subcontract temper the subcontractor's independent authority, reposing approval authority in the Architect. Thus, Article 2.2 states in part:

> The Subcontractor shall undertake and complete the Work under the direction and supervision of the Contractor, *and to the entire satisfaction of the Contractor, the Owner and the Architect.*

(Emphasis added.) Further, § 1C-6(e) of the subcontract's Specifications, Vol. 1 provides:

> *The Architect will be the sole judge* of conformity. No materials shall be installed except in accordance with the plans and specifications or the Architect's written amendments thereto.

(Emphasis in original.) And Article 3-N of the General Conditions provides:

> The Architect, the Owner and the Contractor each will have the *authority to reject subcontractor's work* which does not conform to the Contract Documents.

(Emphasis added.)

Other provisions cover more specific ground. Paragraph 24 of Schedule B of the subcontract states in part:

> Subcontractor will furnish tower cranes for erection of structural steel, metal deck, precast plank, and hoisting of steel stairs. *All load calculations and support methods must be submitted for approval.* . . . All reinforcing of the structure as required for the tower cranes is included by the Subcontractor. *Details and location of reinforcing must be submitted for approval.*

(Emphasis added.) Section 5B-1-05(b)(3) of the Specifications, Vol. 1 states:

> After award [of contract]: . . . (3) Erection procedure (for review and scope): Submit data to illustrate the erection procedure, including the erection, bolting and welding sequence, temporary staying and bracing required, and clarifying information and calculations requested by the Architect/Engineer.

See also Schedule B, para. 29 ("Subcontractor will submit an erection sequence diagram, fabrication and erection Schedule for review."); Schedule B, para. 44 ("Subcontractor shall record the amount of camber that remains after the 1st Vierendeel truss has been erected and loaded with the precast Plank. Fabrication and erection adjustments are to be made for subsequent Vierendeel trusses, subject to the engineer's approval, to insure a level installation of the precast plank within the specified tolerances.")

In the May 12 Order, after considering several of the provisions just cited, Judge Preska wrote: "Read together, these provisions are most naturally understood to mean that while Helena may choose its means and methods, its choices are subject to the approval of the Architect/Engineer." She concluded that "the Architect/Engineer had discretion to reject plans as inconsistent with the contract documents. . . ." We wholly agree with the district court's interpretation.

Our conclusion is not weakened by the "advisory only" language in Article 3-B of the General Conditions (quoted above), much cited by Trinity in its briefs. That language relates only to the Architect's decisions as to the scope of work in the event there is a dispute over the interpretation of the plans and specifications. That is not the issue here. Trinity does not contend that its proposed construction methods were in accordance with the plans but were disapproved nonetheless, a contention that might require an interpretation of the plans; rather, Trinity concedes that its proposed methods contravened the Architect's plans but avers that its methods should have been acceptable because they satisfied industry standards. The issue therefore is not the Architect's exercise of authority in interpreting plans, but its exercise of authority in disapproving Trinity's proposed methods of erecting the trusses and bracing. The subcontract delegates that authority to the Architect.

Whether Trinity's proposed methods for erecting the Vierendeel trusses and temporary bracing were sound and workable, and whether the Architect's demands were unnecessary, are ultimately irrelevant. It was therefore appropriate at trial to preclude Trinity's construction expert from stating his opinions on such questions.

To say the Architect has discretionary authority, of course, is not to say it has unbounded discretion. As noted above, the district court ruled that the Architect's decisions "must be accepted as final and valid under the contract, unless defendants can show such decisions to have been the product of bad faith, fraud, or palpable mistake equivalent to bad faith." This is an accurate statement of controlling New York law. The language derives directly from *Joseph Davis, Inc. v. Merritt-Chapman & Scott Corp.*, 27 A.D.2d 114, 276 N.Y.S.2d 479, 483 (4th Dep't 1967), *aff'd*, 23 N.Y.2d 872, 298 N.Y.S.2d 79, 245 N.E.2d 809 (1969). The same principle is restated in more recent decisions:

> It is established that the contractor cannot recover for additional work required by the architect or engineer in charge of construction where the contract gives the architect or engineer authority to determine the manner of performing the contract. In general, the parties are free to leave certain determinations to the judgment of the engineer and, where this has been done, the determination of the engineer is final as a matter of law, absent a showing of fraud or bad faith. However, if there appears no reasonable basis for the engineer's action, if it is patently erroneous, then the courts have found the equivalent of bad faith and the contractor is not bound by the engineer's decision.

Savin Brothers, Inc. v. State of New York, 62 A.D.2d 511, 405 N.Y.S.2d 516, 519 (4th Dep't 1978) (citations omitted), *aff'd*, 47 N.Y.2d 934, 419 N.Y.S.2d 969, 393 N.E.2d 1041 (1979); *see Thomas Crimmins Contracting Co. v. City of New York*, 138 A.D.2d 138, 530 N.Y.S.2d 779, 782 (lst Dep't 1988), *aff'd*, 74 N.Y.2d 166, 544 N.Y.S.2d 580, 542 N.E.2d 1097 (1989); *see also Brant Constr. Co. v. Metropolitan Water Reclamation Dist. of Greater Chicago*, 967 F.2d 244, 248 (7th Cir. 1992) (jury not appropriate arbiter where contract delegates task to engineer).

2. *The "Inclement Weather" Clause*

Trinity also defended against the charge of late performance by contending that much of the delay was attributable to inclement weather. The subcontract specifically excluded days of inclement weather from the 13-month period required for performance. Schedule B, para. 49; *see also* Art. 6 (time of the essence).

The parties are in substantial agreement that two to three months of the contract period was comprised of bad weather days on which erection work could not proceed. Trinity contends that, as a matter of law, it should not be held accountable for the period of delay attributable to those days. The district court, however, ruled that the term "inclement weather" was ambiguous, and allowed Morse/Diesel to introduce parol evidence that the term referred only to unusually severe weather-that is, weather beyond what one would expect for New York at the time-and that the 13-month period was intended to include "standard" bad weather. The court charged the jury to decide which interpretation was intended by the contracting parties. Trinity argues this was error.

"Ascertaining whether or not a writing is ambiguous is a question of law for the trial court . . . , and we review the trial court's determination de novo." *Sayers v. Rochester Telephone Corp. Supplemental Management Pension Plan*, 7 F.3d 1091, 1094 (2d Cir. 1993) (citing *W.W.W. Assocs. v. Giancontieri*, 77 N.Y.2d 157, 162, 565 N.Y.S.2d 440, 566 N.E.2d 639 (1990)). Under New York law "contract language is ambiguous if it is capable of more than one meaning when viewed objectively by a reasonably intelligent person who has examined the context of the entire integrated agreement and who is cognizant of the customs, practices, usages and terminology as generally understood in the particular trade or business." 7 F.3d at 1095 (internal quotations omitted). Conversely, "no ambiguity exists when contract language has a definite and precise meaning, unattended by danger of misconception in the purport of the [contract] itself, and concerning which there is no reasonable basis for a difference of opinion." *Id.* (internal quotation omitted).

Reasonable people familiar with both this subcontract and the construction industry generally might well differ in their understanding of the term "inclement weather" as used in paragraph 49. Another provision of the subcontract itself casts doubt on Trinity's interpretation of the term; Article 3.4 provides in part: "All loss or damage arising from any of the Work through unforeseen or unusual obstructions, difficulties or delays . . . or through the action of the elements shall be borne by the Subcontractor." Further, Morse/Diesel's evidence of industry usage of the term showed its meaning was not "definite and precise." There was no error in allowing the jury to determine the parties' intent based on extrinsic evidence.

3. *The Notice of Claim Requirement*

Morse/Diesel opposed Trinity's counterclaim at trial by contending that Trinity had not adhered to the subcontract's notice of claim requirements. See General Conditions, Art. 16-F ("If the subcontractor desires to make a claim for an increase in the Subcontract Price or any extension in the time for completion, he shall give the Contractor and Owner written notice thereof within ten (10) days after subcontractor's knowledge of the occurrence of the event giving rise to such claim, together with detailed labor and material costs."); General Conditions, Art. 16-G (four-day notice requirement for extension of time where subcontractor has been obstructed or delayed).[1]

In response, Trinity introduced evidence that it had provided timely written notice, as well as evidence intending to show that Morse/Diesel had actual knowledge of the damages and delays Trinity encountered and that Morse/Diesel had waived strict compliance with the notice of claim procedures by certain representations made to Trinity during construction. Specifically, a witness for Trinity testified that it was often difficult to submit notices of claims within the short

[1] Paragraph 53 does not itself contain a notice of claim requirement, and Articles 16-F and G do not strictly pertain to claims for damages. It is therefore not obvious from the contract which (if any) notice requirement should be read into paragraph 53. The court gave jury instructions on both Articles 16-F and G, but its separate instruction relating to the "ambiguity" of Trinity's right to recover damages for delay under paragraph 53 does not refer to any notice requirement. Trinity, however, concedes it was subject to giving timely notice of its claims for damages, and does not object to the lack of clarity in the court's instructions on the point; its contention on appeal is only that the court ought to have charged the jury that the notice of claim requirement could be waived. Accordingly, that is the only issue we address.

periods required by the subcontract, and that he had explained this problem to a representative of Morse/Diesel, who told him "to do the best you can" and provide "a notification as soon as you can."

Trinity submitted a proposed jury instruction that would permit the jury to find that Morse/Diesel had waived compliance with the notice requirement. The district court declined to give the instruction as requested. However, the court did give the following instruction: "Strict compliance with the written notice terms is not required if you find that there was substantial compliance under the subcontract's notice provisions." Trinity argues the instruction failed to present the waiver theory to the jury.

Although principles of waiver and estoppel generally may be invoked to bar enforcement of notice of claim requirements, *see Safway Steel Products v. Craft Architectural Metals Corp.*, 183 A.D.2d 452, 583 N.Y.S.2d 844, 845 (lst Dep't 1992), here the evidence was insufficient to warrant a waiver instruction. At best, the evidence showed that Morse/Diesel might permit substantial compliance with the notice requirement in instances when strict compliance would be very difficult. As the court gave an instruction allowing "substantial compliance," there was no error. . . .

Aetna's Appeal

Aetna appeals from the $31.8 million judgment entered against it, which represents the full amount of the performance bond it posted to cover Trinity's work. Because Aetna's liability as a surety depends on the liability of its principal, *see Granite Computer Leasing Corp. v. Travelers Indemnity Co.*, 894 F.2d 547, 551 (2d Cir. 1990), our disposition of Trinity's appeal mandates that we also reverse the judgment against Aetna. Morse/Diesel's claim against Aetna, and Aetna's defenses thereto, may be considered anew in subsequent proceedings before the district court. . . .

Conclusion

For the reasons set forth above, the judgment of the district court is reversed and the case is remanded for further proceedings.

[4] Questions

1. What is the role of the owner and architect under the Standard Form of Agreement between the contractor and subcontractor? What legal relationship does the subcontractor have to the owner and architect, if any? AIA Document A201-2007 ¶ 1.1.2 states that the Contract "shall not be construed to create a contractual relationship of any kind . . . (4) between any persons or entities other than the Owner and the Contractor." AIA Document A401-2007 ¶ 2.1 states that the contractor and the subcontractor have the same relationship as do the owner and the contractor under AIA Document A201-2007.

2. Does the owner or architect have any control over the selection of subcontractors? *See* AIA Document A201-2007 ¶ 5.2. Does the owner or architect have any control over the retention of a subcontractor? *See* AIA Document A201-2007 ¶ 5.2.4. Should an owner or architect exercise this

control? *See Meva Corp. v. United States*, 511 F.2d 548 (Ct. Cl. 1975); *Liles Construction Co. v. United States*, 455 F.2d 527 (Ct. Cl. 1972). Can an owner retain a subcontractor if the general contractor is terminated? *See* AIA Document A201-2007 ¶ 5.4.1.

3. Consider the "flow-through" or "conduit" clause between the general contractor and the subcontractor under AIA Document A401-2007 ¶ 2.1, which, as previously stated, puts the contractor and the subcontractor in the same relationship as the owner and contractor have under AIA Document A201-2007. *See also* AIA Document A201-2007 ¶ 5.3.1. AIA Document A401-2007 ¶ 2.2 continues the conduit theory to any sub-subcontractors that the subcontractor might engage. These provisions impose parallel commitments between the general contractor and subcontractor (or subcontractor and sub-subcontractor) as exist between the owner and the general contractor and also extend the rights that the general contractor has against the owner to the subcontractor as against the general contractor. Why should the owner be so concerned with protecting the subcontractors from the general contractor?

4. How is the subcontractor involved when modifications are made to the general contract by change order or construction change directive? AIA Document A401-2007 ¶ 5 requires the subcontractor to make any changes required by the Prime Contract and to promptly submit any claim for adjustment in the subcontract as to price or time so that the contractor can make that part of the contractor's claim under the Prime Contract.

5. How are disputes resolved between the general contractor and subcontractor? The provisions of AIA Document A401-2007 ¶ 6 follow the provisions of AIA Document A201-2007 ¶ 15, with the major change in the 2007 version being that claims by the subcontractor now may be joined into dispute resolution under the Prime Contract.

Part V

LEASING OF THE PROJECT'S RETAIL SPACE

Chapter 14

BUSINESS AND LEGAL ISSUES IN LEASING

§ 14.01 BUSINESS ISSUES

[1] Overview

The commercial lease is the life blood of most real estate developments. The rents paid under the terms of the leases involved will pay for all of the expenses incurred by the lessor, including operation and maintenance expenses, insurance, taxes, and, perhaps most importantly, debt service. As discussed in Part I, any rents in excess of these expenses, as well as any appreciation in the value of the property itself, will provide a return to the lessor. Consequently, the lessor, the lessee, and the permanent lender each will be intensely interested in the terms of the leases and the respective rights and obligations of the lessor and lessee.

As described in the lease, the lessor and lessee will define the terms of their relationship. At a minimum, the lease will describe the premises, the lease term, the rent to be paid during the lease term, and the rights and remedies in the event of default. The lease typically will also contain terms requiring the lessee to pay a share of operating and maintenance expenses for the development, often referred to as common area maintenance or CAM charges, and a share of the local real estate taxes assessed against the development. The lease will also frequently contain terms limiting the lessee's use of the premises and the lessee's ability to transfer the lease, by assignment or subletting. The lease will also detail the lessor's and the lessee's respective obligations to maintain the common areas of the development and the premises, the lessee's obligations to carry both liability and casualty insurance, and the rights of each party in the event of condemnation or casualty. Because the resolution of these issues will affect the financial arrangements between the lessee and lessor and because the lender may find itself in the shoes of the lessor if the project is unsuccessful, the permanent lender is also keenly interested in the manner in which many of these issues are addressed under the lease.

The parties may also address a number of additional issues under the lease. Can the lessee operate a similar business within a certain geographic radius of the premises? Can the lessor lease space within the development to a lessee that operates a similar business as that of an existing lessee? What happens to the lease if the lessee goes bankrupt? What happens to the shopping center should the lessor go bankrupt? Who is liable for the costs of remediating any environmental contamination affecting the property?

All of these specific questions, which should be addressed under the terms of the lease, demonstrate that a commercial lease is, in essence, a risk-allocation and risk-minimizing mechanism between the lessor and lessee. Both lessors and lessees want to reduce the risks that they face individually which might translate into higher costs and reduced income in the future. For example, in a retail mall setting, the lessor will attempt to pass through all costs for the operation of the mall to the lessees so that it does not face the risk that increased costs will reduce its ability to service its debt or its return on investment. At the same time, each lessee will attempt to limit the risk that it faces by limiting its liability for specific costs that the lessor might wish to pass through to the lessees.

The purpose of Part V is to provide you with a broad overview of the issues and concerns that a party must address when entering into a commercial lease. The issues are discussed from the viewpoints of the lessor, the lessee and, where applicable, that of the permanent lender. No single text, much less the two chapters in Part V, could attempt to provide in-depth explanations of all the intricacies of commercial leasing. Nevertheless, Part V provides a starting point from which to explore commercial leasing more fully, first by considering the leasing question from the perspective of a prospective lessee.

[2] Negotiating a Commercial Lease from the Tenant's Perspective

Marisa Manley, *Before You Sign That Lease . . . ,* HARVARD BUSINESS REVIEW (May/June 1988)*

Office space rental is often a big expense for a small company. But it can be unnecessarily expensive if you don't understand the hidden costs and restrictions that are buried in many leases.

The first thing to understand is that when you negotiate an office lease, your landlord probably has the advantage. If you're like most tenants, you negotiate a lease once every five or ten years and you put rent into the same category as other routine, current business expenses, weighing the monthly payment versus your cash flow.

The landlord is in a different position. Its business is leasing space, and buildings are its major asset. The landlord is highly motivated to plan for the long term and to write conservative leases that maximize the return on their assets. A good real estate lawyer can help protect your interests, but often isn't equipped to advise on business points. Legally acceptable arrangements can be bad business deals.

Fortunately, if you're savvy and reserve certain rights, you can turn an office lease into a tremendous asset. Here are some of the more obscure lease provisions that protect landlords at their tenants' expense.

The Space

Office space priced per "rentable" square foot often turns out to be much more expensive than tenants expect because landlords may include space that tenants consider unusable. Normally, you'll be able to use only 75% to 90% of what you pay

---

* Reprinted by permission of *Harvard Business Review. Before You Sign That Lease . . .* by Marisa Manley, May/June 1988.

for. This difference, the loss factor, depends on three things: the physical configuration of your offices, your landlord's method of measuring rentable area, and, increasingly, your landlord's whim.

Rentable area is sure to include a portion of elevators, janitors' closets, lobbies, stairways, and more. Fair enough. Be aware, however, that some buildings have a higher loss factor than others. Fancy curves or sharp angles, elevator banks placed in the center of the building instead of on the side, and an abundance of columns in your space contribute to a higher loss factor.

In addition, landlords often develop their own methods for measuring rentable area. A landlord may measure from the outside of one exterior wall to another, for example, and include questionably "public" areas like air shafts. Some buildings seem to be measured from gargoyle to gargoyle-facade ornaments unrelated to a tenant's usable space.

Beyond this, many landlords create an arbitrary loss factor. Once they've determined how big a space is, they just inflate the number by, say, 25% and then call that the rentable area.

To protect yourself, you might hire an architect to measure the space you plan to lease and tell you whether the usable area will satisfy your business' needs. The architect should use a generally accepted standard, like that adopted by the Building Owners and Managers Association, so you can precisely compare one space with another. Then, whatever number the landlord uses, you'll know how much you'll be paying per usable square foot, and you'll have a more informed basis for negotiation.

On lease renewal, the tenant may also find that the landlord has "remeasured" the space and now claims it's much larger. A well-known Manhattan landlord told a tenant I know that the tenant's space had grown 20%. It also demanded a higher rent per square foot-a double blow.

Operating Expenses — The Trickiest Clause

An operating expense clause lets your landlord recover normal out-of-pocket costs of running a building. That should be all it does. Operating expenses listed in your bill should correspond directly to benefits you gain under the lease, and they ought to meet an objective standard such as GAAP (generally accepted accounting principles), not conventions particular to your landlord.

Insist on a precise and limited definition of the items to be included. Landlords sometimes use the operating expense clause as a profit center. If you approve a catchall clause, which many landlords argue is necessary, it can become a blank check. You may be billed for charges that have little to do with running a building. Ambiguity also increases your risk of litigation.

Exclusions. Certain items should be specifically excluded from operating expenses: electricity that serves tenants' spaces (the landlord recovers this from each tenant individually); executive salaries; consulting fees; market study fees; commissions and advertising costs; initial landscaping costs; structural repairs or replacements; penalties incurred because the landlord fails to pay taxes on time; fees and higher interest charges caused by the landlord's refinancing of the property; money the landlord must pay if it defaults under a lease or other agreement; any legal fees to resolve disputes involving the landlord; any excessive amount the landlord pays a contractor or vendor because of a special relationship.

Capital improvements. Capital expenditures require particular attention when you're negotiating a lease. The operating expense clause should exclude them generally from the operating expenses for which you are billed.

Barclays Bank in New York got a repair bill after its landlord, Panel Realty Company, installed a new air conditioning system. Barclays refused to pay, and the case ended up in court. Barclays' lease required the landlord to make all structural repairs. The bank was responsible for its share of all other building maintenance and repairs, including repairs to the air-conditioning system. The court reasoned that replacing the system goes beyond traditional notions of repair. This was a capital expenditure that Panel Realty couldn't pass on to Barclays. While the bank won, it had taken needless risk because its lease didn't make the landlord responsible for capital expenditures.[1]

Even with an exclusion, substantial capital expenditures — artfully relabeled — can find their way into your operating expense bill if you're not careful. For instance, a lease may require you to pay for equipment rentals. This is a common technique for converting capital expenditures into expenses that are passed on to the tenant. You should agree to pay for equipment rentals only if they're not a substitute for capital equipment the landlord would otherwise have to buy. Tenants should be on the lookout for charges like this because the 1986 Tax Reform Act changed depreciation provisions in the tax law and made equipment leasing more attractive to landlords than buying.

Certain capital improvements, like new, more efficient elevators or a new HVAC system, are supposed to reduce the cost of running the building and thus your portion of operating expenses. Such capital expenditures normally are not included in operating expenses. Landlords often insist, however, that you absorb a portion of the cost. Ask for some demonstration that in fact these capital expenditures will reduce operating expenses. Then if you agree to a lease that allows your landlord to bill you for the annual amortization of these items, make sure your portion is limited to the savings that you realize in a particular year. In other words, your net operating expense should be no higher than it was before the cost-saving installation.

Double dipping. The landlord's costs of running separate income producing parts of the building should be rolled into operating expenses only after the income is deducted from your operating expenses. This goes for sundry shops, coffee shops, observation decks, and so on. If the building has a garage, your landlord probably charges tenants and the public for parking spaces, but the cost of operating the parking garage may also be included among your operating expenses. If your lease doesn't specifically exclude this cost, your landlord has a good argument for billing you.

Electricity. For many tenants, electricity is one of the biggest operating expenses. Landlords that want to augment their revenues without quoting a higher rent often use the electricity clause as a profit center, inflating the already substantial cost for this essential service. Don't let your landlord's profit unnecessarily increase your utility bills. Typically, leases provide that electricity

---

[1] Panel Realty Company v. Barclays Bank, PLC, 130 A.D.2d 427 (N.Y. App. Div. 1987).

will be paid for in one of three ways: direct metering, submetering, or rent inclusion.

Direct metering is straightforward and may be the cheapest for you. When the utility directly meters your electricity, you pay the actual charge for what you use. There's no question of intervening profit for the landlord.

When only one meter in the building connects to the utility, you or your landlord may install a separate meter to measure the electricity you use. Your landlord pays the utility, and you pay the landlord. This method, called submetering, can give you cheaper electricity, provided you know what to ask for. If your landlord can buy electricity at low bulk rates, you should bargain for the benefit of that lower rate. Leases often say the tenant will be billed "in accordance with" a utility's published rate schedule. This may mean the landlord will charge you the highest rate that would apply to your own consumption and pocket the difference.

If a building has only one meter, your electric charges may simply be lumped in with your rent. This method is the riskiest for tenants. The landlord usually estimates your electricity usage by looking at your office equipment and asking how many hours you use each piece in a typical day or week. Such estimates are inherently less certain than measuring the amount of electricity you use; on one Manhattan block, the basic rate landlords charge for electricity varies more than 30%.

Be wary of such estimates for another reason. They may include a substantial "safety factor" that needlessly increases your costs. For instance, suppose your landlord pays $2.25 per square foot for electricity but adds $2.75 a square foot to your basic rent. A 10% rate increase would raise your charges to $3.02, and your landlord's profit would grow from $.50; to $.55; per square foot. If your office were 10,000 square feet, that extra $.05; alone would cost you $5,000 over a ten-year lease term. Your landlord's profit on your electricity bill: $55,000. And that's assuming no further increases.

Can the landlord cut off your electricity? Leases used throughout the country often allow a landlord to do it on short notice — leaving a tenant to deal directly with a utility. Making your own arrangements for electricity can be expensive and time consuming. It may require much interior work — like new risers, conduits, and wiring — which, incidentally, your lease may not give you the right to install. Landlords have used such clauses to gain leverage when dealing with unrelated matters.

Rent Increases

Base year. Office tenants are generally responsible for increased building expenses and real estate taxes over some base point — either a base year or an expense stop. These escalations can easily outstrip the base rent, and courts will generally enforce the provisions in a lease you sign regardless of how much your rent may increase. So it's important to understand the mechanics of escalation formulas.

The base year is generally the first 12 months you occupy your space. The expense "stop" is a number representing average, reasonable operating expenses per square foot during those first 12 months. Because it is the lease's reference point, if you agree to an early base year or an expense stop that's too low, your landlord will get higher profits every year of your lease. Landlords sometimes argue that the base year should be the 12 months preceding occupancy, but that would mean you'd face a rent increase the day you move in.

If your building has been functioning for a while, the previous 12 months' operating expenses are a good basis for estimating the expense stop. Check the estimate with management companies that handle similar buildings to see whether your stop is within the normal range. The experience of comparable buildings is also a good source if your building is new or if for some reason you don't have access to its expense history.

Fair share. Rent escalation formulas, whether tied to direct operating expenses or to indexes (see next section), should limit the tenant's obligation to pay a fair share of a building's total costs. Usually this means you'll be responsible for expenses in proportion to how much of the building you lease.

Watch out. Some leases make the building's "rented" area rather than "rentable" area the denominator in the fraction. This means that you, not the landlord, would pay operating expenses for the building's vacant areas. If your landlord adds floors or converts storage or basement space to office space (thereby adding to the rentable area), the fraction used to determine your share of the building's expenses should reflect this.

And be alert for clauses that don't clearly spell out how the landlord will calculate your share of the building's area. In one case involving a ground-floor tenant whose lease did not contain a formula, a Pennsylvania court decided that the tenant should pay escalations in the same proportion as its rent to the total rent roll.[2] A bad deal for the tenant. Ground-floor space is often more than double the cost per square foot of office space on upper floors.

Indexing the rent. As an alternative to a complex operating expense clause, some landlords index their rents. This lets landlords keep their books private. It also saves tenants from a costly, time-consuming review of expenses that may produce legitimate disagreement.

But be wary. There are a variety of indexes, with many subtle variations in common use, and their behavior can vary substantially. It's surprisingly common for even large, sophisticated companies to be hit by higher rent escalations than they anticipated. In 1969, for instance, Avon Products signed a 27-year lease for nearly half of a 50-story tower in Manhattan. Avon's rent increases were tied to the "porter's wage" — hourly wage and fringe benefit hikes that certain employees receive under a union contract. Because the contract calculated fringe benefits on a weekly or yearly basis, Avon's landlord, Sheldon Solow, had to translate these fringe benefits into an hourly rate.

For ten years, Solow assumed for the purpose of his calculations that the union employees worked a 40 hour week. But in 1980, Solow notified Avon he was revising his calculations to base them on the actual hours employees worked — 31 hours a week. The effect on Avon was dramatic: its rent would jump $780,000 a year, more than $13.5 million over the remaining life of the lease. In 1981, Avon sued Solow over the increase but the case was tossed out. The judge ruled that the lease required the parties to settle by arbitration. Since then, they have been

[2] Pittsburgh Allied Fabrics Inc. v. Habec, 271 A.2d 217 (Penn. 1970).

fighting procedural skirmishes. Seven years after the litigation began, Avon has paid substantial legal fees but still doesn't know its actual rent.[3]

To avoid this predicament, always include a sample calculation in your lease and make sure you understand the implications of any index proposed as the basis for figuring your escalations.

The most common escalation formulas link rent increases to the Consumer Price Index. The CPI measures the cost of food, clothing, recreation, residential rents, and other goods and services, but has no component relating to commercial rents. The components of an index like this may increase far more than the general inflation rate or the cost of running a building.

The CPI-W, a national index, covers only urban wage earners and clerical workers. The CPI-U covers all urban consumers. The CPI-U is generally favored as an index for rent escalation because it covers about twice as many people and is less volatile.

If your city is one of the 28 covered by a metropolitan CPI, your landlord may propose linking your rent to that rather than to the more general CPI-U. But the metropolitan CPIs are much more volatile and, depending on the local economy, may fluctuate in ways entirely unrelated to the cost of running a building.

Another common gauge, the Producer Price Index, is also highly volatile. It measures changes in large quantities of certain commodities at the wholesale level. During the 1970s, when metals and petroleum products made the index rise dramatically, landlords benefitted from the index. One group of Florida tenants sued their landlord, claiming that the use of this index was unconscionable. The court turned them away.[4]

Overlapping escalation formulas. If your landlord indexes base rent in addition to passing through certain operating expenses like fuel, electricity, and real estate taxes, you should negotiate for a partial CPI or Porter's wage formula. Otherwise, you'll pay twice for those increases.[a]

Real Estate Taxes

In general, real estate taxes are the landlord's legal responsibility; you become liable only for the taxes you specifically agree to pay. Like the operating expense clause, however, a real estate tax clause can be used as a catchall to cover additional charges.

Limit your obligation to real estate taxes or taxes a community may impose instead of real estate taxes. Your lease should protect you from paying a landlord's income taxes, corporate taxes, taxes on rents and gross receipts, inheritance taxes, capital gains taxes, and payroll taxes. Be careful about language that tries to make

---

[3] Avon Products, Inc. v. Sheldon H. Solow, dba Solow Building Company, 435 N.Y.S.2d 728 (1981).

[4] Sea Tower Apartments, Inc. v. Century National Bank, 406 So.2d 69 (Fla. 4th Dist. Ct. App. 1981).

[a] [A pass-through of operating expenses coupled with a lease provision indexing rent to cost-of-living increases could result in duplicative treatment because increases in operating expenses are reflected in most indices, and may account for most of the increase in such indices. This duplication has been judicially recognized and nonetheless enforced. 1 M.R. Friedman, Friedman on Leases § 5.404 (3d ed. 1990). Friedman notes that this duplication can be avoided by charging the tenant only a portion of the cost-of-living increase; a limitation of 25% of the cost-of-living increase is not uncommon. — Eds.]

you responsible for undefined taxes that a government authority might impose some time. One tenant who failed to do this many years ago wound up paying its landlord's income taxes after the Sixteenth Amendment initiated them.[5]

Check special assessments to see if they're included with your real estate taxes: charges for new sidewalks, new sewer lines, and so on. Courts have told landlords repeatedly that special assessments aren't real estate taxes. If you're paying assessments as part of your tax bill, you're giving your landlord more than it bargained for.

In some situations, the landlord will contest high taxes in order to enhance the property's value. Make sure your lease entitles you to the benefit of any tax reduction your landlord or other tenants may gain after they've recouped their expenses.

Alterations, maintenance, and repair

Alterations. The alterations-and-improvements clause may give you a false sense of security. It may say that you can make whatever nonstructural changes you like so long as you get your landlord's permission, and that your landlord will be "reasonable." But courts have ruled that things as trivial as lighting fixtures are "structural" components of a building. So a seemingly liberal clause like this could make it impossible for you to move even a single partition.

If you and your landlord disagree about what's structural, it may declare you in default even if you think the changes you've made are reasonable. Consequently, you may be presented with the unpleasant option of paying a big bill at the end of your lease term or restoring so-called structural changes.

So define in the lease what you mean by structural elements. Limit the definitions to components like bearing walls, columns, roof, and facade. And negotiate for the right to make alterations and improvements inside your space, without your landlord's permission, so long as your changes don't affect these few structural elements or the systems that deliver electricity and utilities to other tenants in the building.

Maintenance. In a typical multi-tenant office building, the landlord will be responsible for repairing certain listed items — usually structural elements, the exterior, and parts of the building's common areas. You're responsible for maintaining and repairing everything in your space.

What happens when something outside your space has to be repaired and isn't among the items your landlord promised to take care of? You may have to pay for repairs yourself. Either way, you may have no recourse to the landlord, even if the problem makes your space unusable.

Make sure your responsibilities are specified and limited. Your landlord should be obligated to take care of everything you're not.

Casualties. Many leases have clauses allowing the landlord to terminate the lease after a minor casualty affecting the building, even though your office space remains quite usable. This clause gives the landlord an opportunity to force you out

---

[5] New York Central Railroad Company v. New York and Harlem Railroad Company et al., 56 N.Y.S.2d 712 (1945).

in a rising market or force you to renegotiate unrelated parts of your lease before it will agree to restore the damage.

Make sure your landlord is obligated to restore the building and your space after a casualty if the work can be done in a reasonable time. You should be able to walk if the damage is so severe that your space can't be restored at all or within a time that's reasonable, given your business' needs. Without this right, you could be forced to pay rent even though you have no more office space.

A doctor in Suffolk County, New York signed an eight-year lease for office space. Less than a year later, the building burned down. The landlord sued to keep collecting rent and won, even though he had no obligation to repair the building. New York law would have protected the doctor against this kind of thing, but the lease contained a clause providing that rent wouldn't abate and that his responsibility under the lease would continue even if a casualty destroyed the building. In effect, the doctor signed away his legal rights.[6]

Wear and tear. Your lease should at least stipulate that you're not responsible for repairing normal wear and tear. Some landlords require tenants to "restore" their leased space when they leave. You shouldn't agree to such an arrangement. Since almost every tenant has needs that require modification of the space, restoring the space would cost you a lot without substantial benefit to the landlord. Chances are good that much of the restored carpeting and partitions, and so on, will be torn out to modify space for the next tenant who comes along.

Escapes and Extensions

An assignment is the transfer to a third party of all rights and interests the tenant holds under a lease. In a sublease, the transfer usually covers a portion of the leased space or the entire property for a period shorter than the lease term. If your lease says nothing about subleasing or assignments, you're free to do either. Most landlords, however, are acutely aware of the profit potential this would give you. Usually they're also concerned about controlling the character and quality of tenants in their buildings. Often the landlord's lease flatly prohibits a tenant from assigning or subleasing its space. In a variation that is little better, a landlord will permit subleasing only with their consent, and they'll agree to be "reasonable."

Subleasing. Flexibility could be crucial to your company in a changing and competitive business environment. Unless you have a tiny space or short lease-term, negotiate for the right to sublease part of your space without the landlord's approval. This allows you to warehouse unneeded space but gives you the option of easily regaining it from your subtenant.

If your lease requires the landlord's consent before subleasing and says the landlord must be "reasonable," define what this means. Prospective subtenants probably won't wait while you wrangle with the landlord over the terms under which you can sublease. The landlord's rejection of prospective subtenants should be for limited, objective reasons, like financial inability to handle lease payments or bad reputation. Also limit the landlord's time to decide on any proposed subtenant. A "yes" that comes too late will cost you a subtenant as surely as a "no."

---

[6] José Rodriguez et al. v. Alan Nachamie, 395 N.Y.S.2d 51 (1977).

Whether you're required to turn over 100% of sublease profits or only a portion, define sublease profits to make sure your expenses are covered. You should be able to deduct from rents you receive any expenses like advertising, the cost of negotiating and drafting the lease, and concessions like free rent, carpeting and painting, as well as the unamortized cost of your own improvements in the subleased space. Negotiate, too, to deduct rent you pay while your space sits vacant as you try to sublease it. Agree to pay your landlord only when and if you're paid. If your subtenant defaults, leaving you without a promised income stream, you don't want to be obligated to pay illusory profit to your landlord.

Some landlords will insist on the right to take back space you want to sublease. This allows a landlord to regain space in a rising market and rent it out itself, perhaps negotiating a longer term with another tenant. If your lease contains a clause like this, make sure the landlord is limited to taking back only the space you want to sublease for the time you want to sublease it.

Assignment. Be especially wary of leases that prohibit assignments or give your landlord unfettered discretion to prohibit one. In many cases, a merger or acquisition will result in an assignment because your lease is transferred to a new legal entity. This means you'd be in default and could be forced out — especially in a rising market. The landlord also may try to impose capitalization requirements on an assignee, demanding, for example, that any potential merger partner have assets at least equal to yours. Yet in a merger you may not be in control. Similarly, your landlord may require that any subsidiary to whom you assign your lease have assets as solid as yours. But subsidiaries are seldom as well endowed as their parent companies. A clause like this seriously hampers your business flexibility, especially if your landlord requires you to remain primarily liable even after you assign the lease, and gives the landlord little more protection.

Make sure you can assign to any subsidiary or affiliate as long as you own at least 33%; you're safest to negotiate a deal with no capitalization restrictions on companies with which you may merge. If you think you may be acquired, preserve your flexibility by retaining the right to assign the lease to any acquiring company that meets certain capitalization requirements, for example, that it have a net worth at least equal to yours at the date of acquisition.

Renewals. An extension option can be valuable. Economics aside, it ensures that you can continue operating your business, uninterrupted, at the same location for more than a short three, five, or ten years. If you agree to a fixed rent during the renewal term, both you and the landlord are gambling on a future market. For that reason, leases frequently include a formula — usually tied to the fair market rate — to determine rent during the extended term.

The fair market rate depends on many individual considerations, like a tenant's credit rating (for instance, IBM will probably get a discount over a two-year-old startup because the landlord's risk is lower), the formula for calculating operating expenses, and the lease term. If you agree to a fair market value renewal option, specify factors that would be especially important in your case. Moreover, insist that the space be valued for use as office space, even if that's not its "highest and best use" at renewal time.

Quite a few leases don't require the landlord to commit to the renewal term rental rate until after the term has started. Though the mechanism for determining the renewal rate may be clear, it's unlikely you'll want to commit to pay for space unless you know the cost in advance. Make sure your landlord specifies a firm rate far enough in advance to permit you to shop for alternatives. Otherwise, you give up leverage that could help ensure you a fair renewal rate. An ambiguous arrangement has another hidden cost if you do decide to move: you may have to pay steep holdover rates — 1 to 2 times the normal rent while you shop for new quarters.

Whatever you do, specify the essential terms of your extension option. Don't postpone the decision with a vague lease clause that "agrees to agree." This invites costly litigation and could leave you with no office space.

Dispute Resolution

Leases often include a clause saying that in a dispute over such items as operating costs, electricity, and real estate taxes, the tenant must pay but can take the landlord to court. This is a bad deal for you. It gives you nothing you didn't already have, and the landlord has no incentive to settle. Time-consuming and costly litigation may leave you without an answer for years. Meanwhile, the landlord has your money even if the court eventually finds it wrong and orders repayment.

Provide for dispute resolution in the lease. Here are a few guiding principles:

- Arbitration may be the best method to resolve disputes like disagreement over the fair market rent or whether a tenant's use of space has caused more damage than normal wear and tear. Real estate experts are more qualified than the lay public to say who's right.
- In certain disputes the tenant should have the right to withhold operating expenses — for instance, if the landlord fails to provide essential utilities or repair services.
- The tenant should have convenient access to documentation supporting the landlord's bills and should be given reasonable time to audit the operating expenses. An independent CPA, not the landlord's nephew, should prepare the statement.
- The landlord should share certain audit costs with the tenant.
- If it prevails in a dispute, the tenant should get a prompt refund with interest, plus reimbursement for out-of-pocket expenses and attorneys' fees.

An obvious but essential reminder: once you agree on a way to resolve disputes, follow the procedure to the letter. Paine, Webber, Jackson & Curtis, Inc. (the financial services company that was . . . [the] predecessor [of UBS — Eds.]) took its landlord to court over a dispute about operating expenses, but the case was tossed out by a judge without even a hearing. The company had neglected to start the proceeding within 30 days, as the lease required.[7]

[The Manley article was originally printed in a magazine format, and the following was a boxed separate part of the article which we have chosen to include at the end. — Eds.]

---

[7] Silverstein Properties, Inc. v. Paine, Webber, Jackson & Curtis, Inc., 480 N.Y.S.2d 724 (1984).

Negotiating the Workletter

The work letter is a separate contract that sets out rights and liabilities for finishing off a building's interior space before you move in. It covers installation of interior walls, fixtures, flooring — all the finishing work — and provides a timetable for completion.

Many landlords propose workletters that recognize two kinds of delay: "tenant-caused delay" and "force majeure," or excusable delay. With tenant delays, you pay, usually by reimbursing the landlord for extra out-of-pocket costs and by paying rent even before you can move into your space. But many landlords, concerned about their expenses, try to make tenants responsible for delays they can't control. Similarly, landlords may penalize tenants for delays that are actually part of the normal back-and-forth required to get everyone to sign off on working drawings or unit prices.

To protect yourself, check the definition of tenant-caused delay. It should cover only those situations you can control. Make sure your work letter includes a realistic schedule for producing and reviewing drawings, bidding out the work, and so on. And make sure you're paying only for delays that affect a project's critical path — the schedule of dates that tells your landlord when each task must be finished so that it doesn't interfere with any other.

In addition, see that your work letter allows you enough time to review design drawings and other documents you must approve. A landlord's delay in delivering the documents shouldn't cut into your allotted time.

Force majeure, or excusable delay, is supposed to cover events the landlord can't control — flood, strikes, hurricane. Be sure that it applies only to those few situations the landlord can't reasonably be held responsible for. Otherwise, this becomes a catchall that excuses your landlord from managing the work you've hired it to do.

Your remedy if there's an excusable delay? Landlords normally propose that no matter how long the delay, or how much it costs you to make alternative arrangements, you can't break the contract. You can only push back the date you start paying rent. In other words, you have to wait around. But you need assurance that your business will continue with minimal interruption. Protect yourself with a specific walk date. Except for delays you cause, if your space isn't ready after a reasonable time, you should have the right to terminate your lease and go elsewhere — without having to pay rent on two leases.

Interiors allowance and fit-up. With or without a workletter, tenants often get an interiors allowance for the initial fit-up work: landlords provide a credit of so many dollars per square foot or they provide certain standard items like electrical outlets, doors, latch sets, lighting fixtures, plasterboard, and carpet.

Most tenants prefer better quality or simply need something other than the building standard-but, unless you negotiate it, your lease may permit no credit for items you don't want.

The tenant portion of fit-up can quickly reach $40 to $50 a foot for interiors that aren't lavish. So refuse a clause that obliges you to use resident contractors because you'll likely get a better price by bidding out work to general contractors.

Make sure you understand precisely how the lease distinguishes between "base building," which the landlord pays for, and your premises, which you pay for. Otherwise, you may find you're obligated to pay for expensive wiring, duct work, etc., you hadn't planned on.

[3] Questions

1. The Manley article contains numerous issues to consider when representing a tenant in a lease negotiation. The article points out important instances where a landlord's form lease may contain what appears, on the surface, to be innocuous provisions, but instead contains provisions that from a tenant's perspective inappropriately place risks on the tenant or provides for unwarranted profits for the landlord. Were there any points raised in the article that you did not understand or agree with? When you negotiate a lease on behalf of a tenant, you should consider pulling out this article to check if the landlord's form needs to be negotiated to delete from it the various problematic provisions that Manley points out.

2. Before thinking about specific lease provisions, step back and consider the business objectives of the lessor and lessee in entering into a lease. Importantly, consider the interests of the parties in different lease situations such as a lease for office space in a high-rise office tower, a lease for retail space in a suburban shopping mall, a lease for space to conduct banking operations in an office park, or a lease of warehouse space for a distribution center. What are the principal interests or concerns of the parties in each of these settings? Should these interests or concerns result in specific provisions in the lease? For example, in an industrial lease, the spaces for the tenants are usually larger and often there is only a single user of an entire building. In an office lease, the landlord will not be very concerned about the specific use of the space by the tenants, while in a retail lease the landlord *will* be very concerned about the tenant's use of the space, and may want to preserve the option of combining several spaces for use by a larger retail tenant. If you examine the basic lease terms of the leases for the Fox Valley Auto Care Center in the Document Book you will see that the leases contain special provisions for a "principal use" and "secondary use." Why do you think the FVACC leases provide for these two classifications of uses? As you read through the various permitted principal and secondary uses, do you think the current tenant mix and potential future tenant mix will provide productive synergy or unhealthy competition among the tenants?

3. In the commercial context, long-term leases of five, ten, or fifteen years are not uncommon. How might the fact that the lessor and lessee are entering into a long-term relationship affect the initial negotiating positions of the parties?

4. Commercial leasing is often highly competitive from the lessor's perspective. Lessees with good credit ratings and large space needs are highly desirable. What types of concessions might lessors offer such lessees in addition to favorable rent terms to attract them to rent space in the lessor's buildings? If you examine the basic lease terms of the FVACC leases in the Document Book, you will see that two of the leases have initial rent concessions in them. Why do you think the developer offered

concessions to these two tenants but not the other tenants?

5. Always keep in mind that behind every lessor is a permanent lender. What influence will the lender have on the negotiating position of the lessor, particularly if construction of the project is currently underway?

§ 14.02 REGENT'S LEASING OF THE FOX VALLEY AUTO CARE CENTER

[1] Overview

Although the Fox Valley Auto Care Center is a small development in terms of the number of tenants and the size of the space to be rented, the leasing issues that Regent and its attorneys will confront are very similar to those of a much larger commercial project involving retail tenants. Because of the types of tenants that Regent will be targeting, however, some unusual issues will also arise, as the following article points out. Other portions of the article appear in Chapter 1, but we wanted to wait until now to have you read the article's points on the leasing of a center like the Fox Valley Auto Care Center.

Debra Pogrund Stark,
Rules of the Road for Developing a Successful Auto Service Center,
5 THE JOURNAL OF REAL ESTATE DEVELOPMENT (Summer, 1989)*

SPECIAL ISSUES, CONSIDERATIONS, AND PROBLEMS

A variety of special issues arise in the context of an auto service center. In addition, certain considerations which are general to all shopping center leases become even more important in this context.[8]

Tenant Mix

One of the most important factors behind a successful auto service center is the tenant mix. The goal of the developer and the retailers is to have a mix which creates synergy and not competition. One problem is overlapping uses: although a tenant's primary use of space might be to perform brake work, the tenant might also wish to perform other automotive services or repair work in competition with other tenants in the center. One way to regulate such "secondary" use is through restrictions in the lease. The permitted use section of the lease can contain a

---

* Copyright ©1989 by Debra Pogrund Stark. Reprinted by permission.

[8] This article presumes that the developer is already familiar with the basic lease provisions for a standard general retail shopping center and that the developer or retailer is seeking to convert a standard general retail shopping center lease (such as the International Council of Shopping Centers (ICSC) form) into a special auto service center lease. This article also presumes that the various restrictions upon the retail tenants, as well as the rights with respect to the common areas are covered in the leases as opposed to being covered in a separate document. In the event, however, that the developer sells a portion of the center to a retailer, such restrictions and rights should also be embodied in a Declaration of Restrictions, Easements and Agreements. [Editor's Note: For a review of retail lease provisions, see FRIEDMAN, THE JOURNAL OF REAL ESTATE DEVELOPMENT, Spring 1989.]

defined principal use and a defined secondary use in addition to the standard provision obligating the tenant to use the premises in accordance with its permitted use. The section should prohibit the tenant from increasing its secondary use of the premises to the extent that any of said uses shall become a principal use. . . .

The developer must also keep track of the principal uses specified in the leases to avoid duplicating principal uses and breaching the terms of the leases. [Lease provisions need] not expressly obligate the landlord to prohibit the tenants from engaging in the same principal use as other tenants but instead [only] obligate the landlord not to enter into any leases with a tenant which provides for the same principal use as designated in a prior lease with another tenant.[9]

Aesthetics

A second critical issue to the success of the auto service center is that the center appear neat, clean and aesthetically appealing. Although this is a concern for any shopping center, the ability to achieve this goal is more difficult for auto service centers in light of the uses of the center by some of the tenants. Indeed, a developer might consider not leasing space to certain types of tenants, such as body shops, if it's not possible for that tenant to maintain a neat and clean appearance in its leased space. In order to achieve this goal, the leases should contain a comprehensive set of rules and regulations by which all tenants must abide. . . .

Advertising and Promotion

The advertising and promotion of the auto service center can pose a dilemma for the developer due to the mix of tenants. Tenants who have a franchise from a national franchisor (referred to herein as a "Franchise Tenant") benefit from the extensive advertising by the national franchisor and, in general, would not be interested in contributing to a common advertising and promotion fund for the center. Local retail tenants, however, would probably benefit from common advertising and promotion of the center and might look for same in the leases. In a center with a mix of local retail tenants and Franchise Tenants, a compromise position would be to provide for a contribution from all of the tenants for advertising and promotion only with respect to the opening of the auto service center and other special events rather than on a regular basis.

Relationship Among the Landlord, the Franchise Tenant and the Franchisor

Many of the tenants of an auto service center are franchise tenants which pose additional issues for the developer concerning the leases such as: (1) the

[9] The developer should be aware that clauses restricting the tenant's use of its premises may, under certain circumstances, arguably, (1) violate the anti-trust laws as restraints of trade under Section 1 of the Sherman Act, or attempts to monopolize under Section 2 of said Act, or (2) constitute unfair methods of competition under Section 5 of the Federal Trade Commission Act. *See* Note, *The Anti-Trust Implications of Restrictive Covenants in Shopping Center Leases*, 86 Harv. L. Rev. 1201 (1973). In order for such restrictive covenants to have a real impact on competition, the auto service center would probably have to be much larger than as contemplated herein (e.g., tantamount to a regional shopping center containing not less than 400,000 square feet of leasable area).

consequences of termination of the franchise, (2) the circumstances in which the franchisor may take over the franchise tenant's position under the lease, and (3) the relationship of the [franchisor] with the developer. . . .

Protection Against Environmental Liabilities

One of the most critical provisions which should be addressed in an auto service center lease is the tenant's compliance with environmental laws. Under current federal and state environmental statutes, if a tenant violates such statutes, the landlord as owner of the property, can also be held liable.[10] The fact that a landlord had no knowledge of the tenant's actions and did not participate in such actions generally is no defense to said liability as owner.[11] The practical risk to the landlord for environmental liabilities due to a given tenant will vary based upon the nature of the tenant's use of the premises. While some of the tenants of the auto service center will be engaged in relatively innocuous use of their premises, such as the sale of automotive accessories, other tenants (if the developer elects to lease space to such tenants) may use their premises for more problematic uses, such as transmission work, which requires the storage of large volumes of oil.

In light of the wide range of permitted activities by tenants in a typical auto service center, the standard form of lease for auto service centers should be flexible with respect to the environmental provisions contained therein. The two most basic provisions regarding environmental matters which should be incorporated in the auto service center lease are: one, a covenant and warrant (which should survive termination of the lease) by the tenant not to generate, transport, treat, store nor dispose of any hazardous substances and, two, a covenant and warrant (which should survive termination of the lease) by the tenant to comply with all environmental laws. Since certain tenants might be permitted to generate, transport, treat, store or dispose of hazardous substances, an exception should be created for those tenants and specifically set forth in a separate exhibit to the lease. Moreover, in the rare instances where a tenant is permitted to store hazardous substances in underground or above ground storage tanks, the lease should specifically provide that the tenant shall, on or before the expiration of the term of the lease, remove such tanks in compliance with all environmental laws. . . .

Rather than set forth a separate indemnification paragraph regarding environmental claims (which would cause the environmental section of the lease to be lengthier and, perhaps, more objectionable to the tenants), the developer might wish to rely upon the general indemnification language contained in the ICSC form of lease. Such standard indemnification includes indemnification of any and all claims arising from any default in the performance of any obligation of the tenant under the lease and will, consequently, include a breach of the environmental covenants set forth in the lease.[12] Moreover, a landlord can indirectly and without

---

[10] *See, e.g.*, Stern, *Hazardous Substances in Commercial Leasing (with Forms)*, 13 CMJ ALI-ABA Course Materials Journal 7 (December 1988).

[11] *Id.*

[12] Developers should check their lease to make certain that the tenant's indemnification obligation does not terminate upon termination of the lease. Some forms of lease (such as the ICSC form of lease) fail to provide for survival after termination of the lease, and consequently, do not adequately protect the landlord in the event an environmental liability is discovered after termination of the lease. Tenant

calling attention to the fact, further prohibit the tenant from installing underground or above ground storage tanks when defining the space being demised as specifically excluding the air space above the roof and the space below the floor (such an exclusion is already contained in the ICSC form of lease).

A third provision which should be incorporated in an auto service center lease is the landlord's right to require certain tenants (e.g., those engaging in more risky activity at the center) to obtain insurance (naming landlord as an additional insured) against claims that the tenant's use of the premise violated environmental laws.[13] The lease provision should, on the one hand, allow the landlord flexibility in requiring such insurance, but on the other hand, specify that such insurance may be required only by landlord on a reasonable basis in light of the tenant's permitted use of the premises. A balanced approach is necessary because although the landlord's interest in being protected from environmental liabilities is greater in the context of an auto service center than in a standard retail center, it is currently very difficult and very expensive for tenants to obtain insurance against environmental liabilities.[14]

. . . .

CONCLUSION

This article has addressed some of the special issues which arise in leasing space in an auto service center, the resolution of which are critical to the success of the center. These issues include:

1. Providing a tenant mix which fosters synergy rather than competition;
2. Balancing the conflicting needs of franchise tenants and local retail tenants;
3. Maintaining a neat, clean and aesthetically appealing center;
4. Reducing the developer's exposure to environmental liabilities without losing prospective tenants. . . .

[Lease] provisions [should] attempt to balance the needs of the landlord and tenant in the auto service center in order to make the lease one of the center's "selling points," and consequently, further promote its success.

[2] Developing a Standard Form of Lease

Typically, the attorney for the lessor will develop a standard form of lease that will serve as the starting point for the negotiations between the lessor and potential lessee. This standard form of lease may require the approval of the permanent lender, preferably before the lease is used or perhaps later, if the

---

indemnification of the landlord should be enforceable by the landlord since environmental statutes do not prohibit owners from seeking recovery of their losses from tenants. Owners cannot exculpate themselves from liability to the government under said statutes, but said owners can contract to be indemnified for said losses from their tenants. Stern, *supra* note 10, at 12.

[13] Although there is some question whether insurance policies commonly used in the past (known as GCLs) cover costs incurred by their insured for cleanup of or personal injuries due to hazardous substances, the new insurance policies generally do not cover such damages and contain specific exclusions to such coverage. *See, e.g.*, Stern, *supra* note 10, at 30–34.

[14] *Id.*

permanent lender comes along afterwards. The lessor's attorney will then incorporate the business terms that the lessor and a potential lessee have agreed to, including a description of the demised space and the commencement of the lease term, as well as provisions involving rent, percentage rent, charges for utilities, common area maintenance, property taxes, and insurance. Typically, the lessor and potential lessee will also have agreed to the general terms of any rights of the lessee to expand the demised premises or extend the term of the lease, as well as any use restrictions, radius restrictions, or restrictions on the assignment of the lease. Nevertheless, numerous questions and issues will undoubtedly arise as the general business agreement is translated into specific lease provisions. The resolution of these issues will require the negotiation of the specific language between the attorneys for the parties and the involvement of their clients to the extent that the business terms may be affected.

The following memoranda represent the first step in the leasing process when the lessor's attorney considers the provisions to be contained in the standard form of lease that will serve as the basis for negotiations between the lessor and potential tenant.

[a] Donna Asks Sam to Revise Her Standard Lease Form

MEMORANDUM

TO: Samuel Nader

FROM: Donna Smith

RE: Lease Issues in the Fox Valley Auto Care Center

Our client is beginning some preliminary negotiations with potential tenants for the Auto Care Center development. As you know, our standard retail lease form is quite comprehensive; however, each development has unique issues. Indeed, I recently revised the standard retail lease form to include the concept of "Principal Uses" and "Secondary Uses" for specialty trade centers where the tenants engage in some permitted overlapping uses. I need you to review our standard retail lease and determine what our client should be concerned about during the negotiation process and to suggest any revisions to our standard retail lease form for this project. We then can discuss this further after I read your memo.

Thanks for your help.

[b] Sam Tackles the Auto Care Center Lease Issues

MEMORANDUM

TO: Donna Smith

FROM: Samuel Nader

RE: Lease Issues in the Fox Valley Auto Care Center

You asked me to review our standard retail lease form and to discuss the particular issues Regent should be concerned about during lease negotiations. After reviewing the lease, I believe there are ten potential issues. For each issue, I have provided you with revised language for the relevant sections of the lease and then followed that with additional recommendations and suggestions for our client to consider. The ten issues are:

Going Dark / Continuous Use Provisions

Radius Restrictions

Use Exclusives / Requirements

Assignment and Subletting

CAM Charges

Options to Renew / Cancel

Franchise

Advertising and Promotion

Environmental

Maintenance and Repairs

Going Dark / Continuous Use Provisions and Radius Restrictions

I have reviewed the first paragraph of Section 3.02 of our standard form of lease and suggest that it be revised as follows:

Tenant hereby covenants and agrees: (i) to operate in the Premises only under the Trade Name set forth in Section 1.01, (ii) to continuously and diligently use, occupy and operate the whole of the Premises for the retail sale of its goods or services in accordance with its Permitted Use during such days of the week and such hours as are from time to time designated by local ordinance or the Fox Valley Planned development District, and for no other purpose whatsoever, and (iii) not to own, operate or be financially interested in, either directly or indirectly (by itself or with others), a business like or similar to the business permitted to be conducted hereunder, or which employs the same or similar Trade Name, within a radius of three (3) miles of the perimeter of the Auto Care Center, except for those which Tenant has in operation as of the date hereof. Without limiting Landlord's other available remedies, in the event Tenant should violate this covenant (iii) above, Landlord, may at its option, terminate the Lease upon thirty (30) days written notice to Tenant.

Regent should be aware of whether a potential tenant is currently operating or involved in a similar business, and whether it would fall within the three-mile radius restriction. Furthermore, Regent should study the demographics of the Auto Care Center and decide whether a three-mile radius requirement is adequate.

I am somewhat concerned with the potential impact of the first part of clause (iii) under which the tenant agrees not to "own, operate or be financially interested in, either directly or indirectly (by itself or with others), a business like or similar to the business permitted to be conducted hereunder. . . ." The potential breadth of this provision (which, presumably, makes the provision applicable to related individuals and corporations) along with the vagueness of the "like or similar to" language could present problems in its enforcement.

Use Exclusives / Requirements

The Auto Care Center is a small development in which the tenant mix is important, not only to Regent but to the potential tenants as well. I suggest that the second paragraph of Section 3.02 be revised as follows:

> Tenant covenants and agrees that the Premises shall be used and occupied by Tenant only in accordance with its Permitted Use and for no other purpose or purposes. Tenant also covenants and agrees that Tenant shall not increase its Secondary Use of the Premises to the extent that any said uses shall become a Principal Use. For purposes of this Lease, any use which generates more than twenty-five percent (25%) of the total gross receipts for a particular lease year for the Premises shall be deemed to be a Principal Use of the Premises. Landlord acknowledges that by reason of its character as a full service Auto Service Center, activities of some Tenants may be similar to those of other Tenants, however, Landlord represents that it shall not lease space in the Auto Service Center to any other tenant whose Principal Use as reflected in such Tenant's lease is the same as that of the Tenant's as reflected in this Lease and that all of said leases shall prohibit each tenant thereunder from engaging its Principal Use in the same Principal Use as that of the Tenant as recited above.

It might be wise to attach an entire exhibit or schedule describing the tenant's principal use and any secondary use. This would effectuate a clearer understanding of what is involved with each tenant's operations. Of course, the broad definition contained in the lease should be retained to cover any use that might eventually become a principal use.

I did not draft the last sentence explicitly to require that the landlord enforce a use restriction against another tenant but only to require that the landlord not enter into a lease with another tenant that permits the same principal use. Certainly, prospective tenants will want the lease to contain such a provision. I have not conducted any research to determine if a court might imply such an obligation on the part of the landlord based on such language. The language of this provision could be interpreted as creating exclusive rights for the tenant to engage in the primary use.

Assignment and Subletting

Section 12.01 of our standard lease form, which covers assignment and subletting, currently states:

> Tenant acknowledges that Tenant's agreement to operate in the Premises for the Permitted Use set forth in Section 1.01 hereof for the fully stated

term hereof was a primary inducement and precondition to Landlord's agreement to lease the Premises to Tenant. Accordingly, Tenant's interest in the Premises shall be limited to the use and occupancy thereof in accordance with the provisions hereof and shall be nontransferable. Any attempts by Tenant to sublet the Premises in whole or in part or to sell, assign, lien encumber or in any manner transfer this Lease or an interest therein shall constitute default hereunder, as shall any attempt by Tenant to assign or delegate the management or to permit the use or occupancy of the Premises or any part hereof by anyone other than the Tenant. Notwithstanding anything contained herein to the contrary, Landlord shall consent to such assignment or sublease of the Premises provided (i) the principal use of the assignee or subtenant does not conflict with the Principal Use of any other existing tenant in the Auto Service Center, and (ii) the tangible net worth of the assignee or subtenant is equal to or greater than the tangible net worth of Tenant immediately prior to such assignment or sublease. Landlord and Tenant acknowledge and agree that the foregoing provisions have been freely negotiated by the parties hereto and that Landlord would not have entered into this Lease without Tenant's consent to the terms of this Section 12.01. Any attempt by Tenant to sublet all or any portion of the Premises, to encumber same, or to in any manner transfer, convey, assign Tenant's interest therein, allow the use or management thereof, shall be void ab initio (from the beginning). If this Lease be assigned or the Premises or any part thereof be sublet or occupied by anybody other than the Tenant, the Landlord may collect rent from the assignee, undertenant or occupant and apply the net amount collected of the rent herein reserved, but no such assignment, underletting, occupancy or collection shall be deemed a waiver of this covenant, or the acceptance of the assignee, undertenant or occupancy as Tenant or a release of the Tenant herein contained. Notwithstanding any assignment or sublease, the Tenant shall remain fully liable on this Lease and shall not be released from performing the terms, covenants and conditions of this Lease.

As for this provision, the lease makes little sense when it sets forth the standards allowing subletting and assignments, and then immediately afterwards states that "any attempt by Tenant to sublet all or any portion of the Premises, . . . shall be void ab initio (from the beginning)." We should change the language to state that any attempt to sublet etc., *without the landlord's express written consent*, will be void. Perhaps this is an example of how our retail lease form has over time come to include negotiated points from other deals. Another recommendation is to insert a clause stating that the Landlord will be *reasonable* in allowing assignments or subleases. This approach could prevent future litigation over whether a tenant is allowed to sublease or assign its interests.

While the lease does provide objective criteria to determine when a sublease or assignment shall be allowed, we might talk with Regent about inserting additional criteria. I am particularly concerned with local tenants who may not have significant net worth but to whom Regent is willing to rent space because of prior experience with these tenants or local reputation. If Regent is required to approve an assignment based only on satisfying the use and net worth standards, Regent may be unable to prevent an assignment to a party without adequate assurance of that party's ability to perform.

CAM Charges

Section 4.01 covers CAM charges.

> Commencing upon occupancy of the Premises by Tenant and during each month of the Lease Term, Tenant shall pay without demand, deduction or setoff, as Additional Rent to Landlord, Tenant's proportionate share of all costs incurred by Landlord in maintaining, repairing, operating and insuring the portions of the Auto Service Center which are the responsibility of Landlord. . . .

The lease then gives a detailed list of the operating costs. A partial summary includes:

Lighting

Cleaning

Maintenance

HVAC maintenance

Maintenance reserve charges

Insurance charges

Taxes

Liability insurance

Attorney's fees and other professional fees

After listing the operating costs, this section indicates how the tenant's share of the operating costs will be computed:

> Tenant's proportionate share of Operating Costs shall be computed by multiplying Operating Costs by a fraction, the numerator of which shall be the number of square feet of floor area of the Premises and the denominator of which shall be the number of square feet of gross leasable area of the Auto Service Center. Tenant's proportionate share of all Operating Costs during the Lease Term shall be paid in monthly installments on or before the first day of each calendar month during the Lease Term, in advance, in an amount estimated in writing by Landlord. Upon receipt of all bills attributable to any calendar year during the Lease Term, Landlord shall furnish Tenant with a written statement of the actual amount of Tenant's proportionate share.

If actual costs are more than what the tenant paid, the tenant owes its proportionate amount within ten days. However, if the tenant overpaid, it will receive a credit towards next year's operating expenses.

The language in this section does a nice job listing possible operating expenses. However, to help a tenant understand how its portion will be computed, which would make the provision more user friendly and therefore more easily enforced, we could attach an exhibit that would serve as an example (not a binding portion of the lease) of how, on average, operating costs will be calculated. Additionally, Regent should consider whether it (or its lender) is comfortable with the way the lease computes a tenant's proportionate share of the operating expense. In other words, as currently drafted, Regent will have to cover the portion of operating costs allocable to vacant space. The provision could be redrafted to use only "leased" space as the denominator in the allocation fraction. Of course, prospective tenants will prefer the current provision. If Regent is comfortable with the provision as drafted, we might still draft it from the more landlord favorable perspective and concede it as part of the negotiation.

Finally, the lease might require that any dispute regarding CAM charges be resolved through mandatory arbitration or mediation, thereby reducing possible litigation expenses.

Options to Renew / Cancel

Section 2.05 describes the lease term.

"Within five (5) days after the Rental Commencement Date, Landlord and Tenant shall execute and deliver a written statement in recordable form specifying therein the Rental Commencement Date and termination date of the Lease Term, and Tenant shall acknowledge therein that the Premises (including the building or buildings of which the Premises is a part and the parking facilities and other Common Areas and facilities of the Auto Service Center) are completed in accordance with the terms of the Lease and certify that the lease is in full force and effect.

"Provided that Tenant is not in default hereunder at the time of the commencement of each applicable Option Period, and provided further that Tenant has not assigned or sublet all or any part of the Premises, this Lease shall automatically be extended for each Option Period, upon the same terms and conditions as provided for herein, except that the Fixed Minimum Rent shall be the amount specified for the same for said Option Period(s) in Section 1.01 hereof. Tenant may terminate this Lease at the end of the Initial Term or any subsequent Option Period if tenant shall give written notice to Landlord at least one hundred twenty (120) days (which may be reduced to ninety (90) days provided that Tenant sends a written request for such reduction to Landlord one hundred twenty (120) days prior to the end of the Initial Term or the current Option Period) prior to the end of the Initial Term or the current Option Period that it does not desire to extend this lease.

"Landlord agrees to grant Tenant, at any time throughout the term of this Lease, the right of first refusal to lease adjacent space which may be vacant and available to lease. Said right of first refusal shall be granted provided that in the event Tenant leases only a portion of such adjacent space, the remaining space not leased by Tenant shall have a minimum storefront width of twenty-five (25) feet."

The lease goes on to state that at the end of a designated term, no notice shall be required.

This section is satisfactory, and our client should simply consider how long the initial term would be and the option periods it wishes to allow.

Franchise

Some of the tenants may be franchisees under national franchises. This situation raises several issues, including what should happen in the event that the franchise is terminated and whether the franchisor can take over the lease if the tenant breaches the lease. I suggest that the following provision be included, under which the franchisor may take over the lease with the landlord's permission and the franchisee is obligated to continue in possession of the space despite the bankruptcy or insolvency of the franchisor.

"In the event the Tenant is a franchisee, this leasehold will be deemed conditioned upon the continued good standing of the Tenant's franchise agreement and the termination shall, at the option of the Landlord, constitute a default hereunder. In the event the Tenant's Franchisor, as part of the franchise agreement or through a conditional assignment of Tenant's interest in the Lease, has the right to take over the Premises upon the happening of said event, at the option of Landlord, Tenant's Franchisor may continue business in the Premises. Landlord shall not be a party to any litigation between the Tenant's Franchisor and the Tenant. The Tenant shall agree to indemnify and hold Landlord harmless from any legal or other expenses incurred by Landlord in connection therewith.

"If Tenant is a franchisee, Tenant agrees that Landlord may send to Tenant's Franchisor notice of any default of Tenant under this Lease, without incurring any liability to Tenant in connection therewith. In the event that Tenant's franchise agreement is terminated by the bankruptcy or insolvency of the Tenant's Franchisor, Tenant agrees to thereafter conduct its business and operations in the same manner as they were conducted prior to such termination to the end that the image of Tenant (and therefore the Auto Service Center) shall remain substantially unchanged as a result of the termination of the franchise."

I suspect that any prospective tenant/franchisee will be reluctant to make the lease terminable, at the option of the landlord, on the termination of the franchise. Rather, I imagine that they will want the lease to terminate automatically if the franchise terminates. We should discuss this matter further with Regent to determine how they would like to proceed in situations involving the termination of any tenant's franchise agreement.

Advertising and Promotion

Our lease currently requires that each tenant become a member of the merchant's association and that they pay an initial opening fee along with monthly advertising and promotion fees. I suspect that tenants who are national franchisees will be reluctant to contribute to the advertising and promotion of the center because the franchise fees which they pay already are spent on advertising and promotion. Consequently, Regent will need to negotiate the precise terms for this section of the lease. I have no recommendations other than letting our client know that advertising and promotion must be discussed sometime during the negotiation process.

Environmental

Our standard form of lease contains only one limited provision covering environmental matters, which prohibits the tenant from generating, treating, transporting, and storing hazardous materials. I suggest adding the following provision to provide greater detail in this area and also to recognize that some of the tenants will be using and storing hazardous materials:

"Tenant agrees and covenants that it will not generate, transport, treat, store, nor dispose, nor, in any manner, arrange for the disposal or treatment [within the meaning of the Resource Conservation and Recovery Act, 42 U.S.C. § 6901, et seq. ("RCRA"), the Comprehensive Environmental Response, Compensation and Liability Act, 42 U.S.C. § 9601, et seq. ("CERCLA"), or any applicable federal, state or local law, regulation, ordinance or requirement, as amended or hereafter amended (collectively referred to as "Environmental Laws")] of any hazardous substances as defined below, except as provided in Exhibit ____________. For the substances specifically identified in Exhibit ____________, Tenant agrees and covenants that it will comply with all

Environmental Laws pertaining to the generation, transportation, storage, treatment or disposal, or for in any manner arranging for disposal or treatment.

"Hazardous Substances. "Hazardous Substances," for the purposes of this Lease, means hazardous substances or hazardous wastes, as those terms are defined by the Environmental Laws. "Hazardous Substances" shall also include, but not be limited to, petroleum, including, but not limited to, crude oil or any fraction thereof which is liquid at standard conditions of temperature and pressure (60 degrees Fahrenheit and 14.7 pounds per square inch absolute) and any radioactive material, including, but not limited to, any source, special nuclear or by-product material as defined at 42 U.S.C. § 2011, et seq., as amended or hereafter amended, and asbestos in any form.

"Tenant agrees and covenants that it will comply with all Environmental Laws. At the election of the Landlord (which election shall be exercised by Landlord giving Tenant notice thereof within thirty (30) days before the expiration of the Lease Term), Tenant agrees and covenants to restore the Premises to the condition of the premises upon the execution of this Lease, including, without limitation, removing, in compliance with all Environmental Laws, any and all underground storage or above ground storage tanks installed by Tenant. Tenant represents and warrants to Landlord that there are no pending, or threatened actions or proceedings (or notice of potential actions or proceedings) against Tenant from any governmental agency or any other entity regarding any matter relating to the Environmental Laws or to requirements relating to health, safety and protection of the environmental, except as noted in Exhibit ____________."

Although the descriptions of the demised premises do not currently include any underground areas, the third paragraph provides the flexibility to amend one or more of the leases to permit the installation of underground tanks if necessary.

We could also add some indemnity provisions specifically with respect to hazardous materials, but I believe that the indemnification provision in Section 9.03 is sufficiently broad to cover any breach of the lease in connection with hazardous substances.

Maintenance and Repairs

As a general matter, I am not aware of any maintenance and repair issues that are unique to the Auto Care Center as compared to any other shopping center. Consequently, I have not made any suggestion for changes in this regard in preparing the form of lease for the project. However, I do know that one of the leasable areas has a "lubrication bay." Because I have no idea what is involved in a "lubrication bay," I will talk with Regent to determine if any special lease provisions should be inserted in the lease of that space.

[c] Questions

1. Based on the discussion in the Manley and Stark articles, do you think that Sam has identified the principal leasing issues from the lessor's perspective? From the lessee's perspective? Some lease issues are quite subtle and not so easily identified. For example, how are the leased premises described in the FVACC lease form and why is that description important? Does the description of the leased premises address the type of tenant issues that Manley identified?

2. If you had not known who prepared the lease between Regent and Cellular Communications (landlord's or tenant's counsel), what provisions would have tipped you off and why?

3. Are the terms "fair" to both the lessor and lessee? Are the risks of loss allocated to the party able to prevent or absorb the loss or otherwise insure against the loss? For example, do CAM provisions in § 4 of the FVACC lease just compensate the landlord for expenses or do the lease terms create a profit center for the landlord? Who bears the risk if space at the FVACC is not fully leased up, in terms of payment of CAM expenses? Who do you think should bear those expenses? What about the condition of the premises? Does the FVACC lease strike the right balance between the landlord and tenant positions on this? See in particular §§ 2.03, 2.07 and 17.05 of the FVACC lease.

4. Has Sam identified the appropriate revisions to make to the lease in light of the intended uses at the Fox Valley Auto Care Center? For example, how does the fact that some of the tenants in the FVACC may be franchisees affect the tenant's willingness to contribute to a merchant's association? Do the environmental provisions contained in § 7.07 of the lease adequately address the intended uses at FVACC? What do you think about the assignment and subletting provisions in § 12 of the lease? Many form leases simply prohibit assignment and subletting without the consent of the landlord, but Regent insisted on adding to the form lease the two key conditions to the landlord's consent (the first relating to the permitted uses of the space by the new tenant and the second relating to the creditworthiness of the new tenant). Regent chose to add these terms to the standard form lease rather than require each tenant to negotiate for such clarification on consent in order to reduce the time and cost of negotiating changes to the lease. What do you think about that approach? The first condition covers the competition point, but does it adequately cover the synergy point? Also, what happens if the sublesee breaches the lease? Is the original tenant still liable? What if the new tenant is an "assignee" of the lease?

5. Were any of the lease provisions described thus far not clear and understandable? What suggestions do you have to modify the language to clarify the provisions?

6. Although the provisions relating to the landlord's remedies upon default by the tenant are critical terms in the lease, it is important to note that lease forms typically contain some remedies that may not be enforceable under some state's laws such as (i) election of remedies (in some states, once a landlord takes possession of the premises, she forfeits the right to sue the tenant for future rents) and (ii) re-entry after default (some states require a court action and do not permit even peaceful self-help). In addition, notwithstanding a lease provision to the contrary, upon the filing of a bankruptcy action, (i) an automatic stay prevents collection actions against the tenant during the period of the stay, and (ii) a tenant can reject executory contracts, including leases (if this happens, the landlord is relegated to the bankruptcy code's statutory damages provisions). It is useful to keep these state and federal law limitations in mind when negotiating the terms of the lease. Leases might also contain limitations on

liability that might not be enforceable, for example when a party attempts to exculpate itself from intentional torts or grossly negligent conduct, a topic further discussed in Chapter 15.

Chapter 15

NEGOTIATING AND DRAFTING THE COMMERCIAL LEASE

§ 15.01 BASIC LEASE PROVISIONS

[1] Overview

The negotiation and review of leases on behalf of either lessors or lessees is a routine aspect of practice for most real estate attorneys. Because lessors and lessees are often creating long-term relationships on the order of 5, 10, or 15 years, commercial real estate leases are complicated documents that attempt to anticipate a broad range of events that could confront the parties as well as to delineate the implications of those events should they occur. Successful leases strike a balance between excessive detail regarding every potential event despite its remoteness and a recognition that, in most instances, the lessor and lessee will reach a resolution of most conflicts without resort to their legal rights. In the early 1990s, Bruce Eichner, a developer in New York City, wondered why he spent $200 an hour for legal advice in leasing matters (and think about what the hourly rate would be today!):

> Bruce drew a distinction between his world of "business points" and [his lawyer's] realm of "legal points." The former had to do with money in the here and now: who spent what, who got how much. The latter had to do largely with the what-ifs, the potential for things to go wrong and the remedies and sanctions that could be applied. It wasn't that Bruce didn't believe that things could go wrong. On the contrary, he knew that thousands of things would go wrong, most of them totally unpredictable, unforeseen, and beyond the scope of even the most comprehensive legal draftsmanship. And in that case the solution would be found in the real world and not in the carefully crafted and scrupulously numbered paragraphs of the agreements. Ultimately he would be thrown back on his own resources, to rant and deal as best he could. To spend $200 an hour pretending otherwise struck him as an expensive form of voodoo.

Jerry Adler, High Rise: How 1,000 Men and Women Worked Around the Clock For Five Years And Lost $200 Million Building A Skyscraper 206 (1993). Although Eichner may be correct at the extreme, no lessor or lessee would be willing to enter into a legal relationship without a carefully crafted lease that defines the relationship and allocates to each party the variety of foreseeable financial risks that they confront. Nor would a permanent lender, whose repayment depends on a stable stream of rental income, allow a lessor to avoid paying for the type of insurance that a carefully crafted lease provides.

As you will see while reviewing the lease between Regent and Cellular Communications Corporation which is in the Document Book, leases are long and involved documents that, unfortunately, are often tedious to review. We have saved you the tedium of reviewing all the leases by including in the Document Book the full Cellular Communications lease and just the basic business terms of the others. You will want to compare the business terms of the different leases because Regent made several different deals.

One approach to reviewing a commercial lease is to be an active reader of its terms. With specific questions in mind and a checklist of the important leasing issues from your client's perspective, you can actively seek out the resolution of these issues under the language of the lease rather than passively skimming through the lease from beginning to end.

[2] A Practical Guide

The following article, *A Practical Guide to Reviewing a Commercial Lease*, was written by a team of leasing lawyers from what the American Bar Association now calls its Section of Real Property, Trust and Estates Law. Many of our former students have told us that the "Practical Guide" has been a valuable resource in their leasing law practices.

The Practical Guide describes the principal lease provisions of concern to the lessor, lessee, and permanent lender. You are already familiar with some of these provisions, such as those concerning subordination, nondisturbance, and attornment agreements and estoppel certificates, from the discussion in Chapter 11. Each of the principal lease provisions is subject to negotiation between the lessor and lessee and must be tailored to the particular circumstances involved. As you consider the discussion of each provision, refer to the specific provisions in the lease between Regent and Cellular Communications to see how the parties under that lease resolved their competing interests. In § 15.01(3), we will return to an analysis of the leases at the Fox Valley Auto Care Center in light of the Practical Guide's detailed analysis of key lease terms.

A Practical Guide to Reviewing a Commercial Lease,[*]

19 Real Property, Probate & Trust Journal 891 (1984)[**]

I. INTRODUCTION

Numerous business enterprises occupy their premises pursuant to some type of a commercial lease. Even attorneys who do not specialize in real property law are often asked to review a proposed lease and represent a client in negotiating appropriate changes.

This article considers the more significant provisions of a typical commercial lease from the viewpoint of the landlord, the tenant and a typical lender. It is not intended as a legal treatise on the law of commercial leases, but is written as an aid

[*] Report of the Real Estate Financing Committee, Subcommittee on Commercial Lease Checklist.

[**] "A Practical Guide to Reviewing a Commercial Lease," by the Report of the Real Estate Financing Committee, Subcommittee on Commercial Lease Checklist 1984, Real Property Probate & Trust Journal, 19:4, pp. 891–940. © Copyright 1984 © by the American Bar Association. Reprinted by permission. This information or any or portion thereof may not be copied or disseminated in any form or by any means or stored in an electronic database or retrieval system without the express written consent of the American Bar Association.

to an attorney in reviewing a lease. While it is primarily a checklist of things to consider in the process of reviewing a commercial lease, some of the more important provisions are discussed in more detail.

II. THE DEMISED PREMISES

A. Area

At the outset, the parties should have a clear understanding of the description of the demised premises and the appurtenances thereto. Also, the lender should understand the effect that the demised premises will have on the economics of the lease from both the landlord's and tenant's perspectives. The lease must contain a clear and precise description of the demised premises.

If the demised premises includes the entire project, good form requires that a full legal description of the covered premises be included in the lease. If the demised premises are only a part of the project, it is good practice to attach to the lease a plan of the entire project with the demised premises being defined on the attachment.

The lender should be aware of and understand provisions in the lease which give the parties a right to change or modify the dimensions or location of the demised premises. For example, if the tenant has an option to add space to the demised premises, the lender should be aware of the option and understand the economic impact it may have on the tenant's rental obligations.

If the lease also covers personal property which is situated on, attached to or used in connection with the demised space, a detailed description of the personalty should be attached to the lease. The landlord and the lender should understand the nature and priority of security interests, if any, in the personalty.

The lender should be aware of the tenant's rights which pertain to the demised premises. For example, the lender should be aware of any set-off or termination rights a tenant may have and should understand the tenant's rights and privileges with regard to common areas or equipment which may be provided by the landlord for tenant use. On the other hand, restrictions which limit or restrict the tenant's use of the demised premises must be understood.

The dimensions of the demised premises may have an impact upon the economics of the lease. The parties must determine who has the burden to pay for taxes, utilities, repairs and maintenance, insurance and general operating expenses. The lender should consider the impact on the financial obligations of the parties to the lease if the costs of these items increase (or perhaps decrease). When the demised premises are part of a larger development, the landlord will frequently agree to pay the costs of such items during the base year, but will have the right to assess the tenant for future costs which are in excess of the base costs. This assessment may be determined by relating the size of the demised premises to the size of the larger development. The landlord should understand at the outset how cost increases are to be calculated and thereafter assessed.

B. Condition of Demised Premises

The provisions of the lease relating to the condition of the demised premises and the obligation to maintain and repair the same are extremely important. The tenant should be satisfied that the condition of the demised premises is sufficient to permit the intended use thereof. If the premises prove to be of such poor condition as to be inadequate for tenant's use, the lender can anticipate problems which may ultimately jeopardize the lender's interests.

The lender should understand where the economic burden for maintenance, repair or restoration is placed. This burden will certainly impact on the economics of the lease. Further, the parties should know to whom insurance proceeds, if any, are to be paid if the demised premises are damaged. The tenant must be satisfied that monies will be available to maintain, repair or restore the demised premises.

III. TERM OF THE LEASE

A. Generally

The term of the lease is the period during which the tenant has the exclusive right to possession of the premises and the corresponding obligation to pay rent. Accordingly, the provisions of the lease contract defining the term are of great importance and should be carefully reviewed. A primary concern of all parties should be that the provisions governing the commencement and termination of the term are clear and unambiguous. A lease whose commencement date is uncertain gives a tenant the leverage to bargain for a delay in the payment of rent. A lease whose termination date is uncertain may be found unenforceable as a term of years and converted into a tenancy at will.[1]

B. Duration; Statute of Frauds

Generally there is no limit on the length of the term of a lease and it is not uncommon to find ground leases with terms of 99 years or more (except that in some states, e.g., California, a lease may not extend beyond 99 years). However, a landlord or mortgagee contemplating a long-term lease will want to make certain that the lease is absolutely net to the landlord-i.e., that the tenant pays all costs and expenses, or the lease contains clear escalation provisions governing rent, insurance and other financial covenants to guard against the effects of inflation. . . .

In most American jurisdictions the Statute of Frauds permits enforcement of oral lease agreements, so long as the term is less than a defined period. The most common maximum period for oral leases is one year; however, in some jurisdictions (e.g., Pennsylvania and New Jersey) an oral lease for as much as three years may be enforced.[2] One consequence of the enforceability of oral leases is that unsuccessful negotiations can lead to litigation by the disappointed party claiming that an oral agreement had been breached. Accordingly it is wise to document the essential terms of the lease in writing as early as possible.

---

[1] See Powell, The Law of Real Property ¶ 222[3] (1983); Friedman on Leases § 21.202 (1978).

[2] N.J. Stat. Ann. § 25:1; 68 Pa. Stat. Ann.§ 250.202 (Purdon).

C. Commencement Date

In most leases the commencement date of the term of the lease coincides with the date of the lease agreement, and consequently there is no room for ambiguity. However, in many commercial leases the commencement date of the term depends on the occurrence of another event, usually related to the completion of improvements which the landlord has agreed to build. When the commencement of the term of the lease depends on the occurrence of another event, the following issues are raised:

1. The landlord and the mortgagee will want to insure that the tests to be met for the commencement of the tenant's rental obligation are as objective as possible. Provisions based on potentially ambiguous tests such as "substantial completion in accordance with the plans" should be supplemented, if possible, with more objective tests such as the production of an architect's certificate or a municipal certificate of occupancy.

2. The tenant will want to insure that he retains the leverage of withholding rent until the landlord has substantially performed his undertaking to produce a completed, usable building meeting the requirements of municipal codes.

3. Both landlord and tenant should consider providing for the right to terminate on an outside date if the term has not commenced, in order to avoid tying up the property through lengthy disputes. To protect the tenant's rights, the termination provision should state that the landlord's liability for damages for failure to perform its undertaking will not be affected by such termination. To protect the mortgagee's rights, the mortgagee should be given an opportunity to cure the landlord's default.

4. Since the commencement date of the term is of great importance, there should be a clear mechanism for documenting that date, such as execution of a supplement to the lease.

5. Consideration should be given to whether any of the nonrental obligations of the tenant (such as payment of taxes, maintenance of insurance and indemnities) are intended to commence prior to the commencement date.

6. Under the early common law, a tenant who had entered into a lease agreement but had not yet taken occupancy of the premises was regarded as having an *interesse termini*, or interest in the term, rather than a full leasehold estate or "term of years." Among other things, the holder of a mere *interesse termini* could not bring an action in ejectment to enforce his right of possession. While most American jurisdictions have abandoned this archaic distinction,[3] prudent counsel to the tenant should make certain that it does not still apply.

7. In determining the commencement date, the tenant should make allowance for the period necessary to complete his fix-up work after the landlord has delivered possession.

---

[3] Pennsylvania did not abandon the rule until 1979. See *Soffer v. Beech*, 487 Pa. 255, 409 A.2d 337 (1979).

8. Lease agreements will sometimes give the tenant the right to enter the premises to commence his fix-up work before the landlord has completed work on the building and delivered possession. When this is the case, care should be taken to insure that the tenant does not interfere with the landlord's work. In union-dominated areas, consideration should be given to requiring the tenant to use union labor.

If the leased premises are occupied by another tenant, both the landlord and the new tenant should bargain for protection against the failure of the old tenant to vacate. The lease agreement can condition the commencement of possession and of rent upon such vacancy occurring, and can provide a cut-off date upon which either party may terminate if the old tenant remains in occupancy.

D. Renewals

Lease agreements commonly provide that the tenant may extend the term of the lease for one or more renewal terms. Such provisions are generally enforceable even when the right to renew is perpetual.[4] However, care should be taken to see that the renewal provisions in the lease are clear and unambiguous, including the requirements for notice, the date by which notice must be given, and the rental due during the renewal term. To avoid disputes, the lease should provide that the lease will be renewed on the same terms and conditions (except as modified by the renewal provisions and except for any options then exercised). This is particularly important where the lease contains atypical provisions (such as a covenant by the landlord not to compete) or provisions not favored by the law, such as a confession of judgment. In addition, the landlord should give consideration to requiring special provisions governing financial covenants which may be affected by inflation, such as the level of required insurance coverage. Normally, the tenant's right to renew is conditioned upon the tenant's not being in default.

Because of the general rule that time is always of the essence in an option contract, a tenant should be advised to maintain carefully a calendar for renewal notice dates to avoid losing his right.[5]

A tenant who elects not to renew, but nonetheless remains in occupancy after the expiration of the initial term, may find that the law will hold that the act of holding over constitutes an election to renew for the full additional term.[6]

If the renewal provisions of the lease provide for escalation of the rent, they should not be so ambiguous as to render the renewal option unenforceable. Thus, provisions for rent during the renewal period to be "fixed by agreement" should be avoided in favor of a more objective test, or an appraisal.

---

[4] See *infra* notes [21] and [22] and accompanying text.

[5] In a particularly harsh application of the rule, the tenant mutual savings bank, caught in the middle of a "massive branch expansion program," missed the renewal notice date by four days on a ten-year extension, but the court held for the landlord. *Western Savings Fund Society of Philadelphia v. Southeastern Pennsylvania Transportation Authority*, 285 Pa. Super. 187, 427 A.427 175 (1891); see also Friedman on Leases § 14.2.

[6] See *Cusamano v. Anthony M. DiLucia, Inc.*, 281 Pa. Super. 8, 421 A.2d 1120 (1980).

E. Termination

The term of a lease may be terminated by expiration of the allotted period, or by earlier termination by the parties in accordance with the terms of the lease agreement. In addition, the term of a lease may be terminated by a trustee in bankruptcy or debtor in possession under the power to disaffirm executory contracts granted by the Federal Bankruptcy Code.[7] When the term of a lease ends for any reason, the tenant's right of possession and his obligation to pay rent accruing after the termination date also end. These important consequences necessitate consideration of the following factors:

1. The landlord and the mortgagee will want to provide that if the tenant does hold over, he will owe rent of at least the rate set forth in the lease for each holdover day.

2. The lease should contain provisions governing the tenant's obligation to remove his own property and to restore the premises, and providing remedies to the landlord if the tenant fails to do so. Such remedies might include the right to remove and store property at the tenant's expense, and eventually to dispose of it.

3. Lease agreements often give to the landlord the right, upon the tenant's default, to terminate the lease and regain possession of the premises, and also to accelerate the rent for the balance of the term. Care should be used in exercising these remedies as they are in many ways mutually exclusive. In general, a landlord may not have both possession and rent. If he terminates the lease and removes the tenant, he cannot sue for rent accruing after the date of termination. If he accelerates the rent and obtains a judgment, the tenant may acquire the right of possession for the balance of the term, thereby making it difficult to relet. The exercise of landlord's remedies requires sophisticated analysis of each situation in the light of the laws and practices of each jurisdiction.

Lease agreements often provide for termination in the event that all or part of the leased property is taken by eminent domain. Because such a provision cuts off the tenant's rights in the balance of the term, he will lose his right to claim a share of the condemnation award based on the value of this unexpired portion. To protect himself against such loss, the tenant should bargain for a provision giving him a share of any condemnation award and the right to participate in the proceedings. Such a provision is particularly important to a tenant who has made a substantial investment in improvements to the premises. If the landlord or the lender refuses to allow the tenant a share of the award, the tenant should reserve the right to maintain a separate action against the condemning authority for the costs of leasehold improvements, moving expenses, and loss of business.

F. Persons Deriving Rights Through the Tenant (Subtenants and Leasehold Mortgagees)

A subtenant's rights can be no greater than his sublandlord's; thus, a termination of the prime lease will terminate the sublease. Accordingly, subtenants with bargaining power should consider negotiating an agreement with the prime

---

[7] Bankruptcy Reform Act of 1978, 11 U.S.C. § 365.

landlord to protect their right of possession in the event of a default of the sublandlord.

Similarly, a mortgagee of the tenant's leasehold estate has rights no better than his mortgagor has in the leasehold estate, and a termination of the lease will completely destroy the collateral. At minimum, a leasehold mortgagee should bargain for the right of notice of default from the landlord and an opportunity to cure. In addition, many sophisticated commercial leases give an option to the leasehold mortgagee to enter into a direct lease with the landlord if the original lease is terminated on account of the tenant's default.[8]

IV. RENT

A. Fixed Rent

1. Increases in Fixed Rent

To the extent that the fixed rent does not increase, particularly over a lease term in excess of five years, the landlord's income and the mortgagee's security may be eroded by inflation. Common methods of providing for increased rent include:

> a. *Step-up Rent.* The fixed rent is graduated periodically over the lease term in predetermined amounts.
>
> b. *Indexed Rent.* The fixed rent fluctuates (or only increases) as a function of an external standard or index, usually an economic indicator. . . . The most common index is the Consumer Price Index (often called the CPI or the cost-of-living index), which is published by the Bureau of Labor Statistics of the United States Department of Labor. While this index does not necessarily reflect changes in value of real property (including rental values), it is commonly used because it is widely published and easy to administer. When using an adjustment clause based upon the CPI, the parties should decide between the two versions of the CPI: the index for "Urban Wage Earners and Clerical Workers" or the one for "All Urban Consumers." Separate CPI indices are also published for major urban areas, as well as a nationwide index, and the parties may want to exercise their discretion in this respect.
>
> c. *Appraisal.* The fixed rent is redetermined periodically by appraisal during the lease term. The method of appraisal and instructions to appraisers should be carefully examined. While appraisal can achieve a more accurate result than an index not tied to real property values, it is more time consuming and costly.

2. Rent Abatements and Offsets

The rent stream is of primary importance not only to the landlord but also to the mortgagee. To the extent that it can be reduced or interrupted, the mortgagee's

---

[8] See York, *The Ground Lease and the Leasehold Mortgagee*, 99 Banking L.J. 709 (1982), and Subcommittee on Leasehold Encumbrances, Committee on Leasing, *Model Leasehold Encumbrance Provisions*, 15 Real Prop., Prob. & Tr. J. 395 (1980).

security is reduced as is the market value of the property. Some ways by which rent may be reduced are:

a. *Initial Rent Concession.* How much of the reimbursements or allowances due to tenant by landlord may be offset against monthly rental payments so that the cash flow from the real property is not reduced to such an extent that it would result in a negative cash flow? Too great an offset could create problems for the landlord in that he may not have sufficient cash flow to meet debt service and other expenses for which the landlord is responsible.

b. *Damage by Fire or Other Hazard.* In the event of damage by fire or other hazard to the demised premises, is the fixed rent totally or partially abated, and if so, how is such abatement determined? Can tenant terminate the lease if the demised premises are not restored within a given period or if they are substantially destroyed near the end of the lease term?

c. *Condemnation.* In the event of partial condemnation, is the fixed rent reduced, and if so, how is such reduction determined?

d. *Credit for Tenant Expenditures.* Is the fixed rent abated or reduced to reimburse tenant for expenditures relating to the construction of initial or subsequent leasehold improvements or other costs incurred by tenant?

e. *Interruption of Landlord's Services.* Is the fixed rent abated if landlord's services (HVAC, water, electricity, elevator service) are interrupted for more than a stated number of days?

f. *Landlord's Default.* Is the fixed rent abated or reduced because of violation by landlord of any covenants contained in the lease, such as an exclusivity clause, or by reason of a major tenant's failure to open for business or to continue operation? As with the above examples, are the defaults such that the mortgagee may be unable to cure even after obtaining possession of the property?

g. *Local Law.* Unless waived, does local law provide for rent abatement upon the happening of certain events, such as damage to the demised premises by fire? Does local law allow recoupment or offset by tenant against rents for landlord's default in the performance of its obligations?

h. *Self-help.* Does tenant have the right to cure landlord's default in the performance of its obligations under the lease and deduct the cost of performance from the fixed rent? Can this be done without adequate notice? Can tenant pay real estate taxes or mortgage installments or both to protect its leasehold and deduct the same from the fixed rent? The mortgagee may view this right with respect to delinquent real estate taxes more tolerantly than it might view giving the tenant the right to cure delinquent payments on a subordinate mortgage. In the latter event, a subordinate lien in effect becomes prior to the mortgagee's lien to the extent that fixed rent is diverted by tenant to pay the subordinate mortgage.

i. *Lease Take-over.* If the landlord has taken over the tenant's lease in another building, upon default under the take-over lease by landlord or its assignee, can the tenant offset payments required to be made by it under the take-over lease against the fixed rent?

B. Percentage Rent

1. Generally

In addition to minimum rent and tenant's share of taxes and operating costs, commercial leases often require a tenant to pay an additional rental based upon a percentage of gross sales or revenue. Percentage rent provisions, if properly drafted, are a primary device in making retail commercial real estate investments a reasonable inflation hedge.

Ideally, percentage rent should be based on a net revenue figure, but the problems that arise when the landlord intrudes in the tenant's business and the difficulties in accounting for net revenue have led almost universally to the use of a gross figure. Gross revenue, however, will involve varying amounts of (if any) profit for a tenant, so tenants are concerned with negotiating a figure which is related to the tenant's anticipated profit. As a result, specific percentage figures have evolved over the past several decades, and have become accepted for use depending on the type and volume of the tenant's business. Percentage rents for supermarkets, for example where profit margins are low, may typically range from 1 to 2 percent or less, while motion picture theaters may pay 7 to 14 percent of gross sales in percentage rent. Often the percentage rent is payable only after a minimum threshold amount of sales per annum has been achieved. Sometimes a declining scale of percentages is employed (for example, 4 percent of gross sales between $100,000 and $200,000, and 3 percent of gross sales over $200,000).

2. Definition of "Gross Sales"

Landlords will want the key term "gross sales" (or "gross revenues"), upon which percentage rent is based, to be defined as broadly as possible. For example, the definition normally includes the gross selling price of all merchandise or services sold by tenant (including its subtenants, licensees and concessionaires). Landlords will often seek the following refinements to the definition:

1. The term "sold" should include items leased, licensed or delivered from the premises;

2. Cash and credit transactions should be included (credit transactions including lay-away sales should be treated as a sale for the full price regardless of whether collection occurs);

3. The term should include revenues from orders taken on the premises although filled elsewhere (such as at a branch facility);

4. The term should include sales made by personnel as well as pay telephones, vending machines, stamp machines, amusement machines, and so forth; and

5. Merchandise should include food and beverages.

The tenant will normally insist that a number of items be excluded from gross sales (or deducted to the extent they have been included). These often include the following:

1. The selling price of merchandise returned and accepted for full credit or the amount of discounts and allowances made thereon;

2. Cash refunds made to customers in the ordinary course of business;

3. Discounts given to issuers of credit cards arising out of credit card transactions;

4. Amounts received in settlement of claims for loss or damage to merchandise;

5. Amounts paid to other parties for the rental of pay telephones, vending machines, stamp machines, amusement machines and so forth;

6. Gift certificates until they have been redeemed (unless such certificates are not refundable when sold);

7. Sales taxes, use taxes, luxury taxes, gross receipts taxes and other similar taxes imposed on the sale of merchandise or services (but only if they are added to the selling price, collected separately from the selling price and collected from customers);

8. Sales of fixtures, trade fixtures or personal property that are not stock in trade;

9. Sales made to employees at a discount (although the landlord may insist on a limitation stated as a percentage of tenant's gross annual sales);

10. Refundable deposits;

11. Finance charges received from credit customers;

12. A deduction for bad debts up to a certain stated maximum percentage (at least where a tenant does a large amount of credit business); and

13. Accommodation transfers of goods to branch outlets which may be credited on the books but result in no income to the enterprise.

3. Tenant's Conduct of Business

Percentage rent clauses create an incentive for a landlord to have tenants which are conducting active, profitable businesses. Thus, the landlord will want the tenant to agree to "continuously and uninterruptedly" operate its business and will seek to require hours of operation customary for similar businesses in the area (or, in the case of a shopping center, to the hours maintained by the major department stores).

The landlord will wish to require the tenant to keep the premises adequately stocked with merchandise and trade fixtures to service its customers. The landlord sometimes will request the tenant to agree to "use its best efforts to maximize tenant's gross sales," if the landlord does not wish solely to rely upon the tenant's motivation to make a profit (sometimes a tenant can actually make more profit by reducing sales). Alternatively, the tenant may be required to use "due diligence" to achieve a certain percentage rent. Tenant will obviously wish to spell out circumstances in which it will have the right to close temporarily for reasons such as the taking of inventory, *force majeure*, severe weather, and vacation of the premises at the end of the lease term.

The tenant ordinarily will agree to keep the leased premises in a neat and clean condition. The landlord may often require in the lease that the tenant obtain and maintain at all times all necessary or desirable licenses and the highest available ratings from all applicable government agencies. The landlord may also seek to secure rights of review or approval of standards for employees, the sales area, lighting, display, layout, pricing, and advertising, and may seek to require participation in merchants associations and merchandising events.

In a shopping center, the tenant's duty to conduct an active business is important to the landlord not only because of the percentage rent derived from that tenant, but also because of the effect of the tenant's operations on the entire center-particularly where the tenant is an anchor tenant. Many of the operating duties of such tenants will be embodied not in the lease itself, but in other agreements such as a reciprocal easement agreement.[9]

In order to police operating requirements, leases often contain a specific remedy, in the form of a "recapture" provision, which authorizes the landlord to declare a "recapture," requires the tenant to surrender the premises and terminates the lease in the event of a "closure." Typically "closure" includes such occurrences as closing of business for seven consecutive days; removal by tenant of substantially all of its inventory from the premises; or failure to operate during 75 percent of the hours per day customary in tenant's business. Tenant will seek a right to cure after notification of its breach of such standards. In giving landlord the option to terminate the lease and thus to seek a tenant more willing or able to remain in business, the clause provides greater protection for landlord than a suit for damages or injunctive relief.

4. Frequency of Payment

Landlords normally will want payments of percentage as well as base rent to be as frequent as possible, preferably monthly, in order to take immediate advantage of peak sales periods during the year, such as holiday seasons. If payable monthly or quarterly, such payments are normally subject to adjustment after the end of the lease year or applicable accounting period. Landlords will want a provision to the effect that if there has been an underpayment, the underpayment should be due immediately and should start to bear interest at a specified rate after, for example, ten days. If there has been an overpayment, it is normally credited, without interest to the tenant's credit, to the next payment of rent due.

For partial years, landlord will want threshold or minimum amounts to be prorated. This aspect of the negotiations can be somewhat difficult depending upon how the partial year corresponds to peak sales periods. Conflicts in negotiations will often occur when tenant wants to dovetail the percentage rent period with tenant's accounting periods, while landlord wants such periods to be uniform for all tenants.

5. Statement of Sales

The landlord normally wants statements showing the gross sales and amount of percentage rent due with each monthly or quarterly payment of percentage rent.

---

[9] See Real Estate Financing Committee, *Reviewing a Shopping Center REA*, 18 Real Prop., Prob. & Tr. J. 651 (1983).

These statements are usually not audited, but are certified by an officer of the tenant. At the end of each lease year, the landlord often insists that these statements be audited in order to ensure reliability. Where an audit is required, landlord may want to designate the auditors, normally a firm of certified public accountants. The audit is normally paid for by the landlord unless a deficiency of, for example, 3 percent or more is discovered. If there is a large deficiency (such as 10 percent or more), the landlord may desire to declare a default under the lease.

The tenant will be required to maintain good accounting practices and should be required to maintain cash register receipts or other appropriate records of sales. If a cash register is not used, landlord may request that tenant use consecutively numbered sales slips or some similar procedure. The tenant should make its books and records available for inspection and copying by the landlord at reasonable intervals, and should furnish copies of tenant's sales and use tax returns, together with any reports sent to any franchisor. However, if the tenant leases several different premises, it may object to furnishing tax returns or franchise reports to the landlord because this may reveal confidential information regarding the tenant's overall business which is not relevant to the landlord's concerns.

The tenant should be required to retain its records for at least two or three years following the applicable year. Moreover, this requirement should survive the termination of the lease. The landlord should consider whether the tenant is likely to maintain its books and records at a distant headquarters office which would make inspection by the landlord costly and difficult. The landlord should have the right both to inspect and to copy the tenant's records at landlord's expense (a right which should also continue for several years after termination). The tenant should agree to cooperate with any such request for inspection or copying.

The tenant will want the landlord to agree to keep all financial information confidential. However, the landlord will want an exception as needed for the financing or sale of the premises (although percentage rents are not typically relied upon by a lender in evaluating a loan application). The landlord may also want an exception as needed for litigation or arbitration between the parties or as demanded by a governmental agency.

Occasionally, a tenant will be permitted to occupy premises in advance of full completion of a shopping center with no obligation to pay minimum rent, with the obligation to pay only percentage rent until completion of the center. This is normally acceptable to a lender, provided that the loan is funded only after full completion and that, upon funding, all leases are made pursuant to an approved lease form which contains full minimum rent provisions.

6. Negation of Partnership

Rent derived from a percentage rent clause may be viewed as giving the landlord a form of participation in the tenant's revenues. As described above, implementation of such a clause usually involves other provisions which give the landlord some rights to exercise control over the tenant's operations. For this reason, it is advisable to include a clause in the lease to indicate that the parties do not intend the establishment of a partnership or joint venture.

7. Noncompetition/Radius Restrictions

Noncompetition clauses, frequently found in shopping center and other retail leases, but rarely in office leases, may be classified in several ways. Such clauses may benefit the landlord, restricting the tenant from engaging in a business competitive with another tenant, and thus protecting the rent received by landlord from the other tenant under its percentage rent clause. Such provisions may also benefit the tenant, by forbidding the landlord from leasing to competitors, or by granting the tenant broad rights of approval with respect to other tenants and their activities.

Such clauses may also be classified according to the geographic area which they affect. "Exclusives," which grant to the tenant an exclusive right to engage in a certain line of business on the landlord's premises, restrict competition only on the premises controlled by the landlord. "Radius" restrictions affect competition not only within the premises controlled by the landlord, but also within a geographic area surrounding the premises. Such restrictions may prevent the landlord from leasing premises in a neighboring geographic area to competitors of its tenants, or may prevent tenants from competing with themselves or with other tenants of the landlord within a certain radius of tenant's premises.[10]

Exclusive clauses are normally upheld.[11] However, exclusives are not favored and any ambiguity is to be construed against the restriction.[12] Before granting an exclusive clause, the landlord must examine the rights of existing tenants to use their premises for the purposes sought to be restricted. In this connection, leases often provide that the tenant may use the premises for "any lawful use." One solution is to have the new tenant review all existing leases and to exclude in the new tenant's lease any uses permitted for existing tenants.

Enforcement of clauses protecting the landlord is often effected through a clause which grants the landlord the option to include the gross sales from a competing business in the gross sales made upon the premises for the purpose of computing percentage rent. Such a liquidated damages provision may be more easily enforceable than an attempt to force tenant to close a competing store through injunctive action.

Noncompetition clauses benefitting tenants are most commonly sought by anchor tenants in shopping centers. In the past, these clauses often allowed such tenants the right to review and approve all other leases within the premises and also restricted competition within a radius around the premises, thus preventing landlord from leasing space outside the shopping center to competitors.

Noncompetition clauses benefitting both landlord and tenant have been subject to attack on antitrust grounds in state and federal courts and through action by the Federal Trade Commission.[13] The current trend is against upholding any such

---

[10] See Lentzner, *The Antitrust Implications of Radius Clauses in Shopping Center Leases*, 55 U. Det. J. Urb. L. 1 (1977).

[11] See *Genovese Drugstores, Inc. v. Bercrose Associates*, 1983-2 CCH Trade Cases ¶ 65,605 (D. Conn. 1983); *Borman's, Inc. v. Great Scott Super Markets, Inc.*, 1975-1 CCH Trade Cases ¶ 60,321 (E.D. Mich. 1975); *contrast Pay Less Drug Stores Northwest, Inc. v. City Products Corp.*, 1975-2 CCH Trade Cases ¶ 60,385 (D. Ore. 1975).

[12] See Friedman on Leases § 28.1 at 1239 (2d ed. 1983).

[13] These challenges are often based upon the Sherman Act, 15 U.S.C. §§ 1 *et seq.*, as well as

clauses. There appears to be little or no room for drafting viable provisions benefitting anchor tenants in light of recent FTC actions. The FTC has obtained consent orders in a number of cases against large shopping center owners, developers and/or tenants which prohibit enforcement of clauses granting anchor tenants broad rights to approve and regulate other tenants in shopping centers.

From a lender's perspective, noncompetition clauses which benefit tenants often create problems when they are vaguely worded and grant supposedly exclusive rights to more than one tenant. Care must be taken to review such leases and assure that such exclusive rights neither overlap nor violate state and federal antitrust laws. A lender that can influence negotiation of the leases should seek a provision limiting the tenant's remedies to damages, thereby prohibiting the tenant from canceling its lease or setting off damages against rent because of an anticompetition clause default. Loan documents should provide that a default by the landlord under such noncompetition clauses will constitute a default under the mortgage. The lender may wish to require the landlord to record a short form of the lease evidencing the restriction, in order to minimize the possibility of violation.

Lenders must be aware of situations in which a loan affects only a portion of the premises, but there are noncompetition clauses which are enforceable against the borrower and which affect an area greater than the area subject to the mortgage. An example would be a shopping center where a lender is requested to make a loan secured by only a portion of the center, and the landlord has granted certain tenants noncompetition rights affecting the entire center and possibly an area surrounding the center. In such situations, lenders often require that they be given the right to enforce restrictive clauses against the existing landlord-borrower with respect to portions of the premises not subject to its mortgage.

Another problem arises in cases where the current landlord-borrower has assumed leases from a predecessor landlord which contain noncompetition clauses restricting the landlord from competing with tenants in an area surrounding the premises. The lender will have no practical way to enforce such clauses against the prior landlord, who may wish to develop a competing building or shopping center in violation of such a clause. Such a lender may wish to consider obtaining an estoppel certificate from the tenants in which they agree that they will not seek to enforce such a provision against the current landlord to the extent that the former landlord has committed the actual breach. Thus, where the predecessor has, for example, constructed a nearby mall and has leased space to competitors of its former tenants, those former tenants should be restricted to seeking damages or injunctive relief against their former landlord and should not be able to obtain damages from the current landlord.

8. Prepaid Rent; Security Deposit

Landlords often require that tenants pay one or more months of rent in advance, to be applied to the rent due during the last months of the lease. However, prepaid rent will not by itself provide a fund for the landlord for restoration of the premises in the event the tenant defaults under its obligations to maintain the premises. Therefore, landlords should seriously consider requiring a further security deposit even if rent is prepaid for one or more months.

---

comparable provisions of state law, such as the California Cartwright Act, Cal. Bus. & Prof. Code §§ 16700 (*et seq.*).

If the lease contains an option to extend, the landlord should also make certain that the prepaid rent or security deposit will be carried over to the extended term. Most jurisdictions have particular requirements regarding security deposits, such as an obligation on the part of the landlord to pay interest on the funds, or at least not to commingle them with other assets. The tenant should also consider having the deposit held by an independent escrow agent, particularly if the landlord is not financially strong.

Lenders will generally allow a portion of the rent-usually not in excess of two months' rent-to be prepaid. If the prepaid rent is substantial, a foreclosing lender will be obliged to permit free occupancy of the premises. Where security deposits or prepaid rents are substantial, lenders may require that the security deposits be placed in an escrow account to be available to the lender following foreclosure. In this manner, the foreclosing mortgagee will not have the obligation of paying over to tenants security deposits which it has not been able to collect, in the form of mortgage payments, from the defaulting landlord.

C. Additional Rent

1. Utility Charges

DIRECT

With the exception of office space leases, most occupancy leases require tenant to contract directly for water, steam, gas and electricity. The tenant is usually required to install any necessary meters and, subject to certain limitations, may use the landlord's distribution system. The mortgagee should have no concerns if the tenant contracts directly for utilities.

FROM LANDLORD

In office space leases, the landlord will often provide the tenant with electricity on an electrical inclusion or a submetered basis. In such cases, the tenant will want to be certain that its costs will not be greater than the amount that it would be required to pay if it were to purchase the electricity directly from a public utility.

> 1. *Electrical Inclusion*. Described briefly, the typical electrical inclusion provision includes in the fixed rent an amount (usually determined on a per rentable square foot basis though expressed as part of the fixed rent) representing the value of the tenant's estimated electrical usage. Often the initial "electricity rent" is adjusted by survey after the tenant takes occupancy for the conduct of its business. Thereafter, such rent is usually subject to resurvey if the tenant increases its use of electricity — either through the installation of additional equipment or by longer hours of operation. The survey will express the tenant's usage in terms of kilowatts of demand and kilowatt hours of consumption, to which is then applied the landlord's applicable utility rate schedule, usually at the highest rate bracket. In the event of rate increases, the electricity rent is usually increased in proportion to the increase in the landlord's cost of electricity resulting from such rate increase.

2. *Submetering.* With submetering, the submeter readings of demand and consumption replace the survey. The landlord's applicable utility rate schedule, usually at the highest rate bracket, is then applied to these readings, and often an administration fee is added. The mortgagee should consider:

- Does the electricity rent adequately cover landlord's cost?
- Does the provision contain the proper mechanisms to insure prompt and accurate increases in electricity rent after increases in the utility rate schedule or, with respect to electrical inclusion, in tenant's consumption?
- Can the landlord discontinue furnishing electricity to tenant? If the landlord so elects or is required by law to discontinue furnishing electricity, who pays for meters and all additional panel boards, feeders and risers?
- Utility Escalation. If the lease provides for porter's wage rate escalation rather than escalation based on actual operating expenses, the landlord may require the tenant to pay its proportionate share of any increases in the cost of steam or fuel used in the operation of the building, and any increase in the cost of electricity used in lighting public and service areas and in operating all of the service facilities of the building. As in the case of operating expense escalation, the determination of the base utility amounts and tenant's proportionate share must be examined carefully. The mortgagee will consider the inclusion of such a provision favorably as it is a hedge against operating increases for which landlord may not be adequately protected by porter's wage rate escalation.

2. Real Estate Taxes

a. Determination of Tax

The tenant is customarily required to pay its share of real estate taxes on the building or shopping center in which the demised premises are located or its share of the escalation of such real estate taxes over a base amount.

1. *Definition of Real Estate Taxes.* Usually, the real estate taxes are defined to mean real estate taxes and assessments levied against the building, complex, or shopping center of which the demised premises form a part, and do not include penalties or interest, or income, franchise, transfer, inheritance or capital stock taxes. Increases in the real estate taxes resulting from construction during the term of the lease are often excluded from the definition if such construction is not made for the benefit of tenants in the building generally or does not create additional rentable areas in the building. Special assessments are often specifically addressed so that, to the extent permitted, the same are paid in installments and only installments falling within the lease term are included in the definition of real estate taxes.

2. *Tenant's Share.* The tenant's share of the real estate taxes is usually determined by dividing the rentable area of the demised premises by the entire rentable area of the building complex or shopping center. The tenant's share, often referred to as "tenant's proportionate share," is usually expressed as a percentage and is subject to adjustment if the rentable square footage of the building or the demised premises is changed. In an office building, frequently basement space is either excluded in determining the rentable area of the building, or a percentage of it is excluded. In determining tenant's proportionate share with respect to a shopping center lease, consideration must be given to whether mezzanines, basements, storage areas, outdoor sales areas and drive through porticos are fully or partially included in, or are excluded from, the calculation. Certain out-parcels (parcels with free-standing structures on the periphery of the shopping center) may have a higher per square foot assessment due to construction costs and rent structure.

3. *Base Real Estate Taxes.* If the tenant is required only to pay its share of real estate tax increases, a base for such determination must be set forth in the lease and is usually expressed as the real estate taxes for a specific fiscal tax year or the average for two fiscal tax years. Special problems arise with respect to new construction. Often, the base will be either an assumed amount or the real estate taxes for the first year in which the building is fully assessed as a completed unit. With respect to both methods, significant problems can arise. Without further criteria, it may be difficult to determine the fiscal tax year in which the building is fully assessed as a completed unit.[14]

4. *Tenant's Fixturing and Personal Property.* In the office lease context, the tenant's improvement of the demised premises will not usually increase the assessed value of the building, as assessors customarily determine the assessed value by capitalizing income from the property. However, in other situations, extensive tenant improvements may precipitate an increase in the assessment, for which the tenant should be liable. Many jurisdictions impose personal property taxes on the tenant's personalty and fixtures. The tenant should be required to pay such taxes.

b. Right to Contest

Often, though not always, a major tenant, or tenants of a majority of the space in the building or shopping center, are given the right to require the landlord to contest the real estate taxes or, if the landlord does not institute proceedings or cancels such proceedings, the tenant may bring or carry on such proceedings in its own name or in the landlord's name. The tenant's right so to contest the assessment should not in any way affect its obligations to pay its share of the protested real estate taxes. The provision should not allow the tenant to protest unless the protest stops all proceedings to enforce collection; it will not result in additional penalty or interest; and the landlord is adequately indemnified or secured. Furthermore, a

---

[14] See *Dorothy Stein Shops, Inc. v. Roscon Realty, Inc.*, 59 Misc. 2d 122, 298 N.Y.S.2d 588 (Sup. Ct. 1968), in which a landlord used four slight variations in wording in the "taxes and assessments" clauses of leases involving some 12 different commercial tenants. When it came to allocating the responsibility for taxes, each variation produced a somewhat different outcome.

landlord of a new development may not want the tenant to have the right to contest taxes under any circumstances. If the landlord has entered into an arrangement with the city for fixed taxes over a certain period of time, a tenant's challenge of those taxes could be regarded as terminating that agreement.

c. Obligation for Refunds

If the real estate taxes are reduced and the landlord receives a refund, most leases obligate the landlord to distribute to the tenant its proportionate share of such refund. The landlord should be allowed to reduce such refund by its reasonable costs and expenses, including experts' and attorneys' fees. If the real estate taxes are reduced before the same are paid, the amount of such reasonable costs and expenses should be added to the reduced taxes which the tenant is required to pay.

d. Mortgagee's Considerations

The mortgagee should consider:

- Does the definition of "tenant's proportionate share" adequately insure that 100 percent of the real estate taxes, or of the increase in real estate taxes, will be reimbursed to the landlord?
- Are the mechanics of payment such that the landlord will receive the payments well in advance of the tax payment date or so as to be able to comply with the mortgagee's escrow provisions?
- Can the fixed rent be reduced if real estate taxes are reduced below the base amount? Can the tenant offset its share of real estate taxes against any percentage rents?
- What are the landlord's obligations to the tenant with respect to refunds? How are the costs and expenses of protesting paid?

3. Common Area Charges

In shopping center leases, the costs of maintaining and operating the common areas are customarily passed on to tenants in accordance with their respective proportionate shares. As with the definition of operating expenses in an office space lease, the components of common area maintenance costs should be examined carefully. Questions may arise as to what types of improvements should be excluded as being capital items. The mortgagee should consider:

- Is the definition of common area maintenance broad enough to cover all of the landlord's costs and expenses relating to the normal operation and maintenance of the shopping center's common area?
- Does the definition of "tenant's proportionate share" adequately insure that 100 percent of the cost of common area maintenance is reimbursed to the landlord?
- What are the mechanics of payment? Is there an estimated monthly charge with a year-end adjustment?
- Can the tenant offset its common area charges against percentage rents?

4. Operating and Maintenance Expense

Similar to shopping center leases in their treatment of common area charges, office space leases customarily provide for the tenant to pay its proportionate share of the costs of operating and maintaining the building, or, in the alternative, require the tenant to pay additional rent calculated with respect to increases in the hourly wage rate of porters. The latter approach is frequently used in large metropolitan areas and may result in additional rent payments that do not correspond to the landlord's actual increased costs in maintaining and operating the building.

a. Actual Operating Expenses

Under the customary operating expense escalation clause, the tenant is required to pay its proportionate share of the increase in operating expenses over those expenses for the base period.

1. *Definition of Operating Expenses.* Operating expenses are usually defined to include all costs and expenses paid or incurred by the landlord with respect to the operation, cleaning, repair, management, security and maintenance of the building. Customarily included are: labor costs (often specifically enumerated); materials and supplies; replacement costs of worn out or obsolete tools and equipment; repair and maintenance of building systems (with provisions regarding amortization of new equipment); professional and management fees; contractors' charges for services, materials and supplies; window cleaning and janitorial services; costs for electricity, steam and other utilities (excluding electricity furnished to tenants as a service included in their rents); water charges and sewer rents. Excluded are: cost of correcting initial construction defects; cost of repairs caused by the landlord's negligence; salaries of executives above the grade of building manager; advertising; brokerage fees; legal fees for leasing and enforcement; cost of any item reimbursed by insurance; management fees in excess of those generally charged in comparable first-class buildings; capital expenditures, unless the repair cost warrants capital expenditure or unless the capital expenditure is made to reduce operating expenses. If in the base year or any subsequent year the building is not fully occupied, then the operating expenses are often projected as if the building had been fully occupied during the entire year.

2. *Tenant's Share.* When there are multiple tenants, this share is generally prorated among them. At times, the formula is the square footage of the tenant's space in relation to the square footage of space *leased and occupied*. However, it is preferable to compute the tenant's share by relating its square footage to the *gross leasable area*, thus placing the risk of vacancy upon the landlord. Some landlords prefer to set a flat charge per square foot, which may be indexed in much the same manner as the tenant's base rent.

3. *Base Operating Expenses.* If the operating expenditures for the base year are higher or lower than normal due to an aberration in the expenses of servicing the building during the base period, the amount payable by the tenant over the lease term will be affected. If the landlord is able to reduce operating costs in a subsequent year, the corresponding expenditures in the base year should be adjusted.

The mortgagee considerations with respect to operating expense escalation are similar to those that should be considered with respect to common area charges:

- Is the definition of operating expenses broad enough to cover all of the landlord's costs and expenditures relating to the maintenance and operation of the building?
- Does the definition of "tenant's proportionate share" adequately insure that 100 percent of the increase in the cost of maintaining and operating the building are reimbursed to the landlord?
- What are the mechanics of payment? Is there an estimated monthly payment with a year-end adjustment?

b. Porter's Wage Formula

Frequently in office leases, the landlord, instead of requiring the tenant to pay its proportionate share of increases in operating expenses, will require the tenant to pay as additional rent an amount determined by multiplying the rentable square footage of the demised premises by the increase in the porter's hourly wage rate over the hourly rate as of a given date, usually the commencement of the lease term. The additional rent can be more or less than the incremental increase for each incremental increase in the porter's wage rate. Customarily, the amount is a penny per square foot of rentable area for each penny increase in the porter's wage rate. In a landlord's market the increase may be a penny and one-half for each penny increase in the porter's wage rate. The inclusion of fringe benefits (such as pension, welfare, dental and training fund contributions, mandatory business, mandatory and customary overtime pay, social security, unemployment, disability benefits, and health, life, accident and worker's compensation insurance) and the reduction of hours worked by paid time off (including vacations, holidays, sick days, birthdays, medical check-ups, relief time, jury duty, funeral leave and voting time off), can have a substantial effect on the calculations and result in larger annual increases in the porter's hourly wage rate.

V. OBLIGATIONS OF LANDLORD

A. Maintenance of Premises

1. Free-Standing versus Multi-Tenant Structures

While certain generalizations can be made about the allocation of maintenance obligations, based upon the type of structure being leased and the length of the lease, there are no fixed customs with respect to many of these duties, and they are often the source of extensive negotiations between a landlord and tenant. The extent of the landlord's obligations to maintain a building frequently depends on whether the lease is of a free-standing building or of space within a shopping center or office building, and upon the length of the lease. Leases of freestanding buildings often impose all or most repair and maintenance obligations on the tenant. In a multi-tenant building, however, no one tenant will have control over the entire building. In such situations the landlord will normally be obligated to maintain at least the structural parts of the building, such as the foundations, bearing walls, exterior walls, subflooring and roof. The landlord, however, generally attempts to exclude from such obligations the maintenance of items such as doors, glass, and skylights.

The landlord may also agree to maintain the electrical, plumbing, sewage and air conditioning systems to the extent they are outside the individual premises of the tenant. In a shopping center, the landlord may also be obligated to resurface the parking areas at specified intervals.

Generally, the tenant will have much more extensive obligations under ground leases or other long-term (ten to twenty years or more) leases. Tenants under such leases will often be obliged to undertake all structural as well as nonstructural maintenance and repairs.

2. Shopping Centers

Shopping centers raise special issues because of the significance of their common areas and facilities. Normally the tenant will pay a pro rata share of maintenance costs based on the ratio of the tenant's leased space to the total rentable commercial area in the shopping center. The landlord will estimate such costs and bill monthly, subject to annual adjustment once actual costs are known. In cases where there are buildings on fringe parcels, the tenant may have a different pro rata share for the exterior common areas, including parking areas, than it would have for interior common areas of the central complex.

In some circumstances, tenants will attempt to limit liability for maintenance to a maximum cost per square foot, or to a percentage of gross sales on the demised premises. These limitations are most commonly found in connection with the costs of heating and air conditioning the common areas, which costs are often separated from other maintenance costs. In such cases, the landlord will be obligated to pay maintenance costs beyond such limits. Negotiation frequently centers on the breadth of the definition of such common area maintenance costs. A key issue is the landlord's right to impose a charge to cover management and overhead expenses, and depreciation of maintenance equipment. Fifteen percent of maintenance costs is typical.

Taxes attributable to the common area are frequently decided by negotiation. If the lease contains a normal tax escalation clause, the landlord will prefer to include taxes on the common area within the definition of common area maintenance. If they are not so included, the initial taxes will be borne by the landlord, and only the increase over the base year will be chargeable to the tenant.

B. Tenant Expansion Options

Treatment of tenant expansion needs will vary, depending on the type of structure and business involved. With respect to office space, expansion needs may be met by relatively liberal subleasing provisions which permit a tenant to rent excess space through subleases structured to expire to make space available to meet its anticipated future needs. Alternatively, the landlord may grant the tenant an option to lease additional space in the future.

In shopping centers and free-standing buildings, prime tenants will frequently seek to require the landlord to agree to build expansion space in the future. Definition of such expansion obligations poses a number of problems both for a landlord and its lender. The area in which the expansion will take place should be clearly defined and outlined on a map or diagram attached to the lease. Both the landlord and the lender must be careful that expansion rights of tenants do not conflict and that parking ratios prescribed in various leases are not violated by expansion of other improvements into parking areas. Appropriate rental adjustments must also be made. Where percentage rent clauses are involved, the landlord will frequently seek to condition expansion upon the achievement of certain gross sales figures in the existing premises in order to prevent inefficient expansion by a tenant. Frequently, the landlord will condition its duty to construct additions upon its ability to obtain financing at predetermined rates and terms. Conversely, the tenant may seek the right to perform the construction or provide the necessary financing if the landlord is unable to do so, and to recover the costs thereof out of post-expansion rent.

Lenders will normally oppose provisions requiring a landlord to construct additional improvements for the tenant, because the lender does not want to be required to fulfill these obligations in the event of foreclosure. However, a lender may allow such a provision provided that the tenant agrees that any default by the landlord will not allow the tenant to cancel the lease. The lender may also be protected by providing that it will have an opportunity to foreclose prior to the tenant's taking any action to terminate the lease and that the tenant will not require the lender or any other successor to the property upon foreclosure to perform the work but will do the work itself and recover its costs out of the rentals attributable to the expanded improvements.

C. Contribution to Merchants' Associations and Mall Advertising

Frequently, tenants in a shopping center are required to be members of a tenants' or merchants' association. Such organization may, in cooperation with the landlord, deal with planning, promotional and operating problems of the center, and deal with issues such as achievement of maximum success of promotions through coordinated efforts, decisions regarding store hours and traffic control. Many shopping center leases will require membership in such an association. Participation may be required by obligating the tenant to pay a fixed rate per month, quarterly or yearly as dues to the association. The dues are generally the same for tenants of the same size or sales volume. Alternatively, dues may be left for determination by the tenant members. In such case, a representative committee is often used to make a fair annual determination of the assessment for each tenant. This approach may be objectionable because tenants will not know the amount of their dues in advance. Normally, a lease should provide that a breach of the tenant's covenant to maintain membership in the association constitutes a default as with any other covenant under the lease.

Frequently, the merchants' association has responsibility for mail advertising. Alternatively, some landlords will insist on a fee for arranging and supervising advertising and marketing without the intervention of the merchants' association.

VI. OBLIGATIONS OF TENANT

A. Maintenance of Leased Premises

1. Structure

The lease should clearly state whether it is the obligation of the landlord or the tenant to make structural repairs to the premises, and should define what constitutes the structural portion of the premises. If the lease does not define the term "structural," disagreements could arise as to whether repairs to the various component parts of the premises — such as HVAC, plumbing, electrical and life safety systems — are structural in nature.

In a net lease of a single-tenant building, the tenant is usually required to make all structural repairs. In a multi-tenant building, the landlord is typically obligated to make structural repairs, since it is difficult to apportion the obligation to make structural repairs among the various tenants of the building, although the cost of making the structural repairs may be passed through to the tenants. In any event, a lease should always provide that the tenant is responsible for paying the costs of structural repairs that are required by the acts of the tenant or persons claiming through the tenant, such as subtenants, licensees or visitors.

A lease that gives a tenant the right or duty to make any structural alterations to a building should require the tenant to repair all portions of the building affected by the tenant's alterations.

2. Landlord's Failure to Make Structural Repairs

A tenant may attempt to negotiate the inclusion in a lease of the right to cure the landlord's failure to make structural repairs that are the landlord's obligation. If the landlord agrees that the tenant may make structural repairs that the landlord fails to make, the landlord should be provided a reasonable period to cure its failure after the receipt of notice of such failure from the tenant.

A tenant may want the right to deduct from the rent the costs incurred by it in making any repairs that are the landlord's obligation. A lender, however, usually will not allow any offsets against the rental on account of a default by the landlord. Occasionally, however, lenders have been known to permit a limited tenant's set-off right, which provides for ample notice to the landlord, then sharply restricts the amount of fixed rent (e.g., no more than 25 percent) that the tenant may set off in any one month. In the case of a retail lease in which the tenant is obligated to make percentage rental payments, a lender may agree to allow such an offset against percentage rents, since lenders do not typically rely on such rents in computing the revenue from a building that is available to make debt service payments.

3. Nonstructural Repairs

In a single tenant building, even if a lease does not require the tenant to make structural repairs, it should provide that the tenant will be required to maintain and repair all portions of the premises that are not structural. A multi-tenant building lease will usually provide that the landlord is obligated to make nonstructural repairs, although the cost of any nonstructural repairs will usually be passed through to the tenants.

B. Compliance with Laws

1. General

In general, an owner of real property is required to comply with all laws affecting the property. A landlord or mortgagee will want to pass the obligation to comply with laws to the tenants of the building. The obligation to comply with laws is separate from the duty to repair, since a building may be in good repair but not in compliance with applicable zoning ordinances and other laws — although there is an overlap with respect to laws that relate to the condition of the premises. The lease should provide that the tenant is obligated to comply not only with all laws affecting the premises at the time the lease is executed, but also with all such laws that may be enacted in the future.

2. Limitations

A tenant should attempt to negotiate a provision in the lease stating that it is not responsible for compliance with laws that require structural or other changes to the building, if such changes are not required by the particular use or manner of occupancy of the tenant. If the provisions of a lease relating to the payment by the tenant of maintenance and operating expenses of the building allow the landlord to be reimbursed for costs incurred in connection with the landlord's compliance with laws, the tenant should attempt to limit the costs to be reimbursed by the tenant to those costs relating to laws passed after the date of the lease or the issuance of a certificate of occupancy for the building. On this issue, the tenant's position should be that the landlord is obligated initially to furnish the tenant with premises in a building that is in compliance with all applicable laws.

C. Use Clause

1. General

In order to limit the tenant's use of the premises, a lease must expressly state the purpose for which the tenant is allowed to use the premises and limit the tenant's use to that purpose. In many circumstances, it is to the landlord's benefit to limit the use of the property. For example, in the case of a high quality office building, the landlord may want to limit the tenant to executive or administrative office use or other uses that do not generate a high volume of traffic. With respect to a retail center, the landlord will want the use clause to control the tenant mix at the center, in order to maximize the gross sales of the center as a whole. The mortgagee may prefer a broader use clause than the landlord, in order to ensure that rent will be paid by a contractually obligated tenant.

2. Legality of Use

Prior to execution of a lease, it is important for the tenant to make certain that its intended use of the premises is permitted under applicable laws, particularly with respect to zoning and recorded restrictions. A tenant may want the landlord to represent that the tenant's particular use of the premises under the lease is permitted by law. However, any representation by a landlord that a particular use is permitted should be limited to the time of execution of the lease. A tenant may want the right to cancel the lease if its particular use of the premises is prohibited some time after execution. The landlord, however, will want the tenant to remain liable under the lease, placing the burden of obtaining another lessee on the tenant through its finding a subtenant for the space.

3. Exclusive Use Rights

If exclusive use rights are given to any tenants, the landlord must make certain that there are no conflicts among the leases. If exclusive rights are given to some tenants, the leases of other tenants in the center must clearly restrict such other tenants from that particular use. Lenders will typically object to the giving of exclusive use clauses because of potential defaults, the additional scrutiny required with respect to leases and possible restraint of trade violations.[15]

4. Abandonment

The lease should specify that the tenant's abandonment of the premises is a default. In a retail center, the tenant's failure to operate will affect the gross sales for the rest of the center. In both office and retail space, empty space gives the property an undesirable appearance.

VII. SUBLETTING AND ASSIGNMENT

A. Consent to Assignment

Under common law, absent an express prohibition to the contrary, a tenant may freely assign its lease without obtaining the landlord's consent. Therefore, all landlords and mortgagees will want to make certain that a tenant cannot assign the lease or sublet any portion of the leased premises without the landlord's prior written consent. In some situations an absolute prohibition against assignment or subletting may be appropriate. . . .

In the majority of states, a landlord may withhold its consent to a sublease or assignment arbitrarily and capriciously. [However, other courts have] held that the duty of good faith and fair dealing implicit in a lease requires the lessor to act reasonably in withholding its consent to an assignment, and that a breach of such duty breaches the lease. . . . Courts have looked at factors such as the financial responsibility of the proposed assignee, the identity or business character of the assignee, the legality of the proposed use, and the nature and character of the assignee's occupancy in assessing whether a landlord is acting reasonably in withholding its consent. Therefore, a lease should always provide that the landlord must receive, prior to giving its consent to an assignment or sublease, (i) the name, legal composition and address of any proposed assignee or subtenant, (ii) a complete copy of the proposed assignment agreement or sublease, and (iii) the best

---

[15] See, e.g., *In re Sears, Roebuck & Co.*, 89 F.T.C. 240 (1977) (consent order to cease and desist from enforcing anchor tenant noncompetition clause).

available financial statement of the proposed assignee or subtenant or such other statement acceptable to the landlord and to any beneficiary of a deed of trust or mortgagee of a mortgage affecting the property, audited or certified as correct by a financial officer of the proposed assignee or subtenant. In addition, the landlord must know the nature of the proposed assignee's or subtenant's business to be carried on in the premises and the payments or other consideration to be given on account of the assignment or sublease.

In reviewing a request for assignment, a landlord must always be sure that the assignment will not violate any exclusivity clauses he may have granted in other leases, or any "satellite" clauses providing that one tenant may terminate its lease if another tenant's lease terminates.

Any assignment or subletting without the landlord's prior written consent should be voidable and should constitute a default under the lease, so that the landlord may terminate the lease. In addition, landlords must beware of accepting rent from an assignee, because by doing so in some states they may be deemed to have waived their right to object to the assignment. The lease should also specify that a consent to any one assignment does not constitute a waiver of the right to consent to further assignments.

A tenant's rights to assign its lease will also be limited by the use clauses in the lease. An extremely restrictive use clause obviously limits the tenant's possibilities for assignment.

A tenant should be required to pay the landlord's reasonable attorneys' fees for reviewing and documenting any requested assignment or sublease, regardless of whether the landlord consents thereto.

B. Liability of Original Tenant

If a tenant assigns its interest in a lease, it should remain primarily liable to the landlord for the performance of the tenant's obligations unless the parties agree to release the tenant from any further liability. The landlord should not release any assignor unless the landlord (and the lender, if any) is convinced that the assignee's financial responsibility is equal to or greater than that of the assignor. Any assignee should also be requested to assume and agree to be bound by the tenant's covenants in the lease pursuant to a written assignment and assumption agreement in a form approved by the landlord.

C. Assignments to Related Entities

Often a tenant requests the right to assign to a partnership or corporation which the tenant will form for business or tax purposes. Landlords generally have no objection to such an assignment, provided that the original tenant keeps control of the partnership or corporation to which the lease is assigned, the assignee meets certain net worth requirements and such entity executes an agreement assuming the tenant's obligations under the lease. Landlords may wish to limit the number of times a tenant may make such an assignment.

D. Assignments to Affiliates

In addition, corporate tenants often request the ability to assign a lease to another corporation in the case of a merger or a consolidation of the original tenant. Again, landlords should have no objection to such a clause if the assignee executes an agreement assuming the tenant's obligations under the lease. Landlords sometimes impose net worth tests on the surviving entity.

If a tenant is a partnership, significant change in the status or ownership of the partnership (e.g., any withdrawal or substitution — voluntary, involuntary or by operation of law — of any partner owning 25 percent or more of the partnership), the assignment (even cumulatively) of any interest in the capital or the profits of the partnership or the dissolution of the partnership, should be deemed an assignment of the lease requiring the landlord's prior written consent.

E. Assignment of Subtenant Rent

When subletting is permitted, the landlord should require the tenant to assign to the landlord all rent from subtenants so that the landlord has an immediate right to collect such rent and apply it against the sums owing to the landlord from the tenant. Without such an assignment, because the landlord is usually not in privity with the subtenant the landlord might be prevented from collecting rent directly from the subtenant. The landlord should also require that upon the occurrence of any default by the tenant and so long as such default remains uncured, the landlord may sue for and collect such rent and apply the same — less costs and expenses of operation and collection, including reasonable attorneys' fees — toward the tenant's lease obligations. The landlord should specify that collection of such rent shall not constitute an acceptance by the landlord of attornment by such subtenants.

F. Involuntary Assignment

Leases commonly provide that no interest of the tenant in the lease is assignable by operation of law, including, but not limited to, bankruptcy, assignments for the benefit of creditors, institution of proceedings under the Bankruptcy Act in which the tenant is the bankrupt, or the appointment of a receiver. Section 365(e) of the Bankruptcy Code provides generally that forfeiture and termination clauses contained in leases and conditioned on the insolvency of the tenant are unenforceable. The trustee or tenant-debtor may assume the lease if economic defaults are cured and adequate assurance of future performance is given. With respect to shopping center leases only, the trustee or tenant-debtor may assume and assign such leases only if specific adequate assurance of future performance is given under the provisions of section 365(b)(3). Section 365(b)(3) provides that a shopping center lease cannot be assumed or assigned unless the tenant-debtor or trustee provides adequate assurance (i) of the source of the rent; (ii) that any percentage rent due under the lease will not decline substantially; (iii) that the assumption or assignment of the lease will not breach any covenants regarding radius, location, use or exclusivity provisions in any other lease, financing arrangement or master agreement relating to the shopping center; and (iv) that assumption or assignment of such lease will not disrupt substantially any tenant mix or balance in such shopping center. Since the adoption of the Bankruptcy Reform Act in 1978, some landlords are no longer including prohibitions against involuntary assignment in their leases. The better course is to include such prohibitions to protect the landlord in the event of any change in applicable law, but to advise landlords that such clauses are unenforceable presently.

G. Recapture of Profits or Space

A recapture clause is a lease provision which gives the landlord the opportunity to "recapture" the space that the tenant wishes to assign or sublet, at usually the lower of the lease rent or the current market rent. The recapture may be for the remainder of the lease term or for the term of the proposed subletting or assignment. Any request by a tenant for an assignment of a lease or for a sublease of substantially all of the remainder of the lease term (which is not an exempt transfer, such as one to an affiliate) should constitute an offer to terminate the lease.

A recapture clause may also allow the tenant to assign or sublet on the condition that any profit realized by the tenant from charging a higher rent than the lease rent must be shared with the landlord in accordance with some predetermined formula. For example, such a clause may provide that if the tenant assigns the lease or sublets the premises, the landlord will be entitled to a certain percentage of any rent collected by the tenant under the assignment or sublease in excess of the rent due to the landlord under the master lease. The tenant will usually insist upon sharing such excess rent only after recovery by the tenant of its costs incurred in obtaining such assignment or sublease. Such costs, if allowed to be recovered, should be limited to brokerage commissions, legal fees, and the costs of installing new tenant improvements for the assignee or subtenant, but should not include the unamortized value of any other improvements installed in the premises by the tenant or paid for by the tenant. A clause providing for recapturing space may limit the tenant's rights to sublet to a certain percentage of the premises and give the landlord the right to recapture any space subleased by the tenant in excess of the designated amount.

A lease provision relating to recapture of profits should specify the circumstances under which it will become effective. For instance, such a clause might become operative either upon subleasing or assignment or upon subleasing or assigning without the landlord's written consent. A lease clause providing for the recapture of space should specify (i) the circumstances under which it should become effective; (ii) the percentage of space, if any, the tenant is permitted to sublet; (iii) whether or not the entire lease will terminate upon such recapture; (iv) whether or not the tenant's rent will be reduced in proportion to the premises recaptured; and (v) what notice will be given to the tenant of the landlord's intention to recapture space. All consideration received by the tenant from an assignee or subtenant must be included as rent, including key money, bonus money, payments in excess of fair market value for services, assets, fixtures, inventory, accounts, goodwill, equipment, furniture, general intangibles, capital stock or equity ownership. The validity of recapture clauses has not been determined to date. . . .

VIII. INSURANCE AND CONDEMNATION

A. Insurance

First the parties must determine what interests are to be protected. Among the interests which should be protected are the loss of building and improvements, loss of rental income and loss because of injury or casualty.

The landlord wants its reversion protected. The tenant wants protection for the value or replacement cost of personalty that it has installed on or brought to the property, and the value of the unexpired lease, a coverage that must be obtained by endorsement.

The leasehold mortgagee wants protection coextensive with that of the tenant, protecting it from loss of the security encumbered by the mortgage lien and protecting the flow of funds that services the mortgage debt.

The lease should allocate the responsibility for keeping the property insured. The leasehold mortgagee is concerned that at least its mortgagor will have the obligation to keep the property insured for the leasehold mortgagee's benefit.

The mortgagee wants the casualty policy to include a standard mortgagee clause incorporated into the policy. This clause is many times referred to as the New York form standard mortgagee clause so as to identify the provisions required. This clause creates, in effect, a separate contract between the insurer and the mortgagee that causes the policy to remain outstanding for the mortgagee's benefit even if the mortgagor's acts have caused the insurance to be invalid as to the mortgagor.

A very similar problem is created between the landlord and tenant. A tenant's change of use or breach of other conditions or warranties in the insurance policy may void the landlord's coverage. Special endorsements are needed to cover this contingency.

The leasehold mortgagee wants the casualty insurance proceeds payable to reduce the debt, or, at the election of the mortgagee, to rebuild the leased and mortgaged premises. The lender would not want a clause that allowed the insurance proceeds to go to the landlord. While in the minority, some court decisions infer that if the security is not impaired, proceeds must be used for restoration purposes.

The tenant wants the insurer to waive subrogation so that it will not be ultimately liable to the insurer.

B. Kinds of Insurance

The following are a few of the more common forms of insurance coverage of concern to landlords, tenants and lenders:

1. Fire and Other Property Damage Insurance

The lease should state whether the landlord or the tenant is required to maintain fire insurance on the building and on leasehold improvements to the premises. In addition, the lease should state the types of coverage to be maintained. For example, in addition to the occurrences typically insured by standard fire and extended coverage insurance with vandalism and malicious mischief endorsements, the parties to the lease may desire additional endorsements to be obtained — covering damage from earthquakes, flood, boiler explosion, breakage of glass, and other such perils. The lease should also set forth the requisite amount of the fire and extended coverage insurance, with respect to both occurrences and individual claims. In the case of a retail lease where the tenant is obligated to pay percentage rent, the lease should also require the tenant to carry fire and extended coverage insurance on its merchandise.

In the event of loss, the straight policy will pay the actual cash value of the property at the time of loss, but not more than the cost to replace or repair it. Replacement cost coverage may be added by endorsement. This insurance may also apply to personal property on the premises and may insure the landlord, tenant and lender.

In order to prevent an insurance company from exercising its subrogation rights against one of the parties to a lease, either a waiver of subrogation clause should be included in the lease or both the landlord and the tenant should be named as co-insureds on the policy.

2. Business Interruption Insurance

This policy protects a tenant against lost profits caused by damage to the leased premises. The mortgagee wants the tenant to have this coverage to make the debt service while the business cannot be operated. If a lease does not provide for the abatement of rental during a period in which the tenant's normal business operations are interrupted by casualty damage, the tenant should be responsible for carrying business interruption insurance in order to ensure that the tenant will be able to fulfill its obligations to pay minimum rent.

3. Leasehold Interest Insurance

This policy protects the tenant from the higher cost of rent if alternate quarters must be sought due to destruction of the premises.

4. General Comprehensive Liability Insurance

The lease should require the tenant to maintain public liability insurance. If the tenant is permitted to sell merchandise on the premises, the lease should also require the tenant to carry products liability insurance. In a long-term lease, the landlord will want the liability limits to be redetermined periodically to keep up with the increasing size of personal injury awards. The landlord should be named as a co-insured on the liability insurance policy. If the landlord is so named, in the event of an injury caused by the landlord the insurance company will not be able to collect from landlord through its subrogation rights, since an insurance company cannot seek subrogation against its insured party.

5. Use of Proceeds

In the event of minor damage to leased premises or to the building in which the leased premises are located, insofar as such damage is covered by insurance, the lease should obligate the party receiving the insurance proceeds to use those proceeds to repair the damage.

The lease should also clearly define what constitutes "minor" or "major" damage. This determination can be based either upon the length of time required to repair the damage, the percentage of floor area of the building affected by the damage or the cost of repairing the damage in relation to the total replacement cost of the building. In the event of major damage to the building, both the landlord and the tenant will desire to have the right to terminate the lease.

This termination provision is usually extensively negotiated by the parties to the lease. A lender will usually object to the tenant having the right to terminate the lease as a result of damage to the premises or the building, if the damage can be repaired within a period of six months. A tenant may want to condition the landlord's right to terminate the lease upon the landlord's election also to terminate the leases of all other tenants in the building, in order to prevent the landlord from using casualty damage as an excuse for terminating an unfavorable lease.

C. Condemnation

Ordinarily, a lease will provide that a total taking of the property by eminent domain will terminate the lease. Such a provision brings the tenant's obligation to pay rent to an end but it will also have the effect of precluding the tenant from making a claim for the loss of value of the unexpired portion of the term. Accordingly, the tenant and the mortgagee will want the lease to spell out the tenant's rights to apportionment of the compensation. The tenant will want advance rent payments included in any payment pursuant to the apportionment formula.

When all of the leased premises are taken by eminent domain, the landlord wants to be compensated for the loss of the land and building. The landlord's mortgagee will of course want to be repaid in full before any proceeds are available to the tenant or the leasehold mortgagee. The tenant desires to be compensated for the value of the leasehold and the value of the improvements he has constructed, but the tenant normally waives any right to receive an award for the value of the leasehold if it agrees to termination of the lease upon condemnation.

If the tenant is constructing or adding to improvements, the lease should provide for the tenant's recovery of the unamortized cost of those improvements upon condemnation. An agreement to apportion the award should be made, perhaps capping the tenant's portion at the tenant's unamortized cost. However, if such agreement is not made subject to the rights of a mortgagee, a mortgagee will ordinarily object to it since it might reduce the security (i.e., the condemnation award in lieu of the real property) available to the mortgagee.

If the taking is partial, the parties may want the lease to be automatically terminated, or to be terminable at the option of either party. Often, the parties will negotiate a percentage-of-square-footage condemned as the threshold beyond which the lease will be terminable.

Tenants should be concerned with automatic termination clauses. Termination precludes the tenant from recovering the value of the remaining term and may also impair the tenant's right to recover for the value of leasehold improvements. The tenant usually has the right to maintain a separate action for loss of business, moving and relocation expenses.

In the partial termination setting, issues also arise over the share of the building award to be apportioned between the landlord and tenant and, if reconstruction is to occur, control over the award once paid. The mortgagee will prefer that the award be held by the mortgagee or a trustee.

The lease terms applicable to eminent domain should also be applicable in the instance of a sale in lieu of condemnation, perhaps giving the tenant a right to object to the value offered by the condemning body.

The mortgagee often will require that a condemnation award be applied in full to reduce the mortgage debt. The landlord generally will want the right to apply the award to pay for restoration of the premises in the case of a partial taking, which right is given to the tenant in some court decisions.

IX. DEFAULTS

More than is the case with any other clause in a lease, other than clauses reflecting the business terms, the negotiation of the defaults clause is adversarial. On the one hand, the landlord will want the clause to enable him to act decisively and with dispatch on the occasion of the tenant's failure to comply with the terms and conditions of the lease. On the other hand, the tenant is confronted with a myriad of remedies — not the least of which is the possible loss of his leasehold estate — available to the landlord in the event of his default. The landlord will negotiate this clause from the standpoint of the party who would be injured by the actions or inactions of the tenant. The tenant will want to protect himself, to have the ability to cure his defaults and, in the final analysis, to reduce his exposure and retain his investment as much as is possible under the circumstances.

The tenant agrees to do a significant number of things in a lease, including payment of rent. A well-drafted defaults clause for a landlord will provide that the tenant's failure to comply with his covenants and agreements will result in the landlord having the option to declare the tenant in default under the lease, thereby allowing the landlord to have recourse to his remedies, at law, in equity, or under the lease. The tenant is hard pressed to argue with that approach because it is he who can control his own destiny by complying strictly with the terms and conditions of the lease.

The tenant will want the landlord to notify him in writing of his default and give him an opportunity to cure it. The landlord would prefer to be able to act immediately, if he chooses to do so, without having to give the tenant notice and opportunity to cure. The negotiation of this portion of the default clause will often result in the landlord agreeing to give certain written notices to the tenant of his default and some opportunities to cure the default after notice. Both the landlord and the tenant must be careful to provide for the date when the cure period begins to run-the date of sending of notice or the date of receipt.

If the landlord has agreed to give notice and opportunity to cure, he should insist on there being a difference in the length of the cure period between monetary and nonmonetary defaults. The landlord should only agree to a very short period of time to cure monetary defaults. In certain instances, the landlord may insist on the shorter cure period for nonmonetary defaults. For example, in a shopping center lease where a tenant covenants to be open for business and operate continuously during all required periods, the landlord should insist on the shorter cure period because the tenant's failure so to open for business and to operate continuously would affect adversely the generation of percentage rent under the lease and all other leases at the center, as well as violate the basic premise of shopping center operation that all tenants be open for business and operate continuously, in order to ensure that the buying public can depend on a definitive pattern of shopping days and hours.

The tenant will attempt to have the landlord agree that if it commences to cure a nonmonetary default during the agreed-upon cure period and continues diligently thereafter to effect a cure, even if the curing extends beyond the allowable cure period, the tenant will not be deemed to be in default. This is a negotiable point, but the landlord will need to be careful here because some defaults, such as bankruptcy or insolvency, can take an extremely lengthy period of time to "cure." Of course, the Bankruptcy Code must be considered in negotiating and drafting the defaults clause. This article does not permit a full discussion of the effect of the Bankruptcy Code on leases which are executory contracts under the Code. The landlord's and the tenant's rights are affected by the Code, and each party's attorney must be up to date on the Code in negotiating and drafting a lease-especially the defaults clause.

A good landlord's lease will provide that notwithstanding the fact that a certain default occurs and is cured, if such default and curing occur a certain number of times in a given period, such defaults will be deemed deliberate and not curable on the last occasion thereof, thereby giving the landlord the immediate right to have recourse to all his remedies. This precaution is especially pertinent when rental defaults occur repeatedly and are cured at the last moment. A landlord will be more prone to grant notice and cure period provisions if he can have a "cumulative-is-deliberate" provision such as this one.

When the tenant has committed a default and has failed for whatever reason to cure, the landlord is then at the point of exercising his remedies. The landlord should remember to include any permissible late charges and interest permitted him under the lease or by law in the sums he seeks to collect from the tenant.

At this point, the landlord faces some very critical decisions, some of the ramifications of which he may be unaware. In some jurisdictions, a landlord who takes a certain action against a tenant may be deemed at law to have elected his remedy to the exclusion of all others. In other jurisdictions, the remedies afforded the landlord are cumulative, and recourse to one will not be to the exclusion of others. Many leases will include a "landlord's-remedies-are-cumulative" clause even if the landlord is in a state where the rule is presently election of remedies. One could argue the merits of drafting a lease that only includes reference to remedies available to the landlord on the date of execution. This approach, however, disregards the possible changes in the law of remedies that may occur during the term, often a lengthy one, of the lease. The recommendation here is to be conservative and include all possible remedies, with the understanding that some may not be enforceable. An appropriate severability clause will protect the landlord in this instance.

The classic remedies for default are reentry of the leased premises; dispossession of the tenant from the leased premises; collection of the rentals remaining to be paid under the lease (either presently by acceleration or as they become due); and a suit for damages from the defaulting tenant. There are other remedies, but they are generally derived from the ones listed above.

The landlord will desire to have as many options as possible in the event of default. The defaulting tenant who cannot (or will not) cure his default will want to "cut his losses" as much as possible. The landlord and tenant will probably have negotiated heavily on the duty of the landlord to mitigate damages by reletting the leased premises. Thus the lease and, in some jurisdictions, the law may impose the duty of mitigation of damages on the landlord in such circumstances. If the landlord has agreed (or is required) to mitigate, he should seek to have the lease allow for the expenses of reentering the leased premises; of redecorating and remodeling the leased premises; of amounts other than rent due under the lease such as taxes, insurance and common area maintenance charges; and of brokerage and attorneys' fees of the landlord, all to be "set-off" against the rent collected by the landlord under the new lease before the credit of such new rents is applied against amounts owed to the landlord by the tenant under the old lease. The tenant in default should be obligated to pay any deficiency between the net amount from reletting and the agreed upon rent. The landlord should have minimal accounting requirements to the tenant for such reletting.

The landlord should also be aware of any landlord's liens afforded him by law on the tenant's property in the leased premises that permit such property to be sold and the proceeds applied to amounts (sometimes only to rents) due under the lease. The landlord may attempt to impose an additional lien, perhaps more extensive than the statutory landlord's lien, by means of the lease. The validity and enforceability of this additional lien are of course subject to applicable law.

If the landlord terminates the lease, he will thereby have elected his remedy in some jurisdictions. In all events the landlord should provide in the lease for the immediate payment, as damages, of the present value of future rentals as of the date of termination. Such a calculation will include a discount per annum; the landlord will want a very low percentage discount and the tenant as high a discount as possible. The landlord should agree in such circumstances to account to the tenant for any net amount received from reletting, but only at the end of the lease term as terminated and only to the extent that the tenant has paid such net amount to the landlord, with all surplus from the reletting going to the landlord.

To provide for the possibility that the landlord may need to have recourse to the judicial process regarding its rights and remedies under the lease, the landlord will need to include certain waivers in the lease. He will want the tenant to waive his right to a jury trial, his right to counterclaim, all rights of redemption, and the defense of merger. The landlord should also have the tenant recognize the landlord's right to injunctive relief. The landlord should also seek to have the tenant pay all the costs and expenses, including attorneys' fees, related to efforts to obtain possession of the leased premises and any sums due him under the lease. Such sums should be payable whether or not such litigation goes to judgment. In all events the tenant should be made to agree to the jurisdiction and venue for all legal and equitable actions brought by the landlord under the lease, which jurisdiction and venue should typically be the state and the county or city where the property in question is located.

Obviously, for every right sought by the landlord to be included in the lease, the tenant will oppose the inclusion thereof or try to "water down" the strictness of it. The relative strength of the parties' negotiating positions and their respective negotiating abilities will dictate ultimately the terms and conditions of the lease.

While the landlord may negotiate the tightest of leases, the practicalities of the situation may eventually dictate the way the parties deal with a defaulted lease. Perhaps with the exception of a tenant who defaults under a continuous operation clause (usually because it no longer finds its operation financially viable), a tenant in default who does not contest the default or cannot cure is most probably in substantial economic difficulty. If this is the case, the landlord should consider whether simply taking his space back and terminating the lease may not be his best possible "remedy." This possibility certainly should be considered if bankruptcy of the tenant is a possibility — especially a reorganization type of bankruptcy.

All of the above discussion has involved tenant defaults. What about landlord defaults? Most tenants do not have the "clout" to negotiate a landlord's defaults clause. In the event one is negotiated, a landlord should never allow a tenant to terminate his lease upon the landlord's default; the tenant's sole remedy should be to have recourse to a court of law for specific performance or damages. Lengthy cure periods for the landlord must be provided. No setoffs or abatements of rent will be allowed; such rights on the tenant's part will affect severely the landlord's ability to finance the property involved. In all events, recourse should be limited solely to the interest of the landlord in the property in question (i.e., limited liability), and any such recourse rights should not apply in any event against landlord's mortgagees or their successors and assigns.

X. OPTIONS

An option, in real property dealings is a right, for which consideration has been paid, to buy, lease or sell a particular piece of real estate to or from another at a specified price and within a designated period.[18] In most instances, options have a dual character in that they are rights in real property given to a party, yet also have characteristics of a contract, obligating one party to perform certain acts if requested through the exercise of the option by the other party.

Broadly speaking, there are two types of options — those which simply modify or extend the leasehold interest created by the lease, and those which contemplate a qualitative change in that interest, such as change in interest in real property from leasehold to fee simple. The latter type is somewhat less common; the former is usually included in any thoroughly drafted and negotiated commercial lease.

A. Options to Modify the Leasehold Interest

1. Option to Extend Term

Before we consider options to extend or to renew the term of the lease, it is necessary to state the obvious assumption underlying a lease without such an option: that the parties will enter into fresh negotiations to renew the lease only if they find it mutually convenient to do so. Of the two immediate parties, the landlord would appear to be the more desirous of this option-free situation. As the base term draws to a close, the landlord is free to shop around for new tenants who would be willing to pay the then market rent, safe in the knowledge that as of a relatively certain date the premises will be vacant if the current tenant is not willing to pay the then market rate or if the current tenant does not desire to renew the lease.

On the other hand, a tenant under an optionless lease may see the handwriting on the wall well in advance of the expiration of the lease term: that the landlord will require a substantial increase in rent in order for the current tenant to continue in possession. Even if the tenant is bound by an operating covenant to conduct

[18] Arnold & Kusnet, The Arnold Encyclopedia of Real Estate (1978).

business on the premises, that business may well take on a lame-duck aspect in the final months of the lease term, in that the tenant will not be restocking its store and carrying the latest in inventory — especially if the tenant owns multiple stores in earlier stages of the leasehold lifecycle. If the lease calls for percentage rent, the landlord obviously wishes to avoid this situation. Even if the entire rent is fixed, the premises may be difficult to release if prospective tenants are inspecting them as occupied by a lame-duck tenant.

From another aspect, if new tenants are not readily available, the current tenant would probably exercise its option provided the renewal rent is favorable. If it did not have an option to renew, it would be more likely to negotiate a market rental at another location, thus leaving the landlord with vacant space or a lower rental to hold the tenant. But landlords and mortgagees alike will want to avoid the potential vacancy for as long as possible: first, by seeking the longest possible lease term, provided adequate provisions are made for rent increases so as to protect against inflation; second, by providing in the lease an option to renew during some extended period before the lease term's expiration, or at least for negotiations for renewal. The provision to negotiate is more a covenant (i.e., to negotiate in good faith) than an option, but it provides much the same sort of added incentive for the tenant to innovate late in the lease term as a true option does. Before the concept of "good faith" came into its own, a covenant of this kind had no legal effect, since it was merely an agreement to agree.[19] Occasionally, however, the courts have been willing to enforce such covenants.[20]

A covenant to negotiate for a new or renewal lease will approach the form of an option insofar as certain terms and provisions of the new lease are specified in advance — most commonly, the length of the second lease term and continuation of the same nonmonetary covenants and conditions. The fact that some aspect of the lease — most commonly the rent-remains to be negotiated makes the provision far more uncertain than the usual option. All parties will wish to precisely define the period during which the duty to negotiate exists. In fixing that period, a balance must be struck between the landlord's desire for an ample period in which to find a new tenant should negotiations prove fruitless, and the tenant's desire to keep the economic choices open as late into the lease term as possible.

The landlord desires an increased return which would protect him in inflationary times while, at the same time, not wanting to reduce the rental below the rental paid during the last year of the then-current term. The tenant is desirous of maintaining the present rental payments.

A true option to renew, giving the tenant a yes-or-no proposition setting out all of the terms and conditions of the lease renewal, furnishes greater certainty to all parties as to what may happen as the lease term nears expiration. In exchange for that certainty later on, the parties must play a kind of guessing game in negotiating the option's rental term so far in advance of its exercisability. Where the lease is for a long term in the first place, pegging appropriate future rental value is especially difficult. In order to arrive at an agreement, the landlord is normally willing to limit the increases to one or two relatively short rental periods (say, five years each), but then wants future rentals based upon the then-appraised value of the real

---

[19] See, e.g., *King v. Dalton Motors, Inc.*, 260 Minn. 124,109 N.W.2d 51 (1961); *Joseph Martin, Jr. Delicatessen, Inc. v. Schumacher*, 52 N.Y.2d 105, 436 N.Y.S.2d 247, 417 N.E.2d 541 (1981).

[20] See, e.g., *Chaney v. Schneider*, 92 Cal. App. 2d 88, 206 P.2d 669 (1949).

property-assuring him a certain percentage return on the appraised amount — or else based upon increases in the consumer price index or some other comparable index.

A true option presents the same concerns about timing as does a covenant to negotiate. The landlord will want to ensure ample time to find a substitute tenant, thereby minimizing cash-flow interruptions in the event the option is not exercised by the tenant. The tenant will want to postpone the decision until the last possible moment in order to reduce the risk of being committed to operating at a suddenly unprofitable location and in order to be able to determine what other locations are available in the market area.

The question of who must carry the burden of remembering to exercise the renewal option provision sometimes gives rise to lively negotiations. Acting upon their uniform wish to extinguish the option well in advance of lease term expiration, landlords will insist that the tenant bears the risk of forgetting about the option. This approach leaves open to the landlord the alternative of waiving the option period limitation if no desirable replacement tenant appears after its expiration.

Tenants, for their part, often seek to shift the burden of remembering the option period to the landlord by pressing for the inclusion of a provision "tolling" the option period until the landlord furnishes written notice of its impending expiration. Only tenants with substantial negotiating leverage in a given project are likely to prevail in obtaining such a clause.

By far the most common renewal provision makes some effort to adjust the rent to comport with changing times, but leaves the other terms and conditions of the lease unchanged. This latter choice should not be unthinkingly made. The trend in commercial leases has been in the direction of detailed allocation to the tenant of maintenance costs, taxes and assessments, and insurance coverage. Both parties should consider the lease provision by provision before creating any option to renew under the same terms and conditions. Otherwise the option may prove to be illusory or an economic windfall for the tenant.

In negotiating renewal options, the parties should consult the appropriate jurisdiction's Rule Against Perpetuities and the case law construing it. Although the majority rule is to find the Rule Against Perpetuities inapplicable,[21] some jurisdictions have required that the last option must be exercisable within the perpetuities period; this may be necessary not only to make the option valid, but to keep from voiding the entire lease.[22]

2. Option to Lease Additional Space

Obviously, a leasehold interest can be extended in space as well as in time. The tenant will want to ensure that the premises to which the option attaches are to be so situated that the tenant can make effective use of the additional space should he exercise the option.

---

[21] See *Camerlo v. Howard Johnson Co.*, 545 F. Supp. 395 (E.D. Pa. 1982), *aff'd in relevant part*, 710 F.2d 987 (3d Cir. 1983); *Rose v. Chandler*, 247 Ga. 382, 279 S.E.2d 423 (1981); Friedman on Leases § 4.1, n.11, at 63 (1983).

[22] See, e.g., *Crossroads Shopping Center v. Montgomery Ward & Co.*, 646 P.2d 330 (Colo. 1982) (en banc).

The landlord will need to reserve the "option space" for the option leasehold term, pending exercise or extinguishment of the option. Mutually exclusive options for additional space, or such an option conflicting with some other tenant's occupancy rights during a base term, could easily result in the landlord's liability for damages. Such damages could conceivably be measured according to the out-of-pocket (valuing the option component of rentals over the term of the lease) or benefit-of-the-bargain (valuing the tenant's lost business opportunity) methods.

Options to take additional space present many of the same problems as options to extend, including balancing the parties' needs in setting the option exercise period; projecting a suitable rent; and determining which other clauses in the lease must be specially tailored to reflect the possible extension of the leasehold interest. The landlord will want a short "window period" during which the tenant may exercise its option for additional space. This will give the landlord the opportunity to enter into short leases with other tenants and give them the option to extend their leases provided the first tenant does not exercise its option for such space. Another variation on this option is for the landlord to grant to the tenant the right of first refusal to lease space as it becomes vacant in designated areas. Usually, the tenant has 30 days to elect to take the space or the right is extinguished as to such space. However, in many cases, the right arises each time such space becomes vacant.

The tenant will seek to have the rental per square foot equal to the rental it is paying for the existing space it occupies and to have the term for the new space co-extensive, including any option periods, with that of the existing space. The landlord will attempt to obtain the then-market rent for any additional space, to have the same term which it could obtain from any third person for the space and to cross-default the new lease with the existing lease.

If the parties have recorded the lease or a memorandum thereof, they should file a supplement thereto in order to furnish notice that additional space is subject to the lease between the parties. This is true even though the memorandum of lease includes a reference to the options contained in the lease, which reference should be contained in any properly drafted memorandum.

3. Option to Terminate

Because both the landlord and the mortgagee will wish to view the leasehold as a predictable source of income, the landlord will seek to minimize the number of contingencies which will enable the tenant to cancel the lease. The tenant, on the other hand, will wish to have an option to terminate upon any material change in the conditions for doing business in the leased premises. These changes include damage or destruction to the premises and/or neighboring properties; condemnation (total or partial) of the premises; or, with respect to shopping centers, a high rate of vacancy in, or destruction or condemnation of, neighboring properties.

Insofar as these conditions may be permitted by the mortgagee, the landlord should be willing to grant such options. Beyond that point, the landlord will be reluctant to "insure the tenant's business." The landlord may be somewhat more amenable to extinguishing the operating covenant or abating rent on a pro rata basis so long as the tenant is unable to operate in the premises, since these measures will still assure an income stream from the remaining leasable area of the premises.

When the tenant is to be one of a number of tenants in a shopping mall or other commercial community affording each tenant a broader clientele base, the tenant is correct in insisting that the developer-landlord, who is selling each tenant the community as well as the individual storerooms, should be the insurer that such benefits will continue. Thus, if an "anchor tenant" vacates and cannot be replaced within a reasonable time, or if a certain portion of the mall or strip stores become vacant, the tenant should have the option to terminate.

On the other hand, if the tenant seeks the right to terminate the lease because of a loss of an anchor or of mall or strip stores, the landlord may insist on an option to terminate in the event that percentage rents are not received from the tenant or drop below a certain level for a certain period of time. The outcome on such issues will generally be a function of the market for commercial space.

B. Options to Acquire the Landlord's Interest

1. Option to Purchase

When an option to purchase is exercised, it creates a contract for the sale of land. Thus, although it is embedded within a lease, an option to purchase "clause" should include all the provisions normally contained in a self-contained contract for sale. At a minimum, these should include attention to the risk of loss prior to sale, the requisite evidence of title, and a procedure for dealing with unpermitted title exceptions. The landlord should devote some attention to the methods of payment he would accept. The tenant should insist upon indemnification from the landlord for liabilities or losses resulting from the transfer of title.

In addition to the foregoing matters, the option by its nature gives rise to issues that normally arise in a routine contract for sale. The parties may wish to provide for an adjustment to the purchase price in the event of partial condemnation of the premises before the option is exercised. Also, to avoid uncertainty, they may want to stipulate whether or not the option to purchase may be assignable independently of the leasehold interest.

The mortgagee should insist that any option to purchase should be in terms subordinate to the mortgage. Otherwise, at least in some jurisdictions,[23] the tenant's exercise of the option may extinguish the mortgage.

Even if the tenant does not normally insist on the recording of its lease, or memoranda thereof, it should insist on such recording when the lease contains an option to purchase so as to perfect the option as against subsequent bona fide purchasers for value.[24] The tenant should also take care that the option is sufficiently precise that it only requires assent at the time of exercise. If there are significant gaps to be filled at the time of exercise, an action for specific performance may not lie.

With many commercial properties, the tenant would do well to question precisely what the option to purchase will yield upon its exercise. Rights of ingress and egress, maintenance easements, and so forth may only exist for the tenant by virtue of the landlord's surrounding fee simple estate and the covenants of the lease.

[23] See *Kamas State Bank v. Bourgeois*, 14 Utah 2d 188, 380 P.2d 931 (1963).

[24] See *Connolly v. Des Moines & Central Iowa Ry.*, 246 Iowa 874, 68 N.W.2d 320 (1955).

There may prove to be hidden costs in exercising the option if the tenant is required to have the property subdivided before title may be transferred or if the tenant did not ascertain his rights upon diversity of ownership at the time the lease was executed. Depending on the extent of the landlord's holdings, the tenant should insist that easement rights be protected by the landlord's execution and recording of a declaration of easement or a reciprocal easement agreement, at least before the tenant pays extra for the option.

Although English courts have tended to treat options to purchase contained in leases as subject to the Rule Against Perpetuities,[25] most American courts have recognized the value of remotely exercisable options given with a commercial leasehold estate[26] and have therefore exempted such options from the usual operation of the Rule. However, some recent cases have considered the "clogging of the equity" theory when options are given simultaneously with financing.[27]

2. Right of First Refusal

This option serves to bypass the remote valuation inherent in the appurtenant option to purchase. The landlord can set a price at its leisure, and can time the offer of sale according to its latter-day convenience. The usual first refusal option provides for notice from the landlord to the tenant as to the fair market value of the property, the terms of sale, and a period within which the tenant may elect to purchase at that value and upon those terms. As is the case with standard options to purchase, the tenant must keep in mind that the legal consequences of a counteroffer differ vastly from those of the simple assent that constitutes exercise of the option.

The tenant should seek a provision that would revive the first refusal option in the event that the seller's initial offer is unacceptable and no third party steps in to make the purchase. Although the first refusal option affords less certainty to the tenant than the option to purchase does, the former is nonetheless worth pursuing for its tendency to chill the auction atmosphere that might otherwise exist.

A variation on the right of first refusal is the right or option to match a binding offer. While the holder of this right prefers this method to the right of first refusal, the landlord should not give such right to match a binding offer since this could hamper negotiations. If the landlord must tell a potential buyer that after all terms are agreed upon, he must give his tenant the opportunity to buy the property on the same terms, the potential buyer would be concerned about negotiating all the benefits for the tenant and losing the deal himself.

XI. SUBORDINATION

A. General

The question of lease subordination always comes up in connection with the negotiation of a commercial lease. This is because there is almost always a

---

[25] See, e.g., *Rider v. Ford* [1923] 1 Ch. 541.

[26] See *Quarto Mining Co. v. Litman*, 42 Ohio St. 2d 73, 326 N.E.2d 676 (1975).

[27] See 1 Glenn, Mortgages 279; *cf. Coursey v. Fairchild*, 436 P.2d 35 (Okla. 1967) (oil and gas lease).

permanent lender involved.

A lease is subordinate either because it is later in time than the lender's loan documents or because the lease contains a provision stating that the lease is automatically subordinate to the lender's loan documents. A lease which conditions its subordinate position upon execution of a nondisturbance agreement by the lender is not subordinate, unless the lease is either, in fact, executed later in time than the loan documents, or the lease is actually subordinated by the execution of such an agreement. . . .[a]

XII. ESTOPPEL CERTIFICATES

When a lender looks to a commercial lease as collateral to secure the pay-back of a loan, the lender should be certain that the lease is valid and binding and that the obligations to be performed thereunder by the parties thereto are current. The lender should be satisfied that the parties to the lease have no defenses or offsets as to their respective obligations thereunder. One way for a lender to verify the validity of the lease and the good standing of the parties thereto is to require as a condition precedent to its funding a loan that the parties to the subject lease execute estoppel certificates. . . .

The lease should contain a provision requiring the tenant to deliver an estoppel letter, at the request of landlord, to any mortgagee or purchaser of the interest of landlord. It is recommended that some form of consideration pass to the party executing the estoppel certificate so that the tenant is estopped from denying the validity of the information and/or facts stated therein. Further, the estoppel certificate should clearly state that the lender or purchaser is relying on the execution of the estoppel certificate and on the correctness of the information set out therein as a condition precedent to funding the loan or to purchasing the property, as the case may be.[b]

XIII. CONCLUSION

This article hopefully will serve as a practical guide to reviewing a commercial lease that has been presented to an attorney for a landlord, a tenant or a lender. After obtaining a full understanding of the needs and desires of the client, and after considering carefully the matters discussed in the foregoing article, the attorney should be in a position to negotiate any necessary changes with the other parties.

[3] Notes on Additional Leasing Issues

A Practical Guide to Reviewing a Commercial Lease makes it clear that the lessor and lessee under a commercial lease are almost completely free to structure the terms of their financial and legal relationship so as to promote their mutual advantage. In most jurisdictions, very few laws or judicial decisions restrict the parties or prohibit the use of mutually acceptable provisions. Certainly, no comprehensive set of laws analogous to the Uniform Residential Landlord and Tenant Act applies in the commercial context. Consequently, most disputes between lessors and lessees are resolved by examining the terms of the lease and,

[a] For further discussion of subordination issues, see Chapter 11. — Eds.

[b] For further discussion of estoppel certificates, see Chapter 11. — Eds.

in the absence of specific lease provisions, general common law principles. However, as the following notes indicate, federal and state law may play a part in limiting the terms of the relationship.

[a] Bankruptcy of the Lessee in the Shopping Center Context

When Congress substantially reformed the Bankruptcy Code in 1984, § 365 was amended to require that if a tenant in a shopping center setting files for bankruptcy, the terms of the lease, especially the use clause, must be fully honored by any assignee of the lease so that the tenant mix within the shopping center is not disrupted. *See* Roswick & McEvily, *Use Clauses in Shopping Center Leases: The Effect of the Tenant's Bankruptcy*, 14 Real Est. L.J. 3, 25 (1985). Specifically, § 365(b)(3) of the Bankruptcy Code, as amended, provides:

> adequate assurance of future performance of a lease of real property in a shopping center includes adequate assurance —
>
> (A) of the source of rent and other consideration due under such lease, and in the case of an assignment, that the financial condition and operating performance of the proposed assignee and its guarantors, if any, shall be similar to the financial condition and operating performance of the debtor and its guarantors, if any, as of the time the debtor became the lessee under the lease;
>
> (B) that any percentage rent due under such lease will not decline substantially;
>
> (C) that assumption or assignment of such lease is subject to all the provisions thereof, including (but not limited to) provisions such as a radius, location, use, or exclusivity provision, and will not breach any such provision contained in any other lease, financing agreement, or master agreement relating to such shopping center; and
>
> (D) that assumption or assignment of such lease will not disrupt any tenant mix or balance in such shopping center.

The 1984 amendments were sponsored by the International Council of Shopping Centers (ICSC), presumably in response to the unpredictability of the bankruptcy courts in failing to enforce use restrictions. For example, in 1979, a federal court in Nevada simply categorized the actions of the tenant as "conduct" and refused to enforce the limitations of the use clause contained in the lease. *In re Russell Johns*, 1 C.B.C.2d 174 (Nev. 1979). Beginning with the decision *U.L. Radio Corp.*, 19 Bankr. 537 (S.D.N.Y. 1982), the courts were even willing to modify lease provisions in order to protect the rights of the debtor/tenant. In *U.L. Radio Corp.*, the debtor/tenant assigned the lease to a third party who proposed to operate a bistro instead of the electronic appliance store provided for in the restrictive use provision of the lease. The court, in upholding the assignment, developed the so-called "detriment test" under which the burden of proof was placed on the landlord to show that "actual and substantial detriment would be incurred if the deviation in use was permitted." *Id.* at 544. Courts in jurisdictions ranging from Ohio to Hawaii quickly adopted this test in rendering their decisions.

After the 1984 Code amendments, some courts maintained their pre-amendment attitudes toward restrictive use provisions. In *In the Matter of Goldblatt Bros. Inc.*,

766 F.2d 1136 (7th Cir. 1985), the Seventh Circuit narrowed the definition of what actually constituted a violation of a use clause, in direct derogation of Illinois state law. Illinois state law provided that a use restriction could be violated, not only by the tenant conducting activities specifically prohibited under the use provision, but also by the tenant's failure to operate its business on the leased premises. However, the federal court interpreted the state law as too broad and held that anything less than complete occupancy of rented space did not necessarily constitute a material breach of a use restriction. The court held that it would not enforce a provision that a landlord claims is impliedly present, so long as it does not deny the landlord the benefit of his bargain. Its reasoning was that the landlord had the opportunity to bargain for whatever provisions desired at the inception of the lease. Therefore, so long as the tenant does not violate the explicit requirements of the lease, it is entitled to some discretion in deciding how to operate its business.

Shortly thereafter, a Georgia bankruptcy court delivered a crushing blow to shopping center landlords. The court held that when provisions of unexpired leases conflict with policies of the Bankruptcy Code that prevent or hinder reorganization, bankruptcy courts may find such provisions to be unenforceable. *In re Tobago Bay Trading Company*, 112 B.R. 463 (N.D. Ga. 1990). The court in *Tobago Bay* examined the legislative history behind the 1984 amendments and recognized that the primary problem addressed by § 365 was the assumption and assignment of shopping center leases in a manner that violated the general use provisions and disrupted shopping center tenant mix. However, the court went on to find that nothing in the wording of the Code afforded more protection to shopping centers than other non-residential leases and that the 1984 amendments did not remove the ability of the court to find lease provisions unenforceable if they are contrary to reorganization efforts. Finally, the court noted that, as a court of equity, it had to balance the congressionally expressed public policy of the Bankruptcy Code against the rights of the parties to rely on their bargained for agreement.

Shopping center landlords received their first positive application of the 1984 amendments in *Antwerp Diamond, Inc.*, 138 B.R. 865 (N.D. Ohio 1992), in which the court found that the legislative purpose of the amendments was to prevent an assignment by a lessee that would change the entire nature of the then existing business. The court reasoned that the basic principle of the amendments to § 365 was to protect the landlord and remaining tenants from any economic harm caused by assumption and assignment. Therefore, any deviation from the permitted use provisions in the lease would violate the intent of § 365(b)(3)(C).

Unfortunately, the reprieve for landlords was short-lived. A New York bankruptcy court revived the "detriment test" in 1996 in *In re Martin Paint Stores*, 199 B.R. 258 (S.D.N.Y. 1996). In *Martin*, the court conceded that the intent of § 365 was to protect the economic interests of the landlord rather than those of the tenant. However, the court pointed to the clear congressional policy favoring assumption and assignment of unexpired leases. The court concluded that prevention of an assignment by demanding strict enforcement of a use clause clearly contradicted Congressional policy. The court, citing *U.L. Radio Corp.*, imposed the "detriment test" upon the landlord to show that actual or substantial detriment would be incurred if the deviation in use was permitted.

Although the applicable sections of § 365 appear to provide added protections for shopping center landlords, the majority of cases since the 1984 amendments continue to favor the rights of the commercial tenant. Although a shopping center lease may contain any number of restrictive use clauses designed to protect the landlord directly and the remaining tenants indirectly, their enforcement in bankruptcy is quite speculative. Courts continually hold that the congressional policy favoring assumption and assignment overrides private rights. Any use restriction that is in derogation of that policy and hinders reorganization may be deemed ineffective and unenforceable.

[b] Restrictive Covenants

There are two general types of restrictive clauses used in the commercial context, and more particularly the shopping mall setting; radius clauses and exclusivity clauses. *See* Restatement (Second) of Property § 7.2, *comment a*; FRIEDMAN, FRIEDMAN ON LEASES, §§ 6.701 and 28.1 (1990). Normally, radius clauses protect the lessor's interests by providing that the tenant cannot establish a similar business within a predetermined geographic area during the term of the lease. *See, e.g., Cox v. Simon*, 651 A.2d 476 (N.J. Super. 1995) (in which a restrictive covenant in a commercial lease in a strip mall prohibited the tenant, during the lease and for a period of three years upon its termination, from engaging in its business at any location within two miles of the mall). Exclusivity clauses, on the other hand, favor the tenant and provide that the landlord may not lease space within the shopping center to tenants who carry a similar product line and/or would attract the same type of customer. *See, e.g., Walgreen Co. v. Sara Creek Property Co.*, 775 F. Supp. 1192 (E.D. Wisc. 1991), *aff'd*, 966 F.2d 273 (7th Cir. 1992) (commercial lessee brought action against lessor for breach of lease agreement by renting mall space to another business that would operate a pharmacy and sell health and beauty aids); *Almacs, Inc. v. Drogin*, 771 F. Supp. 506 (D.R.I. 1991) (supermarket tenant in a shopping mall brought an action against the mall owner for leasing to a store that would breach restrictive covenant in lease); *J.C. Penney Co. v. Giant Eagle, Inc.*, 813 F. Supp. 360 (W.D. Penn. 1992), *aff'd*, 995 F.2d 217 (3d Cir. 1993) (shopping center tenant sought preliminary injunction preventing another tenant from operating drugstore at shopping center).

Commentators maintain that radius clauses have a tendency to increase competition within a shopping center. Alan M. DiSciullo, *Geographic and Product Markets for Radius Clauses Under the Rule of Reason*, 19 REAL EST. L.J. 121 (1990) (citing *Continental Television, Inc. v. GTE Sylvania, Inc.*, 433 U.S. 36 (1977)). This view is consistent with the Restatement, which states that using the space in the area for several businesses of the same type cuts down on the space available to provide different types of businesses, and makes it less likely that the shopping center will be able to attract the quality of businesses that may be essential to its financial success. Restatement (Second) of Property § 7.2, *comment d*. Also, the mere presence in a lease of a noncompetition promise by the tenant justifies the conclusion that it is essential that the promise be observed if the landlord is to use his other property in a sufficiently profitable manner. Restatement (Second) of Property § 13.2, *comment b*. Furthermore, lessors may be hesitant to invest substantial sums of money if they have no minimal protection from a lessee starting a business in the near vicinity. Hence, rather than limiting trade, in some instances, restrictive covenants may increase business activity. *Cox*, 651 A.2d at 480; *Acme Markets, Inc. v. Wharton Hardware and Supply Corp.*, 890 F. Supp. 1230 (D.N.J. 1995).

Others challenge this position and conclude that restrictive covenants actually reduce the economic benefits to those involved. Lentzer, *The Antitrust Implications of Radius Clauses in Shopping Center Leases* (Practising Law Institute, Real Estate Law and Practice Handbook Series, 1993). According to these commentators, restrictive covenants should be analyzed from the perspective of an adversarial relationship between the lessor and the lessee, in order to fairly evaluate the validity of the restrictions in light of the economic considerations involved. The assumption that restrictions act as effective competitive or protective devices becomes questionable when such an analysis is applied; instead, reasons for curtailing the use of such clauses becomes apparent. The large amounts of investment capital required to construct shopping malls, secured through financial lending institutions which make stringent demands to insure viability of the project, extensive market analysis to select a suitable site, presence of Triple A tenants committed to long term leases, and percentage rents from tenants all combine to insure that the landlord will receive the benefit of his investment without resort to restrictive covenants. Lentzer, *supra* at 498–499. Furthermore, case studies indicate that radius clauses do not protect either the landlord's competitive position or his percentage rents but result, instead, in an undue restraint on the tenant's expansion. A radius clause neither prevents outside competition nor increases the shopping center's drawing power. Lentzer, *supra* at 506.

Generally, the courts have found restrictive covenants in commercial leases to be valid and enforceable. Restatement (Second) of Property §§ 7.2 and 13.2, *comment a*. Where a radius clause contained in a commercial lease negotiated by the contracting parties is reasonable and serves legitimate business purposes, the covenant will be enforced. *Solari Indus., Inc. v. Malady*, 264 A.2d 53 (N.J. 1970) (adopting a preference to enforce covenant to extent reasonable rather than declaring restriction entirely void); *Cox*, 651 A.2d at 431–432. In addition, exclusivity clauses in shopping center leases have been held presumptively valid and enforceable so long as the restriction is not greater than necessary to protect the tenant and does not cause an undue hardship upon those restricted. *J.C. Penney*, 813 F. Supp. at 367–368.

Two basic methods are considered when evaluating the validity of an activity challenged under the Sherman Act as anti-competitive — the doctrine of per se illegality and the rule of reason. *National Super Markets, Inc. v. Magna Trust Co.*, 570 N.E.2d 1191 (Ill. App. Ct. 1991). Unless the conduct has a pernicious effect on competition and lacks any redeeming value, the analysis will be governed by the rule of reason. *State of New York v. Anheuser-Busch, Inc.*, 811 F. Supp. 848 (E.D.N.Y. 1993). The general consensus of the Federal courts that have considered the validity of restrictive covenants contained in shopping center leases is that the varying terms, conditions, and economic specifications for these covenants render the application of the per se doctrine inappropriate. *National Super Markets*, 570 N.E.2d at 1194. The primary reason that such clauses have not been found to be per se illegal is that they are viewed as encouraging economic development. The clauses are thought to be inducements for tenants to establish stores that in turn attract other tenants who will, it is hoped, enter the marketplace.

To establish that a particular activity is unreasonable under the rule of reason, the claimant must demonstrate that the activity produced anti-competitive effects within the relevant product and geographic markets. *Acme Markets, Inc.*, 890 F.

Supp. at 1239. The courts have developed a multitude of factors to be considered when applying the rule of reason. The relevant factors include the impact of the clause on competition in the relevant market, the availability of alternate sites for the entity excluded by the clause, the scope of the clause, and the economic justification for the inclusion of the clause in the lease. *Id.* In assessing the reasonableness of a covenant and hence its enforceability, the courts have considered an eight factor standard:

(1) The intention of the parties when the covenant was executed and whether the parties had a viable purpose which did not, at that time, interfere with existing commercial laws or public policy,

(2) Whether the covenant was bargained for by the parties in the negotiation of the lease,

(3) Whether the covenant clearly and expressly sets forth the restrictions,

(4) Whether the covenant is in writing and recorded,

(5) Whether the covenant is reasonable with respect to the geographic area affected and its duration,

(6) Whether the covenant imposes an unreasonable restraint of trade or secures a monopoly for the covenantor,

(7) Whether the covenant interferes with the public interest, and

(8) Whether, even if the covenant was reasonable at the time of execution, changed circumstances now make it unreasonable.

Cox, 651 A.2d at 480; *Acme*, 890 F. Supp. at 1242.

In applying the rule of reason, the courts must determine the relevant geographic and product markets. In making this determination, the courts are not free to accept whatever market is suggested by the plaintiff as fitting most persuasively with his contention that his power to compete effectively has been affected. *National Super Markets*, 570 N.E.2d at 1194. The geographic market is defined by most courts by the probable and natural customer base. *Id.* (defining the relevant geographic market as the area in which the seller operates and to which the purchaser can practically turn for supplies); *Anheuser-Busch*, 811 F. Supp. at 871 (defining the relevant geographic market as the area in which the vast bulk of business occurs and not by the area containing fringe or possible customers); *Acme Markets, Inc.*, 890 F. Supp. at 1239 (defining the relevant geographic market as the area in which potential consumers ordinarily look to buy the products offered by the business). In other words, the geographic market used must conform to commercial reality. The relevant product market is also defined by the nature of the product in question. A product market is composed of products that have reasonable interchangeability for the purpose for which they are produced. *Anheuser-Busch*, 811 F. Supp. at 871; *Acme Markets, Inc.*, 890 F. Supp. at 1239. For the purposes of a commercial lease, the relevant product is typically the main product line offered by the tenant in question.

In the event that the court finds the restriction to be invalid, the injured party can request one of two possible remedies — injunctive relief or monetary damages. The courts are split on which remedy is appropriate for violations of restrictive covenants. The court in *Walgreen Co.* held that the lessee was entitled to permanent injunctive relief against lease of space that would include a pharmacy. 775 F. Supp. at 1194. The court reasoned that invalidating the restrictive covenant would cause the plaintiff to suffer irreparable harm by losing its exclusivity rights, an item bargained for in the negotiations and reflected in the value of the lease. In comparison, the court in *8600 Associates v. Wearguard Corp.*, 737 F. Supp. 44 (E.D. Mich. 1990), held that the lessor had an appropriate remedy at law in the form of monetary damages and that injunctive relief would not be awarded. The court, citing *Drabbant Ent. Inc. v. Great Atlantic & Pacific Tea Co.*, 688 F. Supp. 1567 (D. Del. 1988), reasoned that the loss of business and customers that the shopping center allegedly suffered and would continue to suffer in the future without enforcement of the restrictive clause was necessarily economic, and thus compensable through monetary damages.

[c] Environmental Indemnification Agreements

CERCLA specifically provides that the liability of an owner or operator under the statute cannot be avoided through contractual arrangements. See *supra* § 8.01 in Chapter 8 for broader coverage of CERCLA issues. However, CERCLA permits the use of indemnification agreements to shift the liability for the costs of remediating environmental contamination from one party to another once those costs are incurred by a responsible party. Section 107(e) of CERCLA provides:

> Indemnification, hold harmless, etc., agreements or conveyances; subrogation rights.
>
> (1) No indemnification, hold harmless, or similar agreement or conveyance shall be effective to transfer from the owner or operator of any vessel or facility or from any person who may be liable for a release or threat of release under this section, to any other person the liability imposed under this section. Nothing in this subsection shall bar any agreement to insure, hold harmless, or indemnify a party to such agreement for any liability under this section.
>
> (2) Nothing in this title [42 U.S.C. §§ 9601 et seq.], including the provisions of paragraph (1) of this subsection, shall bar a cause of action that an owner or operator or any other person subject to liability under this section, or a guarantor, has or would have, by reason of subrogation or otherwise against any person.

Courts that have considered the issue have generally upheld the use of indemnification agreements. *See Caldwell v. Gurley Refining Co.*, 755 F.2d 645 (8th Cir. 1985); *Versatile Metals, Inc. v. Union Corp.*, 693 F. Supp. 1563 (E.D. Pa. 1988); *Chemical Waste Management v. Armstrong World Industries*, 669 F. Supp. 1285 (E.D. Pa. 1987); *FMC Corp. v. Northern Pump Co.*, 668 F. Supp. 1285 (D. Minn.1987). *But see AM International, Inc. v. International Forging Equipment Corp.*, 743 F. Supp. 525 (N.D. Ohio 1990) (invalidating a release of liability given by a prior owner and operator of property to other potentially responsible parties and allowing the prior owner to seek contribution from these parties). *See, generally,* Howe & Bezold, *Environmental Liability in Leasing, in* AMERICAN COLLEGE OF REAL ESTATE LAWYERS, ENVIRONMENTAL LIABILITY IN COMMERCIAL PROPERTY TRANSACTIONS (1994). Thus, although the issue is not entirely free from doubt, a lease provision that provides for the tenant to indemnify the landlord for any losses, costs, or expenses incurred by the landlord under CERCLA because of the tenant's actions should be enforceable.

[d] Taxation Issues

Several interesting taxation questions arise when considering the landlord/tenant relationship. One such question concerns the treatment of tenant improvement allowances paid by a landlord as an incentive to a prospective tenant to enter into a lease and to assist the tenant in the build out of the tenant's space. In 1998, the Internal Revenue Service concluded that tenant allowances constituted gross income to the tenant unless, under the facts of the case, the improvements were considered the landlord's property. Internal Revenue Service, Industry Specialization Program Settlement Guidelines, Tenant Allowances to Retail Store Operators (Sept. 23, 1998). In addition, the Service concluded that tenant allowances could not be considered rent rebates because the purpose and intent of such payments was not to arrive at a fair market value rent. Rather, "[t]he developer's payment is separate consideration for [the tenant's] decision to locate at the developer's mall and operate a store there. In addition, the fact that the allowance is paid at, or prior to, the execution of the lease, rather than periodically as [the tenant] pays rent, undermines the notion that these payments constitute mechanisms for rent adjustment."

In response to the Service's position, Congress enacted § 110 of the Internal Revenue Code which provides an exclusion from gross income for tenant allowances satisfying certain requirements. Section 110 provides in part:

> (a) IN GENERAL. Gross income of a lessee does not include any amount received in cash (or treated as a rent reduction) by a lessee from a lessor —
>
> (1) under a short-term lease of retail space, and
>
> (2) for the purpose of such lessee's constructing or improving qualified long-term real property for use in such lessee's trade or business at such retail space,
>
> but only to the extent that such amount does not exceed the amount expended by the lessee for such construction or improvement.

For purposes of § 110(a), retail space is defined as "real property leased, occupied, or otherwise used by a lessee in its trade or business of selling tangible personal property or services to the general public." I.R.C. § 110(c)(3). A short-term lease is a lease for 15 years or less as determined under § 168(i)(3). I.R.C. § 110(c)(2). Under § 168(i)(3), options to renew are treated as part of the lease term unless the option to renew is at fair market value determined at the time of renewal, and two or more successive leases that are part of the same transaction for the same or substantially similar property are treated as one lease. Finally, qualified long-term real property is nonresidential real property which is part of, or present at, the retail space and which reverts to the lessor at the termination of the lease. I.R.C. § 110(c)(1). Under Proposed Regulations, no tracing of the tenant allowance to any particular construction expenditure is required, but construction expenditures must be incurred within 8 1/2 months after the end of the taxable year in which the tenant receives the allowance. Prop. Reg. § 1.110-1(b)(4)(ii).

Importantly, any tenant allowance satisfying the requirements of § 110(a) is not currently deductible by the landlord. Instead, any qualified long-term real property is to be treated as nonresidential real property by the landlord for purposes of depreciation under § 168. I.R.C. § 110(b). To ensure consistent treatment, both the tenant and landlord must provide information concerning the amounts excluded from the tenant's gross income under § 110. I.R.C. 110(d); Prop. Reg. § 1.110-1(c).

Another tax issue that frequently arises concerns the proper treatment by the landlord upon expiration of the lease of the value of buildings or other improvements made by the tenant. Section 109 of the Code provides an exclusion from gross income in such a situation:

> Gross income does not include income (other than rent) derived by a lessor of real property on the termination of a lease, representing the value of such property attributable to buildings erected or other improvements made by the lessee.

As an illustration of the application of § 109, the Regulations contain an example in which the tenant leased unimproved real property for a period of 50 years and agreed to erect an office building in addition to the payment of annual rent. The tenant forfeited its lease ten years into the lease term at a time when the building had a value of $100,000. Under § 109, the $100,000 value of the building was excluded from the gross income of the landlord.

Importantly, the exclusion under § 109 does not apply to the value of any improvements if this value is in lieu of rent. Whether the value of any improvements is in lieu of rent depends on the intention of the parties. This question is typically resolved by examining the commercial reasonableness of the rental terms under the lease. *See, e.g., Spera v. Commissioner*, 75 T.C.M. (CCH) 2540, T.C. Memo 1998-225; *Weigel v. Commissioner*, 72 T.C.M. (CCH) 1119, T.C. Memo 1996-485; *Bardes v. Commissioner*, 37 T.C. 1134 (1962).

[4] Questions

1. Perhaps the most significant difference in the lease between Regent and Cellular communications and other retail leases is the absence of a provision for percentage rent. Why do you think such a provision was not included in the lease?

2. The Document Book contains an outline of the basic lease terms for each of the six lessees at the Auto Care Center in addition to Cellular Communications. Review the lease terms and consider what changes or modifications would have to be made to the lease with each of these tenants as compared to the lease with Cellular Communications.

    a. What activities will each of the lessees be engaged in? What are the limitations on any lessee not to engage in similar activities in the immediate vicinity of the Fox Valley Auto Care Center? What are the limitations on the lessor's ability to lease property in the FVACC to future lessees who might compete with existing lessees?

    b. What obligations does the lessor have in preparing the demised premises for the lessees? What obligations do the lessees have? Who pays for lessee improvements to the demised premises? How will delays in constructing lessee improvements affect the commencement of the lease?

c. How are the demised premises defined? What rights do the lessees have in the property outside of the demised premises?

d. How do the lessees exercise their options to extend the term of the lease?

e. How much rent is to be paid by each lessee during the term of the lease and how will the lessor pay the costs of maintaining and operating the Auto Care Center? Who is responsible for the payment of real estate taxes and utilities? Is the real estate tax burden fairly apportioned (consider the different per square foot rents being paid by the different tenants)?

f. How have the lessor and lessee agreed to divide the responsibilities for maintaining the demised premises and common areas? Who is responsible for problems or maintenance of structural and mechanical systems (*i.e.*, plumbing and heating, ventilating and air conditioning)? If the lessor is responsible for maintenance that requires access to the demised premises, under what conditions may the lessor enter the premises?

g. What rules and regulations affect a lessee's ability to operate its business? When must the lessee's business operate?

h. Who is responsible for insurance coverage for the Fox Valley Auto Care Center? What rights do the lessor and lessees have in the event of a casualty involving the Auto Care Center? May the lessor or a lessee terminate the lease in the event of a casualty? What happens in the event of condemnation of the entire FVACC? What happens if only the Turtle Wax car wash is condemned?

i. Under what conditions will the lessee be in default of the lease? What rights does the lessee have to cure any default?

j. Under what conditions may the lessee assign the lease or sublease the demised premises? Under what conditions may the lessor assign its interest in the lease or mortgage its interest in the Fox Valley Auto Care Center? What obligations does the lessee have if the lessor refinances the FVACC?

§ 15.02 STUDENT NEGOTIATION AND DRAFTING EXERCISES

1. Select one of the following sections of the lease between the Regent Real Estate Development Corporation and Cellular Communications Corporation and prepare comments with proposed amendments from the perspective of both the lessor and the lessee:

   a. Section 2.03 — Construction/Possession

   b. Section 7.01 — Installation and Exhibits B and C-Landlord's and Tenant's Work

c. Sections 7.02 through 7.06 — Maintenance and Surrender

d. Article X — Condemnation/Casualty

e. Article XI — Default and Remedies

f. Article XII — Assignment and Subletting

g. Exhibit F — Subordination, Attornment and Non-Disturbance Agreement

Make sure that, in making your proposed amendments, you consider all sections of the lease that may affect the amended provisions.

2. Draft proposed amendments to the lease to incorporate a percentage rent component. As part of the proposed lease terms, specify how the percentage rent will be paid over a given lease year and how any over- or underpayment of percentage rent will be determined and paid at the end of the lease year. What lease terms are necessary to ensure the lessor that the proper percentage rent payments are being made?

3. Section 4.01 of the lease between Regent and Cellular Communications provides that the lessee pay its proportionate share of operating costs based on the ratio of the square footage of the lessee's demised premises to the square footage of the *leasable* area of the Auto Care Center. The permanent lender may complain that, under such a provision, the full amount of operating expenses will not be passed through to the lessees requiring that the lessor make up any shortfall. Consequently, the lender may require that this provision be redrafted to provide that the lessee pay its proportionate share of operating costs based on the ratio of the square footage of the lessee's demised premises to the square footage of the *leased* area of the Auto Care Center. Lessees, in turn, may complain that under such a change they will be paying more than their "fair" share of operating costs if the property is less than fully leased. Draft a compromise provision under which the *leased* area will serve as the denominator only if more than a certain percentage of the leasable area is actually leased.

4. The success of many retail real estate developments like the Auto Care Center requires that all lessees be open for business during designated business hours. However, a lessee will resist the inclusion in the lease of specific operating hours if other lessees are not similarly obligated. Draft a provision requiring the lessee to be open for business during specific hours that will also satisfy the lessee's concerns.

5. Draft a radius clause prohibiting Lube Pros from establishing another service facility in the vicinity of the Auto Care Center. What remedies should the provision contain if the covenant is breached?

6. Review Article IX — Insurance in the lease between Regent Real Estate Development Company and Cellular Communications Corporation. Based on the previous reading, propose revisions to this article from the perspectives of both the lessor and the lessee.

§ 15.03 THE LEASE AFTER THE NEGOTIATION PROCESS

[1] Overview

As previously discussed, the lease will serve to define the relationship between the lessor and lessee. Consequently, when questions arise concerning the rights and obligations of the lessor and lessee, the terms of the lease must be examined. Although the lessor and lessee may be able amicably to resolve any conflicts and disputes without resorting to their legal remedies under the lease, the rights and obligations of the lessor and lessee under the lease provisions will always serve to influence the discussions that will take place. An attorney must be able to advise a client concerning the scope of the client's rights and obligations under the lease but must also understand the business context that the client confronts. Often, the business context provides opportunities for the resolution of disputes or conflicts that should be considered before resorting to legal rights and remedies.

Importantly, an attorney's experience with lessor/lessee disputes involving one client will significantly influence the attorney's concerns when negotiating a future lease on behalf of other clients. For example, in April of 1992, a construction crew working on behalf of the City of Chicago on pilings in the Chicago River mistakenly ruptured a tunnel beneath the river which flooded a network of freight tunnels in the Loop area forcing the closure of office buildings and retail businesses throughout Chicago's financial district, some for several weeks. *See* Gary Washburn, *Flood cripples Loop businesses. Water from the Chicago River breaks through tunnel system at the Kinzie Street bridge, forcing shutdown of electrical power and evacuation of thousands of downtown workers. Construction accident blamed*, Chicago Tribune, p.1 (April 13, 1992); Flynn McRoberts, *Great Chicago Flood . . . so far. Chronology of an ongoing disaster*, Chicago Tribune, p.13 (April 19, 1992). *See also Grubart, Inc. v. Great Lakes Dredge & Dock Co.*, 513 U.S. 527 (1995) (Federal District Court held to have admiralty jurisdiction over claim to limit company's liability for Chicago River piledriving work which allegedly caused flooding of tunnel and buildings). Although attorneys in the Chicago area prior to the flood may not have focused on lease provisions involving damages for business closure following a casualty, the resulting claims by lessees against lessors and insurance companies suggested the need to focus on such provisions in the future.

The importance of the specific language contained in the lease provisions cannot be over-emphasized in delineating the respective rights and obligations of the lessor and lessee. The following memoranda illustrate how the specific terms of the lease must be considered before any definitive legal advice can be offered to either a lessor or lessee.

[2] Lease Problems at the Fox Valley Auto Care Center

[a] Donna's Request to Sam

MEMORANDUM

TO: Samuel Nader

FROM: Donna Smith

RE: Fox Valley Auto Care Center Lease

I just received a call from David Delany at Regent regarding the Fox Valley Auto Care Center development. Apparently they have had a few problems since the Center's opening, and they need our help to straighten out some issues.

First, in late June, Cellular Communications was having a tent sale on its sidewalk when a violent thunderstorm came through the area. Evidently, the wind destroyed one of the tents, and in the process, a tent pole injured an elderly woman. She has brought a negligence claim against Cellular Communications and Regent. Delany has informed me that they did not authorize the tent sale. Delany wants our advice concerning possible liability.

Next, on July 24, the air conditioning unit for the entire Auto Care Center malfunctioned. Somehow, the malfunction caused a problem with one of the Center's main transformers. Many of the tenants were without electricity for several days, and they have demanded that Regent reimburse them for lost profits. Please find out whether the lease covers a situation like this, and whether Regent is liable for the lost profits.

Finally, the Fire Marshall just inspected the auto care center and is requiring additional sprinklers in two of the repair shops. Apparently, the city has just changed the local fire code to require two sets of sprinklers above any area where welding occurs. As you know, this was not the requirement 6 months ago when the development opened. Delany has taken the position that the lease requires the tenants to comply with the new regulations. Please advise.

Thanks for your help with these issues.

[b] Sam's Response

MEMORANDUM

TO: Donna Smith

FROM: Samuel Nader

RE: Lessor Liability Issues
Fox Valley Auto Care Center

Issues Presented

- Whether Regent is liable for injuries that occurred during Cellular Communications' sidewalk sale.
- Whether Regent is liable for its tenants' lost profits due to an electrical malfunction.
- Whether Regent or its tenants are responsible for the installation of additional fire sprinklers as required by changes in the local fire code.

Legal Analysis

I. Introduction

Under Illinois law, "[a] lease is an agreement which gives rise to the relationship of landlord and tenant. It is essentially a type of contract, and, as such, it is governed by the rules which govern contracts generally." *Midland Management Co. v. Helgason*, 158 Ill.2d 98, 103, 630 N.E.2d 836, 839 (1994). When a lease agreement is reduced to writing, the intentions and obligations of the parties must be ascertained from the instrument itself. *Pioneer Trust and Savings Bank v. Zonta*, 74 Ill.App.3d 614, 617, 393 N.E.2d 548, 551 (1979). Consequently, the written lease between Regent and its tenants represents the "private law" that will govern the issues in this case.

II. Negligence Claim

Section 9.03 of the lease is the indemnification clause that governs our first issue. It states:

"Tenant hereby agrees to indemnify and hold Landlord forever harmless from any and all claims, damages, liabilities or expenses arising out of (a) Tenant's use of the Premises or the Auto Service Center, (b) any and all claims arising from any breach or default in performance of any obligation of Tenant, (c) any act, omission or negligence of Tenant, its agents or employees."

Under the facts given, subsection (a) is applicable because the negligence claim arises from Cellular Communication's use of the premises. Additionally, subsection (b) applies because, according to Section 8.01, Cellular Communications violated the lease when it held the sidewalk sale.

"All business conducted by the Tenant including, but not limited to, merchandise sales, vehicle inspection, repair or service of any kind or nature shall be performed within the area of the Premises. Such business shall be strictly prohibited, without limitation, from the common areas including walkways, driveways, fire lanes, landscaped areas and parking areas."

Hence, because Section 9.03 applies, Cellular Communications will be required to indemnify Regent for any damages suffered as result of the negligence claim. This conclusion is supported by additional language in Section 9.03, which states:

"Tenant further releases Landlord from liability for any damages sustained by Tenant or *any other person* claiming by through or under Tenant due to the Premises, the Auto Service Center, or any part thereof or any appurtenances thereto becoming out of repair, or due to the happening of any accident, including, but not limited to, any damage caused by water, snow, *windstorm*, tornado, gas, steam, electrical wiring, sprinkler system, plumbing, heating and air conditioning apparatus and from any acts or omissions of co-tenants or other occupants of the Auto Service Center. Landlord shall not be liable for any damage to or loss of Tenant's personal property, inventory, fixtures, or improvements, from any cause whatsoever, except the affirmative acts of proven gross negligence of Landlord, and then only to the extent not covered by insurance to be obtained by Tenant in accordance with Section 9.01 hereof." (emphasis added).

In conclusion, the lease provisions are clear in stating that Regent has a right of indemnification with respect to the negligence claim.

Cellular Communications, however, may challenge the indemnification clause claiming it violates Illinois law. Under Illinois statutory law, an exculpation clause that seeks to exculpate a landlord for its own negligence is void as against public policy.

"Every covenant, agreement or understanding in or in connection with or collateral to any lease of real property, exempting the lessor from liability for damages for injuries to person or property caused by or resulting from the negligence of the lessor, his or her agents, servants or employees, in the operation or maintenance of the demise premises shall be deemed void as against public policy and wholly unenforceable."

765 ILCS 705/1 (1999). Although our lease does not contain an exculpation clause, courts have broadened the Illinois statute to include indemnification clauses that accomplish the same result. *Economy Mechanical Industries, Inc. v. T.J. Higgins Co.*, 294 Ill.App.3d 150, 154, 689 N.E.2d 199, 202 (1997). Additionally, in *Economy Mechanical Industries*, the court held that such indemnification clauses are void regardless of whether the landlord is actually seeking indemnification for its own negligence. *Id.* at 156. In other words, even if the facts indicate that the landlord was not negligent, the indemnification clause will be struck down.

At first blush, it appears that Section 9.03 may violate the Illinois statute; however, a close reading of the lease reveals that in the context of third party claims, Section 9.03 does not violate the statute. Nowhere in the lease language does Regent seek indemnification for damages to a third party resulting from its own negligence. In other words, Regent is still liable for its negligent acts against third parties. Nevertheless, the Illinois statute may pose a problem in the context of our second issue.

III. Lost Profits

Section 9.03 is very comprehensive and protects Regent against damages that result from the air conditioning system's failure. Accordingly, Regent would not be liable for its tenant's lost profits. Nevertheless, it is in this context of damages suffered by a tenant that Regent is not liable for its own negligence. So far, Illinois case law has not drawn a distinction between third party claims and those brought by a tenant. Without a lengthy analysis of the statute and its legislative purpose, it is difficult to assess how a court would rule on this issue. Nevertheless, one thing is sure, even if the indemnification clause were found to violate the statute, the complaining tenants would still have to present a viable legal theory as to why Regent should reimburse them for their lost profits. More facts are needed in order to discuss this issue thoroughly, but Regent should be aware of the uncertainty surrounding this issue before it relies on the lease and denies the tenant's claims.

IV. Fire Code Changes

This issue is straightforward because Section 8.01(13) specifically requires the tenants to install the additional sprinklers.

"[A]t Tenant's sole cost and expense, comply with all of the requirements of all county, municipal, state, federal and other applicable governmental authorities, now in force, or *which may hereafter be in force* pertaining to the Premises, and shall faithfully observe in the use of the Premises all municipal and county ordinances and state and federal statutes now in force or which may hereafter be in force, and all regulations, orders and other requirements issued or made pursuant to any such ordinances and statutes." (emphasis added)

In addition, Section 7.02, which covers the tenant's maintenance responsibilities under the lease, specifically refers to the tenant's obligation to maintain the sprinkler system as required by law.

"Tenant shall make any and all additions, improvements, alterations, and repairs to or on the Premises (including, without limitation, *all modifications to any fire sprinkler system located within the Premises which Tenant has installed*), other than those required for the structural repair and maintenance of the roof, foundation, or exterior walls, which may at any time during the Lease Term be required or recommended by any lawful authorities, insurance underwriters, Inspection Rating Bureaus, or insurance inspectors designated by Landlord."

Unfortunately, Exhibit C, which details the tenant's work to be performed in the build-out of the premises, does not specifically identify the tenant as responsible for the installation of the sprinkler system. However, it does state that the tenant is responsible for "all additional plumbing and/or water services not covered in items 10 and 13 of Landlord's Work" as described in Exhibit B. Items 10 and 13 of Exhibit B do not refer to the sprinkler systems as falling within the duties of the landlord. In addition, Exhibit C states that "Tenant will obtain and pay for all permits and comply with all building codes, ordinances, regulations and requirements of Fire Insurance Rating Bureau." This provision appears to place the initial obligation to comply with building code requirements on the tenant.

Absent some contractual challenge, such as fraud or duress in the lease negotiations, each individual tenant appears responsible for installing the additional fire sprinklers.

V. Conclusion

The three issues discussed in this memo are the negligence claim, the tenants' claim for lost profits, and the subsequent fire code changes. Regent was astute in drafting a comprehensive lease that covers all these issues. The only uncertainty is whether the tenants' claim for lost profits is strengthened by the ambiguity resulting from the Illinois exculpation statute. As for the other two issues, the lease is clear; Regent is not liable for the negligence claim or the installation of additional fire sprinklers.

[c] Questions About Sam's Memo

1. What do you think of Sam's analysis of the legal issues involving Cellular Communications as described in his memorandum to Donna Smith? Did he overlook any provisions in the lease that may support or undermine his conclusions?

2. Having seen the issues that arose with Cellular Communications, what modifications of the language of the lease would you suggest when negotiating a similar lease on behalf of a lessor in the future?

Part VI

TERMINATION OF THE REAL ESTATE INVESTMENT

Chapter 16

LOANS IN DEFAULT

§ 16.01 INTRODUCTION

This chapter focuses on the remedies and strategies available to lenders when a borrower goes into default on the mortgage loan, as well as the rights and strategies of troubled borrowers, including the special protections a borrower gains by filing a bankruptcy action. Even in the best of economic times, a lender must plan ahead, always considering the possibility of the loan going into default. A complicated "fencing match" between the lender and the borrower begins when a commercial real estate loan goes into default, with supporting roles taken by other combatants such as guarantors, investors, tenants, and junior lien-holders.

The commercial real estate recession which began in earnest in 2008 is different from past ones, because this real estate recession came in the wake of a large securitization of commercial real estate lending with its concomitant use of loan servicers acting on behalf of entities holding large pools of mortgage loans (rather than individual loans being held by banks with experience and expertise in handling loan workouts). Securitization ultimately also let to higher leveraged deals with complicated subordinate interest holders like mezzanine finance lenders. It remains to be seen how these differences will affect the ability of borrowers to work out their defaulted loans, as well as the ability of lenders to realize on their collateral and recover the debt owed to them. In some other important respects, however, this real estate recession was similar to the one that took place in 1990 and 1991, when the Fox Valley Auto Care Center construction loan matured. While some commercial real estate mortgage loans in 2009 were going into default due to the loss of tenants and lower than projected income from the mortgaged property, some loans were still current, but going into default because when they matured with balloon payments due on them; the borrower was unable to obtain financing to pay off the balloon payment due to the current credit crunch and much heightened lending standards. This situation is strikingly similar to what happened to the Fox Valley Auto Care Center construction loan.

Notwithstanding the fact that in most respects the acquisition, leasing and construction of the Fox Valley Auto Care Center occurred as planned, with income from the property adequately paying all expenses, including interest due on the construction loan, by the time the construction loan matured, Regent had still been unable to secure a take-out loan for a variety of reasons. The most important reason was that a real estate recession hit just as the loan was maturing. Lenders were very skittish towards making new real estate loans when so many of the loans on their books were in default. Adding to this problem was the fact that the tenants in the Fox Valley Auto Care Center were not "high-credit" tenants whom lenders were then requiring before they would provide any further real estate financing. In hindsight, Regent should have tried to obtain a take-out commitment before it closed on the acquisition and the construction loan. Regent would have obtained a commitment for a take-out loan if First Mortgage Bank ("FMB") had required them to, but FMB did not require this. Instead, Regent claimed, loan officers of FMB had orally assured David Delany that FMB would "roll over" the loan for another year if Regent did not secure a take-out loan by the time the construction loan matured. Assume, for purposes of this book, that when the construction loan became due, FMB denied making this promise and threatened to exercise its rights under the various loan documents.

As you read through these materials relating to loans in default, think about what rights FMB possesses under these circumstances and what defenses Regent could raise. What options are available to a lender and a borrower when the borrower defaults in this manner and under these circumstances? Can you predict how the default was ultimately resolved? Due to the more unsound general financial situation of many lenders in 2009 compared with in 1990, some lenders in 2009 are unable or unwilling to honor previously agreed to loan commitments and would certainly not entertain agreeing now to provide financing or refinancing even for projects that would ordinarily be considered prudent loans, making the 2009 real estate recession likely to be worse than the situation in the early 1990s.

[1] Overview of the Lender's and Borrower's Options

The article that follows provides a general overview of the lender's and the borrower's rights and options in the situation of a mortgage loan in default. It also addresses the various ways loans can go into default and how the cause of the default will impact the lender's decision making. The article focuses on several potential causes for a loan default in a construction loan setting (such as cost overruns, construction delays, unavailability of permanent financing, and casualty). In a non-construction setting, the most common default situation is when a borrower defaults in making required monthly payments to the mortgage lender. This can occur for a variety of reasons. Under some circumstances, it will make sense for the lender to assist the borrower in curing the default. In such situations, the lender will forbear from exercising its rights and may agree to modify the loan terms and documents so that the borrower will be able to perform. In other circumstances, the lender will want to diligently exercise its remedies to gain control of the income from the property and to protect the property and the lender's interest in the property. This would be the case if the problem is not likely to be cured or if the borrower has acted in bad faith. The article also explains the steps a lender should take once the default occurs to adequately assess the situation and determine which direction to pursue.

Phillip L. Kunkel, *Dealing with the Distressed Real Estate Project,* Probate & Property, March/April, 1989 at 35*

Not every real estate project succeeds. Too often, what at first appears to be a viable project develops into an albatross for all parties to the transaction. In such a case, all parties affected by the transaction must be aware of the options available to deal with the situation presented.

The distressed real estate loan is a loan which, for one reason or another, is not performing up to expectations. Generally, a mortgage is in default. The ultimate causes of default can be numerous. However, when faced with a nonperforming real estate loan, both the borrower and lender must carefully analyze the situation, assess the various options available and implement a plan to deal with the loan to achieve their differing goals.

Cause of Distressed Real Estate

The ultimate cause of a distressed loan may be any combination of different factors. However, it is imperative that both parties attempt to identify the precipitating cause of nonperformance. It is important that this be done as soon as the project begins to experience difficulty. From the lender's point of view, it is not sufficient to rely solely on the explanations of the borrower. Nor, from the borrower's point of view, is it sufficient to rely on the loan officer's assessment and suggestions in formulating a plan for dealing with the troubled loan. In fact, it may often be necessary to seek the counsel of a knowledgeable third party to make an objective evaluation of the situation.

While it is impossible to itemize every conceivable difficulty which may plague a real estate project, the following checklist may be helpful in assessing the underlying problem with a distressed project:

Construction cost overruns

Inadequate income

Construction delays

Neglect

Inadequate financing

Construction defects or errors

Unavailability of permanent financing

Death or sickness of critical individual

Government interference

Fire, flood, collapse or other casualty

Assessment of Loan Status

In addition to identifying the precipitating cause of the nonperforming loan, it is essential for both borrower and lender to further assess the situation. The lender must know whether the borrower can rehabilitate the project. The lender's options are decidedly different in the case of a good loan made to a bad borrower rather than a bad loan to a good borrower. The lender should analyze the feasibility of the project. There should be a new appraisal based on the price that could be obtained for the project on liquidation. It should be decided whether the project can be converted to a higher use and, if so, what is the time value cost for such a conversion. A physical inspection of the property should be made to determine whether the project is complete or if any remedial work is necessary. Similar considerations should be evaluated by the borrower-developer.

In addition to reviewing the factual background of the distressed project, both lender and borrower must analyze their respective legal positions. All notes, deeds of trust or mortgages, security agreements and guaranties must be assembled and reviewed for defects. The lender's file should be reviewed to determine if there are any damaging records which could subject the lender to liability. Finally, it is imperative for the lender to assess any environmental or hazardous waste risks which may be presented by a particular project.

Once the relationship between lender and borrower has been clarified, the parties should determine if there are any other players. Quite often, disputes about rights and liabilities in distressed property will involve questions of priorities among various other parties. Thus all parties having a stake in the outcome must be identified. There may be junior lienholders, mechanic's lienors, taxing authorities, tenants, surety or bonding companies, guarantors or title insurance companies which have a direct financial interest in the project. The respective positions of each must be considered by the borrower and lender in formulating a plan to deal with the project.

Plan Formulation

Once the major participants in the distressed loan have completed their initial assessment of the project, they may begin to analyze the various options available. From the lender's point of view the ultimate objective in any such case is to convert a nonperforming loan into a valuable asset. The lender merely wishes to recover its principal plus accrued interest and expenses, even if this means that such a recovery must be obtained at a later date. In contrast, the borrower generally wishes to avoid losing the property and any related business.

The lender's major threat, ultimately, is the foreclosure of its mortgage. Generally, this is precisely the course of action most dreaded by the borrower. The ultimate threat of the borrower, on the other hand, is a bankruptcy reorganization proceeding. Usually the lender will desire to avoid such a proceeding. However, in some cases the lender may welcome a bankruptcy in order to bring control to a particularly troubled project, especially if the lender's lien is well secured.

The following options are available to the parties:

1. *Loan Restructuring.* Restructuring the debt will usually involve modifying the terms of the debt instruments — for example: reducing the interest rate, extending the maturity date, reducing the face amount of the loan or reducing the accrued interest on the loan. Any loan restructuring plan may involve a combination of these modifications.

Loan restructuring generally will only be available for loans where the relationship between borrower and lender has not completely deteriorated. If the borrower no longer possesses any credibility with the lender, it will be difficult, if not impossible, for the lender to consent to any substantial modification of the loan terms.

It will be necessary for the borrower to demonstrate to the lender that modifications will result in achieving the lender's primary goal, the conversion of the nonperforming loan into a performing loan. However, in cases where the nonperformance is due to a temporary disruption of cash flow, delays in construction that prohibit full occupancy of the premises or similar problems, the modification of payment terms may well be a viable option for both the lender and the borrower.

If a modification involves the charge-off of either principal or interest, it is imperative that the borrower consult tax counsel for an analysis of the implications of such charge-offs under the Internal Revenue Code. Similarly, the lender may find itself constrained by accounting, underwriting or regulatory limitations on such charge-offs.

2. *Sale of Property.* It may be possible for the borrower to convey the distressed project to a third party who, due to greater resources, new financing or negotiation, will be able to complete or rehabilitate the project. If a sale of the property to a third party is contemplated, the lender must be satisfied that the new management is competent to operate the project. The new owner must be credit-worthy if the existing loan is to be assumed. Such sales may require some of the above loan modifications as additional enticements to the prospective new owner. The lender must carefully analyze whether the existing borrower should be released from any residual liability as a result of a sale, or whether any existing guaranties should be modified.

From the borrower's perspective, a sale will carry with it potentially significant income tax consequences which must be assessed. The loss of the project may be devastating to the borrower and any ongoing business. These consequences must also be carefully examined. The loss of a substantial equity investment in the failed project may render the borrower insolvent unless the lender allows the borrower to retain a portion of the investment.

3. *Deed in Lieu of Foreclosure.* In some cases it may be advisable for the borrower to agree to convey all or part of the interest in the property to the lender to fully or partially satisfy the debt. If it becomes evident that the borrower cannot continue to operate the real estate project and fully service the debt, both parties may consider a deed in lieu of foreclosure.

The principal advantage of such a course of action to the lender is avoidance of the costs and delay incurred in the foreclosure process. This will be particularly attractive to a lender who must resort to judicial foreclosure or whose foreclosure sale will be subject to lengthy redemption periods under state law. In addition to avoiding delay, the lender may also obtain the property through a smooth transition. The borrower may agree to provide necessary operating documents and records to facilitate the lender's operation of the project.

A deed in lieu of foreclosure may allow the borrower to avoid any deficiency judgment or personal liability on guaranties. In addition, the borrower will avoid the stigma of a mortgage foreclosure. Finally, it may be possible for a borrower to arrange to be employed by the lender to provide continued management of the project while the lender attempts to market the project.

A deed in lieu of foreclosure will not always be the optimal solution for the lender. One of the major advantages of foreclosing instead of using a deed in lieu of foreclosure is that when a mortgage is foreclosed all junior liens and mortgages are extinguished. As a result, if there are subordinate liens and the lender takes title to the property through a deed in lieu of foreclosure, such junior liens remain on the property. Thus, to insure that there are no junior liens at the date of conveyance, the lender should obtain a new title insurance policy insuring that there are no junior liens.

A second concern for the lender relates to the common law doctrine of "merger." Under the common law, when the greater estate (the borrower-owner's fee title) was combined in the same owner with the lesser estate (the lender's mortgage), the lesser mortgage merged into the fee and the mortgage was extinguished. If a merger occurs, the lender, after accepting the deed in lieu of foreclosure, would have the fee title but no mortgage for the purpose of foreclosing the junior liens. As a general rule, the question of whether a merger has occurred depends on the intent of the parties. If the lender and borrower plan for a deed in lieu of foreclosure and intend that the mortgage should remain so the lender can later foreclose on third party junior lienors, the parties should state their intent that there is to be no merger by acceptance of the deed.

In addition to merger and the effect of the deed on junior lienholders, the lender must be aware of potential challenges to the deed in lieu of foreclosure by either the debtor or third parties seeking to set aside the conveyance due to fraud. Finally, the lender must be careful to protect against the inadvertent loss of liability by any guarantors.

From the borrower's perspective, the deed in lieu of foreclosure often will mean the total loss of the real estate project. The borrower may also lose a principal source of income. The loss of this stream of income in such a transaction may occur more quickly than in the case of a mortgage foreclosure. Finally, the execution and delivery of a deed in lieu of foreclosure to a lender will be a taxable event. Therefore, the borrower must carefully analyze the tax implications of any such conveyance.

4. *Foreclosure.* The lender often will be forced to foreclose on its collateral. Alternatively, the best solution for the parties may be an uncontested foreclosure to extinguish subordinate mortgages, mechanic's liens or tax liens.

If a voluntary agreement proves impossible, the lender will be forced to resort to its state law remedies. In most cases, this will involve the foreclosure of the mortgage or deed of trust. For income properties such as office buildings, shopping centers and apartments, the principal value of the property lies in the rents generated, so it is generally critical that the lender control the disposition of such rents. If a borrower has reached the point of defaulting on the mortgage and risking the loss of the property through foreclosure, the borrower most likely is also being pressured by other creditors. In such a case, the rents may be diverted to the other creditors. The borrower may "milk" the project by offering substantial discounts to existing tenants in exchange for prepayment. By the time the lender is able to obtain possession of the property the borrower will have received the rents and applied them to other debts.

The lender's ability to obtain possession of the property after default, to obtain a receiver or to activate an assignment of rents clause contained in the mortgage or deed of trust will depend on the terms of the agreement between the parties; whether the mortgaged property is in a "title," "intermediate" or "lien theory" state; and whether the effective date of the mortgage is before or after the lease in question. However, the lender's ability to protect itself during the foreclosure process will be a critical issue for the lender in determining its course of action.

Besides considering interim protection, the lender must determine whether it must proceed through a judicial or non-judicial foreclosure process. This issue will be resolved by state law. Judicial foreclosure is available in all jurisdictions and in many states is the only method which may be used. However, in those states which allow non-judicial foreclosure, the process is generally less costly and time consuming than judicial foreclosure.

In some states the lender may choose to judicially foreclose in a particular instance because state law does not permit a deficiency judgment following a non-judicial foreclosure. In other states there is a longer redemption period following a non-judicial foreclosure. As a general rule the requirements for non-judicial foreclosure are statutory, so the statutes must be carefully followed.

A final consideration in assessing the foreclosure of a mortgage relates to the redemption rights, if any, after the foreclosure sale. In all states the borrower has the right, after default and acceleration by the lender, to redeem the property by paying the full debt before the foreclosure sale. However, in about one-half of the states, the borrower also has a statutory redemption right after the foreclosure sale. The purpose of these statutes is to force up the price bid at the foreclosure sale since, if the lender or other purchaser bids less than the value of the property, there is the threat that the borrower or other party will redeem the property during the statutory redemption period. As a result, if the distressed project is located in a state which provides for a statutory period of redemption, the lender must carefully consider the amount bid at the foreclosure sale.

5. *Bankruptcy.* In some cases, a bankruptcy proceeding may be the only realistic course of action for a borrower. If the borrower resorts to the protection of the Bankruptcy Code, the borrower will likely start the case under either Chapter 7 (liquidation) or Chapter 11 (reorganization) of the Bankruptcy Code. In a Chapter 7 case, the debtor's non-exempt property is liquidated and the proceeds distributed to creditors for expenses and claims. As a general rule, fully secured creditors will be able to receive either their collateral or its value following the debtor's Chapter 7 bankruptcy. If, however, the value of the lender's collateral is less than the total amount of the debt, its claim will be separated into a secured claim and an unsecured claim. The lender will not generally receive a substantial amount of its unsecured claim in such a case.

Since the objective of any Chapter 7 liquidation is to liquidate the debtor's property, the Chapter 7 bankruptcy trustee generally will be hesitant to continue operation of the debtor's business for any extended period of time. While it may be expedient to finish work that is in progress, it will be a rare case in which the Chapter 7 trustee continues ongoing operations. The reason is that the business was probably operating at a loss before the bankruptcy proceeding started. If the business had been profitable, the debtor would likely have sought reorganization under Chapter 11.

The Chapter 7 trustee has the power to sell property of the estate even though the property is encumbered. However, if the court has allowed the automatic stay of Section 362 of the Bankruptcy Code to be lifted or if the trustee has not provided for "adequate protection" of the secured creditor, the trustee may not sell encumbered property. The trustee can sell mortgaged property free and clear of the mortgage if the sale price is greater than the mortgage amount. The trustee may also sell the property subject to the mortgage. If mortgaged property is sold, the trustee will be allowed to first deduct the reasonable expenses of disposing of the property from the sale proceeds. The secured lender will be paid the secured portion of its claim. Unsecured creditors will be paid last.

If the debtor believes that the property can be salvaged, the debtor may seek relief under Chapter 11 of the Bankruptcy Code. A debtor need not be insolvent to file for reorganization under Chapter 11. The purpose of Chapter 11 is to allow the debtor to restructure debts in order to continue the business. This restructuring is done by obtaining court confirmation of the debtor's reorganization plan.

As a general rule, the debtor will continue to operate the business and to manage any real property as a "debtor in possession" unless creditors request that a trustee be appointed. The appointment of a trustee has proven to be problematic, at best, in many jurisdictions. As a result, in most cases the debtor in possession will continue to operate the business under the Chapter 11 reorganization.

While filing a bankruptcy petition results in an automatic stay prohibiting a creditor from foreclosing on a mortgage or deed of trust, this automatic stay is not necessarily permanent. If the secured lender can demonstrate that its interest in the property is not being adequately protected, the court may terminate or modify the automatic stay. Issues concerning adequate protection are beyond the scope of this article. However, both lender and borrower must be aware of the Bankruptcy Code rules relating to the protection of the lender under a reorganization proceeding.

Assuming that the debtor in possession has retained control of the property during the proceedings, the debtor will develop a plan of reorganization. The requirements of the Bankruptcy Code for confirmation of a plan, particularly over the objection of a creditor, are complex. In general, however, a plan of reorganization cannot be confirmed over the objection of a secured creditor unless:

a. The plan does not discriminate unfairly; and

b. One of the three following requirements are met:

   (1) the holder of the claim must receive the "indubitable equivalent" of its claim;

   (2) the holder of the claim must retain its lien and receive certain deferred cash payments; or

   (3) the plan provides that the collateral is sold free and clear of the liens and that a lien attaches to the proceeds of the sale.

The possibility of a Chapter 11 proceeding must always be considered by both lender and borrower. The possible ramifications of such a filing should be carefully reviewed at the onset of financial distress. While not every distressed loan will necessarily lead to a reorganization proceeding, such a possibility may be the backdrop against which all future negotiations will be set.

6. *Litigation.* In some cases it may be necessary to litigate certain aspects of the loan transaction in order to resolve the differences between the parties. Such lender liability claims are beyond the scope of this article.

Conclusion

Dealing with the distressed real estate project requires a prompt recognition of the problems presented. Prompt resolution of the nonperforming loan generally will be desirable since neither party is likely to benefit from prolonged confrontations. Once an accurate analysis of the problem has been completed, both parties must formulate and articulate their respective goals. Then, when aided by counsel, both parties may proceed to resolve the situation according to their respective interests.

[2] Questions Regarding the Kunkel Article

1. Kunkel lists several potential causes for a loan default. Which of these causes of default are ones that a lender can address at the outset and how?

2. Kunkel recommends three steps to dealing with default: (a) doing a factual review of the condition of the borrower and the project, (b) reviewing the legal positions of the parties, and (c) determining whether others will have to be included in any workout. How would you apply this to the FVACC (*i.e.*, what will the facts show, what are the legal positions of Regent and FMB, and will others have to be include in any workout)? In determining the value of the mortgaged property, the lender should also consider how that value differs from the value of the property in the hands of the borrower, and to do that must include matters like the costs of recovering the collateral against the borrower's will and any carrying costs the lender will incur. See, James R. Stillman, *Assessing the Value of a Loan Recovery for the Secured Lender*, 19 PRAC. REAL EST. LAW., No. 4, 15 (July 2003).

3. Kunkel notes five different options available to the lender and/or the borrower if the borrower defaults in the performance of the terms of the loan: (a) loan restructuring, (b) sale of the mortgaged property, (c) deed-in-lieu of foreclosure, (d) foreclosure, and (e) bankruptcy. Which of these options are available only upon agreement of both parties? Under what circumstance would each of these remedies make sense or not make sense to pursue versus the other remedies? Among the various factors to consider, each of these options presents different tax consequences. Transfer of the property to the lender will result in taxable gain to the borrower, as discussed in Chapter 3 in *Tufts v. Commissioner*, and in Chapter 17. Restructuring the loan may result in cancellation of indebtedness income, which raises tax issues discussed in depth in Chapter 3, Sections 3.05[3][c] and 3.05[6]. A more detailed description of options available to borrowers and lenders when the borrower files a Chapter 11 bankruptcy is provided later in this Chapter.

4. How does the nature of the default and reasons for the default impact on the decisions a lender is likely to make?

5. What factors might affect how aggressively a borrower fights a foreclosure action?

§ 16.02 THE LENDER'S BASIC REMEDIES

[1] Acceleration of the Debt

A real estate mortgage loan typically includes an acceleration clause in the loan documentation. This clause allows the lender to cause the entire indebtedness to become due after a default in making a required monthly payment or some other event of default such as a prohibited sale of the property or interest in the ownership entity. The case that follows involves a lender's attempt to enforce this type of acceleration clause.

[a] Judicial Acceptance of Acceleration

JACOBSON v. McCLANAHAN
264 P.2d 253 (Wash. 1953)

MALLERY, JUSTICE

On May 21, 1951, the defendants McClanahan gave plaintiffs a promissory note for $13,500, payable in monthly installments of $300 on the twenty-first day of every month thereafter until paid. The note was secured by a chattel mortgage on the "Streamline Tavern" in the city of Seattle.

> The note provided, *inter alia*:
>
> "In case of default in the payment of any installment or any interest which may be due hereon, the aggregate amount of this note remaining unpaid and every installment thereof shall *without notice or demand* at once become due and collectible, at the option of the holder of this note." (Italics ours.)
>
> The mortgage contained an acceleration clause similar to that quoted above, and further provided:
>
> " * * * if the mortgagee deems itself insecure, thereupon the mortgagee may, without notice, declare the whole sum of both principal and interest due and payable, * * *."

The installment due June 21, 1951, was timely paid. The installment due July 21, 1951, was accepted by plaintiffs on August 13, 1951. In August, 1951, defendants McClanahan disposed of the tavern business to defendants Siegel. One Kaczor negotiated the transaction between plaintiffs and defendants McClanahan, and the transaction between defendants McClanahan and defendants Siegel. Kaczor procured the consent of plaintiffs to the transfer of the business and the assumption of the obligation of the McClanahans' note and mortgage by defendants Siegel. He made two copies of the instrument of assumption of the note and mortgage. On the copy given to plaintiffs, defendants Siegel were to pay the August, 1951, installment on August 21, 1951. The copy of the assumption agreement retained by Kaczor, upon which defendants Siegel relied in good faith, provided that the next payment on the note and mortgage would fall due on September 21, 1951. Kaczor was not the agent of plaintiffs, and had no authority to alter the Siegels' copy of the assumption-contract.

Defendants Siegel took possession of the business on or about August 14, 1951. The August installment was paid by defendants Siegel on September 17, 1951. The September installment was not paid on September 21, 1951, and, while still delinquent, plaintiffs gave notice, on October 5, 1951, of their election to accelerate maturity of the note and mortgage upon the grounds (1) that there was a default in payment under the terms of the note and mortgage, and (2) that they deemed themselves insecure. The notice stated that they would accept no further installments.

On October 23, 1951, defendants Siegel tendered the overdue September 21, 1951, installment, and attempted, on October 29, 1951, to pay all the installments in arrears, and thereafter tendered them in court.

Plaintiffs refused the installment tenders, and commenced this action for a decree accelerating the note, and, in default of payment of the judgment, for the foreclosure of their mortgage.

The plaintiffs gave notice of their election to accelerate the payments provided for in the instruments. It was not a notice of their intention to do so after a period of grace during which the defendants could bring their installment payments up to date.

The trial court felt that plaintiffs having accepted late payments of installments, should have given notice of their intention, rather than their election, to accelerate the payments, and, accordingly, entered judgment for defendants. The plaintiffs appeal.

Equity abhors forfeitures and penalties, but an acceleration of payments on a mortgage is not a forfeiture or a penalty. In *Seattle Title Trust Co. v. Beggs*, 146 Wash. 435, 263 P. 598, 599, this court said:

> " * * * Counsel invoke the general rule that forfeitures are not favored in law, and that the courts will, if possible, construe a contract so as to avoid forfeiture or rights thereunder; arguing that this default provision is, in effect, a forfeiture provision, and should accordingly be strictly construed in favor of appellant. We do not think it is in any sense a forfeiture or penalty provision. In the text of 19 R.C.L. 493, we read:
>
> > " 'The proposition is accepted without dispute that a stipulation in a mortgage providing that the whole debt secured thereby shall become due and payable upon failure of the mortgagor to pay the interest annually or to comply with any other condition of the mortgage is a legal, valid, and enforceable stipulation, and is not in the nature of a penalty or forfeiture.
> >
> > "This view of accelerating provisions, such as are here in question, is well supported by the decisions. * * *"

See also Graf v. Hope Building Corporation, 254 N.Y. 1, 171 N.E. 884, 70 A.L.R. 984, and WALSH ON MORTGAGES, 292, § 71.

An election to require an acceleration of payments does not require a notice of intention to accelerate. *Cook v. Strelau*, 127 Wash. 128, 219 P. 846; *Saulsberry v. Millar*, 152 Wash. 290, 277 P. 689. Nor does the fact that a mortgage is not foreclosed on the first default in payment, prevent a foreclosure for a subsequent default, since such indulgence cannot affect a right not yet accrued. 53 A.L.R. 532; 148 A.L.R. 697; 14 C.J.S., Chattel Mortgages, § 360, page 1012; 36 Am.Jur. 887, § 398.

The instruments in question provided that appellants had a right to acceleration (1) if they deemed themselves insecure, and (2) for default in the payments. The trial court found

> "That prior to plaintiffs' election to accelerate, they subjectively deemed themselves insecure; that they were in good faith in so believing, having

heard adverse accounts of falling patronage and having investigated said accounts by looking into the tavern from the street on several occasions, and having checked with the brewery distributor and thereby having determined that there had been a sharp decline in Keggage; that plaintiffs' Exhibit 8 is a true record of the tavern's purchases of draft beer for the months indicated; that although plaintiffs, from their investigation, had probable cause to believe that they were insecure, they were not at anytime in fact insecure prior to their election to accelerate."

We hold that appellants must have reasonable cause to deem themselves insecure, but that they need not be insecure in fact. *Skookum Lumber Co. v. Sacajawea Lumber & Shingle Co.*, 107 Wash. 356, 181 P. 914, 187 P. 410; *Hines v. Pacific Car Co.*, 110 Wash. 75, 188 P. 29; *Rosenthal v. Moses*, 144 Wash. 346, 258 P. 7; 125 A.L.R. 318.

The trial court found there had been a default in payment, but that it was due to a mistake of respondents Siegel in relying, in good faith, upon the unauthorized statement of Kaczor. No fault is imputable to the appellants in the matter. In such a situation, the weight of authority with which this state now aligns itself, is that a mistake of the mortgagor will not excuse compliance with the terms of the mortgage. It is only when the default is attributable to the unconscionable or inequitable conduct of the mortgagee that he cannot avail himself of the benefits of the acceleration clause. *Graf v. Hope Building Corporation*, *supra*, 254 N.Y. 1, 171 N.E. 884, 70 A.L.R. 993; *Glorsky v. Wexler*, 142 N.J.Eq. 55, 59 A.2d 233; *Comellas v. Varicon Corporation*, Sup., 81 N.Y.S.2d 449.

The judgment is reversed.

GRADY, C.J., and HILL, WEAVER, and OLSON, JJ., concur.

[b] Comments and Questions Regarding Acceleration Clauses and *Jacobson*

Jacobson underscores the borrower's need to bargain for the receipt of notice of defaults and adequate cure periods before a lender can exercise the right to accelerate the debt. Had the loan documents in the *Jacobson* case provided for such notice and cure period, then the borrower could have corrected their mistake and avoided acceleration of the loan. How well did Regent negotiate for such rights? *See* Article X of the Loan Agreement in the Document Book. What if the borrower's financial situation has deteriorated but the borrower has not yet made a monetary default? Can the lender still declare a default? Why might a lender want the right to declare a default when the borrower's financial situation has deteriorated, causing the lender to feel "insecure" about repayment of the loan even though the borrower has not yet made a monetary default? Is it fair to the borrower for the lender to make it an event of default if the financial condition of the borrower causes the lender to feel insecure about repayment of the loan and the adequacy of the collateral? If the loan documents provide that the lender has the option to accelerate the debt after any payments are late, and that acceptance of late payments does not terminate the lender's right to accelerate the debt, do you think a court would uphold and enforce this provision? *See LRB Holding Corp. v. Bank of America, N.A.*, 944 So. 2d 1113 (Fla. Ct. App. 3d Dist. 2006).

[2] Appointment of a Receiver/Mortgagee in Possession

After an event of default, a lender often will seek the court appointment of a receiver to manage the mortgaged property in order to prevent the borrower from "milking the project" (*i.e.*, misappropriating money from the project, including siphoning any income from the property into a "war chest" to pay for a legal defense to the lender's foreclosure action). Lenders are reluctant to act as mortgagees in possession due to concerns with potential liability for the actions they take while operating a property (including performing any obligations as the landlord under leases of the mortgaged property). *See United States Fidelity and Guaranty Company v. Old Orchard Plaza Limited Partnership, L.P.*, 284 Ill. App. 3d. 765, 672 N.E.2d 876 (1st Dist. 1996) (holding that the mortgagee's actions in successfully moving for appointment of a receiver were not sufficient to make it a "mortgagee in possession" bound to perform the covenants of the lease, including a covenant to pay a two million dollar termination fee). A second problem with acting as a mortgagee in possession is that in such role the lender will incur expenses in operating the property for which it might not recover full reimbursement. *See, e.g., New York and Suburban Federal Savings and Loan Association v. Sanderman*, 162 N.J. Super. 216, 392 A.2d 635 (Sup. Ct. N.J. 1978). In *Sanderman*, the court held that the lender who was acting as a mortgagee in possession was not entitled to reimbursement for the cost of maintaining a guard on the mortgaged property (a nursing home) 24 hours a day for one year. The court ruled that this action was not that of a provident owner because the mortgagee did not explore whether the vacant nursing home could again be operated as a nursing home, or could otherwise generate income, or if there were other means to appropriately preserve the property.

Each state will have its own statutory requirements which must be met for the court to appoint a receiver. For example, under Illinois law, to be entitled to an appointment of a receiver during the pendency of a foreclosure action, a mortgagee must show two elements: first, that appointment of a receiver was authorized by the terms of the mortgage; and second, that the mortgagee has "good cause" for the appointment. One example of good cause would be if the mortgagor has failed to pay monthly installments of interest, late charges, and real estate tax escrow payments due under the terms of the mortgage. *See Home Life Ins. Co. v. American National Bank and Trust Co*, 777 F. Supp. 629 (N.D. Ill. 1991). If the borrower is maintaining the property and paying real estate taxes but not paying interest/principal on the mortgage lender's debt, would this be "good cause" for court appointment of a receiver? If the borrower is failing to properly maintain the property or is failing to pay real estate taxes, but currently the value of the mortgaged property exceeds the amount of debts secured by the mortgaged property, should a court appoint a receiver to operate the property? What other facts might a court consider to be "good cause" for the appointment of a receiver? What are some reasons why a court should not easily grant a mortgage lender's motion to appoint a receiver?

[3] Foreclosure and Deficiency Actions

Two critical remedies available to a mortgage lender are to foreclose on the real estate mortgage and to sue the borrower for the deficiency (a shortfall between the debt due the lender and the successful bid amount at the foreclosure sale), if any. The following article summarizes the typical foreclosure laws and procedures in the United States, including the special features under Illinois law.

[a] Overview of the Foreclosure Process

Debra Pogrund Stark,
Facing the Facts: An Empirical Study of the Fairness and Efficiency of Foreclosures and a Proposal for Reform*[*]
30 UNIVERSITY OF MICHIGAN JOURNAL OF LAW REFORM 639 (1997)[**]

. . . .

I. Real Estate Foreclosure Law and Procedures

A. Summary of Typical Foreclosure Procedures in the United States

A real estate mortgage is a pledge of the mortgagor's interest in the real estate described in the mortgage document. The pledge secures a specified debt. When a mortgagor defaults in the payment of the debt or the performance of any other obligations which the mortgagor has agreed to perform, an acceleration clause usually causes the entire indebtedness to become immediately due and payable. Theoretically, a lender and borrower could agree that upon default and acceleration, the lender would become the fee title holder of the property pledged. English courts of equity, however, developed the concept of an equitable right of redemption to ameliorate the possible harsh consequences of default and acceleration clauses. Under the equitable right of redemption, a borrower has a certain amount of time to pay off the debt and redeem the property, notwithstanding any agreement to the contrary between the borrower and the lender. The lender can cut off this equitable right of redemption through the foreclosure process governed by state statute in each state.

While each state has its own peculiar foreclosure laws and procedures, certain basic features are present in each statutory scheme. Two dominant forms of foreclosure laws exist in America: a judicial foreclosure sale and a non-judicial foreclosure sale (known as a power of sale). In a judicial sale, the lender must bring a court action to foreclose the borrower's equitable right to redeem the mortgaged property. In a power of sale, the lender (or trustee under a deed of trust) may foreclose the borrower's equitable right to redeem the mortgaged property without bringing a court action.

The following constitutes the typical process followed in a jurisdiction requiring a judicial foreclosure sale:

(i) the mortgagee, or lender, files a foreclosure complaint and serves the mortgagor, or borrower, and any other parties required by statute;[33]

---

[*] Editor's Note: Numerous footnotes have been omitted from this excerpt.

[33] Some jurisdictions statutorily require a written notice of default and acceleration of the loan before filing. For examples of such jurisdictions. See *State-By-State Digest*, [FORECLOSURE LAW & RELATED REMEDIES: A STATE-BY-STATE DIGEST (Sidney A. Keyles ed., 1995) included in the original article at] note 14, at 63 (Colorado), 128 (Georgia), and 167 (Indiana).

(ii) the lender files a lis pendens against the property;[34]

(iii) there is a court hearing and court judgment of foreclosure;[35]

(iv) the lender sends notice of the sale to the borrower and any other parties required by the statute, and advertises the public sale for a certain period of time prior to the sale and in the manner specified in the statute;

(v) the foreclosure sale of the mortgaged property occurs (conducted by the sheriff or other authorized party) in accordance with statutory requirements;

(vi) the successful bidder receives a certificate of sale;

(vii) the court issues an order confirming the sale and after any applicable statutory redemption rights expire, a deed of sale is issued to the successful bidder;

(viii) the borrower relinquishes possession of the property a certain period of time after the court order confirming the sale (in jurisdictions which grant a statutory redemption period after the foreclosure sale, the borrower may sometimes remain in possession after the sale until the expiration of the statutory redemption period); and

(ix) if the amount bid is less than the final judgment, the lender sometimes seeks a deficiency judgment against the borrower following confirmation of the judicial sale (if the jurisdiction's laws do not prohibit or limit a suit for a deficiency through one-action rules, fair value limitations or other anti-deficiency laws).[36]

As previously mentioned, a borrower enjoys an equitable right to redeem the property prior to a foreclosure sale of the property, until such period is extinguished by the foreclosure process. State statutes also provide for a specified period which [either] must expire before the foreclosure sale can occur [or a specified period after the sale during which the borrower can redeem the property by paying the amount bid at the sale] (this period is referred to as the statutory right of redemption). While some statutes permit a waiver of the statutory right of redemption in certain circumstances, a borrower cannot waive the equitable right of redemption when the loan is first made. Many state statutes also provide a time for the borrower to exercise the right of reinstatement between the filing and the foreclosure sale.

---

[34] A lis pendens is a notice of the pending foreclosure litigation that is filed or recorded in the official property records kept by the county where the property is located. See BLACK'S LAW DICTIONARY 932 (6th ed. 1990).

[35] For income-producing properties, lenders commonly seek the appointment of a receiver to handle the revenue and expenses from the property during the pendency of the case.

[36] A one-action rule requires the lender to elect either to foreclose on the mortgage or to sue the guarantor or maker of the note, satisfying any judgment on the note with their assets. A fair value limitation requires the calculation of the deficiency amount by comparing the fair value of the mortgaged property against the final judgment amount instead of comparing the amount bid at the foreclosure sale against the final judgment amount. Another anti-deficiency law is an absolute prohibition from suing borrowers for the difference between the amount bid at a foreclosure sale and the final judgment amount. This prohibition can apply to either an acquisition seller-financed with a purchase money mortgage or a power of sale.

The following is the typical process followed in a jurisdiction permitting a non-judicial foreclosure sale:

(i) the lender or trustee records a notice of default and sends notice of the default and acceleration of the debt to the borrower and any other party required under the applicable statute;

(ii) if the borrower or other party fails to cure the default within the specified statutory period after the notice of default, the lender or trustee sends out a notice of sale within the specified period of time before the date of the sale and advertises the sale;

(iii) the foreclosure sale occurs unless the borrower redeems or reinstates the loan.[42]

Sometimes a borrower is not entitled to any post-sale redemption rights in a non-judicial sale and sometimes the lender is not entitled to seek a deficiency action against the mortgagor in a non-judicial sale.

From the lender's perspective, the non-judicial sale is preferable to the judicial sale because the non-judicial sale is quicker and less expensive.[45] The lender's ability to recover the collateral more quickly saves the lender the costs associated with the time value of money and also may reduce the costs of restoring the property because deterioration occurs for only a short time. From the lender's perspective, the only negative aspects of a non-judicial sale are the usual inability to obtain a deficiency judgment and the greater uncertainty — due to the court's lack of involvement-that the foreclosure action is valid.

From the borrower's perspective, the judicial sale is preferable. First, since it generally takes longer to perform a judicial sale than a power of sale, the borrower has more time to reinstate or redeem the property. Second, the borrower can further delay the foreclosure or have the action dismissed by raising defenses.

In only three jurisdictions (Connecticut, Illinois, and Vermont) can a lender, under certain limited circumstances, recover on the mortgaged property through what is known as a "strict foreclosure." In a strict foreclosure, the lender brings a court action to foreclose on the property and gains full title by decree of the court rather than through bidding at a foreclosure. This is unlike a power of sale, which involves a foreclosure sale without court involvement, or a judicial foreclosure, in which the court is involved both before and after the foreclosure sale. No public or private foreclosure sale of the property occurs in strict foreclosure. In all three of the strict foreclosure jurisdictions, the borrower has a period of time to redeem the property after the court's judgment and decree naming the lender as the owner of the property.

---

[42] Most non-judicial sales are conducted by a trustee under a power of sale. The statutes authorizing this manner of sale do not specify as many details regulating the sale as the statutes requiring a judicial sale. The trustee has more discretion but also has a fiduciary duty to hold the sale in a manner which will yield the highest price possible. See Debra P. Stark, *The Emperor Still Has Clothes: Fraudulent Conveyance Challenges After the* BFP *Decision*, 47 S.C. L. Rev. 563, 594–95 (1996).

[45] Although it is difficult to generalize the timing in different jurisdictions, a power of sale can typically be accomplished in as little as two to four months compared with a typical minimum of 6–12 months for finalizing a judicial sale. See generally *State-By-State Digest, supra* (assessing typical time frames and costs in both judicial and non-judicial foreclosures in each state).

Connecticut and Vermont permit strict foreclosures if it appears that the property is worth less than the debt claimed. In both states, the lender can sue the borrower for a deficiency even after using a strict foreclosure. The deficiency judgment is based on the difference between the amount of debt and the appraised value of the property.

In Illinois, a lender can seek a strict foreclosure if he can show that the borrower is insolvent and the amount of the debt is greater than the value of the mortgaged property. But unlike Connecticut and Vermont, the lender has no right to a deficiency judgment after a strict foreclosure. The process of strict foreclosure in Illinois is rarely utilized, perhaps because of the insolvency requirement and because the Illinois statute offers no guidelines on how to accomplish a strict foreclosure.

B. Basic Features of Illinois Foreclosure Law

Illinois law requires a judicial sale and does not permit a power of sale. In residential mortgages, the Illinois statute provides for a redemption period for the greater of either seven months from the date the court acquires jurisdiction over all mortgagors or three months after the judgment of foreclosure. In non-residential mortgages, the redemption period runs for the greater of either six months from the date the court acquires jurisdiction over all mortgagors or three months after the judgment of foreclosure. A mortgagor in a commercial mortgage may waive the statutory right of redemption at the time the mortgage is made, but a mortgagor under a residential mortgage may not. A residential mortgagor may waive the right to redemption or reinstatement after a foreclosure action is commenced, but only if the lender waives the right to a deficiency judgment. A "residential mortgage" includes mortgages on residential property containing six or fewer dwelling units, at least one unit of which is occupied by the mortgagor or the spouse of the mortgagor as his or her principal place of residence. A "residential mortgage" does not include a single tract of agricultural real estate larger than 40 acres. The mortgagor may exercise the right of redemption, but other interested persons or entities (such as a junior lienholder) ordinarily may not.[67]

The mortgagor also enjoys a right of reinstatement, which is the right to cure the default and reinstate the loan by paying only the amount in default plus costs, rather than paying the entire accelerated loan amount. The right of reinstatement arises upon the filing of the foreclosure action and must be exercised before the earlier of either the entry of the judgment of foreclosure or 90 days after the mortgagor is served.

If the mortgagor fails to redeem or reinstate the loan, a judicial sale occurs following advertising and notice of the sale. It is customary to require the bidding party to deposit 10% of the bid price when making the bid and to require the payment of the balance of the bid within 48 hours. If the amount of the successful bid at the sale is less than the final judgment amount, the lender can sue for a

---

[67] See [735 Ill. Comp. Stat.] 5/15-1402(b), -1603. Under § 1603, only the "owner of redemption," defined in the statute as the mortgagor or other owner, See *Id.* 5/15-1212, may exercise the right of redemption, unless the foreclosure is a consent foreclosure. See *Id.* 5/15-1603. If the foreclosure is a consent foreclosure, a party other than the mortgagor who has an interest in the real estate and who objects to the consent foreclosure may exercise the right of redemption under § 1402 of the statute. See *Id.* 5/15-1402(b).

deficiency; the statute does not prohibit pursuing a deficiency and does not contain a one-action rule or a fair value limitation.

A court must confirm the sale before the lender may sue for a deficiency. The court is required to confirm a sale unless proper notices were not given, the terms of the sale were unconscionable, the sale was conducted fraudulently, or justice was not otherwise served. In addition to these statutory grounds for invalidating a foreclosure sale, the case law implies that a court may set aside a foreclosure sale if there was both a grossly inadequate bid and a noncompliance with the foreclosure process. A residential real estate mortgagor has a 30-day redemption period after the foreclosure sale if the lender elects to sue her for a deficiency. The mortgagor also may be entitled to possession of the home until 30 days after the confirmation of the sale.[77] The mortgagee of residential real estate can seek possession prior to this date if she can satisfy certain requirements.

Due to redemption periods and court calendar delays, Illinois' foreclosure process usually takes nine months to complete even when the mortgagor does not raise any defenses. If there are no court delays, no defenses are raised, and redemption periods are waived, 90 days is the earliest the process can be completed because of the time allowed to answer the complaint (30 days from the service of summons) and the publication requirements prior to the sale.[80]

[b] Comments and Questions Regarding Foreclosure Laws

1. As the article indicates, in each state, the foreclosure process is governed by state statute as well as the common law, and the two can easily be confused. For example, what is the difference between the equitable right of redemption and a statutory right of redemption? What is the difference between a statutory right of redemption and a statutory right of reinstatement? What is the difference between a judicial foreclosure and a power of sale? What is a strict foreclosure?

2. What is the basic foreclosure process in Illinois? What are the special features available under Illinois law? Illinois is among the many states that only permit a judicial foreclosure process, even for non-residential mortgage loans, as contrasted with a non-judicial process, also known as a "power of sale" process. About half of the states permit a "power of sale" process, which is typically a shorter and less expensive process. However, some state statutes permit a waiver of the statutory redemption period (in Illinois the waiver is permitted for commercial mortgage loans, but apparently not for a typical home loan), which can reduce the time period it takes to complete the foreclosure process.

3. In addition to foreclosing on its mortgage and forcing a sale of the property, in most states, the lender also may sue the borrower for the

[77] See *Id.* 5/15-1701. The mortgagee must object during the foreclosure and show good cause to be entitled to possession. See *Id.* 5/15-1701(b). The mortgagee must be entitled to possession according to the loan documents, and the court must be "satisfied that there is a reasonable probability that the mortgagee will prevail on a final hearing of the cause." *Id.*

[80] See *State-By-State Digest*, *supra*, at 155; see also 735 Ill. Comp. Stat. 5/15-1507(c) (1994) (requiring publication of notice in at least three publications, once a week for three consecutive weeks "not less than 7 days prior to the sale").

difference between the amount due to the lender and the amount bid at the foreclosure sale, unless the loan was made as a non-recourse loan. How might the fact that a loan is recourse or non-recourse impact on the borrower's willingness to agree to a deed-in-lieu of foreclosure or other consensual transfer of the property to the lender? The period of the statutory right of redemption in the 50 states varies from as little as no period (with only a few states providing for a period of one month or less) to as long as one year after the foreclosure sale. *See* Stark, *Foreclosing on the American Dream: An Evaluation of Federal Foreclosure Laws*, 51 OKLA. L. REV. 229 (1998). Taking into account any other time delays to the process, the median time period it took to complete a judicial foreclosure was eight months, and two months to complete a power of sale. *Id.* at 257.

4. How do you think a long or short foreclosure process, the availability or limitations on deficiency actions and the existence of one-action rules will impact the lender's decision whether to seek a foreclosure or try to "work out" the loan? The phrase "work out" of a loan usually means modifying the terms of the loan so it can be converted from a non-performing loan into a performing loan. For example, if a loan is accruing interest at 10% per annum, and one of the key tenants has recently abandoned the premises, the borrower may not be able to currently pay the full amount of monthly debt payments to the mortgage lender. Perhaps the borrower is negotiating with a replacement tenant but the new lease will not commence for six months. The mortgage lender might be willing to modify the loan terms so that the loan accrues interest at a lower rate (one the borrower can pay) for six months and then increases to the 10% per annum (with some mechanism for a catch up on the lost interest).

5. Some states grant to borrowers the right to reinstate the loan. Why is the right of reinstatement a more practical right to exercise than the right of redemption? Note that prohibitions on seeking a deficiency action arise in some of the jurisdictions that allow the quicker power of sale process. Why might a jurisdiction prohibit a deficiency action when the lender exercises a power of sale but permit a deficiency action when the lender exercises a judicial sale?

6. One defense that borrowers are more likely to raise today, due to the securitization of real estate loans, is that the current holder of the loan is not entitled to foreclose because it does not have possession of the note and therefore cannot establish a case for foreclosure. Due to the frequent transfers of the notes in a loan pool, and the use of servicers, it is much more likely that the foreclosing lender will have difficulty tracking down the actual physical note that the borrower signed at closing. Although, eventually, the lender is likely to find the original note, the borrower can use this time period as a means to delay the loss of possession of the real estate. In addition, a borrower can also raise the defense that the alleged current holder of the note has failed to present the signed assignment of the note and mortgage documents.

[4] Recovery Under a Guaranty

Another key remedy to the lender is to recover all or a portion of the debt due by suing any guarantors of the debt. Whether the lender pursues this remedy as opposed to the other remedies previously discussed and in what order will depend on a number of variables. These variables include the value of the mortgaged property and the time period it takes to complete the foreclosure process in the jurisdiction where the mortgaged property is located. The lender will also need to know the value of the unencumbered assets of any guarantors, the amount of any letter of credit, and the existence of any anti-deficiency, election of remedies or one-action laws.

[a] Guaranties May Not Be What They Appear to Be

Although guaranties are typically drafted to be absolute and unconditional obligations to pay the guarantied debt, the article which follows identifies and discusses the numerous potential defenses which a guarantor can raise when a lender attempts to enforce the guaranty.

H. Franklin Bloomer, Jr.,
Lenders Beware: Relying on Guaranties,
PROBATE & PROPERTY, July/August, 1990 at 16*

If a borrower's credit is not strong enough, or the value of its available collateral is insufficient, a lender may be willing to rely on the credit or collateral support of another party. Such credit support typically takes the form of a guaranty, which may be unsecured or secured. . . .

Assuming the adequacy of the credit or collateral support from a guarantor, to what extent is the lender's reliance justified? The answer requires the lender and its counsel to consider issues that are not present where reliance is solely on the borrower and its assets.

Consider the following scenario. A commercial bank wishes to make a loan to its customer, a corporation with bright prospects but few assets, provided that the bank receives the guaranty of a second corporation that owns a valuable parcel of unencumbered real estate. The second corporation delivers the guaranty and the bank advances the loan, but, sadly, the borrower's bright prospects subsequently fade. The borrower ultimately seeks protection of the bankruptcy court, and the lender is left to realize what it can under the guaranty.

Was there consideration for the guaranty? Was giving the guaranty permitted by the guarantor's charter and the corporation law under which it is formed? If not, is ultra vires a defense (i.e., does the corporation lack the power or capacity to take certain action)? Assuming the guarantor is permitted to give a guaranty, was it properly authorized? Is the guaranty vulnerable to attack on fraudulent conveyance grounds? If the guarantor were to file in bankruptcy, what rights would a trustee-in-bankruptcy have to upset the guaranty? Would any rights of the borrower's bankruptcy trustee have an impact on recovery under the guaranty? The lender's success will depend on the terms of the guaranty, as well as on

---

additional facts and a variety of issues arising under contract, corporation and creditors' rights laws.

Drafting the Guaranty

A well-drafted guaranty will deal with a number of issues that may arise in connection with its enforcement. A guaranty may state that it is "a guaranty of payment and not of collectibility." The purpose of this language is to ensure that the lender will be able to enforce the guarantor's obligations without first seeking to recover the amount due from the borrower. To overcome the defense that a guaranty is unenforceable if the obligation guarantied is unenforceable, a guaranty may contain provisions either waiving the lack of enforceability of the underlying obligation or creating an independent obligation to pay a sum equal to that owed in the underlying document. A guaranty may state that the guarantor's obligations are not released or otherwise affected by amendment or modification of the loan agreement, by any waiver or extension of any lender rights or by any lender failure by the lender to exercise its rights. These and other provisions typically found in guaranty documents are outside the scope of this article.

Defenses Under Contract Law

A guaranty is a contract. As such, it requires consideration. Under principles of contract law (as opposed to creditor's rights laws), the consideration required to support a guaranty need not benefit the guarantor and the amount of the consideration is not a significant factor — a peppercorn will suffice. In the context of a guaranty, the consideration is the lender's reliance in making the loan to the borrower.

A lender's reliance is most evident when a loan is initially made, but a lender might not obtain a guaranty until later. If there is no new consideration, the guaranty will have been given for a past consideration which, of course, is no consideration for contract law purposes. If, by contrast, the guaranty is given in exchange for an extension of the loan maturity or the lender's forbearance in not exercising remedies otherwise available to it, there is sufficient consideration.

Other contract defenses such as fraud, misrepresentation, duress, undue influence, mistake and illegality may be applied to a contract of guaranty. A guaranty is within the Statute of Frauds and therefore, in states where the common law rule applies, must be in writing.

Defenses Under Corporation Law

Where the guarantor is a corporation, it may assert as a defense that the guaranty is not an obligation of the guarantor because it has not been duly authorized or delivered. Although not unique to guaranties, this is a significant risk in the context of guaranties. The practice of reviewing a corporation's charter, bylaws, minutes and other corporate records and requiring corporate resolutions, incumbency certificates and a legal opinion at the closing enables lender's counsel to guard against this risk.

Modern corporation statutes have greatly limited the ultra vires doctrine. Under the ultra vires doctrine, unless giving a guaranty was one of the powers specifically described in a corporation's charter or the statute under which it is formed, the corporation itself might seek to avoid its obligations under a guaranty on the ground that it lacked the capacity to give a guaranty. Modern corporation statutes approach the ultra vires doctrine in two ways:

1. The corporation statutes of all states contain provisions governing the application of the doctrine. Generally, these provisions abolish the defense of ultra vires while preserving certain rights of stockholders, including a derivative one against the directors and the power of the attorney general to enjoin or dissolve the corporation. Under these provisions, the corporation may not assert the doctrine as a defense to avoid an otherwise lawful obligation.

2. Modern corporation statutes also generally give corporations the power to take various actions, including the power to guaranty the obligations of third parties. Generally, these statutes permit a corporation's powers to be limited by including restrictions in the corporation's charter. Such a restriction would give a corporation a basis on which to assert that a guaranty had not been duly authorized. Lender's counsel will wish to be satisfied that no such restriction exists.

The corporation statutes of certain states include specific provisions on the exercise of a corporation's power to give a guaranty. For example, Section 907 of New York's Business Corporation Law provides that a guaranty by a corporation not in furtherance of its corporate purposes is valid if approved by two-thirds of its shareholders. If a New York guarantor has not obtained shareholder approval, the guarantor may be able to assert that the guaranty has not been duly authorized. For guaranties given by corporations formed under statutes having provisions similar to those of New York — such as California and Rhode Island — lender's counsel will wish to ensure that the corporation has obtained the requisite shareholder approval. Because the New York provision expressly permits securing a guaranty with corporate property "if authorized by a like vote," some practitioners prefer to structure a secured guaranty as a guaranty coupled with a mortgage or security agreement rather than as an accommodation mortgage.

Procedural Constraints

A lender who is owed a duty by a guarantor and a borrower, either or both of which may be secured, enjoys the benefit of having a choice of ways to proceed if the borrower defaults. But this benefit may be limited by some state laws requiring a lender to make an election of remedies or restricting or barring deficiency judgments. The election of remedies laws of certain states do not permit simultaneous proceedings against both a debtor or guarantor and collateral securing such debtor's or guarantor's obligations. These statutes may preclude a secured lender which elects to proceed first against collateral from enforcing rights under a guaranty until after the completion of foreclosure and deficiency judgment proceedings, thus effectively transforming a guaranty from a primary to a deficiency obligation. The situation is particularly acute in California, where statutory and case laws impose a number of significant procedural restrictions.

If required to make an election of remedies, a lender must also weigh practical considerations in determining how to proceed. For example, a lender may choose to proceed against mortgaged property it has had appraised rather than on a guaranty given by a project-related guarantor of questionable liquidity whose balance sheet shows most of its net worth in real estate at market values.

Creditors' Rights Issues

Although lender's counsel needs to address contractual defenses, questions of due authorization and procedural constraints, the principal area of concern is creditors' rights laws. This article considers fraudulent conveyances, the impact of the automatic stay and issues arising under the voidable preference provisions of the Bankruptcy Code.

Before doing so, it should be noted that the title industry recently has proposed to exclude from the coverage of mortgagee title insurance policies the effects of creditors' rights laws. The proposed exclusion reads as follows: "Invalidity, unenforceability or impairment of the lien or priority of the insured mortgage, or claim thereof, by reason of the mortgage being subordinated, or constituting a fraudulent conveyance or preference, under the federal Bankruptcy Code or state insolvency or creditors' rights laws." It appears likely that the title industry will adopt this proposal. If the proposal is adopted, it will resolve the uncertainty that presently exists about the extent to which mortgagee title insurance covers the effect of creditors' rights laws. [Editor's note: The proposed exclusion was adopted; however, it is possible to obtain an endorsement to the loan policy omitting this exclusion in some states if the loan transaction does not involve a "leveraged buy-out" or new security for an antecedent debt. It is not clear whether removal of the printed exclusion means that this risk is now being insured by the title company.]

Fraudulent Conveyances

Of perhaps greatest significance is the ancient doctrine of fraudulent conveyances. Currently this is found in Section 548 of the Bankruptcy Code and in the laws of individual states. Thirty-three states have adopted either the Uniform Fraudulent Conveyance Act (UFCA) or its successor, the Uniform Fraudulent Transfer Act (UFTA). The UFTA, which was approved by the Conference of Commissioners on Uniform State Laws in 1984, follows the Bankruptcy Code in several areas where Section 548 departed from the UFCA.

Modern fraudulent conveyance statutes apply both to transfers or conveyances, such as a mortgage or grant of a security interest, and to obligations, such as a guaranty. Fraudulent conveyance laws generally do not render a transfer or obligation invalid, but permit the transfer to be set aside or avoided by a bankruptcy trustee under Section 548, or by a member of a class of creditors under the UFCA or the UFTA.

The so-called strong arm clause, codified at Section 544(a) of the Bankruptcy Code, gives a bankruptcy trustee certain rights of a creditor of the bankrupt, including the right to assert state fraudulent conveyance laws. Thus in a bankruptcy context a lender is at risk as to the less favorable of two sets of laws.

Because Section 548 applies only to transactions occurring up to one year before a petition is filed and the statutes of limitations under state fraudulent conveyance laws are typically longer, Section 544(a) permits the trustee to attack transactions time-barred under Section 548. In considering state fraudulent conveyance issues, lender's counsel should address not only the law of the jurisdiction chosen as governing in the guaranty document but also the law of the obligor's principal place of business.

Intentional or Constructive Fraud

Modern fraudulent conveyance statutes cover transfers or obligations that are either intentionally fraudulent or constructively fraudulent. In intentional fraud, the tests established by Section 548, the UFCA and the UFTA are substantially the same: that the transfer was made or the obligation was incurred "with actual intent to hinder, delay or defraud" creditors. Where such intent can be shown to exist, it is immaterial that a transfer may have been made for an adequate consideration.

Intentional fraud does not require a state of mind or motive intending to defraud but may be inferred where a transfer or obligation has the effect of hindering or delaying creditors. For example, such an inference was made in *United States v. Tabor Court Realty Corp.*, 803 F.2d 1288 (3d Cir. 1986), where a substantial mortgage was given without receipt of a "fair consideration" at a time when the transferor had inadequate cash reserves but substantial liabilities existed and were to mature shortly. The court reasoned that a party is deemed to have intended the natural consequences of its acts.

A party seeking to avoid or set aside a guaranty under Section 548, the UFCA or the UFTA on the basis of constructive fraud must satisfy a two-pronged test. First, it must be shown that the guaranty was not given for an adequate consideration. If it was not, the issue turns on the financial condition of the guarantor. Because the second prong of the test depends on difficult factual determinations, the best defense for a lender is to show the adequacy of the consideration. In the context of a guaranty, this may not always be possible.

Adequate Consideration

Unlike contract law, in fraudulent conveyance law the consideration must be adequate. The inquiry is whether the consideration is a "fair consideration" within the meaning of the UFCA or is a "reasonably equivalent value" within the meaning of Section 548 or the UFTA. The definition of "fair consideration" contained in the UFCA requires an element of good faith by the lender. This is a subjective standard and, as such, a troublesome one. There is no comparable definition of "reasonably equivalent value" in Section 548 or the UFTA and a demonstration of good faith is not required.

Again unlike contract law, in fraudulent conveyance law the consideration must benefit the party making the transfer or incurring the obligation, i.e., the guarantor. There may be no benefit and thus no consideration to the guarantor at all. This would be the case where a guaranty is given gratuitously by an unrelated party. On the other hand, where a parent corporation guaranties the obligations of its wholly-owned subsidiary incurred in connection with a loan made to the subsidiary, the parent has received a benefit, since the loan presumably benefits the parent's investment in its subsidiary.

Between the extremes of the guaranty given gratuitously by an unrelated party and the guaranty given to benefit a subsidiary, there are guaranties given by parties who are related to the principal obligor, particularly other intercorporate guaran ties. Where a subsidiary guaranties the obligations of its parent or of a sister company, there may be benefit to the guarantor but it is less apparent since it is neither direct nor immediate.

Several courts have held that an indirect benefit is sufficient for fraudulent conveyance purposes. See, e.g., *Rubin v. Manufacturers Hanover Trust Co.*, 661 F.2d 979 (2d Cir. 1981) (up-stream guaranty); *Telefest, Inc. v. VU-TV, Inc.*, 591 F. Supp. 1368 (D.N.J. 1984) (cross-stream guaranty). Indirect benefit may take different forms. For example, some portion of the loan may ultimately reach the guarantor. Or the relationship between the guarantor and the borrower may be such that business opportunities may be created for the guarantor by its use of the loan. Or the guarantor may benefit from the strengthened financial position of the group as a whole. But not all cases find an indirect consideration sufficient. Obviously, much depends on the particular fact situation. As a result, lender's counsel may not be satisfied that an indirect consideration received by the guarantor is adequate.

Financial Condition

If the consideration is inadequate, a guaranty will be subject to attack if any one of the following statements apply to the guarantor's financial condition:

- the guarantor is, or as a result of the guaranty would be rendered, insolvent;
- the guarantor retained an unreasonably small capital following the incurrence of the guaranty; or
- the guarantor intended to incur or believed that it would incur debts beyond its ability to pay as the debts matured.

The Bankruptcy Code, the UFCA and the UFTA define insolvency. The definition of the term in the UFTA is adapted from the definition in the Bankruptcy Code. As stated in Section 2(a) of the UFTA, "[a] debtor is insolvent if the sum of the debtor's debts is greater than all of the debtor's assets at a fair valuation." Under the UFTA, a failure to pay debts as they become due creates a presumption of insolvency; thus the UFTA incorporates both a balance sheet and an equitable test of insolvency. No comparable presumption is contained in either the UFCA or the Bankruptcy Code. The UFCA definition approaches insolvency from the standpoint of the inability, as measured by the "present fair salable value" of a debtor's assets, to pay the probable liability on the debtor's existing debts as they become due.

Because the elements of financial condition that must be present to sustain an attack on constructive fraud grounds are factual in nature, lender's counsel should obtain documentary evidence of the facts. See *Credit Managers Assn. v. Federal Co.*, 629 F. Supp. 175 (C.D. Cal. 1985), where the court upheld a transaction against fraudulent conveyance attack, relying heavily on the analysis of values and cash flow the lender performed at the time of the transaction. Such documentary evidence can take several forms. The borrower's financial statements should have been delivered to the lender. Representations about the financial condition of the guarantor and financial covenants designed to measure its condition should be included in the loan agreement. A certificate of the guarantor's chief financial officer on the guarantor's financial condition with pro forma financial statements and projections of financial performance attached should be delivered at the closing. As evidence of the guarantor's ability to pay its debts as they mature, the chief financial officer's certificate should also state that all accounts payable are current and not overdue. Alternatively or additionally, an opinion of an independent accounting firm, investment banker or valuation consultant on solvency, within the meaning of the relevant fraudulent conveyance law(s), might be obtained at the closing. Most important, the lender should perform its own analysis of the guarantor's projected solvency, capital maintenance and cash flow. . . .

Where a relatively secure analysis of a guarantor's solvency is possible, the guaranty can be limited to an amount that would not result in the guaranty rendering the guarantor insolvent under the financial condition tests of the fraudulent conveyance laws. However, a secure analysis of the guarantor's solvency will not always be possible. Moreover, building a record that the guarantor meets the financial condition tests is a formidable task, subject to second-guessing by a court.

An increasingly popular alternative is to limit the liability of the guarantor to an amount that would meet those tests. A typical formula intended to achieve this provides that the aggregate amount payable by the guarantor shall not exceed at any time 95% of the amount, if any, by which (1) the fair salable value of the property of the guarantor exceeds (2) the total liabilities of the guarantor (including the maximum amounts reasonably expected to come due for contingent liabilities, other than contingent liabilities of the guarantor under the relevant loan documents) from time to time. Another approach is to provide that the aggregate amount payable by the guarantor is limited to the largest amount which would not render its obligation subject to avoidance under Section 548 or to being set aside under any applicable state fraudulent conveyance law. Although a guaranty containing either such provision may withstand attack on fraudulent conveyance grounds, it unfortunately cannot be considered to guaranty a quantifiable amount or, indeed, any amount.

Effect of Automatic Stay

Where bankruptcy proceedings have been filed in respect of the borrower, the automatic stay may impact the lender's ability to enforce a guaranty against the guarantor. In *Guaranty Agreements: The Impact of Bankruptcy*, 3 PROB. & PROP. 17 (May/June 1989), Robin M. Goldman described a line of cases where action by a creditor of a debtor in bankruptcy against a guarantor of the debtor's obligations was stayed because the guarantor had a right of indemnification against the debtor. Goldman recommends, among other things, that the guarantor waive any right of indemnification against the debtor and rely on its right of subrogation to the rights of the lender. As noted below, this may not go far enough to overcome other problems that may arise in a bankruptcy context.

Voidable Preference Issues

A bankruptcy trustee has the right under Section 547 and 550(a) of the Bankruptcy Code to avoid and recover "preferences." [Editor's Note: A preference is defined as a transfer of property on account of an antecedent debt and not in the ordinary course of business. The transfer must be made while the borrower is insolvent or while the debt is causing him to become insolvent. In addition, the transfer must cause the creditor to receive more than it would have under a chapter 7 liquidation. Finally, the transfer must be made within 90 days before the bankruptcy filing or one year before the bankruptcy filing if the transfer is to an "insider."] In the context of the guarantor's bankruptcy filing, a preference issue would exist for payments made within the preference period because such payments clearly are made for an antecedent debt. The trustee would be able to recover any such payments from the lender.

A less obvious application of the preference provisions arises in the context of granting a security interest as security for a guaranty given within the preference period in consideration of the lender's forbearance. This grant would be deemed preferential and might be avoided by the guarantor's trustee. A transfer may not be avoided if it is given for "new value." Although forbearance is sufficient consideration for contract law purposes, it does not fall within the Bankruptcy Code's definition of "new value."

[Discussion of *Levit v. Ingersoll Rand Corp. (In re DePrizio Construction Co.)*, 874 F.2d 1186 (7th Cir. 1989), and the issues raised in it, is omitted since the issues posed by this case have been addressed in the 2005 amendments to the Bankruptcy Code.]

The foregoing is necessarily a brief overview of the issues lender's counsel must consider in connection with guaranties and accommodation collateral. Although this article is not intended to be comprehensive, the author hopes that it has flagged the more significant issues.

[b] Comments and Questions Regarding Guaranties

1. Bloomer raises numerous defenses that guarantors can raise when sued on their guarantees, including: (i) lack of consideration for the guaranty, (ii) if the guarantee is by an entity rather than an individual, lack of authority by the person who signed on behalf of the entity, (iii) if the guarantee is by an entity, that the action of guaranteeing the debt is ultra vires to that entity, (iv) that the giving of the guarantee is a fraudulent conveyance under applicable state law, or either a fraudulent conveyance or a preference under bankruptcy law, if the guarantor has filed or has filed against it a bankruptcy action, (v) that the claim raised is not within the scope of the guaranteed obligations, (vii) that the lender must first seek satisfaction of the claim from the borrower, and (viii) general contract defenses of fraud, misrepresentation, duress, undue influence, mistake and illegality. Which of these defenses might be available to David Delany and the other guarantors of the construction loan for the Fox Valley Auto Care Center in a suit by FMB to enforce the payment guaranty? Which defenses would not be available? Why? What additional information would you need to answer this question?

2. What steps can a lender take to reduce the likelihood that the guarantor can successfully raise some of these defenses? On the issue of fraud, and waiving a claim based on fraud, some case law states that as a policy matter a person cannot waive her right to claim fraud. But some cases make a distinction between a general waiver of any claim of fraud versus a more specific waiver. So, if the agreement (here a guarantee) contains a disclaimer that the other party made a specific representation (for example

a representation that the guarantors could not be shareholders in the entity that owns the mortgage property unless they guaranteed the debt), especially when there is evidence that this disclaimer was specifically negotiated, then some courts enforce the disclaimer and agreement not to raise the representation as having been made. *See Shelby Electric Company, Inc. v. Forbes*, 205 S.W.3d 448, 453–454, 456 (Tenn. 2005). Does this distinction between a general waiver of any claim of fraud versus a disclaimer of a specific representation having been made make sense to you? In light of this distinction in treatment, what drafting implications does it raise when drafting a guarantee on behalf of the mortgage lender?

3. The Bloomer article discusses various possible defenses to enforcement of a guaranty, including defenses tied to bankruptcy law (challenges of the granting of the guaranty by the guarantor as a fraudulent conveyance or a preference). What other "transfers" by a guarantor or by a borrower can be set aside by a bankruptcy trustee as a fraudulent conveyance or a preference? What are the elements set forth in the Bankruptcy Code for a fraudulent conveyance or a preference?

4. We deleted the portion of the Bloomer article that discussed *Levit v. Ingersoll Rand Corp.* (*In re DePrizio Construction Co.*), 874 F.2d 1186 (7th Cir. 1989), and the reaction of lenders to the case because Congress amended Section 547(b) of the Bankruptcy Code to overturn the "*DePrizio* rule." Under the *DePrizio* rule courts had extended the preference rule from 90 days to a full year for transfers to non-insider creditors when the transfers in question nevertheless benefitted an insider (a principal of or entity related to or affiliated with the debtor). The concern raised in *DePrizio* was that it could be argued that when the borrower made a transfer to the mortgage lender, an insider guarantor benefitted from the transfer since the amount of the guaranteed debt decreased and that a bankruptcy trustee could potentially invalidate the transfer under the longer look-back for transfers to insiders and recover the money paid to the mortgage lender. In 2005, Congress amended the Bankruptcy Code in Section 547(b) to provide that if a transfer is made between 90 days and one year before the bankruptcy filing to an entity that is not an insider (like a mortgage lender) but results in a benefit to an insider (like a guarantor of the mortgage debt), the amount transferred is only recoverable from an insider creditor and not from a creditor that is not an insider (like the mortgage lender). Mortgage lenders should be more willing to permit loan guarantees by insiders of debtors after this amendment and should no longer need to require that guarantors waive their right of subrogation against the debtor, in the event the debtor defaults under the loan, as a means to reduce the issue raised in *DePrizio*.

5. The Bloomer article also mentions certain procedural constraints, such as election of remedies restrictions and anti-deficiency laws, as possible defenses to the enforcement of the guaranty. How would an election of remedies limit the lender from recovering from the guarantor if the lender has already begun a foreclosure action against the mortgaged property? How would anti-deficiency laws serve as a defense to enforcement of a guaranty after the lender has begun a foreclosure action against the mortgaged property? Would the guarantors of the Fox Valley Auto Care

Center project be able to successfully raise these procedural constraints as a defense to suit on the payment guaranty after FMB initiated a foreclosure action? If the governing law requires a lender to elect between bringing a suit for payment of the debt against the borrower and guarantors and foreclosing on the property (where the lender can have only one of these two remedies), how should a lender decide which remedy to pursue?

§ 16.03 THE BORROWER'S BASIC DEFENSES, PROTECTIONS AND OPTIONS

[1] State Law Protections

[a] Rights of Reinstatement, Redemption, Anti-Deficiency and One-Action Laws

Portions of Chapter 10 have described rights of reinstatement and redemption, forms of anti-deficiency laws, and one-action laws. These laws are intended to prevent the borrower from losing any equity she may have in her property after she defaults in the performance of her loan obligations or to prevent a "double" loss in bad economic times. The double loss means the loss of the property pledged and the loss of other property she holds. These protections to defaulting borrowers, however, also increase the amount of time it takes lenders to recover on bad debt, increase the costs for such recovery, and increase the lenders' losses. *See* Stark, *Facing the Facts: An Empirical Study of the Fairness and Efficiency of Foreclosures*, 30 U. MICH. J.L. REFORM 639 (1997). These costs and losses are then passed on to all borrowers in the form of higher interest rates or loan fees. Each state has enacted laws that attempt to balance the interest of assisting and protecting defaulting borrowers with the interest of keeping the lenders' costs and losses from bad debts at a minimum to encourage low-cost mortgage lending. No two states' laws are identical. Previous materials described these approaches generally. For a more specific summary of the different approaches among the 50 states, see *Foreclosure and Related Remedies: A Fifty State Digest*, published by the American Bar Association in 1994. [Ed. note: The second edition was forthcoming as this book went to press.] It is very important to know the nuances of each state's laws or the lender may lose the right to recover from all of the collateral pledged or from all of the individuals and entities who would otherwise have liability for the mortgage debt. For example, according to the first edition of the *Fifty State Digest*, if an action is brought under Kansas law to enforce a promissory note without seeking to foreclose on the mortgage securing the note at the same time, it may result in a waiver of the lender's right to enforce the mortgage. Further under Kansas law, if a lender forecloses under the mortgage but does not include an action on the note, all the guarantors are discharged, but so long as the lender does not extinguish the obligation at issue by a foreclosure action, he may separately sue the guarantors. In California, if the lender elects to perform a power of sale rather than a judicial foreclosure, the mortgage lender will not be able to sue the borrower on a deficiency action. Under Montana law, a lender must bring one combined procedural and substantive plenary judicial foreclosure in order to obtain a deficiency judgment. In addition to these "one action" type laws, according to the *Fifty State Digest*, 15 states' statutes provide for limitations on the mortgage lender's ability to seek a deficiency action.

[b] Attacking the Foreclosure Sale as Unconscionable or as a Fraudulent Conveyance

If the amount bid at a foreclosure sale is too low, or if the lender or trustee failed to comply with any of the statutory requirements in the foreclosure action and sale, it is possible for the borrower to successfully petition a court to set aside the foreclosure sale under state law. The possibility of setting aside the foreclosure sale was particularly strong after a bankruptcy case that became famous (some would say "infamous"), *Durrett v. Washington National Insurance Co.*, 621 F.2d 201 (5th Cir. 1980). In *Durrett*, the Fifth Circuit held that a sale could be set aside as a fraudulent conveyance under bankruptcy law if the amount bid at the foreclosure sale was less than 70% of the appraised fair market value of the property. The U.S. Supreme Court in *BFP v. Resolution Trust Corporation*, 114 S. Ct. 1757 (1994), overturned *Durrett* and set a new, more difficult standard to set aside a sale.

[i] Overview

The article that follows explains the *BFP* decision and the grounds courts utilize in determining whether to set aside a foreclosure sale as a "fraudulent conveyance" under bankruptcy law. The article also provides details on the difficult grounds that must be met for a borrower to successfully challenge a foreclosure sale under most state's laws based upon the amount bid, defects in complying with the statutory procedures for the foreclosure action, or defects in the manner in which the foreclosure sale is conducted.

Debra Pogrund Stark,
What* BFP *Really Means for Fraudulent Conveyance Challenges,
THE PRACTICAL LAWYER 55 (1996)*

Durrett may be dead, but fraudulent conveyance challenges aren't.

Can a party now bid a peppercorn for a valuable piece of property? Many people are already familiar with the United States Supreme Court's decision *BFP v. Resolution Trust Corporation*, 114 S. Ct. 1757 (1994), which held that the amount bid at a regularly conducted and non-collusive foreclosure sale will be deemed to constitute the "reasonably equivalent value" necessary to survive attack as a fraudulent conveyance under section 548 of the Bankruptcy Code ("Code") (all section references are to the Code unless otherwise noted). Indeed, the *BFP* decision has caused a great stir in the legal and lending communities and has been both praised and criticized for the perceived impact the decision will have.

Yet many of the decisions' proponents and detractors share the misperception that the case negates any genuine possibility for a borrower or a junior lender to challenge a foreclosure sale as a fraudulent conveyance except in the most egregious cases of fraud or unconscionability. This is not the case.

Based upon a careful review of the *BFP* decision, a review of case law on what types of bidding arrangements or agreements might be deemed collusive and a review of successful challenges to foreclosure sales under state foreclosure laws, some interesting conclusions emerge. This article will summarize the salient practice points gleaned from this review. . . .

CONVENTIONAL WISDOM — AND WHY IT'S WRONG

A conventional interpretation of the *BFP* decision is that:

- A party can now bid a peppercorn for a valuable piece of property (the dissent's interpretation of the majority's holding in *BFP*); and
- A foreclosure sale is only avoidable if there is a showing of fraud or unconscionability.

What *BFP* Really Means

This interpretation of the case is inaccurate. Although the majority decision in *BFP* rejected the application by bankruptcy courts of a federal standard of what constitutes reasonably equivalent value (thus the demise of *Durrett* and other similar approaches to what constitutes reasonably equivalent value), the court shifted the focus of inquiry to whether the sale complied with the applicable state's foreclosure laws.

BASES FOR STATE LAW ATTACKS

In general, under state law, foreclosure sales are subject to attack on three grounds:

- Unconscionability (such as a bid of only 10–20% of value);
- Fraud or collusion which chills bidding (leads to a bid of less than fair value for the property); or
- Grossly inadequate bid amount (which in some cases means a bid of less than 60% of value) and there is some defect in the foreclosure process (such as fraud, collusion, accident, mistake, noncompliance with a foreclosure law requirement or some other "unfairness") which contributed to the grossly inadequate amount bid at the sale.

Grossly Inadequate Bids

It is this third ground which both critics and proponents of the *BFP* decision appear to overlook. Providing an example of how this third ground to challenge a foreclosure sale has been raised will underscore how the *BFP* case has been misconstrued.

An Example

In one case, a trustee under a deed of trust filed a notice of the trustee's sale which incorrectly stated that the property being foreclosed included a 40-acre parcel (the property was actually a four-acre parcel). A third party successfully purchased the property at the sale. The trustor argued that the sale should be set aside because of the misdescription in the notice of sale. The court agreed and set aside the sale, reasoning that the misdescription of the size of the tract would have deterred bidders interested in the smaller parcel from attending the sale (the third party bid $14,975 for property which the person sold three weeks later for $130,000). *Rosner v. Worcester*, 811 F.2d 1224, 1230 (9th Cir. 1987).

Amount of Bid Affects Legitimacy of Process

Although the amount bid in *Rosner* was approximately 11 per cent of the apparent value of the property (which might be deemed not only grossly inadequate but also unconscionable) it is important to note that many courts emphasize that the two factors of the amount bid and a defect in the foreclosure process are interrelated and interdependent. To the extent one exists, it will affect the degree to which the other factor must exist for a court to set aside a sale.

Is Collusion Confined to the Most Egregious Cases of Fraud?

Most courts have rejected claims of collusion in the absence of evidence of an agreement or arrangement made with the purpose of chilling the bidding. However, the dicta in one case alleging collusion suggested the court's willingness to find certain presale arrangements to be collusive based upon whether:

- There was an overlapping of ownership interests between the parties alleged to be collusively chilling bidding;
- The sale between such parties is carried out in the usual and customary manner; and
- The party who purchased the property from the foreclosing lender after the sale regularly engaged in the purchase of real estate.

See *Stockman v. Money, Inc.*, 277 So.2d 504, 508 (La.Ct.App. 1973). Although the court in *Stockman* did not use the phrase "badges of fraud," the factors they mentioned appear to be evidence or badges of fraud rather than smoking-gun evidence of intent to chill bidding.

Are All Defects in Foreclosure Procedure Subject to Attack under Section 548?

Interestingly, some people who have read the *BFP* case have speculated that the decision empowers bankruptcy trustees to invalidate foreclosure sales in the event of any failure to comply with the state's foreclosure laws (even merely technical, nonprejudicial violations). This interpretation of *BFP* is also incorrect.

Reading the Decision

This latter misperception is based upon a portion of the decision in which Justice Scalia states that "so long as all the requirements of the State's foreclosure law" have been complied with, "the amount bid will be deemed reasonably equivalent value." Some authors who have commented on the case have speculated that this seems to suggest that any technical violation of the state's foreclosure procedures can lead to a section 548 challenge. Two points can be raised to counter this speculation.

Irregularity Must Be Sufficient for Invalidation Under State Law

First, in a later portion of the decision Justice Scalia clarifies that "Any irregularity in the conduct of the sale *that would permit judicial invalidation of the sale under applicable state law* deprives the sale price of its conclusive force under Section 548." (emphasis added). Since under the various state foreclosure laws a technical, nonprejudicial defect in complying with the foreclosure procedures will not permit judicial invalidation of the sale, it cannot serve as the basis to challenge the foreclosure sale as a fraudulent conveyance.

Section 548 Does Not Preempt State Foreclosure Laws

Second, much of Justice Scalia's interpretation of section 548 rested on the concept of not preempting state foreclosure laws in the absence of a clearly expressed Congressional intent to do so. Consequently, if a defect does not support invalidation of the sale under the state's foreclosure laws, it will not do so under section 548. Indeed, certain bankruptcy courts have already applied the Supreme Court's ruling in *BFP* in a manner consistent with this interpretation of the case and the latter potion of Justice Scalia's decision. See, e.g., *In re Cummings*, 173 B.R. 959 (Bankr.N.D.Ga. 1994), and *In re Barr*, 170 B.R. 772, 776 (Bankr. C.D.N.Y. 1994).

Start with the State Rules

This being the case, the important focus for borrowers and lenders after the *BFP* decision is to reexamine the state's foreclosure laws and cases involving challenges to foreclosure sales to understand which challenges are likely to be raised.

PRACTICE RECOMMENDATIONS

Based upon a correct interpretation of *BFP* and an exhaustive review of the types of successful challenges which have been made to set aside foreclosure sales under state foreclosure laws, certain practice recommendations become clear, both for senior lenders as well as borrowers or junior lenders.

Recommendations for Senior Lenders

In a nutshell, senior lenders should do the following:

- Scrupulously follow state foreclosure procedure;
- Order an appraisal of the property;
- Approach pre-sale bidding arrangements very carefully;
- Verify the accuracy of statements about the property;
- Consider the advantages of a judicial sale when appropriate;
- Comply with technical requirements;
- Insist on full insurance coverage; and
- Approach the possibility of a deed in lieu of foreclosure very cautiously.

1. Comply with Foreclosure Laws

First, scrupulous compliance with the procedures of the applicable state's foreclosure laws is critical. In the absence of some defect or irregularity in the foreclosure process, a party must show a bid price which shocks the judicial conscience to convince most courts to set aside a sale. If, however, a party is able to show some defect or irregularity, then the party needs to show only that the defect or irregularity led to a grossly inadequate bid or to a chilling of the bidding to the prejudice of a party in interest to convince a court to set aside a sale.

Under *BFP*, if a foreclosure sale could be set aside under the state's foreclosure laws, the sale will lose its presumption of being for reasonably equivalent value and thus a bankruptcy court could set aside the sale as a fraudulent conveyance if the bankruptcy filing is made within one year of the foreclosure sale. By scrupulously complying with state foreclosure laws, you can dramatically reduce the likelihood of a successful fraudulent conveyance challenge to the sale under section 548.

2. Order an Appraisal of the Property

Second, order an appraisal of the property (just before the foreclosure sale) to ensure that you bid an amount which will be deemed adequate. As previously discussed, a party cannot now bid a peppercorn for a valuable piece of property. The amount bid cannot be grossly inadequate (in some cases a bid for less than 60 per cent of the value is considered grossly inadequate). Moreover, if there is fraud, deception, or collusion which has a chilling effect on bidding, perhaps the only valid defense that a successful bidder could raise is that the bidder paid fair value.

3. Approach Pre-sale Bidding Arrangements Carefully

Third, be careful in making any pre-foreclosure sale arrangements regarding bidding. At common law, any agreement not to bid was considered against public policy. Today, any arrangement designed to prevent the free and fair competition among bidders which has a chilling affect on the sale causing the property to be sold for less than market value will cause the sale to be set aside as collusive. For example, if a foreclosing lender and a third party agree before the sale that the lender will bid at the sale and the third party will purchase from the lender after the sale, a court might deem this arrangement to be collusive if the purpose of the arrangement can be shown to chill bidding (which purpose might be proven by certain badges of fraud) and if the arrangement leads to the borrower receiving less than fair value for the property and the lender receiving more than the amount due on the mortgage.

4. Verify Accuracy of Statements About the Property

Fourth, since deception or any form of unfairness can cause a court to set aside the sale, the foreclosing lender (and any of its officers, partners, or agents) must take care not to make any inaccurate statements to the borrower or any potential bidder regarding any aspects of the foreclosure sale.

5. Consider the Advantages of a Judicial Sale

Fifth, do not automatically decide to exercise a power of sale instead of a judicial foreclosure when available. In addition to antideficiency laws which may apply, also factor into the decision that in some jurisdictions challenges can be raised to powers of sale which cannot typically be raised in judicial foreclosure sales. Since a trustee under a power of sale is given more discretion in the procedures for the sale, some courts have imposed a duty on the trustee to exercise that discretion in a manner which will lead to the best bid price possible. Failure to meet this duty can lead to the power of sale being set aside. See, e.g., *Murphy v. Financial Development Corporation*, 495 A.2d 1245, 1249 (N.H. 1985).

6. Comply with Technical Requirements

Sixth, avoid errors in complying with technical requirements which are sometimes overlooked but which can lead to a court invalidating a foreclosure sale, such as:

- Failing to give adequate notice of a postponed sale (a common occurrence when the mortgagor is in bankruptcy);
- Failing to deliver notices as required not only by the foreclosure statute but any applicable civil procedure rules; or
- Making a nominal bid, expecting to be credited for the amount of senior secured debt, without waiving one's right to a deficiency before the sale.

7. Insist on Full Coverage

Seventh, when obtaining a lender's title insurance policy, and when a mortgage loan is first made and when obtaining an owner's policy if the successful bidder at the foreclosure sale, insist on receiving a policy which does not contain the so-called creditor's rights exception (a carve-out of insurance which title insurers added to their policies due to *Durrett* and similar decisions).

8. Approach the Deed-in-Lieu Option Cautiously

Eighth, in deciding whether to pursue a deed in lieu of foreclosure which might otherwise make sense under the circumstances, add the following factor to the risks which a deed in lieu poses: Although the *BFP* presumption of reasonably equivalent value applies to the sale of property under a judicial sale (the type of sale at issue in the *BFP* case) it does not appear to apply to a deed in lieu, except, perhaps, if the deed in lieu is performed according to statutory procedures.

Recommendations for Borrowers or Junior Lenders

Many of the practice points discussed above equally apply to the borrower or any other party challenging the foreclosure sale but from the opposite perspective. There are, however, some particularly important points that the borrower or any other challenger should keep in mind to increase the likelihood of a successful fraudulent conveyance challenge to a foreclosure sale in light of the *BFP* decision.

1. Raise Challenges at the Confirmation Hearing

First, bring any challenges, if possible, at the confirmation hearing rather than after the confirmation hearing. In many jurisdictions, the standard to set aside a foreclosure sale is easier to meet at the confirmation hearing than after the sale is confirmed.

2. Raise Claims as Early as Possible

Second, if you do not discover the basis for the challenge until after the confirmation of the sale, still bring your claim as soon as possible after discovery of the claim. The failure to bring the claim with due diligence may cause you to waive or otherwise lose the right to bring the claim.

3. Demonstrate the Prejudicial Effects of Irregularities

Third, try to find a defect in the manner in which the foreclosure procedures were handled and try to convince the court of how these defects prejudiced the party challenging the sale. Although inadequacy of the amount bid alone will not serve as the basis to set aside a confirmed sale (unless the amount bid is unconscionable) a prejudicial defect leading to a grossly inadequate bid will serve to set it aside.

4. Point Out Lack of Due Diligence

Fourth, if the foreclosure was done through a power of sale, be sure to raise any issues based upon the trustee's or lender's failure to exercise due diligence to obtain a fair price under the circumstances. Some jurisdictions recognize a duty by the trustee and the lender to exercise their rights under the power of sale in good faith and with due diligence.

CONCLUSION

Although *Durrett* may be dead, fraudulent conveyance challenges to foreclosure sales under section 548 will continue, and these challenges will not be confined to the most egregious cases of fraud or unconscionability. The *BFP* decision shifts the source of challenges to foreclosure sales away from a federal standard of what is fair and toward challenges that can be raised under state foreclosure law. Under most states' laws, a foreclosure sale can be set aside when a defect in the foreclosure process leads to a grossly inadequate bid at the sale (and bids as high as 60 per cent of value potentially may be construed as grossly inadequate). The result is that lenders and third-party bidders must still take care not to bid too low and should endeavor to scrupulously comply with state foreclosure procedures. . . .

[ii] Comments and Questions Regarding Challenges to Foreclosure Sales

1. How much protection do courts provide to borrowers to prevent foreclosure sales at prices that are significantly lower than the fair market value of the property? On what basis will courts invalidate foreclosure

sales? Which type of foreclosure sale is more susceptible to challenge after the sale, a judicial foreclosure or a power of sale? Why?

2. In light of the high burden a borrower must meet to have a court set aside a foreclosure sale, do you anticipate that in many instances the borrower will lose its equity in the mortgaged property and be sued for a deficiency? How might the rights of reinstatement, rights of redemption and right to bankruptcy protection affect this issue? *See* Stark, *Facing the Facts: An Empirical Study of the Fairness and Efficiency of Foreclosures*, 30 U. MICH. J.L. REFORM 639 (1997).

[2] Bankruptcy Law Protections

Federal bankruptcy laws provide the most important group of protections (although lenders would probably characterize them as weapons or leverage) available to borrowers who are in default under their mortgage loan transactions. Once a borrower files for bankruptcy law protection, all actions pending against the borrower (including a foreclosure action) are stayed until the bankruptcy court either deals with the action as part of the bankruptcy or dissolves the stay in order to allow the action to move forward in state court. The protections available to a debtor/borrower in a Chapter 11 filing are far greater than in a Chapter 7 filing. In a Chapter 7 liquidation, all of the debtor's non-exempt assets are sold by the trustee in bankruptcy to satisfy the debtor's secured and unsecured creditors. But in a Chapter 11 bankruptcy, the borrower/debtor can attempt to terminate or modify the debt it owes (including the possibility of paying only a fraction of its unsecured debt) so that the borrower/debtor will be able, after the reorganization, to afford to make payments on the revised debts. The possibility of forcing the mortgage lender to modify the mortgage loan is one of the most important benefits to a borrower filing a Chapter 11 bankruptcy when in default and facing a foreclosure action. Examples of typical loan modifications include increasing the period the borrower has to repay the debt, reducing the secured portion of the debt amount, and/or reducing the interest rate at which the debt accrues. However, to make sure that the reorganization plan is equitable and fair to all of the creditors, the plan of reorganization must be approved by at least one impaired class of creditors, must be approved by the bankruptcy court, and otherwise must comply with certain statutory requirements that are described in detail in the article below.

Another important potential benefit to a borrower/debtor to filing a bankruptcy action is that the bankruptcy trustee has the power under bankruptcy law to invalidate certain liens if those liens are not perfected under state law prior to the bankruptcy filing. In addition, to ensure fair treatment to all of the creditors of the borrower/debtor, the bankruptcy trustee also has the power to invalidate as a "preference" any transfer by the borrower/debtor to an "insider" when (i) the transfer is made within one year prior to the bankruptcy filing (or is made within ninety days for certain transfers to a non-insider), (ii) is made for an antecedent debt, (iii) that causes the transferee to recover more than they would under a Chapter 7 filing, or (iv) the debtor was insolvent at the time of the transfer. Similarly, the bankruptcy trustee has the power to invalidate as a "fraudulent conveyance" a transfer by the borrower/debtor when the transfer (i) lacks adequate consideration, (ii) is made while the debtor is insolvent or causes the debtor to become insolvent and, or (iii) takes place within one year (to an insider) or ninety days of the bankruptcy filing (if to a non-insider).

The article that follows briefly notes the purpose of bankruptcy laws and provides an excellent overview of the bankruptcy law process, including the strategies lenders and debtor/borrowers can use at each stage from automatic stay through confirmation of the plan. The article provides a detailed explanation of important issues, like the battle between the debtor/borrower and the mortgage lender over control of the income from the mortgaged property during the pendency of the bankruptcy action, implications from the classification of the creditors' claims, and "cramdown" of modified loan structures. The article also briefly discusses the possibility of a "pre-packaged bankruptcy" (where the debtor and the necessary creditors come to agreement on the reorganization plan before the debtor files the bankruptcy action) that can benefit the borrower/debtor and the mortgage lender in various ways, including potential tax benefits.

[a] An Overview of the Impact of Bankruptcy Laws on the Rights of Borrowers and Lenders

John C. Murray*

The Lender's Guide to Single Asset Real Estate Bankruptcies

INTRODUCTION

. . . .

Once lenders have filed foreclosure proceedings, they will usually seek to immediately obtain a receiver for the real property that is securing the loan. Lenders do this because, assuming the loan is non-recourse, the real property security and the property's rents are the only sources of loan repayment. Facing no alternative to the loss of the property and the risk of the recapture of all or a portion of the tax benefits obtained as a result of the original transaction, borrowers often file for Chapter 11 bankruptcy shortly after the filing of a foreclosure action or on the eve of the scheduled court hearing for the appointment of a receiver.

Although the Bankruptcy Reform Act of 1994 (Reform Act) was widely heralded by Congress and commentators as a victory for secured creditors in connection with single asset Chapter 11 real estate bankruptcy cases, the Act has actually done little to protect secured creditors from single asset filings. This lack of protection results, in part, because the definition of single asset real estate encompasses only a real estate business operation having less than $4 million in secured debt. [Editor's Note: The impact of the 2005 amendment to the Bankruptcy Code is addressed in the Questions and Comments section following this article.]

---

* Vice President-Special Counsel, First American Title Insurance Company, Chicago, Illinois; B.B.A. 1967, University of Michigan; J.D. 1969; University of Michigan. The author expresses his appreciation to Thomas S. Kiriakos, a partner with Mayer, Brown & Platt, Chicago, Illinois for his assistance with this article. [Editor's Note: The full version of this article, including endnotes, as of June 15, 2009, was available on the First American Title Insurance Company website: http://www.firstam.com/list.cfm?id=3106.]

This Article briefly examines the background and purpose of the bankruptcy statutes as well as the process of reorganization under Chapter 11. It then examines in detail the secured creditor's options, strategies, and remedies when faced with a Chapter 11 filing by a single asset real estate debtor. This Article also provides a detailed explanation of the secured creditor's right of election under section 1111(b) of the Bankruptcy Code as well as a time line for a typical Chapter 11 filing. [Editor's Note: The endnotes to this article have been deleted from this excerpt, with a few exceptions, which have been retained as footnotes.]

BACKGROUND AND OSTENSIBLE PURPOSE

. . . .

Bankruptcy encompasses a fresh start policy that enables troubled debtors to restructure their liabilities in an orderly fashion under the protection of the federal court system. One court has stated that a central purpose of the Bankruptcy Code is to provide a procedure by which certain insolvent debtors can reorder their affairs, make peace with their creditors, and enjoy "a new opportunity in life and a clear field for future effort, unhampered by the pressure and discouragement of pre-existing debt." The Bankruptcy Code allows businesses to file for liquidation under Chapter 7 or for reorganization under Chapter 11.

In the Bankruptcy Code, Chapter 7 and Chapter 11 are based on two different valuation approaches. Chapter 7 uses liquidation value and Chapter 11 uses going concern value. In a Chapter 7 proceeding, the bankruptcy strips debtors of their assets and liabilities as of the filing date. The trustee sells the assets and distributes the proceeds to creditors in accordance with their priority. In Chapter 11 proceedings, in which reorganization rather than liquidation is sought, the bankruptcy strips debtors of their liabilities but allows them to keep their assets. The assets are used in the reorganization plan to generate the liquidation value of the assets for pre-petition creditors. The plan of reorganization must include repayment of certain existing liabilities, generally consisting of statutorily defined administrative and priority claims. Post-petition creditors and the debtor receive the excess of the going concern value over the liquidation value. The Bankruptcy Code sets forth specific rules under which the debtor may use either Chapter 7 or Chapter 11.

Because in Chapter 7 bankruptcies, the property is generally abandoned to the lender or sold to pay the lender in full, this Article discusses bankruptcy under Chapter 11.

ECONOMIC BENEFITS TO DEBTOR

Use of Chapter 11 enables a debtor to recognize a variety of economic benefits with almost no downside to the debtor. A debtor may use bankruptcy as a means of obtaining capital discounts, as a means of extending the time to repay, and as a way to modify certain mortgage provisions, such as due-on-sale, default, and prepayment provisions. With the current illiquidity of capital markets, bankruptcy is a convenient way to compel a refinancing. The lender may consent to this refinancing, or, under certain circumstances, the refinancing may be crammed down on the lender when the lender disagrees with the terms.

. . . .

POWERS GRANTED UNDER CHAPTER 11

The Bankruptcy Code assists the debtor in the reorganization process by providing the debtor with many powers that do not exist under state law. For example, section 362(a) of the Bankruptcy Code, which provides for an automatic stay of litigation against the debtor and for the enforcement of liens against the property of the estate, allows the debtor time to reorganize assets and to renegotiate contracts. Under section 362(a) of the Bankruptcy Code, the following actions are stayed by a bankruptcy filing:

(1) the commencement or continuation [of any proceeding (judicial or otherwise)] to recover a claim against the debtor that arose before the commencement of the case . . . ; (2) the enforcement, against the debtor or against property of the estate, of a judgment obtained before the commencement of the case . . . ; (3) any act to obtain possession of the property of the estate . . . ; (4) any act to create, perfect, or enforce any lien against property of the estate; (5) any act to create, perfect, or enforce against property of the debtor any lien to the extent that such lien secures a claim that arose before the commencement of the case . . . ; (6) any act to collect, assess, or recover a claim against the debtor that arose before the commencement of the case . . . ; (7) the setoff of any debt owing to the debtor that arose before the commencement of the case . . . against any claim against the debtor; and (8) the commencement or continuation of a proceeding before the United States Tax Court concerning the debtor.

Section 547(b) of the Bankruptcy Code provides for the recovery of preferential transfers and fraudulent conveyances. When debtors know that their financial problems are worsening, they will often prefer one creditor over another to keep an essential service or to reduce a debt which is personally guaranteed by a partner or shareholder. Therefore, the Bankruptcy Code tries to eliminate the potential for creditors to race to improve their positions shortly before a filing. As a result, under section 547(b), the debtor or a trustee may set aside any transfer to a creditor that was made within ninety days of the filing of the bankruptcy petition on account of an antecedent debt if the debtor was insolvent at the time of the transfer and the transfer gives the creditor more than the creditor would obtain in a Chapter 7 liquidation. A transfer would include a cash payment to the creditor as well as the perfection of a security interest or the obtaining of a lien. If the transfer is made to or benefits an insider, provided that the debtor was insolvent at the time of the transfer and that the transfer gives the creditor more than the creditor would obtain in a Chapter 7 liquidation absent the transfer, the debtor may set aside any such transfer that occurred within one year prior to the bankruptcy filing, subject to the Reform Act amendments regarding DePrizio payments to non-insider creditors. Typically, only unsecured creditors receive preferential transfers because fully secured creditors would receive full payment in a Chapter 7 liquidation unless their security interests were granted during the preference period. If the transfer is set aside, the debtor and the creditor are put back in the positions that they held prior to the transfer.

The Bankruptcy Code also permits the bankruptcy court to subordinate, on equitable grounds, all or part of a lender's allowed claim or interest, to transfer any lien securing a subordinated claim to the bankruptcy estate, or to disallow the claim entirely, in the appropriate circumstances, even if no preferential transfer or fraudulent transfer has occurred. The bankruptcy court generally invokes these sanctions when the lender has engaged in overreaching or lender control, which occurs when the lender steps beyond the traditional role of a lender and participates in the debtor's business or engages in other egregious conduct that justifies the use of the court's equitable powers. In these situations, a court may decide to subordinate or to disallow a transaction that would not constitute a fraudulent transfer under section 548 or a preferential transfer under section 547.

A debtor may transfer assets before the bankruptcy filing, often to relatives or related entities, to protect these assets from the claims of creditors. Under section 548 of the Bankruptcy Code, any transfer by the debtor for inadequate consideration, made within one year (most state laws provide for a longer period) of the bankruptcy filing date, while the debtor was insolvent, or which rendered the debtor insolvent, may be set aside as a fraudulent transfer. The property would then be transferred back to the estate, subject to a lien for whatever price was paid for the asset. Inadequate consideration would not apply to sales at the market price that would generally benefit creditors and are not voidable.

The Bankruptcy Code fraudulent transfer provision applies not only to transfers made by the debtor within one year before the commencement of the bankruptcy case, but also incorporates state law fraudulent conveyance statutes. In Illinois, for example, the period for setting aside a state fraudulent transfer is four years. In single asset real estate cases, fraudulent conveyance or fraudulent transfer statutes may be of particular use when the debtor, during the fraudulent transfer period, makes distributions to partners even though the debtor is otherwise insolvent.

Under Chapter 11, the trustee may reject unexpired leases and executory contracts that are not economically favorable to the debtor. Generally, while the lease or contract will no longer be enforceable, the non-debtor contracting party retains an unsecured claim for damages against the estate.

A Chapter 11 bankruptcy permits debtors to use, in the ordinary course of business, all of their assets, including the collateral of the secured lenders, even though the secured lenders are stayed from collecting their debts or enforcing their rights and remedies. However, a lender's security interests in real estate, cash, and other assets must be adequately protected by the debtor against any decline in value during the bankruptcy case. In a multi-asset, going concern case, a Chapter 11 bankruptcy generally preserves the debtor's assets as a group, allowing the debtor to maintain jobs for the debtor's employees and enhancing the value of the debtor's assets. Chapter 11 bankruptcy allows this type of preservation because assets are generally worth more as part of a going concern.

WHO CONTROLS THE SYSTEM

. . . . [intentionally omitted]

GENERAL OVERVIEW OF THE BANKRUPTCY PROCESS

A. Filing Petitions, Early Motions, and Responses

The debtor begins the process by filing a simple petition for relief under the United States Bankruptcy Protection laws. Immediately, secured creditors of the debtor must consider their responses to the filing or to the debtor's successive motions. A variety of motions are commonly filed.

For example, a debtor can file a motion for the use of cash collateral. When a debtor must continue to operate an ongoing business, usually the debtor immediately files a motion to use cash collateral such as rents and receivables for operating expenses and reorganization costs. Indeed, cash or cash equivalents are the only type of collateral for which the debtor must receive either the secured creditor's consent or the bankruptcy court's approval before the debtor may use it. Immediately following the debtor's motion for the use of cash collateral, a lender who has a security interest in the cash collateral will customarily object on the basis that the security interest is not adequately protected.

Cash collateral is cash or cash equivalents that the debtor receives in which the lender has a security interest. Thus, the debtor is restricted from using the cash unless the lender consents to such use or the court finds that the lender's security interest in the cash is adequately protected. When a mortgagee has previously recorded a mortgage or assignment of rents, the cash should be the mortgagee's collateral in most real estate bankruptcy cases. Prior to the passage of the Reform Act, perfection of the lender's assignment of rents under applicable state law was often an issue for determination under section 552 of the Bankruptcy Code. . . . Section 218 of the Reform Act has eliminated the uncertainty resulting from case law that failed to recognize a creditor's continuing interest in rents subsequent to the commencement of a debtor's bankruptcy case. State law regarding perfection is now inapplicable if the debtor and creditor entered into a pre-petition security agreement covering rents from the debtor's property and if the agreement was properly recorded.[42]

. . . .

In response to a creditor's motion for relief from the automatic stay, the court may grant relief under section 362(d) of the Bankruptcy Code if the debtor cannot provide adequate protection, or if the creditor can successfully argue that there are other reasons for granting relief from the stay. For example, the creditor may argue that the value of the collateral is less than the amount of the debt and that the property is not necessary for a successful reorganization. In other words, the debtor cannot propose a feasible reorganization plan even with the ownership and use of such collateral. Under the Bankruptcy Code, as amended by the Reform Act, the bankruptcy judge assigned to the case must hold a preliminary hearing on a relief-from-stay motion within thirty days of the filing date of the motion for relief. The final hearing on the motion must be concluded within thirty days after the preliminary hearing has ended, unless the parties consent to extend the period or the court orders an extension based on compelling circumstances, such as a participant's bona fide illness or the occurrence of an event beyond the parties' control.

In accordance with the Reform Act, when single asset Chapter 11 real estate cases involve secured debts that do not exceed $4 million, the bankruptcy court must lift the automatic stay within ninety days of the filing date unless the debtor has filed a plan that has a reasonable possibility of being confirmed within a reasonable time or unless the debtor commences paying monthly interest to the secured creditor in an amount equal to the fair market interest rate on the secured claim. The Reform Act also provides that a creditor may maintain or continue the perfection of pre-petition security interests without violating the automatic stay. Therefore, filing a UCC Continuation Statement during bankruptcy will not violate the automatic stay.

The Chapter 11 reorganization can be administered by a court appointed trustee or by the debtor. After filing a Chapter 11 petition, debtors remain in control of their businesses unless creditors or other parties request that a bankruptcy court examine whether the management of the debtors' estates should be transferred to a trustee. Debtors who continue to administer their businesses during the reorganization are referred to as debtors in possession (DIP). A motion for the appointment of a trustee is usually made by one or more creditors and often entails allegations of gross mismanagement, waste, fraud, or incompetence, if, for example, the DIP has failed to protect and conserve the property of the estate for the benefit of its creditors. A trustee may be appointed for cause, or if such appointment is in the interest of creditors. Sufficient cause has been found to include: (1) fraud; (2) the intent to provide inaccurate financial statements; (3) the unauthorized transfer of property of the estate; (4) the debtor's breach of fiduciary duties; (5) failure to seek recovery of avoidable pre-petition transfers; (6) failure to abide by the orders of the bankruptcy court; (7) gross mismanagement of the debtor's finances and financial affairs; and (8) unreasonable delay in presenting a reorganization plan.

Sufficient cause to appoint a trustee has not been found in the following instances: (1) When the debtor's management was knowledgeable, notwithstanding some evidence of mismanagement and the debtor had a good working relationship with employees and suppliers; (2) when the bare allegations of misconduct were not supported by any factual showing; and (3) when the only purpose of the motion was to have someone investigate inter-company transactions.

Like a secured creditor, an unsecured creditor may file an involuntary petition against a debtor. If the debtor has twelve or fewer creditors, only one creditor needs to sign the petition. Otherwise, three creditors must sign the petition and allege that the debtor is generally not paying its debts when they become due. The petitioning creditor or creditors must have valid unsecured debts totalling at least $5,000.[62] The debtor must file an answer within twenty days. Then, the court will hold a hearing within ten days of the answer's due date to determine whether it should enter the order for relief.

B. Exclusive Period: Developing the Plan of Reorganization

During the first 120 days following the voluntary filing of a petition, the debtor has the exclusive right to develop and to file a reorganization plan and a disclosure statement disclosing all of the facts that are relevant to creditors and describing all assumptions that the debtor used in the plan. If the court grants an order for relief in an involuntary filing, the 120-day period commences from the date of the order. If the debtor files a plan within the 120-day period, the debtor is granted an additional sixty days to obtain confirmation of the plan. During this period debtors and creditors ordinarily stake out the value of the collateral and the type and amount of the creditors' claims. As a result of creditors' complaints concerning the tendency of bankruptcy courts to almost routinely grant debtor's extensions of the plan exclusivity period, the Reform Act allows a creditor to appeal as of right to the district court any order that increases or decreases the debtor's exclusivity period.

By the claim bar date, creditors must file a proof of claim that describes the amounts due and summarizes the collateral. The proof of claim describes the status of the loan as of the petition filing date. Often, counsel may recommend distinguishing accrued interest at the contract rate from interest that is charged at the default rate. Default interest and other reasonable charges that are provided in the loan documents, including prepayment charges, will only be allowed post-petition to the extent that the secured creditor has a claim that is oversecured at the time of that filing.

The bankruptcy process treats undersecured creditors differently from secured creditors. Under the Bankruptcy Code, an undersecured creditor, a creditor whose debt exceeds the value of the collateral, has two claims against the debtor's estate: (1) a secured claim in an amount equal to the value of the collateral, and (2) an unsecured recourse claim for the remainder of the debt. Undersecured creditors have both of these claims under the Bankruptcy Code even if the loan is non-recourse. The valuation of the collateral determines the relative size of these two claims and is often disputed by the debtor, who may take varying positions on value throughout the case. Early in the case, the debtor has a minor interest in having a high value on the collateral to stop relief from stay motions by arguing that the secured creditor is adequately protected. Later in the case, however, the debtor has a major interest in having a low value for the collateral for purposes of the Chapter 11 plan and payment of the secured claim, because the debtor will want to argue that the debt must be crammed down.

For claims-payment purposes, debtors use their own valuations of collateral to classify creditors as being secured or undersecured. Often debtors will attempt to create additional claims-voting classes by classifying trade and contingent liabilities separately from other unsecured debt, based on a number of the debt's characteristics. Creating numerous voting classes increases the likelihood that at least one voting class will support the debtor's plan of reorganization. The debtor needs at least one impaired non-insider class to vote in favor of the Chapter 11 plan to have the plan confirmed and crammed down on a dissenting class of impaired claims.

C. Reaching a Consensus for the Plan and Obtaining Confirmation

After the plan and disclosure statement are filed with the court, the judge schedules a hearing on the adequacy of the disclosure statement, usually giving creditors at least twenty-five days advance notice of the hearing. The debtor is responsible for producing a full and complete disclosure statement, and the judge will hear arguments from both sides. The judge can order that certain changes be made to the disclosure statement and approve the disclosure statement concurrently. The judge then schedules a date for a confirmation hearing, again usually providing twenty-five days notice to all creditors. Typically, the debtor will request a postponement of each of these dates. The judge often grants these extensions, even if a creditor objects.

D. Emerging from Bankruptcy

If the bankruptcy court confirms a plan, all impaired debt is modified in accordance with the confirmed plan. Modifications, if approved by the court, are deemed effective as of the plan confirmation or effective date. Some creditors may be left unimpaired either because they were paid in full or because the contractual terms of their debt will not be modified.

If the bankruptcy court does not confirm a plan, the judge may grant relief from the stay, dismiss the case, convert it to a Chapter 7 liquidation proceeding, or give the debtor the opportunity to submit a revised plan.

SECURED CREDITORS' STRATEGIES AND REMEDIES

. . . . [intentionally omitted]

UNDERSTANDING THE SECURED CREDITORS' OPTIONS

A. Asking and Answering Questions

The secured creditor must ask and answer numerous basic questions to obtain the proper position. The most important questions are whether the lender is secured, unsecured, or undersecured, and what is the margin of security or undersecurity. Another important issue is whether the lender took all of the steps necessary to perfect its interest in rents to establish that the rents and receivables are the lender's cash collateral. Furthermore, even if all proper enforcement actions have been taken and the lender or a court-appointed receiver has actually begun collecting rents pre-petition, the lender should take further steps to insure that the rents and receivables are the lender's property and not part of the bankruptcy estate. As discussed previously, cash collateral cannot be used by the debtor without a court order requiring the debtor to furnish adequate protection to the lender. The lender's task in this regard has been made easier as the result of the Reform Act, which provides that a lender's pre-petition security interest in rents also applies to post-petition rents and constitutes cash collateral without regard to applicable state law regarding perfection. . . .

B. Reviewing Loan Files

The lender should review its loan files carefully to determine whether the loan is properly documented and whether security interests in collateral were properly granted and perfected. The Reform Act's revisions to the Bankruptcy Code were intended only to render state law inapplicable to the issue of the enforcement or activation of a secured lender's interest in rents. Consequently, the unperfected security interests may still be subject to the trustee's or DIP's avoidance powers. The Uniform Commercial Code Financing Statements should be checked carefully. Creditors should make sure that these statements were filed correctly and were properly continued, insuring that they are still valid.

If the lender has an assignment of rents, the lender should determine whether applicable state law considers this assignment as automatically activated or if the law requires the lender to take additional action to activate the assignment, such as notifying tenants, filing a court action, requesting the appointment of a receiver, actually obtaining a receiver, or taking possession of the property. Prior to the passage of the Reform Act, it was often too late after the bankruptcy filing date to activate a lender's perfected interest in the rents, although some courts recognized post-petition activation under applicable state law.

The lender must determine whether there had been any preferential transfers or payments to creditors within the ninety-day preference period before the filing of the bankruptcy petition or any fraudulent transfers within the year prior to the filing. Lenders also need to look for preferential transfers or payments to insiders within the one-year (or more, depending on the state) period prior to the filing.

C. Assessing the Property's Value

The key to all strategies and tactics employed by the lender is assessing the value of the collateral. If the secured creditor is over-collateralized, the creditor is probably adequately protected and cannot seek relief from the automatic stay absent special circumstances such as the continued depreciation in the value of the property below the amount of the debt or a bad-faith filing by the debtor. Also, if the debtor's plan does not modify the loan terms in any way, the creditor will not be an impaired class and, therefore, will not have the right to vote for or against a plan. In addition, the debtor may seek to use, sell, or lease a portion of the secured collateral, arguing that the secured creditor is adequately protected by an equity cushion or the availability of other collateral.

If the creditor is undersecured (with a secured claim for the value of the property and an unsecured claim for the balance), the creditor will need valuation information and testimony to prove that the creditor is not adequately protected in order to receive monthly payments to adequately protect the secured portion of the claim. Under a 1988 United States Supreme Court ruling, *United States Ass'n v. Timbers of Inwood Forest Assocs., Ltd.*,[86] [Ed. note: hereinafter referred to as "*Timbers*"] and cases decided thereafter by other courts, undersecured creditors are not entitled to post-petition payments of interest or lost opportunity costs, although they are entitled to adequate protection against diminution in the value of their collateral.

Opinions concerning the value of collateral are always inherently sensitive. One key issue in determining the treatment of secured creditors under the Bankruptcy Code is whether the creditor is less than fully secured or slightly more than fully secured. In many districts, the fully secured creditor is not entitled to adequate protection payments, but the secured claim will accrue interest up to the value of the collateral. The Bankruptcy Code permits an oversecured lender, to the extent that the creditor's claim is oversecured, to collect interest on such claim and any reasonable fees (including attorneys' fees, costs, and charges) that are provided for in the loan documents. Thus, an oversecured lender should be entitled to include, as part of its claim, interest at the default rate on the debt as well as the amount calculated pursuant to its contractual prepayment premium. However, the bankruptcy courts in various jurisdictions have differed as to whether the lender with an oversecured claim should be entitled to a prepayment premium and whether the charge is reasonable under federal or state law. In *In re Skyler Ridge*,[88] a 1987 bankruptcy court decision, the court disallowed a prepayment

[86] 484 U.S. 365 (1988). If the secured collateral is declining in value, the creditor's interest must be protected by periodic payments, substitute liens covering the decline, or by some other means that provide the "indubitable equivalent" of the creditor's interest in the property. 11 U.S.C. § 361 (1993). If such adequate protection is not provided, a creditor whose interest in the secured property is declining is entitled to relief from the automatic stay. *Id.* § 362(d)(1).

[88] 80 B.R. 500 (Bankr. C.D. Cal. 1987). The decision in *Skyler Ridge* has been criticized as a

premium provision as an invalid liquidated damages clause under Kansas law because it was not reasonable. The prepayment premium had not been discounted to present value. However, subsequent bankruptcy court decisions have held that an oversecured lender can collect its actual damages under a prepayment provision when such a provision is enforceable under applicable state law. If the lender is less than fully secured, the lender will be denied payment of interest during the case as well as any payments for lost opportunity costs and will not be entitled to adequate protection payments unless the value of the property is depreciating. The lender should consult its attorney regularly, reporting an up-to-date view of the relationship between the value of the collateral and the amount of the debt.

LIMITING DEBTOR'S CONTROL OVER PROPERTY

If the lender has adequate proof of fraud, misconduct, gross mismanagement, dishonesty, incompetence, or other just cause that does not include mere mismanagement, the lender should consider seeking the appointment of a trustee or examiner. The lender may also consider the conversion of the case to a Chapter 7 liquidation, which automatically requires the appointment of a trustee.

In a voluntary Chapter 11 case, there is a strong presumption that the debtor should remain in possession. The creditor that is moving for the appointment of a trustee must show something more serious than the debtor's mere management indiscretion because all Chapter 11 debtors may have some degree of management problems.

. . . .

OBTAINING AN INTEREST IN CASH COLLATERAL

A. Perfection of Assignment of Rents

. . . . [intentionally omitted]

B. Value of Cash and Pre-Petition Hoarding

One of the first issues facing a debtor after the filing is how to continue in operation. Businesses that plan to continue operations during a Chapter 11 reorganization require cash because it is the key to a successful reorganization. Cash is required by creditors, employees, trade suppliers, the tax authorities, and a myriad of other parties whose cooperation is essential for a debtor to continue operations. Also, the administrative expenses of a Chapter 11 bankruptcy, such as attorneys' and accountants' fees, are extensive. The Illinois Bankruptcy Court held that "[i]t is well established that cash collateral may appropriately be used to pay administrative expenses [only] if the interest secured by the collateral is

---

result-oriented decision in which the court sought to preserve value for junior creditors when the debtor's assets would otherwise have been insufficient to do so. Debra P. Stark, *Prepayment Charges in Jeopardy: The Unhappy and Uncertain Legacy of* In re Skyler Ridge, 24 Real. Prop. Prob. & Tr. J. 191, 193 (1989); *see* Debra P. Stark, *New Developments in Enforcing Prepayment Charges After an Acceleration of a Mortgage Loan*, 26 Real. Prop. Prob. & Tr. J. 213, 234 (1991) ("[B]oth bankruptcy courts and nonbankruptcy courts have recently repudiated the flawed *Skyler Ridge* analysis, which in essence required a perfect estimate of the lender's damages rather than a reasonable one.").

adequately protected [or such expenditures are necessary to preserve or maintain the lender's collateral]."

One of the tests that the debtor must meet under Chapter 11 is to prove to the court that all obligations incurred after the Chapter 11 filing can be paid promptly and in cash. The bankruptcy courts recognize the importance of continued support from suppliers, employees, and other groups and give these groups priority unsecured status for their post-petition claims.

The cash needed by the business during reorganization can be generated internally or it can be borrowed. Only in rare circumstances does a company considering bankruptcy maintain a sufficient war chest to fund the costs of filing and have the remaining cash reserves necessary to continue in operation after the filing. For example, one significant expense for the debtor is the large, up-front retainer required by bankruptcy counsel. In most cases, the debtor who has not been able to hoard pre-petition cash will either need to borrow this cash or to arrange for the use of cash collateral.

A pre-petition debtor holding unencumbered property is in the enviable position of being able to declare a unilateral moratorium on the payment of its debt. Through the collection of receivables or the sale of property, the debtor is able to hoard cash for use during an attempted out-of-court restructuring or ensuing Chapter 11 case. Ways to limit the size of this pre-petition hoard depend on the lender's actions prior to bankruptcy filing.

In the event that a default exists, or in the event that the borrower acknowledges an imminent default, the lender should negotiate a consensual cash management agreement whereby all cash flow is sent by the tenants directly to the lender or to the lender's designated representative and whereby the borrower acknowledges the perfection and enforcement of the lender's interest in the rents. Even though the Reform Act ostensibly makes state laws regarding the perfection of an interest in post-petition rents inapplicable if a properly recorded pre-petition security interest in the rents exists, if bankruptcy is inevitable and the borrower has defaulted, it is still prudent for the lender to move aggressively to perfect or to enforce its security interest in the rents under state law.

Moving aggressively in declaring a default and commencing foreclosure to bring on the bankruptcy filing could limit pre-petition hoarding by the debtor. In many states, if no default exists, the lender is unable to enforce or "activate" its interest in rents. If the borrower files for bankruptcy in those states prior to a default, the unused pre-petition rents may be an unencumbered stream of cash available for the debtor's use.

If the debtor is a general or limited single asset partnership and has made a cash distribution to its partners prior to filing bankruptcy while real estate taxes due on the property remain unpaid, the secured creditor may be able to assert that such action by the debtor constitutes a fraudulent transfer under state or federal law. The lender can argue that the debtor's failure to pay the taxes constitutes the actionable waste of the debtor's collateral. Waste of collateral by the debtor can create an equitable remedy entitling the lender or the bankruptcy estate to recover the distribution payments even if the secured creditor's loan is non-recourse. This tactic was successfully employed by a lender who claimed that the borrower's distribution of cash to its partners while real estate taxes were unpaid constituted a fraudulent transfer under the Uniform Fraudulent Conveyance Act that was in effect in New York. State court decisions in Illinois, Florida, Wisconsin, Missouri, Massachusetts, and Minnesota have also held that a mortgagor's failure to pay real estate taxes can constitute actionable waste.

C. Cash Collateral Motions

The secured creditor should expect the debtor to move for the use of cash collateral. The lender may pre-empt this move by requesting a hearing on a motion to sequester rents. While the lender usually does not object to the debtor's use of cash collateral to pay reasonable operating expenses of the property, this hearing provides an opportunity for the lender to argue its interest in the cash collateral and to pave the way for court-imposed limits on the debtor's use of the cash collateral.

Sometimes the judge will grant a secured party's requested limitations on the use of the cash collateral by the debtor. The judge usually will recognize an interest in the cash collateral in favor of the lender as a secured party. However, this recognition may depend on the existence of a security agreement including rents as well as the perfection of the lender's security interest in the rents. Additionally, the judge may require that the cash, minus operating expenses, be held in escrow in a segregated account subject to a later determination by the court as to the disposition of the net rental proceeds. The lender should be prepared to present operating histories to persuade the judge to cap the use of rents for operating expenses and to persuade the judge to prohibit the use of the rents for the debtor's legal or accounting expenses.

The trustee or DIP is prohibited from using, selling, or leasing generated cash collateral unless each entity with an interest in the collateral consents or unless the court "after notice and a hearing, authorizes such use, sale, or lease."

The debtor must make a motion to use cash collateral. The motion usually includes (1) the amount of cash collateral to be used; (2) the name and address of each entity having an interest in the collateral; (3) the name and address of any entity having control over the collateral; (4) the facts showing the need to use the collateral; and (5) the nature of any adequate protection to be provided vis-Á-vis the cash collateral.

. . . .

Unless the trustee or DIP is permitted to use the cash collateral, he or she is required to segregate and account for any cash collateral in his or her possession, custody, or control. The unauthorized use of cash collateral has been held to be an act in contempt of court on the part of both the debtor and debtor's representative.

Deposit or escrow accounts such as loan holdbacks and tax and insurance escrows held by a secured creditor may be the property of the bankruptcy estate and may be considered cash collateral. The debtor may not use the cash in the account, and the lender may not set off against it unless authorized by the court. If the debtor is authorized to use the cash, the lender should ask to be provided with adequate protection, which should be spelled out in the court order authorizing the use of cash. Also, any set-off occurring within the preference period may be subject to recovery by the trustee or the DIP to the extent that the secured creditor improved its position. The creditor should immediately request adequate protection for any collateral that could be used, sold, or leased by the trustee or the debtor or that is subject to turnover. If such adequate protection later proves inadequate, the former holder of the collateral may be entitled to priority over other administrative claims for the diminution in value.

MOVING FOR RELIEF FROM AUTOMATIC STAY

A. Grounds for Relief

Section 362(d) of the Bankruptcy Code provides two grounds upon which the court may grant relief from the automatic stay. Relief may be granted for cause. Relief may also be granted when the debtor has no equity in the property and the property is not necessary for effective reorganization.

1. Relief Due to Cause

The borrower must provide adequate protection for the lesser of the amount of the creditor's claim or the value of the collateral as of the filing date. Collateral can be hard (the property) or soft (cash). Adequate protection may be afforded to both types of collateral if they exist. In *Timbers*,[18] the United States Supreme Court held that adequate protection is meant only to assure that a secured creditor does not suffer a decline in the value of its interest in the bankruptcy estate's property. Adequate protection is not meant to compensate the creditor for the delay in the ability to enforce rights in the property. In other words, an unsecured creditor whose collateral is not depreciating is not entitled to adequate protection payments.

Cash and cash equivalents are the most liquid of the DIP's assets and, therefore, the most susceptible to dissipation. Adequate protection of cash assets may consist of (1) cash payments to the lender to the extent of a decrease in the value of the lender's interest in cash collateral; (2) additional or replacement liens to the extent of such a decrease; or (3) other relief that will yield the equivalent of the lender's interest in the cash collateral.

In the context of an assignment of rents, the determination of the interests of secured creditors, for purposes of adequate protection, is not directly addressed by the Bankruptcy Code and has produced a large number of conflicting judicial opinions. For example, some courts hold that an undersecured creditor with a pre-petition perfected security interest in rents whose hard collateral is not depreciating is not entitled to payment of net rents. These courts find that to the extent that such payments have been made to the secured creditor prior to confirmation, they consist of pre-payments that reduce the creditor's secured claim. Other courts hold that if a creditor has a perfected pre-petition security interest in the rents, the full amount of the rents is entitled to adequate protection and such rents result in an increase in the creditor's secured claim during the pendency of the bankruptcy. Payment of any such post-petition rents that are not used to preserve the hard collateral of the creditor would then result in a loss in the amount of the increase resulting from each payment. In turn, the total amount of the creditor's claim is decreased, except for the secured portion of the claim as measured by the value of the real estate. Still other courts hold that such rents should first be expended to preserve the real estate and then be seen as increasing

---

[18] *Timbers*, 484 U.S. at 365.

the creditor's secured claim. To the extent that such net rents are paid to the creditor, they decrease the total amount of the creditor's claim but not the secured portion of the claim as measured by the value of the real estate.

2. Adequate Protection of Hard Collateral

If a debtor can argue that the value of the collateral exceeds the amount of the secured creditor's claim, the debtor will maintain that the secured creditor is adequately protected by the equity cushion, however small it may be, in its collateral. Junior lien claims are not considered when determining whether an equity cushion exists. When the debtor has little or no equity in the collateral, and the value of the lender's collateral is decreasing, the bankruptcy courts generally have held that the collateral itself is not sufficient to adequately protect the interest of the secured creditor. In these situations, courts require the debtor to provide other adequate protection, such as monthly payments to the secured creditor or a security interest in additional collateral. The judge, in some cases, will consider the monthly generation of cash collateral as the source of adequate protection of the lender's security interest. However, the lender will not be entitled to adequate protection payments based solely on lost opportunity costs.

The argument concerning adequate protection for hard collateral includes protection from declining market values; however, the decline in value must occur and be demonstrated during the case. Bankruptcy courts differ as to whether, for purposes of adequate protection, the secured creditor's claim is fixed at the date of filing, is entitled to continuous valuation, or is subject to re-valuation only on the confirmation date.

One way to argue the lack of adequate protection is to show loss of value during the case, using appraisal testimony at a preliminary hearing on a motion for relief. More appraisal testimony can be presented to show a decline in value since the last appraisal at a later opportunity, such as the debtor's motion to extend the exclusive period. In cases where market rents have declined dramatically and above-market leases are expiring, the property will decline in value as a result of the expiration of the above-market leases.

Claims against the debtor for unmatured interest on totally unsecured debt are not allowed after the filing of the bankruptcy petition. Unsecured creditors are not entitled to adequate protection. The oversecured lender is entitled to interest on its claim and any reasonable fees, costs, or charges provided for by the terms of the agreement under which the lender's claim arose. An oversecured lender is entitled to continue to accrue interest and to pass through attorneys' fees and all other charges that are not penalties as long as they are provided for under the agreement after the filing of the bankruptcy petition.

To rectify the apparent injustice in cases in which the debtor may use collateral even when there is little equity, early bankruptcy courts allowed secured lenders adequate protection on the basis of lost opportunity costs. Drawing on the indubitable equivalent language, these courts construed the concept of adequate protection as entitling the secured creditor to receive monthly payments approximating the amount that the lender originally bargained for or approximately what the lender would earn if allowed to foreclose, sell the collateral, and reinvest the proceeds. However, this line of reasoning was overruled by the Supreme Court's decision in *Timbers*.[130] The Supreme Court held that an undersecured lender was not entitled to adequate protection for lost opportunity costs, basing its ruling on a section of the Bankruptcy Code that generally prohibits the payment of post-petition interest to unsecured creditors. The Supreme Court was not persuaded by any of the arguments in favor of lost opportunity costs. Timbers reduced the level of adequate protection to which an undersecured lender is entitled and has made it easier for a debtor to avoid modification of the stay. On the other hand, the *Timbers* case may have made it somewhat easier to modify the automatic stay because the debtor has the burden to establish that the collateral is necessary to an effective reorganization. In *Timbers* the Court listed numerous instances where the automatic stay had been lifted within one year after the filing of a bankruptcy petition and expressly noted that the automatic stay should be modified when there is no realistic prospect of an effective reorganization, even if the debtor's exclusive period to file a plan of reorganization has not yet expired.

3. Relief Due to No Equity, and the Property is Unnecessary for a Reorganization

Even if the secured creditor cannot establish cause as a ground for relief from the automatic stay, the stay will be terminated or modified if the mortgage lender can show that the debtor has no equity, and that the property is not necessary for a reorganization.

The secured creditor has the burden of proving that the debtor has no equity in the property. The creditor may prove this with an appraisal, testimony of an appraiser, or by introducing the debtor's own financial information from the filing of claims and liabilities. The court considers not only the debt of the individual secured creditor, but also all secured claims against the collateral as of the date of the bankruptcy case.

The debtor has the burden of proving that the property is necessary for an effective reorganization and that the debtor can propose a feasible and confirmable plan of reorganization. Courts have held property unnecessary for reorganization when there is no reasonable possibility of a successful reorganization within a reasonable period of time. In single asset real estate cases, the debtor has little hope of rehabilitation, even though the property appears to be indispensable to the debtor's survival.

To rebut this appearance, the creditor must establish that the debtor cannot effectively reorganize due to market conditions. The deteriorating condition of the property, the property's inability to generate sufficient cash flow, or other reasons pertinent to the debtor's business operations may also be evidence that the debtor cannot reorganize. One way to argue this, at least where the bankruptcy is truly a two-party dispute is to state that no prospect of settlement exists, that the parties' interests are in conflict, and that considerable efforts to work out the loan have failed. When the lender is undersecured, the lender may also argue that the cash flow is not likely to recover soon, nor is the value of the property.

Again, the determination of these issues may depend on a particular court's interpretation of the pertinent Bankruptcy Code provisions. In the *Timbers* decision, the Supreme Court took the position that the debtor need only prove that

---

[130] *Timbers*, 484 U.S. at 365.

a reorganization plan is likely, in the near future or that it is in prospect. Another court decision in a single asset case used the test of whether a debtor is able to come up with a plan that is not objectively futile.

B. Moving for Dismissal

Subsequent to the *Timbers* decision, a number of courts have recognized the burdens imposed upon the secured creditor in a single asset case. Some courts are responsive to motions to dismiss single asset cases or to modify the stay on the grounds that the case was filed in bad faith. On the other hand, some bankruptcy judges are hostile to the concept of a bad-faith filing and will seldom dismiss a bankruptcy case on such grounds.

However, case law in this area has been less than uniform, and bankruptcy courts often shy away from the concept of bad faith, even if the objective standards are satisfied. Nonetheless, if the court recognizes the filing as having been made in bad faith, it may allow the debtor no more than its 120-day exclusive period in which to propose a plan of reorganization.

The secured creditor should consider moving for dismissal immediately after the debtor files the bankruptcy petition. The creditor's motion for dismissal may be heard simultaneously with the debtor's motion to use cash collateral. This hearing is the creditor's first opportunity to present to the judge the creditor's interests and efforts, or inability, to work out a solution to the case. The creditor might try to persuade the judge that the filing was made in bad faith or that a reorganization is futile. Although it is unlikely that the case will be dismissed at such an early stage, the judge may set a strict time limit for extensions to the exclusivity period and may deny any motions without prejudice.

The creditor's next opportunity to move for dismissal would be when the debtor submits an unconfirmable plan. If the creditor has the good fortune of having the judge rule in the creditor's favor, the debtor will have had its day in court and no more.

THE CHAPTER 11 PLAN

A. Who Can File a Plan

The primary goal of the Bankruptcy Code, and Chapter 11 in particular, is to implement a plan of reorganization that will allow the debtor to continue operating its business and will bind all secured creditors, unsecured creditors, and equity holders. Chapter 11 also permits a liquidating plan of reorganization.

The Bankruptcy Code gives the debtor the exclusive right to file a plan of reorganization until 120 days after the filing of the bankruptcy petition. However, any party in interest may file a plan of reorganization if (1) a trustee has been appointed; (2) the debtor has not filed a plan within 120 days after the filing of the petition; or (3) the debtor has not, within 180 days of the petition filing, filed a plan that has been accepted by each class of claims or interest that is impaired under the plan. Additionally, once the debtor's exclusive period to file a plan expires, creditors have the right to file rival plans.

However, when cause is shown, the court may reduce or extend the 120-day period or the 180-day period. Creditors do not commonly submit plans for reorganization because the debtor seldom relinquishes sole authority to propose a plan within the first 120 days. Furthermore, the bankruptcy judge rarely terminates the debtor's exclusivity early enough in the case to permit a creditor to submit a plan. Additionally, a creditor's plan is also very time-consuming and expensive to propose.

B. The Disclosure Statement and Plan

The plan of reorganization must be submitted to creditors and equity holders for approval, along with a disclosure statement. The burden falls on the debtor to prepare an accurate, fair, and complete disclosure statement. The disclosure statement's adequacy will be tested at a hearing. At the hearing, the plan's proponent will introduce the disclosure materials and other evidence necessary to show that the disclosure is accurate, fair, and complete.

The plan of reorganization enumerates the treatment of each class and sets forth the mechanics of ownership and payment of the debtor's amended obligations. The disclosure statement generally contains a liquidation analysis, to demonstrate that creditors will not be in a worse position upon confirmation of the debtor's plan.

VOTING AND CLASSIFICATION

A. Classes In General

The classification of claims is the foundation of the reorganization plan. The debtor segregates the creditors' claims into various classes, ordered in priority of repayment or consideration. Each class receives a specified treatment or payment schedule. A debtor may place a claim in a particular class only if the claim is substantially similar to other claims in that class.

B. Unimpaired Classes and Their Treatment

Unimpaired classes are not allowed to vote for or against the confirmation of a plan. However, treatment of unimpaired claims must comply with one of the following standards: (1) the plan must not alter the legal, equitable, and contractual rights of claims holders in the class; or (2) the plan must cure all pre-bankruptcy arrearage, reinstate the maturity of the claims, and compensate the claims holders for damages incurred as a result of reasonable reliance on their contractual provisions.

Prior to the passage of the Reform Act, section 1124(3) of the Bankruptcy Code provided that a class was considered to be unimpaired if, on the effective date of the plan, the class members received cash for the allowed amount of their claims. However, section 213 of the Reform Act deleted section 1124(3) of the Bankruptcy Code with the intention of forcing debtors to pay interest to unsecured creditors if the creditors' allowed unsecured claims were paid in full. Congress deleted this section to overrule a 1994 bankruptcy decision holding that, under certain circumstances, the claims of unsecured creditors could be considered paid in full and unimpaired, even though no post-petition interest was to be paid on such claims. Unfortunately, the deletion of this provision may make it easier for a single asset debtor to impair unsecured creditors and confirm a plan.

Arguably a debtor can now pay allowed unsecured claims in full upon confirmation of the plan without paying interest and still treat the class as impaired for voting purposes. Prior to deletion of this provision, the debtor avoided paying interest only by paying less than 100% of such claims or by paying the impaired unsecured creditors in full within an extended period of time — for example, ninety days after the effective date of the plan — and taking a greater risk that the class would reject the plan.

C. Voting of Impaired Classes

The debtor must submit its plan to the creditors holding claims in impaired classes. The creditors may vote to accept or reject the plan. Generally, the creditors do not need to explain or defend their reasons for accepting or rejecting the plan. Certain rules govern creditors' individual and class voting rights. For example, an impaired class of claims is deemed to have accepted the plan if the plan is approved by at least two-thirds in amount and more than one-half in number of those creditors casting ballots. Furthermore, if all classes of impaired claims accept the plan, and the debtor satisfies all of the other requirements under the Bankruptcy Code for confirming a plan of reorganization, the bankruptcy court will confirm the plan and make it binding on all creditors. If, however, the plan does not receive confirmation votes from all impaired classes, but at least one impaired class does accept the plan, the plan may be crammed down on the dissenting classes provided that the court believes that the plan is fair and equitable, and that the plan does not unfairly discriminate against the dissenting classes. In each impaired class of claims, each holder of an impaired claim must either accept the plan or receive property, valued as of the effective date of the plan, that equals at least the amount that the holder would have received if the debtor were liquidated under Chapter 7 of the Bankruptcy Code.

If an undersecured creditor's claim is planned in two different classes, that creditor may be able to cast two votes. If the value of the secured creditor's collateral is less than its claim, the creditor has a secured claim in an amount equal to the value of the collateral and an unsecured claim for the amount of the debt that exceeds the collateral. An unsecured claim that arises in this manner is known as a deficiency claim.

D. Classification Tactics

The Bankruptcy Code provides that a plan may include a claim in a particular class only if the claim is substantially similar to the other claims in that class. Although the case law is not uniform, recent decisions have not required that all similar claims be grouped into one class, but merely that any class contain similar claims. Accordingly, it appears that similar claims may be segregated into separate classes.

Usually, the plan proponent attempts to gerrymander classes of claims to create at least one assenting impaired class. This gerrymandering may involve isolating a large deficiency claim of a secured creditor into its own class. If the deficiency claim votes against the plan, another impaired class of unsecured claims could still vote in favor of it. Several courts have strongly disapproved of attempts by debtors to manipulate unsecured claims or classes. Overall, however, the courts are split over whether this is acceptable or a bad faith classification on the part of the debtor. A majority of courts have denied confirmation of plans that separately classify deficiency claims from other general unsecured claims unless there is a valid reason to do so. Separate classifications are usually deemed invalid when the only apparent purpose of the separate classification is to gerrymander the vote to satisfy the Bankruptcy Code confirmation requirements.

However, the Seventh Circuit, which includes Illinois, Wisconsin, and Indiana, allows the separate classification of deficiency claims. In *In re Woodbrook Associates*,[163] the court held that, at least when the debtor is a partnership comprised of a fully encumbered single asset, the existence of a right by the secured creditor to elect under section 1111(b)(2) of the Bankruptcy Code means that the undersecured real property creditor has different legal rights from other undersecured creditors; therefore, separate classification is required.

Other than a secured lender's deficiency claim, typical gerrymandered classes can be comprised of trade creditors. This is because the nature of trade creditors' debt is allegedly different from other creditors in that trade creditors' debt consists of short-term credit and claims with recourse to the general partner of the debtor. Tenants may be another such class of trade creditors if they are classified as unsecured. This classification might occur by showing that the tenants stand to receive less than they originally bargained for because of the debtor's rejection of their leases.

E. Creditors' Committees

Secured and unsecured creditors are not passive participants in the negotiation of any plan of reorganization, regardless of their voting classifications. If the proposed plan is unacceptable, the holder of an impaired claim may not only vote against the plan, but the holder can encourage others to vote against it. Because the seven largest unsecured or partially unsecured creditors are eligible and are generally asked to become members of a creditors' committee, a secured creditor with an unsecured claim should consider whether or not to participate as a member. Because certain fiduciary obligations arise from membership on a committee, a secured creditor should consult counsel to determine whether the benefits outweigh the burdens.

CONFIRMATION

If all impaired classes vote in favor of the plan of reorganization, the plan will be confirmed under section 1129(a) of the Bankruptcy Code, provided that it is feasible and meets all of the tests. Section 1129(b) allows for confirmation of a plan, notwithstanding the objection of an impaired class, if it is feasible, "fair and equitable," and "does not discriminate unfairly" against the dissenting class. Under Section 1129(b), a plan is fair and equitable to secured creditors if: (1) each secured

[163] 19 F.3d at 319 (noting that the separate classification of the secured creditor's "§ 1111(b) claim neither prevents confirmation of Woodbrooks' plan nor serves as conclusive evidence in this case that Woodbrook manipulated the plan to obtain an affirmative vote."). . . .

creditor retains a lien to the extent of the claim, although the property may be transferred to a third party; (2) each secured creditor receives deferred cash payments that total at least the amount of the secured creditor's claim; and (3) the deferred cash payments have a present value equal to at least the value of the creditor's interest in the collateral. Generally, the only real question here is the discount rate used.

A plan is fair and equitable to unsecured creditors if (1) each creditor receives property with a present value equal to the allowed amount of its claim, or (2) no junior class, including equity holders, (i.e., any class junior to the dissenting class) retains property or receives payment of any kind.

CRAMDOWN PLANS, VARIATIONS, AND ALTERNATIVES

A. The Cramdown

If all of the legal requirements of a reorganization plan are met, with the exception of a successful confirmation vote by creditors, the plan may still be confirmed over the objection of a dissenting class. If the plan does not discriminate unfairly and is fair and equitable to the dissenting class, it can be crammed down on the impaired class that votes against the plan. In a cramdown, the debtor may (1) reduce the principal amount of the secured claim to the value of the collateral; (2) reduce the interest rate; (3) extend the maturity date; or (4) alter the repayment schedule. The debtor may also make a minimal payment on the unsecured claim. Under the Bankruptcy Code a cramdown is permissible when the plan provides a dissenting secured class with consideration equal to the amount of its claim or when no class below the dissenting unsecured class participates under the plan, the plan.

A cramdown is the single biggest workout and bankruptcy threat to a lender. However, the confirmation and other requirements that a debtor must satisfy in order to cram down both a secured and an unsecured claim, particularly in the case of a single asset real estate bankruptcy, impose such burdens on a debtor that few Chapter 11 debtors who propose cramdown plans successfully achieve reorganization by cramming down the lender.

Although a mortgagee may be entitled to retain all of its rights under the mortgage, the mortgagee will not necessarily receive an obligation with level periodic payments. Also, the present value requirement necessitates the use of an interest rate. This rate varies in each jurisdiction and can be either the contract rate or a market rate based on treasury bill rates plus a court determined upward adjustment for risk factors. The debtor's plan may also propose negative amortization of the lender's secured claim. Negative amortization occurs when part or all of the interest on the claim is deferred, allowed to accrue, and added to the principal periodically to be paid at a later date when the income from the property has increased or its value has appreciated. Bankruptcy courts have held that negative amortization is not per se impermissible, but courts will closely scrutinize plans proposing this form of payment on a case-by-case basis.

A class of secured creditors can also be crammed down if each secured creditor receives the indubitable equivalent of the claim. A secured creditor receives the indubitable equivalent of the claim when the secured creditor receives a return of part of its collateral while the remainder of its secured claim continues to be secured by the remaining collateral, and when the debtor proposes to pay the present value of the remaining secured claim over a period of time.

B. New Value Exception to the Absolute Priority Rule

. . . . [intentionally omitted]

C. Survival of the New Value Exception

. . . . [intentionally omitted]

D. The Section 1111(b)(2) Election

Section 1111(b) of the Bankruptcy Code enables an undersecured, non-recourse creditor to avoid being cashed out at the depressed value of the secured collateral and enables the creditor to share in any future appreciation in such value.

As noted above, the claim of an undersecured creditor is divided into two claims: (1) a secured claim equal to the value of its collateral, and (2) an unsecured deficiency claim for the balance. Under section 1111(b)(2), an undersecured creditor may elect to have the entire claim treated as fully secured.

The following are two important aspects of making the section 1111(b)(2) election: (1) the undersecured creditor loses the right to vote regarding the previously unsecured claim; and (2) the unsecured creditor must make the election before the conclusion of the hearing on the disclosure statement. Often, this second requirement forces the undersecured creditor to elect before adequate disclosure has been made concerning the plan and the proponent's intentions. By making a section 1111(b)(2) election, a creditor may significantly affect whether the amount of deferred cash payments proposed under a plan and the present value of those payments satisfy the cramdown confirmation standards of section 1129(b).

For example, assume that a creditor has a $5 million claim secured by collateral worth $3 million. Under section 1129(b), the plan would have to provide the secured creditor with deferred cash payments that total at least $3 million (the amount of the allowed secured claim) and that have a present value of at least $3 million. These cash payments may continue over five years and would total $4.5 million at a 10% rate of interest. Expecting the confirmation of a cramdown, the debtor would be likely to propose some treatment of the $2 million unsecured deficiency claim. Usually, the debtor proposes to pay the deficiency claim at a fraction of the face amount over a period of time, such as 20% over five years.

If, however, the creditor makes the section 1111(b)(2) election, the deferred cash payments for the secured claim must equal $5 million (the allowed amount of the entire claim) and have a present value of $3 million (the value of the collateral). Thus, in this example, if the undersecured creditor makes this election, the creditor is entitled to a total of $2 million of additional deferred cash payments, not just a fraction of this amount. However, this requirement is often met by lengthening the term of the deferred payments. Here, seven years of payments at 10% would total $5.1 million and would satisfy section 1111(b)(2).

Under section 1111(b)(2), the creditor will never get less than the full mortgage amount, but also will never get more than the net present value of the collateral on the plan date. On the other hand, a cramdown plan could provide a market rate of return on the collateral value plus a potential benefit in the form of a share of the excess cash flow, sharp depreciation upon a subsequent sale or refinancing, or a scheduled payment on the unsecured portion of the claim.

By making the section 1111(b)(2) election, the creditor becomes secured and, therefore, loses the right to vote in the unsecured class. In other words, the creditor loses one opportunity to vote against the plan. By foregoing the unsecured claim, the undersecured creditor also foregoes the opportunity to assert any potential classification, unfair discrimination, and fair-and-equitable objections. These objections could prove fatal to the confirmation of the debtor's plan. Thus, the undersecured creditor could be relinquishing major litigation advantages by making the section 1111(b)(2) election.

Nevertheless, a secured creditor should consider making a section 1111(b)(2) election when the deficiency claim is small and unlikely to dominate voting in the secured creditor's class. In this instance, losing a vote as a consequence of making the section 1111(b)(2) election may not be a factor that the creditor needs to consider.

The right to make the section 1111(b)(2) election belongs solely to the secured creditor. This election cannot be made by the debtor on behalf of the secured creditor.

E. Feasibility Requirements of a Cramdown Plan

Before a court confirms a cramdown plan, the court must, among other things, determine whether the plan is feasible. In other words the court must believe that the plan probably will not be followed by an unproposed liquidation or a need for further financial reorganization. According to the United States Supreme Court, "[h]owever honest in its efforts the debtor may be, and however sincere its motives, the District Court is not bound to clog its docket with visionary or impractical schemes for resuscitation."[189]

Although the feasibility requirement does not guarantee the success of the reorganized debtor, it does require that the plan enable the reorganized debtor to emerge solvent and with reasonable prospects of financial stability and success. The burden is on the debtor to prove that the plan is feasible.

Generally, the factors that the court considers in determining feasibility include: (1) the earning power of the business; (2) the sufficiency of the capital structure; (3) the condition of the collateral and any deterioration that may have occurred throughout the bankruptcy process; (4) economic conditions; (5) management efficiency; (6) the availability of credit, if needed; and (7) the debtor's ability to meet capital expenditures. The court is obligated to evaluate past earnings to determine if they are a reliable criterion of future performance and, if not, to make an estimate of future performance by inquiring into foreseeable factors that may affect future prospects. To enable the court to evaluate past earnings and to

---

[189] *Tennessee Publishing Co. v. American Nat'l Bank*, 299 U.S. 18, 22 (1936).

estimate future earnings, the debtor must present competent, concrete, and reliable evidence.

Therefore, although debtors may propose to restructure their debts, debtors have a significant burden to establish that they will be able to satisfy the payments proposed in their plans. In a single asset real estate case, the court will deny confirmation if the debtor cannot demonstrate the plan's feasibility based upon realistic and verifiable projections establishing the existence of adequate cash flow.

F. Purchasing Claims to Block Confirmation and Avoid Cramdown

. . . .

In general, purchasing claims is permitted if full and proper disclosure is made and if the purpose of the purchase is not to increase the creditor's recovery at the expenses of the other creditors. . . .

If the secured creditor's claim is not large enough — at least one-third of the total amount of the claims in the class — to control the class vote, or if the secured creditor's deficiency claim has been classified separately from the other unsecured claims, the creditor may seek to purchase sufficient claims from other class members to force a negative vote by the class or to control one-third of the amount of each non-insider impaired class in order to block confirmation.

Purchasing sufficient claims to confirm a competing plan filed by the creditor is more difficult because the creditor must purchase enough claims to control two-thirds in amount and one-half in number of each non-impaired creditor class. The creditor seeking to purchase claims should also be aware that a court could take the position that an entity that buys multiple claims is then treated as having only one claim for voting purposes. This treatment may prevent the creditor from casting more than 50% of all possible class votes unless the creditor purchases all of the claims in the class. A creditor may also seek to purchase claims in a non-insider impaired class even if the purchase will not enable the creditor to control that class or force a blocking vote. The purchase would require the debtor to comply with the best interests of creditors test under section 1129(a)(7) of the Bankruptcy Code.

Because the bankruptcy court may disallow claims purchased by a creditor not acting in good faith, the question arises as to whether purchasing claims for the purpose of preventing confirmation constitutes bad faith. The emerging test is whether the creditor acted pursuant to an ulterior motive unrelated to the protection of the secured creditor's claims in the case, such as malice, blackmail, intent to destroy the debtor's business in order to advance the interests of a competing business, intent to profit from the purchase or from information obtained thereby, intent to obtain control of the debtor, or intent to obtain an unfair advantage.

. . . .

G. Final Words on Cramdown

The provisions regarding confirmation and cramdown are among the most complicated in the Bankruptcy Code. Although the potential exists for a debtor to restructure debts over the opposition of creditors, the debtor must satisfy numerous interrelated requirements in order to achieve a restructuring. All debtors must overcome, among other things, the feasibility requirement. Additionally, if an undersecured creditor does not make the section 1111(b)(2) election, the debtor, at least in the majority of jurisdictions, may not isolate the deficiency claim and treat it differently from other unsecured claims unless there is a valid reason to do so. Generally a valid reason does not exist for classifying similar claims differently solely to gerrymander an affirmative vote on a reorganization plan. In practice, it is often difficult for a debtor to satisfy all of the necessary requirements in order to effect a cramdown.

H. An Alternative: Pre-Packaged Plans

A pre-packaged bankruptcy plan is a relatively risk-free way to avoid the hazards and expenses of litigation that could result from an unsuccessful workout attempt. It also provides protection down the road for the lender if the borrower fails to perform and title is transferred to the lender. A pre-packaged bankruptcy plan is negotiated by the lender with the borrower and key creditors before, and submitted to the bankruptcy court simultaneously with, a voluntary Chapter 11 filing by the debtor. It is often used in large workouts when there are few significant creditors other than the lender, for example, when only current trade debt exists, and the claims of the other creditors are to be paid substantially or in full as part of the plan. A pre-packaged plan eliminates the risks, costs, and delays of contested bankruptcy proceedings and assures a court-approved and court-supervised plan as well as an orderly transfer of title.

A basic pre-packaged plan might have the following features and components:

(1) The borrower releases the lender form all lender liability claims.

(2) All cash flow is handled in a manner acceptable to the lender and the borrower. Prior to plan confirmation, the lender should obtain acknowledgment of a perfected and presently enforceable rents assignment through a cash collateral agreement. During the implementation of the plan, perfection should continue. The cash management program must not risk loss of perfection or enforcement status for the lender.

(3) Under the Chapter 11 plan that is agreed to by the borrower and the lender before the bankruptcy is filed, the borrower has a set period of time to market and sell the property or to obtain refinancing for a minimum price; the proceeds would be divided according to a set formula.

(4) If no sale or refinancing has occurred at the expiration of the stipulated time period, the lender would have the option to conduct a Bankruptcy Code sale or be granted immediate relief from the automatic stay and proceed with an uncontested foreclosure sale.

(5) Alternatively, the borrower agrees to transfer the property to the lender at the end of the plan if the lender has not been paid, pursuant to a deed and other transfer documents placed in escrow at the time of plan confirmation.

(6) The borrower agrees not to enjoin or otherwise delay any subsequent foreclosure proceedings conducted by the lender.

(7) A liquidated-damages indemnification agreement, or springing guarantee, executed by a solvent third party or parties is delivered to the lender as part of the plan and becomes effective if any attempt is made to prevent, hinder, delay, or obstruct the lender from obtaining title on the final date.

(8) Some or all of the legal costs are normally borne by the lender, such as the costs of drafting the plan, court costs, schedules, solicitation materials, and distribution. The lender also may agree to the payment of all or part of the debtor's costs and attorneys' fees from property income, although these fees are often capped on a negotiated basis.

In short, the lender's normal remedies are safeguarded from future defenses and delays brought by the borrower, including, another adversarial bankruptcy. Having secured concessions from the lender, the borrower gets another chance to perform.

Historically, a pre-packaged plan, referred to as an out-of-court restructuring proposal made by a financially distressed debtor, would qualify as a plan of reorganization in a Chapter 11 case. This stipulation would be signed as an order by the bankruptcy judge and would, therefore, have the force of law. Such bankruptcy stipulations have been judicially upheld as binding on the parties.

The pre-packaged plan avoids the adverse effects of dissension that often accompany a bankruptcy filing, especially if all of the impaired parties in interest accept the plan. If the pre-packaged plan is not overwhelmingly accepted, but is accepted by a majority of each impaired class that would bind that class in a Chapter 11 case, then the pre-packaged plan is filed with the Chapter 11 petition. Depending on factors such as the court's calendar, the plan can be confirmed in as little as thirty to forty-five days after the commencement of the case.

. . . .

One advantage of any Chapter 11 plan in states that have high conveyance taxes, such as Florida, Pennsylvania, and New York, is the applicability of section 1146(c) of the Bankruptcy Code. This section exempts transfers pursuant to a bankruptcy plan from state conveyance taxes provided that the sole purpose of the plan is not tax avoidance.

Borrowers generally cannot legally be prevented from filing serial bankruptcies. . . .

DEBTOR-IN-POSSESSION FINANCING

The authority to continue in business includes the right to obtain credit and incur unsecured debt to fund ordinary operating expenses. To induce creditors to extend any necessary post-petition credit, such credit is allowable as an expense of administration. This provides the credit priority over other claims against the estate.

Two tests should be applied to determine whether a new credit transaction is in the ordinary course of a debtor's business, and, therefore, allowed protection through administrative status. The first test, called the horizontal dimension test, compares the debtor's business to other like businesses. The test is whether the creditor transaction in question is similar to those in which comparable businesses engage in their day-to-day operations. The second test is the vertical dimension test, also called the creditor's expectation test. This test analyzes the credit transaction from the vantage point of a hypothetical creditor and inquires whether the transaction subjects a creditor to atypical economic risks.

If the trustee or the DIP cannot obtain this unsecured credit as an administrative allowance, the court may authorize the trustee or the DIP to obtain credit or incur debt that has priority over all administrative expenses. The court can also authorize debt that is secured by a lien on property of the estate that is not otherwise subject to a lien or is secured by a junior lien on property of the estate that is subject to a lien. Furthermore, the court can authorize debt secured by a senior lien on property of the estate, but only if the trustee or the DIP is unable to obtain such credit otherwise and the existing lienholders' interests are adequately protected.

The burden of proof for both standards is placed upon the trustee or the DIP. Under the prior Bankruptcy Act, a trustee or a DIP could issue certificates of indebtedness supercharging existing liens to secure loans for operating expenses only if there was a high degree of likelihood that there would be a successful reorganization within a reasonable time. This standard has been recently replaced by the adequate protection standard. Accordingly, the trustee or DIP must convince the court (1) that there is sufficient value in the property to satisfy the interest of the primed lender notwithstanding the granting of the new lien; (2) that there is an equity cushion sufficient to adequately protect the prior secured lender; or (3) that the increase in value of the collateral due to capital improvements made as a result of the DIP's financing constitutes adequate protection.

Entities that loan money to debtors without notice and a hearing or a court order act at their own peril. Several courts have held that a creditor who lends money to a DIP without prior court approval is not even entitled to assert a general unsecured claim. On the other hand, a lender has no obligation to continue to extend financing under a pre-petition lending agreement subsequent to the petition date. The pre-petition lender may also enforce its lending agreement regarding termination or modification upon the commencement of a bankruptcy case.

Because most post-petition lenders are generally pre-petition creditors as well, the trustee or the DIP may seek to obtain post-petition financing from such lenders that is secured not only by a post-petition lien, but that also grants additional liens to secure the existing pre-petition indebtedness. Bankruptcy courts generally disfavor such cross-collateralization and require the trustee or DIP to demonstrate (1) that absent the proposed financing, the debtor's business operations will not survive; (2) that the debtor is unable to obtain alternative financing on acceptable terms; (3) that the proposed lender will not agree to less favorable terms; and (4) that the proposed financing is in the best interests of all the creditors.

CONCLUSION

The lender must formulate a coherent and effective course of action when faced with a borrower who has filed a Chapter 11 proceeding to prohibit or delay the exercise of the lender's remedies in connection with a defaulted mortgage loan. To do so, the lender must be aware of and anticipate the tactics likely to be employed by the borrower during the pendency of the case. In furtherance of this goal, the lender and its counsel must be familiar with the background and purpose of the Bankruptcy Code provisions, as amended by the Reform Act, the Federal Rules of Bankruptcy Procedure that apply to Chapter 11 proceedings, the relevant court decisions interpreting and applying such statutes and rules, and the process of reorganization in general.

The lender and its counsel must also be thoroughly aware of a strategy utilizing the powers and alternatives available to the lender in a Chapter 11 proceeding and analyzed in this article, including (1) the purchase of other unsecured claims; (2) the use of cash collateral orders and other rent-perfection and rent-enforcement devices; (3) motions for relief from the automatic stay; (4) motions for dismissal, or for conversion; (5) valuation and feasibility hearings; (6) the section 1111(b) election; (7) the filing of a creditor's plan of reorganization or liquidation; and (8) pre-packaged plans.

Certain issues, such as the borrower's ability to gerrymander claims to create a class of assenting creditors in furtherance of a cramdown plan and the continuing validity of the new value exception to the absolute priority rule, remain subject to conflicting judicial interpretations and may ultimately require final determination by the United States Supreme Court. Lenders and their counsel must closely monitor the continually evolving case law regarding these and other issues affecting Chapter 11 bankruptcy filings by and against single asset real estate entities.

[b] Comments on the Overview of Bankruptcy Law and the Murray Article

1. While one of the goals of the bankruptcy system is to provide a debtor with an opportunity for a "fresh start," another reason why bankruptcy laws permit a "rewriting" of some contractual obligations is that when a debtor becomes insolvent, the insolvency not only impacts the principals of the debtor, but also many others, such as employees of the debtor, causing Congress to wish to step in to protect those employees. When the debtor is a single asset entity like a real estate developer, however, there are very few employees of the debtor who would be affected by the discontinuation of the debtor's business operations. In addition, mortgage lenders claimed that real estate developer debtors were filing Chapter 11 bankruptcies even when there was no real chance for the debtor to propose reorganization plans that were both feasible and in compliance with other bankruptcy law requirements, which meant that the filings were in bad faith and simply to delay foreclosure of the mortgaged property and its resulting negative tax consequences.

   In reaction to these concerns, Congress enacted, in both the 1994 and 2005 bankruptcy acts, additional protection for lenders in the context of a bankruptcy filing by certain "single asset real estate" entities. In 1994, Congress amended § 362(d) of the Bankruptcy Code to add a third criterion for obtaining relief from the automatic stay (the prior two grounds, as previously discussed, were for cause or if the debtor lacked equity in certain property and such property was not necessary to an effective reorganization). Under the new criterion, a secured creditor of a "single asset real estate" entity is entitled to relief from the stay, unless within 90 days of the bankruptcy filing the debtor files a plan of reorganization that "has a reasonable possibility of being confirmed within a reasonable time" or commences monthly payments to the secured creditor "in an amount equal to interest at a current fair market rate on the value of the creditor's interest in the real estate." 11 U.S.C. § 362(d)(3). The definition of "single asset real estate" was limited under the 1994 amendment to "real property constituting a single property or project, [other than residential real property with fewer than four units] which generates substantially all of the gross income of a debtor. . . ." 11 U.S.C. § 101(51B). In addition, single asset real estate was limited to property "on which no substantial business . . . other than the business of operating the real property" is conducted by the debtor. Finally, and most problematically for addressing mortgage lenders' concerns, to fit within the definition of a "single asset real estate" entity, under the 1994 amendment, the property can secure no more than $4,000,000 in "aggregate, noncontingent, liquidated secured debts." If a debtor's property satisfies these requirements, then a lender may seek relief from the bankruptcy stay. Once the lender obtains this relief, it can commence or resume the exercise of its rights under state law, such as a foreclosure action.

In 2005, Congress revised this section to delete the $4 million debt cap that applied to single asset real estate (and also excluded a debtor who is a "family farmer"). The 2005 amendment also provided that to qualify as "single asset real estate," income must not be derived primarily from business operations at the property, which courts have interpreted as excluding hospitals, hotels, casinos, golf courses, manufacturing facilities, ranches, and marinas. *See* John C. Murray, *The New Bankruptcy Act: Observations on Some of the Provisions Affecting Real Estate*, 19 Dec. Prob. & Prop. 43, 43 (2005). Another important change made by Congress in the 2005 amendment to the Bankruptcy Code that relates to the problem of debtors filing a bankruptcy action in bad faith (*i.e.*, with the sole purpose of delaying a foreclosure action) was to prevent courts from having discretion to extend the exclusive period debtors have to get their reorganization plan filed (in place of court discretion on extensions, Congress expanded the debtor's exclusivity period from four months to eighteen months). Similarly, the period for solicitation of acceptances was extended to twenty months (from a prior six months), but Congress prevented courts from being able to extend this filing date.

2. Even prior to these amendments to the Bankruptcy code, a number of courts had dismissed bankruptcy cases involving single asset real estate debtors "for cause" under either § 362(d)(1) or § 1112(b) as lacking good faith. For example, in *In re Little Creek Dev. Co.*, 779 F.2d 1068 (5th Cir. 1986), the Fifth Circuit recognized that a certain class of cases involving real estate ventures may frequently lack good faith:

> Findings of lack of good faith in proceedings based on 362(d) or 1112(b) have been predicated on certain recurring but non-exclusive patterns, and they are based on a conglomerate of factors rather than on any single datum. Several, but not all, of the following conditions usually exist. The debtor has one asset, such as a tract of undeveloped or developed real property. The secured creditors' liens encumber this tract. There are generally no employees except for the principals, little or no cash flow, and no available sources of income to sustain a plan of reorganization or to make adequate protection payments. . . . Typically, there are only a few, if any, unsecured creditors whose claims are relatively small. The property has usually been

> posted for foreclosure because of arrearages on the debt and the debtor has been unsuccessful in defending actions against the foreclosure in state court. Alternatively, the debtor and one creditor may have proceeded to a stand-still in state court litigation, and the debtor has lost or has been required to post a bond which it cannot afford. Bankruptcy offers the only possibility of forestalling loss of the property. . . . Resort to the protection of the bankruptcy laws is not proper under these circumstances because there is no going concern to preserve, there are no employees to protect, and there is no hope of rehabilitation, except according to the debtor's "terminal euphoria."

Id. at 1072–1073. *See also In re Phoenix Piccadilly, Ltd.*, 849 F.2d 1393 (11th Cir. 1988).

Although *In re Little Creek Dev. Co.* pre-dated the enactment of the single asset real estate provisions in 1994, some courts have not retreated from the view that many single asset real estate debtors may be dismissed as lacking good faith based on an objective review of the debtor's financial position. *See In re C-TC 9th Ave. Partnership*, 113 F.3d 1304 (2d Cir. 1997); *In re ACI Sunbow, LLC*, 206 B.R. 213 (Bankr. S.D. Cal. 1997); *In re Midway Investment, Ltd.*, 187 B.R. 382 (Bankr. S.D. Fla. 1995). However, other courts have concluded that the enactment of § 362(d)(3) has expressed Congressional intent regarding single asset real estate debtors and that more than the facts suggested in *In re Little Creek Dev. Co.* are necessary for a finding of bad faith. *See In re Jacksonville Riverfront Dev.*, 215 B.R. 239 (Bankr. M.D. Fla. 1997) ("In determining whether there has been a lack of good faith in this case, the Court will continue to consider factors which evidence an intent to abuse the judicial process and the purposes of the reorganization provisions of the Bankruptcy Code."); *In re Park Forest Development Corp.*, 197 B.R. 388 (Bankr. N.D. Ga. 1996) ("A real estate debtor should not be precluded from availing itself of the rehabilitative provisions of Chapter 11, unless other indications of bad faith are present."). Still other courts have required that "both objective futility and subjective bad faith be shown in order to warrant dismissals for want of good faith in filing." *Carolin Corp. v. Miller*, 886 F.2d 693 (4th Cir. 1989). *See also In re Nursery Land Dev.*, 91 F.3d 1414 (10th Cir. Utah 1996); *In re Dunes Hotel Assocs.*, 188 B.R. 162 (Bankr. D.S.C. 1995).

For further discussion of the issue what is a bad faith filing, see William Thomas Thurman & Brett P. Johnson, *Bankruptcy and the Bad Faith Filing*, 10 UTAH BAR J. 12 (Dec. 1997); Erich J. Stegich, Note, *The National Bankruptcy Review Commission: Proposals for Single Asset Real Estate*, 5 AM. BANKR. INST. L. REV. 530 (1997); Daniel B. Bogart, *Games Lawyers Play: Waivers of the Automatic Stay in Bankruptcy and the Single Asset Loan Workout*, 43 UCLA L. REV. 1117 (1996); Shannon C. Bogle, Note, Bonner Mall *and Single-Asset Real Estate Cases in Chapter 11: Are the 1994 Amendments Enough?* 69 S. CAL. L. REV. 2163 (1996); Paul Deitch, Note, *Expanding the Automatic Stay: Protecting Nondebtors in Single Asset Bankruptcies*, 2 AM. BANKR. INST. L. REV. 453 (1994); Scott Carlisle, *Single Asset Real*

Estate in Chapter 11: Secured Creditors' Perspective and the Need for Reform, 1 AM. BANKR. INST. L. REV. 133 (1993); Carlos J. Cuevas, *Good Faith and Chapter 11: Standard That Should be Employed to Dismiss Bad Faith Chapter 11 Cases*, 60 TENN. L. REV. 525 (1993); H. Miles Cohn, *Single Assets Chapter 11 Cases*, 26 TULSA L.J. 523 (1991); Lawrence Ponoroff & F. Stephen Knippenberg, *The Implied Good Faith Filing Requirement: Sentinel of an Evolving Bankruptcy Policy*, 85 NW. U. L. REV. 919 (1991); H. Miles Cohn, *Good Faith and the Single Asset Debtor*, 62 AM. BANKR. L.J. 131 (1986); Daniel J. Tyukody, Comment, *Good Faith Inquiries Under the Bankruptcy Code: Treating the Symptom, Not the Cause*, 52 U. CHI. L. REV. 795 (1985); Eugene J. Di Donato, *Good Faith Reorganization Petitions: The Back Door Lets the Stranger In*, 16 CONN. L. REV. 1 (1983); Michael Ordin, *The Good Faith Principle in the Bankruptcy Code: A Case Study*, 38 BUS. LAW. 1795 (1983).

3. Another way lenders have sought to be able to continue with a foreclosure action, despite a borrower's filing of a bankruptcy, is by having the borrower sign a "waiver of the automatic stay" in the original loan documents, or in the documents the borrower signs in connection with a work-out of a loan in default. The key issue, of course, is whether a bankruptcy court will enforce the waiver of the automatic stay agreed to by the borrower/debtor before the filing of the bankruptcy petition. The answer is decidedly mixed among the court decisions. "The trend of recent case law . . . is that automatic-lift-of-stay provisions are neither per se enforceable in bankruptcy nor self-executing in favor of the lender. Such provisions will not bind third parties not a party to the agreement when the rights of such parties would be adversely affected and when cause for lift of the stay does not otherwise exist. Instead, bankruptcy courts likely will consider and evaluate the enforceability of such clauses in the context of the fact pattern of each individual case, including the existence, or non-existence, of the relevant factors set forth in recent bankruptcy cases [Ed. note: such as whether the debtor was a single asset real estate holding entity or owned a single parcel of real estate and the debtor had no realistic possibility of reorganization] . . . some courts limit enforcement of such waivers to single-asset real estate cases, and others have held that such waivers are per se enforceable, while still other courts will only enforce the provisions under specified conditions." Judith Greenstone Miller & John C. Murray, *Waivers of Automatic Stay: Are They Enforceable (And Does the New Bankruptcy Act Make A Difference)?* 41 REAL PROP., PROB. & TR. J. 357, 377–378 (Summer 2006).

4. Although Murray's overview article focused on the actions and counter-actions that take place between the debtor/borrower and mortgage lender, other important players are junior lien-holders and other creditors. Mortgage lenders, anticipating this future battleground, require that other proposed lien-holders and creditors of the borrower enter into inter-creditor agreements in which these other creditors agree to subordinate the priority of their liens and assign their voting rights to the senior lender if the mortgagor files, or there is filed against the mortgagor, a bankruptcy proceeding. The inter-creditor agree

ments also cover other related matters such as priority of payment from cash flow, priority of access to insurance and condemnation proceeds, amendments to loan documents, notice of default and cure rights, additional advances, standstill and forbearance agreements, and permitted refinancing. The issue of the enforceability of the subordination of priority and assignment of voting rights provisions in these intercreditors agreements is an important issue and the topic of another article by John C. Murray, *Enforceability of Intercreditor Agreements in Bankruptcy*, 19 No. 1 PRAC. REAL EST. LAW. 27 (Jan. 2003). In that article, Murray notes that the case law on these issues is sparse and contradictory, and concludes, "based on existing case law it is uncertain whether these strategies will be successful." *Id.* at 35. It is anticipated that as the number of mortgage loans that go into default rises in the years to come that more case law will develop on this issue. Do you think that the subordination and assignment of voting rights provisions should be enforced by bankruptcy courts? How do these types of provisions compare with the waiver of the automatic stay provisions?

5. Although Murray's overview article briefly discussed fraudulent conveyances and preferences, it is important to note that the borrower or its other creditors can attempt to invalidate the mortgage lien or foreclosure sale by arguing that it was a "fraudulent conveyance" or a "preference." As previously indicated, a transfer or grant of interest that occurs within one year of the bankruptcy filing must be for "reasonably equivalent value," and as previously discussed, the Supreme Court in *BFP v. Resolution Trust Corporation*, 114 S. Ct. 1757 (1994), ruled that foreclosure sales will be presumed to be for "reasonably equivalent value" only if they are conducted in accordance with state foreclosure laws. Another possible form of attack on the mortgage is to argue that the mortgage is an invalid preference under § 544 of the Bankruptcy Code. One of the elements for a preference is that the transfer is made for an antecedent debt. If the grant of the mortgage or assignment of rents is made contemporaneous with the making of the loan, then this element is not satisfied and the transfer cannot be set aside as a preference. It should also be noted that under § 544(a) (the "strong arm clause") of the Bankruptcy Code, the bankruptcy trustee can convert a secured claim into an unsecured claim if the relevant security interest would be invalid under state law against a hypothetical lien creditor or judgment creditor as of the date of the bankruptcy filing.

6. While the Murray article provides an excellent overview of (i) the bankruptcy process, (ii) the legal issues that arise during this process, (iii) the strategies that borrowers and lenders can use at each stage of the process, and (iv) the possibility of the borrower and key creditors entering into a "pre-packaged bankruptcy," it contains numerous details that are perhaps best understood when applied to an actual case. The materials that follow discuss in detail a famous U.S. Supreme Court bankruptcy law case, *203 North LaSalle Street Partnership*, which addressed two key issues: "cramdown" and the new value exception to the absolute priority rule. Later materials in this chapter also examine how the borrower in the FVACC could potentially use the bankruptcy

laws as a means to regain ground in reaction to a foreclosure action by FMB and provide an opportunity to apply the details in the Murray article (which primarily focuses on the lender's perspective) to an analysis from the borrower's perspective on whether the borrower should file a Chapter 11 Bankruptcy.

[c] More on Chapter 11 Bankruptcies and "Cramdown"

As previously noted, a borrower who files for a Chapter 11 reorganization will be given a certain time period to come up with a plan of reorganization. If the borrower's proposed plan satisfies various statutory requirements and is confirmed by the bankruptcy court, the plan will then govern how the mortgage lender's interest is to be paid and secured. Mortgage lenders complain that oftentimes they are placed in a worse position with respect to repayment of the loan through the confirmation of a reorganization plan that involves the "cramdown" of the mortgage lender's interest.

The following is an example of a potential "cramdown" of a mortgage lender's interest. Assume that the current balance due the lender on a loan is $10 million, but the value of the property has declined to $8 million. In a cramdown, the mortgage lender is classified as a secured creditor for only $8 million (the value of the collateral) and as an unsecured creditor for $2 million. The borrower can then propose a plan in which the mortgage is reduced to $8 million at the prevailing market rate for a similarly secured loan. The remaining debt of $2 million, as an unsecured debt, would be paid out at only a fraction of its full amount (say 10–20 cents on the dollar). In addition, a borrower who puts adequate, additional equity into the property (say $200,000) will be able to retain its interest in the property as well. Whether this type of reorganization plan would be confirmed depends in part on how a court interprets the "absolute priority rule" as well as the "new value corollary" to this rule. The best way to understand the current law on the absolute priority rule and new value exception is to explore a United States Supreme Court decision that addressed these matters in depth.

[i] Limitations on "Cramdown" in a Reorganization

In *Bank of America v. 203 North LaSalle Street Partnership*, 526 U.S. 434 (1999), the debtor/limited partnership proposed a plan of reorganization under Chapter 11 that was objected to by a secured creditor. The question addressed by the Court was the continuing relevance of the judicially created "new value corollary" following the enactment of the Bankruptcy Reform Act of 1978. 203 North LaSalle Street Partnership ("LaSalle") owned 15 floors of office space in a building in the central business district of Chicago. LaSalle owed Bank of America more than $93 million under a nonrecourse loan secured by a mortgage on the property that came due on January 3, 1995. In addition to the debt held by Bank of America, LaSalle had several other debts outstanding: one of the general partners held a second non-recourse mortgage on the property; $2.3 million in real estate taxes remained unpaid; and other non-inside creditors held $90,000 in trade claims. LaSalle was unable to repay Bank of America when the loan matured, and, following default, the bank started a foreclosure action in state court.

In the face of the foreclosure action, LaSalle considered its options. If the mortgage were foreclosed, the partnership would walk away with nothing since the value of the mortgaged property, $54.5 million, was less than the balance due the bank. More significant, however, was the fact that the partners would confront a tax liability estimated at $20 million. Because the loan was nonrecourse, the amount realized on the foreclosure would not be less than the amount of the outstanding loan. IRC § 7701(g); Treas. Reg. § 1.1001-2(a)(1). *See also Commissioner v. Tufts*, 461 U.S. 300 (1983). (*Tufts* also is discussed in § 3.05[2], *supra* and § 18.01 *infra*.) Furthermore, the nonrecourse nature of the debt in this context meant that the discharge of indebtedness provisions under § 108 of the Tax Code were unavailable. Consequently, in response to the foreclosure action, LaSalle filed for bankruptcy under the reorganization provisions of Chapter 11. By filing for bankruptcy rather than having the bank foreclose on the property, LaSalle's partners could postpone the significant tax liability. In addition, by contributing new capital for the partnership's interest in the reorganized debtor, the partners could retain control of the property and perhaps recover their original investment if the value of the property subsequently increased.

Because the value of the mortgaged property was less than the balance due the bank, Bank of America elected to have its secured claim treated as a secured claim and an unsecured claim under § 1111(b) of the Bankruptcy Code. Other than the property, the only asset held by LaSalle was a cash account consisting of pre-petition rents that amounted to $3.1 million. LaSalle proposed the following reorganization:

(1) The Bank's $54.5 million secured claim would be paid in full between 7 and 10 years after the original 1995 repayment date. Payment would consist of a prompt cash payment of $1,149,500 and a secured, 7-year note, extendable at the debtor's option.

(2) The Bank's $38.5 million unsecured deficiency claim would be discharged for an estimated 16% of its present value. This expected yield was based upon the bankruptcy court's projection that a sale or refinancing of the property on the tenth anniversary of the plan's confirmation would produce a $19 million distribution to the Bank.

(3) The remaining unsecured claims of $90,000, held by the outside trade creditors, would be paid in full, without interest, on the effective date of the plan.

(4) Certain former partners of the debtor would contribute $6.125 million in new capital over the course of five years (the contribution being worth some $4.1 million in present value), in exchange for the partnership's entire ownership of the reorganized debtor.

Bank of America objected to the proposed plan, and LaSalle requested that the bankruptcy court impose the plan on the Bank in a process known as a judicial "cramdown" under § 1129(b). The Bank contended that § 1129(b) could not be applied because the plan was not "fair and equitable" as required under § 1129(b)(1), citing § 1129(b)(2)(B)(ii), which imposes the so-called "absolute priority rule." Under the absolute priority rule, a plan is fair and equitable to a class of dissenting creditors only if "the holder of any claim or interest that is junior to the claims of such class will not receive or retain under the plan on account of such junior claim or interest any property." The Bank argued that the partners' ability to retain an equity interest in the property under the reorganization plan was "on account of" their junior interest as partners.

The bankruptcy court disagreed with Bank of America, and the Seventh Circuit Court of Appeals affirmed the bankruptcy court's decision. *Bank of America v. 203 North LaSalle Street Partnership*, 126 F.3d 955 (7th Cir. 1997). The Seventh Circuit ruled that the proposed plan did not run afoul of the absolute priority rule because of the new value corollary developed by the U.S. Supreme Court in *Case v. Los Angeles Lumber Products Co.*, 308 U.S. 106 (1939). According to the Seventh Circuit, the new value corollary provided that the objection of an impaired senior class does not bar junior claim holders from receiving or retaining property interests in the debtor after reorganization if the junior claim holders contribute new capital in money or money's worth, reasonably equivalent to the property's value, and necessary for successful reorganization of the restructured enterprise. The Seventh Circuit held that

> when an old equity holder retains an equity interest in the reorganized debtor by meeting the requirements of the new value corollary, he is not receiving or retaining that interest "on account of" his prior equitable ownership of the debtor. Rather, he is allowed to participate in the reorganized entity "on account of" a new, substantial, necessary and fair infusion of capital.

203 North LaSalle Street Partnership, 126 F.3d at 964. The Seventh Circuit's approach was similar to that adopted by the Ninth Circuit in an earlier decision. *Bonner Mall Partnership v. U.S. Bancorp Mortgage Co.*, 2 F.3d 899 (9th Cir. 1993), *cert. granted*, 510 U.S. 1039 (1994), *appeal dismissed as moot*, 513 U.S. 18 (1994).

The Supreme Court reversed the decision of the Seventh Circuit. Without directly deciding the question, the Court accepted the argument that the new value corollary is not inconsistent with the language of § 1129(b)(2)(B)(ii) and that the "on account of language" could not be interpreted as excluding junior claimants per se from receiving or retaining property under a plan of reorganization unless all senior claimants were paid in full. However, it concluded that the partners' exclusive right to propose a reorganization plan constituted property that they received "on account of" their prior interests. The Court rejected the argument that its approach should be affected by the fact that this type of property had value to the partners alone because of the potential tax liability.

> While it may be argued that the opportunity [to propose an exclusive plan of reorganization] has no market value, being significant only to old equity holders owing to their potential tax liability, such an argument avails the Debtor nothing, for several reasons. It is to avoid just such arguments that the law is settled that any otherwise cognizable property interest must be treated as sufficiently valuable to be recognized under the Bankruptcy Code. . . . Even aside from that rule, the assumption that no one but the Debtor's partners might pay for such an opportunity would obviously support no inference that it is valueless, let alone that it should not be treated as property. And, finally, the source in the tax law of the opportunity's value to the partners implies in no way that it lacks value to others. It might, indeed, be valuable to another precisely as a way to keep the Debtor from implementing a plan that would avoid a Chapter 7 liquidation.

203 North LaSalle Street Partnership, 526 U.S. at 455. The Court concluded that the new value corollary coupled with the absolute priority rule required "some form of market valuation . . . to test the adequacy of an old equity holder's proposed contribution." *Id.* at 458. Unfortunately, the Court did not decide whether a market valuation requirement would be satisfied only by offering an opportunity to others to offer competing plans or to bid for the same interest that the junior claimants were to receive or retain.

[ii] Judicial Requirements for Using Cramdown in a Reorganization

The Court's decision in *203 North LaSalle* reached a result similar to that of the Second and Fourth Circuits in *Coltex Loop Central Three Partners, L.P. v. BT/SAP Pool C Associates, L.P.*, 138 F.3d 39 (2d Cir. 1998), and *Travelers Insurance Co. v. Bryson Properties XVIII*, 961 F.2d 496 (4th Cir. 1992), *cert. denied*, 506 U.S. 866 (1992), both of which refused to confirm a plan of reorganization where the valuation of the retained equity interest was not the result of a competitive bidding process. How this new requirement will be implemented remains to be seen. *See* Barber & Zimmerman, *Refining the Absolute Priority Rule and the New Value Exception*, 29 Colo. Law. 39 (April 2000); Kuney, *The Supreme Court and New Value: The Elusive Search for "True Value" and Neutral Bargaining Devices; Market Value vs. Judicial Value*, 8 J. Bankr. L. & Prac. 505 (1999); Miller & Murray, *The "New Value" Exception: Myth or Reality After* Bank of America National Trust & Savings Association v. 203 N. LaSalle Street Partnership? 104 Com. L. Rev. 147 (1999). One commentator has suggested that the implications of the Supreme Court's decision are vastly overstated in any event, since the reorganization plans in fewer than 3% of the cases involving the new value corollary are ever confirmed. Carlson & Williams, *The Truth About the New Value Exception to Bankruptcy's Absolute Priority Rule*, 21 Cardozo L. Rev. 1303 (2000).

[d] Bankruptcy and the Fox Valley Auto Care Center LLC

Later, Donna Smith will inform Sam Nader that FMB is insisting on repayment of the matured loan and has threatened to exercise all rights and remedies available to it (see § 16.04, *infra*). Sam will be asked to prepare a memorandum that considers whether it would be advantageous for the Fox Valley Auto Care Center LLC to file for bankruptcy law protection. In light of what you have read so far, do you think that Sam should recommend this to his client? There are, of course, other alternatives available to Regent in responding to FMB. The next two sections, loan modification/consensual transfer of the property and lender liability claims, will explore these options as well.

[3] Loan Modification or Consensual Transfer of the Mortgaged Property

As previously addressed in the Kunkel article in § 16.01[1], how a lender will respond to a borrower's default will vary based upon the reason why the borrower defaulted and the nature of the relationship between the lender and the borrower. If the problem can be corrected, and there is still a good relationship between the lender and the borrower, then a lender is more likely to agree to forbear from exercising the rights available to it. Instead, the lender may be willing to modify the loan terms to enable the borrower to perform the loan. Recall the example of the borrower who needed to reduce interest payments for six months until a new tenant could replace a tenant who abandoned its space. Conversely, sometimes both the lender and the borrower realize that the problem cannot be corrected and that the borrower has no equity in the property that it should fight to keep (although tax liabilities may continue to cause the borrower to try to defer the loss of the property). In this circumstance, the borrower and lender may be best off if they agree to a transfer of the mortgaged property to the lender, especially if it can be structured in a way that reduces the tax consequences to the borrower. The lender usually gives the borrower some form of consideration for agreeing to the transfer (such as a release of personal liability on the debt), since the lender can thereby avoid the time and expense of a foreclosure action. In a nutshell, those are the basic reasons why borrowers and lenders enter into loan modifications or consensual transfers of real estate. The next issue to address is what special issues borrowers and lenders should be aware of if they are considering these options.

One key concern is to make certain that there are no liens that have arisen on the mortgaged property. If there are junior liens made without the consent of the senior lender, this is probably a default under the senior loan documents and could be another reason to foreclose rather than do a loan workout. In addition, any modification of the loan without the consent of the junior lienholder that "prejudices" a junior lienholder will lose its priority against the junior lienholder to the extent prejudiced. *See, e.g., Shane v. Winter Hill Federal Savings and Loan Association*, 397 Mass. 479, 492 N.E. 2d 92 (1986); *Lennar Northeast Partners v. Buice and Tahoe Vista Inn and Marina*, 49 Cal. App. 4th 1576, 57 Cal Rptr. 2d 435 (Ct. App. 3d Dist. 1996). To avoid this result, before modifying the loan, the lender should check to make sure there are no junior lienholders. If there are, and the lender still wants to make the loan modification, it should obtain the consent of any junior lienholders to such loan modification. Such consent would not be necessary if the lender is only making an obligatory future advance or, at least according to one court, even if the lender makes a future optional advance without actual knowledge of the existence of the junior lienholder's interest. *See La Cholla Group Inc. v. Timm*, 173 Ariz. 490, 844 P.2d 657 (Ct. App. Ariz. 1992). In a jurisdiction taking this position, and under that circumstance, the mortgage lender could perhaps be better off not checking title before the loan modification, but this seems a risky tactic.

The presence of junior lienholders can also complicate the lender's and borrower's ability to do a consensual transfer of the mortgaged property to resolve the loan default. A foreclosure sale should extinguish a junior lien, but a deed-in-lieu of foreclosure will not. To avoid this problem, lenders do not cancel the note and release the mortgage but instead sign a covenant not to sue the borrower in exchange for a deed to the property. In addition, to avoid the problem of the mortgage extinguishing due to a merger of the mortgage interest with the fee interest, the deed is granted to an entity related to the mortgage lender rather than to the mortgage lender directly.

There are numerous additional considerations that the borrower and lender must address when deciding whether and how to work out a problem loan. Some of these considerations were discussed earlier in this Chapter. For example, once the decision is made to modify the loan or do a form of consensual transfer, there are many options available to the parties to structure the deal in a manner that minimizes adverse income and transfer taxes. Income tax problems posed by cancellation of indebtedness income resulting from a loan modification have been discussed in Chapter 3, Section 3.05[6], and capital gains taxes triggered by a voluntary sale or foreclosure sale are discussed in Chapter 17. For a detailed analysis of the decision-making process generally, the problems that arise, and strategies for resolving these problems, see *Consensual Transfers of Distressed Real Estate* (Debra Stark ed. ABA 1998).

[4] Lender Liability Claims

[a] Overview

In analyzing what options the borrower has after defaulting in the performance of the loan terms, the borrower should also consider whether she has any defenses based on a lender liability claim. Indeed, as the Kunkel article (see § 16.01[1], *supra*) suggests, the lender's assessment of any loan in default requires that the lender examine the records in the file, as well as any allegations of fact concerning the relationship between the borrower and lender that might subject the lender to liability for damages to the borrower. When difficulties arise in the relationship between lender and borrower, the borrower will frequently go on the offensive and allege that the lender, through its agents, took certain actions, or refrained from taking certain actions, to the borrower's detriment. With the mortgage for the Fox Valley Auto Care Center, for example, Regent claimed that the loan officers from First Mortgage Bank had previously told Regent that FMB would extend the loan if no permanent lender had been found by the time the construction loan matured. Borrowers have in some states successfully litigated claims of breach by the lender of such oral contracts. *See, e.g., Landes Construction Co. v. Royal Bank of Canada*, 833 F.2d 1365 (9th Cir. 1987) (awarding the plaintiff $18.5 million for breach of the lender's oral agreement to provide acquisition financing of a real estate project); *Silverdale Hotel Associates v. Lomas & Nettleton Co.*, 677 P.2d 773 (Wash. App. 1984) (lender found liable for disbursements under an oral agreement, the terms of which were not inconsistent with the written construction loan agreement); *Schwachman v. Greenbaum Mortgage Co.*, 450 N.E.2d 750 (Ill. App. Ct. 1983) (lender found liable in the amount of $110,000 in lost profits for failure to provide financing under an oral agreement).

Claims by borrowers against lenders in default and workout situations are frequently referred to as "lender liability" claims. Although these claims may take a variety of forms under the facts of a given situation, they generally fall into one of the following five categories: (1) breach of the duty of good faith and fair dealing implied by most courts as a term in any commercial contract; (2) tortious breach of the duty of good faith and fair dealing; (3) breach of a fiduciary duty owed by the lender to the borrower; (4) intentional interference with contractual duties or economic relations with third parties; and (5) fraud or duress. Lender liability claims such as these were commonly asserted in litigation in the late 1980s and early 1990s during a recession that hit the real estate industry, causing loan defaults across the nation. We think it is likely that lender liability claims are going to be raised as borrowers and lenders work their way through the current real estate recession.

In the face of such claims, lenders fought in both the courts and the legislatures for relief. Appellate courts were sympathetic to lenders and frequently held that the duty of good faith and fair dealing was not violated when the lender proceeded in accordance with the express terms of the loan documents. The decision of the Oregon Supreme Court in *Uptown Heights Associates L.P. v. SeaFirst Corp.*, 891 P.2d 639 (Ore. 1995), is an example of one such decision. *See also Kham & Nate's Shoes No. 2 v. First Bank*, 908 F.2d 1351 (7th Cir. 1990) ("Although courts often refer to the obligation of good faith that exists in every contractual relation, . . . this is not an invitation to the court to decide whether one party ought to have exercised privileges expressly reserved in the document"); *Gaul v. Olympia Fitness Center*, 623 N.E.2d 1281 (Ohio App. 1993) (lender cannot be found to have acted in bad faith where it "did nothing more than stand on its rights to require payment of [the borrower's] contractual obligations according to its terms"); *Gilmore v. Ute City Mortgage Co.*, 660 F. Supp. 437 (D. Colo. 1986) (concluding that, under Colorado law, the implied covenant of good faith and fair dealing cannot override express contractual terms). *But see White Stone Partners, LP v. Piper Jaffray Cos.*, 978 F. Supp. 878 (D. Minn. 1997) (concluding that the duty of good faith and fair dealing may be breached when lender's use of a discretionary term in a loan commitment was pretextual). A number of courts also refused to find that fiduciary duties existed in typical borrower/lender situations or that tort actions were available outside of cases involving outrageous conduct by the lender. *See, e.g., Ed Schory & Sons v. Francis*, 662 N.E.2d 1074 (Ohio 1996); *Batterman v. Wells Fargo Ag. Credit Corp.*, 802 P.2d 1112 (Colo. Ct. App. 1990); *Central Bank of Montana v. Eystad*, 710 P.2d 710 (Mont. 1985); *Wagner v. Benson*, 161 Cal. Rptr. 516 (Cal. Ct. App. 1980). Lenders were also successful in lobbying legislatures to enact statutory provisions requiring that lending and credit arrangements must be in writing to be enforceable. *See, e.g.*, Tex. Bus. & Com. Code Ann. § 26.02 (Vernon 1999); 815 ILCS 160/3 (Smith-Hurd 1999). *See also* John L. Culhane, Jr. & Dean C. Gramlich, *Lender Liability Limitation Amendments to State Statutes of Fraud*, 45 Bus. Law. 1779 (1990).

In the face of a rising tide of lender liability claims, lenders also moved to protect themselves from such claims by including certain provisions in the loan documents. Lenders prudently inserted provisions in loan commitments that such commitments contained the exclusive terms detailing the relationship between the borrower and lender and adopted procedures for careful review of all post-default correspondence with the borrower. Because of a concern that lenders are viewed as "deep pockets" by jurors, lenders have required that loan documents include provisions under which the borrower waives any right to a jury trial. Some lenders have also required that loan documents contain arbitration provisions in order to settle any disputes out of court. In addition, lenders have been cautioned to ensure that all steps taken after default comply with the provisions of the loan documentation and are in conformity with standard and customary lending practices. *See generally* James W. Hubbell, *Defending Lender Liability Suits*, 19 Colo. Law. 2409 (1990).

[b] Judicial Acceptance of Lender Liability Claims

UPTOWN HEIGHTS ASSOCIATES L.P. v. SEAFIRST CORPORATION

891 P.2d 639 (Ore. 1995)

GRABER, J.

This case involves a loan by a bank to a developer. The developer claims that the bank breached its duty of good faith and intentionally interfered with the developer's economic relations. The circuit court dismissed the complaint; the Court of Appeals reversed with respect to the intentional interference claims. We hold that the developer failed to state a claim with respect to the first through fourth claims for relief but that it stated a claim with respect to the fifth claim for relief. . . .

The present controversy arose from a construction loan made to plaintiffs, Uptown Heights Associates Limited Partnership; Leavitt, Shay (Uptown), Inc.; and Leavitt, Shay & Company, Inc. (collectively referred to as "Uptown" in this opinion), by defendant Seattle-First National Bank (Bank).[3]

In 1988 or 1989, Bank learned of Uptown's plans to construct a "high-end" apartment complex in Portland. Bank aggressively solicited Uptown and, on June 20, 1989, Uptown entered into a construction loan agreement with Bank. Uptown borrowed $7,500,000, with interest at one-half of one percent over prime. The loan was secured by a deed of trust on the land and buildings that comprised the apartment complex.

Under the terms of the loan, Uptown was to pay monthly interest until the loan matured. The principal amount was due at maturity, January 1, 1991, with a provision for two six-month extensions until January 1992.

Soon after construction of the apartment complex was completed, the rental market dropped dramatically from Uptown's pre-construction forecasts. For that reason, Uptown encountered difficulty in meeting its obligation to make its monthly interest payments on the loan. In October 1990, Bank agreed to one six-month extension on the loan. Although rental rates improved in late 1990 and early 1991, Uptown was unable to make its full interest payment to Bank in April 1991. Bank had the apartment complex appraised by an independent appraiser; the appraised value was $8,850,000, slightly more than $1 million above the outstanding balance of Bank's loan to Uptown.

Uptown and Bank continued to negotiate concerning the loan. Bank personnel who handled the loan assured Uptown that Bank would work with Uptown to resolve any problems surrounding the loan. Despite those assurances, in June 1991, Bank elected not to grant the second six-month extension. Bank transferred the Uptown account to a department for problem loans known as "Special Credits." Bank also refused to lend money for an unrelated joint venture project involving Uptown (among others) unless Uptown were removed as a participant. Bank

---

[3] According to the complaint, defendant Seattle-First National Bank acted as defendant SeaFirst Corporation's agent in connection with the events at issue. The roles of the two defendants are interconnected, and our references to "Bank" include both.

personnel began to threaten foreclosure on the apartment complex. That pressure forced Uptown to seek a quick sale to try to avoid the harm to its investment and business reputation that would flow from a foreclosure.

Uptown told Bank that it planned to sell the apartment complex and notified Bank that a foreclosure action would damage or destroy Uptown's chances of selling the complex and avoiding a foreclosure sale. Uptown told Bank that potential buyers would have no interest in buying the property from Uptown if they knew that it was threatened with foreclosure, because buyers typically wait to try to buy such a property at a bargain price after foreclosure.

On July 29, 1991, Uptown received an offer to purchase the apartment complex from a buyer in Bend. On July 31, 1991, Uptown notified Bank of that offer. On August 2, 1991, Bank initiated a foreclosure action, filed for appointment of a receiver, and scheduled a trustee's sale for December 20, 1991. Before the hearing on the appointment of a receiver, Uptown provided Bank with the purchase offer that it had received. Bank refused to postpone the hearing to permit further negotiations between Uptown and the offeror and, as a result, the offeror did not proceed further.

The receivership hearing was held on August 16, 1991. The court appointed a receiver chosen by Bank. Uptown continued to look for a buyer for the apartment complex to avoid the harm that would result to its business reputation from a foreclosure sale and to attempt to recover some of its investment. On October 22, 1991, Uptown notified Bank that it had received a second offer for the apartment complex, which would result in a price of between $8.1 and $8.6 million. Uptown also asked that the receiver be replaced immediately. Bank responded to the October 22 notice on November 7, 1991. At that time, Bank refused to extend the foreclosure sale to permit steps to be followed toward closing the sale proposed by Uptown.

Uptown continued to negotiate with the second potential buyer and provided Bank with a copy of a signed purchase agreement. Uptown again asked Bank to postpone the foreclosure sale, this time for the purpose of allowing the second potential buyer to arrange for financing. Bank refused. Uptown and the second potential buyer were unable to work out an agreement under which they could meet Bank's deadline for a full payoff before the foreclosure sale. The foreclosure sale took place on December 20, 1991. Bank bid $7.8 million (the outstanding balance of the loan) and took title to the apartment complex. In January 1992, Bank entered into a purchase and sale agreement with the same second potential buyer for $7.8 million. Uptown received nothing.

Uptown brought this action against Bank, raising one claim for "breach of contractual duty of good faith and fair dealing," one claim for "tortious breach of the duty of good faith and fair dealing," and three claims for intentional interference with economic relations. The circuit court dismissed the complaint . . . on the ground that Uptown failed to state facts sufficient to constitute a claim. The Court of Appeals, sitting *en banc*, affirmed as to the duty of good faith claims, but reversed as to the claims for intentional interference with economic relations. . . .

For the following reasons, we now affirm in part and reverse in part the decision of the Court of Appeals.

IMPLIED CONTRACTUAL DUTY OF GOOD FAITH

(FIRST CLAIM FOR RELIEF)

This court recently addressed the scope of the duty of good faith in *Pacific First Bank v. New Morgan Park Corp.*, 319 Ore. 342, 876 P.2d 761 (1994). *Pacific First Bank* involved a lease agreement that prevented a tenant from transferring the lease without the landlord's approval. In that case, the tenant merged into its wholly owned subsidiary, thus effecting a transfer of the lease requiring the landlord's consent. The landlord refused to grant consent. This court held that, although a duty of good faith applied to the lease agreement, the landlord did not breach that duty, "because the landlord's refusal did not contravene the 'reasonable expectations' of the parties as manifested in the express terms of the lease agreement at issue."

This court reiterated in *Pacific First Bank* that every contract contains an implied duty of good faith. That duty "is to be applied in a manner that will effectuate the reasonable contractual expectations of the parties." But, "it is only the *objectively* reasonable expectations of [the] parties that will be examined in determining whether the obligation of good faith has been met." *Tolbert v. First National Bank*, 312 Ore. 485, 494, 823 P.2d 965 (1991) (emphasis added) (footnote omitted); *see also Pacific First Bank*, 319 Ore. at 352 (quoting *Tolbert* with approval). In *Pacific First Bank*, the court also restated the precept that the duty of good faith cannot serve to contradict an express contractual term:

> This court has emphasized that
>
> "the obligation of good faith does not vary the substantive terms of the bargain . . . , nor does it provide a remedy for an unpleasantly motivated act that is expressly permitted by contract. . . ." *U.S. National Bank v. Boge*, 311 Ore. 550, 567, 814 P.2d 1082 (1991).

Pacific First Bank, 319 Ore. at 352–53.

Under the foregoing established principles, if a written contract between the parties expressly allows for a particular remedy by one of the parties, in the face of a specified breach, the parties' objectively "reasonable expectations" under the contract include the invocation of that remedy in the face of that breach. The party invoking its express, written contractual right does not, merely by so doing, violate its duty of good faith.

The agreement between Uptown and Bank, as pleaded by Uptown, gave Bank the right to foreclose should Uptown default on the loan. Uptown also pleaded that it defaulted on the loan. Uptown did not plead any additional facts that would support a claim for violation of the duty of good faith. For example, Uptown did not plead that Bank *caused the default* to occur, which in turn gave rise to the contractual right to foreclose. Neither did Uptown plead that Bank failed to follow the proper *method* of foreclosure.

Uptown argues that, when a contract gives one party discretion as to when to invoke a bargained-for remedy, the circumstances giving rise to that invocation may permit a claim for breach of the duty of good faith. Uptown argues that this duty was breached when Bank refused to grant the second loan extension and continued to seek foreclosure, because those acts would harm Uptown, while Bank would derive no benefit. In support of its argument, Uptown relies on statements made by this court in *Best v. U.S. National Bank*, 303 Ore. 557, 739 P.2d 554 (1987). Reliance on *Best* is misplaced in this context.

In *Best*, the court considered whether a bank's fees for processing nonsufficient fund (NSF) checks were so high as to violate the bank's duty of good faith in the performance of its account agreement with its depositors. Under the bank's contracts with its customers, the bank "had the contractual discretion to set its . . . fees." Because the court concluded that there was a "genuine issue of material fact whether the Bank set its . . . fees in accordance with the reasonable expectations of the parties," the court held that the defendant's motion for summary judgment should not have been granted on that issue. In reaching that conclusion, the court stated:

> When one party to a contract is given discretion in the performance of some aspect of the contract, the parties ordinarily contemplate that that discretion will be exercised for particular purposes. If the discretion is exercised for purposes not contemplated by the parties, the party exercising discretion has performed in bad faith.

Id. at 563.

Relying on *Best*, Uptown argues that the underlying purpose of Bank's power to foreclose was to secure its loan. That was the reasonable expectation of the parties when they bargained for the foreclosure provision in the contract. Because the value of the property was in excess of the loan balance and because Uptown had located a prospective buyer who was willing to purchase the property for a price in excess of the balance, Uptown argues that "a jury may infer that [Bank] acted for some other purpose not consistent with the parties' expectations when they agreed that [Bank] would have this" contractual right to foreclose.

Best is inapposite, because in that summary judgment case that bank had the discretion to fill in an open price term, and no method of setting the NSF fee was spelled out in the depositors' contracts. "*Assuming that there was no agreement* [about the method of setting the NSF fee], the question before us is whether there is a genuine issue of material fact whether the Bank set its NSF fees in good faith." After examining the evidence before the court on summary judgment, the court concluded that there was a genuine issue of fact concerning the method by which that bank would exercise its discretion to set an NSF fee.

By contrast, in this case, there was a specific agreement. The loan agreement as pleaded by Uptown authorizes foreclosure for any default, not merely for a default that jeopardizes security.

More to the point than *Best* is *Tolbert*, in which the contract contained an express price term. In *Tolbert*, as in *Best*, this court addressed whether a bank had breached its duty of good faith to its depositors in setting and revising the fees that it charged to depositors for NSF checks. *Tolbert* originally was accepted as a companion case to *Best*. In *Tolbert*, the court affirmed the trial court's grant of summary judgment precisely because the bank's customers were apprised of the fees that would be applied to their accounts when they entered their contracts with the bank. The court in *Tolbert* wrote that

> the expectations of [the parties to a contract] are irrelevant if they have agreed to the [express terms of the contract that are at issue]. . . . [T]he

> *Best* court analyzed the reasonable expectations of the parties only after determining that it could not assume the existence of an agreement.

Tolbert, 312 Ore. at 492.

Here, Uptown has pleaded that it defaulted on the interest payments that it was required to make under the loan and that the remedies pursued by Bank are expressly permitted by the parties' written contract in the event of such a default. Uptowns pleading does not suggest that the contract contained any other precondition on Bank's right to foreclose, except for such a default. The contractually described purpose of Bank's power to foreclose was, then, to remedy a default. Thus, "[i]n the present case, the reasonable contractual expectations of the parties are shown, by the unambiguous terms" of the contract as those terms are relayed in Uptown's pleadings. Under those terms, 'the parties agreed to — that is, reasonably expected — a unilateral, unrestricted exercise of discretion" in Bank's choice of foreclosure as a remedy should Uptown breach the contract by failing to make its mortgage payments.

Accordingly, the trial court did not err when it dismissed the first claim for relief. The Court of Appeals properly sustained that dismissal.

TORTIOUS BREACH OF THE DUTY OF GOOD FAITH

(SECOND CLAIM FOR RELIEF)

Uptown next argues that the Court of Appeals erred when it affirmed the circuit court's dismissal of a claim for "tortious breach of the duty of good faith." Uptown alleged that there was "a special relationship of trust and confidence" between Bank and Uptown, imposing on Bank "a duty not to harm [Uptown's] interests by its conduct." Bank allegedly breached that duty by initiating a foreclosure action and seeking a court-ordered receivership when such a remedy would harm Uptown and be of no benefit to Bank.

In *Georgetown Realty v. The Home Ins. Co.*, 313 Ore. 97, 831 P.2d 7 (1992), an insured brought a claim against an insurer, alleging that the insurer was negligent when it failed to settle the third party's claim against the insured. This court held that, when the insurer undertook the responsibility to defend the insured, the law imposed a duty on the insurer, independent of the insurance policy, to use reasonable care; the failure of the insurer to exercise reasonable care thus gave rise to a claim for negligence. The court reasoned:

> The lesson to be drawn from this court's cases . . . is this: When the relationship involved is between contracting parties, and the gravamen of the complaint is that one party caused damage to the other by negligently performing its obligations under the contract, then, and even though the relationship between the parties arises out of the contract, the injured party may bring a claim for negligence *if the other party is subject to a standard of care independent of the terms of the contract*. If the plaintiff's claim is based solely on a breach of a provision in the contract, which itself spells out the party's obligation, then the remedy normally will be only in contract, with contract measures of damages and contract statutes of limitation. That is so whether the breach of contract was negligent, intentional, or otherwise. (emphasis added).

Uptown has pleaded that "[t]here was a special relationship of trust and confidence" between it and Bank, because of their past "course of dealing," which created a standard of care independent of the contract. Uptown's allegations fall into four categories:

(1) Uptown alleged that Bank had a selfish incentive for entering into the loan transaction. (For example, Uptown alleged that "[Bank's] personnel used [Uptown] as a means to satisfy their personal and professional goals" and that Bank "advertised [Uptown] as one of its special customers.")

(2) Uptown alleged that Bank negotiated aggressively toward the loan agreement and, in the course of those negotiations, made assurances to Uptown that Bank wanted Uptown to succeed. (For example, Uptown alleged that Bank "aggressively solicited the . . . loan, by telling the principals of [Uptown] that [Bank] wanted to continue to be its primary bank and lender [and] that they were the kind of customers [Bank] wanted." Uptown also alleged that Bank expressed assurance "that it would work with [Uptown] to make the project a success.")

(3) Uptown alleged that Bank had waived its contractual rights in other contracts with Uptown. (For example, Uptown alleged that, "despite its contractual rights to do so, [Bank] did not enforce reporting and monitoring requirements on several [Uptown] and related entity loans, personal lines of credit or other agreements.")

(4) Uptown alleged that one of the principals and his family had a long personal relationship with Bank, during which Bank "did not strictly enforce its rights, conducted business informally and treated [the principal] as a special customer. [Bank] repeatedly told [the principal] that it would not do this, except for his special relationship with [Bank]."

Reading the allegations of the complaint in the light most favorable to Uptown, and giving Uptown the benefit of all favorable inferences, none of those allegations suggests a standard of care imposed on Bank in favor of Uptown, apart from the contract. The first two kinds of allegations suggest, to the contrary, that Bank had an arm's-length, commercial relationship of creditor to debtor with Uptown. The facts that Bank used aggressive sales tactics, that it made commercial use of its customer relationship with Uptown, and that its employees sought advancement from that commercial relationship do not impose a standard of care on Bank that is higher than that ordinarily applied to debtor-creditor relationships.

The third and fourth kinds of allegations suggest, at most, that Uptown and one of the principals (who is not an individually named plaintiff) had acquired a contractual right to expect forbearance with respect to other contracts, not at issue here. Uptown did not allege that the parties' past course of dealing resulted in any modification to the terms of the loan agreement at issue. Neither did Uptown allege that the parties' past course of dealing was itself of a fiduciary nature.

To summarize, none of Uptown's allegations suggests a standard of care imposed on Bank in favor of Uptown, apart from the loan agreement. In the absence of a standard of care independent of the contract, Bank was under no obligation to refrain from invoking its contractual right to foreclose after default.

The trial court did not err when it dismissed the second claim for relief, and the Court of Appeals properly sustained that dismissal.

TORTIOUS INTERFERENCE WITH ECONOMIC RELATIONS

(THIRD, FOURTH, AND FIFTH CLAIMS FOR RELIEF)

Uptown's third, fourth, and fifth claims for relief are for tortious interference with economic relations. We separate our discussion of the fifth claim from our discussion of the other two, because it raises different issues.

A. *Third and Fourth Claims for Relief*

In its third and fourth claims, Uptown contends that Bank interfered with contractual relations between Uptown and a prospective "buyer for the Uptown Heights Apartments." To state a claim for intentional interference with economic relations, a party must allege: (1) the existence of a valid business relationship or expectancy, (2) intentional interference with that relationship, (3) by a third party, (4) accomplished through improper means or for an improper purpose, (5) a causal effect between the interference and damage to economic relations, and (6) damages. *Straube v. Larson*, 287 Ore. 357, 360–61, 600 P.2d 371 (1979); *Wampler v. Palmerton*, 250 Ore. 65, 73–76, 439 P.2d 601 (1968). The dispositive issue here is the fourth element, the accomplishment of an interference through improper means or for an improper purpose.

It is settled that "[e]ither the pursuit of an improper objective of harming plaintiff or the use of wrongful means that in fact cause injury to plaintiff's contractual or business relationships may give rise to a tort claim for those injuries." *Top Service Body Shop v. Allstate Ins. Co.*, 283 Ore. 201, 205, 582 P.2d 1365 (1978). But, in order to prevail, a plaintiff must establish

> not only . . . that defendant intentionally interfered with his business relationship but also that defendant had a duty of non-interference; i.e., that he interfered for an improper purpose rather than for a legitimate one, or that defendant used improper means which resulted in injury to plaintiff. Therefore, a case is made out which entitles plaintiff to go to a jury only when interference resulting in injury to another is wrongful by some measure beyond the fact of the interference itself.

Straube, 287 Ore. at 361.

Uptown makes no allegation of improper means here. Uptown alleges only an improper purpose. The essence of Uptown's argument is that a party who invokes an express contractual remedy by proper means still may be liable for intentional interference with economic relations if that party simply has a malevolent reason for enforcing its written contract. We disagree. When a party invokes an express contractual remedy in circumstances specified in the written contract — conduct that reflects, by definition, the reasonable expectations of the parties — that party cannot be liable for intentional interference with economic relations based solely on that party's reason for invoking the express contractual remedy. That is because, if the defendant has interfered with the plaintiff's economic relations, the defendant has done so for a "legitimate" purpose, *Straube*, 287 Ore. at 361 — invocation of an express, written contractual remedy — in such circumstances.[5]

---

[5] Our holding is limited to the "improper purpose" prong of the tort.

A contrary ruling would contravene public policy and undermine the stability of contractual relations. As this court's decision in *Pacific First Bank* made clear, courts will not read implied terms into a contract if those terms would contradict the express terms of the contract. It would be anomalous to hold that a party to a contract nonetheless must defend a tort claim when a complaint shows that the party did precisely what the party was entitled to do under the contract. "Economic relations are controlled by contract[,] and the public [as well as the individual contracting party] has an interest in maintaining the security of such transactions." *Wampler*, 250 Ore. at 73.

Uptown's third and fourth claims for relief were properly dismissed by the trial court. The Court of Appeals erred when it reversed that dismissal.

B. *Fifth Claim for Relief*

Uptown's fifth claim for relief alleges that Bank interfered with economic relations between Uptown and Wright Runstad & Co. (WRC), a third party negotiating with Bank for a loan. Uptown alleges that Bank "made funding in a major unrelated project with [WRC] in Bellevue, Washington, contingent on removing [Uptown] as its joint venture partner." Uptown also alleges: "The defendants' motive in such interference was to injure the business relations to the detriment of plaintiffs[,] and defendants acted in bad faith." Bank argues that Uptown did not sufficiently plead improper means or improper purpose.[6]

The general rule is that, ordinarily, one may refuse to deal with another and not be liable in tort for that refusal. See, e.g., *Tolbert*, 312 Ore. at 492–93 (approving of a bank's policy of not entering into a contract with a depositor if the depositor did not agree to the terms offered by the bank). Prior decisions by this court have not addressed the specific question whether a refusal to deal with another can be the basis of liability for the tort of intentional interference with economic relations. However, the Restatement provides some guidance. See *Top Service Body Shop*, 283 Ore. at 205–10 (looking to text and comments in Restatement for assistance in formulating and applying tort of intentional interference with economic relations); *Straube*, 287 Ore. at 361 (same).

The Restatement (Second) of Torts § 766 (1979), defines the tort of "Intentional Interference with Performance of Contract by Third Person." Two comments to that section discuss a "refusal to deal." Comment b states:

> The rule stated in this Section does not apply to a mere refusal to deal. Deliberately and at his pleasure, one may ordinarily refuse to deal with another, and the conduct is not regarded as improper, subjecting the actor to liability.

Restatement (Second) of Torts § 766, comment b at 8. Comment *l* addresses "inducement by refusal to deal":

> A refusal to deal is one means by which a person may induce another to commit a breach of his contract with a third person. Thus A may induce B to break his contract with C by threatening not to enter into, or to sever, business relations with B unless B does break the contract. This situation

---

[6] Bank has not argued that the "third party" element of this tort is lacking with respect to Bank's refusal to deal with the joint venture of which Uptown was a constituent part.

> frequently presents a nice question of fact. While, under the rule stated in this Section, A may not, without some justification induce B to break his contract with C, A is ordinarily free to refuse to deal with B for any reason or no reason. The difficult question of fact presented in this situation is whether A is merely exercising his freedom to select the persons with whom he will do business or is inducing B not to perform his contract with C. That freedom is not restricted by the relationship between B and C; and A's aversion to C is as legitimate a reason for his refusal to deal with B as his aversion to B. If he is merely exercising that freedom, he is not liable to C for the harm caused by B's choice not to lose A's business for the sake of getting C's.

On the other hand, if A, instead of merely refusing to deal with B and leaving B to make his own decision on what to do about it, goes further and uses his own refusal to deal or the threat of it as a means of affirmative inducement, compulsion or pressure to make B break his contract with C, he may be acting improperly and subject to liability under the rule stated in this Section.

> Illustrations
>
> 1. Upon hearing of B's contract with C, A ceases to buy from B. When asked by B to explain his conduct, A replies that his reason is B's contract with C. Thereupon B breaks his contract with C in order to regain A's business. A has not induced the breach and is not subject to liability to C under the rule stated in this Section.
>
> 2. Upon hearing of B's contract with C, A writes to B as follows: "I cannot tolerate your contract with C. You must call it off. I am sure that our continued relations will more than compensate you for any payment you may have to make to C. If you do not advise me within ten days that your contract with C is at an end, you may never expect further business from me." Thereupon B breaks his contract with C. A has induced the breach and is subject to liability under the rule stated in this Section.

Restatement (Second) of Torts § 766, comment *l*, and illustrations 1 and 2 at 13–14.

Applying those principles to the case at hand yields the following discussion. Bank may refuse to deal with WRC for any reason — including WRC's relationship with Uptown. Bank's freedom not to deal with WRC is not restricted by WRC's relationship with Uptown. If WRC decides independently not to continue as a joint venturer with Uptown, having learned of Bank's reason, Bank is not liable to Uptown for the harm caused. This is the scenario envisioned by the first illustration quoted above. For Bank to be liable to Uptown on this tort theory, for refusing to deal with WRC, Bank must have used its own refusal to deal as a form of "affirmative inducement, compulsion or pressure" to make WRC break its contract with Uptown. See Restatement (Second) of Torts § 766, comment *l* at 13 (stating quoted standard). This is the scenario envisioned by the second illustration quoted above.

Assuming the truth of all well-pleaded allegations and giving Uptown the benefit of all favorable inferences that may be drawn therefrom, Uptown's fifth claim for relief is closer to the second illustration than to the first. Uptown alleged more than Bank's mere silent refusal to deal with WRC because of WRC's joint venture with

Uptown; Uptown's complaint can be read to allege, further, that Bank told WRC that a loan would be forthcoming if WRC were to remove Uptown as its joint venturer and that Bank's purpose in telling that to WRC was to injure Uptown's economic relations with WRC. Under the principles discussed above, those allegations suffice to withstand a motion to dismiss the claim, because they describe a form of affirmative inducement for WRC to remove Uptown from the joint venture, without justification.

Therefore, the trial court erred in dismissing Uptown's fifth claim for relief. The Court of Appeals correctly reversed that dismissal.

CONCLUSION

In summary, Uptown failed to state a claim with respect to the first through fourth claims for relief. Uptown stated a claim with respect to the fifth claim for relief.

[c] Comments and Questions About *Uptown Heights Associates*

1. How are the facts in *Uptown Heights Associates* similar to the facts of the construction loan from FMB to Regent? How are they different?
2. Based on the lender liability law articulated in the case, do you think that Regent could survive a motion for summary judgment on a lender liability claim against FMB? What would be the grounds and theories for a lender liability claim against FMB?
3. Sam Nader will be asked to address the topic of potential lender liability of FMB to Regent in the materials that follow. As you will discover, an Illinois statute appears to have a negative impact on any lender liability claims based on the alleged oral agreement from loan officers of FMB to David Delany to extend the term of the loan.

§ 16.04 ADVISING REGENT REGARDING THE LOAN IN DEFAULT

[1] Donna Asks Sam for Advice, One More Time

Following are a memo from Donna to Sam, asking for his views on how Regent should proceed with its loan with FMB on which the Fox Valley Auto Care Center LLC, in which Regent is the manager, is in default, and a memo from Sam in response. The law has changed since the time of Regent's default. We have chosen to give you the current law and we ask your understanding when we present newer cases than the lawyers would have been considering at the time.

MEMORANDUM

TO: Sam Nader

FROM: Donna Smith

RE: Loan from FMB to Regent Real Estate Development Corp.

DATE: April 10, 1991

Our client, Regent Real Estate Development Corp., the developer of the Fox Valley Auto Care Center, has informed me that the construction loan has matured and Regent has been unsuccessful in obtaining a permanent loan to pay off the construction loan. While the project is a success, with the income from the property exceeding the debt payments and expenses of the project, a real estate recession has hit and money to finance real estate projects has dried up. Lenders now are not willing to provide a take-out loan for this type of project because the tenants are not deemed to be of a high enough credit rating.

David Delany has advised me that when the construction loan was first being negotiated with First Mortgage Bank, FMB and Regent discussed whether the bank would require a take-out loan be in place before the funding of the construction loan. It was fairly common in the real estate lending business to require a take-out loan. FMB decided not to require a take-out commitment. Instead, the construction loan was structured to mature approximately seven months after construction was scheduled to be completed, leaving ample time, the parties thought, for Regent to obtain a take-out loan. In addition, one of the bank's loan officers told David (just before he received the term sheet) that if Regent were unable to obtain the permanent loan by the time the construction loan matured, First Mortgage Bank would "roll over" the loan for another year at prime plus 2%.

When the loan matured, First Mortgage Bank notified Regent that if it did not pay off the loan within 30 days, the bank would begin to exercise its rights under the law, including, without limitation, foreclosure proceedings. When Regent requested an extension of the term of the loan for another year, as per the oral agreement with the bank, the bank denied making any agreement and refused to agree to modify the loan in any manner whatsoever. David speculates that the bank wants to take over this healthy project to offset the many unhealthy projects they have recently had to foreclose on so that they can pool this mortgage loan together with the other less healthy ones and sell them to recover their investments.

Regent has now come to us for advice on how to proceed. Please prepare a memorandum to me that answers the following questions:

1. If proved, is the oral agreement to extend the term of the loan enforceable against FMB?

2. Assuming for purposes of this question that the oral agreement to extend the term of the loan is not enforceable, are there any other grounds by which Regent could defend against a foreclosure suit or by which FMB would be liable to Regent?

3. Can Regent improve its position with the lender in fighting the foreclosure action with a bankruptcy filing by the LLC (the shareholders of Regent do not want to file individual bankruptcy actions)? What rights

would Regent have if the LLC filed a bankruptcy action? What rights would FMB have? After taking into account the rights of each party in the event of a bankruptcy filing, what do you predict would be the ultimate outcome if the borrower files a bankruptcy? Will the borrower be successful in confirming a plan by which it is able to retain the mortgaged property over the objection of the bank?

4. What other options are available to Regent besides fighting the lender's foreclosure action (*i.e.*, identify and explain the various ways the parties could "work-out" this problem)? Remember that FMB is not willing to simply modify the loan to extend its term. FMB may require nothing less than Regent and its partners throwing in the towel and turning the property over to the lender. If this is the case, what concessions, if any, should Regent and the investors seek to receive in return from FMB? And what is the impact of any duties Regent owes to the investors in the LLC in structuring the work-out?

5. In light of your conclusions to questions one through four above, and any other matters you deem relevant (and you should consider the tax consequences of the different options as relevant), what do you recommend that Regent do here? Should Regent sue or counterclaim based on the oral agreement? Should Regent raise a lender liability claim or defense to the foreclosure action based on some other ground? Should the Fox Valley Auto Care Center LLC file a bankruptcy petition and invoke various rights under those laws? Should Regent instead try to "work-out" the loan default through a consensual transfer of the property or a pre-packaged bankruptcy?

I have scheduled a meeting with the client next Friday and need to hear back from you before then.

MEMORANDUM

TO: Donna Smith

FROM: Sam Nader

RE: Loan From FMB to Regent Real Estate Development Corp.

QUESTION 1 (Enforcement of the Oral Agreement)

In regard to your question as to the validity of the lender's oral agreement to extend the term of the loan, I have determined that the oral extension is not likely to be upheld as valid. 815 I.L.C.S. 160/2, enacted June 19, 1989, provides that all credit agreements must be in writing. The statute further provides that:

"A debtor may not maintain an action on or in any way related to a credit agreement unless the credit agreement is in writing, expresses an agreement or commitment to lend money or extend credit or delay or forbear repayment of money, sets forth the relevant terms and conditions and is signed by the creditor and the debtor."

Additionally, 815 I.L.C.S. 160/3 provides that an agreement by a creditor to modify or amend an existing credit agreement or to otherwise take certain actions such as rescheduling or extending installments due under an existing credit agreement must meet the requirements of 815 I.L.C.S. 160/2 above. Since the agreement to extend the terms of the loan was made orally, the oral agreement is unenforceable under the statute.

Other cases prior to the enactment of the above statute set forth some of the rationale for the above statute. In *Schwachman v. Greenbaum Mortgage Company*, 115 Ill. App. 3d 234 (1983), the court upheld an oral promise to provide end loan financing. In *Schwachman*, the plaintiffs alleged that the defendants issued a valid loan commitment letter and orally agreed to provide end loan financing if plaintiff could not obtain it elsewhere. The loan commitment letter was issued in April of 1983 and the mortgage loan agreement was signed in August of 1983. The *Schwachman* court determined sufficient evidence existed to prove that the oral agreement was made.

Defendant alleged that the promise to provide end financing was unenforceable because such modification violated the statute of frauds and that there was no consideration for the promise to provide financing. The court disregarded the statute of frauds argument and determined that due to the fact that there was a binding agreement (the Mortgage Loan Agreement), adequate consideration must have existed for the oral contract. The court found that when plaintiff entered into the mortgage loan agreement, adequate consideration existed for both parties, and thus the court determined that consideration existed for the oral contract.

Cases such as *Delcon Group Inc. v. Northern Trust Corporation*, 187 Ill. App. 3d 635 (1989), held that an oral agreement to loan money in the future is recognized in Illinois. The *Delcon* case held that oral agreements to extend loan terms were valid if all material terms of the agreement were reasonably certain. However, if essential terms were missing or were not agreed to, then the court will find that no contract was formed. The *Delcon* court determined that the party claiming such oral contract must show that the alleged agreement contained sufficient definiteness to be enforceable. Cases such as *McErlean v. Union National Bank*, 414 N.E.2d 128 (Ill. App. 1980), held that material terms include duration of the loan, rate, maturity date and type of repayment. Under the *McErlean* test, the *Delcon* court determined that the parties never had a meeting of the minds. Moreover, the *Delcon* loan agreement provided that the agreement was the only agreement between the parties and that the agreement may only be modified in writing. The court held that no written waivers were ever made and that the oral modification was invalid due to the fact that essential terms were not agreed upon and thus no oral contract ever existed.

Based upon 815 I.L.C.S 160/2-3 and *Delcon* and *Schwachman*, it is not likely that the court would uphold the oral agreement that the lender would provide permanent financing to Regent. Although it appears that many material terms were agreed to (interest rate and term of the loan), other material items such as the amount of repayment and timing of repayment were not agreed to. Thus, the lender could cogently argue that no oral contract existed because the oral agreement failed to list all material loan terms as set forth in *McErlean*. Further, Paragraph 12.15 of the Loan Agreement states that:

"This agreement together with the Notes, Loan document and Mortgages constitutes the entire understanding of the parties . . . all prior understandings with respect thereto, whether oral or written shall be of no force or effect."

Due to 815 I.L.C.S. 160/2-3, it is apparent that the lender's oral agreement to extend the loan would not be valid. Moreover, the above provision in the loan agreement and the fact that the lender could argue that no contract was ever agreed to because material terms were omitted would prove to be serious obstacles to Regent.

Regent might have a promissory estoppel argument because it relied on the construction lender's oral promise. However, under the Act, there is no justifiable reliance on an oral credit agreement. *Teachers Insurance and Annuity Association of America v. LaSalle National Bank*, 295 Ill. App. 3d 61, 229 Ill. Dec. 408, 691 N.E.2d 881 (2d Dist. 1998).

QUESTION 2 (Other Grounds in Defense of a Foreclosure Action)

Assuming that the oral agreement to extend the term of the loan is unenforceable, the borrower may bring forth other grounds in defense against a foreclosure suit by the lender. Because foreclosure is an equitable action, Regent may raise equitable defenses. Initially such defenses would be fraud or unclean hands, but, additionally, duress, mistake and laches also might be raised. Moreover, Regent may seek a finding that the lender does not have a right to foreclose on the loan as a result of procedural errors in bringing the action.

To obtain a judgment of foreclosure, the lender must make certain that Regent receives proper notice. It is well-established law in Illinois that mere knowledge of the foreclosure action is insufficient. *Bell Federal Savings and Loan Assoc. v. Horton*, 59 Ill. App. 3d 923, 376 N.E.2d 1029, 17 Ill. Dec. 700 (5th Dist. 1978).

A defense based on fraud must be as to the making of the note, not the consideration for the note. In a defense based on fraud, Regent will have to show the following elements: (1) that the lender, or lender's agent, is commercially sophisticated; (2) the lender misrepresented a material fact; (3) the lender intended to deceive Regent; (4) Regent reasonably relied on the misrepresentation; (5) Regent suffered an injury as a result of its reliance on the misrepresentation; (6) Regent exercised ordinary diligence to discover the truth; and (7) upon discovering the fraud, Regent acted within a reasonable time to rectify the situation.

If Illinois did not have the Act barring actions against oral agreements, Regent would have a valid defense and a lender liability claim based on the exact situation described in the first question — "an oral promise leading the borrower to believe that the loan would be extended or additional credit would be granted." Debra Pogrund Stark, ed., *Consensual Transfers of Distressed Real Estate*, 1998 A.B.A. 6.

Another possible defense is "unclean hands" or inequitable/unconscionable conduct. Examples of such conduct include overreaching: use of unfair, misleading, or intimidating bargaining tactics; or making a loan that violates the lender's lending practices. This defense is also very realistic if the developer could prove that the lending agent violated its lending practices by not requiring a permanent loan commitment. The developer would have to subpoena the manuals and lending guides utilized by the lender.

Furthermore, the lender has a duty to act in good faith in enforcing the loan. If the note incorporates the U.C.C.'s remedies, the lender is subject to the good faith limitation on acceleration and may be held liable for breach of this requirement. The lender may also be liable to the developer if the lender accelerated the loan for an immaterial breach or in violation of a course of dealing with the developer. *Sahadi v. Continental Illinois National Co.*, 706 F.2d 193 (7th Cir. 1983).

If Regent files for bankruptcy within one year of the foreclosure sale, Regent can attempt to argue that the foreclosure sale was a *fraudulent conveyance* under § 548 of the Bankruptcy Code. Foreclosure sales previously were subject to attack if the amount bid at the foreclosure sale was less than 70% of the property's appraised value. However, recent cases have provided that foreclosures will be deemed to be made for reasonably equivalent value if they are conducted in accordance with state foreclosure laws.

Illinois case law provides that a foreclosure sale can be invalidated for an inadequate bid. However, an inadequate bid alone would not typically be sufficient to invalidate a sale. Rather, an inadequate bid must be accompanied by fraud, unfairness, mistake, or oppression (a court might also be influenced to find a fraudulent conveyance if the foreclosure sale was not conducted in a commercially reasonable manner). Courts appear more lenient in setting aside a foreclosure sale before confirmation because the sale is not considered consummated. After the sale is confirmed, it is more difficult to challenge the sale.

Regent could also argue that the foreclosure sale is an invalid *preference* under § 544 of the Bankruptcy Code. The bankruptcy court may also subordinate on equitable grounds all or a part of the lender's allowed claim to any other junior lien holder. Moreover, it may disallow the claim entirely if the court finds that the lender has engaged in overreaching or lender control, or if the lender engages in outlandish conduct that justifies the use of the court's equitable powers.

A borrower may also claim that it received inadequate notice or that the notice did not comply with statutory requirements. Mere de minimis defects in notice may not suffice to invalidate a foreclosure sale. However, if the lender has misinformed the borrower of either the place or time of the sale, the sale may be invalidated.

A borrower may also attempt to assert that the lender has committed fraud or failed to adequately document the transaction. Thus, Regent should review all loan documents including the Note, Mortgage and all U.C.C. filings. For example an analysis of the U.C.C. filings may show that the lender failed to adequately perfect the security interest in the personal property. Alternatively, the Note and Mortgage and the lender's file should be reviewed to determine whether the lender has committed fraud or has made any action to subject the lender to liability.

QUESTION 3 (Bankruptcy Options)

If the developer cannot successfully defend against a foreclosure suit, the only alternative may be to file a bankruptcy petition. Upon the filing of a petition for bankruptcy, there is a temporary automatic stay prohibiting the lender from foreclosing on the mortgage or the deed of trust. The borrower should evaluate whether it is more beneficial to file a case under Chapter 7 or under Chapter 11 of the Bankruptcy Code.

Because the developer desires to maintain ownership and control over the property, a Chapter 7 petition will not be beneficial. In a Chapter 7 case, the debtor's property (that which is non-exempt [it being noted that no property is exempt when a partnership files the Chapter 7 petition]) is liquidated (sold to produce funds) and the proceeds are then used to pay creditors for their allowed claims. Fully secured creditors, such as the construction lender in this situation, will receive the proceeds from a sale of the collateral by the Trustee in Bankruptcy or a modification of the automatic stay permitting the mortgagee to commence or continue the foreclosure.

Moreover, in a Chapter 7 filing, it is unlikely that the developer's business (developing and/or managing the property in question) will continue. If the business is profitable, it is more beneficial for the developer to file a Chapter 11 bankruptcy petition. The goal of a Chapter 11 is reorganization (or orderly liquidation), not liquidation as in Chapter 7 filings.

Generally, in a Chapter 11 proceeding, the debtor (the developer), will be permitted to operate the business and to manage the real property as a "debtor in possession" unless the lender requests a trustee. In order for the lender to convince a court to appoint a trustee, the lender must demonstrate that the borrower has, post-petition, committed acts that diminish the value of the collateral such as fraud, misconduct, gross mismanagement, dishonesty, incompetence, or other cause that does not include mere mismanagement. John C. Murray, *The Lender's Guide to Single Asset Real Estate Bankruptcies*, 31 Real Prop., Prob. & Tr. J., Fall 1996, 393, 431. Under Chapter 11, the debtor must meet post-petition obligations, but does not need to currently pay pre-petition debts on under-secured claims (*i.e.*, claims where the debt exceeds the fair market value of the collateral securing the debt) during the plan formulation. Under the plan, the present value of the secured portion of a creditor's claim will be paid over time and the unsecured portion of a creditor's claim will be paid off at its liquidation value.

One of the greatest benefits to a debtor in a Chapter 11 petition is that it may be used to force the lender to refinance the loan. The lender may consent to this refinance or the bankruptcy court may cramdown the refinance on the lender by confirming the reorganization plan over the lender's objections. If a plan is otherwise confirmable but for an objecting class of creditors, then through a cramdown, the plan will still be confirmed, notwithstanding the objection of that class of creditors. The bankruptcy plan can provide many advantages to debtors such as reducing the amount of a secured claim to the amount of the value of the collateral, reducing the interest rate of the mortgage debt to current market rates, extending the maturity date of the mortgage loan, and altering the repayment schedule.

There are, however, many requirements that must be met in order for the bankruptcy plan to be confirmed. These requirements include that the plan does not discriminate unfairly and that it is fair and equitable to each class of impaired creditors, including those classes that do not accept the plan. Thus, unsecured claimants must at least get what they would have gotten in a liquidation and secured claimants must get the present value of their secured claim over a new specified time period. Another requirement is that if there are any impaired classes, at least one impaired class of creditors must accept the plan. Another requirement is the "absolute priority rule" (equity holders cannot keep an interest in the reorganized entity based only on their prior investment).

In addition, a cramdown is allowed only when the debtor proves that the plan is feasible. The factors a court will consider in determining whether the cramdown is a feasible plan, are:

> ". . . (1) earning power of the business; (2) the sufficiency of the capital structure; (3) the condition of the collateral and any deterioration that may have occurred throughout the bankruptcy process; (4) economic conditions; (5) management efficiency; (6) the availability of credit, if needed; and (7) the debtor's ability to meet capital expenditures."

John C. Murray, *supra* at 472. The debtor will also have to provide concrete and reliable evidence to determine future earnings. *Id.* Even though the debtor seeks to restructure its debt, it has significant burdens of proof to establish that it will be able to satisfy the restructured debt. The debtor must demonstrate an existence of adequate cash flow for the cramdown plan to be considered feasible.

Although Chapter 11 provisions lean toward the debtor's favor, the lender also has a number of rights if the debtor files for bankruptcy. These rights include the lender's right of adequate protection of the secured portion of the collateral, the absolute priority rule mentioned above (although this may be qualified by the "new value" exception) and the requirement that at least one impaired class must approve the plan.

Under the adequate protection right, an undersecured creditor may be able to require cash payments, additional lien rights, or other relief if it can show that the value of the mortgaged property has declined during the pendency of the automatic stay. If the mortgaged property is earning rents (as in Regent's situation), the rents from the property can be considered as "cash collateral" and the borrower is not entitled to use cash collateral without the consent of the lender from whose collateral the rents derive or by court order.

The absolute priority rule prevents the equity interest holders from retaining any ownership until all creditors receive the full value of their claims or have otherwise approved the plan of reorganization. However, courts have recognized a "new value" exception (if the holders of the equity interest contribute new adequate additional capital, then they can obtain an equity interest in the reorganized entity). *See, e.g., In re 203 N. LaSalle St. Partnership*, 119 S. Ct. 1411 (1999) [hereafter "*203 N. LaSalle*"].

The requirement that at least one impaired class must approve the plan might or might not aid the mortgage lender. There is a split of authority among the U.S. Circuit Courts on the ability of the borrower to "create" an impaired class to approve the plan such as was done in the *203 North LaSalle* case by failing to pay interest on the debt of trade creditors.

As previously mentioned, the lender may also seek to limit the debtor's control over property. The lender may seek the appointment of a trustee or examiner to control the property if it can prove that, post-bankruptcy filing, the borrower had engaged in any of the fraud or any of the other bad acts previously enumerated. Given the above rules, Regent should be allowed to retain the property over the objections of FMB. Regent is unlikely to engage in any of the enumerated "wrong" actions post-petition. Moreover, Regent may very realistically be able to prove the feasibility of a cramdown plan to restructure the loan. If the court finds the argument favorable that Regent relied on the extension period before seeking a permanent loan, coupled with all the factors mentioned above that Regent is likely to meet, a cramdown refinance or restructuring may take place.

QUESTION 4 (The Borrower's Alternatives)

The options for the borrower range from selling the property to a deed in lieu of foreclosure or squeeze down. Dependent on the borrower's circumstances, *an outright sale of the property to a third party* with greater resources may make sense. From the borrower's perspective, this option may not be palatable because the borrower may suffer substantial tax ramifications such as cancellation of indebtedness income, recognition of large capital gains on the sale and the possible inability to use the losses generated for tax purposes. Moreover, the investors may object to a sale because they may not profit from it and may claim that the manager owes them a fiduciary duty not to self deal and to use their best business judgment to further the partnership's interests, and not their own.

Many options may be open to the parties. However, these options essentially fall into two categories: last chance deals or walk away deals. In a last chance deal, the borrower is given a last chance to turn the deal around and in return gives the lender substantial concessions such as the removal of foreclosure impediments. In a last chance deal, such as a deed in escrow situation, a structure is set up for a short-term forbearance of debt to enable the borrower to fix its problems. This type of transaction presents difficulties to the lender. These difficulties include the fact that the borrower could renege at the last second and declare bankruptcy or could seek to invalidate the deed on the grounds that the deposit of the deed in escrow to be recorded in the event of a subsequent default would "clog"the borrower's equity of redemption. [The "clogging" rule provides that a borrower cannot waive her equitable right of redemption at the time that the mortgage loan to her is first made. There are some cases that provide that when a borrower enters into the above described transaction, this violates the doctrine against clogging the equity of redemption since under it, the borrower who fails to perform will lose the property without the protections of the foreclosure laws. — Eds.].

Other options could include a *deed in escrow with a repurchase option* where a deed is delivered to the lender and recorded by the lender and the borrower is given a repurchase option. A lender might be reluctant to use this option because some courts view this transaction as an unenforceable clog of the borrower's equitable right of redemption. This option is also problematic because it is laden with up front costs that may prove unnecessary. Additionally, the borrower would potentially recognize gain on the sale and would recognize cancellation of indebtedness income.

Other options include a *Chapter 11 drop dead agreement* or a pre-packaged bankruptcy and a squeeze down. In a Chapter 11 drop dead situation, the parties agree that if the borrower cannot raise a predetermined amount of funds and confirm a plan of reorganization within a specified time; the borrower will agree that the automatic stay lifts and the lender can foreclose. This option may be palatable if the borrower is certain that it can raise the additional money it needs to get approval of the plan, and if the manager is concerned with its fiduciary duties to the investors and wants to give them one more chance to save the project. In Regent's situation, this option probably will not work; because of the current uncertain financial environment, it may not want to be bound to a strict time limit to find new investors. A bankruptcy filing is an effective tool to avoid cancellation of indebtedness income and to shift taxes that would otherwise be payable on the capital gains recognized from foreclosure of the property.

Another possibility is a *squeeze down*. In this situation, the project is converted to a partnership where the borrower and lender are partners. The partnership agreement will provide that the borrower's interest is diluted if performance goals are not met. This method requires a project with equity and substantial upside and parties that believe in each other and trust each other. It also requires a lender that is committed long-term to the property and a borrower willing to see the lender profit substantially from the borrower's work. In this situation, a borrower may recognize gain on the "sale" of its interest to the lender. This situation may prove more palatable to the investors because they will still have an interest in the project and can still profit.

Other options for the borrower may include an *uncontested foreclosure or a bankruptcy 363 sale* to the lender or a third party. In an uncontested foreclosure, the borrower agrees not to contest the foreclosure or file bankruptcy. This method may eliminate any junior lien problems for the lender but can cause many problems with tenants that did not sign attornment or non-disturbance agreements. The 363 sale to the lender may be cheaper than a foreclosure and can be used to keep leases in place where the parties failed to sign non-attornment agreements. However, this method may require consent of any junior lien holders (although you indicated to me that Regent had advised you that they had not obtained any junior financing here).

Another great option may be a *deed in lieu of foreclosure*. A deed in lieu occurs when the borrower agrees to convey all or part of its interest in the property to the lender either to fully or partially satisfy the debt. Thus, the borrower simply gives its deed to the lender. One of the primary advantages of a deed in lieu to the lender is that the lender will avoid the costs and delays involved in a foreclosure. It also eliminates problems with subordinate tenants that did not sign attornment agreements or non-disturbance agreements and may use a foreclosure as a means to walk from their leases. In addition to avoiding delays, the lender will obtain title to the property in a smooth manner. A deed in lieu may allow the borrower to avoid any deficiency judgments or personal liability on guaranties. The deed in lieu is very beneficial to the lender as it allows him to quickly take control of the property and mitigate further losses and halt the further decline in the property's value.

Due to the fact that the deed in lieu is so beneficial to the lender, the borrower should attempt to negotiate major concessions with the lender. These concessions should include release from all personal guaranties for the remaining amount of the debt due if the property alone does not suffice to pay back the loan, or alternatively for a stipulated deficiency claim. The lender may also ask the borrower for a release from lender liability claims.

From a tax perspective, a deed in lieu causes many issues. First, the debtor will recognize gain on the disposition of the property to the extent that the fair market value of the property exceeds the taxpayer's basis in the property. Second, the excess of canceled recourse debt over the fair market value of the property constitutes cancellation of indebtedness income. Thus, an analysis of the property's fair market value and basis is critical to any analysis of possible tax consequences from the transaction. Additionally, the investors may object to a deed in lieu situation because they will likely be forced to relinquish all of their interest in the property.

Another option for the borrower is to file a *pre-packaged bankruptcy*. A pre-packaged bankruptcy is, essentially, an out-of-court restructuring proposal made by a financially distressed debtor that would qualify as a plan of reorganization under Chapter 11. This stipulation would be signed by a bankruptcy judge as an order and would therefore have the force of law. A pre-packaged plan avoids the risks and costs associated with a typical plan of reorganization and assures a quick orderly transfer of title. A pre-packaged plan can be used for tax planning for the borrower by allowing it to transfer gains into a subsequent tax year by manipulating the timing of the transaction. Tax liabilities on pre-petition debts survive bankruptcy under § 523 of the Bankruptcy Code. Thus, the borrower should negotiate for the foreclosure to occur during the bankruptcy rather than before the bankruptcy. Additional tax benefits may include that state transfer taxes can be avoided because the bankruptcy code exempts transfers pursuant to a bankruptcy. The tax code provides that if a debtor is insolvent, any cancellation of indebtedness income that results is excluded from gross income. Rather, any gross income that would be normally recognized must be used to offset any tax attributes such as passive loss carry forwards and other tax credits.

QUESTION 5 (Conclusion)

I would probably advise Regent to either work out the situation with the lender via a deed in lieu of foreclosure transaction or I would file a pre-packaged agreed upon bankruptcy. My analysis would hinge on both Regent's acceptance of the stigma of a bankruptcy and upon an analysis of the tax consequences of the transaction. Regardless of which of these two options is chosen, both present the best opportunity for Regent to enhance its position. By agreeing to a deed in lieu of foreclosure, the lender will be happy because it will obtain the property with minimum delay and costs. Thus, the lender should be willing to negotiate several favorable conditions for Regent. Regent should be able to negotiate the release of personal liability on the remaining debt or negotiate a stipulated deficiency claim pursuant to a favorable repayment schedule. Additionally, an analysis of the fair market value of the property and of Regent's basis in the property must be made. Dependent upon these factors Regent may be forced to recognize cancellation of indebtedness income or capital gains on foreclosure. Regent may prefer capital gains due to the fact that the capital gains rate is lower than the regular corporate rate. Regent may also be subject to paying large state transfer taxes on the deed over to the bank. [This is a problem in some states, but in Illinois, a sheriff's deed after a foreclosure sale, or a deed-in-lieu of foreclosure by the borrower to the lender, are both exempt from transfer taxes. — Eds.] Although a deed-in-lieu of foreclosure is a possible option, if Regent can stomach a bankruptcy filing, they may get more benefits.

An agreed pre-packaged bankruptcy therefore offers business advantages to the project because the borrower (here the LLC) and the lender will agree to the terms of a plan of reorganization and will submit the plan to a judge for approval. This method provides for a quick and orderly transfer of title, and may prevent numerous fights between the manager and the investors that would occur in a deed-in-lieu of foreclosure situation. In bankruptcy, moreover, no state transfer taxes will be due. However, a prepackaged bankruptcy plan will not help the members of the LLC avoid the income tax effects of the transaction, but these can be taken into account in the plan to control how and when the tax effects will apply. The bankruptcy of the LLC (a tax partnership) does not create a separate bankruptcy estate, I.R.C. § 1399, so the tax effects of the transactions done by the LLC will be allocated to the members, as before. Note that this planning might include revision of the distribution provisions of the LLC operating agreement, although any such revision will have to be done with care as the IRS has regulatory authority to disallow allocations when the economic impact of the allocations is not substantial when compared to their tax effect (*see* Treas. Reg. § 1.704-1(b)(2)(iii); Rev. Rul. 99-43, 1999-2 C.B. 506). Therefore, transfer of the property to the lender, either in foreclosure or by deed, results in a taxable transaction with the taxable gain or loss passed through to the members. [Ed. Note: *See* Chapter 17, discussing the effect of an arranged disposition of property by an insolvent debtor (*2925 Briarpark, Ltd v. Commissioner*, 163 F.3d 313 (5th Cir. 1999).] Cancellation of indebtedness income resulting from discharge of the LLC from liability for part of the debt will be allocated to the members of the LLC, and the availability of any exclusion from income under IRC section 108 will then be determined by their individual tax characteristics. [Ed. note: See Section 3.05[6], where these issues are discussed at length.] Discharge will also cause a reduction in members' debt-shares (entity level debt included in the members' outside bases), resulting in deemed distributions to them, which could cause additional tax effects. From a tax perspective, a prepackaged bankruptcy may provide opportunities to plan how and when the tax consequences of the deal with the lender apply, and that does offer some advantages.

[2] Questions and Comments on the Loan in Default Memorandum

1. In July 1989, a loan officer with First Mortgage Bank told David Delany that FMB would roll over the loan for another year if Regent were unable to obtain a take-out loan. It is interesting to note that the Illinois statute that voids oral agreements to make or extend a real estate secured loan was passed in the Illinois General Assembly on June 19, 1989, and made effective on September 1, 1989. Do you think that Donna would have found that information to be relevant? Would it affect Sam's analysis on the enforcement of the oral agreement to extend the loan for another year?

2. Do you think Regent would survive a motion for summary judgment on a lender liability claim or a claim of equitable subordination (if it files a bankruptcy action)? What significance, if any, to such a claim is the fact that First Mortgage Bank did not require as a condition to making the construction loan, a loan commitment from a permanent lender? Do you agree that Regent could challenge a foreclosure sale as a preference under § 544 of the Bankruptcy Code?

3. What if First Mortgage Bank extended the maturity of the loan for one year, but Regent was still unable to obtain a take-out loan during the extension? Consider the remaining questions in light of this scenario and the following assumptions: (i) the fair market value of the Project is $2,169,000 (this assumes a capitalization rate of 10% at the end of 1991, see figure 2.15, and apply the 10% assumption to the net operating income for 1991), (ii) the LLC's adjusted basis in the Project is $2,280,622 (cost of the land ($576,215) plus the cost of the building and land improvements ($1,794.980) (from figure 2.10) less accumulated depreciation ($90,573) (from figure 2.15)); and (iii) although under the current low, floating interest rate, the property was operating at a profit, there is unsecured trade debt of $5,000. Can you guess why there is unsecured trade debt here?

4. How might Regent benefit from filing a Chapter 11 bankruptcy? How would Regent be harmed by such a filing? Note that it would be the LLC/beneficiary of the land trust that would file the bankruptcy action. Regent would have to determine under its LLC operating agreement and under LLC law whether such action would require the consent of its investors. Do you think the investors would agree to a bankruptcy filing here? Why or why not?

5. How does Regent's fiduciary duties to the investors affect its decision making on how to respond to First Mortgage Bank's threats to exercise all remedies available to it?

6. What are the advantages to a "workout" in the form of a Chapter 11 prepackaged bankruptcy as opposed to a "last chance" deed in lieu of foreclosure? What are the disadvantages to a last chance deal in bankruptcy?

7. Note the various "workout" and "fight it out" alternatives Sam raised. Do you agree with Sam's conclusion? Which alternative would you recommend to Regent and why? Be sure to consider the feasibility and terms of a cramdown and the tax ramifications of a simple deed in lieu of foreclosure as you consider those two possible options. These tax ramifications are discussed in Chapter 3, Section 3.05[6] (cancellation of indebtedness), and in Chapter 17.

8. If you were representing First Mortgage Bank, what would you recommend they do here? Of course, in answering this question you need to know what your client's ultimate goals and needs are as well as the borrower's goals, needs, and circumstances. For example, if the borrower believed that it was on the verge of obtaining a take-out loan, would you counsel your client to do a "drop dead chapter 11 agreement"? Why or why not? In representing a lender who has decided to enter any type of settlement with the mortgage borrower, it is critical that a written settlement agreement be entered into that covers all the details (not only what was agreed to, but other matters, like a release of claims against the lender, a covenant not to sue the borrower, not so sweeping a release of the borrower that the debtor becomes a "prevailing party" for attorney's fees purposes, and anticipating that the settlement agreement will be reviewable as a fraudulent conveyance or in bankruptcy as a preference). For a good description of the points that should be covered in a foreclosure settlement agreement, see James R. Stillman, *The Foreclosure Settlement Agreement*, 21 No. 4 Prac. Real Est. Law. 57 (July 2005).

Chapter 17

TAXABLE DISPOSITIONS

§ 17.01 INTRODUCTION TO SALES OR EXCHANGES

In our discussion of the valuation of investment in income producing real estate in Chapter 2, we included proceeds from the disposition of the project at the conclusion of the taxpayer's investment, in that case ten years. These proceeds were projected to have been realized from a sale of the project for a value which we derived from the project's net operating income in the last year of the investment period. This projected transaction resulted in a taxable gain. In this chapter, we explore when and how taxable gain arises on the disposition of income-producing real estate, how it is taxed, and some techniques which offer the opportunity for deferral of the tax which otherwise would result.

[1] Gain or Loss on the Disposition of Property

For an investor, the important determination will be the cash received by the investor net of any income tax which may be incurred in the disposition. Under the income tax, gain from "dealings in property" are included in income. I.R.C. § 61(a)(3). Gain from the "sale or other disposition of property" is the excess of the "amount realized" in the transaction over the taxpayer's "adjusted tax basis" for the taxpayer's interest in the property. I.R.C. § 1001(a). Both are terms of art in the income tax. We have already explored how tax basis is created and then later adjusted as cost recovery deductions are taken. The "amount realized" is defined as the amount of money received plus the fair market value of property received in the transactions. I.R.C. § 1001(b). In this calculation, relief from the obligation to pay an indebtedness is treated as the receipt of money. Moreover, the receipt of property other than money will result in the realization of gain, or, as the case may be, a loss.[1]

A realized gain is taxable, that is, the gain is "recognized," unless the statute provides otherwise. I.R.C. § 1001(c). Realization and recognition are two separate concepts, the latter term referring to when a gain will be taxed or a loss taken into account under other provisions of the Code. The statute provides that a realized gain is, in general, immediately taxable.

---

[1] We discussed the concept of a "realization" in the context of debt modification in Section 3.06(f). A "realization" for purposes of the tax system is a material change in the taxpayer's interest in the property. The Supreme Court in *Cottage Savings Ass'n v. Commissioner*, 499 U.S. 554 (1991), *supra* Section 3.05[6][f], note 41, held that a realization occurred with nominal changes in the taxpayer's investment, even though the taxpayer's economic interest remained the same after the transaction. Although apparently minor shifts can cause a taxable event to occur, the realization concept is fundamental to the income tax. Mere changes in value, without more, are not taxable and permit the deferral of tax on increases in the value of an asset without more.

[2] The Many Flavors of Capital Gains Taxation

The gain from the disposition of property may qualify for treatment as capital gain. A capital gain results from the sale or exchange of a capital asset. Income producing real estate is an asset which is used in the operator's trade or business, and, as such, is not a "capital asset."[2] Gain from the sale or exchange of depreciable real estate, or real estate used in the taxpayer's trade or business, however, usually will be treated as capital gain under the provisions of I.R.C. § 1231, but the application of this provision must be done with care.[3] In a project like Fox Valley Auto Care Center, the entity (the LLC) owns one asset, the project, so that the gain from its sale will treated as a capital gain under I.R.C. § 1231. We will assume that each member of the LLC (investor) will be entitled to treat the gain in this manner.

Capital gain is included in the taxpayer's income. However, the maximum rate which may apply to that gain is, under the current (summer 2009) rules, fifteen percent. I.R.C. § 1(h)(1)(A).[4] This tax is determined by first calculating the tax on the taxpayer's income including the capital gain, then calculating the tax on income excluding the capital gain plus 15% of the capital gain, and comparing the two. The taxpayer is liable to pay the smaller amount. In our discussion, we have assumed that the investors are all taxed at the highest marginal tax rate, which, again under the current rules is, in general, 35%, so that capital gains realized by the taxpayer will be subject to the 15% rate.

A different maximum rate (25%) applies to gain which is a recovery of previously deducted depreciation on real estate assets. I.R.C. § 1(h)(1)(D). Recall that, as depreciation deductions are taken, the tax basis of the project is reduced or "adjusted" by the amount of the deductions. In effect, the taxpayer is writing off a portion of the original tax basis of the property each year. In most cases, disposition of the property will result in an amount realized which exceeds the tax basis of the property as adjusted for the previously deducted depreciation. To the

---

[2] I.R.C. § 1221(a)(2). Assets "primarily held for sale to customers in the ordinary course of the taxpayer's trade or business" are not capital assets either. Much of the discussion of capital gains and losses in the real estate context focuses on this provision, but we will assume for purposes of our discussion that Fox Valley and other operators hold their projects for the purpose of earning income from their operation, so that the "held for sale" issue is not present.

[3] Under I.R.C. § 1231(a), gains and losses from the sales or exchanges of assets subject to I.R.C. § 1231 are netted. If the net is positive, then all gains or losses will be capital; if the net is negative (a net loss), then all gains or loss will be ordinary. The important thing to note here, in the context of a real estate investment, is that the character of gains or losses realized at the entity level flow through to the partners or members, and are reported on their individual returns, where the netting process takes place for all that particular taxpayer's I.R.C. § 1231 gains and losses. In the economic conditions prevalent as this is being written (summer 2009), individual partners or members may have interests in different real estate projects, some of which produce gains and some losses. The ultimate tax consequences to the individual taxpayer, then, will depend on the netting process on that taxpayer's tax returns. In poor economic times, there may be losses, and these losses may be deductible from the taxpayer's ordinary income, assuming that the passive loss limitation does not apply. A net gain from I.R.C. § 1231 assets in any of the ensuing five years will be taxed as ordinary income, however, to the extent of net losses in the earlier year, resulting in a "recapture" of the previously deducted losses. I.R.C. § 1231(c).

[4] *See* Section 2.02[3][b], at notes 41 & 42, *supra*. The 15% rate is subject to a sunset provision under which it will be effective only until the end of 2010. If Congress does not act in the meantime, that rate will revert to 20%, the rate in effect when the 15% rate was first enacted. As you read this, the rate may have reverted to 20%, or Congress may have taken some other action. What we say here should be taken in context.

extent that resulting realized gain does not exceed the depreciation, it will taxed as "unrecaptured section 1250 gain" subject to the 25% rate.[5]

In some projects, cost has been allocated to personal property which is depreciable at higher rates than real estate assets.[6] When the project is sold, the amount realized must be allocated among the assets of the project. Allocation to personal property may result in a gain on these assets, which, to the extent the gain does not exceed the accumulated depreciation previously taken, will be taxed at ordinary income rates as recaptured depreciation. Depreciation recapture, in addition to being taxed at ordinary rates, has other unfavorable tax consequences,[7] which may lead the developer to avoid classification of assets as personal property despite the favorable depreciation methods.

§ 17.02 *COMMISSIONER v. TUFTS*

This subject was introduced in § 3.05, *supra*, with the full opinion in *Commissioner v. Tufts*, 461 U.S. 300 (1983), and an in-depth analysis of the effects of its holding. In that case, the taxpayer and his fellow partners in a partnership which owned an apartment complex sold their partnership interests to an unrelated party, subject to a nonrecourse first mortgage, for, essentially, postage. The apartment complex had been constructed three years earlier with the proceeds of an insured loan. The taxpayer had no equity in the deal. The project was encumbered with a $1,900,000 nonrecourse first mortgage. After the partnership had taken $450,000 in depreciation deductions, the property had an adjusted basis of $1,450,000, was still subject to the original loan but had declined in value to $1,400,000. The Court held that the amount realized on the sale of the partnership interests included the full amount of the mortgage, which still was a lien on the property.

We studied *Tufts* in Chapter 3 because the reasoning in the case was premised squarely on the issues of tax basis and the correct method for computing depreciation. What interested us then was how *Tufts* impacted on the Fox Valley Auto Care Center LLC. Borrowed funds used to purchase or construct an asset are included in the tax basis of the asset for the calculation of depreciation deductions even though the receipt of the proceeds of a loan is not taxable. This arrangement produces tax leverage, in which the depreciation deductions offset or "shelter" income from project rents or from some external source. When the depreciable basis for the asset is derived from borrowed funds, the taxpayer obtains a deferral of tax on the income or gain used to repay the debt.

So it was in *Tufts*. The taxpayer and his colleagues had claimed $450,000 of depreciation deductions, which were derived almost entirely from tax basis created with borrowed funds. The deductions had offset or sheltered income from some other source, professional fees in the taxpayer's case. Repayment of the debt would have been made with after-tax income, and had the partners continued to own the property, income from the apartment complex used to repay the mortgage would

---

[5] For an illustration of the application of these rules, see Section 3.03[3] figure 3.1, *supra*.

[6] *See* Section 3.02[1], at notes 4 & 5.

[7] Recapture income is not eligible for tax deferral under the installment method of reporting income from a sale, I.R.C. § 453(i), and when involved in a nonrecognition exchange under I.R.C. § 1031, must be exchanged for personal property under more restrictive conditions than apply to the underlying real estate assets.

have been taxable to them. And so, on disposition of the property, the full amount of the debt would have to be included in income, that is, in the amount realized, as the natural consequence of this tax system. Otherwise, the taxpayer would realize a double tax benefit: once, when the depreciation deductions were taken; and a second time, when the taxpayer was relieved of his obligation to pay tax on income or gain used to pay the debt. Exclusions and deductions have the same effect on the taxpayer's income, and not including the debt in the amount realized would produce the equivalent of an exclusion and therefore a double deduction. The Court in *Tufts* held that this could not be so, and the Congress agreed. I.R.C. § 7701(g).

The entire tax system for debt financed property is predicated on this result. As you saw in Chapter 4, the operation of the partnership tax rules replicates this system for members in a limited liability company owning leveraged property, creating a circular, self-justifying result which successfully permits the allocation of significant tax benefits to investor-partners, such as the members in the Fox Valley Auto Care Center LLC. Of course, there is a cost to be paid for these benefits, and that is the tax liability at the end of the deferral period. Think of it as a kind of Newton's law of tax leverage: what goes up (tax basis and depreciation deductions), must come down (significant taxable gain at the end of the period).

When there is substantial tax leverage, real estate projects will be encumbered with nonrecourse debt which exceeds the adjusted tax basis of the property. This characteristic feature of real estate investing can be seen as overhanging debt, with significant unrealized gain, which is a real potential tax liability, whatever the value of the property might be. *Any* disposition of the property which shifts responsibility for producing the income used to pay the debt, even to a creditor, will result in realization of the gain. It is for this reason that the difference between the balance due on the mortgage and the adjusted tax basis of the property has been defined to be "minimum gain": it is the minimum amount of gain which *must* be recognized on disposition, whatever the circumstances. When the property has declined in value and is in foreclosure, real estate professionals often refer to the tax effect as "phantom gain" because the taxable gain is not accompanied by cash proceeds. In reality, this event simply marks the end of the deferral period.

§ 17.03 FORECLOSURE

[1] Workout Dispositions

A foreclosure sale is a sale for tax purposes, just like any other sale, despite the compulsion under which such sales take place. There may be dramatic differences in the tax results from such sales, however, if the relief from indebtedness can be characterized in a manner different from inclusion in the "amount realized" on a taxable sale. The following case illustrates how this problem is bound up in workout negotiations.

[a] *2925 Briarpark, Ltd. v. Commissioner*

2925 BRIARPARK, LTD. v. COMMISSIONER
163 F.3d 313 (5th Cir. 1999)

Per Curiam:

I. Factual and Procedural Background

In 1981, Briarpark was organized as a Texas limited partnership ("the partnership"). James C. Motley ("Motley") was a general partner. During 1983 and 1984, the partnership acquired a three-acre parcel of land at 2925 Briarpark Road, Houston, Texas ("the property") and constructed a 12-story office building on it. On September 27, 1983, the partnership borrowed $21,600,000 from InterFirst Bank Houston, N.A. ("InterFirst") to finance the acquisition of the property and the construction of the building. Motley personally guaranteed the principal, interest, penalties and fees on the loan.

By December 31, 1986, the outstanding principal and accrued interest due on the loan was $24,700,000. On May 28, 1987, the partnership and InterFirst modified and extended the original loan pursuant to a modified loan agreement. At the time, InterFirst estimated that the fair market value of the property was approximately $17,000,000. The original loan was converted from a recourse to a nonrecourse obligation, and accrued but unpaid interest in the amount of $3,100,000 was capitalized. Motley's personal obligation under his guarantee was limited to $5,000,000. Also on May 28, 1987, Briarpark obtained a $1,500,000 loan for tenant improvements ("build-out loan") on a nonrecourse basis.

By January 21, 1988, First Republic Bank Houston, N.A. ("First Republic") became the successor in interest to InterFirst. The Federal Deposit Insurance Corporation, as receiver for First Republic, assigned the modified loan and the build-out loan to NCNB Texas National Bank ("NCNB").

During March of 1989, Briarpark submitted an application to NCNB seeking to modify the loans to allow a cash sale of the building. In the summer of 1988, at the suggestion of the bank, Motley placed the building on the market, and in March of 1989, he brought to the bank several similar proposals for the sale of the property. At that time, the bank considered as available options: (1) liquidation in the event of a default (but at that time there was no default); (2) refinancing (which was not an "easily obtained alternative at the level of the debt"); and (3) a sale/settlement, the loan officer expressing the view that "the bank will realize the highest value if the building is sold in 1989." In NCNB's view, the best proposal was a $12,700,000 cash sale offer.

As of July 1989, Briarpark was in default on the loans. On July 21, 1989, the partnership signed a sale agreement to sell the property to Dan Associates. The gross purchase price for the property was $12,200,000. Dan Associates conditioned the purchase of the property upon the partnership's arranging the satisfaction or removal of the encumbrances for consideration paid to NCNB not in excess of $11,490,000. . . .

On November 3, 1989, Briarpark, Motley, Dan Associates, and NCNB entered into a conditional release agreement. NCNB agreed to release the property from all liens and security interests upon satisfaction of the following conditions: (1) the sale of the property to Dan Associates for a minimum gross sales price of $11,600,000; (2) the assignment of the greater of the net sale proceeds or $11,036,000 sale proceeds to the bank, to be applied against the partnership's cash notes; (3) the transfer of the partnership's cash reserves to the bank; and (4) Motley's payment of $175,000 to the bank.

On December 27, 1989, the outstanding balances of the modified and the build-out loan were $24,562,763 and $1,019,418, respectively. Briarpark sold the property to Dan Associates for $11,600,000. Briarpark incurred selling expenses of $554,901. Dan Associates paid the net sales proceeds of $10,936,532 to NCNB. The adjusted basis of the property was $11,105,733.

Also on December 27, 1989, NCNB released the liens against the property and released Motley from his guarantee of the modified loan, in return for his payment of $175,000 in cash. The partnership transferred its cash reserves of $177,495 to NCNB. As of December 31, 1989, Briarpark had no assets and ceased business operations.

On its income tax return for 1989, Briarpark reported cancellation of indebtedness income for $14,468,154 as a result of the November 3, 1989, conditional release agreement. The reported amount was calculated as follows:

Modified loan balance	$24,562,763.
Build-out loan balance	1,019,418.
Total loan Balance	$25,582,181.
Less sale proceed from Dan Associates	(10,936,532.)
Less cash reserves paid to NCNB	(177,495.)
Net cancellation of indebtedness income	$14,468,154.

The partnership also reported a net loss on the sale of the property in the amount of $61,245.

Upon audit, the Commissioner determined that the property incorrectly reported discharge of indebtedness income under I.R.C. § 61(a)(12) on its return. The Commissioner asserts that the partnership realized a gain from dealings in property under I.R.C. § 61(a)(3) because the amount of the discharged debt that had encumbered the property was includable in the amount realized. The Internal Revenue Service mailed to the partnership a Notice of Final Partnership Administrative Adjustment ("FPAA") proposing adjustments to the partnership's return to reflect realized gain from the sale of $13,920,936, rather than the reported loss of $61,245 and to eliminate the reported cancellation of indebtedness income.[1]

---

[1] Generally, where the taxpayer is insolvent immediately after the discharge of a debt, the resulting cancellation of the indebtedness income, ordinarily taxable under I.R.C. § 61(a)(12), is excludable under § 108. Gains from the disposition of property under §§ 61(a)(3) and 1001, however, are not excludable under § 108. Generally, debt-discharge income is recognized at the partnership level, while the exclusion of such income under I.R.C. § 108(a) and the concomitant attribute reduction under § 108(b) are applied at the partner level. *See Gershkowitz v. Commissioner*, 88 T.C. 984 (1987). The tax consequences to an insolvent partner of a partnership's realizing discharge of indebtedness income would therefore become apparent only on the application of such a partnership item to the individual partner's circumstances. However, it bears noting that Motley's distributive share of partnership income and loss was 83%, and,

Pursuant to the parties' stipulation, the Commissioner calculated the partnership's capital gain as follows:

Original loan balance	$24,562,763.35
Build-out loan balance	1,019,417.65
Total loan balance	$25,582,181.00
Less classing proceeds	(10,936,531.90)
Less cash reserves	(177,495.07)
Total amount of debt discharged	$14,468,154.03
Selling price	$11,600,000.00
Total amount realized	$26,068,154.03
Adjusted Basis and selling expenses	(11,660,633.31)
Capital Gain	$14,407,520.72

The Tax Court agreed with the Commissioner that the partnership had realized gains from dealings in property under I.R.C. § 61(a)(3) rather than discharge of indebtedness income under § 61(a)(12). The court noted that, for purposes of §§ 61(a)(3) and 1001(b), "the amount realized from a sale or other disposition of property includes the amount of liabilities from which the transferor is discharged as a result of the sale or disposition." The court found that the sale of the property and the assignment of sale proceeds and transfer of the partnership's cash reserves to NCNB "has the same practical effect as several other transactions which have been held to be a 'sale or exchange.'" According to the court, the transaction at issue "is the functional equivalent of a foreclosure, reconveyance in lieu of foreclosure, abandonment, or repossession" because "the mortgagor in each case is relieved of debt encumbering property and also is relieved of the obligation to pay taxes and assessments against the property."

The court rejected the partnership's argument that NCNB should be regarded as having forgiven, independently of the sale, the excess of the $25,582,181 debt over the $11,114,027 in cash received. Thus, the court disagreed with the partnership's assertion that amount realized on the sale of the property to Dan Associates was only $10,936,532, or less than the partnership's adjusted basis in the property. Far from being "two independent events," as the partnership argued, the court found the record to be "replete with evidence" that the sale and the loan discharges were the "result of a single transaction involving the sale of encumbered property." The court reasoned as follows:

> NCNB conditioned the discharge of the loans upon the sale of the property, and Dan Associates conditioned the purchase upon that discharge. At the end of the day, NCNB had proceeds from the sale, Dan Associates had the property, and Briarpark was relieved of the entire balance of the loans. In the foregoing context, the arrangements among NCNB, Dan Associates, and Briarpark embodied a single transaction to sell the property securing the loans.
>
> This appeal followed.

---

while there is no snapshot of the financial standing immediately after the discharge took place in December of 1989, the record does reflect that he had become insolvent by October of 1989, before the sale took place.

II. Standard of Review

The Tax Court's fact findings are reviewed for clear error because they were based on documentary evidence presented to the court. . . . In reviewing the Tax Court's characterization of the transaction, this Court must determine whether its decision was based on a reasonable interpretation of "sale or exchange." *Yarbro v. Commissioner*, 737 F.2d 479, 483, 486 (5th Cir.1984). Finding that the transaction constitutes a sale or exchange would support the Tax Court's conclusion that the transaction was a gain from dealing in property under § 61(a)(3).

III. Discussion

The question on appeal is whether the Tax Court erred by holding that the partnership realized a gain from dealings in property in the amount of $14,407,520.72, rather than cancellation of indebtedness income in the amount of $14,468,154.

A. *Internal Revenue Code Section 61. Gross Income*

Section 61(a) of the Internal Revenue Code provides that gross income includes all income from whatever source derived, including "gains derived from dealing in property" under § 61(a)(3) and "income from discharge of indebtedness" under § 61(a)(12). Section 1001(a), which governs the computation of gains from dealings in property, provides that "the gain from the sale or other disposition of property shall be the excess of the amount realized therefrom over the adjusted basis provided." Section 1001(b) defines "amount realized" as "the sum of any money received plus the fair market value of the property (other than money) received." The amount realized on a sale or disposition of property includes the amount of the liabilities from which the transferor is discharged as a result of the sale or disposition. Treas. Reg. § 1.1001-2(a)(1); *Commissioner v. Tufts*, 461 U.S. 300, 306 (1983); *Cox v. Commissioner*, 68 F.3d 128, 134 (5th Cir.1995); *Yarbro*, 737 F.2d at 484.

In the case of a property encumbered by nonrecourse indebtedness, the amount realized on disposition includes the entire amount of the mortgage on the property. *Tufts*, 461 U.S. at 312; *Yarbro*, 737 F.2d at 484; See also Treas. Reg. § 1.1001-2(c) *Example* (7). The fact that the fair market value of the security at the time of sale or disposition is less than the amount of the liabilities it secures "does not prevent the full amount of these liabilities from being treated as money received from the sale or other disposition of the property." Treas. Reg. § 1.1001-2(b); *Tufts*, 461 U.S. at 310.

There is a distinction between what constitutes income realized from the "discharge of indebtedness" under § 61(a)(12) and income realized from "gains derived from dealing in property" under § 61(a)(3). Under § 61(a)(12), a debtor may realize income from the discharge of indebtedness where his debt is canceled, forgiven or otherwise discharged for less than the full amount of the debt. The Supreme Court has held that when a nonrecourse debt is forgiven, the debtor's basis in the securing property is reduced by the amount of debt canceled, and realization of income is deferred until the sale of the property. *United States v. Kirby Lumber Co.*, 284 U.S. 1, 3 (1931); *Fulton Gold Corp. v. Commissioner*, 31 B.T.A. 519, 520 (1934). This interpretation attributes income only when assets are freed, therefore, an insolvent debtor realizes income just to the extent his assets exceed his liabilities after the cancellation. *Tufts*, 461 U.S. at 310 n. 11.

Section 61(a)(3) applies when a taxpayer agrees to surrender the property in exchange for the cancellation of a debt. Under this scenario, the transaction may be characterized as a sale or exchange of property giving rise to income under § 61(a)(3) with the whole amount of the canceled nonrecourse indebtedness being includable in the amount realized under § 1001. Therefore, § 61(a)(3) applies if the court determines that the transaction: (1) relieved the taxpayer-owner of his obligation to repay the debt;[2] and (2) the taxpayer is relieved of title of the property. *Yarbro* 737 F.2d at 486.

B. *Whether Briarpark's Transaction Constitutes a Sale or Exchange for Tax Purposes.*

The Commissioner of Internal Revenue asserts that "Congress intended the words 'sale or exchange' to have a broad meaning, not to be limited to the standard transfer of property by one person to another in exchange for a stated consideration in money or money's worth." . . . For example, it has long been established that a foreclosure sale constitutes a "disposition of property" within the meaning of § 1001(b). *Cox*, 68 F.3d at 133. A nonjudicial foreclosure sale is also a transaction that triggers taxable gain. *Chilingirian v. Commissioner*, 918 F.2d 1251, 1253 (6th Cir.1990). It is also well settled that the transfer of property by deed in lieu of foreclosure is the functional equivalent of a "sale or exchange" for federal income tax purposes. *Allan v. Commissioner*, 856 F.2d 1169, 1172 (8th Cir.1988).

The Commissioner asserts that the Tax Court followed the teaching of *Yarbro* and similar cases by considering the "practical effect" of Briarpark's transaction. Under the conditional release agreement, the bank agreed to release the property from all liens and security interests upon satisfaction of the following conditions: (1) the sale of the property to Dan Associates for a minimum gross sales price of $11,600,000; (2) the assignment of the sale proceeds to the bank; (3) the transfer of Briarpark's cash reserves to the bank; and (4) the payment of $175,000 by Motley to the bank. There was no indication that the bank was willing to forgive any part of the partnership's debt except as a condition of sale to Dan Associates. At the end of the transaction NCNB released all liens against the property, released Motley from his guarantee, and Briarpark had no assets and ceased business operations. Unlike § 61(a)(12) cases, where debt forgiveness occurs as a single transaction and the realization of the property income occurs in a later and separate transaction, the debt forgiveness in the case herein was closely intertwined with the terms of the

---

[2] An essential point to remember is that the debt herein is "nonrecourse debt." Nonrecourse debt and recourse debt are treated differently by certain sections of the Code. Case law firmly establishes that when a taxpayer is relieved of nonrecourse debt, his obligation is canceled and he realizes a value. *Tufts*, 461 U.S. at 312. Determining whether that value falls under § 61(a)(3) or § 61(a)(12) will further determine whether the insolvent petitioner herein will have to pay taxes on that value or be absolved under § 108. With a recourse debt, a debtor remains liable for the unpaid balance after a foreclosure sale. Therefore, the unpaid portion is not used to calculate "amount realized" under § 1001(b). Furthermore, if the recourse debt is subsequently forgiven, or the judgement is permitted to lapse uncollected, the recourse debt would then fall under § 61(a)(12). Therefore, if this Court determines that the transaction constituted a "sale or exchange," the value from the nonrecourse debt herein would be governed by § 61(a)(3) and included to calculate "amount realized" under § 1001(b).

agreement. Therefore, this was a single transaction governed by § 61(a)(3). See *Fulton*, 31 B.T.A. at 519.

The partnership correctly asserts that the determination of whether a transaction is governed by § 61(a)(3) or § 61(a)(12) depends on the particular facts of the case. The petitioners assert that in *Gershkowitz v. Commissioner*, 88 T.C. 984, the taxpayer's nonrecourse debt settlement was characterized as § 61(a)(12) income and that the divestment of the property, just three months later, was characterized separately as § 61(a)(3) income. The partnership argues that the fact that Briarpark, NCNB, and Dan Associates accomplished both tasks in a single transaction, rather than in two transactions, should not cause the entire transaction to be categorized as § 61(a)(3) income. The partnership also argues that because the purchaser did not assume the debt, the partnership must be treated as having received discharge of indebtedness income. The Tax Court properly distinguished *Gershkowitz* from this case.

In *Gershkowitz*, the debts were not discharged in connection with the disposition of the property. Since there was no disposition of property upon the discharge of the debts, the Tax Court held that there was no amount realized upon disposition that could be regarded as flowing from the discharge of indebtedness, and, hence, no gain or loss on disposition to be computed. *Id.* at 1016. The Tax Court properly found that the partnership's disposition of the property was conditioned upon the relief of its debt and was therefore the functional equivalent of a foreclosure sale. See *Yarbro*, 737 F.2d at 485–86.

The partnership's argument, that the purchaser did not assume the debt, is also without merit. The language of § 1001-2(a)(1) provides that "the amount realized from a sale or other disposition of property includes the amount of liabilities from which the transferor is discharged as a result of the sale or disposition," and does not consider for its purposes whether the purchaser assumes the debt or not. See also § 1001-2(c) Example (7).

IV. Conclusion

Upon reviewing the factual findings of this case, this Court agrees with the Tax Court's characterization of this transaction. Therefore, we AFFIRM the Tax Court's decision.

[b] Notes and Questions

[i] The Stakes in *Briarpark*

Briarpark is a classic illustration of the failed real estate project. Note that it was heavily debt financed, and over the eight year operating period the partnership wrote off approximately 50% of the project's original cost, as was permitted under the depreciation rules in effect when the Briarpark Office Building was put in service. The debt itself was not significantly curtailed. When the project went into the ditch in the real estate recession in the late 1980s, the debt overhang exceeded $12 million. The parties then commenced negotiations over a "workout," which included an effort to refurbish the building and continue in operation.

There was a significant tax advantage to treating a reduction in the amount of the indebtedness as cancellation of indebtedness ("COD") income. Motley, the principal in *Briarpark*, was bankrupt. COD Income realized by an insolvent taxpayer, or by a taxpayer in Chapter 11, is excluded from income. I.R.C. §§ 108(a)(1)(A) & (B). If the overhang portion of the Briarpark debt could be recharacterized as indebtedness for which Motley, and perhaps other partners, were personally liable, and if it had been "canceled" or reduced by the bank in a transaction separate from the disposition of the property, their tax liabilities could be dramatically less. This explains the effort by the Briarpark partnership to have the bank release its liens before the sale to Dan Associates. In the best judicial tradition, neither court was confused by the maneuvering, and the Fifth Circuit, in particular, points out that the *form* in which the disposition of overleveraged property is cast will not affect the ultimate tax result. Nor was the Fifth Circuit troubled by the General Partner's guarantee, which meant that at least a portion of the debt was recourse. If the release of the indebtedness occurs in a transaction by which the taxpayer disposes of the property, then the full amount of the debt reduction is gain from "dealing in property" within the meaning of section 61(a)(3).

For partners who are not bankrupt or insolvent, the indebtedness probably would have been "qualified real property indebtedness," *see* I.R.C. § 108(a)(1)(D), and the reduction in the debt could have been offset against the tax basis of other depreciable real property, thus achieving further deferral, at least to the extent of the partner's basis in qualifying real property as of the beginning of the taxable year following the discharge. I.R.C. §§ 108(c), 1017.[8] This provision, enacted in 1993 in the wake of the real estate recession of the late 1980s and early 1990s, was specifically intended to permit the further deferral of the tax leverage benefits previously obtained by the taxpayer, at least to the extent of the taxpayer's continuing investment in depreciable real estate. "Qualified real property business indebtedness" is broadly defined to include indebtedness "incurred or assumed . . . *in connection with* real property used in a trade or business and . . . secured by such real property," I.R.C. § 108(c)(3)(A), and if incurred after January 1, 1993 (the effective date of the Omnibus Budget Reconciliation Act ("OBRA") 1993), was incurred or assumed "to acquire, construct, reconstruct or substantially improve such property." I.R.C. § 108(c)(4). Whether the debt is recourse or nonrecourse is not relevant, although the amount of the exclusion is limited to excess of the qualified indebtedness before the restructuring over the net fair market value of the property at that time.[9] There are a variety of special rules and limitations, most of which have not yet been interpreted through regulations. For our purposes, each partner would make the election individually, treating his or her partnership interest as including his or her share of the qualifying real property held by the partnership, and if there is an exclusion, with the accompanying basis adjustment, the amount by which the basis of that partner's interest was reduced is subject to later recapture as ordinary income. I.R.C. § 1017(d). Deferral is almost invariably more valuable than is conversion.

---

[8] Deferral of tax when "qualified real property indebtedness" is reduced was discussed in Section 3.05[6][d], *supra*. For debt-reduction in real estate deals, Congress also enacted an elective deferral of tax on COD income which occurs in 2009 and 2010. *See* Section 3.05[6][f], *supra*.

[9] The amount that can be deferred is also limited to "aggregate adjusted bases of depreciable real property . . . held by the [member] immediately before the discharge," I.R.C. § 108(c)(2B), so to take advantage of this deferral option, the member must already hold investments in depreciable real estate at the time of the discharge.

Because the Fifth Circuit in *Briarpark* held that all of the debt is included in the amount realized from a disposition of the property, nearly $14.5 million of gain had been realized by the partnership and was immediately taxable to its partners without any cash proceeds. The entire amount is phantom gain. The partners may well be dismayed by this prospect, but one should understand that they had previously received significant tax leverage benefits, mostly under the generous pre-1986 tax rules. Once they disposed of the building, it was payback time.

[ii] Calculating the Tax

The Fifth Circuit in *Briarpark* held that the gain was realized in a sale or exchange of the property, essentially to the lender. Gain from the sale or exchange of depreciable property used in the taxpayer's trade or business, in *Briarpark* the business of operating an office building, is capital gain. I.R.C. § 1231.[10] As we observed earlier in this Chapter, the maximum tax rate on capital gain is now subject to a set of upper limits which are significantly less than the maximum rate on ordinary income, such as rents. This was true before Congress adjusted the maximum capital gains tax rates in 1997, and in 1997, it reduced the rates, but, at the same time, significantly complicated these rules. *See* Section 17.01[2], *infra*. In *Briarpark*, the original cost basis for the property (leaving aside issues relating to the tenant build-out) appears to have been around $21.5 million, less the cost of acquiring the land, and depreciation would have been calculated using that tax basis and reducing it as the deductions were taken. Because the mortgage debt at the time the partnership negotiated the transfer included a substantial amount of capitalized interest, the realized gain would have been even larger.

[iii] Strategic Implications of the Deferral

The overhanging debt in *Briarpark* was large, although for projects put in service during a comparable time period, similarly large debt overhangs likely were created. The tax cost of a disposition, particularly in a workout context, can be comparably large, even after the introduction of lower maximum capital gains rates. For the investors, therefore, the stakes involved in a workout can be significant, even when they have no equity remaining in the partnership. The result is an incentive to continue to postpone the day of reckoning as long as possible. This incentive produces strategic moves which may not appear to make much sense in terms of the economic outcome, such as filing for bankruptcy even when the prospects for making a successful reorganization under Chapter 11, and possibly a cramdown of the first mortgagee's interest, seem remote. The issue is whether a voluntary petition filed by the LLC immediately before foreclosure to protect the interests of the members was filed in good faith.[11]

---

[10] In 1989, when this gain was realized, the maximum capital gains rate was capped at 28%, which was also the maximum ordinary income tax rate, apart from the impact of several phase-outs or limitations. There was not much advantage, therefore, in treating the gain as capital gain. In addition, the partnership must have elected an accelerated method of depreciation, which would have resulted in depreciation recapture under I.R.C. § 1250 on disposition of the property. As much as $5 million of the gain would have been taxed as ordinary income for that reason. All around, the result was not good for Moxley.

[11] Note that the use of bankruptcy as a technique to delay or prevent foreclosure has been significantly affected by the use of "bankruptcy remote" entities, where the consent of a partner or member appointed by the lender would be required before a voluntary petition could be filed, or by the practice of including "springing recourse" clauses in otherwise non-recourse debt. In the latter case, the

There are similar incentives in states which have judicial foreclosure procedures. As we saw in Chapter 16, these foreclosure procedures can be time consuming, and sometimes the value of continuing the tax deferral for investors may make it worthwhile for the partnership to stretch out workout negotiations and foreclosure procedures even when the ultimate result appears inevitable.

[iv] Restructuring Transactions

An alternative to foreclosure, or a transaction in lieu of foreclosure, is to restructure the debt and allow the original entity to continue to operate the property. As we discussed earlier, the restructuring transaction may be treated as a taxable exchange under Treas. Reg. § 1.1001-3 (the "*Cottage Savings* regulation").[12] The lender would entertain the possibility of restructuring the loan to avoid taking ownership of the property, a result it might find difficult to manage, for the purpose of realizing at least some of the value from the property. The application of these regulations may complicate negotiations with the lender as delays in the enforcement of the loan could, if the period of negotiation stretches out for more than two years, cause a taxable deemed exchange to occur.[13] Any income that results from the exchange of the new loan for the old loan would be treated as COD income to the borrower, that is, in a compromise or reduction in the amount of the debt. Thus, for example, if the lender agrees to reduce the principal balance on the indebtedness from ten million dollars to eight million dollars in order to convert a non-performing loan into a performing loan, then the borrower will have realized COD income in the amount of two million dollars. If so, the exceptions provided by I.R.C. § 108 could apply to allow members of the borrower to exclude some or all of the COD income, but the correct tax treatment of a change in the *value* of a debt instrument is not entirely clear.[14] These rules are *extraordinarily* complex. They reference, and to some extent rely upon, the "original issue discount" rules,[15] which are even more complicated and which can and do apply to indebtedness created in real property transactions.[16]

---

filing of a voluntary petition would cause the debt to become recourse as to the principals who planned and operated the project. Changes to bankruptcy law for single asset bankruptcies may also have made the use of bankruptcy to obtain delay less available. *See* Section 16.03[2][a], *supra*.

[12] Section 3.05[6][f], *supra*.

[13] *See* Treas. Reg. § 1.1001-3(c)(4)(ii). Continuing "good faith negotiations" between borrower and lender can extend this period.

[14] *See* I.R.C. § 108(e)(10), providing that a reduction in the "issue price" of the debt in a taxable debt-for-debt exchange is COD income. Under I.R.C. § 108(e)(10(B), the "issue price" is computed under the OID rules, see note 16, *infra*, and that amount will be equal to the "stated redemption price at maturity" [the principal due under the loan], as long as the interest rate on the loan equals or exceeds the "Applicable Federal Rate," which is the interest the U.S. Treasury must pay on its long term obligations. *See* I.R.C. §§ 1273(b)(4)(B), 1274(a)(1), and 1274(d)(1)(A). The *Cottage Savings* regulations do not discuss *at all* the effect of a reduction in the principal amount of the debt, presumably because this result is so clearly COD income that the "guidance" of this regulation is unnecessary.

[15] I.R.C. §§ 1271–1275.

[16] "Original issue discount" arises when a debt instrument is issued at a value (the instrument's "present value") which is less than its value at maturity. The difference in values, for interest bearing obligations, arises because the prevailing interest rate in the financial markets is greater than the stated interest on the obligation. The holder will usually have negotiated a price which reflects the present value of all payments to be made under the instrument using a discount rate equal to the prevailing rate. In effect, a portion of the nominal principal amount has been converted to interest. This transaction is fairly common in financial markets, and sometimes in private transactions, particularly when an existing

[c] The Treatment of "Exculpatory Liabilities"

If the loan is recourse as to the LLC, it would nonetheless be treated as nonrecourse as to the members of the LLC. As discussed in Chapter 4, this type of loan is referred to as an "exculpatory liability." While the IRS has taken the position that the personal liability of the LLC would be disregarded for purposes of applying the at risk rules (and, presumably, the debt allocation rules under I.R.C. § 752), the position of the LLC as the debtor might be critical in the application of the holding in *2925 Briarpark, Ltd.*. The court there viewed the debt forgiveness for Motley, the general partner, as dependent upon the sale of the property, and therefore an element of the amount realized in the transaction. But the original debt there was in form nonrecourse, and Motley's guarantee was of a nonrecourse debt. Under those circumstances, the court disregarded the release of Motley's personal liability under the guarantee. If the debt were recourse to begin with, however, albeit to the LLC and not its members, the lender's inability to recover the amount of the debt in excess of the value of the LLC's property might be treated as COD income. While this could be an advantage if the members were individually positioned to take advantage of deferrals or exclusions under I.R.C. § 108, COD income is taxed as ordinary income. It remains unsettled as to how entity-level recourse debt of an LLC which is settled for value less than the amount of the debt will be treated for tax purposes.

[2] The Fox Valley Auto Care Center, LLC

Fox Valley Auto Care Center did not lease up completely during the term of the construction loan. One can only speculate why this was the case. One factor may have been that leasing restrictions imposed on Regent by its contract with Metropolitan sufficiently limited the type of business which the Auto Care Center could have as tenants to prevent leasing to many potentially helpful businesses. This resulted in a shortfall in net operating income and difficulty in negotiating a take-out loan. A second factor was the rise in underwriting standards required by lenders in the fallout from the savings and loan crisis that, without doubt, complicated Regent's task. Eventually, First Mortgage Bank refused to extend the construction loan for another period, and a negotiated settlement was reached in which the Auto Care Center was transferred to FMB in exchange for a release of the shareholders of Regent from personal liability on the guaranty and a release of FMB's right to draw against the letter of credit contributed by the members.

[a] First Mortgage Bank's Position

In deciding whether to refinance the mortgage, FMB would have made its own assessment of value. The *pro forma* called for net operating income in the third year of operation (1993) of approximately $320,000, *see* figure 2.15, *supra*, but the Fox Valley Auto Care Center was only producing $250,000, or about 78% of the forecast level. Assume that the underwriting standards of the take out lender (the "Bank") required application of a capitalization rate of 9.5% in determining the

---

obligation is compromised or adjusted after interest rates have increased. As the obligation matures, this discounted interest ("original issue discount") is accrued for both the lender and borrower. The cited provisions specify how these calculations are to be made, and provide some special rules for cash basis taxpayers. Most real estate partnerships will be required to use the accrual method of taxation. I.R.C. § 448(a)(3), cross referencing I.R.C. § 1256(e)(3)(B) (syndicate is any tax partnership if more than 35% of losses are allocated to limited partners or the equivalent).

75% loan-to-value restriction. Assume further that, for a 9.5% loan with 25-year payment terms (debt constant =.101), the Bank will require a cover ratio of 1.2.

Capitalizing the Fox Valley Auto Care Center's net operating income in its third year of operation results in a value of approximately $2,500,000. The Bank will loan 75% of this amount, or $1,874,000. Calculating the maximum loan amount by the income method, available debt service (the amount permitted with a debt cover of 1.2) is $206,000 approximately, which, at a loan constant of .101, will support a loan of $2,045,000, approximately. These numbers are really just rules of thumb, and the loan committee for FMB, noting that Regent is a good customer, might have been willing to relax underwriting standards somewhat, but the Bank likely would have adhered to them pretty closely. It does seem clear, however, that the price of refinancing would have been a substantial capital infusion, as much as, say, $300,000, and the parties would have negotiated over the minimum necessary to achieve the objective. In the end, the shareholders of Regent lacked the equity and the desire to invest so substantial an amount into this size of an investment and so would probably not have desired to restructure the loan in this manner. In addition, Regent would also have wanted to protect the members in the Fox Valley Auto Care Center, LLC from a draw on the letter of credit, the probability of which might have been increasing as workout discussions proceeded. Thus, transfer by deed-in-lieu of foreclosure with release of Regent's personal liability and a return of the letter of credit may ultimately have become Regent's best alternative.

[b] The Tax Consequences

The Fox Valley Auto Care Center, LLC's transfer of the FVACC to FMB by deed-in-lieu of foreclosure is a taxable exchange. The amount realized is the remaining unpaid balance of the mortgage, in this case $2,300,000. *Briarpark* makes clear that, in that court's view, the full unpaid balance should be included in the amount realized, whether or not there is personal liability on the mortgage. The regulation, Treas. Reg. § 1.1001-2(a)(2), however, provides that the amount realized on a taxable disposition of property does not include income from the discharge of indebtedness, and backstops this statement with an example:

> *Example (8)*. In 1980, F transfers to a creditor an asset with a fair market value of $6,000 and the creditor discharges $7,500 of indebtedness for which F is personally liable. The amount realized on the disposition of the asset is its fair market value ($6,000). In addition, F has income from the discharge of indebtedness of $1,500 ($7,500–$6,000).

The example does not say whether the indebtedness compromised in this transfer was secured by the property, nor that it had been incurred in acquiring or constructing the property. In *Frazier v. Commissioner*, 111 T.C. 243 (1998), the Tax Court applied the example to a foreclosure in which recourse debt secured by the property exceeded the value of the property (which was disputed). The lender did not attempt to enforce the taxpayer's personal liability for the deficiency. The Tax Court held that the excess of the mortgage debt over the value of the property held as security for the debt would be treated as COD income. *Briarpark*, however, took the view that a negotiated workout in which the lender accepted the proceeds of a sale to a third party, plus some additional cash, in satisfaction of a debt which was partially recourse would be treated entirely as a taxable exchange. Unlike the situation in *Frazier*, where the debt was recourse by its terms, it was the *general partner's guarantee* in *Briarpark* which converted a portion of the nominally nonrecourse partnership level debt into a recourse debt for the purpose of I.R.C. § 752. This may have been enough to distinguish *Example (8)*, although neither court in *Briarpark* discussed the example.

The law is not as clear as the *Briarpark* decision might suggest. If the debt had been recourse to the entity, the regulatory example, and *Frazier* which applied the example to a recourse debt, might convert the excess of the amount due over the *value* of the FVACC to COD income. *See* Section 17.02[1][c], *supra*. As discussed above, the value of the property might, in fact, have exceeded the balance due on the loan, even though underwriting restrictions would have limited available financing to, say, 75% of that value, and FMB might have required an additional capital contribution before agreeing to refinance the loan. In that case, the law is rather certain that the full amount of the loan be treated as the amount realized in a taxable transaction. *Cf.* I.R.C. § 7701(g).

If some portion of the loan was COD income to the members in the Fox Valley Auto Care Center, LLC, that might make some difference to the tax result, as both Regent, its stockholders, and possibly the other members were heavily invested in real estate, and some, or all, of them could, presumably, have used the exclusion for qualified real property business indebtedness.[17] Here, however, there does not seem to have been any separate negotiation over the reduction or elimination of Regent's personal liability; it was all involved in the treatment of the property. *Briarpark* makes sense from that standpoint, and it seems to be the better result, at least in the case of the FVACC, that the full unpaid balance of the loan be included in the amount realized. The transfer was made by deed, and that will be taxed as a sale or exchange.

In determining the tax effect of the sale, the adjusted basis for the property is its original cost basis less accumulated depreciation:

Original cost (includes land acquisition)	$2,476,271
Accumulated depreciation (including amortization)	– $279,360
Adjusted tax basis	$2,196,911

The principal on the construction loan had not been curtailed, so the full amount of the loan remained due and was discharged in the transfer by deed. Therefore:

Amount realized (loan balance)	$2,300,000
Adjusted tax basis for the Center	– $2,196,911
Gain realized	$103,089

This gain will be taxed as capital gain which consists entirely of unrecaptured I.R.C. § 1250 gain, taxable under current law at a maximum rate of 25%. Furthermore, the gain should be fully allocated to Regent because Regent bears the "economic risk of loss" on the construction loan. Regent's capital account will

---

[17] Note, however, that the exclusion is available only to the extent that the "outstanding principal amount" of the construction loan exceeded the "fair market value" of the real property which was security for the debt. I.R.C. § 108(c)(2)(A). That seems not to have been true here, so the exclusion would not have been available.

have been reduced below zero by allocations, reallocations and distributions to it.[18] The reallocations occur because tax deductions in excess of the members' capital accounts will end up being deductible by Regent, and, therefore, by Regent's shareholders, a result that ultimately will depend on the tax basis of the shareholders in their stock in Regent. Moreover, there was some distributable cash, and, because the cash distributions to the members would be made at a time when their capital accounts had been reduced to zero, those cash distributions should carry gross income out of the LLC and to the investor-members. This effect, in turn, diverts gross income from Regent, and further increases Regent's deductible losses. Under reasonable assumptions, deductions of about $35,000 would have been shifted from the investor-members to Regent, and gross income allocated to the members from cash distributions made to them of approximately $24,000. The unexpected events that prevented Regent from being able to negotiate a satisfactory nonrecourse loan, therefore, had some unhappy tax effects as well as financial consequences.

[c] Problem

Suppose in the Fox Valley Auto Care Center project that Regent had obtained a nonrecourse loan at 10%, 25 year amortization, and a 10 year term for $2,300,000. In 1997, the property had failed to lease up and rents had remained stagnant. Vacancy was at 32%. What is the "value" of the property? Explain the tax effects for Regent of the following alternative scenarios:

1. The lender takes the position that the loan is non-performing, and that this is ground for acceleration. It demands payment. The balance due on the mortgage at this point is $2,100,000. Regent, having difficulty refinancing the Fox Valley Auto Care Center for the outstanding debt, executes a deed-in-lieu of foreclosure to the lender, which assumes ownership.

2. The lender is willing to write the note down to the current value of the property, as its examiners are requiring, in exchange for Regent's partial guarantee. Assume that the lender insists that the current value of the FVACC, taking into account its then current rental structure and a capitalization rate of 9.5%, is $1,900,000. The parties negotiate a package involving rate adjustments, amortization shifts, principal reduction and guarantees, which results in the value of $1,900,000 for the loan. *See* I.R.C. § 108(e)(10); Reg. § 1.1001-3 (the "*Cottage Savings*" regulation). Because of the tax sensitive nature of indebtedness used in real estate investing, as you have seen from the discussion in this book, adjustment of indebtedness is loaded with tax consequences. You might consider, for example, whether it is possible for the partners to elect to exclude COD income from the compromise of "qualifying real property business indebtedness" and to

[18] The construction loan is assumed to have been recourse to the LLC. It would be nonrecourse as to the members, and therefore an exculpatory indebtedness. However, the guarantees by Regent, and by Regent's shareholders, would put the economic risk of loss on Regent to pay the loan, and this converts the construction loan into partner nonrecourse indebtedness, which means that allocation of losses in excess of the members' equity in the project would be allocated entirely to Regent. These losses would have been increased by an allocation of gross income to the investors to cover cash distributions made to them when their capital accounts had been reduced to zero (net cash flow after payment of operating loans is assumed to have been distributed). The tax and book gain shown on the books of the LLC would be less than the negative balances in Regent's capital account.

reduce tax basis to the value of the property. *See* I.R.C § 108(a)(1)(D), discussed at Sections 3.05[6][d] and 17.02[1][b][i], *supra.*

3. Regent sells the property to Wingding Auto Care REIT, a public company, in exchange for Wingding's assumption of the debt and $5,000 to cover transaction costs.

TABLE OF CASES

[References are to pages]

A

B

C

[References are to pages]

D

[References are to pages]

[References are to pages]

H

I

J

K

[References are to pages]

L

M

[References are to pages]

[References are to pages]

Q

R

S

[References are to pages]

[References are to pages]

Y

Z

INDEX

[References are to pages.]

A

B

C

[References are to pages.]

[References are to pages.]

[References are to pages.]

[References are to pages.]

[References are to pages.]

[References are to pages.]

R

S

[References are to pages.]

[References are to pages.]

W

Z